Fodor's

France

Fodor's Travel Publications • New York, Toronto, London, Sydney, Auckland
www.fodors.com

CONTENTS

3

MAPS

Circled letters in text correspond to letters on the photographs. For more information on the sights pictured, turn to the indicated page number ⒶⓏ on each photograph.

DESTINATION FRANCE

High atop the Musée des Beaux-Arts in Lyon, this statue seems bemused. And who can blame her? After all, she casts a perpetual gaze upon all things French, and for the French, there's no better pursuit than admiring this fabled land and *la civilisation française*. In coming to France, you can join them. Since setting foot on French soil without paying a visit to Paris is barely conceivable, start your visit in this glorious capital. Then savor as much of the rest of this delicious country as your time and budget permit— city streets, village squares, dreamy landscapes, fine art, and that most precious of French gifts, the art of living.

PARIS

Ⓐ⟩45 A quai-side vista that takes in the Seine, a passing boat, the Ile de la Cité, Ⓓ**Notre-Dame,** the mansard roofs, and a few wispy clouds all in one generous sweep is enough to convince you that Paris is indeed the most beautiful and romantic city on earth. The Arc de Triomphe, the Opéra Garnier, and the ©**Place de la Concorde** with its fountains, columns, and statuary, recall the pomp of bygone eras, and their grandeur can leave you breathless, especially on a per-

Ⓑ⟩64

fect sunny day. The sight of the Ⓐ**Eiffel Tower,** the city's enduring symbol, looming and aglow, is an inspiration to leap and run and gallop through the city, taking it all in. And when Paris puts on a display of showiness as modern and brash as the arch at La Défense, Jean Nouvel's Institut du Monde Arabe, or I. M. Pei's hotly debated glass-pyramid entrance to the venerable Ⓔ**Louvre,** it keeps alive what is perhaps its most alluring tradition—an unfailing ability to astonish. Yet, as the nighttime swirl of the Latin Quarter, Place de la Bastille, or Ⓑ**Place du Tertre** in Montmartre shows—even with the august Sacré-Coeur basilica looming behind—Paris is all about people and the pleasure of enjoying its beauty, art, culture, and cuisine. This is, after all, a city where café-sitting is a culture, a simple walk can be an extraordinary experience filled with visual delights, and a meal is an almost sacred ritual.

Ⓐ❯ 129

ILE-DE-FRANCE

Ⓑ❯ 108

Kings, clerics, paupers, and ordinary Parisians have long taken refuge from urban life in Ile-de-France. Most have been content to spend a day in the country amid meandering rivers and lush meadows, while others have left behind spectacular secular and religious monuments. Noble occupants spared no expense in outfitting the Ⓐ**Château de Chantilly** with formal gardens, fountains, a lagoon, and all the other trappings that were standard amenities during the 16th-century château-building craze. Biggest and most ostentatious of these palaces, the Ⓑ**Château de Versailles** is pompous proof that French monarchs lost their heads long before Louis XVI and Marie-Antoinette, the last occupants, walked to the guillotine. All this worldly froth fades in the stained-glass luster of Ⓒ**Chartres Cathedral**, so sublime its soft limestone hulk has brought the faithful to their knees for centuries—an effect it may have on you as well.

Ⓒ❯ 115

Ⓐ 153

LOIRE VALLEY

The valley of the meandering Loire River was for many centuries the favored place to build fine country seats. At the Ⓐ**Château de Chambord** it's easy to imagine the days when King François I arrived with a retinue so large it took 12,000 horses to transport them. At the Ⓒ**Château de Blois**, a refined facade belies the poisonings and other plots that were part of life at court. At the austere Ⓑ**Château d'Angers**, 17 formidable towers recall the days when France and England battled for control of this terrain—which would still be enchanting, if much less intriguing, without its hallmark châteaux.

Ⓒ 156

Ⓑ 170

(A) 197

"Finistère," or "land's end," is what a part of Brittany is called, and the name suits the entire region. A long arm of rocky land stretching into the Atlantic, Brittany is a place unto itself, living to the rhythm of tides and winds, with its own language and legends, personality and geology. The people are Bretons first, rather than French, Celtic rather than Latin, and proud of their difference. They are also proud of their land—with reason. Here you'll find time-defying monuments and customs in awe-inspiring landscapes. The prehistoric standing stones of ⓓ**Carnac** are a gateway to the gorgeous sandy peninsula of the Côte Sauvage, where birds and flowers abound. Harsh, rocky, windswept shores sud-

BRITTANY

(B) 203

denly give way to industrious fishing villages where gray houses of slate and granite withstand the onslaught of the coastal elements. Sweet thatch-roof cottages are the hallmark of the vast inland marshes of Ⓑ**La Grande Brière**. The craftspeople in ⒶQuimper carry on a centuries-old practice of hand-painting delicate-looking faience wares. Tides bathe the foot of St-Malo's impressive fortifications, still haunted by phantom pirates. A trip across the waters to the aptly named Ⓔ**Belle-Ile**, or "beautiful island," will take you to heaths of yellow broom, fine beaches, and quaint towns. When you are finally tired, treat yourself to the freshest of oysters at ⒸCancale. Like them, Brittany is a rare gift from the sea, well worth the trek to land's end.

Ⓐ 232

Normandy is a land of fashionable resorts and austere abbeys, warriors and prolific painters, saints and sinners. At Ⓐ**Bayeux,** the town's famous tapestry provides a scene-by-scene look at the Norman invasion of England in 1066, with William the Conqueror at the head of an army of oarsmen, horsemen, and knights. Not far away, Mont-St-Michel perches dramatically atop its rocky shoreline roost, surrounded on all sides by tidal flats. In Ⓑ**Rouen**, me-

NORMANDY

Ⓑ 216

dieval rue du Gros-Horloge leads to the spot where Joan of Arc was burned at the stake in 1431 (but not before she had routed British troops from Orléans and changed the course of the Hundred Years' War). Off to the west at Ⓔ**Omaha Beach,** vast expanses of empty, windswept sands and grassy dunes pay quiet homage to the 10,000 Allied soldiers who lost their lives during the D-Day invasion of 1944. Elsewhere lovely seascapes and lush fields and orchards have compelled peaceable pursuits. Pretty Ⓒ**Honfleur** made Claude Monet and other Impressionists long to paint the sea and sky. Ⓓ**Étretat** invites a day of ambling along limestone *falaises* (cliffs). Chic Deauville and Trouville beckon you to stroll along their seafront boardwalks. To make your

Ⓒ 221

Normandy experience complete, throw caution to the winds and indulge in the region's cuisine, ruled and inspired by local cream, butter, eggs, and apples, along with fine lamb sweetened by the salty grasses on which the animals graze. Camembert is the best known of Normandy's cheeses. Heady apple brandy, like the Calvados made at the Grandval Calvados Distillery in Ⓕ**Cambremer,** in Pays d'Auge, is often downed with a meal to make a *trou normand* (Norman hole, or room for more rich food). It is guaranteed to evoke pungent reveries of this ageless land.

Ⓔ 234

Ⓕ 227

THE NORTH
AND CHAMPAGNE

"Brother, come quickly, I'm drinking stars," exclaimed Dom Pérignon upon first sipping the bubbling beverage that he invented through luck and alchemy. The blind 17th-century monk put Ⓐ**Hautvillers** and an entire region on the world map; he also ensured that vineyards around ©**Épernay** and elsewhere in the vicinity produce some of the world's finest wine grapes. In towns like Reims—once important enough to host the coronation of French kings, with many an amiable monument and museum as proof of its stature—it's perfectly clear what adds extra sparkle to these parts and gives pleasure to the senses and the stomach, especially at restaurants like Ⓑ**Vigneron** and Boyer. Besides fine food and drink, there's plenty in the north to capture your attention—the bustling city of Lille, the long stretches of empty sand along the Channel coast, and the haunting cemeteries that evoke crucial battles of World War I.

Ⓑ 280

ALSACE, LORRAINE, AND FRANCHE-COMTÉ

Ⓐ 290

Ⓑ 312

"Let them speak German," said Napoléon of the Alsatians, "as long as they think in French." The emperor would be pleased to know that after centuries of conquest and liberation, Alsace and its neighbor Lorraine are now resolutely and proudly French. Yet there are enough imports from beyond the Rhine to make the region fascinating. ©**Strasbourg,** capital of Alsace and the cosmopolitan home of the European Parliament, has sophisticated restaurants and fine museums as well as a lacy-spired cathedral, an old quarter known as La Petite France, beer gardens, and *winstubs.* Ⓐ**Nancy,** capital of Lorraine, adds another element to the region's cultural mix: Much of the elegant, easygoing city was laid out with pomp and grandeur by Stanislas Leszczynski, dethroned king of Poland; it was also a center of Art Nouveau architecture in the late 19th century. The Route du Vin, running through the green foothills of the Vosges mountains, leads to half-timbered, impossibly picturesque wine villages such as Ⓑ**Riquewihr.** Farther south, the verdant folds of Franche-Comté roll seamlessly into yet another world, that of neighboring Switzerland.

© 301

BURGUNDY

Farms, pastures, and fall foliage make Burgundy enticingly, romantically rural. But it's also evident that whether building, ruling, worshiping, dining, or drinking, Burgundians have never embraced life on anything less than a grand scale. From magnificent palaces like the one in the city of Dijon and châteaux like the one at Ⓐ**Tanlay,** dukes more powerful than kings once ruled vast tracts of Western Europe. They left behind mighty medieval cathedrals in Sens and Auxerre, and religious orders built the other Burgundian architectural masterpieces—the Romanesque basilica at Vézelay and even more impressive abbeys, such as the Abbaye de Pontigny, the Abbaye de Fontenay, and the Ⓓ**Abbaye**

Ⓑ 354

de Cluny, the largest church in the world until the construction of St. Peter's in Rome. For centuries this epicenter of European religious and intellectual life was so influential, it was said that "where the wind blows, the Abbey of Cluny owns." The bare, ruined choir still inspires awe. Most likely to evoke a reverential hush, though, is a first sip of one of Burgundy's treasured wines. Follow the Ⓑ**Côte d'Or,** perhaps the world's most famous

Ⓒ 355

wine route, out of Dijon, a gastronomic hub and cultural center; visit the Marché aux Vins in the wine capital of Beaune; tour the highly touted cellars at the Ⓒ**Château du Clos de Vougeot,** once a monastic community, albeit a rather worldly one, that is now hallowed ground for wine lovers from around the world. As you sample the bounty of the highly anticipated annual *vendange* (harvest), you'll be introduced to wines so fine that, as the novelist, playwright, and observer of French life Alexandre Dumas once counseled, they should only be drunk on bended knee.

Ⓓ 360

LYON AND THE ALPS

Ⓐ 397

If the very mention of Lyon teases the taste buds, give credit to this sophisticated city's chefs—masters who can render even a plate of fruit ethereal. Savor their creations—and those of their compatriots at country outposts like La Treille Muscate in ©**Cliousclat**—along with a fine Beaujolais. Lyon's covered passageways, known as *traboules*, lead to treasure-filled museums and a first-class opera house. Near at hand, seek out more *sportif* amusements: a sail from canal-lined, bridge-bedecked Ⓑ**Annecy** across its breezy lake, perhaps, or a gambol through meadows near Ⓐ**Chamonix**, a resort with a reputation for winter pleasures overshadowed only by its Alpine peaks.

© 388

Ⓑ 395

Ⓐ▷ 408

"Early to bed, early to rise," is the rule of thumb in this craggy, rural heartland at the center of France. You'll want to rise early to venture into the spectacular gorges or tackle the slopes of the highest of the region's 80 dormant volcanoes, the ©**Puy-de-Dôme.** The same dictum applies at elegant and infamous Ⓑ**Vichy,**

Ⓑ▷ 412

MASSIF
CENTRAL

a long-favored place to take the waters and get back on the straight and narrow (a path from which the spa town strayed during World War II, when Nazi sympathizers ran their puppet government from here). Early risers in Ⓐ**Bourges,** a medieval city gloriously bypassed by time, have a special reward in store—the sight of the brilliantly hued stained-glass windows of the 13th-century Cathédrale St-Étienne achieving their fullest luster in the morning light.

©▷ 415

Even the cattle and flamingos wallowing in the salty coastal marshes of the ⒟**Camargue** enjoy the sun-drenched good life that Provence provides so gen-

⒜▷**450**

erously. In this smiling landscape and in soft-hued, elegant cities, where life still proceeds at an old-fashioned pace, you'll find no end of pleasures. Aix-en-Provence, Arles, and Avignon have bewitched Roman legionnaires, popes, and Impressionist painters; the tarnished and exotic old port of Marseille continues to intrigue sailors and travelers with its hint of mystery; and dusty Nîmes and sleepy Orange are alluringly littered

PROVENCE

Ⓑ▷**445**   Ⓒ▷**445**

with ancient arches and theaters. The region works its charms most potently in rural places, though, aided in no small part by cypress trees and vineyards, warm breezes scented with wild rosemary and thyme, and by a cooling glass of pastis. In heavenly lavender fields at the foot of ⒜**Mont Ventoux** and in ocher-colored villages—few more enticing than pretty Ⓑ©**St-Rémy-de-Provence,** where sunlight really does dapple lanes of plane trees and where you don't have to look hard to find the bounty for a simple feast—you can't help but fall under the spell of this glorious land.

Ⓓ▷**437**

CÔTE D'AZUR

If only once in your lifetime you want to sip champagne from a slipper or slink up to a roulette table and go for broke, Nice, Monte Carlo, and Antibes are the places to do so. Or you may want to sample the small pleasures of this fabled coast: a session amid scantily but stylishly attired sunbathers on the beach in Ⓑ**Cannes**; an excursion up to medieval St-Paul-de-Vence to see a stunning collection of modern art; or just a flutter with glamour in an enchanted seaside retreat such as Ⓐ**Beaulieu.**

Ⓑ 486

21

Ⓐ⟩ 534

CORSICA

For centuries great powers have fought over this strategically placed piece of Mediterranean real estate, leaving behind both architectural and cultural relics that set the island apart from the rest of France. In Ⓐ**Piana** and other ancient stone villages, news from across the sea still seems far removed—delightfully so. Corsica's capital, Ⓒ**Ajaccio,** hometown of the greatest empire builder of them all, Napoléon Bonaparte, is now a port for launching pleasure craft, not naval fleets. Today's spoils are granite peaks, pine forests, and crystalline waters—those around Ⓑ**Bonifacio,** where Ulysses was besieged, are especially inviting.

Ⓒ⟩ 520

Ⓑ⟩ 527

THE MIDI-PYRÉNÉES AND
THE LANGUEDOC-ROUSSILLON

Ⓐ> 566

Ⓑ> 562

In the vast stretches of south-west France, the strong sun makes fields of flowers glow and renders the brick buildings of Toulouse-Lautrec's native Albi and lively, cosmopolitan, Spanish-flavored Toulouse a rosy pink. It reflects upon walled Ⓐ**Carcassonne** and hilltop Ⓑ**Cordes** (so safely high it's known as Cordes-sur-Ciel or "Cordes in the Sky"), medieval towns with long histories of defending the region. It brightens the cloisters at Moissac and St-Guilhem-le-Désert and warms the vineyards that slope down to the sea near Collioure. It beckons you to climb the the Pyrénées' peaks and then feast on trout that you've caught by fly-fishing in rushing rivers, or on foie gras and cassoulet, two of the region's many culinary specialties.

At its southwesternmost corner, France eases with grace and dignity toward Spain, separated from it in many ways only by the Pyrénées. Napoléon III and his Spanish wife, Empress Eugénie, put the resort towns of Eugénie-les-Bains and Ⓐ**Biarritz** on the map. Ⓑ**Bayonne,** Ainhoa, Ste-Engrâce, and many other towns and villages have a distinctly Basque look and temper-

BASQUE COUNTRY, THE BÉARN, AND THE HAUTES-PYRÉNÉES

ament. The peaks of the Ⓒ**Pyrénées** are breathtaking and are spectacular for hiking. When you come back down, the incomparable local cuisine and the wine produced on the vineyard-clad lower slopes taste all the better.

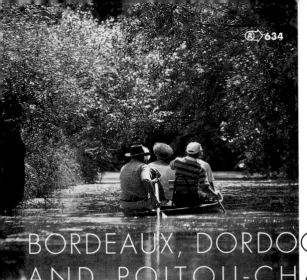

Ⓐ 634

BORDEAUX, DORDOGNE, AND POITOU-CHARENTES

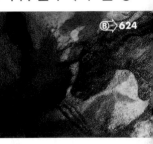

Ⓑ 624

Since prehistoric times, this hinterland near the Atlantic coast has had its appeal, as is apparent when you see the cave paintings at the Ⓑ**Grotte de Lascaux.** In the Middle Ages the French and British fought over the area, leaving behind many castles and cathedrals. The continued allure of the rural landscape lies in an abundance of good food and wine and the opportunity for pleasurable idleness. Float along the waters of Green Venice, as the Ⓐ**Marais Poitevin** near Coulon is known, or explore the vineyards around Bordeaux, perhaps ambling through an estate that rolls right up to the walls of Ⓒ**St-Émilion,** the loveliest of many villages producing wines that are sure to add a memorable note to any day.

Ⓒ 616

GREAT ITINERARIES

So you want to get a taste of France, drink in its beauty, and sample its famous joie de vivre—all in a one-week to 10-day trip? Let's assume that you can start or end your trip in Paris, and you're ready to venture into the countryside. Use these itineraries to help plan the journey, or create your own tour using the suggestions in each chapter.

France from North to South
6 to 9 days

Zoom from Paris to the heart of historic Burgundy, its rolling green hills traced with hedgerows and etched with vineyards. From here, plunge into the arid beauty of Provence and toward the spectacular coastline of the Côte d'Azur.

BURGUNDY WINE COUNTRY
2 or 3 days. Base yourself in the market town of Beaune and visit its famous Hospices and surrounding vineyards. Make a day trip to the ancient hill town of Vézelay, with its incomparable basilica, stopping in Autun to explore Roman ruins and its celebrated Romanesque cathedral. For more vineyards, follow the Côte d'Or from Beaune to Dijon. Or make a beeline to Dijon, with its charming old town and fine museums. From here it's a two-hour drive to Lyon,

where you can feast on this city's famous earthy cuisine. Another three hours' push takes you deep into the heart of Provence.
☞ *Northwest Burgundy and Wine Country in Chapter 8 and Lyon in Chapter 9*

ARLES
2 or 3 days. Arles is the atmospheric, sun-drenched southern town that inspired van Gogh and Gauguin. Make a day trip into grand old Avignon, home to the 14th-century rebel popes, to view their imposing palace. And make a pilgrimage to the Ⓐ Pont du Gard, the famous triple-tiered Roman aqueduct west of Avignon. From here two hours' drive will bring you to the glittering Côte d'Azur.
☞ *Arles, Avignon, and Pont du Gard in Chapter 11*

ANTIBES
2 or 3 days. This historic and atmospheric port town is well positioned for day trips. First head west to glamorous Cannes. The next day head east into Ⓑ Nice, with its exotic old town and its bounty of modern art. There are ports to explore in Villefranche and St-Jean-Cap-Ferrat, east of Nice. Allow time for a walk out onto the tropical paradise–peninsula of Cap d'Antibes, or for an hour or two lolling on the coast's famous pebble beaches.
☞ *Cannes, Nice, Villefranche-sur-Mer, St-Jean-Cap-Ferrat, and Cap d'Antibes in Chapter 12*

By Public Transportation
The high-speed TGV travels from Paris through Burgundy and Lyon then zips through the south to Marseille. Train connections to Beaune from the TGV are easy; getting to Autun from Beaune takes up to two hours, with a change

Ⓐ 431

at Chagny. Vézelay can be reached by bus excursion from Dijon or Beaune. Rail connections are easy between Arles and Avignon; you'll need a bus from Avignon to get to the Pont du Gard. Antibes, Cannes, and Nice are easily reached by the scenic rail line, as are most of the resorts and ports along the coast. To squeeze the most daytime out of your trip, take a night train or a plane from Nice back to Paris.

The Good Life
7 to 10 days

Great châteaux, fine porcelain, superb wine, brandy, truffles, and foie gras sum up France for many. Beginning in château country, head south and west, through Cognac country into wine country around Bordeaux. Then lose yourself in the Dordogne, a landscape of rolling hills peppered with medieval villages, fortresses, and prehistoric caves.

LOIRE VALLEY CHÂTEAUX
2 or 3 days. Base yourself at the crossroads of Blois, starting with its multi-era château. Then head for the huge château in Chambord. ©Amboise's château echoes with history, and the neighboring manor Clos Lucé was Leonardo da Vinci's final home. Heading south, visit the fine Gothic cathedral in the center of Tours.
☞ *The Loire Valley in Chapter 3*

COGNAC COUNTRY
1 or 2 days. Cognac's very air is saturated with evaporations of its heady product, enough to grow mushrooms on its black stone walls; Hennessy and Martell give tasting tours. In neighboring Jarnac you can visit Hine and Courvoisier—and François Mitterrand's grave.
☞ *Charente in Chapter 16*

BORDEAUX WINE COUNTRY
2 days. Pay homage to the great names of Médoc, north of the city of Bordeaux, though the hallowed villages of

©▷ 157

Margaux, St-Julien, Pauillac, and St-Estèphe aren't much to look at. East of Bordeaux, via the prettier Pomerol vineyards, the village of St-Emilion is everything you'd want a wine town to be, with ramparts and medieval streets.
☞ *Bordeaux in Chapter 16*

DORDOGNE AND PÉRIGORD
2 or 3 days. Follow the famous Dordogne River east to the half-timber market town of Bergerac. Wind through the green, wooded countryside into the region where humans' earliest ancestors left their mark, in the caves in Les Eyzies-de-Tayac and the famous Grotte de Lascaux. Be sure to sample the region's culinary specialties: truffles, foie gras, and preserved duck. Then travel north past the stunning château in Hautefort, and continue on to Limoges to admire shops full of France's finest porcelain.
☞ *Dordogne and Poitou-Charente in Chapter 16*

By Public Transportation
It's easy to get to Blois by rail, but you'll need to take a bus excursion to visit other Loire châteaux. Forays farther into Bordeaux country and the Dordogne are difficult by train, involving complex and frequent changes. Limoges, on the other hand, is a railway hub. Further exploration requires a rental car.

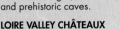

311 km

192.82 mi to Beaune

Vézelay

A6

Dijon

Autun
28 km *38 km*
Beaune

A6

BURGUNDY

155 km

Lyon

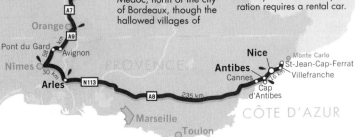
Ⓑ ▷ 498

A7

200 km

A7

Orange
A9

Pont du Gard
Avignon
Nîmes
30 km
Arles
N113

A8
235 km

Marseille

Toulon

Nice
Monte Carlo
Antibes
St-Jean-Cap-Ferrat
Cannes
Villefranche
Cap
d'Antibes

PROVENCE

CÔTE D'AZUR

MEDITERRANEAN
SEA

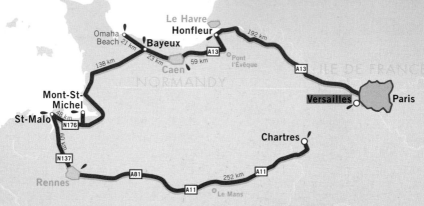

A Child's-Eye View
7 days

Lead your children (and yourself) wide-eyed through the wonders of Europe, instilling some sense of France's cultural legacy. Make your way through Normandy and Brittany, with enough wonders and evocative topics, from William the Conqueror to D-Day, to inspire any child to put down his computer game and gawk. Short daily drives forestall mutiny, and you'll be in crêperie country, satisfying for casual meals.

VERSAILLES
1 day. Here's an opportunity for a history lesson: With its obscene Baroque extravagance, no other monument so succinctly illustrates what inspired the rage of the French Revolution. Louis XIV's eye-popping château of ⒟Versailles pleases the secret monarch in most of us.
☞ *Versailles in Chapter 2*

HONFLEUR
1 day. From this picture-book seaport lined with skinny half-timber rowhouses and salt-dampened cobblestones, the first French explorers set sail for Canada in the 15th century.
☞ *Upper Normandy in Chapter 5*

BAYEUX
2 days. William the Conqueror's extraordinary invasion of England in 1066 was launched from the shores of Normandy. The famous Bayeux tapestry, showcased in a state-of-the-art museum, spins the tale of the Battle of Hastings. From this home base you can introduce the family to the modern saga of 1944's Allied landings with a visit to the Museum of the Battle of Normandy, then make a pilgrimage to Omaha Beach.
☞ *Lower Normandy in Chapter 5*

Ⓔ 238

MONT-ST-MICHEL
1 day. Rising majestically in a shroud of sea mist over vacillating tidal flats, this mystical peninsula is Gothic in every sense of the word. Though its tiny, steep streets are crammed with visitors and tourist traps, no other sight gives you a stronger sense of the worldly power of medieval monasticism than Ⓔ Mont-St-Michel.
☞ *Lower Normandy in Chapter 5*

ST-MALO
1 day. Even in winter you'll want to brave the Channel winds to beachcomb the shores of this onetime pirate base. In summer, of course, it's mobbed with sunseekers who stroll the old streets, restored to quaintness after World War II.
☞ *Northeast Brittany and the Channel Coast in Chapter 4*

CHARTRES
1 day. Making a beeline on the autoroute back to Paris, stop in Chartres to view the loveliest of all of France's cathedrals.
☞ *Versailles, Chartres, and Giverny in Chapter 2*

By Public Transportation
Coordinating a sightseeing tour like this with a limited local train schedule isn't easy, and connections to Mont-St-Michel are especially complicated. Versailles, Chartres, and St-Malo are easy to reach, and Bayeux and Honfleur are doable, if inconvenient. But you'll spend a lot of vacation time waiting along train tracks. It's best to rent a car.

Vintage Sampler
10 days

Tasting wines in a cool, mossy cave redolent of cork gives vintages new dimensions, and you'll meet vintners of every stripe, from gnarled-fingered grandpas in blue aprons to ascoted gentry in cashmere. Along the way, taste the widely varied wines of eastern France, from Champagne to Alsace to the little-known whites of the Jura, then on to Burgundy, Beaujolais, and the Côtes du Rhône. Take it easy on the *dégustations* (tastings) if you're driving.

REIMS
2 days. At the heart of the green panorama of Champagne country lies Reims, with its magnificent Ⓕ cathedral. There's no shortage of downtown sources of bubbly, but you'll probably also want

Map labels:
Reims — 300 km — A4 — Épernay — Hautvillers — Saverne — 83 km — A4 — Strasbourg — Ribeauvillé — Riquewihr — Colmar — 37 km — A83 — 41 km — Belfort — Mulhouse — 90 km — A38 — Dijon — Besançon — A36 — 101 km — 50 km — Arbois — Château-Chalon — 35 km — Beaune — A6 — 84 km — Mâcon — 55-60 km — Villefranche-sur-Saône — 76 km — Lyon — Vienne — A7 — Tournon — Tain-l'Hermitage — 51 km — Valence — 104 km — A7 — Orange — 101 km — Châteauneuf-du-Pape

F→ 278

to venture south down the Route du Vin (Wine Road) to Épernay, home to Moët et Chandon. Just northwest is the old-fashioned village of Hautvillers, which claims Dom Pérignon as its native son.
☞ *Champagne and the Ardennes in Chapter 6*

RIBEAUVILLÉ
2 days. Head east to Franco-Germanic Strasbourg and south down Alsace's Route du Vin. At the foot of forested Vosges foothills, the tiny wine village of Ribeauvillé sums up the spirit of Alsace. Here you'll taste sharp, fruity Rieslings and late-harvest gewürztraminers as sweet as sauternes. Picture-perfect Riquewihr and Colmar are a stone's throw away.
☞ *Alsace in Chapter 7*

ARBOIS
1 day. South of Alsace, follow the Doubs River through the citadel town of Besançon to Arbois. This is the center for the production of the Jura region's obscure and eccentric *vin jaune*: sharp, dry, and sherrylike. Venture to the other-worldly hilltop village of Château-Chalon for some of the finest of the genre.
☞ *Franche-Comté in Chapter 7*

BEAUNE
2 days. Press westward to Beaune, Burgundy's wine-market town (☞ France from North to South itinerary, *above*). Wine shops abound in the center, but you'll want to cruise along the famous Côte d'Or.
☞ *Wine Country in Chapter 8*

VILLEFRANCHE-SUR-SAÔNE
1 day. Head south along the west bank of the Saône. South of Mâcon, home of the last and lightest of the Burgundies, veer westward and follow the winding south-bound Route du Vin through Beaujolais country. Cruise through the famous villages that produce this fruity, Gamay-based red. If you're traveling in autumn, look for the sharp young Beaujolais nouveau: The market-town of Villefranche-sur-Saône celebrates annually with carnival-like festivities.
☞ *Wine Country in Chapter 8 and Beaujolais and La Dombes, and The Rhône Valley in Chapter 9*

CHÂTEAUNEUF-DU-PAPE
2 days. At Lyon you'll merge into the Rhône Valley. Just north of Valence cross the river at Tournon and pay homage to the vineyards at Tain-l'Hermitage. Press on south past Orange to the famous wine region and village of Châteauneuf-du-Pape, named for the Avignon popes who weekended here. You could continue from here into the region of the "sun wines" of the Côtes de Provence and Languedoc, but you might never get home.
☞ *Lyon and the Rhône Valley in Chapter 9, and Avignon and the Vaucluse in Chapter 11*

By Public Transportation
An abbreviated version of this journey can be worked out via train, leaving out the inaccessible vineyards and villages (which serve as lovely scenery through the train window). Start in Reims, move directly on to Colmar (substituting the atmospheric wine-market center for Ribeauvillé); take the train onward to Beaune. From Beaune the train makes stops along the northbound Côte d'Or route, but the best vineyards are hard to reach on foot. To get closer to the sources, look into package excursions or rent a car.

MEDITERRANEAN SEA

(A)

(B)

FODOR'S
CHOICE

(C)

(D)

La Treille Muscate
RESTAURANT

(E)

(F)

(G)

(H)

(I)

(J)

Even with so many special places in France, Fodor's writers and editors have their favorites. Here are a few that stand out.

CHÂTEAUX

Ⓓ **Chenonceau, Loire Valley.** The most romantic of them all. ☞ p. 159

Hautefort, Périgord. Part medieval, part Renaissance, this vast castle arrogantly faces the world. ☞ p. 624

Pierrefonds, Champagne. Viollet-le-Duc restored this huge château. ☞ p. 274

Ⓐ **Vaux-le-Vicomte, Ile-de-France.** The sumptuous gardens and interior made Louis XIV jealous. ☞ p. 134

Ⓗ **Versailles, Ile-de-France.** Undeniably, this is the world's grandest palace. ☞ p. 108

CHURCHES AND ABBEYS

Basilique, Vézelay. This great pilgrim church gazes serenely over the rolling hills. ☞ p. 346

Ⓒ **Cathédrale, Chartres.** Take binoculars to survey the fine stained glass. ☞ p. 115

Cathédrale Notre-Dame, Laon. The hilltop setting is spectacular. ☞ p. 271

Ⓘ **Mont-St-Michel, Normandy.** With its abbey on top, this is truly awe-inspiring. ☞ p. 238

Notre-Dame-du-Haut, Ronchamp. Some say that this free-form chapel is Le Corbusier's masterpiece. ☞ p. 317

FLAVORS

Alain Ducasse. Set in Belle-Epoque salons so stylish even Parisians swoon, this is the stage for the world's most talked-about chef. $$$$ ☞ p. 70

Boyer, Reims. Chef Gérard Boyer's innovative cuisine and opulent setting draw sophisticated diners. $$$$ ☞ p. 280

Le Grand Véfour. Back when Napoléon dined here, this was the most beautiful restaurant in Paris. Guess what? It still is. $$$$ ☞ p. 65

Pierre Gagnaire, Paris. Legendary chef Pierre Gagnaire is sensational here. $$$$ ☞ p. 71

Les Feuillants, Céret. The cuisine underscores the town's superb artistic endowment. $$$ ☞ p. 573

L'Assiette Gourmande, Honfleur. All of Gérard Bonnefoy's food is delectable. $$–$$$ ☞ p. 221

La Corde, Toulouse. This doyen of Toulouse restaurants is hidden in a small 15th-century tower. $$–$$$ ☞ p. 558

La Dame d'Aquitaine, Dijon. The cuisine draws on the best of French regional cooking. $$–$$$ ☞ p. 353

Ⓙ **L'Ami Fritz, Obernai.** The owner-chef serves succulent local specialties at this rustic yet chic spot. $$ ☞ p. 309

Les Muses, Lyon. Dine on Philippe Chavent's inspired dishes atop the opera house. $$ ☞ p. 377

Philippe Detourbe, Paris. The contemporary French cuisine at this glamorous restaurant is spectacular. $$ ☞ p. 73

Chez Yvonne, Strasbourg. This chic *winstub* serves classic Alsatian fare. $ ☞ p. 306

COMFORTS

Costes, Paris. Decorated in *le style Rothschild*, nearly every room at this magnificent hotel is swathed in enough rich fabrics and swags to blanket the Champs-Élysées. $$$$ ☞ p. 76

Ⓑ **La Cour des Loges, Lyon.** This stylish hotel in four Renaissance buildings is a delight. $$$$ ☞ p. 378

La Mirande, Avignon. This hotel at the foot of the Papal Palace is at once grand and intimate. $$$$ ☞ p. 451

Château de la Verrerie, Sancerre. Set in a regal park on the banks of a dreamy lake, this is the very picture of fairytale elegance. $$$–$$$$ ☞ p. 148

Ⓕ **Le Maquis, Porticcio.** It's one of Corsica's finest hotels. $$$–$$$$ ☞ p. 525

Le Vieux Logis, Les Eyzies-de-Tayac. This old Dordogne house is unforgettable; so are the meals. $$$–$$$$ ☞ p. 623

La Maison des Consuls, Mirepoix. This extraordinary hotel is on the medieval central square. $$$ ☞ p. 568

Les Aliberts, Minerve. Don't miss this lovely inn tucked away among the vine-covered hills. $$–$$$ ☞ p. 578

Caron de Beaumarchais, Paris. This Marais hotel is intimate and charming. $$ ☞ p. 80

Ⓔ **La Treille Muscate, Cliousclat.** This gem between Lyon and Avignon has unique rooms and a delightful restaurant. $$ ☞ p. 388

Windsor, Nice. Rooms are decorated by artists; the garden makes this a paradise. $$ ☞ p. 504

MUSEUMS

Fondation Maeght, St-Paul-de-Vence. Mixes a small museum of stunning modern holdings with stylish presentation. ☞ p. 497

Historial de la Grande Guerre, Péronne. An imaginative display of artifacts makes the horror of World War I clear. ☞ p. 268

Louvre, Paris. No matter how many times you've visited, don't miss it. ☞ p. 39

Musée d'Art Moderne, Céret. This modern art museum displays superb French and Catalan works. ☞ p. 572

Ⓖ **Musée Condé, Chantilly.** The illuminated manuscripts, tapestries, and old masters are remarkable. ☞ p. 129

Musée de l'École de Nancy, Nancy. The furniture and glasswork here are classic Art Nouveau. ☞ p. 294

Musée Fesch, Ajaccio. Wonderful works of Italian Old Masters make up the collection. ☞ p. 522

Musée Ingres, Montauban. Works by the French classicist are in the former Bishop's Palace. ☞ p. 562

Palais des Beaux-Arts, Lille. This vast art museum is one of the finest outside Paris. ☞ p. 262

Palais de la Berbie, Albi. A superb Toulouse-Lautrec collection is in this former fortress. ☞ p. 560

1   PARIS

Radiating 2,000 years of history and
culture, Paris intrigues, astonishes, provokes,
overwhelms . . . and gets under your skin.
The City of Light is the apex of architectural
beauty, artistic expression, and culinary
delight, and it knows it. As drop-dead
arrogant as the Arc de Triomphe, as
disarmingly quaint as a lace-curtain bistro, it
seduces newcomers with a Latin-lover
style—and its subtle siren song invites
unhurried exploration of its picture-perfect
streets.

F THERE'S A PROBLEM WITH A TRIP TO PARIS, it's the embarrassment of riches that faces you. No matter which Paris you choose—touristy Paris, historic Paris, fashion-conscious Paris, pretentious bourgeois Paris, thrifty Paris, the legendary bohemian arty Paris of undying attraction—one thing is certain: you will find your own Paris, one that is vivid, exciting, often unforgettable. Wherever you head, your itinerary will prove to be a voyage of discovery. But choosing the Paris of your dreams is a bit like choosing a perfume or cologne. Is it something young and dashing you want, or something elegant and worldly? Something sporty or strictly for glamorous evenings? No matter: they are all here—be it perfumes, famous museums, legendary churches, or romantic cafés. Whether you spend three days or three months in this city, it will always have something new to offer you. This is why the most assiduous explorers of Paris are the Parisians themselves.

Veterans know that Paris is a city of vast, noble perspectives and intimate, ramshackle streets, of formal *espaces vertes* (green open spaces) and of quiet squares. This combination of the pompous and the private is one of the secrets of its perennial pull. Another is its size. Paris is relatively small as capitals go, with distances between many of its major sights and museums invariably walkable.

For the first-timer there will always be several must-dos at the top of the list, but a visit to Paris will never be quite as simple as a quick look at Notre-Dame, the Louvre, and the Eiffel Tower. You'll discover that around every corner, down every *ruelle* (little street) lies a resonance-in-wait. You can stand on the rue du Faubourg St-Honoré at the very spot Edmond Rostand set Ragueneau's pastry shop in *Cyrano de Bergerac*. You can read the letters of Madame de Sévigné in her actual *hôtel particulier*, or private mansion, now the Musée Carnavalet. You can hear Racine resound in the ringing, hair-raising diction of the Comédie Française. You can breathe in the fumes of hubris before the extravagant onyx tomb Napoléon designed for himself. You can try to resist genuflection in the Panthéon, where religion bowed before France's great post-Revolution statesmen. You can gaze through the gates at the school where Voltaire honed his wit and lay a garland on Oscar Wilde's poignant grave at Père Lachaise.

If this is your first trip, there's no harm in taking a guided tour of the city—a perfectly good introduction that will help you get your bearings and provide you with a general impression before you return to explore at leisure the sights that particularly interest you. That route will be marked by your preferences, your curiosity, your guide book, and your state of fatigue. You can wander for hours without getting bored—though not, perhaps, without getting lost. By the time you have quartered the city, you should not only be culturally replete but downright exhausted and hungry, too. Again, take your cue from Parisians, and think out your next move in a sidewalk café. So you've heard stories of a friend who paid $5 for a coffee at a café. That's a bad deal—for only a coffee. But bear in mind that what you're paying for is time—to watch the intricate dramas of Parisian street life unfold in front of you. Hemingway knew the rules; after all, he would have remained just another unknown sportswriter if the waiters of Paris's cafés had hovered around him impatiently.

— Nancy Coons

Pleasures and Pastimes

Cafés

Some would say people-watching is what Paris is all about; and there's no better place to indulge in this pursuit than at a sidewalk café. Favored locales include place St-Michel, boulevard du Montparnasse, and place St-Germain-des-Prés, on the Left Bank; and place de l'Opéra, the Champs-Élysées, and Les Halles, on the Right Bank. But you may enjoy seeking out your own (less expensive) local haunts.

Churches

Paris is rich in churches of two architectural styles: the 15th- to 16th-century overlap of Flamboyant Gothic and Renaissance (at St-Gervais, St-Étienne du Mont, St-Eustache, and St-Séverin) and 17th-century Baroque with domes and two-tiered facades (at Les Invalides, Val de Grâce, and St-Paul–St-Louis). But the city's most enduring religious symbols are medieval (Sainte-Chapelle and the cathedral of Notre-Dame) and 19th-century (Sacré-Coeur and La Madeleine).

Dining

As for dining, well. . . the French wrote the book. Paris is one of the world's great food capitals and a bastion of classic French cuisine. Nonetheless, if you're coming from New York, London, or Los Angeles, where innovative restaurants abound, you may find the French capital a little staid. In fact, a battle is currently being waged between the traditionalists and a remarkable new generation of chefs who are modernizing French cooking—and changing the French culinary landscape. In the end, fads and trends may come and go, but the pragmatic Parisian will always know that this city sets the standards.

Museums

You'll find Leonardos, Monets, and Toulouse-Lautrecs tossed into one bright bouquet when you go museum-hopping in Paris. Alongside the superstars—the Louvre, the Musée d'Orsay, and the newly renovated Centre Pompidou—are such delights as the Musée National du Moyen Age (displaying medieval works of art in the famous Hôtel de Cluny), the regal Louis Quinze splendor of the Musée Nissim de Camondo, and single-artist museums dedicated to the works of Picasso, Rodin, Dalí, and Maillol.

Shopping

Whether you decide to bargain at a flea-market or go whole-snob on the Place Vendôme, shopping opportunities in Paris are endless and geared to every taste. You can spend an afternoon browsing through bookstalls along the Seine, shopping for one of Hermès's famous *foulards* (scarves), touring high-gloss department stores, or bargaining over prices in the sprawling flea markets on the outskirts of town. Everywhere you turn, tastefully displayed wares—luscious chocolates, exquisite clothing, gleaming copper pots—entice the eye and fire the imagination.

EXPLORING PARIS

Revised and updated by Simon Hewitt

As world capitals go, Paris is surprisingly compact. With the exceptions of the Bois de Boulogne and Montmartre, you can easily walk from one major sight to the next. The city is divided in two by the River Seine, with two islands (Ile de la Cité and Ile St-Louis) in the middle. Each bank of the Seine has its own personality; the Rive Droite (Right Bank), with its spacious boulevards and formal buildings, generally has a more genteel feel than the carefree Rive Gauche (Left Bank), to the south. The east–west axis from Châtelet to the Arc de Triomphe, via the rue de Rivoli and the Champs-Élysées, is the Right Bank's principal thoroughfare for sightseeing and shopping.

The city is divided into 20 *arrondissements* (districts). The last two digits of a city zip code (e.g., 75002) will tell you the arrondissement (in this case, the 2e, or 2nd). Although the best method of getting to know Paris is on foot, public transportation—particularly the métro system—is excellent. Buy the *Plan de Paris* booklet, a city map and guide with a street-name index that also shows métro stations. Note that all métro stations have a detailed neighborhood map just inside the entrance (☞ Getting Around *in* Paris A to Z, *below,* for a map of the Paris métro).

Our coverage of Paris is divided into nine neighborhood walks. A few monuments and museums close for lunch, between noon and 2, and many are closed on either Monday or Tuesday: Check before you set off.

Numbers in the text correspond to numbers in the margin and on the Paris and Montmartre maps.

Great Itineraries

A visit to Paris will never be quite as simple as a quick look at a few landmarks. Each *quartier* (neighborhood) has its own treasures, and you should be ready to explore—an enticing prospect in this most elegant of cities. Outlined here are the main areas on which to concentrate, depending on the length of your stay. Bear in mind that the amount of time spent visiting monuments—and museums in particular—is not something you can predict with any certainty, nor would you want to. Just to see the city's large museums, let alone its smaller ones, you probably would need at least a solid week.

IF YOU HAVE 3 DAYS

On your first day begin at the beginning: the Ile de la Cité, settled more than 2,000 years ago and home to the cathedral of Notre-Dame. Take a cue from Victor Hugo and climb the 387 steps of one of its towers to the former haunts of its mythic hunchback, Quasimodo—you'll be rewarded by a great view of Paris framed by the stone gargoyles created by Viollet-le-Duc. Then head several blocks over to marvel at the Sainte-Chapelle, a jewel box of Gothic art shimmering with hundreds of stained-glass panels. After visiting the nearby Conciergerie—the last abode of Queen Marie-Antoinette—walk along the Pont Neuf over the Seine and turn left to reach the greatest museum in the world—the Louvre (keep in mind it's closed Tuesday), home to the *Winged Victory,* the *Venus de Milo,* and the haunting, ironic smile of the *Mona Lisa.* After a lengthy visit, exit into the calm, green Tuileries Gardens, immortalized by the Impressionists, then head west to the city's heart, the place de la Concorde. Walk through the park of the Champs-Élysées, heading over to the Seine and its most Belle Epoque bridge—the Pont Alexandre III—just in time for *l'heure bleu,* or dusk.

On day two tackle picture-postcard Paris, from the Eiffel Tower to the Arc de Triomphe. Start at the Eiffel Tower, then take in some culture at the Palais de Chaillot museums, or the nearby Musée Guimet (for great Asian art) and the Musée d'Art Moderne de la Ville de Paris (for fine modern art). At the place de l'Alma, opt for a ride on the Bateaux Mouches up and down the Seine. Head along avenue Montaigne—home to Dior and numerous other temples of fashion—over to the Champs-Élysées and the Arc de Triomphe. On day three explore the Faubourg St-Honoré, Paris's legendary center of luxe, where world-class shopping and two of Paris's most beautiful urban set pieces—the place Vendome and the Palais Royal—await. Continue north to hit the Grand Boulevards, famed for its sidewalk cafés, the glittering Opéra Garnier—still haunted by the Phantom?—and then enjoy a tranquil afternoon in the chic and rich residential neighborhood around the Parc Monceau, with a stop at the art-filled mansion of the Musée Nissim de Camondo.

IF YOU HAVE 5 DAYS

Follow the three-day itinerary above, then on your fourth day begin at the Musée d'Orsay, home to many of the most famous Impressionist paintings in the world. Pay your respects to Napoléon, at the nearby church of the Invalides, and then to the great sculptor Rodin, at the Musée Rodin, housed in one of the prettiest hôtel particuliers in the city. Head east along the boulevard St-Germain to the picturesque place Furstenberg to visit Atelier Delacroix, the haunt of another great artist. South a few blocks is the Jardin du Luxembourg, perfect for a sylvan time-out. End at Paris's extraordinary Musée National du Moyen-Age, which graces the time-stained Hôtel de Cluny. On your fifth day begin on the Ile St-Louis—the little island sitting next to the larger Ile de la Cité in the Seine. Although there are no major sights to see here, you'll find a charming neighborhood that has more than a touch of the time machine to it. Cross over the Seine to the Marais—one of the city's most venerable quarters, studded with great Baroque and Rococo mansions, many of which are now museums, including the Musée Picasso. Nearby is another mecca for modern-art lovers, the Centre Beaubourg, while those with more traditional tastes will make a beeline for the Musée Carnavalet, or the Paris History Museum, and the magnificent 17th-century Place des Vosges Park.

IF YOU HAVE 7 DAYS

On your sixth day take a vacation from your Paris vacation by heading out for a day trip to Versailles (☞ Chapter 2), built in biceps-flexing Baroque splendor. Don't forget to explore its vast park in order to take in the intimate and charming Petit Trianon and Hameau, which was Marie-Antoinette's toy farm. On your seventh day get up at dawn and hurry up to the Butte (mound) of Montmartre, which graces a dramatic rise over the city. Get here to see the sun rise over the entire city from your perch on the place du Parvis, in front of the basilica of the Sacré-Coeur. Track the spirit of Toulouse-Lautrec through the streets and to the Musée de Montmartre. For your last afternoon, descend back down into the city to either attack some of the city's "other" museums (the Cognacq-Jay and the Maillol), explore Montparnasse, or envy some "permanent" Parisians ensconced in noble marble splendor at the Père Lachaise Cemetery. As an alternative, you can spend your last day on a excursion out to the majestic château in Fontainebleau or the sublime Gothic cathedral in Chartres (☞ Chapter 2).

From Notre-Dame to the Place de la Concorde

No matter how you first approach Paris—historically, geographically, emotionally—it is the River Seine that summons us and that harbors two celebrated islands, the Ile de la Cité and the Ile St-Louis, both at the very center of the city. Of the two, it is the Ile de la Cité that forms the historic ground zero of Paris. It was here that the earliest inhabitants of Paris, the Gaulish tribe of the Parisii, settled in about 250 BC, calling their home Lutetia, meaning "settlement surrounded by water." Today it is famed for the great, brooding cathedral of Notre-Dame, the haunted Conciergerie, and the dazzling Sainte-Chapelle. If Notre-Dame represents Church, another major attraction of this walk—the Louvre—symbolizes State. A succession of French rulers was responsible for filling this immense, symmetrical structure with the world's greatest paintings and works of art, now the largest museum in the world, as well as one of the easiest to get lost in. Beyond the Louvre lies the lovely Tuileries Gardens, the grand place de la Concorde—the very hub of the city—and the Belle Epoque splendor of the Grand Palais and the Pont Alexandre III. All in all, this area comprises some of the most historic and beautiful sights to see in Paris.

A Good Walk

The Place du Parvis Square—regarded by the French as *kilomètre zero*, the spot from which all distances to and from the city are officially measured—makes a fitting setting for **Notre-Dame de Paris** ①, familiar and yet regal, like she (as the priests will tell you) whose name it bears. Explore the interior, then toil up the steps to the towers for a grand view of the heart of Paris. Head behind the cathedral to the Pont de l'Archevêque for the best view of the cathedral, then cross over to the quai de la Tournelle (where Leslie Caron and Gene Kelly so memorably pas-de-deux-ed in *An American in Paris*) for a waterside vista.

Walk along the Seine embankment until the Pont au Double, cross over the Seine once again to the place du Parvis, then head across the square, along rue de la Cité to the rue de la Lutece, where you should make a left and walk to the boulevard du Palais and the imposing **Palais de Justice** ②, the 19th-century Law Court, which harbors the medieval **Sainte-Chapelle** ③—a vision in shimmering stained glass—and the **Conciergerie** ④, the prison where Marie-Antoinette awaited her appointment with Madame Guillotine. At the end of quai de l'Horloge is the place Dauphine, opposite which, on the other side of the Pont Neuf, is the **square du Vert-Galant** ⑤, with its proud equestrian statue of Henri IV. On the quay side of the square, vedette motorboats start their tours along the Seine.

Cross the **Pont Neuf** ⑥—the New Bridge, confusingly so called because it is actually the oldest bridge in Paris—to the Rive Droite and make for the **Louvre** ⑦, the vast museum on the quai du Louvre, entering through the grand East Front and head through the Cour Carrée to the I. M. Pei glass-pyramid entry. After viewing some of the greatest artworks in the world, exit through the **Carrousel du Louvre** ⑧ complex, a posh underground shopping mall, to the manicured lawns of the **Jardin des Tuileries** ⑨, or Tuileries Gardens. Standing sentinel is the **Musée du Jeu de Paume** ⑩, host to outstanding exhibits of contemporary art. To the west lies one of the world's grandest squares, the **place de la Concorde** ⑪, centered by a grand Egyptian Obelisk (with newly gilded top). Continue up the Champs-Élysées to avenue Winston-Churchill to the **Grand Palais** ⑫, whose rear half houses the **Palais de la Découverte** ⑬, with Paris's planetarium and exhibits on science and technology. For a romantic finale, head over to the Seine and the floridly Belle Epoque Pont Alexandre-III.

TIMING

Allowing for toiling up towers, dancing down quays, and musing at the *Mona Lisa*, this walk will take a full day—enabling you to reach Pont Alexandre-III just before sundown. Of course, if you want to do full justice to the vast collections of the Louvre, you could easily spend a week there and not see it all. If you return to ogle the museum, visit in the mornings, when it is less crowded (note that it is closed Tuesday).

Sights to See

⑧ **Carrousel du Louvre.** Part of the early '90s Louvre renovation program, this subterranean shopping complex is centered on an inverted glass pyramid (overlooked by the regional Ile-de-France tourist office) and contains a wide range of stores, spaces for fashion shows, an auditorium, and a huge parking garage. At lunchtime, museum visitors rush to the mall-style food court, where fast food goes international. Note that you can get into or exit from the museum (and avoid some lines) by entering through the mall. ⊠ *Entrances on rue de Rivoli or by Arc du Carrousel. Métro: Palais-Royal.*

❹ Conciergerie. This turreted medieval building by the Seine was originally part of the royal palace on Ile de la Cité. Most people know it, however, as the prison whence Danton, Robespierre, and Marie-Antoinette were bundled off to the guillotine. You can visit Marie-Antoinette's cell, the guardroom, and the monumental Salle des Gens d'Armes (Hall of Men-at-Arms). ⊠ *1 quai de l'Horloge,* ☎ *01–53–73–78–50.* 🎟 *25 frs; joint ticket with Sainte-Chapelle 50 frs.* ☉ *Spring-fall, daily 9:30–6:30; winter, daily 10–5. Métro: Cité.*

⑫ Grand Palais (Grand Palace). With its curved glass roof, the Grand Palais is unmistakable when approached from either the Seine or the Champs-Élysées and forms an attractive duo with the **Petit Palais,** on the other side of avenue Winston-Churchill. Although undergoing renovation until 2002, it also houses the Palais de la Découverte (☞ *below*)—home to the city planetarium—which can be visited. ⊠ *Av. Winston-Churchill,* ☎ *01–42–65–12–73.* 🎟 *27 frs.* ☉ *Tues.–Sun. 10–5:40. Métro: Champs-Élysées–Clemenceau.*

🖐 **❾ Jardin des Tuileries** (Tuileries Gardens). Immortalized in Impressionist canvases by Monet and Pisarro, the Tuileries Gardens are typically French: formal and neatly patterned, with rows of trees, gravel paths, flower beds, and a host of statues from varying eras. This is a delightful place to stroll and survey the surrounding cityscape. *Métro: Concorde, Tuileries.*

❼ Louvre. Leonardo da Vinci's *Mona Lisa* and *Virgin and St. Anne,* Veronese's *Marriage at Cana,* Giorgione's *Concert Champêtre,* Delacroix's *Liberty Guiding the People,* Whistler's *Mother (Arrangement in Black and White)*. . . you get the picture. This is the world's greatest art museum and certainly one of the largest. Today, after three decades of renovations, the Louvre is now a coherent, unified structure, and search parties no longer need to be sent in to bring you out. Originally built by Philippe-Auguste in the 13th century as a fortress, it was not until the reign of pleasure-loving François I, 300 years later, that today's Louvre gradually began to take shape. Through the years Henri IV (1589–1610), Louis XIII (1610–43), Louis XIV (1643–1715), Napoléon (1804–14), and Napoléon III (1852–70) all contributed to its construction. The recent history of the Louvre centers on I. M. Pei's glass pyramid, unveiled in March 1989, and numerous renovations.

The number one attraction is Leonardo da Vinci's enigmatic *Mona Lisa* (*La Joconde,* to the French); be forewarned that you will find it encased in glass and surrounded by a mob of tourists. (You might be better off forsaking her rather dour image and plunking yourself in front of Leonardo's *Virgin and St. Anne,* which contains two of the most beautiful faces the artist ever painted.) The collections are divided into seven sections: Asian antiquities; Egyptian antiquities; Greek and Roman antiquities; sculpture; paintings, prints, and drawings; furniture; and objets d'art. Don't try to see it all at once; try, instead, to make repeat visits—the admission is nearly half price on Sunday and after 3 PM on other days. (Unless you plan on going to a number of museums every day, the one-, three-, and five-day tourist museum passes probably aren't worth your money since you could easily spend a whole day at the Louvre alone.) Some other highlights of the paintings are *Shepherds in Arcadia,* by Nicolas Poussin (1594–1665); *The Oath of the Horatii,* by Jacques-Louis David (1748–1825); and *La Grande Odalisque,* by Jean-Auguste-Dominique Ingres (1780–1867). The French crown jewels (in the objets d'art section of the Richelieu

Wing) include the mind-boggling 186-carat Regent diamond. The Nike, or *Winged Victory of Samothrace,* seems poised for flight at the top of the stairs, and another much-loved piece of sculpture is Michelangelo's pair of *Slaves,* intended for the tomb of Pope Julius II. These can be admired in the Denon Wing, where a new medieval and Renaissance sculpture section is housed partly in the former imperial stables. In 1997 new rooms for Persian, Arab, Greek, and Egyptian art were opened. Come as early as possible to avoid the crowds. ⊠ *Palais du Louvre (other than the main entrance at the Pei pyramid, you can also enter through the East Front and through the Carrousel du Louvre mall on rue de Rivoli),* ☎ *01–40–20–51–51.* ⊑ *45 frs; 26 frs after 3* PM *and on Sun.; free 1st Sun. of month.* ☉ *Thurs.–Sun. 9–6, Mon. and Wed. 9* AM–*9:45* PM. *Some sections open limited days. Métro: Palais-Royal.*

⑩ **Musée du Jeu de Paume.** At the entrance to the Tuileries Garden, this museum is an ultramodern white-walled showcase for excellent temporary exhibits of bold contemporary art. Its adjoining sister museum, the Musé de l'Orangerie—home to Claude Monet's largest *Water Lilies*—is closed for renovation until 2002. ⊠ *1 pl. de la Concorde,* ☎ *01–42–60–69–69.* ⊑ *38 frs.* ☉ *Tues. noon–9:30, Wed.–Fri. noon–7, weekends 10–7. Métro: Concorde.*

★ ❶ **Notre-Dame.** Looming above the large, pedestrian place du Parvis is Notre-Dame Cathedral, the most enduring symbol of Paris. Begun in 1163, it was not completed until 1345. The facade seems perfectly proportioned until you notice that the north (left) tower is wider than the south tower. The south tower houses the great bell of Notre-Dame, as tolled by Quasimodo, Victor Hugo's fictional hunchback. The cathedral interior, with its vast proportions, soaring nave, and soft multicolor light filtering through the stained-glass windows, inspires awe despite the inevitable throngs of tourists. Visit early in the morning, when the cathedral is at its lightest and least crowded. Window space is limited and filled with shimmering stained glass; the circular rose windows in the transept are particularly delicate. The 387-step climb up the towers is worth the effort for a perfect view of the famous gargoyles and the heart of Paris. ⊠ *Pl. du Parvis.* ⊑ *Towers 35 frs.* ☉ *Cathedral 8* AM–*7* PM; *towers summer, daily 9:30–7:30; winter, daily 10–5. Métro: Cité.*

☕ ⑬ **Palais de la Découverte** (Palace of Discovery). A planetarium, working models, and scientific and technological exhibits on such topics as optics, biology, nuclear physics, and electricity make up this science museum behind the Grand Palais. ⊠ *Av. Franklin-D.-Roosevelt,* ☎ *01–56–43–20–21.* ⊑ *30 frs, 15 frs extra for planetarium.* ☉ *Tues.–Sat. 9:30–6, Sun. 10–7. Métro: Champs-Élysées–Clemenceau.*

❷ **Palais de Justice** (Law Courts). In about 1860 the city law courts were built by Baron Haussmann in his characteristically weighty Neoclassical style. You can wander around the buildings, watch the bustle of the lawyers, or attend a court hearing. But the real interest here is the medieval part of the complex, spared by Haussmann: La Conciergerie and Ste-Chapelle (☞ *above* and *below,* respectively). ⊠ *Bd. du Palais. Métro: Cité.*

⑪ **Place de la Concorde.** This majestic square at the foot of the Champs-Élysées was laid out in the 1770s, but there was nothing in the way of peace or concord about its early years. Between 1793 and 1795 more than a thousand victims, including Louis XVI and Marie-Antoinette, were slashed into oblivion at the guillotine, prompting Madame Roland to famously cry, "Liberty, what crimes are committed in thy name." The top of the 107-ft **Obelisk**—a present from the viceroy of Egypt in 1833—was regilded in 1998. *Métro: Concorde.*

❻ Pont Neuf (New Bridge). Crossing the Ile de la Cité, just behind square du Vert-Galant, is the oldest bridge in Paris, confusingly called the New Bridge, or Pont Neuf. It was completed in 1607 and was the first bridge in the city to be built without houses lining either side. *Métro: Pont-Neuf.*

★ **❸ Sainte-Chapelle** (Holy Chapel). One of the most magical sights in European medieval art, this chapel was built by Louis IX (1226–70; later canonized as St. Louis) in the 1240s to house what he believed to be Christ's Crown of Thorns, purchased from Emperor Baldwin of Constantinople. A dark and gloomy lower chapel is the prelude to the shimmering upper one, whose walls consist of little but dazzling 13th-century stained glass. Think of it as an enormous magic lantern, illuminating 1,130 figures from the Bible, to create—as one writer put it—"the most marvelous colored and moving air ever held within four walls." ⊠ 4 *bd. du Palais,* ☎ *01-43-54-30-09 for concert information.* ☎ *35 frs; joint ticket with Conciergerie 50 frs.* ☉ *Apr.–Sept., daily 9:30–6:30; Oct.–Mar., daily 10–5. Métro: Cité.*

❺ Square du Vert-Galant. The equine statue of the Vert-Galant himself—amorous adventurer Henri IV—surveys this leafy square at the western end of the Ile de la Cité. Henri, king of France from 1589 until his assassination in 1610, is probably best remembered for his cynical remark that *"Paris vaut bien une messe"* ("Paris is worth a mass"), a reference to his readiness to renounce Protestantism to gain the throne of predominantly Catholic France. A fine spot to linger on a sunny afternoon, the square is also the departure point for the glass-top vedettes (tour boats) on the Seine (at the bottom of the steps to the right). *Métro: Pont-Neuf.*

From the Eiffel Tower to the Arc de Triomphe

The Eiffel Tower lords it over southwest Paris, and wherever you are on this walk, you can see it looming overhead. Water is the second theme: fountains playing beneath place du Trocadéro and tours along the Seine on a Bateau Mouche. Museums are the third: The area around Trocadéro is full of them. And style is the fourth, but not just because the buildings here are overwhelmingly elegant—this is also the center of haute couture, with the top names in world fashion all congregated around avenue Montaigne, only a brief walk from the Champs-Élysées, to the north.

A Good Walk

The verdant expanse of the Champ de Mars, once used as a parade ground by the École Militaire (still in use as a military academy and therefore not open to the public), then as site of the World Exhibitions, provides a thrilling approach to the iron symbol of Paris, the **Tour Eiffel** (Eiffel Tower) ⑭. As you get nearer, the Eiffel Tower's colossal bulk (it's far bigger and sturdier than pictures suggest) becomes increasingly evident.

Across the Seine from the Eiffel Tower, above stylish gardens and fountains on the heights of place du Trocadéro, is the Art Deco **Palais de Chaillot** ⑮, a cultural center containing three museums: an anthropology museum, a maritime museum, and a museum of French architecture. The area around place du Trocadéro is a feast for museum lovers. The **Musée Guimet** ⑯, on place d'Iéna, contains three floors of Indo-Chinese and Far Eastern art and reopened in fall 2000 after extensive renovation. Farther down the avenue du Président-Wilson is the **Musée d'Art Moderne de la Ville de Paris** ⑰, which has temporary exhibits as well as a permanent collection of modern art.

Montmartre
see detail map

bd. de Clichy
pl. Pigalle
bd. de Rochechouart
bd. Barbès
bd. de la Chapelle

rue d'Amsterdam
rue de Clichy

Gare du Nord

rue La Fayette

Gare de l'Est

Canal St-Martin

av. Jean Jaurès
Canal de l'Ourcq

St-Lazare
rue de Châteaudun

bd. de la Villette

bd. Haussmann
bd. des Italiens
bd. Montmartre
Poissonnière
rue du Fg-Poissonnière
rue Réaumur

bd. de la Madeleine
av. de l'Opéra
rue de Richelieu

rue Étienne Marcel
rue Réaumur
bd. St-Denis
bd. St-Martin
bd. de Strasbourg
bd. de Magenta

rue du Faubourg-du-Temple
pl. de la République
av. de la République

de Rivoli
rue du Louvre
r. Berger
St-Honoré
rue de Rivoli
rue St-Denis
rue St-Martin
rue de Turbigo
rue du Temple
rue Rambuteau
rue des Archives
rue des Francs-Bourgeois

bd. Beaumarchais
bd. Voltaire
bd. Richard-Lenoir
r. de la Roquette
av. Ledru Rollin

Tuileries
Seine
France
pont du Carrousel
l'Université r. Jacob
pont des Arts
pont Neuf
Ile de la Cité
quai du Louvre
quai de l'Hôtel de Ville
pl. du Châtelet
rue de Rivoli
rue St-Antoine

Carrefour de Buci
pl. St-Michel
St-Germain
Ile St-Louis
bd. Henri IV
rue du Faubourg St-Antoine
av. Ledru Rollin

Palais du Luxembourg
Jardin du Luxembourg
pl. Maubert
quai de la Tournelle
pont de Sully
Seine

bd. Rennes
bd. Bonaparte
bd. St-Michel
bd. St-Jacques
rue Monge
rue Descartes
rue Mouffetard
rue Lacépède
av. Ledru Rollin
Daumesnil
bd. Diderot

Gare de Lyon

rue Lacépède
Gare d'Austerlitz

bd. Raspail
av. de l'Observatoire

Continue down to bustling place de l'Alma, where a giant golden torch appears to be saluting the memory of Diana, Princess of Wales, who died in a car crash in the tunnel below in August 1997. Down the sloping side road just beyond the Pont de l'Alma (Alma Bridge) is the embarkation point of the **Bateaux Mouches** ⑱ and their tours of Paris by water. Stylish avenue Montaigne, home to many of the leading Paris fashion houses (☞ Shopping, *below*), runs up from place de l'Alma toward the **Champs-Élysées** ⑲. Local charm is not a feature of this sector of western Paris, though renovation has gone some way toward restoring the avenue's legendary elegance, particularly as you head up the grand promenade to that icon of Paris, the **Arc de Triomphe** ⑳. Through the arch to the west lies Manhattan-on-the-Seine—the skyscraper complex of **La Défense** ㉒. For a more tranquil respite, head southwest from the Arc down the Avenue Foch—one of Paris's most fashionable addresses—to the sylvan glades of Paris's largest park, the **Bois de Boulogne** ㉑.

TIMING

You can probably cover this walk in a couple of hours, but if you wish to ascend the Eiffel Tower, take a trip along the Seine, or visit any of the myriad museums along the way, you'd be best off allowing most of the day.

Sights to See

★ ⑳ **Arc de Triomphe.** This huge arch, standing 164 ft, was planned by Napoléon but not finished until 1836, 20 years after the end of his rule. It is decorated with some magnificent sculptures by François Rude, such as the *Departure of the Volunteers*, better known as *La Marseillaise*, to the right of the arch when viewed from the Champs-Élysées. A small museum halfway up the arch is devoted to its history. France's Unknown Soldier is buried beneath the archway; the flame is rekindled every evening at 6:30. ✉ *Pl. Charles-de-Gaulle*, ☎ *01–55–37–73–77.* 🔳 *40 frs.* ☯ *Spring–autumn, daily 9:30 AM–11 PM; winter, daily 10 AM–10:30 PM. Métro, RER: Charles-de-Gaulle–Étoile.*

⑱ **Bateaux Mouches.** These popular motorboats set off on their hour-long tours of Paris waters regularly (every half hour in summer). ✉ *Pl. de l'Alma*, ☎ *01–40–76–99–99.* 🔳 *40 frs. Métro: Alma-Marceau.*

㉑ **Bois de Boulogne.** Class and style have been associated with this 2,200-acre wood—known to Parisians as Le Bois—ever since it was landscaped into an upper-class playground by Baron Haussmann in the 1850s. Today, the park is home to rowers, joggers, strollers, riders, picnickers, the racetracks of **Longchamp** and **Auteuil,** the **Roland Garros** stadium (where the French Open tennis tournament is held in late May), and—after dark—ladies of the night. *Main entrance at bottom of av. Foch. Métro: Porte Maillot, Porte Dauphine, Porte d'Auteuil; Bus 244.*

⑲ **Champs-Élysées.** The 2-km (1-mi) Champs-Élysées was originally laid out in the 1660s by landscape gardener André Le Nôtre as parkland sweeping away from the Tuileries. In an attempt to reestablish this thoroughfare as one of the world's most beautiful avenues, the city planted extra trees, broadened sidewalks, refurbished Art Nouveau newsstands, and clamped down on garish storefronts. *Métro: George-V, Champs-Élysées–Clemenceau, Franklin-D.-Roosevelt.*

㉒ **La Défense.** This is the skyscraper district of Paris, located just west of Paris (thankfully) across the Seine from Neuilly. Sights here include a spherical IMAX cinema, the **Musée de l'Automobile** for car fans, and, crowning the main plaza, the **Grande Arche de La Défense,** an enormous open cube of a building, where tubular glass elevators whisk you 360 ft to the top. ✉ *Parvis de La Défense*, ☎ *01–49–07–27–57.* 🔳

Arch 43 frs; auto museum 35 frs. ☉ *Arch daily 10–7, auto museum daily 12:35–7:30. Métro, RER: Grande Arche de La Défense.*

⑰ Musée d'Art Moderne de la Ville de Paris (City Museum of Modern Art). Both temporary exhibits and a permanent collection of top-quality 20th-century art can be found at this museum. It takes over, chronologically speaking, where the Musée d'Orsay (☞ *below*) leaves off: Among the earliest works are Fauve paintings by Vlaminck and Derain, followed by Picasso's early experiments in Cubism. ⊠ *11 av. du Président-Wilson,* ☎ *01–53–67–40–00.* 🎫 *27 frs.* ☉ *Tues.–Fri. 10–5:30, weekends 10–6:45. Métro: Iéna.*

⑯ Musée Guimet. This Belle Epoque museum was founded by Lyonnais industrialist Émile Guimet, who traveled around the world in the late 19th century amassing Indo-Chinese and Far Eastern objets d'art, plus a fabled collection of Cambodian art. After a massive renovation, the museum reopened in fall 2000. ⊠ *6 pl. d'Iéna,* ☎ *01–45–05–00–98.* ☉ *Wed.–Mon. 9:45–6. Métro: Iéna.*

⑮ Palais de Chaillot (Chaillot Palace). This honey-color, Art Deco culture center facing the Seine, perched atop tumbling gardens with sculpture and fountains, was built in the 1930s and houses three museums: the **Musée de l'Homme** (Museum of Mankind) with an array of prehistoric artifacts; the **Musée de la Marine** (Maritime Museum), with its salty collection of model ships, marine paintings, and naval paraphernalia; and the **Musée des Monuments Français** (Museum of French Monuments), closed for renovation until 2003. ⊠ *Pl. du Trocadéro,* ☎ *01–44–05–72–72 Museum of Mankind; 01–53–65–69–69 Maritime Museum.* 🎫 *Museum of Mankind 30 frs; Maritime Museum 38 frs.* ☉ *Museum of Mankind Wed.–Mon. 9:45–5:15; Maritime Museum Wed.–Mon. 10–6. Métro: Trocadéro.*

★ ℭ ⑭ Tour Eiffel (Eiffel Tower). Known to the French as La Tour Eiffel (pronounced ef-*el*), Paris's most famous landmark was built by Gustave Eiffel for the World Exhibition of 1889, the centennial of the French Revolution, and was still in good shape to celebrate its own 100th birthday. Such was Eiffel's engineering wizardry that even in the strongest winds his tower never sways more than 4½ inches. If you're full of energy, stride up the stairs as far as the third deck. If you want to go to the top, you'll have to take the elevator. To honor the new millennium, the Tower was transformed into a giant sparkler one second after midnight on January 1st, 2000. The good news is that it will continue to light up every night until January 1st, 2001—every hour on the hour, for ten glittering minutes, from dusk until one AM. ⊠ *Quai Branly,* ☎ *01–44–11–23–23.* 🎫 *By elevator: 2nd floor, 21 frs; 3rd floor, 43 frs; 4th floor, 60 frs. By foot: 2nd and 3rd floors only, 15 frs.* ☉ *July–Aug., daily 9 AM–midnight; Sept.–June, daily 9 AM–11 PM. Métro: Bir-Hakeim; RER: Champ-de-Mars.*

The Faubourg St-Honoré

The Faubourg St-Honoré, north of the Champs-Élysées and the Tuileries, is synonymous with style—as you will see as you progress from the President's Palace, past a wealth of art galleries, to the monumental Madeleine church and on to stately place Vendôme, home to the Ritz and the world's top jewelers. Leading names in modern fashion are found farther east on place des Victoires, close to what was for centuries the gastronomic heart of Paris: Les Halles (pronounced lay-*al*), once the city's main market. In 1969 Les Halles was closed and replaced by a park and a modern shopping mall, the Forum des Halles. The brash modernity of the Forum stands in contrast to the august church of St-

Eustache nearby. Similarly, the incongruous black-and-white columns, an in-situ artwork created by a Minimalist artist in the 1980s, in the classical courtyard of Richelieu's neighboring Palais-Royal present a further case of daring modernity—or architectural vandalism, depending on your point of view.

A Good Walk

Start in front of the most important home in France: the **Palais de l'Élysée** ㉓, or Presidential Palace. Crash barriers and gold-braided guards keep visitors at bay; in fact, there's more to see in the plethora of art galleries and luxury fashion boutiques lining rue du Faubourg–St-Honoré as you head east. Pass the British Embassy and turn left onto rue Boissy-d'Anglas; then cut right through an archway into Village Royal, a restored courtyard with several trendy boutiques. It leads to rue Royale, a classy street lined with jewelry stores. Looming to the left is the **Église de la Madeleine** ㉔, a sturdy Neoclassical edifice.

Cross boulevard de la Madeleine and take rue Duphot down to rue St-Honoré, where you'll pass Notre-Dame de l'Assomption, noted for its huge dome and solemn interior. Continue to rue de Castiglione and then head left to **place Vendôme** ㉕, one of the world's most opulent squares. Return to rue St-Honoré and follow it to the mighty church of **St-Roch** ㉖.

Take the next right onto rue des Pyramides and cross place des Pyramides, with its gilded statue of Joan of Arc on horseback, to the northernmost wing of the Louvre. Stay on arcaded rue de Rivoli to place du Palais-Royal. On the corner of rue de Richelieu and rue de Rivoli is the **Comédie Française** ㉗, the time-honored setting for performances of classical French drama. To the right of the theater is the unobtrusive entrance to the **Palais-Royal** ㉘; its courtyard is a surprising oasis in the heart of the city. Cross through the Palais-Royal gardens and turn right into rue des Petits-Champs to reach circular **place des Victoires** ㉙: That's Louis XIV riding the plunging steed in the center of the square. Head south down rue Croix-des-Petits-Champs, past the nondescript Banque de France on your right, and take the second street on the left to the circular **Bourse du Commerce** ㉚, or Commercial Exchange. Alongside it is the 100-ft-high fluted Colonne de Ruggieri.

You don't need to scale Ruggieri's column to spot the bulky outline of the church of **St-Eustache** ㉛, a curious architectural hybrid of Gothic and classical. The vast site next to St-Eustache is now occupied by a garden, the Jardin des Halles, and the modern **Forum des Halles** ㉜ shopping mall. Rue Berger leads from allée de St-Jean-de-Perse to the Square des Innocents, with its handsome Renaissance fountain. Head south along rue St-Denis from the far end of Square des Innocents to place du Châtelet, with its theaters, fountain, and the Tour St-Jacques, the tower looming up to your left. Turn right along the Seine to reach **St-Germain l'Auxerrois** ㉝, opposite the Louvre, once the French royal family's parish church.

TIMING

With brief visits to churches and monuments, this walk should take from three to four hours. On a nice day you may want to linger in the gardens of the Palais-Royal, and on a cold day you may want to indulge in an unbelievably thick hot chocolate at the Angélina tearoom.

Sights to See

㉚ **Bourse du Commerce** (Commercial Exchange). The 18th-century circular, shallow-dome Commercial Exchange, near Les Halles, began life as a corn exchange; Victor Hugo waggishly likened it to a jockey's cap without the peak. ⊠ *Rue de Viarmes. Métro or RER: Les Halles.*

㉗ Comédie Française. This theater is the setting for performances of classical French drama. The building itself dates from 1790, but the Comédie Française company was created by that most theatrical of French monarchs, Louis XIV, back in 1680. ✉ *Pl. Colette,* ☎ *01–44–58–15–15. Métro: Palais-Royal.*

㉔ Église de La Madeleine (Church of La Madeleine). With its rows of uncompromising columns, this sturdy neoclassical edifice—designed in 1814 but not consecrated until 1842—looks more like a Greek temple than a Christian church. In fact, La Madeleine, as it is known, was nearly selected as Paris's first train station (the site of the Gare St-Lazare, just up the road, was chosen instead). Inside, the walls are richly and harmoniously decorated; gold glints through the murk. The portico's majestic Corinthian colonnade supports a gigantic pediment with a frieze of the Last Judgment. ✉ *Pl. de la Madeleine.* ☉ *Mon.–Sat. 7:30–7, Sun. 8–7. Métro: Madeleine.*

㉜ Forum des Halles. Les Halles, the iron-and-glass halls that made up the central Paris food market, were closed in 1969 and replaced in the late '70s by the Forum des Halles, a mundane shopping mall. Unfortunately, much of its plastic, concrete, glass, and mock-marble exterior is already showing signs of wear and tear. ✉ *Main entrance on rue Pierre-Lescot. Métro: Les Halles; RER: Châtelet–Les Halles.*

NEED A BREAK? Founded in 1903, **Angélina** (✉ 226 rue de Rivoli, ☎ 01–42–60–82–00) is an elegant *salon de thé* (tearoom), famous for its *chocolat africain,* a jug of hot chocolate served with whipped cream (irresistible even in summer).

㉓ Palais de l'Élysée (Élysée Palace). This "palace," known to the French simply as L'Élysée, where the French president lives, works, and receives official visitors, was originally constructed as a private mansion in 1718 and has housed presidents only since 1873. Although you can catch a glimpse of the palace forecourt and facade through the Faubourg St-Honoré gateway, it is difficult to get much idea of the building's size or of the extensive gardens that stretch back to the Champs-Élysées. ✉ *55 rue du Faubourg–St-Honoré.* ☉ *Not open to public. Métro: Miromesnil.*

㉘ Palais-Royal (Royal Palace). The buildings of this former palace—royal only in that all-powerful Cardinal Richelieu (1585–1642) magnanimously bequeathed them to Louis XIII—date from the 1630s. Today the Palais-Royal is home to the French Ministry of Culture and private apartments (Colette and Cocteau were two lucky former owners), and its buildings are not open to the public. You can, however, visit its colonnaded courtyard and classical gardens, a tranquil oasis prized by Parisians. ✉ *Pl. du Palais-Royal. Métro: Palais-Royal.*

㉕ Place Vendôme. Mansart's rhythmic, perfectly proportioned example of 17th-century urban architecture shines in all its golden-stone splendor. The square is a fitting showcase for the deluxe Ritz Hotel and the cluster of jewelry display windows found here. Napoléon had the square's central column made from the melted bronze of 1,200 cannons captured at the Battle of Austerlitz in 1805. There he is, perched vigilantly at the top. *Métro: Opéra.*

㉙ Place des Victoires. This circular square, now home to many of the city's top fashion boutiques, was laid out in 1685 by Jules-Hardouin Mansart in honor of the military victories (*victoires*) of Louis XIV. The Sun King gallops along on a bronze horse in the middle. *Métro: Sentier.*

㉛ St-Eustache. A huge church, it was built as the people's Right Bank reply to Notre-Dame, though St-Eustache dates from a couple of hundred years later. The church is a curious architectural hybrid: With the exception of the feeble west front, added between 1754 and 1788, construction lasted from 1532 to 1637, spanning the decline of the Gothic style and the emergence of the Renaissance. ⊠ *2 rue du Jour,* ☎ *01–46–27–89–21 for concert information.* ☉ *Daily 8–7. Métro: Les Halles; RER: Châtelet–Les Halles.*

③③ **St-Germain l'Auxerrois.** Until 1789 St-Germain was used by the French royal family as its parish church, in the days when the adjacent Louvre was a palace rather than a museum. The facade reveals the influence of 15th-century Flamboyant Gothic style, while the fluted columns around the choir, the area surrounding the altar, demonstrate the triumph of Classicism. ⊠ *Pl. du Louvre. Métro: Louvre-Rivoli.*

②⑥ **St-Roch.** Designed by Lemercier in 1653 but completed only in the 1730s, this huge church is almost as long as Notre-Dame (138 yards) thanks to Hardouin-Mansart's domed Lady Chapel at the far end. ⊠ *Rue St-Honoré. Métro: Tuileries.*

The Grand Boulevards

The focal point of this walk is the uninterrupted avenue that runs in almost a straight line from St-Augustin, the city's grandest Second Empire church, to place de la République, whose very name symbolizes the ultimate downfall of the imperial regime. The avenue's name changes six times along the way, which is why Parisians refer to it as the *Grands Boulevards* (plural). The makeup of the neighborhoods along the Grand Boulevards changes steadily as you head east from the posh 8ᵉ arrondissement toward working-class east Paris. The *grands magasins* (department stores) at the start of the walk epitomize upscale Paris shopping. They stand on boulevard Haussmann, named in honor of the regional prefect who oversaw the reconstruction of the city in the 1850s and 1860s. The opulent Opéra Garnier, just past the grands magasins, is the architectural showpiece of the period (often termed the Second Empire and corresponding to the rule of Napoléon III).

A Good Walk

Take the métro to Monceau and step through gold-top iron gates to enter the enchantingly idyllic **Parc Monceau** ③④ by the domed Chartres Pavilion. At the middle of the park, head left to avenue Velasquez—home to some of the most regal mansions in the city—past the **Musée Cernuschi** ③⑤, home to Chinese art from Neolithic pottery to contemporary paintings, to boulevard Malesherbes. Turn right on boulevard Malesherbes and right again on rue de Monceau to reach the **Musée Nissim de Camondo** ③⑥, whose aristocratic interior reflects the upbeat tone of this haughty part of Paris.

Turn left down rue de Téhéran, left along avenue de Messine, and left again on rue de Laborde to get to the innovative iron-and-stone church of **St-Augustin** ③⑦. Cross the square in front and turn left along boulevard Haussmann to Square Louis-XVI, the original burial spot of Louis XVI and Marie-Antoinette and home to a mausoleum in their honor. Some 300 yards farther down boulevard Haussmann, you'll find the *grands magasins*: Paris's most renowned department stores. First come the cupolas of Au Printemps, then Galeries Lafayette. Opposite looms the massive bulk of the **Opéra Garnier** ③⑧—sumptuous home of the fictional Phantom.

Boulevard des Capucines, lined with cinemas and restaurants, heads left from in front of the Opera, becoming boulevard des Italiens before colliding with boulevard Haussmann. A left here down rue Drouot will take you to the **Hôtel Drouot** ③⑨, Paris's central auction house. Rue

Rossini leads from Drouot to rue de la Grange-Batelière. Halfway along on the right is the Passage Jouffroy, one of the many covered galleries that honeycomb the center of Paris. Head down to boulevard Montmartre and cross to passage des Panoramas, leading to rue St-Marc. Turn right, then left down rue Vivienne to find the foursquare, colonnaded **Bourse** ⑩, the Paris Stock Exchange.

Head east along rue Réaumur, once the heart of the French newspaper industry—stationery shops still abound—and cross rue Montmartre. Take the second left up rue de Cléry, a narrow street that is the exclusive domain of fabric wholesalers. Continue up rue de Cléry as far as rue des Degrés—not a street at all but a 14-step stairway—then look for the crooked church tower of **Notre-Dame de Bonne-Nouvelle** ⑪, hemmed in by rickety housing. The porticoed entrance is around the corner on rue de la Lune, which leads back to the Grand Boulevards, by now going under the name of boulevard de Bonne-Nouvelle.

The newly cleaned Porte St-Denis, a triumphal arch, looms up ahead, and a little farther on is the smaller but similar Porte St-Martin. From here take rue St-Martin south past the Conservatoire National des Techniques, a technical museum housed partly in the former church of St-Martin. Then cross rue Réaumur to the high, narrow, late-Gothic church of **St-Nicolas des Champs** ⑫. Head left on rue de Turbigo, past the cloister ruins and Renaissance gateway that embellish the far side of St-Nicolas. Some 400 yards along on the right is the Baroque church of **Ste-Élisabeth** ⑬; shortly after, you'll reach place de la République. It's a short métro ride from here to the city's most famous cemetery, the **Cimetière du Père Lachaise** ⑭, or to the **Parc de La Villette** ⑮, with its postmodern science and music museums.

TIMING

The distance between Parc Monceau and place de la République is almost 6 km (4 mi), which will probably take you four hours to walk, including coffee breaks and window-shopping. Allot a few additional hours, if not a whole morning or afternoon, to visit the Père Lachaise Cemetery or the Parc de La Villette. Or return to these on another day.

Sights to See

⑩ **Bourse** (Stock Exchange). The Paris Stock Exchange, a serene, colonnaded 19th-century building, is a far cry from Wall Street. Take your passport if you want to tour it. ✉ *Rue Vivienne.* 🎫 *30 frs.* ☉ *Guided tours only (in French), weekdays every ½ hr 1:15–3:45. Métro: Bourse.*

⑭ **Cimetière du Père Lachaise** (Father Lachaise Cemetery). Cemeteries may not be your idea of the ultimate attraction, but this is the largest and most interesting in Paris. It forms a veritable necropolis, with cobbled avenues and tombs competing in pomposity and originality. Leading incumbents include Jim Morrison, Frédéric Chopin, Marcel Proust, Edith Piaf, and Gertrude Stein. Get a map at the entrance and track them down. ✉ *Entrances on rue des Rondeaux, bd. de Ménilmontant, rue de la Réunion.* ☉ *Apr.–Sept., daily 8–6, Oct.–Mar., daily 8–5. Métro: Gambetta, Philippe-Auguste, Père Lachaise.*

⑨ **Hôtel Drouot.** Paris's central auction house has everything from stamps and toy soldiers to Renoirs and 18th-century commodes. The 16 salesrooms make for fascinating browsing, and there's no obligation to bid. ✉ *9 rue Drouot,* ☎ *01–48–00–20–00.* ☉ *Mid-Sept.–mid-July, viewings Mon.–Sat. 11–noon and 2–6, with auctions starting at 2. Métro: Richelieu-Drouot.*

⑤ **Musée Cernuschi.** The collection includes Chinese art from Neolithic pottery (3rd century BC) to funeral statuary, painted 8th-century silks, and contemporary paintings, as well as ancient Persian bronze objects.

✉ *7 av. Velasquez,* ☎ *01–45–63–50–75.* 🎫 *17 frs.* ⏲ *Tues.–Sun. 10–5:40. Métro: Monceau.*

36 **Musée Nissim de Camondo.** The elegant decadence of the last days of the regal Ancien Régime is fully reflected in the lavish interior of this aristocratic Parisian mansion, built in the style of Louis XVI. If you're interested in the luxe of the 18th century, this is a must-see. ✉ *63 rue de Monceau,* ☎ *01–53–89–06–40.* 🎫 *30 frs.* ⏲ *Wed.–Sun. 10–5. Métro: Villiers.*

41 **Notre-Dame de Bonne-Nouvelle.** This wide, soberly Neoclassical church, built 1823–29, is tucked away off the Grand Boulevards. ✉ *Rue de la Lune. Métro: Bonne-Nouvelle.*

★ 38 **Opéra Garnier.** The original Paris Opera, begun in 1862 by Charles Garnier at the behest of Napoléon III, was not completed until 1875, five years after the emperor's abdication. The ornate facade, cleaned 1999–2000, typifies Second Empire architecture: a pompous hodgepodge of styles, with all the subtlety of a Wagnerian cymbal crash. After paying the entrance fee, you can stroll around at leisure. The monumental foyer and staircase are impressive, and the stage is the largest in the world. Marc Chagall painted the ceiling in 1964. The **Musée de l'Opéra**, containing a few paintings and theatrical mementos, is unremarkable. ✉ *Pl. de l'Opéra,* ☎ *01–40–01–22–63.* 🎫 *30 frs, guided tours in English at 3 PM, 60 frs.* ⏲ *Daily 10–5. Métro: Opéra.*

NEED A BREAK? Few cafés in Paris are grander than the Belle Epoque **Café de la Paix** (✉ 5 pl. de l'Opéra, ☎ 01–40–07–30–10).

---

34 **Parc Monceau.** The most picturesque gardens on the Right Bank were laid out as a private park in 1778 and retain some of the fanciful elements then in vogue, including mock ruins and a faux pyramid. ✉ *Entrances on bd. de Courcelles, av. Velasquez, av. Ruysdaël, av. van Dyck. Métro: Monceau.*

45 **Parc de La Villette.** Usually known simply as La Villette, this ambitiously landscaped, futuristic park is home to the **Cité de la Musique** (☞ Nightlife and the Arts, *below*). This giant postmodern musical academy also houses the **Musée de la Musique** (Museum of Musical Instruments). At the **Géode** cinema, which looks like a huge silver golf ball, films are shown on an enormous 180-degree curved screen. The science museum, the **Cité des Sciences et de l'Industrie**, contains dozens of interactive exhibits (though most displays are in French only). ✉ *Science Museum: 30 av. Corentin-Cariou,* ☎ *01–40–05–80–00 for Science Museum.* 🎫 *Museum of Musical Instruments 35 frs; Science Museum 35 frs.* ⏲ *Museum of Musical Instruments Tues.–Sun. noon–6; Science Museum Tues.–Sun. 10–6. Métro: Porte de La Villette, Porte de Pantin.*

37 **St-Augustin.** This domed church was dexterously constructed in the 1860s within the confines of an awkward V-shape site. It represented a breakthrough in ecclesiastical engineering because the use of metal pillars and girders obviated the need for exterior buttressing. ✉ *Pl. St-Augustin. Métro: St-Augustin.*

43 **Ste-Élisabeth.** This studied essay in Baroque (1628–46) has brightly restored wall paintings and a wide, semicircular apse around the choir. ✉ *Rue du Temple. Métro: Temple.*

42 **St-Nicolas des Champs.** The rounded-arch, fluted Doric capitals in the chancel of this church date from 1560 to 1587, a full century later than the pointed-arch nave (1420–80). ✉ *Rue St-Martin. Métro: Arts-et-Métiers.*

The Marais and the Bastille

The Marais is one of the city's most historic and sought-after residential districts. Except for the architecturally whimsical Pompidou Center, the tone here is set by the gracious architecture of the 17th and 18th centuries (the Marais was spared the attentions of Haussmann, the man who rebuilt so much of Paris in the mid-19th century). Today most of the Marais's spectacular *hôtels particuliers*—loosely translated as "mansions," the onetime residences of aristocratic families—have been restored; many are now museums, including the noted Musée Picasso. There are trendy boutiques and cafés among the kosher shops in what used to be a predominantly Jewish neighborhood around rue des Rosiers, and there's an impressive new Jewish Museum on nearby rue du Temple.

On the eastern edge of the Marais is place de la Bastille, site of the infamous prison stormed on July 14, 1789, an event that came to symbolize the beginning of the French Revolution. Largely in commemoration of the bicentennial of the Revolution, the Bastille area was renovated and became one of the trendiest sections of Paris. Galleries, shops, theaters, cafés, restaurants, and bars now fill formerly decrepit buildings and alleys.

A Good Walk

Make your starting point **place de la Bastille** ㊻, easily accessible by métro. Today the square is dominated by the Colonne de Juillet, the curving glass facade of the modern **Opéra de la Bastille.**

Walk down rue St-Antoine to the **Hôtel de Sully** ㊼, home to the Caisse Nationale des Monuments Historiques (National Treasury of Historic Monuments), at No. 62. Cross the road and pause at the mighty Baroque church of **St-Paul–St-Louis** ㊽. Take the left-hand side door out of the church into narrow passage St-Paul; then turn right onto rue St-Paul, past the grid of courtyards that make up the Village St-Paul antiques-shops complex. Wind your way through the small streets to the quai de l'Hôtel-de-Ville.

Turn right on quai de l'Hôtel-de-Ville; *bouquinistes* (booksellers) line the Seine to your left. Pause by the Pont Louis-Philippe to admire the dome of the Panthéon floating above the skyline; then take the next right up picturesque rue des Barres to **St-Gervais–St-Protais** ㊾. Beyond the church stands the **Hôtel de Ville** ㊿, the City Hall. From the Hôtel de Ville, cross rue de Rivoli and go up rue du Temple. On your right you'll pass one of the city's most popular department stores, the Bazar de l'Hôtel de Ville, or BHV, as it is known (☞ Shopping, *below*).

Take rue de la Verrerie, the first street on your left. Cross rue du Renard and take the second right past the ornate 16th-century church of St-Merri. Rue St-Martin, which is lined with stores, restaurants, and galleries, leads to the **Centre Pompidou** ㉑. In front of the Pompidou Center is the **Atelier Brancusi,** the reconstituted studio of sculptor Constantin Brancusi. The adjacent Square Igor-Stravinsky merits a stop for its unusual modern fountain.

Cross rue Beaubourg behind the Pompidou Center to rue Rambuteau, then take the first left onto rue du Temple. A stimulating **Musée d'Art et d'Histoire du Judaïsme** ㉒ opened in the Hôtel de St-Aignan, at No. 71, in 1998. Farther up the street, at No. 79, pause to admire the Hôtel de Montmor, a large-windowed Baroque mansion. Take a right onto rue des Haudriettes. Just to the left at the next corner is the **Musée de la Chasse et de la Nature** ㉓, the Museum of Hunting and Nature, housed in one of the Marais's most stately mansions. Head right on rue des

Archives, crossing rue des Haudriettes, and admire the medieval gateway with two fairy-tale towers, now part of the **Archives Nationales** ⑤④, the archives museum, entered from rue des Francs-Bourgeois around to the left.

Continue past the Crédit Municipal (the city's grandiose pawnbroking concern), the Dôme du Marais restaurant (housed in a circular 18th-century chamber originally used for auctions), and the church of Notre-Dame des Blancs-Manteaux. A corner turret signals rue Vieille-du-Temple: Turn left past the palatial Hôtel de Rohan (now part of the Archives Nationales), then right onto rue de la Perle to the **Musée Bricard** ⑤⑤, occupying a mansion as impressive as the assembly of locks and keys within. From here it is a step down rue de Thorigny (opposite) to the palatial 17th-century Hôtel Salé, now the **Musée Picasso** ⑤⑥.

Backtrack along rue de Thorigny and cross place de Thorigny to rue Elzévir. Halfway along is the **Musée Cognacq-Jay** ⑤⑦, a must if you love 18th-century furniture, porcelain, and paintings. Turn left at the end of the street onto rue des Francs-Bourgeois, then right into rue Pavée, past the cheerfully askew facade of the city history library, to reach rue des Rosiers, with its excellent Jewish bakeries and falafel shops. Double back to rue des Francs-Bourgeois and turn right, then left to find rue de Sévigné and the **Musée Carnavalet** ⑤⑧, the Paris history museum, in perhaps the nicest edifice in the Marais. A short walk along rue des Francs-Bourgeois takes you to one of Paris's most historic squares, the **place des Vosges** ⑤⑨, lined with pink brick and covered arcades.

TIMING

This walk will comfortably take a morning or an afternoon. If you choose to spend an hour or two in any of the museums along the way, allow a full day. Be prepared to wait in line at the Picasso Museum. Note that some of the museums don't open until the afternoon and that most shops in the Bastille and the Marais don't open until the late morning.

Sights to See

⑤④ **Archives Nationales** (National Archives). If you're a serious history buff, you'll be fascinated by the thousands of intricate historical documents, dating from the Merovingian period to the 20th century, at the National Archives. Architecture buffs will also enjoy this place, as it occupies the **Hôtel de Soubise,** one of the grandest of all Parisian mansions, whose salons were among the first to show the Rococo style in full bloom. ⊠ *60 rue des Francs-Bourgeois,* ☎ *01–40–27–62–18.* ☒ *20 frs.* ☉ *Mon. and Wed.–Fri. 10–5:45, weekends 1:45–5:45. Métro: Rambuteau.*

Atelier Brancusi (Brancusi Studio). Romanian-born sculptor Constantin Brancusi settled in Paris in 1898 at age 22. This light, airy museum in front of the Pompidou Center contains four glass-fronted rooms that re-create Brancusi's studio, crammed with smooth, stylized works from all periods of his career. ⊠ *11 rue St-Paul,* ☎ *01–44–78–12–33.* ☒ *20 frs.* ☉ *Wed.–Mon. noon–10. Métro: Rambuteau.*

⑤① **Centre Pompidou.** The futuristic, funnel-top Pompidou Center—known to Parisians as Beaubourg, after the surrounding district—was built in the mid-1970s and named in honor of former French president Georges Pompidou (1911–74). After receiving many more visitors than intended over the years, the center was closed in 1997 for top-to-bottom renovation, reopening at the start of 2000. You approach the center across **place Georges-Pompidou,** a sloping piazza, home to the **Atelier Brancusi** (☞ *above*). The center is most famous for its **Musée National d'Art Moderne** (Modern Art Museum), recently extended to cover two stories: one devoted to figurative works from Fauvism and Cubism onward; the other to postwar abstract art and recent video-based creations.

Also look for rotating exhibits of contemporary art. In addition, there are a public reference library, a language laboratory, an industrial design center, a cinema, a café, a rooftop restaurant, a gift shop, and the famous escalator that snakes up the outside to offer a sweeping panorama of central and western Paris. ⊠ *Pl. Georges-Pompidou,* ☎ *01–44–78–12–33.* ⌷ *50 frs.* ⊙ *Wed.–Mon. 11–10. Métro: Rambuteau.*

47 **Hôtel de Sully.** This late-Renaissance mansion, begun in 1624, has a stately garden and a majestic courtyard with statues, richly carved pediments, and dormer windows. It is the headquarters of the **Caisse Nationale des Monuments Historiques** (National Treasury of Historic Monuments), responsible for administering France's historic monuments. Guided visits to Paris sites and buildings begin here, though all are conducted in French. ⊠ *62 rue St-Antoine,* ☎ *01–44–61–20–00. Métro: St-Paul.*

50 **Hôtel de Ville** (City Hall). During the Commune of 1871, the Hôtel de Ville was burned to the ground. Today's building, based closely on the 16th-century Renaissance original, went up between 1874 and 1884. You can't inspect the lavish interior, but head around left to the traffic-free square, with its fountains and forest of street lamps, to admire the exuberant facade. ⊠ *Pl. de l'Hôtel-de-Ville. Métro: Hôtel-de-Ville.*

52 **Musée d'Art et d'Histoire du Judaïsme** (Museum of Jewish Art and History). With its clifflike courtyard ringed by giant pilasters, Pierre Le Muet's Hôtel St-Aignan—completed 1650—is one of the most awesome sights in the Marais. It opened as a museum in 1998 after a 20-year, $35 million restoration. The interior has been remodeled to the point of blandness, but the displays—including silverware, clothing, and furniture—are carefully presented. ⊠ *71 rue du Temple,* ☎ *01–53–01–86–53.* ⌷ *40 frs.* ⊙ *Sun.–Fri. 11–6. Métro: Rambuteau.*

⟡ **55** **Musée Bricard.** This museum—also called the Musée de la Serrure (Lock Museum)—is housed in a sober Baroque mansion designed in 1685 by the architect of Les Invalides, Libéral Bruand, for himself. If you've got a taste for fine craftsmanship, you will appreciate the intricacy and ingenuity of many of the locks displayed here. ⊠ *1 rue de la Perle,* ☎ *01–42–77–79–62.* ⌷ *30 frs.* ⊙ *Tues.–Fri. 10–noon and 2–5, Mon. 2–5. Métro: St-Paul.*

58 **Musée Carnavalet.** Two adjacent mansions in the heart of the Marais house the Carnavalet Museum, or the Paris History Museum, with material dating from the city's origins to the present. The museum is full of maps and plans, furniture, and busts and portraits of Parisian worthies down the ages. ⊠ *23 rue de Sévigné,* ☎ *01–42–72–21–13.* ⌷ *27 frs.* ⊙ *Tues.–Sun. 10–5:30. Métro: St-Paul.*

NEED A BREAK? **Marais Plus** (⊠ 20 rue des Francs-Bourgeois, ☎ 01–48–87–01–40), on the corner of rue Elzévir and rue des Francs-Bourgeois, is a delightful, artsy gift shop with a cozy *salon de thé* at the rear.

53 **Musée de la Chasse et de la Nature** (Museum of Hunting and Nature). This museum is housed in the Hôtel de Guénégaud, designed around 1650 by François Mansart. There is a series of immense 17th- and 18th-century still lifes (notably by Desportes and Oudry) and a wide variety of swords, guns, muskets, and taxidermy. ⊠ *60 rue des Archives,* ☎ *01–42–72–86–42.* ⌷ *30 frs.* ⊙ *Wed.–Mon. 11–6. Métro: Rambuteau.*

57 **Musée Cognacq-Jay.** Prized by connoisseurs, this museum is devoted to the arts of the 18th century and contains outstanding furniture, porcelain, and paintings (notably by Watteau, Boucher, and Tiepolo). ⊠ *8 rue Elzévir,* ☎ *01–40–27–07–21.* ⌷ *22 frs.* ⊙ *Tues.–Sun. 10–5:40. Métro: St-Paul.*

★ **⑤⑥** **Musée Picasso.** Housed in the 17th-century Hôtel Salé, this museum contains the paintings, sculptures, drawings, prints, ceramics, and assorted works of art given to the government by Picasso's heirs after the painter's death in 1973 in lieu of death duties. There are works from every period of Picasso's life, as well as pieces by Cézanne, Miró, Renoir, Braque, Degas, and Matisse. ⊠ *5 rue de Thorigny,* ☎ *01–42–71–25–21.* 🖾 *30 frs, Sun. 20 frs.* ☉ *Wed.–Mon. 9:30–5:30. Métro: St-Sébastien.*

Opéra de la Bastille. The state-of-the-art Bastille Opera was erected on the south side of place de la Bastille. Designed by Argentine-born Carlos Ott, it opened on July 14, 1989, in commemoration of the bicentennial of the French Revolution. The steep-climbing auditorium seats more than 3,000 and has earned more plaudits than the curving glass facade. ⊠ *Pl. de la Bastille,* ☎ *01–40–01–19–70.* 🖾 *Guided tours 50 frs. Métro: Bastille.*

④⑥ **Place de la Bastille.** Nothing remains of the infamous Bastille prison destroyed at the beginning of the French Revolution. In the midst of the large traffic circle is the **Colonne de Juillet** (July Column), commemorating the overthrow of Charles X in July 1830. As part of the countrywide celebrations for July 1989, the bicentennial of the French Revolution, the Opéra de la Bastille (☞ *above*) was erected, inspiring substantial redevelopment on the surrounding streets, especially along rue de Lappe and rue de la Roquette. What was formerly a humdrum neighborhood rapidly gained art galleries, clubs, and bars. *Métro: Bastille.*

★ **⑤⑨** **Place des Vosges.** Laid out by Henri IV at the start of the 17th century and originally known as place Royale, this square is the oldest and one of the prettiest in Paris. The two larger buildings on either side were originally the king's and queen's pavilions. The statue in the center is of Louis XIII. At No. 6 is the **Maison de Victor Hugo** (Victor Hugo's home), where the workaholic French author, famed for *Les Misérables* and *The Hunchback of Notre-Dame,* lived between 1832 and 1848. ⊠ *Maison de Victor Hugo: 6 pl. des Vosges,* ☎ *01–42–72–10–16.* 🖾 *27 frs.* ☉ *Tues.–Sun. 10–5:45. Métro: St-Paul, Chemin-Vert.*

④⑨ **St-Gervais–St-Protais.** This imposing church near the Hôtel de Ville is named after two Roman soldiers martyred by the emperor Nero in the 1st century AD. The church, a riot of Flamboyant style, went up between 1494 and 1598, making it one of the last Gothic constructions in the country. The facade, constructed between 1616 and 1621, is an early example of French use of classical decoration on the capitals (topmost sections) of the columns. ⊠ *Pl. St-Gervais,* ☎ *01–47–26–78–38 for concert information.* ☉ *Tues.–Sun. 6:30 AM–8 PM. Métro: Hôtel-de-Ville.*

④⑧ **St-Paul–St-Louis.** The leading Baroque church in the Marais, with its elegant dome soaring 180 ft above the crossing, was begun in 1627 by the Jesuits and partly modeled on their Gesu church in Rome. Look for Delacroix's dramatic *Christ on the Mount of Olives* high up in the transept. ⊠ *Rue St-Antoine. Métro: St-Paul.*

The Ile St-Louis and the Latin Quarter

Set behind the Ile de la Cité is one of the most romantic corners of Paris—tiny Ile St-Louis, where clocks seem to have been stopped sometime in the 19th century. South of the Ile St-Louis on the Left Bank of the Seine is the bohemian Quartier Latin (Latin Quarter), with its warren of steep, sloping streets, populated largely by Sorbonne students and academics. The name *Latin Quarter* comes from the old university tradition of studying and speaking in Latin, a tradition that disappeared during the Revolution. The university began as a theological school in the Middle Ages and later became the headquarters of the University of Paris; in 1968 the student revolution here had an explosive effect on French politics, resulting in major reforms in the education system. Most of the district's appeal is less emphatic: Roman ruins, tumbling street markets, the two oldest trees in Paris, and chance glimpses of Notre-Dame all await your discovery.

A Good Walk

Four bridges link the **Ile St-Louis** ⑥, the smaller of the city's two islands, to the mainland. Rue St-Louis-en-l'Ile runs the length of the island, bisecting it in two. Walk down this street and admire the strange, pierced spire of St-Louis-en-l'Ile, and stop off for an ice cream at Berthillon, at No. 31.

Head toward the west end of the island, which gloriously overlooks Notre-Dame, and cross the Pont St-Louis. Just across the bridge on the left, at the eastern tip of the Ile de la Cité, is the Mémorial de la Déportation, a starkly moving modern crypt dedicated to the French people who died in Nazi concentration camps. Head through the gardens to the left of Notre-Dame and take the Pont au Double across the Seine to Square René-Viviani. Behind the square is the church of St-Julien-le-Pauvre, built at the same time as Notre-Dame, and the tiny, elegant streets of the Maubert district. Turn left out of St-Julien, then make the first right, and cross rue St-Jacques to the elegantly proportioned church of **St-Séverin** ⑥. The surrounding streets are pedestrians only. Take rue St-Séverin, a right on rue Xavier-Privas, and a left on rue de la Huchette to reach place St-Michel. Gabriel Davioud's grandiose 1860 fountain, depicting St. Michael slaying the dragon, is a popular meeting spot at the nerve center of the Left Bank.

Turn left up boulevard St-Michel and cross boulevard St-Germain. To your left, behind some forbidding railings, lurks a garden with ruins that date from Roman times. These belong to the **Musée National du Moyen-Age** ⑥, the National Museum of the Middle Ages. The entrance is down rue Sommerard, the next street on the left. Cross place Paul-Painlevé in front of the museum up toward the **Sorbonne** ⑥ university, fronted by a small plaza where the Left Bank's student population congregates after classes. Continue uphill until you are confronted, up rue Soufflot on your left, by the menacing domed bulk of the **Panthéon** ⑥. On the far left corner of place du Panthéon is St-Étienne-du-Mont, a church whose facade is a mishmash of architectural styles. Head down quaint rue de la Montagne-Ste-Geneviève, then turn right onto rue Descartes to reach place de la Contrescarpe. This square looks almost provincial during the day as Parisians flock to the daily market on rue Mouffetard.

Walk down rue Mouffetard to the old church of St-Médard, at the bottom, then head left for 250 yards along rue Censier and turn left again into rue Georges-Desplas to find the beautiful white **Mosquée** ⑥, complete with minaret. On the far side of the mosque, the **Jardin des Plantes** ⑥, a spacious botanical garden, extends down to the Seine. The museums of entomology, paleontology, and mineralogy line the right side of the garden; an old-fashioned zoo, the other.

Take the western exit from the Jardin des Plantes and head up rue Lacépède and turn right into rue de Navarre to reach the **Arènes de Lutèce** ⑥, the remains of a Roman amphitheater. Rue des Arènes and rue Limé lead back down to place Jussieu and its hideous 1960s concrete campus; there's greater refinement around the corner down rue des Fossés-St-Bernard at the glass-facade **Institut du Monde Arabe** ⑥, a center devoted to Arab culture. End your walk here with a cup of mint tea in the rooftop café overlooking Paris.

TIMING

This walk can be fitted into a morning or afternoon or serve as the basis for a leisurely day's exploring—given that several sites, notably the Musée National du Moyen-Age, deserve a lengthy visit.

Sights to See

67 Arènes de Lutèce (Lutetia Amphitheater). This Roman arena was only discovered in 1869 and has since been excavated and landscaped to reveal parts of the original amphitheater. Designed as a theater and circus, the arena was almost totally destroyed by the Barbarians in AD 280, although you can still see part of the stage and tiered seating. ⊠ *Entrances on rue Monge and rue de Navarre.* ⊙ *Daily 8–sunset. Métro: Monge.*

60 Ile St-Louis. One of the more fabled addresses in Paris, this tiny island has long harbored the rich and famous, including Chopin, Helena Rubenstein, Chagall, and the Rothschild family, which still occupies the island's grandest house, the Hôtel Lambert, which is set on the eastern prow of the island. In fact, the entire island displays striking architectural unity, stemming from the efforts of a group of early 17th-century property speculators led by Christophe Marie. The group commissioned leading Baroque architect Louis Le Vau (1612–70) to erect a series of imposing town houses. Other than some elegant facades and the island's highly picturesque quays along the Seine, there are no major sights here—just follow your nose and soak in the atmosphere of old Paris. *Métro: Pont-Marie.*

NEED A
BREAK?   Cafés all over sell Berthillon, the haute couture of ice cream, but the **Berthillon** (⊠ 31 rue St-Louis-en-l'Ile, ☎ 01–43–54–31–61) shop itself is the place to come. More than 30 flavors are served; expect to wait in line. The shop is open Wednesday–Sunday.

68 Institut du Monde Arabe (Institute of the Arab World). Jean Nouvel's striking 1988 glass-and-steel edifice adroitly fuses Arabic and European styles. Note the 240 shutterlike apertures that open and close to regulate light exposure. Inside, the institute tries to do for Arab culture what the Pompidou Center does for modern art, with the help of a sound-and-image center, a vast library and documentation center, and an art museum. The top-floor café provides a good view of Paris. ⊠ *1 rue des Fossés-St-Bernard,* ☎ *01–40–51–38–38.* ▣ *25 frs.* ⊙ *Tues.– Sun. 10–6. Métro: Cardinal-Lemoine.*

66 Jardin des Plantes (Botanical Garden). This enormous swath of greenery contains the botanical garden, the Grande Galerie de l'Évolution, and three natural history museums: the **Musée Entomologique** (15-franc admission), devoted to insects; the **Musée Paléontologique** (30-franc admission), to fossils and prehistoric animals; and the **Musée Minéralogique** (30-franc admission), to rocks and minerals. It also has an alpine garden, an aquarium, a maze, a number of hothouses (15-franc admission), and one of the world's oldest zoos. ⊠ *Entrances on rue Geoffroy-St-Hilaire, rue Cuvier and rue Buffon.* ▣ *Zoo 30 frs.* ⊙ *Garden daily 7:30–sunset; zoo daily 9–6; museums Wed.–Mon. 10–5. Métro: Monge, Jussieu, Gare d'Austerlitz.*

65 Mosquée (Mosque). The city mosque was built from 1922 to 1925, complete with arcades and minaret, and decorated in the style of Moorish Spain. The sunken garden and tiled patios are open to the public (the prayer rooms are not) and so are the *hammams,* or Turkish baths. Venture in and sip a restorative cup of sweet mint tea at the café. ⊠ *2 pl. du Puits-de-l'Ermite,* ☎ *01–45–35–97–33.* ▣ *15 frs guided* *tour, 85 frs Turkish baths.* ☉ *Baths daily 10 AM–9 PM; Tues. and Sun. men only; Mon. and Wed.–Sat. women only. Guided tours of mosque Sat.–Thurs. 9–noon and 2–6. Métro: Monge.*

★ ⑥② **Musée National du Moyen-Age** (National Museum of the Middle Ages). This museum is housed in the famous 15th-century Hôtel de Cluny. The mansion has an intricately vaulted chapel and a cloistered courtyard with mullioned windows that originally belonged to monks of the Cluny Abbey in Burgundy, hence the museum's former name, the Musée de Cluny. A stunning array of tapestries heads its vast exhibition of medieval decorative arts. Alongside the mansion are the city's Roman baths and the *Boatmen's Pillar,* Paris's oldest sculpture. ✉ *6 pl. Paul-Painlevé,* ☎ *01–53–73–78–00.* 🎟 *30 frs, Sun. 20 frs.* ☉ *Wed.–Mon. 9:15–5:45. Métro: Cluny–La Sorbonne.*

⑥④ **Panthéon.** Originally commissioned as a church by Louis XV as a mark of gratitude for his recovery from a grave illness in 1744, the Panthéon is now a monument to France's most glorious historical figures, including Voltaire, Zola, Rousseau, and dozens of French statesmen, military heroes, and other thinkers. Germain Soufflot's building was not begun until 1764; nor completed until 1790, during the French Revolution, whereupon its windows were blocked and it was transformed into the national shrine it is today. A giant pendulum, suspended on a 220-ft steel wire, commemorates Léon Foucault's 1851 experiment to prove the earth's rotation. ✉ *Pl. du Panthéon,* ☎ *01–44–32–18–00.* 🎟 *35 frs.* ☉ *Summer, daily 9:30–6:30; winter, daily 10–6:15. Métro: Cardinal-Lemoine; RER: Luxembourg.*

⑥① **St-Séverin.** This unusually wide, Flamboyant Gothic church dominates a Left Bank neighborhood filled with squares and pedestrian streets. Note the splendidly deviant spiraling column in the forest of pillars behind the altar. ✉ *Rue des Prêtres St-Séverin.* ☉ *Weekdays 11–5:30, Sat. 11–10. Métro: St-Michel.*

⑥③ **Sorbonne.** Named after Robert de Sorbon, a medieval canon who founded a theological college here in 1253, this is one of the oldest universities in Europe. The church and university buildings were restored by Cardinal Richelieu in the 17th century, and the maze of amphitheaters, lecture rooms, and laboratories, along with the surrounding courtyards and narrow streets, retains a hallowed air. You can visit the main courtyard on rue de la Sorbonne and peek into the main lecture hall, a major meeting point during the tumultuous student upheavals of 1968. The square is dominated by the noble university church with cupola and Corinthian columns. Inside is the white-marble tomb of that ultimate crafty cleric, Cardinal Richelieu himself. ✉ *Rue de la Sorbonne. Métro: Cluny–La Sorbonne.*

From Orsay to St-Germain

This walk covers the Left Bank, from the Musée d'Orsay in the stately 7ᵉ arrondissement to the lively and colorful area around St-Germain-des-Prés in the 6ᵉ. The Musée d'Orsay, in a daringly converted Belle Epoque rail station on the Seine, houses one of the world's most spectacular arrays of Impressionist paintings. Farther along the river, the 18th-century Palais Bourbon, home to the National Assembly, sets the tone for the 7ᵉ arrondissement. Luxurious ministries and embassies—including the Hôtel Matignon, residence of the French prime minister—line the surrounding streets, their majestic scale in total keeping with the Hôtel des Invalides, whose gold-leafed dome climbs heavenward above the regal tomb of Napoléon. The Rodin Museum—set in one of the city's prettiest mansions—is only a short walk away.

To the east, away from the splendor of the 7e, the boulevard St-Michel slices the Left Bank in two: on one side, the Latin Quarter (☞ The Islands and the Latin Quarter, *above*); on the other, the Faubourg St-Germain, named for St-Germain-des-Prés, the oldest church in Paris. The venerable church tower has long acted as a beacon for intellectuals, most famously during the 1950s when Albert Camus, Jean-Paul Sartre, and Simone de Beauvoir ate and drank existentialism in the neighborhood cafés. Today most of the philosophizing is done by tourists, yet a wealth of bookshops, art stores, and antiques galleries ensure that St-Germain, as the area is commonly known, retains its highbrow appeal. In the southern part of this district is the city's most famous and colorful park, the Jardin du Luxembourg.

A Good Walk

Start at the **Musée d'Orsay** (69), famed for its collection of art from 1848–1914. A good meeting point is the pedestrian square outside the museum, where huge bronze statues of an elephant and a rhinoceros disprove the idea that the French take their art *too* seriously. Head west along rue de Lille to the **Palais Bourbon** (70), home of the Assemblée Nationale (French Parliament).

Rue de l'Université leads from the Assemblée to the grassy Esplanade des Invalides and an encounter with the **Hôtel des Invalides** (71), founded by Louis XIV to house invalid, or wounded, veterans. The most impressive dome in Paris towers over the church at the Invalides—the Église du Dôme. From the church double back along boulevard des Invalides and take rue de Varenne to the Hôtel Biron, better known as the **Musée Rodin** (72), where you can see a fine collection of Auguste Rodin's emotionally charged statues. The quiet, distinguished 18th-century streets between the Rodin Museum and the Parliament are filled with embassies and ministries.

Continue on to rue du Bac, turn left, then take a right onto rue de Grenelle, to the **Musée Maillol** (73), dedicated to the work of sculptor Aristide Maillol. Continue on rue de Grenelle past Edme Bouchardon's monumental 1730s Fontaine des Quatre Saisons (Four Seasons Fountain) to the carrefour de la Croix-Rouge, with its mighty bronze Centaur by the contemporary sculptor César. Take rue du Vieux-Colombier to place St-Sulpice, a spacious square ringed with cafés. Looming over the square is the enormous church of **St-Sulpice** (74).

Exit the church, head back across the square, and turn right on rue Bonaparte to reach **St-Germain-des-Prés** (75), Paris's oldest church. Across the cobbled place St-Germain-des-Prés is the café Les Deux Magots, one of the principal haunts of the intelligentsia after World War II. Two doors down boulevard St-Germain is the Café de Flore, another popular spot with the likes of Jean-Paul Sartre and Simone de Beauvoir. Follow rue de l'Abbaye, alongside the far side of the church, to rue de Furstenberg. The street opens out into place Furstenberg—a relentlessly picturesque square once used as a backdrop for Louis Jordan's warbling of "Gigi" in the eponymous 1958 Hollywood musical film—where you'll find Eugène Delacroix's studio, the **Atelier Delacroix** (76). Take a left on rue Jacob and turn right down rue Bonaparte to the **École Nationale des Beaux-Arts** (77), whose students can often be seen painting and sketching on the nearby quays and bridges.

Continue down to the Seine and turn right along the quai, past the **Institut de France** (78). With its distinctive dome, curved facade, and commanding position overlooking the Pont des Arts—a footbridge affording delightful views of the Louvre and Ile de la Cité—the institute is one of the city's most impressive waterside sights. Continue along quai de

Conti past the **Hôtel des Monnaies** ⑦, the former national mint. Head up rue Dauphine. Just 150 yards up, it's linked by the open-air passage Dauphine to rue Mazarine, which leads left to the carrefour de Buci, where you can find one of the best food markets in Paris. Rue de l'Ancienne-Comédie, so named because it was the first home of the legendary Comédie Française, leads up to busy place de l'Odéon. Cross boulevard St-Germain and climb rue de l'Odéon to the colonnaded Théâtre de l'Odéon (☞ Nightlife and the Arts, *below*). Behind the theater lies the spacious **Jardin du Luxembourg** ⑧, one of the most stylish parks in the city.

TIMING

This walk could take from four hours to a couple of days, depending on how long you spend in the plethora of museums along the way. Aim for an early start—that way you can hit the Musée d'Orsay early, when crowds are smaller, then get to the rue de Buci street market when it's in full swing, in the late afternoon (the stalls are generally closed for lunch until 3 PM). Note that the Hôtel des Invalides is open daily, but Orsay is closed Monday. You might consider returning to one or more museums on another day or night—Orsay is open late on Thursday evening.

Sights to See

⑦⑥ **Atelier Delacroix** (Delacroix's Studio). The studio of artist Eugène Delacroix (1798–1863) contains only a small collection of his sketches and drawings. But if you want to pay homage to France's foremost Romantic painter, you'll want to visit this museum. Speaking of pictures, don't forget to take some photographs here of place Furstenberg, one of the loveliest corners of 19th-century Paris still extant. ⊠ *6 rue Furstenberg,* ☎ *01–44–41–86–50.* ⊡ *22 frs.* ☉ *Wed.–Mon. 9:30–5. Métro: St-Germain-des-Prés.*

⑦⑦ **École Nationale des Beaux-Arts** (National Fine Arts College). In three large mansions near the Seine, this school—today the breeding ground for painters, sculptors, and architects—was once the site of a convent, founded in 1608. Wander into the courtyard and galleries of the school to see the casts and copies of the statues stored here for safekeeping during the Revolution. ⊠ *14 rue Bonaparte.* ☉ *Daily 1–7. Métro: St-Germain-des-Prés.*

NEED A BREAK? The popular **La Palette** café (⊠ 43 rue de Seine, ☎ 01–43–26–68–15), on the corner of rue de Seine and rue Callot, has long been a favorite haunt of Beaux-Arts students.

★ ⑦⑪ **Hôtel des Invalides.** Les Invalides, as it is widely known, is an outstanding monumental Baroque ensemble, designed by Libéral Bruand in the 1670s at the behest of Louis XIV to house wounded, or *invalid,* soldiers. Although no more than a handful of old-timers live at the Invalides these days, the army link remains in the form of the **Musée de l'Armée,** a military museum. The **Musée des Plans-Reliefs,** also housed here, contains a fascinating collection of old scale models of French towns. The 17th-century **Église St-Louis des Invalides** is the Invalides' original church. More impressive is Jules Hardouin-Mansart's **Église du Dôme,** built onto the end of the church of St-Louis but blocked off from it in 1793. The showpiece is Napoléon's grandiose tomb. ⊠ *Pl. des Invalides,* ☎ *01–44–42–37–72.* ⊡ *38 frs.* ☉ *Apr.–Sept., daily 10–5:45; Oct.–Mar., daily 10–4:45. Métro: Latour-Maubourg.*

⑦⑨ **Hôtel des Monnaies** (Mint). Louis XVI transferred the Royal Mint to this imposing mansion in the late 18th century. Although the mint was moved again, to Pessac, near Bordeaux, in 1973, weights and measures, medals, and limited-edition coins are still made here. The **Musée de la Monnaie** (Coin Museum) has an extensive collection of coins, documents, and engravings, plus a good shop. On Tuesday and Friday at 2 you can catch the coin metal craftsmen at work. ⊠ *11 quai de Conti,* ☎ *01–40–46–55–35.* 🎫 *20 frs.* 🕐 *Tues.–Fri. 11–5:30, weekends noon–5:30. Métro: Pont-Neuf.*

78 **Institut de France** (French Institute). Built to the designs of Louis Le Vau from 1662 to 1674, the institute's curved, dome-top facade is one of the Left Bank's most impressive waterside sights. It also houses one of France's most revered cultural institutions, the Académie Française, created by Cardinal Richelieu in 1635. The interior, unfortunately, is closed to the general public. ⊠ *Pl. de l'Institut. Métro: Pont-Neuf.*

80 **Jardin du Luxembourg** (Luxembourg Gardens). One of the prettiest of Paris's few large parks, the Luxembourg Gardens have fountains, ponds, trim hedges, precisely planted rows of trees, and gravel walks typical of the French fondness for formal landscaping. The 17th-century **Palais de Luxembourg** (Luxembourg Palace), overlooking the gardens, houses the French Senate and is not open to the public. It was built, like the gardens, for Maria de' Medici, widow of Henri IV. *Métro: Odéon; RER: Luxembourg.*

73 **Musée Maillol.** Drawings, paintings, tapestries, and, above all, bronzes by Art Deco sculptor Aristide Maillol (1861–1944)—whose sleek, stylized nudes adorn the Tuileries—can be admired at this handsome town house, lovingly restored by his former muse Dina Vierny. ⊠ *61 rue de Grenelle,* ☎ *01–42–22–59–58.* 🎫 *40 frs.* 🕐 *Wed.–Mon. 11–6. Métro: Rue du Bac.*

★ **69** **Musée d'Orsay.** In a stylishly converted train station, the Orsay Museum—devoted to the arts (mainly French) spanning the period 1848–1914—is one of the city's most popular. The main artistic attraction is the Impressionists: Renoir, Sisley, Pissarro, and Monet are all well represented. The post-Impressionists—Cézanne, van Gogh, Gauguin, and Toulouse-Lautrec—are on the top floor. On the ground floor you'll find the work of Manet, the powerful realism of Courbet, and the delicate nuances of Degas. If you prefer more academic paintings, look for Puvis de Chavannes's larger-than-life classical canvases. And if you're excited by more modern developments, look for the early 20th-century Fauves (meaning "wild beasts," the name given them by an outraged critic in 1905)—particularly Matisse, Derain, and Vlaminck. Thought-provoking sculptures also lurk at every turn. ⊠ *1 rue de Bellechasse,* ☎ *01–40–49–48–84.* 🎫 *40 frs, Sun. 30 frs.* 🕐 *Tues.–Wed. and Fri.–Sat. 10–6, Thurs. 10–9:45, Sun. 9–6. Métro: Solférino; RER: Musée d'Orsay.*

NEED A BREAK? Find respite from the overwhelming collection of art in the **Musée d'Orsay Café** behind one of the giant station clocks, close to the Impressionist galleries on the top floor.

★ **72** **Musée Rodin.** The exquisite 18th-century Hôtel Biron makes a gracious setting for the sculpture of Auguste Rodin (1840–1917). You'll doubtless recognize the seated *Le Penseur* (*The Thinker*), with his elbow resting on his knee, and the passionate *Le Baiser* (*The Kiss*). From the upper rooms, which contain some fine if murky paintings by Rodin's friend Eugène Carrière (1849–1906) and some fine sculptures by Rodin's mistress, Camille Claudel (1864–1943), you can see the large garden behind the house. Don't skip the garden: It is exceptional both for its rosebushes (more than 2,000 of them) and for its sculpture. ⊠ *77 rue de Varenne,* ☎ *01–44–18–61–10.* 🎫 *28 frs, Sun. 18 frs; gardens only*

5 frs. ⊙ Easter–Oct., Tues.–Sun. 9:30–5:45; Nov.–Easter, Tues.–Sun. 9:30–4:45. Métro: Varenne.

⑦ Palais Bourbon. The most prominent feature of the home of the Assemblée Nationale (French Parliament) is its colonnaded facade, commissioned by Napoléon. ⊠ Pl. du Palais-Bourbon. ⊙ During temporary exhibits only. Métro: Assemblée Nationale.

㊄ St-Ge ... ter a
relic ... han-
cel wa ... der
III in 1 ... om
this pe ... ⊠
Pl. St-G ... er-
main-d ...

㊃ St-Sulpi ... us
17th-ce ... in
the first ...
ished, an ... r
design. ⊠

Montmartre

On a dram ...
Basilica ar ...
fabled nigh ...
clubs and ...
charm. W ...
Parisians as ... . They were set up here not
just because ... ill was a good place to catch the wind—at more than
300 ft, it's the highest point in the city—but because Montmartre was
covered with wheat fields and quarries right up to the end of the 19th
century. Today only two of the original 20 windmills remain. Visiting
Montmartre means negotiating a lot of steep streets and flights of steps.
The crown atop this urban peak, the Sacré-Coeur Basilica, is something
of an architectural oddity. It has been called everything from grotesque
to sublime; its silhouette, viewed from afar at dusk or sunrise, looks
more like a mosque than a cathedral.

A Good Walk

Begin at place Blanche, home to the **Moulin Rouge** ㉛, the windmill turned
dance hall, immortalized by Toulouse-Lautrec. Just along boulevard
de Clichy is the **Musée de l'Erotisme** ㉜. Wind your way up rue Lepic
to the **Moulin de la Galette** ㉝, atop its leafy hillock opposite rue
Tholozé, once a path over the hill. Turn right down rue Tholozé, past
Studio 28, the first cinema built expressly for experimental films. Continue
down rue Tholozé to rue des Abbesses and turn left toward the
triangular **place des Abbesses** ㉞. Follow rue Ravignan as it climbs north,
via place Émile-Goudeau, an enchanting little cobbled square, to the
Bateau-Lavoir ㉟, or Boat Wash House, at its northern edge. Painters
Picasso and Braque had studios in the original building; this drab concrete
edifice was built in its place. Continue up the hill via rue de la
Mire to place Jean-Baptiste Clément, where Amedeo Modigliani had
a studio.

The upper reaches of rue Lepic lead to rue Norvins, formerly rue des
Moulins. At the end of the street to the left is stylish avenue Junot. Continue
right past the bars and tourist shops until you reach **place du
Tertre** ㊱. Around the corner on rue Poulbot, the **Espace Dalí** ㊲ houses
works by Salvador Dalí, who once had a studio in the area. Return to
place du Tertre. Looming behind is the scaly white dome of the Basilique

du **Sacré-Coeur** ⑧⑧. The cavernous interior is worth visiting for its golden mosaics; climb to the top of the dome for the view of Paris. Walk back toward place du Tertre. Turn right onto rue du Mont-Cenis and left onto rue Cortot, site of the **Musée de Montmartre** ⑧⑨, which, like the Bateau-Lavoir, once sheltered an illustrious group of painters, writers, and assorted cabaret artists. Another famous Montmartre landmark is at No. 22: the bar-cabaret **Lapin Agile** ⑨⓪. Opposite the Lapin Agile is the tiny Cimetière St-Vincent, where painter Maurice Utrillo is buried.

TIMING

Reserve a morning or afternoon for this walk: Many of the streets are steep and slow. Include half an hour each at Sacré-Coeur and the museums (the Dalí museum is open daily, but the Montmartre museum is closed Monday). From Easter through September Montmartre is besieged by tourists. Two hints for avoiding the worst of the rush: Come on a gray day, when Montmartre's sullen-tone facades suffer less than most others in the city; or visit during the afternoon and return to place du Tertre (maybe via the funicular) by the early evening, when the tourist buses will have departed.

Sights to See

⑧⑤ **Bateau-Lavoir** (Boat Wash House). Montmartre poet Max Jacob coined the name for the original building on this site (which burned down in 1970), saying it resembled a boat and that the warren of artists' studios within was perpetually paint-splattered and in need of a good hosing down. It was here that Pablo Picasso and Georges Braque made their first bold stabs at the concept of Cubism. The new building also contains art studios, but is the epitome of poured-concrete drabness. ⊠ *13 pl. Émile-Goudeau. Métro: Abbesses.*

⑧⑦ **Espace Dalí** (Dalí Center). Some of Salvador Dalí's less familiar works are among the 25 sculptures and 300 prints housed in this museum with an atmosphere that is meant to approximate the surreal experience. ⊠ *11 rue Poulbot,* ☎ *01–42–64–40–10.* 🖾 *40 frs.* ☉ *Daily 10– 6:30. Métro: Abbesses.*

⑨⓪ **Lapin Agile.** This bar-cabaret, originally one of the raunchiest haunts in Montmartre, got its curious name—the Nimble Rabbit—when the owner, André Gill, hung up a sign of a laughing rabbit jumping out of a saucepan clutching a bottle of wine. Locals christened it the *Lapin à Gill,* meaning "Gill's rabbit." When, in 1886, it was sold to cabaret singer Jules Jouy, he called it the Lapin Agile, a French homonym of "Lapin à Gill." In 1903 the premises were bought by the most celebrated cabaret entrepreneur of them all, Aristide Bruand, depicted by Toulouse-Lautrec in a series of famous posters. ⊠ *22 rue des Saules,* ☎ *01–46–06–85–87.* 🖾 *130 frs.* ☉ *Tues.–Sat. 9 PM–2 AM. Métro: Lamarck-Caulaincourt.*

⑧③ **Moulin de la Galette** (Biscuit Windmill). This is one of two remaining windmills in Montmartre. It was once the focal point of an open-air cabaret (made famous in a painting by Renoir). Rumor has it that in 1814 the miller Debray, who had struggled in vain to defend the windmill from invading Cossacks, was then strung up on its sails and spun to death by the invaders. Unfortunately, it is privately owned and can only be admired from the street below. ⊠ *Rue Tholozé. Métro: Abbesses.*

⑧① **Moulin Rouge** (Red Windmill). This world-famous cabaret was built in 1885 as a windmill, then transformed into a dance hall in 1900. Those wild, early days were immortalized by Toulouse-Lautrec in his posters and paintings. It still trades shamelessly on the notion of Paris as a city of sin: If you fancy a Vegas-style night out, this is the place to go. ⊠

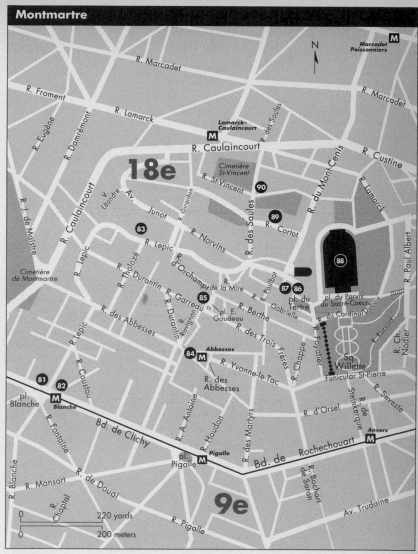

Montmartre

82 bd. de Clichy, ☏ *01–53–09–82–82.* 🎫 *360–550 frs.* ⏲ *Shows nightly at 9 and 11. Métro: Blanche.*

(82) **Musée de l'Erotisme** (Erotic Art Museum). Opened in 1997, this museum claims to offer "a prestigious showcase for every kind of erotic fantasy." Its 2,000 works of art—some might question that term—range from Peruvian potteries, African carvings, and Indian miniatures to Nepalese bronzes, Chinese ivories, and Japanese prints. ✉ *72 bd. de Clichy,* ☏ *01–42–58–28–73.* 🎫 *40 frs.* ⏲ *Daily 10 AM–2 AM. Métro: Blanche.*

(89) **Musée de Montmartre** (Montmartre Museum). In its turn-of-the-century heyday, Montmartre's historical museum was home to an illustrious group of painters, writers, and assorted cabaret artists. Foremost among them were Renoir and Maurice Utrillo. The museum also provides a view of the tiny **vineyard**—the only one in Paris—on neighboring rue des Saules. A token 125 gallons of wine are still produced every year. ✉ *12 rue Cortot,* ☏ *01–46–06–61–11.* 🎫 *25 frs.* ⏲ *Tues.–Sun. 11–6. Métro: Lamarck-Caulaincourt.*

(84) **Place des Abbesses.** This triangular square is typical of the picturesque, slightly countrified style that has made Montmartre famous. The entrance to the Abbesses métro station, a curving, sensuous mass of delicate iron, is one of only two original Art Nouveau entrance canopies left in Paris. *Métro: Abbesses.*

(86) **Place du Tertre.** This tumbling square (*tertre* means "hillock") regains its village atmosphere only in the winter, when the branches of the plane trees sketch traceries against the sky. At any other time of year you'll be confronted by crowds of tourists and a swarm of third-rate artists clamoring to do your portrait (if one of them produces an unsolicited portrait, you are not obligated to buy it). **La Mère Catherine,** on one corner of the square, was a favorite with the Russian Cossacks who occupied Paris in 1814. They couldn't have suspected that, by banging on the table and yelling "*bistro*" (Russian for "quickly"), they were inventing a new breed of French restaurant. *Métro: Abbesses.*

NEED A BREAK?

Patachou (✉ 9 pl. du Tertre, ☏ 01–42–51–06–06), serving exquisite if expensive cakes and teas, sounds the one classy note on place du Tertre.

(88) **Sacré-Coeur.** The Sacred Heart Basilica was erected as a sort of national guilt offering in expiation for the blood shed during the Paris Commune and Franco-Prussian War in 1870–71 and was largely financed by French Catholics fearful of an anticlerical backlash under the new republican regime. The basilica was not consecrated until 1919. Stylistically, the Sacré-Coeur borrows elements from Romanesque and Byzantine models. The gloomy, cavernous interior is worth visiting for its golden mosaics; climb to the top of the dome for the view of Paris. ✉ *Pl. du Parvis-du-Sacré-Coeur. Métro: Anvers.*

DINING

Revised and updated by Alexander Lobrano and Brandy Whittingham

Whether you get knee-deep in white truffles at Les Ambassadors or merely discover pistacchioed sausage (the poor man's caviar) at a classic corner bistro, you'll discover that food in Paris is an obsession, an art, a subject of endless debate. From the edible genius of haute cuisine wizard Alain Ducasse—whose turbot with "marmalade" of asparagus will make you purr—to brilliant bistro chef Yves Camdeborde's red mullet with chestnuts and cèpes, dining in Paris can easily leave you in a pleasurable stupor. And when it all seems a bit overwhelming, you can slip away to a casual little place for an earthy, bubbling

HOW TO USE THIS GUIDE

Think of this guide as your tool kit for a perfect trip. It's packed with everything you need—color photos, insider advice on hotels and restaurants, practical tips, essential maps, and more.

COOL TOOLS

As you're planning your trip, be on the lookout for our favorite features.

Fodor's Choice Look for entries marked with a star. Although all listings in this guide come highly recommended, these deserve special mention.

Great Itineraries Not sure what to see in the time you have? Mix and match our easy-to-follow itineraries to create a trip that suits you.

Good Walks Let us be your guide to the must-see sights. Follow the numbered bullets and you won't miss a thing.

Need a Break? Looking for a quick bite to eat or a spot to rest? These sure bets are along the way.

Off the Beaten Path Some lesser-known sights are definitely worth a special trip. We tell you which to detour for.

POST-IT® FLAGS

Note your favorite spots with these handy Post-it® flags.

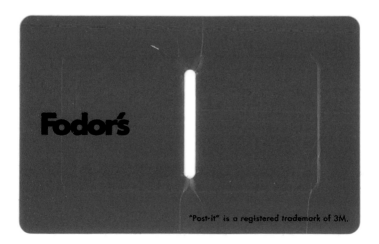

"Post-it" is a registered trademark of 3M.

ICONS AND SYMBOLS

Look for these icons and symbols throughout the guide. Price charts for dining and lodging are strategically located—check the index to find the one you want.

★   Our special recommendations
✕   Restaurant
🏠   Lodging establishment

✕🏠   Lodging establishment whose restaurant warrants a special trip
☺   Good for kids
☞   Sends you to another section of the guide for more information
✉   Address
☎   Telephone number
◷   Opening hours
💰   Admission prices
🖰   Sends you to www.fodors.com/urls for up-to-date links to the property's Web site

VACATION COUNTDOWN

Your checklist for a perfect journey

WAY AHEAD

- Devise a trip budget.
- Write down the five things you want most from this trip. Keep this list handy before and during your trip.
- Make plane or train reservations. Book lodging, rental cars, and other transportation.
- Arrange for pet care.
- Submit your passport application, or check that your existing passport is valid.
- Photocopy important documents and store in a safe place.

A MONTH BEFORE

- Make restaurant reservations and buy theater and concert tickets. Visit fodors.com for links to local events and news.
- Familiarize yourself with the local language or lingo.

TWO WEEKS BEFORE

- Replenish your supply of medications and contact lenses if necessary.
- Create your itinerary.
- Enjoy a book or movie set in your destination to get you in the mood.

- Develop a packing list. Shop for missing essentials. Repair and launder or dry-clean your clothes.

A WEEK BEFORE

- Stop newspaper and mail deliveries and pay bills.
- Acquire local currency and traveler's checks.
- Stock up on film and batteries.
- Label your luggage.
- Finalize your packing list— always take less than you think you need.
- Create a toiletries kit filled with travel-size essentials.
- Get lots of sleep. You don't want to get sick or run-down before your trip.

A DAY BEFORE

- Drink plenty of water.
- Check your necessary travel documents.
- Get packing!

DURING YOUR TRIP

- Keep a journal/scrapbook as a personal souvenir.
- Spend time with locals.
- Take time to explore. Don't plan too much. Let yourself get lost and use your Fodor's guide to get back on track.

cassoulet, have a midnight feast of the world's silkiest oysters, or even opt out of Gaul altogether for superb pasta, couscous, or an herb-bright Vietnamese stir-fry. Once you know where to go, Paris is a city where perfection awaits at all levels of the food chain.

Generally, restaurants are open from noon to about 2 and from 7:30 or 8 to 10 or 10:30. It's best to make reservations, particularly in summer, although the reviews only state when reservations are absolutely essential. If you want no-smoking seating, make this clear; the mandatory no-smoking area is sometimes limited to a very few tables. Brasseries have longer hours and often serve all day and late into the evening; some are open 24 hours. Assume a restaurant is open every day unless otherwise indicated. Surprisingly, many prestigious restaurants close on Saturday as well as Sunday. July and August are the most common months for annual closings, although Paris in August is no longer the wasteland it once was. For help with the vocabulary of French cooking, *see* the Menu Guide at the end of this book. Although prices include tax and tip by law, pocket change left on the table in simple places, or an additional 5% in better restaurants, is appreciated. Places where a jacket and tie are de rigueur are noted. Otherwise, use common sense—jeans and T-shirts are not suitable in Paris restaurants, nor are shorts or running clothes, except in the most casual bistros and cafés.

CATEGORY	COST*
$$$$	over 550 frs
$$$	300 frs–550 frs
$$	175 frs–300 frs
$	under 175 frs

per person for a three-course meal, including 20.6% tax and service but not drinks

≪ *following the text of a review is your signal that the property has a Web site, where you will find details and, usually, images; for a link, visit www.fodors.com/urls.*

1ᵉʳ Arrondissement (Louvre/Les Halles)

FRENCH

$$$$ ✕ **Le Grand Véfour.** Victor Hugo could stride in and still recognize this ★ place—then, as now, a contender for the prize for the most beautiful restaurant in Paris. Originally built in 1784, set in the arcades of the Palais-Royal, it has welcomed everyone from Napoléon to Colette to Jean Cocteau—nearly every seat bears a plaque commemorating famous patrons, and you can request to be seated at your idol's table. The mirrored ceiling and Restauration-era glass paintings of goddesses are most beguiling, as so are the dishes of chef Guy Martin. He hails from the mountains of Savoie, so you can find some peasant-luxe dishes among all the foie gras–stuffed ravioli and truffled veal sweetbreads. ⊠ *17 rue Beaujolais,* ☎ *01–42–96–56–27. Reservations essential 1 wk in advance. Jacket and tie. AE, DC, MC, V. Closed weekends and Aug. Métro: Palais-Royal.*

$$ ✕ **Restaurant du Palais-Royal.** Tucked away in the northern corner of the magnificent Palais-Royal garden, this pleasant bistro has a lovely terrace and good food. John Dory sautéed with red peppers and onions is among the interesting contemporary dishes. Since this is a wonderful spot for a romantic tête-à-tête, be sure to book in advance, especially during the summer when the terrace tables are hotly sought after. ⊠ *Jardins du Palais-Royal, 110 Galerie Valois,* ☎ *01–40–20–00–27. AE, MC, V. Closed Sun. No lunch Sat. Métro: Palais-Royal.*

$–$$ ✕ **Aux Crus de Bourgogne.** This delightfully old-fashioned bistro, with its bright lights and red-check tablecloths, attracts a lively crowd. It opened in 1932 and quickly became popular by serving two luxury items—foie gras and cold lobster with homemade mayonnaise—at surprisingly low prices, a tradition that happily continues. ⊠ *3 rue Bachaumont,* ☎ *01–42–33–48–24. V. Closed weekends and Aug. Métro: Sentier.*

$ **L'Ardoise.** This minuscule storefront, painted white and decorated with enlargements of old sepia postcards of Paris, is the very model of the new contemporary bistros making waves in Paris. Chef Pierre Jay trained at Tour d'Argent, and his creations are first rate: a flan of crab in creamy emulsion of parsley, fresh cod with grilled chips of chorizo sausage, and a *feuillantine au citron*—sugar-glazed, cinammon sprinkled pastry leaves filled with lemon cream and lemon sections—are all enticing. No wonder L'Ardoise is often crowded. ⊠ *28 rue du Mont Thabor,* ☎ *01–42–96–28–18. Reservations essential. MC, V. Closed Mon. Métro: Concorde.*

2ᵉ Arrondissement (La Bourse)
FRENCH

$$ ✕ **Chez Georges.** When you ask sophisticated Parisians—bankers, aristocrats, or antiques dealers—to name their favorite bistro, many choose Georges. The traditional bistro cooking is good—herring, sole, kidneys, steak, and *frites* (fries)—but the atmosphere is better. A wood-paneled entry leads you to an elegant and unpretentious dining room where one long, white-clothed stretch of table lines the mirrored walls. ⊠ *1 rue du Mail,* ☎ *01–42–60–07–11. AE, DC, MC, V. Closed Sun. and Aug. Métro: Sentier.*

$$ ✕ **Le Vaudeville.** One of Jean-Paul Bucher's seven Parisian brasseries, Le Vaudeville is filled with well-dressed Parisians (many from the Stock Exchange across the street) and is a good value, thanks to its assortment of prix-fixe menus. Shellfish, house-smoked salmon, and desserts such as profiteroles are particularly fine. Enjoy the handsome 1930s decor and joyful dining until 2 AM daily. ⊠ *29 rue Vivienne,* ☎ *01–40–20–04–62. AE, DC, MC, V. Closed Dec. 24. Métro: Bourse.*

3ᵉ Arrondissement (Beaubourg/Marais)
FRENCH

$ **Le Pamphlet.** Chef Alain Carrere's modern take on the hearty cooking of the Basque Country and Bearn region of southwestern France has made this Marais bistro popular with an arty local crowd. Beyond the delicious, homey food, what many Parisians love here is that this place feels like a restaurant in the provinces, with its beamed ceiling, homey lamps, generously spaced tables, polite service, and faience that looks like its on loan from *grandmère*. ⊠ *38 rue Debelleyme,* ☎ *01–42–72–39–24. MC, V. Closed Sun. No lunch Sat. Métro: St-Sebastien-Froissart.*

NORTH AFRICAN

$ ✕ **Chez Omar.** Popular with a high-voltage fashion crowd—yes, that is Vivienne Westwood having dinner with Alexander McQueen—this is the place to come for couscous, whether you're a die-hard fan or have yet to taste this signature North African dish in all its glory. Proprietor Omar Guerida is famously friendly and speaks English. ⊠ *47 rue de Bretagne,* ☎ *01–42–72–36–26. MC, V. No lunch Sun. Métro: Filles du Calvaire.*

4ᵉ Arrondissement (Marais/Ile St-Louis)
FRENCH

$$ ✕ **Le Grizzli.** It's said that this turn-of-the-century bistro used to have
★ dancing bears out front—thus the name. A real charmer, this is one of the last of the unself-consciously old-fashioned bistros left in Paris (right down to the creaky spiral staircase leading up to the restroom). The owner gets many of his ingredients—especially the wonderful ham and cheeses—from his native Auvergne. Several dishes are cooked on a hot slate, including the salmon and the lamb. There's an interesting selec-

tion of wines from southwest France. ✉ *7 rue St-Martin,* ☎ *01–48–87–77–56. MC, V. Closed Sun. Métro: Châtelet.*

$$ ✕ **Le Vieux Bistro.** Despite the obvious location next to Notre-Dame and the corny name, "the Old Bistro" still pulls a worldly crowd of Parisians, including the likes of Leslie Caron, for home-style Paris comfort food like the sublime slow-simmered *boeuf Bourguignon* (beef stewed in wine). This place really *is* generations old, and its menu is full of bistro classics, such as beef fillet with marrow, éclairs, and tart Tatin. The decor is nondescript, but the frequently fancy crowd doesn't seem to notice. ✉ *14 rue du Cloître-Notre-Dame,* ☎ *01–43–54–18–95. MC, V. Métro: Hôtel de Ville.*

$–$$ ✕ **Bofinger.** One of the oldest, most beautiful, and most popular brasseries in Paris has generally improved since brasserie maestro Jean-Paul Bucher took over. Settle in to one of the tables dressed in crisp white linens, under the gorgeous Art Nouveau glass cupola, and enjoy fine classic brasserie fare, such as oysters, grilled sole, or fillet of lamb. ✉ *5–7 rue de la Bastille,* ☎ *01–42–72–87–82. AE, DC, MC, V. Métro: Bastille.*

5e Arrondissement (Latin Quarter)
FRENCH

$$$$ ✕ **La Tour d'Argent.** Set in a townhouse aerie overlooking Notre-Dame (with prices that are even higher), this temple of *la grande cuisine* is not what it used to be—but what is? Still, a meal here can be an event, with its view of Notre-Dame (its nighttime illumination is partly footed by your check and, mind you, many tables are not window-side). The food, though often good, rarely reaches the same heights as this view. But who can resist *caneton Tour d'Argent* (pressed duck; order it crispy, as the French like it rare), which famously comes with numbered certificate. Nouvelle creations are also featured, along with the best wine cellar in all France. ✉ *15 quai de la Tournelle,* ☎ *01–43–54–23–31. Reservations essential at least 1 wk in advance. Jacket and tie at dinner. AE, DC, MC, V. Closed Mon. Métro: Cardinal Lemoine.*

$$ **Bistrot. . . Côte Mer.** A local hit for the professionalism of its staff and its very delicious food, this reasonably priced fish house warms the eye with warm exposed stone walls, marble-top tables, a long brick-color velvet banquette, and old-fashioned tile floors. The dishes warm the stomach, and best bets include a tomato sauté of shrimps with orecchiette pasta and grilled sea bass with black-olive polenta. End it all with crêpes flamed in Grand Marnier—which gives the waiters a chance to ham it up a bit. ✉ *16 bd. St-Germain,* ☎ *01–43–54–59–10. AE, MC, V. Métro: Maubert-Mutualité.*

$$ ✕ **Chez René.** Cozy and appealingly shabby, this reliable address at the eastern end of boulevard St-Germain has satisfied three generations of Parisians, who count on finding dishes from Burgundy, such as *boeuf Bourguignon* (beef stewed in wine) and coq au vin. The dining rooms are cozy, with red-leatherette banquettes and white honeycomb-tile floors. ✉ *14 bd. St-Germain,* ☎ *01–43–54–30–23. MC, V. Closed Sun., Aug., and late Dec.–early Jan. No lunch Sat. Métro: Cardinal Lemoine.*

$ ✕ **Chantairelle.** Delicious south-central Auvergne cuisine is the specialty here, but the owners of this friendly, good-value spot also want you to fully experience the region, hence the recycled barn timbers, little stone fountain, and oils diffusing scents from the Auvergne. ✉ *17 rue Laplace,* ☎ *01–46–33–18–59. MC, V. Closed Sun. No lunch Sat. Métro: Maubert-Mutualité.*

6e Arrondissement (St-Germain)
FRENCH

$$ ✕ **Alcazar.** Englishman Sir Terence Conran's stunning, large new
★ brasserie is one of the chicest and liveliest spots in town. To take in the scene—and quite a scene it is, as this place seats 300 under a sky-

68

light roof—opt for a table on the mezzanine, where a long brushed-steel bar gives you a bird's-eye view. Chef Guillaume Lutard has created an appealingly classic menu. ⊠ *62 rue Mazarine,* ☎ *01–53–10–19–99. Reservations essential. AE, DC, MC, V. Métro: Odéon.*

$–$$ ✕ **Le Bouillon Racine.** Originally a *bouillon*—a Parisian soup restaurant popular at the turn of the century—this two-story place is now a lushly renovated Belle Epoque oasis featuring a good Belgian menu. In honor of Belgium's some 400 brews, it has a wonderful selection of beers. ⊠ *3 rue Racine,* ☎ *01–44–32–15–60. Reservations essential. AE, MC, V. Closed Sun. Métro: Odéon.*

$ ✕ **La Table d'Aude.** Rive Gauche students, senators, and book editors who dine here are on to a good thing, since this jolly restaurant serves some of the best *cuisine regionale* in Paris. Owner Bernard Patou and his wife, Veronique, take a contagious pleasure in serving up the best of their home turf—the Aude, that long narrow region in the Languedoc-Roussillon, which includes Carcacassonne, and Castelnaudry, which is famed for its cassoulet. ⊠ *8 rue de Vaugirard,* ☎ *01–43–26–36–36. MC, V. Closed Sun. Métro: Odeon.*

SEAFOOD

$$ ✕ **L'Espadon Bleu.** Chef Jacques Cagna's moderately priced seafood restaurant is a good spot to drop anchor in St-Germain. Yellow walls, blue beams, and mosaic tables with the restaurant's namesake, a blue swordfish, create a stylish nautical feel. The prix-fixe menu is a great deal. ⊠ *25 rue des Grands Augustins,* ☎ *01–46–33–00–85. Reservations essential. AE, MC, V. Closed Sun. and Mon. No lunch Sat. Métro: Odéon.*

7e Arrondissement (Invalides/École Militaire)

FRENCH

$$$$ ✕ **Jules Verne.** Top-ranked chef Alain Reix's cuisine—not to mention a location at 400 ft up, on the second level of the Eiffel Tower—make the Jules Verne one of the hardest dinner reservations to get in Paris. Reix's cooking, like the service, has its ups and downs. Come for lunch—a table is easier to snag—and be prepared for the distinctive all-black decor, a rather strange hybrid of Star Trek and '70s disco. ⊠ *Eiffel Tower,* ☎ *01–45–55–61–44. Reservations essential. Jacket and tie. AE, DC, MC, V. Métro: Bir-Hakeim.*

$–$$ ✕ **Au Bon Accueil.** If you want to see what well-heeled Parisians like to eat these days, book a table at this popular bistro as soon as you get to town. The excellent, reasonably priced *cuisine du marché* (daily menu based on what's in the markets) has made it a hit. Be sure to call first, as the owners are planning a major renovation so a temporary closing is in the works. ⊠ *14 rue de Montessuy,* ☎ *01–47–05–46–11. Reservations essential. MC, V. Closed Sun. Métro, RER: Pont de l'Alma.*

$ ✕ **Thoumieux.** Delightfully Parisian, this place vibes with red-velour banquettes, yellow walls, and bustling waiters in long, white aprons. Budget prices for decent food like duck confit and cassoulet make this place—owned by the same family for three generations—popular. ⊠ *79 rue St-Dominique,* ☎ *01–47–05–49–75. MC, V. Métro: Invalides.*

8e Arrondissement (Champs-Élysées)

FRENCH

$$$$ ✕ **Alain Ducasse.** Mega-starred chef Alain Ducasse recently took over
★ the restaurant of the Hotel Plaza-Athénée (beloved of yankee glitterati). You may need to instantly book a Concorde seat to actually catch him at this particular stove—Ducasse now has restaurants around the globe (and never cooks on weekends)—but it will probably be worth it: he's France's top chef. When you taste the *bisque d'homard* (lob-

ster bisque) or the $56 pork belly, you know you are getting the real thing—each is made from as many elements (shell, skin, juice, pan drippings) as possible and offers the absolute quintessence of each dish. Still, for these astronomical prices you might wish for more multi-culti fireworks from the kitchen and a less distant staff. ⊠ *Hotel Plaza-Athénée, 27 ave. Montaigne,* ☏ *01–53–67–66–65. Reservations essential weeks in advance. AE, DC, MC, V. Closed Sun. Métro: Alma-Marceau.*

$$$$ ✕ **Les Ambassadeurs.** Looking as if Madame de Pompadour might stroll
★ in the door any moment, Les Ambassadeurs offers a setting of uniquely ancien régime splendor, with dramatic black-and-white diamond floor, glittering chandeliers, and honey-color marble walls. Chef Dominique Bouchet likes to mix up luxe with more down-to-earth flavors: potato pancakes topped with smoked salmon, caviar-flecked scallops wrapped in bacon with tomato and basil, duck with rutabaga, turbot with cauliflower. It's difficult to fault the distinguished service or the memorable wine list. ⊠ *10 pl. de la Concorde,* ☏ *01–44–71–16–16. Reservations essential. Jacket and tie at dinner. AE, DC, MC, V. Métro: Concorde.*

$$$$ ✕ **Les Élysées.** Chef Alain Solivères is a passionate cook whose repu-
★ tation continues to grow in Paris gourmet circles. Come here when you want to treat yourself, since not only is the southern French food of chef Alain Solivères exquisite, but service is also impeccable and the intimate dining room, under a beautiful turn-of-the-century *verrière* (glass ceiling), is the kind of place where you want to linger. Note, though, that it's very busy at midday, so unless you're coming for the good-value lunch menu, dinner is a calmer option. ⊠ *In Hôtel Vernet, 25 rue Vernet,* ☏ *01–47–23–43–10. AE, DC, MC, V. Reservations essential. Closed weekends. Métro: George V.*

$$$$ ✕ **Ledoyen.** Whether you want to eat light or hearty, young chef Chris-
★ tian Le Squer's elegant, beautifully realized menu is a treat. The elegant restaurant tucked away in the quiet gardens flanking the avenue as it runs into the place de la Concorde is a study in the grandiose style of Napoleon III, as revisited by decorator Jacques Grange, with gilded ceilings and walls, plush armchairs, and tables with candelabra. ⊠ *1 av. Dutuit, on the Carré des Champs-Élysées,* ☏ *01–47–42–23–23. Reservations essential. AE, DC, MC, V. Closed weekends. Métro: Place de la Concorde, Champs-Élysées–Clemenceau.*

$$$$ ✕ **Pierre Gagnaire.** In a single dish, legendary chef Pierre Gagnaire sen-
★ sationally brings together unexpected tastes and textures. Two intriguing dishes from a recent menu—it changes seasonally—included duck foie gras wrapped in bacon, and sea bass in herbs with tiny clams. The only negatives are the amateurish service and the brief wine list. ⊠ *6 rue de Balzac,* ☏ *01–44–35–18–25. Reservations essential. AE, DC, MC, V. Closed Sun. Métro: Charles-de-Gaulle–Étoile.*

$$$$ ✕ **Taillevent.** Perhaps the most traditional—and this is meant as high
★ praise—of all Paris's luxury restaurants, this grande dame is suddenly the object of a certain uncharacteristic buzz since the arrival of new chef Michel Del Burgo, who has a reputation for food that is at once earthy yet refined. Now he's judiciously revising the menu here, while classics like the *boudin d'homard*—an airy sausage-shape soufflé of lobster—offer continuity with the fabled past. Service is exceptional, the setting—19th-century paneled salons now accented with abstract paintings—is luxe, and the wine list probably one of the top 10 in the world. ⊠ *15 rue Lamennais,* ☏ *01–45–63–39–94. Reservations 3–4 wks in advance essential. Jacket and tie. AE, MC, V. Closed weekends and Aug. Métro: Charles-de-Gaulle–Étoile.*

$$ ✕ **Sébillon.** The original Sébillon has nurtured chic residents of the fashionable suburb of Neuilly for generations; this elegant, polished branch off the Champs-Élysées continues the tradition. The menu includes lob-

ster salad, lots of shellfish, and—the specialty—roast leg of lamb sliced table-side and served in unlimited quantity. Service is notably friendly. ⊠ *66 rue Pierre Charron,* ☎ *01–43–59–28–15. AE, DC, MC, V. Métro: Franklin-D.-Roosevelt.*

CONTEMPORARY

$$ ✕ **Spoon, Food and Wine.** Star chef Alain Ducasse's blueprint of a bistro for the 21st century has been packed ever since it opened in late 1998. What draws the trendy crowd is the playful Asian- and American-inspired menu, the great decor—at night the large white-linen shades on the walls are rolled up to reveal plum upholstery—and that it's so hard to get a reservation. Try the Thai soup, the pasta dishes, and the roast salmon with béarnaise sauce. ⊠ *14 rue de Marignan,* ☎ *01– 40–76–34–44. Reservations essential. AE, MC, V. Métro: Franklin-D.-Roosevelt.*

9ᵉ Arrondissement (Opéra)

FRENCH

$ ✕ **Chartier.** People come to this cavernous turn-of-the-century restaurant more for the bonhomie than the food, which is often rather ordinary. You may find yourself sharing a table as you study the long, old-fashioned menu of such favorites as steak tartare and roast chicken with fries. ⊠ *7 rue du Faubourg-Montmartre,* ☎ *01–47–70–86–29. Reservations not accepted. No credit cards. Métro: Rue Montmartre.*

10ᵉ Arrondissement (République/Gare du Nord)

FRENCH

$$ ✕ **Brasserie Flo.** Though it's hard to find—down a passageway near Gare de l'Est—it's worth the effort, for both food and decor. The rich wood and stained glass are typically Alsatian, service is enthusiastic, and brasserie standards such as shellfish and *choucroute* (sauerkraut and sausage) are savory. It's open until 1:30 AM, with a special night-owl menu from 10 PM. ⊠ *7 cour des Petites Écuries,* ☎ *01–47–70– 13–59. AE, DC, MC, V. Métro: Château d'Eau.*

$–$$ ✕ **Chez Michel.** Chef Thierry Breton pulls a stylish crowd—despite the drab decor and neighborhood—with his wonderful cuisine du marché and dishes from his native Brittany. Typical of Breton's kitchen are the lasagna stuffed with chèvre and the artichokes and tuna steak with pureed peas. ⊠ *10 rue Belzunce,* ☎ *01–44–53–06–20. Reservations essential. MC, V. Closed Sun.–Mon. No lunch Sat. Métro: Gare du Nord.*

11ᵉ Arrondissement (Bastille/République)

CHINESE

$$ ✕ **Wok.** Design-it-yourself Oriental stir-fry in a slick, minimalist setting has made this spot a hit with the pennywise hipsters who hang out in the clubs around party-hearty Bastille. You select what type of noodle you want, the waiter brings you a bowl, and then you load up at a buffet with bins of chicken, white fish, shrimp, salmon, beef, vegetables. Mobbed on weekends, this place is fun, nourishing, and cheap. ⊠ *23 rue des Taillandiers,* ☎ *01–55–28–88–77. MC, V. Métro: Breguet Sabin, Bastille, or Ledru Rollin.*

FRENCH

$$ ✕ **Le Repaire de Cartouche.** Near the Cirque d'Hiver, in the Bastille,
★ this split-level, '50s-style bistro with dark wood decor is the latest good-value bistro sensation in Paris. Young chef Rodolphe Paquin is a creative and impeccably trained cook who does a stylish take on earthy French regional dishes. The wine list is excellent, with bargains like a Pernand-Vergelesses (red Burgundy) for $20. ⊠ *99 rue Amelot,* ☎ *01– 47–00–25–86. AE, MC, V. Reservations essential. Closed Sun. No dinner Mon. Métro: Filles du Calvaire.*

12e Arrondissement (Bastille/Gare de Lyon)

FRENCH

$$$ ✕ **Au Trou Gascon.** At this successful Belle Epoque establishment off place Daumesnil, owner Alain Dutournier serves his version of the cuisine of Gascony—a region of outstanding ham, foie gras, lamb, and poultry—and his now-classic white-chocolate mousse. ⊠ *40 rue Taine,* ☎ *01–43–44–34–26. AE, DC, MC, V. Closed Sun., Christmas wk, and Aug. No lunch Sat. Métro: Daumesnil.*

$$ ✕ **Le Square Trousseau.** Since fashion designer Jean-Paul Gaultier moved his headquarters nearby, this charming turn-of-the-century bistro has become very chic. You might see a supermodel or two—Claudia Schiffer often comes in when in town—while dining on the homemade foie gras and tender baby chicken with mustard and bread-crumb crust. The house wine is a good value, especially the fruity red Morgon. ⊠ *1 rue Antoine Vollon,* ☎ *01–43–44–06–00. MC, V. Métro: Ledru-Rollin.*

13e Arrondissement (Les Gobelins)

FRENCH

$ ✕ **Le Terroir.** A jolly crowd of regulars makes this little bistro festive. The solidly classical menu, based on first-rate ingredients from all over France, includes salads with chicken livers or fresh marinated anchovies, calves' liver or monkfish with saffron, and pears marinated in wine. ⊠ *11 bd. Arago,* ☎ *01–47–07–36–99. Closed Sun. No lunch Sat. Métro: Les Gobelins.*

14e Arrondissement (Montparnasse)

FRENCH

$$ ✕ **Contre-Allée.** Students and professors crowd this large restaurant, simply decorated with bullfighting posters. The menu has selections such as squid salad with mussels and roast cod with Parmesan; homemade pasta accompanies many dishes. A sidewalk terrace enlivens shady avenue Denfert-Rochereau in summer. The restaurant serves until 11:30 PM. ⊠ *83 av. Denfert-Rochereau,* ☎ *01–43–54–99–86. AE, DC, MC, V. No lunch Sat. Métro: Denfert-Rochereau.*

$$ ✕ **La Coupole.** This world-renowned, cavernous place practically defines the term *brasserie.* Many find it too large, too noisy, and too expensive, and no one likes the long wait at the bar before being seated. Still, it has been popular since the days Jean-Paul Sartre and Simone de Beauvoir were regulars, although there are now more bourgeois grandmothers dining here than existential philosophers. ⊠ *102 bd. du Montparnasse,* ☎ *01–43–20–14–20. AE, DC, MC, V. Métro: Vavin.*

15e Arrondissement (Motte-Picquet/Balard)

FRENCH

$$ ✕ **Bistrot d'Hubert.** In a studied environment that might have sprung from the pages of *Elle Décor,* this popular bistro—frequented by a stylish crowd—serves food that perfectly expresses the countercurrents of the Parisian culinary landscape. The prix-fixe menu is split into two: "tradition" and "innovation." You might have the tuna steak in a "caramel" of balsamic vinegar, or go for the more classic roast lamb. ⊠ *41 bd. Pasteur,* ☎ *01–47–34–15–50. Reservations essential. AE, DC, MC, V. Métro: Pasteur.*

$$ ✕ **Philippe Detourbe.** Amid black lacquer, mirrors, and burgundy-vel-
★ vet upholstery, sample Detourbe's spectacular contemporary French cooking. The menu changes with every meal and may include smoked salmon filled with cabbage *rémoulade* (cabbage in a creamy dressing) or cod steak with white beans and caramelized endives; desserts are fantastic. The wine list is brief but well chosen; service is friendly and efficient. ⊠ *8 rue Nicolas Charlet,* ☎ *01–42–19–08–59. Reservations essential. MC, V. Closed Sun. No lunch Sat. Métro: Pasteur.*

16e Arrondissement (Arc de Triomphe)

FRENCH

$$–$$$ ✕ **Prunier.** Founded in 1925, this seafood restaurant is one of the best—and the prettiest—in Paris. The famous Art Deco mosaics glitter, and the white-marble counters shine with impeccably fresh shellfish. The kitchen not only excels at classic French fish dishes but has added some interesting options, like a *Saintongeaise* plate—raw oysters with grilled sausages. ✉ *16 av. Victor-Hugo,* ☎ *01–44–17–35–85. Reservations essential in upstairs dining room. Jacket and tie. AE, DC, MC, V. Closed Sun.–Mon. Métro: Charles-de-Gaulle–Étoile.*

$$ ✕ **La Grande Armée.** Jacques Garcia, France's most talked-about dec-
★ orator, has unleashed here an exotic Napoléon-III bordello decor—think black lacquered tables, leopard upholstery, Bordeaux velvet, plus, of course, a carefully tousled clientele picking at those dishes that chic Parisians like best these days. ✉ *3 av. de la Grande Armée,* ☎ *01–45–00–24–77. AE, DC, MC, V. Métro: Charles de Gaullle-Étoile.*

$$ ✕ **Le Relais du Parc.** This bistro-annex is the place to try a lighter version of Alain Ducasse's cooking for less. Two delicious starters—the lobster salad, and the baby potatoes with black truffles in a creamy oxtail-stock sauce—make good meals, followed by cheese or dessert. Main courses are also excellent, but the desserts could be better, and wine is overpriced. ✉ *55 av. Raymond-Poincaré,* ☎ *01–44–05–66–10. Reservations essential. AE, DC, MC, V. Métro: Victor Hugo.*

$ ✕ **Le Petit Rétro.** Two types of clientele—men in expensive suits at noon and well-dressed couples in the evening—frequent this little bistro with Art Nouveau tiles and bentwood furniture. You can't go wrong with the daily special written on the chalkboard. Come when you want a good solid meal, like the perfect *pavé de boeuf* (thick steak). ✉ *5 rue Mesnil,* ☎ *01–44–05–06–05. MC, V. Closed Sun. No lunch Mon. Métro: Victor Hugo.*

17e Arrondissement (Monceau/Clichy/Arc de Triomphe)

FRENCH

$$$$ ✕ **Guy Savoy.** Top chef Guy Savoy's other five bistros have not dis-
★ tracted him too much from his handsome luxury restaurant near the Arc de Triomphe. The oysters in aspic and grilled pigeon reveal the magnitude of his talent, and the mille-feuille is a contemporary classic. ✉ *18 rue Troyon,* ☎ *01–43–80–40–61. Reservations essential. AE, MC, V. Closed Sun. No lunch Sat. Métro: Charles-de-Gaulle–Étoile.*

ITALIAN

$$ ✕ **Il Baccello.** Young chef Raphael Bembaron's talent is pulling crowds to this outpost for first-rate contemporary Italian food. Bembaron trained at Lucas Carton in Paris, Enoteca Pinchiorri in Florence, and at Joia, the gourmet vegetarian restaurant in Milan, and his background comes through in superb dishes like the risotto cooked with Barolo wine and garnished with duck breast and aged Mimolette cheese or langoustines on toothpicks with almond-stuffed green olives on a bed of spelt and broccoli in a pumpkin coulis. This is also a good address for vegetarians. The dining room is done in a sleek (if noisy) minimalist style. ✉ *23 rue des Taillandiers,* ☎ *01–55–28–88–77. MC, V.. Métro: Breguet Sabin, Bastille, or Ledru Rollin.*

NORTH AFRICAN

$$ ✕ **Le Timgad.** For a stylish evening out and a night off from French food, try this elegant North African restaurant. Start with a savory *brick* (crispy parchment pastry filled with meat, eggs, or seafood), followed by tasty couscous or succulent *tagine* (meat or poultry that's slowly braised inside a domed pottery casserole). ✉ *21 rue de Brunel,* ☎ *01–45–74–23–70. MC, V. Métro: Argentine.*

18ᵉ Arrondissement (Montmartre)

FRENCH

$ ✕ **Le Moulin à Vins.** The atmosphere at this popular wine bar/bistro is sepia toned—both it and the surrounding neighborhood evoke old Paris. It's perfect for lunch while touring Montmartre. In the evening it's livelier, when devoted regulars come for the daily short list of hot dishes. ✉ *6 rue Burq,* ☎ *01–45–52–81–27. MC, V. Closed Mon. Métro: Abbesses.*

Cafés and Salons de Thé

Cafés can be found at every bend in Paris; following is a small selection of cafés and *salons de thé* (tearooms) to whet your appetite. **Au Père Tranquille** (✉ 16 rue Pierre Lescot, 1ᵉʳ, ☎ 01–45–08–00–34, métro Les Halles) is one of the best places in Paris for people-watching. **Café Beaubourg** (✉ 43 rue St-Merri, 4ᵉ, ☎ 01–48–87–63–96, métro Hôtel-de-Ville), near the Pompidou Center, is a slick, modern spot. **Café Marly** (✉ Cour Napoléon du Louvre, 93 rue de Rivoli, 1ᵉʳ, ☎ 01–49–26–06–60, métro Palais-Royal), overlooking the main courtyard of the Louvre, is perfect for an afternoon break or a nightcap and offers a spectacular Belle Epoque decor. **La Crémaillère** (✉ 15 pl. du Tertre, 18ᵉ, ☎ 01–46–06–58–59, métro Anvers) is a veritable monument to fin-de-siècle art in Montmartre. **Ma Bourgogne** (✉ 19 pl. des Vosges, 4ᵉ, ☎ 01–42–78–44–64, métro St-Paul) is a calm oasis for a coffee or a light lunch away from the noisy streets. **Mariage Frères** (✉ 30 rue du Bourg-Tibourg, 4ᵉ, ☎ 01–42–72–28–11, métro Hôtel-de-Ville) is an outstanding tea shop serving 500 kinds of tea, along with delicious tarts. **Salon de Thé du Palais Royal** (✉ Jardins du Palais Royal, 110 Galérie de Valois, 1ᵉʳ, ☎ 01–40–20–00–27, métro Palais-Royal) serves tea on a terrace overlooking the gardens of the Palais Royal. **Le Vieux Colombier** (✉ 65 rue de Rennes, 7ᵉ, ☎ 01–45–48–53–81, métro St-Sulpice) is just around the corner from St-Sulpice and the Vieux Colombier Theater.

Wine Bars

Wine bars are a good place to sample a glass (or bottle) of French wine and have an excellent, simple hot meal or just a plate of cheese or charcuterie. Hours can vary widely, so it's best to check ahead; many close around 10 PM. **Aux Bons Crus** (✉ 7 rue des Petits-Champs, 1ᵉʳ, ☎ 01–42–60–06–45, métro Bourse) is a cramped, narrow venue with an authentically Parisian feel. **Le Baron Rouge** (✉ 1 rue Théophile-Roussel, 12ᵉ, ☎ 01–43–43–14–32, métro Ledru-Rollin) is a noisy and convivial haunt. **Jacques Mélac** (✉ 42 rue Léon-Frot, 11ᵉ, ☎ 01–43–70–59–27, métro Charonne) is named after the jolly owner who bottles several of his own wines—try the chewy red Lirac.

LODGING

Revised and updated by Christopher Mooney

Winding staircases, flower-filled window boxes, concierges who seem to have stepped from a 19th-century novel—all of these still exist in Paris hotels. So do grand rooms with marble baths, Belle Epoque lobbies, and polished staff at your beck and call. In Paris there are wonderful hotels for every taste and budget.

Our criteria when selecting the hotels reviewed below were quality, location, and character. Fewer hotels are listed in outlying arrondissements (the 10ᵉ to the 20ᵉ) because these are farther from the major sights. Generally, there are more hotels on the Right Bank offering luxury— or at any rate formality—than there are on the Left Bank, where hotels are frequently smaller and richer in old-fashioned ambience. In Paris's oldest quarters hotel rooms are generally much smaller than their American counterparts. Although air-conditioning has become de rigueur in middle- to higher-price hotels, it is generally not a prerequisite for comfort (Paris's hot weather season doesn't usually last long).

Despite the huge choice of hotels, you should always reserve well in advance, especially if you're determined to stay in a specific place. You can do this by telephoning or faxing ahead, then asking for written or faxed confirmation of your reservation, detailing the duration of your stay, the price, the location and type of your room (single or double, twin beds or double), and the bathroom (shower—*douche*—or bath—*baignoire*—private or shared).

Almost all Paris hotels charge extra for breakfast, with prices ranging from 30 francs to more than 200 francs per person in luxury establishments. For anything more than the standard Continental breakfast of café au lait and croissants, the price will be higher. You may be better off finding the nearest café. A nominal *séjour* (lodging) tax of 7 francs per person, per night is charged to pay for promotion of tourism in Paris.

CATEGORY	COST*
$$$$	over 1,750 frs
$$$	1,000 frs–1,750 frs
$$	600 frs–1,000 frs
$	under 600 frs

All prices are for a standard double room, including 20.6% tax and service.

1er Arrondissement (Louvre/Les Halles)

$$$$ ⊞ **Costes.** Jean-Louis and Gilbert Costes's sumptuous hotel is the darling of the fashion and media set. Conjuring up the palaces of Napoléon III, salons are swathed in rich garnet and bronze tones and contain a luxurious mélange of patterned fabrics, heavy swags, and enough brocade and fringe to blanket the Champs-Élysées. The seductive, go-for-baroque bar, with its labyrinth of little rooms and secluded nooks, is *the* place in Paris to be seen trying not to be seen. Thanks to decorating genius Jacques Garcia, this hotel is the tops for taste in Paris. ⊠ *239 rue St-Honoré, 75001,* ☎ *01–42–44–50–50,* FAX *01–42–44–50–01,. 85 rooms. Restaurant, bar, air-conditioning, in-room data ports, in-room safes, room service, indoor pool, sauna, exercise room, laundry service. AE, DC, MC, V. Métro: Tuileries.* ✍

$$$$ ⊞ **Meurice.** One of the finest hotels in the world has become even finer—thanks to the millions of the sultan of Brunei, the fabled restaurant and the elaborately gilded 18th-century Rococo salons have been entirely restored, and the rooms—adorned with Persian carpets, marble mantelpieces, and ormolu clocks—are now more opulent and soigné than ever, if that's possible (book well in advance for a room or a suite overlooking the Tuileries Gardens). The hotel's restaurant is set in one of the most lavishly opulent rooms in the city. ⊠ *228 rue de Rivoli, 75001,* ☎ *01–44–58–10–10,* FAX *01–44–58–10–15. 160 rooms, 36 suites. 2 Restaurants, bar, air-conditioning, in-room data ports, in-room safes, minibars, concierge, sauna, no-smoking rooms, room service, laundry service, business services. AE, DC, MC, V. Métro: Tuileries, Concorde.* ✍

$$$$ ⊞ **Régina.** In the handsome place des Pyramides, this 100-year-old Art Nouveau gem oozes old-fashioned grandeur in both public spaces and guest rooms. There are a sublime Belle Epoque lounge and fine antiques throughout. Request a room on rue de Rivoli facing the Louvre and the Tuileries Gardens. ⊠ *2 rue des Pyramides, 75001,* ☎ *01–42–60–31–10,* FAX *01–40–15–95–16. 129 rooms, 15 suites. Restaurant, bar, air-conditioning, in-room safes, no-smoking rooms, room service, laundry service, meeting rooms. AE, DC, MC, V. Métro: Tuileries.* ✍

$$$$ 🏨 **Ritz.** Founded as a temple of luxury by Cesar Ritz, this legendary place has been regilded at a cost of $150 million by owner Mohammed al-Fayed (whose son Dodi, with Diana, Princess of Wales, set out on their fatal car ride after dining here in August 1997). Of course, there are really two Ritzes. The first is the gilded place Vendôme wing—this is where Gary Cooper serenaded Audrey Hepburn in *Love in the Afternoon* and features the legendary suites named after former residents, such as Marcel Proust and Coco Chanel. The newer wing, off the back of the building, remains surprisingly (disappointingly?) intimate. Don't miss the famous Hemingway Bar (which the writer claimed to have "liberated" in 1944). ⊠ *15 pl. Vendôme, 75001,* ☎ *01–43–16–30–30,* ℻ *01–43–16–36–68. 142 rooms, 45 suites. 3 restaurants, 2 bars, air-conditioning, in-room safes, room service, indoor pool, beauty salon, health club, shops, laundry service, meeting rooms, parking (fee). AE, DC, MC, V. Métro: Opéra.* ✎

$$$–$$$$ 🏨 **Vendôme.** This hotel has the best guest-to-staff ratio in Paris and
★ every luxury perk imaginable. Rooms are in sumptuous, Second Empire style and bathrooms are over the top. Best of all, besides a videophone for checking out visitors at the door, is the fully automated bedside console that controls the lights, curtains, and electronic do-not-disturb sign. ⊠ *1 pl. Vendôme, 75001,* ☎ *01–42–60–32–84,* ℻ *01–49–27–97–89. 19 rooms, 10 suites. Restaurant, bar, air-conditioning, room service, in-room safes, in-room modem lines, laundry service. AE, DC, MC, V. Métro: Concorde, Opéra.*

$$ 🏨 **Britannique.** Open since 1870, the Britannique blends courteous English service with old-fashioned French elegance. It has retained its handsome winding staircase and has well-appointed, soundproof rooms in chic, warm tones. ⊠ *20 av. Victoria, 75001,* ☎ *01–42–33–74–59,* ℻ *01–42–33–82–65. 40 rooms. Bar, in-room safes. AE, DC, MC, V. Métro: Châtelet.*

$ 🏨 **Louvre Forum.** This hotel is a find: Smack in the center of town, it
★ has a friendly feel and clean, comfortable, well-equipped rooms (minibars, satellite TV). ⊠ *25 rue du Bouloi, 75001,* ☎ *01–42–36–54–19,* ℻ *01–42–33–66–31. 27 rooms. Bar, minibars. AE, DC, MC, V. Métro: Louvre.*

2ᵉ Arrondissement (La Bourse)

$$ 🏨 **Grand Hôtel de Besançon.** This terrific hotel, with its very Parisian cream-color facade and wrought-iron balconies, has it all—intimacy, comfort, affordability, and a location on a delightful, pedestrian market street near Les Halles, the Pompidou Center, and the Marais. Rooms are classically decorated with French upholsteries and period reproductions, and despite the busy area nearby, they are quiet. ⊠ *56 rue Montorgueil, 75002,* ☎ *01–42–36–41–08,* ℻ *01–45–08–08–79. 11 rooms, 14 suites. In-room modem lines, in-room safes, laundry service AE, DC, MC, V. Métro: Etienne-Marcel, Les Halles.*

$$ 🏨 **Hôtel de Noailles.** With a nod to the work of postmodern designers like Putman and Starck, this new-wave inn (part of the Tulip Inn group) is a star among Paris's new crop of well-priced, style-driven boutique hotels. Though not to everyone's taste, rooms are imaginatively decorated with funky furnishings and contemporary details. ⊠ *9 rue de Michodière, 75002,* ☎ *01–47–42–92–90,* ℻ *01–49–24–92–71. 58 rooms. Bar, air-conditioning, laundry service. AE, DC, MC, V. Métro: Opéra.*

3ᵉ Arrondissement (Beaubourg/Marais)

$$$$ 🏨 **Pavillon de la Reine.** On lovely place des Vosges, this magnificent mansion, reconstructed from original plans, is filled with Louis XIII–style fireplaces and antiques. Ask for a duplex with French windows overlooking the first of two flower-filled courtyards behind the historic Queen's Pavilion. Breakfast is served in the vaulted cellar, *digestifs* in front of the

Paris Lodging

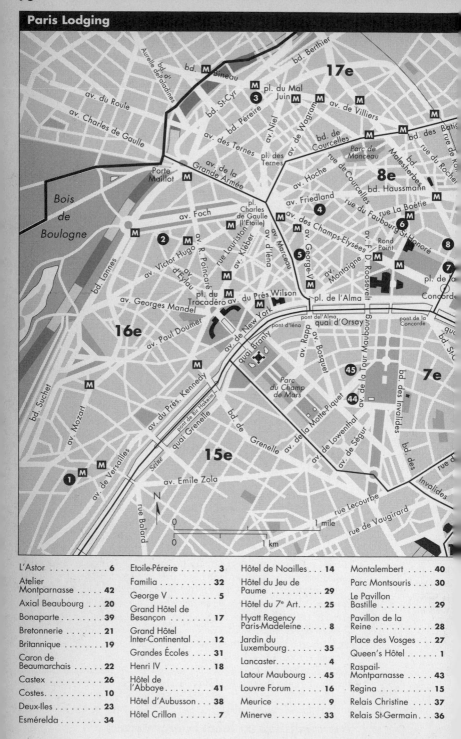

salon's gargantuan fireplace. ⊠ *28 pl. des Vosges, 75003,* ☎ *01–40–29–19–19; 800/447–7462 in the U.S.,* FAX *01–40–29–19–20. 30 rooms, 25 suites. Bar, breakfast room, air-conditioning, room service, laundry service, parking (free). AE, DC, MC, V. Métro: Bastille, St-Paul.*

4ᵉ Arrondissement (Marais/Ile St-Louis)

$$$ ⊡ **Hôtel du Jeu de Paume.** The showpiece of this lovely 17th-century hotel on the Ile St-Louis is the stone-walled, vaulted lobby–cum–breakfast room. It stands on an erstwhile court where French aristocrats once played *jeu de paume,* an early version of tennis using palm fronds. The bright rooms are nicely done up in butter yellow, with rustic antiques, tasteful objets and bric-a-brac, beamed ceilings, and damask upholsteries. The little garden is a haven of sun-drenched tranquillity. ⊠ *54 rue St-Louis-en-l'Ile, 75004,* ☎ *01–43–26–14–18,* FAX *01–40–46–02–76. 30 rooms, 1 junior suite. Bar, baby-sitting, laundry service, sauna, health club, meeting rooms. AE, DC, MC, V. Métro: Pont-Marie.* ✍

$$ ⊡ **Axial Beaubourg.** A solid bet in the Marais, this hotel in a 16th-century building has beamed ceilings in the lobby and in the six first-floor rooms. Most have pleasant if functional decor, and all have satellite TV. The Pompidou Center and the Picasso Museum are five minutes away. ⊠ *11 rue du Temple, 75004,* ☎ *01–42–72–72–22,* FAX *01–42–72–03–53. 39 rooms. Air-conditioning, in-room data ports, in-room safes, no-smoking rooms. AE, DC, MC, V. Métro: Hôtel de Ville.*

$$ ⊡ **Bretonnerie.** This small hotel is in a 17th-century *hôtel particulier* (town house) on a tiny street in the Marais, a few minutes' walk from the Pompidou Center. Rooms are done in Louis XIII style, complete with upholstered walls; they vary considerably in size from spacious to cramped. ⊠ *22 rue Ste-Croix-de-la-Bretonnerie, 75004,* ☎ *01–48–87–77–63,* FAX *01–42–77–26–78. 27 rooms, 3 suites. In-room safes. MC, V. Métro: Hôtel de Ville.*

$$ ⊡ **Caron de Beaumarchais.** The theme of this intimate jewel is the work **★** of Caron de Beaumarchais, who wrote *The Marriage of Figaro* in 1778. Rooms faithfully reflect the taste of 18th-century French nobility. The second- and fifth-floor rooms with balconies are the largest; those on the sixth floor have beguiling views across Right Bank rooftops. ⊠ *12 rue Vieille-du-Temple, 75004,* ☎ *01–42–72–34–12,* FAX *01–42–72–34–63. 19 rooms. Air-conditioning, in-room safes, laundry service. AE, DC, MC, V. Métro: Hôtel de Ville.*

$$ ⊡ **Deux-Iles.** This converted 17th-century mansion on the Ile St-Louis has long won plaudits for charm and comfort. The delightfully old-fashioned rooms, blessed with exposed beams, are small but airy; ask for one overlooking the little garden courtyard. In winter a roaring fire warms the lounge. ⊠ *59 rue St-Louis-en-l'Ile, 75004,* ☎ *01–43–26–13–35,* FAX *01–43–29–60–25. 17 rooms. Air-conditioning, in-room safes, baby-sitting. AE, MC, V. Métro: Pont-Marie.*

$–$$ ⊡ **Hôtel du 7ᵉ Art.** The theme of this hip Marais hotel ("Seventh Art" is what the French call filmmaking) is Hollywood from the '40s to the '60s. Rooms are small and spartan but clean, quiet, and equipped with cable TV. There's no elevator, but there is a pleasant bar. The clientele is young, trendy, and primarily American. ⊠ *20 rue St-Paul, 75004,* ☎ *01–44–54–85–00,* FAX *01–42–77–69–10. 23 rooms. Bar, in-room safes. AE, DC, MC, V. Métro: St-Paul.*

$ ⊡ **Castex.** This Marais hotel in a Revolution-era building is a bargain hunter's dream. Rooms are low on frills but squeaky clean and up to date, the owners are extremely friendly, and the prices are rock bottom, which ensures the hotel is often booked months ahead. There's no elevator, and the only TV is in the ground-floor salon. ⊠ *5 rue Castex, 75004,* ☎ *01–42–72–31–52,* FAX *01–42–72–57–91. 29 rooms, 23 with shower. MC, V. Métro: Bastille.*

$ ⌂ **Place des Vosges.** A loyal, eclectic clientele swears by this small, historic Marais hotel on a delightful street just off place des Vosges. The Louis XIII–style reception area and rooms with oak-beamed ceilings, rough-hewn stone, and a mix of rustic finds from secondhand shops evoke old Marais. ⊠ *12 rue de Birague, 75004,* ☎ *01–42–72–60–46,* FAX *01–42–72–02–64. 16 rooms. Breakfast room. AE, DC, MC, V. Métro: Bastille.*

5ᵉ Arrondissement (Latin Quarter)

$$$ ⌂ **Jardin du Luxembourg.** Blessed with a charming staff and a stylish look, this hotel is one of the most sought after in the Latin Quarter. Rooms are a bit small (common for this neighborhood) but intelligently furnished for optimal space and warmly decorated in ocher, rust, and indigo à la Provençal. Ask for one with a balcony overlooking the street; the best, No. 25, has a peekaboo view of the Eiffel Tower. ⊠ *5 impasse Royer-Collard, 75005,* ☎ *01–40–46–08–88,* FAX *01–40–46–02–28. 27 rooms. Air-conditioning, in-room safes, no-smoking rooms, sauna. AE, DC, MC, V. Métro: Luxembourg.*

$$ ⌂ **Esméralda.** Once any *Vogue* editor's best-kept secret, this place used
★ to be the ultimate Left Bank *hôtel de charme.* Set in a fusty 17th-century building across from Notre-Dame, it has long been cherished for its quirky, cozy, eccentric charm. Some closet-size rooms are nearly overpowered by gaudy imitation antiques or 1970s fabrics, while others could be cleaner. The tiny lobby—adorned with silk flowers, daub and wood moldings, and snoozing cats—is right out of a Flaubert novel. ⊠ *4 rue St-Julien-le-Pauvre, 75005,* ☎ *01–43–54–19–20,* FAX *01–40–51–00–68. 15 rooms with bath, 4 without. No credit cards. Métro: St-Michel.*

$ ⌂ **Familia.** The hospitable Gaucheron family, the owners, bends over
★ backward for you. About half the rooms feature romantic sepia frescoes of celebrated Paris scenes; others are appointed with exquisite Louis XV–style furnishings or have nice mahogany pieces. Book a month ahead for one with a walk-out balcony on the second or fifth floor. ⊠ *11 rue des Écoles, 75005,* ☎ *01–43–54–55–27,* FAX *01–43–29–61–77. 30 rooms. AE, MC, V. Métro: Cardinal Lemoine.*

$ ⌂ **Grandes Écoles.** This delightfully intimate place looks and feels like a country cottage dropped smack in the middle of the Latin Quarter. It's off the street and occupies three buildings on a beautiful leafy garden. Parquet floors, Louis-Philippe furnishings, lace bedspreads, and the absence of TV all add to the rustic ambience. ⊠ *75 rue du Cardinal Lemoine, 75005,* ☎ *01–43–26–79–23,* FAX *01–43–25–28–15. 51 rooms. Parking (fee). MC, V. Métro: Cardinal Lemoine.*

$ ⌂ **Minerve.** Fans of the Gaucheron family—and they are legion—will
★ be delighted to learn that the Minerve is now part of the Familia (see *above*) fold. Just next door to the Familia, and twice as big, the hotel has been completely refurbished in the inimitable Gaucheron style: flowers and breakfast tables on the balconies, frescoes in the spacious lobby, tapestries on the walls and cherry-wood furniture in the rooms. It's less intimate than the Familia —but just as charming. ⊠ *13 rue des Écoles, 75005,* ☎ *01–43–26–26–04,* FAX *01–44–07–01–96. 54 rooms. In-room data ports, breakfast room. AE, MC, V. Métro: Cardinal Lemoine.*

6ᵉ Arrondissement (St-Germain/Montparnasse)

$$$$ ⌂ **Relais Christine.** On a quiet street between the Seine and boulevard St-Germain, this luxurious and popular hotel, occupying 16th-century abbey cloisters, oozes romantic ambience. Rooms are spacious (particularly the duplexes on the upper floors) and well appointed in old Parisian style; the best have exposed beams and overlook the garden. ⊠ *3 rue Christine, 75006,* ☎ *01–40–51–60–80; 800/447–7462 in the U.S.,* FAX *01–40–51–60–81. 31 rooms, 18 suites. Bar, air-conditioning,* no-smoking rooms, room service, baby-sitting, laundry service, meeting rooms, parking (free). AE, DC, MC, V. Métro: Odéon.

$$$$ ★ **Relais St-Germain.** The interior-designer owners of this outstanding hotel have exquisite taste and a superb respect for tradition and detail. Moreover, the rooms are at least twice the size of those in other hotels in the area for the same price. Much of the furniture was selected with a knowledgeable eye from the city's *brocantes* (secondhand dealers), and every room has unique treasures. Breakfast is included. ⊠ *9 carrefour de l'Odéon, 75006,* ☎ *01–43–29–12–05,* FAX *01–46–33–45–30. 21 rooms, 1 suite. AE, DC, MC, V. Métro: Odéon.*

$$$–$$$$ ★ **Hôtel d'Aubusson.** This good-value hotel keeps prices in check while offering original Aubusson tapestries, Versailles-style parquet floors, a chiseled stone fireplace, and restored antiques. Even the smallest rooms are a good size by Paris standards, and all are decked out in rich burgundies, greens, or blues. The 10 best rooms have canopied beds and ceiling beams. ⊠ *33 rue Dauphine, 75006,* ☎ *01–43–29–43–43,* FAX *01–43–29–12–62. 49 rooms. Bar, air-conditioning, in-room safes, baby-sitting, laundry service. AE, MC, V. Métro: Odéon.*

$$$ **Hôtel de L'Abbaye.** This delightful hotel near St-Sulpice was transformed from an erstwhile convent. The blend of stylishly rustic antiques and earthy apricot and ocher tones makes for a calm, cozy atmosphere. The first-floor rooms open onto the garden; most of those on the upper floors have oak beams and sitting alcoves. The four duplexes with private terraces are more expensive. Breakfast is included. ⊠ *10 rue Cassette, 75006,* ☎ *01–45–44–38–11,* FAX *01–45–48–07–86. 42 rooms, 4 suites. Bar, air-conditioning, room service, baby-sitting, laundry service. AE, MC, V. Métro: St-Sulpice.*

$$ **Atelier Montparnasse.** This Art Deco–inspired gem of a hotel was designed with style and comfort in mind. Rooms are tastefully decorated and spacious, and all the bathrooms feature mosaic reproductions of famous French paintings. One of the rooms sleeps three. The hotel is within walking distance of the Luxembourg Garden and St-Germain-des-Prés. ⊠ *49 rue Vavin, 75006,* ☎ *01–46–33–60–00,* FAX *01–40–51–04–21. 17 rooms. Bar, room service, baby-sitting, laundry service. AE, DC, MC, V. Métro: Vavin.*

$$ **Bonaparte.** The congenial staff only makes staying in this intimate place more of a treat. Old-fashioned upholsteries, 19th-century furnishings, and paintings create a quaint feel in the relatively spacious rooms. And the location in the heart of St-Germain is nothing short of fabulous. ⊠ *61 rue Bonaparte, 75006,* ☎ *01–43–26–97–37,* FAX *01–46–33–57–67. 29 rooms. Air-conditioning, in-room safes, refrigerators, laundry service. MC, V. Métro: St-Germain-des-Prés.*

7e Arrondissement (Invalides/École Militaire)

$$$$ **Montalembert.** This place is one of Paris's most originally voguish boutique hotels. Whether appointed with traditional or contemporary furnishings, rooms are all about simple lines and chic luxury. Ask about special packages if you're staying for more than three nights. ⊠ *3 rue de Montalembert, 75007,* ☎ *01–45–49–68–68; 800/628–8929 in the U.S.,* FAX *01–45–49–69–49. 50 rooms, 6 suites. Restaurant, bar, air-conditioning, in-room data ports, in-room safes, in-room VCRs, room service, baby-sitting, meeting rooms. AE, DC, MC, V. Métro: Rue du Bac.*

$$–$$$ ★ **Le Tourville.** Here is a rare find: an intimate, upscale hotel at an affordable price. Each room has crisp, virgin-white damask upholstery set against pastel or ocher walls, a smattering of antiques, original artwork, and fabulous old mirrors. The staff couldn't be more helpful. ⊠ *16 av. de Tourville, 75007,* ☎ *01–47–05–62–62; 800/528–3549 in the U.S.,* FAX *01–47–05–43–90. 27 rooms, 3 junior suites. Bar, break-*

*fast room, air-conditioning, laundry service. AE, DC, MC, V. Métro:
École Militaire.* ✒

$$ 🖭 **Latour Maubourg.** In the residential heart of the ritzy seventh, a stone's throw from Invalides, this hotel with a friendly staff has been inked into many a traveler's journal. Decor is homey and unpretentious, and with just 10 rooms, the accent is on intimacy and personalized service. ✉ *150 rue de Grenelle, 75007,* ☎ *01–47–05–16–16,* FAX *01–47–05–16–14. 9 rooms, 1 suite. In-room safes. MC, V. Métro: Latour Maubourg.* ✒

8e Arrondissement (Champs-Élysées)

$$$$ 🖭 **L'Astor.** Following a top-to-bottom makeover by the Westin-Demeure group, L'Astor has been reborn as a bastion of highly stylized, civilized chic, thanks to the Sofitel chain. The lobby is Art Deco; rooms are testimonials to the sober Regency style, with weighty marble fireplaces and mahogany furnishings. The hotel's restaurant is supervised by the celebrated chef Joël Robuchon. ✉ *11 rue d'Astorg, 75008,* ☎ *01–53–05–05–05; 800/937–8461 in the U.S.,* FAX *01–53–05–05–30. 134 rooms, 5 suites. Restaurant, bar, air-conditioning, in-room data ports, in-room safes, no-smoking rooms, room service, massage, health club, baby-sitting, laundry service. AE, DC, MC, V. Métro: Miromesnil, St-Augustin.* ✒

$$$$ 🖭 **Hôtel Crillon.** Home away from home for movie stars and off-duty
★ celebrities, this is one of Paris's most famous palace hotels. The Crillon is in two 18th-century town houses on place de la Concorde. Rooms are lavish, with Rococo and Directoire furnishings and crystal and gilt wall sconces. The sheer quantity of marble downstairs— especially in Les Ambassadeurs restaurant—is staggering. ✉ *10 pl. de la Concorde, 75008,* ☎ *01–44–71–15–00; 800/888–4747 in the U.S.,* FAX *01–44–71–15–02. 115 rooms, 45 suites. 2 restaurants, 2 bars, tea shop, air-conditioning, in-room safes, in-room data ports, no-smoking rooms, room service, exercise room, baby-sitting, laundry service, meeting rooms. AE, DC, MC, V. Métro: Concorde.* ✒

$$$$ 🖭 **George V.** Two years and $125 million in renovations later, the George V has finally reopened its glittering gold doors. General Eisenhower's headquarters during the liberation of Paris is now owned by a Saudi prince (who gets first dibs on the $8,500 a night Royal Suite) and managed by the Four Seasons group. The original Art Deco detailings and 17th century tapestries have been restored, the bas-reliefs releafed in gold, and the marble-floor mosaics rebuilt stone by stone. New additions include private health club facilities and the super-luxe Le V restaurant. ✉ *31 av. George V, 75008,* ☎ *01–49–52–70–00,* FAX *01–49–52–70–10. 184 rooms and 61 suites. Restaurant, bar, air-conditioning, in-room safes, in-room data ports, no-smoking rooms, indoor swimming pool, beauty salons, saunas, health club, business center, meeting rooms. AE, DC, MC, V. Métro: George V.* ✒

$$$$ 🖭 **Hyatt Regency Paris–Madeleine.** This stunning Haussmann-esque building near the Opéra Garnier feels more like a boutique hotel than an international business chain, thanks to stylized details like cherry paneling and mismatched bedside tables. Book a room on the seventh or eighth floor facing boulevard Malesherbes for a view of the Eiffel Tower. ✉ *24 bd. Malesherbes, 75008,* ☎ *01–55–27–12–34; 800/223–1234 in the U.S.,* FAX *01–55–27–12–35. 81 rooms, 5 suites. Restaurant, bar, air-conditioning, in-room data ports, in-room safes, no-smoking floors, room service, sauna, exercise room, laundry service, meeting rooms. AE, DC, MC, V. Métro: St-Augustin.*

$$$$ 🖭 **Lancaster.** The Lancaster—one of Paris's most venerable institutions,
★ now owned by the Savoy group—has been meticulously transformed into one of the city's most modish luxury hotels. The clubby decor seamlessly

blends the traditional with the contemporary to evoke an overall feeling of timeless elegance. ⊠ *7 rue de Berri, 75008,* ☎ *01–40–76–40–76; 877/ 75–PARIS in the U.S.,* ℻ *01–40–76–40–00. 50 rooms, 10 suites. Restaurant, bar, air-conditioning, in-room data ports, in-room safes, in-room VCRs, room service, sauna, exercise room, baby-sitting, laundry service, meeting rooms, parking (fee). AE, DC, MC, V. Métro: George-V.*

9ᵉ Arrondissement (Opéra)

$$$$ ⊞ **Grand Hôtel Inter-Continental.** Open since 1862, Paris's biggest luxury hotel has a facade that seems as long as the Louvre. The grand salon's Art Deco dome and the restaurant's painted ceilings are registered landmarks. The Art Deco rooms are spacious and light (ask for one on the top floors). Its famed Café de la Paix is one of the city's great people-watching spots. ⊠ *2 rue Scribe, 75009,* ☎ *01–40–07– 32–32; 800/327–0200 in the U.S.,* ℻ *01–42–66–12–51. 475 rooms, 39 suites. 3 restaurants, 2 bars, air-conditioning, in-room data ports, in-room safes, in-room VCRs, no-smoking rooms, room service, sauna, health club, laundry service, business services, meeting rooms. AE, DC, MC, V. Métro: Opéra.*

12ᵉ Arrondissement (Bastille/Gare de Lyon)

$$–$$$ ⊞ **Le Pavillon Bastille.** The transformation of this 19th-century *hôtel particulier* (across from the Opéra Bastille) into a mod, colorful, high-design hotel garnered architectural awards and a fiercely loyal, hip clientele. ⊠ *65 rue de Lyon, 75012,* ☎ *01–43–43–65–65; 800/233–2552 in the U.S.,* ℻ *01–43–43–96–52. 24 rooms, 1 suite. Bar, air-conditioning, in-room safes, minibars, room service. AE, DC, MC, V. Métro: Bastille.*

14ᵉ Arrondissement (Montparnasse)

$$ ⊞ **Raspail-Montparnasse.** Rooms in this hotel are named after the artists who made Montparnasse the art capital of the world in the '20s and '30s. All are decorated in pastels and contemporary blond-wood furniture. Most are at the low end of this price category; five have spectacular panoramic views of Montparnasse and the Eiffel Tower. ⊠ *203 bd. Raspail, 75014,* ☎ *01–43–20–62–86,* ℻ *01–43–20–50–79,* ℻ *01– 43–20–50–79. 38 rooms. Bar, air-conditioning, in-room safes, meeting rooms. AE, DC, MC, V. Métro: Vavin.* ✎

$ ⊞ **Parc Montsouris.** This modest hotel in a 1930s villa is on a quiet residential street next to the lovely Parc Montsouris. Attractive oak pieces and high-quality French fabrics embellish the small but clean rooms; satellite TV is another plus. Those with shower are very inexpensive; suites sleep four. ⊠ *4 rue du Parc-Montsouris, 75014,* ☎ *01–45–89– 09–72,* ℻ *01–45–80–92–72. 28 rooms, 7 suites. Air-conditioning, no-smoking rooms, laundry service. AE, MC, V. Métro: Montparnasse-Bienvenue.*

16ᵉ Arrondissement (Arc de Triomphe/Le Bois)

$$$$ ⊞ **Saint James Paris.** Touted as the "only château-hôtel" in Paris, this gracious late-19th-century Neoclassical mansion is surrounded by a lush private park. The lavish Art Deco interior was created by designer Andrée Putman. Ten rooms on the third floor open onto a winter garden. The restaurant is reserved for guests; in warm weather meals are served in the garden. ⊠ *43 av. Bugeaud, 75016,* ☎ *01–44–05–81–81; 800/447–7462 in the U.S.,* ℻ *01–44–05–81–82. 24 rooms, 24 suites. Restaurant, bar, air-conditioning, in-room data ports, in-room safes, no-smoking rooms, room service, sauna, health club, baby-sitting, laundry service, meeting rooms, parking (free). AE, DC, MC, V. Métro: Porte Dauphine.*

$ ⊞ **Queen's Hôtel.** One of only a handful of hotels in the tony residential district near the Bois de Boulogne, Queen's is a small, comfortable hotel with a high standard of service. Each room focuses on a different

20th-century French artist. The rooms with baths have Jacuzzis. ✉ *4 rue Bastien-Lepage, 75016,* ☎ *01–42–88–89–85,* FAX *01–40–50–67– 52. 21 rooms. Air-conditioning, in-room safes, minibars, no-smoking rooms. AE, DC, MC, V. Métro: Michel-Ange–Auteuil.* ✇

17e Arrondissement (Monceau/Clichy)

$$ 🏨 **Étoile-Péreire.** Behind a quiet, leafy courtyard in this chic residential district is this unique, intimate hotel, consisting of two parts: a fin-de-siècle building on the street and a 1920s annex overlooking an interior courtyard. Rooms and duplexes are done in deep shades of rose or blue with crisp, white damask upholstery; only suites have air-conditioning. ✉ *146 bd. Péreire, 75017,* ☎ *01–42–67–60–00,* FAX *01–42–67– 02–90. 21 rooms, 5 duplex suites. Bar, in-room safes, no-smoking rooms, laundry service. AE, DC, MC, V. Métro: Péreire.*

NIGHTLIFE AND THE ARTS

With a heritage that includes the Can-Can, the Folies-Bergère, the Moulin Rouge, Mistinguett, and Josephine Baker, Paris is one city where no one has ever had to ask, "Is there any place exciting to go to tonight?" Today the city's nightlife and arts scenes are still filled with pleasures. Hear a chansonnier belt out Piaf, take in a *Victor/Victoria* show, catch a Molière play at the Comédie Française, or perhaps spot Madonna at the Buddha Bar. Information about what's going on in the city can be found in the weekly magazines (published every Wednesday) *Pariscope* (which has an English section), *L'Officiel des Spectacles,* and *Figaroscope* (a supplement to *Le Figaro* newspaper). The **Paris Tourist Office** (☞ Visitor Information *in* Paris A to Z, *below*) has a 24-hour hot line in English (☎ 08–36–68–31–12) and a Web site (✇) listing events.

The best place to buy tickets is at the venue itself; try to purchase in advance, as many of the more popular performances sell out. Also try your hotel or a travel agency, such as **Paris-Vision** (✉ 1 rue Auber, 9e, ☎ 01–40–06–01–00, métro Opéra). Tickets for most concerts can be bought at **FNAC** (especially ✉ 1–5 rue Pierre Lescot, Forum des Halles, 3rd level down, 1er, ☎ 01–49–87–50–50, métro Châtelet–Les Halles). The **Virgin Megastore** (✉ 52 av. des Champs-Élysées, 8e, ☎ 08–03– 02–30–24, métro Franklin-D.-Roosevelt) also sells theater and concert tickets. Half-price tickets for many same-day theater performances are available at the **Kiosques Théâtre** (✉ Across from 15 pl. de la Madeleine, métro Madeleine and Montparnasse-Bienvenüe; and ✉ Outside Gare Montparnasse on pl. Raoul Dautry, 15e, métro Madeleine métro Montparnasse-Bienvenüe); both are open Tuesday–Saturday 12:30–8 and Sunday 12:30–4. Expect to pay a 16-franc commission per ticket and to wait in line.

The Arts

Classical Music

Classical- and world-music concerts are held at the **Cité de la Musique** (✉ 221 av. Jean-Jaurès, 19e, ☎ 01–44–84–44–84, métro Porte de Pantin). The **Salle Pleyel** (✉ 252 rue du Faubourg–St-Honoré, 8e, ☎ 01–45–61–53–00, métro Ternes) is Paris's principal home of classical music. The **Théâtre des Champs-Élysées** (✉ 15 av. Montaigne, 8e, ☎ 01–49–52–50–50, métro Alma-Marceau), an Art Deco temple, hosts concerts and ballet. Paris has a never-ending stream of inexpensive lunchtime and evening concerts in churches, some scheduled as part of the **Festival d'Art Sacré** (☎ 01–44–70–64–10 for information) between mid-November and Christmas. **Churches** with classical concerts (often free) include (☞ Exploring, *above*, for addresses): **Notre-Dame,**

Sainte-Chapelle, St-Eustache, St-Germain-des-Prés, St-Julien-Le-Pauvre, St-Louis-en-l'Ile, and St-Roch.

Dance

The **Opéra Garnier** (⊠ Pl. de l'Opéra, 9ᵉ, ☏ 08–36–69–78–68, www.opera-de-paris.fr, métro Opéra) is home to the reputable Paris Ballet. The **Opéra de la Bastille** (⊠ Pl. de la Bastille, 12ᵉ, ☏ 08–36–69–78–68, www.opera-de-paris.fr, métro Bastille) occasionally hosts major dance troupes, often modern and avant-garde in tenor. Both here and at the Opéra Garnier venue, ballet production ticket prices usually range from about 45 to 270 francs. At the **Théâtre de la Bastille** (⊠ 76 rue de la Roquette, 11ᵉ, ☏ 01–43–57–42–14, métro Bastille), innovative modern dance companies perform. The **Théâtre de la Ville** (⊠ 2 pl. du Châtelet, 4ᵉ, ☏ 01–42–74–22–77 for both, métro Châtelet; ⊠ 31 rue des Abbesses, 18ᵉ, métro Abbesses) is Paris's temple of contemporary dance.

Film

Parisians are far more addicted to the cinema as an art form than even Londoners or New Yorkers, as revealed by the number of movie theaters in the city. Many theaters, especially in principal tourist areas such as the Champs-Élysées, St-Germain-des-Prés, Les Halles, and the boulevard des Italiens near the Opéra, show first-run films in English. Check the weekly guides for a movie of your choice. Look for the initials *v.o.*, which mean *version originale*, that is, not dubbed. Cinema admission runs from 37 to 51 francs; many theaters reduce rates slightly on Monday and for some morning shows. Most theaters will post two show times: The first is the *séance*, when commercials, previews, and sometimes short films start, and the second is the actual feature presentation time, which is usually 10–20 minutes later. Paris has many small cinemas showing classic and independent films, especially in the Latin Quarter. Screenings are often organized around retrospectives (check "Festivals" in weekly guides). One of the best venues for classic French and international films (Wednesday–Saturday) is the **Cinémathèque Française** (⊠ 42 bd. de Bonne-Nouvelle, ☏ 01–47–04–24–24, métro Bonne-Nouvelle and ⊠ Palais de Chaillot, 7 av. Albert de Mun, ☏ 01–55–73–16–80, métro Trocadéro). The **Max Linder Panorama** (⊠ 24 bd. Poissonnière, 9ᵉ, ☏ 01–48–24–88–88, métro Rue Montmartre) frequently shows classics on its big screen.

Opera

Getting tickets to the opera can be difficult on short notice, so it's a good idea to plan ahead. For the season's schedule, contact the **Opéra de la Bastille** (⊠ 120 rue de Lyon, Paris 75012) in advance. Bookings by mail begin roughly two months before the date of performance. Buying from scalpers is not recommended, as they have been known to sell counterfeit tickets. The **Opéra de la Bastille** (⊠ Pl. de la Bastille, 12ᵉ, ☏ 08–36–69–78–68, www.opera-de-paris.fr, métro Bastille), a modern auditorium, has taken over the role as Paris's main opera house from the Opéra Garnier (☞ Dance, *above*). However, nothing beats seeing a grand production of a Verdi or Mozart opera within the splendor of Opéra Garnier, and the good news is that this historic house still hosts a limited number of Opéra National de Paris productions every season. Note that if a *Don Giovanni* is presented, it is only mounted for a minirun of one to two weeks, not in a repertory schedule throughout the season. At both the Bastille and Garnier houses, opera price tickets range from about 70 to 625 francs; cheaper seats in the Garnier house are sometimes view-obstructed. The **Opéra Comique** (⊠ 5 rue Favart, 2ᵉ, ☏ 01–42–44–45–46, métro Richelieu-Drouot) is a lofty old hall where comic operas are often performed.

Better known as the Théâtre du Châtelet, the **Théâtre Musical de Paris** (⊠ Pl. du Châtelet, 1ᵉʳ, ☎ 01–40–28–28–40, métro Châtelet) has built up a strong reputation for opera and other productions.

Theater

A number of theaters line the Grand Boulevards between Opéra and République, but there is no Paris equivalent to Broadway or the West End. Shows are mostly in French. **Bouffes du Nord** (⊠ 37 bis bd. de la Chapelle, 10ᵉ, ☎ 01–46–07–34–50, métro La Chapelle) is the wonderfully atmospheric theater that is home to English director Peter Brook. The **Comédie-Française** (⊠ Pl. André-Malraux, 1ᵉʳ, ☎ 01–44–58–15–15, métro Palais-Royal) is a distinguished venue that stages classical French drama. The **Théâtre de la Huchette** (⊠ 23 rue de la Huchette, 5ᵉ, ☎ 01–43–26–38–99, métro St-Michel), a tiny Left Bank theater, has been staging Ionesco's *The Bald Soprano* every night since 1950. **Théâtre de l'Odéon** (⊠ Pl. de l'Odéon, 6ᵉ, ☎ 01–44–41–36–36, métro Odéon) has made pan-European theater its primary focus.

Nightlife

The City of Light truly lights up after dark. So, if you want to paint the town *rouge* after dutifully pounding the parquet in museums all day, there's a dazzling array of options to discover. The hottest spots are around Ménilmontant, the Bastille, and the Marais. The Left Bank is definitely a lot less happening. The Champs-Élysées is making a comeback, though the clientele remains predominantly foreign. Take note: The last métro runs between 12:30 AM and 1 AM (you can take a taxi, but they can be hard to find, especially on weekend nights).

Bars and Clubs

It helps to be famous—or look like a model—to get into **Les Bains** (⊠ 7 rue du Bourg-l'Abbé, 3ᵉ, ☎ 01–48–87–01–80, métro Étienne-Marcel), a forever-trendy club (closed Monday). **Barrio Latino** (⊠ 46/48 rue du Faubourg St-Antoine, 11ᵉ ☎ 01–55–78–84–75, métro Bastille) is the latest addition to the Bastille party district, with a decor that is a lush cross of Casbah, old Havana, and Soho Loft. **Batofar** (⊠ 11 quai François Mauriac, 11ᵉ, 01–56–29–10–00, métro Bibliothèque) is an old lighthouse tug, now refitted to include a bar, a club, and a concert venue that's become one of the hippest spots in town. **Buddha Bar** (⊠ 8 rue Boissy d'Anglas, 8ᵉ, ☎ 01–53–05–90–00, métro Concorde) offers a knockout setting, with its towering gold-painted Buddha contemplating enough Dragon Empress screens and colorful chinoiserie for five MGM movies. When it opened several years ago, Madonna used to make this scene, along with a lot of other glitterati. **Le Cabaret** (⊠ 68 rue de Charonne, 8ᵉ, ☎ 01–42–89–44–14, métro Franklin-D.-Roosevelt) used to be just that; now there are still cabaret acts, as well as dancing to soul and funk. **Café Charbon** (⊠ 109 rue Oberkampf, 11ᵉ, ☎ 01–43–57–55–13, métro St-Maur, Parmentier) is a beautifully restored 19th-century café with a trendsetting crowd. **Le Comptoir** (⊠ 5 rue Monsieur-Le-Prince, 6ᵉ, ☎ 01–43–29–12–05, Odéon) is a traditional wine bar serving Burgundy and Bordeaux by the glass. **L'Élysée Montmartre** (⊠ 72 bd. de Rochechouart, 18ᵉ, ☎ 01–44–92–45–45, métro Anvers) hosts the hottest club nights in Paris on Saturday (during the week it's a concert hall). **Finnegan's Wake** (⊠ 9 rue des Boulangers, 5ᵉ, ☎ 01–46–34–23–65, métro Jussieu) attracts a mixed Franco-British clientele with its Guinness on tap and Irish music. If you ever get homesick to hear English, Paris has quite a few other pubs, including the Auld Alliance, Connolly's Corner, and the Cricketeer. **Le Fumoir** (⊠ 6 rue Amiral de Coligny, 1ᵉʳ, ☎ 01–42–92–00–24, métro Louvre), a fashionable spot for cocktails, has a large bar, library, and comfy leather couches. **Man Ray** (⊠ 34 rue Marbeuf, 8ᵉ, ☎ 01–56–88–36–36, métro Franklin-D.-Roosevelt), owned by Sean Penn, Johnny Depp, and Mick Hucknall, has a spacious mezzanine bar overlooking an Asian-inspired dining room. **Le What's Up Bar** (⊠ 15 rue Daval, 11ᵉ, ☎ 01–48–05–88–33, métro Bastille) is a hip, modern spot where trendy DJs play house and garage music after 10:30 PM; on weekends there's a 50-franc cover.

GAY AND LESBIAN BARS AND CLUBS

Gay and lesbian bars and clubs are mostly concentrated in the Marais and include some of the most happening addresses in the city. **Le Dépôt** (⊠ 10 rue aux Ours, 3ᵉ, ☎ 01–44–54–96–96, métro Etienne Marcel) is a bar, club, and back room for men. The mostly male crowd at **L'Open Café** (⊠ 17 rue des Archives, 4ᵉ, ☎ 01–42–72–26–18, métro Hôtel-de-Ville) comes for the sunny decor and convivial ambience. **Le Pulp!** (⊠ 25 bd. Poissonnière, 2ᵉ, ☎ 01–40–26–01–93, métro Grands Boulevards) is one of the few lesbian-only nightclubs in Paris. **Queen** (⊠ 102 av. des Champs-Élysées, 8ᵉ, ☎ 01–53–89–08–90, métro George-V) is one of the hottest nightspots in Paris: Although it's predominantly gay, everyone else lines up to get in, too.

HOTEL BARS

Paris's hotel bars are highly popular nostalgic spots as well as quiet, elegant places to talk. **Bristol** (⊠ 112 rue du Faubourg–St-Honoré, 8ᵉ, ☎ 01–53–43–43–42, métro Miromesnil). **Lutétia** (⊠ 45 bd. Raspail, 6ᵉ, ☎ 01–49–54–46–09, métro Sèvres-Babylone). **Ritz Hemingway Bar** (⊠ 15 pl. Vendôme, 1ᵉʳ, ☎ 01–43–16–33–65, métro Opéra).

Cabaret

Paris's cabarets are household names, though mostly tourists go to them these days. Prices range from 200 francs (simple admission plus one drink) to more than 800 francs (dinner plus show). **Crazy Horse** (⊠ 12 av. George-V, 8ᵉ, ☎ 01–47–23–32–32, métro Alma-Marceau) is one of the best-known cabarets, with pretty dancers and raunchy routines. **Au Lapin Agile** (⊠ 22 rue des Saules, 18ᵉ, ☎ 01–46–06–85–87, métro Lamarck-Caulaincourt), in Montmartre, considers itself the doyen of cabarets and is a miraculous survivor from the early 20th century. You'll find no frou-frou here, just a chunk of Montmartre history. Picasso immortalized the place in a painting that was sold for $48 million and now is in New York's Metropolitan Museum. Prices here are lower than elsewhere, but then it is more a large bar than a full-blown cabaret. **Lido** (⊠ 116 bis av. des Champs-Élysées, 8ᵉ, ☎ 01–40–76–56–10, métro George-V) stars the famous Bluebell Girls; the owners claim that no show in Las Vegas can rival it for special effects. That old favorite at the foot of Montmartre, **Moulin Rouge** (⊠ Pl. Blanche, 18ᵉ, ☎ 01–53–09–82–82, métro Blanche), mingles the Doriss Girls, the cancan, and a horse in an extravagant spectacle. **Paradis Latin** (⊠ 28 rue du Cardinal Lemoine, 5ᵉ, ☎ 01–43–25–28–28, métro Cardinal Lemoine) is the liveliest and trendiest cabaret on the Left Bank.

Jazz Clubs

For nightly schedules consult the specialty magazines *Jazz Hot* or *Jazz Magazine*. Nothing gets going till 10 PM or 11 PM; entry prices vary widely from about 40 francs to more than 100 francs. At the Méridien Hotel, near Porte Maillot, the **Lionel Hampton Jazz Club** (⊠ 81 bd. Gouvion-St-Cyr, 17ᵉ, ☎ 01–40–68–30–42, métro Porte Maillot) hosts a roster of international jazz players. **New Morning** (⊠ 7 rue des Petites-Écuries, 10ᵉ, ☎ 01–45–23–51–41, métro Château-d'Eau) is a premier spot for serious fans of avant-garde jazz, as well as folk and world music. The greatest names in French and international jazz have been playing at **Le Petit Journal** (⊠ 71 bd. St-Michel, 5ᵉ, ☎ 01–43–

26–28–59, RER Luxembourg) for decades; it now specializes in Dixieland jazz (it's closed Sunday).

Rock, Pop, and World Music Venues

Upcoming concerts are posted on boards in FNAC and Virgin Megastores. **Le Bataclan** (⊠ 50 bd. Voltaire, 11ᵉ, ☎ 01–48–06–28–12, métro Oberkampf) is an intimate venue for live rock, rap, and reggae. **L'Élysée Montmartre** (☞ Bars and Clubs, *above*) is one of the prime venues for emerging French and international rock groups. **L'Olympia** (⊠ 28 bd. des Capucines, 9ᵉ, ☎ 01–47–42–25–49, métro Madeleine), a legendary venue once favored by Jacques Brel and Edith Piaf, still plays host to leading French vocalists. **Zenith** (⊠ Parc de la Villette, 19ᵉ, ☎ 01–42–08–60–00, métro Porte-de-Pantin) stages large rock shows.

OUTDOOR ACTIVITIES AND SPORTS

Participant Sports

Bicycling

Paris has been making valiant efforts to become more bicycle-friendly. More than 150 km (94 mi) of bicycle lanes now cross the city, notably along rue de Rivoli and boulevard St-Germain. Certain roads are banned to cars altogether on Sunday (including the banks of the Seine along quai de la Tournelle from 9 to 6 mid-March to late fall and the roads alongside the Canal St-Martin from noon to 6 year-round) Paris's two large parks, the Bois de Boulogne (☞ Exploring, *above*) and the Bois de Vincennes (métro Porte Dorée, Château de Vincennes) are also good places for biking. Bikes can be rented from the following: **Pariscyclo** (⊠ Rond Point de Jardin d'Acclimatation, in the Bois de Boulogne, 16ᵉ, ☎ 01–47–47–76–50, métro Les Sablons); and **Paris à Vélo, C'est Sympa** (⊠ 37 bd. Bourdon, 4ᵉ, ☎ 01–48–87–60–01, métro Bastille); **Paris Vélo Rent a Bike** (⊠ 2 rue Fer à Moulin, 5ᵉ, ☎ 01–43–37–59–22, métro Censier-Daubenton).

Health Clubs and Swimming Pools

A number of hotels, gyms, and clubs in the city offer one-day or short-term memberships. **Aquaboulevard de Paris** (⊠ 4 rue Louis-Armand, 15ᵉ, ☎ 01–40–60–10–00, métro Balard) has a gym, Turkish baths, and the city's best swimming pool, complete with giant slide and wave machine (150 francs per day). **Club Quartier Latin** (⊠ 19 rue de Pontoise, 5ᵉ, ☎ 01–55–42–77–88, métro Maubert Mutualité) has a 30-meter skylighted pool, a climbing wall, squash courts, and exercise equipment (85 francs per day and 75 francs per 40 minutes of squash). **Espace Vit'Halles** (⊠ 48 rue Rambuteau, 3ᵉ, ☎ 01–42–77–21–71, métro Rambuteau) has a broad range of aerobics classes (100 francs a class), exercise machines, a sauna, and a steam bath. **Pilates Studio** (⊠ 39 rue du Temple, 4ᵉ, ☎ 01–42–72–91–74, métro Hôtel de Ville) may just be based in a three-room apartment, but it attracts numerous celebrities, such as actress. Kristin Scott Thomas and French *Vogue* editor Joan Juliet Buck. A one-hour private class costs 310 francs; classes for two are 210 francs per person. The **Piscine des Halles** (⊠ Entrance on pl. de la Rotonde, in Forum des Halles, 1ᵉʳ, ☎ 01–42–36–98–44) is a 50-meter public pool; admission is 25 francs; call for hours. The **Ritz Health Club** (⊠ Hotel Ritz, pl. Vendôme, 1ᵉʳ, ☎ 01–43–16–30–60, métro Opéra), as fancy as the hotel, has a swimming pool, sauna, steam room, Jacuzzi, exercise machines, and aerobics classes (all for 600 francs on weekdays, 700 francs on weekends). **Sofitel Paris Vitatop Club** (⊠ 8 rue Louis-Armand, 15ᵉ, ☎ 01–45–54–79–00, métro Balard) has a 15-meter pool, a sauna, a steam room, and a Jacuzzi, plus a stunning view of the Paris skyline (200 francs per day and free to hotel guests).

Rollerblading

A popular site for rollerblading is along the promenade Plantée, running along the former viaduct in the 12ᵉ arrondissement, as well as along the Seine and the Canal St-Martin (☞ Bicycling, *above*). Every Friday night starting at 10, thousands of advanced skaters gather at place de l'Italie to rollerblade together through Paris (roads are blocked off); for details check the Web site (www.pari-roller.com). A more leisurely three-hour route is organized on Sunday at 2:30 PM and leaves from Roller Locations Nomades near the place de la Bastille. Rollerblades can be rented from **Bike'n'Roller** (⊠ 6 rue St-Julien le Pauvre, 5ᵉ, ☎ 01–44–07–35–89) for 30 francs for three hours and 60 francs per day. **Roller Location Nomades** (⊠ 37 bd. Bourdon, 4ᵉ, ☎ 01–44–54–07–44) rents skates for 50–60 francs per day.

Spectator Sports

Information on upcoming events can be found in the weekly guide *Pariscope,* on posters around the city, or by calling the ticket agencies of **FNAC** (☎ 08–03–80–88–03) or the **Virgin Megastore** (☎ 08–03–02–30–24). A wide range of sporting events takes place at the **Palais Omnisports de Paris-Bercy** (⊠ 8 bd. de Bercy, 12ᵉ, ☎ 08–03–03–00–31, métro Bercy). Details of events are also on their Web site: www.bercy.com The **Parc des Princes** (⊠ 24 rue du Cdt. Guilbaud, 16ᵉ, ☎ 01–42–88–02–76, métro Porte d'Auteuil) is where the city's soccer team, Paris St-Germain, plays its home matches. **Roland-Garros** (⊠ 2 av. Gordon Bennett, 16ᵉ, ☎ 01–47–43–48–00, métro Porte d'Auteuil) is the venue for the French Open tennis tournament in May. **Stade de France** (⊠ St-Denis, ☎ 01–55–93–00–00, RER La Plaine–Stade de France) was built for the World Cup in 1998 and is now home to the French national soccer and rugby teams.

SHOPPING

Revised and updated by Ian Phillips

In the most beautiful city in the world, it's no surprise to discover that the local greengrocer displays his tomatoes as artistically as Cartier does its rubies. The capital of style, Paris has an endless array of delights to tempt shop-till-you-droppers, from grand couturiers like Dior to the funkiest flea markets. Today every neighborhood seems to reflect a unique attitude and style: Designer extravagance and haute couture characterize avenue Montaigne and rue Faubourg St-Honoré; classic sophistication pervades St-Germain; avant-garde style dresses up the Marais; while a hip feel suffuses the area around Les Halles.

Bargains are surprisingly elusive—it's good to be aware of the slings and arrows of international exchange rates and to know prices at home before you arrive, but if you're hunting for bargains, watch for the word *soldes* (sales): The two main sale seasons are January and July. For nice gifts try the shops in Paris's museums, especially the Louvre, the Musée Carnavalet, the Opéra Garnier, and the Musée des Arts Décoratifs.

If you're from outside the European Union, age 15 and over, and stay in France and/or the European Union for less than six months, you can benefit from Value Added Tax (VAT) reimbursements, known in France as TVA or *détaxe*. To qualify, non-EU residents must spend at least 1,200 francs in a single store on a single day. Refunds vary from 13% to 20.6% and are mailed to you by check or credited to your charge card.

Shopping by Neighborhood

Avenue Montaigne

Shopping doesn't come much more chic than on the avenue Montaigne, with its graceful town mansions, which house some of the top names in international fashion: **Chanel, Dior, Nina Ricci, Valentino, Escada, Hanae Mori, Prada, Dolce & Gabbana,** and many more. Neighboring rue François 1er and avenue George V are also lined with many designer boutiques: **Versace, Yves St-Laurent,** and **Balenciaga.**

Champs-Élysées

Cafés and movie theaters keep the once-chic Champs-Élysées active 24 hours a day, but the invasion of exchange banks, car showrooms, and fast-food chains has lowered the tone. Four glitzy 20th-century arcade malls—**Galerie du Lido, Le Rond-Point, Le Claridge,** and **Élysées 26**—capture most of the retail action, not to mention the **Gap** and the **Disney Store.** The opening of a new Peter Marino–designed **Louis Vuitton** boutique and the cosmetic wonder store **Sephora** have reintroduced a touch of elegance.

The Faubourg St-Honoré

This chic shopping and residential street is also quite a political hub. It is home to the Élysée Palace as well as the official residences of the American and British ambassadors. The Paris branches of **Sotheby's** and **Christie's** and renowned antiques galleries such as **Didier Aaron** add artistic flavor. Boutiques include **Hermès, Lanvin, Gucci, Chloé,** and **Christian Lacroix.**

Left Bank

After decades of clustering on the Right Bank's venerable shopping avenues, the high-fashion houses have stormed the Rive Gauche. The first to arrive were **Sonia Rykiel** and **Yves St-Laurent** in the late '60s. Some of the more recent arrivals include **Christian Dior** and **Louis Vuitton.** Rue des St-Pères and rue de Grenelle are lined with designer names.

Louvre–Palais Royal

The elegant and eclectic shops clustered in the 18th-century arcades of the Palais-Royal sell such items as antiques, toy soldiers, cosmetics, jewelry, and vintage designer dresses. The glossy, marble **Carrousel du Louvre** mall, beneath the Louvre Museum, is lighted by an immense inverted glass pyramid. Shops are accompanied by a lively international food court, and all are open on Sunday—still a rare convenience in Paris.

Le Marais

Between the pre-Revolution mansions and tiny kosher food shops that characterize this area are scores of trendy gift and clothing stores, with couturier **Azzedine Alaïa** heading the list of chic boutiques. The Marais is one of the few neighborhoods where shops are open on Sunday.

Opéra to La Madeleine

Three major department stores—**Au Printemps, Galeries Lafayette,** and the British **Marks & Spencer**—dominate boulevard Haussmann, behind Paris's ornate 19th-century Opéra Garnier. Place de la Madeleine is home to two luxurious food stores, **Fauchon** and **Hédiard.**

Place Vendôme and Rue de la Paix

The magnificent 17th-century place Vendôme, home of the Ritz Hotel, and rue de la Paix, leading north from Vendôme, are where you can find the world's most elegant jewelers: **Cartier, Boucheron, Bulgari,** and **Van Cleef and Arpels.** The most exclusive, however, is the discreet **Jar's.**

Rue St-Honoré

A fashionable set makes its way to rue St-Honoré to shop at Paris's most trendy boutique, **Colette.** The street is lined with numerous designer names, while on nearby rue Cambon, you'll find the wonderfully elegant **Maria Luisa** and the main **Chanel** boutique.

Department Stores

Paris's top department stores offer both convenience and style. Most are open Monday through Saturday from 9:30 AM to 7 PM, and some are open until 10 PM one weekday evening.

Au Bon Marché (✉ 22 rue de Sèvres, 7ᵉ, ☎ 01–44–39–80–00, métro Sèvres-Babylone), the only department store on the Left Bank, is an excellent hunting ground for housewares, men's clothes, and gifts. On the Right Bank, **Bazar de l'Hôtel de Ville** (✉ 52–64 rue de Rivoli, 4ᵉ, ☎ 01–42–74–90–00, métro Hôtel de Ville), better known as BHV, has minimal fashion offerings but is noteworthy for its enormous basement hardware store. **La Samaritaine** (✉ 19 rue de la Monnaie, 1ᵉʳ, ☎ 01–40–41–20–20, métro Pont-Neuf or Châtelet) has the Toupary restaurant with magnificent views of the Seine. The Grand Boulevards are lined with three major department stores: **Au Printemps** (✉ 64 bd. Haussmann, 9ᵉ, ☎ 01–42–82–50–00, métro Havre-Caumartin, Opéra, or Auber); **Galeries Lafayette** (✉ 40 bd. Haussmann, 9ᵉ, ☎ 01–42–82–34–56, métro Chaussée d'Antin, Opéra, or Havre-Caumartin); and the British outlet **Marks & Spencer** (✉ 35 bd. Haussmann, 9ᵉ, ☎ 01–47–42–42–91, métro Havre-Caumartin, Auber, or Opéra).

Budget

Monoprix and **Prisunic** are French dime stores—with scores of branches throughout the city—that stock inexpensive everyday items like toothpaste, groceries, toys, and paper—a little of everything. Both chains carry inexpensive children's clothes and makeup of surprisingly good quality.

Markets

The **Marché aux Puces,** on Paris's northern boundary (métro Porte de Clignancourt), which takes place from Saturday through Monday, is a century-old labyrinth of alleyways packed with antiques dealers' booths and junk stalls spreading for more than a square mile; arrive early.

The lively atmosphere that reigns in most of Paris's open-air food markets makes them a sight worth seeing even if you don't want or need to buy anything. Every neighborhood has one, though many are open only a few days each week. Sunday morning till 1 PM is usually a good time to go; Monday the markets are likely to be closed. Many of the better-known markets are in areas you'd visit for sightseeing: **boulevard Raspail** (✉ Between rue de Rennes and rue du Cherche-Midi, 6ᵉ, métro Rennes), with a Sunday organic market; **rue de Buci** (✉ 6ᵉ, métro Odéon), closed Sunday afternoon and Monday; **rue Mouffetard** (✉ 5ᵉ, métro Monge), best on weekends, near the Jardin des Plantes; **rue Montorgueuil** (✉ 1ᵉʳ, métro Châtelet–Les Halles), closed Monday; **boulevard Richard Lenoir** (✉ 11ᵉ, métro Bastille); and **rue Lepic** in Montmartre (✉ 18ᵉ, métro Blanche or Abbesses), best on weekends.

Shopping Arcades

Paris's 19th-century commercial arcades, called *passages* or *galeries* are the forerunners of the modern mall. Glass roofs, decorative pillars, and mosaic floors give the passages character. The major arcades are on the Right Bank in central Paris. **Galerie Vivienne** (✉ 4 rue des Petits-

Champs, 2ᵉ, métro Bourse) is home to a range of interesting shops, an excellent tearoom, and a quality wine shop. **Passage Jouffroy** (⊠ 12 bd. Montmartre, 2ᵉ, métro Montmartre) is full of shops selling toys, postcards, antique canes, and perfumes. **Passage des Panoramas** (⊠ 11 bd. Montmartre, 2ᵉ, métro Montmartre), built in 1800, is the oldest of them all. The elegant **Galerie Véro-Dodat** (⊠ 19 rue Jean-Jacques Rousseau, 1ᵉʳ, métro Louvre) has shops selling old-fashioned toys, contemporary art, and stringed instruments. It is best known, however, for its antiques stores.

Specialty Stores

Accessories, Cosmetics, and Perfumes

Christian Louboutin (⊠ 19 rue Jean-Jacques Rousseau, 1ᵉʳ, ☎ 01–42–36–05–31, métro Louvre) is famous for his wacky but elegant shoes, trademark blood-red soles, and impressive client list (Caroline of Monaco, Catherine Deneuve, Liz Taylor). **Philippe Model** (⊠ 33 pl. du Marché St-Honoré, 1ᵉʳ, ☎ 01–42–96–89–02, métro Tuileries) started off making hats favored by fashionable society ladies and has since added shoes and housewares in two adjacent shops. **Sabbia Rosa** (⊠ 73 rue des Sts-Pères, 6ᵉ, ☎ 01–45–48–88–37, métro St-Germain-des-Prés) sells French lingerie favored by celebrities like Catherine Deneuve and Claudia Schiffer. **Sephora** (⊠ 70 av. de Champs-Elysées, 8ᵉ, ☎ 01–53–93–22–50, métro Franklin-D.-Roosevelt; 1 rue Pierre Lescot, in the Forum des Halles, 1ᵉʳ, ☎ 01–40–13–72–25, métro Châtelet–Les Halles) is the leading chain of perfume and cosmetics stores in France. Choose from 365 colors of lipstick, browse through the "Cultural Gallery" at the Champs-Élysées store, and even send e-mails for free from the in-store computers.Bookstores (English-Language)

The scenic open-air bookstalls along the Seine sell secondhand books (mostly in French), prints, and souvenirs. Numerous French-language bookstores—specializing in a wide range of topics, including art, film, literature, and philosophy—are found in the Latin Quarter and around St-Germain-des-Prés. For English-language books try these stores: **Brentano's** (⊠ 37 av. de l'Opéra, 2ᵉ, ☎ 01–42–61–52–50, métro Opéra) is stocked with everything from classics to children's titles. **Galignani** (⊠ 224 rue de Rivoli, 1ᵉʳ, ☎ 01–42–60–76–07, métro Tuileries) is especially known for its extensive range of art and coffee-table books. **Village Voice** (⊠ 6 rue Princesse, 6ᵉ, ☎ 01–46–33–36–47, métro Mabillon) hosts regular literary readings.

Clothing

MENSWEAR

Berluti (⊠ 26 rue Marbeuf, 8ᵉ, ☎ 01–53–93–97–97, métro Franklin-D.-Roosevelt) has been making the most exclusive shoes for men for more than a century. **Charvet** (⊠ 28 pl. Vendôme, 1ᵉʳ, ☎ 01–42–60–30–70, métro Opéra) is the Parisian equivalent of a Savile Row tailor. **Le Printemps de l'Homme** (⊠ 61 rue Caumartin, 9ᵉ, ☎ 01–42–82–50–00, métro Havre-Caumartin) has six floors of designer suits, sportswear, coats, ties, and accessories. **Panoplie** (⊠ 7 rue d'Argout, 2ᵉ, ☎ 01–40–28–90–35, métro Louvre) is one of the best addresses in town for men's designer fashions.

WOMENSWEAR

No matter, say the French, that fewer and fewer of their top couture houses are still headed by compatriots. It's the chic elegance, the classic ambience, the *je ne sais quoi,* that remains undeniably Gallic. Here are some top meccas for Paris chic. **Azzedine Alaïa** (⊠ 7 rue de Moussy, 4ᵉ, ☎ 01–42–72–19–19, métro Hôtel-de-Ville) is the undisputed "king of cling" and the supermodel favorite. **Chanel** (⊠ 42 av. Montaigne,

8ᵉ, ☎ 01–47–23–74–12, métro Franklin-D.-Roosevelt; ⊠ 31 rue Cambon, 1ᵉʳ, ☎ 01–42–86–28–00, métro Tuileries) is helmed by Karl Lagerfeld, a master at updating Coco's signature look with fresh colors and free-spirited silhouettes. **Christian Dior** (⊠ 30 av. Montaigne, 8ᵉ, ☎ 01–40–73–54–00, métro Franklin-D.-Roosevelt) installed flamboyant British designer John Galliano as head designer after his triumphant run at Givenchy. **Colette** (⊠ 213 rue St-Honoré, 1ᵉʳ, ☎ 01–55–35–33–90, métro Tuileries) is the most fashionable, most hip, and most hyped store in Paris (and possibly in the world). The ground floor, which stocks design objects, gadgets, and makeup, is generally packed with fashion victims and the simply curious. Upstairs are handpicked fashions, accessories, magazines and books, all of which ooze trendiness. **Sonia Rykiel** (⊠ 175 bd. St-Germain, 6ᵉ, ☎ 01–49–54–60–60, métro St-Germain-des-Prés; ⊠ 70 rue du Faubourg St-Honoré, 8ᵉ, ☎ 01–42–65–20–81, métro Concorde) is the queen of French fashion. Since the '60s she has been designing stylish knit separates and has made black her color of predilection.

L'Absinthe (⊠ 74–76 rue Jean-Jacques Rousseau, 1ᵉʳ, ☎ 01–42–33–54–44, métro Les Halles) is a magical address with clothing that's new but looks vintage. **Antik Batik** (⊠ 18 rue de Turenne, 4ᵉ, ☎ 01–48–87–95–95, métro St-Paul) sells hippie-chic, ethnic-inspired clothing, bags, and shoes, which has made the label a hit with in-the-know Parisians and supermodels. **Isabel Marant** (⊠ 16 rue de Charonne, 11ᵉ, ☎ 01–49–29–71–55, métro Ledru-Rollin) is one of the Paris press's favorite designers. French fashionistas flock to her Bastille boutique for her youthful and feminine designs. **Réciproque** (⊠ 88, 89, 92, 95, 101, and 123 rue de la Pompe, 16ᵉ, ☎ 01–47–04–30–28, métro Rue de la Pompe) is Paris's largest and most exclusive swap shop; savings on designer wear—Hermès, Dior, Chanel—are significant. **Ventilo** (⊠ 27 bis, rue du Louvre, 2ᵉ, ☎ 01–44–76–83–00, métro Louvre) sells ethnic-inspired fashions to savvy Parisians; On the third floor are housewares and a café serving what is perhaps the best chocolate cake in the world. **Zara** (⊠ 44 av. des Champs-Élysées, 8ᵉ, ☎ 01–45–61–52–80, métro Franklin-D.-Roosevelt) is where smart Parisians pick up the latest trends at bargain prices.

Food and Wine

À la Mère de Famille (⊠ 35 rue du Faubourg-Montmartre, 9ᵉ, ☎ 01–47–70–83–69, métro Cadet) is well versed in French regional specialties and old-fashioned bonbons, sugar candy, and more. **Les Caves Augé** (⊠ 116 bd. Haussmann, 8ᵉ, ☎ 01–45–22–16–97, métro St-Augustin) has been one of the best wine shops in Paris since 1850. **La Maison du Chocolat** (⊠ 56 rue Pierre-Charron, 8ᵉ, ☎ 01–47–23–38–25, métro Franklin-D.-Roosevelt; ⊠ 8 bd. de la Madeleine, 9ᵉ, ☎ 01–47–42–86–52, métro Madeleine; ⊠ 225 rue du Faubourg–St-Honoré, 8ᵉ, ☎ 01–42–27–39–44, métro Ternes) is the place for chocolate; take home some or go to the tearoom at rue Pierre Charron or Madeleine.

Housewares and Gifts

Catherine Memmi (⊠ 32–34 rue St-Sulpice, 6ᵉ, ☎ 01–44–07–22–28, métro St-Sulpice; ⊠ 43 rue Madame, 6ᵉ, ☎ 01–45–48–18–34, métro St-Sulpice) sells wonderfully chic bed linens, bath products, lamps, table settings, furniture, and casual wear—all in elegantly neutral colors. **Christophe Delcourt** (⊠ 76 bis rue Vieille-du-Temple, 3ᵉ, ☎ 01–42–78–44–97, métro Rambuteau/St-Paul) attracts fashion designers and French film stars, who go mad for his lamps based on old-fashioned drawing tools, pared-down waxed-steel furniture, and sleek wooden tables. **Diptyque** (⊠ 34 bd. St-Germain, 5ᵉ, ☎ 01–43–26–45–27, métro Maubert-Mutualité) sells the best scented candles in Paris. **Sentou Ga-**

lerie (✉ 24 rue du Pont Louis-Philippe, 4ᵉ, ☎ 01–42–71–00–01, métro St-Paul) has lights created by artists, furniture made by young designers, and funky tableware.

PARIS A TO Z

Arriving and Departing

By Bus

Long-distance bus journeys within France are uncommon, which may be why Paris has no central bus depot. *See* Bus Travel *in* Smart Travel Tips A to Z for information on traveling to and from Paris by bus.

By Car

In a country as highly centralized as France, it's no surprise that expressways converge on the capital from every direction: A1 from the north (225 km [140 mi] from Lille); A13 from Normandy (225 km [140 mi] from Caen); A4 from the east (500 km [310 mi] from Strasbourg); A10 from the southwest (580 km [360 mi] from Bordeaux); and A7 from the Alps and the Riviera (465 km [290 mi] from Lyon). Each connects with the *périphérique*, the beltway, whose exits into the city are named (as *portes*), not numbered.

By Plane

Paris is served by two international airports: **Charles de Gaulle,** also known as Roissy, 26 km (16 mi) northeast; and **Orly,** 16 km (10 mi) south. Major carriers fly daily from the United States; Air France, British Airways, British Midland, and Air U.K. fly regularly from London. *See* Air Travel *in* Smart Travel Tips A to Z for details.

BETWEEN THE AIRPORT AND DOWNTOWN

From Charles de Gaulle, the **RER-B,** the suburban commuter train, beneath Terminal 2, has trains to central Paris (Les Halles, St-Michel, Luxembourg) every 15 minutes; the fare is 49 francs, and the journey lasts 30 minutes. Note that you have to carry your luggage up from and down to the platform and that trains can be crowded during rush hour. **Buses** operated by Air France (you need not have flown with the airline) run every 15 minutes between Roissy and western Paris (Porte Maillot and the Arc de Triomphe). The fare is 60 francs, and the trip lasts about 40 minutes, though rush-hour traffic may make it longer. Additionally, the **Roissybus,** operated by the RATP, runs directly between Roissy and rue Scribe by the Opéra every 15 minutes and costs 48 francs. **Taxis** are readily available; the fare will be around 200–250 francs, depending on traffic. **Aeroports Limousine Service** (☎ 01–40–71–84–62 can meet you on arrival in a private car and drive you to your destination; reservations should be made two or three days in advance; MasterCard and Visa are accepted.

The **RER-C** line is one way to get to Paris from Orly Airport; there's a free shuttle bus from the terminal building to the train station, and trains leave every 15 minutes. The fare is 33 francs (métro included), and the train journey takes about 45 minutes. The **Orlyval** service is a shuttle train that runs direct from each Orly terminal to the Antony **RER-B** station every seven minutes; a one-way ticket for the entire trip into Paris is 57 francs. **Buses** operated by Air France (you need not have flown with the airline) run every 12 minutes between Orly Airport and the Air France air terminal at Les Invalides, on the Left Bank; the fare is 45 francs, and the trip can take from 30 minutes to an hour, depending on traffic. RATP also runs the **Orlybus** between the Denfert-Rochereau métro station and Orly every 15 minutes, and the trip costs 35 francs.

A 25-minute **taxi** ride costs about 130–180 francs. With reservations, **Aeroports Limousine Service** (☞ *above*) can pick you up at Orly.

By Train

Paris has five international train stations: **Gare du Nord** (northern France, northern Europe, and England via Calais or the Channel Tunnel); **Gare St-Lazare** (Normandy and England via Dieppe); **Gare de l'Est** (Strasbourg, Luxembourg, Basel, and central Europe); **Gare de Lyon** (Lyon, Marseille, the Riviera, Geneva, Italy); and **Gare d'Austerlitz** (Loire Valley, southwest France, Spain). The **Gare Montparnasse** is used by the TGV-*Atlantique* bound for Nantes or Bordeaux. For information contact the **RATP** (✉ 54 quai de la Rapée, ☎ 08–36–68–77–14).

Getting Around

To help you find your way around, buy a *Plan de Paris par Arrondissement,* a city guide available at most kiosks, with separate maps of each district, including the whereabouts of métro stations and an index of street names. Maps of the métro/RER network are available free from any métro station and from many hotels. They are also posted on every platform, as are maps of the bus network. Bus routes are also marked at bus stops and on buses. The extensive public transportation system is the best way to get around.

By Bicycle

Despite the recent introduction of bike lanes, bicycling in central Paris is not very safe; wear a helmet. Bicycles can be rented at various locations throughout the city (☞ Outdoor Activities and Sports, *above*).

By Bus

Paris buses are marked with the route number and destination in front and with major stopping places along the sides. Most routes operate from 6 AM to 8:30 PM; some continue until midnight. Ten *Noctambus,* or night buses, operate hourly (1 AM to 6 AM) between Châtelet and various nearby suburbs. The brown bus shelters, topped by red-and-yellow circular signs, contain timetables and route maps. You can use your métro ticket on the buses; if you have individual tickets (as opposed to weekly or monthly tickets), state your destination and be prepared to punch one or more tickets in the red-and-gray machines onboard.

By Car

Don't use a car in Paris unless you have to. Parking is difficult—and expensive—and traffic, except late at night, is awful. Meters and ticket machines (pay and display) are common; make sure you have a supply of coins.

By Métro

The métro is by far the quickest and most efficient way of getting around. Trains run from 5:30 AM until 1:15 AM (and be forewarned—this means the famous "last métro" can pass your station anytime after 12:30 AM). Stations are signaled either by a large yellow M within a circle or by their distinctive curly green Art Nouveau railings and archway entrances bearing the subway's full title (Métropolitain). You must know the name of the last station on the line you take, as this appears on all signs. A connection (you can make as many as you like on one ticket) is called a *correspondance.* At junction stations, illuminated orange signs bearing the name of the line terminal appear over the correct corridors for correspondance. Illuminated blue signs marked SORTIE indicate the station exit. In general, the métro is safe, although try to avoid Lines 2 and 13 if you're alone late at night. Access to métro platforms is through an automatic ticket barrier. Slide your ticket in and pick it up and retrieve it as it pops up. Keep your ticket during your journey; you will need it to leave the RER system, and you'll be glad you have it in case you run into any green-clad inspectors when you are leaving—they can be very nasty and will impose a big fine on the spot if you do not have a ticket.

All métro tickets and passes are valid for RER and bus travel as well; tickets cost 8 francs each, but it makes more sense to buy a *carnet* (10 tickets) for 55 francs. If you're staying for a week or more, the best deals are the weekly *coupon jaune* (yellow ticket) or monthly *carte orange* (orange card), sold according to zone. Zones 1 and 2 cover the entire métro network; tickets cost 82 francs a week or 279 francs a month. If you plan to take suburban trains to visit places in the Ile-de-France, consider a four-zoner (Versailles, St-Germain-en-Laye; 137 francs a week) or a six-zoner (Rambouillet, Fontainebleau; 187 francs a week). Weekly and monthly passes are available from rail and major métro stations; the monthly pass requires a passport-size photograph.

An alternative is to purchase two, three, or five-day unlimited-travel tickets (*Paris Visite*). Unlike the coupon jaune, good from Monday morning to Sunday evening, the unlimited ticket is valid starting any day of the week and gives you discounts on a limited number of museums and tourist attractions. The prices are, respectively, 90, 120, and 175 francs for Paris only; 175, 245, and 300 francs for Paris and the suburbs. The equivalent one-day ticket is called *mobilis* and costs 32 francs (Paris only) or 50–90 francs (Paris plus suburbs).

By RER

RER trains travel between Paris and the suburbs. When they go through Paris, they act as a sort of supersonic métro—they connect with the métro network at several points—and can be great time-savers. Access to RER platforms is through the same type of automatic ticket barrier (if you've started your journey on the métro, you can use the same ticket), but you'll need to have the same ticket handy to put through another barrier when you leave the system.

By Taxi

You are best off asking hotel or restaurant staff to call for a taxi; cruising cabs are difficult to spot, especially late at night. Note that taxis seldom take more than three people at a time. There is a basic charge of 13 francs for all rides and a 6-franc charge per piece of luggage. Daytime rates (from 7 AM to 7:30 PM) are around 2.80 francs per kilometer, and nighttime rates are around 4.50 francs. Rates are about 40% higher in the suburbs than in the city.

Contacts and Resources

Baby-Sitters

Baby-sitting services can provide English-speaking baby-sitters on just a few hours' notice. The hourly rate is approximately $6 (three-hour minimum) plus an agency fee of around $10. **Ababa** (✉ 8 av. du Maine, 15e, ☎ 01–45–49–46–46). **Allo Maman Poule** (✉ 7 Villa Murat, 16e, ☎ 01–45–20–96–96). **Baby Sitting Services** (✉ 18 rue Tronchet, 8e, ☎ 01–46–21–33–16).

Car Rentals

Cars can be rented at both airports, as well as at locations throughout the city, including the following. **Avis** (✉ 60 rue de Ponthieu, 8e, ☎ 01–43–59–03–83, métro St-Philippe du Roule). **Citer** (✉ 18 rue de Dunkerque, 10e, ☎ 01–53–20–04–75, métro Gare du Nord). **Europcar** (✉ 202 rue de Rivoli, 1er, ☎ 01–40–15–96–98, métro Tuileries). **Hertz** (✉ 193 rue de Bercy, 12e, ☎ 01–43–44–06–00, métro Gare de Lyon).

Paris Métro

Gabriel Péri (Asnières-Gennevilliers) 13

Carrefour Pleyel
St-Denis Porte de Paris
St-Denis Basilique
Mairie de St-Ouen
St-Ouen
Porte de Clignancourt 4
Garibaldi
Mairie de Clichy
Porte de St-Ouen
Jules Joff
Lamarck-Caulaincourt
Abbesses
Guy Môquet
Pigalle
Anvers
Porte de Clichy
Brochant
Blanche
Saint-Georges
La Fourche
Notre-Dame-de-Lorette
Cadet
Pont de Levallois-Bécon 3
Place de Clichy
Liège
Trinité
Le Peletier
Richelieu-Drouot
Grand Boulevo
Anatole-France
Rome
St-Lazare
Chaussée-d'Antin La Fayette
Louise-Michel
Wagram
Malesherbes
Villiers
Europe
Havre-Caumartin
Grands-Boulevards
Porte de Champerret
Péreire
4 Septembre
Bou
Monceau
Auber
Opéra
Grande Arche de La Défense
Courcelles
St-Augustin
Méteor 14
Pyr
Esplanade de La Défense
Charles de Gaulle Etoile
Ternes
St-Philippe-du-Roule
Miromesnil
Madeleine
RER LINE A
Concorde
Palais-R Musée du L 1
Pont de Neuilly
Les Sablons
Porte Maillot
Argentine
Victor Hugo
George V
F.D. Roosevelt
Champs-Elysées Clemenceau
Tuileries
Porte Dauphine 2
Kléber
Boissière
Alma-Marceau
Seine
Av. Foch
Iéna
Invalides
Musée d'Orsay
Rue de la Pompe
Trocadéro
Assemblée Nationale
St-Germa des-Pré
Av. Henri Martin
Passy
Pont de l'Alma
Varenne
Solférino
La Muette
La Tour-Maubourg
Rue du Bac
Boulainvilliers
Kennedy Radio France
St-François Xavier
Sèvres-Babylone
Ma
Ranelagh
Bir-Hakeim
Duroc
Rennes
Vaneau
St-Sul
Jasmin
Michel-Ange Auteuil
Champ-de-Mars Tour Eiffel
Ségur
St-Placide
Porte d'Auteuil
Eglise d'Auteuil
Ecole Mil.
Falguière
Boulogne Jean-Jaurès
Dupleix
Cambronne
Sèvres-Lecourbe
Boulogne Pt. de St-Cloud 10
Michel-Ange-Molitor
Chardon-Lagache
Mirabeau
Javel
Javel André Citroën
Charles Michels
Av. Emile Zola
La Motte-Picquet-Grenelle
Pasteur
Montparnasse Bienvenüe
E Q
Exelmans
Commerce
Volontaires
Gaîté
Porte de St-Cloud
Boulevard Victor
Félix Faure
Boucicaut
Vaugirard
Pernety
Plaisance
Marcel Sembat
Lourmel
Convention
Porte de Vanves
Billancourt
Balard 8
Porte de Versailles
Malakoff-Plateau de Vanves
Pont de Sèvres 9
Issy Plaine
Corentin Celton
Malakoff-Rue Etienne Dolet
Mairie d'Issy 12
Châtillon-Montrouge 13

N

Seine

RER LINE C

RER LINE C

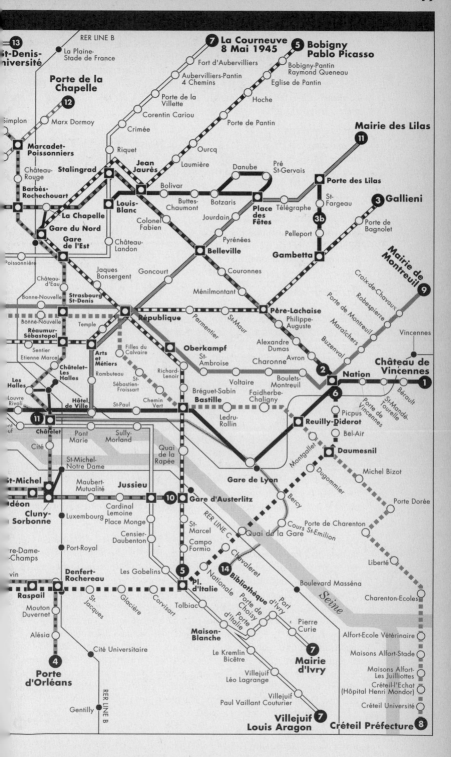

Embassies

Australia (✉ 4 rue Jean-Rey, 15ᵉ, ☎ 01–40–59–33–00, métro Bir Hakeim). **Canada** (✉ 35 av. Montaigne, 8ᵉ, ☎ 01–44–43–29–00, métro Franklin-D.-Roosevelt). **United Kingdom** (✉ 35 rue du Faubourg–St-Honoré, 8ᵉ, ☎ 01–44–51–31–00, métro Concorde). **United States** (✉ 2 av. Gabriel, 8ᵉ, ☎ 01–43–12–22–22, métro Concorde). **New Zealand** (✉ 7 ter rue Léonardo da Vinci, 16ᵉ, ☎ 01–45–00–24–11, métro Victor-Hugo).

Emergencies

Ambulance (☎ 15 or 01–45–67–50–50). **Dentist** (☎ 01–43–37–51–00). **Doctor** (☎ 01–43–37–77–77). **Police** (☎ 17). A 24-hour emergency service is available at **American Hospital** (✉ 63 bd. Victor-Hugo, Neuilly, ☎ 01–47–45–71–00). **Hertford British Hospital** (✉ 3 rue Barbès, Levallois-Perret, ☎ 01–47–58–13–12) also has all-night emergency service.

LATE-NIGHT PHARMACIES

Pharmacie Les Champs (✉ 84 av. des Champs-Élysées, 8ᵉ, ☎ 01–45–62–02–41, métro George-V) is open 24 hours a day, 365 days a year. **Pharmacie Européenne** (✉ 6 pl. Clichy, 9ᵉ, ☎ 01–48–74–65–18, métro Place de Clichy) is also open around the clock.

Guided Tours

BY BOAT

Hour-long boat trips on the Seine can be fun if you're in Paris for the first time; the cost is 40–50 francs. Some boats serve lunch and dinner (for an additional cost); make reservations in advance. **Bateaux Mouches** (✉ Pont de l'Alma, 8ᵉ, ☎ 01–40–76–99–99, métro Alma-Marceau) boats depart daily 11–10 in summer, 11–9 in winter. **Bateaux Parisiens** (✉ Pont d'Iéna, 7ᵉ, ☎ 01–44–11–33–44, métro Trocadéro) boats depart every half hour in summer and every hour in winter, starting at 10 AM; the last boat departs at 10 PM (11 PM in summer). **Canauxrama** (Boats depart from: ✉ 13 quai de la Loire, 19ᵉ, métro Jaurès; ✉ Bassin de l'Arsenal, 12ᵉ, opposite 50 bd. de la Bastille, métro Bastille; ☎ 01–42–39–15–00 for information) organizes half- and full-day barge tours along the canals of east Paris. **Vedettes du Pont-Neuf** (✉ Below Sq. du Vert-Galant, 1ᵉʳ, ☎ 01–46–33–98–38, métro Pont Neuf) depart every half hour 10–noon, 1:30–6:30, and 9–10:30 from March to October, and every 45 minutes 10–noon and 2–6:30 from November to February.

BY BUS

Cityrama (✉ 4 pl. des Pyramides, 1ᵉʳ, ☎ 01–44–55–61–00, métro Tuileries) and **Paris Vision** (✉ 214 rue de Rivoli, 1ᵉʳ, ☎ 08-00–03–02–14, métro Tuileries) both organize a number of different tours, from two hours on a double-decker bus with live or tape-recorded commentary (English is available) to day trips to sights in the Paris region. Tours generally cost about 150 francs. For a more intimate—albeit expensive—tour of the city, **Paris Bus** (✉ 22 rue de la Prévoyance, 94300 Vincennes, ☎ 01–43–65–55–55, métro St-Mandé–Tourelle) runs several minibus excursions per day; the bus can take eight people and can pick up or drop off at hotels; the cost is 270 francs for a 2½-hour tour, 335 francs for four hours. For sightseeing at your own pace, Paris Bus also runs a red double-decker with nine pickup and drop-off points around Paris. Tours start from Trocadéro at 10:20 AM and every 50 minutes until 5. Tickets are good for two days and cost 120 francs.

BY PRIVATE CAR

Paris Major Limousine (✉ 14 rue Atlas, 19ᵉ, ☎ 01–44–52–50–00) arranges private tours of Paris in luxury cars or minibuses (holding up to seven passengers) with English-speaking drivers. The price starts at

1,400 francs but varies with time (a minimum of three hours) and number of passengers. Reservations are essential.

WALKING TOURS

Plenty of guided walking tours of specific areas of Paris are available, often concentrating on a historical or architectural topic. Guides are enthusiastic but not always English speaking; costs range from 40 to 60 francs, and tours last about two hours. Details are published in the weekly magazines *Pariscope* and *L'Officiel des Spectacles* under "Conférences." Walking tours are also organized by the **Caisse Nationale des Monuments Historiques,** Bureau des Visites (✉ Hôtel de Sully, 62 rue St-Antoine, 4ᵉ, ☎ 01–44–61–20–00, métro St-Paul).

Travel Agencies

Air France (✉ 119 av. des Champs-Élysées, 8ᵉ, ☎ 01–42–99–21–01, métro Charles-de-Gaulle–Étoile). **American Express** (✉ 11 rue Scribe, 8ᵉ, ☎ 01–47–77–77–07, métro Opéra; ✉ 38 av. de Wagram, 8ᵉ, ☎ 01–42–27–58–80, métro Charles-de-Gaulle–Étoile). **Nouvelles Frontières** (✉ 5 ave. de l'Opéra, 1ᵉʳ, ☎ 08–03–33–33–33, métro Pyramides). **Soltours** (✉ 46 rue de Rivoli, 4ᵉ, ☎ 01–42–71–24–34, métro Hôtel-de-Ville). **Wagon-Lits** (✉ 32 rue du Quatre-Septembre, 2ᵉ, ☎ 01–42–66–15–80, métro Opéra).

Visitor Information

The **Office de Tourisme de Paris** (Paris Tourist Office; ✉ 127 av. des Champs-Élysées, 75008, ☎ 01–49–52–53–54; 01–49–52–53–56 for recorded information in English, métro Charles-de-Gaulle–Étoile) is open daily 9–8. It has branches at all main-line train stations except Gare St-Lazare.

2 ILE-DE-FRANCE

Appearing like all France in miniature, the
Ile-de France region is the heartland of the
nation. Here Louis XIV willed the construction
of Versailles, the world's most vainglorious
palace. Nearby, *la vie de château* continues
to dazzle at Chantilly, Fontainebleau, and
Vaux-le-Vicomte. More spiritual concerns
are embodied nearby in Chartres Cathedral,
the soaring pinnacle of Gothic architecture.
Not far away are Giverny and Auvers—
immortalized by Monet and van Gogh,
respectively. What more can you ask for?
How about Mickey Mouse on parade
at Disneyland Paris?

Updated by
Simon Hewitt

F OR VISITORS THE ILE-DE-FRANCE is the most heartwarming of all the French provinces. First, there is the pleasure of imagination satisfied: there is something strangely familiar about the look of lanes bordered with silvery poplar trees, the golden haze in the air, the gray stone of a village steeple. And no wonder, for scores of painters have immortalized them. Corot began with the forest of Fontainebleau and the village of Barbizon. Pissarro worked at Pontoise; Sisley's famous riverside canvases were painted at Moret-sur-Loing near Fontainebleau; Monet painted the Epte River; and van Gogh died in Auvers.

What, in fact, makes the Ile-de-France so visionary: its proximity to Paris—or that it's so far removed? Had there not been a great city—the hub of a world-class culture—within spitting distance, would Monet have retreated to his Japanese gardens at Giverny? Cézanne and van Gogh to bucolic Auvers? Counts and kings to the game-rich forests of Fontainebleau, Rambouillet, Dampierre? Would medieval castles and palaces have sprouted in the towns of Vincennes and St-Germain-en-Laye? Would abbeys and cathedrals have sprung skyward in Chartres, Senlis, and Royaumont?

If you'd asked Louis XIV, he wouldn't have minced words at all: Paris was *over*, my dear. The new power base was going to be Versailles—one of the most spectacular sights in the Ile-de-France. From this gigantic château, the Sun King's rays (Louis XIV was known as *le roi soleil*) could radiate, unfettered by rebellious rabble and European arrivistes. But his heirs kept the lines open and restored the grandiose palace as the country retreat it was meant to be—and commuted to Paris, well before the high-speed RER.

That is, of course, the dream of most Parisians: to keep a foot in both worlds. Paris may be small as capital cities go, with slightly more than 2 million inhabitants, but Ile-de-France, the region around Paris, contains more than 10 million people—one-sixth of France's entire population. That's why on closer inspection the once pastoral villages of Ile-de-France reveal cosseted gardens, stylishly gentrified cottages, and extraordinary country restaurants no farmer could afford. And that's why Ile-de-France retains a sophisticated air not found in France's other pockets of verdure and has more than a touch of history.

The Ile-de-France is the ancient heartland of France, the core from which the French kings gradually extended their power over the rest of a rebellious, individualistic nation. From the time when it was first wrested from savage Gauls in 52 BC by Julius Caesar, the region has played an intimate role in French history. No major coronation and few battles of supreme importance took place outside its boundaries. Its towns and villages have been entwined in the course of national fact and legend. Charlemagne confirmed his power in France after generations had fought against the Romans near Soissons; Joan of Arc battling for her king's supremacy was finally captured at Compiègne. There is Versailles from which the three Louis gloriously reigned until the Revolution dealt the French monarchy its death blow. And Napoléon ruled for a time from Malmaison and abdicated in the courtyard at Fontainebleau.

It's not really an *île* (island), of course. This green-forested buffer that wraps around Paris is only vaguely surrounded by the three rivers that meander through its periphery. But France's capital city seems to crown an atoll of genteel verdure, peppered with pretty villages, anchored by grandiose châteaux. The spokes of railway and freeway that radiate every which way from the Paris ring roads all merge gently into countryside.

All in all, Ile-de-France strikes a balance, offering visitors a rich and varied cross section of Gallic culture . . . a minisampling of everything we expect from France, and all within easy day trips out of Paris. With cathedrals, châteaux, and places immortalized by great painters, what more could you wish for? Well, how about Goofy on parade along Main Street U.S.A.? Pirates of the Caribbean? And Disney's own answer to Versailles, the bubble-gum pink turrets of Sleeping Beauty's Castle? Yes, the much-maligned, now recherché Disneyland Paris has taken root, drawing sellout crowds of Europeans wanting a taste of the American Dream—and of Americans with children in tow, bargaining against a day at the Louvre. It is just another epic vision realized against the green backdrop of Ile-de-France.

— Nancy Coons

Pleasures and Pastimes

Artists' Residences

At Giverny, Claude Monet's house and garden, with its famous lily pond, is a moving visual link to Impressionist painting. In Auvers-sur-Oise, Vincent van Gogh had a final burst of creativity before taking his life. André Derain lived in Chambourcy; Camille Pissarro, in Pontoise; Alfred Sisley, in Moret-sur-Loing. Earlier, Rousseau, Millet, and Corot paved the way for Impressionism with their penchant for outdoor landscape painting in the town of Barbizon.

Châteaux

Ile-de-France never lost favor with the powerful, partly because its many forests—large chunks of which still stand—harbored sufficient game to ensure a regular kill, even for bloated, pampered monarchs. First Fontainebleau, in manageable Renaissance proportions, then Versailles reflected the royal desire to transform hunting lodges into palatial residences. Other châteaux that exude almost comparable grandeur are at Vaux-le-Vicomte and Chantilly. And there are another dozen châteaux almost as grand—led by Dampierre, Rambouillet, Maintenon, Maisons-Laffitte, and Thoiry.

Dining

Ile-de-France's fanciest restaurants can be just as pricey as their Parisian counterparts. Little wonder—unlike Normandy's cider, creams, and chicken or Périgord's truffles and foie gras, Ile-de-France cuisine mirrors that of the big capital. Textbook "local delicacies"—lamb stew, *pâté de Pantin* (pastry filled with meat), or pig's trotters—tend to be obsolete; instead, look for sumptuous game and asparagus in season in the south of the region and the soft, creamy cheese of Meaux and Coulommiers to the east. However, in smaller towns or if you venture off the beaten tourist path, well-priced meals are not hard to find. Reservations are a must at all restaurants in summer.

CATEGORY	COST*
$$$$	over 500 frs
$$$	250 frs–500 frs
$$	125 frs–250 frs
$	under 125 frs

per person for a three-course meal, including tax (20.6%) and tip but not wine

✍ *following the text of a review is your signal that the property has a Web site, where you will find details and, usually, images; for a link, visit www.fodors.com/urls.*

Lodging

In summer hotel rooms are at a premium and making reservations essential; almost all accommodations in the swanker towns—Versailles, Rambouillet, and Fontainebleau—are on the costly side. Take nothing for granted. Picturesque Senlis, for instance, does not have a single hotel in its historic downtown area.

CATEGORY	COST*
$$$$	over 900 frs
$$$	600 frs–900 frs
$$	300 frs–600 frs
$	under 300 frs

All prices are for a standard double room for two, including tax (20.6%) and service charge.

Exploring Ile-de-France

A great advantage to exploring Ile-de-France is that all its major monuments are within a half day's drive from Paris. Though small, the Ile-de-France is so rich in treasures that a whole day of fascinating exploration may take you no more than 36 km (60 mi) from the capital. The four tours suggested below detail the major points of interest and skip the pedantic: southwest from Paris to Versailles and Chartres; northwest along the Seine to St-Germain and Giverny; north and east along the Oise Valley via Chantilly to Disneyland; and southeast from Vaux-le-Vicomte to Fontainebleau.

Numbers in the text correspond to numbers in the margin and on the Ile-de-France, Versailles, and Fontainebleau maps.

Great Itineraries

With so many legendary sights—each a rewarding human experience rather than a guidebook necessity—in the Ile-de-France, you could spend weeks visiting the dozens of châteaux and historic towns in the region. But if you don't have that much time, try one of the following shorter itineraries. Spend from two to eight days exploring the area or take day trips from Paris—most sites are within easy reach of the capital by car or train.

IF YOU HAVE 2 DAYS

Head west from Paris to nearby **St-Germain-en-Laye** ㉚ and visit either the château or the Prieuré Museum. Try to reach 🏛 **Versailles** ①–⑰ for lunch and then visit the château and the park. The next morning spend more time in Versailles or leave early and visit **Rambouillet** ⑳ or **Maintenon** ㉑ on your way to 🏛 **Chartres** ㉒; spend half a day exploring the cathedral and the old town.

IF YOU HAVE 5 DAYS

Take the expressway north from Paris to **Senlis** ㊷, visit the old town and cathedral, then head to 🏛 **Chantilly** ㊶ for the afternoon. The next morning follow the Oise Valley, stopping briefly in **Auvers-sur-Oise** ㊴ en route to 🏛 **Versailles** ①–⑰. Spend the morning of your third day in Versailles or **Rambouillet** ⑳; try to be in 🏛 **Chartres** ㉒ by early afternoon. Spend the night there and drive to 🏛 **Fontainebleau** ㊽–㊼ the following morning, perhaps visiting **Barbizon** ㊷ on your way. On day five make sure to visit **Vaux-le-Vicomte** ㊻.

When to Tour Ile-de-France

With its extensive forests, Ile-de-France is especially beautiful in the fall, particularly October. June and July are good months, too, while August can be sultry and crowded. On a Saturday night in summer you can see son-et-lumière shows in Moret-sur-Loing and make can-

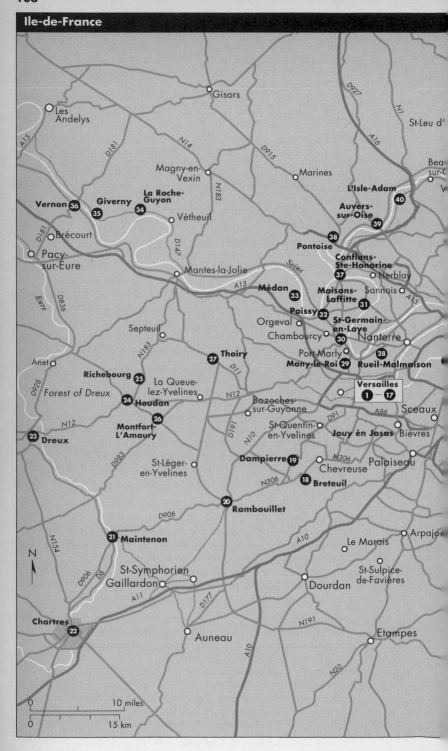

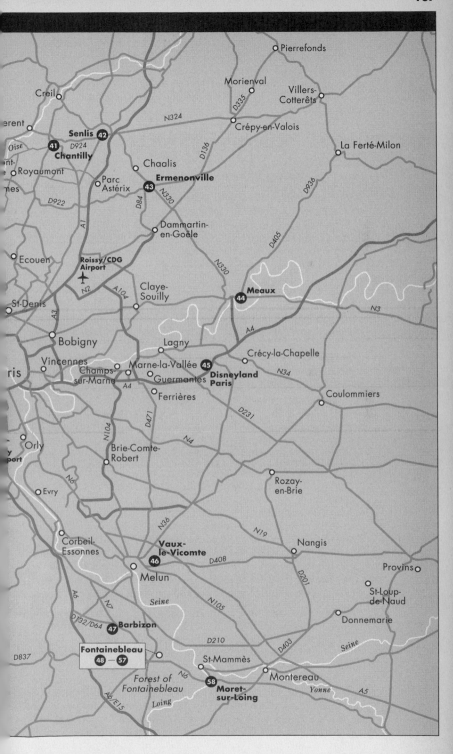

dlelight visits to Vaux-le-Vicomte. Be aware when making your travel plans that some places are closed one or two days a week: The châteaux of Versailles and Auvers are closed on Monday; the Prieuré Museum in St-Germain is closed both Monday and Tuesday; and the châteaux of Chantilly and Fontainebleau are closed Tuesday. Disneyland Paris gets really crowded on summer weekends. So does Giverny (Monet's garden), which is at its best in May–June and, like Vaux-le-Vicomte, is closed November–March.

SOUTHWEST FROM VERSAILLES TO CHARTRES

Not only is majestic Versailles one of the most unforgettable sights in Ile-de-France, but it is also within easy reach of Paris, less than 30 minutes by either train (☞ Arriving and Departing *in* Ile-de-France A to Z, *below*) or car (A13 expressway from Porte d'Auteuil). It's also the starting point for a visit to southwestern Ile-de-France, anchored by Chartres to the south and the old town of Dreux to the west.

Versailles

16 km (10 mi) west of Paris via A13.

You'll need no reminding that you're in the world's grandest palace when you arrive at Versailles. Gold, gold, and more gold, multicolor marbles, acres of Le Brun painted ceilings, and hallways still spirit-warm with the ghosts of Louis XIV, Madame de Pompadour, and Marie-Antoinette remind you that such insensate glory foreshadowed the blood-stained French Revolution. Less a monument than an entire world unto itself, its mere immensity is such that some travelers still consider it more an ordeal than a pleasure. That's understandable—even the Bourbon kings needed to escape it and did so by building one of Europe's largest and most sylvan parks to surround the palace. So take a cue from them and remember: if the grandeur ever becomes too much, the park outside is the best place to get your breath back.

Psychologically, historically, Versailles may be regarded as the result of a childhood shock suffered by the young king Louis XIV. With his mother, Anne of Austria, he was forced to flee Paris and was captured temporarily by a group of nobles, known as the Frondeurs. Louis developed a hatred for Paris and of the Parisians who had sided with the conspirators. He lost no time in casting his cantankerous royal eye over Ile-de-France in search of a new power base. Marshy, inhospitable Versailles became the place of his dreams. Down came his father's modest royal hunting lodge and up, up, and up rose a swanky new palace.

★ ❶ The **Château de Versailles** seems monstrously huge, but it wasn't big enough for the army of 20,000 noblemen, servants, and sycophants who moved in with Louis XIV. Hence, a new city had to be constructed from scratch to accommodate them. Town planners dreamed up vast mansions and avenues broader than the Champs-Élysées, all in minion-crushing, bicep-flexing Baroque, which the 23-year-old Louis took a liking to just after the blow to his pride caused by an earlier visit to the just-built château of Vaux-le-Vicomte (☞ *below*), where his own finance minister had built a lavishly Baroque Xanadu. It's hardly surprising that Louis XIV's successors felt out of sync with their architectural inheritance. Louis XV traded in the heavy, gilded red-and-gold Baroque style (actually a transplant from Italy) for the newer, lighter pastel-hued Rococo mode. In doing so, he transformed the royal apartments into places to live rather than to pose. The hapless Louis XVI

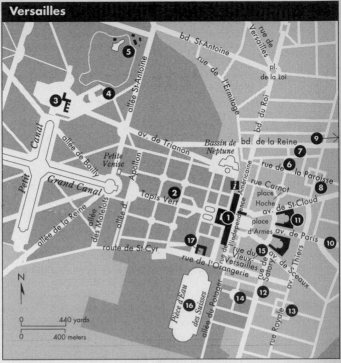

cowered in the Petit Trianon, in the leafy depths of Versailles's gardens, out of the mighty château's shadow. His queen, Marie-Antoinette, lost her head well before her trip to the guillotine in 1793, pretending to be a peasant shepherdess amid the ersatz rusticity and perfumed flocks of sheep of her **Hameau,** a mock farm and village she had built just beyond the precincts of the Petit Trianon.

You enter the château—built between 1662 and 1690 by architects Louis Le Vau and Jules Hardouin-Mansart—through the gilt iron gates from huge place d'Armes. On the first floor of the château, dead center across the sprawling cobbled forecourt beyond the Sun King's statue, is **Louis XIV's bedchamber.** The two wings were occupied by the royal children and princes of the blood, while courtiers had to make do in the attics. One of the palace's trademark sights is the sparkling **Galerie des Glaces** (Hall of Mirrors). It was here, after France's capitulation, that Otto von Bismarck proclaimed the unified German Empire in 1871; and here that the Treaty of Versailles, asserting Germany's responsibility for World War I, was signed in 1919. The **Grands Appartements** (state apartments), which flank the Hall of Mirrors, retain much of their original Baroque decoration: gilt stucco, painted ceilings, and marble sculpture. Perhaps the most extravagant is the **Salon d'Apollon** (Apollo Chamber), the former throne room, dedicated to the sun god Apollo, Louis XIV's mythical hero. Equally interesting are the **Petits Appartements** (private apartments), where the royal family and friends lived in (relative) privacy.

In the north wing of the château is the solemn white-and-gold **chapelle** (chapel), completed in 1710; the intimate **Opéra Royal** (Opera House), the first oval hall in France, built by Jacques-Ange Gabriel for Louis XV in 1770; and, connecting the two, the 17th-century **Galeries,** with exhibits retracing the château's history. The south wing contains the bombastic **Galerie des Batailles** (Hall of Battles), lined with gigantic canvases extolling French military glory. In 1997 the former state rooms and sumptuous debate chamber of the **Aile du Midi** (South Wing) were opened to the public, with infrared headphones (English commentary available) explaining Versailles's parliamentary history. ☎ 01–30–84–76–18. ▭ *Château 45 frs, parliament exhibition 25 frs extra.* ☉ *Tues.–Sun. 9–6:30, 9–5:30 in winter (Galerie des Glaces 9:45–5; Opéra Royal 9:45–3:30). Tours of Opéra Royal and Petits Appartements every 15 mins.*

★ ❷ After the awesome feast of interior decor, the **Parc de Versailles** (Versailles Park) is an ideal place to catch your breath. The gardens were designed by André Le Nôtre, whose work here represents classical French landscaping at its most formal and sophisticated. The 250-acre grounds include woods, lawns, flower beds, statues, artificial lakes, and fountains galore. An extensive tree-replacement scheme—necessary once a century—was launched at the start of 1998 to recapture the full impact of Le Nôtres's artful vistas; new plantings became all the more necessary after thousands of trees were uprooted during the major storm over the Christmas 1999 holiday. The distances are vast—the Trianons themselves are more than a mile from the château—so you might want to rent a bike from the **Grille de la Reine** near the Trianon Palace Hotel (27 francs per hour) or from the **Petite-Venise** building at the top of the Grand Canal (32 francs per hour, or 160 francs for six hours). You can also drive to the Trianons and Canal through the Grille de la Reine (28 francs per car). The park is at its golden-leafed best in the fall but is also enticing in summer—especially on Sunday afternoons from mid-April through mid-October, when the fountains are in full flow. ▭ *Park free (32 frs for fountains).* ☉ *Daily 7 AM–8 PM or dusk.*

❸ The **Grand Trianon,** built by Hardouin-Mansart in 1687, is a pink-marble pleasure palace occasionally used to entertain visiting heads of state. But most of the time it is open to visitors, who can admire its lavish interior and early 19th-century furniture. ☎ 01–30–84–75–43. ▭ *25 frs, joint ticket with Petit Trianon 30 frs.* ☉ *Tues.–Fri. 10–12:30 and 2–5:30; weekends 10–5:30.*

Was Marie-Antoinette a luxury-mad butterfly flitting from ball to costume ball? Or was she a misunderstood queen who suffered a loveless marriage and became a prisoner of etiquette at Versailles? Historians now believe the answer was the latter and point to the comparatively
★ ❹ dainty **Petit Trianon** as proof. Although the exterior was built by Gabriel from 1762 to 1768 for Marie-Antoinette's predecessor, Madame de Pompadour, the interior was fashioned according to the queen's eye—and what a surprisingly modern one it was. No overwhelming gilt or shot silk here—rather sober Neoclassical *boiseries* (carved wall panels), distinguished Riesener and Carlin bureaus, and a subdued palette reveal there had been a sea change in taste at that historical juncture. This is a mansion, not a palace—modest by Versailles standards. Today it is furnished and stuffed with mementos of Marie-Antoinette; Look for her initials wrought into the iron railings of the main staircase, as well as her own private boudoir. In a life that took her from royal cradle to the throne of France to the guillotine, her happiest days were spent here. ▭ *15 frs, joint ticket with Grand Trianon 30 frs.* ☉ *Tues.–Fri. 10–noon and 2–5:30; weekends 10–5:30.*

❺ Beyond the Petit Trianon and across the Petit Lac—which looks more like a wriggly stream—is the queen's fairytale **Hameau** (hamlet). Here, dressed in the new and expensive fabric called cotton, outfitted as a Dresden shepherdess, with a Sevres porcelain crook and a flock of perfumed sheep, Marie-Antoinette lived out her romanticized dreams of peasant life. With its water mill, genuine lake (Grand Lac), houses built in the Normandy daub-and-wattle style (where gaming parties and balls were often held for close friends), pigeon loft, and vegetable plots, this make-believe village is pure enchantment.

The town of Versailles itself—the capital of France from 1682 to 1789 and again from 1871 to 1879—is easily underestimated, despite its broad, leafy boulevards and majestic buildings. You may feel too tired from exploring the palace and park to spend time visiting the town—but it's worth the effort. Leave the château park by the Bassin de Neptune and turn right onto rue des Réservoirs, past the classical Théâtre Montansier, and pause at the Office de Tourisme. Up ahead you can make out Louis XIV's equestrian statue in the château courtyard; away in the other direction is the church spire of neighboring Le Chesnay. Rue Carnot, opposite the tourist office, leads past the stately Écuries de la Reine, once the queen's stables, now a law court, to octagonal place Hoche.

⑥ Down rue Hoche to the left is the powerful Baroque facade of **Notre-Dame,** built from 1684 to 1686 by Jules Hardouin-Mansart as the parish church for Louis XIV's brand-new town. Around the back of Notre-Dame, on boulevard de la Reine (note the regimented lines of trees), is the elegant Hôtel de Neyret, now used by the Banque de France, and

⑦ the **Musée Lambinet,** a sumptuous mansion from 1751, furnished with paintings, weapons, fans, and porcelain. ⊠ *54 bd. de la Reine,* ☎ *01–39–50–30–32.* ✎ *25 frs.* ☾ *Tues.–Sun. 2–5.*

Take a right onto rue Le Nôtre, then go left and right again into passage de la Geôle, a cobbled alley lined with quaint antiques shops that

⑧ climbs up to **place du Marché-Notre-Dame,** whose open-air morning market on Tuesday, Friday, and Sunday is famed throughout the region; there are also four 19th-century timber-roofed halls with fish, meat, and spice stalls. Cross the square and head up rue de la Paroisse to av-

⑨ enue de St-Cloud. Around to the left is the **Lycée Hoche,** whose domed, colonnaded chapel was once part of a convent built for Louis XV's queen, Marie Leszczynska, in 1767.

⑩ Cross avenue de St-Cloud and head along rue Montbauron to **Avenue de Paris**; at 120 yards across, it's wider than the Champs-Élysées, and its buildings are just as grand and more historic. Note the mighty doorway at the Hôtel de Police on your left and then, at No. 21, the pretty Hôtel du Barry. Cross the avenue and return toward the château, past the Hôtel des Menus-Plaisirs, where the States General held its first session in May 1789. Just opposite, behind an imposing grille, is the elaborate 19th-century Prêfecture (the local government building), confronting the even bigger—but uglier—stone-and-brick Hôtel de Ville (Town Hall). Avenue de Paris leads down to place d'Armes, a vast sloping plaza usually filled with tourist buses. Facing the château are

⑪ the Trojan-size royal stables. One wing of the **Grandes Écuries** (Great Stables), to the left, houses a distinguished parade of royal and imperial carriages in what is known as the **Musée des Carrosses** (Carriage Museum). ⊠ *1 av. de Paris,* ☎ *01–30–21–54–82.* ✎ *20 frs.* ☾ *Weekends 2–6.*

Cross avenue de Sceaux, pass the imposing chancellery on the corner, and take rue de Satory—a cute pedestrian shopping-street—to the

⑫ domed **Cathédrale St-Louis** with its twin-towered facade, built from 1743 to 1754 and endowed with a fine organ and paintings.

Turn left down narrow rue du Marché to reach the ramshackle but pho-

⑬ togenic **Carrés St-Louis,** a prototype 18th-century housing development.

⑭ Rue d'Anjou leads down to the **Potager du Roi,** the lovingly restored, split-level royal fruit-and-vegetable garden created in 1683 by Jean-Baptiste de la Quintinye. ⊠ *Entrance at 4 rue Hardy,* ☏ *01–39–24–62–62.* ⊡ *40 frs.* ⊘ *Guided tours Apr.–Oct., Wed.–Sun. at 2:30; June–Sept., Wed.–Fri. at 2:30, weekends at 2:30 and 4:30.*

From the Potager du Roi, return up rue de Satory and take rue du Vieux-Versailles, just as old—in parts, decrepit—and full of character as its name suggests. The **Salle du Jeu de Paume,** the indoor sports hall (built ⑮ in 1686) where the Third Estate swore to transform absolutist France into a constitutional monarchy on June 20, 1789, is off to the right. ⊠ *1 rue du Jeu-de-Paume.* ⊘ *June–Sept., Wed. 2–5.*

Rue de l'Indépendence-Américaine leads from the top of rue du Vieux-Versailles up to the château, where Louis XIV, quite uncoincidentally, is clearly visible on his prancing steed. Admire the sculpted porticoes and gilded Sun King emblems on the 17th- and 18th-century state build-⑯ ings lining the street. In the other direction, it leads down to the **Pièce d'Eau des Suisses,** a large artificial lake. Opposite the lake is the stately ⑰ **Orangerie,** erected by Hardouin-Mansart from 1684 to 1686. From November through Easter the Orangerie serves as a hothouse, when it is packed with orange and palm trees, which are artfully arranged in front in summer. Two monumental flights of steps lead up to the château terrace above.

Dining and Lodging

$$$$ ✕ **Les Trois Marches.** The restaurant at the Trianon Palace hotel (☞
★   *below*) is recognized as one of the best in Ile-de-France and one of the grandest in France. It's hard to wait for your meal after perusing Gérard Vié's menu, which may include lobster bisque, salmon with fennel, and turbot *galette* (cake). When it's nice out, you can eat on the huge terrace. ⊠ *1 bd. de la Reine,* ☏ *01–39–50–13–21. Reservations essential. Jacket and tie. AE, DC, MC, V. Closed Aug.*

$$–$$$ ✕ **Café Trianon.** In the Hôtel Trianon Chef Benoist Bambaud serves traditional French cuisine: salmon, roast bream, confit of canard, and lamb with rosemary. The prix-fixe menus are your best bet. ⊠ *1 bd. de la Reine,* ☏ *01–30–84–38–47. AE, DC, MC, V.*

$$ ✕ **Quai No. 1.** Fish and seafood rule supreme amid the sails, barometers, and model ships of this quaintly decked-out restaurant. Home-smoked salmon and sauerkraut with fish are specialties. Eating à la carte isn't too expensive, and there are good-value prix-fixe menus. ⊠ *1 av. de St-Cloud,* ☏ *01–39–50–42–26. MC, V. Closed Mon. No dinner Sun.*

$$$$ ▥ **Trianon Palace.** This deluxe hotel, a turn-of-the-century creation of
★   imposing size, is in a huge garden close to the château park. Its once-faded charm was given a thorough overhaul by its new Japanese owners, and the results are spectacular: The health club alone is worth the price of admission, while the restaurant is one of France's best. ⊠ *1 bd. de la Reine, 78000,* ☏ *01–30–84–38–00,* ꜰᴀx *01–39–49–00–77. 190 rooms, 25 suites. Restaurant, pool, health club, business services. AE, DC, MC, V.*

$$ ▥ **Le Cheval Rouge.** This unpretentious old hotel, built in 1676, is in the corner of the town market square, close to the château and recommended if you plan to explore the town on foot. Some rooms around the old stable courtyard have their original wood beams. ⊠ *18 rue André-Chénier, 78000,* ☏ *01–39–50–03–03,* ꜰᴀx *01–39–50–61–27. 38 rooms. MC, V.*

$ ▥ **Home St-Louis.** This family-run three-story brick hotel is a good, cheap, quiet bet—close to the cathedral and not too far from the château. ⊠ *28 rue St-Louis, 78000,* ☏ *01–39–50–23–55,* ꜰᴀx *01–39–21–62–45. 25 rooms. AE, MC, V.*

Nightlife and the Arts

The largest fountain in the château park, the Bassin de Neptune, becomes a spectacle of rare grandeur during the **Fêtes de Nuit,** a light-and-fireworks show every Saturday evening in July and September (☎ 01–30–83–78–88 for details). The **Mois Molière** (☎ 01–30–97–84–48) in June heralds a program of concerts, drama, and exhibits inspired by the famous playwright. A **music festival,** with concerts and operas in the town and château, runs May–June; call the tourist office (☎ 01–30–97–81–03) for info. The **Automne Musical** (☎ 01–39–20–78–00) presents concerts of Baroque music in the château each fall.

Shopping

Aux Colonnes (✉ 14 rue Hoche) is a highly rated *confiserie* (candy shop) with an astounding array of chocolates and candies; it's closed Monday. **Les Délices du Palais** (✉ 4 rue du Maréchal-Foch) has everything for the makings of an impromptu picnic (cold cuts, cheese, salads); it's also closed Monday. **Le Gall** (✉ 15 rue Ducis) has a huge choice of cheeses—including one of France's widest selection of goat cheeses; it's closed Sunday afternoon and Monday. **Passage de la Geôle,** which is open Friday–Sunday 9–7 and is close to the town's stupendous market, houses several good antiques shops.

Breteuil

⑱ *27 km (17 mi) southwest of Versailles, 40 km (35 mi) southwest of Paris.*

The steep-roofed **Château de Breteuil** has been owned by the same family since the 17th century. Interior highlights range from Swedish porcelain to Gobelin tapestries and a richly inlaid Teschen table encrusted with pearls and precious stones—an 18th-century present from Austrian empress Maria Theresa. The vast wooded park has picnic areas and playgrounds. Life-size wax figures—including English king Edward VII and novelist Marcel Proust (a onetime guest)—lurk in many rooms. ☎ *01–30–52–05–11.* ✉ *Château and grounds 57 frs, grounds only 38 frs.* ☉ *Château Mon.–Sat. 2:30–6, Sun. 11–6; grounds daily 10–6.*

Dampierre

⑲ *5 km (3 mi) northwest of Breteuil via D906 and D149, 21 km (13 mi) southwest of Versailles via D91.*

The unspoiled village of Dampierre is home to one of the most charming family seats in Ile-de-France. The stone-and-brick **Château de Dampierre,** surrounded by a moat and set well back from the road, was rebuilt in the 1670s by Hardouin-Mansart for the Duc de Luynes. Much of the interior has kept its 17th-century decoration—portraits, wood paneling, furniture, and works of art. But the main staircase, with its trompe l'oeil murals, and the richly gilded **Salle des Fêtes** (ballroom) date from the last century. This second-floor chamber contains a huge wall painting by the celebrated artist Jean-Auguste Ingres (1780–1867) that is a mythical evocation of the Age d'Or (Golden Age). The large park was planned by Versailles designer André Le Nôtre. ✉ *2 Grande-Rue,* ☎ *01–30–52–52–83.* ✉ *55 frs, grounds only 36 frs.* ☉ *Apr.–Oct., Mon.–Sat. 2–6, Sun. 11–noon and 2–6.*

Rambouillet

⑳ *16 km (10 mi) southwest of Dampierre via D91 and D906, 32 km (20 mi) southwest of Versailles, 42 km (26 mi) southwest of Paris.*

Haughty Rambouillet, once favored by kings and dukes, is now home to affluent gentry and, occasionally, the French president. The **Château**

de Rambouillet is surrounded by a magnificent 30,000-acre forest that, although severely battered in the horrific storms of late 1999, remains a great place for biking and walking. Most of the château dates from the early 18th century, but the brawny **Tour François-Ier** (François I Tower), named for the king who died here in 1547, was part of the 14th-century fortified castle that first stood on this site. Highlights include the wood-paneled apartments, especially the **Boudoir de la Comtesse** (Countess's Dressing Room); the marble-walled **Salle de Marbre** (Marble Hall), dating from the Renaissance; and the **Salle de Bains de Napoléon** (Napoléon's Bathroom), adorned with Pompeii-style frescoes. The lakeside facade of the château is a sight of unsuspected serenity and, as more flowers spill from its balconies, cheerful informality. ☎ 01–34–94–28–00. 🖼 27 frs. ⊙ Daily 10–11:30 and 2–5:30.

An extensive **park,** with a lake with small islands, stretches behind the château; its exotic, storybook beauty once inspired Fragonard to paint one of the greatest landscape paintings of the 18th century, the *Fête at Rambouillet* (now in the Gulbenkian Museum in Lisbon). Also in the park is the **Laiterie de la Reine** (Queen's Dairy), built for Marie-Antoinette, who, inspired by the romantic back-to-nature novels of Jean-Jacques Rousseau, escaped here from the pressures of Versailles and pretended to be a simple milkmaid. It has a small temple, grotto, and the shell-lined Chaumière des Coquillages (Shell Pavilion). The **Bergerie Nationale** (National Sheepfold), is the site of a more serious agricultural venture: The merinos reared here, prized for the quality and yield of their wool, are descendants of sheep imported from Spain by Louis XVI in 1786. A museum alongside tells the tale and evokes shepherd life. 🖼 *Queen's Dairy 15 frs; National Sheepfold 25 frs.* ⊙ *Queen's Dairy Wed.–Mon. 10–11:30 and 2–4:30 (until 4 Nov.–Easter); National Sheepfold mid-Jan.–mid-Dec., Wed.–Sun. 2–5.*

Some 4,000 models dating to 1885 and more than 1,300 ft of track make the **Musée Rambolitrain** France's leading model-train museum. It has historic steam engines, old-time stations, and a realistic points and signaling system. ⊠ *4 pl. Jeanne-d'Arc,* ☎ *01–34–83–15–93.* 🖼 *22 frs.* ⊙ *Wed.–Sun. 10–noon and 2–5:30.*

Dining

$–$$ ✕ **Poste.** You can bank on traditional, unpretentious cooking at this former coaching inn right in the center of town. Service is good, as is the selection of prix-fixe menus. Game is a specialty in season. ⊠ *101 rue du Général-de-Gaulle,* ☎ *01–34–83–03–01. AE, MC, V. Closed Mon. No dinner Sun.*

Maintenon

㉑ *23 km (14 mi) southwest of Rambouillet via D906, 65 km (41 mi) southwest of Paris.*

Vestiges of Louis XIV, both atmospheric and architectural, make Maintenon an intriguing stopover on the road to Chartres. The **Château de Maintenon** once belonged to Louis XIV's second wife, Françoise Scarron—better known as Madame de Maintenon—whom he married morganatically in 1684 (as social inferiors, neither she nor her children could claim a royal title). She had acquired the château as a young widow 10 years earlier, and her private apartments form the hub of the interior visit. A round brick tower (16th century) and square 12th-century keep give the ensemble a muscular dignity at odds with the picturesque back garden with its lawns, canal, and prim hedges. ⊠ *Pl. Aristide Briand,* ☎ *02–37–23–00–09.* 🖼 *38 frs.* ⊙ *Apr.–Oct., Wed.–Mon. 2–6; Nov.–mid-Dec. and late Jan.–Mar., weekends 2–5.*

Looming at the back of the château garden and extending through the village almost from the train station to highway D6 are the unlikely ivy-covered arches of a ruined **aqueduct,** one of the Sun King's most outrageous projects. The original scheme aimed to provide the ornamental lakes in the gardens of Versailles (some 50 km [31 mi] away) with water from the River Eure. In 1684, 30,000 men were signed up to construct a three-tiered, 5-km (3-mi) aqueduct as part of the project. Many died in the process, and construction was called off in 1689.

Dining and Lodging

$$$–$$$$ ✕▥ **Château d'Esclimont.** The 16th-century château is well worth seeking out if you wish to eat and sleep like royalty. On luxurious grounds, with lawns, a lake, and a heliport, this member of the Relais & Châteaux group is a regular spot for Parisian power brokers. Rooms are luxuriously furnished with reproduction 18th-century French pieces. The cuisine is sophisticated and varied: Quail, lamb, lobster, and game in season top the menu. Dinner reservations are essential, and a jacket and tie are required. ⊠ *2 rue du Château-d'Esclimont, 28700 St-Symphorien-le-Château (19 km [12 mi] southeast of Maintenon: take D116 to village of Gaillardon, keep an eye out for church, then turn left),* ☎ *02–37–31–15–15,* FAX *02–37–31–57–91. 47 rooms, 6 suites. Restaurant, pool, 2 tennis courts, fishing, helipad. AE, DC, MC, V.*

Chartres

  ㉒   *19 km (12 mi) southwest of Maintenon via D906, 88 km (55 mi) southwest of Paris.*

As Versailles is the climax of French secular architecture, so Chartres is the religious apogee. All the descriptive prose and poetry that have been lavished on this supreme cathedral can only begin to suggest the glory of its 12th- and 13th-century sculpture and stained glass, the strange sense of the numinous that the whole ensemble imparts even to non-believers. Notre-Dame de Chartres is an extraordinary fusion of Romanesque and Gothic elements brought together at a moment when the flame of medieval faith burned brightest. The stone and glass of this cathedral are somehow suffused with that same burning mysticism. Chartres is more than a church; it's a religious experience—so say its most fervent admirers.

If you arrive via the Ablis road across the Beauce, one of the most extraordinary plains in France, you can see Chartres's spires rising up from oceans of wheat (at least between early June and late July). In fact, the whole town—with its old houses and picturesque streets—is worth leisurely exploration. Ancient streets tumble down from the cathedral to the river; from rue du Pont-St-Hilaire is a lovely view of the rooftops beneath the cathedral. Each year on August 15, pilgrims and tourists flock here for the Procession du Voeu de Louis XIII, a religious procession through the streets commemorating the French monarchy's vow to serve the Virgin Mary.

★ Worship on the site of the **Cathédrale Notre-Dame,** better known as Chartres Cathedral, goes back to before the Gallo-Roman period; the crypt contains a well that was the focus of Druid ceremonies. In the late 9th century Charles II (known as the Bald) presented Chartres with what was believed to be the tunic of the Virgin Mary, a precious relic that attracted hordes of pilgrims. The current cathedral, the sixth church on the spot, dates mainly from the 12th and 13th centuries and was erected after the previous building, dating to the 11th century, burned down in 1194. A well-chronicled outburst of religious fervor followed the discovery that the Virgin Mary's relic had miraculously survived unsinged. Princes and paupers, barons and bourgeois gave their money and their labor to built the new cathedral. Ladies of the manor came to help monks and peasants on the scaffolding in a tremendous resurgence of religious faith that followed the Second Crusade. Just 25 years were needed for Chartres Cathedral to rise again, and it has remained substantially unchanged since.

The lower half of the facade is a survivor of the earlier Romanesque church: This can be seen most clearly in the use of round arches rather than the pointed Gothic type. The **Royal Portal** is richly sculpted with scenes from the life of Christ—these sculpted figures are among the greatest created during the Middle Ages—and the flanking towers are also Romanesque. The taller of the two spires (380 ft versus 350 ft) was built at the start of the 16th century, after its predecessor was destroyed by fire; its fanciful Flamboyant intricacy contrasts sharply with the stumpy solemnity of its Romanesque counterpart. The **rose window** above the main portal dates from the 13th century, and the three windows below it contain some of the finest examples of 12th-century stained glass in France.

The interior is somber, and your eyes will need time to adjust. The reward is seeing the gemlike richness of the stained glass, with the famous deep Chartres blue predominating. The oldest window is arguably the most beautiful: **Notre-Dame de la Belle Verrière** (Our Lady of the Lovely Window), in the south choir. The cathedral's windows are being gradually cleaned—a lengthy, painstaking process—and the contrast with those still covered in the grime of centuries is staggering. It's worth taking a pair of binoculars to pick out the details. If you wish to know more about stained-glass techniques and the motifs used, visit the small exhibit in the gallery opposite the north porch. For even more detail, try to arrange a tour (in English) with local institution Malcolm Miller, who has a formidable knowledge of the cathedral's windows. (He leads tours twice a day Monday through Saturday; the cost is 30 francs. You can reach him at the telephone number below.) The vast black-and-white labyrinth on the floor of the nave is one of the few to have survived from the Middle Ages; the faithful were expected to travel along its entire length (some 300 yards) on their knees. Guided tours of the **Crypte** start from the Maison de la Crypte opposite the south porch. You can also see a 4th-century Gallo-Roman wall and some 12th-century wall paintings. ⊠ *16 cloître Notre-Dame,* ☎ *02–37–21–56–33.* 🎫 *Crypt 10 frs.* ☉ *Church 8–6. Guided tours of crypt Easter–Oct., daily at 11, 2:15, 3:30, 4:30, 5:15; Nov.–Easter, daily at 11 and 4.*

The **Musée des Beaux-Arts** (Fine Arts Museum) is in a handsome 18th-century building just behind the cathedral that used to serve as the bishop's palace. Its varied collection includes Renaissance enamels, a portrait of Erasmus by Holbein, tapestries, armor, and some fine (mainly French) paintings of the 17th, 18th, and 19th centuries. There's also a room devoted to the forceful 20th-century land- and snowscapes of Maurice de Vlaminck, who lived in the region. ⊠ *29 cloître Notre-Dame,* ☎ *02–37–36–41–39.* 🎫 *10 frs (20 frs for special exhibitions).* ☉ *Apr.–Oct., Wed.–Mon. 10–6; Nov.–Mar., Wed.–Mon. 10–noon and 2–5.*

The Gothic church of **St-Pierre** (⊠ Rue St-Pierre), near the Eure River, has magnificent medieval windows from a period (circa 1300) not represented at the cathedral. The oldest stained glass here, portraying Old Testament worthies, is to the right of the choir and dates from the late 13th century. Exquisite 17th-century stained glass can be admired at the church of **St-Aignan** (⊠ Rue des Grenets), around the corner from St-Pierre.

Dining and Lodging

$$–$$$ ✕ **La Vieille Maison.** Just 100 yards from the cathedral, in a pretty 14th-century building with a flower-decked patio, this restaurant is a fine choice for either lunch or dinner. The menu changes regularly but invariably includes regional specialties, such as asparagus, rich duck pâté, and superb homemade foie gras. Prices, though justified, can be steep, but the 165-franc lunch menu is a good bet. ✉ *5 rue au Lait,* ☎ *02–37–34–10–67. AE, MC, V. Closed Mon. No dinner Sun.*

$$ ✕ **Buisson Ardent.** In an attractive, old oak-beam building almost
★ within sight of the cathedral's south portal, this popular restaurant has inexpensive prix-fixe menus (especially on weekdays) and a choice of imaginative à la carte dishes. Try the chicken ravioli with leeks or the rolled beef with spinach. Service is gratifyingly attentive. ✉ *10 rue au Lait,* ☎ *02–37–34–04–66. MC, V. No dinner Sun.*

$$$ ☷ **Grand Monarque.** The most popular rooms in this 18th-century coaching inn, part of the Best Western chain, are in a separate turn-of-the-century building overlooking a garden. The most atmospheric are tucked away in the attic. The restaurant has a variety of prix-fixe menus for 163, 235, and 295 francs. ✉ *22 pl. des Épars, 28000,* ☎ *02–37–21–00–72,* ℻ *02–37–36–34–18. 53 rooms, 5 suites. Restaurant. AE, DC, MC, V.*

Shopping

Vitrail (stained glass) being the key to Chartres's fame, you may want to visit the **Galerie du Vitrail** (✉ 17 cloître Notre-Dame, ☎ 02–37–36–10–03), which specializes in the noble art. Pieces range from small plaques to entire windows, and there are books on the subject in English and French.

Dreux

㉓ *35 km (22 mi) north of Chartres via N154, 74 km (46 mi) west of Paris.*

Dreux, center of an independent province during the Middle Ages, enjoyed an upsurge in prosperity after being united to the French crown in 1556 (shortly after completion of the beefy belfry on the main square). The early 19th century conferred lasting glory on the town in the form of the burial chapel of the royal House of Orléans.

In 1816 the Orléans family, France's ruling house from 1830 to 1848,
★ began the construction of a circular chapel-mausoleum on the hill behind the town center. The **Chapelle Royale St-Louis** is built in sugary but not unappealing neo-Gothic: superficial ornament rather than structure recalls the medieval style. The magnificent interior can be visited only with a guided tour (in French only), though an English text is provided. And no linguistic explanations are needed to prompt wonder at either the Sèvres-manufactured "stained glass"—thin layers of glass coated with painted enamel (an extremely rare, fragile, and vivid technique)—or the funereal statuary. Some of the **tombs**—an imploring hand reaching through a window to a loved one or an infant wrapped in a cloak of transparent gauze—may evoke morbid sentimentality, but their technical skill and compositional drama belie this mawkishness. ✉ *2 Sq. d'Aumale,* ☎ *02–37–46–07–06.* ▦ *34 frs.* ☉ *Apr.–Nov., Wed.–Mon. 9–11:30 and 2:30–6.*

The church of **St-Pierre,** across the road from the belfry, is an interesting jumble of styles with pretty stained glass and a 17th-century organ loft. It presents a curious silhouette, with its unfinished classical towers cut off midway. ✉ *Pl. Métezeau,* ☎ *02–37–42–06–89.*

Lodging

$$ ⊞ **Beffroi.** This modest country hotel is on the historic square that links the church to the belfry. Ask for a room with a view. ⊠ *12 pl. Métezeau, 28100,* ☎ *02–37–50–02–03,* FAX *02–37–42–07–69. 16 rooms. AE, DC, MC, V.*

Houdan

❷❹ *20 km (12 mi) east of Dreux via N12, 54 km (34 mi) west of Paris.*

Although fast N12 now skirts Houdan, the town grew up as a busy stop on the Paris–Dreux road. It's protected by a mighty 12th century donjon rising from the hilltop above two small rivers, the Opton and the Vesgre. Timber-frame houses along the main street (rue de Paris), including several former inns, recall Houdan's bygone status, as does the ornate church, which retains many of its original 17th- and 18th-century elements, including the pulpit, altarpiece, lectern, pews, and organ case. Houdan was also famed for its poultry market, and a succulent local breed of chicken—the *poularde de Houdan*—still exists.

Dining

$$–$$$ ✕ **La Poularde.** This comfortable restaurant at the foot of the town is named for the local breed of chicken, often served here with truffles or morels. Braised beef and smoked fish salad are other specialties, and there's a good-value lunch menu. The airy, pastel-shaded dining room turns its back on the highway outside, looking out on a trim lawn. ⊠ *24 av. de la République,* ☎ *01–30–59–60–50. Reservations essential. MC, V. Closed Wed. No dinner Tues.*

Richebourg

❷❺ *5 km (3 mi) northeast of Houdan on D983.*

The village of Richebourg has a newly restored *lavoir* (washhouse) and a fine 16th-century church, the **Église St-Georges.** The church's sturdy bell tower is topped by a slender spire with four small, spiky steeples in each corner like witches' hats. Chimeras, lizards, demons, and battling rats make up the gargoyles beneath the slate-and-tile roof. The Renaissance stained glass includes a *Tree of Jesse* and an *Adoration of the Magi.*

Montfort-L'Amaury

❷❻ *18 km (11 mi) east of Houdan via N12 and D76, 40 km (25 mi) west of Paris.*

Montfort-L'Amaury, with its 17th-century houses and twisting, narrow streets clustered around an old church, is one of the prettiest towns in Ile-de-France. It has a ruined hilltop castle, remnants of medieval ramparts, and a cloister-lined cemetery. Dominating the town square is the bulky Renaissance tower of the church of **St-Pierre–St-Paul.** Note the gargoyles around the far end and, inside, the 37 splendid Renaissance stained-glass windows.

Composer Maurice Ravel lived in Montfort from 1921 until his death in 1937; he composed his famous *Bolero* in 1928 in his Japanese-style garden. His house, now the **Musée Ravel** (Ravel Museum), has been reconstituted with many of his souvenirs and furnishings (including his piano). ⊠ *Le Belvédère, 5 rue Maurice-Ravel,* ☎ *01–34–86–00–89.* ☎ *25 frs.* ☉ *Guided visits only, weekends at 10, 11, 2:30, 3:30 and 4:30, Wed.–Fri. by appointment 2:30–5.*

Shortly after moving into his attractive, thatched house 5 km (3 mi) east of Montfort-L'Amaury, politician Jean Monnet (1888–1979), often called the Father of Europe, is said to have conceived the idea of the "United States of Europe" in 1950. He lived here until his death in 1979 and was accorded the supreme state accolade of burial in the Paris Panthéon. The **Maison Jean-Monnet** (Jean Monnet's Home), where Monnet once hobnobbed with world leaders (including Dwight D. Eisenhower), is now owned by the European Parliament and displays information on the present European Union, Monnet mementos, and a film on his life and ideas—all in 11 languages, in time-honored "Eurocrat" tradition. ✉ *Houjarray (take D13 east from Montfort and turn right at entry to Bazoches-sur-Guyonne),* ☎ *01–34–86–12–43.* 🎫 *Free.* ☉ *Wed.–Sun. 2–6.*

Lodging

$–$$ 🏨 **Voyageurs.** This small, homey hotel at the bottom of Montfort's
★ cobbled main street is a handy base for exploring Thoiry, Dreux, or Rambouillet. It has rooms with wood beams, a well-priced restaurant (menus from 80 to 140 francs), and a cheerful bar with incongruous but appealing '50s decor. ✉ *49 rue de Paris, 78490,* ☎ *01–34–86–00–14,* ⚏ *01–34–86–14–56. 7 rooms. Restaurant, bar. MC, V. Closed mid- to late Aug.*

Thoiry

㉗ *11 km (7 mi) north of Montfort-L'Amaury via D76 and D11, 44 km (28 mi) west of Paris.*

Thoiry is most famous for its 16th-century château with beautiful gardens, a wild animal reserve, and a gastronomy museum. The village makes an excellent day trip from Paris, especially if you're traveling with children.

♺ Built by Philibert de l'Orme in 1564, the **Château de Thoiry** has a handsome Renaissance facade set off by gardens landscaped in the disciplined French fashion by Le Nôtre, in this case with unexpected justification: The château is positioned directly in line with the sun as it sets in the west at the winter solstice (December 21) and as it rises in the east at the summer solstice (June 21). Heightening the effect, the central part of the château appears to be a transparent arch of light because of its huge glass doors and windows.

Owners Vicomte Paul de La Panouse and his American wife, Annabelle, have restored the château and park, opening both to the public. The distinguished history of the La Panouse family—a Comte César even fought in the American Revolution—is retraced in the **Musée des Archives** (Archives Museum), where papal bulls and Napoleonic letters mingle with missives from Thomas Jefferson and Benjamin Franklin. The neighboring pantries house a **Musée de la Gastronomie** (Gastronomy Museum), with *pièces montées*—virtuoso banquet showpieces—re-creating the designs of famed 19th-century chef Antoine Carême. Early recipe books, engravings, and old copper pots are also displayed.

Other highlights of the château interior include the grand staircase, the **Escalier d'Honneur,** with its 18th-century Gobelin tapestries; the **Salon Vert** and **Salon Blanc** (Green Salon and White Salon), with their antique painted harpsichord and portraits; and the **Salon de la Tapisserie** (Tapestry Salon), with its monumental Don Quixote tapestry bearing the rather gruesome arms (three severed raven's heads) of former owner Machault d'Arnouville. An authentic, homey, faded charm pervades these rooms, especially when fires crackle in their enormous hearths on damp afternoons.

The viscountess is a keen gardener and enjoys experimenting in the less formal **Jardin Anglais** (English Garden) and in her late-flowering **Jardin d'Automne** (Autumn Garden). You're allowed to wander at leisure, although it's best not to stray too far from the official footpath through the **Parc Zoologique** (animal reserve). Note that the parts of the reserve that contain the wilder beasts—deer, zebra, camels, hippos, bears, elephants, and lions—can be visited only by car. Tigers can be seen from the safety of a raised footbridge. Nearby is a children's play area with a burrow to wriggle through and a huge netted cobweb to bounce around in. ☎ 01–34–87–52–25. ⊠ *Château only, 30 frs; Château, park, and game reserve, 105 frs.* ⊙ *Summer, weekdays 10–6, weekends 10–6:30; winter, daily 10–5.*

Dining and Lodging

$ ✕ **Commerce.** This bar on Thoiry's main street has an attractive upstairs dining room where locals come for hearty weekday lunches. Start with the extensive buffet—pâté, salami, and carrot salad are favorites—followed by a sturdy dish of the day such as steak-frîtes or beef Wellington. ⊠ *28 rue de la Porte-St-Martin,* ☎ *01–34–87–40–18. No credit cards. Closed Sat. No dinner.*

$ ✕🛏 **Étoile.** This dowdy hotel-restaurant, just 300 yards from the château along the main street, is more convenient than appealing. Rooms need redecorating, but the fine restaurant serves a good *menu touristique* (special tourist menu, a term that doesn't mean you should go running the other way) of robust French dishes. ⊠ *38 rue de la Porte-St-Martin, 78770,* ☎ *01–34–87–40–21,* 🖷 *01–34–87–49–57. 12 rooms. Restaurant. MC, V. Closed Mon.*

NORTHWEST TO GIVERNY ALONG THE SEINE

Renowned for its beauty as it weaves through Paris, the Seine River is no less appealing as it flows gently northwest toward Normandy. The terrace at the château of St-Germain-en-Laye, home to the French kings before Versailles, provides a memorable view of the valley, soon to break into a series of chalky cliffs beyond Mantes. Farther on, tucked away on the banks of the Epte (a tributary of the Seine), is Monet's home and fabled garden in Giverny.

Rueil-Malmaison

㉘ *8 km (5 mi) west of Paris on N13 via La Défense.*

Rueil-Malmaison is a slightly dreary western suburb of Paris, but the memory of the legendary pair Napoléon and Joséphine still haunts its ★ château. Built in 1622, **La Malmaison** was bought by the future empress Joséphine in 1799 as a love nest for Napoléon and herself (they had married three years earlier). After the childless Joséphine was divorced by the heir-hungry emperor in 1809, she retired to La Malmaison and died here on May 29, 1814. The château has 24 rooms furnished with exquisite tables, chairs, and sofas of the Napoleonic period; of special note are the library, game room, and dining room. The walls are adorned with works by artists of the day, such as Jacques-Louis David, Pierre-Paul Prud'hon, and Baron Gérard. Take time to admire the clothes and hats that belonged to Napoléon and Joséphine, particularly the empress's gowns. Their carriage can be seen in one of the garden pavilions, and another pavilion contains a unique collection of snuffboxes donated by Prince George of Greece. The gardens themselves are delightful, especially the regimented rows of spring tulips. ⊠ *15 av. du Château,* ☎ *01–41–29–05–55.* ⊠ *30 frs (including Bois*

Préau; ☞ *below).* ◷ *Wed.–Fri. and Mon. 10–12:30 and 1:30–5:15; weekends 10–5:45.*

The **Bois Préau,** a smaller mansion dating from the 17th century, is close to La Malmaison (and can be visited on the same admission ticket). It was acquired by Joséphine in 1810, after her divorce, but was subsequently reconstructed in the 1850s. Today its 10 rooms, complete with furniture and objects from the Empire period, are devoted mainly to souvenirs of Napoléon's exile on the island of St. Helena. ⊠ *Av. de l'Impératrice,* ☎ *01–47–08–37–67.* ▧ *16 frs, or 30 frs including La Malmaison (*☞ *above).* ◷ *Thurs.–Sun. 12:30–6.*

Festivals

Ile-de-France was once a wine-producing center—though there's little evidence these days—and one of the few places where the tradition lingers is in the hilly neighboring suburb of Suresnes, where a **Fête des Vendanges** (Grape Harvest Festival) is held the first weekend of October.

Marly-le-Roi

㉙ *9 km (6 mi) west of Rueil-Malmaison via N13 and N186, 17 km (11 mi) west of Paris.*

Marly-le-Roi, halfway between St-Germain and Versailles, was once home to yet another royal château. Nothing of it remains, but a tumbling park, ruined aqueduct, and massive pipes snaking up the hillside from the Seine offer spectacular evidence of the Sun King's crazy attempts to nail nature.

As you head west along the Seine from Rueil-Malmaison toward St-Germain, pause on quai Rennequin-Sualem, opposite the Ile de le Loge. To the left are the engine rooms of the vanished **Machine de Marly,** a mind-boggling construction of 14 giant waterwheels, each 40 ft in diameter, built 1681–84 to pump water from the Seine to Marly, 2 km (1½ mi) away—and 500 ft above the level of the river. The Machine was dismantled in 1965, but you can still see the water pipes as they scramble up the hillside through a gap in the trees. Now continue along the Seine and turn left up N186 to Louveciennes, where you can meet the pipes as they complete their climb at the end of chemin de la Machine. There's a fine view of the Seine from here, too. Next, to find out what happened to the water once it left the pipes, double back to N186 and take a first right. The answer is right above: a 700-yard aqueduct, needed to provide the extra height and pressure for the water to service the fountains in Louis XIV's new park. Follow the arches left to the park entrance.

St-Germain-en-Laye

㉚ *4 km (2½ mi) north of Marly-le-Roi via N186 and N13, 9 km (6 mi) west of Rueil-Malmaison, 17 km (11 mi) west of Paris.*

The elegant town of St-Germain-en-Laye, on a hill above the Seine and encircled by forest, has lost little of its original cachet, despite the invasion of wealthy former Parisians who commute to work on the RER.

If you're fond of the swashbuckling novels of Alexandre Dumas, then you'll enjoy the **Château de Monte-Cristo** (Monte Cristo Castle), at Port-Marly on the southern fringe of St-Germain (signposted to your left as you arrive from Marly-le-Roi). You may find that its fanciful exterior, where pilasters, cupolas, and stone carvings compete for attention, has crossed the line from opulence to tastelessness, but—as in the novels, *The Count of Monte Cristo* and *The Three Musketeers*—swagger, not subtlety, is what counts. Dumas built the château after his books' surging popularity made him rich in the 1840s. Construction costs and lavish partying meant he went broke just as quickly, and he skedaddled to a Belgian exile in 1849. The château contains pictures, Dumas mementos, and the luxurious Moorish Chamber, with spellbinding, interlacing plasterwork executed by Arab craftsmen (lent by the Bey of Tunis) and restored by a donation from Moroccan king Hassan II. There's also a miniature version of the Château d'If in Marseille—scene of the Count of Monte Cristo's great escape—in a miniature lake in the park. ⊠ *Av. du Président-Kennedy,* ☎ *01–39–16–49–49.* ⊠ *30 frs.* ☉ *Apr.–Oct., Tues.–Fri. 10–12:30 and 2–6, weekends 10–6; Jan.–Mar, Sun. 2–5.*

Next to the St-Germain RER train station is the stone-and-brick **Château de St-Germain,** with its dry moat and intimidating circular towers; it dates from the 16th and 17th centuries. A royal palace has existed here since the early 12th century, when Louis VI—known as Le Gros (the Fat)—exploited St-Germain's defensive potential in his bid to pacify Ile-de-France. A hundred years later Louis IX (St. Louis) added the elegant **Sainte-Chapelle,** the château's oldest remaining section. The figures on the tympanum (the inset triangular area over the main door) are believed to be the first known representations of French royalty, portraying Louis with his mother, Blanche de Castille, and other members of his family. Charles V (1364–80) built a powerful defensive keep in the mid-14th century, but from the 1540s François I and his successors transformed St-Germain into a palace with more of a domestic than warlike vocation. Louis XIV was born here, and it was here that his father, Louis XIII, died. Until 1682—when the court moved to Versailles—it remained the country's foremost royal residence outside Paris. Since 1867 the château has housed the impressive **Musée des Antiquités Nationales** (Museum of Ancient History), holding a trove of artifacts, figurines, brooches, and weapons from the Stone Age to the 8th century. ⊠ *Pl. Charles-de-Gaulle,* ☎ *01–34–51–53–65.* ⊠ *25 frs, 17 frs on Sun.* ☉ *Wed.–Mon. 9–5:15.*

★ The quaint **Musée du Prieuré** (Priory Museum) is devoted to the work of the artist Maurice Denis (1870–1943) and his fellow Symbolists and to Nabis—painters opposed to the naturalism of their 19th-century Impressionist contemporaries. Denis found the calm of the former Jesuit priory, set above tiered gardens, ideally suited to his spiritual themes, which he expressed in stained glass, ceramics, and frescoes, as well as oils. ⊠ *2 bis rue Maurice-Denis,* ☎ *01–39–73–77–87.* ⊠ *25 frs.* ☉ *Wed.–Fri. 10–5:30, weekends 10–6:30.*

In the village of Chambourcy, 3 km (2 mi) northwest of St-Germain-en-Laye via N13, is the stately **Maison André-Derain** (André Derain's House). This 17th-century building is where the versatile Derain (1880–1954), best known for his pioneering, hotly colored Fauve paintings, lived from 1935 until his death. You can admire his well-preserved studio and a smattering of his works and watch a 12-minute film about his career. ⊠ *64 Grande-Rue,* ☎ *01–30–74–70–04.* ⊠ *20 frs.* ☉ *Guided tours 4th weekend of each month at 3 and 4:30.*

Dining and Lodging

$$ ✕ **La Feuillantine.** Friendly service and an imaginative, good-value prix-fixe menu have made this restaurant a success. Gizzard salad, salmon with endive, and herbed chicken fricassee with morels are among the specialties. ⊠ *10 rue des Louviers,* ☎ *01–34–51–04–24. AE, MC, V.*

$$$–$$$$ ⊞ **La Forestière.** Opened in 1928, this hotel is St-Germain's most
★ stylish and a member of the Relais & Châteaux chain. Its forest setting, 18th-century-style furniture, and fine restaurant, the Cazaudehore (closed Monday), contribute to a sense of well-being. ⊠ *1 av. du Prési-*

*dent-Kennedy, 78100, ☎ 01–39–10–38–38, ℻ 01–39–73–73–88. 25
rooms, 5 suites. Restaurant. AE, DC, MC, V.*

Nightlife and the Arts

The **Fête des Loges** (Loges Festival) is a giant fair and carnival held in
the Forest of St-Germain from July to mid-August. Nearly 4 million
fans of cotton candy, roller coasters, and Ferris wheels turn up every
year.

Maisons-Laffitte

③ *8 km (5 mi) northeast of St-Germain-en-Laye via D157, 16 km (10
mi) northwest of Paris.*

The riverside suburb of Maisons-Laffitte has an unusually high proportion of elegant villas, many of which were built with profits from
the town's racetrack by the Seine (with its famous 2,200-yard straight)
and training stables; 14 races are held between July and September.

★ The early Baroque **Château de Maisons,** constructed by architect
François Mansart from 1642 to 1651, is one of the least-known but
most elegant of châteaux in Ile-de-France. This was not always the case:
Sun King Louis XIV came to the housewarming party, and Louis XV,
Louis XVI, the 18th-century writer Voltaire, and Napoléon all stayed
here. The interior clearly met their exacting standards, thanks to the
well-proportioned entrance vestibule with its rich sculpture; the winding **Escalier d'Honneur,** a majestic staircase adorned with paintings and
statues; and the royal apartments, above them, with their parquet
floors and elegant wall paneling. The Musée du Cheval de Course (Racehorse Museum), in the basement, evokes the world of the turf. ⊠ 2
av. Carnot, ☎ 01–39–62–01–49. ☜ 32 frs. ☉ Château Wed.–Mon.
10–noon and 1:30–5; Racehorse Museum Sun. 1:30–5.

Poissy

㉜ *8 km (4 mi) west of Maisons-Laffitte via D308, 21 km (13 mi) northwest of Paris.*

Three museums and its historic significance as the birthplace of France's
saintly king, Louis IX, help Poissy—the name comes from *poisson* (fish),
as you may deduce from the town's ubiquitous emblem—defy its reputation as an unfashionable industrial town.

The remains of the font in which Louis was baptized in 1214 can still
be seen in the **Église Notre-Dame,** a medieval church with two striking octagonal towers. The **Musée d'Art et d'Histoire** (Art and History
Museum), in a stern brick mansion opposite the church, is packed with
tools, sculptures, old postcards, and paintings tracking Poissy's history
from its 6th-century origins to its medieval prosperity as a cattle market and vine-growing center to its latter-day position as home to auto
plants. ⊠ 12 rue St-Louis, ☎ 01–39–65–06–06. ☜ Free. ☉ Wed.–Sun.
9:30–noon and 2–5:30.

Housed behind the turreted facade of the 14th-century royal priory,
the **Musée du Jouet** (Toy Museum) has a collection of historical toys,
games, automatons, puppets, electric trains, rocking horses, tin soldiers,
and dollhouses. ⊠ 1 enclos de l'Abbaye, ☎ 01–39–65–06–06. ☜ 20
frs. ☉ Tues.–Sun. 9:30–noon and 2–5:30.

Rising on what look like stilts—in fact, slender concrete pillars—above
an extensive lawn that stretched over 15 acres until a (not undistin-
★ guished) school was built alongside in the 1950s, the **Villa Savoye** is
considered one of Le Corbusier's most accomplished designs. Indus-

trialist Pierre Savoye and his wife spent weekends here beginning in 1931 but stopped coming in 1938—fed up with the leaky flat roof. The villa was commandeered by the Germans during World War II and only fully restored to its original glory in 1997 after years of neglect. The villa appears as an austere white block; this is intentionally misleading—the ground floor, in fact, curves around to the entrance, at the back. An oval funnel emerges from the roof, harboring a solarium. Inside, the visual teasing continues, with a spiral staircase whose vertical emphasis clashes with the gently sloping ramp that serves as the principal transition from floor to floor. Light floods in through the long horizontal windows—bouncing off the white walls to be absorbed by unexpected coats of brown and electric blue paint. Be warned: the villa's delights are hidden in more ways than one, and signposting is terrible. Head up from the Toy Museum and turn right at the lights opposite the cemetery: the villa is 700 yards up, at the crest of the hill on the right. ✉ *82 rue de Villiers,* ☎ *01–39–65–01–06.* ✍ *25 frs.* ☉ *Apr.–Oct., Wed.–Mon. 9:30–12:30 and 1:30–6; Nov.–Mar., 9:30–12:30 and 1:30–4:30.*

Médan

㉝ *8 km (5 mi) southwest of Poissy, 32 km (20 mi) northwest of Paris.*

Médan is home to the **Musée Émile-Zola,** overlooking the Paris–Le Havre railroad Zola smokily evokes in *La Bête Humaine.* Zola moved here in 1877, and you can now visit the spacious rooms (including the study where he wrote many of his novels) furnished in the surprisingly ostentatious, bourgeois taste of one of France's most rebellious writers, renowned for his defense of the working classes and for taking up the cause of the Dreyfus case. ✉ *26 rue Pasteur,* ☎ *01–39–75–35–65.* ✍ *30 frs.* ☉ *Weekends 2–6.*

En Route   Cross the Seine at Vernouillet and follow D190 to **Mantes-la-Jolie,** approaching across the old bridge from Limay, once painted by Corot. Another painter, the neo-Impressionist Maximilien Luce, is the hero of the fine town museum alongside the vast, 12th-century **Église Notre-Dame,** whose twin-towered facade is strikingly similar to that of Notre-Dame in Paris. The small, circular windows ringing the east end of the church are an unusual local architectural characteristic—you can also see them 11 km (7 mi) north, at the church in **Vétheuil,** where the road regains the riverbank beneath impressive chalk cliffs.

La Roche-Guyon

㉞ *7 km (4 mi) northwest of Vetheuil on D913, 45 km (28 mi) northwest of Poissy via D190 and D147, 69 km (43 mi) northwest of Paris.*

Ruins of a medieval cliff-top castle look down on the quaint village of La Roche-Guyon and its classical **Château,** constructed mainly in the 18th century. The château, by the highway overlooking the Seine, has impressive iron gates incorporating the arms of the owners, the La Rochefoucauld family; the main château building is one story higher than ground level, behind an arcaded terrace that towers above the stables and grassy forecourt. ✉ *1 rue de l'Audience,* ☎ *01–34–79–74–42.* ✍ *40 frs.* ☉ *Mid-Jan.–mid-Dec., Sat.–Thurs. 10–6.*

Giverny

㉟ *8 km (5 mi) west of La Roche-Guyon on D5, 70 km (44 mi) northwest of Paris.*

The small village of Giverny, just beyond the Epte River, which marks the official boundary of Ile-de-France, has become a place of pilgrimage for art lovers. It was here that Claude Monet lived for 43 years, until his death in 1926 at the age of 86. Although his house is now prized by connoisseurs of 19th-century interior decoration, it is his garden, with its Japanese-inspired water lily pond and bridge, that remains the high point for many—a veritable 5-acre, three-dimensional Impressionist painting through which you can walk.

★ The **Maison et Jardin Claude-Monet** (Monet's House and Garden) has been lovingly restored. Monet was brought up in Normandy and, like many of the Impressionists, was sold on the soft light of the Seine Valley. After several years in Argenteuil, just north of Paris, he moved downriver to Giverny in 1883 along with his two sons, his mistress, Alice Hoschedé (whom he later married), and her six children. By 1890 a prospering Monet was able to buy the house outright. With its pretty pink walls and green shutters, the house has a warm feeling that may come as a welcome break after visiting stately French châteaux. Rooms have been restored to Monet's original designs: the kitchen with its blue tiles, the buttercup-yellow dining room, and Monet's bedroom on the second floor. Reproductions of his works, and some of the Japanese prints he avidly collected, crowd the walls.

Three years after buying his house, Monet purchased another plot of land, across the lane, to continue his gardening experiments, even diverting the Epte to make a pond. The resulting garden, with flowers spilling out across the paths, is as cheerful and natural as the house. The famous Japanese bridge and water lily pond, flanked by a mighty willow and rhododendrons, are across the lane that runs to the side of the house and can be reached through a tunnel (which goes under a roadway that rather distressingly cuts through the property). Images of the bridge and the water lilies during various seasons appear in much of Monet's later work. Looking across the pond, it's easy to conjure up the grizzled, bearded painter dabbing at his canvases—capturing changes in light and pioneering a breakdown in form that was to have a major influence on 20th-century art. Note that during the height of spring, when the flowers are in full bloom, the place can be packed with tourists. ⊠ *84 rue Claude-Monet,* ☎ *02–32–51–28–21.* 🎟 *Gardens and home, 35 frs; gardens only, 25 frs.* ☉ *Tues.–Sun. 10–6.*

The airy **Musée Américain** (American Museum), endowed by Chicago art patrons Daniel and Judith Terra, displays works by American Impressionists who were influenced by—and often studied with—Claude Monet. ⊠ *99 rue Claude-Monet,* ☎ *02–32–51–94–65.* 🎟 *35 frs.* ☉ *Apr.–Oct., Tues.–Sun. 10–6.*

Dining

$$–$$$ ✕ **Moulin de Fourges.** Nestled in verdant countryside by the River Epte, 9 km (6 mi) northeast of Giverny on D5, this converted 17th-century water mill has a sitting that alone will make you ravenous. Cuisine varies from meat dishes with creamy Normandy sauces to fish from the Mediterranean. ⊠ *38 rue du Moulin, Fourges,* ☎ *02–32–52–12–12. Reservations essential. AE, MC, V. Closed Mon. (except July–Aug.) and Jan. No dinner Sun., or Wed. in winter.*

$$ ✕ **Les Jardins de Giverny.** This restaurant, with a tile-floor dining room overlooking a rose garden, is a few minutes' walk from Monet's house. Enjoy the 130-franc lunch menu or choose from a repertoire of inventive dishes such as foie gras spiked with Calvados or scallops with wild mushrooms. ⊠ *1 rue Milieu,* ☎ *02–32–21–60–80. AE, MC, V. Closed Mon. and Feb. No dinner Sun.–Fri.*

Vernon

36 *5 km (3 mi) northwest of Giverny on D5, 73 km (46 mi) northwest of Paris.*

The old town of Vernon, on the Seine, has a medieval church, which was often painted by Claude Monet, and several fine medieval timber-frame houses (the best, on rue Carnot, houses the tourist office).

The church of **Notre-Dame** (⊠ Rue Carnot), across from the tourist office, has an arresting rose-window facade that, like the high nave, dates from the 15th century. Rounded Romanesque arches in the choir, however, attest to the building's 12th-century origins. The church is a fine sight when viewed from behind: Monet liked to paint it from across the Seine.

A few minor Monet canvases, along with other late-19th-century paintings, can be admired in the town museum, the **Musée Poulain.** This rambling old mansion is seldom crowded, and the helpful curators are happy to explain local history. ⊠ *12 rue du Pont,* ☎ *02–32–21–28–09.* ⛬ *15 frs.* ☉ *Tues.–Fri. 11–1 and 2–6, weekends 2–6.*

Dining and Lodging

$$$ ✕🏨 **Château de Brécourt.** This 17th-century stone-and-brick château,
★ outside Vernon, has high-pitched roofs, an imposing forecourt, and extensive grounds. Guest rooms follow the same exuberant turn-of-the-century lines. Even if you're not staying here, you can dine on the inventive food in the august restaurant, Le Grand Siècle. Dishes such as lobster mousse and veal with truffles make it a popular spot—and it's even easy to get to from Giverny, which is just across the Seine from Vernon. As such châteaux-hotels go, a stay here is a relatively good value. ⊠ *27120 Brécourt (8 km [5 mi] southwest of Vernon on D181/D75),* ☎ *02–32–52–40–50,* 🇫🇦🇽 *02–32–52–69–65. 33 rooms. Restaurant, pool, tennis court. AE, DC, MC, V.*

THE OISE VALLEY AND EAST TO DISNEYLAND PARIS

This area covers a broad arc, beginning northwest of Paris in Conflans–Ste-Honorine, where the Oise joins the Seine, then heading east along the Oise Valley to Chantilly, and continuing southeast through Meaux. In addition to being the old stomping grounds for several world-famous artists, the area is now the domain of Disneyland Paris.

Conflans–Ste-Honorine

37 *28 km (3 mi) northwest of Paris via A15 and D48.*

Conflans is the capital of France's inland waterway network. Barges arrive from as far afield as the ports of Le Havre and Dunkerque, on the Channel coast, and are often moored as many as six abreast along the 1½-km-long (1-mi-long) quayside, near the *conflans* (confluence) of the Rivers Seine and Oise. From the hilltop church of St-Maclou is a spectacular view of the boats. The **Musée de la Batellerie** (Waterways Museum) explains the historic role of the barges and waterways with the help of pictures and scale models. ⊠ *3 pl. Jules-Gévelot,* ☎ *01–39–72–58–05.* ⛬ *15 frs.* ☉ *Tues. 1:30–6, Wed.–Fri. 9–noon and 1:30–6, weekends 3–6 (summer) or 2–5 (winter).*

Pontoise

㊳ *8 km (5 mi) north of Conflans-Ste-Honorine via N184 and N14, 29 km (19 mi) northwest of Paris via A15.*

A pleasant old town on the banks of the Oise, Pontoise is famous for its link with the Impressionists.

The small **Musée Pissarro,** high up in the old town, pays tribute to one of Pontoise's most illustrious past residents: Impressionist painter Camille Pissarro (1830–1903). The collection of prints and drawings is of interest mainly to specialists, but the view across the valley from the museum gardens will appeal to all. ✉ *17 rue du Château,* ☎ *01–30–32–06–75.* ⌨ *Free.* ☉ *Wed.–Sun. 2–6.*

The **Musée Tavet-Delacour,** housed in a turreted mansion in the center of Pontoise, stages good exhibitions and has a permanent collection that ranges from street scenes and landscapes by Norbert Goenutte and other local painters to contemporary art and the intriguing abstractions of Otto Freundlich. ✉ *4 rue Lemercier,* ☎ *01–30–38–02–40.* ⌨ *25 frs.* ☉ *Wed.–Sun. 10–12:30 and 1:30–6.*

Auvers-sur-Oise

㊴ *7 km (4 mi) east of Pontoise via D4, 33 km (21 mi) northwest of Paris via N328.*

The tranquil Oise River valley, which runs northeast from Pontoise, retains much of the charm that attracted Camille Pissarro, Paul Cézanne, Camille Corot, Charles-François Daubigny, and Berthe Morisot to Auvers-sur-Oise in the second half of the 19th century. But it is the shadow of Vincent van Gogh that haunts every nook and cranny of this pretty riverside village.

Van Gogh moved here from Arles in 1890 to be with his brother, Theo. Little has changed since the summer of 1890, during the last 10 weeks of van Gogh's life, when he painted no fewer than 70 pictures and then shot himself behind the village château. He is buried next to his brother in a simple ivy-covered grave in the village cemetery. The whole village is peppered with plaques marking the spots that inspired his art. The plaques bear reproductions of his paintings, enabling you to compare his final works with the scenes as they are today. After years of indifference and neglect, his last abode has been turned into a shrine. You can also visit the medieval village church, subject of one of van Gogh's most famous paintings, *L'Église d'Auvers,* and admire Osip Zadkine's powerful modern statue of van Gogh in the village park.

The Auberge Ravoux, the inn where van Gogh stayed, is now the **Maison de van Gogh** (van Gogh House). A dingy staircase leads up to the tiny, spartan wood-floor attic where van Gogh stored some of modern art's most famous pictures under his bed. A short film retraces van Gogh's time at Auvers, and there is a well-stocked souvenir shop. Stop for a drink or for lunch at the ground-floor restaurant. ✉ *8 rue de la Sansonne,* ☎ *01–30–36–60–60.* ⌨ *30 frs.* ☉ *Daily 10–6.*

★ ♧ The elegant 17th-century village château, set above split-level gardens, is home to the **Voyage au Temps des Impressionistes** (Journey Through the Impressionist Era). You'll receive a set of infrared headphones (English available), with commentary that guides you past various tableaux illustrating life in the Impressionist era. Although there are no Impressionist originals—500 reproductions pop up on screens interspersed between the tableaux—this is one of France's most imaginative, enjoyable, and innovative museums. Some of the special effects—

talking mirrors, computerized cabaret dancing girls, and a simulated train ride past Impressionist landscapes—are worthy of Disney at its best. ✉ *Rue de Léry,* ☎ *01–34–48–48–48.* ✆ *60 frs.* ☉ *May–Oct., daily 10–6; Nov.–Apr., Tues.–Sun. 10–4:30.*

The landscapist Charles-François Daubigny, a precursor of the Impressionists, lived in Auvers from 1861 until his death in 1878. You can visit his studio, the **Atelier Daubigny,** and admire the remarkable array of mural and roof paintings by Daubigny and fellow artists Camille Corot and Honoré Daumier. ✉ *61 rue Daubigny,* ☎ *01–34–48–03–03.* ✆ *25 frs.* ☉ *Tues.–Sun. 2–6:30.*

You may also want to visit the modest **Musée Daubigny** to admire the drawings, lithographs, and occasional oils by local 19th-century artists, some of which were collected by Daubigny himself. The museum is opposite the Maison de van Gogh, above the tourist office. ✉ *Manoir des Colombières, rue de la Sansonne,* ☎ *01–30–36–80–20.* ✆ *20 frs.* ☉ *May–Oct., Wed.–Sun. 2:30–6:30; Nov.–Apr., Wed.–Sun. 2–5:30.*

The small **Musée de l'Absinthe** (Absinthe Museum), near the château, contains publicity posters and other Belle Epoque artifacts evoking the history of absinthe—a forerunner of today's anise-based aperitifs like Ricard and Pernod. Before it was banned in 1915 because of its negative effects on the nervous system, absinthe was France's national drink. A famous painting by Edgar Degas shows two absinthe drinkers; van Gogh probably downed a few glasses at the Auberge Ravoux (☞ *below*). ✉ *44 rue Callé,* ☎ *01–30–36–83–26.* ✆ *25 frs.* ☉ *Oct.–May, weekends 11–6; June–Sept., Wed.–Sun. 11–6.*

Dining

$$ ✕ **Auberge Ravoux.** For total van Gogh immersion, have lunch in the
★   same restaurant he patronized more than 100 years ago. The 185-franc, three-course menu changes regularly, but it's the setting that makes eating here special, with glasswork, lace curtains, and wall decor carefully modeled on the original designs. ✉ *52 rue Général-de-Gaulle,* ☎ *01–30–36–60–60. Reservations essential. AE, MC, V. Closed Mon. No dinner Sun.*

L'Isle-Adam

⓵ *6 km (4 mi) northeast of Auvers-sur-Oise via D4, 40 km (25 mi) north of Paris via N1.*

Residentially exclusive L'Isle-Adam is one of the most picturesque towns in Ile-de-France. Paris lies just 40 km (25 mi) south, but it could be 100 mi and as many years away. The town has a sandy beach along one stretch of the River Oise (via rue de Beaumont); a curious pagoda-like folly, the Pavillon Chinois de Cassan; and an unassuming local museum. The **Musée Louis-Senlecq,** on the main street, often stages painting exhibitions and contains numerous attractive works by local landscapists. ✉ *46 Grande-Rue,* ☎ *01–34–69–45–44.* ✆ *15 frs.* ☉ *Wed.–Mon. 2:30–6.*

Dining and Lodging

$$–$$$ ✕⊞ **Le Cabouillet.** The riverside Cabouillet aptly reflects the quiet charm of L'Isle-Adam, thanks to its pretty views over the Oise. You can savor these from each of its eight rooms or from the chic restaurant (closed Wednesday), where the cooking can be inspired—have the crawfish in Sauternes sauce, if it's on the menu. ✉ *5 quai de l'Oise, 95290,* ☎ *01–34–69–00–90,* 𝙵𝙰𝚇 *01–34–69–33–88. 8 rooms. Restaurant. AE, DC, MC, V. Closed late Dec.–early Feb.*

Chantilly

④ *10 km (6 mi) northeast of Royaumont via D909, 23 km (14 mi) east of L'Isle-Adam via D4, 37 km (23 mi) north of Paris via N16.*

Famous for lace, cream, and the most beautiful medieval manuscript in the world—*Les Très Riches Heures du Duc de Berry* (The Very Rich Hours of the Duke of Berry)—romantic Chantilly has a host of other attractions: a faux Renaissance château with an eye-popping art collection, splendid Baroque stables, a classy racecourse, and a 16,000-acre forest. Yet it remains relatively neglected by sightseers. As former U.S. president Richard Nixon once exclaimed: "Why have I been taken to Versailles seven times, and never here?"

★ Although its lavish exterior may be 19th-century Renaissance pastiche, the **Château de Chantilly,** sitting snugly behind an artificial lake, houses the outstanding **Musée Condé,** with illuminated medieval manuscripts, tapestries, furniture, and paintings. The most famous room, the **Santuario** (sanctuary), contains two celebrated works by Italian painter Raphael (1483–1520)—the *Three Graces* and the *Orleans Virgin*—plus an exquisite ensemble of 15th-century miniatures by the most illustrious French painter of his time, Jean Fouquet (1420–81). Farther on, in the *Cabinet des Livres* (library), is the world-famous Book of Hours whose title translates as "The Very Rich Hours of the Duc de Berry," which was illuminated by the Brothers Limbourg with magical pictures of early 15th-century life as lived by one of Burgundy's richest lords. Other highlights of this unusual museum are the **Galerie de Psyché** (Psyche Gallery), with 16th-century stained glass and portrait drawings by Flemish artist Jean Clouet II; the **Chapelle,** with sculptures by Jean Goujon and Jacques Sarrazin; and the extensive collection of paintings by 19th-century French artists, headed by Jean-Auguste Ingres. ☎ *03–44–62–62–62.* ▦ *39 frs (including park).* ☉ *Mar.–Oct., Wed.–Mon. 10–6; Nov.–Feb., 10:30–12:45 and 2–5.*

Le Nôtre's **park** is based on that familiar combination of formal (neatly planned parterres and a mighty straight-banked canal) and romantic eccentricity (the waterfall and the make-believe village that inspired Marie-Antoinette's version at Versailles). The **Aérophile,** the world's largest tethered balloon, floats you 450 ft up for a bird's-eye view; the **Hydrophile,** an electric-powered boat, glides you for 30 minutes down the Grand Canal. ☎ *03–44–57–35–35.* ▦ *Park only 17 frs, Hydrophile and Aérophile 45 frs each (65 frs joint ticket).* ☉ *Mar.–Oct., daily 10–6; Nov.–Feb., daily 10:30–12:45 and 2–5.*

★ ℭ The palatial 18th-century **Grandes Écuries** by the racetrack, built by Jean Aubert in 1719 to accommodate 240 horses and 500 hounds for stag and boar hunts in the forests nearby, are the grandest stables in France. They're still in use, as the home of the **Musée Vivant du Cheval** (Living Horse Museum), with 30 breeds of horses and ponies housed in straw-lined comfort—in between dressage displays in the courtyard or beneath the awe-inspiring central dome. The 31-room museum has a comprehensive collection of equine paraphernalia: everything from saddles, bridles, and stirrups to rocking horses, anatomy displays, and old postcards. There are explanations in English throughout. ⊠ *7 rue du Connétable,* ☎ *03–44–57–40–40.* ▦ *40 frs.* ☉ *Easter–Sept., Wed.–Mon. 10:30–5:30; Oct.–Easter, Wed.–Fri. and Mon. 2–5, weekends 10:30–5:30.*

Dining and Lodging

$$ ✕ **La Ferme de Condé.** Opposite the racetrack, in a building that originally served as an Anglican chapel, is one of the classiest restaurants in Chantilly. Elegant dishes include duck with honey and spices and lobster terrine. A reasonably priced menu makes it a suitable lunch spot. There is a good wine list. ✉ *42 av. du Maréchal-Joffre,* ☎ *03–44–57–32–31. Reservations essential. AE, MC, V. Closed Tues.*

$ ✕ **Capitainerie.** This self-service restaurant is in the château's medieval basement, adorned with old kitchen utensils. The buffet is available non-stop from 10:30 through 6:30; you'll find salads, cheeses, and desserts, along with a few hot dishes. ✉ *In Château de Chantilly,* ☎ *03–44–57–15–89. Reservations not accepted. No credit cards. Closed Tues.*

$$$–$$$$ 🏨 **Domaine de Chantilly.** This large hotel with a pink facade, 1½ km (1 mi) northeast of the château, is surrounded by forest and overlooks its own 18-hole golf course. The marble-floor reception hall creates a glitzy impression not quite matched by the guest rooms, which are functional, modern, and a bit small. The De Par En Par brasserie, in the golf clubhouse, serves lunch for 90 francs, and the deluxe Carmontelle has formal dining (pastry chef Hugues Lenté is a master at *crème de Chantilly*). ✉ *Rte. d'Apremont, 60500 Vineuil–S,* ☎ *03–44–58–47–77,* 🖷 *03–44–58–50–11. 111 rooms. 2 restaurants, golf course, pool, tennis courts. AE, DC, MC, V.*

$–$$ 🏨 **Campanile.** This functional, modern motel is in quiet Les Huit Curés, just north of Chantilly, on the edge of the forest (which compensates for the lack of interior atmosphere). There's a grill room for straightforward meals, with a buffet for appetizers, cheese, and desserts. You can dine outside on the terrace in summer. ✉ *Rte. de Creil (on N16 toward Creil), 60500,* ☎ *03–44–57–39–24,* 🖷 *03–44–58–10–05. 47 rooms. Grill. AE, DC, MC, V.*

Outdoor Activities and Sports

Since 1834 Chantilly's fabled racetrack has come into its own each June with two of Europe's most prestigious events: the **Prix du Jockey-Club** (French Derby), on the first Sunday of the month, and the **Prix de Diane** for three-year-old fillies, the Sunday after.

Senlis

㊷   *10 km (6 mi) east of Chantilly via D924, 45 km (28 mi) north of Paris via A1.*

Senlis is an exceptionally well-preserved medieval town with crooked, mazelike streets dominated by the svelte, soaring spire of its Gothic cathedral. Be sure to also inspect the moss-tile church of St-Pierre, with its stumpy crocketed spire. Two museums—one on hunting and the other on art and archaeology—are also worth a visit. You can enjoy a 40-minute tour of the old town in a horse-and-carriage, which departs from in front of the cathedral, daily April–December (180 francs for up to three people).

★   The **Cathédrale Notre-Dame** (✉ Pl. de Parvis), one of France's oldest and narrowest cathedrals, dates from the second half of the 12th century and has recently been cleaned and restored. The superb spire— arguably the most elegant in France—was added around 1240, and the majestic transept, with its ornate rose windows, in the 16th century.

The **Musée de la Vénerie** (Hunting Museum), across from the cathedral in the picturesque grounds of the ruined royal castle ringed by the medieval town walls, is one of France's few full-fledged hunting museums. Displayed are artifacts, prints, and paintings, including excellent works by 18th-century animal portraitist Jean-Baptiste Oudry. ✉ *Château Royal,* ☎ *03–44–53–00–80.* 🎫 *15 frs.* ⊘ *Mid-Jan.–mid-Dec. for guided tours only, Thurs.–Mon. at 10, 11, 2, 3, 4, and 5, Wed. at 2, 3, 4, and 5.*

The town's excellent **Musée d'Art et Archéologie** (Museum of Art and Archaeology), built atop an ancient Gallo-Roman residence, displays some excellent finds, from Gallo-Roman votive objects, unearthed in the neighboring Halatte Forest, to the building's own excavated foundations (found in the basement), including an array of macabre stone heads bathed in half light. Paintings upstairs include works by Manet's teacher Thomas Couture (who lived in Senlis), and a whimsical fried-egg still life by 19th-century realist Théodule Ribot. ⊠ *Palais Épiscopal, pl. du Parvis-Notre-Dame,* ☎ *03–44–53–00–80.* ☜ *15 frs.* ☉ *Thurs.–Mon. 9–noon and 1:30–5:30.*

OFF THE
BEATEN PATH

PARC ASTÉRIX – Great for kids of all ages, this Gallic theme park, 10 km (6 mi) south of Senlis via A1, takes its cue from a French comic-book figure whose adventures are set during the Roman invasion of France 2,000 years ago. Highlights include a mock Gallo-Roman village, a dolphin lake, and a giant roller coaster. ☎ *03–44–62–34–34.* ☜ *170 frs.* ☉ *Apr.–Aug., daily 10–6; Sept.–mid-Oct., Wed. and weekends 10–6.*

Dining and Lodging

$$ ✕ **Le Bourgeois Gentilhomme.** This cozy restaurant in old Senlis serves some interesting fish dishes: mullet with dill, fricassee of burbot with mushrooms, and crab lasagna with cress, to name but three. ⊠ *3 pl. de la Halle,* ☎ *03–44–53–13–22. MC, V. Closed Mon. and 3 wks in Aug. No dinner Sun.*

$–$$ ▥ **Hostellerie de la Porte-Bellon.** This is the closest you'll get to spending a night in the historic center of Senlis. This modest hotel is just a five-minute walk from the cathedral and close to the bus station. ⊠ *51 rue Bellon, 60300,* ☎ *03–44–53–03–05,* FAX *03–44–53–29–94. 19 rooms. Restaurant. MC, V. Closed mid-Dec.–mid-Jan.*

Ermenonville

⑬ *13 km (8 mi) southeast of Senlis via N330, 43 km (27 mi) northeast of Paris.*

A ruined abbey and children's amusement park, both nearby, add to the appeal of the village of Ermenonville, best known as the final haunt of the 18th-century French philosopher Jean-Jacques Rousseau.

The Cistercian **Abbaye de Chaalis,** just off N330 as you arrive from Senlis, has photogenic 13th-century ruins, a landscaped park, an orangery, and an 18th-century château. Inside is an eclectic collection of Egyptian antiquities and medieval paintings and three rooms displaying manuscripts and other mementos of Jean-Jacques Rousseau. ⊠ *Just off N330,* ☎ *03–44–54–04–02.* ☜ *Abbey and park 35 frs, park only 15 frs.* ☉ *Mar.–Oct., daily 10:30–12:30 and 2–6; Nov.–Feb., Sun. 10:30–12:30 and 1:30–5:30.*

The **Mer de Sable** (Sea of Sand) amusement park, opposite the abbey of Chaalis, is a cheerful place for children, with its miniature train, giant slide, small zoo, and curious natural "desert" of sand. ⊠ *Parc d'Attractions Jean-Richard,* ☎ *03–44–54–00–96.* ☜ *90 frs.* ☉ *Apr.–May and Sept., Wed. and weekends 10:30–6:30; June, weekdays 10–6, weekends 11–7; July–Aug., daily 10:30–6:30, weekends 10:30–7.*

The elegant **Parc Jean-Jacques Rousseau,** in the center of Ermenonville, is famous as the initial resting place of the influential writer, who spent the last three months of his life in Ermenonville in 1778 and was buried on the Ile des Peupliers in the middle of the lake. Rousseau's ideas about natural equality made him a hero of the French Revolution, and in 1794 his body was removed to the Panthéon in Paris. A few years later Napoléon came to Ermenonville to pay homage to Rousseau, saying: "It would have been better for the peace of France if this man had never existed; he paved the way for the French Revolution." When it was pointed out that he could hardly complain about the turn of revolutionary events, Napoléon is said to have replied: "Time will tell whether it would have been better for peace on earth if Rousseau and I had never lived."

Dining and Lodging

$$$–$$$$ ✕⊡ **Château d'Ermenonville.** This turreted 18th-century château, opposite the Parc Jean-Jacques Rousseau, has great style—it's surrounded by a lake, the main courtyard has a sculpted pediment and wrought-iron balconies, and the rooms are furnished with Grand Siècle grand fin-de-siècle opulence. The menu changes regularly at the restaurant, *La Table du Poète.* ⊠ *60950 Ermenonville,* ☎ *03–44–54–00–26,* ℻ *03–44–54–01–00. 49 rooms. Restaurant. AE, DC, MC, V.*

Meaux

㊹   *24 km (15 mi) southeast of Ermenonville via N330, 40 km (25 mi) east of Paris via N3.*

A sturdy cathedral and well-preserved bishop's palace embellish Meaux, a dignified old market town on the banks of the Marne River. An excellent variety of Brie is produced locally.

Above the Marne sits the **Cathédrale St-Étienne,** which took more than 300 years to complete and stylistically is a bit of a hodgepodge. The stonework in the soaring interior becomes increasingly decorative as you approach the west end, culminating in a notable Flamboyant Gothic rose window. The exterior is somewhat eroded and looks sadly battered—or pleasingly authentic, according to taste. A son-et-lumière show replete with medieval costumes is staged outside the cathedral most weekends in June and July. ⊠ *Rue St-Étienne,* ☎ *01–60–23–40–00 for details about son-et-lumière show.* ☉ *Daily 8–noon and 2–6.*

The former bishop's palace next to the cathedral, overlooking a trimly patterned garden with remains of the town wall, now houses the **Musée Bossuet.** The museum combines French old masters with a quirky collection of medals commemorating the Paris Commune and Franco-Prussian War, along with documents and mementos detailing the life of former bishop Jacques Bossuet, a noted 17th-century theologian. ⊠ *Ancien Palais Épiscopal,* ☎ *01–64–34–84–45.* ▣ *15 frs, free Wed.* ☉ *Wed.–Mon. 10–noon and 2–5.*

Disneyland Paris

㊺   *20 km (13 mi) southwest of Meaux via A140 and A4, 38 km (24 mi) east of Paris via A4.*

Disneyland Paris (originally called Euro Disney) is probably not what you've traveled to France to experience. But if you have a child in tow, the promise of a day here may get you through an afternoon at Versailles or Fontainebleau. If you're a dyed-in-the-wool Disney fan, you'll want to make a beeline for the park to see how it has been molded to appeal to the tastes of Europeans (Disney's "Imagineers" call it their most lovingly detailed park). And if you've never experienced this particular form of Disney showmanship, you may want to put in an appearance, if only to see what the fuss is all about. When it opened, few turned up to do so; today the place is jammed with crowds, and Disneyland Paris looks like it is here to stay.

The theme park is made up of five "lands": Main Street U.S.A., Frontierland, Adventureland, Fantasyland, and Discoveryland. The central theme of each land is relentlessly echoed in every detail, from attractions to restaurant menus to souvenirs. The park is circled by a railroad, which stops three times along the perimeter.

Main Street U.S.A. goes under the railroad and past shops and restaurants toward the main plaza; the Disney Parades are held here every afternoon and—during holiday periods—every evening.

Top attractions at **Frontierland** are the chilling Phantom Manor, haunted by holographic spooks, and the thrilling runaway mine train of Big Thunder Mountain, a roller coaster that plunges wildly through floods and avalanches in a setting meant to evoke Utah's Monument Valley.

Whiffs of Arabia, Africa, and the West Indies give **Adventureland** its exotic cachet; the spicy meals and snacks served here rank among the best food in the park. Don't miss the Pirates of the Caribbean, an exciting mise-en-scène populated by eerily humanlike, computer-driven figures, or Indiana Jones and the Temple of Doom, a breathtaking ride that relives some of this luckless hero's most exciting moments.

Fantasyland charms the youngest park goers with familiar cartoon characters from such classic Disney films as *Snow White, Pinocchio, Dumbo,* and *Peter Pan.* The focal point of Fantasyland, and indeed Disneyland Paris, is Le Château de la Belle au Bois Dormant (Sleeping Beauty's Castle), a 140-ft, bubble-gum-pink structure topped with 16 blue- and gold-tipped turrets. Its design was allegedly inspired by illustrations from a medieval *Book of Hours*—if so, it was by way of Beverly Hills. The castle's dungeon conceals a 2-ton scaly, green dragon that rumbles in its sleep and occasionally rouses to roar—an impressive feat of engineering, producing an answering chorus of shrieks from younger children.

Discoveryland is a futuristic setting for high-tech Disney entertainment. Robots on roller skates welcome you on your way to Star Tours, a pitching, plunging, sense-confounding ride based on the *Star Wars* films. In Le Visionarium, a simulated space journey is presented by 9-Eye, a staggeringly realistic robot. Space Mountain pretends to catapult riders through the Milky Way. ☎ *08–03–30–60–30.* 🎟 *Apr.–Oct. and Christmas period 220 frs (425 frs for 2-day Passport, 595 frs for 3-day Passport); Nov.–Mar., except Christmas period, 165 frs (320 frs for 2-day Passport, 445 frs for 3-day Passport); includes admission to all individual attractions within the park but not meals.* ⊙ *Mid-June–mid-Sept., daily 9* AM*–10* PM*; mid-Sept.–mid-June, Sun.–Fri. 10–6, Sat. 9–8; Dec. 20–Jan. 3, daily 9–8. AE, DC, MC, V.*

Dining and Lodging

$–$$ ✕ **Disneyland Restaurants.** Disneyland Paris is peppered with places to eat, ranging from snack bars and fast-food joints to five full-service restaurants—all with a distinguishing theme. In addition, Disney Village (☞ *below*) and Disney hotels have restaurants open to the public. But since these are outside the park, it is not recommended that you waste time traveling to them for lunch. Disneyland Paris has relaxed its no-alcohol policy and now serves wine and beer in the park's sit-down restaurants, as well as in the hotels and restaurants outside the park. Eateries serve nonstop as long as the park is open. ☎ *01–60–45–65–40. AE, DC, MC, V accepted at sit-down restaurants; counter-service restaurants do not accept credit cards.*

$$–$$$$ 🏨 **Disneyland Hotels.** The resort has 5,000 rooms in six hotels, all a short distance from the park, ranging from the luxurious Disneyland Hotel to the not-so-rustic Camp Davy Crockett. Free transportation

to the park is available at every hotel. Packages including Disneyland lodging, entertainment, and admission are available through travel agents in Europe. ⊠ *Centre de Réservations, B.P. 100, 77777 Marne-la-Vallée cedex 4,* ☎ *01–60–30–60–30; 407/934–7639 in U.S.,* 𝖥𝖠𝖷 *01–49–30–71–00. All hotels have at least 1 restaurant, bar, café, indoor pool, sauna, exercise facilities, and free parking. AE, DC, MC, V.*

Nightlife and the Arts

Nocturnal entertainment outside the park centers on **Disney Village,** a vast pleasure mall designed by American architect Frank Gehry. Featured are American-style restaurants (crab shack, diner, deli, steak house), including **Billybob's Country Western Saloon** (☎ 01–60–45–70–81) and the disco **Hurricane's** (☎ 01–60–45–70–70), which has a giant video screen. Also in Disney Village is **Buffalo Bill's Wild West Show** (☎ 01–60–45–71–00 for reservations), a two-hour dinner extravaganza with a menu of sausages, spareribs, and chili; performances by a talented troupe of stunt riders, bronco busters, tribal dancers, and musicians; plus some 50 horses, a dozen buffalo, a bull, and an Annie Oakley–style sharpshooter, with a golden-maned "Buffalo Bill" as emcee. A re-creation of a show that dazzled Parisians 100 years ago, it's corny but great fun if you can manage the appropriate suspension of disbelief. There are two shows nightly, at 6:30 and 9:30; the cost is 325 francs.

Outdoor Activities and Sports

A 27-hole **golf course** (☎ 01–60–45–68–04) is open to the public at Disneyland; rental clubs are available, and some special golf packages are available through travel agents.

En Route   Three châteaux just west of Disneyland merit a stop if you have time. The **Château de Ferrières** (just off the expressway, 8 km [5 mi] west of Disneyland) was built by the Rothschilds in the 19th century; it's open afternoons only, Wednesday–Sunday in summer, weekends only in winter. The 17th-century **Château de Guermantes** (5 km [3 mi] north of Ferrières via D35) has Italianate decor and is open weekends from March through November. The 18th-century **Château de Champs-sur-Marne** (8 km [5 mi] west of Guermantes) has gardens with an assortment of ingeniously trimmed hedges; it's open daily except Tuesday.

SOUTHEAST TO FONTAINEBLEAU

Fontainebleau forms the hub of this heavily wooded southeast region of Ile-de-France, but no one will want to bypass the grandeur of Vaux-le-Vicomte, a masterpiece of 17th-century architecture and garden design; or the pretty painters' villages of Barbizon and Moret-sur-Loing.

Vaux-le-Vicomte

★ ㊽   *56 km (35 mi) southeast of Paris via A6, N104, A5, and N36; 5 km (3 mi) northeast of Melun via N36 and D215; 48 km south (30 mi) of Disneyland Paris via N36.*

The quintessence of French 17th-century splendor, the **Château de Vaux-le-Vicomte** was built between 1656 and 1661 for finance minister Nicolas Fouquet. The construction of this château was monstrous even for those days: Entire villages were razed, 18,000 workmen called in, and architect Louis Le Vau, painter Charles Le Brun, and landscape architect André Le Nôtre were hired to prove that Fouquet's refined tastes matched his business acumen. The housewarming party was so lavish that star guest Louis XIV, tetchy at the best of times, threw a jealous fit. He hurled Fouquet in the slammer and promptly began building Versailles to prove just who was boss.

The high-roofed château, partially surrounded by a moat, is set well back from the road behind iron railings topped with sculpted heads. A cobbled avenue stretches up to the entrance, and stone steps lead to the vestibule, which seems small, given the noble scale of the exterior. There is no grand staircase, either—the stairs are tucked away in the left wing and lead to the private apartments, rooms designed on an intimate scale for daily living. Charles Le Brun's captivating decoration includes the ceiling of the **Chambre du Roi** (Royal Bedchamber), depicting *Time Bearing Truth Heavenward,* framed by stuccowork by sculptors François Girardon and André Legendre. Along the frieze you can make out small squirrels, the Fouquet family's emblem—even now squirrels are known as *fouquets* in local dialect. But Le Brun's masterwork is the ceiling in the **Salon des Muses** (Hall of Muses), a brilliant allegorical composition painted in glowing, sensuous colors that surpasses his work at Versailles.

On the ground floor the impressive **Grand Salon** (Great Hall), with its unusual oval form and 16 caryatid pillars symbolizing the months and seasons, possesses harmony and style despite its unfinished state. In fact, the lack of decoration only points up Le Vau's architectural genius. In the basement, whose cool, dim rooms were used to store food and wine and house the château's staff, you'll find rotating exhibits about the château's past and life-size wax figures illustrating its history. The **Cuisine** (kitchen), a cheerful sight with its gleaming copperware and old menus, is also down here.

There is no mistaking the grandeur of Le Nôtre's carefully restored **gardens**, at their best when the fountains are turned on (the second and last Saturdays of each month from April through October 3 PM–6 PM). Also visit the **Musée des Équipages** (Carriage Museum), in the stables, and inspect a host of carriages and coaches in wonderful condition. ☎ 01–64–14–41–90. 🎫 *Château and grounds 63 frs, grounds and museum only 30 frs, candlelight visits 82 frs.* ☼ *Mid-Mar.–Nov. 11, daily 10–6 candlelight visits May–Oct., Sat. 8 PM–midnight.*

Dining

$ ✕ **L'Écureuil.** An imposing barn to the right of the château entrance has been transformed into this self-service cafeteria, where you can enjoy fine steaks (insist yours is cooked enough), coffee, or a snack beneath the ancient rafters of a wood-beam roof. The restaurant is open daily for lunch and tea, and for dinner during candlelight visits. ✉ *Château de Vaux-le-Vicomte,* ☎ 01–60–66–95–66. MC, V.

Barbizon

🔴 *17 km (11 mi) southwest of Vaux-le-Vicomte via Melun and D132/ D64, 52 km (33 mi) southeast of Paris.*

On the western edge of the 62,000-acre Fontainebleau forest, the village of Barbizon retains its atmosphere despite the intrusion of art galleries, souvenir shops, and busloads of tourists. The group of landscape painters known as the Barbizon School—Camille Corot, Jean-François Millet, Narcisse Diaz de la Peña, and Théodore Rousseau, among others—lived here from the 1830s on. They paved the way for the Impressionists by their willingness to accept nature on its own terms, rather than use it as an idealized base for carefully structured compositions. Sealed to one of the famous sandstone rocks in the forest—which starts, literally, at the far end of the main street—is a bronze medallion by sculptor Henri Chapu, paying homage to Millet and Rousseau.

Corot and company would often repair to the Auberge Ganne after painting; the inn is now the **Musée de l'École de Barbizon** (Barbizon

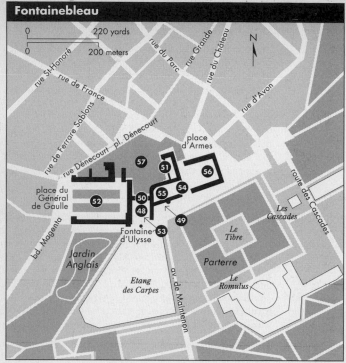

Fontainebleau

School Museum). Here you'll find documents of the village as it was
in the 19th century, as well as a few original works. The Barbizon artists
painted on every available surface, and even now you can see some
originals on the upstairs walls. Two of the ground-floor rooms have
been reconstituted as they were in Ganne's time—note the trompe l'oeil
paintings on the buffet doors. There's also a video on the Barbizon
School. ⊠ *92 Grande-Rue,* ☎ *01–60–66–22–27.* 🔳 *25 frs (joint admission with Maison-Atelier Théodore-Rousseau).* ⊙ *Mon. and Wed.–
Fri. 10–12:30 and 2–5, weekends 10–5.*

Though there are no actual Millet works, the **Atelier Jean-François Millet** (Millet's Studio) is cluttered with photographs and mementos evoking his career. It was here that Millet painted some of his most renowned
pieces, including *The Gleaners.* ⊠ *27 Grande-Rue,* ☎ *01–60–66–21–
55.* 🔳 *Free.* ⊙ *Wed.–Mon. 9:30–12:30 and 2–5:30.*

By the church, beyond the extraordinary village war memorial featuring
a mustached ancient Gaul in a winged helmet, is the **Maison-Atelier
Théodore-Rousseau** (Rousseau's house-cum-studio), in a converted
barn. It doubles as the tourist office and exhibition space for temporary shows. ⊠ *55 Grande-Rue,* ☎ *01–60–66–22–38.* 🔳 *25 frs (joint
ticket with Barbizon School Museum).* ⊙ *Mon. and Wed.–Fri. 10–12:30
and 2–5, weekends 10–5.*

Dining and Lodging

$–$$ ✕ **Le Relais de Barbizon.** French country specialties are served at this
rustic restaurant, with a big open fire and a large terrace shaded by
lime and chestnut trees. The four-course weekday menu is a good
value, but wine here is expensive and cannot be ordered by the *pichet*
(pitcher). ⊠ *2 av. Général-de-Gaulle,* ☎ *01–60–66–40–28. Reservations essential on weekends. MC, V. Closed Wed. No dinner Tues.*

$$ ✕▥ **Auberge des Alouettes.** This delightful, family-run 19th-century
★ inn is on 2 acres (which the better rooms overlook). The interior is '30s
style, but many rooms still have their original oak beams. The popu-
lar restaurant (reservations essential; October through March, no Sun-
day dinner), with its large open terrace, serves light cuisine and
barbecued beef in summer. ✉ *4 rue Antoine-Barye, 77630,* ☎ *01–60–
66–41–98,* ℻ *01–60–66–20–69. 22 rooms. Restaurant, tennis court.
AE, DC, MC, V.*

Fontainebleau

*9 km (6 mi) southeast of Barbizon via N7, 61 km (38 mi) southeast
of Paris via A6 and N7.*

Like Chambord in the Loire Valley or Compiègne to the north,
Fontainebleau was a favorite spot for royal hunting parties long be-
fore the construction of one of France's grandest residences. Although
not as celebrated as Versailles, Vaux-le-Vicomte, or Chenonceau, this
palace is almost as spectacular as those other sights.

The **Château de Fontainebleau** you see today dates from the 16th cen-
tury, although additions were made by various royal incumbents
through the next 300 years.

The palace was begun under the flamboyant Renaissance king, François
I, the French contemporary of England's Henry VIII. The king hired
Italian artists Il Rosso (a pupil of Michelangelo) and Primaticcio to em-
bellish his château. In fact, they did much more: By introducing the
pagan allegories and elegant lines of Mannerism to France, they rev-
olutionized French decorative art. Their extraordinary frescoes and stuc-
cowork can be admired in the **Galerie François-I** (Gallery Francis I)
and the jewel of the interior, the **Salle de Bal** (ballroom). Here in the
ceremonial ballroom, which is nearly 100 ft long, you can admire the
dazzling 16th-century frescoes and gilding. Completed under Henri II,
François's successor, it is luxuriantly wood paneled, with a gleaming
parquet floor that reflects the patterns on the ceiling. Like the château
as a whole, the room exudes a sense of elegance and style—but on a
more intimate, human scale than at Versailles: This is Renaissance, not
Baroque. The decorative interlaced initials found throughout the
château were also added by Henri II. You might expect to see the royal
H woven with a *C* (for Catherine de Médicis, his wife). Instead you'll
find a *D*—indicating his mistress, Diane de Poitiers.

Napoléon's apartments occupied the first floor. You can see a lock of
his hair, his Légion d'Honneur medal, his imperial uniform, the hat he
wore on his return from Elba in 1815, and one bed in which he defi-
nitely did spend a night (almost every town in France boasts a bed in
which the emperor supposedly snoozed). There is also a throne room—
Napoléon spurned the one at Versailles, a palace he disliked, establishing
his imperial seat in the former King's Bedchamber—and the Queen's
Boudoir, also known as the Room of the Six Maries (occupants included
ill-fated Marie-Antoinette and Napoléon's second wife, Marie-Louise).

The sweeping **Galerie de Diane**, built during the reign of Henri IV (1589–
1610), was converted to a library in the 1860s. Other salons have 17th-
century tapestries, marble reliefs by Jacquet de Grenoble, and paint-
ings and frescoes by Primaticcio, Niccolò dell'Abbate, and other
members of the Fontainebleau School.

Although Louis XIV's architectural fancy was concentrated on Versailles,
he commissioned Mansart to design new pavilions and had André Le
Nôtre replant the gardens at Fontainebleau, where he and his court

returned faithfully in the fall for the hunting season. But it was Napoléon who made a Versailles, as it were, out of Fontainebleau, spending lavishly to restore it to its former glory. He held Pope Pius VII prisoner here in 1812, signed the second church–state concordat here in 1813, **❷** and, in the cobbled **Cour des Adieux** (Farewell Courtyard), said goodbye to his Old Guard in 1814 as he began his brief exile on the Mediterranean island of Elba. The famous Horseshoe Staircase that dominates the Cour des Adieux, once the Cour du Cheval Blanc (White Horse Courtyard), was built by Androuet du Cerceau for Louis XIII (1610– **❸** 43). Another courtyard—the **Cour de la Fontaine** (Fountain Courtyard)—was commissioned by Napoléon in 1812 and adjoins the Étang des Carpes (Carp Pond). Ancient carp are alleged to swim here, though Allied soldiers drained the pond in 1915 and ate all the fish, and, in the event they missed some, Hitler's hordes did likewise in 1940. Across from the pond, is the formal Parterre (Flower Garden), and on the other side, the leafy Jardin Anglais (English Garden).

❹ The **Porte Dauphine** is the most beautiful of the various gateways that connect the complex of buildings; its name commemorates the christening of the dauphin—the heir to the throne, later Louis XIII—under its arch- **❺** way in 1606. The gateway fronts the **Cour Ovale** (Oval Court), shaped **❻** like a flattened egg. Opposite the courtyard is the **Cour Henri IV** (Henry IV Court), a large, severe square built at the same time as place des Vos- **❼** ges in Paris (1609). Around the corner is the informal **Jardin de Diane** (Diana's Garden), with peacocks and a statue of the hunting goddess surrounded by mournful hounds. ⊠ *Pl. du Général-de-Gaulle,* ☎ *01–60– 71–50–70.* 🎫 *35 frs; gardens free.* ☉ *Wed.–Mon. 9:30–12:30 and 2–5; gardens Apr.–Sept., daily 8–8:30, Oct.–Mar., daily 8–5.*

Dining and Lodging

$ ✕ **La Route du Beaujolais.** The food is cheap and the atmosphere cheerful at Giorgio's jolly eatery near the château, where Lyonnais-style cold cuts and bottles of Beaujolais are the mainstays. For something a little more upscale, try the beef fillet with Brie or choose from the wide choice of fish dishes. Prix-fixe meals are priced at 85 and 100 francs. ⊠ *3 rue Montebello,* ☎ *01–64–22–27–98. AE, DC, MC, V.*

$$$$ ✕🏨 **Aigle Noir.** This may be Fontainebleau's costliest hotel, but you ★ can't go wrong if you request one of the rooms overlooking either the garden or the château. They have late-18th- or early 19th-century re-production furniture, evoking a Napoleonic mood. The restaurant, Le Beauharnais, serves subtle, imaginative cuisine—lamb with thyme and gentian, for instance. There's a tranquil garden for alfresco dining in summer. Reservations are essential and jacket and tie are required. ⊠ *27 pl. Napoléon-Bonaparte, 77300,* ☎ *01–60–74–60–00,* 𝔽𝔸𝕏 *01–60– 74–60–01. 56 rooms. Restaurant, pool, sauna, exercise room, convention center. AE, DC, MC, V.*

$$$ ✕🏨 **Napoléon.** Opposite the château, this is surely one of the best local hotels. Pastel-color rooms have modern furniture and marble baths and look out onto terraces or the indoor garden. The restaurant, La Table des Maréchaux, serves satisfying, deftly prepared classics, and the 125-franc menu is an excellent deal. ⊠ *9 rue Grande, 77300,* ☎ *01–60–39– 50–50,* 𝔽𝔸𝕏 *01–64–22–20–87. 57 rooms. Restaurant. AE, DC, MC, V.*

$$ 🏨 **Londres.** Established in 1850, the Londres is a tranquil, family-style hotel with Louis XV decor. Some balconies overlook the château and the Cour des Adieux, where Napoléon bade his troops an emotional farewell. The austere 19th-century facade is a registered landmark. ⊠ *1 pl. du Général-de-Gaulle, 77300,* ☎ *01–64–22–20–21,* 𝔽𝔸𝕏 *01–60– 72–39–16. 22 rooms. Restaurant, bar. AE, DC, MC, V. Closed mid-Dec.–early Jan.*

Outdoor Activities and Sports

The Forest of Fontainebleau is laced with hiking trails; for more information ask for the *Guide des Sentiers* (trail guide) at the tourist office (☞ Visitor Information *in* Ile-de-France A to Z, *below*). Bikes can be rented at the Fontainebleau-Avon train station. The forest is also famed for its fascinating rock formations, where many a novice alpinist first caught the climbing bug; for more information contact the **Club Alpin Français** (✉ 24 av. Laumière, 75019 Paris, ☎ 01–53–72–88–00).

Moret-sur-Loing

58 *10 km (6 mi) southeast of Fontainebleau via N6, 72 km (45 mi) southeast of Paris.*

Close to the confluence of the Seine and Yonne rivers is the village of Moret-sur-Loing. It was immortalized by Impressionist painter Alfred Sisley, who lived here for 20 years at 19 rue Montmartre (not open to the public), around the corner from the church. A narrow bridge, one of the oldest in France, leads across the Loing River and provides a view of the village walls, rooftops, and church tower. If you've got a sweet tooth, take note: Moret is renowned for its barley sugar.

Truculent World War I leader Georges Clemenceau (1841–1929), known as the Tiger, is the subject of a cozy museum at **La Grange-Batelière,** the thatched house in which he used to live. His taste for Asian art and his friendship with Impressionist Claude Monet are evoked here. ✉ *Access via rue du Peintre-Sisley,* ☎ *01–60–70–51–21.* ▣ *Guided tours only 35 frs.* ☉ *Easter–mid-Nov., weekends 3–6.*

Nightlife and the Arts

A good time to visit the town is on a Saturday evening in summer (from late June through early September) for the riverside **Festival,** when 600 locals stage son-et-lumière pageants illustrating the town's history. ☎ *01–60–70–41-66.* ▣ *80–100 frs.*

ILE-DE-FRANCE A TO Z

Arriving and Departing

By Car

A13 links Paris (from the Porte d'Auteuil) to Versailles. You can get to Chartres on A10 from Paris (Porte d'Orléans). For Fontainebleau take A6 from Paris (Porte d'Orléans), or for a more attractive route through the Forest of Sénart and the northern part of the Forest of Fontainebleau, take N6 from Paris (Porte de Charenton) via Melun. A4 runs from Paris (Porte de Bercy) to Disneyland.

By Plane

Major airports in the Ile-de-France area are **Charles de Gaulle** (☎ 01–48–62–22–80), commonly known as Roissy, 25 km (16 mi) northwest of Paris, and **Orly** (☎ 01–49–75–15–15), 16 km (10 mi) south. Shuttle buses link Disneyland to the airports at Roissy, 56 km (35 mi) away, and Orly, 50 km (31 mi) distant; buses take 45 minutes and run every 45 minutes from Roissy, every 60 minutes from Orly (less frequently in low season), and cost 80 francs.

By Train

Many sights can be reached by train from Paris. Both regional and mainline (Le Mans–bound) trains leave the **Gare Montparnasse** for Chartres (50–70 minutes); the former also stop at Versailles, Rambouillet, and Maintenon. Gare Montparnasse is also the terminal for trains to Dreux

(Granville line) and for the suburban trains that stop at Montfort-L'Amaury, the nearest station to Thoiry (35 minutes).

Some mainline trains from **Gare St-Lazare** stop at Mantes-la-Jolie (30 minutes) and Vernon (50 minutes) on their way to Rouen and Le Havre. Suburban trains leave the **Gare du Nord** for L'Isle-Adam (50 minutes). Chantilly is on the main northbound line from **Gare du Nord** (the trip takes 25 minutes; Senlis can be reached by bus from Chantilly) on a suburban line from **Gare de l'Est**. Fontainebleau—or, rather, neighboring Avon, 2 km (1½ mi) away (there is frequent bus service)— is 45 minutes from **Gare de Lyon**.

St-Germain-en-Laye is a terminal of the **RER-A** (commuter train) that tunnels through Paris (main stations at Étoile, Auber, and Les Halles). The RER-A also accesses Possy and Maisons-Laffitte and, at the other end, the station for Disneyland Paris (called Marne-la-Vallée–Chessy), within 100 yards of the entrance to both the theme park and Disney Village. Journey time is around 40 minutes, and trains operate every 10–30 minutes, depending on the time of day. The handiest of Versailles's three train stations is the one reached by the **RER-C** line (main stations at Austerlitz, St-Michel, Invalides, and Champ-de-Mars); the trip takes 25–40 minutes.

A mainline **TGV** (*Trains à Grande Vitesse*) station links Disneyland to Lille, Lyon, Brussels, and London (via Lille and the Channel Tunnel).

Getting Around

Although a comprehensive rail network ensures that most towns in Ile-de-France can make comfortable day trips from Paris, the only way to crisscross the region without returning to the capital is by car. There is no shortage of expressways or fast highways, but be prepared for delays close to Paris and during the morning and evening rush hours.

Contacts and Resources

Car Rentals
Cars can be rented from agencies in Paris (☞ Contacts and Resources *in* Paris A to Z *in* Chapter 1) or at Orly or Charles de Gaulle airports (☞ Car Rental *in* Smart Travel Tips A to Z).

Emergencies
Ambulance (☎ 15). **Regional hospitals: Chartres** (⊠ 34 rue du Dr-Maunoury, ☎ 02–37–30–30–30). **Melun** (⊠ 2 rue Fréteau-de-Pény, ☎ 01–64–71–60–00). **Versailles** (⊠ 177 rue de Versailles, in neighboring Le Chesnay, ☎ 01–39–63–91–33). Hospitals closer to Paris: **American Hospital** in Neuilly (⊠ 63 bd. Victor-Hugo, ☎ 01–47–45–71–00). **British Hospital** in Levallois-Perret (⊠ 3 rue Barbès, ☎ 01–47–58–13–12).

Guided Tours
Alliance Autos (⊠ 10 bis rue Jeanne-d'Arc, St-Mandé, métro St-Mandé–Tourelle, ☎ 01–43–28–20–20) has bilingual guides who can take you on a private tour around the Paris area in a luxury car or minibus for a minimum of four hours for about 500 francs an hour (call to check details and prices).

Guided excursions to Giverny are organized by **American Express** (⊠ 11 rue Scribe, Paris, 9ᵉ, ☎ 01–47–77–77–07) from April through October. **Cityrama** (⊠ 4 pl. des Pyramides, Paris 1ᵉʳ, ☎ 01–44–55–61–00) and **Paris Vision** (⊠ 214 rue de Rivoli, Paris 1ᵉʳ, ☎ 08–00–03–02–14) run half- and full-day trips to Versailles (195–395 francs) and guided trips to Chartres and Fontainebleau/Barbizon (275–330 francs), some combined with Versailles (500–650 francs).

Visitor Information

Contact the **Espace du Tourisme d'Ile-de-France,** under the inverted pyramid in the Carrousel du Louvre (⊠ 99 rue de Rivoli, 75001 Paris, ☎ 01–44–50–19–98) ⊙ Wednesday–Monday 10–7. Information on Disneyland is available from the **Disneyland Paris Reservations Office** (⊠ B.P. 100, 77777 Marne-la-Vallée cedex 4, ☎ 01–60–30–60–30; 407/824–4321 in the U.S.).

Local tourist offices: **Barbizon** (⊠ 55 Grande-Rue, ☎ 01–60–66–41–87). **Chantilly** (⊠ 60 av. du Maréchal-Joffre, ☎ 03–44–57–08–58). **Chartres** (⊠ Pl. de la Cathédrale, ☎ 02–37–21–50–00). **Fontainebleau** (⊠ 4 rue Royale, ☎ 01–60–74–99–99). **Rambouillet** (⊠ 1 pl. de la Libération, ☎ 01–34–83–21–21). **St-Germain-en-Laye** (⊠ 38 rue au Pain, ☎ 01–34–51–05–12). **Senlis** (⊠ Pl. du Parvis Notre-Dame, ☎ 03–44–53–06–40). **Versailles** (⊠ 7 rue des Réservoirs, ☎ 01–39–50–36–22).

3 THE LOIRE VALLEY

Strung like precious gems along the peaceful Loire and its tributaries, the royal and near-royal châteaux of this region are among the most storied sights in France. From magical Chenonceau—improbably suspended above the river itself—to mighty Chambord, from the Sleeping Beauty abode of Ussé to the famed gardens of Villandry, this parade of châteaux magnificently captures France's golden age of monarchy. In Orléans, too, you can see the country's history: It was here that Joan of Arc had her most rousing successes against the English.

Updated by
Simon Hewitt

CAUGHT IN A DIAPHANOUS WEB OF SUBTLY SHIFTING LIGHT, with a countryside both luxuriant and fertile, running thick with game, mild of climate, and with shipping access from the Languedoc to the Atlantic, the Loire Valley has always been prime real estate. But when the dust from the Hundred Years' War began to settle and the bastions of the Plantagenet kings lost a bit of their utility, the victorious Valois dynasty began to see the territory in a new light. Just the spot for a holiday home! they thought. Sketching, no doubt, on the back of a tavern napkin at Blois, Louis XII dreamed of turrets and gargoyles, a tasteful blend of symmetry and fantasy, all the while Anne of Bretagne breathing down his neck for closet space. In no time at all, the neighboring Joneses had kept up, and by the 16th century the neighborhood was bristling with fabulous châteaux *d'agrément*, or pleasure castles—palaces for royalty, yes, but also love nests for mistresses and status statements for arrivistes (Chenonceau was built by a tax collector). There were vast boxwood gardens retreating toward perspective points, moats floating with swans, parades of delicate cone-topped towers, frescoes and fancywork ceilings. The glories of the Italian Renaissance, witnessed by the Valois while making war on their neighbor, graced these new megamonuments with all the elegance and proportion of antiquity.

By the time François I was in charge, the extravagance knew no bounds: On a 13,000 acre forest estate, hunting parties at Chambord drew A-list crowds from the far reaches of Europe—and the 430 rooms made weekend entertainment a snap. Queen Claudia hired only the most recherché Italian artisans: Chambord's famous double-helix staircase may, in fact, have been Leonardo da Vinci's design (he was a frequent houseguest, holding forth in a manor on the Amboise grounds). From massive kennels teeming with hunting hounds at Cheverny to luxurious stables at Chaumont-sur-Loire, from endless allées of pollarded lime trees at Villandry to the fairy-tale towers of Ussé—worthy of Sleeping Beauty herself—the Loire Valley was the power base and social center for the New France, and the monarchy was strutting its stuff.

All for good reason. Charles V of Spain, at the age of 19, inherited the Holy Roman Empire in 1519, leaving François and his New France—as well as England's Henry VIII—out in the cold. In a grand gesture of face-saving, it was perhaps no coincidence that in 1519 François commenced construction of his ultimate declaration of dominion, the gigantic château of Chambord. After a few skirmishes (the Low Countries, Italy) and a few power breakfasts, François was cozy enough to entertain the emperor on his lavish Loire estates, and, by 1539 he had married Charles V's sister.

Location is everything, as you realize when you think of Hyannisport, Kennebunkport, or Balmoral: all homesteads redolent of dynasty, where natural beauty, idyllic views, an invigorating hunt with the boys, and a barefoot stroll in the great outdoors liberate the mind to think great thoughts and make history's decisions. Perhaps this is why the have-nots sacked many of the châteaux of the Loire Valley in the French Revolution. Nowadays most of them have fallen into public domain and are restored and maintained as museums—although they are testimony to France's golden age of monarchy, their pleasures are now shared by the common man. Yet the Revolution and latter-day socialists have not erased a certain lingering gentility in the region, an air of refined assurance in its residents far removed from gesticulating, shoulder-shrugging, chest-tapping French stereotypes. Here life goes on at a gentle, pleasant pace, and you'll find a winning concentration of gracious country inns and discerning chefs, a cornucopia of local produce and game, and the famous, fruity wines of Sancerre—all regional blessings still truly fit for a king.

— Nancy Coons

Pleasures and Pastimes

Châteaux

Loire and *château* are almost synonymous; even the word *château*—part fortress, part palace, part mansion—has no English equivalent. More than 20 are described in this chapter, from grandiose Chambord and Saumur to the more intimate Cheverny and Azay-le-Rideau to the rousingly scenic Chenonceau and Ussé. There are genuine castles to admire, too—either preserved in intimidating glory, such as Langeais, Loches, and Angers, or gloriously ruined, like Chinon. Still, this is but the crème de la crème—indeed, there are almost 400 châteaux in the region.

Dining

The Loire region, known as the Garden of France, produces a cornucopia of fine victuals–from beef, poultry, game, and fish to butter, cream, wine, fruits, and vegetables (especially asparagus and mushrooms). It sends its early crops to the best Parisian tables yet keeps more than enough for local use. Loire wines can be extremely good—and varied. Among the best are Savennières and Cheverny, dry whites; Coteau du Layon and Montlouis, sweet whites; Cabernet d'Anjou, rosé; Bourgueil, Chinon, and Saumur-Champigny, reds; and Vouvray, white—dry, sweet, or sparkling.

CATEGORY	COST*
$$$$	over 500 frs
$$$	250 frs–500 frs
$$	125 frs–250 frs
$	under 125 frs

per person for a three-course meal, including tax (20.6%) and tip but not wine

✆ *following the text of a review is your signal that the property has a Web site, where you will find details and, usually, images; for a link, visit www.fodors.com/urls.*

Lodging

Even before the age of the train, the Loire Valley drew visitors from far and wide, and so there are hundreds of hotels of all types. At the higher end are converted châteaux. At the lower end are small, traditional inns in towns and villages, usually offering terrific value for the money. The Loire Valley is a very popular destination, so make reservations well in advance.

CATEGORY	COST*
$$$$	over 800 frs
$$$	600 frs–800 frs
$$	300 frs–600 frs
$	under 300 frs

All prices are for a standard double room for two, including tax (20.6%) and service charge.

Outdoor Activities

The Loire Valley offers a great variety of outdoor activities, from bicycling to picnicking to walking through rolling hills and along riverbanks. The short distances between châteaux and other attractions make for pleasant bicycling even if you don't want to spend all day pedaling. Bicycles can be rented from many train stations.

Son-et-Lumière

In summer, concerts, music festivals, fairs, and celebrated son-et-lumière (sound-and-light) extravaganzas held on the grounds of many châteaux. Dramatic spectacles mounted after dark, these son-et-lumière shows can take the form of historical pageants—with huge casts of people, all in period costume, and caparisoned horses, all floodlighted (some shows dramatically feature the shadows of flickering flames to conjure up the mobs of the French Revolution) and backed by music and commentary, sometimes in English. They also can be shows with spoken commentary and dialogue but no visible figures, as at Chenonceau. The most magnificent, with more than 100 performers, is at Le Lude.

Exploring the Loire Valley

Pick up the Loire River halfway along its course from central France to the Atlantic Ocean. Châteaux and vineyards will accompany you throughout your 340-km (210-mi) westbound course from the hilltop wine town of Sancerre to the bustling city of Angers. Lively towns punctuate the route at almost equal distances—Orléans, Blois, Tours, and Saumur—and are useful bases if you're relying on public transportation. Although you may be rushing around to see as many famous châteaux as possible, try to make time to walk through the poppy-covered hills, picnic along the riverbanks, and sample the local wines. If you want an escape from the usual tourist track, explore the lakes and forests of Sologne or wend your way back along the gentle (but confusingly spelled) Loir Valley.

Great Itineraries

You need a fortnight to cover the Loire Valley region in its entirety. But even if you don't have that long, you can still see many of the Loire's finest châteaux in three days by concentrating on the area between Blois and Amboise. Six days will give you time to explore these châteaux as well as visit Tours and Angers, two of the region's major cities. In 10 days you can follow the Loire from Orléans to Angers.

Numbers in the text correspond to numbers in the margin and on the Loire Valley, Orléans, and Tours maps.

IF YOU HAVE 3 DAYS

Begin in **Blois** ⑰—one of the earliest of the great châteaux—and move inland through the forest to spend the night at ⛫ **Chambord** ⑭—such a vast marble pile it seems more a city than a palace. The next day take in nearby **Cheverny** ⑮—one of the last châteaux to be built—and return to the river at ⛫ **Chaumont-sur-Loire** ⑱. Two attractions await just downstream at **Amboise** ⑲: the château and the Clos-Lucé mansion, devoted to Leonardo da Vinci. Afterward, take in the dreamiest abode of them all: the Château de Chenonceau (spelled without the *x*), in the town of **Chenonceaux** ⑳, for a fitting climax for a visit to this area.

IF YOU HAVE 6 DAYS

Start by following the three-day itinerary through **Blois** ⑰, ⛫ **Chambord** ⑭, **Cheverny** ⑮, ⛫ **Chaumont-sur-Loire** ⑱, and **Amboise** ⑲, spending your third night in either ⛫ **Chenonceaux** ⑳ or the region's major city, ⛫ **Tours** ㉒–㉗. On the fourth day head west to see three more spectacular châteaux—**Azay-le-Rideau** ㉚, **Ussé** ㉜, and ⛫ **Chinon** ㉝. The next day continue downstream to the venerable abbey at **Fontevraud** ㊱ and spend the fifth night in ⛫ **Saumur** ㊲. On day six end up in **Angers** ㊴, a lively city with a dramatic castle and good museums and shops.

IF YOU HAVE 10 DAYS

Stop in **Orléans** ⑧–⑪ on your way west along the Loire if you are coming from Paris. From there head to ⛫ **Blois** ⑰ for the night. Over the

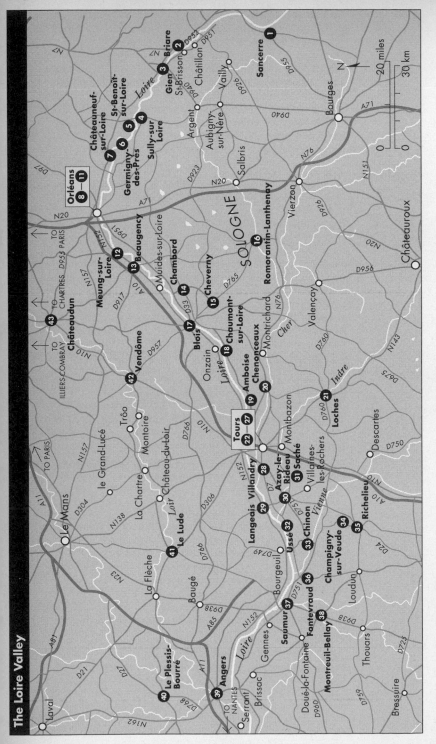

The Loire Valley

20 miles
30 km
N

1 Sancerre

2 Briare
3 Gien
St-Brisson-sur-Loire
Châtillon
Vailly
Bourges
A71

4 Sully-sur-Loire
5
6 Germigny-des-Prés
7 Châteauneuf-sur-Loire
St-Benoît-sur-Loire
Argent
Aubigny-sur-Nère
Salbris

8 – 11 Orléans
Meung-sur-Loire
12 Beaugency
13
Muides-sur-Loire
Chambord

14
15 Cheverny

16 Romorantin-Lanthenay
SOLOGNE
Vierzon
Châteauroux

17 Blois
Onzain
18 Chaumont-sur-Loire
Montrichard
Chenonceaux
Valençay
Cher
Indre

42 Vendôme
Trôo
Montoire
Château-du-Loir

43 Châteaudun

Amboise
19
20
21 Loches
Descartes

Tours 22 – 27

le Grand-Lucé
le Lude
28 Azay-le-Rideau
Saché
31
Villaines-les-Rochers
Richelieu
34
35

Le Mans
La Chartre
29 Langeais Villandry
30
Ussé 32
33 Chinon
Champigny-sur-Veude
Loudun

41 Le Lude
La Flèche
Baugé
Bourgueil

36
37 Saumur
38 Fontevraud
Montreuil-Bellay
Thouars

40 Le Plessis-Bourré
39 Angers
Brissac
Gennes
Doué-la-Fontaine
Bressuire

Laval

TO PARIS
TO NANTES

next two days explore **Cheverny** ⑮, **▦ Chambord** ⑭, **Chaumont-sur-Loire** ⑱, **Amboise** ⑲, and **▦ Chenonceaux** ⑳. On day four detour south to the mighty citadel of **Loches** ㉑, before an overnight stop in **▦ Tours** ㉒–㉗. Take in the reconstituted gardens at **Villandry** ㉘ en route to see the Renaissance pleasure palace of **▦ Azay-le-Rideau** ㉚. The following day head to the château of **Ussé** ㉜ and the castle at **▦ Chinon** ㉝. From Chinon a short excursion south brings you to the chapel in **Champigny-sur-Veude** ㉞ and the unchanged 17th-century town of **Richelieu** ㉟. Continue west on day eight from Chinon to **Fontevraud** ㊱ and **▦ Saumur** ㊲. Spend the next night in **▦ Angers** ㊳, with a detour to the imposing Château de Serrant if you have time. Finish with a leisurely drive east through the other Loir Valley, from the grand and seignorial chateau of **Le Lude** ㊶ to the historic town of **Vendôme** ㊷.

When to Tour the Loire Valley

The Loire, the last great river of Europe left undammed, is at its best in May and June, when it still looks like a river; come midsummer, the water level drops, marooning unsightly sandbanks. The valley divides France in two, both geographically and climatically: north of the Loire, France has the moist, temperate climate of northern Europe; southward lies the drier climate of the Mediterranean. It's striking how often the weather can change as you cross the Loire. The valley can be sultry, stuffy, and crowded in July and August, although most of the son-et-lumière shows take place at this time. October is a good off-season option, when all is mist and mellow fruitfulness along the Loire and the mysterious pools of the Sologne, and the trees are turning russet and gold. The fall is also the best time to sample regional specialties such as wild mushrooms and game. On Sunday try to avoid the main cities—Orléans, Tours, and Angers—because most shops are closed.

THE LOIRE VALLEY

Halfway along the route of the Loire—the longest river in France—and just outside the city of Orléans, the river makes a wide, westward bend, gliding languidly through low, rich country known as the Val de Loire—the Loire Valley. In this temperate region—a 225-km (140-mi) stretch between Orléans and Angers—scores of châteaux built of local *tufa* (white limestone) rise from the rocky banks of the Loire and its tributaries: the rivers Cher, Indre, Vienne, and Loir (with no *e*).

The Loire is liquid history. For centuries the river was the area's principal means of transportation and an important barrier against invading armies. Towns arose at strategic bridgeheads, and fortresses—the earliest châteaux—appeared on towering slopes. The Loire Valley was hotly disputed by France and England during the Middle Ages; it belonged to England (under the Anjou Plantagenet family) between 1154 and 1216 and again during the Hundred Years' War (1337–1453). It was the example of Joan of Arc, the Maid of Orléans (scene of her most stirring victories), that crystallized French efforts to expel the English.

The Loire Valley's golden age came under François I (1515–47), flamboyant contemporary of Henry VIII. His salamander emblem can be seen in many châteaux, including Chambord, the mightiest one. Although the nation's power base shifted to Paris around 1600, aristocrats continued to erect luxurious palaces along the Loire until the end of the 18th century.

Although Orléans is considered the gateway to the Loire—especially if you're coming from Paris—you may want to start exploring this area farther east. Take in the hilltop wine town of Sancerre, the hunting and ceramics center of Gien, and the ancient abbey of St-Benoît. A string of fine châteaux dominates the valley west of Orléans—Blois, Chaumont, and Amboise lead the way—but the area's most stunning monuments lie inland: romantic Chenonceau, with its arches half-straddling the River Cher, and colossal Chambord, its forest of chimneys and turrets visible above the treetops. Tours, the largest and most central of the cities in the Loire Valley, leads to Ussé and Azay-le-Rideau and the more muscular castles of Chinon and Saumur. At Angers you can drive northeast to explore the winding, intimate Loir Valley all the way to Châteaudun, just south of Chartres and the Ile-de-France; or continue along the Loire as far as Nantes, the gateway to Brittany.

Sancerre

❶ *200 km (125 mi) south of Paris via A6 and N7, 120 km (75 mi) southeast of Orléans, 46 km (29 mi) northeast of Bourges.*

The hilltop town of Sancerre is a maze of old cobbled streets offering dramatic views of the mountainous vineyards producing lively white wines and flinty, lesser-known rosés and reds. Forget about the Loire's reputation for soft pastures and gentle hills: The vineyards of Sancerre (like the town itself) stand on rugged, towering mounds and are among the most scenic in France. The main square, Nouvelle Place, was once the site of the grain market; here you'll find the tourist office, which has information about a walking tour of town.

From Sancerre visit **Chavignol,** 3 km (2 mi) away, a wine village with a number of producers that have tastings and vintages for sale. Chavignol is also home to a delicious small, round goat cheese, Crottin de Chavignol, which comes in both hard and soft varieties, depending on the time of year. This famous goat cheese, along with other local cheeses, is celebrated in Sancerre every April during the Fête du Crottin.

Dining and Lodging

$$$–$$$$ ✕⊞ **Château de la Verrerie.** If you dream of *la vie de château,* this is
★   your place. The very picture of fairy-tale elegance, this turreted and towered abode lies by the banks of its own lake, creating a storybook image that would have made any 19th-century painter set up shop here in a minute. Dating from the 15th century, set in the Forêt d'Ivoy 32 km (20 mi) northwest of Sancerre, this was once owned by the royal Stuarts of Scotland, who were granted the nearby town of Aubigny-sur-Nère by King Charles VII in 1423. It has been transformed into an elegant hotel by Comte Béraud de Vogüé, whose ancestors acquired the place in 1842 (another branch of the family owns Vaux-le-Vicomte). Rooms are spacious (six have twin beds, six are doubles) with high ceilings, family heirlooms, and sweeping views of the estate. Breakfast is served in your room or in a flower-decked salon. A half-timber 17th-century cottage on the estate has been transformed into La Maison d'Helene restaurant, an excellent spot for light lunches and sumptuous dinners. Don't forget to visit the château's delightful Renaissance chapel, with frescoes dating from 1525. ⊠ *18700 Oizon,* ☎ *02–48–81–51–60 for château; 02–48–58–24–27 for restaurant,* FAX *02–48–58–21–25. 12 rooms. Restaurant. MC, V. Closed mid-Dec.–mid-Jan.*

Briare

❷ *40 km (25 mi) north of Sancerre via D955 and D951, 39 km (24 mi) northeast of La Verrerie.*

The **Pont-Canal de Briare** is one of France's most famous bridges—in fact, a lamp-lined 700-yard aqueduct, held together by a mind-boggling 7 million bolts, built by Gustave Eiffel in 1890 (the year after his Parisian tower) to transport the Canal Latéral de la Loire (Loire Side

Canal) across the river to join the Canal de Briare. Walk along the top and admire the colorful riverboats along Briare's pretty quay. (If you're interested in waterways, make a detour 10 mi [6 km] north of Briare to admire the abandoned but spectacular seven-tiered 17th-century locks at **Rogny-les-Sept-Écluses.**)

Just downstream on the opposite bank of the Loire from Briare you'll find the 12th-century castle of **St-Brisson,** whose collection of 13th-century mangonels (giant catapults) is activated by local strongmen every Sunday in summer. The biggest catapult, known as a *couillard,* sends rocks that weigh 45 pounds spinning as high as the castle roof before crashing 150 yards away. ☒ ☎ 02–38–36–71–29. ☜ 30 frs. ☉ June–Sept., Sun. 2–6.

Gien

❸ *6 km (4 mi) northwest of St-Brisson; 67 km (42 mi) southeast of Orléans.*

Ceramics and hunting are the twin historical attractions of the pleasant riverside town of Gien. Its redbrick château, completed in 1484, ★ houses the unexpectedly fine **Musée International de la Chasse** (International Hunting Museum). Exhibits trace the various types of hunt—shooting, trapping, fox hunting with hounds—and the display of firearms ranges from harquebuses to rifles. Vast 18th-century hunting pictures by François Desportes and Jean-Baptiste Oudry line the stately hall with its superb beamed roof. ☒ *Pl. du Château,* ☎ *02–38–67–69–69.* ☜ *35 frs.* ☉ *Apr.–Oct., daily 9:30–6:30; Nov.–Mar., daily 9–noon and 2–5.*

At the **Musée de la Faïencerie** (Earthenware Factory Museum), in an old paste store, admire local Gien earthenware (both old and new), with its distinctive deep blue glaze and golden decoration. Call ahead to arrange a tour of the factory; there's also a shop. ☒ *78 pl. de la Victoire,* ☎ *02–38–67–00–05.* ☜ *20 frs.* ☉ *Apr.–Sept., daily 9–11:45 and 2–5:45; Oct.–Mar., daily 2–6.*

Dining and Lodging

$$ ✕☏ **Rivage.** Jolly *patron* Christian Gaillard, unmistakable behind his huge Gallic mustache, presides over the finest hotel in Gien. Rooms are large and airy, breakfasts are copious, and the piano bar, with its terrace overlooking Loire, is the ideal spot to relax before or after a dinner. Fish and herbs are likely to figure in your meal at the restaurant (no lunch Monday, and from November through March, no dinner Sunday), unless you opt for the snails or veal kidneys with fresh pasta. Menus start at 145 francs, and there is an extensive wine cellar. ☒ *1 quai de Nice, 45500,* ☎ *02–38–37–79–00,* FAX *02–38–38–10–21. 16 rooms, 3 suites. Restaurant. AE, DC, MC, V. Closed most of Feb., 2 wks in June.*

Sully-sur-Loire

❹ *24 km (15 mi) northwest of Gien via D951, 48 km (30 mi) southeast of Orléans.*

An imposing castle with a park, moat, and spectacular medieval roof makes Sully-sur-Loire worth visiting. The **Château de Sully** dates from the first half of the 14th century. It has a sturdy keep with the finest chestnut roof anywhere along the Loire—a vast structure in the form of an upturned boat, constructed in 1400. ☎ *02–38–36–36–86.* ☜ *30 frs.* ☉ *June–Aug., daily 10–6; Sept.–May, daily 10–noon and 2–5.*

St-Benoît-sur-Loire

❺ *8 km (5 mi) northwest of Sully-sur-Loire via D60, 40 km (30 mi) south-east of Orléans.*

The highlight of St-Benoît-sur-Loire is its ancient abbey, often called the greatest Romanesque church in France. Village signposts refer to it as LA BASILIQUE.

★ St-Benoît (St. Benedict) was the founder of the Benedictine monastic order. In AD 650 a group of monks chose this safe and fertile spot for their new monastery, then returned to Monte Cassino, Italy, to retrieve the bones of St. Benedict with which to bless the site. Despite demands from priests at Monte Cassino for the return of the bones, some of the relics remain here in the 11th-century **Abbaye St-Benoît.** Following the Hundred Years' War in the 14th and 15th centuries, the monastery fell into a decline, and the Wars of Religion (1562–98) wrought further damage. During the French Revolution the monks dispersed, and all the buildings were destroyed, except the abbey church itself, which became the parish church. Monastic life here began anew in 1944, when the monks rebuilt their monastery and regained the church for their own use. The pillars of the tower porch are noted for their intricately carved capitals, and the choir floor is a gaudy patchwork of multicolor marble. Gregorian chants can be heard daily, at mass or at vespers, and Sunday services attract worshipers and music lovers from all around. You are welcome to explore the church crypt. ☎ 02–38–35–72–43. ☉ *Mass and vespers Sun. 11 AM and 6:15 PM, Mon.–Sat. noon and 6:15 PM. Guided English-language tours of the monastic bldgs. can be arranged; inquire at the monastery shop.*

Germigny-des-Prés

❻ *6 km (4 mi) northwest of St-Benoît-sur-Loire via D60, 34 km (21 mi) southeast of Orléans.*

The village of Germigny-des-Prés is famous for its church, one of the oldest in France. Around AD 800, Theodulf, an abbot of St-Benoît, built the tiny **Église de Germigny-des-Prés**—a Byzantine arrangement of round arches on square pillars, with indirect light filtering from smaller arches above the central square. The church was carefully restored to its original condition during the last century. Though Theodulf himself brought most of the original mosaics from Italy, only one—covered by plaster and not discovered until 1848—survives. Made of 130,000 cubes of colored glass, it shows the Ark of the Covenant transported by angels with golden halos. The Latin inscription asks us not to forget Theodulf in our prayers. ☉ *Daily 9–noon and 2–5.*

Châteauneuf-sur-Loire

❼ *5 km (3 mi) northwest of Germigny-des-Prés.*

The village of Châteauneuf-sur-Loire has a delightful public park with giant tulip trees, magnolias, weeping willows, and rhododendrons and is especially beautiful in late May and early June. Little streams on their way to the Loire snake their way across the parkland, past benches, shady copses, and scenic picnic spots.

The Loire was a working river until the railroad arrived 130 years ago, with boats transporting everything from wheat, salt, wine, and stone to slate, wood, coal, and pottery. The **Musée de la Marine** (Maritime Museum), housed since 1998 in the former château stables, chronicles that halcyon era with documents, old photos and a reconstituted 19th-century fishing boat equipped with ropes, nets, chests, eel pots and harpoons. ⊠ *1 pl. Aristide-Briand,* ☎ *02–38–46–84–46.* 🎫 *20 frs.* ☉ *Apr.–Oct., Wed.–Mon. 10–6; Nov.–Mar., Wed.–Mon. 2–6.*

Orléans

125 km (78 mi) south of Paris; 112 km (70 mi) northeast of Tours.

Once hallowed by Joan of Arc, Orléans is a thriving commercial city; sensitive urban renewal has done much to bring it back to life, especially the medieval streets between the Loire and the cathedral. The city has quite a history; as a natural bridgehead over the Loire, it has long been the focus of hostile confrontations and invasions. In 52 BC Julius Caesar slaughtered its inhabitants and burned it to the ground. Five centuries later Attila and the Huns did much the same. Next came the Normans; then the Valois kings turned it into a secondary capital. The story of the Hundred Years' War, Joan of Arc, and the Siege of Orléans is widely known. In 1429 France had reached the nadir of its long and varied history. The English and their Burgundian allies were carving up the kingdom. Besieged by the English, Orléans was one of the last towns about to yield, when a young peasant girl, Joan of Arc, arrived to rally the troops and save the kingdom. During the Wars of Religion (1562–98), much of the cathedral was destroyed. A century ago ham-fisted town planners razed many of the city's fine old buildings. Both German and Allied bombs helped finish the job during World War II.

❽ The **Cathédrale Ste-Croix** is a riot of pinnacles and gargoyles, both Gothic and pseudo-Gothic, embellished with 18th-century wedding-cake towers. After most of the cathedral was destroyed in the 16th century during the Wars of Religion, Henry IV and his successors rebuilt it. Novelist Marcel Proust (1871–1922) called it France's ugliest church, but most find it impressive. Inside are vast quantities of stained glass and 18th-century wood carvings, plus the modern **Chapelle de Jeanne d'Arc** (Joan of Arc Chapel), with plaques in memory of the British and American war dead. ⊠ *Pl. Ste-Croix.* ☉ *Daily 9–noon and 2–6.*

❾ The modern **Musée des Beaux-Arts** (Fine Arts Museum) is across from the cathedral. Take the elevator to the top of the five-story building; then make your way down to see works by such artists as Tintoretto, Velázquez, Watteau, Boucher, Rodin, and Gauguin. The museum's richest collection is its 17th-century French paintings. ⊠ *1 rue Ferdinand-Rabier,* ☎ *02–38–79–21–55.* 🎫 *20 frs.* ☉ *Tues.–Sun. 11–6.*

❿ The **Musée Historique** (History Museum) is housed in the **Hôtel Cabu,** a Renaissance mansion restored after World War II. It contains both "fine" and "popular" works of art connected with the town's past, including a remarkable collection of pagan bronzes of animals and dancers. These bronzes were hidden from zealous Christian missionaries in the 4th century and discovered in a sandpit near St-Benoît in 1861. ⊠ *Pl. de l'Abbé-Desnoyers,* ☎ *02–38–79–25–60.* 🎫 *15 frs.* ☉ *July–Aug., Tues.–Sun. 10–6; Sept.–June, Wed. and weekends 2–6.*

⓫ During the 10-day Siege of Orléans in 1429, 17-year-old Joan of Arc stayed on the site of the **Maison de Jeanne d'Arc** (Joan of Arc's House). This faithful reconstruction of the house she knew contains exhibits about her life and costumes and weapons of her time. Several dioramas modeled by Lucien Harmey recount the main episodes in her life: from the audience at Chinon to the coronation at Reims, her seizure at Compiègne, and the stake at Rouen. ⊠ *3 pl. du Général-de-Gaulle,* ☎ *02–38–52–99–89.* 🎫 *13 frs.* ☉ *May–Oct., Tues.–Sun. 10–noon and 2–6; Nov.–Apr., Tues.–Sun. 2–6.*

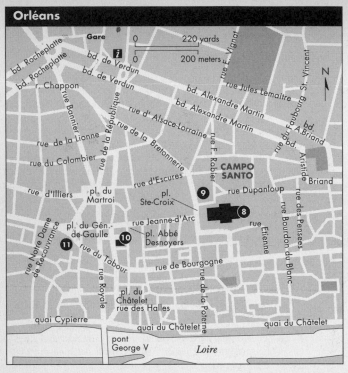

Dining and Lodging

$$$ ✕ **Les Antiquaires.** The understated elegance of this cozy, wood-beamed restaurant close to the river, with its red walls, cane-backed chairs, and brass chandeliers, is a telling contrast to Philippe Bardau's penchant for colorfully presented dishes with a Mediterranean flavor: mullet with eggplant, for instance, or sea bass with artichokes and fennel. ⊠ *2 rue au Lin,* ☎ *02–38–53–52–35. AE, MC, V. Closed early Jan. No dinner Sun.*

$$ ✕⊡ **Rivage.** This small, white-walled hotel south of Orléans makes a pleasant base. Each of the compact rooms has a little balcony with a view of the tree-lined Loiret River; the bathrooms are tiny. There is no elevator. The dining room (no lunch Saturday; no dinner Sunday November through March) opens onto a terrace facing the river. The menu changes with the season—if you're lucky, chef François Tassain's memorable crayfish, lamb marinated in paprika, and glazed green-apple soufflé with apple marmalade will be on it. ⊠ *635 rue de la Reine-Blanche, 45160 Olivet (5 km [3 mi] south of Orléans),* ☎ *02–38–66–02–93,* FAX *02–38–56–31–11. 17 rooms, 11 with shower, 6 with bath. Restaurant, tennis court. AE, DC, MC, V. Closed late Dec.–mid-Jan.*

Nightlife and the Arts

The two-day **Fête de Jeanne d'Arc** (Joan of Arc Festival), on May 7 and 8, celebrates the heroic Maid of Orléans with a military parade and religious procession.

Meung-sur-Loire

⑫ *16 km (10 mi) southwest of Orléans via N152.*

Intimate Meung-sur-Loire is not as commercial as Amboise or Azay-le-Rideau. The town's most famous citizen was Jehan de Meung, born in 1260 and author of the best-selling *Roman de la Rose* (Geoffrey

Chaucer produced the English translation). Give yourself time to wander down rue Jehan-de-Meung, the street leading off the main square away from the château, to see the half-timber houses.

The **Château de Meung** is part 12th-century fortress, part 18th-century residence. From the 12th century to the French Revolution, it served mainly as the official residence of the bishops of Orléans, although in 1429 Lord Salisbury used it as his headquarters during the Siege of Orléans. (When he was killed in the fray, Lord Talbot took over but could not prevent Joan of Arc from capturing the château.) It was sold after the French Revolution and had stood empty and derelict for years before private restoration began in the early 1970s. It has since been furnished with a diverse collection of items that range from 12th-century antiques to medieval crossbows, World War II submachine guns, and military helmets from the Middle Ages to 1945. The most unexpected part of the hour-long tour is the underground network of tunnels, dungeons, and storehouses, with a chapel and torture chamber. ⊠ *16 pl. du Martroi,* ☎ *02–38–44–36–47.* ⌨ *35 frs.* ☉ *Apr.–Oct., daily 9:30– 5; Nov.–Mar., daily 10:30–noon and 2:30–4:30; guided visits only.*

Dining and Lodging

$–$$ ✕▤ **St-Jacques.** This inn, on Meung's busy main road, is just a five-minute walk from the château and the river. At the family-run restaurant (closed Monday), excellent fresh food is served without fuss at deliciously low prices. The prix-fixe menus might include oysters, fillet of duck in a raspberry vinaigrette, lamb or fish, cheese, and dessert. The clean, simple rooms either have a shower or, for 20 francs more, a full bath. ⊠ *60 rue du Général-de-Gaulle, 45130,* ☎ *02–38–44–30– 39,* ℻ *02–38–45–17–02. 12 rooms. Restaurant. AE, MC, V. Closed last 2 wks in Jan.*

Beaugency

⑬ *7 km (4 mi) southwest of Meung.*

A clutch of historic towers and buildings around a 14th-century bridge over the Loire lend Beaugency its charm. The buildings include the massive 11th-century **donjon** (keep), the Romanesque church of **Notre-Dame**, and the **Tour du Diable** (Devil's Tower), overlooking the river. The **Château Dunois** contains a regional museum with traditional costumes and peasant furniture. ⊠ *2 pl. Dunois,* ☎ *02–38–44–55–23.* ⌨ *22 frs.* ☉ *Apr.–Oct., Wed.–Mon. 10–noon and 2–5.*

Chambord

★ ⑭ *24 km (15 mi) southwest of Beaugency via D925, D951, and D112; 19 km (12 mi) east of Blois; 45 km (28 mi) southwest of Orléans; 175 km (109 mi) southwest of Paris.*

☾ The largest of the Loire châteaux, the **Château de Chambord** is the kind of place William Randolph Hearst might have built if he'd had more money. Variously dubbed "megalomaniac" and "an enormous film-set extravaganza," this is one of the most extraordinary structures in Europe. It is set in the middle of a royal game forest, with a cluster of buildings—barely a village—across the road.

A few facts about the château set the tone: The facade is 420 ft long, there are 440 rooms and 365 chimneys, and a wall 32 km (20 mi) long encloses the 13,000-acre forest (you can wander through 3,000 acres of it; the rest is reserved for wild boar and other game). Under François I, building began in 1519, a job that took 12 years and required 1,800 workers. His original grandiose idea was to divert the Loire to form a moat, but someone (perhaps his adviser, Leonardo da Vinci) persuaded him to make do with the River Cosson. François I used the château only for short stays; yet when he came, 12,000 horses were required to transport his luggage, servants, and entourage! Later kings also used Chambord as an occasional retreat, and Louis XIV, the Sun King, had Molière perform here. In the 18th century Louis XV gave the château to Maréchal de Saxe as a reward for his victory over the English and Dutch at Fontenoy (southern Belgium) in 1745. When not indulging himself with wine, women, and song, the marshal stood on the roof to oversee the exercises of his own regiment of 1,000 cavalry. Now, after long neglect—all the original furnishings vanished during the French Revolution—Chambord belongs to the state.

You can wander freely through the vast rooms, filled with a variety of exhibits (including a hunting museum)—not all concerned with Chambord, but interesting nonetheless. The enormous double-helix staircase looks like a single staircase, but an entire regiment could march up one spiral while a second came down the other, and they would never meet. Also be sure to visit the roof terrace, whose forest of towers, turrets, cupolas, gables, and chimneys was described by 19th-century novelist Henry James as "more like the spires of a city than the salient points of a single building." The château is sumptuously illuminated at night, and a short son-et-lumière show in French, English, and German, successively, is held on many evenings from mid-May to mid-October; admission is 50 francs. ☎ 02–54–50–40–28. ⊟ 40 frs. ☉ Apr.–Aug., daily 9–6:15; Sept.–Mar., daily 9–5:15.

Dining and Lodging

$$ ✕⊞ **Grand St-Michel.** Enjoy simple and comfortable quarters in this re-
★ vamped country house at the edge of the woods, across from the château. A few rooms have spectacular views, the restaurant serves hearty local fare (including game in the fall), and there's a pleasant café-terrace—just the place for contemplation while sipping a drink. ⊠ 103 pl. St-Michel, 41250, ☎ 02–54–20–31–31, ℻ 02–54–20–36–40. 39 rooms, 31 with bath. Restaurant, tennis court. MC, V. Closed mid-Nov.–mid-Dec.

Outdoor Activities and Sports

Rent a horse from the former stables of the **Maréchal de Saxe** (⊠ On grounds of Château de Chambord, ☎ 02–54–20–31–01) and ride through the vast national park surrounding the château. From March through October you can hire a boat to explore the château moat and the **Grand Canal** linking it to the River Cosson (☎ 02–54–56–00–43 for details).

Cheverny

⑮   *17 km (11 mi) south of Chambord via D112 and D102, 13 km (8 mi) southeast of Blois via D765.*

Cheverny has become synonymous with its restrained, classical château, although the village is officially named Cour-Cheverny.

One of the last in the area to be built, the **Château de Cheverny** was finished in 1634. Its white, elegantly proportioned classical facade greets you across manicured lawns. The interior—with its painted and gilded rooms, splendid furniture, and rich tapestries depicting the *Labors of Hercules*—is one of the grandest in the Loire region. In the gallery there's a bronze of George Washington alongside a document that bears his signature.

Unfortunately, the gardens are off-limits, as is the orangery, where the *Mona Lisa* and other masterpieces were hidden during World War II.

But you are free to contemplate the antlers of 2,000 stags in the Trophy Room. Hunting, called "venery" in the leaflets, continues vigorously here, with red coats, bugles, and all. In the château's kennels, hordes of hungry hounds lounge about, dreaming of their next kill. Feeding times—*la soupe aux chiens*—are posted on a notice board, and you are welcome to watch the dogs wolf down their dinner. You can visit the château grounds by either boat or electric buggy, or get a bird's-eye view from 500 ft up in a hot-air balloon; purchase tickets on the spot. ☎ 02–54–79–96–29. ☎ 35 frs. ☉ Mar.–Sept., daily 9–6:30; Oct.–Feb., daily 9:30–noon and 2:15–5.

Dining and Lodging

$$$ ✕ **Le Relais.** Chef Bernard Robin produces fine nouvelle cuisine in his
★ gleaming kitchens, but connoisseurs savor his simpler dishes: carp, game in season, and salmon with beef marrow. The attentive staff brings delicious tidbits to keep you busy between courses. ⊠ *1 av. de Chambord, Bracieux (9 km [6 mi] northeast of Cour-Cheverny on road to Chambord),* ☎ 02–54–46–41–22, FAX 02–54–46–03–69. *Reservations essential. Jacket and tie. AE, DC, MC, V. Closed Jan. and Wed., Sept.–June. No dinner Tues.*

$$ ✕🏠 **Château de Bois Minhy.** You can expect a warm welcome from Ingeborg Tartière and her husband, Jean-Pierre, at this inn south of Cheverny. With its turrets and steep-tiled roof, their 19th-century neo-Renaissance château, on 15 acres of wooded parkland, has a fortresslike air. The old-fashioned rooms have floral-pattern wallpaper, sturdy wooden furniture, and brass bedsteads and chandeliers. You can have dinner with the Tartières if you book ahead (the suite has its own kitchen). ⊠ *41700 Chémery (18 km [11 mi] south of Cheverny),* ☎ 02–54–79–51–01, FAX 02–54–79–06–26. *3 rooms, 1 suite. Pool. MC, V.*

Romorantin-Lanthenay

16 *41 km (25 mi) southeast of Blois, 67 km (42 mi) south of Orléans, 73 km (46 mi) northwest of Bourges.*

Silence rules in the flat, wooded Sologne region, famed for its game, mushrooms, asparagus, and hidden lakes. Pretty Romorantin-Lanthenay is the area's main town, whose heyday harks back to the early 16th century and the turbulent youth of François I. Some of the great Renaissance houses, including the Hôtel St-Pol where François had his head shaved by doctors after being hit by a burning log, are on rue du Milieu and rue de la Résistance.

Dining and Lodging

$$$–$$$$ ✕🏠 **Grand Hôtel du Lion d'Or.** The Barrat family has owned this exceptionally comfortable mansion for four decades. Pale greens, blues, pinks, old stones, and warm wood dominate. Guest rooms have large beds, couches, and marble bathrooms; choose one overlooking the delightful courtyard (where lunch and aperitifs are served in summer), perhaps No. 7. Chef Didier is famous for his prawns with the unusual medieval spice called paradise seed. Other dishes are more modern, such as the delicate duck with exotic herbs. ⊠ *69 rue Georges-Clemenceau, 41200,* ☎ 02–54–94–15–15, FAX 02–54–88–24–87. *16 rooms. Restaurant. AE, DC, MC, V. Closed mid-Feb.–mid-Mar.*

Blois

★ **17** *13 km (8 mi) northwest of Cour-Cheverny via D765, 54 km (34 mi) southwest of Orléans, 58 km (36 mi) northeast of Tours.*

Perched on a steep hillside overlooking the Loire, bustling Blois is a convenient base, well served by train and highway. A signposted route leads you on a walking tour of the Vieille Ville (Old Town)—maps are available from the tourist office. The best view of the town, with its château and numerous church spires rising sharply above the river, can be had from across the Loire.

The massive **Château de Blois** spans several architectural periods and is among the valley's finest. Your ticket entitles you to a guided tour—in English when there are enough visitors who don't understand French—but you are more than welcome to roam around without a guide if you visit between mid-March and August. Before you enter, stand in the courtyard to admire four centuries of architecture. On one side stand the 13th-century hall and tower, the latter offering a stunning view of the town and countryside. The Renaissance begins to flower in the Louis XII wing (built between 1498 and 1503), through which you enter, and comes to full bloom in the François I wing (1515–24). The masterpiece here is the openwork spiral staircase, painstakingly restored. The fourth side consists of the classical Gaston d'Orléans wing (1635–38).

At the bottom of the spiral staircase is an audiovisual display that traces the château's history. Upstairs is a series of enormous rooms with tremendous fireplaces decorated with the gilded porcupine, emblem of Louis XII; the ermine of Anne of Brittany; and, of course, François I's salamander, breathing fire and surrounded by flickering flames. Many rooms have intricate ceilings and carved, gilded paneling; there is even a sad little picture of Mary, Queen of Scots. In the council room the duke of Guise was murdered on the orders of Henri III in 1588. In the **Musée des Beaux-Arts** (Fine Arts Museum), in the Louis XII wing, you'll find royal portraits, including Rubens's puffy portrayal of Maria de' Medici as France personified. Most evenings from April through September, **son-et-lumière** shows in French and English are staged. Call the château or the tourist office (☞ The Loire Valley A to Z, *below*) for details; admission is 50 francs. ☎ *02–54–90–33–33.* ▨ *35 frs.* ☼ *Apr.–Aug., daily 9–6; Sept.–Mar., daily 9–12:30 and 2–5:30.*

Dining and Lodging

$$–$$$ ✕ **Espérance.** In a bucolic setting overlooking the Loire, chef Raphaël Guillot serves up inventive cuisine, like fried mangoes with lavender and five different kinds of scallop dishes. ▨ *189 quai Ulysse-Besnard,* ☎ *02–54–78–09–01. AE, MC, V.*

$$ ✕ **Au Rendez-Vous des Pêcheurs.** This modest restaurant near the
★ Loire has simple decor but offers excellent value for its creative cooking. Chef Eric Reithler studied under Guy Savoy in Paris and has brought inventiveness to his fish and seafood specialties. ▨ *27 rue de Foix,* ☎ *02–54–74–67–48. Reservations advised. MC, V. Closed Sun. and Aug. No lunch Mon.*

$$ ✕▥ **Médicis.** Rooms at this smart little hotel not far from the château are comfortable, air-conditioned, and soundproof; all share a joyous color scheme but are individually decorated. If you wish to splurge, the suite has a whirlpool. The restaurant alone makes a stay here worthwhile. Chef-owner Christian Garanger turns his innovative classical dishes into a presentation—*coquilles St-Jacques* (scallops) with a pear fondue and thin slices of roast hare with a black-currant sauce. The staff is cheerful (the restaurant doesn't serve dinner Sunday off-season). ▨ *2 allée François-Ier, 41000,* ☎ *02–54–43–94–04,* ☏ *02–54–42–04–05. 12 rooms. Restaurant, air-conditioning. AE, DC, MC, V. Closed Jan.*

$$ ▥ **Anne de Bretagne.** Although this simple pension—on a small square across from the cathedral—is nothing to rave about, the rooms, up rather steep stairs, are clean and neat, with bright bedspreads and curtains. There's space to keep your car on the street, which is a plus, and a small bar next door, a congenial spot for a nightcap. ⊠ *31 av. du Dr- Jean-Laigret, 41000,* ☎ *02–54–78–05–38,* 🖷 *02–54–74–37–79. 29 rooms, 24 with bath. AE, DC, MC, V. Closed Jan. and 1st half of Mar.*

Chaumont-sur-Loire

⑱ *21 km (13 mi) southwest of Blois via D751.*

Chaumont is best known for its sturdy castle with its famous stables and magnificent panorama of the Loire. Built between 1465 and 1510, the **Château de Chaumont** was given to Henri II's mistress, Diane de Poitiers, by his wife, Catherine de' Medici, to get her out of the Château de Chenonceau. Benjamin Franklin was a regular visitor here. The interior has been extensively restored but still has less cachet than the majestic stables, where purebreds lived like royalty. ☎ *02–54–51–26–26.* 🖾 *32 frs.* ☉ *Mid-Mar.–Oct., daily 9:30–6.*

Dining and Lodging

$$$$
★
✕🖻 **Domaine des Hauts-de-Loire.** Across the river from Chaumont is this exquisite hotel in an 18th-century turreted, vine-covered hunting lodge on 180 acres. Rooms in the main house are furnished with antiques, creating an aristocratic air; those in the adjacent carriage houses have a mix of old and modern furnishings that harmonize with the exposed brick walls and gabled ceilings. Service is relaxed and unpretentious; the restaurant (closed Monday and no lunch Tuesday off-season) is first class. ⊠ *Rte. de Mesland, 41150 Onzain (across the Loire from Chaumont),* ☎ *02–54–20–72–57,* 🖷 *02–54–20–77–32. 25 rooms, 10 suites. Restaurant, pool, tennis court, fishing, helipad. AE, DC, MC, V. Closed Dec.–Feb.*

$
🖻 **Ferme de la Quantinière.** This ivy-covered farmhouse southwest of Chaumont was built in 1855. You can enjoy an excellent dinner with English-speaking hosts Annie and Daniel Doyer in their wood-beamed, tile-floored dining room, complete with monumental fireplace. Then repair to one of the comfortable rooms, modernized in 1999, and enjoy the view over the spacious garden. ⊠ *La Quantinière, 41400 Vallières-les-Grandes (8 km [5 mi] southwest of Chaumont),* ☎ 🖷 *02–54–20–99–53. 5 rooms. No credit cards.*

Amboise

★ ⑲ *17 km (11 mi) southwest of Chaumont-sur-Loire via D751, 26 km (16 mi) east of Tours.*

Artifacts from the life of Leonardo da Vinci, a château overlooking the Loire, bustling markets, narrow medieval streets, and plenty of hotels and restaurants make Amboise a superb base.

The **Château d'Amboise** stands on a flattened hill that was originally a Stone Age settlement, fortified in the Iron Age by a ditch and a rampart. An early bridge gave the stronghold strategic importance. In AD 503, Clovis, king of the Franks, met with Alaric, king of the Visigoths, at Amboise. But the 15th and 16th centuries were Amboise's golden age, when the château, enlarged and embellished, became a royal palace. Charles VII stayed here, as did the unfortunate Charles VIII, best remembered for banging his head on a low doorway (you will be shown it) and dying as a result. François I, whose long nose appears in so many château paintings, based his court here. In 1560 his son, François II, settled here with his wife, Mary Stuart (otherwise known as Mary, Queen of Scots), and his mother, Catherine de' Medici. The castle was also the setting for the Amboise Conspiracy, an ill-fated Protestant plot organized against François II; you are shown where the corpses of 1,200 conspirators dangled from the castle walls. Decline and demolition occurred before and after the Revolution; today only about a third of the original building remains.

The château's interior is partly furnished, though not with the original objects; these vanished when the building was converted into a barracks and then a button factory. The great round tower has a spiral ramp rather than a staircase; designed for horsemen, it is wide enough to accommodate a small car. You are free to explore the grounds at your own pace, including the little chapel of St-Hubert with its carvings of the Virgin and Child, Charles VIII, and Anne of Brittany. **Son-et-lumière** pageants take place at the château daily in July and August. ☎ 02–47–57–00–98. ⊡ 39 frs; son-et-lumière 40 frs–90 frs. ⊙ Oct.–Mar., daily 9–noon and 2–5:30; Apr.–June and Sept., daily 9–noon and 2–6:30; July–Aug., daily 9–6:30.

The **Clos Lucé,** a few hundred yards up rue Victor-Hugo from the château, is a handsome Renaissance manor where Leonardo da Vinci spent the last four years of his life and died in 1519. The basement contains working models built by IBM engineers (using the detailed sketches in his notebooks) of some of Leonardo's extraordinary inventions. Mechanisms on display include three-speed gearboxes, a military tank, a clockwork car, and even a flying machine complete with designs for parachutes. ⊠ 2 rue du Clos-Lucé, ☎ 02–47–57–62–88. ⊡ 39 frs. ⊙ Sept.–June, daily 9–6; July–Aug., daily 9–7.

Dining and Lodging

$$$ ✕ **Manoir St-Thomas.** Between the château and the Clos Lucé, this restaurant occupies a fine Renaissance building with a statue-lined garden. Chef François Le Coz serves elegant, regional dishes such as eels in wine and *suprême de pintade farci* (stuffed guinea-fowl breast). The list of Touraine wines is enticing. ⊠ 1 mail St-Thomas, ☎ 02–47–57–22–52. *Jacket and tie.* AE, DC, MC, V. Closed Mon. and mid-Jan.–mid-Mar. No lunch Tues., no dinner Sun. out of season.

$$$ ✕▥ **Choiseul.** Classical elegance and a formal pink-and-gold restaurant characterize this Relais & Châteaux hotel on the bank of the Loire, just below the château. Though rooms are modern, they retain an old and distinctive feel. The highly rated young chef, Pascal Bouvier, cooks up such specialties as lobster in pastry and beef with truffles. Prix-fixe menus start at 190 francs at lunch and 290 francs at dinner. ⊠ 36 quai Charles-Guinot, 37400, ☎ 02–47–30–45–45, ⒻⒶⓍ 02–47–30–46–10. 29 rooms, 3 suites. Restaurant, pool. AE, DC, MC, V. Closed Dec.–mid-Jan.

$ ✕▥ **Le Blason.** Behind the château and a five-minute walk from the
★ town center, this delightful, small hotel is enlivened by its enthusiastic owners. The old building has rooms of different shapes and sizes: No. 229, for example, has exposed beams and a cathedral ceiling; No. 109 is comfortably spacious and has a good view of the square. In the restaurant, superior, reasonably priced seasonal fare is served—roast lamb with garlic and salmon carpaccio with mustard dressing, for instance. ⊠ 11 pl. Richelieu, 37400, ☎ 02–47–23–22–41, ⒻⒶⓍ 02–47–57–56–18. 28 rooms. Restaurant. AE, DC, MC, V. Closed Jan.

$$ ✕▥ **Auberge Forestière de Marcheroux.** This small, friendly inn is in the forest just south of Amboise, on the road to Chenonceaux. The modernized rooms have comfortable beds and large showers. Good, fresh food (foie gras and wild duck are specialties) and excellent wines are served in the restaurant. ⊠ Rte. de Chenonceaux, 37400, ☎ 02–47–57–27–57, ⒻⒶⓍ 02–47–57–32–50. 9 rooms. Restaurant, pool. MC, V. Closed Jan.

En Route Just 3 km (2 mi) south of Amboise on the road to Chenonceaux, pause
★ at the **Pagode de Chanteloup,** an extraordinary 140-ft, seven-story Chinese-style pagoda built for the duke of Choiseul in 1778.

Chenonceaux

20 *12 km (8 mi) south of Amboise via D81 and D40; 32 km (20 mi) east of Tours.*

★ The small village of Chenonceaux, on the River Cher, is best known as the site of the **Château de Chenonceau** (without the *x*). From historical figures like Diane de Poitiers, Catherine de' Medici, and Mary, Queen of Scots, to a host of modern travel writers, many have called it the "most romantic" of all the Loire châteaux. Its site, straddling the river, is the prettiest and most unusual in France. You could happily spend half a day wandering through the château and grounds. During the peak summer season the château is open—unlike many others—all day. The only drawback is its popularity: If you want to avoid a roomful of schoolchildren, take a stroll on the grounds and come back at lunchtime.

More pleasure palace than fortress, the château was built in 1520 by Thomas Bohier, a wealthy tax collector. When he went bankrupt, it passed to François I. Later, Henri II gave it to his mistress, Diane de Poitiers. After his death, Henri's not-so-understanding widow, Catherine de' Medici, expelled Diane to nearby Chaumont and took back the château. It is to Catherine that we owe the lovely gardens and the handsome three-story extension whose arches span the River Cher.

Before you go inside, pick up an English-language leaflet at the gate. Then walk around to the right of the main building to see the harmonious, delicate architecture beyond the formal garden, with the river gliding under the arches. You may want to rent a rowboat and spend an hour just drifting. Inside the château are splendid ceilings, colossal fireplaces, authentic furnishings, and paintings by Rubens, del Sarto, and Correggio. As you tour the rooms, be sure to pay your respects to former owner Madame Dupin, tellingly captured in Nattier's charming portrait: Thanks to the great affection she inspired among her proletarian neighbors, the château and its treasures survived the Revolution intact. The château's history is illustrated with wax figures in the **Musée des Cires** (Waxwork Museum), in one of the château's outbuildings. Every night from mid-June to mid-September, an excellent **son-et-lumière** is performed in the illuminated château gardens. ☎ *02–47–23–90–07.* 🎫 *Château 50 frs; Waxwork Museum 15 frs; son-et-lumière 40 frs.* ☉ *Feb.–May and Oct.–mid-Nov., daily 9–5:30; June–Sept., daily 9–7.*

OFF THE BEATEN PATH

VALENÇAY – Although 49 km (31 mi) southeast of Chenonceaux, Valençay may entice you with its lusciously furnished château (with excellent audiovisual presentation), collection of vintage cars, son-et-lumière shows, and eccentric outdoor appeal: The grounds include statues, manicured hedges, peacocks, llamas, and intrepid kangaroos. ☎ *02–54–00–15–69.* 🎫 *48 frs.* ☉ *Mid-Mar.–mid-Nov., daily 9–noon and 2–dusk or 2–8; mid-Nov.–mid-Mar., weekends 2–5.*

Dining and Lodging

$$–$$$ ✕🏨 **Bon Laboureur & Château.** In 1882 this ivy-covered inn won Henry James's praise as a simple, rustic place. Since then, through four generations of the Jeudi family, it has become an elegantly modern hotel. Rooms in the old house are comfortably traditional; those in the former stables are larger and more contemporary; the biggest and most elegant are in the manor house across the street. For romantics, there's a small separate house. A large garden supplies vegetables and herbs for the kitchen. The food is commendable—try the excellent turbot with hollandaise or the braised rabbit with dried fruits. Make your dinner reservations early for a table in the original dining room rather than in the annex. ⊠ *6 rue du Dr-Bretonneau, 37150,* ☎ *02–47–23–90–02,* FAX *02–47–23–82–01. 22 rooms, 5 suites. Restaurant, pool, bicycles. AE, DC, MC, V. Closed mid-Nov.–mid-Dec.

$$ ✕ 🏨 **Roseraie.** What the Roseraie may lack in style, compared to its
★ illustrious neighbor the Bon Laboureur, it makes up for with the joyful welcome of its English-speaking hosts, Laurent and Sophie Fiorito. Rooms are simple but spacious and quiet—especially those overlooking the garden—and copious meals are served in the rustic dining-room. ⊠ *7 rue du Dr-Bretonneau, 37150,* ☎ *02–47–23–90–09,* FAX *02–47–23–91–59. 15 rooms. Restaurant, pool. AE, DC, MC, V. Closed Dec.–Jan.*

Loches

㉑ 27 km (17 mi) south of Chenonceaux via D40, D80, and D31; 49 km (31 mi) west of Valençay; 39 km (24 mi) southeast of Tours.

On a rocky spur just beside the River Indre is small, picturesque, medieval Loches. The town is dominated by the **Citadelle.** Unlike Chinon's, which is a ruined shell, much of Loches's defensive walls are well preserved and function as part of the town. At one end is the castle, whose terrace provides a fine view of the roofs and river below and the towers and swallows' nests above; on the other end is the keep.

Inside the **Logis Royaux** (château), on the north end of the citadel, look for the vicious two-man crossbow that could pierce an oak door at 200 yards. There are some interesting pictures, too, including a copy of the well-known portrait showing a disgruntled Charles VII with one of his mistresses, Agnès Sorel, poised as a virtuous Virgin Mary (though semi-topless). Her alabaster image decorates her tomb, guarded by angels and lambs. Agnès died in 1450 at age 28, probably poisoned by Charles's son, the future Louis XI. The little chapel was built by Charles VIII for his queen, Anne of Brittany, and is lavishly decorated with sculpted ermine tails, the lady's emblem. In the donjon (keep), on the south side of the citadel, one 11th-century tower, half-ruined and roofless, is open for exploration; the others require guided supervision. These towers contain dungeons and will delight anyone who revels in prison cells and torture chambers. The citadel church of **St-Ours** has a striking roof formed of octagonal pyramids, which dates from the 12th century; a doorway sculpted with owls, monkeys, and mythical beasts; and a baptismal font converted from a Roman altar. ⊠ *Pl. Charles-VII,* ☎ *02–47–59–01–32.* 🎫 *32 frs.* ◷ *Jan.–mid-Mar. and Sept.–Nov., daily 9:30–noon and 2–5; mid-Mar.–June, daily 9–noon and 2–6; July–Aug., daily 9–6.*

Tours

39 km (24 mi) northwest of Loches via N143; 112 km (70 mi) southwest of Orléans; 240 km (150 mi) southwest of Paris.

Little remains of Tours's château—one of France's finest cathedrals more than compensates—but the city makes an ideal center from which to tour the Loire Valley's attractions by public transportation. Trains from Tours run along the river in both directions, and regular bus services radiate from here; in addition, the city is the starting point for a variety of organized bus excursions (many with English-speaking guides). The formerly small town has mushroomed into a city of a quarter of a million inhabitants, with an ugly modern sprawl of factories, high-rise blocks, and overhead expressway junctions cluttering up the outskirts. But the timber-frame houses in Le Vieux Tours (Old Tours), the attractive medieval center around place Plumereau, were smartly restored after extensive damage in World War II. Tours is easy to get around by public bus. If you have a car, you may prefer to base yourself in any of a dozen smaller towns within a half-hour drive.

22 The **Musée des Beaux-Arts** (Fine Arts Museum), in what was once the archbishop's palace, has an eclectic selection of treasures: furniture, sculpture, wrought-iron work, and pieces by Rubens, Rembrandt, Boucher, Degas, and Calder—and even Fritz the Elephant, stuffed in 1902. ⊠ *18 pl. François-Sicard,* ☎ *02–47–05–68–73.* ▦ *30 frs.* ☉ *Wed.– Mon. 9–12:45 and 2–6.*

★ **23** The **Cathédrale St-Gatien,** built between 1239 and 1484, reveals a mixture of architectural styles. The richly sculpted stonework of its majestic, soaring, two-tower facade betrays the Renaissance influence among local château-trained craftsmen. The stained glass dates from the 13th century (if you have binoculars, bring them). Also take a look at the little tomb with kneeling angels built in memory of Charles VIII and Anne of Brittany's two children. ⊠ *Rue Lavoisier.* ☉ *Daily 8–noon and 2–6.*

24 Alongside the château ruins you will find the **Historial de Touraine** (Regional History Museum)—a group of more than 150 waxwork models that represent historic figures like St. Martin and Joan of Arc, whose deeds helped shape this region for more than 15 centuries. There's also a small aquarium (open daily 2–6) next door. ⊠ *Quai d'Orléans,* ☎ *02–47–61–02–95.* ▦ *Wax museum 35 frs, aquarium 30 frs.* ☉ *Mid-Mar.–June and Sept.–Oct., daily 9–noon and 2–6; Nov.–mid-Mar., daily 2–5:30; July–Aug., daily 9–6:30.*

25 The **Musée du Compagnonnage** (Guild Museum) and the **Musée du Vin** (Wine Museum) are both in the cloisters of the 13th-century church of St-Julien. *Compagnonnage* is a sort of apprenticeship–cum–trade union system, and here you see the masterpieces of the candidates for guild membership: virtuoso craft work, some of it eccentric (an Eiffel Tower made of slate, for instance, or a varnished noodle château). These stand as evidence of the devotion to craftsmanship that is still an important feature of French life. ⊠ *8 rue Nationale,* ☎ *02–47–61–07– 93.* ▦ *Musée du Compagnonnage 25 frs, Musée du Vin 15 frs.* ☉ *Wed.– Mon. 9–noon and 2–6.*

26 The **Musée du Gemmail,** in the imposing 19th-century Hôtel Raimbault, contains an unusual collection of three-dimensional colored-glass window panels. Depicting patterns, figures, and even portraits, the panels are both beautiful and intriguing, since most of the gemlike fragments of glass come from broken bottles. Incidentally, Jean Cocteau coined the word *gemmail* by combining *gemme* (gem) with *émail* (enamel). ⊠ *7 rue du Mûrier,* ☎ *02–47–61–01–19.* ▦ *30 frs.* ☉ *Apr.–mid-Oct., Tues.–Sun. 10–noon and 2:30–6; mid-Oct.–Feb., weekends 10–noon and 2–6:15.*

27 Only two sturdy towers—the Tour Charlemagne and the Tour de l'Horloge (Clock Tower)—remain of the medieval abbey, the **Collégiale St-Martin,** that once dominated the heart of the city. Old wall paintings and Romanesque sculptures are on display in the small museum, housed in a restored 13th-century chapel that once adjoined the abbey cloisters. Here, the life of St. Martin and the history of the abbey, destroyed in 1802 and since replaced by a bombastic neo-Byzantine basilica, are retraced. ⊠ *3 rue Rapin,* ☎ *02–47–64–48–87.* ▦ *15 frs.* ☉ *Mid-Mar.–mid-Nov., Wed.–Sun. 9:30–12:30 and 2–5:30.*

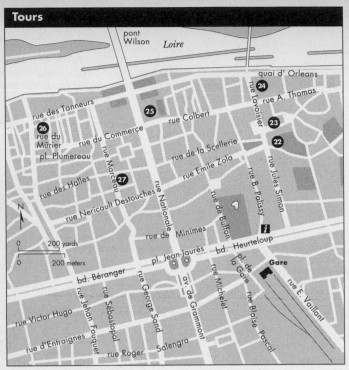

Tours

Dining and Lodging

$$ ✕ **Les Tuffeaux.** This restaurant, between the cathedral and the Loire, is the city's best value for the money. Chef Gildas Marsollier wins customers with delicious fennel-perfumed salmon, oysters in an egg sauce seasoned with Roquefort, and remarkable desserts. Gentle lighting and a wood-beamed, stone-walled decor provide a soothing background. ⊠ *19 rue Lavoisier,* ☎ *02–47–47–19–89. MC, V. Closed Sun. No lunch Mon.*

$$$$ ✕🛏 **Château d'Artigny.** The ambience of this Relais & Châteaux hotel—built by the Coty perfume tycoon in 1912 as a vast pseudo–Louis XV house—recalls a perfume ad: Gilt, marble, and plush abound, creating a perfect backdrop for the frequent celebrity guests. The spacious rooms have 18th-century-style French furnishings. The nouvelle restaurant is excellent but expensive. You can jog away the calories in the 60-acre park overlooking the Indre River. ⊠ *Rte. d'Azay-le-Rideau, 37250 Montbazon (13 km [8 mi] south of Tours, west of Montbazon on D17),* ☎ *02–47–34–30–30,* 🖷 *02–47–34–30–39. 40 rooms, 4 suites. Restaurant, pool, tennis court. AE, DC, MC, V. Closed Dec.–early Jan.*

$$$$ ✕🛏 **Jean Bardet.** Bardet, one of France's top 20 chefs, showcases pro-
★ duce from his own rare herb and exotic vegetable garden in the eight-course *menu dégustation* (tasting menu) for 620 francs and in the à la carte menu that might include baby eel in red wine or oysters poached in Muscadet on a puree of watercress. Reservations are essential, and the restaurant doesn't serve lunch Monday nor, November through March, dinner Sunday and Monday. Rooms and suites at this stately mansion, though luxurious, are on the exorbitant side. For real style, hire Bardet's Rolls-Royce Silver Shadow II to take you on a tour of the Loire. ⊠ *Château de Belmont, 57 rue Groison, 37100,* ☎ *02–47–41–41–11,* 🖷 *02–47–51–68–72. 16 rooms, 5 suites. Restaurant, pool. AE, DC, MC, V.*

$$$ ✕🛏 **Domaine de la Tortinière.** Subtle elegance exudes from this little 19th-century château south of Tours. Rooms in the main building convey quiet, rustic luxury; those in the modern annex are less desirable. Some negatives in the old house: the morning gurgle of the water pipes and the sound of doors shutting; No. 15, however small, is pleasant and quieter. Anyway, most of the beds are so comfy it's a pleasure to wake up in them. Dinner is a delightful occasion, even if some of the fare does not quite live up to its reputation. The pigeon in a rich wine sauce, and the lobster bisque with a pastry top are excellent, however. ⊠ *10 rte. de Ballan, 37250 Veigné (12 km [7 mi] south of Tours)*, ☎ *02–47–34–35–00,* ℻ *02–47–65–95–70. 21 rooms. Restaurant, pool, tennis court. AE, MC, V. Closed mid-Dec.–Mar.*

$$$ 🏨 **Univers.** The Univers is the best hotel in central Tours. Murals in
★ the lobby depict some of the famous people who have stayed here since it opened in 1846: Winston Churchill, Sarah Bernhardt, Maurice Chevalier, Rudyard Kipling, Ernest Hemingway, Edith Piaf, and the Duke of Windsor. Wood panels and soft colors add traditional warmth to the air-conditioned rooms, of which only 10 face the street; the others look onto a flower garden. ⊠ *5 bd. Heurteloup, 37000,* ☎ *02–47–05–37–12,* ℻ *02–47–61–51–80. 77 rooms, 8 suites. Restaurant, bar, meeting room. AE, DC, MC, V.*

Villandry

㉘ *16 km (10 mi) west of Tours via D7.*

Villandry is renowned for its extravagant terraced gardens—the finest in the Loire Valley—reconstituted according to original plans. In 1906 Spanish doctor Joachim Carvalla and his wife, American heiress Ann
★ Coleman, bought the **Château de Villandry** and began a long process of restoration. Both the château and the gardens are from the 16th century, but over the years they had fallen into disrepair. The château has a remarkable gilded ceiling—imported from Toledo, Spain—and a collection of fine Spanish paintings. The **gardens** are unquestionably the main attraction, replanted according to their original rigorous, geometric design, with zigzagging hedges around flower beds, vegetable plots, and gravel walks. The result is an aristocratic 16th-century *jardin à la française* (French-style garden). Below an avenue of 1,500 precisely pruned lime trees lies an ornamental lake filled with swans: Not a ripple is out of place. The aromatic and medicinal garden, its plots neatly labeled in three languages, is especially appealing. The quietest time to visit is usually during the two-hour French lunch break. ☎ *02–47–50–02–09.* 🎫 *Château and gardens 45 frs, gardens only 33 frs.* ☉ *June–Sept., daily 9–6, gardens 9–8; Oct.–Dec. and Feb.–May, daily 9:30–5, gardens 9–dusk.*

Dining and Lodging

$–$$ ✕🏨 **Cheval Rouge.** Rooms at this fine, old-fashioned hotel are spacious—ask for one of the quieter ones at the back. The restaurant (closed Monday) is popular with locals, who come for the surprisingly good classical food—considering its touristy location next to the château—and wine. Best bets are the terrine of foie gras, the calf sweetbreads, and the wood-fired-grill fare. ⊠ *9 rue de la Mairie, 37510 Villandry,* ☎ *02–47–50–02–07,* ℻ *02–47–50–08–77. 18 rooms. Restaurant. MC, V. Closed Feb.–mid-Mar.*

Langeais

㉙ *8 km (5 mi) west of Villandry.*

Across the Loire from Villandry is the small, old town of Langeais, with a Renaissance church-tower and some 16th-century houses dwarfed by its massive castle. The **Château de Langeais,** built in the 1460s and never altered, contains a superb collection of fireplaces, tapestries, chests, and beds. Outside, tidy gardens nestle behind sturdy walls and battlements. ☎ 02–47–96–72–60. ✉ 40 frs. ☼ Easter–Oct., Tues.–Sun. 9–6:30; Nov.–Easter, daily 9–noon and 2–5.

Dining and Lodging

$$ ✕🏠 **Castel de Bray et Monts.** In the tiny wine village of Bréhémont, on the south bank of the Loire, Maxime and Eliane Rochereau have converted this handsome 18th-century manor into a hotel with a difference—Maxime, once a chef at the Paris Ritz, holds weeklong cooking classes. But you don't need to take the course to sample Maxime's cooking (with local fish at the fore), showcased in three prix-fixe menus starting at 125 francs. Other standouts include the magnificent hotel staircase, with its neo-Gothic iron banisters; the shady rose garden; and the duplex bedroom in the converted former chapel. ✉ 10 rue Ridet, 37130 Bréhémont (5 km [3 mi] southwest of Langeais), ☎ 02–47–96–70–47, FAX 02–47–96–57–36. 9 rooms. Restaurant, bicycles. AE, MC, V. Closed mid-Nov.–mid-Feb.

Azay-le-Rideau

㉚ 10 km (6 mi) southeast of Langeais via D57, 24 km (15 mi) southwest of Tours.

In a sylvan setting on the banks of the River Indre, the pleasant village of Azay-le-Rideau is famed for its white-walled Renaissance pleasure
★ palace. The 16th-century **Château d'Azay-le-Rideau** was never a serious fortress. It certainly offered no protection to its builder, royal financier Gilles Berthelot, when a financial scandal forced him to flee France shortly after the château's completion in 1529. For centuries the château passed from one private owner to another and was finally bought by the state in 1905. Though the interior contains an interesting blend of furniture and artwork, you may wish to spend most of your time exploring the enchanting private park, complete with a moatlike lake. Delightful son-et-lumière shows are held on the château grounds at 10:30 PM from May through September. ☎ 02–47–45–42–04. ✉ Château 35 frs, son-et-lumière 60 frs. ☼ Apr.–Sept., daily 9:30–6; Nov.–Mar., daily 9:30–12:30 and 2–5:30.

Dining and Lodging

$$ ✕🏠 **Grand Monarque.** Near the château, this old hotel has a captive audience, which shows in its offhand service. However, rooms, which vary in size and style, have character; most are simple, with an antique or two, and many have exposed beams. The restaurant (closed Monday and dinner Sunday) serves good, traditional food and an extensive selection of Loire wines; the 99-franc lunch menu is a particularly good value. Weekend stays must include dinner. ✉ 3 pl. de la République, 37190, ☎ 02–47–45–40–08, FAX 02–47–45–46–25. 24 rooms. Restaurant. AE, MC, V. Closed mid-Dec.–end of Jan.

Outdoor Activities and Sports

Rent bikes from **Leprovost** (✉ 13 rue Carnot, ☎ 02–47–45–40–94) to ride along the Indre.

Shopping

Osier (wicker) products have been made for centuries in Villaines-les-Rochers, 6 km (4 mi) southeast of Azay-le-Rideau via D57. Willow reeds are cultivated in nearby fields and dried in the sun each May, before being transformed into sofas, cat baskets, or babies' rattles. In 1849, when the craft was threatened with extinction, the parish priest persuaded 65 small groups of basket weavers to form France's first agricultural workers' cooperative. The **Coopératif de la Vannerie** (✉ 1 rue de la Cheneillère, ☎ 02–47–45–43–03), which is open Saturday 10–

noon and 2–7 and Sunday 2–7, is still going strong and has a wide choice of wicker goods for sale.

Saché

③¹ *7 km (4 mi) east of Azay-le-Rideau via D17.*

Saché is best known for its associations with the novelist Honoré de Balzac (1799–1850), who lived and wrote in its **Château.** If you've never read Balzac and don't understand spoken French, you may find little of interest here; but if you have, and do, you'll return to the novels with fresh enthusiasm and understanding. The present château, built between the 16th and 18th centuries, is more of a comfortable country house than a fortress. Balzac came here—to stay with his friends, the Margonnes—during the 1830s, both to write and to escape his creditors. The château houses the substantial **Musée Balzac,** where exhibits range from photographs to original manuscripts to the coffeepot Balzac used to help keep him writing up to 16 hours a day. As the great author once wrote about the area around Tours: "It is no use asking me why I am in love with Touraine. It is not only the love one has for one's birthplace, nor the love one might have for an oasis in the desert; it is the lover of the artist for his art." ☎ *02–47–26–86–50.* ✍ *24 frs.* ◷ *Feb.–mid-Mar. and Oct.–Nov., Thurs.–Tues. 9:30–12:30 and 2–5; mid-Mar.–Sept., daily 9–noon and 2–6.*

Ussé

★ **③²** *14 km (9 mi) west of Azay-le-Rideau via D17 and D7, 36 km (23 mi) southwest of Tours.*

As you approach the **Château d'Ussé** (actually in the village of Rigny-Ussé), between the Forest of Chinon and the Loire, an astonishing array of delicate towers and turrets greets you. Literature describes this château as the original *Sleeping Beauty* castle—the inspiration for Charles Perrault's beloved 17th-century tale. Though parts of the castle are from the 1400s, most of it was completed two centuries later. It is a flamboyant mix of Gothic and Renaissance styles—stylish and romantic, built for fun, not for fighting. Its history supports this playful image: It suffered no bloodbaths—no political conquests or conflicts. And a tablet in the chapel indicates that even the French Revolution passed it by.

After admiring the château's luxurious furnishings and 19th-century French fashion exhibit, climb the spiral stairway to the tower to view the River Indre through the battlements. Here you will also find a waxwork effigy of Sleeping Beauty herself. Before you leave, visit the 16th-century chapel in the garden; its door is decorated with pleasingly sinister skull-and-crossbones carvings. ☎ *02–47–95–54–05.* ✍ *59 frs.* ◷ *Mid-Feb.–mid-Nov., daily 10–noon and 2–5:30.*

Dining

$$
★ ✕ **Atlantide.** This restaurant is worth seeking out. The small dining room, dressed in white tablecloths, potted plants, and a Grecian statue, has a classic simplicity that allows you to focus on the food. ⊠ *17 rue Nationale, Avoine (8 km [5 mi] southwest of Ussé),* ☎ *02–47–58–81–85. MC, V. Closed Mon. and 1st ½ half July. No dinner Sun.*

Chinon

★ **③³** *13 km (8 mi) southwest of Rigny-Ussé via D7 and D16, 44 km (28 mi) southwest of Tours.*

The town of Chinon—birthplace of author François Rabelais (1494–1553)—is dominated by the towering ruins of its medieval castle, perched high above the River Vienne. Though the main tourist office is in the town below, in summer a special annex operates from the castle grounds. The town is a warren of narrow, cobbled streets (some are pedestrians only) lined with half-timber medieval houses. Since both the village and the château are on steep, cobbled slopes, it's a good idea to wear comfortable walking shoes.

The vast **Château de Chinon,** a veritable fortress with walls 400 yards long, is from the time of Henry II of England, who died here in 1189 and was buried at Fontevraud. Two centuries later the castle witnessed an important historic moment: Joan of Arc's recognition of the disguised dauphin, later Charles VII. In the early 17th century the castle was partially dismantled by Cardinal Richelieu (1585–1642), who used many of its stones to build a new palace 21 km (13 mi) to the south, in Richelieu.

At Chinon everything is open to the elements, except the **Logis Royal** (Royal Chambers). Here there is a small museum containing a model of the castle when it was intact, various old tapestries, and precious stones. For a fine view of the region, climb the **Tour Coudray** (Coudray Tower), where in 1307 leading members of the crusading Knights Templar were imprisoned before being taken to Paris, tried, and burned at the stake. The **Tour de l'Horloge** (Clock Tower), whose bell has sounded the hours since 1399, contains the **Musée Jeanne d'Arc** (Joan of Arc Museum). There are sensational views from the ramparts over Chinon and the Vienne Valley. ☎ 02–47–93–13–45. ✆ *Château 29 frs.* ⊙ *Mid-Mar.–June and Sept., daily 9–6; July and Aug., daily 9–7; Oct., daily 9–5; Nov.–mid-Mar., daily 9–noon and 2–5.*

The **Musée du Vin** (Wine Museum), in a vaulted cellar beneath one of Chinon's fine medieval streets, has a fascinating presentation about vine growing and wine and barrel making. English commentary is available, and the admission charge entitles you to a sample of the local product. ⊠ *12 rue Voltaire,* ☎ *02–47–93–25–63.* ✆ *22 frs.* ⊙ *Apr.–Oct., Fri.–Wed. 10–noon and 2–6.*

Dining and Lodging

$$$ ✕ **Au Plaisir Gourmand.** Jean-Claude Rigollet's tufa-stone restaurant by the Vienne River is the finest in Chinon. Specialties served in the Renaissance-style dining room include snails in garlic, jellied rabbit, *sandre* (perch) with butter sauce, and braised oxtail in red wine. ⊠ *2 rue Parmentier,* ☎ *02–47–93–20–48. Reservations essential. AE, MC, V. Closed Mon. and mid-Feb.–mid-Mar. No dinner Sun.*

$$$–$$$$ ✕⌘ **Château de Marçay.** A fashionable clientele stays at this picturesque
★   hotel outside Chinon. The spacious rooms in the château have beams and cables and a cozy warmth; those in the separate Pavilion are pleasant and less expensive but have little charm. Chef Pascal Bodin serves excellent carpaccio *de canard* (thin slices of marinated cold duck), tournedos of salmon in a Chinon wine sauce, an extensive cheese board (sample the Ste-Marie chèvre), and a big wine list. There's no dinner Sunday in winter. ⊠ *37500 Marçay (8 km [5 mi] south of Chinon),* ☎ *02–47–93–03–47,* ℻ *02–47–93–45–33. 30 rooms, 4 suites. Restaurant, pool, tennis court. AE, DC, MC, V. Closed Feb.–mid-Mar.*

$$ ✕⌘ **Gargantua.** This small, quiet hotel in the center of town was a bailiff's palace in the 15th century. Rooms come in various sizes and styles, but simple good taste prevails throughout; Nos. 7 and 9 have views of the château and are good choices. In the restaurant sample such delicious local specialties as fillet of *barbue* (brill) with a marmalade, thyme, and lemon sauce. On Friday and Saturday evenings the staff dresses up in medieval costume; in summer you can dine outside and admire the castle. ⊠ *73 rue Voltaire, 37500,* ☎ *02–47–93–04–71,* ℻

02–47–93–08–02. *8 rooms, 4 with bath. AE, DC, MC, V. Closed Wed. and Feb.*

$$ ⌐⌐ **France.** Just off the main square is this hotel in the town's oldest buildings. Built in the 16th century, it was home to many notables until the Revolution, when it became known as the Hôtel de France. Rooms are all comfortable, but ask for one of the more refurbished ones with a view of the castle. The ground-floor restaurant (closed Tuesday and no lunch Wednesday) serves Italian cuisine and doubles as a bar, making it a congenial spot to regroup your energies before your next adventure. ⊠ *47 pl. du Général-de-Gaulle, 37500,* ☎ *02–47–93–33–91,* FAX *02–47–98–37–03. 27 rooms. Restaurant. AE, DC, MC, V. Closed 2nd ½ Nov.*

Nightlife and the Arts

Chinon stages a **Marché Médiéval** (Medieval Market) during the first weekend of August. The streets are decked with flags and bunting, craftsmen ply their wares, ancient recipes are resurrected, and locals dress up in medieval costumes.

Champigny-sur-Veude

③④ *15 km (9 mi) south of Chinon via D749.*

★ Some of the best Renaissance stained glass in the world is in the village of Champigny-sur-Veude. In the dainty white-stone **Sainte-Chapelle,** the 16th-century windows relate scenes from the Passion, Crucifixion, and the life of the 13th-century French king St. Louis; note the vividness and harmony of the colors, especially the purplish blues. The church was originally part of a château built between 1508 and 1543, but it was razed a century later by order of jealous neighbor Cardinal Richelieu. ☎ *02–47–95–71–46.* ⊠ *20 frs.* ◔ *Apr.–Sept., Wed.–Mon. 9–noon and 2–6.*

Richelieu

③⑤ *6 km (4 mi) south of Champigny-sur-Veude.*

The eerie town of Richelieu was founded by Cardinal Richelieu in 1631, along with a megalomaniac château intended to be one of the most lavish in Christendom. The town remains a rare example of rigid, symmetrical, and unspoiled classical town planning, with 28 identical mansions lining the main street. Its bombastic scale and state of preservation are unique; the severe, straight streets have not changed for 350 years, give or take the odd traffic sign. All that's left of the cardinal's vainglorious country palace, however, are a few outbuildings and parkland.

Fontevraud

③⑥ *20 km (12 mi) northwest of Chinon via D751, 15 km (9 mi) southeast of Saumur.*

The small village of Fontevraud is famous for its large medieval abbey, of central importance in the history of both England and France. Founded in 1099, the **Abbaye Royale de Fontevraud** had separate churches and living quarters for nuns, monks, lepers, "repentant" female sinners, and the sick. Between 1115 and the French Revolution in 1789, 39 abbesses—among them a granddaughter of William the Conqueror—directed its operations. The great 12th-century **Église Abbatiale** (Abbey Church), one of the most eclectic architectural structures in France, contains the tombs of Henry II of England; his wife, Eleanor of Aquitaine; and their son, Richard Coeur de Lion—Richard the Lionhearted. Though their bones were scattered during the Revolution, their effigies remain. Napoléon turned the abbey church into a prison, and so it remained until 1963, when historical restoration work—still under way—began. The **Salle Capitulaire** (Chapter House), adjacent to the church, with its collection of 16th-century religious wall paintings (prominent abbesses served as models), is unmistakably Renaissance; the paving stones bear the salamander emblem of François I. Next to the long refectory is the unusual, octagonal **Cuisine** (kitchen), topped by 20 scaly-looking stone chimneys led by the **Tour d'Evrault.** ⊠ *Pl. des Plantagenêts,* ☎ *02–41–51–71–41.* ⌾ *32 frs.* ⊘ *May–mid-Sept., daily 9–noon and 2–6:30; mid-Sept.–Apr., daily 9:30–noon and 2–5.*

Saumur

★ ㉗ *15 km (9 mi) northwest of Fontevraud via D947, 65 km (41 mi) west of Tours, 46 km (29 mi) southeast of Angers.*

The ancient town of Saumur, dominated by its mighty turreted château, high above town and river, makes an excellent base for exploring the western Loire. It's also known for its riding school and flourishing mushroom industry, which produces 100,000 tons per year. The same cool tunnels in which the mushrooms grow provide an ideal storage place for the local *mousseux* (sparkling wines).

If you arrive in the evening, the sight of the elegant, floodlighted, white 14th-century **Château de Saumur** takes your breath away. Look familiar? Probably because you've seen it in countless reproductions from the famous *Très Riches Heures* Book of Hours, painted for the Duc de Berri in 1416 (now in the Musée Condé at Chantilly). Inside it's bright and cheerful, with a fairy-tale gateway and plentiful potted flowers. There are two museums: the **Musée des Arts Décoratifs** (Decorative Arts Museum), with its fine collection of medieval objets d'art and 18th- and 19th-century porcelain, and the **Musée du Cheval** (Horse Museum). Afterward, climb the **Tour de Guet** (watchtower) for an impressive view. ⊠ *Esplanade du Château,* ☎ *02–41–40–24–40.* ⌾ *38 frs.* ⊘ *July–Sept., daily 9–6:30; Oct. and Apr.–June, daily 9–11:30 and 2–6; Nov.–Mar., Wed.–Mon. 9:30–noon and 2–5:30.*

In the old powder house at the château is the **Musée de la Figurine-Jouet** (Toy Figurine Museum), with more than 2,000 toy figurines on display. ☎ *02–41–67–39–23.* ⌾ *12 frs.* ⊘ *June and Sept., Wed.–Mon. 2–6; July–Aug., Wed.–Mon. 10–6.*

At the **Musée du Champignon** (Mushroom Museum), on the outskirts of Saumur, take an intriguing subterranean tour through fossil-filled caverns where the edible fungi are grown. ⊠ *Rte. de Gennes, St-Hilaire-St-Florent,* ☎ *02–41–50–31–55.* ⌾ *40 frs.* ⊘ *Mid-Feb.–mid-Sept., daily 10–7.*

Dining and Lodging

$$–$$$ ✕ **Les Ménestrels.** Chef Lucien Von cooks fine fare in a restored 18th-
★ century white-stone mansion up against the castle cliff. Specialties include pheasant casserole, fried mushrooms, perch with spring-onion fondue, and beef in local red-wine sauce. ⊠ *11 rue Raspail,* ☎ *02–41–67–71–10.* AE, DC, MC, V. *No dinner Sun. (except July–Aug.).*

$$ ⊞ **Loire.** This member of the Best Western chain wins no prizes for charm or friendly service, but it is clean, spacious, and functional. It's also inconveniently located across the river from the main part of town, though this makes parking easier and affords a stunning view of the château from its restaurant (closed Saturday and, November through March, no dinner Friday). ⊠ *Rue de Vieux-Pont, 49400,* ☎ *02–41–67–22–42; 800/ 528–1234 for U.S. reservations; 0181/541–0033 for U.K. reservations;* FAX *02–41–67–88–80. 44 rooms. Restaurant. AE, DC, MC, V.*

$$ **Anne d'Anjou.** Close to the center of town, this hotel facing the river has a view of the château above. Inside the 18th-century building is an astounding staircase, which circles up to the top floor to an impressive mural. Most rooms are simple; most likely, owners Yves and Anne-Marie Touzé will point you to their best, No. 102 (650 frs), with wood-panel paintings and Empire furnishings. ✉ *32 quai Mayaud, 49400,* ☎ *02–41–67–30–30,* FAX *02–41–67–51–00. 50 rooms. Restaurant. AE, DC, MC, V.*

Outdoor Activities and Sports

If you want to ride through the rolling hills or take a weeklong equestrian tour of the Loire Valley, head to the **Centre Équestre de Saumur** (✉ Petit Souper, St-Hilaire–St-Florent, ☎ 02–41–50–29–90), 3 km (2 mi) northwest of town.

Shopping

Loire wine is not a practical buy—except for instant consumption—but if wine-tasting tours of vineyards inspire you, enterprising wine makers will arrange shipments. For sparkling wine try **Ackerman** (✉ 19 rue Léopold-Palustre, St-Hilaire, ☎ 02–41–53–30–20) or **Veuve Amiot** (✉ 21 rue Jean-Ackerman, St-Hilaire, ☎ 02–41–83–14–14). Just southeast of Saumur in Dampierre-sur-Loire, stop in at the **Château de Chaintres** (✉ 54 rue de la Croix-de-Chaintre, ☎ 02–41–52–90–54), where gravel-voiced Krishna Lester, an English eccentric, produces the region's finest red and enjoys lecturing visitors about fermentation and vinification.

Montreuil-Bellay

38 *18 km (11 mi) south of Saumur via N147.*

Montreuil-Bellay is a small riverside town with many 18th- and 19th-century houses, lovely public gardens, and a leafy square next to its castle. The 15th-century **Château de Montreuil-Bellay** has a grandiose exterior—majestic towers and pointed roofs—and a fascinating interior, with fine furniture and tapestries, a fully equipped medieval kitchen, and a chapel adorned with frescoes of angelic musicians. For a memorable view, take a stroll in the gardens; graceful white turrets tower high above the trees and rosebushes, and down below, the little River Thouet winds its lazy way to the Loire. ✉ *Pl. des Ormeaux,* ☎ *02–41–52–33–06.* *45 frs.* *Apr.–Oct., Wed.–Mon. 10–noon and 2–5:30.*

En Route From Montreuil-Bellay take D761 northwest to Doué-la-Fontaine, 12 km (8 mi) away. The town is home to the **Zoo de Doué** (✉ 103 rte. de Cholet, ☎ 02–41–59–18–58) where deer, emus, and monkeys roam happily, surrounded by golden limestone quarries. It's open May–September, daily 9–7, and October–mid-November and mid-February–April, daily 9–12:30 and 2–6; admission is 60 francs. From the zoo return to D761 to continue to Angers, pausing along the way to admire the towering and picturesque **Château de Brissac.**

Angers

39 *51 km (28 mi) northwest of Montreuil-Bellay via D761, 10 km (69 mi) west of Tours, 88 km (55 mi) east of Nantes.*

The bustling city of Angers, on the banks of the Maine River, just north of the Loire, is famous for its towering castle filled with extraordinary tapestries. But it also has a fine Gothic cathedral, a selection of art galleries, and a network of pleasant, traffic-free streets around place Ste-Croix, with its half-timber houses. The town's principal sights lie within a compact square formed by the three main boulevards and the Maine.

The banded black-and-white **Château d'Angers,** built by St. Louis (1228–38), glowers over the town from behind turreted moats, now laid out as gardens and overrun with flowers and deer. As you explore the grounds, note the startling contrast between the thick, defensive walls, defended by a drawbridge and 17 massive round towers in a distinctive pattern, and the formal garden, with its delicate white-tufa-stone chapel, erected in the 16th century. For a sweeping view of the city and surrounding countryside, climb one of the castle towers. A well-integrated modern
★ gallery on the castle grounds contains the great **Tenture de l'Apocalypse** (Apocalypse Tapestry), woven in Paris in the 1380s for the duke of Anjou and restored to almost pristine glory in 1996. Measuring 16 ft high and 120 yards long, it shows a series of 70 horrifying and humorous scenes from the Book of Revelation. In one, mountains of fire fall from heaven while boats capsize and men struggle in the water. Another has the beast with seven heads. ⊠ *Pl. du Président-Kennedy,* ☎ *02–41–87–43–47.* 🎫 *35 frs.* ☉ *July–Aug., daily 10–7; Sept.–June, daily 10–5.*

The **Cathédrale St-Maurice** (⊠ Pl. Freppel) is a 12th- and 13th-century Gothic cathedral noted for its curious Romanesque facade and original stained-glass windows; bring binoculars to appreciate both fully.

The **Musée David d'Angers,** in a refurbished glass-roof medieval church, has a collection of dramatic sculptures by Jean-Pierre David (1788–1859), the city's favorite son. ⊠ *33 rue Toussaint,* ☎ *02–41–87–21–03.* 🎫 *10 frs.* ☉ *Tues.–Sun. 10–noon and 2–6.*

To learn about the heartwarming liqueur made in Angers since 1849, head to the **Distillerie Cointreau,** east of the city. There are a museum and a guided visit of the distillery, which starts with an introductory film; moves through the bottling plant and alembic room, with its gleaming copper-pot stills; and ends with a tasting. ⊠ *Carrefour Molière, Blvd. Bretonnières, St-Barthélémy d'Anjou,* ☎ *02–41–31–50–50.* 🎫 *20 frs.* ☉ *Tours June–Sept., weekdays every hr at 10, 11, and 2–5, weekends at 3 and 4:30; tours Oct.–May, Mon.–Sat. at 3, Sun. at 3 and 4:30.*

OFF THE
BEATEN PATH

CHÂTEAU DE SERRANT – This sumptuous château 17 km (11 mi) southwest of Angers on N23, flanked by stately lawns and a moat, dates from 1546, with additions from the 17th and 18th centuries. The lush, paneled interior is hung with tapestries; the magnificent library is lined with 10,000 books. ☎ *02–41–39–13–01.* 🎫 *45 frs.* ☉ *Apr.–Oct., Wed.–Mon. 9–11:30 and 2–6.*

Dining and Lodging

$$–$$$ ✕ **La Salamandre.** Carefully prepared classical cuisine is served in this restaurant in the Anjou Hotel (☞ *below*). Lamb, duck with cranberries, and calamari with crab sauce are just a few of the dishes served amid the Renaissance-style decor and stained-glass windows. Opt for one of the reasonably priced prix-fixe menus. ⊠ *1 bd. du Maréchal-Foch,* ☎ *02–41–88–99–55. AE, DC, MC, V. Closed Sun.*

$$ ✕ **Toussaint.** Chef Michel Bignon serves nouvelle versions of traditional
★ regional dishes, plus fine wines and tasty desserts. Local river fish with beurre blanc is a particular specialty. The ground-floor dining room is less formal; upstairs, it's more Neoclassical, with a better view of the castle. Reserve your table accordingly. ⊠ *7 pl. du Président-Kennedy,* ☎ *02–41–87–46–20. Reservations essential. Jacket required. AE, MC, V. Closed Mon. and 1st ½ of Sept; no dinner Sun.*

$ ✕ **La Boucherie.** If you have an appetite for steak and good value, this place is for you. The various menus feature different cuts of beef, but for 55 francs you can get a sirloin, a small salad, bread, and a ¼-liter carafe of wine. If there is a wait for a table, don't despair: The action is fast. Tables are close together, and lively conversation adds to the robust atmosphere. ⊠ *27 bd. du Maréchal-Foch,* ☎ *02–41–25–39–25. Reservations not accepted. MC, V.*

$ ✕ **La Treille.** For traditional, simple fare at affordable prices, try this small, two-story mom-and-pop restaurant, off place Ste-Croix and across from Maison d'Adam, Angers's finest timber house. The prix-fixe menu may start with a *salade au chèvre chaud* (warm goat-cheese salad), followed by confit of duck and an apple tart. The upstairs dining room draws a lively crowd; downstairs is quieter. ⊠ *12 rue Montault,* ☎ *02–41–88–45–51. MC, V. Closed Sun.*

$$–$$$ ⊞ **Anjou.** In business since 1846, the Anjou, now part of the Best Western chain, has a vaguely 18th-century style, including stained-glass windows in the lobby. The spacious rooms have high ceilings, double doors, and modern bathrooms with terry-cloth bathrobes. ⊠ *1 bd. du Maréchal-Foch, 49000,* ☎ *02–41–88–24–82; 800/528–1324 in the U.S.,* FAX *02–41–87–22–21. 53 rooms. Restaurant. AE, DC, MC, V.*

$ ⊞ **Mail.** A stately lime tree stands sentinel outside this converted 17th-century convent, on a calm street near the Hôtel de Ville. The small-ish rooms were individually redecorated in 1997 in pastel shades with striped wallpaper. ⊠ *8 rue des Ursules, 49100,* ☎ *02–41–25–05–05,* FAX *02–41–86–91–20. 26 rooms. Breakfast room AE, DC, MC, V.*

Nightlife and the Arts

For four weeks beginning in mid-June, the **Fête d'Anjou** (Anjou Festival) enlivens the area around Angers with music, theater, and dance. Call the tourist office (☞ The Loire Valley A to Z, *below*) for details.

Outdoor Activities and Sports

Go canoeing, sailing, fishing, and windsurfing at the **Centre Nautique du Lac de Maine** (Maine Lake Nautical Center; ⊠ 75 av. du Lac-de-Maine, ☎ 02–41–22–32–20), 5 km (3 mi) southwest of the city.

Le Plessis-Bourré

④⓿ *20 km (12 mi) north of Angers via D107, off D508 south of Écuillé.*

The reason to visit Le Plessis-Bourré is to see its Renaissance castle. The **Château du Plessis-Bourré,** built between 1468 and 1473 by Jean Bourré (one of Louis XI's top-ranking civil servants), looks like a traditional grim fortress: The bridge across its moat is nearly 50 yards long. Once you step into the central courtyard, however, the gentler mood of the Renaissance takes over. What makes this place special is the painted wooden ceiling in the **Salle des Gardes** (Guards' Room). Jean Bourré's hobby was alchemy—an ancient branch of chemistry with more than a touch of the occult—and the ceiling's 24 hexagonal panels are covered with scenes illustrating the craft. Some have overtones of the nightmare world of late-medieval Dutch painter Hieronymus Bosch, while others illustrate folktales or proverbs. A few must have been painted just for fun: A topless lady steers a land yacht with wooden wheels (thought to be an allegory of spirit and matter); people urinate ceremoniously (ammonia was extracted from urine); an emaciated wolf takes a bite out of a startled lady (according to folk legend, the wolf's diet consisted of faithful wives, apparently in short supply); and Thurberesque dogs gambol in between. You may want to ignore the guide's lecture on furniture and spend your time gazing upward. ☎ 02–41–32–06–72. ☒ 45 frs. ☉ Apr.–Aug., Thurs.–Tues. 10–noon and 2–6; Sept.–Nov. and Feb.–Mar., Thurs.–Tues. 2–6.

Le Lude

④① *62 km (39 mi) east of Le Plessis-Bourré via D74, D766, and D305; 47 km (29 mi) northeast of Saumur; 44 km (28 mi) south of Le Mans.*

★ One of France's most spectacular son-et-lumière shows takes place at the **Château du Lude** in the Loir Valley. Of its three wings, the north, or Louis XII, wing is the earliest, dating from the early 16th century; it houses a ballroom and a spacious, 19th-century library. The François I wing, facing the park, combines round fortress towers with dainty Renaissance detail and contains Flemish and Gobelin tapestries and a chimneypiece with the king's carved salamander emblem. The 18th-century Louis XVI wing overlooking the river displays severe, classical symmetry. Highlights (guided tours only) include the oval saloon, ornate bedroom, and murals by followers of Raphael. On Friday and Saturday evenings from mid-June to mid-September, more than 130 costumed performers, assisted by fountains and fireworks, take part in Le Lude's son-et-lumière pageant chronicling the history of the château and the region from the Hundred Years' War onward. ⊠ *Pl. François-de-Nicolaÿ,* ☎ *02–43–94–60–09.* ☞ *40 frs, park only 30 frs, son-et-lumière 90 frs.* ☉ *Château Apr.–Sept., daily 2–6; park Apr.–Sept., daily 10–noon.*

OFF THE BEATEN PATH	**LE MANS –** Best known for its 24-hour automobile race in the second half of June, Le Mans (44 km [28 mi] north of Le Lude via D307) is a bustling city with Gallo-Roman ramparts, a well-preserved old quarter, and a magnificent cathedral—part Gothic, part Romanesque—perched precariously on a hilltop overlooking the River Sarthe.

En Route As you head east from Le Lude on D305, the gentle **Loir Valley** serves up troglodyte dwellings; the sedate little towns of **Château-du-Loir** and **La Chartre-sur-le-Loir** (home to a fine dry white wine, Jasnières); hilltop **Trôo,** with its feudal burial mound; and **Montoire,** whose disused train station, where Hitler met Pétain in 1940, still stands, overlooking a tangle of weed-covered tracks.

Vendôme

㊷ *80 km (50 mi) east of Le Lude via D305 and D917, 32 km (20 mi) northwest of Blois, 70 km (44 mi) west of Orléans.*

The enchanting town of Vendôme may not be on your itinerary, but its picturesque appeal—the Loir River splits here into numerous arms, creating a canal-like effect—merits a visit. Take time to stroll along the narrow streets, through the 15th-century Porte St-Georges gateway, and climb up to the gardens of the ruined hilltop castle for stunning views of the town.

★ The former Benedictine abbey church of **La Trinité** (⊠ Rue de l'Abbaye), dominated by a solemn, 12th-century, 260-ft bell tower that served as a model for the elder spire at Chartres, has a dramatic Flamboyant Gothic front on its west side, with lacy, petal-like stonework by Jean de Beauce. The earliest part of the interior dates from the 11th century. Note the amusingly carved choir stalls and fine stained glass. The adjacent cloisters lead to the chapter house, whose wall paintings depict the life of Christ, and to the **Musée du Cloître** and its tidy collection of paintings, religious art, ceramics, and archeological findings. There's a fine view of the church from the top floor. ☎ 02–54–77–26–13. ☞ 10 frs. ☉ Wed.–Mon. 10–noon and 2–6.

Dining and Lodging

$–$$ ✕▥ **Vendôme.** This traditional hotel, a few minutes' walk from the town center, has pleasant rooms in pastel colors, although they are a bit on the small side. The restaurant, La Cloche Rouge, exudes hushed provincial formality, as local gentry concentrate reverentially on their crayfish mousse or *lapin à la solognote* (rabbit cooked in wine with onions and mushrooms). The wine list is strong on local vintages. ⊠

15 Faubourg Chartrain, 41100, ☎ *02–54–77–02–88,* ℻ *02–54–73–90–71. 35 rooms. Restaurant. AE, MC, V.*

Châteaudun

㊸ *45 km (28 mi) northeast of Vendôme via N10, 44 km (28 mi) south of Chartres, 29 km (18 mi) southeast of Illiers-Combray.*

The small town of Châteaudun, on the only hill for miles around, grew up as the market center for grain produced from the flat farmlands of the Beauce. Although the town took a battering from the Prussians in 1870, a well-indicated pedestrian circuit enables you to admire the 16th- and 17th-century houses that line the tumbling streets between the colossal castle and the 12th-century church of La Madeleine.

The **Château de Châteaudun** stands resplendent on a steep promontory 200 ft above the Loir. The courtyard presents a stylistic clash between cheerful 16th-century buildings and the 12th-century circular **Grosse Tour** (Great Tower), with its pointed roof like a witch's hat—one of France's bulkiest and best-preserved keeps, with walls more than 12 ft thick. Originally, the ground floor was used solely to store food. Reinforcing its defensive impregnability, the only way in was through a hole in the ceiling; the entrance to the tower itself was halfway up, through a door in a gallery above the chapel. The Sainte-Chapelle (Holy Chapel) has a noted collection of 15th-century statues. The other château buildings, with their unsteady brick flooring, host a smattering of tapestries and architectural exhibitions. There are also some vaulted medieval kitchens and two fine stone staircases: one Gothic, the other Renaissance. ✉ *Pl. Jehan-du-Dunois,* ☎ *02–37–94–02–90.* 🎫 *32 frs.* ☉ *Mid-Mar.–Sept., daily 8–11:45 and 2–6; Oct.–mid-Mar., daily 10–12:30 and 2–5. Guided tours (in English in summer) at 10:30 and 3.*

En Route　From Châteaudun, fast N10 heads a half hour north to Chartres. If you're a fan of author Marcel Proust, you may want to make a pilgrimage northwest to **Illiers-Combray** to visit the house where he spent his summers as a boy, painstakingly evoked in *Swann's Way* and *The Guermantes' Way* in his grand opus *In Search of Lost Time.*

THE LOIRE VALLEY A TO Z

Arriving and Departing

By Car
The Loire Valley is an easy drive from Paris. A10 runs from Paris to Orléans—a distance of 130 km (80 mi)—and on to Tours, with exits at Meung, Blois, and Amboise. After Tours, A10 veers south, toward Poitiers and Bordeaux. A11 links Paris to Angers via Le Mans. Slower but more scenic routes run from the Channel ports down through Normandy into the Loire region.

By Plane
The closest international airports are Paris's Charles-de-Gaulle and Orly (☞ Air Travel *in* Smart Travel Tips A to Z.

By Train
Tours and Angers are both served by the superfast TGV (*Trains à Grande Vitesse*) from Paris (Gare Montparnasse); three TGVs daily reach Vendôme in 40 minutes. Express trains run every two hours from Paris (Gare d'Austerlitz) to Orléans (usually you must change at Les Aubrais) and Blois. Note that trains for Gien leave from Paris's Gare de Lyon (direction Nevers) and that the nearest station to Sancerre is across the Loire at Tracy.

Getting Around

By Bus

Local bus services are extensive and reliable and are a link between train stations and scenic areas off the river. Inquire at tourist offices for information about routes and timetables.

By Car

By far the easiest way to visit the Loire châteaux is by car; N152 hugs the riverbank and is excellent for sightseeing. You can rent a car in all the large towns in the region, or at train stations in Orléans, Blois, Tours, or Angers, or in Paris.

By Train

The Loire region's local train network is good but not great: although it's possible to reach many of the châteaux by train, it's not that easy if you have limited time (having a car makes getting around much easier). The main line follows the Loire from Orléans to Blois, Tours, Langeais, Saumur, and Angers, with trains every two hours. There are branch lines with less frequent trains from Tours to Loches, Azay-le-Rideau and Chinon, and to Vendôme and Châteaudun. Ask the SNCF for the brochure *Les Chateaux de la Loire en Train* for more detailed information.

Contacts and Resources

Car Rental

Avis (⊠ 6 rue Jean-Moulin, Blois, ☎ 02–54–74–48–15; ⊠ 13 rue Sansonnières, Orléans, ☎ 02–38–62–27–04; ⊠ Pl. Gal-Leclerc, Tours, ☎ 02–47–20–53–27). **Europcar** (⊠ 81 rue André-Dessaux, Fleury-les-Aubrais, near Orléans, ☎ 02–33–73–00–40; ⊠ 76 rue Bernard-Palissy, Tours, ☎ 02–47–64–47–76). **Hertz** (⊠ Chaussée St-Victor [on N7], Blois, ☎ 02–54–74–03–03; ⊠ 57 rue Marcel-Tribut, Tours, ☎ 02–47–75–50–00).

Emergencies

Ambulance (☎ 15). **Regional hospitals: Angers** (⊠ 4 rue Larrey, ☎ 02–41–35–36–37); **Orléans** (⊠ 14 av. de l'Hôpital, ☎ 02–38–51–44–44); **Tours** (⊠ 2 bd. Tonnellé, ☎ 02–47–47–47–47).

Guided Tours

CHÂTEAU TOURS

Most châteaux insist that you follow one of their tours; try to get a booklet in English before joining, as most are in French. Bus tours of the main châteaux leave daily in summer from Tours, Blois, Angers, Orléans, and Saumur: Ask at the relevant tourist office for latest times and prices (☞ Visitor Information, *below*).

PERSONAL GUIDES

The tourist offices in Tours and Angers (☞ Visitor Information, *below*) arrange city and regional excursions with personal guides.

WALKING TOURS

A walking tour of Tours sets out from the tourist office (☞ Visitor Information, *below*) every morning at 10 AM from mid-April through October (40 francs). English-speaking guides show you around Blois on a tour that starts from the château at 4 (30 francs).

Travel Agencies

Havas–American Express (⊠ 19 av. des Droits-de-l'Homme, Orléans, ☎ 02–38–22–15–45). **Carlson-Wagonlit** (⊠ 9 rue Marceau, Tours, ☎ 02–47–20–40–54).

Visitor Information

The Loire region has two area tourist offices, for written inquiries only. For Chinon and points east, contact the **Comité Régional du Tourisme Centre-Val de Loire** (✉ 15 rue Parisie, 45000 Orléans). For Fontevraud and points west, contact the **Comité Régional du Tourisme des Pays-de-Loire** (✉ 2 rue de la Loire, 44200 Nantes).

Other main tourist offices are as follows. **Amboise** (✉ Quai Général-de-Gaulle, ☎ 02–47–57–01–37). **Angers** (✉ 1 pl. du Président-Kennedy, ☎ 02–41–23–51–11). **Blois** (✉ 3 av. du Dr-Jean-Laigret, ☎ 02–54–90–41–41). **Orléans** (✉ Pl. Albert-Ier, ☎ 02–38–24–05–05). **Saumur** (✉ Pl. de la Bilange, ☎ 02–41–40–20–60). **Tours** (✉ 78 rue Bernard-Palissy, ☎ 02–47–70–37–37).

4 BRITTANY

Even the French feel they are in a foreign land when they visit Brittany, the bulbous portion of western France jutting far out into the Atlantic. Cut off from mainstream culture, the Bretons have closer cultural affinities with the Celts across the Channel than with Parisians. There are delights by the score here—village fêtes, prehistoric megaliths, picturesque medieval towns. Little wonder Brittany remains a favorite vacation getaway for Brits—but don't worry about overcrowding: its vast beaches aren't easily crowded, and there are enough castles to go around.

Y OU FEEL IT EVEN BEFORE THE SHARP SALT AIR hits your face from the west—a subliminal rhythm looming in the mist, a subsonic drone somewhere between a foghorn and a heartbeat, seemingly made up of bagpipes, drums, and a thin, haunting filigree of a tin-whistle tune. This is Brittany, land of the Bretons, where Celtic bloodlines run as deep as a Druid's roots into the rocky, sea-swept soil. Wherever you wander here—along jagged coastal cliffs, through cobbled seaport streets, into burnished-oak cider pubs—you'll hear the primal pulse of Celtic music. France's most fiercely and determinedly ethnic people, the Bretons celebrate their primeval culture often and well: dancing in a ring at street fairs, sporting starched lace bonnet *coiffes* and striped fishermen's shirts at the least sign of a regional celebration. They name their children Erwan and Edwige, carry sacred statues in ceremonial religious processions called *pardons,* pray in hobbit-scaled stone churches decked with elfin moon-faced gargoyles. And scattered over the mossy hillsides stand Stonehenge-like dolmen and menhirs (prehistoric standing stones), eerie testimony to a primordial culture that predated and has long outlived Frankish France.

Any similarities in character, situation, or culture to certain islands across the Channel are by no means coincidental. Indeed, the Celts thatmigrated to this westernmost outcrop of the French landmass spent much of the Iron Age on the British Isles, introducing the indigenes to innovations like the potter's wheel, the rotary millstone, and the compass. This first influx of Continental culture to Great Britain was greeted with typically mixed feelings, and by the 6th century AD the Saxon hordes had sent the Britons packing southward to the peninsula that still bears their name. So completely did they dominate their new, Cornwall-like peninsula (appropriately named Finistère from *finis terrae,* or "land's end") that when in 496 they allied themselves with Clovis, the king of the Franks, he felt as if he'd just claimed a little bit of England. Nonetheless the Britons remained independent of France until 1532, only occasionally hiring out as wild and woolly warrior-allies to the Norsemen of Normandy.

Yet the cultural exchange flowed two ways over the Channel. From their days on the British isles the Britons brought a folklore that shares with England the bittersweet legend of Tristan and Iseult; that weaves mystical tales of the Cornwall/Cornouaille of King Arthur and Merlin. They brought a language that still renders village names unpronounceable: Aber-Wrac'h, Tronoën, Locmariaquer, Poldreuzic, Kerhornaouen. And with them, too, they brought a way of life: half-timbered seaside cider bars, their blackened-oak tables softened with prim bits of lace; stone cottages watercolored with hollyhocks, foxgloves, and hydrangea, with damp woolens and rows of rubber boots dripping on flagstone entryway floors; chin-bearded fishermen in yellow oilskins heaving the day's catch onto weather-beaten boats, terns and seagulls wheeling in the wake. It's a way of life that feels deliciously exotic to the Frenchman and—like the primordial drone of the bagpipes—comfortably, delightfully, even primally familiar to the Anglo-Saxon.

This cozy regional charm extends inland to Rennes, Bretagne's biggest city at 200,000 inhabitants, as well as to Dinan, Vannes, Quimper, and seaside St-Malo. Though many towns took a beating during the Nazi retreat in 1944, most have been gracefully restored. And the countryside retains the heather-and-emerald moorscape, peppered with sweet whitewashed cottages, framed in forests primeval, and bordered by open sea, that first inspired wandering peoples to their pipes.

— Nancy Coons

Revised and updated by Simon Hewitt

Pleasures and Pastimes

Beaches

Wherever you go in Brittany, the coast is close by: In winter the frenzied, cliff-bashing Atlantic pounds the shore; in summer the sprawling beaches and bustling harbors are filled with frolicking bathers and boaters. Dozens of islands, many inhabited and within easy reach of the mainland, spangle the coastal waters. The best sandy beaches and a multitude of water sports are found in Dinard, Perros-Guirec, Trégastel-Plage, Douarnenez, Carnac, La Trinité-sur-Mer, and La Baule.

Dining

Not surprisingly, Breton cuisine is dominated by seafood—often lobster, grilled or prepared in a cream sauce. Brittany is the land of *homard à l'armoricaine* (lobster with cream), a name derived from the ancient name for Brittany—Armorici—and not to be confused with Américane. Other popular meals include smoked ham and lamb, frequently served with green kidney beans. Fried eel is a traditional dish in Nantes. Brittany is particularly famous for its crepes, served with savory fillings. Accompanied by a glass of local cider, they are an ideal light, inexpensive meal; as *crêpes dentelles* (lace crepes) they make a delicious dessert.

CATEGORY	COST*
$$$$	over 400 frs
$$$	250 frs–400 frs
$$	125 frs–250 frs
$	under 125 frs

per person for a three-course meal, including tax (20.6%) and tip but not wine

✎ *following the text of a review is your signal that the property has a Web site, where you will find details and, usually, images; for a link, visit www.fodors.com/urls.*

Lodging

Brittany has plenty of small, appealing family-run hotels with friendly and personal service, as well as a growing number of luxury hotels and châteaux. Dinard, on the English Channel, and La Baule, on the Atlantic, are the area's two most expensive resorts. In summer, expect large crowds, so make reservations far in advance and reconfirm.

CATEGORY	COST*
$$$$	over 400 frs
$$$	250 frs–400 frs
$$	125 frs–250 frs
$	under 125 frs

per person for a three-course meal, including tax (20.6%) and tip but not wine

Exploring Brittany

Brittany can be divided into two basic areas. The first is the northeast, stretching from Rennes—the traditional capital of Brittany—to St-Malo and along the Channel coast. Here, mighty medieval castles survey the land and quaint resort towns line the seacoast. In addition to the cosmopolitan pleasures of Rennes and St-Malo, highlights include the splendid triangular-gable wooden houses of Dinan; Chateaubriand's home at Combourg; and Dinard, the elegant Belle Epoque resort once favored by British aristocrats. The second region is the Atlantic coast between Brest and Nantes, where frenzied surf crashes against the cliffs, alternating with sprawling beaches and bustling harbors. Here is lively Quimper, with its fine cathedral and museum; Pont-Aven, a former artists' colony made famous by Gauguin; the pretty island of Belle-Ile; the prehistoric menhirs of Carnac; the medieval castle at Josselin; the 19th-century resort of La Baule; and the thriving city of Nantes.

Great Itineraries

If you only have three days or so, concentrate on northeast Brittany. With five days you can explore the region in greater depth, including Rennes. With 10 days you can cover the entire region, if you don't spend too much time in any one place. A car is necessary for getting to the small medieval towns and deserted coastline.

Numbers in the text correspond to numbers in the margin and on the Brittany and Nantes maps.

IF YOU HAVE 3 DAYS

Make either the fortified port of ⊞ **St-Malo** ⑨—surrounded on four sides by walls and on three sides by sea—or the medieval town of ⊞ **Dinan** ⑤ your base for exploring northeast Brittany. Be sure to visit seaside **Dinard** ⑩, ancient **Dol-de-Bretagne** ⑦, Chateaubriand's boyhood home at **Combourg** ⑥, or the 16th-century castle in **La Bourbansais,** all within a 30-km (20-mi) radius. In addition, the magnificent rock island of **Mont-St-Michel** (☞ Chapter 5) is only 50 km (30 mi) away, in Normandy.

IF YOU HAVE 5 DAYS

Follow the three-day itinerary, then spend your fourth day in ⊞ **Rennes** ③, the region's capital and yet the least typical of Breton cities. Visit the formidable castle in **Vitré** ② and the medieval military town of **Fougères** ① on day five.

IF YOU HAVE 10 DAYS

Make ⊞ **Rennes** ③ your base for exploring the castles, châteaux, and fortresses in **Vitré** ②, **Fougères** ①, and **Montmuran** ④, making an excursion to the Château de Caradeuc if you have time. On day three stop in **La Bourbansais, Combourg** ⑥, or **Dol-de-Bretagne** ⑦ on your way to ⊞ **Dinan** ⑤ or ⊞ **St-Malo** ⑨ for the night. Head west the following day on a scenic tour of the coast and spend the night in ⊞ **Trébeurden** ⑫, on the tip of the Corniche Bretonne. Start early the next day for quaint **Morlaix** ⑬. Continue west and briefly visit the market town of **St-Pol-de-Léon** ⑭, the fortified château of **Kerjean,** or the splendid basilica at **Le Folgoët.** Eat lunch in **Brest** ⑮, a huge, modern port town. By late afternoon plan on being in **Locronan,** where sails used to be made for French fleets. Try to reach picturesque ⊞ **Douarnenez** ⑰ by evening. On the sixth day head to **Audierne** ⑱ and then on to the rugged Pointe du Raz; then double back to **Quimper** ⑲, with its lovely river bank and cathedral. Stop briefly to see the offshore stronghold at **Concarneau** ⑳ and aim to reach ⊞ **Pont-Aven** ㉑ by the end of the day; then dine on oysters in nearby **Riec-sur-Belon.** On day seven drive down the Atlantic seaboard to the beaches of **Quiberon** ㉓ and catch the ferry to the pretty island of ⊞ **Belle-Ile** ㉔. On day eight return to the mainland and meander along the coast through the beach resorts of **Carnac** ㉕ and La Trinité-sur-Mer, stopping in the medieval town of **Vannes** ㉗ and exploring the marshy parkland of **La Grande Brière.** Spend the night in seaside ⊞ **La Baule** ㉘. The following day head to tranquil, prosperous ⊞ **Nantes** ㉙–㉟.

When to Tour Brittany

The tourist season is short in Brittany. Long, damp winters keep visitors away, and many hotels are closed until Easter. Brittany is particularly crowded in July and August, when most French people are on vacation, so choose crowd-free June, September, or early October,

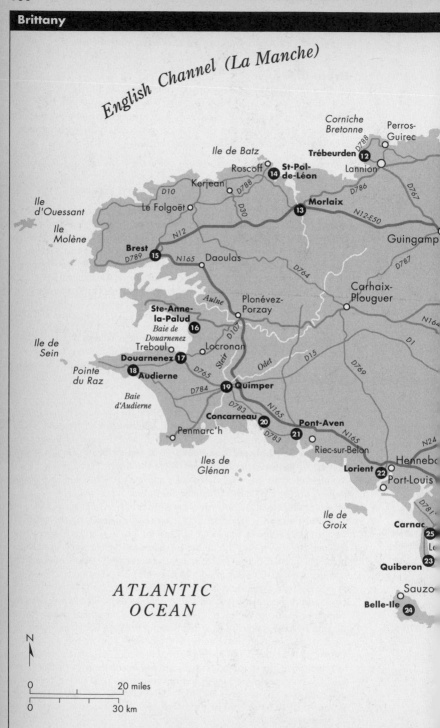

English Channel (La Manche)

*Corniche
Bretonne*

Perros-
Guirec

Ile de Batz

Trébeurden 12

Roscoff **St-Pol-
de-Léon**

14

Lannion

Kerjean

D788

D786

D767

D10

Le Folgoët

D30

Morlaix

13

N12-E50

*Ile
d'Ouessant*

N12

Guingamp

*Ile
Molène*

Brest 15

D789

N165

Daoulas

D764

**Carhaix-
Plouguer**

D787

Aulne

Plonévez-
Porzay

N164

**Ste-Anne-
la-Palud**

16

*Baie de
Douarnenez*

D107

Locronan

D1

*Ile de
Sein*

Treboul

Steir

Odet

D15

D769

Douarnenez 17

18 **Audierne**

D765

19 **Quimper**

*Pointe
du Raz*

D784

Concarneau

20

Pont-Aven

21

N165

N24

*Baie
d'Audierne*

D783

D783

Riec-sur-Belon

Penmarc'h

Hennebo

*Iles de
Glénan*

Lorient 22

Port-Louis

D781

*Ile de
Groix*

Carnac

25

L

Quiberon 23

**ATLANTIC
OCEAN**

Sauzo

Belle-Ile 24

N

0   20 miles

0   30 km

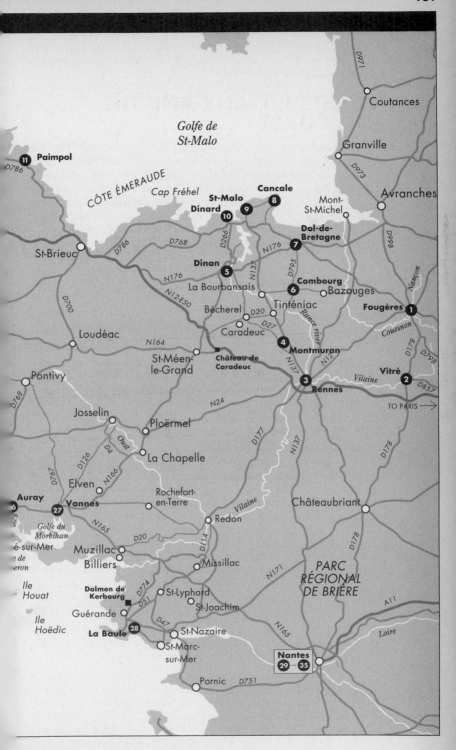

Golfe de St-Malo

CÔTE ÉMERAUDE

Cap Fréhel

Paimpol ⑪

Cancale ⑧

St-Malo

Dinard ⑩ ⑨

Mont-St-Michel

Avranches

Coutances

Granville

Dol-de-Bretagne ⑦

St-Brieuc

Dinan ⑤

La Bourbansais

Combourg ⑥

Bazouges

Fougères ①

Bécherel

Tinténiac

Caradeuc

Montmuran ④

Vitré ②

Loudéac

St-Méen-le-Grand

Château de Caradeuc

⑤ **Rennes**

TO PARIS ➝

Pontivy

Josselin

Ploërmel

N24

La Chapelle

Rochefort-en-Terre

Auray

Elven

Vannes ㉗

Golfe du Morbihan

Redon

Châteaubriant

é-sur-Mer
e de
eron

Muzillac

Billiers

Missillac

PARC RÉGIONAL DE BRIÈRE

Ile Houat

Dolmen de Kerbourg

St-Lyphard

St-Joachim

Ile Hoëdic

Guérande

La Baule ㉘

St-Nazaire

St-Marc-sur-Mer

Loire

Pornic

Nantes ㉙—㉟

when autumnal colors and crisp evenings make for a particularly invigorating visit. Late summer, however, is the most festive time in Brittany: The two biggest pardons take place on July 26 (Sainte-Anne d'Auray) and the last Sunday in August (Sainte-Anne-la-Palud); the Celtic Festival de Cornouaille is held in Quimper in late July.

NORTHEAST BRITTANY AND THE CHANNEL COAST

Northeast Brittany extends from the city of Rennes to the coast. The rolling farmland around Rennes is strewn with mighty castles in Vitré, Fougères, and Dinan—remnants of Brittany's ceaseless efforts to repel invaders during the Middle Ages and a testimony to the wealth derived from pirate and merchant ships. The beautiful Côte d'Émeraude (Emerald Coast) stretches west from Cancale to St-Brieuc, and the dramatic Côte de Granit Rose (Pink Granite Coast) extends from Paimpol to Trébeurden and the Corniche Bretonne. Follow the coastal routes D786 and D34—winding, narrow roads that total less than 100 km (62 mi) but can take five hours to drive; the spectacular views make it worthwhile.

Fougères

❶ *320 km (200 mi) west of Paris via A11, A81, and D30; 47 km (29 mi) southeast of Mont-St-Michel; 48 km (30 mi) northeast of Rennes.*

For many centuries Fougères, a traditional cobbling and cider-making center, was a frontier town, valiantly attempting to guard Brittany against attack. One of the reasons for its conspicuous lack of success is the site of its castle: Instead of sitting high up on the hill, it spreads out down in the valley, though the sinuous River Nançon does make an admirable moat. A number of medieval houses line rue de la Pinterie, which leads directly from the castle up to the undistinguished heart of town.

The 13-tower **Château de Fougères,** one of the largest in Europe, covers more than 5 acres. Although largely in ruins, it's an excellent example of the military architecture of the Middle Ages, impressive both inside and out. The thick walls—20 ft across in places—were intended to resist 15th-century artillery fire, but the castle proved vulnerable to surprise attacks and sieges. A visit inside the castle walls reveals three lines of fortification, with the keep at their heart. From the **Tour Mélusine** (Mélusine Tower) are memorable views of Fougères; in the **Tour Raoul** is a small shoe museum. The second and third stories of the **Tour de Coigny** were transformed into a chapel during the 16th century. ⊠ *Pl. Symon,* ☎ *02–99–99–79–59.* ☚ *23 frs.* ⊙ *Feb.–Mar. and Oct.–Dec., daily 10–noon and 2–5; Apr.–mid-June, daily 9:30–noon and 2–6; mid-June–Sept., daily 9–7.*

The town's oldest streets are alongside the castle, clustered around the elegant slate spire of **St-Sulpice** (⊠ Rue Le Bouteiller), a Flamboyant Gothic church with several fine altarpieces.

In the 1790s Fougères was a center of Royalist resistance to the French Revolution. Much of the action in 19th-century writer Honoré Balzac's bloodcurdling novel *Les Chouans* takes place hereabouts. The novel's heroine, Marie de Verneuil, had rooms close to the church of **St-Léonard** (⊠ Rue de la Porte-St-Léonard), overlooking the Nançon Valley. To get there from the cathedral, follow the river south. Both the footpath leading to the building and the church, with its ornate facade and 17th-century tower, have changed little; the park through which the path leads is known today as the **Jardin Public** (Public Garden).

Also inspired by the scenery of Fougères was locally born Emmanuel de La Villéon (1858–1944), a little-known Impressionist painter. More than 100 paintings, pastels, watercolors, and drawings—revealing a serene, underestimated talent—are on display at the **Musée La Villéon.** It is in one of the oldest surviving houses (dating from the 16th century) in Fougères. The artist's work ranges from compassionate studies of toiling peasants to pretty landscapes where soft shades of green melt into hazy blue horizons. To reach it from the Jardin Public, head left past St-Léonard and cross the square into the adjacent rue Nationale. ⊠ *51 rue Nationale,* ☎ *02–99–99–19–98.* 🖾 *Free.* ☉ *Wed.–Sun. 10–noon and 2–5.*

Dining and Lodging

$$ ✕🖾 **Voyageurs.** The refined cuisine—local foie gras and sweetbreads in Madeira sauce—has made this hotel-restaurant a favorite. Save room for the dessert cart loaded with homemade pastries (the restaurant is closed for lunch Saturday and for dinner Sunday). Some rooms have been pleasantly redecorated in light colors and chintzes; ask for one of these. ⊠ *10 pl. Gambetta, 35300,* ☎ *02–99–99–08–20,* 𝔽𝔸𝕏 *02–99–99–99–04. 37 rooms. Restaurant. AE, MC, V. Closed mid-Dec.–early Jan.*

Vitré

❷ *30 km (19 mi) south of Fougères via D798 and D178, 36 km (22 mi) east of Rennes.*

Built high above the Vilaine Valley, Vitré (pronounced vee-*tray*) is one of the age-old gateways to Brittany: There's still a feel of the Middle Ages about its formidable castle, tightly packed and half-timber houses, remaining ramparts, and dark, narrow alleys. The castle stands at the west end of town, facing narrow, cobbled streets as picturesque as any in Brittany— rue Poterie, rue d'Embas, and rue Beaudrairie, originally the home of tanners (the name comes from *baudoyers,* or leather workers).

★ Rebuilt in the 14th and 15th centuries to protect Brittany from invasion, the 11th-century **Château de Vitré**—shaped in an imposing triangle with fat, round towers—proved to be one of the province's most successful fortresses: During the Hundred Years' War (1337–1453), the English repeatedly failed to take it, even though they occupied the rest of the town. It's a splendid sight, especially from the vantage point of rue de Fougères across the river valley below. Time, not foreigners, came closest to ravaging the castle, which was heavily though tastefully restored during the past century. The **Hôtel de Ville** (Town Hall), however, is an unfortunate 1913 accretion to the castle courtyard. Visit the wing to the left of the entrance, beginning with the **Tour St-Laurent** and its museum, which contains 15th- and 16th-century sculptures, Aubusson tapestries, and engravings. Continue along the walls via the **Tour de l'Argenterie** (Silverware Tower)—which contains a macabre collection of stuffed frogs and reptiles preserved in glass jars—to the **Tour de l'Oratoire** (Oratory Tower). ☎ *02–99–96–76–51.* 🖾 *20 frs.* ☉ *Apr.–June, Wed.–Mon. 10–noon and 2–5:30; July–Sept., daily 10–12:30 and 2–6:15; Oct.–Mar., Mon. 2–5:30, Wed.–Fri. 10–noon and 2–5.*

Fragments of the town's medieval ramparts include the 15th-century **Tour de la Bridolle** (⊠ Pl. de la République), five blocks up from the castle. The church of **Notre-Dame** (⊠ Pl. Notre-Dame), with its fine, pinnacled south front, was built in the 15th and 16th centuries.

Dining and Lodging

$$ ✗▥▦ **Le Petit Billot.** Carved wood paneling and faded pastels give this hotel a delightful French Provincial atmosphere. The staff is friendly, and the restaurant serves good food: Try the vegetable terrine with a chopped tomato sauce or the grilled fresh mackerel. ⊠ *5 pl. du Général-Leclerc, 35500,* ☎ *02–99–75–02–10,* FAX *02–99–74–72–96. 22 rooms, 5 with bath. Restaurant. MC, V. Closed last wk of Dec. No dinner Sat.*

Rennes

❸ *6 km (22 mi) west of Vitré via D857 and N157, 348 km (216 mi) west of Paris, 107 km (66 mi) north of Nantes.*

Rennes (pronounced ren) is the traditional capital of Brittany. It has a different flavor from other towns in the region, mainly because of a terrible fire in 1720, which lasted a week and destroyed half the city. The remaining cobbled streets and 15th-century half-timber houses form an interesting contrast to the classical feel of the cathedral and Jacques Gabriel's disciplined granite buildings, broad avenues, and spacious squares. Many of the 15th- and 16th-century houses in the streets surrounding the cathedral have been converted into shops, boutiques, restaurants, and *crêperies* (crepe restaurants).

A late-18th-century building in classical style that took 57 years to construct, the **Cathédrale St-Pierre** looms above rue de la Monnaie at the west end of the old town, bordered by the Rance River. Stop in to admire its richly decorated interior and outstanding 16th-century Flemish altarpiece. ⊠ *Pl. St-Pierre.* ⊗ *Mon.–Sat. 8:30–noon and 2–5, Sun. 8:30–noon.*

The **Palais de Justice** (Law Courts; ⊠ Rue Nationale), the palatial original home of the Breton Parliament and now the Rennes law courts, was designed in 1618 by Salomon de Brosse, architect of the Luxembourg Palace in Paris. It was the most important building in Rennes to escape the 1720 fire, but in 1994, following a massive demonstration by Breton fishermen demanding state subsidies, a disastrous fire broke out at the Parliament building, which left it just a charred shell. Much of the artwork—though damaged—was saved by firefighters, who arrived at the scene after the building was already engulfed in flames. It was a case of the fire bell that cried "fire" once too often; a faulty bell, which rang regularly for no reason, had led the man on duty to ignore the ringing. Restoration was expected to be completed in 2001, and the building was partly reopened for legal business (and guided tours [☎ 02–99–67–11–11 for details]) in early 2000.

The **Musée des Beaux-Arts** (Fine Arts Museum) contains works by Georges de La Tour, Jean-Baptiste Chardin, Camille Corot, Paul Gauguin, and Maurice Utrillo, to name a few. ⊠ *20 quai Émile-Zola,* ☎ *02–99–28–55–85.* ▦ *20 frs.* ⊗ *Wed.–Mon. 10–noon and 2–6.*

★ Take a stroll through the lovely **Jardin du Thabor** (⊠ Rue de Paris), east of the Palais des Musées. It's a large, formal French garden with regimented rows of trees, shrubs, flowers, and a notable view of the church of **Notre-Dame-en-St-Melaine.**

Dining and Lodging

$ ✗ **Piccadilly Tavern.** Around the corner from the Palais de Justice and next to the municipal theater is this oddly named tavern. Its huge, sunny terrace is the perfect place to people-watch while downing a half-dozen fresh oysters and an aperitif. ⊠ *15 Galeries du Théâtre,* ☎ *02–99–78–17–17. MC, V.*

$$$ ✕⊞ **Lecoq-Gadby.** A 19th-century mansion with huge fireplaces and
★   antiques sets the stage for this cozy hotel-restaurant. Rooms have a homey
feel and four-poster beds with floral covers; some have fireplaces.
French presidents have come here to dine on traditional Breton spe-
cialties—*biscuit de langoustines aux olives noires* (puff pastry filled with
langoustines and black olives) and *frigousse aux trois volailles* (poul-
try stew). It's a popular spot, so reserve ahead; there's no dinner Sun-
day. ⊠ *156 rue d'Antrain, 35300,* ☎ *02–99–38–05–55,* 𝖥𝖠𝖷 *02–99–
38–53–40. 11 rooms. Restaurant. AE, DC, MC, V.*

$$ ⊞ **Garden.** This picturesque hotel has an age-old wooden gallery overlooking the sunny inner courtyard where breakfast is served. Rooms
are small but nice, with bright colors and antiques. ⊠ *3 rue Duhamel,
35000,* ☎ *02–99–65–45–06,* 𝖥𝖠𝖷 *02–99–65–02–62. 24 rooms. AE,
MC, V.*

$$ ⊞ **Mercure Centre.** This stately 19th-century hotel is centrally located
on a quiet, narrow backstreet close to the cathedral. Rooms overlook
the street or a courtyard; all are modern and functional. ⊠ *6 rue Lan-
juinais, 35000,* ☎ *02–99–79–12–36,* 𝖥𝖠𝖷 *02–99–79–65–76. 43 rooms.
AE, DC, MC, V.*

Nightlife and the Arts

Dance the night away at **L'Espace** (⊠ 45 bd. de la Tour d'Auvergne,
☎ 02–99–30–21–95) or the **Pym's Club** (⊠ 27 pl. du Colombier, ☎
02–99–67–30–00).

Brittany's principal theater is the **Opéra de Rennes** (⊠ Pl. de la Mairie,
☎ 02–99–78–48–78). All kinds of performances are staged at the
Théâtre National de Bretagne (⊠ 1 rue St-Hélier, ☎ 02–99–31–12–
31). The famous, annual international rock-and-roll festival, **Les Trans-
musicales** (☎ 02–99–31–12–10 for information), happens the second
week of December in bars around town and at the Théâtre National
de Bretagne. The first week of July sees **Les Tombées de la Nuit,** the
Nightfall Festival, featuring ballet, music, and theater performances
staged in old historic streets and churches (☎ 02–99–67–11–11 for in-
formation).

Shopping

A lively **market** is held on place des Lices on Saturday morning.

Montmuran

❹ *24 km (15 mi) northwest of Rennes via N137 and D221.*

The **Château de Montmuran** was once home to one of France's finest
knights, Bertrand du Guesclin (1320–80). Commemorated in count-
less squares and hostelries across the province, du Guesclin sprang to
prominence at the age of 17, when he entered a jousting tournament
in disguise and successfully unseated several hoarier knights. He went
on to lead the onslaught against the English during the Hundred Years'
War. An alley of oak and beech trees leads up to the main 17th-cen-
tury building, which is surrounded by a moat and flanked by four tow-
ers, two built in the 12th century, two in the 14th. You can visit the
towers and a small museum devoted to the castle's history. The château
also has two pleasant guest rooms, which are open from May to Oc-
tober. Call to reserve. ⊠ *Les Iffs,* ☎ *02–99–45–88–88.* 🎟 *25 frs.* ☯
June–Sept., daily 2–7.

OFF THE   **CHÂTEAU DE CARADEUC** – Ambitiously dubbed the Versailles of Brittany,
BEATEN PATH   this château, 8 km (5 mi) west of Montmuran just beyond Bécherel, is
privately owned and not open to the public. But you can explore the
statues, flower beds, and leafy alleys in the surrounding park—Brittany's

largest. ⊠ *Rte. de Chateaubriand,* ☎ *02–99–66–77–76.* 💳 *15 frs.* ☉ *Apr.–Oct., daily 10–6; Nov.–Mar., weekends 2–6.*

Dinan

★ ❺ *29 km (18 mi) northwest of Montmuran via D27 and D68, 24 km (15 mi) south of Dinard.*

Like Montmuran (☞ *above*), Dinan has close links with warrior-hero Bertrand du Guesclin, who won a famous victory here in 1359 and promptly married a local girl, Tiphaine Raguenel. When he died in the siege of Châteauneuf-de-Randon in Auvergne (central France) in 1380, his body was dispatched home to Dinan. Owing to the great man's popularity, only his heart completed the journey (it rests in the basilica); the rest of him was confiscated by devoted followers along the way.

On place des Merciers, rue de l'Apport, and rue de la Poissonnerie, note the splendid triangular-gable wooden houses. Rue du Jerzual, which leads down to Dinan's harbor, is also a beautifully preserved medieval street, divided halfway down by the town walls and the massive Porte du Jerzual gateway and lined with boutiques and crafts shops in 15th- and 16th-century houses. A few restaurants brighten the area around the harbor, and boats sail up the Rance River in summer, but the abandoned warehouses mostly bear witness to the town's vanished commercial activity. Above the harbor, near Porte St-Malo, is the leafy Promenade des Grands Fossés, the best-preserved section of the town walls, which leads to the castle. The **tourist office** (⊠ 6 rue de l'Horloge) is housed in a 16th-century building in the old town.

For a superb view of town, climb to the top of the medieval **Tour de l'Horloge** (Clock Tower). ⊠ *Rue de l'Horloge.* 💳 *10 frs.* ☉ *July–Sept., daily 10:45–1:15 and 3–6.*

Du Guesclin's heart lies in the north transept of the **Basilique St-Sauveur** (⊠ Pl. St-Sauveur). The church's style ranges from the Romanesque south front to the Flamboyant Gothic facade and Renaissance side chapels. The old trees in the **Jardin Anglais** (English Garden) behind the church provide a nice frame. More spectacular views can be found at the bottom of the garden, which looks down the plummeting Rance Valley to the river below.

The **Château,** at the end of the Promenade des Petits Fossés, has a two-story tower, the **Tour du Coëtquen,** and a 100-ft, 14th-century **donjon** (keep), containing a museum with varied displays of medieval effigies and statues, Breton furniture, and local lace coiffes. ⊠ *Porte de Guichet,* ☎ *02–96–39–45–20.* 💳 *25 frs.* ☉ *Mar.–May and mid-Sept.–mid-Nov., daily 10–11:30 and 2–5:30; June–mid-Sept., daily 10–5:30; mid-Nov.–Feb., Wed.–Mon. 1:30–5:30.*

Dining and Lodging

$ ✕ **Relais des Corsaires.** This riverbank spot is named, it is said, after the old-time pirates who sporadically plundered Dinan and the Rance Valley. The midrange prix-fixe menu provides an ample four-course meal of traditional French cuisine, with an emphasis on steak and fish. The welcoming proprietors, Jacques and Barbel Pauwels, also have a more informal grill, *Au Petit Corsair,* in the 15th-century building next door. ⊠ *7 rue du Quai,* ☎ *02–96–39–40–17. AE, DC, MC, V. Closed Jan.–Feb.*

$$$ 🏠 **Avaugour.** Opposite the castle tower, this hotel has a sunny flower ★   garden where breakfast and afternoon tea are served. Most rooms are cozy and look out onto either the garden or the castle. Start the day

with the full buffet breakfast. Owner Nicolas Caron enjoys speaking English and helping plan day trips. ⊠ *1 pl. du Champ-Clos, 22100,* ☎ *02–96–39–07–49,* FAX *02–96–85–43–04. 27 rooms. Restaurant, breakfast room. AE, DC, MC, V.*

$$ 🖭 **Arvor.** The cobbled streets of the old town are visible from this comfortably converted 18th-century convent across from the tourist office. It's run by the convivial Brigitte Urvoy and is a good value without frills. ⊠ *5 rue Auguste-Pavie, 22100,* ☎ *02–96–39–21–22,* FAX *02–96–39–83–09. 23 rooms. AE, MC, V.*

Nightlife and the Arts

Every two years (next in 2002), on the first weekend in September, medieval France is re-created with a market, parade, jousting tournament, and street music for **La Fête des Remparts** (Ramparts Festival), one of the largest medieval festivals in Europe.

Shopping

The cobbled, sloping **rue de Jerzual** is lined with medieval houses containing shops selling crafts by local wood-carvers, jewelers, leather workers, glass specialists, and silk painters.

En Route Halfway between Dinan and Combourg is the castle of **La Bourbansais,** built in the 1580s. Most of the interior furnishings date from the 18th century, including the fine collection of porcelain and tapestries. Its extensive gardens contain a small zoo and a pack of hunting hounds. ⊠ *Just north of D75,* ☎ *02–99–69–40–07.* 🖭 *Castle 55 frs, park 55 frs, castle and park 68 frs.* ☉ *Castle Apr.–Oct., daily 2–6; Nov.–Mar., Sun. 3:30–5; park daily 10–noon and 2–6.*

Combourg

❻ *24 km (15 mi) southeast of Dinan via D794, 39 km (24 mi) north of Rennes.*

The pretty lakeside village of Combourg is dominated by the boyhood home of Romantic writer Viscount René de Chateaubriand (1768–1848), the thick-walled, four-tower **Château de Combourg.** The castle dates mainly from the 14th and 15th centuries. The Chateaubriand archives and the writer's austere bedroom are in the **Tour du Chat** (Cat's Tower). Chateaubriand was a leading light of Romanticism and the return-to-nature movement—his novel *Atala and René,* about a tragic love affair between a French solider and a Native American maiden, was a international sensation in the mid-19th century. The château grounds—ponds, woods, and cattle-strewn meadowland—are suitably mournful and can seem positively desolate under leaden skies. ☎ *02–99–73–22–95.* 🖭 *25 frs, park only 8 frs.* ☉ *Castle open Apr.–June and Sept., Tues.–Sun. 2–5:30; July–Aug., daily 11–12:30 and 1:30–5:30; Oct., Tues.–Sun. 2–4:30; park also open Apr.–Oct., Tues.–Sun. 10–noon.*

OFF THE
BEATEN PATH

CHÂTEAU DE LA BALLUE – This castle, 18 km (11 mi) east of Combourg, dates to 1620. The stylish interior has some of the original wood paneling and a huge granite staircase. The 19th-century writers Alfred de Musset, Honoré Balzac, and Victor Hugo all stayed here, and exhibitions of contemporary art maintain the cultural tradition today. In the garden is sculpture, along with leafy groves, a labyrinth, and the Temple of Diana. You can stay the night, too, in one of the five large guest rooms (each with a four-poster bed), and dine with the dynamic English-speaking owners Alain Schrotter and Marie-France Barrère. ⊠ *Bazouges-la-Pérouse,* ☎ *02–99–97–47–86,* FAX *02–99–97–47–70.* 🖭 *35 frs.* ☉ *Mid-Mar.–mid-Nov., daily 10:30–5:30.*

Dining

$-$$ ✕ **L'Ecrivain.** Inventive, light cuisine and good fixed-price menus (start-
★ ing at just 80 francs) have made this unpretentious restaurant the best
in town. Ask for a table in the intimate, wood-paneled dining room,
with candles on the tables, rather than in the bustling larger hall. ⊠ *1
pl. St-Gilduin,* ☎ *02–99–73–01–61. MC, V. Closed Thurs. and first
½ Mar. No dinner Wed.*

Dol-de-Bretagne

❼ *17 km (11 mi) north of Combourg via D795, 56 km (35 mi) north of
Rennes.*

The ancient town of Dol-de-Bretagne, which still has its original ramparts, looks out over the Marais de Dol, a marshy plain stretching across
to Mont-St-Michel, 21 km (13 mi) northeast. For extensive views of
the Marais as well as Mont-Dol, a 200-ft windmill-topped mound 3
km (2 mi) north and the legendary scene of combat between St. Michael
and the devil, walk along the **Promenade des Douves,** on the northern part of the original ramparts. Dol's picturesque main street is
Grande-Rue des Stuarts, lined with medieval houses; the oldest, the **Maison des Palets,** at No. 17, has a chunky row of Romanesque arches.

The **Cathédrale St-Samson** (⊠ Pl. de la Cathédrale) is a damp, soaring, fortresslike bulk of granite dating mainly from the 12th to the 14th
centuries. This mighty building shows just how influential the bishopric
of Dol was in days gone by. The richly sculpted Great Porch, carved
wooden choir stalls, and stained glass in the chancel warrant scrutiny.

The new **Cathéfraloscope** (Cathedral Museum), opposite the cathedral,
uses models, frescoes, ground plans, and special lighting effects to explain the construction of France's cathedrals, their feats of engineering, and the development of the soaring Gothic style that characterizes
them. There are also sections on church liturgy and stained glass. ⊠
Pl. de la Cathédrale, ☎ *02–99–48–35–30.* ☜ *40 frs.* ☉ *May–Sept.,
daily 9–7; Oct.–mid–Jan. and mid-Feb.–Apr., daily 10–6.*

The small, cheerfully managed **Musée Historique** (History Museum),
by the cathedral, houses costumes, weapons, and models retracing life
in Dol since prehistoric times. The pride of the museum is its assembly of wooden religious statues. ⊠ *2 pl. de la Trésorerie,* ☎ *02–99–
48–33–46.* ☜ *20 frs.* ☉ *Easter–Sept., daily 9:30–12:30 and 1:30–6.*

Dining and Lodging

$$ ✕🏨 **Bresche Arthur.** With its crisp outlines, white walls, and glassed-
in terrace, this hotel doesn't look as historic as it sounds. But it is cozy,
and rooms are inexpensive if functional. Character and indulgence are
reserved for the restaurant (closed Monday, no dinner Sunday), where
chef-owner Philippe Martel serves classically inspired dishes such as
roast pigeon with blackcurrant and ginger and ravioli stuffed with *pe-
tits gris* (small snails). ⊠ *36 bd. Deminiac, 35120,* ☎ *02–99–48–01–
44,* ᖴᎯᚷ *02–99–48–16–32. 24 rooms. Restaurant. MC, V. Closed Feb.*

$$ ✕🏨 **Domaine des Ormes.** The former country retreat of the bishops of
Dol, south of town, serves as the backdrop for this complex with a camp-
site, rental chalets, golf course, artificial lakes, outdoor pool, archery
concourse, cricket ground, and modern hotel with spacious rooms and
a bilingual staff. Decor throughout, however, is nondescript. But the
restaurant's menu is inventive, with a fine array of meats, shellfish, and
pâtés for 95 francs and up. The salads at the golf club are a good
lunchtime bet. ⊠ *35120 Épiniac (7 km [4 mi] south of Dol-de-Bretagne),*
☎ *02–99–73–43–33,* ᖴᎯᚷ *02–99–73–40–84. 32 rooms. Restaurant, bar,
pool, 19-hole golf course, 2 tennis courts, archery. AE, DC, MC, V.*

Cancale

⑧ *22 km (14 mi) northwest of Dol via D155 and D76.*

If you enjoy eating oysters, be sure to get to Cancale, a picturesque fishing village renowned for its offshore *bancs d'huîtres* (oyster beds). You can sample the little brutes at countless stalls or restaurants along the quay. The **Musée de l'Huître et du Coquillage** (Oyster and Shellfish Museum) explains everything you ever wanted to know about farming oysters. ⊠ *Les Parcs St-Kerber, Plage de l'Aurore,* ☏ *02–99–89–69–99.* ☉ *Guided 1-hr tours mid-June–mid-Sept., daily 11 and 3–5; mid-Feb.–mid-June and Oct., daily 3.*

Dining and Lodging

$$$$ ✕⊞ **Château Richeux.** One of three hotels owned by the Roellingers of the Bricourt (☞ *above*), the Château Richeux occupies an imposing turn-of-the-20th-century waterfront mansion, built on the ruins of the du Guesclin family's 11th-century château, 4 mi (2½ km) south of Cancale. Request one of the tower rooms, which have stunning views of Mont-St-Michel Bay. Le Coquillage, the small restaurant (closed mid-November through mid-December) majors in local oysters. ⊠ *Le Point du Jour, St-Méloir des Ondes, 35350,* ☏ *02–99–89–25–25,* ℻ *02–99–89–18–49. 13 rooms. Restaurant. AE, DC, MC, V.*

$$$–$$$$ ✕⊞ **Bricourt.** This large 18th-century stone house where chef Olivier Roellinger grew up is now home to one of the region's best restaurants. Murals, stone fireplaces, and antique tiles create an imposing yet cozy atmosphere. Local seafood dishes seasoned with exotic spices are the specialty; don't skip dessert. The restaurant is closed Tuesday and Wednesday in winter. If you wish to stay the night, attractive rooms (with views across the bay toward Mont-St-Michel) are available in the annex on rue des Rimains, a short walk away. ⊠ *1 rue Du-Guesclin, 35260,* ☏ *02–99–89–64–76,* ℻ *02–99–89–88–47. 6 rooms. Restaurant. AE, DC, MC, V.*

En Route   Heading north from Cancale, past the attractive beach of Port-Mer, takes you to the jagged rock formations rising from the sea at the **Pointe de Grouin.** From here follow D201 along the coast to St-Malo.

St-Malo

★ **⑨** *23 km (14 mi) west of Cancale via coastal D201, 69 km (43 mi) north of Rennes.*

Facing Dinard across the Rance Estuary lies the ancient walled town of St-Malo. The stone ramparts of this onetime pirate base have withstood the Atlantic since the 12th century. They were considerably enlarged and modified in the 18th century and now extend from the castle for more than 1½ km (1 mi) around the old town—known as the *intra-muros* (within the walls). The views are stupendous, especially at high tide.

The town itself has proved less resistant: A weeklong fire in 1944, kindled by retreating Nazis, wiped out nearly all the old buildings. Restoration work was more painstaking than brilliant, but the narrow streets and granite houses of the old town were satisfactorily re-created, enabling St-Malo to regain its role as a busy fishing port, seaside resort, and tourist destination. Battalions of tourists invade this quaint town, so if you want to avoid crowds, don't come here in summer.

At the edge of the ramparts is the **Château,** whose great keep and watchtowers command an impressive view of the harbor and coastline. It houses the **Musée d'Histoire de la Ville** (Town History Museum), devoted to local history, and the **Galerie Quic-en-Grogne,** a museum in a tower, where various episodes and celebrities from St-Malo's past are recalled by way of waxworks. ⊠ *Hôtel de Ville,* ☎ *02–99–40–71–57.* 🎫 *27 frs.* ☉ *Tues.–Sun. 10–noon and 2–6.*

Five hundred yards offshore is the **Ile du Grand Bé,** a small island housing the somber military tomb of the great Romantic writer Viscount René de Chateaubriand, who was born in St-Malo. The islet can be reached by a causeway at low tide.

The **Fort National,** also offshore and only accessible by causeway at low tide, is a massive fortress with a dungeon constructed in 1689 by that military-engineering genius Sébastien de Vauban. ☎ *02–99–56–64–48.* 🎫 *20 frs.* ☉ *Easter–Oct.; call ahead. Times of ½-hr guided tours depend on tides.*

You can pay homage to Jacques Cartier, who set sail from St-Malo in 1535 on a voyage in which he would discover the St. Lawrence River and found Québec, at his tomb in the church of **St-Vincent** (⊠ At top of Grande-Rue). His statue looks out over the town ramparts, four blocks away, along with that of swashbuckling corsair Robert Surcouf (hero of many daring 18th-century raids on the British navy), wagging an angry finger over the waves at England.

Dining and Lodging

$$ ✕ **Chalut.** Locals and tourists come to this simple, casual, friendly restaurant where the emphasis is on fish. You can inspect the night's fare, on ice in front or in the large tank in the dining room. ⊠ *8 rue de la Corne-de-Cerf,* ☎ *02–99–56–71–58. AE, MC, V. Closed Mon. No dinner Sun. Sept.–June.*

$ ✕ **Café de la Bourse.** Prawns and oysters are downed by the shovelful in this bustling brasserie in the old town. Replete with wooden seats, ships' wheels, and posters of grizzled old sea dogs, it's hardly high design. But the large L-shape dining room makes amends with friendly service and a seafood platter for two that includes tanklike crabs flanked by an army of cockles, snails, and periwinkles. ⊠ *1 rue de Dinan,* ☎ *02–99–56–47–17. MC, V. Closed Wed. Nov.–Easter.*

$$–$$$ 🛏 **Atlantis.** The view of the sea is magnificent from the hotel's terrace and rooms. The largest and most luxurious rooms are pricey, but others are quite reasonable. The bar, overlooking the water, and the *salon de thé* (tea shop) add to the hotel's charm. ⊠ *49 chaussée du Sillon, 35400,* ☎ *02–99–56–09–26,* FAX *02–99–56–41–65. 53 rooms. Bar, tea shop. AE, V. Closed Jan.*

$$ 🛏 **Elisabeth.** In a town house built into the ramparts of the city wall, ★   the Elisabeth, near the Porte St-Louis, is a little gem of sophistication in touristy St-Malo. Rooms are generally small but tastefully furnished; rates vary with size. ⊠ *2 rue des Cordiers, 35400,* ☎ *02–99–56–24–98,* FAX *02–99–56–39–24. 17 rooms. AE, DC, MC, V.*

$$ 🛏 **Jean-Bart.** This clean, quiet hotel next to the ramparts is done in cool blues. Beds are comfortable and bathrooms modern, but the rooms, some with sea views, are somewhat small. ⊠ *12 rue de Chartres, 35400,* ☎ *02–99–40–33–88,* FAX *02–99–40–33–88. 18 rooms. MC, V. Closed mid-Nov.–Mar.*

Nightlife and the Arts

Bar de L'Univers (⊠ Pl. Chateaubriand) is a nice spot to sip a drink in a pirate's lair setting. **La Belle Époque** (⊠ 11 rue de Dinan) is a popular hangout for all ages till the wee hours. **L'Escalier** (⊠ La Buzardière, rue de la Tour-du-Bonheur) is the place for dancing the night away.

In summer performances are held at the **Théâtre Chateaubriand** (⊠ 6 rue Groult-de-St-Georges, ☎ 02–99–40–98–05). Bastille Day (July 14) sees the **Fête du Clos Poulet,** a town festival with traditional dancing. August brings a religious music festival, the **Festival de la Musique Sacrée.**

Outdoor Activities and Sports

The **Club Hippique La Cravache** (⊠ In St-Coulomb, 8 km (5 mi) east of St-Malo on D255), ☎ 02–99–81–65–03) is the source for horses. The harbor and area outside the breakwater are popular sailing spots; boats are available from **Étoile Marine** (⊠ 6 av. Louis-Martin, ☎ 02–99–40–48–72).

Shopping

A lively outdoor **market** is held in the streets of old St-Malo every Tuesday and Friday.

Dinard

🔟 *13 km (8 mi) west of St-Malo via D168, 71 km (44 mi) north of Rennes.*

Dinard is the most elegant resort town on this stretch of the Brittany coast. Its picture-book setting on the Rance Estuary opposite the walled town of St-Malo lured the English aristocracy here in droves toward the end of the 19th century. What started out as a small fishing port soon became a seaside mecca of lavish Belle Epoque villas, grand hotels, and a bustling casino. A number of modern establishments punctuate the landscape, but the town still retains something of an Edwardian tone. To make the most of Dinard's beauty, head down to the Pointe de la Vicomte, at the town's southern tip, where the cliffs give panoramic views across the Baie du Prieuré and Rance Estuary, or stroll along the narrow promenade.

The **Promenade Clair de Lune** hugs the seacoast on its way toward the English Channel and passes in front of the small jetty used by boats crossing to St-Malo. It really hits its stride as it rounds the **Pointe du Moulinet** and heads toward the sandy **Plage du Prieuré,** named after a priory that once stood here. River meets sea in a foaming mass of rock-pounding surf: Be careful as you walk along the slippery path to the calm shelter of the **Plage de l'Écluse,** an inviting sandy beach, bordered by the casino and numerous stylish hotels. The coastal path picks up on the west side of Plage de l'Écluse, ringing the Pointe de la Malouine and the Pointe des Étêtés before arriving at the **Plage de St-Énogat.**

At the **Musée de la Mer** (Marine Museum and Aquarium), almost every known species of Breton bird and sea creature is on display in two rooms and 24 pools. Another room is devoted to the polar expeditions of explorer Jean Charcot, one of the first men to chart the Antarctic. ⊠ *17 av. George-V,* ☎ *02–99–46–13–90.* ☒ *15 frs.* ☉ *mid-May–mid-Sept., daily 10:30–12:30 and 3:30–7:30.*

Dining and Lodging

$$ ✕ **Présidence.** Imaginatively prepared fish and seafood are the credo of this green-front restaurant near the casino. Fillet of John Dory cooked in sherry and scallops with lentils in curry sauce are just two choice examples from the menu. ⊠ *29 bd. du Président-Wilson,* ☎ *02–99–46–44–27. AE, MC, V. Closed Mon. No dinner Sun.*

$$ ✕ **Salle à Manger.** Chef Jacques Gonthier moved to Dinard in 1997 and immediately established his new restaurant as one of the best in town. His English-speaking wife, Marie-Claire, chose the crisp blue-and-yellow color scheme, offset by the starched white tablecloths and old furniture. Her unflappable presence makes sure that a casual, unstuffy ambience prevails in the small dining room. But that shouldn't stop you from paying reverential attention to the succulent foie gras, grilled swordfish with warm oysters and citrus butter, and pigeon with

cumin and rosemary. ⊠ *25 bd. Féart,* ☎ *02–99–16–07–95. MC, V. Closed Jan. and Mon. except June–Sept.*

$$ 🏨 **Printania.** This white-walled, family-run hotel is on the Clair de Lune Promenade. Rooms have regional furnishings and pictures of local scenes; the best have balconies and a sea view (ask for Rooms 101, 102, 211, or 311). ⊠ *5 av. George-V, 35800,* ☎ *02–99–46–13–07,* ℻ *02–99–46–26–32. 59 rooms. Restaurant, bar. AE, MC, V. Closed mid-Nov.–mid-Mar.*

Nightlife

The main nightlife activity in town is at the **casino** (⊠ 4 bd. du Président-Wilson, ☎ 02–99–16–30–30).

Outdoor Activities and Sports

You can go horseback riding at the **Centre Équestre de la Côte d'Émeraude** (⊠ Le Val Porée, ☎ 02–99–46–23–57). For windsurfing, wander over to the **Wishbone Club** (⊠ Digue de l'Écluse, ☎ 02–99–88–15–20). Boats can be rented from the **Yacht Club** (⊠ Promenade Clair de Lune, ☎ 02–99–46–14–32).

En Route Forty kilometers (25 miles) west of Dinard along the coast is the **Cap Fréhel,** where dramatic pink cliffs rise vertically from the sea. The colors are best in the evening, but at any time of day the sight is formidable. Pick your way through the seagulls and cormorants, and if you're not afraid of heights, walk down past the small restaurant for a vertiginous glimpse of the rocks below. Then climb up to the lighthouse, whose beam winks at ships 100 km (over 60 mi) away. If you've got time, check out the **Fort de Latte** nearby, a 17th-century fort linked to the mainland by a drawbridge. Then head west, past fine beaches at Pléhérel and Sables-d'Or-les-Pins, to pick up D786 and skirt around the Bay of St-Brieuc.

Paimpol

⑪ *92 km (57 mi) west of Cap Fréhel via D786, 45 km (28 mi) northwest of St-Brieuc.*

Paimpol is one of the best fishing ports in the area and a good base for exploring this part of the coast. The town is a maze of narrow streets lined with local shops, a number of restaurants, and the inevitable souvenir shops. The harbor is its main focal point: Fishermen used to unload their catch from far-off seas; today, most fish is caught in the Channel. From the sharp cliffs you can see the coast's famous pink-granite rocks.

For centuries, but no longer, Breton fishermen sailed to Newfoundland each spring to harvest cod—a long and perilous journey. The **Fête des Terres-Neuvas** is a celebration of the traditional return from Newfoundland of the Breton fishing fleets on the third Sunday in July.

Dining and Lodging

$$–$$$ ✕🏨 **Repaire de Kerroc'h.** This delightful hotel overlooks the harbor
★   and has spacious rooms with artfully used odd angles. A favorite, Les Sept Isles, faces the street and has a view of the boats. Chef Louis Le Roy prepares delicious seafood dishes—skate with zesty beurre blanc and sea trout—as well as *lapereau confit* (young rabbit confit). Be sure to have breakfast, if just for the homemade confitures of bananas and green tomatoes. The restaurant is closed Tuesday and Wednesday, except in July and August. ⊠ *29 quai Morand 22500,* ☎ *02–96–20–50–13,* ℻ *02–96–22–07–46. 12 rooms. Restaurant. MC, V. Closed early Jan.–mid-Feb.*

Trébeurden

⑫ *42 km (26 mi) west of Paimpol via D786 and D65, 9 km (6 mi) northwest of Lannion.*

A small, pleasant fishing village that is now a summer resort town, Trébeurden makes a good base for exploring the pink-granite cliffs of the Corniche Bretonne, starting with the rocky point at nearby Le Castel. Take a look at the profile of the dramatic rocks off the coast near Trégastel and Perros-Guirec and use your imagination to see La Tête de Mort (Death's Head), La Tortoise, Le Sentinel, and Le Chapeau de Wellington (Wellington's Hat). The scene changes with the sunlight and the sweep and retreat of the tide, which strands fishing boats among islands that were, only hours before, hidden beneath the sea.

Dining and Lodging

$$$–$$$$ ✕🛏 **Manoir Lan Kerellec.** The beauty of the Breton coastline is embraced by this Relais & Châteaux hotel. Choose from a range of comfortable accommodations. The restaurant, whose circular dining room has a delightful model of the *St-Yves* ship suspended from its ceiling, mostly serves seafood, but the roast lamb is also good; it offers no lunch Tuesday and is closed Monday off-season. ⊠ *11 allée Centrale, 22560,* ☎ *02-96-15-47-47,* 𝖥𝖠𝖷 *02-96-23-66-88. 18 rooms. Restaurant, tennis court. AE, DC, MC, V. Closed mid-Nov.–mid-Mar.*

Morlaix

⑬ *45 km (28 mi) southwest of Trébeurden via D65 and D786, 60 km (37 mi) east of Brest.*

An unforgettable sight is the 19th-century stone railroad viaduct of Morlaix (pronounced mor-*lay*). At 300 yards long and 200 ft high, it spans the entire town. The old town is an attractive mix of half-timber houses and shops that deserve unhurried exploration. At its commercial heart is the pedestrian Grand'Rue, lined with quaint 15th-century houses. Look for the 16th-century three-story Maison de la Reine Anne (Queen Anne's House), on the adjacent rue du Mur—it's adorned with statuettes of saints.

The town's museum, known as the **Musée des Jacobins** because it is in a former Jacobin church (note the early 15th-century rose window at one end) is just off rue d'Aiguillon, parallel to Grand'Rue; it has an eclectic collection ranging from religious statues to archaeological finds and modern paintings. ⊠ *Pl. des Jacobins,* ☎ *02-98-88-68-88.* 🎟 *26 frs.* ☉ *Apr.–Oct., daily 10–12:30 and 2–6:30; Nov.–Mar., Mon. and Wed.–Fri. 10–noon and 2–5, Sat. 2–5.*

Beer at the **Brasserie des Deux Rivières** (Two Rivers Brewery—named for the two rivers, the Jarlo and the Queffleuth, that flow through Morlaix) is brewed according to traditional English methods. You complete your visit to the brewery—whose long, narrow building was originally a rope factory—with a glass of dark, cask-conditioned *Coreff* ale. ⊠ *1 pl. de la Madeleine,* ☎ *02-98-63-41-92.* 🎟 *Free.* ☉ *July–Aug., tours Mon.–Wed. 10:30, 2, and 3:30. Call ahead to book a tour in English.*

Dining and Lodging

$–$$ ✕🛏 **Europe.** Although rooms here—as in many old French hotels—are in need of renovation, they're large and the hotel is centrally located. It also has a welcoming, many-mirrored restaurant with a low-cost prix-fixe menu that might include lobster (try the fricassee of Breton lobster with chervil and garlic confit), warm oysters, and smoked salmon. ⊠ *1 rue d'Aiguillon, 29600,* ☎ *02-98-62-11-99,* 𝖥𝖠𝖷 *02-98-88-83-38. 60 rooms, 41 with bath. Restaurant. AE, DC, MC, V.*

St-Pol-de-Léon

⑭ *18 km (11 mi) northwest of Morlaix via D58.*

St-Pol-de-Léon is a lively market town famous for its cauliflowers, artichokes, and three spires: Two belong to the cathedral, the highest to the chapel.

The pleasingly proportioned **Ancienne Cathédrale** (⊠ Rue Général-Leclerc) was built between the 13th and 16th centuries and has finely carved 16th-century choir stalls that warrant a trip inside.

The **Chapelle Notre-Dame du Kreisker,** once used for meetings by the town council, has a magnificent 250-ft 15th-century granite spire, flanked at each corner by tiny spires known as *fillettes* (literally, "girls"): the prototype for countless bell towers in Brittany. From the top there is a resounding view across the Bay of Morlaix toward the English Channel. ⊠ *Rue du Général-Leclerc,* ☎ *02–98–69–01–15.* ⊠ *Tower 5 frs.* ☉ *Mid-June–mid-Sept., daily 10–noon and 2–5.*

THE ATLANTIC COAST

What Brittany offers in the way of the sea handsomely makes up for its shortage of mountain peaks and passes. Its hundreds of miles of sawtooth coastline reveal the Atlantic Ocean in its every mood and form—from the peaceful cove where waders poke about hunting seashells to the treacherous bay whose waters swirl over quicksands in unpredictable crosscurrent; from the majestic serenity of the breakers rolling across La Baule's 6 mi of white-sand beaches to the savage fury of the gigantic waves that fling their force against jagged rocks 340 dizzy ft below the cliffs of Pointe du Raz. Brittany's Atlantic coast runs southeast from the down-to-earth port of Brest to the tony city of Nantes, at the mouth of the Loire River. The wild, rugged creeks around the little-visited northwestern tip of Finistère (Land's End) gradually give way to sandy beaches south of Concarneau. Inland, the bent trees and craggy rocks look like they've been bewitched by Merlin in a bad mood.

Brest

⑮ *75 km (47 mi) southwest of Morlaix, 244 km (151 mi) west of Rennes.*

Brest's enormous, sheltered bay is strategically positioned close to the Atlantic and the English Channel. You need not spend much time here: World War II left the city in ruins. Postwar reconstruction, resulting in long, straight streets of reinforced concrete, has given latter-day Brest the unenviable reputation of being one of France's drabber cities. Its waterfront, however, is worth visiting for the few old buildings, its castle, and its museums, as well as for dramatic views across the bay toward the Plougastel Peninsula. The Pont de Recouvrance, which crosses the Penfeld River, is Europe's longest lift bridge, at 95 yards.

Begin your visit at one of the town's oldest monuments, the **Tour Tanguy,** next to the bridge. This bulky, round 14th-century tower, once used as a lookout post, contains a museum of local history with scale models of the Brest of yore. ⊠ *Free.* ☉ *Oct.–May, Wed.–Sun. 2–6; June–Sept., daily 10–noon and 2–7.*

The medieval **château** across the bridge from the Tour Tanguy, is home to the **Musée de la Marine** (Naval Museum), containing boat models, sculpture, pictures, and naval instruments. A section is devoted to the castle's 700-year history. The dungeons can also be visited. ☎ *02–98–22–12–39.* ⊠ *29 frs.* ☉ *Wed.–Mon. 10–noon and 2–6.*

French, Flemish, and Italian paintings, spanning the period from the 17th to the 20th centuries, make up the collection at the **Musée Municipal** (City Museum). ⊠ *22 rue Traverse,* ☎ *02–98–00–87–96.* 🖼 *25 frs.* ⊘ *Mon. and Wed.–Sat. 10–11:45 and 2–6, Sun. 2–6.*

The fauna and flora of the world's three ocean climates—temperate, polar, and tropical—are the themes of the exhibits at **Océanopolis,** a marine complex that was expanded in 2000 to become one of the largest in Europe, complete with an extensive aquarium. ⊠ *Rue Alain-Colas,* ☎ *02–98–34–40–40.* 🖼 *90 frs.* ⊘ *July–Sept., daily 9:30–6; Oct.–June, Mon. 2–5, Tues.–Fri. 9:30–5, weekends 9–6.*

OFF THE
BEATEN PATH

LE FOLGOËT – Pilgrims come from afar to Le Folgoët, 24 km (15 mi) northeast of Brest, to attend the pardon in early September and to drink from the Fontaine de Salaün, a fountain behind the church, whose water comes from a spring beneath the altar. The splendid church, known as the Basilique, has a sturdy north tower that serves as a beacon for miles around and, inside, a rare, intricately carved granite rood screen, separating the choir and nave.

Dining

$–$$ ✕ **Maison de l'Océan.** This giant split-level brasserie by the waterfront mirrors the city of Brest: all earnest bustle with no frills. It serves the freshest seafood at top value—two prix-fixe menus are under 100 francs, and the 149-franc menu includes a seafood platter. In the finest French tradition, the service remains hectically unflappable. ⊠ *2 quai de la Douane,* ☎ *02–98–80–44–84. AE, MC, V.*

Nightlife and the Arts

The **Festival des Trois Mers** (Three Seas Festival), in July and August, is famous for its sacred and choral music performances.

Outdoor Activities and Sports

Sailboats are available for rent at the **Centre Nautique Municipal** (⊠ Port de Plaisance Moulin Blanc, ☎ 02–98–34–64–64).

En Route Stop in **Daoulas,** 16 km (10 mi) east of Brest, to admire its still-functioning 12th-century Romanesque abbey, with cloisters and herbal garden. Then head south on N165 and D7 to the old weaving town of **Locronan,** 46 km (29 mi) away, and visit the 5th-century Église St-Ronan and the adjacent **Chapelle du Penity,** dominating the magnificently preserved ensemble of houses and main square.

Ste-Anne-la-Palud

⓰ *64 km (40 mi) south of Brest.*

It has been said that there are as many Breton saints as there are stones in the ground. One of the great attractions of the region is the celebration of a religious festival known as a village *pardon*: Banners and saintly statues are borne in colorful parades, accompanied by hymns, and the whole event is rounded off by a feast. The seaside village of Ste-Anne-la-Palud has one of the finest and most authentic age-old pardons in Brittany, held on the last Sunday in August.

Dining and Lodging

$$$–$$$$ ✕🖾 **Plage.** This former private house sits nestled in a cove on a quiet strip of sandy beach around the bay—a remote setting perfect for long, restorative walks. Some of the comfortably furnished rooms face the sea. The hotel, however, has less of a feeling of Brittany than you might want. The food in the restaurant is consistently good, especially the seafood dishes, but not very innovative; reservations are essential,

and a jacket is required. ✉ *Ste-Anne-la-Palud 29550,* ☎ *02–98–92–50–12,* FAX *02–98–92–56–54. 26 rooms, 4 suites. Restaurant, tennis court, beach. AE, DC, MC, V. Closed mid-Oct.–early Apr.*

Douarnenez

⓱ *10 km (6 mi) west of Locronan via D7, 86 km (54 mi) south of Brest.*

Douarnenez is a quaint old fishing town of quayside paths and zigzagging narrow streets. Boats come in from the Atlantic to unload their catches of mackerel, sardines, and tuna. Just over the Port-Rhu Estuary is Tréboul, a seaside resort town favored by French families.

☾ One of the three town harbors is home to the unique **Port-Musée** (Port Museum). Along the wharves, you can visit the workshops of wooden-boat wrights, sail makers, and other old-time craftspeople, then go aboard the historic trawlers, lobster boats, Thames barges, and a former lightship anchored alongside. On the second weekend of May you can sail on an antique fishing boat. ✉ *quai de Port-Rhu,* ☎ *02–98–92–65–20.* ☞ *40 frs June–Sept., 30 frs Oct.–May.* ☉ *June–Sept., daily 10–7; Oct.–Dec. and May, Tues.–Sun. 10–12:30 and 2–6.*

Dining and Lodging

$$ ✕⊞ **Ty Mad.** In the 1920s artists and writers such as Picasso and Bre-
★ ton native Max Jacob frequented this small hotel, in a quiet residential area. Rooms are not big, but the sea views are great. Delicious food is served in the glass-enclosed restaurant, including skate pâté with mint sauce and monkfish flambéed with tarragon. ✉ *3 rue St-Jean, 29100,* ☎ *02–98–74–00–53,* FAX *02–98–74–15–16. 23 rooms. Restaurant. MC, V. Closed Oct. –Easter.*

$–$$ ✕⊞ **Manoir de Moëllien.** This lovely 15th-century manor house, filled with precious antiques, is famous for its local seafood dishes. Sample the *terrine de poisson chaud* (warm seafood terrine) or the *duo de truites de mer* (poached sea trout). Rooms have terraces overlooking the garden, which makes for a peaceful, country atmosphere. ✉ *29550 Plonévez-Porzay (12 km [7 mi] northeast of Douarnenez),* ☎ *02–98–92–50–40,* FAX *02–98–92–55–21. 10 rooms. Restaurant. AE, DC, MC, V. Closed Jan.–Mar.*

Outdoor Activities and Sports

Sailboats can be rented from **Les Voiles d'Iroise** (✉ 19 quai de Port-Rhu, ☎ 02–98–92–76–25), on the bay.

Audierne

⓲ *22 km (14 mi) southwest of Douarnenez via D765.*

In summer the small working port of Audierne, where the fishermen come daily bearing the day's catch of langoustines, is a busy pleasure-boat center that is never overcrowded. Most visitors are locals, which makes for a nontouristy, welcoming atmosphere.

West of Audierne is the Cap Sizun Peninsula, whose dramatic, jagged coastline culminates with the 300-ft drop at the **Pointe du Raz,** the westernmost tip of France.

Dining and Lodging

$$–$$$ ✕⊞ **Le Goyen.** In the early morning you can watch the activity in the
★ bustling fishing port from the balcony of your very pretty room (or ultramodern suite) in this modern hotel. In the evening aperitifs are served while you wait for chef Freddy Reault's adroit Breton cuisine. Watch the port as you dine on baked turbot with a beef stock sauce, Breton lobster, or aromatic *ris de veau* (veal sweetbread). The restau-

rant is closed Monday off-season. ✉ *Pl. Jean-Simon, 29770,* ☎ *02–98–70–08–88,* FAX *02–98–70–18–77. 24 rooms, 3 suites. Restaurant AE, MC, V. Closed mid-Nov.–Easter.*

Quimper

⑲ *35 km (22 mi) east of Audierne via D784, 72 km (45 mi) south of Brest.*

Lively, commercial Quimper is the ancient capital of the Cornouaille province, founded, it is said, by King Gradlon 1,500 years ago. Quimper (pronounced cam-*pair*) owes its strange name to its site at the confluence (*kemper* in Breton) of the Odet and Steir rivers. Stroll along the banks of the Odet and through the old town, with its cathedral. Then walk along the lively shopping street, rue Kéréon, and down narrow medieval rue du Guéodet (note the house with caryatids), rue St-Mathieu, and rue du Sallé.

The **Cathédrale St-Corentin** (✉ Pl. St-Corentin) is a masterpiece of Gothic architecture and the second-largest cathedral in Brittany (after Dol-de-Bretagne's). Legendary King Gradlon is represented on horseback just below the base of the spires, harmonious mid-19th-century additions to the medieval ensemble. The 15th-century stained glass is luminous. Behind the cathedral is the stately **Jardin de l'Évêché** (Bishop's Garden).

Works by major masters, such as Rubens, Corot, and Picasso, mingle with pretty landscapes from the local Gauguin-inspired Pont-Aven school in the **Musée des Beaux-Arts** (Fine Arts Museum), next to the cathedral. ✉ *40 pl. St-Corentin,* ☎ *02–98–95–45–20.* 🎫 *25 frs.* ☉ *July–Aug., daily 9–7; Sept.–June, Wed.–Mon. 10–noon and 2–6.*

Local furniture, ceramics, and folklore top the bill at the **Musée Départemental Breton** (Breton Regional Museum). ✉ *1 rue du Roi-Gradlon,* ☎ *02–98–95–21–60.* 🎫 *25 frs.* ☉ *June–Sept., daily 9–6; Oct.–May, Tues.–Sun. 9–noon and 2–5.*

In the mid-18th century Quimper sprang to nationwide attention as a pottery manufacturing center when it began producing second-rate imitations of Rouen faience, or ceramics with blue motifs. Today's more colorful designs, based on floral arrangements and marine fauna, are still often hand-painted. Guided tours are available at the **Musée de la Faïence** (Earthenware Museum). ✉ *14 rue Jean-Baptiste-Bousquet,* ☎ *02–98–90–12–72.* 🎫 *26 frs.* ☉ *Mid-Apr.–Oct., Mon.–Sat. 10–6.*

Dining

$$ ✕ **Ambroisie.** With its yellow walls, huge contemporary paintings, and different settings at every table, this restaurant looks modern. But the food remains resolutely old-style Breton, such as rolled buckwheat crepes with smoked salmon and crab crepes. ✉ *49 rue Élie-Fréron,* ☎ *02–98–95–00–02. Reservations essential. MC, V. Closed early Jul. and part of Feb. and Nov. No dinner Sun.*

Nightlife and the Arts

The Celtic **Festival de Cornouaille** (☎ 02–98–55–53–33 for information) is held in Quimper in late July.

Shopping

Keep an eye out for such typical Breton products as woven and embroidered cloth, woolen goods, brass and wooden items, puppets, dolls, and locally designed jewelry. When it comes to distinctive Breton folk costumes, Quimper is the best place to look. The streets around the cathedral, especially **rue du Parc,** are full of shops selling the woolen goods (notably thick marine sweaters). Faience and a wide selection of hand-painted pottery can be purchased at the **Faïencerie d'Art Breton** (✉ 16 bis rue du Parc, ☎ 02–98–95–34–13).

Concarneau

⓴ *21 km (13 mi) south of Quimper via D783, 93 km (58 mi) southeast of Brest.*

Concarneau is the third-largest fishing port in France. A busy industrial town, it has a grain of charm and an abundance of tacky souvenir shops. But it's worth visiting to see the fortified islet in the middle of the harbor. Entered by a quaint drawbridge is the **Ville Close,** which was regarded as impregnable from early medieval times on. The fortifications were further strengthened by the English under John de Montfort during the War of Succession (1341–64). Three hundred years later Sébastien de Vauban remodeled the ramparts into what you see today: 1 km (½ mi) long, with splendid views across the two harbors on either side. Held here during the second half of August is the **Fête des Filets Bleus** (Blue Net Festival), a weeklong folk celebration in which Bretons in costume swirl and dance to the wail of bagpipes. ▦ *Ramparts 5 frs.* ☉ *Easter–Sept., daily 10–7:30; Oct.–Easter, daily 10–noon and 2–5.*

The **Musée de la Pêche** (Fishing Museum), close to the island gateway, has aquariums and exhibits on fishing techniques from around the world. ✉ *3 rue Vauban,* ☎ *02–98–97–10–20.* ▦ *36 frs.* ☉ *July–Aug., daily 9:30–7:30; Sept.–June, daily 10–noon and 2–6.*

Dining

$$ ✕ **Chez Armande.** Rather than opting for one of the various tourist haunts in the Ville Clos, you might like to wander 300 yards down the waterfront for an excellent fish or seafood meal at Chez Armande, where good value set menus start at around 100 francs. ✉ *15 bis av. du Dr-Nicolas,* ☎ *02–98–97–00–76. AE, DC, MC, V. Closed Wed., and mid-Dec.–early Jan., and part of Feb. No dinner Tues.*

Pont-Aven

㉑ *14 km (9 mi) east of Concarneau via D783, 91 km (56 mi) northwest of Vannes.*

Pont-Aven is a former artists' colony where Paul Gauguin lived before he headed off to the South Seas. While you're here, visit the museum dedicated to the Pont-Aven School—whose many adherents painted Breton landscapes in a dreamy, pastel-hued style now considered one of the prettier branches of Postimpressionism— cool off (in summer) with a boat trip down the estuary, or take a walk in the hills among the pastures to the Trémalo Chapel, where there is a crucifix attributed to Gauguin. While in Brittany, Gauguin painted many of his earliest masterpieces, now holding pride of place in great museums around the world. At the **Musée Municipal** (Town Museum), a permanent photography exhibition documenting the Pont-Aven School, are works by its participants. ✉ *Pl. de l'Hôtel-de-Ville,* ☎ *02–98–06–14–43.* ▦ *25 frs July–Aug., 20 frs Feb.–June and Sept.–Dec.* ☉ *July–Aug., daily 9:30–7:30; Feb.–June and Sept.–Dec., Tues.–Sun. 10–12:30 and 2–6.*

Dining and Lodging

$$$ ✕ **La Taupinière.** On the road from Concarneau, 2 mi (1 km) west of Pont-Aven, is this roadside inn with an attractive garden. The food isn't cheap, but chef Guy Guilloux's fish, crab, crayfish, and Breton ham (grilled over the large, open fire) are worth it. And his wine cellar is renowned. ✉ *Croissant St-André,* ☎ *02–98–06–03–12. Reservations* *essential. Jacket required. AE, DC, MC, V. Closed Tues. and mid-Sept.–mid-Oct. No dinner Mon.*

$$$ ✕⊞ **Moulin de Rosmadec.** The Sébilleaus' old water mill sits in the middle of the rushing, rocky Aven River. You can hear the sound of water gently spilling over the stones beneath your window. In the rustic-looking restaurant enjoy such dishes as lobster and langoustine ravioli and opt for the prix-fixe menus. Reservations are essential and a jacket recommended; the restaurant doesn't serve dinner Sunday and Wednesday from mid-September to mid-June. ⊠ *Pl. Paul-Gauguin, 29930,* ☎ *02–98–06–00–22,* FAX *02–98–06–18–00. 4 rooms. Restaurant. MC, V. Closed mid-Nov.–late Nov. and Feb.*

$$ ✕⊞ **Roz Aven.** Built into a rock face on the banks of the Aven, this efficiently run hotel has simple, clean rooms. The owner, Yann Souffez, speaks excellent English. He describes the furnishings as Louis XVI, but, at best, they appear petit bourgeois. The restaurant has a limited selection of fine prix-fixe menus and wines, priced 20% less than some fancier restaurants. ⊠ *11 quai Théodore-Botrel, 29930,* ☎ *02–98–06–13–06,* FAX *02–98–06–03–89. 24 rooms. Restaurant. MC, V.*

Lorient

㉒ *36 km (22 mi) southeast of Pont-Aven via D24.*

France's most exotically named town—founded by Colbert in 1666 as a base for the spice-seeking vessels of France's East India Company (Compagnie des Indes) bound for the Orient (thus the name)—was smashed into semi-oblivion during World War II. A handful of Art Deco mansions survived, and you may want to visit the brazen concrete church of Notre-Dame-de-Victoire for its modern frescoes and stained glass.

Fish and submarines have fueled Lorient's resurrection: This is France's leading Atlantic submarine base, and the fishing port is second only to that of Boulogne. Both types of vessel rub shoulders along the mile-long quay, and the choice at the fish market (the Halles de Merville) is unsurpassed. The town itself is at its liveliest during the Celtic Festival in August (☞ *below*).

Dining and Lodging

$$$ ✕⊞ **Château de Locguénolé.** This imposing Neoclassical château emerges from lawns and woods above the Blavet Estuary. Tapestries and 19th-century furnishings adorn public spaces and guest rooms; ask for one with a view of the river, or you may find yourself exiled to one of the rustic, cozy rooms in the renovated stables, 3 km (2 mi) away. Philippe Peudenier is one of France's most creative chefs, as his crab ravioli with coriander proves. The restaurant is closed Monday. ⊠ *Rte. de Port-Louis, 56700 Kervignac (10 km [6 mi] east of Lorient via D194),* ☎ *02–97–76–76–76,* FAX *02–97–76–82–35. 24 rooms, 4 suites. Restaurant, pool, sauna. AE, DC, MC, V. Closed Jan.–mid-Feb.*

Nightlife and the Arts

The **Festival Interceltique** (☎ 02–97–21–24–29 for information), held in the first half of August, is a jamboree of Celtic culture—music, drama, poetry, dance—with fellow Celts pouring into Lorient from all over northwestern Europe (Cornwall, Wales, Ireland, and Galicia) to celebrate.

Outdoor Activities

There's a nice beach, **Larmor-Plage,** 5 km (3 mi) south of Lorient. Or you could take a ferry to the rocky **Ile de Groix** or go across the bay to **Port-Louis,** a harbor renowned for tuna fishing and its 17th-century fort and ramparts.

Quiberon

㉓ *40 km (25 mi) southeast of Lorient via D781 and D768.*

Quiberon is a spa town with pearl-like beaches on the eastern side of the 16-km-long (10-mi-long) Presqu'île de Quiberon (Quiberon Peninsula), a stretch of rough coastal cliffs and beaches joined to the mainland by a hairbreadth of sand. Its dramatic western coast is dubbed the Côte Sauvage (Wild Coast), a mix of crevices, coves, and rocky grottoes lashed by the sea. The coast is extremely dangerous, and swimming is prohibited. Quiberon's best beach is the Grande Plage (Great Beach), on the protected side of the peninsula. Boats for nearby Belle-Ile (☞ *below*) leave from the harbor of Port-Maria.

Nightlife
The **casino** (✉ 2 bd. René-Cassin, ☎ 02–97–50–23–57) has the standard games of chance, as well as shows in summer.

Outdoor Activities and Sports
An 18-km (11-mi) footpath follows the Côte Sauvage, as does the boulevard de la Côte Sauvage, which is perfect for cycling. Bicycles are for rent at **Cyclomar** (✉ 47 pl. Hoche, ☎ 02–97–50–26–00).

Shopping
In a country where gourmandism is virtually a cultural pursuit, **Henri Le Roux** (✉ 18 rue du Port-Maria, ☎ 02–97–50–06–83) has taken the art of chocolatiering to dizzy heights.

Belle-Ile-en-Mer

㉔ *45 mins by boat from Quiberon.*

At 18 km (11 mi) long, Belle-Ile is the largest of Brittany's islands. It also lives up to its name: It's beautiful and much less commercialized than Quiberon. Because of the cost and inconvenience of reserving car berths on the ferry, cross over to the island as a pedestrian and rent a car—or, if you don't mind the hilly terrain, a bicycle.

The ferry lands at **Le Palais,** where there is a Vauban citadelle. From Le Palais head northwest to **Sauzon,** the prettiest fishing harbor on the island; from here you can see across to the Quiberon Peninsula and the Gulf of Morbihan. Continue on to the **Grotte de l'Apothicairerie,** which derives its name from the local cormorants' nests, said to resemble apothecary bottles. At Port Goulphar is the **Grand Phare** (Great Lighthouse). Built in 1835, it rises 275 ft above sea level and has one of the most powerful lights in Europe, visible from 120 km (75 mi) across the Atlantic. If the keeper is available, you may be able to climb to the top.

Dining and Lodging
$$$–$$$$ ✕▨ **Castel Clara.** This modern hotel is perched on a cliff overlooking
★ the surf and the narrow Anse de Goulphar Bay. Ask for a room with a view. In the bright, airy restaurant, chef Christophe Hardouin specializes in seafood, literally caught just offshore. The St-Pierre fish baked in sea salt, and the grilled sea bream are simple but delicious. ✉ *Port-Goulphar, 56360,* ☎ *02–97–31–84–21,* ☏ *02–97–31–51–69. 33 rooms, 10 suites. Restaurant, indoor pool, spa, tennis court. AE, DC, MC, V. Closed mid-Nov.–mid-Feb.*

Carnac

㉕ *16 km (10 mi) northeast of Quiberon via D768/D781, 32 km (20 mi) southeast of Lorient.*

At the north end of Quiberon Bay, Carnac is known for its fabulous beaches but is especially famous for its ancient stone monuments. Dating from around 4500 BC, the origin of Carnac's **menhirs** remains as obscure as those of their English contemporary, Stonehenge, although religious beliefs and astronomy were doubtless an influence. The 2,395 megalithic monuments that make up the three **Alignements**—Kermario, Kerlescan, and Ménec—form the largest megalithic site in the world and are positioned with astounding astronomical accuracy in semicircles and parallel lines over about 1 km (½ mi). The site is fenced off for protection, and you can only examine the menhirs up close October through March; in summer you must join a guided tour (some in English, costing 25 francs; call 02–97–52–29–81 for details). More can be learned at the **Archéoscope**, a visitor center, where a 30-minute presentation involving slides, a video, and models explains the menhirs' history and significance. ⊠ *Alignement du Ménec,* ☎ *02–97–52–07–49.* ▣ *45 frs.* ☉ *Daily 10–4:30, English presentations at 10:30 and 2:30.*

Carnac also has smaller-scale dolmen ensembles and three *tumuli* (mounds or barrows), including the 130-yard-long, 38-ft-high **Tumulus de St-Michel,** topped by a small chapel with views of the rock-strewn countryside. ▣ *10 frs.* ☉ *Easter–Oct.; guided tours of tumulus Apr.–Sept., daily 10, 11, 2, and 3:30.*

Nightlife and the Arts
A cosmopolitan crowd goes dancing at **Les Chandelles** (⊠ 24 av. des Druides).

Outdoor Activities and Sports
Windsurfing equipment is available at **Bernard de Petigny** (⊠ 90 rue du Pô, ☎ 02–97–52–02–41). Horseback-riding tours can be arranged through the **Centre Équestre des Menhirs** (☎ 02–97–55–73–45).

Auray

26 *14 km (12 mi) north of Carnac via D119/D768, 38 km (24 mi) southeast of Lorient.*

The ancient town of Auray grew up along the banks of the Loch River, best admired from the Promenade du Loch overlooking the quayside. Cross the river to explore the old, cobbled streets of the St-Goustan neighborhood. Across the old bridge at the harbor is the **Goélette St-Sauveur,** an old sailing ship tied alongside the quay. In its hold is a sailing museum with many unusual nautical artifacts. ☎ *02–97–40–37–05.* ☉ *July–Aug., daily 10–noon; Sept.–June, by appointment.*

Dining
$$–$$$ ✗ **Closerie de Kerdrain.** Chef Fernand Corfmat presides over the kitchen in this large Breton house draped in wisteria. Inventively blending traditional and contemporary cuisines, he creates such combinations as vegetable and langoustine tart and ravioli stuffed with seafood. ⊠ *20 rue Louis-Billet,* ☎ *02–97–56–61–27. AE, DC, MC, V. Closed Mon., last 2 wks of Nov., part of Feb., and 1st 2 wks of Mar.*

Outdoor Activities and Sports
Take a cruise down the Auray River on the **Navix-Vedettes du Golfe** (☎ 02–97–56–59–47); along the way you'll discover the lovely 16th-century Château du Plessis-Kaer and the tiny, tidal fishing port of Bono tucked between the steep banks and the oysters beds of the Pô estuary.

Vannes

★ ❷ *16 km (10 mi) east of Auray via N165, 108 km (67 mi) southwest of Rennes.*

Scene of the declaration of unity between France and Brittany in 1532, historic Vannes is one of the few towns in Brittany to have been spared damage during World War II. Be sure to saunter through the Promenade de la Garenne, a colorful park, and admire the magnificent gardens nestled beneath the adjacent ramparts. Also visit the medieval wash houses and the cathedral; browse in the small boutiques and antiques shops in the pedestrian streets around pretty place Henri-IV; check out the Cohue, the medieval market hall now used as an exhibition center; and take a boat trip around the scenic Golfe du Morbihan.

Inside the **Cathédrale St-Pierre** is a 1537 Renaissance chapel, a Flamboyant Gothic transept portal, and a treasury. ⊠ *Pl. de la Cathédrale.* ☞ *5 frs.* ☉ *Treasury mid-June–mid-Sept., Mon.–Sat. 2–6.*

The **Musée d'Archéologie** (Archaeology Museum) houses a collection of ancient tools and artifacts dating from the Paleolithic Age to the Middle Ages. ⊠ *2 rue Noé,* ☎ *02–97–42–59–80.* ☞ *20 frs.* ☉ *Apr.–Sept., Mon.–Sat. 9:30–noon and 2–6; Oct.–Mar., Mon.–Sat. 2–6.*

Dining and Lodging

$$–$$$ ✕ **Régis Mahé.** Step off the train and right into this popular spot, a haven of refinement where seafood reigns. The chef's delicate poached snapper and grilled sea bass garnished with vegetables are so fresh you can still smell the sea. The prix-fixe menus are your best bet. ⊠ *24 pl. de la Gare,* ☎ *02–97–42–61–41. AE, MC, V. Closed Mon., late Nov., and part of Feb. No dinner Sun.*

$$$$ ✕🏠 **Domaine de Rochevilaine.** At sunset on summer evenings, the view of the sea is magnificent. Parisians come to this resort in summer to relax; businesspeople come for seminars in winter. Rooms are arranged on two sides of a courtyard, surrounded by terraced gardens; all have modern furnishings but vary in size; not all face the ocean. Chef Patrice Caillaut's cuisine is creative, but the prices are somewhat inflated. ⊠ *16 rue du Phare, 56190 Billiers (30 km [19 mi] southeast of Vannes, at tip of Pointe de Pen-Lan),* ☎ *02–97–41–61–61,* FAX *02–97–41–44–85. 33 rooms, 7 suites. Restaurant, pool, meeting rooms. AE, DC, MC, V.*

$$ ✕🏠 **A L'Image Sainte-Anne.** A varied foreign clientele stays in this hotel in an old, rustic building in town. The comfortable rooms and welcoming staff make the price of a night here seem more than acceptable. Mussels, sole in cider, and duck are featured in the restaurant, which has a very reasonable prix-fixe menu; no dinner is served Sunday, November through March. ⊠ *8 pl. de la Libération, 56000,* ☎ *02–97–63–27–36,* FAX *02–97–40–97–02. 33 rooms. Restaurant. AE, DC, MC, V.*

La Baule

❷ *72 km (45 mi) southeast of Vannes via N165 and D774.*

One of the most fashionable—and pricey—resorts in France, La Baule has a 5-km (3-mi) seafront promenade lined with hotels. Like Le Touquet and Dinard, it is a 19th-century creation, founded in 1879 to make the most of the excellent sandy beaches that extend around the broad, sheltered bay between Pornichet and Le Pouliguen. A pine forest, planted in 1840, keeps the shifting local sand dunes firmly at bay.

Dining and Lodging

$$$ ✕ **La Marcanderie.** This warm, yellow-walled restaurant run by cheerful Jean-Luc Giraud is considered the best in town. Potato and scampi tart, lobster salad, monkfish in cider, and scallops in endive top the

menu. ⊠ *5 av. d'Agen,* ☎ *02–40–24–03–12. Reservations essential. Jacket and tie. AE, DC, MC, V. Closed Mon. No dinner Sun.*

$$ ✕ **Ferme du Grand Clos.** At this lively restaurant in an old farmhouse, wafer-thin crepes are served with every imaginable filling, from sweet to savory—mussels, fish, chicken, or chocolate. Come early for a table; it's a popular place. ⊠ *52 av. du Maréchal-de-Lattre-de-Tassigny,* ☎ *02–40–60–03–30. MC, V. Closed Wed. Sept.–June.*

$$ 🏨 **Concorde.** This establishment numbers among the least expensive good hotels in pricey La Baule. It's calm, comfortable, modernized, and a short block from the beach (ask for a room with a sea view). ⊠ *1 bis av. de la Concorde, 44500,* ☎ *02–40–60–23–09,* FAX *02–40–42– 72–14. 47 rooms. AE, DC, MC, V. Closed Oct.–Easter.*

$$ 🏨 **Hôtel de la Plage.** One of the few hotels on the beach in St-Marc-sur-Mer, this comfortable lodging was the setting for Jacques Tati's classic comedy *Les Vacances de Monsieur Hulot.* It has been updated since and, *hélas,* the swinging door to the dining room is no longer there. But the view of the sea and the sound of the surf remain. ⊠ *37 rue du Commandant-Charcot, 44600 St-Marc-sur-Mer (10 km [6 mi] southeast of La Baule),* ☎ *02–40–91–99–01,* FAX *02–40–91–92–00. 33 rooms. Restaurant. MC, V. Closed Jan.*

Nightlife

Occasionally you see high stakes on the tables at La Baule's **casino** (⊠ 6 av. Pierre-Loti, ☎ 02–40–11–48–28).

En Route   Just north of La Baule is **Guérande,** an appealing 15th-century walled town with towers and moat, surrounded by salt flats. From here follow D51 northeast to the curious **Dolmen de Kerbourg,** a table-shape megalith. Continue to the village of **St-Lyphard** and climb up the church tower for a panoramic view of the regional park known as **La Grande Brière.** With its peat marshes crisscrossed by reed-lined canals, the park is a bird-watcher's delight. The best way to explore it is to take a boat trip organized by the **Maison du Parc Naturel Régional de Brière** (⊠ 177 rte. de Fédrun, ☎ 02–40–91–68–68), in St-Joachim—a few miles east of St-Lyphard as the wild duck flies but, along the highway, a tortuous 19 km (12 mi) waddle via D51 and D50.

Nantes

72 km (45 mi) east of La Baule via N171 and N165, 108 km (67 mi) south of Rennes, 114 km (71 mi) southeast of Vannes.

The tranquil, prosperous city of Nantes seems to pursue its existence without too much concern for what's going on elsewhere in France. Cobbled streets surround its castle and cathedral in the town's medieval sector. Across the broad boulevard, Cours des 50-Otages, is the 19th-century city. Although Nantes is officially part of the Pays de la Loire, its historic ties with Brittany are embodied in its imposing castle.

29   Built by the dukes of Brittany, who had no doubt that Nantes belonged in their domain, the **Château des Ducs de Bretagne** is a massive, well-preserved 15th-century fortress with a moat. François II, the duke responsible for building most of it, led a hedonistic existence here, surrounded by ministers, chamberlains, and an army of servants. Numerous monarchs later stayed in the castle, where in 1598 Henri IV signed the famous Edict of Nantes advocating religious tolerance.

The Harnachement (saddlery)—a separate building inside the castle walls—is home to the **Musée des Salorges** (Naval Museum), devoted principally to the history of seafaring; a separate section outlines the triangular trade that involved transportation of Africans to America to be sold as slaves. As you cross the courtyard to the Grand Gouverne-

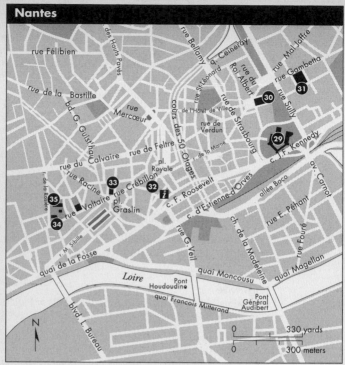

ment wing, home to the **Musée d'Art Breton Régional** (Regional Folk Art Museum), look for the old well, where the ducal coat of arms is entwined in a magnificent wrought-iron decoration. The **Musée d'Art Populaire** (Folk Art Museum) features an array of armor, furniture, 19th-century Breton costumes, and reconstituted interiors illustrating the former life of the Vendée region, to the south. ⊠ *4 pl. Marc-Elder,* ☎ *02–40–41–56–56.* ▣ *20 frs.* ⊙ *Castle and museums July–Aug., daily 10–noon and 2–6; Sept.–June, Wed.–Mon. 10–noon and 2–6.*

③0 The **Cathédrale St-Pierre** is one of France's last Gothic cathedrals, begun in 1434, well after most other medieval cathedrals had been completed. The facade is ponderous and austere, in contrast to the light, wide, limestone interior, whose vaults rise higher (120 ft) than those of Notre-Dame in Paris. In the transept, notice Michel Colombe's early 16th-century tomb of François II and his wife, Marguerite de Foix; the tomb is one of France's finest examples of funerary sculpture. ⊠ *Pl. St-Pierre,* ☎ *02–51–88–95–47.* ▣ *20 frs.* ⊙ *Crypt Mon.–Sat. 10– 12:30 and 2–6, Sun. 2–6:30.*

③1 A fine collection of paintings from the Renaissance, including works by Jacopo Tintoretto, Georges de La Tour, Jean-Auguste Ingres, and Gustave Courbet, is at the **Musée des Beaux-Arts** (Museum of Fine Arts). ⊠ *10 rue Georges-Clemenceau,* ☎ *02–40–41–65–65. é* ▣ *20 frs.* ⊙ *Mon., Wed.–Thurs., and Sat. 10–6, Fri. 10–9, Sun. 11–6.*

③2 Erected in 1843, the **Passage Pommeraye** (⊠ Rue Crébillon) is an el-
③3 egant shopping gallery in the 19th-century part of town. The **Grand Théâtre** (⊠ Pl. Graslin), down the block from the Passage Pommeraye, was built in 1783.

㉞ The 15th-century **Manoir de la Touche** (✉ Rue Voltaire) was once home
㉟ to the bishops of Nantes. The mock Romanesque **Musée Dobrée,** off-
setting the medieval silhouette of the Manoir de la Touche, across the
way, was built by arts connoisseur Thomas Dobrée during the past century. Among the treasures within are miniatures, tapestries, medieval
manuscripts, and enamels; one room is devoted to the Revolutionary
War in Vendée. ✉ *Rue Voltaire,* ☎ *02–40–71–03–50.* 🎟 *20 frs, free
Sun.* ☉ *Tues.–Sun. 10–noon and 1:30–5:30.*

Dining and Lodging

$$ ✕ **L'Embellie.** The cuisine at this small, modern bistro is serious and
traditional and makes the most of herbs to bring out the natural fla-
vors in seafood and game dishes. The lunchtime menu is a particularly
good value. ✉ *14 rue Armand-Brossard,* ☎ *02–40–48–20–02. MC,
V. Closed Sun. and 2nd wk in Aug. No lunch Sat.*

$$ ✕ **Villa Mon Rêve.** This cozy little restaurant is in delightful parkland
★ outside Nantes. Chef Gérard Ryngel concocts elegantly inventive re-
gional fare (the duck or rabbit in muscadet are good choices), with which
you can sample one of more than 50 varieties of Muscadet, the local
wine. ✉ *Levée Divatte, 506 bd. de la Loire, Basse-Goulaine (8 mi [5
mi] east of Nantes),* ☎ *02–40–03–55–50. AE, DC, MC, V. Closed part
of Feb., last wk of Oct.*

$–$$ ✕ **Cigale.** Miniature palm trees, gleaming woodwork, colorful enamel
tiles, and painted ceilings have led to the official recognition of La Cigale
(built in 1895) as a *monument historique* (historic monument). You
can savor its Belle Epoque ambience without spending a fortune—the
prix-fixe lunch menus are a good value. But the banks of fresh oysters
and well-stacked dessert cart may tempt you to order à la carte. ✉ *4
Pl. Graslin,* ☎ *02–51–84–94–94. Reservations essential. MC, V.*

$$ 🛏 **La Pérouse.** Bare parquet floors, plain off-white walls, simple high-
tech lighting, and minimal contemporary furnishings make rooms feel
spacious; bathrooms are equally modern. The amiable staff speaks flu-
ent English. A pedestrian zone full of boutiques and restaurants is right
outside the door, and place Royale is just 300 yards away. ✉ *3 allée
Dusquesne, 44000,* ☎ *02–40–89–75–00,* 📠 *02–40–89–76–00. 47
rooms. AE, DC, MC, V.*

Nightlife and the Arts

For live jazz, the informal **Pub Univers** (✉ 16 rue Jean-Jacques Rousseau)
is the spot. **Le Tie Break** (✉ 1 rue des Petites-Écuries) is a popular piano
bar. The **Théâtre Graslin** (✉ 1 rue Molière, ☎ 02–40–69–77–18) is
Nantes's principal concert hall and opera house.

Outdoor Activities and Sports

You can take a 100-minute cruise along the pretty Erdre River, past a
string of gardens and châteaux, with the **Bateaux Nantais.** There are
also four-course lunch and dinner cruises (☎ 250–285 frs.). ✉ *Port
de la Motte Rouge, pl. Waldeck-Rousseau,* ☎ *02–40–14–51–14.* 🎟
50 frs. ☉ *June–Aug., Mon. and Fri. at 3, weekends at 3 and 5; May
and Sept.–Oct., weekends at 3.*

Shopping

The commercial quarter of Nantes stretches from place Royale to
place Graslin. Various antiques shops can be found on rue Voltaire.
The Devineau family has been selling wax fruit and vegetables at
Devineau (✉ 2 pl. Ste-Croix) since 1803; for 75 francs, you can take
home a basket of purple grapes or a cauliflower, as well as handmade
candles and wildflower honey. For chocolate, head to **Gautier-Debotté**
(✉ 9 rue de la Fosse); try the local Muscadet grapes dipped in brandy
and covered with chocolate.

BRITTANY A TO Z

Arriving and Departing

By Car
Rennes, the gateway to Brittany, is 310 km (195 mi) west of Paris. It can be reached in about three hours via Le Mans and A81 and A11 (A11 continues southwest from Le Mans to Nantes).

By Train
Numerous high-speed TGVs (*Trains à Grande Vitesse*) depart daily from Paris (Gare Montparnasse) for both Nantes and Rennes, making this region easily accessible. The trip to either city takes about 2¼ hours. There is also regular train service up the west coast to Nantes from La Rochelle and Bordeaux.

Getting Around

By Bus
Les Courriers Bretons (⊠ 13 rue d'Alsace, St-Malo, ☎ 02–99–19–70–80) has daily service from St-Malo and Rennes to Mont-St-Michel.

By Car
Rennes, a strategic base for penetrating Brittany, is linked by good roads to Morlaix and Brest (E50), Quimper (N24/N165), and Vannes (N24/N166). A car is a good idea if you want to see more out-of-the-way places.

By Plane
Rennes, Brest, Nantes, Quimper, Dinard, and Lorient all have domestic airports. **Air France** (☞ Air Travel *in* Smart Travel Tips A to Z) flies to them all, except Dinard.

By Train
Most towns in this region are accessible by train, though you need a car to get to some of the more secluded spots. Some trains from Paris stop in Vitré before forking at Rennes on their way to either Brest (via Morlaix) or Quimper (via Vannes). Change at Rennes for Dol-de-Bretagne and St-Malo; at Dol-de-Bretagne for Dinan and Dinard (bus link); at Morlaix for Roscoff; at Rosporden, 19 km (12 mi) south of Quimper, for Concarneau (bus link); and at Auray for Quiberon.

Contacts and Resources

Bicycling
Bikes can be rented at most major train stations.

Car Rental
Avis (☎ 01–46–10–60–60 national reservations number in Paris; ⊠ Pl. Rhin-et-Danube, La Baule, ☎ 02–40–60–36–28; ⊠ 20 bis rue de Siam, Brest, ☎ 02–98–44–63–02; ⊠ Aéroport, Dinard, ☎ 02–99–46–25–20; ⊠ Rue Lourmel, Nantes, ☎ 02–40–89–25–50; ⊠ Gare SNCF, Quimper, ☎ 02–98–90–31–34). **Europcar** (⊠ 65 mail François-Mitterrand, Rennes, ☎ 02–99–14–33–33). **Hertz** (⊠ Rte. de Trégastel, Lannion, ☎ 02–96–05–82–82; ⊠ 53 rue de la Gare, St-Brieuc, ☎ 02–96–94–25–89).

Guided Tours
Information about organized tours of Brittany is available from the very helpful **Maison de la Bretagne** (⊠ 203 bd. St-Germain, 75007 Paris, ☎ 01–53–63–11–50, FAX 01–53–63–11–57). The following regional offices also have information about guided tours of Brittany: **Quimper** (⊠ 11 rue Théodore-le-Hac, ☎ 02–98–76–20–70) and **St-Brieuc** (⊠

29 rue des Promenades, ☎ 02–96–62–72–00). **France Tourisme** (✉ 3 rue d'Alger, 75001 Paris, ☎ 01–44–50–44–20) organizes three-day tours of Normandy and Brittany from April through October.

Travel Agencies

Havas (✉ 33 rue Jean-Macé, Brest, ☎ 02–98–80–05–43; ✉ 14 rue Ville-Pépin, St-Malo, ☎ 02–99–19–79–90). **Carlson-Wagonlit** (✉ 22 rue du Calvaire, Nantes, ☎ 02–40–08–29–18; ✉ 2 rue Jules-Simon, Rennes, ☎ 02–99–79–45–96).

Visitor Information

The principal regional tourist offices follow. **Brest** (✉ 8 av. Georges-Clemenceau, ☎ 02–98–44–24–96). **Nantes** (✉ 2 allée Baco, ☎ 02–51–72–95–30). **Rennes** (✉ 11 rue St-Yves, ☎ 02–99–67–11–11).

The following smaller towns also have tourist offices: **Carnac** (✉ 74 av. des Druides, ☎ 02–97–52–13–52). **Concarneau** (✉ Quai d'Aiguillon, ☎ 02–98–97–01–44). **Dinan** (✉ 6 rue de l'Horloge, ☎ 02–96–39–75–40). **Dinard** (✉ 2 bd. Féart, ☎ 02–99–46–94–12). **Dol-de-Bretagne** (✉ 3 Grande-Rue, ☎ 02–99–48–15–37). **Douarnenez** (✉ 1 rue du Dr-Mével, ☎ 02–98–92–13–35). **La Baule** (✉ 8 pl. de la Victoire, ☎ 02–40–24–34–44). **Lorient** (✉ Maison de la Mer, quai de Rohan, ☎ 02–97–21–07–84). **Morlaix** (✉ Pl. des Otages, ☎ 02–98–62–14–94). **Quiberon** (✉ 14 rue de Verdun, ☎ 02–97–50–07–84). **Quimper** (✉ 7 rue Déesse, ☎ 02–98–53–04–05). **St-Malo** (✉ Esplanade St-Vincent, ☎ 02–99–56–64–48). **Vannes** (✉ 1 rue Thiers, ☎ 02–97–47–24–34). **Vitré** (✉ Pl. St-Yves, ☎ 02–99–75–04–46).

5 NORMANDY

Named for the Norsemen who claimed this corner of Gaul and sent a famous conqueror over the Channel in 1066, and eternally tied in our memory with the D-Day landings, Normandy has always played shuttle diplomat in Anglo-French relations. From its half-timber houses to its green apple orchards to its rich dairy cream, it seems to mirror the culture of its English neighbor across the water. Even the island-abbey of Mont-St-Michel is a looking-glass reflection of its over-the-Channel counterpart, St. Michael's Mount in Cornwall. Other treasures beckon: elegant Deauville, Rouen's great cathedral and museums, the legendary Bayeux Tapestry . . . and those warming glasses of calvados.

S AY THE WORD **NORMANDY** and which channel-side scenario comes to mind first? Long ships bristling with oars scudding into the darkness toward Hastings? Those very ships immortalized in the Bayeux Tapestry, which traces step by step the epic tale of William the Conqueror, who in 1066 sailed across the Channel to claim his right to England's throne. Or do you think of iron gray battleships amassing silently along the shore at dawn, lowering tailgates to pour troop after troop of young Allied infantry into German machine-gun fire? At Omaha Beach you may marvel at the odds against the handful of soldiers who, in June 1944, were able to rise above the carnage on the waterfront to take the hill and pave the way for the Allies to reclaim Europe.

Updated by Simon Hewitt

Or do you think of Joan of Arc—imprisoned by England but burned by the Church she believed in—tethered to the stake at Rouen? In a modern chapel in Rouen, you may light a candle on the spot where in 1431 Joan the Maiden Warrior met her ultimate defeat at the hands of panicky politicians and church bureaucrats, a moment that marked a turning point in the Hundred Years' War.

Or are you reminded of the romantic spires of Mont-St-Michel, looming above the tidal flats, its cobbled streets echoing with the footfalls of medieval scholars? You may make a latter-day pilgrimage to the famous island-abbey, one of the most evocative and best-preserved monuments in Europe. Even when its crow's-nest ramparts are flooded with tourists, it offers mute testimony to the worldly power and wide-ranging influence of medieval monasticism. From the Norman conquest to D-Day, Normandy resonates with history in our collective memories, a history inextricably woven with that of its neighbor over the Channel.

The destinies of England and Normandy (or Normandie, as the French spell it) have long been intertwined. A history of royal relations between the two territories led William, duke of Normandy, to lay grounds for the cross-channel cultural flow that continues today. Convinced that Edward I of England owed him the succession to the English crown (young Edward had been raised in exile in Normandy and may have made rash promises), William was incensed when the royal council anointed the Anglo-Saxon Harold Godwinsson king instead. To claim the English crown he believed his right, William took action, setting sail across the Channel with some 7,000 well-equipped archers, well-mounted knights, and well-paid Frankish mercenaries. They landed en masse at Pevonsey Bay and built a stronghold at Hastings— only to face a ragtag mix of battle-weary English troops hastily reinforced with drafted peasants swinging stones tied to sticks. William and his men made short work of them and left Harold in a field with an arrow through his eye. English powers in London saw the writing on the wall: William the Conqueror was crowned king of England on Christmas Day 1066.

There followed nearly 400 years of Norman sovereignty in England: In fact, the world began to view Normandy as an English possession under a Norman-English king. For generations England and Normandy vacillated and blurred, merged and emerged. Today you'll still feel the strong flow of English culture over the channel, from the Deauville horse races frequented by highborn ladies in gloves to the silver spoon mounded high with thick cream at teatime; from the bowfront, slope-roof shops along the boat port at Honfleur to the black-and-white half-timber row houses of Rouen, which would seem just as much at home in *David Copperfield* as they would in *Madame Bovary*.

And, just as in the British Isles, no matter how you concentrate on history and culture, sooner or later you'll find yourself beguiled by the countryside, by Normandy's rolling green landscape peppered with dairy cows and half-timber farmhouses, by the spray of sea breezes off the Channel. Like the locals, you'll be tempted by seafood fresh off the boat, by sauces rich with Isigny crème fraîche, by cheese redolent of farm and pasture. And perhaps with cheeks pink from the apple-scented country air, you'll eventually succumb to the local antidote to northern damp and chill: a mug of tangy hard cider by the crackling fire, and the bracing tonic of Normandy's famous apple brandy, calvados.

— Nancy Coons

Pleasures and Pastimes

The Coast

Normandy has 600 km (375 mi) of coastline bordering the English Channel. There are major ports—Le Havre, Dieppe, and Cherbourg—plus coastal towns with seafaring pasts, like Honfleur, and fishing villages, like Fécamp. Sandwiched between are beaches and fashionable resort towns—Cabourg, Deauville, Étretat—where you might find yourself succumbing to a deck chair. Though the waters are chilly, you might be tempted to take a dip on a hot, sunny day.

Dining

The Normans are notoriously big eaters: On festive occasions in the olden days, they wouldn't bat an eye at tucking away 24 courses. Between the warm-up and the main course there was a *trou Normand* (Norman hole), a break often lasting several hours, during which an abundance of calvados (apple brandy) was downed. And Norman food isn't light; many dishes are prepared with cream sauces and apple flavoring—hence *à la normande* (with cream sauce or apples). Rich local milk makes excellent cheese: Pont-l'Évêque (known since the 13th century) is made in the Pays d'Auge with milk still warm and creamy; Livarot (also produced for centuries) uses milk that has stood a while—don't be put off by its pungent smell. The excellent Pavé d'Auge is a firm, square-shape cheese with a strong flavor. Best known of them all is creamy Camembert, a relative newcomer, invented by a farmer's wife in the late 18th century. Although Normandy is not a wine-growing area, it produces excellent hard cider (the best comes from the Vallée d'Auge) and calvados.

Local specialties differ from place to place. Rouen is famous for its canard *à la rouennaise* (duck in blood sauce); Caen, for its *tripes à la mode de Caen* (tripe cooked with carrots in a seasoned cider stock); Mont-St-Michel, for *omelettes Mère Poulard* (a secret recipe first made by a local hotel manager in the late 19th century) and *pré-salé* (lamb from the salt marshes). Try *andouille de Vire,* a delicate chitterling sausage (sometimes smoked), served in thin slices like salami. Fish and seafood lovers can feast on oysters, lobster, shrimp, and sole *dieppoise* (sole poached in a sauce with cream and mussels). In summer be sure to make reservations for meals at restaurants.

CATEGORY	COST*
$$$$	over 400 frs
$$$	250 frs–400 frs
$$	125 frs–250 frs
$	under 125 frs

*per person for a three-course meal, including tax (20.6%) and tip but not wine

🖉 *following the text of a review is your signal that the property has a Web site, where you will find details and, usually, images; for a link, visit www.fodors.com/urls.*

Lodging

Accommodations to suit every taste can be found in Normandy. The beach resort season is very short—July and August only—but weekends are busy most of the year, especially during school holidays. In June and September lodging is usually available on short notice, and good discounts are given off-season, particularly for stays of more than one night.

CATEGORY	COST*
$$$$	over 800 frs
$$$	600 frs–800 frs
$$	300 frs–600 frs
$	under 300 frs

*All prices are for a standard double room for two, including tax (20.6%) and service charge.

Exploring Normandy

You won't want to miss medieval Rouen, seaside Deauville, or magnificent Mont-St-Michel. But if you get away from these popular spots, you can lose yourself along the cliff-lined coast and the green spaces inland, where the closest thing to a crowd is a farmer with his herd of brown-and-white cows. From Rouen northeast to the coast—the area known as Upper Normandy—medieval castles and abbeys stand guard above rolling countryside, while resort and fishing towns line the white cliffs of the Côte d'Alabâtre. Popular seaside resorts and the D-Day landing sites occupy the sandy beaches along the Côte Fleurie; apple orchards and dairy farms sprinkle the countryside of the area known as Lower Normandy. The Cotentin Peninsula to the west juts out into the English Channel. Central Normandy encompasses the peacefully rural, hilly region of La Suisse Normande, along the scenic Orne River.

Numbers in the text correspond to numbers in the margin and on the Normandy and Rouen maps.

Great Itineraries

With three days you can get a feel for the region. Five days gives you time to meander through the countryside and down the coast. And with nine days, if you don't spend much time in any one place, you can see most of Normandy.

IF YOU HAVE 3 DAYS
Head straight to 🔟 **Rouen** ⑤–⑭ and spend a day and a half in the region's cultural capital. Then follow the Seine Valley past the abbeys of **Jumièges** ⑮ and **St-Wandrille** ⑯ and head west to 🔟 **Honfleur** ⑱, the fishing port that caught the Impressionists' eye.

IF YOU HAVE 6 DAYS
Follow the Seine as it snakes through the gentle rolling countryside on your way from Paris to Rouen. Stop at the formidable fortress in **Les Andelys** ④ before going to 🔟 **Rouen** ⑤–⑭ for two nights and a day. On the third day continue along the Seine Valley on the route des Abbayes to the **Abbaye de Jumièges** ⑮ and the **Abbaye de St-Wandrille** ⑯. Cross the Pont de Normandie and spend the night in 🔟 **Honfleur** ⑱. Next day, travel along the Côte Fleurie to the fashionable resort towns of **Deauville-Trouville** ㉖, and **Cabourg** ㉘. By early afternoon try to reach 🔟 **Caen** ㉙, site of some of World War II's fiercest fighting and home to William the Conqueror's fortress. Next day explore **Arromanches** ㉚

0 | 20 miles
0 | 30 km

N

TO
ROSSLARE
TO
POOLE
TO
PORTSMOUTH
TO
CAP DE
LA HAGUE

English Channel
(La Manche)

TO PORTS.
TO ROSSLARE
TO CORK
TO PORTSMOUTH

Cotentin
Péninsula
Barfleur

Cherbourg 36
St-Vaast
la Hougue
Quinéville
Iles
St-Marcouf

Valognes
N13

Carteret
Portbail
La Madeleine
Utah
Beach 35
Grandcamp-
Maisy
Pointe du Hoc
Vierville-
sur-Mer
Omaha
Beach
Port-en-Bessin-
Huppain
Côte
Fleur

Ste-Mère-
Église 34
33
St-Laurent-sur-Mer
32
Gold Beach 30
Juno Beach
Cabourg

La Haye-
du-Puits
D903
Carentan
Isigny-
sur-Mer
Colleville-
sur-Mer
31
Arromanches
Courseulles
Riva Bella
28

Lessay
D971
Bayeux
N13
Bénouville
D513

Coutances
D972
St-Lô 37
D572
Balleroy
Caen 29
Troarn

38
N174
N175
Laize-la-Ville
Orne
D212
N158

D990
Le Chefresne
LA SUISSE
NORMANDE
D562
Thury-Harcourt

Percy
Clécy
Pont
d'Ouilly
Falaise 41

Granville 39
Villedieu-
les-Poêles
Vire
D577
Roche d'
Oëtre
Georges de
St-Aubert
Rabodanges
D909

D973
N175
A84
Conde-sur-
Noireau
Flers
Putanges-
Pont-Ecrépin

Avranches
PARC REGIONAL NORMANDIE-MAINE
Bagnoles-
de-l'Orne

Mont-St-Michel 40
N175
Mortain
D907
Domfront
D916
N176

Dol-de-Bretagne
N176
D795
D155
Antrain
D177
D23
Pré-en-Pail

Combourg
D998
Fougères
N12
Mayenne
D35

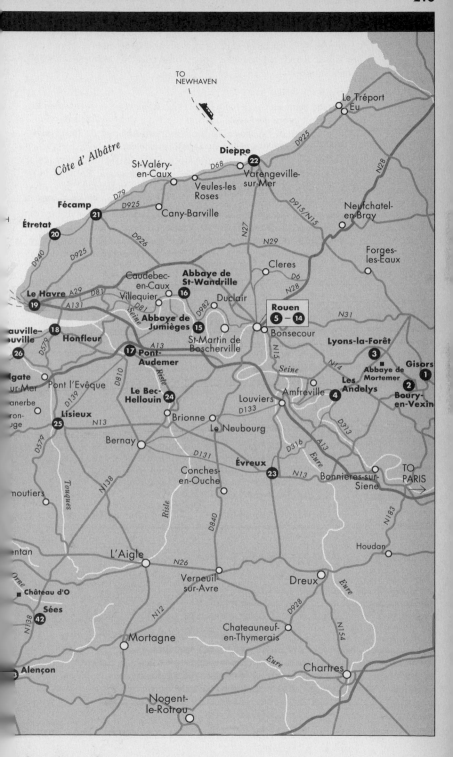

TO NEWHAVEN

Côte d' Albâtre

Le Tréport
Eu

Dieppe

St-Valéry-
en-Caux

Varengeville-
sur-Mer

Veules-les-
Roses

D68

D925

N28

Neufchatel-
en-Bray

Fécamp **21**

D79

D925

Cany-Barville

N27

N29

D915/N15

Forges-
les-Eaux

Étretat

20

D926

D940

D925

Caudebec-
en-Caux
Villequier

**Abbaye de
St-Wandrille**

16

Duclair

Cleres

D6

N28

Le Havre

19

A29

D81

A131

D81

D982

**Abbaye de
Jumièges**

15

Seine

Rouen

5 — **14**

N31

Bonsecours

Lyons-la-Forêt

-auville-
-ouville

18

26

D579

Honfleur

17 **Pont-
Audemer**

St-Martin de
Boscherville

Seine

3

Abbaye de
Mortemer

**Les
Andelys**

Gisors

1

-lgate
-ur-Mer

D139

Pont l'Evêque

Risle

D810

**Le Bec-
Hellouin**

24

Louviers

Amfreville

N14

4

2

**Boury-
en-Vexin**

-anerbe
-ron-
-uge

Lisieux

25

N13

Brionne

Le Neubourg

D133

N15

D313

-moutiers

Bernay

D131

D316

A13

Eure

Conches-
en-Ouche

Évreux

23

N13

Bonnières-sur-
Siene

**TO
PARIS**

Touques

N138

Risle

D840

Houdan

N183

-ntan

L'Aigle

N26

Verneuil-
sur-Avre

Dreux

Eure

Orne

Château d'O

D928

N154

D579

N138

Sées

42

N12

Mortagne

Chateauneuf-
en-Thymerais

Eure

Alençon

Chartres

Nogent-
le-Rotrou

and the **D-Day beaches** ㉜–㉞, then spend the night in 🎭 **Bayeux** ㉛, famous for its medieval tapestry. On the sixth day head southwest to **Coutances** ㊳, with its elegant cathedral, and **Granville** ㊴, an old harbor town. Reach the majestic abbey on a rock, 🎭 **Mont-St-Michel** ㊵, before sundown.

IF YOU HAVE 9 DAYS
Follow the Seine en route from Paris to 🎭 **Rouen** ⑤–⑭, visiting **Les Andelys** ④ and **Lyons-la-Forêt** ③ along the way. On the third day wind along the route des Abbayes to the abbeys of **Abbaye de Jumièges** ⑮ and **Abbaye de St-Wandrille** ⑯. Drive northwest to the fishing town of **Fécamp** ㉑, then head down the Côte d'Alabâtre to the spectacular beach resort of **Étretat** ⑳. Continue south, cross the Pont de Normandie, and spend the night in 🎭 **Honfleur** ⑱. On the next day travel along the Côte Fleurie to the seaside resorts of **Deauville-Trouville** ㉖ and **Cabourg** ㉘, reaching 🎭 **Caen** ㉙ by midafternoon. The following day visit Gold, Juno and Sword beaches and historic **Arromanches** ㉚, then stay in 🎭 **Bayeux** ㉛ overnight. Visit the storied tapestry and continue your exploration of the **D-Day beaches** ㉜–㉞ before continuing up the Cotentin coast to 🎭 **Cherbourg** ㊱. On day seven ramble south to the cathedral town of **Coutances** ㊳ and on to seafaring **Granville** ㊴, then continue to the majestic 🎭 **Mont-St-Michel** ㊵. Next morning hurry east to the Suisse Normande's rocky expanse of hills, passing through Clécy before stopping for a picnic lunch at the Roche d'Oëtre, a rock with a spectacular view of the Orne Valley. If time allows, take in William the Conqueror's castle at **Falaise** ㊶.

When to Tour Normandy

July and August—when French families vacation—are the busiest months but also the most activity filled: Concerts are held every evening at Mont-St-Michel, and the region's most important horse races are held in Deauville in the second half of August. June 6, the anniversary of the Allied invasion, is the most popular time to visit the D-Day beaches. If you're trying to avoid crowds, your best bet is late spring and early autumn, when it is still fairly temperate. Some of the biggest events of the region take place during these seasons: in Rouen, at the end of May, Joan of Arc is honored at a festival named for her; the first week of September in Deauville is the American Film Festival. Though it's chilly, winter gives you the pleasures of Normandy without the crowds (most places remain open throughout the year, except for January).

UPPER NORMANDY

Upper Normandy is delineated by the Seine, which winds northwest out of Paris through the rolling hills around Rouen, the region's cultural and commercial capital, on its way to meet the English Channel. Between Rouen and Le Havre, the Seine snakes its way along the route des Abbayes, past ancient abbeys and small towns. The impressive chalky cliffs and pebbly beaches of the Côte d'Alabâtre stretch from Le Havre to the fishing town of Dieppe. In the 19th century the bathing resorts along the coast attracted writers and artists like Maupassant, Monet, and Braque, who were inspired by the dramatic scenery.

Gisors

❶ *64 km (40 mi) northwest of Paris via A15 and D915, 35 km (24 mi) northeast of Vernon.*

Gisors, a peaceful market town evoked by Impressionist painter Camille Pissarro (who lived just to the north in Eragny-sur-Epte), has several half-timber houses along the sloping rue de Vienne and a fine hilltop castle standing sentinel at the confines of Normandy. The town church, lovingly restored after damage in World War II, is a jumble of styles; the elaborate, two-towered 16th-century facade and florid vaulting in the side chapels clash with the sober choir consecrated in 1249. The royal fleur-de-lis emblem keeps cropping up unexpectedly—carved on a spiral-patterned pillar, in a modern stained-glass window, or woven into the stone balustrade above the side chapels outside.

The **Château Fort** was begun in 1097 by the English king William Rufus, son of the Conqueror. The castle has two parts. One is the drumlike ring of curtain walls with a dozen towers, surrounded by a big ditch and enclosing a park filled with flowers and evergreens. The park is open daily without charge and offers a fine view of the church above the roofs of the old town. The other is the 70-ft artificial mound in the middle, the foursquare keep, with a staircase leading to the top—and down to the dungeon. ⊠ *Pl. Blanmont,* ☎ *02–32–55–59–36.* ☒ *25 frs.* ◷ *Apr.–Sept., Wed.–Mon. 10–noon and 2–6; Oct.–Nov. and Feb.–Mar., weekends 10–noon and 2–5.*

Boury-en-Vexin

❷ *8 km (5 mi) southwest of Gisors.*

In the pretty village of Boury-en-Vexin, the steep-roofed **Château de Boury,** built in 1685 by Jules Hardouin-Mansart, displays the same monumental dignity as the architect's work at Versailles. The two-tiered facade, with arched ground-flower windows and Ionic pilasters above, surveys a trim lawn with cone-shape topiary bushes. The château has remained in the same family since it was built and has a homey, lived-in feel to complement its grand furniture, portraits, and crystal chandeliers. ⊠ *Boury-en-Vexin,* ☎ *02–32–55–15–10.* ☒ *25 frs.* ◷ *July–Aug., Wed.–Mon. 2:30–6:30; mid-Apr.–June and Sept.–mid-Oct., weekends 2:30–6:30.*

Lyons-la-Forêt

★ ❸ *34 km (21 mi) northwest of Gisors, 36 km (23 mi) east of Rouen.*

Few villages in France are as pretty as Lyons-la-Forêt, built in a verdant clearing surrounded by a noble beech forest. Lyons has entire streets full of rickety half-timber houses and a venerable market hall built of robust medieval oaks on its main square. In fact, the square is more of a tumbling triangle—all bustle in summer but, come winter, when most hotels and restaurants are shut, as forlorn as the leafless beech trees all around. Lyons is built on two levels, and if you arrive from Gisors, take care not to miss the lower road—a black-and-white quilt of medieval frontages, leading to the village church and its life-size wooden statues.

The scenic ruins of the Cistercian **Abbaye de Mortemer** are by a small lake in the heart of the forest, 5 km (3 mi) south of Lyons-la-Forêt. The 100-yard-long church was built at the start of the 13th century but destroyed during the Revolution. Some of the abbey buildings survive, including the large 15th-century pigeon loft that was also used as a prison. A small museum evokes aspects of monastic life. ⊠ *Rue de Mortemer, Lisors,* ☎ *02–32–49–54–37.* ☒ *25 frs.* ◷ *Easter–Oct., daily 2–6:30; Nov.–Easter, Sun. 2–6.*

Dining and Lodging

$$–$$$ ✕☷ **Licorne.** This venerable inn at the top of the village square has comfortable rooms with rustic wooden furniture. The colorful garden at the back of the hotel is a nice spot for a predinner drink before repairing

to the dining room (no meals Monday), where a fire crackles in the hearth on cooler evenings. For a main course, try grilled salmon or guinea fowl with peaches. ⊠ *Pl. du Marché, 27480,* ☎ *02–32–49–62–02,* 𝔽𝔸𝕏 *02–32–49–80–09. 12 rooms, 6 suites. Restaurant. AE, DC, MC, V. Closed mid-Dec.–late Jan.*

Les Andelys

❹ *20 km (13 mi) southwest of Lyons-la-Forêt, 88 km (55 mi) northwest of Paris, 40 km (25 mi) southeast of Rouen.*

In one of the most picturesque loops of the Seine, the small town of Les Andelys, birthplace of France's leading classical painter, Nicolas Poussin, is set against magnificent chalky cliffs. The **Château Gaillard,** a formidable fortress built by England's King Richard the Lionhearted in 1196, overlooks Les Andelys from the cliff tops, with spectacular views in both directions. Despite its solid defenses, the castle fell to the French in 1204. It suffered considerable damage during the assault, and sections were eventually torn down at the end of the 16th century; only one of its five main towers remains intact, but the location and the ruins bring alive a history long forgotten. ⊠ *rue Richard-Coeur-de-Lion,* ☎ *02–32–54–04–16.* 🎫 *20 frs.* ☉ *Apr.–Oct., Thurs.–Mon. 10–noon and 2–5, Wed. 2–5.*

Dining and Lodging

$$$ ✕🏠 **Hostellerie St-Pierre.** This hotel, west of Les Andelys on the road to Rouen, is a great place to stay in the Seine Valley. Room 27 has the best view of the river and French windows that open onto a terrace; its size, like that of most others, is modest; all have comfortingly traditional decor. At dinner sample the *rable de lapin farci* (saddle of rabbit) stuffed with mushrooms in a cider sauce, or the *boudin de poisson* (fish mousse) in beurre blanc. Desserts are generally good, though the *assiette tout chocolat* (all-chocolate plate) is less satisfying than expected. ⊠ *6 chemin de la Digue, 27430 St-Pierre-du-Vauvray (11 km [7 mi] west of Les Andelys),* ☎ *02–32–59–93–29,* 𝔽𝔸𝕏 *02–32–59–41–93. 14 rooms. Restaurant. AE, MC, V. Closed mid-Nov.–mid-Mar.*

En Route From Les Andelys stay on the right bank of the Seine for 24 km (15 mi) to Amfreville; then turn right up steep D508 to what is known as the **Côte des Deux Amants** (Lovers' Mount) for a spectacular view of the Seine Valley and its chalky cliffs. Follow the road to Pont St-Pierre (St. Pierre Bridge) and then head northwest on D138 toward Rouen, pausing in the suburb of **Bonsecours** to check out its **Basilique Notre-Dame.** This fine neo-Gothic church was built in 1840 on a hilltop overlooking the Seine.

Rouen

★ *40 km (25 mi) northwest of Les Andelys, 86 km (53 mi) east of Le Havre, 132 km (82 mi) northwest of Paris.*

"O Rouen, art thou then to be my final abode!" was the agonized cry of Joan of Arc as the English dragged her out to be burned alive on May 30, 1431. The exact spot of the pyre is marked by a new church, the Église Jeanne d'Arc, just off rue Jeanne-d'Arc. This is just one of the many landmarks that make Rouen a fascinating destination for the traveler. The city has a surprising wealth of medieval buildings, despite the fact that a large part of the city was destroyed during World War II and subsequently rebuilt. But even before its massive reconstruction, Rouen had expanded with the development of industries spawned by its increasingly busy port, now the fifth largest in France. Cobblestone streets lined with ancient Norman buildings—like rue d'Amiette, a pedes-

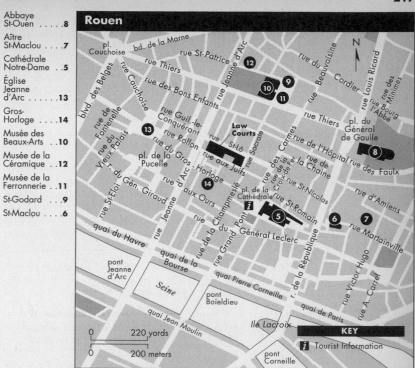

Rouen

KEY

i Tourist Information

0   220 yards

0   200 meters

trians-only street harboring restaurants and small shops—fan out from
place St-Maclou, an attractive square surrounded by picturesque half-
timber houses.

Rouen is known as the City of a Hundred Spires because many of its
important edifices are churches. Lording it over them all is the magnificent **Cathédrale Notre-Dame.** If you are familiar with the works of
Impressionist artist Claude Monet, you will immediately recognize
the cathedral's immense west facade, rendered in an increasingly hazy
fashion in his series *Cathédrales de Rouen*. The original 12th-century
construction was replaced after a terrible fire in 1200; only the left-
hand spire, the **Tour St-Romain** (St. Romanus Tower), survived the
flames. Construction on the imposing 250-ft steeple on the right,
known as the **Tour de Beurre** (Butter Tower), was begun in the 15th
and 16th centuries and completed in the 17th, when a group of wealthy
citizens donated large sums of money for the privilege of eating butter during Lent. Interior highlights include the 13th-century choir,
with its pointed arcades; vibrant stained glass depicting the crucified
Christ (restored after heavy damage during World War II); and massive stone columns topped by some intriguing carved faces. The first
flight of the famous **Escalier de la Librairie** (Booksellers' Stairway), attributed to Guillaume Pontifs (also responsible for most of the 15th-
century work seen in the cathedral), rises from a tiny balcony just to
the left of the transept. ⊠ *Pl. de la Cathédrale*, ☎ *02–35–71–00–48.*
☺ *Mon.–Sat. 8–7, Sun. 8–6.*

The late-Gothic church of **St-Maclou,** across rue de la République behind Cathédrale Notre-Dame, bears testimony to the wild excesses of
Flamboyant architecture; take time to examine the central and left-hand
portals on the main facade, covered with little bronze lion heads and
pagan engravings. Inside, note the 16th-century organ, with its Re-

naissance wood carving, and the fine marble columns. ⊠ *Pl. St-Maclou,* ☎ *02–35–71–71–72.* ☉ *Mon.–Sat. 10–noon and 2:30–6, Sun. 3–5:30.*

❼ A former ossuary (a charnel house used for the bodies of plague victims), the **Aître St-Maclou** (⊠ 184 rue Martainville) is one of the last reminders of the plague that devastated Europe during the Middle Ages; these days it holds Rouen's School of Art and Architecture. French composer Camille Saint-Saëns (1835–1921) is said to have been inspired by the ossuary when he was working on his *Danse Macabre.* The building's massive double frieze is carved with some graphic skulls, bones, and grave diggers' tools.

❽ A fine example of late Gothic architecture is the **Abbaye St-Ouen** on the square at the end of rue de la République. The stained-glass windows, dating from the 14th to the 16th centuries, are the most spectacular features of the otherwise spare abbey. The church's 19th-century pipe organs have few equals in France. ⊠ *Pl. du Général-de-Gaulle.* ☉ *Mid-Mar.–Oct., Wed.–Mon. 8–noon and 2–6; Nov.–mid-Dec. and mid-Jan.–mid-Mar., Wed. and weekends 10–12:30 and 2–6.*

❾ A painted wooden ceiling and fine medieval stained glass, especially the *Tree of Jesse* dating from 1506, distinguish the church of **St-Godard.** ⊠ *Pl. St-Godard,* ☎ *02–35–71–47–12.*

❿ One of Rouen's cultural mainstays is the **Musée des Beaux-Arts** (Fine Arts Museum). It contains a good collection of French paintings from the 17th and 19th centuries, including works by Claude Monet, Alfred Sisley, Auguste Renoir, Eugène Delacroix, and Théodore Chassériau. An entire room is devoted to Rouen-born Théodore Géricault. ⊠ *Sq. Verdrel, off rue Thiers,* ☎ *02–35–71–28–40.* 🖃 *20 frs.* ☉ *Wed.–Mon. 10–6.*

⓫ The **Musée de la Ferronnerie** (Wrought-Iron Works Museum), behind the Musée des Beaux-Arts, claims to possess the world's finest collection of wrought iron, with exhibits spanning the 3rd through the 19th centuries. Displays include a range of items used in daily life, accessories, and professional instruments used by surgeons, barbers, carpenters, clock makers, and gardeners. ⊠ *Sq. Verdrel,* ☎ *02–35–88–42–92.* 🖃 *15 frs.* ☉ *Wed.–Mon. 10–1 and 2–6.*

⓬ A superb array of local faience is in the **Musée de la Céramique** (Ceramics Museum), near the Musée des Beaux-Arts. ⊠ *rue Faucon,* ☎ *02–35–07–31–74.* 🖃 *10 frs.* ☉ *Wed.–Mon. 10–1 and 2–6.*

⓭ Dedicated to Joan of Arc, the modern **Église Jeanne d'Arc** (Joan of Arc Church), a few blocks from rue Thiers, just off rue Jeanne-d'Arc, was built on the spot where she was burned to death in 1431. Not all is new, however: The church incorporates some remarkable 16th-century stained-glass windows taken from the former Église St-Vincent, destroyed in 1944. ⊠ *Pl. du Vieux-Marché.* ☉ *Mon.–Thurs. and Sat. 10–12:15 and 2–6, Fri. and Sun. 2–6.*

⓮ The name of the pedestrian rue du Gros-Horloge, Rouen's most popular street, comes from the **Gros-Horloge** itself, a giant Renaissance clock. In 1527 the Rouennais had a splendid arch built especially for it, and today its golden face looks out over the street. You can see the clock's inner workings from the 15th-century belfry. Though the street is crammed with boutiques and fast-food joints, a few old houses, dating from the 16th century, remain. Wander through the surrounding old town, a warren of tiny streets lined with more than 700 half-timber houses, many artfully transformed into fashionable shops. ⊠ *Rue du Gros-Horloge.* 🖃 *Clock 10 frs.* ☉ *Wed.–Mon. 10–1 and 2–6.*

Dining and Lodging

$$$ ✕ **Auberge de la Butte.** This former 18th-century post house, in the
★ suburb of Bonsecours, is well worth seeking out (you'll need a car).
Chef Pierre Hervé is renowned for his subtle fish and seafood dishes,
such as poached oysters wrapped in spinach leaves and fricasseed fil-
let of sole. The magnificent Norman dining room has exposed beams
and half-timber walls adorned with paintings and shining copper pots.
✉ *69 rte. de Paris, Bonsecours (3 km [2 mi] east of city center),* ☎
*02–35–80–43–11. Jacket and tie. AE, DC, MC, V. Closed Sun.–Mon.
and Aug.*

$$–$$$ ✕ **La Couronne.** In what is claimed to be the "oldest inn in France,"
dating to 1345, this restaurant is crammed with leather-upholstered
chairs and a scattering of sculpture. The traditional Norman cuisine—
crayfish salad with foie gras and caviar, duck with orange sauce—makes
few modern concessions. ✉ *31 pl. du Vieux-Marché,* ☎ *02–35–71–
40–90. Jacket and tie. AE, DC, MC, V.*

$$ ✕ **La Toque d'Or.** Next to the market and the Église Jeanne d'Arc, this
large, bustling bistro has a helpful staff and a huge menu. Excellent
specialties include oysters, mussels, and tripe. ✉ *11 pl. du Vieux-
Marché,* ☎ *02–35–71–46–29. AE, DC, V.*

$$ ✕🏨 **Dieppe.** Dating from the late 19th century, the Dieppe remains
up to date thanks to the strong management by four generations of
one family. The staff, too, is helpful and speaks English. The compact
rooms are cheerful and modern; street noise can be a problem, how-
ever, despite double-glazed windows. The restaurant, Les Quatre
Saisons, has a well-earned reputation and serves English-style roasts,
as well as traditional Norman dishes. ✉ *Pl. Bernard-Tissot, 76000,*
☎ *02–35–71–96–00; 800/528–1324 for U.S. reservations,* FAX *02–35–
89–65–21. 42 rooms. Restaurant, breakfast room. AE, DC, MC, V.*

$$ 🏨 **Mercure Centre.** In the jumble of streets near the cathedral—a nav-
igational challenge if you arrive by car—this modern chain hotel has
small, comfortable rooms in breezy pastels. The location makes this
hotel ideal for exploring the old streets of the city center. ✉ *7 rue de
la Croix-de-Fer, 76000,* ☎ *02–35–52–69–52,* FAX *02–35–89–41–46. 125
rooms. Bar. AE, DC, MC, V.*

$–$$ 🏨 **Cathédrale.** This hotel is in a medieval building on a narrow pedes-
trian street behind the cathedral. (You can sleep soundly, though: The
cathedral bells do not boom out the hour at night.) Rooms are petite
but neat and comfortable. Breakfast is served in the beamed dining room.
✉ *12 rue St-Romain, 76000,* ☎ *02–35–71–57–95,* FAX *02–35–70–15–
54. 24 rooms. Breakfast room, parking (fee). MC, V.*

Nightlife and the Arts

The **Fête Jeanne d'Arc** (Joan of Arc Festival) takes place on the Sunday nearest to May 30, with parades, street plays, concerts, and exhibitions. Evening **concerts** and organ recitals are held at St-Maclou in
August and at St-Ouen throughout the year; get details from the Rouen
Tourist Office (☞ Visitor Information *in* Normandy A to Z, *below*).
Operas are staged at the **Théâtre des Arts** (✉ 7 rue du Dr-Rambert,
☎ 02–35–71–41–36).

Abbaye de Jumièges

★ ⑮ *24 km (15 mi) west of Rouen: Head west on D982 through St-Martin de Boscherville and then turn off left on D143 to get to the Abbaye de Jumièges.*

Imposing ruins are all that is left of the once mighty Benedictine Abbaye de Jumièges, founded in 654 by St-Philbert, plundered by Vikings
in 841, then rebuilt by William Longswood, duke of Normandy, around

940, though not consecrated until 1067. The French Revolution forced the evacuation of the remaining 16 monks, whereupon the abbey was auctioned off to a timber merchant, who promptly demolished part of the building to sell the stones. What remains is impressive enough. ⊠ *24 rue Guillaume-le-Conquérant,* ☎ *02–35–37–24–02.* 🎫 *32 frs.* ☉ *Apr.–Sept., daily 9–7; Oct.–Mar., daily 9:30–1 and 2:30–5:30.*

Abbaye de St-Wandrille

⑯ *14 km (9 mi) north of the Abbaye de Jumièges via D982, 37 km (23 mi) northwest of Rouen.*

The Benedictine Abbaye de St-Wandrille is still active today. Founded in the 7th century, the abbey was sacked by the Normans and rebuilt in the 10th century—although what you see today is an ensemble of styles from the 11th century through the early 18th century (mainly the latter). You can hear the monks sing their Gregorian chants at morning mass if you arrive early (9:25 weekdays and 10 on Sunday and holidays). Be sure to visit the abbey shop down the hill. Everything it sells—from floor polish to spiritual aids—is monk-made. ☎ *02–35–96–23–11.* 🎫 *25 frs.* ☉ *Guided tour weekdays at 3:30, Sun. at 11:30.*

Pont-Audemer

⑰ *32 km (20 mi) southwest of St-Wandrille, 50 km (31 mi) west of Rouen.*

Pont-Audemer, on the banks of the Risle River in the heart of calvados country, luckily escaped destruction by warfare and bulldozers. Today many of its buildings are still as they were in the 16th century, when the town made its mark as an important trading center. Stroll along impasse St-Ouen and impasse de l'Épée, narrow streets by the church that are lined with timber-frame medieval houses. The pleasingly dilapidated church of **St-Ouen** has an unfinished single-tower facade and an entertaining clash of modern stained-glass windows and exuberant late medieval stonework. ⊠ *Rue de la République,* ☎ *02–32–41–12–88.*

Dining and Lodging

$$$ ✕🏨 **Belle-Isle sur Risle.** It's hard not to feel like a guest of this private
★ manor—an impression somehow heightened by a few rough edges. The newer, more modern rooms have wall-to-wall carpeting and department-store furniture, but the older ones have wood floors with rugs and assorted traditional pieces; those on the first floor have balconies. In the restaurant, chef Laurent Matuit turns out tasty foie gras blinis, *coquilles St-Jacques* (scallops) with a coulis (thick sauce) of mushrooms, and light pastry tarts. ⊠ *112 rte. de Rouen, 27500,* ☎ *02–32–56–96–22,* 🖷 *02–32–42–88–96. 15 rooms, 4 suites. Restaurant, pool, sauna, tennis court. MC, V.*

$$–$$$ ✕🏨 **Auberge du Vieux Puits.** Gustave Flaubert, an early admirer of this hotel in a trellised and beamed 17th-century cottage, gave it a few lines in his celebrated novel *Madame Bovary.* The quiet rooms, with heavy wooden pieces and pretty curtains, overlook the courtyard. The restaurant serves first-rate, rich, innovative Norman cuisine—trout in champagne sauce, duckling stew with sour cherries, local cheeses, and fresh fruit tarts. Since this place is first and foremost a restaurant (it is closed Monday and Tuesday dinner off-season), you are expected to have dinner here when you stay. ⊠ *6 rue Notre-Dame-du-Pré, 27500,* ☎ *02–32–41–01–48,* 🖷 *02–32–42–37–28. 12 rooms. Restaurant. MC, V. Closed mid-Dec.–late Jan.*

Honfleur

★ ⑱   *24 km (15 mi) northwest of Pont-Audemer via N175 and D80, 80 km (50 mi) west of Rouen.*

The colorful port of Honfleur on the Seine estuary has become increasingly crowded since the Pont de Normandie suspension bridge—providing a direct link with Le Havre and Upper Normandy—opened in 1995. The town, full of half-timber houses and cobbled streets, was once an important departure point for maritime expeditions, including the first voyages to Canada in the 15th and 16th centuries. The 17th-century harbor is fronted on one side by two-story stone houses with low, sloping roofs and on the other by tall, narrow houses whose wooden facades are topped by slate roofs.

Soak up the seafaring atmosphere by strolling around the old harbor and paying a visit to the wooden church of Ste-Catherine, which dominates the harbor's northern side. It was built by townspeople to show their gratitude for the departure of the English at the end of the Hundred Years' War (1453). ☒ *Rue des Logettes,* ☎ *02–31–89–11–83.*

Dining and Lodging

$$$ ✗ **Absinthe.** A 16th-century dining room in a former presbytery, with stone walls and beamed ceilings, is the magnificent setting for chef Antoine Ceffrey's restaurant. He creates masterly seafood and fish dishes, such as *barbet* (freshwater cod) with ginger. On sunny days the terrace is ideal. ☒ *10 quai de la Quarantaine,* ☎ *02–31–89–39–00. DC, MC, V. Closed mid-Nov.–mid-Dec. No dinner Mon.*

$$–$$$ ✗ **Assiette Gourmande.** At one of Honfleur's top restaurants, chef Gérard
★   Bonnefoy offers a seasonal menu. You might find succulent *noix de St-Jacques* (scallops with hazelnut risotto) or roast lamb from the salt marshes. ☒ *2 quai des Passagers,* ☎ *02–31–89–24–88. AE, DC, MC, V. Closed Mon. except July–Aug.*

$$ ✗ **Ancrage.** Massive seafood platters top the bill at this delightful old restaurant in a two-story 17th-century building overlooking the harbor. The cuisine is authentically Norman—simple but good. If you want a change, try the succulent calf sweetbreads. ☒ *12 rue Montpensier,* ☎ *02–31–89–00–70. Reservations essential. MC, V. Closed Wed., mid-Nov.–early Dec. and mid-Jan.–early Feb. No dinner Tues. except July–Aug.*

$$$$ 🏨 **Ferme St-Siméon.** The story goes that this 19th-century manor house was the birthplace of Impressionism and that its park inspired Claude Monet and Alfred Sisley. Rooms are opulent, with pastel colors, floral wallpaper, antiques, and period decor. Those in the converted stables are quieter but have less character. Be aware, however, that the high prices have more to do with the hotel's reputation than with what it offers. The sophisticated restaurant specializes in fish; the cheese board does justice to the region. ☒ *Rue Adolphe-Marais, on D513 to Trouville, 14600,* ☎ *02–31–81–78–00,* ☏ *02–31–89–48–48. 31 rooms, 3 suites. Restaurant, pool, tennis court. AE, MC, V.*

$$ 🏨 **Cheval Blanc.** Alain Petit, the owner of this friendly inn by the harbor, is a humorous and helpful Frenchman who speaks excellent English. Rooms have fine views of the port; No. 34 is larger, better furnished, with a couch, queen-size bed, gabled ceilings, and Jacuzzi—and it's twice as expensive as the others. ☒ *2 quai des Passagers, 14600,* ☎ *02–31–81–65–00,* ☏ *02–31–89–52–80. 33 rooms. MC, V. Closed Jan.*

$$ 🏨 **Hostellerie Lechat.** This typical 18th-century Norman building is in a pretty square just behind the harbor. The well-maintained, spacious rooms are filled with French provincial prints—ask for one with a view of Ste-Catherine's Church. Hearty Norman cuisine is served in the rustic, beamed restaurant. ☒ *13 pl. Ste-Catherine, 14600,* ☎ *02–31–14–*

49–49, FAX *02–31–89–28–61. 22 rooms. Restaurant, bar. AE, DC, MC, V. Closed Jan.*

Nightlife and the Arts

The two-day **Fête des Marins** (Marine Festival) is held on Pentecost Sunday and Monday. On Sunday all the boats in the harbor are decked out in flags and paper roses, and a priest bestows his blessing at high tide. The next day model boats and local children head a musical procession.

En Route   Three kilometers (2 miles) east of Honfleur is the turnoff to the elegant **Pont de Normandie,** a suspension bridge (toll 35 francs) across the Seine. This is the world's largest cable-stayed bridge, supported by two concrete pylons taller than the Eiffel Tower, and it is designed to resist winds of 160 mph. To reach Le Havre, continue west for 16 km (10 mi) on A131.

Le Havre

⑲   *23 km (14 mi) northwest of Honfleur via the Pont de Normandie, 88 km (55 mi) west of Rouen, 200 km (125 mi) northwest of Paris.*

Le Havre, France's second-largest port (after Marseille), was bombarded no fewer than 146 times during World War II. You may find the rebuilt city, with its uncompromising recourse to reinforced concrete and open spaces, bleak and uninviting; on the other hand, you may admire its rational planning and audacious modern architecture. The **Musée André-Malraux,** the city art museum, is an innovative early '60s metal-and-glass structure surrounded by a moat; it was renovated 1997–99 and now boasts an attractive sea-view café. Two local artists are showcased here—Raoul Dufy (1877–1953), with a remarkable collection of his brightly colored oils, watercolors, and sketches on the ground floor; and, upstairs, Eugène Boudin (1824–98), a forerunner of Impressionism, whose compelling beach scenes and landscapes tellingly evoke the Normandy coast and skyline. ⊠ *23 bd. Clemenceau,* ☎ *02–35–19–62–62.* ⌺ *25 frs.* ☉ *Wed.–Mon. 11–6.*

★   The other outstanding building in Le Havre and one of the most impressive 20th-century churches in France is the **Église St-Joseph,** built to the plans of Auguste Perret in the 1950s. The 350-ft tower powers into the sky like a fat rocket. The inside is just as thrilling. No frills here: The 270-ft octagonal lantern soars above the crossing, filled almost to the top with abstract stained glass that hurls colored light over the bare concrete walls. ⊠ *Bd. François-Ier,* ☎ *02–35–42–20–03.*

The hilly suburb of **Ste-Adresse** just west of town is resplendent with Belle Epoque villas and an old fortress. It's also worth a visit for its beach, often painted by Raoul Dufy, and for its fine views of the sea and port.

Dining and Lodging

$$$ ✕ **Odyssée.** With the port and fish market within netting distance, fresh seafood is guaranteed. It's a no frills place—the visual appeal is on your plate, in the pinks and greens of the smoked salmon and avocado sauce that accompany the chef's homemade fish terrine. Other inventive dishes include fried sole with lemon sabayon and grilled turbot with poppy seeds in cream sauce. ⊠ *41 rue du Général-Faidherbe,* ☎ *02–35–21–32–42. AE, MC, V. Closed Mon. and mid-Aug.–early Sept. No dinner Sun., no lunch Sat.*

$$ ⊞ **Bordeaux.** The central location is this hotel's main plus—along with the welcoming owners. The light, airy rooms have modern furniture; the best have views of the port. As at all other hotels in Le Havre,

prices are high for room size. ⊠ *147 rue Louis-Brindeau, 76600,* ☎ *02–35–22–69–44,* FAX *02–35–42–09–27. 31 rooms. Parking (fee). AE, DC, MC, V.*

Étretat

②⓪ *28 km (17 mi) north of Le Havre via D940, 88 km (55 mi) northwest of Rouen.*

Although the promenade running the length of the town's pebble beach has been marred by a proliferation of seedy cafés and french-fry stands, this town is justly famous for the magnificent tall rock for-

★ mations that extend out into the sea. The **Falaises d'Étretat** are white cliffs that are as famous in France as Dover's are in England—they have been painted by many artists, Claude Monet among them. At low tide it's possible to walk through the huge archways formed by the rocks to neighboring beaches. The biggest arch is at the **Falaise d'Aval,** to the south. For a breathtaking view of the whole bay, take the path up to the Falaise d'Aval, from which you can hike for miles across the Manneporte Hills. . . or play a round of golf on one of Europe's windiest, and most scenic, courses. Farther south is the **Aiguille** (Needle), a 300-ft spike of rock jutting into the air just off the coast; to the north towers the **Falaise d'Amont.**

Dining and Lodging

$$ ✕ **Roches Blanches.** The exterior of this family-owned restaurant off the beach is a post–World War II concrete eyesore. But take a table by the window with a view of the cliffs, order Georges Trézeux's superb fresh seafood (try the mussels), and you'll be glad you came. ⊠ *Rue de l'Abbé-Cochet,* ☎ *02–35–27–07–34. Reservations essential for Sun. lunch. MC, V. Closed Tues.–Thurs. (Wed. only July–early Sept.), Jan., and Oct.*

$$–$$$ ✕🖭 **Donjon.** This endearing little château has lovely views of the bay

★ and town. Rooms, individually furnished with flair, are huge, comfortable, and quiet. Prix-fixe menus and reliable French cuisine—scallops and a seafood platter with lobster—are served in the cozy restaurant. ⊠ *Chemin de St-Clair, 76790,* ☎ *02–35–27–08–23,* FAX *02–35–29–92–24. 10 rooms, 7 with bath. Restaurant, pool. AE, DC, MC, V.*

Outdoor Activities and Sports

Don't miss the chance to play on the breathtaking course at the **Golf d'Étretat** (⊠ Rte. du Havre, ☎ 02–35–27–04–89), 6,580 yards long (par 72) across the cliff tops of the Falaise d'Aval; it's closed Tuesday.

Fécamp

②① *17 km (11 mi) northeast of Étretat via D940, 42 km (26 mi) northeast of Le Havre.*

The ancient cod-fishing port of Fécamp was—until Mont-St-Michel stole the limelight—Normandy's primary pilgrimage site. The magnificent abbey-church, the **Église de La Trinité** (Trinity Church; ⊠ Rue Leroux) bears witness to Fécamp's religious past. The Benedictine abbey was founded by the duke of Normandy in the 11th century and became the home of the monastic order of the Précieux Sang et de la Trinité (Precious Blood of the Trinity—referring to Christ's blood, which supposedly arrived here in the 7th century in a reliquary from the Holy Land).

Fécamp is also the home of Benedictine liqueur. The **Palais de la Bénédictine** (Benedictine Palace), seven blocks from La Trinité and across from the tourist office, is in a building dating from 1892. A florid mixture of neo-Gothic and Renaissance styles, it's one of Normandy's most popular attractions. You can drop in for a sample—at 12 francs a shot—or browse through the shop selling Benedictine products and souvenirs. ⊠ *110 rue Alexandre-le-Grand,* ☎ *02–35–10–26–10.* 🖾 *29 frs (including tasting).* ☉ *Feb.–Dec., daily 10–11:15 and 2–5.*

Dining and Lodging

$ ✕ **L'Escalier.** This delightfully simple little restaurant overlooking the harbor serves traditional Norman cuisine. The prix-fixe menus, beginning at 60 francs, consist mainly of fish and seafood dishes. ⊠ *101 quai Bérigny,* ☎ *02–35–28–26–79. Reservations essential in summer. DC, MC, V. Closed Mon. and 2 wks in Nov.*

$$$ ✕🏨 **Les Hêtres.** One of the most highly rated chefs in Normandy, Bertrand Warin, runs this restaurant in Ingouville, east of Fécamp. Reservations are essential—as are jacket and tie—for the elegant 17th-century dining room (closed Sunday dinner and Monday), where half-timber walls and Louis XIII chairs contrast with sleek, modern furnishings. The four pretty guest rooms are for diners only; they have old wooden furniture and engravings; the largest has a terrace overlooking the garden. ⊠ *Rue des Fleurs, 76460 Ingouville (28 km [17 mi] east of Fécamp),* ☎ *02–35–57–09–30,* ℻ *02–35–57–09–31. 4 rooms. Restaurant. MC, V. Closed 1st ½ Jan., last 2 wks in Aug.*

$$ ✕🏨 **Auberge de la Rouge.** In a little hamlet just south of Fécamp is
★ this small inn with simple rooms and modern amenities (such as TVs). In the restaurant (closed Sunday dinner and Monday), the menu features a mix of classic and modern dishes and local specialties; the lobster is good, but the *coquilles St-Jacques* (scallops) with herbs and the wild pressed duck are the true temptations. ⊠ *1 rue du Bois-de-Boclion, 76400 St-Léonard (1 km [½ mi] south of Fécamp),* ☎ *02–35–28–07–59,* ℻ *02–35–28–70–55. 8 rooms. Restaurant, minibars. AE, DC, MC, V. Closed mid-Jan.–early Feb.*

En Route From Fécamp take the scenic coastal road (D79) via the quaint harbor of **St-Valery-en-Caux.** Before you reach Dieppe, look for the tiny hilltop church in **Varengeville-sur-Mer**; the 20th-century painter Georges Braque (1882–1963)—who, with Picasso, is credited with inventing Cubism—is buried in its graveyard. The nearby **Parc Floral des Moustiers** (Moustiers Flower Garden), laid out by Gertrude Jekyll around a house designed by Sir Edward Lutyens in 1898, has a colorful collection of rare flowers and giant 100-year-old rhododendrons. ⊠ *La Haie des Moustiers,* ☎ *02–35–85–10–02.* 🖾 *40 frs.* ☉ *Mid-Mar.–mid-Nov., daily 10–noon and 2–6.*

Dieppe

㉒ *11 km (7 mi) east of Varengeville-sur-Mer via D75, 64 km (40 mi) northeast of Fécamp, 64 km (40 mi) north of Rouen.*

Bustling Dieppe, beneath its cliff-top castle, is part fishing and commercial port and part Norman seaside town—though its era in the fashionable spotlight is past, its hotels have seen better days, and the ferries across the Channel to Newhaven, near Brighton, have now been replaced by a faster, but less frequent, jetfoil. The seafront promenade, boulevard du Maréchal-Foch, separates an immense lawn from an unspoiled pebble beach where in 1942 many Canadian soldiers were killed during the so-called Jubilee Raid. You might like to continue along the coast from Dieppe to Le Tréport (☞ Chapter 6, The North and Champagne).

The 15th-century **Château,** overlooking the Channel at the western end of the bay, contains a museum, well known for its collection of ivories. In the 17th century Dieppe imported vast quantities of elephant tusks from Africa and Asia, and as many as 350 craftsmen settled here to work the ivory; their efforts can be seen in the form of ship models, nautical accessories, religious artifacts, and day-to-day objects. The museum also has a room devoted to sketches by Georges Braque. ⊠ *Sq. du Canada,* ☎ *02–35–84–19–76.* 🎫 *15 frs.* ☉ *Wed.–Sat. and Mon. 10–noon and 2–5, Sun. 10–noon and 2–6.*

Dining and Lodging

$$ ✕🏠 **Auberge du Clos Normand.** This 15th-century inn in the tiny village of Martin-Église, 4 mi (7 km) southeast of Dieppe, is best known for its pretty, nearly Chekhovian garden, complete with stream and flower-strewn balconies. Even the bedrooms—which may seem a little chilly out of season—have flowery wallpaper, in the time-honored rural French tradition. The kitchen, all agleam with copper pots, is actually in the same long wood-beamed room as the restaurant, so you can glimpse the chef at work on his sturdy Norman dishes, with chicken a specialty. ⊠ *22 rue Henri-IV, 76370,* ☎ *02–35–04–40–34,* ﬁ𝐗 *02–35–04–48–49. 8 rooms. Restaurant. AE, MC, V. Closed Tues. and mid-Nov.–mid-Dec. No dinner Mon.*

Nightlife and the Arts

At night the **casino** at the Grand Hotel (⊠ 3 bd. de Verdun, ☎ 02–35–82–33–60) comes alive with shows and gambling. If you love jazz, come for the **Festival Européen de Jazz Traditionnel** (European Traditional Jazz Festival), held in mid-June in Luneray, 8 km (5 mi) southwest of Dieppe. For information contact the Dieppe tourist office (☞ Visitor Information *in* Normandy A to Z, *below*).

Outdoor Activities and Sports

Bicycles can be rented from Dieppe's train station for around 50 francs a day; the flat terrain around the city is great for biking. For information on routes, check with the tourist office (☞ Visitor Information *in* Normandy A to Z, *below*).

LOWER NORMANDY: ON THE ROAD TO MONT-ST-MICHEL

Lower Normandy encompasses the Cotentin Peninsula, jutting out into the English Channel, and the sandy Côte Fleurie (Flower Coast), stretching from the D-Day landing sites of Omaha and Utah Beaches to the resort towns of Trouville and Deauville. Inland, lush green meadows and apple orchards cover the countryside from west of the market town of Lisieux—the heart of calvados country. After the World War II D-Day landings, some of the fiercest fighting took place around Caen and Bayeux, as many monuments and memorials testify. To the south, in the prosperous Pays d'Auge, dairy farms produce the region's famous cheeses. The hilly Suisse Normande provides the region's most rugged scenery. Rising to the west is the fabled Mont-St-Michel.

Évreux

㉓ *102 km (63 mi) northwest of Paris via A13 and N13, 50 km (31 mi) south of Rouen via N15 and N154.*

From the 5th century on, Évreux, capital of the Eure *département* (province), was ravaged and burned by a succession of armies—first the Vandals, then the Normans, the English, and various French kings. World War II played its part as well. But the town has been restored and is now embellished by gardens and calm, overgrown footpaths.

Évreux's principal historic site is the **Cathédrale Notre-Dame,** in the heart of town just off rue Corbeau. Unfortunately, it was an easy vic-tim of the many fires and raids that took place over the centuries; all that's left of the original 12th-century construction are the nave arcades. The lower parts of the chancel date from 1260, the chapels from the 14th century. Yet it's an outstanding example of Flamboyant Gothic inside and out. Don't miss the choir triforium and transept, the 14th-century stained-glass windows in the apse, and the entrance to the fourth chapel. ⊠ *Pl. Notre-Dame,* ☎ 02–32–33–06–57.

En Route   Just outside the village of Le Neubourg, and clearly signposted as you head west from Évreux along N13, is the 17th-century stone-and-brick **Château du Champ de Bataille.** The interior is lavishly furnished, and the 40-acre park combines formal gardens (currently being restored to their original 18th-century design) with a golf course and wild forest. ☞ *60 frs.* ☉ *May–mid-Sept., daily 2–6; mid-Sept.–mid-Nov. and Mar.–Apr., weekends 2–6.*

Le Bec-Hellouin

❷❹ *46 km (29 mi) northwest of Évreux via N13 and D130, 39 km (24 mi) southwest of Rouen.*

Although it has an attractive sloping green and tasteful, modern stained glass in the village church, you're probably coming to Le Bec-Hellouin to see its once-powerful abbey. Dating from 1034 when the knight Herluin exchanged his charger for a donkey and took up the simple life, the original **Abbaye Notre-Dame du Bec** was demolished during the French Revolution. All that remains of the original abbey is part of the south transept, the bases of some of the 11th-century pillars, and the mighty 15th-century **Tour St-Nicolas** (St. Nicholas Tower), with its plaque commemorating the abbey's historic links with the archbishops of Canterbury. During the guided tour you'll learn more about both the abbey's history and the life of today's monks. In addition, it's hard to beat the tranquil riverside setting. ⊠ ☎ *02–32–43–72–60.* ☞ *25 frs.* ☉ *Guided tours June–Sept., Wed.–Mon. at 10, 11, 3, 4, and 5; Sun. at 12:15, 3:30, 4, and 6; Oct.–May, Wed.–Mon. at 11 and 3:15; Sun. at noon, 3, and 4.*

Dining and Lodging

$$ ✕🏠 **Auberge de l'Abbaye.** You can enjoy traditional Norman cooking (including an exceptional apple tart) at this rustic inn with a classic *colombage* (exposed timber in stucco walls) facade. Inside, the beamed ceilings and stone walls are hung with ornamental copper pans. (Off-season the restaurant is closed Tuesday, and there's no dinner Monday; lunch is not served before 12:30.) The delightfully old-fashioned, small guest rooms are reserved for diners only (though you don't have to stay to eat). ⊠ *Pl. Guillaume-le-Conquérant, 27800,* ☎ *02–32–44–86–02,* ᶠᴬˣ *02–32–46–32–23. 10 rooms. Restaurant. AE, MC, V. Closed Jan.*

Lisieux

❷❺ *47 km (29 mi) west of Le Bec-Hellouin via D130, N138, and N13; 82 km (51 mi) southwest of Rouen.*

Lisieux is the main market town of the prosperous Pays d'Auge, an agricultural region famous for cheeses named after such towns as Camembert, Pont l'Évêque, and Livarot. It is also a land of apple orchards, used for the finest calvados. Although Lisieux emerged relatively unscathed from World War II, it has few historic monuments beyond the 12th- and 13th-century **Cathédrale St-Pierre.** (The tower to the left of the imposing facade is later than it looks—it's a rare example of 17th-century neo-Gothic reconstruction.) ⊠ *Pl. François-Mitterrand,* ☎ *02–31–62–09–82.*

The town's fame stems from St. Theresa (1873–97), who came to Lisieux as a child, joined a convent at 15, and spent the last 10 years of her life as a Carmelite nun. Theresa was canonized in 1925, and in 1954 the **Basilique Ste-Thérèse**—one of the world's largest 20th-century churches, with a huge dome and an interior of colored marble—was built in her honor. From the cathedral walk up avenue Victor-Hugo and branch left onto avenue Jean-XXIII. A **son-et-lumière** show, running through 2,000 years of history, is presented at the basilica Monday–Saturday nights at 9:45 from June to September. The **Procession de la Vierge** (Virgin's Procession) is held on August 15. The **Procession de la Fête Ste-Thérèse** (St. Theresa's Day Parade) is on the last Sunday in September. ✉ *Av. Jean-XXIII,* ☎ *02–31–78–52–62.* ✉ *Son-et-lumières 35 frs.*

En Route   For apple brandy, head through the region known as the **Pays d'Auge,** between Lisieux and Beuvron-sur-Auge, 27 km (17 mi) west. This is the heart of calvados country: You don't need a fixed itinerary; just follow your nose and the minor roads, keeping an eye out for local farmers selling calvados. One good distillery to seek out, however, is the Grandval Calvados Distillery in **Cambremer.** From Beuvron nearby A13 speeds to Deauville, 40 km (25 mi) away, in about half an hour.

Deauville–Trouville

㉖ *29 km (17 mi) north of Lisieux via D579 and N177, 92 km (57 mi) west of Rouen.*

The twin seaside resorts of Deauville and Trouville are separated by the estuary of the River Touques and joined by a bridge. The two towns have distinctly different atmospheres, but it's easy (and common) to shuttle between them. Trouville—whose beaches were immortalized in the 19th-century paintings of Eugene Boudin—is the oldest seaside resort in France. In the days of Louis-Phillipe, it was discovered by artists and the upper crust; By the end of the Second Empire, it was the beach à la mode. Then the Duc de Morny, half brother of Napoléon III, and other aristos who were looking for something more exclusive built their villas along the deserted beach across the Touques. Thus was launched Deauville, a vigorous grande dame who started kicking up her heels during the Second Empire, kept swinging through the Belle Epoque, and is still frequented by a fair share of millionaires, princes, and French movie stars. None of them ever goes near the water here, since other attractions—casino, theater, music hall, polo, galas, racecourse, marina and regattas, palaces and gardens, and place Vendôme jewelry shops—compete. The Promenade des Planches—the boardwalk extending along the seafront and lined with deck chairs, bars, and striped cabanas—is the place for celebrity spotting. With high-price hotels, designer boutiques, and one of the smartest gilt-edge casinos in Europe, Deauville's fashionable image still attracts the wealthy throughout the year.

Trouville is now considered an overflow town for its more prestigious neighbor—it remains more of a family resort, with few pretensions. If you'd like to see a typical French holiday spot rather than look for glamour, stay in Trouville. It, too, has a casino and boardwalk, a bustling fishing port, and a native population that makes it a livelier spot out of season than Deauville.

Dining and Lodging

$$$$ ✕🏨 **Normandy.** Since it opened in 1912, the fashionable and moneyed from Paris have been attracted to this hotel, with its traditional Norman facade and underground passage to the casino. A luxurious sense of well-being pervades the chandeliers and columns of the public areas.

Request a room with a sea view. Breakfast (96 francs) is served around the indoor pool. The gourmet restaurant serves mouthwatering variations of Norman cuisine, with creamy sauces much in evidence. ⊠ *38 rue Jean-Mermoz, 14800 Deauville,* ☎ *02–31–98–66–22; 800/ 223–5652 for U.S. reservations,* FAX *02–31–98–66–23. 252 rooms, 28 suites. Restaurant, indoor pool, sauna. AE, DC, MC, V.*

$$–$$$ 🏨 **Beach.** Although it lacks character, this hotel, one of the newer ones in town, is handy because of its location behind the casino. Print fabrics add color to the pristine white rooms; most overlook the sea or the harbor. Public rooms are designed for the flow of guests arriving with tour groups, so expect efficiency rather than personal service. ⊠ *Quai Albert-I, 14360 Trouville,* ☎ *02–31–98–12–00,* FAX *02–31–87–30–29. 110 rooms, 8 suites. Restaurant, pool, meeting rooms. AE, DC, MC, V.*

$$ 🏨 **Continental.** One of Deauville's oldest buildings is now this provincial hotel, four blocks from the sea and within easy walking distance of the town center and downtown Trouville. Rooms are small but simple, pristine, and reasonably priced for Deauville. ⊠ *1 rue Désiré-Le-Hoc, 14800 Deauville,* ☎ *02–31–88–21–06,* FAX *02–31–98–93–67. 42 rooms. AE, DC, MC, V. Closed mid-Nov.–mid-Mar.*

$–$$ 🏨 **Carmen.** This straightforward, unpretentious little hotel is around the corner from the casino and a block from the sea. Rooms range from plain and inexpensive to comfortable and moderate. The owners, the Bude family, are on hand to give advice. ⊠ *24 rue Carnot, 14360 Trouville,* ☎ *02–31–88–35–43,* FAX *02–31–88–08–03. 18 rooms. Restaurant. AE, DC, MC, V. Closed Jan.–mid-Feb. and 10 days in Oct.*

Nightlife and the Arts

One of the biggest cultural events on the Norman calendar is the **American Film Festival,** held in Deauville during the first week of September. Formal attire is required at Deauville's **casino** (⊠ 2 rue Edmond-Blanc, ☎ 02–31–14–31–14). Trouville's **casino** (⊠ Pl. du Maréchal-Foch, ☎ 02–31–87–75–00) is slightly less highbrow than Deauville's. Night owls enjoy the smoky ambience of the **Snake Pit Club** (⊠ 13 rue Albert-Fracasse, Deauville); it's open until 5 AM. The **Y Club** (⊠ 14 bis rue Désiré-le-Hoc, Deauville) is the place to go out dancing.

Outdoor Activities and Sports

At the **Club Nautique de Deauville** (⊠ Quai de la Marine, ☎ 02–31–88–38–19), hiring the smallest boat (16 ft) costs 140 francs, while a day on an 80-ft yacht will set you back about 600 francs per person. Sailing boats large and small can also be rented from the **Club Nautique de Trouville** (⊠ Digue des Roches Noires, ☎ 02–31–88–13–59). Deauville becomes Europe's horse capital in August, when breeders jet in from around the world for its yearling auctions and the races at its two attractive **hippodromes** (racetracks).

Houlgate

㉗ *14 km (9 mi) southwest of Deauville via D513, 27 km (17 mi) northeast of Caen.*

Cheerful Houlgate, bursting with wood-beamed, striped-brick Belle Epoque villas and thatched-roof houses, is a personable alternative to its pricier neighbors Deauville and Cabourg. The setting is prettier, too, with the steep **Falaise des Vaches Noires** (Black Cow Cliffs) providing a rocky backdrop to the town's enormous sandy beach.

Dining and Lodging

$–$$ ✕🏨 **1900.** Don't be misled by the tacky glass veranda: A wonderful
★ dining room lurks behind, with Art Nouveau lamps and a fine carved bar almost as old as the regiment of varied-size calvados bottles that

parade across the top. Claire is the good-humored *patronne*; her husband, André, is a deft cook with a penchant for fish and seafood. Service from the young trainees, impeccable in their black-and-white aprons, is discreet and helpful. You can stay the night here, too: rooms were modernized in 1998, and there is an annex with an attractive courtyard 100 yards down the street. ⊠ *17 rue des Bains, 14510,* ☎ *02–31–28–77–77,* ℻ *02–31–28–08–07. 28 rooms. Restaurant. MC, V. Closed Jan.*

En Route As you drive west along the seafront toward Cabourg, pause to visit historic **Dives-sur-Mer,** with its oak-beamed medieval market hall, rickety square, and chunky Gothic church.

Cabourg

㉘ *4 km (2 mi) west of Houlgate via D513, 25 km (16 mi) northeast of Caen.*

Cabourg retains a certain frowsy 19th-century elegance. Its streets fan out from a central hub near the seafront and the casino and Grand Hôtel. Writer Marcel Proust vacationed here, and one of the volumes in his epic *In Search of Lost Time* paints an evocative picture of life in the resort (named Balbec in the novel); Cabourg responded by naming its magnificent seafront promenade after him.

Lodging

$$$–$$$$ **Pullman Grand Hôtel.** This luxurious white-stucco hotel, on the seafront in the heart of town, is connected to the casino and has a lively piano bar in summer. Many rooms have balconies overlooking the sea; Proust used to stay in No. 147. In the restaurant (open November through March, closed Monday and Tuesday), Le Balbec, you can dine on traditional French cuisine of a high standard but no great sophistication. ⊠ *Promenade Marcel-Proust, 14390,* ☎ *02–31–91–01–79,* ℻ *02–31–24–03–20. 68 rooms. Restaurant, piano bar. AE, DC, MC, V.*

Caen

㉙ *24 km (15 mi) southwest of Cabourg, 120 km (75 mi) west of Rouen, 150 km (94 mi) north of Le Mans.*

With its abbeys and castle, Caen, a busy commercial city and the capital of Lower Normandy, is very different from the coastal resorts. William of Normandy ruled from Caen in the 11th century before he conquered England. Nine hundred years later, the two-month Battle of Caen in 1944 devastated the town. Much of the city burned in a fire that raged for 11 days, and the downtown area was almost entirely—yet tastefully—rebuilt after the war.

A good place to begin exploring Caen is the **Hôtel d'Escoville,** a stately mansion in the city center, built by wealthy merchant Nicolas Le Valois d'Escoville in the 1530s. The building was badly damaged during the war but has since been restored; the austere facade conceals an elaborate inner courtyard, reflecting the Italian influence on early Renaissance Norman architecture. The city **tourist office** is housed here and is an excellent resource. ⊠ *Pl. St-Pierre,* ☎ *02–31–27–14–14.*

Across the square is the late-Gothic church of **St-Pierre,** a riot of ornamental stonework. Looming on a mound ahead of the church is the **Château**—the ruins of William the Conqueror's fortress, built in 1060 and sensitively restored after the war. The castle gardens are a perfect spot for strolling, and the ramparts afford good views of the city. The citadel also contains two museums (☞ *below*) and the medieval Chapelle St-Georges.

The **Musée des Beaux-Arts,** within the castle's walls, is a heavyweight among France's provincial fine-arts museums. Its old-master collection includes works by Poussin, Rembrandt, Titian, Tintoretto, van der Weyden, and Paolo Veronese. ✉ *Entrance by castle gateway,* ☏ *02–31–30–47–70.* 🎫 *20 frs, free Wed.* ☼ *Wed.–Mon. 9:30–6.*

The **Musée de Normandie** (Normandy Museum), in the former keep of the castle governor, is dedicated to regional arts, such as ceramics and sculpture, plus some local archaeological finds. ✉ *Entrance by castle gateway,* ☏ *02–31–30–47–50.* 🎫 *10 frs, free Wed.* ☼ *Wed.–Mon. 9:30–12:30 and 2–6.*

★ Caen's finest church, of cathedral proportions, is part of the **Abbaye aux Hommes** (Men's Abbey), a monastery built by William the Conqueror. The abbey was begun in Romanesque style in 1066 and added to in the 18th century. Note the magnificent yet spare facade of the abbey church of **St-Étienne,** whose spareness is enhanced by two 11th-century towers topped by octagonal spires. Inside, what had been William the Conqueror's tomb was destroyed by 16th-century Huguenots during the Wars of Religion. However, the choir still stands; it was the first to be built in Norman Gothic style, and many subsequent choirs were modeled after it. ✉ *Pl. Louis-Guillouard,* ☏ *02–31–30–41–00.* 🎫 *Free, guided tours 10 frs.* ☼ *Tours daily at 9:30, 11, 2:30, and 4.*

The **Abbaye aux Dames** (Ladies' Abbey) was founded by William the Conqueror's wife, Matilda, in 1062. Once a hospital, the abbey—rebuilt in the 18th century—was restored in the 1980s by the Regional Council, which promptly requisitioned it for office space; however, its elegant arcaded courtyard and ground-floor reception rooms can be admired during a (free) guided tour. You can also visit the squat **Église de la Trinité** (Trinity Church), a fine example of 11th-century Romanesque architecture, though its original spires were replaced by bulky balustrades in the early 18th century. The 11th-century crypt once held Matilda's tomb, destroyed during the French Revolution. Note the intricate carvings on columns and arches in the chapel. ✉ *Pl. de la Reine-Mathilde,* ☏ *02–31–06–98–98.* 🎫 *Free.* ☼ *Guided tours daily at 2:30 and 4.*

★ The **Mémorial,** erected in 1988 in the north side of the city, is a must-see if you're interested in World War II history. The stark, flat facade, with a narrow doorway symbolizing the Allies' breach in the Nazi's supposedly impregnable Atlantic Wall, opens onto an immense foyer containing a café, brasserie, shop, and British Typhoon aircraft suspended overhead. The museum itself is down a spiral ramp, lined with photos and documents charting the Nazi's rise to power in the 1930s. The idea—hardly subtle but visually effective—is to suggest a descent into the hell of the war. The extensive displays ranges from wartime plastic jewelry to scale models of battleships, with scholarly sections on how the Nazis tracked down radios used by the French Resistance and on the development of the atomic bomb. A room commemorating the Holocaust, with flickering candles and twinkling overhead lights, provides a jarring, unfortunately artificial note. The D-Day landings are evoked by a tabletop Allied map of the theater of war and by a split-screen presentation of the D-Day invasion from both the Allied and Nazi standpoints. Four-hour minibus tours of the D-Day beaches are run daily April–September. ✉ *Esplanade Dwight-D.-Eisenhower,* ☏ *02–31–06–06–44.* 🎫 *74 frs.* ☼ *Feb.–Oct., daily 9–7; Nov.–Dec. and late-Jan., daily 9–6.*

Dining and Lodging

$$$ ✕ **Bourride.** On one of Caen's oldest streets near the castle is one of
★ the region's best restaurants. Chef Michel Bruneau's specialties include
baked *St-Pierre* (whitefish) with green mango, and baby pigeon in a
salted bean crust. The small dining room is typically Norman—stone
walls, beamed ceilings, and a large fireplace. ⊠ *15 rue de Vaugueux,*
☎ *02–31–93–50–76. Reservations essential. Jacket and tie. AE, DC,
MC, V. Closed Mon., most of Jan., and 2nd ½ Aug. No dinner Sun.*

$$$ ✕ **La Pommeraie.** Chef-owner José Aparicio's celebrated restaurant is
in a 17th-century former priory in the small village of Bénouville,
northeast of Caen. The excellent fish and seafood come off without a
hitch. If you eat here, you can stay overnight in one of the 15 cozy rooms
at the adjoining hotel, Le Manoir d'Hastings. ⊠ *18 av. de la Côte-de-
Nacre, 14970 Bénouville (10 km [6 mi] northeast of Caen),* ☎ *02–
31–44–62–43. Reservations essential. Jacket and tie. AE, DC, MC, V.
Closed Mon. and mid-Nov.–mid-Dec. No dinner Sun.*

$$ ⌂ **Dauphin.** Right in the center of town, this hotel, in a former 12th-
century priory, is surprisingly quiet. Rooms are smallish and modern;
those overlooking the street are soundproof; the ones in back look out
on the courtyard. Service is friendly and efficient in the hotel and in
the excellent though expensive restaurant (closed Saturday). ⊠ *29 rue
Gémare, 14000,* ☎ *02–31–86–22–26,* ☎ *02–31–86–35–14. 21 rooms.
Restaurant. AE, DC, MC, V.*

Shopping

A **marché aux puces** (flea market) is held on Friday morning on place
St-Saveur and on Sunday morning on place Courtonne. In June col-
lectors and dealers flock to Caen's bric-a-brac and **antiques fair.**

En Route Early on June 6, 1944, the British 6th Airborne Division landed by glider
and captured the **Pegasus Bridge** (named for the division's emblem,
showing Bellerophon astride his winged horse, Pegasus). This proved
the first symbolic step toward the liberation of France from Nazi oc-
cupation. To see this symbol of the Allied invasion, from Caen take
D514 north and turn right at Bénouville. The central section of the orig-
inal bridge—erected in 1935 but replaced by a similar but slightly wider
bridge in 1993—was moved to a nearby field, where it lay neglected
until an airy new structure was built to protect it in 2000. The café by
the bridge—the first building recaptured on French soil—is still stand-
ing and houses a small museum. A 40-minute son-et-lumière show lights
up the bridge and the café at nightfall between June and September.

Five kilometers (3 miles) north of here, just beyond the Ouistreham
Port, near Riva Bella, are some of the D-Day landing beaches: **Sword
Beach** extends to Luc-sur-Mer; **Juno Beach,** to Courseulles; and **Gold
Beach,** to Arromanches. These flat, sandy beaches, stormed by British
(Gold and Sword) and Canadian (Juno) troops, extend beneath pretty
resort towns like Lion-sur-Mer, Langrune, and St-Aubin. Inland, slen-
der church spires patrol the vast, flat horizon.

Arromanches-les-Bains

㉚ *31 km (19 mi) northwest of Caen, 10 km (6 mi) northeast of Bayeux.*

Little remains to mark the furious fighting waged hereabouts after D-
Day. In the bay off Arromanches, however, some elements of the float-
ing harbor are still visible. Head up to the terrace alongside Arromanches
360 (☞ *below*), high above the town on D65, to contemplate the seem-
ingly insignificant hunks of concrete that form a broken offshore semi-
circle—and try to imagine the extraordinary technical feat involved in
towing them across the Channel from England.

The **Musée du Débarquement,** on the seafront, has models, mock-ups, and photographs depicting Operation Overlord—the code name for the invasion of Normandy. Five beachheads (dubbed Utah, Omaha, Gold, Juno, and Sword) were established along the coast to either side of Arromanches (☞ *above* and *below*). Preparations started in mid-1943, and British shipyards worked furiously through the following winter and spring building two artificial harbors (called "mulberries"), boats, and landing equipment; the other harbor, moored off Omaha Beach, was destroyed on June 19, 1944, by a violent storm. The British and Canadian troops that landed on Sword, Juno, and Gold on June 6, 1944, quickly pushed inland and joined with parachute regiments previously dropped behind German lines, before encountering fierce resistance at Caen, which did not fall until July 9. ⊠ *Pl. du 6-Juin,* ☎ *02–31–22–34–31.* ⊑ *35 frs.* ☉ *May–Sept., daily 9–7; Oct.–Dec. and Feb.–Apr., daily 10–12:30 and 1:30–4:30.*

Arromanches 360 is a striking modern movie theater with a 360-degree circular screen—actually nine curved screens synchronized to show an 18-minute film (screenings at 10 past and 20 to the hour) entitled *Le Prix de la Liberté* (*The Price of Freedom*). The film, which tells the story of the D-Day landings, is a mix of archival and more recent footage from major sites and cemeteries. Evocative music and sound effects mean there's no need for spoken commentary. ⊠ *Chemin du Calvaire,* ☎ *02–31–22–30–30.* ⊑ *24 frs.* ☉ *June–Aug., daily 9–6:30; Sept.–May, daily 10–5.*

Bayeux

③ *10 km (6 mi) southwest of Arromanches via D516, 28 km (17 mi) north-west of Caen.*

Bayeux, the first town to be liberated during the Battle of Normandy, is steeped in history—home to a Norman-Gothic cathedral, a museum dedicated to the Battle of Normandy, and the world's most celebrated piece of needlework: the Bayeux Tapestry. Bayeux's medieval atmosphere makes it a popular base, especially among British travelers, for day trips to other towns in Normandy. The old-world mood is at its most boisterous during the Fêtes Médiévales, a market-cum-carnival held in the streets around the cathedral on the first weekend of July.

★ Really a 225-ft-long embroidered scroll stitched in 1067, the **Bayeux Tapestry,** known in French as the Tapisserie de la Reine Mathilde (Queen Matilde's Tapestry), depicts, in 58 comic-strip-type scenes, the epic story of William of Normandy's conquest of England in 1066. The tapestry was probably commissioned from Saxon embroiderers by the count of Kent—who was also the bishop of Bayeux—to be displayed in his newly built cathedral, the Cathédrale Notre-Dame (☞ *below*). Despite its age, the tapestry is in remarkably good condition; the extremely detailed, often homey scenes provide an unequaled record of the clothes, weapons, ships, and lifestyles of the day. It's showcased in the **Musée de la Tapisserie** (Tapestry Museum), in an 18th-century building; for 5 francs you can rent headphones and listen to an English commentary on the tapestry, scene by scene. ⊠ *Centre Guillaume le Conquérant, 13 bis rue de Nesmond,* ☎ *02–31–51–25–50.* ⊑ *40 frs (joint ticket with Musée Baron-Gérard and the Conservatoire de la Dentelle;* ☞ *below).* ☉ *May–mid-Sept., daily 9–6:30; mid-Sept.–Apr., daily 9:30–12:30 and 2–6.*

Housed in the Bishop's Palace beneath the cathedral, and fronted by a majestic plane tree planted in March 1797 and known as the Tree of Liberty, the **Musée Baron-Gérard** contains a fine collection of Bayeux porcelain and lace, ceramics from Rouen, a marvelous collection of apothecary jars from the 17th and 18th centuries, and 16th- to 19th-century furniture and paintings by local artists. ⊠ *1 pl. de la Liberté,* ☏ *02–31–92–14–21.* ⊡ *40 frs (joint ticket with Tapestry Museum and Conservatoire de la Dentelle; ☞ above and below).* ☼ *June–mid-Sept., daily 9–7; mid-Sept.–May, 10–12:30 and 2–6.*

Bayeux's mightiest edifice, the **Cathédrale Notre-Dame** is a harmonious mixture of Norman and Gothic architecture. Note the portal on the south side of the transept that depicts the assassination of English archbishop Thomas à Becket in Canterbury Cathedral in 1170, following his opposition to King Henry II's attempts to control the church. ⊠ *Rue du Bienvenue,* ☏ *02–31–92–01–85.*

Handmade lace is a specialty of Bayeux. The best place to learn more about it and to buy some is the **Conservatoire de la Dentelle.** ⊠ *Hôtel du Doyen, rue Lambert-Leforestier,* ☏ *02–31–92–73–80.* ⊡ *40 frs (joint ticket with Tapestry Museum and Musée Baron-Gérard; ☞ above).* ☼ *Daily 9–12:30 and 2–6.*

At the **Musée de la Bataille de Normandie** (Battle of Normandy Museum) detailed exhibits trace the story of the Battle of Normandy from June 7 to August 22, 1944. This modern museum near the British War Cemetery, sunk partly beneath the level of its surrounding lawns, contains an impressive array of war paraphernalia, including uniforms, weapons, equipment, 150 waxworks, and a film depicting scenes and tactics of the invasion. ⊠ *Bd. du Général-Fabian-Ware,* ☏ *02–31–92–93–41.* ⊡ *32 frs.* ☼ *May–mid-Sept., daily 9–6:30; mid-Sept.–Apr., daily 10–noon and 2–6.*

Dining and Lodging

$ ✕ **Amaryllis.** This small restaurant has a prix-fixe menu with a variety of dishes. The three-course dinner, with six selections per course, may include a half-dozen oysters, fillet of sole with a cider-based sauce, and pastries for dessert. ⊠ *32 rue St-Patrice,* ☏ *02–31–22–47–94. MC, V. Closed Mon. and mid-Dec.–mid-Jan.*

$$$$ ✕⊡ **Château d'Audrieu.** This family-owned château fulfills a Holly-★ wood notion of a palatial property: An avenue leads to the imposing, elegant 18th-century facade that sets the tone for what lies within—old-world opulence, wall sconces, overstuffed chairs, and antiques. Rooms 50 and 51 have gabled ceilings with exposed-wood beams. The restaurant (closed Monday, and no lunch is served Tuesday) has an extensive wine list, and chef Alain Cornet keeps to a classical repertoire of dishes. ⊠ *14250 Audrieu (13 km [8 mi] southeast of Bayeux off N13),* ☏ *02–31–80–21–52,* ⊞ *02–31–80–24–73. 25 rooms. Restaurant, bar, pool, helipad. AE, MC, V. Closed mid-Dec.–mid-Feb.*

$$–$$$ ✕⊡ **Grand Hôtel du Luxembourg.** The Luxembourg, a Best Western affiliate renovated in 1999, has small but adequate rooms; all but two face the courtyard garden. It has one of the town's best restaurants, Les Quatre Saisons, with a seasonal menu; depending on the time of year, you might have a salmon *galette* (buckwheat pancake) or chicken roasted with cider. ⊠ *25 rue des Bouchers, 14400,* ☏ *02–31–92–00–04; 800/528–1234 for U.S. reservations,* ⊞ *02–31–92–54–26. 19 rooms, 3 suites. Restaurant, bar, dance club. AE, DC, MC, V.*

$$ ⊡ **Manoir du Carel.** Archives suggest that the Manoir du Carel, an ideal ★ spot halfway between Bayeux and the Normandy beaches, was constructed as a fortified manor by an Englishman during the Hundred Years' War. Certainly the narrow slits serving as windows on the tower suggest a defensive stance. Current owner Jacques Aumond offers comfortable rooms with modern furnishings. The cottage on the grounds has a kitchen plus a fireplace that masks a brick oven where villagers once

had their bread baked. The lounges have turn-of-the-century furniture and are perfect places for a glass of wine before going out to dinner. ⊠ *14400 Maisons (5 km [3 mi] northwest of Bayeux),* ☎ *02–31–22–37–00,* ℻ *02–31–21–57–00. 3 rooms, 1 cottage. Breakfast room.*

Outdoor Activities and Sports

Bicycles can be rented from **Family Home** (⊠ 39 rue Général-de-Dais, ☎ 02–31–92–15–22) for about 50 francs a day. Ask the tourist office for information about trails (☞ Visitor Information *in* Normandy A to Z, *below*). The **Rassemblement International de Ballons** (International Balloon Festival; ☎ 02–31–21–60–61 for information) takes place in mid-June, 16 km (10 mi) southwest of Bayeux at the early 17th-century Château de Balleroy (bought by Malcolm S. Forbes in 1970). The château's Musée des Ballons (Balloon Museum) is open Thursday–Tuesday from April though October. Whether or not you're interested in balloons, try to visit this chateau, one of the most elegant buildings of the late 17th century. With ceilings painted by Pierre Mignard and a moat, this is a masterpiece of the French Baroque and one of the earliest buildings designed by Jules-Hardouin Mansart, who went on to build a little thing called Versailles.

The D-Day Beaches

You won't be disappointed by the rugged terrain and windswept sand of **Omaha Beach,** 16 km (10 mi) northwest of Bayeux. Here you'll find the **Monument du Débarquement** (Monument to the Normandy Landings) and nearby, in Vierville-sur-Mer, the **Monument to the Members of the U.S. National Guard** who fought in both world wars. In Colleville-sur-Mer is the hilltop **American Cemetery and Memorial,** designed by the landscape architect Markley Stevenson. It is a moving tribute to the fallen, with its Wall of the Missing (in the form of a semicircular colonnade), drumlike chapel, and avenues of holly oaks trimmed to resemble open parachutes. The crisply mown lawns are studded with 9,386 marble tombstones; this is where Stephen Spielberg's fictional hero, Captain John Miller, was supposed to have been buried in *Saving Private Ryan.* You can look out to sea across the landing beach from a platform on the north side of the cemetery.

The most spectacular scenery along the coast is at the **Pointe du Hoc,** 13 km (8 mi) west of St-Laurent. Wildly undulating grassland leads past ruined blockhouses to a cliff-top observatory and a German machine-gun post whose intimidating mass of reinforced concrete merits chilly exploration. Despite Spielberg's cinematic genius, it remains hard to imagine just how Colonel Rudder and his 225 men—only 90 survived—managed to scale the jagged cliffs with rope ladders and capture the German defenses in one of the most heroic and dramatic episodes of the war.

Head west around the coast on N13, pause in the town of **Carentan** to admire its modern marina and the mighty octagonal spire of the Église Notre-Dame, and continue northwest to **Sainte-Mère-Église.** At 2:30 AM on the morning of June 6, 1944, the 82nd Airborne Division was dropped over Ste-Mère, heralding the start of D-Day operations. Famously, one parachutist got stuck on the church tower (memorably recreated in the 1960 film *The Longest Day*); a dummy is strung up each summer to recall the event, and a stained-glass window inside the church honors American paratroopers. After securing their position at Ste-Mère, U.S. forces pushed north, then west, cutting off the Cotentin Peninsula on June 18 and taking Cherbourg on June 26. German defense proved fiercer farther south, and St-Lô was not liberated until July 19. Ste-Mère's symbolic importance as the first French town to be liberated from the Nazis is commemorated by the Borne 0 (Zero) outside the Town Hall—a large, domed milestone marking the start of the Voie de la Libertè (Freedom Way), charting the Allies' progress across France.

The **Musée des Troupes Aéroportées** (Airborne Troops Museum), built behind the church in 1964 in the form of an open parachute, houses documents, maps, mementos, and one of the Waco CG4A gliders used to drop troops. ⊠ *Pl. du 6-juin-1944,* ☎ *02–33–41–41–35.* 🎟 *20 frs.* ☉ *Apr.–Nov., daily 9–noon and 2–7.*

③⑤ Head east from Ste-Mère on D67 to **Utah Beach,** which, being sheltered from the Atlantic winds by the Cotentin Peninsula and surveyed by lowly sand dunes rather than rocky cliffs, proved easier to attack than Omaha. In **La Madeleine** inspect the modern museum (⊠ Plage de La Madeleine, ☎ 02–33–71–53–35) devoted to the battle of Utah Beach; it's open April–June and September–October, daily 9:30–noon and 2–6; and July–August, daily 9:30–6:30. Continue north to the **Dunes de Varreville,** home to a monument to French hero General Leclerc, who landed here. Offshore you can see the fortified **Iles St-Marcouf.** Continue to **Quinéville,** at the far end of Utah Beach, with its **museum** (⊠ Rue de la Plage, ☎ 02–33–21–40–44) evoking life during the German Occupation; the museum is open April–May and October, daily 10–noon and 2–6; and June–September, daily 9:30–6:30.

Dining and Lodging

$$$–$$$$ ✕⊡ **Chenevière.** This grand 19th-century manor, just inland from Port-en-Bessin, to the east of Omaha Beach, has rooms with modern furnishings, floor-to-ceiling windows, and flowered bedspreads. The restaurant lives up to its surroundings; Claude Esprabens's roasted scampi with sesame seeds and fresh chanterelles is delicious, as is the warm sliced duck liver with raspberry sauce. ⊠ *Les Escures, 14520 Commes,* ☎ *02–31–51–25–25,* 🅵🅰🆇 *02–31–51–25–20. 18 rooms. Restaurant. AE, DC, MC, V. Closed Jan.*

$$ ✕⊡ **Casino.** You can't get closer to the action: This handsome, postwar stone hotel, renovated in 1999, looks directly onto Omaha Beach. Fish and regional cuisine with creamy sauces predominate in the restaurant. ⊠ *Rue de la Percée, 14710 Vierville-sur-Mer,* ☎ *02–31–22–41– 02,* 🅵🅰🆇 *02–31–22–41–12. 12 rooms. Restaurant. MC, V. Closed mid-Nov.–Feb.*

En Route From Quinéville head north up the coast to the bustling harbor town of **St-Vaast-la Hougue,** with its Vauban citadel. Just offshore is the **Ile de Tatihou,** with its sturdy round fort. Continue up the coast on D1, stopping first in **Montfarville** to visit its granite church, with gaudy ceiling frescoes on the Life of Christ by local 19th-century artist Guillaume Fouace, then in **Barfleur,** renowned for its picturesque waterfront. The 230-ft lighthouse at nearby **Gatteville-le-Phare** is one of the tallest in France, surveying a stretch of coast notorious for its treacherous crosscurrents. Head west to **St-Pierre-Église** and its fortified church, again with a painted roof, then go northwest via D210 to **Cap Lévy,** a quaint little cove affording fine views across the bay to Cherbourg.

Cherbourg

③⑥ *37 km (23 mi) northwest of Ste-Mère-Église via N13.*

Perhaps best known for Michel Legrand's haunting theme from the 1960s film musical *Les Parapluies de Cherbourg* (The Umbrellas of Cherbourg), Cherbourg is no longer the thriving transatlantic port of a Belle Epoque heyday symbolized by the hyperelaborate facade of its 1882 **theater,** one of the few old monuments to survive World War II. Umbrellas are hardly the sunniest of city symbols, but the climate, though gusty, is generally mild, and it's fun to stroll around the grid of narrow lanes (many pedestrians only) between the theater and the ramshackle **Église de la Trinité** by the seafront—especially on Tuesday, Thursday, or Saturday, when the street market is in full action.

It was back in 1686 that Vauban first spotted Cherbourg's potential as a defensive port beneath the rocky, 360-ft Montagne du Roule, but it took the completion of a massive breakwater, in 1853, for Cherbourg to be able to harbor ocean-going ships. The first transatlantic liner docked in 1869; these days ferries ply the Channel to England (Portsmouth and Poole) and Ireland (Rosslare). You can take a short sea cruise around the bay any afternoon from April through September (call 02–33–93–75–27 for details). Cherbourg is also a major submarine base: More than 90 have been built here since 1899, and one of them will be on display at the new **Cité de La Mer** (Marine Center), slated to open in 2001.

Uniforms, photographs, maps, flags, posters, and medals at the **Musée de la Libération** (Liberation Museum), on the hill above the town (excellent sea views), recall Cherbourg's pivotal role at the end of World War II, when it was the Allies' major bridgehead to France after the D-Day landings, and the French terminal for the PLUTO sea-bed pipeline that pumped troop-needed fuel under the Channel from the Isle of Wight. ⊠ *Fort du Roule,* ☎ *02–33–20–14–12.* 🎟 *20 frs.* ☉ *Apr.–Sept., daily 10–6; Oct.–Mar., Tues.–Sun. 9:30–noon and 2–5:30.*

Thirty works by local-born François Millet (of *Angélus* fame) can be seen at the **Musée Thomas-Henry,** the city art museum, along with works by Murillo, Velvet Brueghel, David, and talented 19th-century regional artists like Guillaume Fouace and Félix Bahot. Sculpture and ceramics complete the collection. ⊠ *Rue Vartel,* ☎ *02–33–23–02–23.* 🎟 *15 frs.* ☉ *Tues.–Sun. 9–noon and 2–6.*

Dining and Lodging

$$ ✕ **Faitout.** This cozy, paneled bistro in the shopping district near the Trinité church packs in locals with its friendly service and traditional French cuisine. Stews, steaks, and mussels are usually high on the menu. ⊠ *25 rue de la Tour-Carree,* ☎ *02–33–04–25–04. MC, V. Closed Sun. and 1 wk in Jul. No lunch Mon.*

$$ 🏨 **Hôtel Ambassadeur.** This modernized quayside hotel offers good value, a central location, and an English-speaking staff. The better, and more expensive, rooms have bathtubs rather than showers and look out over the harbor. The Vauban restaurant, right next door, makes for a calmer dinnertime alternative to the bustling Faitout (☞ *above*). ⊠ *22 quai de Caligny, 50100,* ☎ *02–33–43–10–00,* 🗚 *02–33–43–10–01. 40 rooms. MC, V.*

En Route   Speed south on N13 and pause in the elegant old town of **Valognes.** Despite the ravages of World War II—witness the reconstructed church with its unusual octagonal lantern—the town retains several opulent 18th-century mansions, notably the majestic **Hôtel de Beaumont** with its grand staircase and stately gardens. Continue from Valognes to Carentan and head south on N174 to St-Lô.

St-Lô

㊲   *78 km (49 mi) southeast of Cherbourg, 36 km (22 mi) southwest of Bayeux.*

St-Lô, perched dramatically on a rocky spur above the Vire Valley, was a key communications center that suffered so badly in World War II that it became known as the "capital of ruins." The medieval **Église**

Notre-Dame bears mournful witness to those dark days: Its imposing, spire-topped west front was never rebuilt, merely shored up with a wall of greenish stone. Reconstruction elsewhere, though, was wholesale. Some of it was spectacular, like the slender, spiral-staircased tower outside city hall; the circular theater; or the openwork belfry of the church of Ste-Croix. The city was freed by American troops, and its rebuilding was financed with U.S. support, notably from Baltimore. The **Hôpital–Mémorial France–États-Unis** (France–United States Memorial Hospital), designed by Paul Nelson and featuring a giant mosaic by Fernand Léger, is named to honor those links.

St-Lô is capital of the Manche *département* and, less prosaically, likes to consider itself France's horse capital. Hundreds of breeders are based in its environs, and the **Haras National** (National Stud) was established here in 1886 (call 02–33–77–88–77 for details on how to visit on a summer afternoon).

★ The city art museum, the **Musée des Beaux-Arts,** opened in 1989. It's the perfect French provincial museum: airy, seldom busy, not too big, yet full of varied exhibits—including an unexpected masterpiece: *Gombault et Macée,* a set of nine silk-and-wool tapestries woven in Bruges around 1600, relating a famous tale about a shepherd couple and exquisitely showcased in a special circular room. Other highlights include brash modern tapestries by Jean Lurçat; paintings by Corot, Boudin, and Géricault; court miniatures by Daniel Saint (1778-1847); and the Art Deco pictures of Slovenian-born Jaro Hilbert (1897-1995), inspired by ancient Egypt. Photographs, models, and documents evoke the city's wartime devastation. ⊠ *Centre Culturel, pl. du Champ-de-Mars,* ☎ *02–33–72–52–55.* ⌸ *10 frs.* ⊙ *Wed.–Mon. 10–noon and 2–6.*

Coutances

㊳ *27 km (18 mi) southwest of St-Lô via D972*

If you're interested in cathedral architecture, you'll want to stop off in
★ Coutances. The largely 13th-century **Cathédrale Notre-Dame,** with its famous octagonal lantern rising 135 ft above the nave, is considered the most harmonious Gothic building in Normandy. On the outside, especially the facade, note the obsessive use of turrets, spires, slender shafts, and ultranarrow pointed arches squeezed senseless in their architectural pursuit of vertical takeoff.

Lodging

$ 🏠 **Moulin Girard.** If you have a hankering for English hospitality, cheerful conversation, and inexpensive accommodations, Roger and Jasmine Albon's inn is the place to head. The main house has three very small rooms, and the Norman-style cottage has a two-bedroom suite—for 350 francs, including breakfast, it's ideal for a family or two couples. ⊠ *50410 Le Chefresne (26 km [16 mi] southeast of Coutances; from Villedieu-les-Poêles take a right on D98 as you enter Percy in the direction of Tessy-sur-Vire and then go right on D452 for Le Chefresne),* ☎ FAX *02–33–61–62–06. 3 rooms, 1 suite. No credit cards.*

Granville

㊴ *30 km (19 mi) south of Coutances via D971, 107 km (67 mi) southwest of Caen.*

Proud locals like to call Granville the "Monaco of the North." It's perched on a rocky outcrop and has a sea-water therapy center, and. . . the similarities end there. Free of casinos and sequins, Granville instead has a down-to-earth feel. Granite houses cluster around the church in the old town, and the harbor below is full of working boats. From the ramparts there are fine views of the English Channel; catamarans breeze over to Jersey and the Iles Chausey daily in summer. Drive a few miles down the coast to find sandy beaches and a view of distant Mont-St-Michel.

Nightlife and the Arts

The rambunctious **Carnaval de Granville** involves four days of parades and festivities, culminating each year on Shrove Tuesday. The **Grand Pardon des Corporations de la Mer,** a *pardon,* or religious festival, devoted to the sea, is celebrated on the last Sunday of July with a military parade, regatta, and platefuls of shellfish.

Outdoor Activities and Sports

Granville is a center for aquatic sports; inquire about sailboat jaunts at the **Centre Régional de Nautisme de Granville** (⊠ Bd. des Amiraux, ☎ 02–33–91–22–60). **Lepesqueux** (⊠ 3 rue Clément-Desmaisons, ☎ 02–33–50–18–97) also rents boats and yachts.

Shopping

It is said that every French kitchen worth its salt buys its pans from **Villedieu-les-Poêles,** 28 km (18 mi) east of Granville. The town is famous for its copperware (and its bells), and shops line the main street, rue Carnot, but you can find smaller outlets, with better buys, on the parallel rue du Dr-Harvard. Note that Tuesday is market day, so parking can be a bit of a problem.

Mont-St-Michel

★ *44 km (27 mi) south of Granville via D973, N175, and D43; 123 km (77 mi) southwest of Caen; 67 km (42 mi) north of Rennes; 325 km (202 mi) west of Paris.*

Wrought by nature plus centuries of man's tireless toil, this sea-surrounded mass of granite, adorned with the soul-lifting silhouette of the abbey of Mont-St-Michel, may well be your most lasting image of Normandy. The abbey is perched on a 264-ft rock a few hundred yards off the coast: It's surrounded by water during the year's highest tides and by desolate sand flats the rest of the time. Be warned: tides in the bay are dangerously unpredictable. The sea can rise up to 45 ft at high tide and rushes in at incredible speed—more than a few ill-prepared tourists over the years have drowned. Also, be warned there are patches of quicksand.

Because of its legendary origins and the sheer exploit of its construction, the abbey is known as the *Merveille de l'Occident* (Wonder of the Western World): The granite used to build it was transported from the nearby Isles of Chausey and hauled up to the site. The abbey's construction took more than 500 years, from 1017 to 1521. Legend has it that the Archangel Michael appeared to Aubert, bishop of Avranches, inspiring him to build an oratory on what was then called Mont Tombe. The original church was completed in 1144, but new buildings were added in the 13th century to accommodate the monks, as well as the hordes of pilgrims who flocked here even during the Hundred Years' War, when the region was in English hands. The Romanesque choir was rebuilt in Gothic style during the 15th and 16th centuries. The abbey's monastic vocation was undermined during the 17th century, when the monks began to flout the strict rules and discipline of their order, drifting into a state of decadence that culminated in their dispersal and the abbey's conversion into a prison, well before the French Revolution. In 1874 the former abbey was handed over to a governmental agency responsible for the preservation of historic monuments. Emmanuel Frémiet's great gilded statute of St. Michael was added to the spire in 1897 and skillfully restored (after being removed by helicopter) in the early 1990s. Monks now live and work here again, as in medieval times: you can join them for daily mass at 12:15.

A causeway—to be replaced in 2001 by a bridge, thus allowing the bay waters to circulate freely—links Mont-St-Michel to the mainland. Leave your car in the parking lot (15 francs) along the causeway, outside the main gate. Just inside you'll find the tourist office, to the left, and a pair of old cannons (and cannonballs) to the right. If you're staying the night on Mont-St-Michel, take what you need in a small suitcase; you cannot gain access to your hotel by car.

The climb to the abbey is hard going—by the time you have mounted the celebrated **Escalier de Dentelle** (Lace Staircase) to the gallery around the roof of the abbey church, you will have climbed no fewer than 900 steps—but it's worth it. Stop off halfway up Grande-Rue at the medieval parish church of St-Pierre to admire the richly carved side chapel with its dramatic statue of St. Michael slaying the dragon. The **Grand Degré**, a steep, narrow staircase, leads to the abbey entrance, from which a wider flight of stone steps climbs to the **Saut Gautier Terrace** (named after a prisoner who jumped to his death from it), outside the sober, dignified church. After visiting the arcaded cloisters alongside, which offer vertiginous views of the bay, you can wander at leisure, and probably get lost, among the maze of rooms, staircases, and vaulted halls that make up the abbey. In July and August evening concerts are held here during the **Heures Musicales** (Musical Hours), and there's a **son-et-lumière** every night Monday through Saturday, June through September. The island village, with its steep, narrow streets, is best visited out of season, from September to June. In summer the hordes of tourists and souvenir sellers can be stifling. Give yourself at least half a day here, and follow your nose. The mount is full of nooks, crannies, and little gardens, and there are fine views from along the ramparts. Best of all, when the day-trippers depart, the centuries-old peace and quiet of the mount return, and you can truly appreciate the frightening grandeur of this solitary spot. With this in mind, consider an overnight stay here, even though the hotels have somewhat inflated prices. If possible, time your visit a couple of days after the full moon—then the sunsets over this part of the Atlantic can be of incredible beauty. ☎ 02–33–60–14–14. ⊠ 40 frs. ☉ May–Sept., daily 9:30–11:30 and 1:30–6; Oct.–Apr., Wed.–Mon. 9:30–4:30.

Dining and Lodging

$$$–$$$$ ✕▥ **Mère Poulard.** The hotel of the most celebrated restaurant on the mount consists of adjoining houses with small, simple, clean rooms, up three steep flights of narrow stairs. The restaurant's reputation derives partly from Mère Poulard's famous fluffy omelet and partly from its location right by the gateway. The owners trade on a captive market—prices are exorbitant, service obsequious, and you are charged for extras. Room prices start low but ratchet upward the bigger they get; the smallest rooms are bearable for an overnight stay, not longer. Walls throughout are plastered with posters and photographs of illustrious guests. You are usually requested to book two meals with the room. Reservations are essential for the restaurant in summer. ⊠ Grande-Rue, 50116, ☎ 02–33–60–14–01, ℻ 02–33–48–52–31. 27 rooms. Restaurant, piano bar. AE, DC, MC, V.

$$ ✕▥ **Roche Torin.** Run by the Barraux family, this small, ivy-clad manor ★ house on 4 acres of parkland is a delightful alternative to the high price of staying on Mont-St-Michel. Rooms are pleasantly old-fashioned, and the bathrooms modern. The pleasant restaurant (closed Monday) has an open fireplace and serves superb *pré-salé* (salt-marsh lamb). In summer aperitifs are served in the garden, facing a view of Mont-St-Michel. ⊠ *34 rte. de la Roche-Torin, 50220 Courtils (9 km [5 mi] from Mont-St-Michel),* ☎ *02-33-70-96-55,* FAX *02-33-48-35-20. 11 rooms, 1 suite. Restaurant. MC, V. Closed mid-Nov.–mid-Mar.*

\$\$–\$\$\$ 🍴 **Terrasses Poulard.** Hordes of tourists come to this ensemble of buildings clustered around a small garden in the middle of the mount. Rooms at this hotel are some of the best—with views of the bay and rustic-style furnishings—and the most spacious on the mount, although many require you to negotiate a labyrinth of steep stairways first. ⊠ *Grande-Rue, opposite the parish church, 50116,* ☎ *02-33-60-14-09,* FAX *02-33-60-37-31. 29 rooms. Restaurant, billiards, library. AE, DC, MC, V.*

Falaise

❹① *132 km (82 mi) northeast of Mont-St-Michel, 32 km (20 mi) south of Caen.*

The memory of William the Conqueror, born here in 1027 as the illegitimate child of Duke Robert of Normandy and local girl La Belle Arlette, haunts the lively town of Falaise. William can be admired on a rearing bronze steed in the main square, and you can see the fountain where Robert is said to have first laid eyes on the lovely Arlette as she washed her clothes. Although Falaise was badly mauled during the Battle of Normandy, parts of the original town walls remain, as do the impressive medieval churches of St-Gervais, La Trinité, and Notre-Dame de Guibray.

The foursquare **Château Guillaume-le-Conquérant** (Castle of William the Conqueror) glowers down from a spur above the town. Little has survived from the original building where William was born—but what remains is old enough: the main keep, built by English king Henry I in 1123; a smaller keep, erected by his grandson Henry II around 1180; and the sturdy round Talbot Tower, built by French king Philippe-Auguste after seizing Falaise in 1204. You can climb to the top of the tower for a panoramic view of the town and countryside. The castle's most recent addition is also its most controversial: a somber entrance block in dark gray concrete that went wrong during mixing (it was meant to be blue). The castle interior, rescued from ruin in the 1990s, is equally startling. The glass-paneled floor of the *aula* (main hall) enables you to peer down into what seems to be the bowels of the earth. It's an optical illusion—you're actually looking at the rocky foundations 30 ft below. ⊠ *Pl. Guillaume-le-Conquérant,* ☎ *02-31-41-61-44.* 🎫 *30 frs.* ☉ *Apr.–Sept., daily 9:30–5; Oct.–Mar., Thurs.–Tues. 10–noon and 2–5.*

☾ At **Automates Avenue,** 300 clockwork toys and automatons, from the turn of the century to the 1950s, are artfully presented in display windows evoking the streets of Paris. ⊠ *Bd. de la Libération,* ☎ *02-31-90-02-43.* 🎫 *30 frs.* ☉ *Apr.–Sept., daily 10–6; Oct.–mid-Jan. and Feb.–Mar., weekends 10–12:30 and 1:30–6.*

OFF THE   **LA SUISSE NORMANDE** — Swiss Normandy is a striking, rocky expanse of
BEATEN PATH hills and gullies southwest of Falaise. One of the most dramatic sights in
the area is the Gorges de St-Aubert, 11 km (7 mi) southwest of Falaise via D44 and D21. From the gorge continue on D301 to the Roche d'Oëtre, a rock with spectacular views of the craggy hills that give the region its name. Head northwest to Rouvrou, then turn right to Point-des-Vers, and left on D167 to reach the riverside town of Pont d'Ouilly. From here take D1 west to Le Fresne, then follow D562 north for just over 3 km (2 mi) to Clécy, the area's main town. From the cliffs overlooking the

Orne, there are lovely views of the woods on the other bank. Stop for a snack at La Potinière café, on the riverbank (it's closed October–April). Farther north is the town of Thury-Harcourt, which is famous for the beautiful gardens of its ruined castle.

Dining and Lodging

$$ ✕ **Fine Fourchette.** Chef Gilbert Costil attracts local devotees with
★ dishes combining color, flavor, and quantity. Salmon and tuna gazpacho, foie gras with hazelnut dressing, grilled turbot with lemon, and chocolate cake with pistachio cream number among his specialties. Madame Costil provides a gracious welcome. ⊠ *52 rue Georges-Clemenceau,* ☎ *02–31–90–08–59. AE, MC, V. Closed Wed. and Feb. No dinner Tues.*

$$–$$$ ▦ **Hôtel de Souza.** This hotel in an 18th-century town house has a magnificent iron-railing staircase and museum-quality paintings, china, and furniture, many evoking the memory of Adelaïde de Souza Bothello (1761–1836), who lived here in the early 19th century. De Souza Bothello was a writer and society hostess whose circle of intimates included Governor Morris—who played a key role in drafting the U.S. Constitution and adopting decimal coinage in the United States. Owner Patrick Laprée is only too happy to provide more historical background during a guided tour (20 francs for nonguests). You can experience the Ancien Regime ambience firsthand by booking the small but sumptuous two-room suite, which overlooks the garden and town walls. The guest room at the front of the house, in cheerful yellow and white, is a cheaper alternative. ⊠ *26 rue du Camp-Fermé, 14700,* ☎ *02–31–40–84–25. 1 room, 1 suite. No credit cards.*

Sées

㊷ *44 km (28 mi) southeast of Falaise via N158.*

With old houses, churches, a stately town hall, a majestic bishop's palace and former abbey, and a quaint circular market hall—all paying tribute to its onetime importance as the religious center of southern Normandy—the small town of Sées exudes faded charm.

★ The **Cathédrale St-Latrium** rises from the sleepy heart of Sées, its 200-ft spires visible for miles around. Apart from the tower, the main external feature is the huge porch, reinforced by extra buttressing when it started leaning on the sloping ground in the 16th century. The elegant interior has an airy east end, with exquisite late-13th-century stained glass in the soaring choir and the two rose windows in the transepts. ⊠ *Pl. du Général-de-Gaulle.*

The turrets and improbably steep slate roofs of the **Château d'O** rise above rich meadowland near Mortrée, 7 km (4 mi) northwest of Sées. The three-winged château, surrounded by a moat patrolled by regal swans, has checkerboard brick-and-stone walls and an interior refurbished in the 18th century; look out for the sculpted ermine emblem of the O family, distinguished both as royal courtiers and for possessing the shortest family name in France. ☎ *02–33–35–34–69.* ▦ *35 frs.* ☉ *Mar.–Nov., Wed.–Mon. 2–5.*

Alençon

㊸ *22 km (16 mi) south of Sées via N138, 49 km (31 (mi) north of Le Mans.*

Historic Alençon, an attractive town with many old buildings and an impressive late-Gothic church, is south of the Écouves Forest on the eastern edge of the Normandie-Maine Regional Park.

The town has been a lace-making center since 1665; by the end of the 17th century *point d'Alençon* (Alençon needlepoint lace) was de rigueur on women's and men's clothing and in interior decor in all fashionable circles. The **Musée des Beaux-Arts et de la Dentelle** (Museum of Fine Arts and Lace) contains a sophisticated collection of lace from Italy, Flanders, and France, along with paintings from the French school that span the 17th to the 20th centuries. ⊠ *Rue du Capitaine-Charles-Aveline,* ☎ *02–33–32–40–07.* ⊠ *18 frs.* ⊘ *Tues.–Sun. 10–noon and 2–6.*

Shopping
Handmade lace is a rarity, and prices are high, though this kind of labor-intensive, superior-quality creation never comes cheap: The **Musée de la Dentelle** (⊠ 31 rue du Pont-Neuf, ☎ 02–33–26–27–26) has an excellent selection.

NORMANDY A TO Z

Arriving and Departing

By Boat
A number of ferry companies sail between the United Kingdom and ports in Normandy. **Brittany Ferries** (☎ 08–03–82–88–28) travels between Caen (Ouistreham) and Portsmouth and between Poole and Cherbourg. **Hoverspeed** (☎ 08–20–00–35–55) goes between Dieppe and Newhaven daily in summer, weekends only in winter (and not at all Januar–mid-February). **P&O** (☎ 08–03–01–30–13) goes between Le Havre and Portsmouth and between Cherbourg and Portsmouth.

By Car
From Paris A13 slices its way to Rouen in 1½ hours (toll 37 francs) before forking to Caen (an additional hour, toll 31 francs) or Le Havre (45 minutes on A131). N13 continues from Caen to Cherbourg via Bayeux in another two hours.

By Plane
Paris's Charles de Gaulle (Roissy) and Orly airports are the closest international links with the region. **Air France** (☎ 08–02–80–28–02 for information) flies to Caen from Paris. From London there are regular flights to Caen (☎ 02–31–71–20–10 for airport information) and Deauville (☎ 02–31–65–65–65 for airport information) on Air France; and from Southampton and the Channel Islands to Cherbourg (☎ 02–33–88–57–60 for airport information).

By Train
From Paris (Gare St-Lazare), separate train lines head to Upper Normandy (Rouen and Le Havre or Dieppe) and Lower Normandy (Caen, Bayeux, and Cherbourg, via Évreux and Lisieux). Taking the train from Paris to Mont-St-Michel is not easy: Connections are complicated, and it could take you all day to get there (☞ Getting Around By Train *below* for more information).

Getting Around

By Car
The 1995 opening of the Pont de Normandie, between Le Havre and Honfleur, has effectively united Upper and Lower Normandy and made driving between the two regions a lot easier. A13/N13, linking Rouen to Caen, Bayeux, and Cherbourg, is the backbone of Normandy. If you have extra time, taking Normandy's scenic minor roads can be very rewarding.

By Train

Unless you are content to stick to the major towns (Rouen, Le Havre, Dieppe, Caen, Bayeux), visiting Normandy by train may prove frustrating. You can reach several smaller towns (Fécamp, Deauville, Cabourg), and even Mont-St-Michel (sort of—it's a 15-minute taxi ride from Pontorson), on snail-paced branch lines, but the intricacies of what is said to be Europe's most complicated regional timetable will probably have driven you nuts by the time you get there.

Contacts and Resources

Bike Rental

You can rent bicycles at most major train stations for about 45 francs per day.

Car Rental

Avis (⊠ 44 pl. de la Gare, Caen, ☎ 02–31–84–73–80; ⊠ 32 av. de Caen, Rouen, ☎ 02–35–72–64–32). **Europcar** (⊠ 6 rue du Docteur-Piasecki, Le Havre, ☎ 02–35–25–21–95).

Emergencies

Ambulance (☎ 15). **Regional hospitals: Caen** (⊠ Av. de la Côte-de-Nacre, ☎ 02–31–06–31–06); **Le Havre** (⊠ 29 av. Pierre-Mendès-France, Montivilliers, ☎ 02–32–73–32–32); **Rouen** (⊠ 1 rue Germont, ☎ 02–32–88–89–90).

Guided Tours

The following companies run full-day bus excursions from Paris to Mont-St-Michel for around 975 francs, meals and admission included. **Cityrama** (⊠ 4 pl. des Pyramides, 75001 Paris, ☎ 01–44–55–61–00). **Paris-Vision** (⊠ 214 rue de Rivoli, 75001 Paris, ☎ 08–00–03–02–14).

Cars Périer (⊠ 130 rue Martainville, 76000 Rouen, ☎ 02–35–98–59–00) arranges personalized driving tours with an English-speaking driver. **Viking Voyages** (⊠ 16 rue du Général-Giraud, 14000 Caen, ☎ 02–31–27–12–34) specializes in two-day packages by car, with overnight stays in private châteaux, as well as bike trips around the region and the Normandy Antiques tour by car. They can also meet travelers at Orly or Roissy airports.

In Caen the **Mémorial** (☎ 02–31–06–06–44 for information) organizes four-hour English-language minibus tours of the D-Day landing beaches, daily from April through September. The cost is 370 francs, including entrance fees. **Bus Fly** (⊠ 25 rue des Cuisiniers, 14400 Bayeux, (☎ 02–31–22–00–08) run trips to the D-Day beaches and Mont-St-Michel.

Outdoor Activities and Sports

To find out about hiking trails in the region, contact the **Comité Départemental de la Randonnée Pédestre de Seine-Maritime** (⊠ 18 rue Henri-Ferric, 76210 Gruchet-le-Valasse, ☎ 02–35–31–05–51). For information about horseback riding, contact **Ligue de Normandie des Sports Équestres** (⊠ 181 rue d'Auge, 14000 Caen, ☎ 02–31–84–61–87).

Travel Agencies

Havas–American Express (⊠ 1 pl. Jacques-Le-Lieur, Rouen, ☎ 02–32–08–19–20; ⊠ 57 quai George-V, Le Havre, ☎ 02–32–74–75–76); ⊠ 25 Grande-Rue, Alençon, ☎ 02–33–82–59–00; ⊠ 80 rue St-Jean, Caen, ☎ 02–31–27–10–50.

Visitor Information

Each of Normandy's five *départements* has its own central tourist office. **Alençon** (⊠ 88 rue St-Blaise, ☎ 02–33–28–88–71) for Orne. **Caen** (⊠ Pl. du Canada, ☎ 02–31–27–90–30) for Calvados. **Évreux**

(✉ Bd. Georges-Chauvin, ☎ 02–32–31–51–51) for Eure. **Rouen** (✉ 6 rue de la Couronne, Bihorel-les-Rouen, ☎ 02–35–12–10–10) for Seine-Maritime. **St-Lô** (✉ Maison du Département, Rte. de Villedieu, ☎ 02–33–05–98–70) for Manche.

Other major Norman towns with tourist offices include the following. **Bayeux** (✉ 3 rue St-Jean, ☎ 02–31–51–28–28). **Cherbourg** (✉ 2 quai Alexandre-III, ☎ 02–33–93–52–02). **Dieppe** (✉ Pont Jehan-An, ☎ 02–35–84–11–77). **Fécamp** (✉ 113 rue Alexandre-le-Grand, ☎ 02–35–28–51–01). **Falaise** (✉ Le Forum, Bd. de la Libération, ☎ 02–31–90–17–26). **Le Havre** (✉ 186 bd. Clemenceau, ☎ 02–32–74–04–04). **Honfleur** (✉ 9 rue de la Ville, ☎ 02–31–89–23–30). **Lisieux** (✉ 11 rue d'Alençon, ☎ 02–31–62–08–41). **Mont-St-Michel** (✉ Corps de Garde, ☎ 02–33–93–52–02).

6 THE NORTH AND CHAMPAGNE

France's northernmost out-thrust shows its Flemish roots in a Brueghelesque landscape, cozy old-master interiors, and a violent history worthy of the images of Hieronymus Bosch, from the battle of Agincourt to the Somme. Add a concentration of six spectacular Gothic cathedrals, fine Flemish art in Lille, broad beaches, the fairytale forests of the Ardennes, and Reims—the capital of bubbly—and you'll find this overlooked region merits discovery.

Revised and
updated by
Simon Hewitt

F LAT AS CREPE AS FAR AS THE EYE CAN SEE and shimmering with
hoarfrost, magpies wheeling over gnarled-fingered trees, and
white-brick cottages punctuating an otherwise uninterrupted
sight line to the horizon: This is the landscape of the north of France,
an evocative canvas that both conjures up the great 16th-century paintings of Pieter Brueghel and reflects, as no history book can, how closely
married this corner of France was—and is—to Flanders. Here, as in
Belgium and the Netherlands, the iron grip of the Spanish Inquisition
sent thinkers and threshers alike scrambling for cover. Here, also, numerous woolen mills spun the stuff of epic tapestries. And here, as well,
the ill humors of the flatland air drove a people and a culture into golden,
firelit Vermeer interiors to seek comfort, as did their brothers to the
east, in a steaming platter of *moules-frîtes* (mussels and french fries),
a mug of amber beer, and a belly-warming swallow of juniper gin.

The landscape recalls images relentlessly epic: In the region's industrial
areas the hollow-eyed miners immortalized in Zola's *Germinal* once descended into hellish black coal portals, while earlier medieval stone workers in fingerless gloves raised radically new Gothic arches to improbable
heights—and ran for cover when the naves collapsed. In Compiène, Joan
of Arc languished, wounded, in a prison after falling in mounted battle
to the English. While at Agincourt, Henry V rallied the British to gory
victory, reversing William the Norseman's four-century conquest. And in
the Somme, wave upon wave of doughboy infantry slogged through the
bomb-torn countryside to gain, lose, and ultimately regain a scrap of land.

Most people give the north of France wide berth, roaring through the
Channel ports at Boulogne and Calais on a beeline for Paris, seeking
the south for a sunshine cure. But this region, with its chiaroscuro of
bleak exteriors and interior glow, conceals treasures of art, architecture, history, and natural beauty that reward slow and pleasurable study.
Just a hour trip from Paris on the TGV, Lille beckons with its Musée
des Beaux Arts, whose collections of old masters are worthy in scale
of the capital's. There are no less than six cathedrals, all still standing
(though you might want to hover near the exits at Beauvais). You may
choose to wander battlefields and ponder World War I cemeteries of
imponderable scale, or relax on the relatively uncrowded beaches that
wrap the coast from Dunkerque to the Bay of Somme.

And then you can celebrate with Champagne. Head southeast toward
Reims, and the sky clears, the landscape loosens and undulates, and
the hills tantalize with the vineyards that produce the world's antidote
to gloom, *à la méthode champagnoise*. Between tasting tours at Reims
and Epernay, you can contemplate Reims Cathedral, where Clovis
was baptized and St. Joan dragged a recalcitrant dauphin to be crowned.
Or lose yourself in the dense forests of the Ardennes—Ozark-like highlands concealing châteaux, fortresses, and succulent game. No wonder more and more British are using the Channel Tunnel to visit
northern France for day and weekend trips.

— Nancy Coons

Pleasures and Pastimes

Beaches

From Dunkerque to the Bay of the Somme is the Côte d'Opale, one
long, sandy beach. It's sometimes short of sun, but not of space or beach
sports, like *char à voile* (sand sailing), involving windsurfing boards
on wheels that race along the sands at up to 110 kph (70 mph). The
climate is bracing, often windy, but there are wonderfully scenic spots

along the cliffs south of Calais: Cap Gris Nez and Cap Blanc Nez. Le Touquet is one of France's fanciest coastal resort towns; Le Crotoy, Wimereux, and Hardelot are more family oriented.

Champagne

The world's most famous sparkling wine comes from France's northernmost vineyards, along the towering Marne Valley between Épernay and Château-Thierry and on the slopes of the Montagne de Reims between Épernay and Reims. Champagne firms, in these two towns and in Ay, welcome you into their chalky, mazelike cellars. You can also visit the tomb of Dom Pérignon, the inventor of champagne, in Hautvillers.

Churches and Cathedrals

Northern France contains many of France's most remarkable Gothic cathedrals: Amiens, the largest; Beauvais, the highest; Noyon, the earliest; Abbeville, the last; Reims, the most regal; and Laon, with the most towers (and the most spectacular hilltop setting). The region's smaller churches are also admirable—the intricate stonework of Rue and L'Épine; the ruined drama of Mont St-Eloi; the modern stained glass of Mézières; and the Baroque brickwork of Asfeld.

Dining

The cuisine of northern France is robust and hearty. In Flanders beer is often used as a base for sauces. French fries and mussels are featured on most menus; vans selling fries and hot dogs are a common sight; and large quantities of mussels and fish, notably herring, are consumed. Smoked ham and, in season, boar and venison are specialties of the Ardennes. In the eastern part of the region, sample creamy cheeses like the soft, square *Maroilles,* with its orange rind, and the spicy, pyramid-shape *boulette d'Avesnes*. To satisfy your sweet tooth, try the macaroons and *bêtises de Cambrai* (minty lollipops) in Flanders. Ham, pigs' feet, gingerbread, and champagne-based mustard are specialties of the Reims area, as is ratafia, a sweet aperitif made from grape juice and brandy. To the north, a glass of *genièvre* (gin flavored with juniper berries, which is sometimes added to black coffee to make a *bistouille*) is the classic way to finish a meal.

CATEGORY	COST*
$$$$	over 500 frs
$$$	250 frs–500 frs
$$	125 frs–250 frs
$	under 125 frs

*per person for a three-course meal, including tax (20.6%) and tip but not wine

✎ *following the text of a review is your signal that the property has a Web site, where you will find details and, usually, images; for a link, visit www.fodors.com/urls.*

Lodging

Northern France is overladen with old, rambling hotels, often simple rather than pretentious; there are also luxurious châteaux with fine restaurants. Top quality is hard to come by, except in major cities such as Lille and Reims, or in Le Touquet, where the Westminster Hotel numbers among the country's best.

CATEGORY	COST*
$$$$	over 800 frs
$$$	600 frs–800 frs
$$	300 frs–600 frs
$	under 300 frs

*All prices are for a standard double room for two, including tax (20.6%) and service charge.

War Memorials

Cemeteries and war memorials may not be the most cheerful items on your itinerary, but they do have a melancholy, thought-provoking beauty. Northern France was in the frontline of battle during World War I and suffered heavily. The city of Reims was shelled incessantly, and such names as the Somme and Vimy Ridge evoke the bloody, dead-locked battles that raged between 1914 and 1918.

Exploring the North and Champagne

The region commonly referred to as northern France stretches from the Somme River up to the Channel Tunnel and includes the vibrant city of Lille, to the northeast. Champagne encompasses Reims and the surrounding vineyards and chalky plains. Picardy, to the south of the region, is traversed by the Aisne and Oise rivers. The hills and forests of the Ardennes lead northeast toward Belgium.

The north of France has a shared history with Flemish-speaking territories. Lille, France's northern metropolis, is the capital of what is known as French Flanders, which stretches northwest from the city to the coastal areas around Dunkerque and Gravelines. West and north of Lille extends the Côte d'Opale, the Channel coastline so named for the color of its sea and sky. To the southeast the grapes of champagne flourish on the steep slopes of the Marne Valley and the Montagne de Reims, really more of a mighty hill than a mountain. Reims is the only city in Champagne—and one of France's richest tourist venues.

Great Itineraries

Count on at least a week to do justice to this vast and varied region, starting at Beauvais, north of Paris, and ending in the Ardennes. Five days will give you time to explore Lille and Arras, before heading south to Reims. If you only have three days, just concentrate on the most scenic attractions of Picardy and Champagne.

IF YOU HAVE 3 DAYS
Numbers in the text correspond to numbers in the margin and on the North; Champagne and the Ardennes; Lille; and Reims maps.

Start in **Compiègne** ㊽ at its elegant palace, and then head to **Pierrefonds** ㊾ to see its storybook castle. By dinnertime be in the hilltop cathedral town of ☷ **Laon** ㊸. After visiting Laon the next morning, drive to ☷ **Reims** ㊽–㊻ for the afternoon, the night, and maybe part of the third morning. Make the champagne vineyards to the south—on the Montagne de Reims, along the Route du Vin, and in the steeply terraced Marne Valley west of **Épernay** ㊶—your final destination.

IF YOU HAVE 5 DAYS
Begin with a day in the vibrant city of ☷ **Lille** ⑮–㉖. The next morning take in stately **Arras** ㉝ and the moving war cemeteries nearby en route to ☷ **Compiègne** ㊽. Devote day three to **Pierrefonds** ㊾ and ☷ **Laon** ㊸ and day four to ☷ **Reims** ㊽–㊻. Spend your last day touring the Montagne de Reims and the Route du Vin, and then head east from **Épernay** ㊶ to the historic town of **Châlons-en-Champagne** ㊷.

IF YOU HAVE 8 DAYS
Venture along the cliffs from the Channel Tunnel to **Boulogne-sur-Mer** ⑩. If want to go to the beach, head down the coast to **Le Touquet** ⑨ and rejoin the itinerary at Amiens. If you prefer history and culture, head inland from Boulogne to ☷ **Lille** ⑮–㉖ for the night and following morning. That afternoon go south to ☷ **Arras** ㉝. On day four cross the **Somme battlefields** via **Albert** ㊳, ending the day in the cathedral city of ☷ **Amiens** ②. The next day visit **Beauvais** ①, home to another

cathedral as well as a fine tapestry museum; then go east to 🏛 **Compiègne** ㊽. Spend day six in **Pierrefonds** ㊾ and 🏛 **Laon** ㊸. On day seven head northeast into the Ardennes to explore historic 🏛 **Reims** ㊄–㉒, which has one of the most magnificent cathedrals in France. On day eight head to the champagne vineyards south of Reims en route to **Châlons-en-Champagne** ㊲ and the fine hotel-restaurant by the basilica in nearby 🏛 **L'Épine** ㊳.

When to Tour the North and Champagne

Compared to many other regions of France, the north remains relatively uncrowded in July and August, and the huge Channel beaches have room for everyone. The liveliest time in Lille is the first weekend in September during its three-day street fair, La Grande Braderie. Other local fairs include the Dunkerque Carnival, in February, and the Giants' Carnival, in Douai in July. Make sure to plan a visit to Reims and Champagne between May and October; the region's ubiquitous vineyards are a dismal, leafless sight the rest of the year. The wooded Ardennes are attractive in fall, when local game highlights menus.

THE NORTH

Starting in Beauvais and Amiens—easily accessible by expressway from Paris—follow the Somme Valley to the Channel. Unfortunately the ports of Calais and Dunkerque are among France's uglier towns, but the old sections of Boulogne-sur-Mer have scenic appeal, as do the narrow streets of ancient Montreuil and the posh avenues of fashionable Le Touquet. After wheeling inland to Lille, head south to the World War I battlefields between Arras and Albert, continuing southeast into Picardy and its hilltop castles and cathedrals.

Beauvais

❶ *80 km (50 mi north of Paris.*

Beauvais and its neighbor Amiens have been rivals since the 13th century, when they locked horns over who could build the bigger cathedral. Beauvais lost—gloriously.

A work-in-progress preserved for all time, soaring above the characterless modern blocks of the town center, is the tallest cathedral in France: ★ the **Cathédrale St-Pierre.** You may have an attack of vertigo just gazing up at its vaults, 153 ft off the ground. It may be the tallest, but it's not the biggest. Paid for by the riches of Beauvais's wool industry, the choir collapsed in 1284, shortly after completion, and was only rebuilt with the addition of extra pillars. This engineering fiasco proved so costly that the transept was not attempted until the 16th century. It was obviously worth the wait: The transept is an outstanding example of Flamboyant Gothic, with ornate rose windows flanked by pinnacles and turrets. It is also still standing—which is more than can be said for the megalomaniac 450-ft spire erected at the same time. This lasted precisely four years; when it came crashing down, the transept was damaged, all remaining funds were hurled at an emergency consolidation program, and Beauvais's dream of having the largest church in Christendom vanished forever. Now the cathedral is starting to lean, and cracks have appeared in the choir vaults because of shifting water levels in the soil. No such problems bedevil the **Basse Oeuvre** (Lower Edifice; closed to the public), which juts out impertinently where the nave should have been. It has been there for 1,000 years. Fittingly donated to the cathedral by the canon Étienne Musique, the oldest surviving **chiming clock** in the world, a 1302 model with a 15th-century painted wooden face and most of its original clockwork,

The North and Champagne

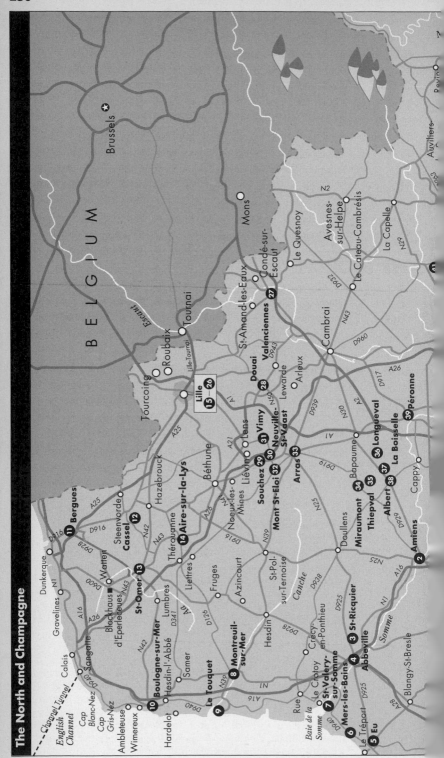

English Channel
Channel Tunnel
Calais
Cap Blanc-Nez
Cap Gris-Nez
Sangatte
Gravelines
Dunkerque
N1
A16
Ambleteuse
Wimereux
Hardelot
Boulogne-sur-Mer **10**
Hesdin-l'Abbé
Samer
Le Touquet
9
Rue
Baie de la Somme
Le Tréport
5 Eu
6 Mers-les-Bains
7 St-Valery-sur-Somme
Le Crotoy
Blangy-St-Bresle
4 Abbeville
3 St-Ricquier
Crécy-en-Ponthieu
Hesdin
Montreuil-sur-Mer **8**
Fruges
Azincourt
St-Pol-sur-Ternoise
Lumbres
Blockhaus d'Éperlecques
St-Omer **13**
Lieftres
Thérouanne
Wotten
Steenvoorde
Cassel **12**
Bergues **11**
A25
Hazebrouck
Aire-sur-la-Lys **14**
Béthune
Noeux-les-Mines
Lens
Liévin **29** Souchez
30 Neuville-St-Vaast
32 Mont St-Éloi
31 Vimy
Arras **33**
Bapaume
Doullens
Miraumont **34** **35**
Thiepval **37** Albert
38
Cappy
La Boisselle **36**
Longueval **39** Péronne
Cambrai
Amiens **2**
Doué
28 Lille **15—26**
Lille-Tournai
Roubaix
Tourcoing
Lys
Tournai
Escaut
B E L G I U M
Brussels
Mons
Le Quesnoy
Condé-sur-Escaut
St-Amand-les-Eaux
Valenciennes **27**
Arleux
Lewarde
Avesnes-sur-Helpe
Le Cateau-Cambrésis
La Capelle

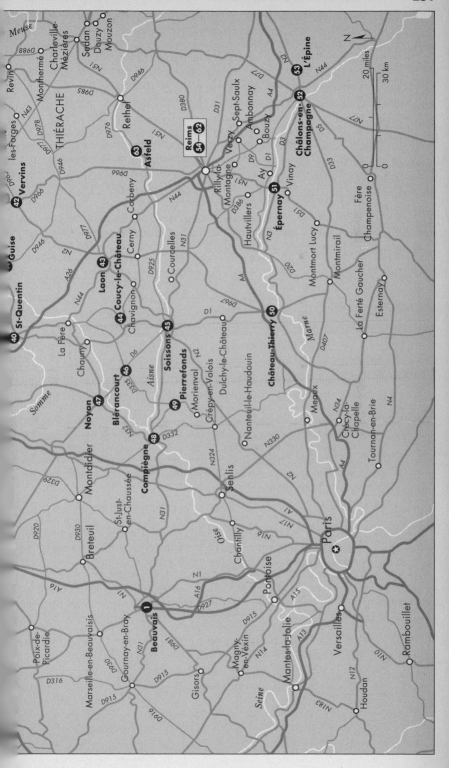

is built into the wall of the cathedral. Perhaps Auguste Verité drew his inspiration from this humbler timepiece when, in 1868, he made a gift to his hometown of the gilded, templelike **astrological clock.** Animated religious figurines surrounded by all sorts of gears and dials emerge for their short program at erratic times, although there is a schedule for commentated visits. ⊠ *Rue St-Pierre.* ⊙ *May–Oct., daily 9–12:15 and 2–6:15; Nov.–Apr., daily 9–12:15 and 2–5:30.*

From 1664 to 1939 Beauvais was one of France's leading tapestry centers; it reached its zenith in the mid-18th century under the gifted artist Jean-Baptiste Oudry, known for his hunting scenes. Examples from all periods are in the modern **Galerie Nationale de la Tapisserie** (National Museum of Tapestry). ⊠ *1 rue St-Pierre,* ☎ *03–44–05–14–28.* ▧ *25 frs.* ⊙ *Apr.–Sept., Tues.–Sun. 9:30–11:30 and 2–6; Oct.–Mar., Tues.–Sun. 10–11:30 and 2:30–4:30.*

One of the few remaining testaments to Beauvais's glorious past, the old Bishop's Palace is now the **Musée Départemental de l'Oise** (Oise Museum). Don't miss the beautifully proportioned top floor; Thomas Couture's epic canvas of the French Revolution; the 14th-century frescoes of instrument-playing sirens on a section of the palace's vaults; or the 1st-century brass *Guerrier Gaulois* (Gallic Warrior). ⊠ *1 rue du Musée,* ☎ *03–44–11–43–83.* ▧ *10 frs, free Wed.* ⊙ *Wed.–Mon. 10–noon and 2–6.*

Amiens

❷ *58 km (36 mi) north of Beauvais via N1 or A16.*

Although Amiens showcases some pretty brazen postwar reconstruction, epitomized by Auguste Perret's 340-ft Tour Perret, a soaring concrete stump by the train station, the city is still worth exploring. It has lovely Art Deco buildings in its traffic-free city center, as well as elegant, older stone buildings like the 18th-century Beffroi (belfry) and Neoclassical prefecture. The great Gothic cathedral has survived the ages intact, and the nearby waterfront quarter of St-Leu, with its small, colorful houses, rivals the old city center in Lille as the cutest city district north of Paris.

★ By far the largest church in France, the **Cathédrale Notre-Dame** could fit Paris's Notre-Dame inside twice. It may lack the stained glass of Chartres or the sculpture of Reims, but for architectural harmony, engineering proficiency, and sheer size, it has no peer. The soaring, asymmetrical facade of the cathedral has a notable Flamboyant Gothic rose window. Inside, the overwhelming sensation is one of space; there is no stylistic disunity to mar the perspective. Construction took place between 1220 and 1264, a remarkably short period in cathedral-building terms. One of the highlights of a visit here is hidden from the eye, at least until you lift up some of the 110 choir stall seats and admire the humorous, skillful misericord (seat) carvings executed between 1508 and 1518. ⊠ *Pl. Notre-Dame,* ☎ *03–22–92–77–29; 03–22–91–83–83 for son-et-lumière information.* ▧ *60 frs.*

The **Hôtel de Berny,** near the cathedral, is a steep-roof stone-and-brick mansion built in 1633. It's filled with 18th-century furniture, tapestries, and objets d'art. ⊠ *34 rue Victor-Hugo,* ☎ *03–22–91–81–12.* ▧ *20 frs.* ⊙ *Oct.–mid-Apr., Sun. 10–12:30 and 2–6; mid-Apr.–Sept., Thurs.–Sun. 1–6.*

★ Behind an opulent columned facade, the **Musée de Picardie,** built 1855–67, looks like just another pompous offering from the Second Empire. Initial impressions are hardly challenged by its grand staircase lined with monumental frescoes by local-born Puvis de Chavannes, or its central hall with huge canvases, like Gérôme's 1855 *Siècle d'Auguste* and Maignon's 1892 *Mort de Carpeaux,* with flying muses wresting the dying sculptor from his earthly clay. One step beyond, though, and you're in a rotunda painted top to bottom in modern minimalist fashion by Sol LeWitt in 1992. The basement is filled with subtly lighted archaeological findings and Egyptian artifacts beneath masterly brick vaulting. On the top floor, El Greco leads the old masters, along with a humorous set of hunting scenes like Boucher's Rococo-framed *Crocodile Hunt,* from 1736. ✉ *48 rue de la République,* ☎ *03–22–97–14–00.* ✆ *20 frs.* ☉ *Tues.–Sun. 10–12:30 and 2–6.*

Jules Verne (1828–1905) lived in Amiens for some 35 years, and his former home has become the **Centre de Documentation Jules Verne** (✉ 2 rue Charles-Dubois, ☎ 03–22–45–37–84). It contains some 15,000 documents about Verne's life as well as original furniture and a reconstruction of the writing studio where he created his science fiction classics. If you're a true Verne fan, you might want to visit his last resting place, in the **Cimetière de la Madeleine** (✉ 2 rue de la Poudrière), where he is melodramatically portrayed pushing up his tombstone as if enacting his own sci-fi resurrection.

The **Hortillonnages,** on the east side of town, are commercial water gardens—more than 700 acres—where vegetables have been grown since Roman times. They're best visited by boat. ✉ *Boats leave from 54 bd. Beauvillé,* ☎ *03–22–92–12–18.* ✆ *28 frs.* ☉ *Apr.–Oct., daily 2–6.*

Dining and Lodging

$$ ✕ **Joséphine.** Despite its unprepossessing facade and drab front room, this good-value restaurant in central Amiens is a reliable choice. It serves solid fare and has decent wines and a back room overlooking a garden courtyard. ✉ *20 rue Sire-Firmin-Leroux,* ☎ *03–22–91–47–38. AE, MC, V. Closed Mon. and 3rd wk in Aug. No dinner Sun.*

$$ ✕ **Les Marissons.** In the scenic St-Leu section of Amiens, beneath the
★ cathedral, this picturesque waterside restaurant serves creative takes on regional ingredients: burbot with apricots, rabbit with mint and goat cheese, and pigeon with black currants. To avoid pricey dining à la carte, order from the prix-fixe menus. ✉ *68 rue des Marissons,* ☎ *03–22–92–96–66. Jacket and tie. AE, DC, MC, V. Closed Sun. No lunch Sat.*

$$ 🏨 **Carlton.** This hotel near the train station has a stylish Belle Epoque facade. In contrast, rooms are sober and functional, though light and airy, with spacious bathrooms. Foreign guests are common, and English is spoken. The brasserie-style restaurant, Le Baron, doesn't serve dinner Sunday. ✉ *42 rue de Noyon, 80000,* ☎ *03–22–97–72–22,* FAX *03–22–97–72–00. 24 rooms. Restaurant. AE, MC, V.*

Nightlife and the Arts

The **Théâtre de Marionnettes** (✉ 31 rue Edouard-David, ☎ 03–22–22–30–90) presents a rare glimpse of the traditional Picardy marionettes, known locally as *Chès Cabotans d'Amiens*. Shows are performed (in French), usually on Friday evening and Sunday afternoon (daily in August), with plot synopses in English.

St-Riquier

➌ *37 (23 mi) northwest of Amiens via N1 and D32.*

The tumbling village of St-Riquier is dominated by its imposing abbey
★ church. Magnificent **St-Riquier** has a majestic Flamboyant Gothic facade with a superbly sculpted 160-ft tower (illuminated on Friday and Saturday evenings), a 100-yard-long nave, and handsome 17th-century wrought-iron gates at the front of the choir.

Lodging

$$$ 🏠 **Jean de Bruges.** The 1473 abbot's house next to the church has been transformed into a small, stylish hotel owned by the Stubbe-Martens. Decor is refined: gleaming marble floors, white stonework, cream-color curtains, designer lighting, old carved furniture, and impressive modern art throughout. Ask for airy Room 2, or Room 8, with a small terrace; all are named for former abbots. The glass-roof breakfast room leads to a patio used for afternoon tea. Unfortunately there's no restaurant—either here or in the village. ⊠ *18 pl. de l'Église, 80135,* ☎ *03–22–28–30–30,* 🖷 *03–22–28–00–69. 8 rooms. Breakfast room, parking. AE, MC, V. Closed Jan.*

Abbeville

➍ *9 km (6 mi) southwest of St-Riquier via D925, 43 km (27 mi) northwest of Amiens.*

The historic town of Abbeville was heavily reconstructed after being reduced to rubble in 1940. Its most admirable building is its Gothic church. Begun in 1488, **St-Vulfran** (⊠ Rue St-Vulfran) was the last cathedral-size church to be constructed in the Gothic style. According to 19th-century art historian John Ruskin, it was here that Gothic "lay down and died." After decades of restoration, the riotous tracery and ornament of its much-mauled facade have been revived. The tall, elegant nave retains fine medieval stained glass. Work is still in progress on the 17th-century choir.

With typical Gallic flair, the derelict, war-ravaged Gothic church of **St-Sépulcre** was given a new lease on life in 1993, when local artist Alfred Manessier was commissioned to fit it out with 20 windows of psychedelic stained glass. The effect is glorious. ⊠ *Pl. St-Sépulcre.* 🖾 *Free.* ☉ *June–Sept., daily 2–6.*

The **Musée Boucher de Perthes,** housed in a beefy medieval belfry, contains an eclectic array of Gallo-Roman items, Vron earthenware, Camille Claudel bronzes, ornithological displays, and old-master altarpieces. ⊠ *24 rue Gonthier-Patin,* ☎ *03–22–24–08–49.* 🖾 *Free.* ☉ *Wed.–Mon. 2–6.*

Dining

$ ✗ **Étoile du Jour.** Abbeville is no great gastronomic shakes, so you might as well check out the town's prettiest restaurant, with its open beams and split-level floors. A hearty steak is your best bet, with the local delicacy, a béchamel-smothered pancake, called *ficelle picarde,* served piping hot as an appetizer. ⊠ *2 chaussée Marcadé,* ☎ *03–22–24–06–90. MC, V. Closed Mon.*

Eu

➎ *28 km (18 mi) southwest of Abbeville via D925.*

Slightly inland from the English Channel, hilltop Eu is home to France's last royal residence: The stone-and-brick Renaissance **Château d'Eu,** built between 1578 and 1665, was used as a summer palace by France's last king, Louis-Philippe of Orléans, who ruled from 1830 to 1848. In the château, along with the town hall, is the **Musée Louis-Philippe.** It evokes Eu's regal heyday—including two visits by Queen Victoria—amid a welter of souvenirs, furniture, pictures, porcelain, and local glasswork. ☎ *02–35–86–44–00.* 🖾 *20 frs.* ☉ *Mid-Mar.–Oct., Wed.–Mon. 10–noon and 2–6.*

On the old streets of town, clustered around the stately Gothic **Collégiale** (Collegiate Church), are two outstanding 17th-century buildings, the **Chapelle des Jésuites** (Jesuit Chapel) and the **Hôtel-Dieu** (hospital)

Mers-les-Bains

❻ *4 km (3 mi) northwest of Eu via D1015.*

Like Cabourg or Le Touquet farther up the coast, Mers (pronounced *mairce*) sprang to prominence in the late 19th century, when the railroad brought the seaside within reach of weekending Parisians. Those fashionable days are long gone, but Mers still deserves a visit for its magnificent sandy beach and lengthy *front de mer* (seafront) with gaily painted villas decorated with Belle Epoque enameled tiles.

Stairs behind the town church lead up to the cliff-top statue of **Notre-Dame de la Falaise,** with its bas-reliefs devoted to the three *villes soeurs* (sister towns) of Mers, Eu, and Le Tréport, the latter a gritty fishing port and boat-trip center just down the coast.

Dining and Lodging

$ ✗🖬 **Bellevue.** This pink-front hotel, in business since 1920, is the only hotel on the historic Mers beachside promenade. The staircase creaks a bit, and some of the rooms are on the small side, but others have been modernized in pastel colors; ask for one facing the sea. The restaurant, decked out in nautical white and blue, with nets and knots on the walls, duly focuses on fish. ✉ *24 esplanade du Général-Leclerc, 80350,* ☎ *02–35–86–12–89,* ℻ *02–35–50–88–62. 25 rooms. Restaurant, bar. MC, V.*

St-Valery-sur-Somme

❼ *27 km (17 mi) north of Mers-les-Bains via D940.*

St-Valery-sur-Somme is a pretty fishing harbor (squid and shellfish are specialties) on the Baie de la Somme, with a shady seaside promenade, medieval fortifications, and the remains of St-Valery. The flint-and-sandstone-checkerboard 18th-century **Chapelle des Marins** (Mariners' Chapel), at the far end of the town's bay-side promenade (where there are views of the Somme Estuary), houses the tomb of St-Valery.

The wide sand flats of the **Baie de Somme** (Bay of the Somme) are a haven for wildlife—especially birds and sheep, which graze peacefully on the salt marshes.

☕ A good overview of the Baie de Somme is provided by the **Chemin de Fer de la Baie de Somme** (steam railway). It chugs around the bay between St-Valery and Le Crotoy on an hour-long trip driven by a 130T locomotive that was used during construction of the Panama Canal. ✉ *Departs from St-Valery-sur-Somme and Le Crotoy train stations,* ☎ *03–22–26–96–96.* 🎫 *60 frs.* ☉ *Apr.–June and Sept., departure 3:30 and return 5:30 Wed. and weekends; July–Aug., departure 3:30 and return 5:30 Tues.–Sun.; early Oct.– late Oct., departure 3:30 and return 5:30 Sun.*

☕ The **Maison de l'Oiseau** (Bird Sanctuary), just west of St-Valery on D204 (in the direction of Cayeux-sur-Mer), has a collection of 400 stuffed birds, a video presentation about their local habitats, and occasional special appearances by live and happily obedient birds of prey. ✉ *Carrefour du Hourdel,* ☎ *03–22–26–93–93.* 🎫 *59 frs.* ☉ *Mid-Feb.–June and Sept.–mid-Nov., daily 10–6; July–Aug., daily 10–7.*

Dining

$–$$ ✗ **Parc aux Huîtres.** This large-windowed restaurant in Le Hourdel, on the south side of the bay, is an honest, unpretentious place to have a lunch of fresh seafood, starring oysters, scallops, turbot, and lobster. Service is brisk and matter of fact: you're treated like a local, and that's a compliment. ✉ *Le Hourdel (8 km [5 mi] from St-Valery),* ☎ *03–22–26–61–20. MC, V. Closed Wed. No dinner Tues.*

En Route   The small town of **Rue,** 7 km (4 mi) north of St-Valery, is famed for its extravagantly sculpted **Chapelle du St-Esprit,** with lacelike stonework and star-patterned vaulting.

Montreuil-sur-Mer

8   *38 km (24 mi) northeast of Le Crotoy via D940 and D917, 45 km (28 mi) northeast of St-Valery.*

Despite its seaside-sounding name, Montreuil-sur-Mer is 18 km (11 mi) inland. It was once a port, but the Canche River silted up and left it high and dry. The ancient town has majestic walls and ramparts, as well as a faded charm to which various authors, notably Victor Hugo, have succumbed; an episode of *Les Misérables* is set here.

Wherever citadels and city walls loom in France, it's a fair bet that Vauban had a hand in their construction. Montreuil is no exception. First Errard de Bar-le-Duc and then Vauban supplemented the existing 16th-century towers of the **Citadelle.** ⊠ *Rue Carnot,* ☎ *03–21–06–10–83.* ▣ *10 frs.* ☉ *Nov.–Sept., Wed.–Mon. 9–11:30 and 2–5:30.*

OFF THE   **AZINCOURT –** The Battle of Agincourt (Azincourt in French) took place
BEATEN PATH   30 km (19 mi) east of Montreuil in October 1415 when Henry V's long-bowmen defeated Charles VI's more numerous and heavily armored French troops. There are a museum, an orientation map, and a clearly marked 3-km (2-mi) trail.

Dining and Lodging

$$$$ ✕▣ **Château de Montreuil.** At this manor house facing the citadel, rooms
★   are furnished with 18th- and 19th-century antiques. No. 208 has a large sitting area and a view of the garden. The less expensive rooms, in the converted stables, are also pleasantly furnished but smaller. Owner Lindsay Germain is English. Her husband, Christian, is an excellent chef: His forte is bringing out the natural flavor in such dishes as lightly sautéed scallops served with *pompadour* (a variety of potato) and lamb chops with a wine-sauce glaze. (The restaurant is closed Monday, September–June; there's no lunch on Thursday.) ⊠ *Chaussée des Capucins, 62170,* ☎ *03–21–81–53–04,* FAX *03–21–81–36–43. 13 rooms. Restaurant. MC, V. Closed mid-Dec.– early Feb.*

Le Touquet

9   *15 km (9 mi) northwest of Montreuil via N39.*

At the mouth of the Canche Estuary, Le Touquet is an elegant Victorian seaside resort town. First transformed into a sandy pine forest by Alphonse Daloz in the mid-19th century, the town was developed by Yorkshire businessman John White to attract English vacationers. On the Paris end, the newspaper *Le Figaro* baptized it "Paris-Plage" (Paris-Beach) and launched a huge advertising campaign to lure well-to-do Parisians. A cosmopolitan atmosphere remains, and many French people, attracted by the airy, elegant avenues and invigorating climate, have moved here for good (many are retirees). On one side is a fine sandy beach; on the other, the flourishing pine forest. There are also a casino, golf courses, and a racetrack.

Dining and Lodging

$$$ ✕ **Flavio.** Fish is the star at this elegant spot near the casino. Chef Guy Delmotte specializes in lobster (for which he charges whale-size prices). The other two prix-fixe menus are more reasonable (wine is included in the 250-franc weekday menu). Cut glass and Oriental carpets add a note of dated glamour. ⊠ *1 av. du Verger,* ☎ *03–21–05–10–22. Reser*

vations essential. Jacket and tie. AE, DC, MC, V. Closed Jan.–Feb., 2nd ½ Nov., and Mon. Sept.–June.

$$$ ✕⊞ **Westminster.** The Westminster's mammoth redbrick facade looks
★ as if it were built just a few years ago; in fact, it dates from the 1930s and, like the rest of the hotel, has been extensively restored. The enormous double rooms are a good value, and the bridal suite is the last word in thick-carpeted extravagance. The hotel's brasserie, Le Coffee-Shop, is modestly priced (lunch and dinner); the Pavillon restaurant serves inventive French cuisine (it's closed Tuesday and in February). ⊠ *Av. du Verger, 62520,* ☎ *03–21–05–48–48,* FAX *03–21–05–45–45. 115 rooms. Restaurant, bar, brasserie, indoor pool, hot tub, sauna, squash. AE, DC, MC, V. Closed Jan.*

Outdoor Activities and Sports

Aqualud, a water park on the beachfront, has numerous water-sports facilities, half outdoors, half in, including a giant pool with wave machine. ⊠ *Bd. Thierry-Sabine,* ☎ *03–21–05–90–96.* 🎫 *65 frs for 3 hrs, 82 frs all day.* 🕑 *Apr.–June and Sept., Wed.–Sun. 10–6; July–Aug., daily 10–7.*

The **Enduro** in February sees thousands of motorbikes converge on Le Touquet for an epic race through the dunes.

Boulogne-sur-Mer

➓ *24 km (15 mi) north of Le Touquet via D940.*

Boulogne-sur-Mer, famous for its smoked herring, is France's largest fishing port. The rebuilt concrete streets around the port are ugly and unpleasant, but the old town on the hill is a different world—pretty, well kept, and full of character. Perhaps this is why Napoléon chose Boulogne as his base in 1803 while making his fruitless plans to cross the Channel with 2,000 boats and 180,000 men.

The four main streets of the **Ville Haute** (Upper Town) intersect at place Godefroy-de-Bouillon. The square is flanked by the 18th-century rosebrick **Hôtel de Ville,** the 12th- to 13th-century **belfry;** the cloistered **Annonciades** (a former convent, now a library); and the **Hôtel Desandrouins,** Napoléon's imperial palace. Dominating them all is the formidable **Basilique Notre-Dame,** its distinctive elongated dome visible from far out at sea.

Inside the 13th-century ramparts, studded with four gateways and 17 watch towers, is the polygonal castle, today known as the **Château-Musée.** Built for the counts of Boulogne, the castle dates in part from the 13th-century and houses a fine collection of Egyptian artifacts donated by the celebrated Louvre Egyptologist Auguste Mariette, who was born in Boulogne in 1821. The museum's collection of Greek vases is considered second only to that in the Louvre. ⊠ *Rue de Bernet,* ☎ *03–21–10–02–20.* 🎫 *20 frs.* 🕑 *Wed.–Mon. 10–12:30 and 2–5, Sun. 10–12:30 and 2:30–5:30.*

★ ♻ **Nausicaä,** the Centre National de la Mer (National Marine Center), has a battery of aquariums containing more than 4,000 fish. Highlights include sharks, sea lions, a Plexiglas column of shimmering jellyfish, and playful rays. It also has a coral reef, 3-D films, swimming pool, weather center, library, large bookstore, and classy restaurant. ⊠ *Bd. Ste-Beuve,* ☎ *03–21–30–99–99.* 🎫 *65 frs.* 🕑 *Sept.–June, daily 9:30–6:30, July–Aug., daily 9:30–8.*

The **Colonne de la Grande Armée,** a 160-ft marble column begun in 1804 to commemorate Napoléon's invasion of England, is north of the town just off the road to Calais. The idea was shelved in 1805, and the column (closed for restoration at press time, spring 2000) was only finished 30 years later under Louis-Philippe. The 263 steps take you to the top and a wide-reaching panoramic view; if the weather is clear, you may be able to make out the distant cliffs of Dover. ⊠ *Off A6, the road to Calais,* ☎ *03–21–80–43–69.* 🎫 *20 frs.* ☉ *Apr.–Sept., Thurs.–Mon. 9–noon and 2–6; Oct.–Mar., Thurs.–Mon. 9–noon and 2–5.*

Dining and Lodging

$$ ✕ **Matelote.** The name of this restaurant, across the way from Nausicaä, means "the Sailor's Wife." Here in the bright yellow interior, you can enjoy seafood specialties such as roast fillet of turbot with thyme. ⊠ *80 bd. Ste-Beuve,* ☎ *03–21–30–17–97. AE, DC, V. No dinner Sun., Sept.–June.*

$$ ✕ **Epicure.** This intimate, 20-seat restaurant in neighboring Wimereux
★ serves an outstanding three-course, 125-franc menu that might include duck terrine, salmon with parsley and horseradish butter, and hot pear and chocolate cake. There's a monumental cheese board and an imaginative wine list. Chef Philippe Carrée works alone in the kitchen and is entitled to foibles like refusing diners who turn up "too late"—after 9 PM. Claudette Carrée anxiously surveys the dining room. ⊠ *1 rue de la Gare Wimereux (6 km [4 mi] north of Boulogne),* ☎ *03–21–83–21–83. AE, DC, V. Closed Wed. and late Dec.–mid-Jan. No dinner Sun.*

$$ ✕🏠 **Cléry.** It was at this 18th-century château that Napoléon decided to abandon his plans to invade England. As you bask in the peace and quiet of the beautiful grounds, you'll understand why. Extensive lawns and an avenue of trees lead to this stylish hotel set in the tiny village of Hesdin-l'Abbé. Rooms vary in price and decor; those in the former stables have been converted into light, spacious, and modern spaces. No luncheon is offered in the restaurant, which is closed weekends. ⊠ *Rue du Château, 62360 Hesdin-l'Abbé (8 km [5 mi] inland from Boulogne via N1),* ☎ *03–21–83–19–83,* FAX *03–21–87–52–59. 22 rooms. Restaurant, tennis court. AE, DC, MC, V. Closed Dec.–Jan.*

$$ 🏠 **Métropole.** This small hotel is handy for hovercraft passengers but, like most of the Ville Basse (Lower Town), no great architectural shakes (it's a rather faceless '50s building). The small garden is pleasant for breakfast in summer, however, and rooms are adequately furnished. ⊠ *51 rue Adolphe-Thiers, 62200,* ☎ *03–21–31–54–30,* FAX *03–21–30–45–72. 25 rooms. AE, DC, MC, V. Closed late Dec.–early Jan.*

Outdoor Activities and Sports

The coast is a popular spot for speed sailing and sand sailing. For details contact the **Drakkars** club (⊠ Base Nautique Sud, 62152 Hardelot-Plage, ☎ 03–21–83–27–93), 14 km (9 mi) south of Boulogne.

En Route   Just north of Boulogne is **Wimereux,** a cheerful Belle Epoque resort town, and **Ambleteuse,** with its small seashore fort built by Vauban in the 1680s. Mighty cliffs survey the Channel as D940 continues toward Calais: **Cap Gris-Nez,** home to a lighthouse and a World War II concrete bunker; and **Cap Blanc-Nez,** with its obelisk war memorial. There's little to warrant a stop at either the entrance to the **Channel Tunnel,** near Coquelles, or in **Calais,** which was flattened in World War II—although its reconstructed 240-ft belfry is visible from far inland. **Gravelines,** at the mouth of the Aa River, warrants a brief stop for Vauban's moated ramparts. **Dunkerque** doesn't: Like Calais, it's a working port of little scenic appeal, although it spurts into life with a rambunctious three-day carnival at the beginning of Lent.

Bergues

★ ⓫   *9 km (6 mi) south of Dunkerque via D916.*

One of France's most scenic walled towns, Bergues was first fortified back in the 7th century. Between the 9th and 13th centuries it was sacked seven times, prompting Philip the Bold to rebuild the **ramparts**—over 5 km (3 mi) of them—in the distinctive shape of an eight. In the 1690s Vauban erected the Baroque **Porte de Cassel** (Cassel Gateway) and perfected the system of moats and canals around the walls, including the triple-ditched, crown-shape **Couronne d'Hondschoote.** Inside the walls, the 160-ft medieval belfry disputes skyline supremacy with the square and pointed towers of the ruined **Abbaye de St-Winoc.**

Nightlife and the Arts

The end of May is the time for Bergues's **beer festival.** The first Sunday of December brings the **Fête St-Nicolas,** a Christmas celebration.

Cassel

⑫ *18 km (11 mi) south of Bergues via D916.*

In Cassel the north's ubiquitous image as Le Plat Pays (the Flat Land) is given a nasty jolt by a 580-ft mound, the **Mont-Cassel,** towering over the plain like a land-bound Mont-St-Michel. Sailors use it as a landmark from the Channel—27 km (17 mi) away. It's the highest of a series of outcrops known as the Monts de Flandre, although the 520-ft Mont des Récollets (to the east) runs a close second. At its top is a wooden windmill. The views from the surrounding gardens extend over roofs to a patchwork quilt of wheat fields. Nearby, the sloping town square, more than 200 yards long, hosts a lively carnival on Easter Monday, when giants Reuze-Papa and Reuze-Maman lead the parade.

Dining

$ ✕ **T'Kasteelhof.** An outdoor staircase opposite Cassel's hilltop windmill leads up to this traditional *estaminet*—a cozy, old-fashioned pub-style café-restaurant, where beer (50 kinds) and platters of cheese and meats are served. T'Kasteelhof claims to be the highest eatery in Flanders, so grab a table by the window to admire the view. ⊠ *8 rue St-Nicolas,* ☎ *03–28–40–59–29. MC, V. Closed Mon.–Tues.*

St-Omer

⑬ *23 km (14 mi) southwest of Cassel via D933, 64 km (40 mi) northwest of Lille.*

Hilly St-Omer is not your archetypal northern industrial town. With its yellow-brick buildings it looks different from its neighbors. Its Belle Epoque train station is modeled on a Loire château, and the romantic ruins of the Abbaye de St-Bertin recall the town's medieval preeminence as a religious center.

★ The **Basilique Notre-Dame** (⊠ Rue Henri-Dupuis), surrounded by narrow streets at the top of the town, is a homely cathedral-size church. Its lowish vaults and broad windows with geometric tracery bear testimony to the local influence of the English Perpendicular style during the 15th century. Look for the early 18th-century organ case, with its carved angel musicians; the astronomical clock in the north transept; and the majestic **Grand Dieu de Thérouanne,** a 13th-century sculpture of *Christ in Judgment,* gleefully transported here when Charles V razed the rival cathedral of Thérouanne (14 km [9 mi] south of St-Omer) in 1553.

The **Hôtel Sandelin,** a 1776 mansion, houses the town museum. Here you'll find period furnishings and paintings and an exceptional collection of porcelain and faience, with more than 700 pieces of delftware. At press time the museum was undergoing restoration, with a view to reopening during the second half of 2001. ⊠ *14 rue Carnot,* ☎ *03–21–38–00–94.* ▨ *20 frs.* ☉ *Wed. and weekends 10–noon and 2–6, Thurs.–Fri. 10–noon and 2–5.*

Vestiges of World War I pepper the north of France, but few are as grisly as the Nazi specter in the forest near Watten, 13 km (8 mi) north of St-Omer. The **Blockhaus d'Eperlecques** is a bunker of monstrous size and intent, 80 ft high with concrete walls 20 ft thick. It was erected in 1943 by 35,000 slave laborers as the secret base for the assembly and launch of the V2 rocket bomb, whose destination would have been London. The structure is so secret, in fact, that you can't even see it from the entrance 100 yards away. Yet it was not secret enough to escape Allied reconnaissance: RAF bombers destroyed the bunker and saved London from being blown to smithereens. Strategic loudspeakers fire out French commentary as you walk around—but the site's message is essentially unspeakable. ⊠ *Off D205 west of Watten,* ☎ *03–21–88–44–22.* 💷 *35 frs.* ☉ *Mar. and Oct., Sun. 2:15–6; Apr.–June and Sept., daily 2:15–6; July–Aug., daily 10–7.*

★ Another chilling episode of World War II lurks beneath the moss-covered 55,000-ton concrete dome of **La Coupole,** 5 km (3 mi) south of St-Omer. Hitler earmarked this former quarry as a more secure launch site than Eperlecques for his V2 rockets, which were meant to flatten London, 200 km (125 mi)—and only a couple of minutes—away. The rockets were built in central Germany and would have been railroaded to St-Omer had the Nazis not started to lose the war. The cupola, built in 1943 by Russian and Polish prisoners to protect the missile chamber, is 75 yards in diameter and 16 ft thick; after the war Allied forces reckoned the amount of dynamite needed to destroy it would have blown up most of St-Omer as well, so they didn't bother. The site lay neglected for more than 50 years until tourist authorities restored it; in fact, they did far more, equipping the huge space beneath the dome with a 45-ft V2 and a battery of movie and TV screens outlining the history of the rocket. Infrared headsets guide you through dank galleries and up to the dome; you end your two-hour visit in the unfinished missile chamber. ⊠ *5 mi (3 mi) south of St-Omer between Helfaut and Wizernes,* ☎ *03–21–93–07–07.* 💷 *55 frs.* ☉ *Apr.–Oct., daily 9–7; Nov.–Mar., daily 10–6.*

Dining and Lodging

$$$ ✕🏨 **Moulin de Mombreux.** Huge cogs and waterwheels reflect the 18th-century water-mill origins of the Moulin, west of St-Omer in Lumbres. Silver candlesticks and original wood beams lend atmosphere to the dining room, with poached oysters in fennel, lamb in foie gras sauce, and raspberry soufflé often among the chef's selections. The discreet if unoriginal charm of pastel-painted guest rooms is augmented by a spacious breakfast room with large windows and wicker chairs. ⊠ *Rte. de Bayenghem, 62380 Lumbres (9 km [6 mi] west of St-Omer),* ☎ *03–21–39–62–44,* 𝐅𝐀𝐗 *03–21–93–61–34. 24 rooms. Restaurant, breakfast room. AE, DC, MC, V.*

Shopping

Founded in 1825 in Arques, 3 km (2 mi) east of St-Omer, the **Verrerie-Cristallerie d'Arques** is France's biggest glassworks, producing 4 million items a day—most famously Cristal d'Arques wineglasses. You can visit the spacious showroom and take a 90-minute tour of the factory (30 francs). ⊠ *On N43 just south of Arques,* ☎ *03–21–95–46–96.* ☉ *Sat.–Mon. 10–6:30.*

En Route Take D77 south from St-Omer to **Thérouanne**—once the leading religious center of northern France, with a population of 20,000 when it was flattened by Charles V in 1553. All that remains are the foundations of the cathedral, in a field to the north of today's unremarkable town. Follow D341 to Estrée-Blanche and then turn left toward **Liet-**

tres. Pop in at the pretty, moated Château de Créminil. The beefier Château de Liettres is farther along the Lacquette Valley; the first written mention of the sport of *criquet* (cricket), in a manuscript now in the Archives Nationales in Paris, refers to a mortal dispute between a player and spectator here in October 1478—an event commemorated by a brass plaque near the village bridge.

Aire-sur-la-Lys

⑭ *20 km (12 mi) southeast of St-Omer via N43.*

An unspoiled town center and the proximity of A26 have made Aire, once a busy market town and army base, a favored stopover for tourists arriving from England. The grandiose **Hôtel de Ville** (Town Hall), with its sculpted pediment, giant pilasters, and 145-ft cupola-topped belfry, dominates the Grand'Place, the main square. It was built 1717–21 as a symbol of the town's resurgence after being partially destroyed by the duke of Marlborough in 1710. The town center contains many other Neoclassical 18th-century buildings—you can get details of a numbered trail from the tourist office, which is housed in a notable survivor from the 17th century: the arcaded stone-and-brick *bailliage* (guard house), on the corner of Grand'Place. The Jesuit **Chapelle St-Jacques,** built in the 1680s, is another survivor from the 17th century.

The 210-ft stone tower of the **Collégiale St-Pierre** (⊠ Pl. St-Pierre) dominates the land for miles around. Despite all the pinnacles at the top, this is not a strictly Gothic tower—it was only completed in 1634, and pilasters and rounded arches betray the stylistic influence of the Renaissance. At over 110 yards, the interior is impressively long but has suffered heavily down the ages—most recently from bombs in 1944—and its flaking 19th-century paintwork makes it look messy and disjointed. The highlight is the carved organ case made in 1633.

Dining and Lodging

$$–$$$ ✕☲ **Trois Mousquetaires.** No language problems here—some days Brits make up more than 90% of the guests. It's no surprise that they feel at home in this spacious, timber-frame-and-brick late-19th-century hotel on the outskirts of town (set well back from N43 behind a large garden). It has the feel of a baronial mansion, especially when a log fire is blazing in the wood-paneled lobby. Rooms have heavy brass lamps, plush carpeting, and floral-patterned quilts. The restaurant looks out across the fields and serves regional dishes. ⊠ *Château du Fort de la Redoute, 62120,* ☎ *03–21–39–01–11,* ☎ *03–21–39–50–10. 31 rooms, 2 suites. Restaurant. AE, DC, MC, V. Closed mid-Dec.–mid-Jan.*

Lille

60 km (37 mi) east of Aire-sur-la-Lys, 220 km (137 mi) north of Paris, 100 km (63 mi) southeast of Calais, 100 km (62 mi) west of Brussels.

For a big city supposedly reeling from the problems of its main industry—textiles—Lille (the name comes from *l'isle,* the island, in the Deûle River, where the city began) is remarkably dynamic and attractive. After experiencing Flemish, Austrian, and Spanish rule, Lille passed into French hands for good in 1668. Since the launch of the city's own métro system and the arrival of the TGV in 1994, Lille is again a European crossroads—one hour by train from Paris and Brussels, just two from London. The shiny glass towers of the Euralille complex, a high-tech commercial center of dubious aesthetic merit, greet travelers arriving at the new TGV station, Lille-Europe.

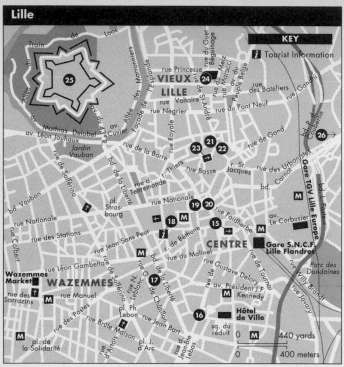

⑮ The sumptuous church of **St-Maurice** (⊠ Rue de Paris), just off place de la Gare, is a large, five-aisle structure built between the 14th and
⑯ 19th centuries. The majestic **Porte de Paris** (⊠ Rue de Paris), overlooked by the 340-ft brick tower of the **Hôtel de Ville**, is a cross between a mansion and a triumphal arch. It was built by Simon Vollant in the 1680s in honor of Louis XIV and was originally part of the city walls.

★ ⑰ The **Palais des Beaux-Arts** is the country's largest fine arts museum outside Paris. It houses a noteworthy collection of Dutch and Flemish paintings (Anthony Van Dyck, Peter Paul Rubens, Flemish Primitives, and Dutch landscapists) as well as some charmingly understated still lifes by Chardin, works by the Impressionists, and dramatic canvases by El Greco, Tintoretto, Paolo Veronese, and Goya (including two of his most famous—*Les Jeunes* and the ghastly *Les Vieilles*). A ceramics section displays some fine examples of Lille faience (earthenware), and there's a superbly lighted display of *plans reliefs* (18th-century scale models of French towns) in the basement, with binoculars provided to help you admire all the intricate detail. ⊠ *Pl. de la République*, ☎ *03–20–06–78–00.* ☞ *30 frs.* ☺ *Wed.–Thurs. and weekends 10–6, Fri. 10–7, Mon. 2–6.*

⑱ The late-15th-century **Palais Rihour** (Rihour Palace; ⊠ Pl. Rihour), built for Philippe le Bon, duke of Burgundy, is famed for its octagonal turret and staircase with intricate swirling-pattern brickwork. The city **tourist office** is housed in the vaulted former guardroom on the ground floor.

⑲ Lille's most famous square, Grand'Place, is just one block from place Rihour and is now officially called **place du Général-de-Gaulle.** The *Déesse* (Goddess), atop the giant column, clutching a linstock (used to fire a cannon), has dominated the square since 1845; she commemorates Lille's heroic resistance to an Austrian siege in 1792. Other landmarks include the handsome, gabled 1936 facade of *La Voix du Nord* (the main regional newspaper), topped by three gilded statues symbolizing the three historic regions of Flanders, Artois, and Hainaut; and the Furet du Nord, which immodestly claims to be the world's largest bookstore.

❷⓪ The elegant **Vieille Bourse** (Old Commercial Exchange), on one side of Grand'Place, was built in 1653 by Julien Destrées as a commercial exchange to rival those of the Low Countries. Note the bronze busts, sculpted medallions, and ornate stonework of its arcaded quadrangle.

The Vieux Lille (Old Lille) neighborhood dates mainly from the 17th and 18th centuries; most of its richly sculpted facades, often combining stone facings with pale pink brickwork, have been restored. Perhaps the most ornate building is the **Maison de Gilles de La Boë** (⊠ Pl. Louise-de-Bettignies), built in 1636 for a rich grocer.

❷② The **Hospice Comtesse** (Countess Hospital), founded as a hospital in 1237 by Jeanne de Constantinople, countess of Flanders, was rebuilt in the 15th century after a fire destroyed most of the original. Local artifacts from the 17th and 18th centuries form the backbone of the museum now housed here, but its star attraction is the **Salle des Malades** (Sick Ward), featuring a majestic wooden ceiling. ⊠ *32 rue de la Monnaie,* ☎ *03–28–36–84–00.* ▦ *15 frs (5 frs Sat. afternoon and Wed.).* ☉ *Wed.–Thurs. and weekends 10–6, Fri. 10–7, Mon. 2–6.*

❷③ The cathedral of **Notre-Dame de la Treille** (⊠ rue des Trois-Mollettes) stands on the spot of a medieval church dismantled during the Revolution. The present building was begun—in a suitably neo-Gothic style—in 1854. Building was halted from 1869 to 1893, and by World War I only the choir was finished. The roof vaults were only finished in 1973, and the west front, with its dismal expanses of gray concrete, remained despairingly incomplete until a translucent marble facade was finally added in 1999.

President and General Charles de Gaulle (1890–1970) was born in Lille.
❷④ His birthplace, the **Maison Natale du Général de Gaulle,** is now a museum. ⊠ *9 rue Princesse,* ☎ *03–28–38–12–05.* ▦ *15 frs.* ☉ *Wed.–Sun. 10–noon and 2–5.*

❷⑤ Lille's gigantic **Citadelle** patrols the northwest of the city from the enchanting Bois de Boulogne Gardens, whose leafy walkways alongside photogenic streams attract hordes of strollers, cyclists, and joggers. The colossal walls of the citadel are immaculately preserved, no doubt because the site is still inhabited by the French military (you can only visit the interior on Sunday afternoon). It was constructed rapidly between 1667 and 1670; of course, that genius of military engineering Sébastien de Vauban got the commission. Some 60 million bricks were baked in record time, and the result is a fortified town in its own right. ☎ *03–20–21–94–21 for tourist office to arrange tours.* ▦ *40 frs.* ☉ *Guided tours only Sun. 3–5.*

❷⑥ The **Musée d'Art Moderne** in the eastern suburb of Villeneuve d'Ascq is a modern, sober brick building ringed by trim lawns alive with boxing bronze hares by Barry Flanagan and a giant Calder mobile. The picture collection ranges from the Cubists, Modigliani and the Surrealists to Chaissac, Soulages, and postwar abstraction. ⊠ *1 allée du Musée,* ☎ *03–20–19–68–68.* ▦ *43 frs.* ☉ *Wed.–Mon. 10–6.*

Dining and Lodging

$$$ ✕ **Huîtrière.** Behind a magnificent Art Deco fish store lined with local Desvres tiles, this elegant seafood restaurant serves fresh, local seafood, simply prepared in regional (Flemish) style—turbot hollandaise, *wa-terzoï* (a mild, creamy fish stew), braised eel, scallops, and oysters. The clientele is well heeled and the prices justifiably high. ⊠ *3 rue des Chats-Bossus,* ☎ *03–20–55–43–41. AE, DC, MC, V. Closed mid–July–late Aug. No dinner Sun.*

$$ ✕ **Lion Bossu.** Old bricks and beams distinguish the 17th-century interior of this restaurant in the heart of Old Lille. This cozy, old-fashioned spot serves simple, homey regional food. ⊠ *1 rue St-Jacques,* ☎ *03–20–06–06–88. AE, V. Closed Sun. No lunch Mon.*

$ ✕ **Les Brasseurs.** This dark, wood-paneled brasserie beside the Lille-Flandres station brews its own beer. Four types—blond (lager), amber, dark (stout), and white (wheat beer)—are available, and La Palette du Barman lets you sample all for 24 francs. *Carbonnade flamande* (Flemish-style beef cooked in a sweet and sour sauce) and *flammekueches* (flattened bread dough topped with bacon and onions) are served. ⊠ *22 pl. de la Gare,* ☎ *03–20–06–46–25. AE, V.*

$$–$$$ ▦ **Bellevue.** The former Hôtel de Bourbon, home to Mozart in 1765, is now an elegante central lodging near Grand'Place. Large, comfortable Art Deco rooms and modern bathrooms are complemented by the sort of deferential service you can no longer take for granted. The leather-lined bar is a good spot at which to rendezvous. ⊠ *5 rue Jean-Roisin, 59800,* ☎ *03–20–57–45–64,* ℻ *03–20–40–07–93. 61 rooms. Piano bar. AE, DC, MC, V.*

Nightlife and the Arts

Jazz clubs, piano bars, nightclubs, and all kinds of performances are listed in *Lille by Night,* available at the Lille tourist office. Lille is at its liveliest during the first weekend of September, when the **Grande Braderie** summons folk from miles around to what is theoretically a street market but is better described as one giant beer- and mussel-swilling party.

The **Opéra de Lille** (⊠ Pl. du Théâtre, ☎ 03–20–14–48–61) has performances October–June. The **Orchestre National de Lille** (⊠ 30 pl. Mendès-France, ☎ 03–20–12–82–40) is a well-respected symphony orchestra. The **Théâtre du Nord** (⊠ 4 pl. Général-de-Gaulle, ☎ 03–20–14–24–24) is one of Lille's most prominent theaters.

En Route   En route to Valenciennes, stop in **St-Amand-les-Eaux,** 35 km (23 mi) southeast of Lille on D955, to admire the riotous stonework of its 270-ft 17th-century Baroque abbey tower, topped by a cupola.

Valenciennes

㉗   *45 km (28 mi) southeast of Lille via D955 or A23.*

The industrial city of Valenciennes was once known as the Athens of the North because of the number of artists and sculptors born here. The greatest painter of the Rococo style, Antoine Watteau, is the most famous, followed by the 19th-century sculptor Jean-Baptiste Carpeaux; works by both can be seen at the **Musée des Beaux-Arts** (Fine Arts Museum), along with local archaeological findings and an impressive array of Flemish old masters, led by Rubens, Van Dyck, and Jordaens. ⊠ *Bd. Watteau,* ☎ *03–27–22–57–20.* ◫ *20 frs.* ☉ *Wed. and Fri.–Mon. 10–6, Thurs. 10–8.*

OFF THE   **LE QUESNOY –** The partly moated fortifications of this small town, 16 km
BEATEN PATH   (10 mi) southeast of Valenciennes, were first built by Charles V in 1536, then modernized by Vauban in 1676, and have been remarkably preserved.

Douai

28 *32 km (20 mi) west of Valenciennes, 35 km (22 mi) south of Lille.*

The industrial town of Douai still has several imposing mansions recalling its 18th-century importance as a commercial capital of the French province of Flanders.

The town is most noteworthy as the home of northern France's most famous *beffroi* (belfry), whose turrets and pinnacles are immortalized in a painting by Camille Corot, now in the Louvre. The sturdy tower, completed in 1410, rises 210 ft from the ground and is topped by a huge weather vane in the form of a Flanders Lion. The peal of bells—62 of them!—sounds the quarter hour with a variety of tunes. Climb the 193 steps to the top for a view of the town and the Scarpe River. ⊠ *Rue de la Mairie,* ☎ *03–27–87–26–63.* ⊙ *Sept.–June, Mon.–Sat. at 2, 3, 4, and 5, Sun. at 10, 11, 3, 4, and 5; July–Aug., daily at 10, 11, 2, 3, 4, and 5.*

The abandoned mine in Lewarde, 7 km (4 mi) east of Douai on the road from Valenciennes, has been skillfully converted into the **Centre Historique Minier,** a museum charting the history of the local coal industry. You can admire beefy machinery, stroll around an interesting photographic exhibit, and take a mine-car ride through reconstructed coal galleries. Wear sturdy shoes and allow two hours for the visit. ☎ *03–27–95–82–82.* ⊠ *66 frs.* ⊙ *Nov.–Feb., Mon.–Sat. 1–5, Sun. 10–5; Mar.–Oct., daily 9–5:30.*

OFF THE BEATEN PATH
ARLEUX – Few herbs are more readily associated with France than *ail* (garlic), and France's unofficial garlic capital is Arleux, 11 km (7 mi) south of Douai; smoked garlic cloves are the local specialty. On the first weekend of September a Fête d'Ail (Garlic Festival) is held here. Just south of Arleux, the ponds and small lakes known as the Étangs de la Sensée provide a scenic backdrop for strolls and picnics.

Nightlife and the Arts

Giants and processions go together in northern France, most famously during the **Fêtes de Gayant** (Festival of the Giant), which has been held in Douai on the first Sunday after July 5 ever since Flanders and France signed a peace treaty in 1530. A family of five giants, more than 25 ft tall, are borne through the streets. At 11 the city bells ring out, and hundreds of pigeons are released from the Town Hall.

The Artois Battlefields

The most poignant memories of World War I are evoked in the war cemeteries in the countryside between Lens and Arras, all of which are superbly cared for.

Take A21 west from Douai to Lens and head through Liévin and Angres to **Souchez.** Standing on a windswept hill 500 ft above the Artois plain is **Notre-Dame de Lorette,** a 30-acre cemetery with endless rows of white crosses, a mock-Byzantine church, an ossuary, and a huge tower with a small war museum. From the top there are extensive views of the surrounding countryside.

30 From Souchez head south on D937, past the beautiful circular cemetery of Cabaret Rouge, to **Neuville-St-Vaast,** whose Art Deco church is a stately example of 1920s reconstruction. Just off D937 is gently sloping **La Targette,** one of the most serene and beautiful of all French war cemeteries. At the nearby crossroads of D937 and D49, opposite a stark war memorial in the form of a giant torch, is the small **Musée**

de la Guerre 1914–18 (World War I Museum), with a musty collection of posters, documents, costumes, and weapons.

★ ③ From Neuville take D55 to **Vimy,** where there's a park commemorating the epic Canadian victory during World War I. With its woods and lush grass, it has become a popular picnic spot—yet the preserved trenches and savagely undulating terrain are harsh reminders of the combat waged here in April 1917. The simple, soaring white-stone **Canadian War Memorial,** a cleft rectangular tower adorned with female figures in tearful lament, was designed by Walter Seymour Allward. Its base is inscribed with the names of the 11,285 Canadians who fell in battle here.

③ Some 4 km (2½ mi) west on D49, the ghostly towers of **Mont-St-Eloi** peer mournfully over the tiny village and surrounding countryside, visible for miles around. Once part of a vast abbey razed during the French Revolution, they were one story higher before World War I, when their lookout potential invited constant bombardment.

Arras

③ *9 km (6 mi) south of Mont-St-Eloi via D341, 178 km (105 mi) north of Paris, 113 km (70 mi) southeast of Calais, 54 km (34 mi) southwest of Lille.*

At first glance you might not guess that Arras, the capital of the historic Artois region between Flanders and Picardy, was badly mauled during World War I. In the Middle Ages Arras was an important trading and tapestry-weaving center, its wealth reflected in two of the finest squares in the country—now home to lively markets on Wednesday and Saturday mornings. Other landmarks include the 18th-century theater, the Palais des États (former regional parliament), the octagonal place Victor-Hugo, and the former home of revolutionary firebrand Maximilien Robespierre. An hour-long audio guided tour of the city is available from the tourist office (35 francs).

Start your visit at the arcaded place des Héros, the smaller of the two main squares and dominated by the richly worked—and much restored—**Hôtel de Ville** (Town Hall). You can take an elevator to the top of its ornate 240-ft **belfry** (14 francs) for a view that stretches as far as the ruined towers of Mont St-Eloi, 10 km (6 mi) northwest, and you can join a guided tour through the **Boves** (20 francs), a maze of underground chalk galleries quarried out back in the 10th century and then transformed into an underground city by 10,000 British troops during World War I. The tunnels run for miles in all directions—even, it is said, as far as Mont-St-Eloi. The tour lasts about an hour, and you'll need sturdy footwear to negotiate all the steep, slimy stairs. ⊠ *Pl. des Héros.* ⊙ *May–Sept., Mon.–Sat. 9–6:30, Sun. 10–1 and 2–6:30; Oct.–Apr., Mon.–Sat. 9–noon and 2–6, Sun. 10–12:30 and 3–6:30.*

★ **Grand'Place,** linked to place des Héros by rue de la Taillerie, is a grand, harmonious showcase of 17th- and 18th-century Flemish architecture. The gabled facades recall those in Belgium and Holland and are a reminder of the unifying influence of the Spanish colonizers of the Low Country during the 17th century—though the oldest house here, the *Trois Luppars* hotel, at No. 49, actually dates to 1467.

The 19th-century **Cathédrale St-Vaast** (⊠ Rue des Teinturiers) is a stately classical building in cool white stone, every bit as vast as its name (pronounced *va*) almost suggests. It was built between 1775 and 1830 to the designs of Contant d'Ivry; although it was half-razed during World War I, restoration was so diligent that you'd never know.

The **Musée des Beaux-Arts** (Fine Arts Museum), in the massive, regimented 18th-century abbey next to the cathedral, has a rich collection of objects and pictures, including cobalt-blue Arras porcelain; 19th-century landscapes by Camille Dutilleux and other local artists inspired by Camille Corot (also represented), who frequently visited the region; and two smiling 13th-century gilded wooden angels, the *Anges de Saudémont.* ⊠ *20 rue Paul-Doumer,* ☎ *03–21–71–26–43.* 🎫 *20 frs.* ☉ *Wed.–Fri. and Mon., 10–noon and 2–5; weekends 10–noon and 3–6.*

Dining and Lodging

$$$ ✕ **Faisanderie.** In a former stable, this splendid restaurant serves memorable variations on international fare: *pied de veau* (calves' feet), pike baked with frogs' legs, and cod with local Arleux garlic. A loyal clientele supports its longstanding gastronomic reputation. ⊠ *45 Grand'-Place,* ☎ *03–21–48–20–76. Reservations essential. Jacket and tie. AE, DC, MC, V. Closed Aug. and Mon. No dinner Sun.*

$ ✕ **Rapière.** This lively bistro dishes up distinctly local cuisine, including andouillettes (a kind of chitterling sausage) and *poule à la bière* (hen in beer), as well as specialties like *flan aux maroilles* (flan made with regional cheese) and homemade foie gras, all in a casual setting. ⊠ *44 Grand'Place,* ☎ *03–21–55–09–92. AE, MC, V. No dinner Sun.*

$$ ⌸ **Univers.** Once an 18th-century Jesuit monastery, this stylish hotel has a pretty garden, charming restaurant, and pale pink brickwork. Although centrally located, it's set well back from the main street and is an oasis of calm. The interior has been modernized but retains rustic provincial furniture. ⊠ *3 pl. de la Croix-Rouge, 62000,* ☎ *03–21–71–34–01,* ℻ *03–21–71–41–42. 37 rooms. Restaurant. AE, MC, V.*

Outdoor Activities and Sports

Three former mining towns a dozen miles north of Arras have placed sports firmly on their rejuvenation agendas. **Lens** has the top soccer team and the biggest sports stadium in northern France—used for the 1998 World Cup—with a seating capacity (41,000), larger than the town's entire population. The Stade Couvert, in neighboring **Liévin,** is France's premier indoor athletics stadium. And, crazy as it may seem in this least mountainous of regions, **Noeux-les-Mines** (⊠ Loisinord, rue Léon-Blum, ☎ 03–21–26–84–84) has made a name for itself as France's leading ski center between the Alps and the Channel by transforming its giant *terril* (slag heap) into an artificial ski run.

The Somme Battlefields

32 km (20 mi) south of Arras near Albert.

The Battle of the Somme—a name forever etched into history as site of one of the bloodiest battle campaigns of World War I—raged south of Arras, near Albert, from July through November 1916, leaving a million dead. During those five futile months, the Allies, including Irish, Canadian, Australian, and South African soldiers, progressed about 8 km (5 mi) along the hills above the Ancre River north of Albert.

㉞ From Arras take D919 through gently rolling farmland, to Puisieux, then follow D107 to **Miraumont** and turn right on D50 along the north bank of the Ancre River. Follow signs to the memorial of **Beaumont-Hamel,** where a bronze caribou—emblem of the Newfoundland regiments that fought here—gazes accusingly over trenches and undulating, still shell-shocked terrain. Across the Ancre and up the hill on the other side is the **Tour Ulster** (Ulster Tower), commemorating the troops from Belfast.

㉟ From the village of **Thiepval,** follow signs to the bombastic brick **British War Memorial,** a disjointed triumphal arch that looks as if it were made of giant Lego blocks.

③⑥ Take D73 and then D147 to Bazentin and continue on to **Longueval,** site of the **Delville Wood Memorial:** A long lawn framed by a stately avenue of oaks leads to an airy white-stone pentagon, modeled on the Castle of Good Hope in Cape Town. Here giant photographs and etched-glass panels evoke the memories of South Africans who fought in the war.

③⑦ Return to Bazentin and continue west on D20 to **La Boisselle** and its awesome **Lochnagar Crater,** 300 ft across and 90 ft deep, the fruit of 27 tons of Allied explosives detonated on July 1, 1916.

Albert

③⑧ *3 km (2 mi) southwest of La Boiselle on D929, 41 km (25 mi) south of Arras.*

The dour brick town of Albert has little going for it apart from poignant war memories. Even now, 80 years later, shells and grenades still rise to the surface of the fields here; 90 tons of these dormant time bombs are collected and destroyed near here every year.

The **Musée des Abris** (Underground Shelter Museum) uses photographs, costumes, guns, and sandbags to evoke the soldiers' life in the trenches. The museum is almost entirely underground (wear a sweater), and by the time you come up for air, you've tunneled your way through to a tranquil park 100 yards from where you started. ⊠ *Rue Anicet-Godin,* ☎ *03–22–75–16–17.* 🎫 *20 frs.* ☉ *Jan.–June and Sept.–mid-Dec., daily 9:30–noon and 2–6; July–Aug., daily 9:30–6.*

The neo-Byzantine, brick **Basilique Notre-Dame-de-Brébières** is an ostentatious country cousin of churches like Fourvière in Lyon and Sacré-Coeur in Paris. Its wealth derives from an 11th-century statue of the Virgin Mary, still venerated by pilgrims. The stone sculpture was discovered "miraculously," the story goes, by a shepherd whose obstinate sheep (*brébis*) wouldn't budge from the spot where the statue was buried. But it's another miraculous statue of the Virgin—the one on top of the 220-ft tower—that captivates most visitors. When the basilica was nearly reduced to rubble in 1916, this mighty gold Virgin, holding aloft the infant Jesus, was left dangling from the tower at right angles, as if held in place by a magic thread. Postcards showing this astonishing scene look like primitive examples of trick photography; in fact, they capture one of the most poignantly symbolic images of World War I. ⊠ *Pl. d'Armes,* ☎ *03–22–75–09–54.*

Dining

$$ ✕ **Escale.** This vine-covered restaurant in the tiny village of Cappy, southeast of Albert, is worth seeking out: With its antiques and needlework tablecloths and menu illustrated with poems and old photos, it has the feel of a country cottage. The seasonal, regional dishes (smoked eel, duck, and black pudding) are accompanied by subtle, refined sauces. ⊠ *22 chaussée Léon-Blum, Cappy (10 km [6 mi] southeast of Albert),* ☎ *03–22–76–02–03. MC, V. No dinner Sun.–Wed.*

Péronne

③⑨ *23 km (14 mi) southeast of Albert via D938.*

The small, brick town of Péronne was almost entirely razed in 1916. It's
★ now home to a fine World War I museum, the **Historial de la Grande Guerre.** Integrated into a ruined brick castle, this spacious modern museum has a thought-provoking variety of exhibits, from TV monitors playing old newsreels to soldiers' uniforms strung out on the floor surrounded

by machine guns and a dim roomful of nightmarish war lithographs by Otto Dix. It also has a good gift shop, with books in English, and a café with views of a leafy-banked lake. Walk around to the end, and you'll find the Somme River, strewn with islands, languidly colliding with its tributary, the Cologne. ⊠ *Pl. du Château,* ☎ *03–22–83–14–18.* 🎫 *39 frs.* ☉ *May–Sept., daily 10–6; Oct.–Apr., Tues.–Sun. 10–6.*

St-Quentin

④⓪ *28 km (18 mi) southwest of Péronne via N44 and N29.*

Bustling St-Quentin, an industrial town rebuilt with considerable Art Deco panache after World War I (ask about a guided tour at the tourist office), is famed as the birthplace of 18th-century pastelist Maurice Quentin de La Tour—his work can be admired at the town museum.

Appearing to survey the town's sloping, pedestrians-only main square is the riotously sculpted, early 16th-century facade of the **Hôtel de Ville** (Town Hall; ⊠ Pl. de l'Hôtel de Ville), complete with arcades and gables and topped by an 18th-century campanile with an attractive peal of bells. The town's cathedral-size hilltop **Basilique** (⊠ Pl. de la Basilique) at the top of rue St-André is topped by a 270-ft flèche, reconstructed in 1976. Most of the building, however, is resolutely medieval: the elegant 13th-century choir retains some original stained glass; the soaring nave, rising 112 ft from the ground, was added 200 years later (note the black-and-white-labyrinth pattern embedded in the floor); the ornate organ case was designed by Berain in 1690.

Guise

④① *27 km (17 mi) northeast of St-Quentin via N29.*

Creeping up the dark and ominous covered passageway to the **Château-Fort de Guise** on a gloomy day will give you the decided impression you've entered the guarded domain of the Ducs de Guise, the closest allies of François I. This influential line of dukes produced the throne-coveting Henri I, known as Le Balafré (Scarface), who plotted the St. Bartholomew's Day massacre of August 1572, the great slaughter of Paris's Protestant notables. The imposing remains of the fortress were fortified in the style of Italian Renaissance military architecture to defend the northeastern route from Paris against the ambitious Habsburg emperor Charles V. Heavy French bombardment in 1917 chased the Germans out of the town of Guise but also destroyed much of the complex. The fortress is being slowly restored by volunteers, and you can book a fascinating hour-long visit (wear sweater and flat shoes) by calling ahead and asking for Welsh guide Rosalind Guillemin. Tours take in the slimy dungeons and 11th- to 13th-century donjon (keep), one of the best preserved in Picardy. ☎ *03–23–61–11–76.* 🎫 *30 frs.* ☉ *Mid-Jan.–Nov., daily 10–noon and 2–6.*

Guise has long been famous for the cast-iron stoves made by the Godin Company. An early example of industrial philanthropy is evident at the **Familistère Godin** (Godin Phalanstery), an ideal "town within a town" built for factory workers in 1859. The largely untouched brick complex includes a school, theater, library, shop, park, and three tenement buildings with glass-roof courtyards, still home to 300 families. The guided tour includes a visit to a worker's apartment furnished in the style of 1880. ⊠ *265 Familistère Aile Droite,* ☎ *03–23–61–35–36.* 🎫 *20 frs.* ☉ *Guided tours (English available), Tues.–Sat. at 2:30 and 4, Sun. at 3.*

OFF THE   **MUSÉE MATISSE** – Artist Henri Matisse (1869–1954) was born in Le
BEATEN PATH   Cateau-Cambrésis, 25 km (16 mi) north of Guise. The Matisse Museum,
               housed in the **Palais Fénelon** (former home to the archbishops of Cam-
               brai), contains a number of early oil paintings and sculptures, plus a su-
               perb collection of 50 drawings selected by Matisse himself. Call ahead
               for a guided visit. ⊠ *Palais Fénelon,* ☎ *03–27–84–13–15.* ▨ *16 frs.*
               ☼ *Mon. and Wed.–Sat. 10–12:30 and 2–6, Sun. 10–12:30 and*
               2:30–6. Free guided tour Sun. at 3.

Vervins

㊷   *25 km (16 mi) southeast of Guise.*

Snugly tucked behind crumbling ramparts, Vervins is worth exploring
for its tumbling cobbled streets and the church of **Notre-Dame,** which
has a 13th-century choir, wall paintings (notably Jouvenet's vast 1699
Le Repas Chez Simon), and a 16th-century tower propped up by bulky
corner buttressing.

Vervins is the largest town in the **Thiérache** region, commonly referred
to as the "Pays des Églises Fortifiées" (Land of Fortified Churches) because of the redbrick village churches that were fortified in the 16th
century when Habsburg emperor Charles V and French king François
I were fighting for supremacy. There are about 60 of these proud,
fortresslike places of worship in the area, each with its own peculiar-
ities; a list and a map of the **Route des Églises Fortifiées** can be acquired
★   from local tourist offices. Among the most noteworthy: **Plomion,** with
its massive facade and three witch-hat towers; **Englancourt,** perched
above the Oise Valley; **Jeantes,** with its postwar frescoes by Charles
Eyck; **Parfondeval,** with a stone gateway and surrounded by a pretty
village; and **Burelles,** whose 16th-century towers were added to a
13th-century nave—so that menaced locals could seek refuge in the right-
hand tower (to which you have free access).

Dining and Lodging

$ ✕ **Huteau.** This rustic inn on the sloping, ramshackle village square in
Plomion, a stone's throw from a medieval market hall and the most
impressive of the Thiérache churches, makes an ideal lunch spot. *Tarte
maroille* (local cheese flan) and breast of duck are both featured on
the 100-franc four-course set menu, a good value. ⊠ *21 pl. de l'Église,
Plomion (9 km [6 mi] southeast of Vervins; 46 km [29 mi] northeast
of Laon),* ☎ *03–23–98–81–21. MC, V. Closed Wed. No dinner Sun.*

$$$ ✕▣ **Tour du Roy.** This pink-and-blue hotel in Vervins, built of stone
from the town's ramparts, is run by garrulous Claude Desvignes. His
wife, the self-styled "Dame Annie," holds sway in the kitchen. Her clas-
sical dishes emphasize seasonal produce, including *sanglier* (wild boar)
in a cream and peppercorn sauce. There's no dinner Sunday and no
lunch Monday. Rooms display the character of the owners, a blend of
French traditional and charming kitsch. ⊠ *45 rue du Général-Leclerc,
02140,* ☎ *03–23–98–00–11,* ⊠AX *03–23–98–00–72. 13 rooms, 5 suites.
Restaurant. AE, DC, MC, V.*

Laon

★ **㊸**   *36 km (22 mi) southwest of Vervins on N2.*

Thanks to its awesome hilltop site and the forest of towers sprouting
from its ancient cathedral, Laon basks in the title of the "crowned moun-
tain." The medieval ramparts, virtually undisturbed by passing traf-
fic, provide a ready-made itinerary for a tour of enchantingly venerable

Laon. Panoramic views, sturdy gateways, and intriguing glimpses of the cathedral lurk around every bend. There's even a funicular, which makes frequent trips (except on Sunday in winter) up and down the hillside between the station and the old town.

★ The **Cathédrale Notre-Dame,** constructed between 1150 and 1230, is a superb example of early Gothic. The light interior gives the impression of order and immense length, and the first flourishing of Gothic architecture is reflected in the harmony of the four-tiered nave: From the bottom up, observe the wide arcades, the double windows of the *tribune,* the squat windows of the *triforium,* and, finally, the upper windows of the clerestory. The majestic towers can be explored during the guided visits that leave from the tourist office, housed in a 12th-century hospital on the cathedral square. The filigreed elegance of the five towers is audacious and rare. Look for the 16 stone oxen protruding from the tops: a tribute to the stalwart 12th-century beasts that carted up blocks of stone from quarries far below. Medieval stained glass includes the rose window dedicated to the liberal arts in the left transept, and the windows in the flat east end, an unusual feature for France although common in England. ⊠ *Pl. du Parvis.* ▣ *Guided tours 35 frs.* ☉ *Daily 8:30–6:30; guided tours Apr.–Sept., daily at 3* PM.

The **Musée de Laon,** the town museum, has some fine antique pottery and work by the local-born Le Nain brothers. But its chief pull is the **Chapelle des Templiers** in the garden—a small, octagonal 12th-century chapel topped by a shallow dome. It houses fragments of the cathedral's gable and the chilling effigy of Guillaume de Harcigny, doctor to the insane king Charles VI, whose death from natural causes in 1393 did not prevent his memorializers from chiseling a skeletal portrait that recalls the Black Death. ⊠ *32 rue Georges-Ermant,* ☎ *03–23–20–19–87.* ▣ *20 frs.* ☉ *Apr.–Sept., Wed.–Mon. 10–noon and 2–6; Oct.–Mar., Wed.–Mon. 10–noon and 2–5.*

Dining and Lodging

$$ ✕▣ **Bannière de France.** In business since 1685, this old-fashioned, uneven-floored hostelry is just five minutes from the cathedral. Madame Lefèvre, the German patronne, speaks fluent English. Rooms are cozy and quaint. The restaurant's venerable dining room features sturdy cuisine (trout, lemon sole, guinea fowl) and good-value prix-fixe menus. ⊠ *11 rue Franklin-Roosevelt, 02000,* ☎ *03–23–23–21–44,* FAX *03–23–23–31–56. 18 rooms, 14 with bath or shower. Restaurant. AE, DC, MC, V. Closed mid-Dec.–mid-Jan.*

Coucy-le-Château

★ ㊹ *28 km (18 mi) southwest of Laon via N2 and D5.*

The majestic hilltop fortress, or **château,** in Coucy-le-Château is but a glimmer of its former self—but it still casts a pretty intimidating shadow over the lush, rolling countryside of eastern Picardy. The 30-acre site, ringed with nearly 3 km (2 mi) of walls and no fewer than 31 towers, was developed by all-powerful warlords, the Enguerrands de Coucy, in the 12th century. They also erected the largest keep in Christendom, more than 210 ft high (Barbara Tuchman's *A Distant Mirror* provides fascinating background reading). The fortifications were partially dismantled by Mazarin in 1650 to prevent their use by rebels during the Fronde, then used as an open quarry after the Revolution, and then dynamited by retreating Germans in 1917. You can visit what's left of the keep and the vaulted cellars, and follow a path around the still-imposing town walls. ☎ *03–23–52–71–28.* ▣ *25 frs.*

⏲ *Apr.–Sept., daily 9–noon and 2–6; Oct.–Mar., Wed.–Mon. 10–noon and 1:30–4.*

Dining and Lodging

$ ✕▣ **Bellevue.** Rooms in this small old hotel just inside the town walls have been unfussily modernized, and although hardly the lap of luxury—none has a bathtub—they are light, clean, cheap, and have gleaming wooden floors. Room 8 is the largest, accommodating four people. The old-fashioned dining room has a cozy, slightly faded charm, and some of the fixed-price menus showcase regional cuisine. ✉ *2 Porte de Laon, 02380,* ☎ *03–23–52–69–70,* FAX *03–23–52–69–79. 8 rooms. Restaurant. MC, V. Closed late Dec.–early Feb.*

Soissons

45 *19 km (12 mi) south of Coucy via D1.*

Although much damaged in World War I, Soissons commands attention for its two huge churches: one intact, one in ruins.

The Gothic **Cathédrale Notre-Dame** was appreciated by Rodin, who famously declared that "there are no hours in this cathedral, but rather eternity." The interior, with its pure lines and restrained ornamentation, creates a more harmonious impression than the asymmetrical, one-towered facade. The most remarkable feature, however, is the rounded two-story transept, a feature more frequently found in the German Rhineland than in France. Rubens's freshly restored *Adoration of the Shepherds* hangs on the other side of the transept. ✉ *Pl. Fernand-Marquigny.* ⏲ *Daily 9:30–noon and 2:30–5:30.*

The twin-spire facade, arcaded cloister, and airy refectory, constructed from the 14th to the 16th centuries, are all that is left of the hilltop abbey church of **St-Jean-des-Vignes,** which was largely destroyed just after the Revolution. Its stones were used to restore the cathedral and neighboring homes. But the church remains the most impressive sight in Soissons, its hollow rose window peering out over the town like the eye of some giant Cyclops. ✉ *Cours St-Jean-des-Vignes.* 🎫 *Free.* ⏲ *Mon.–Sat. 9–12:30 and 1:30–6, Sun. 10–12:30 and 1:30–7.*

Partly housed in the medieval church of St-Léger, the **Musée de Soissons,** the town museum, has a varied collection of local archaeological findings and paintings, with fine 19th-century works by Gustave Courbet and Eugène Boudin. ✉ *2 rue de la Congrégation,* ☎ *03–23–59–15–90.* 🎫 *Free.* ⏲ *Wed.–Mon. 10–noon and 2–5.*

Dining and Lodging

$$$$ ★ ✕▣ **Château de Courcelles.** East of Soissons, along the Vesle River on the Champagne border, is this luxurious and refined château run by easygoing Frédéric Nouhaud. Its pure, classical Louis-XIV facade harmonizes oddly well with the sweeping brass and pewter main staircase attributed to Jean Cocteau and the red teapot-pattern wallpaper on the upper floors. Rooms vary in size and grandeur; the former outbuildings have been converted into large family-size suites. Wind down in the cozy, antechamber-like bar next to a roaring fire while anticipating excellent fare, including seasonal game, prepared by chef Pascal Mottet and served up in the stately dining room. A formal garden and pool are the gateway to 40 acres of parkland and a tree-shaded canal. ✉ *8 rue du Château, 02220 Courcelles-sur-Vesle (20 km [12 mi] east of Soissons via N31),* ☎ *03–23–74–13–53,* FAX *03–23–74–06–41. 13 rooms, 5 suites. Restaurant, bar, pool, sauna, tennis court, horseback riding. AE, DC, MC, V.*

Blérancourt

46 *23 km (14 mi) northwest of Soissons via D6.*

The village of Blérancourt is home to the **Musée National de la Coopéra-
tion Franco-Américaine** (Museum of French-American Cooperation).
Two pavilions and monumental archways are all that remain of the
original château, built 1612–19 by Salomon de Brosse but largely demolished during the French Revolution. American Anne Morgan
founded the museum in 1924. The airy, modern museum contains art
and documents charting Franco-American relations, with a section on
American involvement in World War I. A beguiling female portrait by
Missouri Postimpressionist Richard Miller stands out: an American
Mona Lisa. The trim gardens host a bronze casting of the statue of George
Washington by Jean-Antoine Houdan and an arboretum. ⊠ *Off D939*,
☎ *03–23–39–60–16.* ⊡ *16 frs, 12 frs Sun.* ☉ *Wed.–Mon. 10–12:30
and 2–5:30.*

Noyon

47 *14 km (9 mi) northwest of Blérancourt, 37 km (23 mi) northwest of
Soissons.*

Noyon is an often overlooked cathedral town that owed its medieval
importance to the cult of 7th-century St. Eloi, patron of blacksmiths
and a former town bishop. Its second famous son, the Protestant the-
ologian John Calvin, was born here in 1509. The old streets around the
cathedral are at their liveliest during the Saturday-morning market.

Constructed between 1140 and 1290, the **Cathédrale St-Eloi** was one
of the earliest attempts at building a full-fledged Gothic cathedral. This
feat is evident in the four-story nave; the intermittent use of rounded
as well as pointed arches; and the thin, pointed lancet (as opposed to
rose) windows in the austere facade. Pause for a wry smile at the "piazza" in front of the cathedral, with its elegant town houses arranged
in a semicircle in bashful imitation of St. Peter's in Rome; then head
down the cobbled lane to the left of the facade to admire the timber-
front 16th-century library behind the cathedral. ⊠ *Pl. du Parvis.* ☉
Daily 8–noon and 2–6.

Lodging

$$ 🏨 **St-Eloi.** Between the train station and the cathedral, this hotel charms
with its provincial elegance. The redbrick and timber Victorian exte-
rior, marble-lined reception area, and airy dining room are staunchly
French bourgeois. The spacious, pastel rooms have high ceilings; sev-
eral have views of the interior courtyard. Avoid, however, the chain-
hotel-like annex. Affordable prix-fixe menus are available in the
restaurant, which doesn't serve Sunday dinner. ⊠ *81 bd. Carnot,
60400,* ☎ *03–44–44–01–49,* 🖷 *03–44–09–20–90. 22 rooms. Bar,
restaurant. AE, MC, V. Closed part of Aug.*

Compiègne

48 *24 km (15 mi) southwest of Noyon via N32.*

Compiègne, a bustling town of some 40,000 people, is at the north-
ern limit of the Forêt de Compiègne, on the edge of the misty plains
of Picardy: prime hunting country, a sure sign there's a former royal
hunting lodge in the vicinity. The one here enjoyed its heyday in the
mid-19th century under upstart emperor Napoléon III. But the town's
history stretches farther back—to Joan of Arc, who was captured in
battle and held prisoner here, and to its 15th-century Hôtel de Ville
(Town Hall), with its exceptional Flamboyant Gothic facade; and far-

ther forward—to the World War I armistice, signed in Compiègne Forest on November 11, 1918.

★ The 18th-century **Palais de Compiègne** was restored by Napoléon I and favored for wild weekends by his nephew Napoléon III. The first Napoléon's legacy is more keenly felt: His state apartments have been refurnished using the original designs for hangings and upholstery, and bright silks and damasks adorn every room. Much of the mahogany furniture gleams with ormolu, and the chairs sparkle with gold leaf. Napoléon III's furniture looks ponderous in comparison, but fans of the Second Empire style love its lavish opulence. Behind the palace is a gently rising 4-km (2½-mi) vista, inspired by the park at Schönbrunn, in Vienna, where Napoléon I's second wife, Empress Marie-Louise, grew up. Also here is the **Musée du Second Empire**, a collection of Napoléon III–era decorative arts, including works by the caricaturist
ⓒ Honoré Daumier. Make time, too, for the **Musée de la Voiture** and its display of carriages, coaches, and old cars, including the *Jamais Contente* (*Never Satisfied*), the first car to reach 100 kph (62 mph). ⊠ *Pl. du Général-de-Gaulle,* ☎ *03–44–38–47–00.* ☞ *35 frs.* ☉ *Wed.–Mon. 10–5:45.*

A collection of 85,000 miniature soldiers—fashioned out of lead, cardboard, and other materials—that depicts military uniforms through the
ⓒ ages is found in the **Musée de la Figurine Historique** (Toy Soldier Museum). ⊠ *28 pl. de l'Hôtel-de-Ville,* ☎ *03–44–40–72–55.* ☞ *12 frs.* ☉ *Mar.–Oct., Tues.–Sat. 9–noon and 2–6, Sun. 2–6; Nov.–Feb., Tues.–Sat. 9–noon and 2–5, Sun. 2–5.*

Some 7 km (4 mi) east of Compiègne via N31 and D546, off the road to Rethondes, is the **Wagon de l'Armistice** (Armistice Railcar), a replica of the one in which the World War I armistice was signed, in 1918. In 1940 the Nazis turned the tables and made the French sign their own surrender in the same place—accompanied by Hitler's famous jig for joy—then tugged the original car off to Germany, where it was later destroyed. The car is part of a small museum in a leafy clearing. ⊠ *Clairière de l'Armistice,* ☎ *03–44–40–09–27.* ☞ *10 frs.* ☉ *Apr.–Oct., Wed.–Mon. 9–noon and 2–6:30; Nov.–Mar., Wed.–Mon. 9:30–11:45 and 2–5:30.*

Dining and Lodging

$$ ✕☰ **France.** A former 17th-century posting inn, the hotel is central, cheap, and the epitome of French Provincial—rooms have creaky, uneven floors, and the prim *patronne,* Madame Robert, appears seemingly from nowhere as you cross the threshold. The labyrinth of rooms, with their matching fruit-and-flower wallpaper and bedspreads, ranges from nooks and crannies to family sleepers. The restaurant's name, La Rôtisserie du Chat Qui Tourne (the Cat That Turns the Spit), recalls a legendary street performance involving a cat roasting a chicken. With its brass lights and plush curtains and waiters in black tie, it tries valiantly to be upper crust. The scallops in pastry soufflé and the langoustines in cream try hard, too. ⊠ *17 rue Eugène-Floquet, 60200,* ☎ *03–44–40–02–74,* ℻ *03–44–40–48–37. 20 rooms. Restaurant, bar. MC, V.*

Pierrefonds

★ ㊾ *14 km (9 mi) southeast of Compiègne via D973.*

Dominating the attractive lakeside village of Pierrefonds is its huge ersatz medieval castle. Built on a mound in the 15th century, the **Château de Pierrefonds** was comprehensively restored and re-created in the 1860s to imagined former glory at the behest of upstart emperor Napoléon

III, then seeking to cash in on the fashion for neo-Gothic and the 19th-century craze for the Middle Ages. Architect Viollet-le-Duc left a crenellated fortress with a fairy-tale silhouette, although, like the fortified town of Carcassonne, which he also restored, Pierrefonds is more a construct of what Viollet-le-Duc thought it should have looked like than what it really was. A visit takes in the chapel, barracks, and the majestic keep holding the lord's bedchamber and reception hall, which is bordered by a spiral staircase whose lower and upper sections reveal clearly what is ancient and modern in this former fortress. Don't miss the plaster casts of tomb sculptures from all over France in the cellars, and the **Collection Monduit**—industrially produced, larger-than-life lead decorations made by the 19th-century firm that brought the Statue of Liberty to life. ☎ 03–44–42–72–72. ⬚ 32 frs. ☉ Mar.–Apr. and Sept.–Oct., Mon.–Sat. 10–noon and 2–6, Sun. 10–6; May–Aug., daily 10–6; Nov.–Feb., Mon.–Sat. 10–11:45 and 2–5:15, Sun. 10–5:15 (last admission ¼ hr before closing).

OFF THE BEATEN PATH

MORIENVAL – This village, 6 km (4 mi) south of Pierrefonds via D335, is known for its modest 11th-century Romanesque church, one of the key buildings in architectural history. It was here, in the 1120s, that masons first hit on the idea of using stone vaults supported on "ribs" springing diagonally from column to column, an architectural breakthrough that formed the structural basis of the Gothic style. The trend was soon picked up at the great basilica of St-Denis near Paris and swept through northern France during the years that followed.

Dining and Lodging

$$ ✕⌂ **Relais Brunehaut.** Just down the valley from Pierrefonds, in the hamlet of Chelles, is this quaint hotel-restaurant, with a view of the abbey church next door. It's made up of a tiny ensemble of stucco buildings, bordered by several acres of pleasant park and a small duck-populated river. An old wooden water mill in the dining room and the good, simple seasonal fare make eating here a pleasure. The dining room is closed Monday and Tuesday. ✉ 3 rue de l'Église, 60350 Chelles (3 km [2 mi] east of Pierrefonds), ☎ 03–44–42–85–05, FAX 03–44–42–83–30. 7 rooms. Restaurant. MC, V.

CHAMPAGNE AND THE ARDENNES

Champagne, a place name that has become a universal synonym for joy and festivity, is a word of humble origin. Like *campagna,* its Italian counterpart, it is derived from the Latin *campus,* which means "open field." In French, campus became *champ,* with the old language extending this to *champaign,* for "battlefield," and *champaine,* for "district of plains." *Battlefield* and *plains* both accurately describe the province, as Champagne is crisscrossed by Roman roads along which defenders and invaders have clashed for two millennia.

Today, of course, the province is best known for its champagne vineyards, which start just beyond Château-Thierry, 96 km (60 mi) northeast of Paris, and continue along the towering Marne Valley to Epernay. Cheerful villages line the Route du Vin (Wine Road), which twines north to Reims, the capital of bubbly. As you head farther northeast, rolling chalk hills give way to the rugged Ardennes Forest, close to the Belgian border and Lorraine (☞ Chapter 7).

Château-Thierry

🔟 94 km (59 mi) northeast of Paris via A4, 51 km (32 mi) southeast of Pierrefonds.

Built along the Marne River beneath the ruins of a hilltop castle that dates to the time of Joan of Arc, and within sight of the American **Belleau Wood** War Cemetery, Château-Thierry is best known as the birthplace of the French fable teller Jean de La Fontaine (1621–95). The 16th-century mansion where de La Fontaine was born is now a museum, the **Musée Jean de La Fontaine,** furnished in the style of the 17th century. It contains de La Fontaine's bust, portrait, and baptism certificate, plus editions of his fables magnificently illustrated by Jean-Baptiste Oudry (1755) and Gustave Doré (1868). ✉ *12 rue Jean-de-La-Fontaine,* ☎ *03–23–69–05–60.* ✉ *19 frs.* ☉ *Wed.–Mon. 10–noon and 2–6.*

Épernay

🟤 *50 km (31 mi) east of Château-Thierry via N3 or D3 and D1.*

Unlike Reims with its numerous treasures, the town of Épernay, on the south bank of the Marne, appears to live only for champagne. Unfortunately, no relation exists between the fabulous wealth of Épernay's illustrious wine houses and the drab, dreary appearance of the town as a whole. Most champagne firms are spaced out along the long, straight avenue de Champagne, and although their names may provoke sighs of wonder, their facades are either functional or overdressy. The attractions are all underground.

Of the various champagne houses open to the public, **Mercier** offers the best deal; its sculpted, labyrinthine cellars contain one of the world's largest wooden barrels (with a capacity of more than 215,000 bottles). A tour of the cellars takes 45 minutes in the relative comfort of a small train. A glass of champagne is your postvisit reward. ✉ *75 av. de Champagne,* ☎ *03–26–51–22–22.* ✉ *30 frs.* ☉ *Jan.–late Dec., weekdays 9:30–11:30 and 2–4:30, weekends 9:30–11:30 and 2–5.*

To understand how the region's still wine became sparkling champagne, head across the Marne to **Hautvillers.** Here the monk Dom Pérignon (1638–1715)—for whom, legend has it, his blindness conferred the gifts of exceptional taste buds and sense of smell—invented champagne as we know it by using corks for stoppers and blending wines from different vineyards. Dom Pérignon's simple tomb, in a damp, dreary Benedictine abbey church (now owned by Moët et Chandon), is a forlorn memorial to the hero of one of the world's most lucrative drink industries.

Dining and Lodging

$$$–$$$$ ✕🏨 **Briqueterie.** Épernay is short on good hotels, so it's worth driving south to Vinay to find this luxurious manor. The spacious rooms are modern; ask for one overlooking the extensive gardens. The chef has the Mediterranean on his mind: hence the lobster and prawns in citrus sauce. For more regional fare try the Champagne snails with herbed butter and, for dessert, the *crêpe soufflée au marc de champagne* (a crepe filled with pastry cream and flavored with brandy). ✉ *4 rte. de Sézanne, 51530 Vinay (6 km [4 mi] south of Épernay),* ☎ *03–26–59–99–99,* ☎ *03–26–59–92–10. 40 rooms, 2 suites. Restaurant, indoor pool, sauna, exercise room. AE, MC, V. Closed late Dec.*

Nightlife and the Arts

The leading wine festival in the Champagne region is the **Fête St-Vincent** (named for the patron saint of vine growers), held on either January 22 or the following Saturday in Ambonnay, 24 km (15 mi) east of Épernay.

Châlons-en-Champagne

52 *34 km (21 mi) east of Épernay via N3.*

Strangely enough, the official administrative center of the champagne industry is not Reims or Épernay but Châlons-en-Champagne. Yet this large town is of significant interest for its vast cathedral and smaller, early Gothic church.

★ With its twin spires, Romanesque nave, and early Gothic choir and vaults, the church of **Notre-Dame-en-Vaux** bears eloquent testimony to Châlons's medieval importance. The small **museum** beside the excavated cloister contains outstanding medieval statuary. ☒ *Rue Nicolas-Durand,* ☎ *03–26–64–03–87.* ☒ *25 frs.* ☉ *Apr.–Sept., Wed.–Mon. 10–noon and 2–6; Oct.–Mar., Wed.–Fri. 10–noon and 2–5, weekends 10–noon and 2–6.*

The 13th-century **Cathédrale St-Étienne** (☒ Rue de la Marne) is a harmonious structure with large nave windows and tidy flying buttresses; the exterior effect is marred only by the bulky 17th-century Baroque west front.

Dining and Lodging

$$–$$$ ✕☷ **Angleterre.** Rooms at this stylish spot in central Châlons have elaborate decor and marble bathrooms; those in the back are quietest. Particularly standing apart is the restaurant (closed Sunday; no lunch Saturday): Chef Jacky Michel's creations include *sandre* (perch-pike) cooked in champagne and seasoned roast duck, as well as the seasonal dessert *tout-pommes,* featuring five variations on the humble apple. Breakfast is a superb buffet. ☒ *19 Pl. Monseigneur-Tissier, 51000,* ☎ *03–26–68–21–51,* ℻ *03–26–70–51–67. 18 rooms. Restaurant. AE, DC, MC, V. Closed mid-July–early Aug. and late Dec.–early Jan.*

En Route The grapes of Champagne flourish on the steep slopes of the Montagne de Reims—more of a forest-topped plateau than a mountain—northwest of Châlons. Take D1 northwest, then turn right on D37 to Ambonnay to join the Route des Vins (Wine Road). This winds around the vine-entangled eastern slopes of the Montagne through such pretty wine villages as the aptly named **Bouzy** (home to a fashionable but overpriced still red wine), **Verzy, Mailly-Champagne, Chigny-les-Roses,** and **Rilly-la-Montagne.**

L'Épine

53 *7 km (4 mi) east of Châlons.*

The tiny village of L'Épine is dominated by its church, the twin-towered Flamboyant Gothic **Basilique de Notre-Dame de l'Épine.** The church's facade is a magnificent creation of intricate patterns, spires, and an interior that exudes elegance and restraint.

Dining and Lodging

$$$ ✕☷ **Aux Armes de Champagne.** The highlight of this cozy former coach-★ ing inn, opposite the church, is the restaurant, with its renowned champagne list and imaginative, often spectacular cuisine by chef Gilles Blandin. Among his specialties are artichokes with local goat cheese, and red mullet prepared with juice from roast veal. Ask for a table by the window, with a view of the church. (The restaurant is closed Monday in winter; no dinner is served Sunday.) Rooms are furnished with solid, traditional reproductions; wall hangings; and thick carpets. No. 21, with wood beams, is especially nice. ☒ *31 av. du Luxembourg, 51460,* ☎ *03–26–69–30–30,* ℻ *03–26–66–92–31. 37 rooms. Restaurant, tennis court. AE, DC, MC, V. Closed Jan.–mid-Feb.*

Reims

11 km (7 mi) north of Rilly-la-Montagne, 44 km (27 mi) northwest of Châlons via N44, 144 km (90 mi) east of Paris.

Although most of its historic buildings were flattened in World War I and replaced by drab, modern architecture, those that do remain are of royal magnitude. Top of the list goes to the city's magnificent cathedral, in which the kings of France were crowned until 1825, while the Musée des Beaux-Arts has a stellar collection, including the famed Jacques-Louis David painting of Marat in his bath. Reims sparkles with some of the biggest names in champagne production, and the thriving industry has conferred wealth and sometimes an arrogant reserve on the region's inhabitants. Nevertheless, the maze of champagne cellars constitutes another fascinating sight of the city. Several champagne producers organize visits to their cellars, combining video presentations with guided tours of their cavernous, chalk-hewn underground warehouses. For a complete list of champagne cellars, head to the **tourist office** (⊠ 2 rue Guillaume-de-Machault, ☎ 03–26–77–45–25), next to the cathedral.

★ ⑤④ The tour of the **Taittinger** cellars is the most spectacular of the champagne producer visits. It includes a champagne *dégustation* (tasting) afterward. ⊠ *9 pl. St-Nicaise,* ☎ *03–26–85–45–35.* 🎫 *35 frs.* ☽ *March–Nov., weekdays 9:30–noon and 2–4, weekends 9–11 and 2–4:45; Dec.–Feb., weekdays 9:30–noon and 2–4:15.*

⑤⑤ The 11th-century **Basilique St-Rémi** honors the 5th-century saint who gave his name to the city. St-Rémi is nearly as long as the cathedral, and its interior seems to stretch into the endless distance, an impression created by its relative murk and lowness. The airy four-story Gothic choir contains some fine original 12th-century stained glass. Like its sister cathedral, the basilica puts on indoor **son-et-lumière** shows every Saturday evening at 9:30 from late June to early October. They are preceded by a tour of the building and are free. ⊠ *53 rue St-Rémi,* ☎ *03–26–85–31–20.* ☽ *Sun.–Wed. 8–6 or 8–7, Thurs. and Sat. 8–9.*

⑤⑥ The **Palais du Tau** (formerly the Archbishop's Palace), alongside the cathedral, houses an impressive display of tapestries and coronation robes, as well as several statues rescued from the cathedral facade before they fell off. The second-floor views of Notre-Dame are terrific. ⊠ *2 pl. du Cardinal Luçon,* ☎ *03–26–47–81–79.* 🎫 *32 frs.* ☽ *July–Aug., daily 9:30–6:30; mid-Mar.–June and Sept.–mid-Nov., daily 9:30–12:30 and 2–6; mid-Nov.–mid-Mar., weekdays 10–noon and 2–5, weekends 10–noon and 2–6.*

⑤⑦ The **Musée des Beaux-Arts** (Museum of Fine Arts), two blocks southwest of the cathedral, has an outstanding collection of paintings: no fewer than 27 Corots are here, as well as Jacques-Louis David's celebrated and unforgettable portrait of the revolutionary polemicist Jean-Paul Marat, stabbed in his bath by Charlotte Corday. ⊠ *8 rue Chanzy,* ☎ *03–26–47–28–44.* 🎫 *10 frs.* ☽ *Wed.–Mon. 10–noon and 2–6.*

★ ⑤⑧ The **Cathédrale Notre-Dame** was the age-old setting for the coronations of the French kings. Clovis, king of the Franks in the 6th century, was baptized in an early structure on this site; Joan of Arc led her recalcitrant dauphin here to be crowned King Charles VII; Charles X's coronation, in 1825, was the last. The high, solemn nave is at its best in summer, when the light shows up the plain lower walls. The east-end windows have stained glass by Marc Chagall. Admire the vista toward the west end, with an interplay of narrow pointed arches. The glory of Reims's cathedral is its facade: It's so skillfully proportioned that initially you have little idea of its monumental size. Above the north (left) door hov-

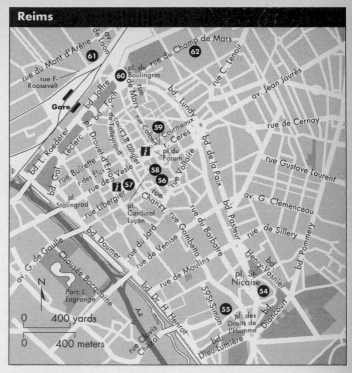

Reims

ers the *Laughing Angel,* a delightful statue whose famous smile threatens to melt into an acid-rain scowl. Pollution has succeeded war as the ravager of the building's fabric. Restoration is an ongoing process. With the exception of the 15th-century towers, most of the original building went up in the 100 years after 1211. A stroll around the outside reinforces the impression of harmony, discipline, and decorative richness. The east end presents an idyllic sight across well-tended lawns. Spectacular **son-et-lumière** shows are performed both inside (50 francs) and outside (free) the cathedral on Friday and Saturday evenings from July to mid-September. ⊠ *Pl. du Cardinal-Luçon.* ☺ *Daily 7:30–7:30.*

59 The Gallo-Roman **Cryptoportique,** an underground gallery and crypt, now a semisubterranean passageway, was constructed around AD 200 under the forum of what was Reim's predecessor, the Roman town of Durocortorum. ⊠ *Pl. du Forum,* ☎ *03–26–85–23–36.* ☺ *Mid-June–mid-Sept., Tues.–Sun. 2–6.*

60 The **Porte Mars** (⊠ Rue de Mars), an unlikely but impressive 3rd-century Roman arch adorned by faded bas-reliefs depicting Jupiter, Romulus, and Remus, looms up across from the train station.

61 The **Salle de Reddition** (Surrender Room), near the train station, also known as the Salle du 8 mai 1945, is a well-preserved map-covered room used by General Eisenhower as Allied headquarters at the end of World War II. It was here that General Alfred Jodl signed the German surrender at 2:41 AM on May 7, 1945. Fighting officially ceased at midnight the next day. ⊠ *12 rue Franklin-Roosevelt,* ☎ *03–26–47–84–19.* ⊡ *10 frs.* ☺ *Wed.–Mon. 10–noon and 2–6.*

62 **Mumm** is one of the few champagne houses to give out free samples after a tour. ⊠ *34 rue du Champ-de-Mars,* ☎ *03–26–49–59–70.* ⊡ *25 frs.* ☺ *Mar.–Oct., daily 9–11 and 2–5; Nov.–Feb., daily 2–5.*

Dining and Lodging

$$ ✕ **Vigneron.** This little brasserie in a 17th-century mansion is cozy and cheerful, with two tiny dining rooms displaying a jumble of champagne-related paraphernalia. The food is delightful as well: relatively cheap, distinctly hearty, and prepared with finesse. Try the pigs' feet or andouillettes slathered with delicious mustard made with champagne. ✉ *1 pl. Paul-Jamot,* ☎ *03–26–79–86–86. MC, V. Closed Sun., late Dec.–early Jan. and most of Aug. No lunch Sat.*

$$$$ ✕🏠 **Boyer.** This hotel—a late 19th-century château surrounded by a hilly
★ park—has pomp and style; the opulent decor is typified by ornate chandeliers, towering ceilings, and gilt mirrors. But the top attraction here is Gérard Boyer, one of the country's most highly rated chefs, with delectable dishes ranging from wild mushrooms in cream to scallops with endive confit. The extensive wine list pays homage to Reims's champagne heritage. The restaurant is closed Monday and no luncheon is offered Tuesday; reservations and jacket and tie are all essential. ✉ *Les Crayères, 64 bd. Henri-Vasnier, 51100,* ☎ *03–26–82–80–80,* ℻ *03–26–82–65–52. 19 rooms. Restaurant. AE, DC, MC, V. Closed late Dec.–mid-Jan.*

$$–$$$ ✕🏠 **La Paix.** A modern eight-story hotel, 10 minutes' walk from the cathedral, La Paix has stylish rooms with 18th- and 19th-century reproductions, a pretty garden, and a rather incongruous chapel. Its brasserie-style restaurant serves good, though not inexpensive, cuisine (mainly grilled meats and seafood). ✉ *9 rue Buirette, 51100,* ☎ *03–26–40–04–08,* ℻ *03–26–47–75–04. 106 rooms. Restaurant, bar, pool. AE, DC, MC, V.*

$$ ✕🏠 **Cheval Blanc.** This hotel, owned for five generations by the hospitable Robert family, is in the small village of Sept-Saulx, southeast of Reims. Rooms are across the road in a parklike setting—with swings for kids and a tennis court—on the small Vesle River. Some rooms are quite small, but opening the French doors onto the garden helps. The newer suites are larger and have modern furnishings. Restaurant specialties include St-Pierre fish seasoned with Chinese pepper and pigeon with dried raisins. ✉ *Rue du Moulin, 51400 Sept-Saulx (24 km [15 mi] southeast of Reims via D8),* ☎ *03–26–03–90–27,* ℻ *03–26–03–97–09. 25 rooms. Restaurant, tennis court, fishing, playground. AE, DC, MC, V. Closed late Jan.–mid-Feb.*

Asfeld

63 *28 km (18 mi) north of Reims via D966 and D926.*

The tiny village of Asfeld is home to one of France's most surprising churches. The **Église St-Didier,** designed by Father François Romain for Comte d'Avaux in 1683, is a whimsical essay in Roman Baroque, with curves, cupolas, a rotunda, colonnades, oval side chapels, and hardly a straight line in sight. The ground plan is said to be based on a viola, and the individual bricks are not rectangular but concave or convex. The church would look great in a tony sector of Rome; in this scruffy village it hovers between the sublime and the ridiculous. ☎ *03–24–72–95–46.* ☉ *Daily noon–7.*

THE NORTH AND CHAMPAGNE A TO Z

Arriving and Departing

By Car

Two highways head north from Paris. Busy A1 passes close to Compiègne and Arras (where A26 branches off to Calais) before reaching Lille. Journey time is about 1 hour and 40 minutes to Arras and 2½ hours to Lille. The new, often empty A16 leads from L'Isle-Adam, north of

Paris, up to Beauvais and Amiens, before veering northwest to Abbeville and around the coast to Boulogne, Calais, and Dunkerque. Journey time is about 90 minutes to Amiens and 2½ hours to Boulogne. If you're arriving by car via the Channel Tunnel, you'll disembark at Coquelles, near Calais, and join A16 not far from its junction with A26, which heads to Arras (75 minutes) and Reims (2½ hours). A4 heads east from Paris to Reims; allow 90 minutes to two hours, depending on traffic.

By Ferry

Ferry and hovercraft companies travel between northern France and the United Kingdom. Companies traveling between Calais and Dover include **Hoverspeed, P&O Stena,** and **Seafrance.** The sole operator of the route between Boulogne and Folkestone is **Hoverspeed.** For more information *see* Boat & Ferry Travel *in* Smart Travel Tips A to Z.

By Plane

If you are coming from the U.S. and most other destinations, count on arriving at Paris's Charles de Gaulle or Orly airports. Charles de Gaulle offers easy access to the northbound A1 and the TGV line for Lille. If coming from London, consider the occasional direct flights from Heathrow to Lille-Lesquin and from Gatwick to Beauvais.

By Train

TGV (*Trains à Grande Vitesse*) speed from Paris (Gare du Nord) to Lille (255 km [165 mi]) in just one hour. A separate TGV service links Paris (Gare du Nord) to Arras (50 minutes) and Dunkerque (two hours). The Paris–Boulogne–Calais train chugs unhurriedly around the coast, taking nearly three hours to cover 300 km (185 mi) via Amiens. There is also frequent daily service from Paris (Gare du Nord) to Compiègne and Noyon, as well as to Laon (taking up to two leisurely hours to cover 140 km [87 mi]). Regular trains cover the 170 km (105 mi) from Paris (Gare de l'Est) to Reims in 1½ hours. Eurostar trains, via the Channel Tunnel, link London to Lille in two hours; some stop at Calais.

Getting Around

By Car

A26 heads inland from Calais and St-Omer to Arras (where it intersects with A1), Laon, and Reims, which is directly linked to Paris by A4. A16 follows the railroad around the coast from Belgium and Dunkerque past Calais, Boulogne, Le Touquet, Abbeville, Amiens, and Beauvais to Paris.

By Train

It's easy to get around this region by train. Most sites can be reached by regular train service, except for the war cemeteries and the château in Pierrefonds. The Lille–Calais regional line (TER) stops at St-Omer. From Calais it follows the coast to Boulogne, Montreuil, Étaples (with a bus link to Le Touquet 6½ km [4 mi] away), Abbeville, and Amiens, where a change is needed to reach Beauvais or Reims (via Laon). Trains leave Reims for Épernay and Châlons.

Contacts and Resources

Car Rentals

Be aware that the Avis offices at the Calais car ferry and Hoverport terminals may not always be staffed. Look for instructions on how to use the red phones provided in these offices to reach the central office in the town of Calais, which will handle your rental.

Avis (✉ 36 pl. d'Armes, Calais, ☎ 03–21–34–66–50; ✉ Calais car ferry terminal, ☎ 03–21–34–66–50; ✉ Calais Hoverport, ☎ 03–21–96–66–

52; ⊠ Cour de la Gare, Reims, ☎ 03–26–47–10–08). **Europcar** (⊠ 32 pl. de la Gare, Lille, ☎ 03–20–78–18–18). **Hertz** (⊠ 5 bd. d'Alsace-Lorraine, Amiens, ☎ 03–22–91–26–24; ⊠ 10 bd. Daunou, Boulogne, ☎ 03–21–31–53–14).

Emergencies

Ambulance (☎ 15). **Hospitals: Amiens** (⊠ 1 pl. Victor-Pauchet, ☎ 03–22–66–80–00). Compiègne (⊠ 8 av. Henri-Adnot, ☎ 03–44–23–60–00). Lille (⊠ 51 bd. de Belfort, ☎ 03–20–87–48–48). **Reims** (⊠ American Hospital, 47 rue Cognac-Jay, ☎ 03–26–78–78–78).

Guided Tours

The **Lille Tourist Office** (⊠ 42 pl. Rihour, ☎ 03–20–21–94–21) is a mine of information about companies that give bus tours of northern France. **Loisirs-Accueil Nord** (⊠ 6 rue Gauthier-de-Châtillon, Lille, ☎ 03–20–57–59–59) organizes bus trips to Boulogne and Flanders and can arrange fishing, walking, and beer-tasting tours. The **Service des Visites Guidées** in Boulogne's Château-Musée (⊠ Rue Bernet, Boulogne-sur-Mer, ☎ 03–21–80–56–78) arranges trips to Boulogne's old town and port for groups of up to 30 people; the cost for two hours totals 400 francs for two or more.

Travel Agencies

Carlson–Wagonlit (⊠ 1 rue Paul-Bert, Calais, ☎ 03–21–34–79–25; ⊠ 9 rue Faidherbe, Lille, ☎ 03–20–55–05–76).

Visitor Information

The principal regional tourist offices in Amiens, Lille, and Reims are good sources of information about the region. Other, smaller towns also have their own tourist offices: **Abbeville** (⊠ 1 pl. de l'Amiral-Courbet, ☎ 03–22–24–27–92). **Amiens** (⊠ 6 bis rue Dusevel, ☎ 03–22–71–60–50). **Arras** (⊠ Hôtel de Ville, pl. des Héros, ☎ 03–21–51–26–95). **Beauvais** (⊠ 1 rue Beauregard, ☎ 03–44–45–08–18). **Boulogne** (⊠ Forum Jean-Noël, quai de la Poste, ☎ 03–21–31–68–38). **Calais** (⊠ 12 bd. Clemenceau, ☎ 03–21–96–62–40). **Compiègne** (⊠ Pl. de l'Hôtel-de-Ville, ☎ 03–44–40–01–00). **Eu** (⊠ 41 rue Paul-Bignon, ☎ 02–35–86–04–68). **Laon** (⊠ Pl. du Parvis, ☎ 03–23–20–28–62). **Le Touquet** (⊠ Palais de l'Europe, pl. de l'Hermitage, ☎ 03–21–06–72–00). **Lille** (⊠ 42 pl. Rihour, ☎ 03–20–21–94–21). **Montreuil-sur-Mer** (⊠ 21 rue Carnot, ☎ 03–21–06–04–27). **Noyon** (⊠ Pl. de l'Hôtel-de-Ville, ☎ 03–44–44–21–88). **Pierrefonds** (⊠ Rue Louis-d'Orléans, ☎ 03–44–42–81–44). **Reims** (⊠ 2 rue Guillaume-de-Machault, ☎ 03–26–77–45–25). **St-Omer** (⊠ Hôtel de Ville, pl. du Maréchal-Foch, ☎ 03–21–98–08–51).

7 ALSACE, LORRAINE, AND FRANCHE-COMTÉ

Only the Rhine separates Germany from Alsace-Lorraine, a region that often looks German and even sounds German. But its heart—after all, its natives were the first to sing the "Marseillaise"—is passionately French. In Alsace, wind along the Route du Vin through vineyards and storybook villages, then explore Strasbourg, which for all its medieval charms rivals Paris in history and haute cuisine. In mellow Lorraine, trace Joan of Arc's childhood, then discover elegant 18th-century Nancy. Art treasures—the great Grünewald altarpiece at Colmar, for one—also entice, as do hikes in the forested wilds of Franche-Comté.

Updated by
Nancy Coons

W HO PUT THE HYPHEN IN ALSACE-LORRAINE? The two regions, long at odds physically and culturally, were bonded when Kaiser Wilhelm, Dr. Frankenstein-like, sliced off the Moselle chunk of Lorraine and sutured it to Alsace, claiming the unfortunate graft as German turf. Though the names to this day are often hyphenated, Alsace and Lorraine have always been two separate territories, with strong individual styles. It is only their recent German past that ties them together—it wasn't until 1879, as a concession after France's surrender in 1871, that a newly hyphenated "Alsace-Lorraine" became part of the enemy's spoils. At that point the region was systematically Teutonized—architecturally, linguistically, culinarily (" . . . ve haff our own vays of cookink sauerkraut!"), and two generations grew up culturally torn. Until, that is, 1918, when France revenged its defeat and reclaimed its turf. Until, that is, 1940, when Hitler snatched it back and reinstated German textbooks in the primary schools. Until, that is, 1945, when France once again raised the *bleu-blanc-et-rouge* over Strasbourg.

But no matter how forcefully the French tout its hard-won Frenchness, Alsace's German roots go deeper than the late 19th century, as one look at its storybook medieval architecture will prove. In fact, this strip of vine-covered hills squeezed between the Rhine and the Vosges mountains was called Prima Germania by the Romans, and belonged to the fiercely germanic Holy Roman Empire for more than 700 years.

Yet west of the Vosges, Lorraine served under French and Burgundian lords as well as the Holy Roman Empire, coming into its own under the powerful and influential dukes of Lorraine in the Middle Ages and Renaissance. Stanislas, the duke of Lorraine who transformed Nancy into a cosmopolitan Paris-of-the-East, was Louis XV's father-in-law. Thus, the Lorraine culture evolved as decidedly less German than its neighbor to the southeast.

But that's why these days most travelers find Alsace more exotic than Lorraine: Its pointed, half-timber houses, ornate wells and fountains, oriels (upstairs bay windows), stork's nests, and carved-wood balustrades would serve well on a stage set for the tale of William Tell and satisfy a visitor's deepest craving for old-world atmosphere preserved intact. Strasbourg, perhaps France's most fascinating city outside Paris, offers all this atmosphere, and urban sophistication as well. And throughout Alsace, hotels are well scrubbed, with tile bathrooms, good mattresses, and geraniums spilling from every windowsill; although the cuisine leans toward sausage and sauerkraut, sophisticated spins on tradition have earned it a reputation—perhaps ironic, in some quarters—as one of the gastronomic centers of France. In fact, it has been crudely but vividly put that Alsace combines the best of the French and Germanic worlds: One dines in France but washes up, as it were, in Germany.

Lorraine, on the other hand, has suffered in recent years, and a decline in its northern industry and the miseries of its small farmers have left much of it tarnished, neglected—and, as some might say, unspoiled. Yet Lorraine's rich caches of verdure, its rolling countryside dotted with *mirabelle* (plum) orchards and crumbling-stucco villages, abbeys, fortresses, and historic cities (majestic Nancy, war-ravaged Verdun) offer a truly French view of life in the north. Its borders flank Belgium, Luxembourg, and Germany's mellow Mosel (also known as Moselle). Home of Baccarat and St-Louis crystal (thanks to limitless supplies of firewood from the Vosges Forest), the origin of the Gregorian chant, birthplace of Art Nouveau and Joan of Arc, Lorraine-the-underdog has long had something of its own to contribute. Although it may lack the Teutonic comforts of Alsace—it subscribes to the more Latin laissez-faire school of innkeeping (concave mattresses, dusty bolsters, creaky floors)—it serves its regional delicacies with flair: *tourte Lorraine* (a pork-and-beef pie), madeleines (shell-shape butter cakes), mirabelle plum tarts, and the famous local quiche.

There's even more novelty to be found south of Alsace and Lorraine: folkloric Franche-Comté. With its forested pre-Alpine mountains, weathered-wood and stone chalets, green-velvet pastures, and cheese cooperatives, it reminds visitors of a certain cuckoo-clock country just over the border. In the misty Jura Mountain range, sturdy shoes and topographical maps are de rigueur, with a decidedly un-Swiss reward at the end of a hiker's day: superb and eccentric Jura wines, a panoply of subtly smoked sausages, and the discreet hospitality that makes this the *bouche à l'oreille* (word of mouth) retreat of ski-weary Parisians.

— Nancy Coons

Pleasures and Pastimes

Dining

If Alsace cooking tends to be heavy—*choucroute* (sauerkraut served with ham and sausages) and *baeckoffe* (a hearty meat-and-potato casserole) are two mainstays—there is sophistication, too: foie gras accompanied by a glass of *vendange tardive* (late-harvested) gewürztraminer and trout and chicken cooked in Riesling, the classic wine of Alsace. Snails and seasonal game are other favorites, as are Muenster cheese, salty *bretzel* loaves, and briochelike *kouglof* bread. Carp fried in bread crumbs is a specialty of southern Alsace. Lorraine, renowned for quiches, is also famous for its madeleines, *dragées* (almond candies), macaroons, and the lovely little *mirabelle,* a small yellow plum filled with heady, perfumed nectar. Lorraine shares the Alsatian love of pastry and fruit tarts, served as often with coffee at 4 in the afternoon as after dinner as a dessert. Restaurant prices tend to be lower in Lorraine than in Alsace, but only in German-influenced Alsace will you find *winstubs* (pronounced *veen*-shtoob), cozy, paneled inns serving hearty regional specialties or, between meals, wine and snacks. Mountain-smoked hams and sausages, mushrooms, and freshwater fish are menu mainstays in the Jura. Hard, flavorsome Comté and Beaufort are the choice local Gruyère-style cheeses, along with blue-stripe Morbier, satiny Vacherin (often served melted in its box), and Cancaillotte, its flavor milder than its reek. *Tartiflettes* (diced potatoes in bacony cheese sauce) is a rib-sticking mainstay.

CATEGORY	COST*
$$$$	over 400 frs
$$$	250 frs–400 frs
$$	125 frs–250 frs
$	under 125 frs

*per person for a three-course meal, including tax (20.6%) and tip but not wine

✑ *following the text of a review is your signal that the property has a Web site, where you will find details and, usually, images; for a link, visit www.fodors.com/urls.*

Lodging

Accommodations are easier to find in Lorraine and the Jura than in Alsace, where advance reservations are essential in summer. Alsace is rich in *gîtes,* country houses that can be rented. Throughout Alsace hotels are well scrubbed, with tile bathrooms, good mattresses, and geraniums spilling from every window sill. Lorraine tends to lack the Teutonic comforts of Alsace but is coming around as renovations get under way.

CATEGORY	COST*
$$$$	over 800 frs
$$$	500 frs–800 frs
$$	300 frs–500 frs
$	under 300 frs

**All prices are for a standard double room for two, including tax (20.6%) and service charge.*

Outdoor Activities and Sports

The region is ideal for a variety of outdoor activities: bicycling along the banks of rivers in Lorraine, horseback riding through the forests, fishing in the angler's paradise of Franche-Comté, or hiking in the Vosges and Jura mountains.

Exploring Alsace, Lorraine, and Franche-Comté

Most visitors begin exploring this region to the west—nearest Paris—where the battlegrounds of Verdun provide a poignant introduction to Lorraine. Linger in the artistic city of Nancy and then head east to Strasbourg (146 km [91 mi]), a city of such historic and cultural importance that it is worth exploring in depth. From here tour the rest of Alsace, following the photogenic Route du Vin (Wine Road) to Mulhouse. Finally, head south to Besançon and the spectacular scenery of Franche-Comté and the Jura.

Great Itineraries

You can cover most of Alsace-Lorraine and Franche-Comté in about nine days. With six days you can see the northern part of Lorraine, from Verdun to Nancy, and most of Alsace. Three days will give you just enough time to explore Alsace, including the cosmopolitan city of Strasbourg.

Numbers in the text correspond to numbers in the margin and on the Lorraine, Alsace, Franche-Comté, Nancy, and Strasbourg maps.

IF YOU HAVE 3 DAYS

Explore Alsace, beginning with a day and night in the delightful city of **Strasbourg** ㉗–㊵. The next day start out early, cruising south along the Route du Vin to pretty **Obernai** ㊸; the charming villages of **Barr** ㊺, **Andlau** ㊻, and **Dambach-la-Ville** ㊼; and the dramatic castle in **Haut-Koenigsbourg** ㊾. Spend the night in the wine town of **Ribeauvillé** ㊿ or medieval **Riquewihr** (51). On day three soak up the art and atmosphere in **Colmar** (52)—whose museum is home to a world-famous Grünewald altarpiece—or tour industrial museums in **Mulhouse** (55).

IF YOU HAVE 6 DAYS

Coming from Paris, start at the moving **Verdun** ⑲ battlefields; then head east to the cathedral city of **Metz** ⑳. On day two concentrate on **Nancy** ①–⑱, home to some of the most elegant 18th-century architecture in France. Spend your third evening in **Strasbourg** ㉗–㊵ and your fourth in or around **Obernai** ㊸, visiting **Barr** ㊺ and environs en route. Take in bustling **Sélestat** ㊽, with its fine churches, on day five, along with **Haut-Koenigsbourg** ㊾ and **Ribeauvillé** ㊿, ending up in **Riquewihr** (51). On day six head to **Colmar** (52) or **Mulhouse** (55).

IF YOU HAVE 9 DAYS

Begin in **Verdun** ⑲ and **Metz** ⑳; then head south through Lorraine to the crumbling cathedral town of **Toul** ㉒ and to Joan of Arc's birth-

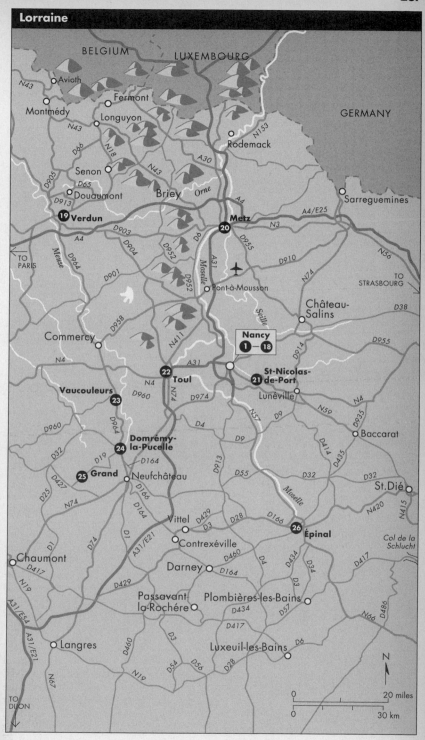

Lorraine

BELGIUM

LUXEMBOURG

GERMANY

N43

Avioth

Fermont

Montmédy

Longuyon

N43

Rodemack

N153

N118

D66

D205

Senon

D65

Douaumont

D913

19 Verdun

Briey

Orne

Metz

20

Sarreguemines

A30

A4

A4/E25

N3

N56

TO
PARIS

A4

Meuse

D903

D904

D952

D952

D6

D955

D910

D74

N56

TO
STRASBOURG

D964

D901

Moselle

A31

Pont-à-Mousson

Château-
Salins

D38

D958

Commercy

N411

Seille

Nancy

1 — 18

D914

D955

N4

A31

22 Toul

St-Nicolas-
de-Port

21

Vaucouleurs

23

N4

D960

N74

D974

Lunéville

D9

N59

N4

D835

Baccarat

D960

D964

**Domrémy-
la-Pucelle**

24

D4

D9

D414

D435

D32

St.Dié

D32

D19

D164

25 Grand

Neufchâteau

D913

D55

D166

Moselle

D32

N420

N415

D32

D427

D166

D429

D28

26 Épinal

Col de la
Schlucht

N74

D164

Vittel

D3

D460

D434

D34

D417

D1

A31/E21

Contrexéville

D4

D3

Chaumont

D417

Darney

D164

Passavant-
la-Rochère

Plombières-les-Bains

D434

D57

N66

D486

D429

D417

N19

A31/E54

Langres

D460

D3

Luxeuil-les-Bains

D6

N67

D54

D56

D28

N19

TO
DIJON

N

0   20 miles

0   30 km

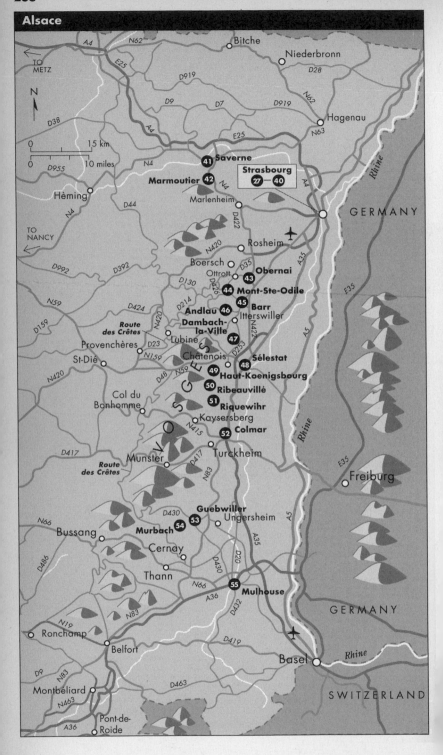

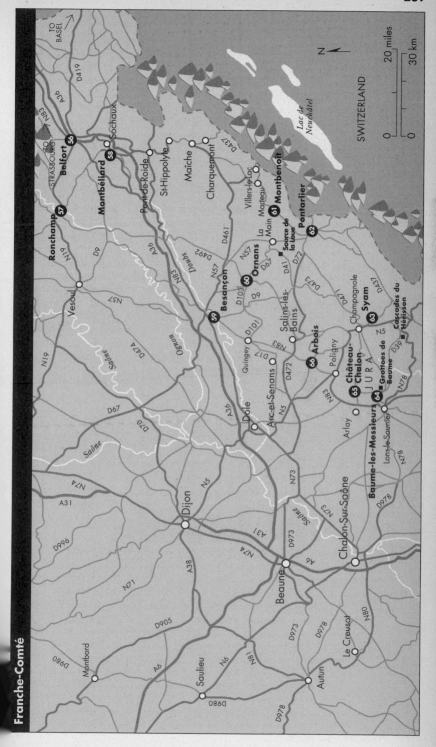

TO
BASEL

N

20 miles

30 km

SWITZERLAND

Lac de Neuchâtel

D419

A36

N83

TO
STRASBOURG

56 Belfort

Sochaux

58 Montbéliard

Pont-de-Roide

St-Hippolyte

Maîche

Charquemont

D437

Villers-le-Lac

La
Moteau
Main

61 Montbenoît

57 Ronchamp

62 Pontarlier

Vesoul

D9

Doubs

D492

D57

D461

N57

Besançon **60** Ornans

Source de
la Loue

D67

D41

D72

D473

D471

D437

Source de
la Loue

Champagnole

63 Syam

Cascades du
Hérisson

N19

N57

N83

Ognon

Saône

D474

59

D103

D9

Salins-les-
Bains

66 Arbois

Poligny

D472

N5

N83

65 Château-
Chalon

64 Grottes de
Baume

Quingey

D17

Arc-et-Senans

Dole

Arlay

Baume-les-Messieurs

Lons-le-Saunier

D39

N78

N5

JURA

D267

Saône

D70

N74

A31

D67

A36

N5

Dijon

N71

A38

D905

Saône

N73

N73

D973

A6

Beaune

Chalon-Sur-Saône

D978

N78

D980

Montbard

Saulieu

N6

N81

D978

Autun

le Creusot

N80

D980

D973

D978

place in **Domrémy-la-Pucelle** ㉔. Spend day three in **Nancy** ①–⑱. On day four make **Strasbourg** ㉗–㊵ your goal. The next day follow the Route du Vin to **Obernai** ㊸, **Mont-Ste-Odile** ㊹, and **Barr** ㊺. Continue south to **Sélestat** ㊽, **Haut-Koenigsbourg** ㊾, **Ribeauvillé** ㊿, and **Riquewihr** (51). On day seven head to one of the following cities: **Colmar** (52), to see its splendid Unterlinden Museum; **Mulhouse** (55), if you're interested in visiting museums of industry and technology; or **Belfort** (56), for its monuments. Spend the night in Colmar or Belfort, or head that night to **Besançon** (59). Explore this historic Franche-Comté town on the morning of day eight; then head to scenic riverside **Ornans** (60) before wheeling west to the wine town of **Arbois** (66). Use Arbois as a base to explore the grandiose Jura scenery at the Reculée des Planches, the Cirque du Fer-à-Cheval, **Baume-les-Messieurs** (64), and the hilltop village of **Château-Chalon** (65).

When to Tour Alsace-Lorraine and Franche-Comté

Outside tourist-packed high summer, June and September are the warmest and sunniest months. Many regional towns and villages, especially the wine villages of Alsace, stage summer festivals, including the spectacular pagan-inspired burning of the three pine trees in Thann (late June), the Flower Carnival in Sélestat (mid-August), and the wine fair in Colmar (first half of August). Some of the region's top sights, however—notably Haut-Koenigsbourg—can be besieged by tourists in July and August, so if you're there then, try to visit early in the morning. Although Lorraine is a lusterless place in winter, the Vosges and Jura mountains make attempts at being ski venues—plentiful snow cannot always be guaranteed—while Strasbourg pays tribute to the Germanic tradition with a Christmas fair.

NANCY

For architectural variety, few French cities match Nancy, which is in the heart of Lorraine, 146 km (91 mi) east of Paris. Medieval ornament, 18th-century grandeur, and Belle Epoque fluidity rub shoulders in the town center, where commercial bustle mingles with stately elegance. Its majesty derives from a long history as home to the powerful dukes of Lorraine, whose double-barred crosses figure prominently on statues and buildings. Never having fallen under the rule of the Holy Roman Empire or, more recently, the Germans, this Lorraine city retains an eminently Gallic charm.

The city is at its most sublimely French in its harmoniously constructed squares and buildings, which, as vestiges of the 18th century, have the quiet refinement that's always associated with the best in French architecture. Curiously enough, it was a Pole, and not a Frenchman, who was responsible for much of what is beautiful in Nancy. Stanislas Leszczynski, ex-King of Poland and father of Marie Leczinska (who married Louis XV of France) was given the kingdom of Lorraine-Habsburg by his royal son-in-law on the understanding that on his death it should revert to France. Stanislas installed himself in Nancy and devoted himself to the glorious embellishment of the city. Today the place Stanislas remains one of the loveliest and most perfectly proportioned squares in the world, with the place de la Carrière, reached through Stanislas's Arc de Triomphe, its close rival with its elegant, homogeneous 18th-century houses.

The Historic Center

Concentrated northeast of the train station, this neighborhood—rich in architectural treasures as well as museums—includes classical place Stanislas and the shuttered, medieval *vieille ville* (old town).

A Good Walk

Begin your walk at the symbolic heart of Nancy, **place Stanislas** ①. On the western corner is the **Musée des Beaux-Arts** ②, the fine arts museum. Cross place Stanislas diagonally and head south down rue Maurice Barrès to the Baroque **Cathédrale** ③. On leaving, turn left on rue St-Georges and right up rue des Dominicains, stopping to admire the elegant stonework on No. 57, the Maison des Adams, named for the sculptors who lived in (and decorated) the edifice in the 18th century.

Recross place Stanislas and go through the monumental Arc de Triomphe, entering into peaceful **place de la Carrière** ④. At the colonnaded Palais du Gouvernement, former home of the governors of Lorraine, turn right into the vast, formal city park known as **La Pépinière** ⑤. From the park's entrance at the foot of place de la Carrière, head straight under the arches and into the vieille ville. Dominating the square is the basilica of **St-Epvre** ⑥, clearly constructed to make up for the absence of a Gothic cathedral in Nancy.

Head immediately right up the picturesque Grande-Rue, with its antiques shops, bookstores, and artisanal bakeries behind brightly painted facades. On your right is the **Palais Ducal** ⑦. Here is the main branch of the Musée Historique Lorraine, a marvelous complex that covers art as well as regional lore. The neighboring **Musée des Arts et Traditions Populaires** ⑧ holds forth in the Couvent des Cordeliers, combining a folk arts museum and a Gothic chapel. At the end of Grande-Rue is the **Porte de la Craffe** ⑨, the last of Nancy's medieval fortifications.

TIMING

Depending on how much time you spend in the museums, this walk could take an hour or a whole day. Note that all the museums are closed on Tuesday.

Sights to See

❸ **Cathédrale.** This vast, frigid edifice was built in the 1740s in a ponderous Baroque style eased in part by florid ironwork by Jean Lamour. Its most notable interior feature is a murky 19th-century fresco in the dome. The **Trésor** (treasury) contains minute 10th-century splendors in carved ivory and gold. ⊠ *Rue St-Georges.*

★ ❽ Just up the street from the Palais Ducal, the quirky, appealing **Musée des Arts et Traditions Populaires,** (Museum of Folk Arts and Traditions) is housed in the **Couvent des Cordeliers** (Convent of the Franciscans, who were known as Cordeliers until the Revolution). It re-creates how local people lived in preindustrial times, using a series of evocative rural interiors. Craftsmen's tools, colorful crockery, stark stone fireplaces, and dark waxed-oak furniture trim the tableaulike settings. Also within the religious complex, the dukes of Lorraine are buried in the crypt of the adjoining **Église des Cordeliers,** a Flamboyant Gothic church; the *gisant* (reclining statue) of Philippa de Gueldra, second wife of René II, is a moving example of Renaissance portraiture, executed in limestone in flowing detail. The octagonal Ducal Chapel was begun in 1607 in the classical style, modeled on the Medici Chapel in Florence. ⊠ *66 Grande-Rue,* ☎ *03–83–32–18–74.* 🖼 *20 frs.* ⊙ *May–Sept., Wed.–Mon. 10–6; Oct.–Apr., Wed.–Sat. and Mon. 10–noon and 2–5, Sun. 10–noon and 2–6.*

★ ❷ **Musée des Beaux-Arts** (Fine Arts Museum). In a splendid building, which now spills over into a spectacular new wing, a broad and varied collection of art treasures live up to the noble white Héré facade. Most striking are the freeze-the-moment realist tableaux painted by native son Emile Friant at the turn of the 20th century. A sizable collection of Lipschitz sculptures includes portrait busts of Gertrude Stein, Jean Cocteau, and Coco Chanel. You'll also find 19th- and 20th-century

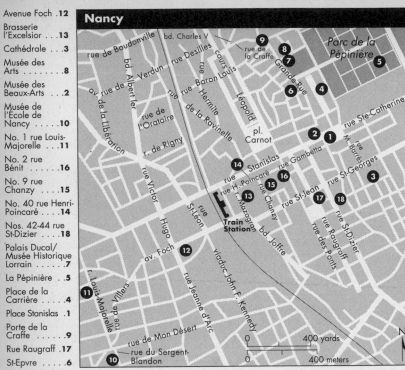

Nancy

paintings by Monet, Manet, Utrillo, and Modigliani; a Caravaggio *An-nunciation* and a wealth of old masters from the Italian, Dutch, Flemish, and French schools; and impressive glassworks by Nancy native Antonin Daum. The showpiece is Rubens's massive *Transfiguration*. Good commentary cards in English are available in every hall. ⊠ *Pl. Stanislas*, ☎ *03–83–85–30–72.* ☞ *30 frs.* ☉ *Wed.–Mon. 10:30–6.*

7 Palais Ducal (Ducal Palace). This palace was built in the 13th century and completely restored at the end of the 15th century and again after a fire at the end of the 19th century. The main entrance to the palace, and the **Musée Historique Lorrain** (Lorraine History Museum), which it now houses, is 80 yards down the street from the spectacularly flamboyant Renaissance portal. A spiral stone staircase leads up to the palace's most impressive room, the **Galerie des Cerfs** (Stags Gallery). Exhibits here (including pictures, armor, and books) recapture the Renaissance mood of the 16th and 17th centuries—one of elegance and merrymaking, though not devoid of stern morality: An elaborate series of huge tapestries, *La Condemnation du Banquet* (Condemnation of the Banquet), expounds on the evils of drink and gluttony. Exhibits feature Stanislas and his court, including "his" oft-portrayed dwarf; a section on Nancy in the revolutionary era; and works of Lorraine native sons, including a collection of Jacques Callot engravings and a handful of Georges de La Tours. ⊠ *64 Grande-Rue*, ☎ *03–83–32–18–74.* ☞ *20 frs.* ☉ *May–Sept., Wed.–Sat. and Mon 10–noon and 2–5, Sun. 10–noon and 2–6.*

5 La Pépinière. This lovely, landscaped city park has labeled ancient trees, a rose garden, playgrounds, a carousel, and a small zoo. ⊠ *Entrance off pl. de la Carrière.*

4 Place de la Carrière. Lined with pollarded trees and handsome 18th-century mansions (another successful collaboration between Stanislas and Héré), this elegant rectangle leads from place Stanislas to th colonnaded facade of the **Palais du Gouvernement** (Government Palace), former home of the governors of Lorraine.

★ ❶ **Place Stanislas.** With its severe, gleaming-white Classical facades given a touch of Rococo jollity by fanciful wrought gilt-iron railings, this perfectly proportioned square will probably remind many of Versailles. The square is named for Stanislas Leszczynski, twice dethroned as king of Poland but offered the throne of Lorraine by Louis XV (his son-in-law) in 1736. Stanislas left a legacy of spectacular buildings, undertaken between 1751 and 1760 by architect Emmanuel Héré and ironwork genius Jean Lamour. The sculpture of Stanislas dominating the square went up in the 1830s, when the square was named after him. Framing the exit is the **Arc de Triomphe**, erected in the 1750s to honor Louis XV. The facade features the gods of war and the gods of peace; Louis's portrait is here.

❾ **Porte de la Craffe.** The only remains of Nancy's medieval fortifications loom at one end of the Grande-Rue. Built in the 14th and 15th centuries, this arch served as a prison through the Revolution. The thistle and cross are symbols of Lorraine.

❻ **St-Epvre.** A 275-ft spire towers over this splendid neo-Gothic church rebuilt in the 1860s. Most of the 2,800 square yards of stained glass were created by the Geyling workshop in Vienna; the chandeliers were made in Liège, Belgium; many carvings are the work of Margraff of Munich; the heaviest of the eight bells was cast in Budapest; and the organ, though manufactured by Merklin of Paris, was inaugurated in 1869 by Austrian composer Anton Bruckner. ⊠ *Pl. de la Carrière.*

Art Nouveau Nancy

Nancy was a principal source of the revolution in decorative arts that produced Art Nouveau and Jugendstil (the German version of Art Nouveau). Inspired and coordinated by the glass master Émile Gallé, the local movement, formalized in 1901 as L'École de Nancy, nurtured the floral *pâte de verre* (literally, glass dough) works of Antonin Daum and Gallé; the Tiffany-esque stained-glass windows of Jacques Gruber; the fluid furniture of Louis Majorelle; and the sinuous architecture of Lucien Weissenburger, Émile André, and Eugène Vallin. Thanks to these artists, Nancy's downtown architecture flows and flowers above the sidewalks like a living garden.

A Good Walk

The **Musée de l'École de Nancy** ⑩ is the best place to immerse yourself in the fanciful style that crept into interiors and exteriors throughout Nancy. To get to the museum from the busy shopping street rue St-Jean (just up rue des Dominicains from place Stanislas), take Bus 5 or 25 uphill and get off at place Pain-Levée. From the museum turn left down rue du Sergent Blandan and walk about four blocks to **No. 1 rue Louis-Majorelle** ⑪. Cut east to place de la Commanderie and head up **avenue Foch** ⑫ to admire the colorful structures at Nos. 71, 69, and 41. Hike over the Viaduct Kennedy and the *gare* (train station), turn left past the department store Printemps, and follow rue Mazagran to the **Brasserie l'Excelsior** ⑬. Turn right toward **No. 40 rue Henri-Poincaré** ⑭. Turn right and walk past **No. 9 rue Chanzy** ⑮ (now the Banque Nationale de Paris). Head left to find **No. 2 rue Bénit** ⑯, with its ornate metal structure. Head south to rue St-Jean; at the corner of **rue Raugraff** ⑰ are two bay windows, remnants of stores that were once here. Continue down rue St-Jean and turn right to find **Nos. 42–44 rue St-Dizier** ⑱. Many more Art Nouveau addresses are scattered throughout the city; you can get a detailed map at the tourist office.

TIMING

Allow a full morning to linger in the Musée de l'École de Nancy and then, during the course of about an hour and a half, wander back circuitously toward the vieille ville, stopping to admire Art Nouveau masterworks along the way.

Sights to See

⑫ Avenue Foch. This busy boulevard lined with mansions was built for Nancy's affluent 19th-century middle class. At No. 69, the occasional pinnacle suggests Gothic influence on a house built in 1902 by Émile André, who designed the neighboring No. 71 two years later. No. 41, built by Paul Charbonnier in 1905, bears ironwork by Majorelle.

⑬ Brasserie l'Excelsior. This bustling brasserie has a severely rhythmic facade that is invitingly illuminated at night. The popular restaurant continues to evoke the turn of the century, both in its historic decor and its fin-de-siècle ambience. ⊠ *5 rue Mazagran.*

★ ⑩ Musée de l'École de Nancy (School of Nancy Museum). The only museum in France devoted to Art Nouveau is housed in an airy turn-of-the-century garden–town house. It was built by Eugène Corbin, an early patron of the School of Nancy. There isn't a straight line in the house; pianos ooze, bedsteads undulate; the wood itself, hard and burnished as it is, seems to have melted and re-formed. ⊠ *36 rue du Sergent-Blandan,* ☎ *03–83–40–14–86.* 🖾 *30 frs, 40 frs for joint ticket with Musée des Beaux-Arts (☞ below).* ☉ *Mon. 2–6, Wed.–Sun. 10:30–6.*

⑪ No. 1 rue Louis-Majorelle. This villa was built in 1902 by Paris architect Henri Sauvage for Majorelle himself. Sinuous metal supports seem to sneak up on the unsuspecting balcony like swaying cobras, and there are two grand windows by Gruber: one lighting the staircase (visible from the street) and the other the dining room on the south side of the villa (peek around from the garden side).

⑯ No. 2 rue Bénit. This elaborately worked metal exoskeleton, the first in Nancy (1901), is as functional as it is beautiful. The fluid decoration reminds you of the building's past as a seed supply store. Windows were worked by Gruber; the builders were Henry-Barthélemy Gutton (architect) and Henri Gutton (engineer); Victor Schertzer conceived the metal frame.

⑮ No. 9 rue Chanzy. Designed by architect Émile André, this lovely structure—now a bank—can be visited during business hours. You can still see the cabinetry of Majorelle, the decor of Paul Charbonnier, and the stained-glass windows of Gruber.

⑭ No. 40 rue Henri-Poincaré. The Lorraine thistle and brasserie hops weave through this undulating exterior, designed by architects Émile Toussaint and Louis Marchal. Victor Schertzer conceived this metal structure in 1908, after the success of No. 2 rue Bénit. Gruber's windows are enhanced by the curving metalwork of Majorelle.

⑱ Nos. 42–44 rue St-Dizier. Eugène Vallin and Georges Biet left their mark on this graceful 1903 bank structure, open weekdays 8:30–5:30.

⑰ Rue Raugraff. Once there were two stores here, both built in 1901. The bay windows are the last vestiges of the work of Charles Vallin, Émile André, and Eugène Vallin. ⊠ *At corner of rue St-Jean.*

Dining and Lodging

$$$ ✕ Capucin Gourmand. With a chic new decor making the most of Nancy's Art Nouveau pâté de verre, including a giant chandelier and glowing mushroom lamps on the tables, this landmark puts its best foot forward under chef Hervé Fourrière. Soigné specialties include a light lobster lasagna with mushrooms, beef marrow served in the bone with truffles and white beans, and a trio of fresh mango desserts. The list of Toul wines is also most admirable. ✉ *31 rue Gambetta,* ☎ *03–83–35–26–98. Reservations essential. V. Closed Mon., Aug., and end Feb.–early March. No dinner Sun.*

$$ ✕ **Comptoir du Petit Gastrolâtre.** Under the inspired direction of chef Patrick Tanesy, this stylish checked-cloth bistro off place Stanislas serves sophisticated regional cooking. Combinations include baeckoffe with foie gras, mullet with pigs' feet, and authentic *bouchée à la reine* (pastry shell with creamed meat) complete with cock's comb, sweetbreads, and morel mushrooms. Reserve for summer terrace dining. ✉ *1 pl. Vaudemont,* ☎ *03–83–35–51–94. MC, V. Closed Sun. No lunch Mon.*

$ ✕ **Au P'tit Cuny.** If you were inspired by the rustic exhibits of the Musée
★ des Arts et Traditions Populaires, cross the street and sink your teeth into authentic Lorraine cuisine in the form of choucroute, *tête de veau* (veal head), or tangy veal *tourte* (pie). ✉ *97–99 Grande-Rue,* ☎ *03–83–32–85–94. MC, V. Closed Sun.–Mon.*

$$$ ✕🏨 **Grand Hôtel de la Reine.** This hotel is every bit as grand as place
★ Stanislas, on which it stands; the magnificent 18th-century building is officially classified as a historic monument. Rooms are in a suitably flamboyant Louis XV style; the most luxurious look out onto the square. The restaurant, Le Stanislas, features ambitious Eric Cizeron in the kitchen; his sophisticated touch bodes well: beef carpaccio with truffles, *dorade* crisped in sesame seeds, and poached plums stuffed with Roquefort. ✉ *2 pl. Stanislas, 54000,* ☎ *03–83–35–03–01,* 🅵🅰🆇 *03–83–32–86–04. 48 rooms. Restaurant, bar. AE, DC, MC, V.* ✎

$ 🏨 **Carnot.** This somewhat generic downtown hotel, with 1950s-style comforts and mostly tiny rooms, is handy to cours Léopold parking and backs up on the old town. Corner rooms are sizable, back rooms quiet. ✉ *2 cours Léopold, 54000,* ☎ *03–83–36–59–58,* 🅵🅰🆇 *03–83–37–00–19. 28 rooms. Breakfast room. MC, V.*

$ 🏨 **Hôtel de Guise.** Deep in the shuttered old town, this hotel is in a formerly noble mansion with a magnificent stone-floor entry. Unfortunately, the dramatic sweeping stairs wind up to a shabby, creaky renovation job. Breakfast on the once-grand main floor and an excellent location make this a good choice if you're a bargain-hunting romantic. ✉ *18 rue de Guise, 54000,* ☎ *03–83–32–24–68,* 🅵🅰🆇 *03–83–35–75–63. 42 rooms. MC, V. Closed 2 wks in Dec. and Aug.*

Nightlife and the Arts

On summer evenings (June–September) at 10 PM, place Stanislas comes alive with a **sound-and-light show,** and the doors of the magnificent Hôtel de Ville are opened to the public (15 francs). Nancy's **Orchestre Symphonique et Lyrique** (✉ 1 rue Ste-Catherine, ☎ 03–83–85–30–65) is a highly rated classical orchestra.

Le Chat Noir (✉ 63 rue Jeanne-d'Arc, ☎ 03–83–28–49–29) draws a thirtysomething crowd to retro-theme dance parties. The **Majéstic** (✉ 22 rue St-Dizier, ☎ 03–83–32–83–42) has a bar, dance floor, and occasional live music. **Métro** (✉ 1 rue du Général-Hoche, ☎ 03–83–40–25–13) is a popular dance club. **La Place** (✉ 9 pl. Stanislas, ☎ 03–83–35–24–14) attracts a young upscale crowd that comes to dance.

Shopping

Daum (✉ 17 rue des Cristalleries, ☎ 03–83–30–80–20) sells deluxe crystal and examples of the city's traditional Art Nouveau pâte de verre.**Librairie Lorraine** (✉ 93 Grande-Rue, ☎ 03–83–36–79–52), across from the Musée des Arts et Traditions, is an excellent bookstore devoted entirely to Lorraine history and culture.

LORRAINE

In long-neglected Lorraine there are hidden treasures worth digging up. You can study the evolution of Gregorian chant in the municipal museum in Metz, where it was first codified. You can observe the luster of Baccarat crystal at its ancient factory, and the grace of Daum glassware in Nancy (☞ *above*), where it sprung from the roots of Art Nouveau. You can hear the church bells in which Joan of Arc heard voices challenging her to save Orléans, and stand on the wounded earth of Verdun. And throughout Lorraine you'll find the statue of the region's patron saint, St. Nicholas—old St. Nick himself—with three children in a *saloir* (salting tub). Every December 6 Lorraine schoolchildren reenact the legend: A greedy butcher slaughters and salts down three children as hams, but when St. Nicholas drops by his place for a meal, he discovers the deed and brings them back to life.

Verdun

⑲ *66 km (41 mi) west of Metz, 93 km (58 mi) northwest of Nancy, 262 km (164 mi) east of Paris.*

A key strategic site along the Meuse Valley, Verdun is famous, above all, for the 10-month battle between the French and the Germans in World War I. It left more than 350,000 dead and nine villages wiped off the map. Both sides fought with suicidal fury, yet no significant ground was gained or lost. The French declared victory once they regained the 10 km (6 mi) the Germans had taken, but bloody scrapping continued until the Armistice, leaving a total of more than 700,000 dead. To this day, the scenes of battle are scarred by bomb craters, stunted vegetation, and thousands of unexploded mines and shells, rendering the area permanently uninhabitable.

The most shocking memorial of the carnage is the **Ossuaire de Douaumont,** 10 km (6 mi) north of the city. The bizarre, evocative structure— a little like a cross, a lot like a bomb—rears up over an endless sea of graves, its ground-level windows revealing undignified heaps of human bones harvested from the killing fields. Climb to the top of the tower (6 francs) for a view of the cemetery. In the basement is the shown film that dwells on the agony of the futile butchery. ☎ 03–29–84–54–81. ▤ *Slide show 17 frs.* ⊙ *Mar. and Oct., daily 9–noon and 2–5:30; Apr., daily 9–6; May–Aug., daily 9–6:30; Sept., daily 9–noon and 2–6; Nov., daily 9–noon and 2–5.*

The square, modern **Mémorial de Verdun** (Verdun Memorial), in the town of Fleury-devant-Douaumont, is a World War I museum with emotionally charged texts and video commentary, as well as uniforms, weapons, and the artwork of soldiers (Art Nouveau vases hammered from artillery shells). ☎ 03–29–84–35–34. ▤ *30 frs.* ⊙ *Mid-Apr.–Dec., daily 9–6; Feb.–Mar., daily 9–noon and 2–6.*

Dining and Lodging

$$$ ✕▥ **Coq Hardi.** This large, steep-roof, half-timber hotel, built in 1827 on the banks of the Meuse, is a Lorraine landmark, with comfy, unpretentious rooms and a familial welcome. Now young new chef Frédéric Engel brings a breath of fresh air to the place. His training at Bueheriesel and Crocodile in Strasbourg shows, blending fashionable Mediterranean touches with Lorraine tradition: frothy pea soup "cappuccino" with Spanish ham, pig's foot stuffed with foie gras, and raspberry-lemon gratin. ⌧ *8 av. de la Victoire, 55100,* ☎ *03–29–86–36–36,* FAX *03–29–86–09–21. 32 rooms. Restaurant. AE, DC, MC, V.*

Metz

★ ❷ *66 km (41 mi) east of Verdun, 53 km (33 mi) north of Nancy, 160 km (100 mi) northwest of Strasbourg.*

Despite its industrial background, Metz, the capital of the Moselle region, is one of France's greenest cities: Parks, gardens, and leafy squares frame an imposing mix of military and classical architecture, all carved out of the region's yellow sandstone. At the old town's heart is one of the finest Gothic cathedrals in France.

The **Musée d'Art et d'Histoire** (Museum of Art and History), two blocks up from the cathedral in a 17th-century former convent, has a wide-ranging collection of French and German paintings from the 18th century on; military arms and uniforms; and religious works of art stored in the **Grenier de Chèvremont,** a granary built in 1457. Best by far are the stelae, statuary, jewelry, arms, clothing, and plumbing evoking the city's Gallo-Roman and Merovingian past. Not to be missed: the ethereal reconstruction of the ancient chapel of St-Pierre-aux-Nonnains (☞ *below*). Unfortunately, the museum's labyrinth of stairways excludes wheelchairs, strollers, and poor navigators. ⌧ *2 rue du Haut-Poirier,* ☎ *03–87–75–10–18.* 🎫 *30 frs.* ☉ *Daily 10–noon and 2–6.*

★ At 137 ft from floor to roof, the **Cathédrale St-Étienne** (⌧ Pl. des Armes) is one of France's tallest; and thanks to nearly 1½ acres of window space, one of the brightest. The narrow 13th- to 14th-century nave channels the eye toward the dramatically raised 16th-century choir, whose walls have given way to huge sheets of richly colored, gemlike glass by masters old and modern, including artist Marc Chagall (1887–1985). The oldest windows—on the right rear wall of the transepts above the modern organ—date from the 12th century and, in their dark, mosaiclike simplicity, are a stark contrast to the ethereal new stained glass. A pair of symmetrical 290-ft towers flank the nave, marking the division between the two churches that were merged to form the cathedral. The great Christmas windstorms of 1999 ripped a stone spire from the cathedral roof and sent it hurtling, point down, through the roof and into the sacristy, where it missed the custodian thanks to a few sturdy beams; repairs have temporarily closed from view the treasures displayed within. The **Grand Portal,** beneath the large rose window, was reconstructed by the Germans at the turn of the century; the statues of the prophets include, on the right, *Daniel,* sculpted to resemble Kaiser Wilhelm II (his unmistakable upturned mustache was shaved off in 1940).

The lively **Marché Couvert** (Market Hall; ⌧ Pl. de la Cathédrale) was built as a bishop's palace at the end of the 18th century, but the Revolution nipped this decadence in the bud, and it was converted to its current, more sensible use. The right flank offers artisanal farm-cured cheeses and still-flopping seafood. At the bottom of the hill that slopes down rue d'Estrées from the market, veer left and cut right over the rushing river for picturesque views of bridges and balconies laden with flowers.

Take in the broad perspective of grand classical symmetry on the **place de la Comédie,** with its turn-of-the-century Protestant temple. The curving sandstone buildings date from the 18th century and include the opera, theater, and département seat.

The small, heavily restored church of **St-Pierre-aux-Nonnains** (⌧ rue Poncelet) has round stones and rows of red bricks thought to date from the 4th century, predating Attila the Hun's sacking of Metz; thus, Metz claims the oldest church in France.

But you may want to skip the church itself: The best of the rare Merovingian ornaments salvaged from the 6th-century version of the chapel are displayed in a full reproduction in the Museum of Art and History (☞ *above*), demonstrating as chronologies never can how early Christian times mixed the culture and tastes of Celts, Romans, and Gauls.

Dining and Lodging

$$$ ✕ **La Dinanderie.** Chef Claude Piergiorgi serves inventive cuisine—scallops with delicate bacon threads, farm pigeon in salt crust, and pear gratin with gingerbread ice cream—with dependable flair. The intimate restaurant is across the Moselle, a 10-minute hike from the cathedral. ⊠ *2 rue de Paris,* ☎ *03–87–30–14–40. AE, MC, V. Closed Sun.–Mon.*

$$ ✕ **La Baraka.** Below the cathedral, this classic French-Moroccan couscous spot offers a fiery but delicious and digestible break from French cooking. ⊠ *24 pl. de Chambre,* ☎ *03–87–36–33–92. MC, V. Closed Wed.*

$$ ✕ **Pont St-Marcel.** Murals, dirndl skirts, and rib-sticking old-style cuisine make this a culinary plunge into Lorraine culture. There's quiche, of course, but also stewed rabbit, *potée* (boiled pork and cabbage), and carp. The list of Lorraine wines (from Toul) is encyclopedic, with the oak-cured red from Laroppe worth the splurge. In summer reserve on the tiny terrace on the river. ⊠ *1 rue du Pont St-Marcel,* ☎ *03–87–30–12–29. AE, DC, MC, V.*

$ ✕ **La Dauphiné.** Come to this unpretentious barrel-vaulted lunch spot for *tourte Lorraine* (meat pie), a plat du jour with delicious gratin potatoes and a generous slice of fruit tart. Locals claim permanent lunch stations, but there's room upstairs, too. It's between the cathedral and the museum. ⊠ *8 rue du Chanoine-Collin,* ☎ *03–87–36–03–04. MC, V. Closed Sun. No dinner Mon.–Thurs.*

$ ✕ **Le Grand Café.** Catercorner from the cathedral entrance, this stylish Belle Epoque–style brasserie has tables spilling onto place d'Armes. Lorraine specialties include *cochon de lait* (suckling pig), local lamb and rabbit, and succulent lard-roasted potatoes. ⊠ *14 pl. d'Armes,* ☎ *03–87–75–35–09. MC, V.*

$$–$$$ ☷ **Royal Bleu Marine.** This fully modernized hotel, taken over and buffed up by the Campanile chain, occupies a sumptuous Belle Epoque building not far from the train station. Rooms come in a choice of styles (old-fashioned luxury versus simpler modernity); all are soundproof. ⊠ *23 av. Foch, 57011,* ☎ *03–87–66–81–11,* FAX *03–87–56–13–16. 61 rooms. Restaurant, bar, sauna, exercise room. AE, DC, MC, V.* ✍

$$ ☷ **Cathédrale.** From its waxed plank floors, ironwork banister, beamed
★   ceilings, and French windows to its views of the cathedral, this gem of a hotel is reason enough to spend the night in Metz. The country-chic bedspreads, linen drapes, and hand-painted furniture are the work of the friendly owner; she collected all the antiques, too. Breakfast is served in the Baraka, downstairs (☞ *above*). ⊠ *25 pl. de Chambre, 57000,* ☎ *03–87–75–00–02,* FAX *03–87–75–40–75. 20 rooms. Restaurant. AE, DC, MC, V.*

St-Nicolas-de-Port

㉑   *20 km (12 mi) southeast of Nancy.*

The small industrial town of St-Nicolas-de-Port is saved from mediocrity by its colossal basilica. Legend has it that a finger of St. Nicholas was brought to the town during the 11th-century Crusades. Holding such a priceless relic, the **Basilique de St-Nicolas-de-Port** (1495–1555) was rapidly besieged by pilgrims (including Joan of Arc, who came to ask St. Nicolas's blessings on her famous journey to Orléans). The simplified column capitals and elaborate rib vaulting are shining examples of Flamboyant Gothic enjoying a final fling before the gathering impetus of the Renaissance, as are the 280-ft onion-dome towers, almost symmetrical but, as was the Gothic wont, not quite. Inside, the slender, freestanding 90-ft pillars in the transept are the highest in France.

Toul

㉒ *23 km (14 mi) west of Nancy.*

The old town of Toul, nestled behind mossy, star-shape ramparts, has been a bishopric since AD 365 and merited visits from the Frankish king Clovis to study the Christian faith; from Charlemagne in passing; and from a young, premilitary Joan of Arc, who was sued in the Toul court for breach of promise when she threw over a beau for the voice of God. In 1700, under Louis XIV, the military engineer Vauban built the thrusting ramparts around the town.

The ramshackle streets of central Toul haven't changed much for centuries—not since the embroidered twin-tower facade, a Flamboyant Gothic masterpiece, was woven onto the **Cathédrale St-Étienne** in the second half of the 15th century. The cathedral's interior, begun in 1204, is long (321 ft), airy (105 ft high), and more restrained than its exuberant facade. On one side of the cathedral are the 14th-century **cloisters,** and on the other is a pleasant **garden** behind the **Hôtel de Ville** (Town Hall), built in 1740 as the Bishop's Palace. ⊠ *Pl. d'Armes.* ☉ *Summer, daily 9–6; winter, daily 9–dark.*

The **Musée Municipal** (Town Museum), in a former medieval hospital, has a well-preserved *Salle des Malades* (Patients' Ward) dating from the 13th century. Archaeological finds, ceramics, tapestries, and medieval sculpture are on display. ⊠ *25 rue Gouvion-St-Cyr,* ☎ *03–83–64–13–38.* 🎫 *17 frs.* ☉ *Apr.–Oct., Wed.–Mon. 10–noon and 2–6; Nov.–Mar., Wed.–Mon. 2–6.*

Dining

$$$ ✕ **Le Dauphin.** In a bleak industrial neighborhood and a dated decor, this grand restaurant seems out of place in humble Toul. But the modern and imaginative cooking of Christophe Vohmann draws kudos for its exotic touches and balance of flavor—opt for the langoustines with ginger and radishes or the local foie gras with artichokes. ⊠ *65 allée Gaumiron,* ☎ *03–83–43–13–46. AE, DC, MC, V. Closed Mon. No dinner Sun.*

Vaucouleurs

㉓ *24 km (15 mi) southwest of Toul on D960.*

Below the medieval walls and ruins of Robert de Baudricourt's ancient château, in the modest market town of Vaucouleurs, you can see the **Porte de France,** through which Joan of Arc led her armed soldiers to Orléans. The barefoot Maid of Orléans spent a year within these walls, first wheedling an audience with Baudricourt and then, having convinced him of her mission, learning to ride and to sword-fight.

Dining and Lodging

$ ✕🏠 **Relais de la Poste.** On the main street, this simple hotel has quiet rooms and a pleasant, intimate restaurant (closed Monday; no dinner Sunday). The good regional menu is served noon and night. A friendly family cooks, serves the meals, and checks you in. ⊠ *12 av. André Maginot, 55140,* ☎ *03–29–89–40–01,* 𝖥𝖠𝖷 *03–29–89–40–93. 9 rooms. Restaurant. MC, V. Closed end Dec.–Jan.*

Domrémy-la-Pucelle

㉔ *40 km (25 mi) southwest of Toul, 19 km (12 mi) south of Vaucouleurs.*

Joan of Arc was born in a stone hut in Domrémy-la-Pucelle in either 1411 or 1412. You can see it (though Luc Besson had it burned to the ground in his wildly fictionalized 1999 film), as well as the church where she was baptized, the actual statue of St. Marguerite before which she prayed, and the hillside where she tended sheep and first heard voices telling her to take up arms and save France from the English.

The humble stone-and-stucco **Maison Natale Jeanne d'Arc** (Joan of Arc Birthplace)—an irregular, slope-roofed former cowshed—has been preserved with some reverence. Now an inspired new museum called the Centre Johannique has been built, complete with a film and mannequins in period costume, to tell Joan of Arc's amazing story. After she heard mystical voices, Joan walked 19 km (12 mi) to Vaucouleurs (☞ *above*). Dressed and mounted like a man, she led her forces to lift the siege of Orléans, defeated the English, and escorted the unseated Charles VII to Reims, to be crowned king of France. Military missions after Orléans failed—including an attempt to retake Paris—and she was captured at Compiègne. The English turned her over to the Church, which sent her to be tried by the Inquisition for witchcraft and heresy. She was convicted, excommunicated, and burned at the stake in Rouen (☞ Chapter 5)—but was she? A new historical theory surmises she was never actually burned, for she was actually a distant relative of the royal family and not quite the "peasant" she was made out to be. ⊠ *2 rue de la Basilique,* ☎ *03–29–06–95–86.* ⊡ *20 frs.* ☉ *Apr.–Sept., daily 9–noon and 2–6:30; Oct.–Mar., Wed.–Mon. 9:30–noon and 2–5.*

The ornate late-19th-century **Basilique du Bois-Chenu** (Aged-Forest Basilica), a pleasant walk up a country road from Joan of Arc's birthplace, has enormous painted panels telling her story in glowing Pre-Raphaelite tones. Here you can see Joan's budding role as symbol of French nationalist pride, passionately illustrated in the shadow of Prussian defeat.

Lodging

$ 🏨 **Jeanne d'Arc.** Stay next door to Joan of Arc's childhood church and wake to the bells that summoned her voices. Accommodations are considerably less evocative, in jazzy '60s tile and paneling, but bathrooms are spotless and breakfasts (in-room only) generous. ⊠ *1 rue Principale, 88630,* ☎ *03–29–06–96–06. 12 rooms. No credit cards. Closed mid-Nov.–Mar.*

Grand

㉕ *15 km (9 mi) northwest of Domrémy-la-Pucelle: From Domrémy follow signs down country roads west toward Grand.*

In the tiny, enigmatic hamlet of Grand, a spring developed into a center for the worship of the Gallo-Roman sun god Apollo-Grannus. It was important enough to draw the Roman emperors Caracalla and Constantine. Thus, Grand today is a treasure trove of classical ruins.

At the entry to the village the remains of a large **amphitheater** that once seated 20,000 are being reconstructed as an outdoor theater; displays illustrate its history. In a tiny museum in the upper village there is a marvelously expressive floor **mosaic** with realistic animal details. Surrounding the mosaic are scraps of exotic stone and relics transported from across two continents, bearing witness to this isolated village's opulent past. ☎ *03–29–06–63–43.* ⊡ *Amphitheater and mosaic 20 frs.* ☉ *Apr.–Sept., daily 9–noon and 2–7; Oct.–mid-Dec. and mid-Jan.–Mar., Wed.–Mon. 10–noon and 2–5.*

Épinal

㉖ *84 km (53 mi) southeast of Domrémy, 69 km (43 mi) south of Nancy, 97 km (61 mi) north of Belfort.*

On the Moselle River at the feet of the Vosges, Épinal, a printing center since 1735, is famous throughout France for boldly colored prints, popular illustrations, and hand-colored stencils. **L'Imagerie Pellerin,** the artisanal workshop, has a slide show tracing the history of local printing. ✉ *42 bis quai de Dogneville,* ☎ *03–29–31–28–88.* 🎫 *Free; guided tour with slide show 30 frs.* ⊙ *Tours at 9:30, 11, 3, and 4:30 for 45 mins. Gallery-salesroom open between tours Sept.–June Mon.–Sat. 9–noon and 2–6:30, Sun. 2–6:30; July–Aug. Mon–Sat. 9–7, Sun. 2–7.*

On an island in the Moselle in the center of Épinal, the spectacular **Musée Départemental d'Art Ancien et Contemporain** (Museum of Ancient and Contemporary Art) is in a renovated 17th-century hospital, whose classical traces are still visible under a dramatic barrel-vaulted skylight. It contains France's fourth-largest collection of contemporary art, as well as Gallo-Roman artifacts; rural tools and local faience; and old masters, including some fine drawings and watercolors by Fragonard and Boucher. ✉ *1 pl. Lagarde,* ☎ *03–29–82–20–33.* 🎫 *30 frs.* ⊙ *Wed.–Mon. 10–6.*

The small but bustling old town is anchored by the lovely old **Basilique St-Maurice,** a low gray-stone basilica blending Romanesque and Gothic styles. Its deep 15th-century entry porch prepares you for passing into dark, holy space. ✉ *Pl. St-Goëry,* ☎ *03–29–82–58–36.*

STRASBOURG

Though centered in the heart of Alsace 490 km (304 mi) east of Paris, and drawing appealingly on Alsatian gemütlichkeit (friendliness), the city of Strasbourg is a cosmopolitan French cultural center and, in many ways, the unofficial capital of Europe. Against an irresistible backdrop of old half-timber houses, waterways, and the colossal single spire of its red-sandstone cathedral, which seems to insist imperiously that you pay homage to its majestic beauty, Strasbourg is an incongruously sophisticated mix of museums, elite schools (including that notorious hothouse for blooming politicos, the École Nationale d'Administration, or National Administration School), international think tanks, and the European Parliament.

The Romans knew Strasbourg as Argentoratum before it came to be known as Strateburgum, or City of (Cross) Roads. After centuries as part of the Germanic Holy Roman Empire, the city was united with France in 1681, but retained independence regarding legislation, education, and religion under the honorific title Free Royal City. Since World War II Strasbourg has become a symbolic city, embodying Franco-German reconciliation and the wider idea of a united Europe. The city center is effectively an island within two arms of the River Ill; most major sites are found here, but the northern districts also contain some fine buildings erected over the last 100 years, culminating in the Palais de l'Europe.

Note to drivers: The new configuration of downtown streets makes it difficult to approach the center via the autoroute exit marked STRASBOURG CENTRE. Instead, hold out for the exit marked PLACE DE L'ÉTOILE and follow signs to CATHÉDRALE/CENTRE VILLE. At place du Corbeau, veer left across the Ill, and go straight to the place Gutenberg parking garage, a block from the cathedral.

The Historic Heart

This central area, from the cathedral to picturesque Petite France, concentrates the best of old Strasbourg, with its twisting backstreets, flower-lined courts, tempting shops, and inviting winstubs (wine taverns).

A Good Walk

Begin at place Gutenberg and head up rue des Hallebardes. To see a bit of Strasbourg's appealing combination of cozy winstubs, medieval alleys, and chic shops, turn left up rue des Orfevres (marked RUE PITTORESQUE); then circle right down rue Chaudron and again down rue du Sanglier. Head back right down rue des Hallebardes and onto place de la Cathédrale, passing the landmark Maison Kammerzells (☞ Dining and Lodging, *below*).

Emerging from this close-packed warren of dark-timber buildings and narrow streets, you'll confront the magnificent **Cathédrale Notre-Dame** ㉗. Continue across the square to the **Musée de l'Oeuvre Notre-Dame** ㉘, with its collection of statuary. Leaving the museum, turn right and approach the vast neighboring palace, the **Palais Rohan** ㉙. Once the headquarters of the powerful prince-bishops, the Rohans, it now houses the art and archaeology museums.

Once out of the château's entry court, double back left and turn left again, following rue des Rohan to the river. From here you can take a boat tour (☞ Outdoor Activities, *below*) of the old town. Veer right away from the water and cross place du Marché aux Cochons de Lait (Suckling Pig Market Square) and place de la Grande Boucherie (Grand Slaughterhouse Square) to reach the **Musée Historique** ㉚, with its collection of paintings, weapons, and furniture from Strasbourg (reopening in mid-2001 after renovations). Across the street is the modern glass entrance to the **Ancienne Douane** ㉛, the former customs house, now a vast venue for temporary exhibitions. Over the Ill, cross Pont du Corbeau and veer right to the **Musée Alsacien** ㉜, where you can get a glimpse of how Alsatian families used to live.

Now cross back over the river on the Pont St-Nicolas and follow the riverside promenade west to the picturesque quarter of **Petite France** ㉝. At Pont St-Martin, take rue des Dentelles to rue du Bain aux Plantes. Explore the alleys, courtyards, cafés, and shop windows as you work your way west. Eventually you'll reach the four monumental **Ponts Couverts** ㉞. Just beyond the bridges lies the grass-roof dam, the **Barrage Vauban** ㉟. Climb to the top; from here you'll see a gleaming glass-frame building, the new **Musée d'Art Moderne et Contemporain** ㊱.

TIMING

Allow at least a full day to see Strasbourg—perhaps visiting the old town and cathedral in the morning, ending at 12:30 with the astronomical clock, and then lunch on a nearby backstreet. The afternoon might allow a museum stop and time to wander through Petite France. Two days would allow more museum time; a third day would allow you to take in the monumental sights on place de la République and the Palais de l'Europe (☞ *below*).

Sights to See

㉛ Ancienne Douane (Old Customs House). The airport-hangar scale and flexible walls lend themselves to enormous expositions of old-master paintings as well as archaeology and history at this gallery in a former customs house on the Ill River. ✉ *1 rue de Vieux-Marché-aux-Poissons,* ☎ *03–88–52–50–00.* ▣ *30 frs.* ◷ *Daily 11–6:30.*

㉟ Barrage Vauban (Vauban Dam). Just beyond the Ponts Couverts is the grass-roof Vauban Dam, built by its namesake in 1682. Climb to the

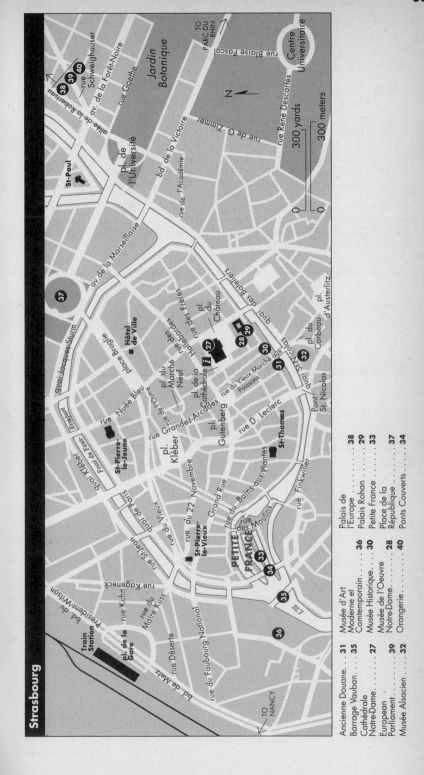

Strasbourg

St-Paul

Jardin Botanique

TO PARC DU RHIN

rue Blaise Pascal

Centre Universitaire

rue René Descartes

rue Schweighauser

av. de la Forêt-Noire

rue Goethe

allée de la Robertsau

pl. de l'Université

bd. de la Victoire

rue de G. Zimmer

rue de l'Académie

300 yards

300 meters

av. de la Marseillaise

Hôtel de Ville

place Broglie

pl. du Château

quai des Bateliers

pl. du Corbeau

pl. d'Austerlitz

quai Jacques-Sturm

rue des Hallebardes

rue des Frères

rue des Juifs

Nuée Bleu

pl. du Marché Neuf

pl. de la Cathédrale

rue Mercière

rue du Vieux Marché aux Poissons

Pont St. Nicolas

quai aux St-Nicolas

Rempart

rue Grandes-Arcades

Gutenberg

rue D. Leclerc

St-Pierre-le-Jeune

pl. Kléber

rue du 22 Novembre

Grand Rue

St-Thomas

rue Finkwiller

Fossé des Faux

quai Kléber

quai de Paris

rue du Vieux

St-Pierre-le-Vieux

rue des Bains-aux-Plantes

rue des Moulins

PETITE FRANCE

L'Ill.

rue St-Jean

quai de Metz

rue Kageneck

rue Kuhn

rue du Maire Kuss

rue Déserte

rue du Faubourg-National

bd. du Président-Wilson

Train Station

pl. de la Gare

bd. de Metz

TO NANCY

top for wide-angle views of the Ponts Couverts and, on the other side, the Museum of Modern Art. Then stroll through its echoing galleries, where magnificent cathedral statuary lies scattered in pigeon droppings. ⊠ *Ponts Couverts.* ✆ *Free.* ⊙ *Mid-Oct.–mid-Mar., daily 9–7; mid-Mar.–mid-Oct., daily 9–8.*

★ ㉗ **Cathédrale Notre-Dame.** Rosy, ornately carved Vosges sandstone masonry covers the facade of this most novel and Germanic of French cathedrals, a triumph of Gothic art begun in 1176. Not content with the outlines of the walls themselves, medieval builders encased them in a lacy exoskeleton of slender shafts of stone. The off-center **spire,** finished in 1439, looks absurdly fragile as it tapers skyward some 466 ft; you can nonetheless climb its 330 steps to the top to take in sweeping views of the city, the Vosges Mountains, and the Black Forest.

The interior presents a stark contrast to the facade: It is older (mostly finished by 1275), and the nave's broad windows emphasize the horizontal rather than the vertical. Note Hans Hammer's ornately sculpted pulpit (1484–86) and the richly painted 14th- to 15th-century organ loft that rises from pillar to ceiling. The left side of the nave is flanked with richly colored Gothic windows honoring the early leaders of the Holy Roman Empire—Otto I and II, and Heinrich I and II. The **choir** is not ablaze with stained glass but framed by chunky Romanesque masonry. The elaborate 16th-century **Chapelle St-Laurent,** to the left of the choir, merits a visit; turn to the right to admire the **Pilier des Anges** (Angels' Pillar), an intricate column dating from 1230.

Just beyond the pillar, the Renaissance machinery of the 16th-century ㋡ **Horloge Astronomique** (Astronomical Clock) whirs into action daily at 12:30 PM (but the line starts at the south door at 11:45 AM): Macabre clockwork figures enact the story of Christ's Passion. ⊠ *Pl. de la Cathédrale.* ✆ *Clock 5 frs; spire 20 frs.*

㉜ **Musée Alsacien** (Alsatian Museum). In this labyrinthine half-timber home, with layers of carved balconies sagging over a cobbled inner courtyard, local interiors have been faithfully reconstituted. The diverse activities of blacksmiths, clog makers, saddlers, and makers of artificial flowers are explained with the help of old-time artisans' tools and equipment. ⊠ *23–25 quai St-Nicolas,* ☎ *03–88–52–50–00.* ✆ *20 frs.* ⊙ *Mon. and Wed.–Sat. 10–noon and 1:30–6, Sun. 10–5.*

㊱ **Musée d'Art Moderne et Contemporain** (Modern and Contemporary Art Museum). A magnificent sculpture of a building that sometimes dwarfs its contents, this spectacular museum frames a relatively thin collection of new, esoteric, and unsung 20th-century art. Downstairs, a permanent collection of Impressionists and modernists up to 1950 is heavily padded with local heroes but happily fleshed out with some striking furniture; all are juxtaposed for contrasting and comparing, with little to no chronological flow. Upstairs, harsh, spare new works must work hard to live up to their setting; few contemporary masters are featured. Drawings, aquarelles, and paintings of Gustave Doré, a native of Alsace, are enshrined in a separate room. ⊠ *1 pl. Hans-Jean Arp,* ☎ *03–88–23–31–31.* ✆ *30 frs.* ⊙ *Tues.–Wed. and Fri.–Sun. 11–7, Thurs. 12–10.*

㉚ **Musée Historique** (Local History Museum). This museum, in a step-gabled slaughterhouse dating to 1588, was temporarily closed for extensive renovations at press time; it is expected to reopen by mid-2001. It contains a collection of maps, armor, arms, bells, uniforms, traditional dress, printing paraphernalia, and two huge relief models of Strasbourg. ⊠ *2 rue du Vieux-Marché-aux-Poissons,* ☎ *03–88–52–00–00.*

★ ㉘ **Musée de l'Oeuvre Notre-Dame** (Museum of Works from Notre-Dame). There is more to this museum than the usual assembly of dilapidated statues rescued from the local cathedral before they fell off the walls (*those* you'll find rotting in the Barrage Vauban). Sacred sculptures stand in churchlike settings, and secular exhibits are enhanced by the building's fine old architecture. Subjects include a wealth of Flemish and Upper Rhine paintings, stained glass, gold objects, and massive heavily carved furniture. ⊠ *3 pl. du Château,* ☎ *03–88–52–50–00.* ▨ *20 frs.* ☉ *Tues.–Sat. 10–noon and 1:30–6, Sun. 10–5.*

㉙ **Palais Rohan** (Rohan Palace). The exterior of Robert de Cotte's massive Neoclassical palace (1732–42) is starkly austere. But the glamour is inside, in Robert le Lorrain's magnificent ground-floor rooms, led by the great **Salon d'Assemblée** (Assembly Room) and the book- and tapestry-lined **Bibliothèque des Cardinaux** (Cardinals' Library). The library leads to a series of less august rooms that house the **Musée des Arts Décoratifs** (Decorative Arts Museum) and its elaborate display of ceramics. This is a comprehensive presentation of works by Hannong, a porcelain manufacturer active in Strasbourg from 1721 to 1782; dinner services by other local kilns reveal the influence of Chinese porcelain. The **Musée des Beaux-Arts** (Fine-Arts Museum), also in the château, features masterworks of European paintings from Giotto and Memling to El Greco, Rubens, and Goya. Downstairs, the **Musée Archéologique** (Archaeology Museum) displays regional archaeological finds, including gorgeous Merovingian treasures. ⊠ *2 pl. du Château,* ☎ *03–88–52–50–00.* ▨ *40 frs all museums; 20 frs each museum.* ☉ *Mon. and Wed.–Sat. 10–noon and 1:30–6, Sun. 10–5.*

★ ㉝ **Petite France.** With its gingerbread half-timber houses that seem to lean precariously over the canals of the Ill, its shops, and inviting little restaurants, this is the most magical neighborhood in Strasbourg. Wander up and down the tiny streets that connect rue du Bain aux Plantes and rue des Dentelles to Grand' Rue, and stroll the waterfront promenade.

㉞ **Ponts Couverts** (Covered Bridges). These three bridges, distinguished by their four stone towers, were once covered with wooden shelters. Part of the 14th-century ramparts that framed old Strasbourg, they span the Ill as it branches into four fingerlike canals.

Beyond the Ill

If you've seen the center and have time to strike out in new directions, head across the Ill to view two architectural landmarks unrelated to Strasbourg's famous medieval past: place de la République and the Palais de l'Europe.

A Good Walk

North of the cathedral, walk up rue des Hallebardes and turn left on rue du Dôme. Take a right onto place Broglie and continue up this main thoroughfare across the river to the striking circle of red-sandstone buildings on **place de la République** ㊲. Back at the river, head for a bus stop on avenue de la Marseillaise and take Bus 23 to the **Palais de l'Europe** ㊳ for a guided tour (by appointment, arranged in advance). You may also want to visit the sleek new digs of the **European Parliament** ㊴, just across the river. From here plunge into the greenery of the **Orangerie** ㊵. Indulge in a three-hour lunch at the stellar Buerehiesel (☞ Dining and Lodging, *below*) or have a picnic on a bench.

TIMING
Basing your schedule on your tour appointment at the Palais de l'Europe, allow about a half day for this walk; if need be, you can while away the wait in the Orangerie.

Sights to See

③⑨ European Parliament. This sleek new building testifies to the growing importance of the governing body of the European Union, which used to make do with rental offices in the Palais de l'Europe. Eurocrats continue to commute between Brussels, Luxembourg, and Strasbourg, hauling their staff and files with them. One week per month, individuals can slip into the hemicycle and witness the tribune in debate, complete with simultaneous translation. ⊠ *Behind the Palais de l'Europe, 03–88–17–52–85.* 🎫 *Free.* ⊙ *Call ahead to see if Parliament is in session.*

④⓪ Orangerie. Like a private backyard to the Eurocrats in the Palais de l'Europe, this delightful park is laden with flowers and punctuated by noble copper beeches. It contains a lake and, close by, a small reserve of rare birds, including flamingos and noisy local storks. ⊠ *Av. de l'Europe.*

③⑧ Palais de l'Europe. Designed by Paris architect Henri Bernard in 1977, this Continental landmark is headquarters to the Council of Europe, founded in 1949 and independent of the European Union. A guided tour introduces you to the intricacies of their workings and may allow you to eavesdrop on a session. Arrange your tour by telephone in advance; appointments are fixed according to language demands and usually take place in the afternoon. Note: You must provide a *pièce d'identité* (ID) before entering. ⊠ *Av. de l'Europe,* ☎ *03–90–21–49–40 for appointments.* 🎫 *Free.* ⊙ *Guided tours by appointment weekdays.*

③⑦ Place de la République. The spacious layout and ponderous architecture of this monumental *cirque* (circle) have nothing in common with the old town, except for the local red sandstone. A different hand was at work here—that of occupying Germans, who erected the former Ministry (1902); the Academy of Music (1882–92); and the Palais du Rhin (1883–88). The handsome neo-Gothic church of **St-Paul** and the pseudo-Renaissance **Palais de l'Université** (University Palace), constructed between 1875 and 1885, also bear the German stamp. Heavy turn-of-the-century houses, some betraying the whimsical curves of the Art Nouveau style, frame **allée de la Robertsau,** a tree-lined boulevard that would not look out of place in Berlin.

Dining and Lodging

$$$$ **✕ Buerehiesel.** This lovely Alsatian farmhouse, reconstructed in the Orangerie, warrants a pilgrimage if you are willing to pay for the finest
★   cooking in Alsace. Antoine Westermann stands in the upper echelon of chefs while remaining true to the ingredients and specialties of his native Alsace: *schniederspaetzle* (onion-perfumed ravioli) with frogs' legs, duck braised and caramelized in Asian spices, and plum tart Tatin with vanilla ice cream. European *parlementaires* come on foot; others might come on their knees. ⊠ *4 parc de l'Orangerie,* ☎ *03–88–45–56–65. Reservations essential. AE, DC, MC, V. Closed Tues.–Wed.*

$$$$ **✕ Crocodile.** Chef Émile Jung is celebrated throughout the region for
★   his Alsatian dishes prepared with urbane finesse: truffle turnover, warmed goose liver with rhubarb, and bitter-chocolate cherry cake. The restaurant's opulent decor makes a sophisticated backdrop for a sensual meal. It's more central than the Buerehiesel and nearly as revered. ⊠ *10 rue de l'Outre,* ☎ *03–88–32–13–02. Reservations essential. Jacket and tie. AE, DC, MC, V. Closed Sun.–Mon.*

$$ **✕ Chez Yvonne.** Behind red-checked curtains, you'll find artists,
★   tourists, lovers, and heads of state sitting elbow-to-elbow in this classic winstub. All come to savor steaming platters of local specialties: Watch for duck confit on choucroute, and *tête de veau* (veal head) in white wine. Warm Alsatian fabrics dress tables and lamps, the china is regional, the photos historic, and the ambience all chic—and no kitsch.

✉ *10 rue du Sanglier,* ☎ *03–88–32–84–15. AE, DC, MC, V. Closed Sun. No lunch Mon.*

$$ ✕ **Maison Kammerzell.** This restaurant glories in its richly carved, half-timber 16th-century building—probably the most familiar house in Strasbourg. Fight your way through the tourist hordes on the terrace and ground floor to one of the atmospheric rooms above, with their gleaming wooden furniture and stained-glass windows. Foie gras and choucroute are best bets, though you may want to try the chef's pet discovery, choucroute with freshwater fish. ✉ *16 pl. de la Cathédrale,* ☎ *03–88–32–42–14. AE, DC, MC, V.*

$$ ✕ **Suzel.** This cozy little tearoom in Petite France mixes rustic-chic decor
★ (blue gingham, artfully arranged bric-a-brac, rows of potted boxwood) with excellent and unpretentious regional food. There's rabbit stew with dumplings, fresh trout, baeckoffe, fruit tarts, and good wines. It's also marvelous for an atmospheric afternoon tea break. Too bad it's closed nights. ✉ *2 rue des Moulins at rue Bain-aux-Plantes,* ☎ *03–88–23–10–46. MC, V. Closed Mon. No dinner.*

$ ✕ **St-Sépulcre.** Shared plank tables, a jovial red-vested patron (with a nose to match), and a wisecracking waitstaff enhance the convivial atmosphere at this no-frills, down-home winstub. A massive ham sits casually on the counter, and slabs of it find their way onto every platter—even the salads. A crock of crunchy pickles, chewy bread, and a cereal bowl heaped with fresh horseradish accompany every order except dessert. ✉ *15 rue des Orfèvres,* ☎ *03–88–32–39–97. MC, V.*

$$$$ 🏨 **Régent-Contades.** This sleek, modern hotel is in a revamped mansion in a residential turn-of-the-century district close to the Ill (ask for a room with a view of St-Paul's). It's intimate, quiet, and homey in an aristocratic way. First-class amenities add to the appeal of the spacious rooms. ✉ *8 av. de la Liberté, 67000,* ☎ *03–88–15–05–05,* 🖷 *03–88– 15–05–15. 45 rooms. Bar, air-conditioning, sauna. AE, DC, MC, V.* ✑

$$$$ 🏨 **Régent-Petite France.** Opposite the Ponts Couverts and surrounded by rushing canals, this boldly modern luxury hotel holds forth in a former ice factory in the heart of Strasbourg's quaintest quarter. A spacious marble vestibule, vivid graffiti art, and sculptural room furnishings contrast sharply with the half-timber houses and roaring river viewed from nearly every room. The restaurant, Le Pont Tournant, offers summer tables over the torrent. ✉ *5 rue des Moulins, 67000,* ☎ *03– 88–76–43–43,* 🖷 *03–88–76–43–76. 72 rooms. Restaurant, piano bar, air-conditioning. AE, DC, MC, V.* ✑

$$$ 🏨 **Cathédrale.** Expansion and renovation have brought this superbly positioned hotel more than up to par, with a sleek marble lobby, with lounges, bar, and breakfast room rich with ancient beams and sandstone. Rooms feature dark timbers, and most have windows framing a view of the Maison Kammerzell or the cathedral. For summer drinks and breakfast, there's a garden courtyard cloistered from the outside world. ✉ *12–13 pl. de la Cathédrale, 67000,* ☎ *03–88–22–12–12,* 🖷 *03–88–23–28–00. 44 rooms. Bar, air-conditioning, parking (fee). AE, DC, MC, V.* ✑

$$$ 🏨 **Rohan.** Across from the cathedral on a picturesque pedestrian street, this modest little hotel has a welcoming atmosphere and a marvelous sense of French style, from the Louis XV furniture to the gilt mirrors. Though swagged in rich fabrics, rooms are fully modern, with impeccable all-tile baths. ✉ *17–19 rue Maroquin, 67000,* ☎ *03–88–32–85– 11,* 🖷 *03–88–75–65–37. 36 rooms. Air-conditioning, parking (fee). AE, DC, MC, V.* ✑

$$ 🏨 **Gutenberg.** In a 200-year-old mansion just off place Gutenberg, this sturdy urban hotel has rooms with fresh, old-fashioned wallpaper and built-in wood cabinetry. Charming little fifth-floor lofts reveal roof timbers; most rooms have air-conditioning. ✉ *31 rue des Serruriers,*

67000, ☎ 03–88–32–17–15, FAX 03–88–75–76–67. *42 rooms. Breakfast room. MC, V. Closed 1st 2 wks in Jan.*

Nightlife and the Arts

The annual **Festival de Musique** (Music Festival) is held from June to early July at the Palais des Congrès and at the cathedral; contact the Amis de la Musique (✉ 1 av. de la Marseillaise, ☎ 03–88–39–64–10) for information. The **Opéra du Rhin** (✉ 19 pl. Broglie, ☎ 03–88–75–48–23) has a sizable repertoire. Classical concerts are staged by the **Orchestre Philharmonique** (✉ Palais des Congrès, ☎ 03–88–15–09–09).

The old-town neighborhood east of the cathedral, along rue des Frères, is the nightlife hangout for university students and twentysomethings; among its handful of heavily frequented bars is **Le Velvet** (✉ 6 rue Tonnelet Rouge, ☎ 03–88–37–95–84). **Le Chalet** (✉ 376 rte. de la Wantzenau, ☎ 03–88–31–18–31) is the biggest and most popular disco, but it is some 10 km (6 mi) northeast of the city center.

Outdoor Activities

The **Port Autonome de Strasbourg** (☎ 03–88–84–13–13) organizes 75-minute boat tours four times a day in winter and up to every half hour from 9:30 to 9, April–October, along the Ill. Boats leave from behind the Palais Rohan; the cost is 41 francs.

Shopping

The lively city center is full of boutiques, including chocolate shops and delicatessens selling locally made foie gras. Look for warm paisley linens and rustic homespun fabrics, Alsatian pottery, and local wines. **Rue des Hallebardes,** next to the cathedral; **rue des Grandes Arcades,** with its shopping mall; and **place Kléber** form the city's commercial heart. An **antiques market** takes place behind the cathedral on rue du Vieil-Hôpital, rue des Bouchers, and place de la Grande Boucherie every Wednesday and Saturday morning.

ALSACE

The Rhine River forms the eastern boundary of both Alsace and France. But the best of Alsace is not found along the Rhine's industrial waterfront. Instead it's nestled in the Ill Valley at the base of the Vosges, southwest of cosmopolitan Strasbourg (☞ *above*). Northwest is Saverne and the beginning of the Route du Vin, the great Alsace Wine Road, which winds its way south through the Vosges foothills, fruitful vineyards, and medieval villages that would serve well on an opera set for William Tell. Signs for the road help you keep your bearings on the twisty way south, and you'll find limitless opportunities to stop at wineries and sample the local wares. At the industrial town of Mulhouse, you leave behind the charms of Alsace and head into the historic wilds of Franche-Comté.

Saverne

㊶ *37 km (23 mi) northwest of Strasbourg.*

Saverne, gateway to the northern Vosges, has a stately castle and an exuberant rose garden. Built of red sandstone, the 18th-century **Château** is renowned for its majestic north facade, lined by fluted pilasters and a Corinthian colonnade. In the right wing is a museum devoted to archaeology, religious statuary, and local history. ☎ 03–88–91–06–28. 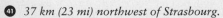 *Museum 19 frs.* ☉ *Mar.–mid-June, Wed.–Mon. 2–5; mid-June–mid-*

Sept., Wed.–Mon. 10–noon and 2–6; mid-Sept.–Nov., Wed.–Mon. 2–5; Dec.–Feb., Sun. 2–5.

Don't miss the **Roseraie** (Rose Garden), on the western side of town (off N4). It has some 8,000 roses of 550 varieties, in glorious bloom from June through October. ⊠ ☏ *03–88–71–83–33.* ⬚ *15 frs.* ☉ *Sunrise–sunset.*

Marmoutier

④② *6 km (4 mi) south of Saverne, 41 km (25 mi) northwest of Strasbourg.*

Marmoutier is worth a stop to see its handsome Romanesque **Église Abbatiale** (Abbey Church). The facade, dating from the 11th and 12th centuries, is pure Lombard Romanesque, built of local Vosges sandstone. Inside, you'll find a handsome 1710 organ, made by Silbermann (organ maker to J. S. Bach).

Obernai

④③ *35 km (22 mi) south of Saverne, 27 km (17 mi) southwest of Strasbourg.*

Obernai is a thriving, colorful Renaissance market town with a medieval belfry, a Renaissance well, and a late-19th-century church.

Place du Marché, in the heart of town, is dominated by the stout, square 13th-century **Kapelturm Beffroi** (Chapel Tower Belfry), topped by a pointed steeple flanked at each corner by frilly openwork turrets added in 1597. An elaborate Renaissance well near the belfry, the **Puits à Six-Seaux** (Well of Six Buckets), was constructed in 1579; its name recalls the six buckets suspended from its metal chains. The twin spires of the parish church of **St-Pierre-St-Paul** compete with the belfry for skyline preeminence. They date, like the rest of the church, from the 1860s, although the 1504 Holy Sepulchre altarpiece in the north transept is a survivor from the previous church, along with some 15th-century stained glass.

Dining and Lodging

$$ ✕⊞ **L'Ami Fritz.** In the hilltop village of Ottrott, west of Obernai, this
★ welcoming inn combines style, rustic warmth, and three generations of family tradition. For winter dining head for the firelighted stone-and-beam *caveau* (cellar) or the formal but unstuffy dining room; in summer dine on the tree-shaded terrace. The chef-owner's sophisticated twists on regional specialties include feather-light blood sausage in flaky pastry, a delicate choucroute of grated turnips, and freshwater fish. Don't miss the fruity red wine, an Ottrott exclusive. Pretty, impeccable rooms decked in toile de jouy and homespun checks are available in the historic house, with breakfast in a beamed parlor; avoid the less appealing residence across the village. ⊠ *8 rue des Châteaux, 67530 Ottrott (3 km [2 mi] from Obernai),* ☏ *03–88–95–80–81,* ℻ *03–88–95–84–85. 39 rooms. Restaurant. AE, DC, MC, V.* ✍

$ ✕⊞ **La Cloche.** Leaded glass, dark oak, and Hansi-like murals set the tone in this sturdy, half-timber 14th-century landmark on Obernai's market square. Standard local dishes and blackboard specials draw locals on market days. Rooms are well equipped and country-pretty; two double-decker duplex rooms accommodate four. ⊠ *90 rue Général-Gouraud, 67210,* ☏ *03–88–95–52–89,* ℻ *03–88–95–07–63. 20 rooms. Restaurant. AE, DC, MC, V. Closed 1st 2 wks Jan.* ✍

Shopping

Dietrich (⊠ 58 and 74 rue du Général-Gouraud, ☏ 03–88–95–57–58) has a varied selection of Beauvillé linens, locally hand-blown Alsatian wine glasses, and Obernai-patterned china.

Mont-Ste-Odile

④④ *12 km (8 mi) southwest of Obernai, 42 km (26 mi) southwest of Stras-bourg.*

★ Mont-Ste-Odile, a 2,500-ft hill, has been an important religious and military site for 3,000 years. The eerie 9½-km-long (6-mi-long) **Mur Païen** (Pagan Wall), up to 12 ft high and, in parts, several feet thick, rings the summit; its mysterious origins and purpose still baffle archaeologists.

The Romans established a settlement here, and at the start of the 8th century, Odile, daughter of Duke Etichon of Obernai, who had been born blind, founded a convent on the same spot after recovering her sight while being baptized. The relatively modern convent is now a workaday hostelry for modern pilgrims on group retreats. Odile—who is the patron saint of Alsace—died here in AD 720; her sarcophagus rests in the 12th-century **Chapelle Ste-Odile.** The spare, Romanesque **Chapelle de la Croix** adjoins St-Odile.

Barr

④⑤ *11 km (7 mi) southeast of Mont Ste-Odile, 8 km (5 mi) south of Ober-nai, 33 km (20 mi) southwest of Strasbourg.*

Barr is a thriving, semi-industrial town surrounded by vines, with some charming narrow streets (notably rue des Cigognes, rue Neuve, and the tiny rue de l'Essieu), a cheerful Hôtel de Ville, and a decorative arts museum. Most buildings date from after a catastrophic fire in 1678; the only medieval survivor is the Romanesque tower of St-Martin, the Protestant church.

Admire original furniture, local porcelain, earthenware, and pewter at the **Musée de la Folie Marco,** in a mansion built by local magistrate Félix Marco in 1763. One section of the museum explains the traditional process of *schlittage*: Sleds, bearing bundles of freshly sawed tree trunks, once slid down the forest slopes on a "corduroy road" made of logs. ⊠ *30 rue du Dr-Sultzer,* ☎ *03–88–08–94–72 (winter 03–88–08–66–65).* ⊡ *20 frs.* ☉ *End June–Sept., Wed.–Mon. 10–noon and 2–6; early June, Oct., and Dec., weekends 10–noon and 2–6.*

Andlau

④⑥ *3 km (2 mi) southwest of Barr, 37 km (23 mi) southwest of Strasbourg.*

Andlau has long been known for its magnificent abbey. Built in the 12th century, the **Abbaye d'Andlau** has the richest ensemble of Romanesque sculpture in Alsace. Sculpted vines wind their way around the doorway as a reminder of wine's time-honored importance to the local economy. A statue of a female bear, the abbey mascot—bears used to roam local forests and were bred at the abbey until the 16th century—can be seen in the north transept. Legend has it that Queen Richarde, spurned by her husband, Charles the Fat, founded the abbey in AD 887 when an angel enjoined her to construct a church on a site to be shown to her by a female bear.

Dambach-la-Ville

④⑦ *5 km (3 mi) southwest of Andlau, 42 km (26 mi) southwest of Stras-bourg. From Andlau take D253 to the junction with D603; keep right; about 1 km (½ mi) later, turn right, then left through Itterswiller be-fore turning right toward Dambach-la-Ville.*

Dambach-la-Ville is a fortified medieval town protected by ramparts and three powerful 13th-century gateways. It is particularly rich in half-timber, high-roof houses from the 17th and 18th centuries, clustered mainly around **place du Marché** (Market Square). Also on the square is the 16th-century **Hôtel de Ville** (Town Hall).

En Route Just south of Dambach is the imposing **Château d'Ortenburg,** constructed in 1000 by Wernher d'Ortenburg and restored in 1258 by Rodolphe de Habsbourg, a reigning Hapsburg.

Sélestat

🔴 *9 km (5 mi) southeast of Dambach, 19 km (12 mi) south of Barr, 47 km (29 mi) southwest of Strasbourg.*

Sélestat, midway between Strasbourg and Colmar, is a lively, historic town with a Romanesque church and a library of medieval manuscripts. Head directly to the vieille ville and explore the quarter on foot.

The church of **St-Foy** (⊠ Pl. du Marché-Vert) dates from between 1155 and 1190; its Romanesque facade remains largely intact (the spires were added in the 19th century), as does the 140-ft octagonal tower over the crossing. Sadly, the interior was mangled during the centuries, chiefly by the Jesuits; their most inspired legacy is the Baroque pulpit of 1733 depicting the life of St. Francis Xavier. Note the Romanesque bas-relief next to the baptistery, originally the lid of a sarcophagus.

Among the precious medieval and Renaissance manuscripts on display at the **Bibliothèque Humaniste** (Humanist Library), a major library founded in 1452 and installed in the former Halle aux Blés, are a 7th-century lectionary and a 12th-century Book of Miracles. ⊠ *1 rue de la Bibliothèque,* ☎ *03-88-58-07-20.* ⊡ *20 frs.* ☉ *Sept.–June, Mon. and Wed.–Fri. 9–noon and 2–6, Sat. 9–noon; July–Aug., Mon. and Wed.–Fri. 9–noon and 2–6, weekends 9–noon and 2–5.*

Dining

$$$$ ✕ **L'Auberge de l'Ill.** With its windows opening over the swans on the
★ river and an entire family carrying on tradition, this is the ultimate Alsatian inn. It happens to be among the best restaurants in France, too, vying with Strasbourg's Buerehiesel and Crocodile for top honors. Firmly fixed in culinary tradition, master chef Paul Haeberlin creates his famous foie gras terrine, a delicate salmon soufflé, and lamb chops in dainty strudel; in short, regional tours de force with no surprises—unless you're surprised by consistent excellence. ⊠ *2 rue de Collonges, Illhaeusern (12 km [7 mi] south of Sélestat),* ☎ *03-89-71-89-00,* FAX *03-89-71-82-83. AE, DC, MC, V. Closed Mon.–Tues. and Feb.*

Nightlife and the Arts

The colorful **Corso Fleuri** (Flower Carnival) takes place on the second Sunday in August, when the town decks itself—and the floats in its vivid parade—with a magnificent display of dahlias.

Haut-Koenigsbourg

🔴 *12 km (8 mi) west of Sélestat, 59 km (36½ mi) southwest of Strasbourg.*

One of the most popular spots in Alsace is the romantic, crag-top castle of Haut-Koenigsbourg, originally built as a fortress in the 12th cen-
★ ☾ tury. The ruins of the **Château du Haut-Koenigsbourg** were presented by the town of Sélestat to German emperor Wilhelm II in 1901. The château looked just as a kaiser thought it should, and he restored it with some diligence and no lack of imagination—squaring the main tower's original circle, for instance. The site, panorama, drawbridge, and amply fur-

nished imperial chambers may lack authenticity, but they are undeniably dramatic. ☎ 03–88–92–11–46. 🏛 *Château 40 frs.* ☉ *Jan.–Feb. and Nov.–Dec., daily 9:30–noon and 1–4:30; Mar.–Apr. and Oct., daily 9–noon and 1–5:30; May–June and Sept., daily 9–6; July–Aug., daily 9–6:30.*

Ribeauvillé

🟤 *14 km (9 mi) southwest of Sélestat, 63 km (39 mi) southwest of Strasbourg.*

The beautiful half-timber town of Ribeauvillé, surrounded by rolling vineyards and three imposing châteaux, produces some of the best Riesling in Alsace. (The Trimbach family has made Riesling and superb gewürztraminer here since 1626.) The town's narrow main street, crowded with winstubs, pottery shops, bakeries, and wine sellers, is bisected by the 13th-century **Tour des Bouchers,** a clock-belfry completed (gargoyles and all) in the 15th century. Storks' nests crown several towers in the village.

Dining and Lodging

$$ ✕ **Zum Pfifferhüss.** This is a true-blood winstub, with yellowed murals, glowing lighting, and great local wines by the glass. The cooking is pure Alsace, with German-scale portions of choucroute, ham hock, and fruit tarts. ⊠ *14 Grand-Rue,* ☎ *03–89–73–62–28. MC, V. Closed Wed.–Thurs.*

$$$ 🏨 **Hostellerie des Seigneurs de Ribeaupierre.** On the edge of Ribeauvillé's old quarter, this gracious half-timber inn offers a warm regional welcome with a touch of flair. It has exposed timbers in pastel tones, sumptuous fabrics, and slick bathrooms upstairs, as well as a fire crackling downstairs on your way to the generous breakfast. ⊠ *11 rue du Château, 68150,* ☎ *03–89–73–70–31,* 🆇 *03–89–73–71–21. 10 rooms. Breakfast room. AE, MC, V. Closed Feb.*

$$ 🏨 **Hôtel de la Tour.** In the center of Ribeauvillé and across from the Tour des Bouchers, this hotel, with an ornate Renaissance fountain outside its front door, is a good choice for experiencing the atmospheric town by night. Rooms and amenities are modern; those on the top floor have exposed timbers and wonderful views of ramshackle rooftops. ⊠ *1 rue de la Mairie, 68150,* ☎ *03–89–73–72–73,* 🆇 *03–89–73–38–74. 35 rooms. Breakfast room, hot tub, sauna. AE, DC, MC, V.* 🐾

Shopping

Find rich paisley Alsatian tablecloths discounted at the factory outlet for **Beauvillé** (⊠ *19 rte. de Ste-Marie-aux-Mines,* ☎ *03–89–73–74–74*), at the foot of forested hills just past the town center.

Riquewihr

★ 🟤 *5 km (3 mi) south of Ribeauvillé, 68 km (42 mi) south of Strasbourg.*

Riquewihr is a living museum to the quaint architecture and storybook atmosphere of old Alsace. Its steep main street, ramparts, and winding back alleys have scarcely changed since the 16th century and could easily serve as a film set. Merchants cater to the sizable influx of tourists with a plethora of kitschy souvenir shops; bypass them to peep into courtyards with massive wine presses, to study the woodwork and ornately decorated houses, to stand in the narrow old courtyard that was once the Jewish quarter, or to climb up a narrow wooden stair to the ramparts. You would also do well to settle into a winstub to sample some of Riquewihr's famous wines.

Dining and Lodging

$$ ✕🏨 **Sarment d'Or.** This cozy little hotel stands apart for its irreproachable modern comforts tactfully dovetailed with stone, dark tim-

bers, and thick walls. For a price ($$$) the restaurant downstairs of-
fers firelight romance and delicious cuisine—foie gras, frogs' legs in
garlic cream, and breast of duck in pinot noir; it is closed Monday and
doesn't serve dinner Sunday or lunch Tuesday. ⊠ *4 rue du Cerf, 68340,*
☎ *03–89–86–02–86,* 𝖥𝖠𝖷 *03–89–47–99–23. 9 rooms. Restaurant. MC,*
V. Closed Jan.

Colmar

🔢 *16 km (10 mi) southeast of Riquewihr, 71 km (44 mi) southwest of*
Strasbourg.

Much of Colmar's architecture is modern because of the destruction of
World Wars I and II. But the heart of this proud merchant town—an
atmospheric maze of narrow streets lined with Renaissance houses re-
stored to the last detail—outcharms Strasbourg. Old-town streets fan
out from the beefy towered church of **St-Martin.** Each shop-lined back-
street winds its way to the 15th-century customs house, the **Ancienne
Douane,** and the square and canals that surround it. The **Maison Pfis-
ter** (Pfister House; ⊠ 11 rue Mercière), built in 1537, is the most strik-
ing of Colmar's many old dwellings. Note its decorative frescoes and
medallions, carved balcony, and ground-floor arcades. Up the street from
the Ancienne Douane on the Grand'Rue, the **Maison aux Arcades** (Ar-
cades House) was built in 1609 in high Renaissance style and features
a series of archèd porches (arcades) anchored by two octagonal towers

Calm canals wind through **La Petite Venise** (Little Venice), an area of
bright Alsatian houses with colorful shutters and window boxes that's
south of the center of town.

★ The **Musée d'Unterlinden,** once a medieval convent, is now an impor-
tant museum. The star attraction is the *Retable d'Issenheim* (Issenheim
Altarpiece; 1512–16), by Matthias Grünewald, majestically displayed in
the convent's Gothic chapel. Originally painted for the Antoine convent
at Issenheim, 32 km (20 mi) south of Colmar, the multipaneled altar-
piece was believed to have miraculous healing powers over ergotism, a
widespread disease in the Middle Ages caused by the ingestion of fun-
gus-ridden grains. With its leprous bodies, raw emotional drama, and
hallucinogenic fantasies, the enormous work moves sharply away from
the stilted restraint of earlier styles. In doing so, Grünewald made a di-
rect appeal to the pain-racked victims living out their last days at the
convent. Modern art, stone sculpture, ancient wine presses and barrels,
and local crafts cluster around the enchanting 13th-century cloister. Up-
stairs, there are fine regional furniture and a collection of Rhine Valley
paintings from the Renaissance. ⊠ *1 rue Unterlinden,* ☎ *03–89–20–15–*
50. 🎫 *35 frs.* ☉ *Apr.–Oct., daily 9–6; Nov.–Mar., Wed.–Mon. 10–5.*

The **Église des Dominicains** (Dominican Church) houses the Flemish-
influenced *Madonna of the Rosebush* (1473), by Martin Schongauer
(1445–91). This work, stolen from St-Martin's in 1972 and later re-
covered and hung here, has almost certainly been reduced in size from
its original state but retains enormous impact. The grace and intensity
of the Virgin match that of the Christ child; yet her slender fingers dent
the child's soft flesh (and his fingers entwine her curls) with immedi-
ate intimacy. Schongauer's text for her crown is: ME CARPES GENITO TUO
O SANTISSIMA VIRGO ("Choose me also for your child, o holiest Virgin").
⊠ *Pl. des Dominicains,* ☎ *03–89–24–46–57.* 🎫 *8 frs.* ☉ *Apr.–Dec.,*
daily 10–1 and 3–6.

The **Musée Bartholdi** (Bartholdi Museum) is the birthplace of Frédéric-
Auguste Bartholdi (1834–1904), the local sculptor who designed the
Statue of Liberty. Exhibits of Bartholdi's works claim the ground floor;

a reconstruction of the artist's Paris apartments and furniture are upstairs; and, in adjoining rooms, the creation of Lady Liberty is explored. ⊠ *30 rue des Marchands,* ☎ *03–89–41–90–60.* ☜ *23 frs.* ☉ *Mar.–Dec., Wed.–Mon. 10–noon and 2–6.*

Dining and Lodging

$$$ ✕ **À l'Échevin.** This restaurant in Le Maréchal hotel (☞ *below*) is an old-fashioned romantic's delight, with candles, canal views, elegant food, and discreet service. Choose from such dishes as terrine of rouget, leeks, and truffles, and pigeon breast and foie gras crisped in pastry; and from the series of sommelier-selected wines by the glass. ⊠ *5 pl. des Six-Montagnes-Noires,* ☎ *03–89–41–60–32. MC, V.*

$$ ✕ **Caveau Hansi.** Named for the Rockwell-like illustrator whose beclogged folk children adorn most of the souvenirs of Alsace, this hypertraditional beamed tavern in the old town serves excellent down-home classics such as choucroute and pot-au-feu, prepared and served with a sophisticated touch despite the waitresses' dirndls. ⊠ *23 rue des Marchands,* ☎ *03–89–41–37–84. MC, V. Closed Wed.–Thurs. and Jan.*

$ ✕ **Au Koïfhus.** Not to be confused with the shabby little Koïfhus on rue des Marchands, this popular landmark serves huge portions of regional standards, plus a variety of changing specialties: roast quail and foie gras on salad, game stews with spaetzle (dumplings), and freshwater fish. Choose between the big, open dining room, glowing with wood and warm fabric, and a shaded table on the broad, lovely square. ⊠ *2 pl. de l'Ancienne-Douane,* ☎ *03–89–23–04–90. DC, MC, V. Closed Thurs. and Jan.*

$$$ 🛏 **Le Maréchal.** A maze of narrow, creaky corridors connects the se-
★   ries of Renaissance houses that make up this romantic riverside inn. Rooms are small but lavished with extravagant detail, from glossy rafters to rich fabrics to four-poster beds. A vivid color scheme—scarlet, sapphire, candy pink—adds to the Vermeer atmosphere. Bathrooms have been upgraded; many now include whirlpools. But this is not a high-tech luxury hotel: It's an endearing, quirky, lovely old place hanging over a Petite Venise canal. ⊠ *5 pl. des Six-Montagnes-Noires, 68000,* ☎ *03–89–41–60–32,* 𝖥𝖠𝖷 *03–89–24–59–40. 30 rooms. Restaurant, air-conditioning. AE, DC, MC, V.* ☜

$$ 🛏 **Rapp.** In the old town, just off the Champ de Mars, this solid, modern hotel has business-class comforts, a professional and welcoming staff, and good German-scale breakfast. There's even an extensive indoor-pool complex, including sauna, steam bath, and workout equipment—all included in the low price. ⊠ *1–5 rue Weinemer, 68000,* ☎ *03–89–41–62–10,* 𝖥𝖠𝖷 *03–89–24–13–58. 42 rooms. Restaurant, breakfast room, indoor pool, sauna, steam room, exercise room. AE, DC, MC, V.* ☜

The Arts

During the first half of August Colmar celebrates with its annual **Foire Régionale des Vins d'Alsace,** an Alsatian wine fair in the Parc des Expositions. Events include folk music and theater performances and, above all, the tasting and selling of wine.

Guebwiller

🗺 *26 km (16 mi) southwest of Colmar, 25 km (16 mi) north of Mulhouse, 94 km (58 mi) south of Strasbourg.*

Despite its admirable churches, fine old buildings, and pleasantly authentic feeling, Guebwiller is often overlooked.

The **Église St-Léger** (⊠ Pl. St-Léger), built 1180–1280, is one of the most harmonious Romanesque churches in Alsace, though its original choir was replaced by the current Gothic one in 1336. The bare, solemn interior is of less interest than the three-tower exterior. The towers match—almost: The one on the left has small turrets at the base of its steeple, while the one on the right is ringed by triangular gables. The octagonal tower over the crossing looms above them both, topped by a seldom-visited stork's nest. The surrounding square is home to a lively weekly market.

The **Église Dominicaine** (✉ rue de l'Hôpital) has an unmistakable silhouette thanks to the thin, lacy lantern that sticks out of its roof like an effeminate chimney. Its large 14th-century nave is adorned with frescoes and contains a fine rood screen.

Guebwiller's third and largest church, **Notre-Dame** (✉ Rue de la République), possesses a Baroque grandeur that would not be out of keeping in Paris—a reflection of the wealth of the Benedictine abbey in nearby Murbach, whose worldly friars, fed up with country life, opted for the bright lights of Guebwiller in the mid-18th century. The monks—who needed a noble pedigree of four generations to qualify for the cloth—outmaneuvered church authorities by pretending to take temporary exile in Guebwiller while "modernizing" Murbach Abbey, thus circumnavigating the papal permission required before abbeys could move. As a token gesture, the crafty clerics smashed the nave of Murbach Abbey but failed to replace it and refused to budge from their "temporary" home. Instead, they commissioned Louis Beuque to design this new church in Guebwiller (1762–85). The interior is majestic but not overbearing. The gold-and-marble high altar fits in better, perhaps, than does the trick 3-D-effect stucco Assumption (1783), an example of Baroque craftsmanship at its most outlandish.

The **Musée du Florival** is in one of the 18th-century canon's houses alongside Notre-Dame. It has a fine collection of ceramics designed by Théodore Deck (1823–91), a native of Guebwiller and director of the renowned Sèvres porcelain factory near Paris. It also contains archaeological treasures, artifacts from everyday life, and religious sculpture. ✉ *1 rue du 4-Février*, ☎ *03–89–74–22–89.* 🎟 *15 frs.* ☉ *Mon. and Wed.–Fri. 2–6, weekends 10–noon and 2–6.*

OFF THE
BEATEN PATH
☺ **ECOMUSÉE DE HAUTE-ALSACE –** Great for kids, this open-air museum near Ungersheim, southeast of Guebwiller (via D430), is really a small village created from scratch in 1980, including 70 historic peasant houses and buildings typical of the region. The village is crisscrossed by donkey carts and wagons, and behind every door lie entertaining demonstrations of the old ways. An off-season visit is a study in local architecture; in high season the place comes alive. Small restaurants, snack bars, a playground, and a few amusement rides are scattered about for breaks. Inexpensive lodging is available on-site. ☎ *03–89–74–44–74.* 🎟 *78 frs.* ☉ *July–Aug., daily 9–7; Apr.–June and Sept., daily 9:30–6; Mar. and Oct., daily 10–5; Nov.–Feb. and Dec.–Jan., daily 10:30–4:30.*

Murbach

➎ *5 km (3 mi) west of Guebwiller, 23 km (14 mi) northwest of Mulhouse.*

In the tiny village of Murbach, a vast structure—the east end of the church of **St-Léger**—towers above the hillside. This is all that remains of what was once part of the most powerful abbey in Alsace. Roofs and towers create a geometric interplay of squares and triangles, lent rhythm and variety by those round-arched windows and arcades so loved by Romanesque architects. Note the tympanum above the door to the south transept: Its elongated lions, seen in profile, resemble stone images found more commonly in the Middle East.

Mulhouse

⑤ *23 km (14 mi) southeast of Guebwiller, 35 km (22 mi) south of Colmar.*

An unremarkable industrial town, Mulhouse nonetheless rates a visit for its superb car and train museums, as well as for its art and fabric museums.

Some 500 vintage and modern cars, dating from the steam-powered Jacquot of 1878 and spanning 100 different makes, are housed at the **Musée National de l'Automobile** (National Car Museum). ⊠ *192 av. de Colmar,* ☎ *03–89–33–23–23.* ⊡ *57 frs.* ☉ *Mar.–Oct., daily 9–6; Nov.–Feb., daily 10–5.*

A reconstructed Stephenson locomotive of 1846 sets the wheels rolling at the **Musée Français du Chemin de Fer** (National Train Museum). Stock is spread over 12 tracks, including a vast array of steam trains and the BB 9004 electric train. ⊠ *2 rue Alfred-de-Glehn,* ☎ *03–89–42–83–33.* ⊡ *46 frs.* ☉ *Apr.–Sept., daily 9–6; Oct.–Mar., daily 9–5.*

Dutch and Flemish masters of the 17th to 18th centuries—including Brueghel, Teniers, and Ruisdael—top the bill at the **Musée des Beaux-Arts** (Fine Arts Museum), complemented by French painters such as Boudin, Courbet, and Bouguereau. ⊠ *4 pl. Guillaume-Tell,* ☎ *03–89–45–43–19.* ⊡ *21 frs.* ☉ *Oct.–mid-May., Wed. and Fri.–Mon. 10–noon and 2–5, Thurs. 10–lunch; mid-May–Sept., Wed. and Fri.–Mon. 10–noon and 2–6, Thurs. 10–lunch.*

The **Musée de l'Impression sur Étoffes** (Museum of Fabric Printing) traces the history and development of industrial cloth printing in Alsace. Like the more famous Provençal cottons, these fine floral and geometric prints were first imported from India; feast your eyes on a variety of ancient samples and presses. ⊠ *14 rue Jean-Jacques Henner,* ☎ *03–89–46–83–00.* ⊡ *36 frs.* ☉ *Daily 10–6.*

FRANCHE-COMTÉ

The name of the Jura Mountains—that huge natural barrier some 240 km (150 mi) long that throws its curved length between France and Switzerland—was known to Julius Caesar, who referred to them in his *Commentaries* as the Mons Jura. Jura is derived from *juria,* which means "forest," and no more fitting phrase could be found to describe this region than that of "the forested mountains." It is the name by which the region of the Franche-Comté—the "free country"—is best known among foreign visitors. The Franche-Comté extends from Belfort to Besançon, then clockwise through the Jura's great expanses of quiet, untouched land with rivers, waterfalls, and its challenging range of mountains, where you can climb, ski, and enjoy the solitude. From this region it is an easy trip to Burgundy (☞ Chapter 8) and the Rhône Valley (☞ Chapter 9).

Belfort

⑤ *40 km (25 mi) southwest of Mulhouse, 146 km (90½ mi) southwest of Strasbourg.*

A beefy citadel and colossal stone lion bear witness to the distinguished military history of the stubborn warrior-town of Belfort. In the heart of town is a 36-ft-high **Lion,** sculpted in red sandstone by Frédéric-Auguste Bartholdi, best known as the sculptor of the Statue of Liberty in New York harbor. The lion was commissioned to celebrate Belfort's heroic resistance during the Franco-Prussian War (1870–

71), when the town of Belfort, under the leadership of General Den-fert-Rochereau, withstood a 103-day siege, surrendering only after the rest of France had capitulated. The Prussian leader Otto von Bismarck was so impressed by Belfort's plucky resistance that he granted Belfort independent status. Although Alsace was returned to France in 1918, Belfort maintained its special status—meaning that the Territoire de Belfort (Belfort Territory) remains by far the smallest *département* (province) in France. ⊠ *Pl. des Bourgeois.* 🎫 *To climb up to see statue of lion 6 frs.*

Belfort's Lion sits proudly at the foot of Vauban's impregnable hilltop château, now home to the **Musée d'Art et d'Histoire** (Museum of Art and History), containing Vauban's 1687 scale model of the town plus a detailed section on military history. There's also a collection of paint-ings and sculpture from the 16th through 19th centuries. From the ram-parts you can look out over the old town, toward the Vosges Mountains to the north and the Jura to the south. ☎ *03–84–54–25–52.* 🎫 *Château free, museum 18 frs (free Wed.).* ⊙ *May–Sept., daily 10–7; Oct.–Apr., Wed.–Mon. 10–noon and 2–5.*

Dining and Lodging

$$ ✕ **Pot-au-Feu.** This rustic bistro, tucked in a 16th-century *cave* (cel-lar) at the foot of the citadel, serves good regional specialties, such as Jura sausages and *coq au vin jaune* (chicken in Jura wine) and features—of course—a savory, long-simmered pot-au-feu. ⊠ *27 bis Grande-Rue,* ☎ *03–84–28–57–84. AE, MC, V. Closed 2 wks in Aug. No lunch Sat. and Mon., no dinner Sun.*

$$ ✕🏨 **Château Servin.** Off the street in an intimate garden, this hotel was built in 1885 and maintains that era's stuffy grandeur, although a somewhat creepy, frayed Gothic air has entered the picture, under-scored by a sometimes preoccupied staff. Dark polished woodwork, heavy floral carpets, fringe, gilt, and lace close you in, whether in the velour-beswagged rooms or the stately restaurant. Chef Dominique Mathy creates classic dishes—sole soufflé in lobster sauce, fresh foie gras with poppy seeds, and hot cherry soufflé. The restaurant (in the $$$ category) is closed Friday and doesn't serve dinner Sunday. ⊠ *9 rue du Général-Négrier, 90000,* ☎ *03–84–21–41–85,* FAX *03–84–57–05–57. 10 rooms. Restaurant. AE, DC, MC, V.*

Ronchamp

⑤⑦ *21 km (13 mi) west of Belfort via N19.*

The little town of Ronchamp, in the windswept Haute-Saône dé-partement, was once renowned for having France's deepest coal mine shaft (3,300 ft). The mine's huge chimney still towers above the val-ley, but Ronchamp is now the site of one of Europe's most famous post-★ war buildings. The hilltop chapel of **Notre-Dame-du-Haut** was designed by Swiss-born French architect Le Corbusier in 1951 to replace a church destroyed during World War II. The chapel's curved, sloping white walls; small, irregularly placed windows; and unadorned, slug-shape gray-concrete roof are unique. Many consider it Le Corbusier's masterpiece. ☎ *03–84–20–65–13.* 🎫 *10 frs.* ⊙ *Mid-Mar.–Oct., Wed.–Mon. 9:30–6:30; Nov.–mid-Mar., Wed.–Mon. 10–4.*

Montbéliard

⑤⑧ *16 km (10 mi) south of Belfort.*

Montbéliard is an industrial town that is home to the giant Peugeot automobile company and a stately castle. Only the two round towers of the **Château** remain from the heyday of the princes of Würstemberg, who once ruled this Renaissance principality; its more classical portions, dating to the 18th century, contain a museum devoted to insects, geological and archaeological finds, and local clocks and musical boxes. ⊠ *Rue du Château,* ☎ *03–81–99–22–61.* ≊ *May–Sept. 30 frs, Oct.–Apr. 10 frs.* ⊘ *Wed.–Mon. 2–6.*

Across the rail line in the neighboring suburb of Sochaux, Peugeot's production methods and colorful history can be explored at the **Musée de l'Aventure Peugeot** (Peugeot Adventure Museum). You can also tour the factory (children under 14 are not allowed). ⊠ *Carrefour de l'Europe,* ☎ *03–81–94–48–21; 03–81–33–27–46 to arrange factory tours.* ≊ *Museum 30 frs, factory tour free.* ⊘ *Museum daily 10–6; factory tours 8:30* AM *weekdays (English-speaking guides available).*

Besançon

⑤⑨ *80 km (50 mi) southwest of Montbéliard, 238 km (147 mi) southwest of Strasbourg.*

The former capital of the Franche-Comté, Besançon is a graceful, old gray-stone city nestled in a vast bend of the River Doubs. Its defensive potential was quickly realized by Vauban, whose imposing citadel remains the town's architectural focal point. The town has long been a clock-making center and, more recently, was the birthplace of the rayon industry. Famous offspring include Auguste and Louis Lumière, the inventors of a motion-picture camera, and the poet Victor Hugo, born in 1802 while his father was garrisoned here.

☾ A 75-minute **boat trip** along the Doubs River provides a good introduction to Besançon. Boats leave from Pont de la République and take in a lock and the 400-yard tunnel under the citadel. ☎ *03–81–68–13–25.* ≊ *49 frs.* ⊘ *July–early Sept., weekdays 10, 2:30, 4:30, weekends 10, 2:30, 4:30, 6; May–June, weekends 2:30 and 4:30.*

Wander around the quayside to the **Musée des Beaux-Arts et d'Archéologie** (Museum of Fine Arts and Archaeology) to see its collection of tapestries, ceramics, and paintings by Bonnard, Renoir, and Courbet. ⊠ *1 pl. de la Révolution,* ☎ *03–81–82–39–89.* ≊ *21 frs.* ⊘ *June–Oct., Wed.–Mon 9:30–6; Nov.–May, Wed.–Mon. 9:30–noon and 2–6.*

Besançon was once a great watch- and clock-making center, and the **Musée du Temps** (Museum of Time) houses an extensive collection of fine old timepieces. Even if you're not interested in watches, you can still enjoy touring the lovely Renaissance **Palais Granvelle** (1540), the museum's home. ⊠ *Palais Granvelle, Grande-Rue,* ☎ *03–81–81–45–14.* ≊ *Prices and hrs unavailable at press time.*

Besançon's oldest street, **Grande-Rue,** leads from the river toward the citadel, past fountains, wrought-iron railings, and stately 16th- to 18th-century mansions. Hugo was born at No. 140, the Lumière brothers just opposite.

☾ The **Horloge Astronomique,** at the foot of the citadel, is a stupendous 19th-century astronomical clock with 62 dials and an array of automatons that spring into action just before the hours are sounded. ⊠ *2 rue du Chapitre,* ☎ *03–81–81–12–76.* ≊ *15 frs.* ⊘ *Apr.–Sept., tours hourly Wed.–Mon. 9:50–11:50 and 2:50–5:50; Oct.–Mar., tours hourly Thurs.–Mon. 9:50–11:50 and 2:50–5:50.*

The **Citadelle,** perched on a rocky spur 350 ft above the town, has a triple ring of ramparts now laid out as promenades and peppered with Vauban's original watchtowers. Inside are museums devoted to natural history, regional folklore, agricultural tools, and the French Resistance during World War II. There also are shops and restaurants. ☎ 03–81–65–07–54. 🖪 *Joint ticket with citadel and museums 40 frs.* ☉ *Late Mar.–June and Sept.–Oct., daily 9–6; July–Aug., daily 9–7; Nov.– Mar., daily 10–5.*

Dining and Lodging

$$$ ✕ **Mungo Park.** This former warehouse on the banks of the Doubs is now a bright, glassed-in restaurant. Chefs Jocelyne Choquart and Benoît Rotschi bring local ingredients into this century—Jura snails in horseradish cream, chicken breast with morel mushrooms and vin jaune, and a sweet, hot dessert soup of walnuts, vin jaune, and nutmeg. ⊠ *11 rue Jean-Petit,* ☎ *03–81–81–28–01. Reservations essential. AE, MC, V. Closed Sun., 1 wk in Feb., and 2 wks in Aug. No lunch Mon.*

$$ ✕ **Poker d'As.** Carved-wood tables and cowbells counterbalanced by
★ swagged tulle and porcelain capture the ethnic-chic of this landmark restaurant's cuisine. Earning kudos for his *cuisine du terroir* (regional cooking), chef Raymond Ferreux animates his upscale experiments with splashes of local color: Jura *morteau* (sausage) sautéed with artichokes and cèpes, and pressed partridge with wild mushrooms. ⊠ *14 Clos St-Amour,* ☎ *03–81–81–42–49. AE, DC, MC, V. Closed Mon. and late July–early Aug. No dinner Sun.*

$ ✕ **Bistrot du Jura.** In an intimate, downscale setting of checkered tiles and bentwood, sample home-cooked regional specialties such as herring with steamed potatoes and andouillette in Jura wine—a fine selection of which is served by the glass. The owner keeps proud standards but irregular hours; call in advance. ⊠ *35 rue Charles-Nodier,* ☎ *03– 81–82–03–48. MC, V. Closed weekends.*

$$$ 🏨 **Castan.** Just below the citadel, in a courtyard behind a tangle of an-
★ cient trees and crumbling Roman pillars, this noble 17th- and 18th-century mansion has become a chic *relais* (inn). Rooms are atmospheric and exquisitely decorated: Regency moldings, period fabrics, luxurious baths, and a private collection of regional bibelots set the tone. ⊠ *6 sq. Castan, 25000,* ☎ *03–81–65–02–00, FAX 03–81–83–01–02. 10 rooms. Breakfast room, free parking. AE, MC, V.*

$$ 🏨 **Paris.** Extensive renovations have given this standby a sleek new look, with a mahogany-lined lobby and freshly decorated and enlarged rooms, all with full baths. Rooms overlook the quiet, tree-lined courtyard, though it's in the commercial heart of Besançon. It's well run and unpretentious. ⊠ *33 rue des Granges, 25000,* ☎ *03–81–81–36–56, FAX 03–81–61–94–90. 48 rooms. Breakfast room. AE, DC, MC, V.*

$ 🏨 **Granvelle.** Convenient to the citadel and set back from old-town streets, this modest, straightforward lodging has freshly decorated rooms, including some bargains with shared bathrooms. ⊠ *13 rue du Général-Lecourbe, 25000,* ☎ *03–81–81–33–92, FAX 03–81–81–31–77. 30 rooms, 26 with bath. Breakfast room. DC, MC, V.*

Ornans

60 *26 km (16 mi) south of Besançon.*

In the pretty village of Ornans, you can enjoy the views of the steep-roof old houses lining the Loue River and see the birthplace of Gustave Courbet (1819–77).

Gustave Courbet, the pioneering French Realist painter who influenced Édouard Manet, was an assertive, full-bearded radical who spent his last years in Swiss exile after toppling Napoléon's column on place Vendôme during the Paris Commune in 1871. The **Musée de la Maison Natale de Courbet** (Courbet's Birthplace Museum)—a rambling 18th-century mansion—hardly goes with his tempestuous image and provides a sedate setting for souvenirs, documents, drawings, sculptures, and paintings. Courbet is best known for his *Burial at Ornans* (now in the Musée d'Orsay in Paris; ☞ Chapter 1), with its procession of somber peasants. ✉ *Pl. Robert-Fernier,* ☎ *03–81–62–23–30.* 🎫 *20 frs.* ⏲ *July–Aug., daily 10–6; Apr.–June and Sept.–Oct., daily 10–noon and 2–6; Nov.–Mar., Wed.–Mon. 10–noon and 2–6.*

Montbenoît

㊱ *40 km (25 mi) southeast of Ornans.*

The tiny village of Montbenoît is dominated by its **Ancienne Abbaye,** which dates from the 11th century. The vast cloisters, conservative for their flamboyant times, were added in the 15th century. Take time to study the superbly carved wooden **choir stalls** (1525–27), which give a Renaissance interpretation of biblical tales. Samson, for instance, wears natty hose and a lace ruff collar as Delilah takes to his flowing locks with a pair of oversize scissors. ☎ *03–81–38–10–32.* 🎫 *15 frs.* ⏲ *July–Aug., Mon.–Sat. 10–noon and 2–6, Sun. 11:15–noon and 2–6; Sept.–June, check at tourist office (route de Pontarlier, tel. above). Guided tours with kitchen and refectory July–Aug. by request.*

Dining and Lodging

$$ ✕🏨 **France.** Swiss gourmets flock across the border, just two minutes away, to Villers-le-Lac, to savor chef Hugues Droz's exotic but earthy cuisine: lobster in vanilla and escargots in Pernod (the restaurant is closed Monday and doesn't serve dinner Sunday or lunch Tuesday). The spare, modern rooms are somewhat noisy. Breakfast, however, is bountiful. ✉ *8 pl. Maxime-Cupillard, 25130 Villers-le-Lac (24 km [15 mi] northeast of Montbenoît),* ☎ *03–81–68–00–06,* ℻ *03–81–68–09–22. 14 rooms. Restaurant. AE, DC, MC, V. Closed Jan.*

Pontarlier

㊲ *14 km (9 mi) southwest of Montbenoît.*

Pontarlier, with its old streets, churches, and gateways, was once France's main center for manufacturing absinthe—a notorious anise-based aperitif, the forerunner of Ricard and Pernod. It was banned in 1915 for inducing alcoholism and even madness. The **Musée Municipal** has a section on the history of the *fée verte* (green fairy), as absinthe was called. Porcelain and local paintings are also on display. ✉ *2 pl. d'Arçon,* ☎ *03–81–38–82–14.* 🎫 *15 frs.* ⏲ *Wed.–Mon. 10–noon and 2–6, Sat. 2–6, Sun. 3–7.*

OFF THE BEATEN PATH   **CHÂTEAU DE JOUX –** Just south of Pontarlier via N57, this fortress perched on a steep hill glowers across the Jura landscape toward the Swiss border. Founded in the 11th century, it retains its round medieval towers, drawbridges, and 17th-century ramparts. The dungeon holds a sturdy collection of old guns and weapons (guided tours only; allow one hour). ☎ *03–81–69–47–95.* 🎫 *32 frs.* ⏲ *July–Aug., daily 9–6; Feb.–June and Sept., daily 10–11:30 and 2–4:30; Oct.–Jan., daily tours at 10, 11:15, 2, and 3:30.*

Syam

㊳ *48 km (30 mi) southwest of Pontarlier: Take D72 and D471 to Champagnole, then N5 south (toward Geneva) before bearing left on D127.*

Syam, nestled in the lush Ain Valley, forged into the limelight in the second decade of the 19th century as an ironworks center. The **Forges de Syam** (Syam Ironworks) was built in 1813; iron was hauled in by train, then dragged down to the riverside by oxen. Simple lodging was

ONE LAST TRAVEL TIP:

Pack an easy way to reach the world.

123 456 7891 2345
J.D. SMITH

Wherever you travel, the MCI WorldCom Card℠ is the easiest way to stay in touch. You can use it to call to and from more than 125 countries worldwide. And you can earn bonus miles every time you use your card. So go ahead, travel the world. MCI WorldCom℠ makes it even more rewarding. For additional access codes, visit www.wcom.com/worldphone.

MCI WORLDCOM.

EASY TO CALL WORLDWIDE

1. Just dial the WorldPhone® access number of the country you're calling from.

2. Dial or give the operator your MCI WorldCom Card number.

3. Dial or give the number you're calling.

Austria ◆	0800-200-235
Belgium ◆	0800-10012
Czech Republic ◆	00-42-000112
Denmark ◆	8001-0022
Estonia ★	800-800-1122
Finland ◆	08001-102-80
France ◆	0-800-99-0019
Germany	0800-888-8000
Greece ◆	00-800-1211
Hungary ◆	06▼-800-01411

Ireland	1-800-55-1001
Italy ◆	172-1022
Luxembourg	8002-0112
Netherlands ◆	0800-022-91-22
Norway ◆	800-19912
Poland ÷	800-111-21-22
Portugal ÷	800-800-123
Romania ÷	01-800-1800
Russia ◆ ÷	747-3322
Spain	900-99-0014
Sweden ◆	020-795-922
Switzerland ◆	0800-89-0222
Ukraine ÷	8▼10-013
United Kingdom	0800-89-0222
Vatican City	172-1022

◆ Public phones may require deposit of coin or phone card for dial tone. ★ Not available from public pay phones.
▼ Wait for second dial tone. ÷ Limited availability.

EARN FREQUENT FLIER MILES

Bureau de change

Cambio

外国為替

In this city, you can find money on almost any street.

NO-FEE FOREIGN EXCHANGE

The Chase Manhattan Bank has over 80 convenient locations near New York City destinations such as:

    Times Square
    Rockefeller Center
    Empire State Building
    2 World Trade Center
    United Nations Plaza

Exchange any of 75 foreign currencies

 CHASE

THE RIGHT RELATIONSHIP IS EVERYTHING.®

built on-site, now occupied by the nearly 50 people who still work here, making nails, locks, tools, and machinery. "Hot-rolling" and "hard-drawing" techniques are explained at the museum (with video presentation). ☎ 03–84–51–61–00. 🎫 12 frs. ☾ July–Aug., Wed.–Mon. 10–6; May–June and Sept., weekends 10–6.

The founder of the forge, Alphonse Jobez, was clearly flushed with pride when he built the **Château de Syam,** a sturdy, square, yellow-front neo-Palladian villa. Finished in 1818, this grandiose self-homage has out-size Ionic pilasters at each corner and, inside, a theatrical colonnaded rotunda ringed with balconies and Pompeiian grotesques. Guided tours take you through restored rooms. ☎ 03–84–51–61–25. 🎫 25 frs. ☾ July–Sept., Fri.–Mon. 2–6.

Baume-les-Messieurs

64 *33 km (21 mi) west of Syam.*

A rambling little stone village in a breathtaking setting of cliffs and forests, Baume-les-Messieurs has a venerable medieval abbey and an underground network of caves. Its Romanesque stonework resonant with history, the 12th-century **Abbaye** has time-worn courtyards and a tenderly painted 16th-century Flemish altarpiece donated by the Belgian town of Ghent. ☎ 03–81–84–27–98. 🎫 Free. ☾ Daily 9–8.

The **Grottes de Baume,** 2 km (1 mi) outside town, consists of 650 yards of skillfully lighted galleries 400 ft underground, containing a river, a lake, and weird-shape stalactites and stalagmites (the temperature is chilly, so take a sweater). The largest cave is more than 200 ft high, and classical music blasts out to heighten the dramatic effect. The ceilings are clustered with hundreds of tiny mink-brown bats. ⊠ Chalet de Guide, ☎ 03–84–44–61–58. 🎫 25 frs. ☾ Apr.–Sept., daily 9:30–noon and 2–6.

Five kilometers (3 miles) outside Baume-les-Messieurs (south on D4 and then west on D71) is the **Belvédère des Roches de Baume** (Baume Rocks Overlook); watch for signs. The plummeting view of the ring of chalky cliffs hemming the village is spectacular. You can also hike the rim of the cirque, following the Grand Randonée (national hiking trail, GR59).

Dining and Lodging

$ ✕🏠 **Chambre d'Hôte/Étape Gourmande.** This bed-and-breakfast and
★ casual restaurant is nestled in the abbey itself, featuring groin-vaulted stonework, a vast Gothic fireplace, and a weathered refectory table for breakfast. Enjoy salads, Charolais beef with morels, and regional cheese dishes melted in the fireplace. If you're lucky, you can even stay in one of the three vast, beamed rooms furnished casually with mismatched collectibles and woodstoves. Views defy description. ⊠ Abbaye de Baume-les-Messieurs, 39210, ☎ 03–84–44–64–47. 3 rooms. Restaurant, breakfast room, deli. MC, V.

Château-Chalon

★ **65** *13 km (8 mi) north of Baume-les-Messieurs.*

The medieval village of Château-Chalon, on a rocky promontory high above vertiginous local vineyards, is renowned for its legendary vin jaune, said to keep for 200 years without losing its vigor (an 1857 bottle sold at auction in 1999 for 9,500 francs). Though there's very little to "do" here, you could easily lose yourself for a day in its atmosphere: The restored stonework, restrained shop fronts, and archaic street signs help to keep out the 20th century. You can sample the nutty, sherrylike flavor of vin jaune, opposite the 10th-century St-Pierre church, at the **Fruitière Vinicole.** Walk off any aftereffects with a stroll through the narrow, twisting streets.

<table>
<tr><td>OFF THE
BEATEN PATH</td><td>CHÂTEAU D'ARLAY – This 18th-century château, 8 km (5 mi) west of Château-Chalon, contains sumptuously carved regional furniture dating from the same period. The outstanding wine produced here can be sampled (and purchased) in the château's cellar, open Monday–Saturday 8–noon and 2–6. Combine your visit with a walk around the magnificent park, with its grotto, medieval ruins, and alley of ancient tilleuls (lime trees). Stop at the Volerie des Rapaces, where (at 4 PM and 5 PM) trained eagles and other birds of prey perform wide-winged acrobatics overhead. The Jardin des Jeux (Garden of Games) is a manicured vegetable garden designed on a parlor-game theme and is great fun for kids. ⊠ Rue Haute-du-Bourg, ☎ 03–84–85–04–22. ⊠ Château and volerie: 52 frs. ⊙ Mid-June–mid-Sept., Mon.–Sun. 2–6. Volerie also open Apr.–Oct., weekends 2–6.</td></tr>
</table>

Arbois

66 *24 km (15 mi) north of Château-Chalon.*

The pretty wine market town of Arbois is worth a stop for its fine restaurant, Jean-Paul Jeûnet (☞ Dining and Lodging, *below*). It also has a museum dedicated to the vine and to Louis Pasteur (1822–95), the famous bacteriologist and father of pasteurization, who grew up in Arbois.

The **Maison de Pasteur,** Louis Pasteur's family home, is fully furnished in authentic style, containing many of his possessions. ⊠ *83 rue de Courcelles,* ☎ *03–84–66–11–72.* ⊠ *32 frs.* ⊙ *Guided tours on the ½ hr June–Sept., daily 9:45–11:45 and 2:15–5:15; Apr.–May and early Oct. afternoons only.*

The Arbois vineyard is one of the finest in eastern France; to learn more about it, visit the **Musée de la Vigne et du Vin** (Vineyard and Wine Museum) and peruse its collection of tools and documents. ⊠ *Château Pécauld,* ☎ *03–84–66–26–14.* ⊠ *21 frs.* ⊙ *Mar.–Oct., Wed.–Mon. 10–noon and 2–6; Nov.–Feb., Wed.–Mon. 2–6.*

A short excursion south along D469 takes you into the magnificent **Reculée des Planches,** a dramatic rocky valley created by glacial erosion and peppered with caves and waterfalls. ☎ *03–84–66–07–96 cave access information.* ⊠ *Caves 33 frs.* ⊙ *Apr.–June and Sept., daily 10–noon and 2–5; July–Aug., daily 9:30–6.*

Continue along D469 from the Reculée des Planches to the beautiful, rocky **Cirque du Fer à Cheval** (Horseshoe Cirque), with its panoramic view of U-shape cliffs (10 minutes' walk from parking.) Watch for signs.

Dining and Lodging

$ ✕ **La Finette.** In a kitschy log-cabin setting, you can find hot, hearty local cooking at all hours: tripe in a casserole, sausage with lentils, and fondue. ⊠ *22 av. Pasteur,* ☎ *03–84–66–06–78. MC, V.*

$$$ ✕⊞ **Jean-Paul Jeûnet.** One of the most lauded eateries in the Jura holds
★   forth in an ancient stone convent, its massive beams enhanced with subtle lighting and contemporary art. Chef Jeûnet's devotion to local flora and fauna has evolved into a bold, earthy, flavorful cuisine: crayfish sausage, prawns with heather flowers, and even sheep's-milk sorbet. The chef's father, once an award-winning sommelier, has established a worthy cellar. (The restaurant is closed Tuesday, September to June; there is no lunch Wednesday.) Guest rooms have pleasant modern decor and pretty pine furniture. ⊠ *9 rue de l'Hôtel-de-Ville, 39600*

☎ *03–84–66–05–67,* 🖷 *03–84–66–24–20. 17 rooms. Restaurant. DC, MC, V. Closed Dec.–Jan.*

$$ 🖃 **Hôtel des Messageries.** This dignified, vine-covered inn on Arbois's main street has moderate rooms with flossy Baroque decor and a warm public ambience enhanced by grand spaces full of old wood and stone. ⊠ *2 rue des Courcelles, 39600,* ☎ *03–84–66–15–45,* 🖷 *03–84–37–41–09. 26 rooms. Breakfast room. MC, V. Closed Dec.–Jan.*

Outdoor Activities and Sports

Contact **Le Petit Cheval Blanc** (⊠ 39800 Fay-en-Montagne, ☎ 03–84–85–32–07) for details on renting horses, whether for an afternoon promenade or for an eight-day farm-to-farm self-guided circuit (available April–October).

ALSACE, LORRAINE, AND FRANCHE-COMTÉ A TO Z

Arriving and Departing

By Car

A4 heads east from Paris to Strasbourg, via Verdun, Metz, and Saverne. It is met by A26, descending from the English Channel, at Reims. A31 links Metz to Nancy, continuing south to Burgundy and Lyon. The quickest route from Paris to Besançon and the Jura is on A6 (to Beaune) and then A36; A5 from Paris to Besançon is swift and direct.

By Plane

Most international flights to Alsace land at **Mulhouse-Basel Airport,** on the Franco-Swiss border. Strasbourg, Metz-Nancy, and Mirecourt (Vittel/Épinal) also have tiny airports for charter and private plane landings.

By Train

Mainline trains leave Paris (Gare de l'Est) every couple of hours for the four-hour, 504-km (315-mi) journey to Strasbourg. Some stop in Toul, and all stop in Nancy, where there are connections for Épinal and Gérardmer. Trains run three times daily from Paris to Verdun and more often to Metz (around three hours to each). Mainline trains stop in Mulhouse (four to five hours) en route to Basel. Three high-speed TGV (*Trains à Grande Vitesse*) leave Paris (Gare de Lyon) daily for Besançon (2½ to 3 hours).

Getting Around

By Car

N83/A35 connects Strasbourg, Colmar, and Mulhouse. A36 continues to Belfort and Besançon. A4, linking Paris to Strasbourg, passes through Lorraine via Metz, linking Lorraine and Alsace. Picturesque secondary roads lead from Nancy and Toul through Joan of Arc country and onto Épinal. Several scenic roads climb switchbacks over forested mountain passes through the Vosges, connecting Lorraine to Alsace and Alsace to Belfort. And Alsace's Route du Vin, winding from Marlenheim, in the north, all the way south to Guebwiller, is the ultimate touring experience.

By Train

Several local trains a day run between Strasbourg and Mulhouse, stopping in Sélestat and Colmar. Several continue to Belfort and Besançon. Local trains link Besançon to Lons-le-Saunier, occasionally stopping in Arbois. Other towns, such as Arbois, Montbenoît, and Pontarlier, are accessible, with planning, by train. But you'll need a car to visit smaller villages and the region's spectacular natural sights.

Contacts and Resources

Car Rentals

Avis (⊠ 7 pl. Flore, Besançon, ☎ 03–81–80–91–08; ⊠ Pl. de la Gare, Strasbourg, ☎ 03–88–32–30–44). **Europcar** (⊠ 18 rue de Serre, Nancy, ☎ 03–83–37–57–24). **Hertz** (⊠ 7 pl. Thiers, Nancy, ☎ 03–83–32–13–14; ⊠ Pl. Flore, Besançon, ☎ 03–81–47–43–23).

Guided Tours

Walking tours of Strasbourg's old town are given by a tourist office guide at 2:30 every Saturday afternoon in low season, daily at 10:30 in July and August (38 francs). For information contact the **tourist office** (⊠ Pl. de la Cathédrale, ☎ 03–88–52–28–28). **Minitrain tours** (☎ 03–88–77–70–03) of the old town with commentary leave from place du Château from April through October (29 francs). In Besançon you can take a minitrain tour from the center up to the citadel, including recorded commentary and access to the various museums at the top (☎ 03–81–65–07–50 for info).

Outdoor Activities and Sports

A guide to bicycling in the Lorraine is available from the **Comité Départemental de Cyclisme** (⊠ 33 rue de la République, 54950 Laronxe). The **Comité Régional de Tourisme** (⊠ 9 rue de Pontarlier, 25000 Besançon) provides full details on hiking and biking in Franche-Comté. The **Fédération Jurassienne de Randonnée Pédestre** (⊠ Hôtel du Département, B.P. 652, 39021 Lons-le-Saunier) publishes a brochure on trails in the Jura. For a list of signposted trails in the Vosges foothills, contact the **Sélestat Tourist Office** (☞ *below*). A brochure on fishing is available by writing to **Agence de Developpement Deconomique du Doubs)** ⊠ Av. de la Gare d'Eau, 25031 Besançon). For information on horseback riding in the area, contact the **Délégation Départementale de Tourisme Équestre** (⊠ 4 rue des Violettes, 67201 Eckbolsheim, ☎ 03–88–77–39–64).

Travel Agencies

Havas Voyages (⊠ 23 rue de la Haute-Montée, Strasbourg, ☎ 03–88–32–99–77). **Carlson Wagons-Lits** (⊠ 30 pl. Kléber, Strasbourg, ☎ 03–88–32–16–34; ⊠ 2 rue Raymond-Poincaré, Nancy, ☎ 03–83–35–06–97).

Vacation Rentals

Contact **Gîtes de France** (⊠ 8 rue Louis Rousseau, 39016 Lons-le-Saunier, ☎ 03–84–87–08–88) for its brochure on "Gîtes de France" in the Jura. The list includes both bed-and-breakfasts and houses for rent.

Visitor Information

The principal regional tourist offices are in the following towns: **Besançon** (⊠ 2 pl. de la 1ᵉ–Armée Française, ☎ 03–81–82–80–77). **Nancy** (⊠ 14 pl. Stanislas, ☎ 03–83–35–22–41). **Strasbourg** (⊠ 17 pl. de la Cathédrale, ☎ 03–88–52–28–28), there is also a city tourist office at the train station; ⊠ Pl. de la Gare, ☎ 03–88–32–51–49).

Other local tourist offices are as follows: **Belfort** (⊠ 2 bis bd. Clemenceau, ☎ 03–84–55–90–90). **Colmar** (⊠ 4 rue Unterlinden, ☎ 03–89–20–68–95). **Guebwiller** (⊠ 73 rue de la République, ☎ 03–89–76–10–63). **Lons-le-Saunier** (⊠ 1 rue Louis-Pasteur, ☎ 03–84–24–65–01). **Metz** (⊠ Pl. d'Armes, ☎ 03–87–55–53–76). **Mulhouse** (⊠ 9 av. du Maréchal-Foch, ☎ 03–89–35–48–48). **Obernai** (⊠ 59 rue du Général-Gouraud, ☎ 03–88–95–64–13). **Saverne** (⊠ 37 Grand'Rue, ☎ 03–88–91–80–47). **Sélestat** (⊠ 10 bd. Leclerc, ☎ 03–88–58–87–20). **Toul** (⊠ Parvis de la Cathédrale, ☎ 03–83–64–11–69). **Verdun** (⊠ Pl. de la Nation, ☎ 03–29–86–14–18).

8 BURGUNDY

Producing a rarefied concentration of what many pronounce the world's greatest wines and harboring a knee-weakening concentration of magnificent Romanesque abbeys, Burgundy hardly needs to be beautiful—but it is. Its green-hedgerowed countryside and dense forests of the Morvan, its manor houses, scattered villages, and lovely (as well as stellar) vineyards deserve to be rolled on the palate and savored. Like glasses filled with Clos de Vougeot, the sights here—from the stately hub of Dijon to the medieval sanctuaries of Cluny and Clairvaux—invite us to tarry and partake of their mellow splendor.

Updated by
Christopher
Mooney

DRAIN TO THE DREGS BURGUNDY'S FULL-BODIED VISTAS: Rolling hillsides carpeted in emerald green, each pasture finely etched with hedgerows, peppered with cows, crosshatched with vineyards. Behind a massive quarried-stone wall, a château looms untouched by time, feather beds airing from the casement windows, a flock of sheep mowing the grounds. Tight-clustered villages, slate roofs still ringed from the days when they protected against brigands, encircle one central church spire, a lightning rod of local faith. On a hilltop high over the patchwork of green lords is a pale, patrician edifice of white rock, a Romanesque church of such austerity, such concentrated architectural purity, that it harks back to the Roman temples on which it first was modeled. And deep in a musty *cave* or in a wine cellar, redolent of cork and sour grapes, a row of glasses gleams like a garnet necklace, waiting to be swirled, sniffed, and savored.

You may often fall under the influence of extraordinary wine during a sojourn in Burgundy, but the beauty around you is not a boozy illusion. Passed over by the revolutions, both republican and industrial, unscarred by the world wars, relatively inaccessible thanks to circuitous country roads, it still reflects the pastoral prosperity it enjoyed under the Capetian dukes and kings.

Those were the glory days, the era of a Burgundy self-sufficient enough to hold its own against budding France and the fading Holy Roman Empire, the period of the expansive influence of the dukes of Bourgogne. Consider the Capetians, history-book celebrities all: There was Philippe the Bold, with his power-broker marriage to Marguèrite of Flanders. There was Jean sans Peur, who murdered Louis d'Orléans in a cloak-and-dagger affair in 1407 and was himself murdered in 1419 on a dark bridge while in a secret treaty negotiation with the future Charles VII. There was Philippe le Bon, who threw in with the English against Joan of Arc, and of course Charles the Bold, whose temerity stretched the territories of Bourgogne—already bulging with Flanders, Luxembourg, and Picardie—to include most of Holland, Lorraine, Alsace, and even French Switzerland. He met his match in 1477 at the battle of Nancy, where he and his boldness were parted. Nonetheless, you can still see Burgundian candy-tile roofs in Fribourg, Switzerland, his easternmost conquest.

Yet the Capetians in their acquisitions couldn't hold a candle to the Light of the World: The great Abbaye de Cluny, founded in 910, grew to such overweening ecclesiastic power that it dominated the European Church on a papal scale for some four centuries. It was Urban II himself who dubbed it *"la Lumière du Monde."* And like the Italian popes, Cluny, too, indulged a weakness for worldly luxury and knowledge, both sacred and profane. In nearby Clairvaux, St-Bernard himself spoke up in outrage, chiding the monks who, sworn to chastity and poverty, kept mistresses, teams of horses, and a library of unfathomable depth that codified classical and Eastern wisdom for all posterity—that is, until it was burned in the War of Religions and its knowledge lost for all time. The abbey itself followed after, destroyed for quarry stone after the French Revolution.

Neighboring abbeys, perhaps less glorious than Cluny but with more humility than hubris, faired better. The stark geometry of the Cistercian abbeys—Clairvaux, Cîteaux—stand as silent rebuke to Cluny's excess. The basilicas at Autun, Vézelay, and Paray le Monial remain today in all their noble simplicity yet manifest some of the finest Romanesque sculpture in the world; the tympanum at Autun stands outside all time frames in its visionary daring. And anchored between Autun and Vézelay the broad massif of the Morvan rises up, its dewy green flanks densely wooded in oak and beech. Hidden streams, rocky escarpments, dark forests, and meadows alive with hoopoes and falcons are protected today by the Parc Naturel Régional du Morvan—a hiker's dream.

It's almost unfair to the rest of France that all this history, all this art, all this natural beauty comes with refreshments. As if to live up to the extraordinary quality of its Chablis, its Chassagne-Montrachet, its Nuits-St-Georges, its Gevrey-Chambertin, Burgundy flaunts some of the best good, plain food in the world. Take two poached eggs in a savory wine sauce, a slab of ham in aspic, a platter of beef stew, a humble half-dozen snails: No frills, just the chill of pleasure that something so simple could resonate on the tongue—and harmonize so brilliantly with the local wine. This is simplicity carried to Gallic heights, with the poetry of one perfect glass of pinot noir married to a licensed and diploma'd *poulet de Bresse* (Bresse chicken), which sputters in unvarnished perfection on your white-china plate.

Thus you'll find that that food and drink take as much space in your travel diary as the sights you see. And that's as it should be in such well-rounded, full-bodied terrain.

— Nancy Coons

Pleasures and Pastimes

Abbeys

From the sober beauty of splendid and well-preserved Fontenay to the majestic ruins of Cluny and the isolated remains of Pontigny and Clairvaux—all presently ghosts of their former glory—the abbeys of Burgundy are an evocative part of the region's history. Reminders of medieval religious luminaries—notably Thomas à Becket and Bernard of Clairvaux—are everywhere, and they inject a sense of living history into a visit to the region.

Dining

Dijon ranks with Lyon as one of the unofficial gastronomic capitals of France, and Burgundy's hearty traditions help explain why. Parisian gourmets think nothing of driving three hours to sample the cuisine of Beaune's Jean Crotet or Vézelay's Marc Meneau. Game, freshwater trout, garlicky *jambon persillé* (ham flavored with parsley), coq au vin, snails, and, of course, beef Bourguignon number among the region's specialties. Sadly, mustard production is no longer the mainstay of Dijon (it has been displaced by the more profitable colza plant, from which cooking oil is made), but one or two people continue to make it by hand (importing the grain from Canada). *Pain d'épices,* a dense spice cake, is the delectable dessert staple of the region.

Like every other part of France, Burgundy has its own cheeses. The Abbaye de Cîteaux, birthplace of Cistercian monasticism in Burgundy, has produced a mild cheese for centuries. Chaource and strong, melt-in-your-mouth Époisses are also treats—as are Bleu de Bresse and Meursault. Meat and poultry—including Charolais beef from the regional breed of cattle and *poulet de Bresse,* the only regionally certified breed of chicken in France—are often served in rich wine-based sauces.

CATEGORY	COST*
$$$$	over 400 frs
$$$	250 frs–400 frs
$$	125 frs–250 frs
$	under 125 frs

per person for a three-course meal, including tax (20.6%) and tip but not wine

📧 *following the text of a review is your signal that the property has a Web site, where you will find details and, usually, images; for a link, visit www.fodors.com/urls.*

Hiking and Horseback Riding

The Parc Naturel Régional du Morvan, with its rocky escarpments, hidden valleys, rushing streams, thick forests, and wooded hills, is marvelous for hiking and horseback riding, especially in spring and fall.

Lodging

Burgundy is seldom deluged by tourists, so finding accommodations is not hard. But it is still wise to make advance reservations, especially in the wine country (from Dijon to Beaune). If you intend to visit Beaune for the Trois Glorieuses wine festival in November, make your hotel reservation several months in advance. Note that nearly all country hotels have restaurants, and you are usually expected to eat at them. Some towns have a large number of inexpensive hotels. In Dijon you can find them around place Émile Zola; in Beaune look around place Madeleine; in Auxerre they're tucked away in the streets down from Cathédrale St-Étienne; in Tournus and Avallon check out their old towns.

CATEGORY	COST*
$$$$	over 800 frs
$$$	550 frs–800 frs
$$	300 frs–550 frs
$	under 300 frs

All prices are for a standard double room for two, including tax (20.6%) and service charge.

Wine

Geography and centuries of tradition have given the wines of Burgundy a worldwide fame, each region producing a wine of distinctive quality: Chablis (dry white wine), Côte de Nuits (rich and full-flavored red wine), Côte de Beaune (delicately flavored red and white wines), Côte Chalonnaise (full-flavored red, white, and sparkling wines), Mâcon (earthy flavored white wines), or Beaujolais (fresh and fruity wine). The famous vineyards south of Dijon—the Côte de Nuits and Côte de Beaune—are among the world's most distinguished and picturesque. You can sample a selection at the Marché aux Vins in Beaune, an old town clustered around the patterned-tile roofs of its medieval hôtel-Dieu (hospital). Or go directly to the vineyards (though, of course, the hope is that you'll purchase a case). Don't expect to unearth many bargains, however. Less expensive Burgundies can be found between Chalon and Mâcon.

Exploring Burgundy

The best way to enter Burgundy is southeast from Paris by car. First, explore the northwest part of the region, from Sens to Autun, with a rewarding detour to the town of Troyes, in Champagne, and the Loire, in the west, around the Parc du Morvan. Go next to Burgundy's wine country, which begins at Dijon and stretches south down the Saône Valley through charming Beaune to Mâcon.

Great Itineraries

You could easily spend two weeks in Burgundy—visiting the sights, tasting the wine, and filling up on the rich food. If, however, you only have three days, you can take in two of Burgundy's most interesting cities—Dijon and Beaune. With five days you can explore the northeast part of the region, from Sens to Beaune. Eight days will give you time to get to the Parc du Morvan and the Côte d'Or—home to Burgundy's finest vineyards.

Numbers in the text correspond to numbers in the margin and on the Burgundy, Troyes, and Dijon maps.

IF YOU HAVE 3 DAYS

Start with Burgundy's two most interesting cities: First, the age-old capital of Burgundy, **Dijon** ㉞–㊺—former home to the dukes of Burgundy, who were among the richest people in the late Middle Ages and bequeathed to the city a dazzling legacy of art, goldsmithery, and tapestry. Second, move on to medieval **Beaune** ㊽ to view its majestic Hospice, founded by Chancellor Rolin, the great patron of Jan van Eyck and Rogier van der Weyden, whose *Last Judgement* altarpiece takes pride of place here. Between the two towns, visit the famous Burgundy vineyards around **Clos de Vougeot** ㊻—if you're lucky, you'll catch one of the *vendages* (or grape harvests).

IF YOU HAVE 5 DAYS

Make your first stop out of Paris the small town of **Sens** ①, with its vast cathedral and its 13th-century Palais Synodal. Then head for the serene abbey in **Pontigny** ⑯ and the Ancien Hôpital in **Tonnerre** ⑲. End the day tasting the famous white wine in **Chablis** ⑱ and spend the night there. Begin day two with a visit to **Auxerre** ⑰ and its cathedral before going on to ancient **Clamecy** ㉚ and the world-famous basilica in **Vézelay** ㉛. Stay overnight in dramatic **Avallon** ㉜, with its medieval church of St-Lazarus. By day three get to **Dijon** ㉞–㊺ and stay two nights. On day five take a short run down the wine-producing Côte d'Or to **Beaune** ㊽.

IF YOU HAVE 9 DAYS

Make **Troyes** ②–⑭, with its medieval pedestrian streets, your first stop. On day two head south to see **Tonnerre** ⑲, the Renaissance châteaux of **Tanlay** ⑳ and **Ancy-le-Franc** ㉑, and the Cistercian **Abbaye de Fontenay** ㉒. End the day in **Dijon** ㉞–㊻. Give yourself two days and nights in Dijon and then go to **Beaune** ㊽ for another night. While you're in the vicinity, drive south down the Saône River to medieval **Tournus** ㊿ and the abbey of St-Philibert, as well as the ruined abbey of **Cluny** (51). The next day drive north to see the cathedral and Roman remains in **Autun** ㉖, the **Château de Sully** ㉕, the hilltop town of **Châteauneuf-en-Auxois** ㉔, and the basilica in **Saulieu** ㉓; end up in **Avallon** ㉜. On day six drive through the **Parc Naturel Régional du Morvan** ㉝ and visit the village of **Château-Chinon** ㉗, the imposing cathedral in **Nevers** ㉘, and the abbey-church in **La Charité-sur-Loire** ㉙, before returning to Avallon. Spend the next two days and nights around **Auxerre** ⑰, **Chablis** ⑱, or **Sens** ①. These make good bases for exploring unspoiled **Clamecy** ㉚, the vineyards around Chablis, the abbey in **Pontigny** ⑯, and the basilica in **Vézelay** ㉛.

When to Tour Burgundy

May in Burgundy is especially nice, as are September and October, when the sun is still warm on the shimmering golden trees and the grapes are ready for harvesting scenting the air with anticipation. Many festivals also take place around this time.

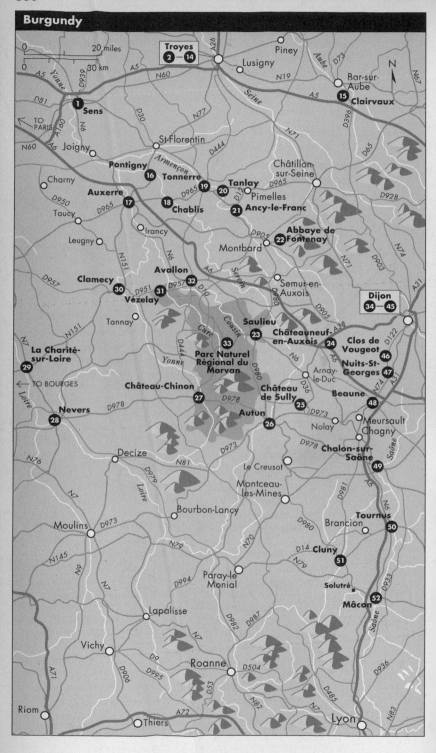

Troyes ②—⑭

① Sens

⑮ Clairvaux

⑯ Tonnerre

⑰ Auxerre

⑱ Chablis

⑲

⑳ Tanlay

㉑ Ancy-le-Franc

㉒ Abbaye de Fontenay

㉛ Vézelay

㉚

㉜

㉝ Parc Naturel Régional du Morvan

㉓ Saulieu

Châteauneuf-en-Auxois ㉔

Dijon ㉞—㊺

Clos de Vougeot ㊻

Nuits-St-Georges ㊼

㉗ Château-Chinon

㉕ Château de Sully

㉖ Autun

Beaune ㊽

Chalon-sur-Saône ㊾

Tournus ㊿

㉘ Nevers

㉙ La Charité-sur-Loire

Cluny 51

Mâcon 52

mid-19th century by medieval monument restorer Viollet-
six grand windows and vaulted Synodal Hall are outst
tectural features, but the building is now an exhibition
to the Palais Synodal is an ensemble of Renaissance b
courtyard there is a fine view of the cathedral's Fl
transept, constructed by master stonemason
start of the 16th century (rose windows
appreciate here). Inside is a museum
the Gallo-Roman period, includin
of bronze popular jewelry une
exceptional stelae depicting
Roman baths discovered
now on the museum's
parable to that of C
the shrouds of S
the star of th
ver-edged
displa
Sep

—can give you a false im-
in a hurry. The streets leading off it near the cathedral (notably rue Abelard and rue Jean-Cousin) are full of half-timber
medieval houses. On Monday the cathedral square is crowded with
stalls, and the beautiful late-19th century Baltard-style market throbs
with people buying meat and produce. A smaller market is held on Friday morning.

Begun around 1140, the cathedral used to have two towers; one was
topped in 1532 by an elegant though somewhat incongruous Renaissance campanile that contains two monster bells; the other collapsed
in the 19th century. Note the trilobed arches decorating the exterior
of the remaining tower. The gallery, with statues of former archbishops of Sens, is a 19th-century addition, but the statue of St. Stephen,
between the doors of the central portal, is thought to date from the
late 12th century. The vast, harmonious interior is justly renowned for
its stained-glass windows; the oldest (circa 1200) are in the north
transept and include the stories of the Samaritans and the Prodigal Son;
those in the south transept were manufactured in 1500 in Troyes and
include a much-admired *Tree of Jesse*. Stained-glass windows in the
north of the chancel retrace the story of Thomas à Becket: Becket fled
to Sens from England to escape the wrath of Henry II before returning to his cathedral in Canterbury where, in 1170, he was murdered.
Below the window (which shows him embarking on his journey in a
boat, and at the moment of his death) is a medieval statue of an archbishop said to have come from the site of Becket's Sens home. Years
of restoration have permitted the display of his *aube* (vestment) in the
annex to the Palais Synodal (☞ *below*). ⊠ *Pl. de la République,* ☎
03–86–64–15–27, www.musees£mariežsens.fr.

The roof of the 13th-century **Palais Synodal** (Synodal Palace), alongside Sens's cathedral, is notable for its Burgundian yellow, green, and
red diamond-tile motif—misleadingly (and incongruously) added in the

e-Duc. Its
nding archi-
space. Annexed
uildings from whose
mboyant Gothic south
Martin Chambiges at the
were his specialty, as you can
with archaeological finds from
g the *trésor de Villethierry*, a cache
rthed during the construction of A5,
various professions, and the remains of
n situ 20 years ago. The cathedral treasury,
econd floor, is one of the richest in France, com-
onques. It contains a collection of miters, ivories,
. Sivard and St. Loup, and sumptuous reliquaries. But
e collection is Thomas à Becket's restored brown- and sil-
linen robe. His chasuble, stole, and sandals, too fragile to
, await similar help. ☎ *03–86–64–46–27.* ⌷ *20 frs.* ☉ *June–*
.., daily 10–noon and 2–6; Oct.–May, Wed. and weekends 10–noon
nd 2–6, Mon. and Thurs.–Fri. 2–6.

Dining and Lodging

$–$$ ✕ **Le Clos des Jacobins.** With its pale orange walls and exceptional fish
★ specialties, this restaurant in the center of town strikes a happy balance between elegant and casual. Try the 100-franc lunch *menu du*
marché, which may include *matelotte d'oeufs pochés à l'Irancy* (poached
eggs in Irancy wine sauce), and *blanc de turbot au Noilly-Prat* (turbot
with Noilly-Prat vermouth). ✉ *49 Grande-Rue,* ☎ *03–86–95–29–70.*
AE, MC, V.

$$$ ✕⊞ **La Lucarne aux Chouettes.** There's nothing Hollywoodesque about
actress Leslie Caron's charmingly rustic riverside hotel and restaurant,
the Owl's Nest. The whitewashed brick dining room, with its ingenious
twisted rope chandeliers and cloth-covered chairs, has a homey-meets-
elegant feel, as do the rooms. There are only four, and the legendary
hostess is often on hand to greet her guests—so book early. In sum-
mer enjoy the terrace on the Yonne. The town itself, a *bastide* (forti-
fied town, built on a grid pattern), is entered and exited via sturdy, angular
13th- and 14th-century gateways. ✉ *Quai Bretoche, 89500 Villeneuve-*
sur-Yonne (12 km [7 mi]) south of Sens on N6), ☎ *03–86–87–18–26,*
FAX *03–86–87–22–63. 4 rooms. Restaurant. AE, MC, V.*

$$–$$$ ✕⊞ **Hôtel de Paris et de la Poste.** Owned for the last several decades
★ by the Godard family, the modernized Paris & Poste, which began life
as a post house in the 1700s, is a convenient and pleasant stopping
point. Rooms are clean and well equipped; No. 42, facing the inner
courtyard, is especially nice. But it's the traditional red-and-gold restau-
rant (with great homemade smoked salmon), padded green-leather arm-
chairs in the lounge, and little curved wooden bar that give this place
its comfy charm. ✉ *97 rue de la République, 89100,* ☎ *03–86–65–*
17–43, FAX *03–86–64–48–45. 25 rooms. Restaurant. AE, DC, MC, V.*

$$$–$$$$ ⊞ **Château de Prunoy.** Though it's a little out of the way, you may want
to venture southwest to this vast château and park built by one of Louis
XVI's finance ministers. It can seem a little haphazard, but if you
don't expect prompt service or mind Labradors running around, you'll
enjoy it. The comfortable rooms have idiosyncratic flair verging on kitsch:
One has a pair of carved, 7-ft-tall gilded wings guarding an 18th-cen-
tury ivory-and-pearl-inlaid jewelry stand; another is designed as a Jap-
anese teahouse. Dinner is not especially grand, but there are few
options nearby. ✉ *89120 Charny (40 km [25 mi] southwest of Sens,*
40 km/25 mi northwest of Auxerre on N6 to D943 to D18), ☎ *03–*

86–63–66–91, FAX *03–86–63–77–79. 19 rooms. Restaurant, pool, sauna, exercise room, meeting rooms. AE, DC, MC, V.*

Nightlife and the Arts

Sens is known throughout France for **Les Synodales,** an annual dance festival held in late June and July, which features distinguished dancers and other artists from around the world. Events are held in front of the cathedral and in surrounding streets; contact the tourist office for information (☞ Visitor Information *in* Burgundy A to Z, *below*).

Troyes

★ *64 km (40 mi) northeast of Sens, 150 km (95 mi) east of Paris.*

The inhabitants of Troyes would be insulted if you mistook them for Burgundians. Troyes is the historic capital of the Counts of Champagne; as if to prove the point, its historic town center is shaped like a champagne cork, the rounded top enclosed by a loop of the Seine. It was also the home of the late 12th-century writer Chrétien (or Chrestien) de Troyes, who, in seeking to please his patrons Count Henry the Liberal and Marie de Champagne, penned the first Arthurian legends. Few, if any, French town centers contain so much to see and do. A web of enchanting pedestrian streets with timber-frame houses, magnificent churches, fine museums, and a wide choice of restaurants make Troyes appealing. Keep in mind, however, that you're looking at a model of historical preservation. Despite its being one of the first French towns to be classed a *secteur sauvegardé* (protected zone) by then–Minister of Culture André Malraux, modern development and several major fires have removed large chunks of Troyes (brace yourself for the '70s concrete of the Quartier du 14 Juillet, intersected by the boulevard of the same name).

The center of Troyes is divided by quai Dampierre, a broad, busy boulevard. On one side is the quiet cathedral quarter, on the other the more upbeat commercial part. Keep your eyes peeled for the delightful architectural accents that make Troyes unique: *essentes,* geometric chestnut tiles that keep out humidity and are fire resistant; and sculpted *poteaux* (in Troyes they are called *montjoies*), carvings at the joint of corner structural beams. There's a lovely one of Adam and Eve next door to the hotel Les Comtes de Champagne (☞ Dining and Lodging, *below*). Along with its neighbors Provins and Bar-sur-Aube, Troyes was one of Champagne's major fair towns in the Middle Ages. The wool trade gave way to the cotton textile trade in the 18th century, and today Troyes draws busloads of visitors from all over Europe to its outlet clothing stores (☞ Shopping, *below*).

The **tourist office** (✉ 16 bd. Carnot, ☎ 03–25–82–62–70)www.ot-troyes.fr has information and sells museum passes that admit you to the four major museums for 60 francs—a 50% savings.

② Although Troyes is on the Seine, it is the capital of the Aube *département* (province), run from the elegant **Préfecture.** The building looks out across both an arm of the Seine, known as the Bassin de la Préfecture, and the place de la Libération from behind its gleaming gilt-iron railings.

③ Across the Bassin is the **Hôtel-Dieu** (hospital), fronted by superb wrought-iron gates (from the 18th century) and topped with the blue-and-gold fleurs-de-lis emblems of the French monarchy. Around the corner is the entrance to the **Apothicairie de l'Hôtel-Dieu Le Comte,** the former medical laboratory, the only part of the Hôtel-Dieu open to visitors. Inside, time has been frozen: Floral painted boxes and ceramic jars containing medicinal plants line the antique shelves. ✉ *quai*

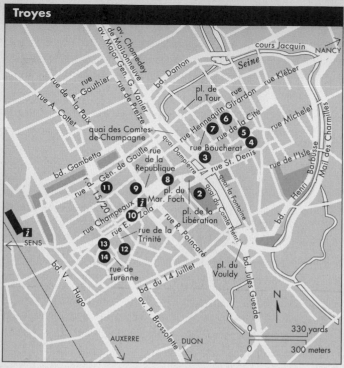

des Comtes-de-Champagne, ☎ *03–25–80–98–97.* 🖼 *20 frs.* ⊙ *July–Aug., Wed.–Mon. 10–6; Sept.–June, Wed. and weekends 2–6.*

④ The **Musée d'Art Moderne** (Modern Art Museum) is housed in the 16th-to 17th-century former Bishop's Palace. Its magnificent interior, with a wreath-and-cornucopia carved oak fireplace, ceilings with carved wood beams, and a Renaissance staircase, is home to the Lévy Collection of modern art—including an important group of works by Claude Derain. In the back are formal gardens. ⊠ *Palais Épiscopal, pl. St-Pierre,* ☎ *03–25–76–26–80.* 🖼 *30 frs.* ⊙ *Tues.–Sun. 11–6.*

⑤ The Flamboyant Gothic **Cathédrale St-Pierre–St-Paul** dominates with its 200-ft towers (undergoing restoration at press time); note the incomplete one-tower facade, the small Renaissance campaniles on top of the tower, and the artistry of Martin Chambiges, who worked on Troyes's facade (with its characteristic large rose window) around the same time as he did the transept of Sens. At night the floodlighted features are thrown into dramatic relief. The cathedral's vast five-aisle interior, refreshingly light thanks to large windows and the near-whiteness of the local stone, dates mainly from the 13th century. It has fine examples of 13th-century stained-glass in the choir, such as the *Tree of Jesse* (a popular regional theme), and richly colored 16th-century glass in the nave and facade rose window. The choir stalls and organ were requisitioned from Clairvaux Abbey. One of the chapels contains black-basalt tombstones marking the remains of Count Henry I of Champagne, carved in 1792 after the counts' palace was destroyed, and the cathedral treasury displays such curiosities as a piece of St. Bernard of Clairvaux's skull. The arcaded triforium above the pillars of the choir was one of the first in France to be glazed rather than filled with stone. Across the street from the cathedral, behind an iron fence, is an unusual, lopsided, late-medieval **grange aux dîmes** (tithe barn) with a peaked roof. It is used as a warehouse by the

wine maker next door. ⊠ *Pl. St-Pierre.* ☎ *03–25–76–98–18.* 🎟 *Free.*
🕓 *July–mid-Sept., daily 9–1 and 2–7; mid-Sept.–Feb., daily 10–noon and
2–4; Mar.–June, daily 10–noon and 2–5.*

⑥ Facing the cathedral square, the buildings of the former Abbaye St-Loup
now house the **Musée St-Loup,** an arts and archaeology museum. Exhibits are devoted to natural history, with impressive collections of
birds and meteorites; local archaeological finds, especially gold-mounted
5th-century jewelry and a Gallo-Roman bronze statue of Apollo; medieval statuary and gargoyles; and paintings from the 15th to the 19th
centuries, including works by Rubens, Anthony Van Dyck, Antoine Watteau, François Boucher, and Jacques-Louis David. ⊠ *1 rue Chrestien-
de-Troyes,* ☎ *03–25–76–21–60.* 🎟 *30 frs.* 🕓 *Sept.–June, Wed.–Mon.
10–noon and 2–6; July–Aug. Wed.–Mon. 10–noon and 2–7*

⑦ The **Hôtel du Petit Louvre** (⊠ Rue Boucherat) is a handsome, former
16th-century *relais de diligence* (coaching inn).

⑧ The **Basilique St-Urbain** was built between 1262 and 1286 by Pope Urban
IV, who was born in Troyes. St-Urbain is one of the most remarkable
churches in France, a perfect culmination of Gothic's quest to replace
stone walls with stained glass. Its magnificently long and narrow porch
frames a 13th-century *Last Judgment* tympanum, whose highly worked
elements include a frieze of the dead rising out of their coffins (note
the grimacing skeleton) and an enormous crayfish, a testament to the
local river culture. Inside, a chapel on the south side houses the *Vièrge
au Raisin* (*Virgin with Grapes*), clutching Jesus with one hand and a
bunch of Champagne grapes in the other. ⊠ *Pl. Vernier,* ☎ *03–25–
73–37–13.* 🎟 *Free.* 🕓 *July–Aug., daily 10:30–7; 1st 2 wks in Sept.,
daily 10:30–5; mid-Sept.–June, daily 10–noon and 2–4.*

⑨ Place du Maréchal-Foch, the main square of central Troyes, is flanked
by cafés, shops, and the delightful facade of the **Hôtel de Ville** (Town
Hall). In summer the square is filled from morning to night.

⑩ The clock tower of the church of **St-Jean** is an unmistakable landmark.
England's warrior king, Henry V, married Catherine of France here in
1420. The church's tall 16th-century choir contrasts with the low
nave, constructed earlier. ⊠ *Pl. du Marché au Pain.* ☎ *03–25–73–06–
96.* 🎟 *Free.* 🕓 *July–Aug., daily 10:30–7; 1st 2 wks in Sept., daily 10:30–
5; mid-Sept.–June, daily 10–noon and 2–4.*

⑪ **Ste-Madeleine,** the oldest church in Troyes, is best known for its elaborate triple-arched stone rood screen separating the nave and the choir.
Only six other such screens still remain in France—most were dismantled
during the French Revolution. This filigreed Flamboyant Gothic beauty
was carved with panache by Jean Gailde between 1508 and 1517. ⊠
Rue de la Madeleine. ☎ *03–25–73–82–90.* 🎟 *Free.* 🕓 *July–Aug.,
daily 10:30–7; 1st 2 wks in Sept., daily 10:30–5; mid-Sept.–June, daily
10–noon and 2–4.*

🐾 ⑫ There's a practical reason that the windows of the **Maison de l'Outil**
(Tool and Craft Museum) are filled with bizarre and beautiful outsize
models—like a winding staircase and a globe on a swivel. It's the display venue for the "final projects" created by apprentice Compagnons
de Devoir, members of the national craftsmen's guild whose school is
in Troyes. The museum, in the 16th-century Hôtel de Mauroy, also contains a collection of paintings, models, and tools relevant to such traditional wood-related trades as carpentry, clog making, and barrel
making—including a medieval anvil, called a *bigorne.* ⊠ *7 rue de la
Trinité,* ☎ *03–25–73–28–26.* 🎟 *30 frs.* 🕓 *Weekdays 9–1 and 2–6:30,
weekends 10–1 and 2–6.*

⑬ The 16th- to 18th-century church of **St-Pantaléon** primarily serves the local Polish community. A number of fine canopied stone statues, many of them the work of the Troyen Dominique le Florentin, decorator to François I, are clustered around its pillars. ⊠ *Rue de Turenne,* ☎ *03–25–73–06–99.* ⚏ *Free.* ☉ *July–Aug., daily 10:30–12:30 and 2:30–6:30; 1st 2 wks in Sept., daily 10:30–12:30 and 2:30–5:30; mid-Sept.–June, daily 10–noon and 2–4.*

🐚 ⑭ The 16th- to 17th-century **Hôtel de Vauluisant** houses two museums: the **Musée de Vauluisant** (History Museum) and the **Musée de la Bonneterie** (Textile Museum). The former traces the development of Troyes and southern Champagne, with a section devoted to religious art; the latter outlines the history and manufacturing process of the town's 18th- to 19th-century textile industry. ⊠ *4 rue Vauluisant,* ☎ *03–25–76–21–60.* ⚏ *Joint ticket for both museums 30 frs.* ☉ *Sept.–June, Wed.–Sun. 10–noon and 2–6; July–Aug., Wed.–Mon. 10–6.*

Dining and Lodging

The pleasure of Troyes is its old town, Vieux Troyes. This is where you want your hotel to be or at least within walking distance of it. If you want to dine informally, it's also the area to find a restaurant, especially rue Champeaux.

$$$ ✕ **Le Clos Juillet.** The best restaurant in Troyes, Le Clos Juillet also fea-
★ tures one of the largest wine cellars in Champagne. Chef Philippe Collin concentrates his considerable skills on local produce and practices but also throws in some exotic curveballs—oysters poached in cider, sea bream and caramelized leek tart, lobster couscous and fruit-filled Vietnamese rolls served with balsamic vinegar syrup. ⊠ *22 bd. du 14-Juillet,* ☎ *03–25–73–31–32. AE, MC, V. Closed Sun.–Mon. (summer), Feb., and last 2 wks of Aug.*

$$$ ✕ **Valentino.** Across the back courtyard from the Relais St-Jean (☞ *below*), is this comfortable, sea green–painted restaurant with a glassed-in terrace (tables are set outside in summer). Oysters are served as a complement to the menu's fish specialties—try them *en gelée d'eau de mer* (sea water aspic), chilled and served on a bed of *crème fraîche* with rock salt on the side. ⊠ *11 cour de la Rencontre,* ☎ *03–25–73–14–14. AE, MC, V. Closed Mon., last wk of Aug., and early Jan. No lunch Sat.*

$–$$ ✕ **La Taverne de l'Ours.** This popular, convivial brasserie has faux Art Nouveau and Gothic decor, brass globe lamps, and plush seating alcoves. It also has delicious, hearty cuisine, such as roast *cochon de lait* (suckling pig) straight off the spit. The 69-franc lunch menu is a real bargain, and even more heavenly when accompanied by the grapy, dark pink rosé *des Riceys* from the Champagne–Burgundy border. Happily, this place is open year-round. ⊠ *2 rue Champeaux,* ☎ *03–25–73–22–18. AE, MC, V.*

$$$ 🏨 **Le Champ des Oiseaux.** Idyllically situated in Troyes' oldest quar-
★ ter, this is the finest hotel in town—an ensemble of pink and yellow 15th- and 16th-century houses (their bright colors part of a town campaign to "medievalize" half-timber facades). Inside are stylish floral prints and 15th-century scrollwork panels. The biggest room, the Suite Médiévale, is under the oak-beamed eaves. Downstairs is a lovely breakfast room with a stone fireplace, as well as a vine-clad inner courtyard for summer mornings. ⊠ *20 rue Linard Gonthier, 10000,* ☎ *03–25–80–58–50,* 🖷 *03–25–80–98–34. 12 rooms. AE, MC, V.*

$$$ 🏨 **Relais St-Jean.** This calm, half-timbered hotel, in the pedestrian zone near St-Jean, has fully equipped, good-size rooms—some connected by a path through the second floor's tree-filled atrium. Black-leather chairs and mirrored walls make for incongruous bar decor, particularly because it's juxtaposed with the wicker and plants of the adjoining room. But have a drink here, and good-natured owner Monsieur Rinaldi will gladly chat. The hotel has no restaurant, but next door is the friendly **Valentino** (✉ 11 cour de la Rencontre, ☎ 03–25–73–14–14), with dining in its courtyard. ✉ *49 rue Paillot-de-Montabert, 10000,* ☎ *03–25–73–89–90,* FAX *03–25–73–88–60. 25 rooms. Bar, air-conditioning. AE, DC, MC, V. Closed mid-Dec.–early Jan.*

$$ 🏨 **Royal.** This modern hotel benefits by being less than a five-minute walk from Vieux Troyes and from the train and bus station (with windows open, you can hear the passing TGV—close them and it's quieter). Rooms are standard for a refurbished hotel: smallish, with either double or single beds, a desk, and a couple of chairs. The comfy bar, with its black-leather chairs, is a good evening hangout. ✉ *22 bd. Carnot, 10000,* ☎ *03–25–73–19–99,* FAX *03–25–73–47–85. 37 rooms. Restaurant, bar. AE, DC, MC, V.*

$ 🏨 **Les Comtes de Champagne.** In Vieux Troyes's former mint is this bargain hotel. The topsy-turvy building, with its solid, squat staircase and faded floral wallpaper, has a nice inner courtyard with large vines and a philodendron. The two couples who co-manage, the Gribourets and the Picards, are friendly. ✉ *56 rue de la Monnaie, 10000,* ☎ *03–25–73–11–70,* FAX *03–25–73–06–02. 35 rooms, 5 with bath. Parking. MC, V.*

Shopping

If there's an ideal place for a shopping spree, it's Troyes. Many clothing manufacturers are just outside town, clustered together in two large suburban malls: **Marques Avenue,** in St-Julien-les-Villas (take N71 toward Dijon); and **Marques City** and the American outlet store **McArthur Glen,** in Pont-Ste-Marie (take N77 toward Chalons-sur-Marne). Ralph Lauren and Calvin Klein at McArthur Glen face off with Laura Ashley at Marques Avenue and Doc Martens at Marques City, to name a few of the shops. The malls are open Monday 2–7, Tuesday–Friday 10–7, and Saturday 9:30–7.

Clairvaux

⑮ *55 km (34 mi) east of Troyes via N19.*

Although much of it has been replaced by a sprawling 19th-century prison, the **Abbaye de Clairvaux,** once the Cistercian mother abbey of Champagne and northern Burgundy, is well worth the detour from Troyes. St. Bernard, a native of Fontaine-les-Dijon, founded Clairvaux (meaning "bright valley") only two years after his entry into Cîteaux, in 1115, and three years before setting up the community of Fontenay, in 1118. Henceforward known as Bernard of Clairvaux, he went on to condemn Peter Abelard, preach the Second Crusade in Vézélay, and decry the lavish decor of Cluny. The 12th-century vaulted halls of the lay brothers' dormitory remain, as do parts of the once-flourishing 18th-century abbey. ✉ *Off of N19; watch for signs,* ☎ *03–25–27–88–17.* ⊙ *May–Oct., Sat. only. Guided tours at 2, 3, 4 and 5. Bring ID.*

Pontigny

⑯ *60 km (37 mi) south of Troyes, 56 km (35 mi) southeast of Sens.*

Pontigny can easily be mistaken for another drowsy, dusty village, but the once-proud **Abbaye de Pontigny** is as large as many cathedrals. In the 12th and 13th centuries it sheltered three archbishops of Canterbury, including St. Thomas à Becket (from 1164 to 1166). His path to refuge from the king of England was followed by his successor, Stephen Langton (here from 1207 to 1215), and, lastly, Edmund of Abingdon—whose body, naturally mummified in the years following his death in

1240, has been venerated by centuries of English pilgrims to Pontigny (as St. Edmund). His Baroque tomb, whose occupant is supposedly very much intact, can be seen at the rear of the church, although peeking through one of the openings is now strictly forbidden. The abbey was founded in 1114, but the current church was finished around 1150. By Burgundian standards the church and lay brothers' quarters (all that remain) were precociously Gothic—the first buildings in the region to have rib vaults. Inside, it is surprisingly Baroque—particularly beautiful are the late-17th-century wooden choir stalls, carved with garlands and angels. On the grassy lawn adjacent to the church is a large, plate-shape 12th-century **fountain** with 31 spigots and sculpted Gothic feet—one of the few functional medieval abbey fountains remaining in Europe. ☎ 03–86–47–54–99. 🖼 *Free, 20 frs for a guided tour.* ☉ *June–Oct., daily 9–7; Nov.–May, daily 10–5, except during services.*

Auxerre

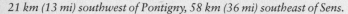 *21 km (13 mi) southwest of Pontigny, 58 km (36 mi) southeast of Sens.*

Auxerre is the jewel of Burgundy's Yonne region—a beautifully laid-out town with three imposing and elegant churches climbing the large hill on which it's perched over the Yonne River. Its steep, undulating streets are full of half-timbered houses in every imaginable style and shape. Although, as late medieval towns go, it is much more harmonious and architecturally interesting than flat, half-destroyed Troyes, Auxerre is underappreciated—perhaps because of its location, midway between Paris and Dijon.

The town's dominant feature is the ascending line of three magnificent churches—St-Pierre, St-Étienne, and St-Germain—and the **Cathédrale St-Étienne,** in the middle, rising majestically from the squat houses around it. The 13th-century choir, the oldest part of the edifice, contains its original stained glass, dominated by dazzling reds and blues. Beneath the choir, the frescoed 11th-century Romanesque crypt keeps company with the treasury, which features medieval enamels, manuscripts, and miniatures. A 75-minute son-et-lumière show focusing on Roman Gaul is presented every evening from June to September. ⊠ *Pl. St-Étienne,* ☎ *03–86–52–31–68.* 🖼 *Crypt and treasury 10 frs each; 25-fr Passport Ticket allows entry to crypt and treasury plus St-Germain (☞ below).* ☉ *Easter–Nov., Mon.–Sat. 9–noon and 2–6, Sun. 2–6.*

Fanning out from Auxerre's main square, **place des Cordeliers** (just up from the cathedral), are a number of venerable, crooked, steep streets lined with half-timber and stone houses, all gems. The best way to see them is to start from the riverside on the quai de la République, where the tourist office is (where a handy local map can be obtained), and continue along the quai de la Marine. The medieval arcaded gallery of the **Ancien Evêché** (Old Bishop's Palace), now an administrative building, is just visible on the hillside beside the tourist office. At No. 9 **rue de la Marine** (which leads off one of several riverside squares) are the two oldest houses in Auxerre, dating from the end of the 14th century. Continue up the hill to rue de l'Yonne, which leads into the **rue Cochois.** Here, at No. 23, is the appropriately topsy-turvy home and shop of *maître verrier* (lead-glass maker) P. Defert. Closer to the center of town, the most beautiful of Auxerre's many *poteaux* (the carved tops of wooden corner posts) can be seen at No. 8 **rue Joubert:** it dates from the late 15th century and its Gothic tracery windows, acorns, and oak leaves are an open-air masterpiece.

North of place des Cordeliers is the former **Abbaye de St-Germain,** which stands parallel to the cathedral some 300 yards away. The church's earliest section above ground is the 12th-century Romanesque bell tower, but the extensive underground crypt was inaugurated by Charles the Bald in 859 and contains its original Carolingian frescoes and Ionic capitals. It's the only monument of its kind in Europe, a labyrinth retaining the plan of the long-gone church built above it, and was a place of pilgrimage until Huguenots burned the remains of its namesake—a Gallo-Roman governor and bishop of Auxerre—in the 16th century. Several hundred years of veneration had already seen the burial of 33 bishops of Auxerre as close to the central tomb of St-Germain as they could physically get. The frescoes are a testimony to the brief artistic sophistication of the Carolingian Renaissance: witness St. Stephen running from a stone-hurling crowd towards the disembodied hand of God, a date-bearing palm tree, and the reversed images of a young and an old bishop teaching each other. ⊠ *Pl. St-Germain,* ☎ *03–86–51–09–74.* ▦ *22 frs.* ☉ *Guided tours of crypt, Oct.–Apr., daily 10, 11, and 2–5; May–Sept., daily every ½ hr between 10 and 5:30.*

Dining and Lodging

$$ ✕ **La Chamaille.** This restaurant, behind the church in the small village of Chevannes, south of Auxerre, is remarkably low-key for its culinary aspirations. The mood is set by the babbling brook running through the garden and the exposed brick walls in the dining room. Try the rabbit in a rich brown sauce and pastry. You'll be hard-pressed to find room for the apple flan, but you must—it's delectable. Prices are reasonable, especially the four-course menu, which includes a half bottle of regional wine, for 210 francs. ⊠ *4 rte. de Boiloup, Chevannes (10 km [6 km] south of Auxerre),* ☎ *03–86–41–24–80. AE, MC, V. Closed Mon.–Tues.*

$$ ✕ **Jardin Gourmand.** As its name implies, this restaurant in a former manor house has a pretty garden (*jardin*) where you can eat in summer. Inside is accented by sea green and yellow panels and is equally congenial and elegant. Terrine of pheasant breast is a specialty, and hope that the superb snails with barley and chanterelles is available. The staff is discreet and friendly. ⊠ *56 bd. Vauban,* ☎ *03–86–51–53–52. AE, MC, V. Closed Mon.*

$$ ▦ **Château de Ribourdin.** Retired farmer Claude Brodard began build-
★ ing his *chambres d'hôtes* (bed-and-breakfast) in an old stable six years ago, and the result is cozy, comfortable, and reasonably priced. Château de la Borde, named for another small manor (and former family-run establishment) nearby, is the smallest, sunniest, and most intimate room; all overlook Monsieur Brodard's fields. Homemade preserves—cassis, quince, and carrot—are served at breakfast. ⊠ *89240 Chevannes (8 km [5 mi] southwest of Auxerre on D1),* ☎ *03–86–41–23–16,* FAX *03–86–41–23–16. 5 rooms. No credit cards.*

$–$$ ▦ **Normandie.** The grand-looking, vine-covered Normandie is in the center of Auxerre, a short walk from the cathedral. Rooms are unpretentious and clean. The terrace is a nice place to relax after a long day of sightseeing. ⊠ *41 bd. Vauban, 89000,* ☎ *03–86–52–57–80,* FAX *03–86–51–54–33. 47 rooms. Bar, sauna, exercise room. AE, DC, MC, V.*

Chablis

⑱ *16 km (10 mi) east of Auxerre, 70 km (44 mi) south of Troyes, 183 km (114 mi) southeast of Paris.*

The pretty little village of Chablis, famous for its white wine, nestles on the banks of the River Serein and is protected by the massive, round, turreted towers of the Porte Noël gateway. Although in America Chablis has become a generic name for cheap white wine, it's not so in France: There it's a sharp, slightly acacia-tasting wine of tremendous character, with the Premier Cru and Grand Cru wines standing head to head with the best French whites. Prices in the local shops tend to be inflated, so your best bet is to buy directly from a vineyard; keep in mind that most are closed Sunday.

Dining and Lodging

$$–$$$ ✕⊞ **Hostellerie des Clos.** The moderately priced, simple yet comfort-
★ able rooms at this inn have floral curtains and wicker tables with chairs. But most of all, come here for chef Michel Vignaud's cooking, some of the best in the region. The restaurant is closed Wednesday. ⊠ *18 rue Jules-Rathier, 89800,* ☎ *03–86–42–10–63,* 🅵🅰🆇 *03–86–42–17–11. 26 rooms. Restaurant. AE, MC, V. Closed late Dec.–mid-Jan.*

$ ⊞ **Domaine de Montpierreux.** This private manor on a truffle farm south of Chablis has five immaculate rooms on its top floor. All are delight-ful, with paisley fabrics and at least one piece of antique furniture. The friendly owners help to make this a very comfortable base for explor-ing the area. Breakfast is served. ⊠ *89290 Venoy (6 km [4 mi] south of Chablis, 10 km [6 mi] north of Auxerre on D965),* ☎ *03–86–40–20–91,* 🅵🅰🆇 *03–86–40–28–00. 5 rooms. No credit cards.*

Tonnerre

⑲ *16 km (10 mi) northeast of Chablis, 60 km (37 mi) south of Troyes.*

The small town of Tonnerre was mostly rebuilt after a devastating fire in 1556. A good spot to survey the 16th-century reconstruction and the Armançon Valley is from the terrace of the church of **St-Pierre.**

The town's chief attraction, the high-roofed **Ancien Hôpital,** or hôtel-Dieu (hospital), was built in 1293 and has survived the passing cen-turies—flames and all—largely intact. The main room, the **Grande Salle,** is 280 ft long and retains its oak ceiling; it was conceived as the hos-pital ward and after 1650 served as the parish church. The original hospital church leads off from the Grande Salle; in the adjoining **Chapelle du Revestière,** a dramatic 15th-century stone group represents the *Burial of Christ.* Look for good finds at the **Salon des Antiquaires** (Antiques Fair), held here on All Saints weekend (the second weekend in November). ⊠ *Rue du Prieuré,* ☎ *03–86–54–33–00.* ⊡ *26 frs.* ☉ *June–Sept., Wed.–Mon. 10–noon and 1:30–6:30; Apr.–May and Oct.–Nov., weekends 1:30–6:30.*

Tanlay

⑳ *10 km (6 mi) east of Tonnerre, 45 km (28 mi) northeast of Auxerre.*

Tanlay is best known for its castle, the **Château de Tanlay.** Built around 1550, it is an example of the influence of the classical on Renaissance design. The vestibule, framed by wrought-iron railings, leads to a wood-paneled salon and dining room filled with period furniture. A graceful staircase climbs to the second floor, which has a frescoed gallery and or-nate fireplaces. A small room in the tower above was used as a secret meeting place by Huguenot Protestants during the 1562–98 Wars of Re-ligion; note the cupola with its fresco of scantily clad 16th-century reli-gious personalities. ☎ *03–86–75–70–61.* ⊡ *Guided tours 36 frs; grounds only 16 frs.* ☉ *Apr.–Nov. 15, Wed.–Mon. 9:30–11:30 and 2:15–5:15.*

Lodging

$ ⊞ **Chez Batreau.** The lovely little farming village of Cruzy-le-Chatel, on a hillside close to Tanlay, is home to this inn in a walled garden. Rooms are large and filled with family furnishings; beds sag a little. Nonetheless, the rooms are good value for the money, especially the one at the end of the hall, whose exposed timbers and cross beams form a sort of loft. ✉ 89740 *Cruzy-le-Chatel (12 km [7 mi] from Tanlay),* ☎ *03–86–75–22–78. 4 rooms, 2 with bath. No credit cards.*

Ancy-le-Franc

㉑ *14 km (9 mi) southeast of Tanlay, 63 km (40 mi) northeast of Auxerre, 51 km (32 mi) north of Avallon.*

Ancy-le-Franc is famous for its Renaissance châteaux. Built from Sebastiano Serlio's designs with interior decor by Primaticcio, both of whom worked at the court of François I (1515–47), the **Château d'Ancy-le-Franc** has an Italian flavor. The plain, majestic exterior contrasts with the sumptuous rooms and apartments, many—particularly the magnificent Chambre des Arts (Art Gallery)—with carved or painted walls and ceilings and their original furniture. Such grandeur won the approval of the Sun King, Louis XIV, no less, who once stayed in the Salon Bleu (Blue Room). Adjoining the château is a small **Musée de l'Automobile.** ✉ *Pl. Clermont-Tonnerre,* ☎ *03–86–75–14–63.* 🎫 *Château and museum 42 frs, museum only 20 frs.* ☉ *Early Apr.–mid-Nov., guided château tours at 10, 11, 2, 3, 4, 5, and 6 (last one at 5, mid-Sept.–mid-Nov.).*

Abbaye de Fontenay

★ **㉒** *46 km (29 mi) southeast of Tonnerre, 104 km (75 mi) southeast of Auxerre.*

Just east of Montbard is the best preserved of the Cistercian abbeys, the Abbaye de Fontenay, founded in 1118 by St. Bernard. The same Cistercian criteria applied to Fontenay as to Pontigny (☞ *above*): no-frills architecture and an isolated site—the spot was especially remote, for it had been decreed that these monasteries could not be established anywhere near "cities, feudal manors, or villages." The monks were required to live a completely self-sufficient existence, with no contact whatsoever with the outside world. By the end of the 12th century the buildings were finished, and the abbey's community grew to some 300 monks. Under the protection of Pope Gregory IX and Hughes IV, duke of Burgundy, the monastery soon controlled huge land holdings, vineyards, and timberlands. It prospered until the 16th century, when religious wars and administrative mayhem hastened its decline. Dissolved during the French Revolution, the abbey was used as a paper factory until 1906. Fortunately, the historic buildings emerged unscathed. The abbey is surrounded by extensive gardens dotted with the fountains that gave it its name. The church's solemn interior is lighted by windows in the facade and by a double row of three narrow windows, representing the Trinity, in the choir. A staircase in the south transept leads to the wood-roofed dormitory (spare a thought for the bleary-eyed monks, obliged to stagger down for services in the dead of night). The chapter house, flanked by a majestic arcade, and the scriptorium, where monks worked on their manuscripts, lead off from the adjoining cloisters. Fontenay retains one of the oldest forges in Europe, dating from the 13th century (including the massive fireplace) and once powered by the river. ✉ *Marmagne,* ☎ *03–80–92–15–00.* 🎫 *50 frs.* ☉ *Mid-Mar.–mid-Nov., daily 9–noon and 2–6; mid-Nov–mid-Mar., daily 2–5.*

Saulieu

㉓ *46 km (29 mi) south of Fontenay, 62 km (37 mi) northwest of Beaune, 77 km (49 mi) west of Dijon.*

Saulieu's reputation belies its size: It is renowned for good food (Rabelais, that roly-poly 16th-century man of letters, extolled its gargantuan hospitality) and Christmas trees (a staggering million are packed and sent off from the area each year).

The town's **Basilique de St-Andoche** (⊠ Pl. du Docteur Roclore) is almost as old as that of Vézelay, though less imposing and much restored. Note the Romanesque capitals. The **Musée François Pompon,** adjoining the basilica, is a museum devoted, in part, to the work of animal-bronze sculptor Pompon (1855–1933), whose smooth, stylized creations seem contemporary but predate World War II. The museum also contains Gallo-Roman funeral stones, sacred art, and a room devoted to local gastronomic lore. ⊠ *Rue Sallier,* ☎ *03–80–64–19–51.* 🖾 *22 frs.* ☉ *Apr.–Sept., Wed.–Mon. 10–12:30 and 2–6 (until 5:30, Oct.–Mar.).*

Dining and Lodging

$$$$ ✕🖫 **La Côte d'Or.** Chef Bernard Loiseau is one of France's culinary
★   superstars. Come here for dishes like foie gras and fowl in a pureed truffle sauce, served in the chapel-like wood-beamed dining room with a lush flower garden radiating around it. Rooms and suites likewise combine exposed beams and glass panels, with cheerful traditional furnishings. ⊠ *2 rue d'Argentine (off N6), 21210 Saulieu,* ☎ *03–80–90–53–53,* 🖾X *03–80–64–08–92. 15 rooms. Restaurant. AE, DC, MC, V.*

$$ ✕🖫 **Chez Camille.** Small, quiet, and friendly sum up this hotel in a 16th-century house with an exterior so ordinary you might easily pass it by. Rooms have period furniture and original wooden beams; ask for No. 22 or No. 23, the most dramatic, with a beamed ceiling that looks like spokes in a wheel. Traditional Burgundian fare—duck and boar are specialties—makes up the menu in the glass-roofed restaurant. ⊠ *1 pl. Édouard-Herriot, 21230 Arnay-le-Duc (on N6 between Saulieu and Beaune),* ☎ *03–80–90–01–38,* 🖾X *03–80–90–04–64. 11 rooms. Restaurant. AE, DC, MC, V.*

Châteauneuf-en-Auxois

㉔ *41 km (25 mi) east of Saulieu, 35 km (22 mi) northwest of Beaune.*

The tiny hilltop town of Châteauneuf-en-Auxois catches your eye from A6. Turn off at Pouilly-en-Auxois and take any one of the three narrow, winding roads up, and you'll suddenly feel you've entered the Middle Ages. The town's modest 15th-century church was the salvation for perhaps as many as 500 souls when the village was at its zenith. In the last few years tourists have discovered the charm of this village, so try to avoid it on weekends.

The **château,** built in the 12th and 15th centuries (with some later modifications), commands a breadth of view over rolling farmland as far as the eye can see. Clustered behind the château are houses for ordinary folk, at least a score of them notable for their 14th- and 15th-century charm, where today only about 80 people live. One of them, the charming **Monsieur Simon** (☎ 03–80–49–21–59), is so proud of his village that he gladly takes small groups on tours of the sights. ☎ *03–80–49–21–89.* 🖾 *21 frs.* ☉ *Apr.–May and Sept., Thurs.–Mon. 9:30–12:30 and 2–6; June–Aug., Thurs.–Mon. 9:30–12:30 and 2–7; Oct.–Mar., Thurs.–Mon. 10–noon and 2–4.*

Dining and Lodging

$$$$ ✕🖫 **Château la Chassagne.** Feel like a king or a queen for a night at this former country estate where you can even arrive by private plane or helicopter and be picked up in a Rolls-Royce. Rooms have high ceilings and are spacious—their best attributes; for although the modern wrought-iron and cane furnishings are obviously expensive, they are of disputable taste. The extensive grounds include a golf driving range, tennis courts, and a swimming pool. The restaurant, managed separately,

is quite formal. Nouvelle cuisine is served, but the chef seems to focus more on artistic presentation than creative tastes; still it's enjoyable. ✉ *21410 Pont-de-Pany (12 km [7 mi] from Châteauneuf-en-Auxois off A38, shortly after the junction with A6),* ☎ *03–80–49–76–00,* FAX *03–80–49–76–19. 12 rooms. Restaurant, pool, driving range, 2 tennis courts, helipad, private airstrip. AE, DC, MC, V. Closed Nov.–Mar.*

$$ ✕⊞ **Hostellerie du Château.** This hotel is in an ancient timbered building in the shadow of the castle. The restaurant serves classical Bourgogne fare—roasted Époisses (local cow's-milk cheese) on a salad bed with walnuts, noisettes of lamb with thyme, and coq au vin; it is closed Tuesday and doesn't serve dinner Monday, except in July and August. Rooms vary considerably—from small to much more commodious; the best have a view of the castle. ✉ *Châteauneuf-en-Auxois, 21320 Pouilly,* ☎ *03–80–49–22–00,* FAX *03–80–49–21–27. 17 rooms. Restaurant. AE, DC, MC, V. Closed late Nov.–early Feb.*

Château de Sully

㉕ *37 km (28 mi) south of Châteauneuf-en-Auxois, 43 km (27 mi) southeast of Saulieu.*

The turreted Renaissance Château de Sully stands in a stately park, surrounded by a moat. A monumental staircase leads to the broad terrace. Marshal MacMahon, president of France from 1873 to 1879, was born here in 1808. ☎ *03–85–82–10–27.* 🎫 *Guided tours 35 frs, grounds 15 frs.* ☉ *Château 45-min guided tours June–Sept. (call for times). Grounds daily 10–noon and 2–6.*

Autun

㉖ *20 km (12 mi) southwest of Sully, 41 km (25 mi) south of Saulieu, 49 km (30 mi) west of Beaune.*

Autun is an underrated mecca for fans of both Gallo-Roman and Romanesque art. It has been an important town since Roman times, as you can detect from the well-preserved archways, Porte St-André and Porte d'Arroux, and the Théâtre Romain, once the largest arena in Gaul. Not known for their modesty, the Autunois went so far as to declare their hometown (then called Augustodonum) "sister and rival of Rome itself." In the 12th century master sculptor Gislebertus left his precocious mark on the cathedral. Several centuries later, Napoléon and his brother Joseph studied here at the military academy.

★ Autun's principal monument is the **Cathédrale St-Lazarus,** built from 1120 to 1146 to house the relics of St. Lazarus; the main tower, spire, and upper reaches of the chancel were added in the late 15th century. Lazarus's tricolor tomb was dismantled in 1766 by canons: vestiges of exquisite workmanship can be seen in the neighboring Musée Rolin. The same canons also did their best to transform the Romanesque-Gothic cathedral into a classical temple, adding pilasters and classical ornaments willy-nilly. Fortunately, the lacy Flamboyant Gothic organ tribune and some of the best Romanesque stonework, including the inspired nave capitals and the tympanum above the main door, emerged unscathed. Jean-Auguste Ingres's painting depicting the *Martyrdom of St. Symphorien* has been relegated to a dingy chapel in the north aisle of the nave. The *Last Judgment,* above the main door, was plastered over in the 18th century, which preserved not only the stylized Christ and elongated apostles but also the inscription GISLEBERTUS HOC FECIT— Gislebertus did this. Christ's head, which had disappeared, was found by a local canon shortly after World War II. Make sure to visit the cathedral's **Salle Capitulaire,** which houses Gislebertus's original capitals, distinguished by their relief carvings. The cathedral provides a stunning setting for **Musique en Morvan,** a classical music festival in July. ✉ *Pl. St-Louis.*

The **Musée Rolin,** across from the cathedral, was once home to Chancelor Nicholas Rolin, an important Burgundian administrator and art patron. The museum is noteworthy for its Dutch Renaissance paintings and sculpture. But the collection's star is a Gislebertus masterpiece, the *Temptation of Eve,* which originally topped one of the side doors of the cathedral. Try to imagine the missing elements of the scene: Adam on the left and the devil on the right. ✉ *3 rue des Bancs,* ☎ *03–85–52–09–76.* 🎫 *20 frs.* ☉ *Oct.–Mar., Wed.–Sat. 10–noon and 2–4, Sun. 10–noon and 2:30–5; Apr.–Sept., Wed.–Mon. 9:30–noon and 1:30–6.*

The **Théâtre Romain,** at the edge of town on the road to Chalon-sur-Saône, is a historic spot for lunch. Pick up the makings for a picnic in town and eat it on the stepped seats where as many as 15,000 Gallo-Roman spectators sat during performances two millennia ago. In August a Gallo-Roman performance—the only one of its kind—is put on by locals in period costume. The peak of a Gallo-Roman pyramid can be seen in the foreground.

The **Temple of Janus,** in a field at the edge of town as you leave for Château-Chinon, is a Celtic temple built in the Roman style by the local Eduan tribe. It may have honored the horse goddess Eponna, a maternal figure, or Cernunnos, a war god.

Dining and Lodging

$$–$$$$ ✕☗ **Hôtel St-Louis.** Autun's best hotel, in a former post house, is more noteworthy for its history than its pretensions to elegance. It has Mexican wrought-iron furnishings and a remarkable family-size suite—it was while making a speech from this room's balcony in 1815 on his way back to Paris that Napoléon was rebuffed by crowds; George Sand also stayed here. The staff is friendly and helpful, and the restaurant, La Rotonde, is one of Autun's best. ✉ *6 rue de l'Arbalète, 71400,* ☎ *03–85–52–01–01,* 🅵🅰🆇 *03–85–86–32–54. 39 rooms. Restaurant. AE, DC, MC, V.*

$$–$$$$ ☗ **Hôtel des Ursalines.** Placed above the Roman ramparts of the old city, this converted 17th-century convent offers spacious, well-kept rooms overlooking a charming French garden. The restaurant, run by Paul Bocuse protégée Bruno Schlewitz, is worth a trip in itself, especially for the escargots with dried tomatoes and garlic *confit.* ✉ *14 rue Rivault,* ☎ *03–85–86–58–58,* 🅵🅰🆇 *03–85–86–23–07. 35 rooms, 8 apartments. Restaurant, air-conditioning. AE, DC, MC, V.*

Château-Chinon

㉗ *37 km (23 mi) west of Autun, 62 km (38 mi) south of Avallon.*

The late president François Mitterrand was a former mayor of the small town of Château-Chinon, the capital of the Morvan. One of his legacies is the brash, colorful, and controversial **Fontaine de Niki de St-Phalle,** in front of the Hôtel de Ville.

At the **Musée du Septennat** (Septannate Museum)—the name refers to the seven-year French presidency—is an astonishing variety of gifts Mitterrand received while president. ✉ *6 rue du Château,* ☎ *03–86–60–67–62.* 🎫 *26 frs.* ☉ *Early Feb.–Apr. and Oct.–Dec., Wed.–Mon. 10–1 and 2–7; May–June and Sept., daily 10–1 and 2–6; July–Aug., daily 10–1 and 2–7.*

☺ The **Musée du Costume** (Clothing Museum) exhibits French clothing from the 18th century. ✉ *4 rue du Château,* ☎ *03–86–85–18–55.* 🎫

25 frs. ⊙ *Oct.–Apr., Wed.–Mon. 10–1 and 2–6; May–June and Sept., Wed.–Mon. 10–1 and 2–6; July–Aug., daily 10–1 and 2–7.*

$$ ⊞ **Le Vieux Morvan.** This family-run pension was Monsieur le Présidènt François Mitterrand's unofficial headquarters during his 14-year reign, and it still attracts its share of presidential pilgrims. The rooms are simple and clean, and the 130-seat restaurant, with its panoramic view of the Morvan, is worth a trip in itself. Try the very copious *tête de veau* (calf's head) —which just happens to be the favorite dish of Mitterrand's successor, Jacques Chirac. ⊠ *8 pl. Gudin,* ☎ *03–86–85–05–01,* ⅢⅩ *03–86–85–05–01. 24 rooms. MC,V. Closed Jan.*

Nevers

㉘ *64 km (40 mi) west of Château-Chinon, 119 km (74 mi) south of Auxerre, 239 km (149 mi) southeast of Paris.*

Burgundy's western outpost, Nevers, on the banks of the Loire, has been producing earthenware since the late 16th century. Promoted initially by Italian craftsmen, the industry suffered during the French Revolution, but five or six traditional manufacturers remain. An extensive selection of Nevers earthenware, retracing its stylistic development, can be admired at the **Musée Municipal** (Town Museum). ⊠ *Promenade des Remparts,* ☎ *03–86–71–67–90.* ⅢⅩ *15 frs.* ⊙ *May–Sept., daily 10–6:30; Oct.–Apr., Wed.–Sat. 1–5:30, Sun. 10–noon and 2–5:30.*

Part of Nevers's medieval walls extend behind the Town Museum, culminating in the intimidating gateway known as the **Porte du Croux** (built in 1393), which, thanks to its turrets and huge, sloping roof, resembles a small castle.

The **Cathédrale** (⊠ Rue du Cloître-St-Cyr) has a 170-ft square tower, two apses, and two choirs—one Romanesque, one Gothic—in place of a narthex. The **Palais Ducal** (⊠ Pl. de la République), beyond the cathedral, has a sumptuous, large-windowed Renaissance facade but, unfortunately, is closed to the public.

Across the park that can be entered from place Carnot is the **Couvent St-Gildard,** the convent where St. Bernadette of Lourdes (1844–79) spent the last 13 years of her life. A small museum contains mementos and outlines her life story (she claimed to have seen the Virgin several times in 1858 and was canonized in 1933). ⊠ *Rue St-Gildard,* ☎ *03–86–71–99–50.* ⅢⅩ *Free.* ⊙ *Apr.–Oct., daily 7 AM–7:30 PM; Nov.–Mar., daily 7:30–noon and 2–7.*

Dining

$–$$ ✕ **La Cour St-Étienne.** The food is delicious, exquisitely presented, and an excellent value, and the ambience is serene. Enjoy lunch on the terrace overlooking the courtyard or in one of the cozy dining rooms. Farm-raised veal medallions with morels is just one of the specialties. ⊠ *Rue St-Etienne,* ☎ *03–86–36–74–57. Reservations essential. MC, V. Closed Aug. and 1st 2 wks of Jan. No dinner Sun.–Mon.*

The Arts

Jazz à Nevers is just that—a jazz festival that takes place in Nevers in the spring (☎ 03–86–57–88–51 for more information).

La Charité-sur-Loire

㉙ *24 km (15 mi) northwest of Nevers, 94 km (58 mi) south of Auxerre.*

La Charité-sur-Loire is best known for its medieval church. Unlike those of Pontigny and Fontenay, the abbey church of **Ste-Croix-Notre-Dame** was dependent on Cluny; when it was consecrated by Pope Pascal II in 1107, it was the country's second-largest church. Fire and neglect have taken their toll on the massive original edifice, and these days the church is cut in two, with the single-tower facade separated from the imposing choir and transept by pretty place Ste-Croix (where the nave used to be). A fine view of the church's exterior can be seen from Square des Bénédictins, just off Grande-Rue.

Clamecy

 51 km (32 mi) northeast of La Charité-sur-Loire, 44 km (27 mi) south of Auxerre.

Slow-moving Clamecy is not on many tourist itineraries, but its tumbling alleyways and untouched ancient houses epitomize *la France profonde* (the French heartland). The multishape roofs, dominated by the majestic square tower of the church of **St-Martin,** are best viewed from the banks of the Yonne River. The river played a crucial role in Clamecy's development; trees from the nearby Morvan Forest were chopped down and floated to Paris in huge convoys. The history of this form of transport (*flottage*), which lasted until 1923, is detailed in the Musée Municipal (Town Museum), also known as the **Musée d'Art et d'Histoire Romain Rolland** (Romain Rolland Museum of Art and History). Native son Rolland, Nobel Laureate of literature in 1915, spent his final years in a small literary community in nearby Vézelay. Faïence and paintings from the 17th–19th centuries are also on display. ✉ *Av. de la République,* ☎ *03–86–60–67–61.* 🎫 *15 frs.* ☉ *Easter–Oct., Wed.–Mon. 10–noon and 2–6; Nov.–Easter, Mon. and Wed.–Sat. 10–noon and 3–6.*

In homage to the logs that were once floated downriver, *bûchette* (a log-shape sugared-almond candy) has long been a favorite of Clamecyçois. Sample it at **Avignon** (✉ 22 rue de la Monnaie, near steps leading to St-Martin), a pastry shop and tearoom.

Dining and Lodging

$–$$ ✕🏨 **Hostellerie de la Poste.** This family-run hotel, in an old coaching stop in the heart of Clamecy, has a welcoming feel. The old-fashioned rooms are small and worn but tidy and clean. It's a popular place for lunching locals, who all seem to be greeted warmly by name at the desk. Regional fare is served; menus start at 100 francs. ✉ *4 pl. Émile Zola, 58500,* ☎ *03–86–27–01–55,* 📠 *03–86–27–05–99. 16 rooms. Restaurant, bar, meeting rooms. AE, MC, V.*

Vézelay

 24 km (15 mi) east of Clamecy, 51 km (32 mi) south of Auxerre, 13 km (8 mi) southwest of Avallon.

The somewhat isolated, picturesque village of Vézelay is on a peak, with one main street, rue St-Étienne, climbing steeply to its summit and its medieval basilica, with its world-famous Romanesque sculpture. In summer you have to leave your car at the bottom and walk up. Off-season you can drive up and look for a spot to park in the square.

It's easy to ignore this tiny village, but don't: hidden under its narrow *ruelles* (small streets) are Romanesque cellars that once sheltered pilgrims and are now opened to visitors by homeowners in summer. Sections of several houses have arches and columns dating to the 12th and 13th centuries: don't miss the hostelry across from the tourist office and, next to it, the house where Louis VII, Eleanor of Aquitaine, and the king's adviser Suger stayed when they came to hear St. Bernard preach the Second Crusade in 1146.

★ In the 11th and 12th centuries the celebrated **Basilique Ste-Madeleine** was one of the focal points of Christendom. Pilgrims poured in to see the relics of St. Mary Magdalene (in the crypt) before setting off on the great trek to the shrine of St. James at Santiago de Compostela, in northwest Spain. Several pivotal church declarations of the Middle Ages were made from here, including St. Bernard's preaching of the Second Crusade (which attracted a huge French following) and Thomas à Becket's excommunication of English king Henry II. By the mid-13th century the authenticity of St. Mary's relics was in doubt; others had been discovered in Provence. The basilica's decline continued until the French Revolution, when the basilica and adjoining monastery buildings were sold by the state. Only the basilica, cloister, and dormitory escaped demolition and were falling into ruin when ace restorer Viollet-le-Duc, sent by his mentor Prosper Merimée, rode to the rescue in 1840 (he also restored the cathedrals of Laon and Amiens and Paris's Notre-Dame).

Today the basilica, under the patrimony of UNESCO, has recaptured some of its glory and is considered to be one of France's most prestigious Romanesque showcases. The exterior tympanum was redone by Viollet-le-Duc (have a look at the eroded original as you exit the cloister), but the narthex (circa 1150) is a Romanesque masterpiece. Note the interwoven zodiac signs and depictions of seasonal crafts along its rim, similar to those at Troyes and Autun. The pilgrims' route around the building is indicated by the majestic flowers over the left-hand entrance, which metamorphose into full-blown blooms on the right; a yearly procession is still held on July 22. Among the most beautiful of the nave capitals is one of Moses grinding grain—symbolizing the Old Testament—into the flour—the New Testament—which St. Paul collects in a sack.

The basilica's exterior is best seen from the leafy terrace to the right of the facade. Opposite, a vast, verdant panorama encompasses lush valleys and rolling hills and hedgerows. In the foreground is the Flamboyant Gothic spire of St-Père-sous-Vézelay, a tiny village 3 km (2 mi) away that is the site of Marc Meneau's famed restaurant (☞ Dining and Lodging, *below*). ⊠ *Pl. de la Basilique,* ☎ 03–86–33–39–50. 🖾 *Free; donation of 20 frs for guided visit.* ⊙ *Daily 8–8, except during offices Mon.–Sat. 12:30–1:15 and 6–7, Sun. 11–12:15.*

Just 10 km (6 mi) out of Vézelay in the small town of Bazoches-du-Morvan is the **Château de Bazoches,** the former home of Maréchal de Vauban. Built in the 12th century in the form of a trapezium with four towers and a keep, the building was bought by Vauban in 1675 with the money Louis XIV awarded him for devising the parallel trenches successfully used in the siege of Maastricht. Vauban transformed the building into a fortress and created many of his military engineering designs here. These and furnishings of his day are on display. ⊠ *Bazoches-du-Morvan,* ☎ 03–86–22–10–22. 🖾 *Free.* ⊙ *Late Mar.–early Nov., daily 9:30–noon and 2:15–6.*

Dining and Lodging

$$$$ ✕🖬 **L'Espérance.** Chef Marc Meneau is not the most modest of men—his monogram appears everywhere—but he is renowned for his subtle, original creations, such as roast veal in a bitter caramel-based sauce and turbot in a salt-crust *croûte.* The setting—by a stream and a large, statue-filled garden with Vézelay in the background—is delightful. Reservations are essential, and a jacket is required for the restaurant; the restaurant is closed Tuesday and doesn't serve lunch Wednesday. Rooms are in different buildings and vary in price and style. ⊠ *89450 St-Père-sous-Vézelay,* ☎ 03–86–33–39–10, FAX 03–86–33–26–15. *44 rooms. Restaurant. AE, DC, MC, V. Closed Feb.*

$$ ✕⊞ **Hôtel de la Poste et du Lion d'Or.** On a small square in the lower part of town is this old-fashioned, rambling hotel. A terrace out front welcomes you; the good-size rooms have traditional chintzes. The comfortable restaurant is a popular spot with locals, who come for the regional fare, such as roast partridge in black currant sauce and rabbit casserole. ⊠ *Pl. du Champ de Foire, 89450,* ☎ *03–86–33–21–23,* FAX *03–86–32–30–92. 39 rooms. Restaurant, bar. AE, MC, V. Closed mid-Nov.–mid-Mar.*

$$$ ⊞ **Résidence Hôtel Le Pontot.** With Vézelay's limited lodging you would do well to book ahead, especially for this historic fortified house with sumptuous little rooms and a lovely garden. Another advantage is the hotel's location, in the center of the village halfway up the hill. ⊠ *Pl. du Pontot, 89450,* ☎ *03–86–33–24–40,* FAX *03–86–33–30–05. 10 rooms. DC, MC, V. Closed mid-Oct.–mid-Apr.*

Avallon

㉜ *13 km (8 mi) east of Vézelay, 105 km (65 mi) northeast of Nevers, 52 km (42 mi) southeast of Auxerre.*

Avallon is on a spectacular promontory jutting over the Vallée du Cousin. Its old streets and ramparts are pleasant places to stroll, and its medieval market-town ambience is appealing. It has enough cafés, bars, and shops to make it interesting, yet it's small enough that you can quickly become familiar with it and turn it into your base for exploring the rest of the region.

The main sight to see in town is the work of Romanesque stone carvers whose imaginations ran riot on the portals and 15th-century belfry of the venerable church of **St-Lazarus.**

Dining and Lodging

$$ ✕⊞ **Moulin des Ruats.** Once an old flour mill, the Moulin des Ruats became a family hotel in 1924 and is now a comfortable country inn run by Monsieur Rossi. Rooms have pretty country-French decor; some have balconies overlooking the Cousin River. Ask for one that has been renovated; No. 11, for instance, with its exposed beams and a cozy alcove. The restaurant (closed November through February), fronting the river, serves traditional Bourgogne fare with a strong Provençal accent. The best option is the 235-franc menu (try the distinctive foie gras salad), but be warned that dishes can be uneven: You're better off choosing simple rather than complex dishes. ⊠ *Vallée du Cousin, 89200 (4 km [2 mi] southwest of Avallon),* ☎ *03–86–34–97–00,* FAX *03–86–31–65–47. 25 rooms. Restaurant. AE, DC, MC, V.*

$–$$ ✕⊞ **Les Capucins.** On a peaceful square 10 minutes from the town cen-
★   ter, this intimate hotel has rooms in a range of prices. It's better known for its lovely restaurant, however, whose mirrored walls set off the hosts' collection of painted-glass cookie jars, *seaux à biscuits,* dating from the early part of the century. The prix-fixe menus are dominated by regional fare—pike perch, snails and the *oeufs en meurette* (eggs poached in broth and red wine). For dessert, the spice cake is a treat. There are a pleasing garden for breakfast and aperitifs and small cozy rooms for a postprandial drink. ⊠ *6 av. Paul-Doumer (also known as avenue de la Gare), 89200,* ☎ *03–86–34–06–52,* FAX *03–86–34–58–47. 8 rooms, 7 with bath. Restaurant. AE, MC, V. Closed Dec.–Jan.*

Parc Naturel Régional du Morvan

㉝ *Take D944 out of Avallon and then turn left on D10 to Quarré-les-Tombes.*

The vast Parc du Morvan encompasses a 3,500-square-km (1,290-square-mi) chunk of Burgundy. A network of roads and *Grandes Randonnées* (GRs, or Long Trails) winds around the park's lush forests, granite outcroppings, photogenic lakes, idyllic farms, and tiny villages. Hiking in the Morvan is not strenuous, but it is enchanting: Every turn down a trail provides a new country scene. Numerous itineraries through the park are mapped and marked (maps for specific trails are available from local tourist offices). About fifty 5- to 15-km (3- to 9-mi) routes are good for day hikes; another 10 or so trails of around 110 km (68 mi) each are good for much longer walks.

Quarré-les-Tombes, one of the best little villages peppering the park, is so named because of the empty prehistoric stone tombs discovered eerily arrayed in a ring around its church. Eight kilometers (5 miles) south of Quarré-les-Tombes is the **Rocher de la Pérouse,** a mighty outcrop worth scrambling up for a view of the park and the Cure and Cousin valleys.

Some 25 **gîtes d'étapes** (simple bed-and-breakfasts, also known as *chambres d'hôte*) en route provide for overnight stays (to make reservations, call ☎ 03–86–78–74–93). Twenty-one gîtes have facilities for you and your horse to stay overnight. For the pamphlet "Le Morvan à Cheval," which lists stables and gîtes for overnight accommodations, contact the **Parc Natural Régional du Morvan** (✉ Maison du Parc, St-Brisson, ☎ 03–86–78–79–00, FAX 03–86–78–74–22). Horses can be rented from several stables: **La Ferme des Ruats** (✉ Off N6, between St-Émilion and Bussières, ☎ 03–86–33–16–57); **Le Triangle** (✉ Usy, ☎ 03–86–33–32–78); and **La Vieille Diligence** (✉ Rive Droite, Lac des Settons, 58230 Montsauche, ☎ 03–86–84–55–22).

DIJON

314 km (195 mi) southeast of Paris, 100 km (62 mi) east of Avallon.

Dijon, linked to Paris by expressway (A6/A38) and the high-speed TGV (Train à Grande Vitesse), is the age-old capital of Burgundy. Throughout the Middle Ages, Burgundy was a duchy that led a separate existence from the rest of France, culminating in the rule of the four "Grand Dukes of the West"—Philippe le Hardi (the Bold), Jean Sans Peur (the Fearless), Philippe le Bon (the Good), and the unfortunate Charles le Téméraire (the Foolhardy, whose defeat by French king Louis XI at Nancy spelled the end of Burgundian independence)—between 1364 and 1477. A number of monuments date from this period, including the Palais des Ducs (Ducal Palace), now largely converted into an art museum. The city has magnificent half-timbered houses and *hôtels particuliers*, rivaling those in Paris. But the most striking ensemble of buildings is its three central churches, built one following the other for three distinct parishes—St-Bénigne, its facade distinguished by Gothic galleries; St-Philibert, the only Romanesque church (with Merovingian vestiges) of Dijon; and St-Jean, an asymmetrical building now used as a theater.

Dijon's fame and fortune outlasted its dukes, and the city continued to flourish under French rule from the 17th century on. It has remained the major city of Burgundy—the only one, in fact, with more than 150,000 inhabitants. Its site, on the major European north–south trade route and within striking distance of the Swiss and German borders, has helped maintain its economic importance. It's also a cultural center—a few of its half-dozen museums are mentioned below. And many of the gastronomic specialties that originated here are known worldwide, although unfortunately the Dijon traditions have largely passed into legend. They include snails (now mainly imported from Czechoslovakia), mustard (no longer handmade), and cassis (a blackcurrant liqueur often mixed with white wine—preferably Burgundy Aligoté—to make *kir,* the popular aperitif).

The Historic Center

A Good Walk

Begin at the **Palais des Ducs** ㉞, Dijon's leading testimony to bygone splendor; these days it's home to an art museum. Cross to the left side of place de la Libération and take rue des Bons-Enfants, where you'll find the **Musée Magnin** ㉟, with exhibits of furniture and paintings. Continue on to rue Philippe Pot to see the elegant **Chambre des Métiers** ㊱. Just south of here is the **Palais de Justice** ㊲, with its elaborate Baroque facade. Turn onto rue Jean-Baptiste-Liégeard, where the imposing pink-and-yellow limestone Hôtel Legouz de Gerland watches over the street from its distinctive *échauguettes* (faceted towers). Return to rue de la Liberté to get to the church of **St-Michel** ㊳. West of here, behind the palace, is **Notre-Dame** ㊴, one of the city's oldest churches. The rue Verrerie, behind Notre-Dame and the Palais des Ducs, is lined with half-timbered houses. Facing the church on rue de la Chouette is the elegant **Hôtel de Vogüé** ㊵. Walk from here to the somewhat plain **Cathédrale St-Bénigne** ㊶. In the former abbey of St-Bénigne is the **Musée Archéologique** ㊷. The former Cistercian convent houses two museums, the **Musée d'Art Sacré** and **Musée de la Vie Bourguignonne** ㊸. Behind the train station is the **Musée d'Histoire Naturelle** ㊹, in the lovely Jardin de l'Arquebuse, the botanical garden. More links with Dijon's medieval past can be found west of the town center, beyond the train station, just off avenue Albert-1er, including the gateway to the **Chartreuse de Champmol** ㊺ and the Puits de Moïse.

Sights to See

㊶ **Cathédrale St-Bénigne.** The chief glory of this comparatively austere cathedral is its 11th-century crypt—a forest of pillars surmounted by a rotunda. ⊠ *Pl. St-Bénigne.*

㊱ **Chambre des Métiers.** This stately mansion with Gallo-Roman *stelae* incorporated into the walls (a quirky touch) was built in the 19th century. ⊠ *Rue Philippe Pot.*

★ ㊺ **Chartreuse de Champmol.** All that remains of this former charter house is the exuberant 15th-century gateway and the **Puits de Moïse** (Well of Moses), one of the greatest—perhaps the greatest—examples of late Netherlandish sculpture. The Well was designed by Flemish master Claus Sluter, who also created several other masterpieces during the late 14th and early 15th centuries, including the tombs of the dukes of Burgundy. Set on a hexagonal base in the center of a basin, the Well features six large statues that are the most compellingly realistic figures ever crafted by a medieval sculptor.

㊵ **Hôtel de Vogüé.** This stately 17th-century mansion has a characteristic red, yellow, and green Burgundian tile roof—a tradition whose disputed origins lie either with the Crusades and the adoption of Arabic tiles or with Philip the Bold's wife, Marguerite of Flanders. ⊠ *Rue de la Chouette.*

㊷ **Musée Archéologique** (Archaeological Museum). This museum, in the former abbey buildings of the church of St-Bénigne, traces the history of the region through archaeological discoveries. ⊠ *5 rue du Dr-Maret,* ☎ *03–80–30–88–54.* ▨ *11 frs.* ⊘ *June–Sept., Wed.–Mon. 9:30–6; Oct.–May, Wed.–Mon. 9–noon and 2–6.*

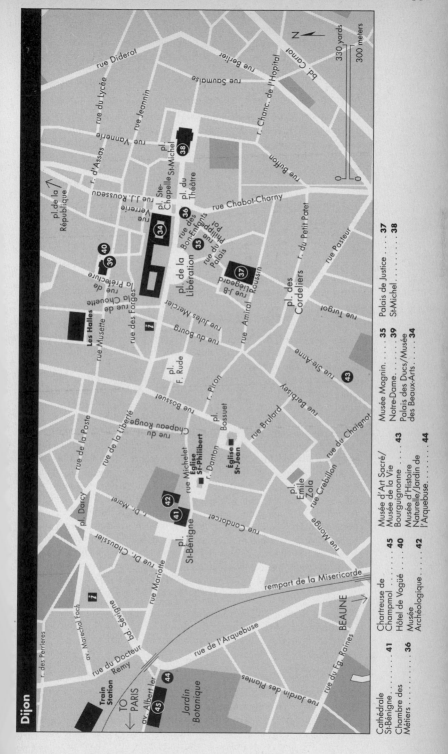

㊽ Musée d'Art Sacré and Musée de la Vie Bourguignonne (Museum of Religious Art and Museum of Burgundian Traditions). In the former Cistercian convent, one museum contains religious art and sculpture; the other has crafts and artifacts from Burgundy, including old storefronts saved from the streets of Dijon that have been reconstituted to form an imaginary street. ⊠ *17 rue Ste-Anne,* ☎ *03–80–30–65–91.* ⌦ *8 frs.* ⊙ *Wed.–Mon. 9–noon and 2–6.*

㊹ Musée d'Histoire Naturelle (Natural History Museum). The museum is in the impressive botanical garden, the **Jardin de l'Arquebuse,** a pleasant place to stroll amid the wide variety of trees and tropical flowers. ⊠ *1 av. Albert-1er,* ☎ *03–80–76–82–76 for museum; 03–80–76–82–84 for garden.* ⌦ *Museum 11 frs, garden free.* ⊙ *Museum Wed.–Mon. 9–noon and 2–6; garden daily 7:30–6 (until 8 PM in summer).*

㉟ The Musée Magnin. In a 17th-century mansion, this museum showcases a private collection of original furnishings and a variety of paintings from the 16th to the 19th centuries. ⊠ *4 rue des Bons-Enfants,* ☎ *03–80–67–11–10.* ⌦ *16 frs.* ⊙ *Tues.–Sun. 10–noon and 2–6.*

㊴ Notre-Dame. One of the city's oldest churches, Notre-Dame stands out with its spindlelike towers, delicate arches gracing its facade, and 13th-century stained glass. Note the windows in the north transept tracing the lives of five saints, as well as the 11th-century Byzantine cedar Black Virgin. ⊠ *Rue de la Préfecture.*

★ ㉞ Palais des Ducs. The elegant, classical exterior of the former palace can best be admired from the half-moon place de la Libération and the Cour d'Honneur. The **kitchens** (circa 1450), with their six huge fireplaces and (for its time) state-of-the-art aeration funnel in the ceiling, and the 14th-century **chapter house** catch the eye, as does the 15th-century **Salle des Gardes** (Guards' Room), with its richly carved and colored tombs and late-14th-century altarpieces. The palace is now home to one of France's major art museums, the **Musée des Beaux-Arts** (Fine Arts Museum), where the tombs sculpted by celebrated artist Claus Sluter for dukes Philip the Bold and his son John the Fearless are the center of a rich collection of medieval objects and Renaissance furniture. Marguerite of Flanders, wife of Philip the Bold, brought to Burgundy not only her dowry, which was Flanders itself, but also a host of distinguished artists—including Rogier van der Weyden, Jan van Eyck, and Claus Sluter. Their artistic legacy can be seen in this collection, as well as at several other of Burgundy's museums and monuments. Among the paintings are works by Italian old masters and French 19th-century artists, such as Théodore Géricault and Gustave Courbet, and their Realist and Impressionist successors, notably Édouard Manet and Claude Monet. ⊠ *Cour de Bar du Palais des Etats,* ☎ *03–80–74–52–70.* ⌦ *22 frs.* ⊙ *Wed.–Mon. 10–6.*

㊲ Palais de Justice. The meeting place for the old regional Parliament of Burgundy serves as a reminder that Louis XI incorporated the province into France in the late 15th century. ⊠ *Rue du Palais.*

㊳ St-Michel. This church, with its chunky Renaissance facade, takes you forward 300 years from when Notre-Dame was built. ⊠ *Pl. St-Michel.*

Dining and Lodging

As one of the longtime culinary capitals of France, Dijon has many superb restaurants, with three areas popular for casual dining. One is around place Darcy, a square catering to all tastes and budgets: Choose from the bustling Concorde brasserie, the quiet bar of the Hôtel de la Cloche, the underground Caveau de la Porte Guillaume wine-and-snack bar, or—for your sweet tooth—the Pâtisserie Darcy. For a really inexpensive meal, try the cafeteria Le Flunch on boulevard de Brosses (near place Darcy).

Two other areas for casual dining in the evening are place Émile Zola and the old market (Les Halles), along rue Bannelier.

$$$–$$$$ ✕ **Billoux.** A local celebrity, Jean-Pierre Billoux is a noted name in the annals of modern Burgundian cooking. He made his name as chef for other establishments, but for the past three years he's owned this spot in the center of Dijon. Today this bright and beautiful restaurant draws the cognoscenti. The house specialties are inventive, the welcome always convivial, and the wine list reads like a who's who of the region's best—but not necessarily best-known—wine makers. The lunch menu, at 200 francs (including wine), is a terrific introduction to modern Burgundian cuisine. ⊠ *13 pl. de la Libération,* ☎ *03–80–38–05–05. Reservations essential. AE, DC, MC, V. Closed Mon. No dinner Sun.*

$$$–$$$$ ✕ **Thibert.** The refined menu at this Art Deco restaurant changes regularly and is highly acclaimed. Specialties include perch with blood pudding and apple sauce and are a remarkable value for the money. ⊠ *10 pl. Wilson,* ☎ *03–80–67–74–64. Reservations essential. Jacket and tie. MC, V. Closed Sun., early Jan., and Aug. No lunch Mon.*

$$$ ✕ **Central Grill Rôtisserie.** This grill room, attached to the Central Ibis Hotel (☞ *below*), is a good alternative to the gastronomic sophistication of Dijon. There are carpaccio and smoked salmon in addition to heavier *abats* (organ meats) dishes. ⊠ *3 pl. Grangier,* ☎ *03–80–30–44–00. AE, DC, MC, V. Closed Sun.*

$$–$$$ ✕ **La Dame d'Aquitaine.** In a happy marriage between two of France's
★ greatest gastronomic regions, chef Monique Saléra, of Pau, and her Dijonnais husband create a wonderful blend of regional cuisines. The foie gras and duck, in confit or with cèpes, come from Saléra's native region; the coq au vin, snails, and *lapin à la moutarde* (rabbit with mustard) from her husband's Burgundy; the *magret de canard aux baies de cassis* (duck breast with cassis berries) is a hybrid. The moderate prix-fixe menus are good value, and the dramatic dining room, in a medieval crypt with a large, modern stained-glass window as its centerpiece, is atmospheric. ⊠ *23 pl. Bossuet,* ☎ *03–80–30–45–65. Reservations essential. AE, DC, MC, V. Closed Sun. No lunch Mon.*

$$ ✕ **Toison d'Or.** A collection of superbly restored 16th-century build-
★ ings belonging to the Burgundian Company of Wine Tasters forms the backdrop to this pleasant restaurant. It's lavishly furnished and quaint (candlelight is de rigueur in the evening). The food is good, especially the langoustines with ginger and the nougat-and-honey dessert. After dinner you can visit the small wine museum in the cellar. ⊠ *18 rue Ste-Anne,* ☎ *03–80–30–73–52. Reservations essential. Jacket required. AE, DC, MC, V. No dinner Sun.*

$ ✕ **Bistrot des Halles.** Of the many restaurants in the area, this one is the best value. Well-prepared dishes range from escargots to beef bourguignonne with braised endives. Dine either at the sidewalk tables or inside, where traditional French decor—mirrors and polished wood—dominates. ⊠ *8 rue Bannelier,* ☎ *03–80–49–94–15. MC, V. No dinner Sun.*

$ ✕ **Les Moules Zola.** If you love mussels, this is the place. Mussels and only mussels—prepared a half-dozen ways, from traditional *moules marinières* (mussels cooked with white wine) to mussels with Dijon mustard—are served. Large picture windows look over the square, and the ambience is jovial—conversation hums to the music of empty shells clattering into bowls. ⊠ *3 pl. Émile Zola,* ☎ *03–80–58–93–26. Reservations essential. MC, V.*

$$$–$$$$ ✕🖬 **Chapeau Rouge.** A player piano in the bar and elegant staircase give this hotel a certain charm that the rooms, though clean and well appointed, lack. The restaurant, renowned as a haven of classic regional cuisine, serves snails cooked in basil and stuffed pigeon. The staff and owner Patrick Lagrange are attentive. ⊠ *5 rue Michelet, 21000,* ☎ *03–80–30–28–10,* FAX *03–80–30–33–89. 30 rooms. Restaurant, bar. AE, DC, MC, V.*

$$$–$$$$ 🏨 **Hôtel Sofitel Dijon–La Cloche.** In use since the 19th century, La Cloche is a successful cross between a luxury chain and a Grand Hotel. The entry hall is imposing, and the sophisticated, gleaming bar has stylish leather-covered chairs. Rooms are large and plush and have attractive chintzes and modern fabrics; try to get one overlooking the tiny, tranquil back garden with its reflecting pool. The garden is also the backdrop for La Rotonde restaurant; unfortunately, the staff is not quite up to snuff. The more relaxed Les Caves de la Cloche, in the cellar, offers French sing-alongs to accompany food and a choice of Burgundies. ⊠ *14 pl. Darcy, 21000,* ☎ *03–80–30–12–32,* FAX *03–80–30–04–15. 53 rooms, 15 suites. 2 restaurants, bar, sauna, exercise room, meeting rooms. AE, DC, MC, V.*

$$ 🏨 **Central Ibis.** This central, old hotel, now part of a national chain, offers comfort in excess of price. Rooms are clean if ordinary. ⊠ *3 pl. Grangier, 21000,* ☎ *03–80–30–44–00,* FAX *03–80–30–77–12. 90 rooms. Restaurant, air-conditioning. AE, DC, MC, V.*

$$ 🏨 **Hôtel Wilson.** This hotel in a 17th-century post house is connected by a walkway to the Thibert restaurant (☞ *above*). Rooms are modern and comfortable. ⊠ *Pl. Wilson, 21000,* ☎ *03–80–66–82–50,* FAX *03–80–36–41–54. 27 rooms. AE, MC, V.*

Nightlife and the Arts

Dijon stages **L'Été Musical** (the Musical Summer), a predominantly classical music festival in June; the tourist office (☞ Burgundy A to Z, *below*) can supply the details. For three days in June the city hosts **Arts in the Streets** (☎ 03–80–65–91–00 for information), an event at which dozens of painters exhibit their works. During the **Bell-Ringing Festival,** in mid-August, St-Bénigne's bells chime and chime. In September Dijon puts on the **Festival International de Folklore.** November in Dijon is the time for the **International Gastronomy Fair.**

L'An Fer (⊠ 8 rue Pierre-Marceau, ☎ 03–80–70–03–69) caters to a slightly youngish clientele. **Bahia Brazil** (⊠ 39 rue des Godrans, ☎ 03–80–30–90–19), a piano bar, is pleasant for a romantic drink. **L'Endroit** (⊠ Centre Dauphine, ☎ 03–80–30–60–63) is a popular Dijon disco. **Le Messire** (⊠ 3 rue Jules-Mercier, ☎ 03–80–30–16–40) bar attracts an older crowd.

Shopping

The auction houses in Dijon are good places to prospect for antiques and works of art. Tempting food items—mustard, snails, and candy (including snail-shape chocolates—escargots de Bourgogne) can easily be found in the heart of Dijon's pedestrian streets.

En Route   A31 connects Dijon to Beaune, 40 km (25 mi) south. But if you prefer a leisurely route through the vineyards, chug along D122, the **route des Grands Crus,** past venerable properties such as Gevrey-Chambertin, Chambolle-Musigny, and Morey-St-Denis, to Clos de Vougeot

THE WINE COUNTRY

Burgundy, Bourgogne to the French, has given its name to one of the world's great wines. Although many people will allow a preference for Bordeaux, Alsatian, Loire, or Rhône Valley wines, the great French gourmands often confess that the precious red nectars of Burgundy have no rivals, and they treat them with religious reverence. So, for some travelers, a trip to Burgundy's Wine Country takes the nature of a pilgrimage. East of the Parc du Morvan the low hills and woodland gra ually open up, and vineyards, clothing the contour of the land in orderly beauty, even in winter, appear on all sides. The vineyards' steeply banked hills stand in contrast to the region's characteristic gentle slopes. Burgundy's most famous vineyards run south from Dijon through Beaune to Mâcon along what has become known as the Côte d'Or (*or* doesn't mean gold here, but is an abbreviation of *orient*, or east). Here you can go from vineyard to vineyard, tasting the various samples (both the powerfully tannic aged reds and the less tannic younger ones). Purists will remind you that you're not supposed to drink them but simply taste them, then spit them into the little buckets discreetly provided. But who wants to be a purist?

Clos de Vougeot

46 *17 km (11 mi) south of Dijon.*

The reason to come to Vougeot is to see its *grange viticole* (wine-making barn), surrounded by its famous vineyard—a symbolic spot for all Burgundy viticulturists. The **Château du Clos de Vougeot** was constructed in the 12th century by Cistercian monks from neighboring Cîteaux—who were in need of wine for mass and also wanted to make a diplomatic offering—and completed during the Renaissance. It's best known as the seat of Burgundy's elite company of wine lovers, the Confrérie des Chevaliers du Tastevin, who gather here in November at the start of an annual three-day festival, Les Trois Glorieuses. Josephine Baker sampled wine here once. You can admire the château's cellars, where ceremonies are held, and ogle the huge 13th-century grape presses, true marvels of medieval engineering. ☎ *03–80–62–86–09.* ✆ *20 frs.* ◷ *Apr.–Sept., daily 9–6:30; Oct.–Mar., weekdays and Sun. 9–11:30 and 2–5:30, Sat. 9–5.*

Near Clos de Vougeot is the **Abbaye de Cîteaux,** where the austere Cistercian order was founded in 1098 by Robert of Molesmes. The abbey, still functional, recently celebrated its 900th birthday and has just reopened to visitors. ✉ *Off D996 (signs point the way along a short country road that breaks off from the entry road to Château de Gilly; ☞ Dining and Lodging, below),* ☎ *03–80–62–15–00.* ✆ *45 frs.* ◷ *May–Oct., Mon. and Wed.–Sat. 9:15–noon and 1:45–4:45; Sun. after 10:30 mass. Guided tours available.*

Dining and Lodging

$$$–$$$$ ✕⊞ **Château de Gilly.** Formerly an abbey and a government-run avantgarde theater, the château is today part of the Relais & Châteaux group. Vestiges of the abbey remain, including painted ceilings and a vaulted crypt, now the dining room. Rooms have magnificent beamed ceilings and lovely views, but the fabric-covered walls, reproduction furniture, and disappointingly ordinary marble-tile bathrooms will greatly benefit from planned renovations. The restaurant's menu includes pastries made with Cîteaux's famous handmade cheese and pike perch with a *pain d'épices* (spice bread) crust. "An elegant form of dress" at dinner is requested. ✉ *Gilly-les-Cîteaux, 21640,* ☎ *03–80–62–89–98,* ℻ *03–80–62–82–34. 48 rooms. Restaurant, pool, tennis court, meeting rooms. AE, DC, MC, V.*

Nuits-St-Georges

47 *27 km (17 mi) south of Dijon, 20 km (12 mi) north of Beaune, 5 km (3 mi) south of Clos de Vougeot.*

Wine has been made in Nuits-St-Georges since Roman times; its "dry, tonic, and generous qualities" were recommended to Louis XIV for medicinal use. There isn't much to see or do here—it mostly serves as a good stop while visiting the surrounding area.

Dining and Lodging

$ ✕ **Au Bois de Charmois.** Three kilometers (2 miles) out of Nuits-St-Georges, on the way toward Meuilley, is this marvelous little inn serving local fare at great prices—a three-course lunch (sample the huge plate of garlicky frogs' legs) is only 62 francs. An even less expensive menu is available at weekday lunch. It's especially pleasant to sit in the courtyard under the ancient trees, though even on chilly, gray days the small dining room is full of good cheer. ⊠ *Rte. de la Serrée,* ☎ *03–80–61–04–79. MC, V. Closed Mon.*

$$$ 🏨 **Domaine Comtesse Michel de Loisy.** Comtesse Christine de Loisy is an institution unto herself in the Nuits-St-Georges area: an internationally traveled, erudite *dame d'un certain âge,* who is also a well-known enologist and local historian. Rooms in her eclectic hôtel particulier are furnished with fine antiques, tapestries, chintz wallpaper, and Oriental carpets, making for a grandeur tempered by old-fashioned charm. Four of the five have a view of the flower-filled courtyard or the magnificent winter garden. The countess offers an optional two-day program of wine tastings, Burgundy-focused meals, and vineyard excursions (including Clos de Vougeot). If you're passing through in winter, stop by and try your luck—Madame de Loisy may be around. ⊠ *B.P. 1, 28 rue Général de Gaulle, 21701,* ☎ *03–80–61–02–72,* FAX *03–80–61–36–14. 5 rooms. AE, MC, V. Mid-Nov.–mid-Mar.*

Beaune

🔴 *26 km (16 mi) south of Clos de Vougeot, 40 km (25 mi) south of Dijon, 315 km (197 mi) southeast of Paris.*

Beaune is sometimes considered the wine capital of Burgundy because it is at the heart of the region's vineyards, with the Côte de Nuits to the north and the Côte de Beaune to the south. In late November the famous wine auction at the Hospices de Beaune pulls in connoisseurs and the curious from France and abroad. Despite the hordes, Beaune remains one of France's most attractive provincial towns.

★ Some of the region's finest vineyards are owned by the **Hospices de Beaune** (also known as the hôtel-Dieu), founded in 1443 as a hospital to provide free care for men who had fought in the Hundred Years' War. A visit to the Hospices (across from the city's tourist office) is one of the highlights of a stay in Beaune; its tiled roofs and Flemish architecture have become icons of Burgundy, and in fact the same glowing colors and intricate patterns are seen throughout the region. Misleadingly appearing to be medieval, the interior was repainted by 19th-century Gothic restorer Viollet-le-Duc. The Hospices carried on its medical activities until 1971—its nurses still wearing their habitlike uniforms—and the hospital's history is retraced in the museum, whose wide-ranging collection contain some weird and wonderful medical instruments from the 15th century. You can also see a collection of tapestries that belonged to the repentant founder of the Hospices, ducal chancellor Nicolas Rolin, who hoped charity would relieve him of his sins—one of which was collecting wives. Outstanding are both the tapestry he had made for Madame Rolin III, with its repeated motif of "my only star," and one relating the legend of St. Eloi and his miraculous restoration of a horse's leg. But the star of the collection is Rogier Van der Weyden's stirringly composed 15th-century Flemish masterpiece, *The Last Judgment.* A son-et-lumière show is presented every evening from April to mid-November. ⊠ *Rue de l'Hôtel-Dieu,* ☎ *03–80–24–45–00.* 🎟 *32 frs.* ☉ *Late Mar.–mid-Nov., daily 9–6:30; mid-Nov.–Mar., daily 9–11:30 and 2–5:30.*

A series of tapestries, relating the life of the Virgin, are in Beaune's main church, the 12th-century **Collégiale Notre-Dame.** ⊠ *Just off av. de la République.*

In the candlelighted cellars of the **Marché aux Vins** (Wine Market), you can taste several regional wines. (You can also visit most of the Burgundian vineyards themselves and get free tastings of their wines, which may be more interesting than those available at the Marché aux Vins; of course, they hope that you'll buy a case or two.) Perhaps the best reason to visit the Marché aux Vins is to see the building's Burgundian Romanesque architecture mixed with Gothic additions. Even Viollet-le-Duc left his mark by adding the galleries to the right of the portal. ⊠ *Rue Nicolas Rolin,* ☎ *03–80–25–08–20.* ⊡ *Entry and tasting 50 frs.* ⊘ *Daily 9:30–noon and 2–6.*

For a break and a snack of handmade pain d'épices in all shapes and incarnations, stop by **Mulot and Petitjean** (⊠ Pl. Carnot).

Dining and Lodging

$$ ✕ **L'Écusson.** Don't be put off by its unprepossessing exterior: this is a comfortable, friendly, thick-carpeted restaurant with good value prix-fixe menus. Showcased is chef Jean-Pierre Senelet's sure-footed culinary mastery with dishes like boar terrine with dried apricot and juniper berries, and roast crayfish with curried semolina and ratatouille. ⊠ *Pl. Malmédy,* ☎ *03–80–24–03–82. Reservations essential. AE, DC, MC, V. Closed Sun., Feb., and early July. No dinner Mon.*

$–$$ ✕ **Le Gourmandin.** In the center of Beaune, chef Alain Billard and Isabelle Crotet (daughter of Jean) serve regional fare at their intimate bistro. It's simple, in the style of a 1930s café, with black-and-white tabletops and art posters on the walls. Pork shank and shoulder stewed with beans and cabbage—*potée Bourguignonne*—is a delicious staple, accompanied by a good range of wines from small vineyards. ⊠ *8 pl. Carnot,* ☎ *03–80–24–07–88. MC, V. Closed Nov.–Feb., Tues., no lunch Wed.; Mar.–Oct., closed Tues., no dinner Mon.; Jan.–Feb. variable.*

$–$$ ✕ **La Grilladine.** Chef Pierre Lenko's cuisine, though not elaborate, is good, hearty Burgundy fare: beef Bourguignon and oeufs en meurette. The prix-fixe menus are extremely reasonable. The ambience is warm and cheerful: rose-pink tablecloths, exposed stone walls, and an ancient beam supporting the ceiling. One room is for nonsmokers. ⊠ *17 rue Maufoux,* ☎ *03–80–22–22–36. Reservations essential. MC, V. Closed Mon. and end Nov.–mid-Dec.*

$$$$ ✕▣ **Hostellerie de Levernois.** The Crotets' hotel-restaurant, a Relais & Châteaux property, gleams with light from its large picture windows. It's a shame that though the cuisine is still of the highest standard, the lodgings are beginning to show signs of age and neglect. Some rooms are traditionally furnished and have a comfortably elegant feel; those in the modern building in the landscaped garden are more up to date. In the kitchen Jean works with his sons, Christophe and Guillaume, who have a more nouvelle approach. Meals are occasions to be savored, but they are also expensive; menus begin at 345 francs (200 francs at lunch) and may feature pigeon with foie gras and truffles or smoked salmon with vine shoots. ⊠ *Rte. de Verdun-sur-le-Doubs, 21200 Levernois (3 km [2 mi] east of Beaune),* ☎ *03–80–24–73–58,* ℻ *03–80–22–78–00. 15 rooms, 1 suite. Restaurant, air-conditioning, babysitting, in-room data ports. AE, DC, MC, V. Closed 1st 2 wks of Aug.*

$$$–$$$$ ✕▣ **Lameloise.** This small, unpretentious hotel on the outskirts of Chagny, south of Beaune, may be the only Relais & Châteaux property to stock crayons for kids. But don't be misled: The clientele is well heeled. Rooms are fresh and deluxe, with token rustic touches. Confident and consistent, chef-owner Jacques Lameloise cooks luxurious

but not stuffy dishes, such as roast pigeon with minced truffles and snails in garlic-flavored bouillon. The restaurant is closed Wednesday and doesn't serve lunch Thursday, except in July and August. ⊠ *36 pl. d'Armes, 71150 Chagny (14 km [9 mi] south of Beaune),* ☎ *03–85–87–08–85,* FAX *03–85–87–03–57. 17 rooms. Restaurant. AE, MC, V. Closed late Dec.–late Jan.*

$$ ✕🏨 **Central.** A well-run establishment with several modernized rooms, the Central lives up to its name. The stone-walled restaurant is cozy—some might say cramped—and the consistently good cuisine is popular with locals, who come to enjoy oeufs en meurette and coq au vin. Service is efficient, if a little hurried. Dinner is obligatory in July and August. ⊠ *2 rue Victor-Millot, 21200,* ☎ *03–80–24–77–24,* FAX *03–80–22–30–40. 20 rooms. Restaurant. MC, V. Closed late Nov.–mid-Dec.*

$$–$$$ 🏨 **Château de Chorey-les-Beaune.** To really soak up the flavor of the vineyards, stay at the Germain family's winery and B&B, north of Beaune. Guest rooms are up a circular stone staircase; furnishings are from the attic. Though it's a bit rustic and casual, it's the kind of place where you can open the windows and let the country air, perfumed by grapes, waft in. A good breakfast is served but no dinner; you may have a chance to try their wine before going out to eat in Beaune. ⊠ *21200 Chorey-les-Beaune (1½ km [1 mi] north of Beaune),* ☎ *03–80–22–06–05,* FAX *03–80–24–03–93. 7 rooms. Breakfast room. MC, V. Closed Dec.–Apr.*

$$ 🏨 **Hôtel de la Cloche.** In a 15th-century residence in the heart of town, this hotel has rooms furnished with care by owners Monsieur and Madame Lamy, both of whom are always on hand to assist. The best rooms, those with a full bath, are more expensive; the smaller yet delightful attic rooms, each with a shower and separate toilet, are less. Breakfast is served on the garden terrace in summer. ⊠ *40–42 rue Faubourg-Madeleine, 21200,* ☎ *03–80–24–66–33,* FAX *03–80–24–04–24. 22 rooms. Restaurant. AE, MC, V. Closed late Dec.–mid-Jan.*

The Arts

In July Beaune celebrates its annual **International Festival of Baroque Music,** which draws big stars of the music world. On the third Sunday in November at the Hospices is Beaune's famous wine festival, **Les Trois Glorieuses.**

Chalon-sur-Saône

49 *29 km (18 mi) south of Beaune, 127 km (79 mi) north of Lyon.*

Chalon-sur-Saône's medieval heart is close to the banks of the Saône River, around the former Cathédrale St-Vincent (now a parish church), which displays a jumble of styles. This area was reconstructed to have an old-world charm, but the rest of Chalon is a modern, commercial, cosmopolitan city—the cultural and shopping center of southern Burgundy. Chalon is the birthplace of Nicéphore Niepce (1765–1833), whose early experiments, developed further by Jacques Daguerre, qualify him as the father of photography.

The **Musée Nicéphore Niepce,** occupying an 18th-century house overlooking the Saône, retraces the early history of photography and motion pictures with the help of some pioneering equipment. It also includes a selection of contemporary photographic work and a lunar camera used during the U.S. *Apollo* program. But the star of the museum is the primitive camera used to take the first photographs in 1816 ⊠ *28 quai des Messageries,* ☎ *03–85–48–41–98.* 🎫 *10 frs, free Wed* ⊙ *Sept.–June, Wed.–Mon. 9:30–11:30 and 2:30–5:30; July–Aug. Wed.–Mon. 10–6.*

Dining and Lodging

$$–$$$ ✕🏨 **Moulin d'Hautrive.** Once a mill built by Cistercian monks in the
★ 12th century, it's now a comfortable hotel in the country. Every room
has blackened ancient beams, antiques, and bric-a-brac. The restaurant's four-course, 240-franc menu may include frogs' legs in cream
with basil and pigeon with semolina and spices. The restaurant is
closed Sunday dinner and Monday. ⊠ *Hameau de Chaublanc, 71350
St-Gervais-en-Vallière (24 km [15 mi] north of Chalon, 12 km [7 mi]
south of Beaune),* ☎ *03–85–91–55–56,* FAX *03–85–91–89–65. 22
rooms. Restaurant, pool, sauna, tennis court. AE, MC, V.*

$$ ✕🏨 **St-Georges.** Close to the train station and town center, this friendly,
white-walled hotel is tastefully modernized and has many spacious rooms.
Its cozy restaurant is known locally for its efficient service and menus
of outstanding value, with such specialties as veal kidney with mustard. ⊠ *32 av. Jean-Jaurès, 71100,* ☎ *03–85–48–27–05,* FAX *03–85–
93–23–88. 48 rooms. Restaurant. AE, DC, MC, V.*

The Arts

For two weeks in July all of Chalon becomes a stage as street theater
groups from around the world come to perform in the annual **Chalon
in the Streets Festival.**

Tournus

㊿ *27 km (17 mi) south of Chalon-sur-Saône, 30 km (18 mi) north of
Mâcon.*

Tournus, which retains much of the charm of the Middle Ages and the
Renaissance and has one of Burgundy's most spectacular and best-preserved Romanesque buildings, has long been overshadowed as a tourist
attraction by other Burgundian medieval towns. But it's worth a stop,
and it's also a great spot for a picnic, especially along the left bank (*rive
gauche*) of the Saône River. The **tourist office** (⊠ 2 pl. Carnot, ☎ 03–
85–51–13–10) has a map of the town's many *traboules*—its hidden,
covered walkways, which are fun to explore.

The 17th-century **Hôtel-Dieu** (hospital) reopened in mid-1999 after extensive renovation. Particularly noteworthy is its pharmacy. In one wing
is the **Musée de Greuze,** displaying the work of painter Jean-Baptiste
Greuze (1725–1805), a native of Tournus, as well as pieces by other
painters past and present, sculpture, and archaeological finds; it's set
to open in 2001. ⊠ *Rue de l'Hôpital,* ☎ *03–85–51–23–50.* ⊡ *25 frs.*
☉ *Apr.–Oct., Wed.–Mon. 11–6.*

The abbey church of **St-Philibert,** despite its massiveness—unadorned
cylindrical pillars more than 4 ft thick support the nave—is spacious
and light. No effort was made to decorate or embellish the interior,
whose sole hint of frivolity is the alternating red and white stones in
the nave arches. The crypt—with its chapels containing 12th-century
frescoes of *Christ in Majesty* and the *Virgin with Child*—and former
abbey buildings, including the cloister and magnificent 12th-century
refectory, can also be visited. ⊠ *Pl. de l'Abbaye.*

Dining and Lodging

$$ ✕🏨 **Aux Terrasses.** For an enjoyable meal of the region's products at
★ reasonable prices—such as chef Michel Carrette's fricassee of rabbit
with pepper—this is the place. (The restaurant is closed Sunday dinner and Monday.) Many French, German, and Dutch travelers stop here
for dinner and a night's rest. Rooms are reasonably large and comfortable, with standard floral decor. ⊠ *18 av. du 23-Janvier, 71700,*
☎ *03–85–51–01–74,* FAX *03–85–51–09–99. 18 rooms. Restaurant.
MC, V. Closed early Jan.–early Feb.*

$$ ✕⊞ **Le Rempart.** This hotel, originally a 15th-century guardhouse built on the town ramparts, has an elegant foyer and dining room incorporating Romanesque pillars. Rooms are modern, functional, and kept up. Double-glazed windows keep out traffic noise. At the restaurant, prix-fixe dinners begin at 165 francs; the cooking, though competently prepared by chef Daniel Rogie, doesn't live up to its reputation; you may wish to dine elsewhere. ⊠ *2–4 av. Gambetta, 71700,* ☎ *03–85–51–10–56,* FAX *03–85–40–77–22. 32 rooms, 6 suites. Restaurant, bar, air-conditioning. AE, DC, MC, V.*

$ ✕⊞ **Le Coq d'Or.** For inexpensive prix-fixe menus, this cheerful hotel-restaurant is the spot. The traditional fare is reliable, from onion soup and steak to poulet de Bresse and fruit tarts, and many dishes are cooked on an open-hearth grill. The exposed beams, peach tablecloths, and friendly service create a cozy atmosphere. Rooms are bare bones but clean. The best, No. 8, is at the quiet back of the building. ⊠ *1 rue Pasteur, 71700,* ☎ *03–85–51–35–91. 6 rooms. Restaurant. MC, V.*

En Route The best way to reach Cluny from Tournus is to use picturesque D14. Along the way, you pass the fortified hilltop town of **Brancion,** with its old castle and soaring keep, before turning left at Cormatin.

Cluny

❺❶ *36 km (22 mi) southwest of Tournus, 50 km (31 mi) south of Chalon-sur-Saône, 24 km (15 mi) northwest of Mâcon.*

The village of Cluny is famous for its medieval abbey, once the center of a vast Christian empire and today one of the most spectacular of medieval ruins—unfortunately, not a great deal of this church (nor little evidence of its fundamental influence of its architecture in the development of early Gothic style) remains standing, thanks to the mobs of the French Revolution. Founded in the 10th century, the **Ancienne Abbaye** was the biggest church in Europe until the 16th century, when Michelangelo built St. Peter's in Rome. Cluny's medieval abbots were as powerful as popes; in 1098 Pope Urban II (himself a Cluniac) assured the head of his old abbey that Cluny was the "light of the world." That assertion, of dubious religious validity, has not stood the test of time—after the Revolution the abbey was sold as national property and much of it used as a stone quarry. Today Cluny stands in ruins, a reminder of the limits of human grandeur. The ruins, however, suggest the size and glory of the abbey at its zenith, and piecing it back together in your mind is part of the attraction.

In order to get a clear sense of what you are looking at, start at the **Porte d'Honneur,** the entrance to the abbey from the village, whose classical architecture is reflected in the pilasters and Corinthian columns of the **Clocher de l'Eau-Bénite** (a majestic bell tower), crowning the only remaining part of the abbey church, the south transept. Between the two are the reconstructed monumental staircase, which led to the portal of the abbey church, and the excavated column bases of the vast narthex. The entire nave is gone. On one side of the transept is a national horse-breeding center *(haras)* founded in 1806 by Napoléon and constructed with materials from the destroyed abbey; on the other is an elegant pavilion built as new monks' lodgings in the 18th century. The gardens in front of it once contained an ancient lime tree (destroyed by a 1982 storm) named after Abélard, the controversial philosopher who sought shelter at the abbey in 1142. Off to the right is the 13th-century *farinier* (flour mill), with its fine oak-and-chestnut roof and collection of exquisite Romanesque capitals from the disappeared choir. The **Musée Ochier,** in the abbatial palace, contains Europe's foremost Romanesque lapidary museum. Vestiges of both the abbey and the village constructed around it are conserved here, as well as part of the Bibliothèque des Moines (Monks' Library). ☎ 03–85–59–12–79. 🎫 *Abbey and museum 32 frs, museum only 14 frs.* ☉ *Abbey and museum Nov.–mid-Feb., daily 10–noon and 2–4; mid-Feb.–Mar., daily 10–noon and 2–5; Apr.–June, daily 9:30–noon and 2–6; July–Aug., daily 9–7; Sept., daily 9–6; Oct., daily 9:30–noon and 2–5.*

The village of Cluny was built to serve the abbey's more practical needs, and several fine Romanesque houses around the rue d'Avril and the rue de la République, including the so-called **Hôtel de la Monnaie** (Abbey Mint; ✉ 6 rue d'Avril, ☎ 03–85–59–25–66) are prime examples of the period's different architectural styles. Parts of the town ramparts, the much-restored 11th-century defensive **Tour des Fromages** (✉ 6 rue Mercière, ☎ 03–85–59–05–34), now home to the tourist office, and several noteworthy medieval churches also remain.

Dining and Lodging

$$–$$$ ✕🏨 **Bourgogne.** Get into Cluny's medieval mood at this old-fashioned hotel, dating from 1817, where parts of the abbey used to be. It has a small garden and an atmospheric restaurant with sober pink decor and comfort cuisine, such as *volaille de Bresse au Noilly et morilles* (Bresse chicken with Noilly Prat and morels. The evening meal is mandatory in July and August, and lunch is not served on Tuesday or Wednesday. ✉ *Pl. de l'Abbaye, 71250,* ☎ *03–85–59–00–58,* 📠 *03–85–59–03–73. 15 rooms. Restaurant. AE, DC, MC, V. Closed mid-Nov.–early Mar.*

$–$$ ✕🏨 **Hôtel de l'Abbaye.** This modest hotel is a five-minute walk from the center. The three rooms to the right of the dining room are the most recently redone and the best value. The restaurant serves rich, hearty local fare that's less elaborate than at the Bourgogne (☞ *above*) but better; if you're feeling adventurous, try the *pâté en croûte de grenouilles au Bleu de Bresse* (frog and Bresse blue cheese pie). The prix-fixe menus are very reasonable, and the restaurant is closed Monday and doesn't serve dinner Sunday. ✉ *Av. Charles-de-Gaulle, 71250,* ☎ *03–85–59–11–14,* 📠 *03–85–59–09–76. 14 rooms, 9 with bath. Restaurant. AE, MC, V. Closed mid-Jan.–mid-Feb.*

The Arts

The ruined abbey of Cluny forms the backdrop of the **Grandes Heures de Cluny** (☎ 03–85–59–05–34 for details), a classical music festival held in August.

Mâcon

🔵52 *25 km (16 mi) southeast of Cluny, 58 km (36 mi) south of Chalon-sur-Saône, 69 km (43 mi) north of Lyon.*

Mâcon is a bustling town, best known for its wine fair in May and for its pesky stone bridge across the Saône, whose low arches are a headache for the pilots of large river barges. The Romantic poet Alphonse de Lamartine (1790–1869) was born in Mâcon. The two octagonal towers of the ruined **Cathédrale de St-Vincent** loom over the wide quays along the river in the old part of town. The **Maison du Bois,** near the cathedral, is a fine example of an ancient timbered house.

BURGUNDY A TO Z

Arriving and Departing

By Car

A6 heads southeast from Paris through Burgundy, passing Sens, Auxerre, Chablis, Avallon, Saulieu, Beaune, and Mâcon before continuing on to Lyon and the south. A38 leads from A6 to Dijon, 290 km (180 mi) southeast of Paris; the trip takes 2½–3½ hours, depending on traffic. If you have more time, take N6 to Sens, just 110 km (68 mi) southeast of Paris; then continue southeast.

By Plane

The **Dijon Airport** (☎ 03–80–67–67–67) serves domestic flights between Paris and Lyon.

By Train

The TGV zips out of Paris (Gare de Lyon) to Dijon (75 minutes), Mâcon (100 minutes), and on to Lyon (two hours). Trains run frequently, though the fastest Paris–Lyon trains do not stop at Dijon or go anywhere near it. Some TGVs stop at Le Creusot, between Chalon and Autun, 90 minutes from Paris. There is also TGV service directly from Roissy Airport to Dijon (1 hour, 50 minutes). Sens is on a mainline route from Paris (45 minutes).

Getting Around

By Car

Burgundy is best visited by car because its meandering country roads invite leisurely exploration. A6 is the main route through the region; N6 is a slower, prettier option. A38 provides a quick link between A6 and Dijon; A31 heads down from Dijon to Beaune, a distance of 45 km (27 mi). Troyes and Dijon are linked via A5 and A31. Other smaller roads lead off the main routes to the little villages.

By Train

The region has two local train routes: one linking Sens, Joigny, Montbard, Dijon, Beaune, Chalon, Tournus, and Mâcon and the other connecting Auxerre, Avallon, Clamecy, Autun, and Nevers. If you want to get to smaller towns or to vineyards, you would be better off renting a car.

Contacts and Resources

Car Rental

Avis (✉ 5 av. du Maréchal Foch, Dijon, ☎ 03–80–43–60–76). **Europcar** (✉ 47 rue Guillaume-Tell, Dijon, ☎ 03–80–43–28–44). **Hertz** (✉ 18 bis av. Foch, Dijon, ☎ 03–80–43–55–22).

Guided Tours

For general information on tours in Burgundy, contact the regional tourist office, the **Comité Régional du Tourisme** (✉ B.P. 1602, 21035 Dijon Cedex, ☎ 03–80–50–90–00). From April to November **Air Escargot** (✉ 71150 Remigny, ☎ 03–85–87–12–30) arranges hot-air balloon rides over the countryside. Tours of Beaune with a guide and a wine tasting can be arranged in advance through the **Beaune tourist office** (✉ Rue de l'Hôtel-Dieu, ☎ 03–80–26–21–30). Gastronomic weekends, including wine tastings, are organized by **Bourgogne Tour** (✉ 11 rue de la Liberté, 21000 Dijon, ☎ 03–80–30–49–49). Details about recommended bike routes and where to rent bicycles (train stations are a good bet) can be found at most tourist offices. **La Peurtantaine** (✉ Accueil Morvan Environment, École du Bourg, 71550 Anost, ☎ 03–85–82–77–74) arranges bicycle tours of Burgundy.

Travel Agencies

Air France (✉ 29 pl. Darcy, Dijon, ☎ 03–80–42–89–90). **Wagons-Lits** (✉ 8 av. du Maréchal-Foch, Dijon, ☎ 03–80–45–26–26).

Visitor Information

Following are principal regional tourist offices: **Dijon** (✉ 29 pl. Darcy, close to cathedral, ☎ 03–80–44–11–44, ✍). **Auxerre** (✉ 1 quai de la

République, ☎ 03–86–52–06–19, ✉). **Mâcon** (✉ 1 pl. St-Pierre, ☎ 03–85–21–07–07).

Addresses of other tourist offices in towns mentioned in this chapter: **Autun** (✉ 2 av. Charles-de-Gaulle, ☎ 03–85–86–80–38, www.autun.com). **Avallon** (✉ 4 rue Bocquillot, ☎ 03–86–34–14–19). **Beaune** (✉ Rue de l'Hôtel-Dieu, ☎ 03–80–26–21–30,✉). **Clamecy** (✉ Rue du Grand-Marché, ☎ 03–86–27–02–51). **Cluny** (✉ 6 rue Mercière, ☎ 03–85–59–05–34,✉). **Sens** (✉ Pl. Jean-Jaurès, ☎ 03–86–65–19–49). **Tournus** (✉ 2 pl. Carnot, ☎ 03–85–51–13–10). **Troyes** (✉ 16 bd. Carnot, ☎ 03–25–82–62–70, www.ot-troyes.fr; ✉ Rue Mignard, ☎ 03–25–73–36–88). **Vézelay** (✉ Rue St-Pierre, ☎ 03–86–33–23–69).

9 LYON AND THE ALPS

In this diverse region—where the local chefs rival their Parisian counterparts—earthly pleasures have been perfected. You can ski in the shadow of Mont Blanc, hike along trails over Alpine slopes, sail across stunningly idyllic Lake Annecy, and generally enjoy the cultural treasures of Lyon. You can visit the Roman sites and medieval towns—reminders of other eras—or take a trip along the Beaujolais Wine Road to discover what refreshingly unaffected vintages the region has to offer today.

A S THE NOBLE RHÔNE COURSES ITS WAY DOWN from Switzerland, flowing out of Lake Geneva and being nudged east and south by the flanking Jura Mountains and the Alps, it meanders through France at its wholesome best. Here you'll find the pretty towns and fruity purple wines of Beaujolais, the brawny, broad-shouldered cuisine of Lyon, the extraordinary beauty of the Alps, and the friendly wine villages that loom high on the steep hills flanking the Rhône on its long, low roll to the Mediterranean. Deep gorges carve the Ardèche to its west, beckoning you to lose yourself in a no-man's-land of ragged stone and pine. Yes, there is history here, but it weighs none too heavy: The sweet medieval hill town of Pérouges offers diverting charms, and the ruins at Vienne mark the region's Gallo-Roman roots with more grace than pomp.

Updated by
George Semler

So relax and dig into the *terroir,* or earth. Strike up a flirtation with saucy Beaujolais, a pink-cheeked country girl of a region, blushing voluptuously next to its noble neighbor, Burgundy. The very names of Beaujolais's robust wines make up a bouquet of country wildflowers: Fleurie, Chiroubles, Juliénas, St-Amour. Glinting purple against red-checked linens in a Lyonnais *bouchon* they flatter every delight on the blackboard menu: a salty chew of sausage, a crunch of bacon, a spurt of boudin noir bursting from its skin, a tang of crisp country greens in mustard vinaigrette, or a taste of crackling roast chicken.

If you are what you eat, then Lyon itself is real and hearty, as straightforward and unabashedly simple as a *poulet de Bresse.* Yet world-class opera, theater, and classical music thrive happily here in Lyon's gently patinaed urban milieu, one strangely reminiscent of 1930s Paris—lace curtains in overpainted storefronts, elegant bourgeois town houses, deep-shaded parks, and low-slung bridges lacing back and forth over the broad, lazy rivers of the Saône and the Rhône. Far from Paris's snootiness, here you can immerse yourself in old urban France.

Then pack a picnic to tide yourself over and take to the hills. If you head west, the Gorges de l'Ardèche swallow you up in a craggy world of chasms and stone villages; if you head northeast, you'll ease slowly into the Alps, a world of green-velvet slopes and cold, icy mist, ranging from the modern urban Oz of Grenoble to the ethereal crystal lake of Annecy to the state-of-the-art ski resorts of Chamonix, Megève, and former Olympic site Albertville. The grand finale: awe-inspiring Mont-Blanc, at 15,700 ft Western Europe's tallest peak. End your day's exertions on the piste or the trail with a bottle of gentian-perfumed Suze, repair to your fir-lined chalet, and dress down for a hearty mountain-peasant supper of raclette, fondue, or cheesy *ravioles,* all by a crackling fire.

— Nancy Coons

Pleasures and Pastimes

Dining

Food lovers around the world celebrate Lyon's cuisine. Robust specialties like *saveloy* (sausage) and quenelles (poached fish dumplings) appear on tables in restaurants from the elegant on down. Traditional *bouchons* (taverns) with homey wooden benches, zinc counters, and paper tablecloths serve salads, pork products like garlicky *rosette* sausage, and sturdy main courses such as tripe, veal stew, and andouillette (chitterling sausage). The Dombes is rich in game and fowl; the chicken is famous, especially *poulet de Bresse,* usually cooked with cream. Thrush, partridge, and hare star along the Rhône. Local cheeses include St-Marcellin, Roquefort, Beaufort, Tomme, and goat's-milk Cabecou. Privas has its *marrons glacés* (candied chestnuts), Montélimar its nougats. Alpine rivers and lakes teem with pike and trout. In the Alps try a raclette, melted cheese over potatoes. Mountain herbs yield liqueurs and aperitifs such as tangy, dark Suédois; sweet, green Chartreuse; and bittersweet Suze (made from gentian).

CATEGORY	COST*
$$$$	over 400 frs
$$$	250 frs–400 frs
$$	125 frs–250 frs
$	under 125 frs

per person for a three-course meal, including tax (20.6%) and tip but not wine

🐾 *following the text of a review is your signal that the property has a Web site, where you will find details and, usually, images; for a link, visit www.fodors.com/urls.*

Lodging

Hotels, inns, bed-and-breakfasts, *gites d'étapes* (hikers' way stations) and tables d'hôte run the gamut from grande luxe to spartan rustic in this ample region. At many places you are expected to have your evening meal there, especially in summer. In winter Alpine travelers are generally free to choose breakfast only, *demi-pension,* with breakfast and dinner, or *pension complète,* with three meals a day.

CATEGORY	COST*
$$$$	over 800 frs
$$$	550 frs–800 frs
$$	300 frs–550 frs
$	under 300 frs

All prices are for a standard double room for two, including tax (20.6%) and service charge.

Skiing

The area's most famous ski venue is Chamonix. Chic, expensive Megève, Courchevel, and fashionable Méribel are also world-class spots. Val d'Isère is one of Europe's poshest. Nearby Tignes and novice-friendly Morzine are also good bets. L'Alpe d'Huez is near Grenoble. The ski season lasts from December through April.

Exploring Lyon and the Alps

East-central France can be divided into two areas: the Alps and "not the Alps." The second group includes Lyon, the country's "second city," a magnet for the surrounding region, including the vineyards of Beaujolais; and the area south of Lyon, dominated by the mighty Rhône as it flows toward the Mediterranean.

Great Itineraries

As you plan your trip, remember that although you can make good time along the highways, you'll have to slow down on smaller roads and in the Alps. In more rural and mountainous regions don't make your daily itineraries too ambitious.

Numbers in the text correspond to numbers in the margin and on Lyon and the Alps and Lyon maps.

IF YOU HAVE 3 DAYS

To enjoy some of France's best cooking, best museums, and best theater, concentrate on 🏠 **Lyon** ①–㉗, but take a day to head down the Rhône to see the Roman ruins in **Vienne** ㉞. If you prefer the countryside

ar○
using
merge t

IF YOU HAV
Stay in 🏨 **Lyo**
to travel up the
Wine Road, and th
Pérouges ㉝ for the nig
dieval old town, your d
lovely Talloires; stay in ei
row roads connecting small
Stop in the fashionable mounta
drive to elegant 🏨 **Chambéry** ㊻.
Chartreuse ㊺; then either go to **Gr**
seum's fabulous collection or zip via
view the old town's cathedral and art mus
the spectacular Ardèche Gorge, if you are
make a stop in **Privas** ㊶. Or you can return t
with a stop along the way at **Vienne** ㉞ to see t

When to Tour Lyon and the Alps

The best time of year in Lyon and the Rhône Valley
the lakes are still warm, grape harvesting is under way,
tivals are taking place. Note, however, that many of Lyon'
early for September and October, when delegates attend co
Midsummer can be hot and sticky. Winter tends to be dreary,
the crystal mist hovering over the Rhône can be beautiful. In the
summer is the time to hike, explore isolated villages, and admire
vistas; in winter the focus is snow and skiing. In early spring and l
autumn many hotels in the Alps are closed.

LYON

Lyon and Marseille both claim to be France's "second city." In ter
of size and industrial importance, Marseille probably grabs that ti
But for tourist appeal, Lyon, 462 km (287 mi) southeast of Paris
the clear winner. It's easily accessible by car or by train. Its scale is hum
It has historic buildings and quaint *traboules*—passageways un
buildings dating from the Renaissance (in Vieux Lyon) and the 1
century (in Croix Rousse). (During World War II these passagew
were used by the French Resistance to elude German street patro
The city's setting at the confluence of the Saône and Rhône is sp
tacular. And it has more good restaurants per square mile than any ot
European city except Paris.

Lyon's development owes much to its riverside site halfway betw
Paris and the Mediterranean and within striking distance of Swit
land, Italy, and the Alps. Lyonnais are proud that their city has b
important for more than 2,000 years: Romans made it the capita
Gaul around 43 BC. Its name derives from the Latin *lugdunum* (hi
the crow).

In the middle of the city is Presqu'île, a fingerlike peninsula betw
the rivers, only half a dozen blocks wide and about 10 km (6 mi) lo
where modern Lyon throbs with shops, restaurants, museums, theat
and an opera house. Across the Saône is Vieux Lyon (Old Lyon); ab
it is the old Roman district of Fourvière. To the north is the hilly C
Rousse District, where there are more museums. Across the Rhôn
the east is a mix of older residential areas and the ultramodern P

ver the city, as an alternative, either spend a leisurely three days und the lake in ⊞ **Annecy** ㊽ or in the dramatic Alpine mountains, e skiing—as your base.

⊞ **Megève** ㊾—where the après-ski amusements tend to sub-

6 DAYS

①–㉗ for two days. If you love wine, leave a day early aône Valley, through the villages along the **Beaujolais** en head to ⊞ **Bourg-en-Bresse** ㉛ or medieval ⊞ ht. On day three make ⊞ **Annecy** ㊽, with its me-estination; be sure to drive around the lake to the nar-her one. The next day travel along the villages via mountain passes in the Alps. in resort town of **Megève** ㉞ before you

On day five visit the abbey of **Grande** enoble ㊸ to see the Grenoble Mu-he autoroute to ⊞ **Valence** ㊴ to um. The next day drive through heading for Provence, and Lyon via **Montélimar** ㊷, e Roman sites.

is autumn, when and many fes-hotels book ventions. through e Alps the

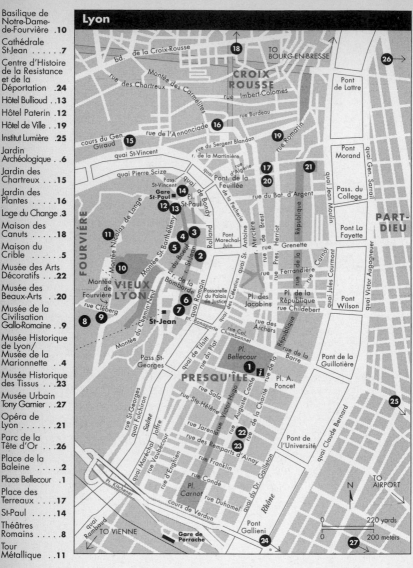

Dieu business and office district. Consider taking advantage of the Clés de Lyon (Keys to Lyon), a three-day museum pass costing 90 francs.

Vieux Lyon and Fourvière

Vieux Lyon—one of the richest groups of urban Renaissance dwellings in Europe—has narrow cobblestone streets, 17th- and 18th-century mansions, small museums, and the city's cathedral. When the city developed as an important silk weaving town, Italian merchants and bankers built town houses in the area; the influence of Italian Renaissance architecture still dominates. Above Vieux Lyon, in hilly Fourvière, are the remains of Roman theaters and the Basilique de Notre-Dame, visible from all over the city.

A Good Walk

Start your walk armed with free maps from the Lyon tourist office on Presqu'île's **place Bellecour** ①. Cross the square and head north along lively rue du Président-Herriot; turn left onto place des Jacobins and explore rue Mercière and the small streets off it. Cross the Saône on the Passerelle du Palais de Justice (Palace of Justice Footbridge); now you are in Vieux Lyon. Facing you is the old Palais de Justice. Turn right and then walk 200 yards along quai Romain Rolland to No. 36, where there is a traboule that leads to rue des Trois Maries. Take a right to get to small **place de la Baleine** ②. Exit the square on the left (north) side and go right on historic **rue St-Jean.** Head up to cobblestoned place du Change; on your left is the **Loge du Change** ③ church. Take rue Soufflot and turn left onto rue de Gadagne. The Hôtel de Gadagne is home to two museums: the **Musée Historique de Lyon** ④, with medieval sculpture and local artifacts, and the Musée de la Marionnette, a puppet museum.

Walk south along **rue du Boeuf,** which runs parallel to rue St-Jean. Just off tiny place du Petit-Collège, at No. 16, is the **Maison du Crible** ⑤, with its pink tower. Use the traboule at 1 rue du Boeuf to lead you to 24 rue St-Jean. Turn right and then left onto rue de la Bombarde to get to the **Jardin Archéologique** ⑥, a small garden with two excavated churches. Alongside the gardens is the solid **Cathédrale St-Jean** ⑦, itself an architectural history lesson. The *ficelle* (funicular railway) runs from the cathedral to the top of Colline de Fourvière (Fourvière Hill). Take the Montée de Fourvière to the **Théâtres Romains** ⑧, two ruined Roman theaters. Overlooking the theaters is the semisubterranean **Musée de la Civilisation Gallo-Romaine** ⑨, a repository for Roman finds. Continue up the hill and take the first right to the mock-Byzantine **Basilique de Notre-Dame-de-Fourvière** ⑩.

Return to Vieux Lyon via the Montée Nicolas-de-Lange, which are stone stairs at the foot of the metal tower, the **Tour Métallique** ⑪. You will emerge alongside the St-Paul train station. Venture onto rue Juiverie, off place St-Paul, to see two splendid Renaissance mansions, the **Hôtel Paterin** ⑫, at No. 4, and the **Hôtel Bullioud** ⑬, at No. 8. On the northeast side of place St-Paul is the church of **St-Paul** ⑭. Behind the church, cross the river on the Passarelle St-Vincent and take a left on quai St-Vincent; 200 yards along on the right is the **Jardin des Chartreux** ⑮, a small park. Cut through the park up to cours du Général Giraud and then turn right to place Rouville. Rue de l'Annonciade leads from the square to the **Jardin des Plantes** ⑯, botanical gardens.

TIMING

Spend the morning ambling around Vieux Lyon and Fourvière, and then eat lunch in one of Vieux Lyon's many restaurants or have a picnic in the Jardin des Plantes. In the afternoon explore the Croix Rousse District (☞ *below*) and its many museums. Note that most museums are closed Monday.

Sights to See

⑩ **Basilique de Notre-Dame-de-Fourvière.** The pompous late-19th-century basilica, at the top of the ficelle, is—for better or worse—the symbol of Lyon. Its mock-Byzantine architecture and hilltop site make it a close cousin of Paris's Sacré-Coeur. Both were built to underline the might of the Roman Catholic Church after the Prussian defeat of France in 1870 gave rise to the birth of the anticlerical Third Republic. The excessive gilt, marble, and mosaics in the interior underscore the wealth of the church, although they masked its low-grade political clout at that time. One of the few places in Lyon where you can't see the basilica is the adjacent terrace, whose panorama reveals the city—with the cathedral of St-Jean in the foreground and the glass towers of the reconstructed Part-Dieu business complex glistening behind. For a yet more sweeping view, climb the 287 steps to the basilica observatory. ⊠ *Pl. de Fourvière.* 🎟 *Observatory 10 frs.* ☉ *Observatory Easter–Oct., daily 10–noon and 2–6; Nov.–Easter, weekends 2–6. Basilica daily 8–noon and 2–6.*

❼ Cathédrale St-Jean. Solid and determined—it withstood the sieges of time, revolution, and war—the cathedral's stumpy facade is stuck almost bashfully onto the nave. Although the mishmash inside has its moments—the fabulous 13th-century stained-glass windows in the choir and the varied window tracery and vaulting in the side chapels—the interior lacks drama and harmony. Still, it is an architectural history lesson. The cathedral dates from the 12th century, and the chancel is Romanesque, but construction continued over three centuries. The 14th-century astronomical clock, in the north transept, is a marvel of technology. It chimes a hymn to St. John on the hour at noon, 2, 3, and 4 as a screeching rooster and other automatons enact the Annunciation. To the right of the Cathédrale St-Jean stands the 12th-century **Manécanterie** (choir school). ⊠ *70 rue St-Jean,* ☎ *04–78–92–82–29.*

⓭ Hôtel Bullioud. This Renaissance mansion, close to the Hôtel Paterin, is noted for its courtyard, with an ingenious gallery (1536) built by Philibert Delorme, one of France's earliest and most accomplished exponents of classical architecture. He worked on the Loire Valley châteaux of Fontainebleau and Chenonceau. ⊠ *8 rue Juiverie, off pl. St-Paul.*

⓬ Hôtel Paterin. This splendid Renaissance mansion is a fine example of one of many notable buildings in the area. ⊠ *4 rue Juiverie, off pl. St-Paul.*

❻ Jardin Archéologique (Archaeological Garden). This garden contains the excavated ruins of two churches that succeeded one another on this spot. The foundations of the churches were unearthed during a time when apartment buildings—constructed here after churches had been destroyed during the Revolution—were being demolished. One arch still remains and forms part of the ornamentation in the garden. ⊠ *Entrance on rue de la Bombarde.*

⓯ Jardin des Chartreux. This garden is just one of several small, leafy parks in Lyon. It's a peaceful place to take a break while admiring the splendid view of the river and Fourvière Hill. ⊠ *Entrance on quai St-Vincent.*

⓰ Jardin des Plantes (Botanical Garden). In the peaceful, luxurious Botanical Garden are remnants of the once-huge **Amphithéâtre des Trois Gauls** (Three Gauls Amphitheater), built in AD 19. ⊠ *Entrance on rue de la Tourette.* ☉ *Dawn to dusk.*

❸ Loge du Change. Germain Soufflot (architect of Paris's Panthéon; ☞ Chapter 1) constructed this church (originally known as the Église Reformée) in 1747–50. Money changers used to hang out on this square, thus the name. ⊠ *Pl. du Change.*

❺ Maison du Crible. This 17th-century mansion is one of Lyon's oldest. In the courtyard you can glimpse a charming garden and the original Tour Rose—an elegant pink tower. The higher the tower in those days, the greater the prestige; this one was owned by the tax collector. ⊠ *16 rue du Boeuf (off pl. du Petit-Collège).* 🎟 *Free.* ☉ *Daily 10–noon and 2–6.*

❾ Musée de la Civilisation Gallo-Romaine (Gallo-Roman Civilization Museum). Since 1933 systematic excavations have unearthed vestiges of Lyon's opulent Roman precursor. The statues, mosaics, vases, coins, and tombstones are excellently displayed in this semisubterranean museum next to the Roman Theaters (☞ *below*). The large, bronze Table Claudienne is inscribed with part of Emperor Claudius's speech to the Roman Senate in AD 48, conferring senatorial rights on the Roman citizens of Gaul. ⊠ *17 rue Clébert*, ☎ *04–72–38–81–90.* ☒ *20 frs.* ☉ *Wed.–Sun. 9:30–noon and 2–6.*

🦢 ❹ **Musée Historique de Lyon** (Lyon Historical Museum). This museum is housed in the city's largest ensemble of Renaissance buildings, the Hôtel de Gadagne, built between the 14th and 16th centuries. Medieval sculpture, furniture, pottery, paintings, and engravings are on display. Also housed here is the **Musée de la Marionnette** (Puppet Museum), tracing the history of marionettes beginning with Guignol and Madelon (Lyon's Punch and Judy, created by Laurent Mourguet in 1795). ⊠ *1 pl. du Petit-Collège*, ☎ *04–78–42–03–61.* ☒ *25 frs.* ☉ *Wed.–Mon. 10:45–6.*

❷ **Place de la Baleine.** This small square is lined with 17th-century houses once owned by those merchants who became rich from the silk trade.

❶ **Place Bellecour.** Shady, imposing place Bellecour is one of the largest squares in France and Lyon's fashionable center, midway between the Saône and the Rhône. Classical facades erected along its narrower sides in 1800 lend architectural interest. The large, bronze equestrian Louis XIV, installed in 1828, is by local sculptor Jean Lemot. On the south side of the square is the **tourist office** (☎ *04–72–77–69–69*).

Rue du Boeuf. At the corner of place Neuve St-Jean and rue du Boeuf is one of Vieux Lyon's most famous signs, portraying the bull for which rue du Boeuf is named; it's by renowned French sculptor Jean de Bologne (1529–1608), trained in Renaissance Italy.

Rue St-Jean. Once Vieux Lyon's major thoroughfare, this street leads north from place de la Baleine to place du Change, where money changers operated during medieval trade fairs. Its elegant houses were largely built for illustrious Lyonnais bankers and silk merchants during the French Renaissance. No. 27 has an especially lovely courtyard. The houses once had just four stories; upper floors were added in the last century. Many area streets were named for their shops, which are still heralded by intricate iron signs.

⑭ **St-Paul.** The 12th-century church of St-Paul is noted for its octagonal lantern, its frieze of animal heads on the chancel, and its Flamboyant Gothic chapel. ⊠ *Pl. St-Paul.*

❽ **Théâtres Romains** (Roman Theaters). Two ruined, semicircular Roman-built theaters are tucked into the hillside, just down from the summit of Fourvière. The **Grand Théâtre,** the oldest Roman theater in France, was built in 15 BC to seat 10,000. The smaller **Odéon,** with its geometric flooring, was designed for music and poetry performances. Lyon International Arts Festival performances are held here each September. ⊠ *Colline Fourvière.* ☒ *Free.* ☉ *Daily 9–dusk.*

⑪ **Tour Métallique** (Metal Tower). Beyond Fourvière Basilica is this skeletal metal tower built in 1893 and now a television transmitter. The stone staircase, the **Montée Nicolas-de-Lange,** at the foot of the tower, is a direct but steep route from the basilica to the St-Paul train station. ⊠ *Colline Fourvière.*

Presqu'île and the Croix Rousse District

Presqu'île, the peninsula flanked by the Saône and the Rhône, is the modern center of Lyon with fashionable shops, an array of restaurants and museums, and squares with fountains and 19th-century buildings. This is the core of Lyon, where you'll be tempted to wander the streets from one riverbank to the other and to explore the area from place Bellecour to place des Terreaux.

The hilly district north of place des Terreaux, the Croix Rousse District, is flanked by the Jardins des Plantes on the west and the Rhône on the east. It once resounded to the clanking of looms churning out the silk and cloth that made Lyon famous. By the 19th century more than 30,000 *canuts* (weavers) worked on looms on the upper floors of the houses. So tightly packed were the houses that the only way to transport fabrics was through the traboules, which had the additional advantage of protecting the fine cloth in bad weather.

A Good Walk

Armed with a detailed map available from the Lyon Tourist Office (☞ Guided Tours *in* Lyon and the Alps A to Z, *below*), you could spend hours "trabouling" in the area, which is still busy with textile merchants despite the demise of the old-style cottage industry of silk weaving. In the very northern part of the Croix Rousse District you can see old-time looms at the **Maison des Canuts** ⑱. For an impromptu tour of the area, walk along rue Imbert-Colomès. At No. 20, turn right through the traboule that leads to rue des Tables Claudiennes and right again across place Chardonnet. Take the Passage Mermet alongside the church of St-Polycarpe; then turn left onto rue Leynaud. A traboule at No. 32 leads to the Montée St-Sébastien. Here is a transfixing trompe l'oeil on the Mur des Canuts, a large wall painted with depictions of local citizens sitting and walking up a passageway of steps. Exit the Croix Rousse District by taking rue Romarin down to **place des Terreaux** ⑰.

The sizable place des Terreaux has two notable buildings: On the north side is the **Hôtel de Ville** ⑲, the Town Hall; on the south side is the elegant **Musée des Beaux-Arts** ⑳, the art museum. To reach the barrel-vaulted **Opéra de Lyon** ㉑, walk west across place des Terreaux and through the ground floor of the Hôtel de Ville (go around if it's closed). For a look at Lyon's fashionable shops, walk down the pedestrians-only rue de la République and cross place Bellecour. Continue 300 yards farther (now rue de la Charité) to the **Musée des Arts Décoratifs** ㉒, a decorative arts museum. Next door is the **Musée Historique des Tissus** ㉓, a textiles museum.

Walking south along quai du Dr. Gailleton, crossing the Rhône at Pont Galliéni, and going up avenue Berthelot will get you to the **Centre d'Histoire de la Resistance et de la Déportation** ㉔, which is focused on Lyon's Resistance movement during World War II. If you're a film buff, head to the **Institut Lumière** ㉕. From the center walk east along avenue Berthelot to avenue Jean-Jaurès; take a right and then a left on grande rue de Guillotière, then another right on rue Premier-Film. To return to Presqu'île, walk west to Pont de la Guillotière.

If you've seen all of Lyon's main cultural sights and want to indulge your children, take the métro from Perrache train station to Masséna and the **Parc de la Tête d'Or** ㉖, which has a small zoo and pony rides. If you're an architecture buff, take the métro from place Bellecour to Monplaisir-Lumière (it's a bit of a long trip) and walk 10 minutes south along rue Antoine to the **Musée Urbain Tony Garnier** ㉗, usually referred to as the Cité de la Création.

TIMING

It will probably take you an hour to explore Presqu'île and the Croix Rousse District. The Musée des Beaux-Arts deserves at least two hours, the Musée des Arts Décoratifs and the Musée Historique des Tissus another couple of hours. You may want to leave these until the following day. Note that most museums are closed Monday, and the Musée des Beaux-Arts is also closed Tuesday.

Sights to See

㉔ Centre d'Histoire de la Résistance et de la Déportation (Museum of the History of the Resistance and the Deportation). During World War II, especially after 1942, Lyon played an important role in the Resistance movement against the German occupation of France. Displays include equipment, such as radios and printing presses, photographs, and exhibits recreating the clandestine lives and heroic efforts of Resistance members. ⊠ *14 av. Berthelot,* ☎ *04–78–72–23–11.* ≊ *25 frs.* ⊙ *Wed.–Sun. 9–5:30.*

⑲ Hôtel de Ville (Town Hall). Architects Jules Hardouin-Mansart and Robert de Cotte redesigned the very impressive facade of the Town Hall after a 1674 fire. The rest of the building dates from the early 17th century. ⊠ *Pl. des Terreaux.*

㉕ Institut Lumière. On the site where the Lumière brothers invented the first cinematographic apparatus, this museum has daily showings of early films and contemporary movies as well as a permanent exhibit about the Lumières. Researchers can have access to the archives, which contain numerous films, books, periodicals, director and actor information, photos files, posters, and more. ⊠ *25 rue Premier-Film,* ☎ *04–78–78–18–95.* ≊ *25 frs.* ⊙ *Tues.-Fri. 9–12:30 and 2–6; weekends 2–6.*

🖐 ⑱ Maison des Canuts (Silk Weavers' Museum). Despite the industrialization of silk and textile production, old-time Jacquard looms are still in action at this historical house in the Croix Rousse. The weavers are happy to show children how to operate a miniature loom. ⊠ *12 rue d'Ivry,* ☎ *04–78–28–62–04.* ≊ *20 frs.* ⊙ *Sept.–Jul., weekdays 8:30–noon and 2–6:30, Sat. 9–noon and 2–6; Aug., Tues.–Fri. 8:30–noon and 2–6:30, Sat. 9-noon and 2–6;.*

★ ㉒ Musée des Arts Décoratifs (Decorative Arts Museum). Housed in an 18th-century mansion, this museum has fine collections of silverware, furniture, objets d'art, porcelain, and tapestries. ⊠ *34 rue de la Charité,* ☎ *04–78–38–42–00.* ≊ *30 frs (joint ticket with the nearby Musée Historique des Tissus;* ☞ *below).* ⊙ *Tues.–Sun. 10–5:30.*

⑳ Musée des Beaux-Arts (Fine Arts Museum). In the elegant 17th-century Palais St-Pierre, once a Benedictine abbey, this museum has one of France's largest collections of art after the Louvre, including Rodin's *Walker,* Byzantine ivories, Etruscan statues, and Egyptian artifacts. Amid old master, Impressionist, and modern paintings are works by the tight-knit Lyon School, characterized by exquisitely rendered flowers and overbearing religious sentimentality. Note Louis Janmot's *Poem of the Soul,* immaculately painted visions that are by turns heavenly, hellish, and downright spooky. ⊠ *Palais St-Pierre, 20 pl. des Terreaux,* ☎ *04–72–10–17–40.* ≊ *25 frs.* ⊙ *Wed.–Sun. 10:30–6.*

㉓ Musée Historique des Tissus (Textile History Museum). On display is a fascinating exhibit of intricate carpets, tapestries, and silks, including Asian tapestries from as early as the 4th century, Turkish and Persian carpets from the 16th to the 18th centuries, and 18th-century Lyon silks. ⊠ *34 rue de la Charité,* ☎ *04–78–38–42–00.* ≊ *30 frs (joint ticket with Musée des Arts Décoratifs;* ☞ *above).* ⊙ *Tues.–Sun. 10–5:30.*

㉗ Musée Urbain Tony Garnier (Tony Garnier Urban Museum). Also know as the Cité de la Création (City of Creation), this project was France's first attempt at low-income housing. In recent years the tenants have tried to bring some art and cheerfulness to their environment: Twenty-two giant murals depicting the work of Tony Garnier, the turn-of-the-20th-century Lyon architect, are painted on the walls of huge housing projects built in 1920 and 1933. Artists from around the world, with the support of UNESCO, have added their vision to the creation of the ideal housing project. To get there, take the métro from place Bellecour to Monplaisir-Lumière and walk 10 minutes south along rue Antoine. ⊠ *Bd. des États-Unis, 7ᵉ.*

㉑ Opéra de Lyon. The barrel-vaulted Lyon Opera, a reincarnation of a moribund 1831 building, was built in the early '90s to the tune of 478 million francs. It incorporates a columned exterior, soaring glass vaulting, Neoclassical public spaces, and the latest backstage magic. High above, looking out between the heroic statues lined up along the parapet, is a small restaurant, Les Muses (☞ Dining and Lodging, *below*). ⊠ *Pl. de la Comédie,* ☎ *04–72–00–45–00; 04–72–00–45–45 for tickets.*

㉖ Parc de la Tête d'Or (Golden Head Park). On the banks of the Rhône, this 300-acre park has a lake, pony rides, and a small zoo. It's ideal for an afternoon's outing with children. Take the métro from Perrache train station to Masséna. ⊠ *Pl. du Général-Leclerc, quai Charles-de-Gaulle.* ⊠ *Free.* ☉ *Dawn–dusk.*

⑰ Place des Terreaux. The four majestic horses rearing up from a monumental 19th-century fountain in the middle of this large square are by Frédéric-Auguste Bartholdi, who also sculpted New York's Statue of Liberty. The two notable buildings sitting on either side are the Hôtel de Ville and the Musée des Beaux-Arts (☞ *above*).

Dining and Lodging

$$$$ ✕ Léon de Lyon. Chef Jean-Paul Lacombe's innovative uses of the re-
★ gion's butter, cream, and foie gras put this restaurant at the forefront of the city's gastronomic scene. Dishes such as fillet of veal with celery and leg of lamb with fava beans are memorable; suckling pig comes with foie gras, onions, and a truffle salad. Alcoves and wood paneling in this 19th-century house add to the atmosphere. ⊠ *1 rue Pléney,* ☎ *04–72–10–11–12. Reservations essential. Jacket required. AE, MC, V. Closed Sun.–Mon. and 1st 3 wks Aug.*

$$$$ ✕ Paul Bocuse. In this culinary shrine north of Lyon in Collonges-au-
★ Mont-d'Or, the grand dining room makes a fitting backdrop for the creations of star chef Paul Bocuse. Elegantly dressed food lovers throng here to feast on his truffle soup and sea bass, although he is often away. Call ahead if you want to find out whether Bocuse or one of his chefs will be cooking, and book far in advance. ⊠ *50 quai de la Plage, Collonges-au-Mont-d'Or,* ☎ *04–72–42–90–90. Reservations essential. Jacket required. AE, DC, MC, V.*

$$$–$$$$ ✕ Orsi. Pierre Orsi's lavish restaurant, a pink-stucco wonder, is by a tiny tree-lined square. Marble floors, brocade draperies, bronze nudes, and gilt-frame paintings make it glamorously festive. The foie gras ravioli with truffles and the mesclun with goat cheese are hard acts to follow, though the dessert of sliced figs with pistachio ice cream holds its own. ⊠ *3 pl. Kléber,* ☎ *04–78–89–57–68. Reservations essential. Jacket required. AE, MC, V. Closed Sun.*

$$ ✕ Brasserie Georges. This inexpensive brasserie at the end of rue de la Charité is one of the city's largest and oldest, founded in 1836 but now in a palatial Art Deco building. Meals range from hearty veal stew or sauerkraut and sausage to more refined fare. ⊠ *30 cours de Verdun,* ☎ *04–72–56–54–54. AE, DC, MC, V.*

$$ ✕ Café des Fédérations. For 80 years this sawdust-strewn café with homey red-checked tablecloths has reigned as one of the city's friendliest spots. Raymond Fulchiron not only serves deftly prepared local classics like *boudin blanc* (white-meat sausage) but also stops by to chat with you, making you feel at home. ⊠ *8 rue du Major-Martin,* ☎ *04–78–28–26–00. DC, MC, V. Closed weekends and Aug.*

$$ ✕ **Les Muses.** High up under the glass vault of the Opéra de Lyon is
★ this small restaurant run by Philippe Chavent. Look out the glass front
between statues of the Muses to the Hôtel de Ville. The nouvelle cuisine makes it hard to choose between the choices offered, but don't
pass up the salmon in butter sauce with watercress mousse. Pricewise,
the best value for dinner is the 159-franc menu. ⊠ *Opéra de Lyon,* ☎
04–72–00–45–58. Reservations essential. AE, MC, V. Closed Sun.

$$ ✕ **Le Nord.** Should you want to keep some change in your pocket and
still sample cooking by Paul Bocuse–trained chefs (☞ Paul Bocuse,
above), lunch at his bistro in downtown Lyon. Be sure to order the *frites*
(fries)—they are some of the country's best. ⊠ *18 rue Neuve,* ☎ *04–72–10–69–69. AE, DC, MC, V.*

$$ ✕ **Le Vivarais.** Robert Duffaud's simple, tidy restaurant is an outstanding culinary value. Don't expect napkins folded into flower
shapes—the excitement is on your plate, with dishes like *lièvre royale*
(hare rolled and stuffed with foie gras and a hint of truffles). ⊠ *1 pl.
du Dr-Gailleton,* ☎ *04–78–37–85–15. Reservations essential. AE,
MC, V. Closed Sun. and 1st 2 wks in Aug.*

$–$$ ✕ **Anticipation.** Light, creative dishes using the region's famed specialties
(such as poulet de Bresse) are carefully prepared here by John Rosiak,
a former cook at Georges Blanc (☞ Dining and Lodging *in* Bourg-en-Bresse, *below*). John's wife, Nathalie, speaks English and is helpful at
translating the menu. The homey feel makes it a place where you can
settle in for an evening of good fare and fun. ⊠ *7 rue Chavanne,* ☎
04–78–30–91–92. AE, MC, V. Closed Mon. No dinner Sun.

$–$$ ✕ **Maison Villemanzy.** A former cook from Léon de Lyon (☞ *above*)
owns this delightful restaurant on the Croix Rousse hills, from which
there are outstanding views. The cuisine is a modern, lighter version
of Lyonnais fare, though you can still expect veal and chicken cooked
in butter and cream to be on the menu. ⊠ *5 Montée St-Sébastien,* ☎
04–78–39–37–00. MC, V. Closed Sun. and 1st 2 wks in Jan.

$ ✕ **Brunet.** Tables are crammed together in this tiny *bouchon* (tavern)
where the decor is limited to past menus inscribed on mirrors and a
few photographs. The food is good, traditional Lyonnais fare; besides
the mandatory andouillette sausage and tripe, there is usually excellent roast pork on the 98-franc menu. On a busy night expect it to be
crowded—but it's all part of the fun. ⊠ *23 rue Claudia,* ☎ *04–78–37–44–31. MC, V. Closed Sun.–Mon. and Aug.*

$ ✕ **Hugon.** This typical, tiny bouchon with red-checked tablecloths is
behind the Musée des Beaux-Arts. The owner drinks with patrons while
madame chops away in back. Go for a hunk of homemade pâté and
stewed chicken in wine vinegar sauce or a plate of *ris de veau* (sweetbreads)—good, inexpensive food and plenty of it. ⊠ *12 rue Pizay,* ☎
04–78–28–10–94. MC, V. Closed weekends and Aug.

$ ✕ **Le Jura.** The rows of tables, the mosaic tile floor, and the absence
of anything pretty gives this place the feel of a men's club. The mustachioed owner, looking as if he stepped out of the turn-of-the-century
prints on the walls, acts gruffly but with a smile, as his wife rushes around.
The game and steak dishes are robust, as is the *cassoulet des escargots*
(stew of beans, mutton, and snails). Desserts are mediocre, so order
the cheese. ⊠ *25 rue Tupin,* ☎ *04–78–42–20–57. MC, V. Closed
weekends in summer and Aug. No lunch Sun.–Mon.*

$ ✕ **Les Lyonnais.** This popular brasserie, decorated with local celebrities' photos, is particularly animated. The simple food—chicken simmered for hours in wine, meat stews, and grilled fish—is served on bare
wood tables. A blackboard announces plats du jour, which are less ex-

pensive than items on the printed menu. ✉ *1 rue Tramassac,* ☎ *04–78–37–64–82. MC, V. Closed Aug. and the 1st wk Jan.*

$$$$ ✕⊠ **La Tour Rose.** Philippe Chavent's silk-swathed Vieux Lyon hotel occupies several houses around a courtyard under a rose-washed tower; the glass-roof restaurant occupies a former chapel. Each room is named for an old silk factory and decorated in its goods; taffetas, plissés, and velvets cover walls, windows, and beds in daring, even startling styles. Dinner is an occasion and can be expensive, but if you limit yourself to the prix-fixe 295-franc menu of rabbit braised with olives and port wine or some similar dish, you'll have a memorable (and affordable) dinner. ✉ *22 rue du Boeuf, 69005,* ☎ *04–78–37–25–90,* FAX *04–78–42–26–02. 12 rooms. Restaurant, bar. AE, DC, MC, V.* ⊛

$$$$ ⊠ **La Cour des Loges.** Young Lyonnais architects teamed with Italian
★ designers to transform four Renaissance mansions into one of Lyon's most stylish hotels. It has an immense courtyard, spiral stone staircases, and exposed beams. Rooms range from fairly small to comfortably large and are either classic or contemporary in design. There is a cellar-level wine bar and a tapas bar. Concierge Gérard Ravet is not only a character, but also knows Lyon inside out. ✉ *6 rue du Boeuf, 69005,* ☎ *04–72–77–44–44,* FAX *04–72–40–93–61. 63 rooms. Restaurant, bar, breakfast room, indoor pool, hot tub, sauna, health club, library, meeting room. AE, DC, MC, V.* ⊛

$$$$ ⊠ **Hôtel Saxe Lafayette.** There are times when a good chain hotel is needed: This one, owned by the Accord group, has super king-size beds, large bathrooms and towels, uniformity without problems, and an English-speaking staff. It's in Part-Dieu, the business section of town, not far from the train station (a shuttle is available), though this means it's a little less convenient for shopping or hanging out in Vieux Lyon. ✉ *29 rue de Bonnel, 69003,* ☎ *04–72–61–90–90,* FAX *04–72–61–17–54. 156 rooms. Restaurant, bar, in-room modem lines, health club, parking (fee). AE, DC, MC, V.* ⊛

$$$$ ⊠ **Villa Florentine.** High above the old town, near the Roman theater
★ and basilica, this pristine hotel was once a convent. It has beamed and vaulted ceilings, terraces, marvelous views, and an excellent restaurant, Les Terraces de Lyon, with distinguished cuisine. ✉ *25–27 Montée St-Barthélémy, 69005,* ☎ *04–72–56–56–56,* FAX *04–72–40–90–56. 11 rooms, 8 suites. Restaurant, bar, breakfast room, pool, meeting rooms. AE, DC, MC, V.* ⊛

$$$ ⊠ **Grande Hôtel Concorde.** This Belle Epoque hotel off place de la République has a courteous and efficient staff. Rooms have high ceilings, mostly modern furnishings, and one special piece such as an armoire or writing desk. ✉ *11 rue Grôlée, 69002,* ☎ *04–72–40–45–45,* FAX *04–78–37–52–55. 140 rooms. Restaurant, air-conditioning, meeting rooms. AE, DC, MC, V.* ⊛

$$$ ⊠ **Hôtel des Artistes.** This intimate hotel on an elegant square opposite the Théâtre des Célestins has long been popular among stage and screen artists; black-and-white photographs of actors and actresses adorn lobby walls. Rooms are smallish but modern and comfortable, and the friendly reception and great location appeal to all comers. ✉ *8 rue Gaspard-André, 69002,* ☎ *04–78–42–04–88,* FAX *04–78–42–93–76. 45 rooms. AE, DC, MC, V.* ⊛

$$–$$$ ⊠ **Grand Hôtel des Beaux-Arts.** Half the rooms at this hotel are termed "inspired worlds," where an artist has developed a decorating theme through his paintings, some of which are on display in the room. In Room 309, for instance, the paintings of Carmelo Zagari are used to lead you into the world of the theater. Should you want a more conventional sleeping environment, other rooms are traditionally furnished. A buffet breakfast is served. ⊠ *rue du Président Édouard-Herriot, pl. des Jacobins, 69002,* ☎ *04–78–38–09–50,* FAX *04–78–42–19–19. 75 rooms. AE, DC, MC, V.* 🐾

$ 🖭 **Bed et Breakfast à Lyon.** This nonprofit agency can house you for one night or several: singles are 120–290 francs; doubles are 170–390 francs. The agency is open weekdays 9:30 AM–8 PM. ⊠ *3 bis rue de la Garenne, 69005,* ☎ *04–72–16–95–01,* FAX *04–78–59–58–62. No credit cards.*

$ 🖭 **Hôtel Bayard.** Rooms at this hotel in the heart of town each have a distinctive look. One favorite, No. 2, overlooks the large square and has a canopied bed. For a group, opt for No. 15, which sleeps four. Only breakfast is served, but there are dozens of restaurants nearby. ⊠ *23 pl. Bellecour, 69002,* ☎ *04–78–37–39–64,* FAX *04–72–40–95–51. 22 rooms. MC, V.*

$ 🖭 **Hôtel du Théâtre.** The friendly and enthusiastic owner is sufficient enough reason to recommend this small hotel. But its location and reasonable prices make it even more commendable. Rooms are simple but clean; those overlooking place des Célestins not only have a theatrical view but also a bathroom with a tub (330 francs). Those facing the side have a shower only. Breakfast is included. ⊠ *10 rue de Savoie, 69002,* ☎ *04–78–42–33–32,* FAX *04–72–40–00–61. 21 rooms. MC, V.*

Nightlife and the Arts

Lyon is the region's liveliest arts center; check the weekly *Lyon-Poche*, published on Wednesday and sold at newsstands, for cultural events and goings-on at the dozens of discos, bars, and clubs.

For darts and pints and jazz on weekends, head to the **Albion Public House** (⊠ 12 rue Ste-Catherine, 1ᵉʳ, ☎ 04–78–28–33–00), where they even accept British pounds. The low-key, chic **L'Alibi** (⊠ 13 quai Romain-Roland, 5ᵉ, ☎ 04–78–42–04–66) has a laser show along with the music. **Bar Live** (⊠ 13 pl. Jules Ferry, ☎ 04–72–74–04–41) is in the old Brotteaux train station and is the current drinking haunt. Romantics rendezvous at the **Bar de la Tour Rose** (⊠ 22 rue du Boeuf, 5ᵉ, ☎ 04–78–37–25–90).

Bouchon aux Vin (⊠ 64 rue Mercière, 2ᵉ, ☎ 04–78–42–88–90) is a wine bar with 30-plus vintages. Computer jocks head into cyberspace at **Le Chantier** (⊠ 18–20 rue Ste-Catherine, 1ᵉʳ, ☎ 04–78–39–05–56) while their friends listen to jazz and nibble on tapas. Caribbean and African music pulses at **Le Club des Iles** (⊠ 1 Grande-Rue des Feuillants, 1ᵉʳ, ☎ 04–78–39–16–35). Live jazz is played in the stone-vaulted basement of **Hot Club** (⊠ 26 rue Lanterne, 1ᵉʳ, ☎ 04–78–39–54–74). A gay crowd is found among the 1930s decor at **La Ruche** (⊠ 22 rue Gentil, 2ᵉ, ☎ 04–78–39–03–82). **Villa Florentine** (⊠ 25 Montée St-Barthélémy, 5ᵉ, ☎ 04–72–56–56–56) is a quiet spot for a drink accompanied by a harpist, who plays on Friday and Saturday.

Café-Théâtre de L'Accessoire (⊠ 26 rue de l'Annonciade, ☎ 04–78–27–84–84) and **Espace Gerson** (⊠ 1 pl. Gerson, ☎ 04–78–27–96–99) are two café-theaters where you can eat and drink while watching a revue. The **Opéra de Lyon** (⊠ 1 pl. de la Comédie, ☎ 04–72–00–45–45) presents plays, concerts, ballets, and opera from October to June. Lyon's Société de Musique de Chambre performs at **Salle Molière** (⊠ 18 quai Bondy, ☎ 04–78–28–03–11).

Early fall sees the renowned **Biennale de la Danse** (Dance Biennial; in even years). September is the time for the **Foire aux Tupiniers** (☎ 04–78–37–00–68), a pottery fair. October brings the **Festival Bach** (☎ 04–

78–72–75–31). The **Biennale d'Art Contemporain** (Contemporary Art Biennial; ☎ 04–78–30–50–66) is held in odd years in October. The **Festival du Vieux Lyon** (☎ 04–78–42–39–04) is a musical festival in November and December. On December 8 the Fête de La Immaculée Conception (Feast of the Immaculate Conception) lights go on city-wide for the marvelous **Fête de Lumière**, Lyon's Festival of Lights.

Shopping

Lyon has the region's best shopping; it is still the nation's silk-and-textiles capital, and all big-name designers have shops here. For chic clothing try the stores on rue du Président Édouard-Herriot and rue de la République in the center of town. Lyon's biggest shopping mall is the **Part-Dieu Shopping Center** (✉ Rue du Dr-Bouchut, ☎ 04–72–60–60–62), where there are 14 movie theaters and 250 shops. France's major department stores are well represented in Lyon, including **Galeries Lafayette** (✉ In Part-Dieu Shopping Center, ☎ 04–72–61–44–44; ✉ 6 pl. des Cordeliers, ☎ 04–72–40–48–00; ✉ 200 bd. Pinel, ☎ 04–78–77–82–12). There's also a **Printemps** (✉ 42 rue de la République, ☎ 04–72–41–29–29).

Captiva (✉ 10 rue de la Charité, ☎ 04–78–37–96–15) is the boutique of a young designer who works mainly in silk. **Les Gones** (✉ 33 rue Leynaud, ☎ 04–78–28–40–78), in the Croix Rousse District, is a boutique carrying the silk creations of several young designers. The workshop of **Monsieur Georges Mattelon** (✉ Rue d'Ivry, ☎ 04–78–28–62–04) is one of the oldest silk-weaving shops in Lyon. Lyonnais designer **Clémentine** (✉ 18 rue Émile-Zola) is good for well-cut, tailored clothing. **Étincelle** (✉ 34 rue St-Jean) has trendy outfits for youngsters.

For antiques, wander down **rue Auguste-Comte** (from place Bellecour to Perrache). **Image en Cours** (✉ 26 rue du Boeuf) sells superb engravings. **La Maison des Canuts** (✉ 10–12 rue d'Ivry, Croix Rousse) carries local textiles. Fabrics can be also found at the **Boutique des Soyeux Lyonnais** (✉ 3 rue du Boeuf).

For arts and crafts there are several places where you can find irresistible objects. Look for Lyonnais puppets on **place du Change.** Or try the **Marché des Artistes** (Artists' Market; ✉ Quai Romain Rolland, 5ᵉ), every Sunday morning from 7 to 1. Also held on Sunday morning is the **Marché des Artisans** (Crafts Market; ✉ Quai Fulchiron, 5ᵉ). A **Marché des Puces** (Flea Market; ✉ 1 rue du Canal in Villeurbanne; take Bus 37) takes place on Thursday and Saturday mornings 8–noon and on Sunday 6–1. For **secondhand books** try the market along quai de la Pêcherie (2ᵉ) near place Bellecour, held every Saturday and Sunday 10–6.

Food markets are held from Tuesday through Sunday on boulevard de la Croix-Rousse (4ᵉ), at Les Halles on cours Lafayette (3ᵉ), on quai Victor Augagneur (3ᵉ), and on quai St-Antoine (2ᵉ). A wine shop with an excellent selection is **À Ma Vigne** (✉ 18 rue Vaubecour, ☎ 04–78–37–05–29). **Cave de la Côte** (✉ 5 rue Pleney, ☎ 04–78–39–93–20) also has good wines. For chocolates head to **Bernachon** (✉ 42 cours Franklin-Roosevelt); some say it is the best *chocolaterie* in France. **La Boîte à Dessert** (✉ 1 rue de l'Ancienne-Préfecture) makes luscious peach turnovers. For culinary variety, shop **Les Halles** (✉ 102 cours Lafayette). **Pignol** (✉ 17 rue Émile-Zola) is good for meats and sandwich makings. **Reynon** (✉ 13 rue des Archers) is the place for charcuterie.

BEAUJOLAIS AND LA DOMBES

North of Lyon along the Saône are the vineyards of Beaujolais, a thrill for any oenophile. East of the Saône is the fertile land of La Dombes, where ornithologists flock to see migratory bird life. North of La Dombes and east of the Beaujolais wine villages is Bourg-en-Bresse, home to a marvelous church and poultry that delights gourmets; it makes a good base after Lyon. South toward the Rhône, the great river of southern France, is the well-preserved medieval village of Pérouges.

L'Arbresle

28 *16 km (10 mi) northwest of Lyon.*

If you love modern architecture, don't miss Éveux, outside L'Arbresle. Here the stark, blocky Dominican convent of **Ste-Marie de la Tourette** protrudes over the hillside, resting on slender pillars that look like stilts and revealing the minimalist sensibilities of architect Le Corbusier, who designed it in 1957–59. ☎ 04–74–01–01–03. ⊠ 22 frs. ☉ July–Aug., daily 9–noon and 2–6; Sept.–June, weekends 2–6.

Ars-sur-Formans

29 *30 km (19 mi) northeast of L'Arbresle; 36 km (22 mi) north of Lyon via A6, Villefranche exit.*

Each year 400,000 pilgrims invade this village (population 719) to honor the Curé d'Ars, Jean-Baptiste Vianney (1786–1859), patron saint of parish priests. Arriving in Ars in 1818, he was soon known as a charismatic confessor of unparalleled godliness and was thought of as a saint well before his death in 1859 and his actual canonization in 1925. The village church, enlarged to accommodate pilgrims, retains Vianney's confessional and his embalmed body; his Saint's Day is August 4. Seventeen tableaux chart Vianney's life at the **Historial du St-Curé-d'Ars.** ⊠ Le Tonneau, ☎ 04–74–00–70–22. ⊠ 25 frs. ☉ Mar.–Oct., daily 10–noon and 2–6; Nov.–Feb., weekends 2–7.

Villefranche-sur-Saône

30 *6 km (4 mi) east of Ars-sur-Formans, 31 km (19 mi) north of Lyon.*

The lively industrial town of Villefranche-sur-Saône is the capital of the Beaujolais region and is known for its *vin nouveau* (new wine). Thanks to marketing hype, this youthful, fruity red wine is eagerly gulped down around the world every year on the third Thursday of November.

Dining and Lodging

$$$$
★ ✕⌂ **Château de Bagnols.** This exquisite, small medieval castle, southwest of Villefranche, began life in the 13th century. Period glassware, fabrics, and porcelain were copied to complement the antique furniture. Adorning the walls are 17th- and 18th-century murals inspired by Lyon's textile industry. Rooms are huge, as are the regal bathrooms. Those in the main château evoke the 18th century; the ones in the converted stables and carriage houses known as La Résidence are, while rustic, furnished in a more contemporary mode. Wine tastings are held (if requested) in the beautiful stone *cuvage* (wine-pressing room). ⊠ 69620 Bagnols (15 km [9 mi] southwest of Villefranche on D38 to Tarare), ☎ 04–74–71–40–00, FAX 04–74–71–40–49. 20 rooms (12 in the castle, 8 suites in the carriage houses). Restaurant, library, meeting rooms. AE, DC, MC, V. ✆

Beaujolais Route du Vin

16 km (10 mi) north of Villefranche-sur-Saône, 49 km (30 mi) north of Lyon.

Not all Beaujolais wine is promoted as vin nouveau—that's just a marketing gimmick celebrated in full force on the third Thursday in November every year in this region (and around the world). Wine classed as "Beaujolais Villages" is higher in alcohol and produced from a clearly defined region northwest of Villefranche. Beaujolais is made from one single variety of grape, the gamay. However, there are 12 different appellations: Beaujolais, Beaujolais Villages, Brouilly, Chénas, Chiroubles, Côte de Brouilly, Fleurie, Juliénas, Morgon, Moulin à Vent, Régnié, and St-Amour. The Beaujolais Route du Vin (Wine Road), a narrow strip just 23 km (14 mi) long, is home to nine of these deluxe Beaujolais wines, also known as *crus*. Most villages have a *cave* (communal cellar) or *coopérative* where you can taste and buy. The **École Beaujolaise des Vins** (Beaujolais School of Wine; ⊠ Villefranche, ☎ 04–74–02–22–81) organizes lessons in wine tasting and on setting up your own cellar.

In the southernmost and largest vineyard of the Beaujolais crus is **Odenas,** producing Brouilly, a soft, fruity wine best drunk young. In the vineyard's center is towering Mont Brouilly, a hill whose vines produce a tougher, firmer wine, classified as Côte de Brouilly. From Odenas take D68, via St-Lager to **Villié-Morgon,** in the heart of the Morgon vineyard; robust wines that age well are produced here. At Monternot, east of Villié-Morgon, you will find the 15th-century **Château de Corcelles,** noted for its Renaissance galleries, canopied courtyard well, and medieval carvings in its chapel. The guardroom is now an atmospheric tasting cellar. ⊠ *Off D9 from Villié-Morgon,* ☎ *04–74–66–72–42.* ☉ *Mon.–Sat. 10–noon and 2:30–6:30.*

From Villié-Morgon D68 wiggles north through several more wine villages, including **Chiroubles,** where a rare, light wine best drunk young is produced. The wines from **Fleurie** are elegant and flowery. Well-known **Chénas** is home to two crus: the robust, velvety, and expensive Moulin à Vent, and the fruity and underestimated Chénas. The wines of **Juliénas** are sturdy and a deep color; sample them in the cellar of the town church (closed Tuesday and lunchtime), amid bacchanalian decor. **St-Amour,** west of Juliénas, produces light but firm reds and a limited quantity of whites. The famous white Pouilly-Fuissé comes from the area around **Fuissé.**

Bourg-en-Bresse

③ *43 km (27 mi) east of St-Amour on N79, 65 km (40 mi) northeast of Lyon.*

Cheerful Bourg-en-Bresse is esteemed among gastronomes for its fowl—striking-looking chickens with plump white bodies and bright blue feet, the *poulet de Bresse.* The town's southeasternmost district, Brou, is its most interesting and the site of a singular church. This is a good place to stay before or after a trip along the Beaujolais Wine Road (☞ *above*).

The **Église de Brou,** a marvel of Flamboyant Gothic, is no longer in religious use. The church was built between 1506 and 1532 by Margaret of Austria in memory of her husband, Philibert le Beau, the duke of Savoy, and their finely sculpted tombs highlight the rich interior. Son-et-lumière shows—on Easter and Pentecost Sunday and Monday, and on Thursday, Saturday, and Sunday from May through September—are magical. A massive restoration of the roof was completed in 1998 and has brought it back to its 16th-century state with the same gorgeous, multicolor, intricate patterns found throughout Burgundy. The museum in the nearby **cloister** stands out for its paintings: 16th- and 17th-century Flemish and Dutch artists keep company with 17th- and 18th-century French and Italian masters, 19th-century artists of the Lyon School, Gustave Doré, and contemporary local painters. ⊠ *63 bd. de Brou,* ☎ *04–74–22–83–83.* ⌑ *Church and museum 35 frs.* ⊙ *Apr.–Sept., daily 9–12:30 and 2–6:30; Oct.–Mar., daily 9–noon and 2–5.*

Dining and Lodging

$$$ ✕ **L'Auberge Bressane.** The location, looking out on the Brou church,
★ makes this modern, polished spot a good bet. Chef Jean-Pierre Vullin's preparations are becoming more and more consistent and always interesting. Frogs' legs and Bresse chicken with morel mushroom cream sauce are specialties; also try the *quenelles de brochet* (poached fish dumplings). Jean-Pierre wanders through the dining room ready for a chat while his staff provides excellent service. Don't miss the house aperitif, a champagne cocktail with fresh strawberry puree. The wine list has 300 vintages. ⊠ *166 bd. de Brou,* ☎ *04–74–22–22–68. Reservations essential. Jacket and tie. AE, DC, MC, V.*

$$–$$$ ✕ **La Petite Auberge.** This cozy flower-decked inn is in the countryside on the outskirts of town. Motherly Madame Bertrand provides games for children. Chef Philippe Garnier has a subtle way with mullet (he grills it in saffron butter) and Bresse chicken (browned in tangy cider vinegar). ⊠ *St-Just, rte. de Ceyzeriat,* ☎ *04–74–22–30–04. MC, V. Closed Jan. and Tues. No dinner Mon.*

$$$$ ✕⌑ **Georges Blanc.** This simple 19th-century inn, full of beautiful rugs, grandfather clocks, and antique country furniture, makes a fine setting for innovative preparations. Indulge in frogs' legs, wine from the extensive list, and superb desserts. The restaurant is closed Wednesday and Thursday (except for dinner June to mid-September). The 30 guest rooms range from (relatively) simple to downright luxurious. It's worth the trip from Bourg-en-Bresse, though only if you have money to burn and are making your way through every luxury restaurant in France. ⊠ *Pl. du Marché, 01540 Vonnas (19 km [12 mi] from Bourg-en-Bresse),* ☎ *04–74–50–90–90,* 🖷 *04–74–50–08–80. 48 rooms. Restaurant, pool, tennis court, helipad. AE, DC, MC, V. Reservations essential. Closed Jan.–mid-Feb.* ✎

$$$ ✕⌑ **Hôtel de France.** This new Best Western acquisition is centrally located and impeccably renovated. Rooms are comfortable and equipped with the full range of the most modern amenities, from hair dryers to minibars. The adjoining restaurant has been taken over by Georges Blanc and, as expected, is steaming to the top of local gastronomical charts. ⊠ *19 pl. Bernard, 01000,* ☎ *04–74–23–30–24,* 🖷 *04–74–23–69–90. 44 rooms, 2 suites. Restaurant. AE, DC, MC, V.*

Villars-les-Dombes

㉜ *29 km (18 mi) south of Bourg-en-Bresse, 37 km (23 mi) north of Lyon.*

Villars-les-Dombes is the unofficial capital of La Dombes, an area once covered by a glacier. When the ice retreated, it left a network of lakes and ponds that draws anglers and bird-watchers today. The 56-acre **Parc des Oiseaux,** one of Europe's finest bird sanctuaries, is home to 400 species of birds (some 2,000 from five continents); 435 aviaries house species from waders to birds of prey; and tropical birds in vivid hues fill the indoor birdhouse. Allow two hours. ⊠ *Off N83,* ☎ *04–74–98–05–54.* ⌑ *38 frs.* ⊙ *Easter–Sept., daily 9–7; Oct.–Easter, daily 9–dusk.*

En Route N83 skirts the Dombes region's largest lake, the **Grand Étang de Birieux,** en route from Villars-les-Dombes to St-André de Covey.

Pérouges

★ ㉝ *21 km (13 mi) southeast of Villars-les-Dombes, 36 km (22 mi) north-east of Lyon.*

Wonderfully preserved (though a little too precious), hilltop Pérouges, with its medieval houses and narrow cobbled streets surrounded by ramparts, is just 200 yards across. Hand weavers first brought it prosperity; the industrial revolution meant their downfall, and by the late 19th century the population had dwindled from 1,500 to 12. Now the government has restored the most interesting houses; a potter, bookbinder, cabinetmaker, and weaver have given the town a new lease on life. A number of restaurants make Pérouges a good lunch stop.

Encircling the town is **rue des Rondes**; from this road you can get fine views of the countryside and, on clear days, the Alps. Park your car by the main gateway, **Porte d'En-Haut,** alongside the 15th-century fortress-church. Rue du Prince, the town's main street, leads to the **Maison des Princes de Savoie** (Palace of the Princes of Savoie), formerly the home of the influential Savoie family that once controlled the eastern part of France. Note the fine watchtower. **Place de la Halle,** a pretty square with great charm, around the corner from the Maison des Princes de Savoie, is the site of a lime tree planted in 1792. The **Musée de Vieux Pérouges** (Old Pérouges Museum), to one side of the place de la Halle, contains local artifacts and a reconstructed weaver's workshop. The medieval **garden** alongside has an array of rare medicinal plants. ⊠ *Pl. du Tilleul,* ☎ *04–74–61–00–88.* ▢ *20 frs.* ☉ *May–Sept., daily 10–noon and 2–6.*

Lodging

$$$–$$$$ ▣ **Hostellerie du Vieux Pérouges.** Extraordinary even by French standards, this historic inn has antiques, glossy wood floors and tables, and gigantic stone hearths. Rooms in the geranium-decked 15th-century manor are more spacious (but also nearly twice the cost) than those in the annex and have marble bathrooms and period furniture. In the restaurant, dishes are served on pewter plates by waitresses in folk costumes; the crayfish is particularly good. Prices are high: The various menus range from the simple three-course choice at 180 francs to the gourmet 400-franc option. Fortunately, there are several places to dine that are on or near the square, so if the Hostellerie's offerings are not tempting, there are other good options at hand. ⊠ *Pl. du Tilleul, 01800 Pérouges,* ☎ *04–74–61–00–88,* ℻ *04–74–34–77–90. 28 rooms. Restaurant, meeting rooms. AE, DC, MC, V.* ✎

THE RHÔNE VALLEY

At Lyon, the Rhône, joined by the Saône, truly comes into its own, plummeting south in search of the Mediterranean. The river's progress is often spectacular, as steep vineyards conjure up vistas that are more readily associated with the river's Germanic cousin, the Rhine. All along the way, small-town vintners invite you to sample their wines. Roman towns like Vienne and Valence reflect the Rhône's importance as a trading route. To the west is the rugged, rustic Ardèche *département* (province), where time seems to have slowed to a standstill.

Vienne

㉞ *27 km (17 mi) south of Lyon via A7.*

One of Roman Gaul's most important towns, Vienne became a religious and cultural center under its count-archbishops in the Middle

Ages and retains considerable historic charm despite being a major road and train junction. The tourist office anchors cours Brillier in the leafy shadow of the Jardin Public (Public Garden). The 30-franc Passport admits you to most local monuments and museums; it's available at the tourist office and at the first site that you visit.

On quai Jean-Jaurès, beside the Rhône, is the church of **St-Pierre.** Note the rectangular 12th-century Romanesque bell tower with its arcaded tiers. The lower church walls date from the 6th century. Although religious wars deprived the cathedral of **St-Maurice** of many statues, much original decoration is intact; the portals on the 15th-century facade are carved with Old Testament scenes. The cathedral was built between the 12th and 16th centuries, with later additions, such as the splendid 18th-century mausoleum, to the right of the altar. A frieze of the zodiac adorns the entrance to the vaulted passage that once led to the cloisters but now opens onto place St-Paul.

Place du Palais is the site of the remains of the **Temple d'Auguste et de Livie** (Temple of Augustus and Livia), accessible via place St-Paul and rue Clémentine; they probably date in part from Vienne's earliest Roman settlements (1st century BC). The Corinthian columns were walled in during the 11th century, when the temple was used as a church; in 1833 Prosper Mérimée intervened to have the temple restored. The last vestige of the city's sizable Roman baths is a **Roman gateway** (⊠ Rue Chantelouve) decorated with delicate friezes.

The **Théâtre Romain** (Roman Theater), on rue de la Charité, is one of the largest in Gaul (143 yards across). It held 13,000 spectators and is only slightly smaller than Rome's Theater of Marcellus. Rubble buried Vienne's theater until 1922; excavation has uncovered 46 rows of seats, some marble flooring, and the frieze on the stage. Concerts take place here in summer. ⊠ *7 rue du Cirque,* ☎ *04–74–85–39–23.* ▧ *15 frs.* ☉ *Apr.–Aug., daily 9–12:30 and 2–6; Sept.–mid-Oct., Tues.– Sun. 9–12:30 and 2–6; mid-Oct.–Mar., Tues.–Sat. 9:30–12:30 and 2– 5, Sun. 1:30–5:30.*

Rue des Orfèvres (off rue de la Charité) is lined with Renaissance facades and distinguished by the church of **St-André-le-Bas,** once part of a powerful abbey. If possible, venture past the restoration now in progress to see the finely sculpted 12th-century capitals (made of Roman stone) and the 17th-century wood statue of St. Andrew. It's best to see the cloisters during the music festival held here and at the cathedral from June to August. ⊠ *Cour St-André,* ☎ *04–74–85–18– 49.* ▧ *15 frs.* ☉ *Apr.–mid-Oct., Tues.–Sun. 9:30–1 and 2–6; mid-Oct.– Mar., Tues.–Sat. 9:30–12:30 and 2–5, Sun. 2–6.*

Across the Rhône from the town center is the excavated **Cité Gallo-Romaine** (Gallo-Roman City), covering several acres. Here you can find villas, houses, workshops, public baths, and roads built by the Romans. ▧ *30 frs.* ☉ *Daily 9–6.*

Dining

$$ ✕ **Le Bec Fin.** An inexpensive weekday menu makes this unpretentious eatery opposite the cathedral a good choice for lunch and dinner. The steak and freshwater fish seldom disappoint and occasionally display a deft touch (turbot cooked with saffron). The dining room has an understated elegance. ⊠ *7 pl. St-Maurice,* ☎ *04–74–85–76–72. Reservations essential at dinner. Jacket required at dinner. MC, V. Closed Mon. No dinner Sun.*

Serrières

③⑤ *32 km (20 mi) south of Vienne, 59 km (37 mi) south of Lyon.*

Riverboats traditionally stop at little Serrières, on the Rhône's west bank. Life on the water is depicted at the **Musée des Mariniers du Rhône** (Boatmen's Museum), in the wooden-roof Gothic chapel of St-Sornin. ☎ *04–75–34–01–26. ⬚ 15 frs. ⊘ Apr.–Oct., weekends 3–6.*

Dining and Lodging

$$–$$$ ✕⊡ **Schaeffer.** In a sophisticated setting, chef Bernard Mathé dishes up inventive variants of traditional French dishes: smoked duck cutlet in lentil stew or lamb with eggplant in anchovy butter. The number of desserts is overwhelming, but pistachio cake with bitter chocolate is the clear winner. Reservations are essential, and a jacket is required at the restaurant, which is closed Sunday night and Monday. Guest rooms are decorated in contemporary style. ⊠ *Quai Jules Roche, 07340,* ☎ *04–75–34–00–07, Ⅸ 04–75–34–08–79. 11 rooms. Restaurant. AE, DC, MC, V. Closed 1st 3 wks Jan.*

Hauterives

③⑥ *28 km (17 mi) east of Serrières, 40 km (25 mi) south of Vienne.*

Hauterives would be just another quaint village on the eastern side of the Rhône if not for the **Palais Idéal,** one of Western Europe's weirdest constructions. A fantasy constructed entirely of stones (called *galets*) from the nearby Galaure River, it was the life's work of a local postman, Ferdinand Cheval (1836–1924), who was haunted by visions of faraway mosques and temples. One of many wall inscriptions reads "1879–1912: 10,000 days, 93,000 hours, 33 years of toil." ☎ *04–75–68–81–19, Ⅸ 04–75–68–88–15. ⬚ 30 frs. ⊘ mid-Apr.–mid-Sept., daily 9–7; mid-Sept.–mid-Apr., 9:30–5:30.*

Dining and Lodging

$$ ✕⊡ **Le Relais.** A stone's throw from the Palais Idéal, this rustic inn is a good place for a meal—and a night's stay, if desirable. Rooms are small and could use refurbishing in the not-too-distant future. Owner Roland Graillat is better as a chef—roast partridge and delicately seasoned frogs' legs are good bets. The restaurant is closed Sunday dinner and Monday, except for July and August. ⊠ *Pl. de l'Église, 26390,* ☎ *04–75–68–81–12, Ⅸ 04–75–68–92–42. 13 rooms. Restaurant. AE, DC, V. Closed Jan.–Feb.*

Annonay

③⑦ *44 km (27 mi) south of Vienne, 43 km (27 mi) southeast of St-Étienne.*

The narrow streets and passageways of central Annonay are full of character. The town, which grew up around the leather industry, is best known as the home of Joseph and Étienne Montgolfier, who, in 1783, invented the hot-air balloon (known in French as a *montgolfière*). The first flight was on June 4, 1783, from place des Cordeliers (although a commemorating obelisk is on avenue Marc-Seguin); the flight lasted a half hour and reached 6,500 ft.

Local history and folklore are evoked at the **Musée Vivarais César Filhol,** between the Mairie (Town Hall) and the church of Notre-Dame. ⊠ *15 rue Béchetoille,* ☎ *04–75–33–24–51. ⬚ 15 frs. ⊘ July–Aug., Tues.–Fri. 3–6; weekends 3–6; Sept.–June, Wed. and weekends 3–6.*

Tournon

38 *37 km (23 mi) southeast of Annonay, 59 km (37 mi) south of Vienne.*

Tournon is on the Rhône at the foot of granite hills. Its hefty **Château,** dating from the 15th and 16th centuries, is the chief attraction. The castle's twin terraces have wonderful views of the old town, the river, and—towering above Tain-l'Hermitage across the Rhône—the steep vineyards that produce Hermitage wine, one of the region's most refined—and costly—reds. In the château is a museum of local history, the **Musée Rhodanien** (or du Rhône), which explores the life of Annonay-born engineer Marc Seguin (1786–1875), who, in 1825, built the first suspension bridge over the Rhône at Tournon (demolished in 1965). ⊠ *Pl. Auguste-Faure,* ☎ *04–75–08–10–23.* ▧ *25 frs.* ☉ *June–Aug., Wed.–Mon. 10–noon and 2–6; Apr.–May and Sept.–Oct., Wed.–Mon. 2–6.*

A ride on one of France's last steam trains, the **Chemin de Fer du Vivarais,** makes an adventurous two-hour trip 33 km (21 mi) along the narrow, rocky Doux Valley to Lamastre and back to Tournon. ⊠ *Departs from Tournon station,* ☎ *04–78–28–83–34.* ▧ *Round-trip 115 frs.* ☉ *June–Aug., daily 10 AM; May and Sept., weekends 10 AM.*

Dining and Lodging

$$ ✕ **Jean-Marc Reynaud.** Tain-l'Hermitage, across the Rhône from Tournon, is home to this fine restaurant with a comfortable, traditional dining room and a magnificent river view. The classic cuisine is excellent; specialties include poached egg with foie gras and pigeon fillet in black-currant sauce. ⊠ *82 av. du Président-Roosevelt, Tain-l'Hermitage,* ☎ *04–75–07–22–10. AE, DC, MC, V. Closed Mon., Jan., and 1 wk in Aug. No dinner Sun.*

$$$ ✕▣ **Michel Chabran.** This sophisticated hotel-restaurant is decidedly modern in its use of stone and wood in the Drôme style, its floral displays, its airy picture windows overlooking the garden, and its guest rooms with a touch of contemporary Danish influence. Note that since the hotel is on the main road, sleeping with the windows open can make for a noisy night. The restaurant (closed from Sunday dinner through Monday November through March) serves such imaginative and light fare as mille-feuille de foie gras with artichokes and lamb from Rémuzat. ⊠ *29 av. du 45ᵉ Parallèle, 26600 Pont de l'Isère (on left [east] bank of the Rhône, 10 km [6 mi] south of Tournon via N7 and 7 km [4 mi] north of Valence),* ☎ *04–75–84–60–09,* 𝐅𝐀𝐗 *04–75–84–59–65. 12 rooms. Restaurant, pool, meeting rooms. AE, MC, V.* ✎

En Route From Tournon's place Jean-Jaurès, slightly inland from the château, follow signs to narrow, twisting **Route Panoramique**; the views en route to the old village of **St-Romain-de-Lerps** are breathtaking. In good weather the panorama at St-Romain includes 13 départements, Mont Blanc to the east, and arid Mont Ventoux to the south. D287 winds down to St-Péray and Valence; topping the **Montagne de Crussol,** 650 ft above the plain, is the ruined 12th-century **Château de Crussol.**

Valence

39 *17 km (11 mi) south of Tournon, 92 km (57 mi) west of Grenoble, 127 km (79 mi) north of Avignon.*

Largish Valence, the Drôme département capital, is the region's market center. Steep-curbed alleyways called *côtes* extend into the old town from the Rhône. At the center of the old town is the cathedral of **St-Apollinaire.** Although begun in the 12th century in the Romanesque style, it is not as old as it looks: Parts of it were rebuilt in the 17th century, with the belfry rebuilt in the 19th. The **Musée des**

Beaux-Arts (Fine Arts Museum), next to the cathedral of St-Apollinaire, in the former 18th-century Bishops' Palace, displays archaeological finds as well as sculpture and furniture along with drawings by landscapist Hubert Robert (1733–1808). ⊠ *Pl. des Ormeaux,* ☎ *04–75–79–20–80.* 🎫 *20 frs.* 🕐 *Mon.–Tues. and Thurs.–Fri. 2–6, Wed. and weekends 9–noon and 2–6.*

Dining and Lodging

$$$$ ✕🍴 **Pic.** Serving up subtle and original cuisine, such as truffle-fla-
★   vored *galettes* (pancakes) and asparagus with caviar, the Pic family is the undisputed king among Drôme restaurateurs. And you pay for it (the best bargain is the lunch-only 290-franc menu). Dine in the peach dining room on the comfortable, embroidered armchairs or, in summer, on the shaded terrace (a jacket is required, and reservations are essential; there is no Sunday dinner). Elegant guest rooms and two opulent suites are available if you want to stay the night; book in advance. ⊠ *285 av. Victor-Hugo, 26000,* ☎ *04–75–44–15–32,* FAX *04–75–40–96–03. 13 rooms, 2 apartments. Restaurant. AE, MC, DC, V.* 🍽

Shopping

In the small town of Romans, 15 minutes east of Valence via D532, are a score of retail outlets for designer shoes. Romans, with its tradition of leather making, has become the major factory center for the production of high-quality shoes. Many of the top European designers are represented, and their products may be had at bargain prices from any number of stores, such as **Charles Jourdan** (⊠ Galerie Fan Halles, ☎ 04–75–02–32–36), **Chaussures Tchlin** (⊠ Quai Chopin, ☎ 04–75–72–51–41), and **Stephane Kelian** (⊠ 11 pl. Charles-de-Gaulle, ☎ 04–75–05–23–26).

En Route   The prettiest route between Valence and Privas is N86, on the right bank of the Rhône; after 16 km (10 mi) and just before La Voulte, turn onto the scenic D120, which follows the Eyrieux Valley as far as Les Ollières-sur-Eyrieux; then turn south along D2, under the thick canopy of horse chestnut trees.

Cliousclat

④   *21 km (13 mi) south of Valence, 27 km (17 mi) north of Montélimar.*

Less than 10 km (6 mi) off A7 and N7, the roads running south from Valence to Montélimar and on to Provence, is the delightful, tiny village of Cliousclat. It's built on a side of hill, with just one narrow street running through it. There's not much to do or see, but its charming atmosphere and its gorgeous views make it very appealing. While you're here, however, drop in at the small **Histoires de Poteries** (Pottery History Museum) to see the work of local potters. You might want to buy some of the lovely wares, too. ☎ *04–75–63–15–60.* 🎫 *15 frs.* 🕐 *Apr.–June, Tues.–Sun. 2–7; July–Aug., daily 10–1 and 2–8; Sept., Tues.–Sun. 10–noon and 2–7; Oct., Tues.–Sun. 2–6.*

Dining and Lodging

$$–$$$ ✕🍴 **La Treille Muscate.** Between Lyon and Avignon there is no better
★   place to spend a night than at this gem of a hotel. Each room is made unique by items lovingly collected from antiques shops. Clay-tile floor covered with throw rugs add to the provincial charm. The most delightful is No. 11, which has a huge terrace looking over fields to the Rhône. Dinner is a pleasure. It's inexpensive (135 francs for four courses), tasty, and made from top-quality products, such as Sisteron lamb, Mediterranean fish, and homemade foie gras. The wine list is also extremely reasonable. The friendly owner, Madame de Laître, speaks English fluently but politely refrains from doing so until you have ex-

hausted your French. ⊠ *26270 Cliousclat,* ☎ *04–75–63–13–10,* FAX *04–75–63–10–79. 12 rooms. Restaurant. MC, V. Closed mid-Dec.–Feb.*

Privas

🔳 *41 km (25 mi) southwest of Valence.*

The capital of the spectacular Ardèche département, renowned for its caves and rocky gorges, Privas makes a good base for exploring the region. The tourist office, just off place Charles-de-Gaulle, can provide details. A Protestant stronghold during the 16th-century Wars of Religion, Privas was razed by Louis XIII in 1629, following a 16-day siege. The Pont Louis XIII (Louis XIII Bridge), over the River Ouvèze, commemorates the town's return to royal good graces. It eventually became a peaceful administrative town, best known for the production of that French delicacy known as *marrons glacés* (candied chestnuts).

Dining

$–$$ ✕ **Lous Esclos.** This strikingly modern restaurant has more windows than walls—all overlooking the wild Ardèche landscape. The chef's masterpieces include goose and snail in flaky pastry—at prices that are too good to be true. ⊠ *Alissas (5 km [3 mi] southeast of Privas on D2),* ☎ *04–75–65–12–73. MC, V. Closed late-Dec.–mid-Jan.*

The Ardèche Valley

Aubenas is 30 km (18 mi) south of Privas on N104, 74 km (46 mi) northeast of Alés; Pont-St-Esprit is 43 km (27 mi) south of Montélimar, 45 km (28 mi) north of Avignon.

For the 120 km (75 mi) that the Ardèche River flows from its source to the Rhône, there is a spectacular variety of nature—basins of orchards, vertical cliffs, and spectacular gorges—plus medieval villages guarded by castles perched high up on rocky promontories. A good base is in or near the small town of **Aubenas,** which has a thriving silk industry and a 12th-century castle (with later additions) that is now the town hall. The Ardèche River's source can be traced at the **Col de la Chavade** (4,154 ft); take N102 west from Aubenas toward **Mayres,** 38 km (24 mi) upstream.

East of Aubenas via D104 and D579 is a 40-km (25-mi) stretch known as **La Valée Moyenne** (Middle Valley), where you'll find a number of small villages and a dramatic gorge. Pass through Rochecolombe and Balazuc to get to the small medieval village of **Voqüssmé.** Just before Ruoms, make a detour right on D245 for 3½ km (2 mi) en route to the tiny village of **Labesume.** The houses here are all built out of natural stone and, as if camouflaged, seem unnoticeable except for their balconies. Labesume is at the southern end of the **Gorges de la Beaume,** a 40-km (25-mi) gorge cut through by the Beaume River as it tumbles down from the Tanarque Massif to join the Ardèche River at Ruoms.

The last 58 km (35 mi) of the valley, from Vallon-Pont-d'Arc to Pont-St-Esprit, are particularly magnificent. Here you'll find another dramatic gorge, the 41-km-long (26-mi-long) **Gorges de l'Ardèche.** Route D290 runs from Vallon-Pont-d'Arc along the edge of the gorge on the side of the Gras Plâteau; stop periodically to look down. Your first stop should be at the **Pont d'Arc,** where the river flows under a natural arch 112 ft high and 194 ft wide. From here on, the river makes some spectacular bends and varies from tumbling through rapids to a gentle meander. The most dramatic view of the gorge is from **Serre de Toure Belvédère,** about 11 km (7 mi) from Vallon, where you can peer down 750 ft to the river. Another 11 km (7 mi) along, the **Gournier Belvédère** gives you a view of the river tumbling its way through the Gournier Toupine Rocks. All along the gorge are caverns and grottoes. The best is **Marzal Aven,** with its large variety of calcite formations. To reach it, turn left onto D590 just after the Gournier Belvédère and drive about 5 km (3 mi); the entrance to the main cave is down 743 steps to the **Salle du Tombeau** (Tomb Cave), where translucent sheets of stalactites seem like shielding drapes to bear and deer bones. Spend a fascinating hour underground being guided through the fantastic caves, but be sure to take a sweater, as it can be chilly. ⊡ *33 frs.* ⊘ *Mid-Apr.–Sept., daily 9–6; mid-Mar.–mid-Apr. and Oct.–Nov., weekends 11, 3, and 5.*

Take one last look at the gorge at the **Ranc-Pointu Belvédère,** where the Le Louby River joins the Ardèche. This viewpoint overlooks the river's last enclosed bend, so don't pass up a stop here. The gorge then ends, and the countryside opens up to a fertile valley. Cross over the suspension bridge at **Pont-St-Esprit** and turn left on D941 to reach the Rhône and the north–south route A7 heading toward Montélimar.

Lodging

$$ ⊞ **Les Cedres.** A friendly husband-and-wife team (she speaks English) efficiently manages this moderate hotel. Rooms are functional, small, and clean; ask for one overlooking the garden (though they are among the smaller and more expensive) instead of the parking lot. Half have small terraces; only those without these outdoor areas are air-conditioned. Dinner is moderately priced and enjoyable though nothing fancy—just simple, good fare of sautéed fish, regional stews, and meats with Provençal sauces. Breakfasts are a little disappointing. ⊠ *07260 Joyeuse (20 km [12 mi] southwest of Aubenas),* ☎ *04–75–39–40–60,* FAX *04–75–39–90–16. 40 rooms. Restaurant, pool, fishing. AE, DC, MC, V. Closed mid-Oct.–mid-Apr.*

$$$ ✕⊞ **La Bastide du Soleil.** This recent addition to the fine cuisine and hostelry of the Ardèche is nestled in a 17th-century castle in the heart of the medieval village of Vinezac. The rooms are modern and charming, while the excellent restaurant specializes in an ever-changing seasonal menu based on fresh local produce. Menus range from an economical 100-france choice to the 265-franc gourmet taster's menu. ⊠ *07110 Vinezac (off rte. D104 10 km [6 mi] southwest of Aubenas),* ☎ *04–75–36–91–66,* FAX *04–75–36–91–59. 6 rooms. Restaurant. AE, DC, MC, V. Closed Jan. 1–Feb. 29.*

Outdoor Activities and Sports

If you're interested in kayaking or canoeing through the Gorges de l'Ardèche, contact **Alpha Bateaux** (⊠ 07150 Vallon Pont d'Arc, ☎ 04–75–88–08–29). A two-person canoe costs about 350 francs per day, and a one-person kayak is about 220 francs.

Montélimar

㊷ *43 km (27 mi) north of Pont-St-Esprit, 35 km (22 mi) southeast of Privas, 83 km (52 mi) north of Avignon.*

The town got its name from the 12th- to 14th-century fortress, the **Château des Mont Adhémar,** situated in a park surveying the town and valley. ⊠ *24 rue du Château,* ☎ *04–75–01–07–85.* ⊡ *35 frs.* ⊘ *Apr.–Oct., daily 9:30–11:30 and 2–5:30; Nov.–Mar., Wed.–Mon. 9:30–11:30 and 2–5:30.*

At the **Musée de la Miniature** (Miniatures Museum), a collection of very small pieces (a little *Mona Lisa,* a tiny chess game, a minimicroscope, etc.) from all over the world is displayed. ⊠ *19 rue Pierre Julien,* ☎ *04–75–53–79–24.* ⊡ *30 frs.* ⊘ *June–mid-Sept., daily 10–6; mid-Sept.–Dec. and Feb.–May, Wed.–Sun. 2–6.*

Montélimar's nougat candy has been famous since the end of the 17th century, soon after the first almond trees were introduced to the area. Almonds mixed with honey replaced the then-traditional walnut cake known as *nux gatum,* or *nougo.* The nougat is made with melted honey and sugar and whipped egg whites. The addition of more sugar at high temperatures creates a paste that characterizes Montélimar's nougat. Vanilla, almonds, and pistachios are then added, and the paste is poured in molds lined with unleavened bread. The nougat must have a minimum of 30% almonds (or 28% almonds and 2% pistachios) and 25% honey; ordinary nougat needs to have only a minimum of 15% almonds or hazelnuts. At least a dozen shops specialize in the candy, among them **Nougat Chabert & Guillot** (⊠ 9 rue Ch. Chalbert, ☎ 04–75–00–82–00) and **Nougat Diane de Poyters** (⊠ 99 av. Jean-Jaurès, ☎ 04–75–01–04–95).

Dining and Lodging

$$$ ✕⊞ **Les Hospitaliers.** This tasteful, modern hotel with sweeping views is in tiny hilltop Le Poët-Laval, east of Montélimar. With its stone walls and red-tile roof, the hotel is perfect in its medieval setting. In cold weather, escape from the large but tacky rooms to the immense stone hearth in the sitting room. The airy restaurant serves local specialties; the thrush pâté with truffles is especially good. ⊠ *Le Vieux Village, 26160 Le Poët-Laval (22 km [14 mi] east of Montélimar),* ☎ *04–75–46–22–32,* FAX *04–75–46–49–99. 20 rooms, 2 suites. Restaurant, pool. AE, DC, MC, V. Closed mid-Nov.–mid-Mar.*

$$ ⊞ **Sphinx Hôtel.** The best bargain in Montélimar is this privately owned hotel in a former 17th-century residence in the heart of town. Though rooms are on the small side, they are neat; most overlook the courtyard, which minimizes traffic noise—ask for one of these. Bathrooms are modest and adequate. The owner, who speaks English fluently, can recommend good places to eat in town. ⊠ *19 bd. Marre-Desmarais, 26200,* ☎ *04–75–01–86–64,* FAX *04–75–52–34–21. 24 rooms. Parking (free) MC, V.*

Outdoor Activities and Sports

If you're interested in going riding, horses can be rented from the **Centre Equestre** (⊠ Montchinal ☎ 04–75–01–23–32). A pleasant par-72 **golf course** is found at Château Le Monard (⊠ Montboucher-sur-Labron, Montélimar).

GRENOBLE AND THE ALPS

In winter some of the world's best skiing is found in the Alps; in summer chic spas, shimmering lakes, and hilltop trails come into their own. The Savoie and Haute-Savoie départements occupy the most impressive territory; Grenoble, in the Dauphiné, is the Alps' gateway and the area's only city. It's all at the nexus of highways from Marseille, Valence, Lyon, Geneva, and Turin.

Grenoble

43 *104 km (65 mi) southeast of Lyon, 138 km (86 mi) northeast of Montélimar.*

Cosmopolitan Grenoble's skyscrapers seem intimidating by homey French standards. But along with the city's nuclear research plant, they bear witness to the fierce local desire to move ahead with the times. Grenoble is also home to a large university and is the birthplace of the great French novelist Stendhal. All around are proud mountains, dramatic gorges, and hidden valleys.

☺ A **cable car,** starting at quai St-Stéphane-Jay, on the north side of the River Isère, whisks you up to the hilltop and its **Fort de la Bastille,** where there are splendid views. ☒ *40 frs round-trip.* ☉ *Apr.–Oct., daily 9 AM–midnight; Nov.–Dec. and Feb.–Mar., daily 10–6.*

Rue Maurice-Gignoux is home to gardens, cafés, mansions, and a 17th-century convent that contains the **Musée Dauphinois,** a lively museum with local folk art. The *Premiers Alpins* explores the evolution of the Alps and its inhabitants. ☒ *30 rue Maurice-Gignoux,* ☎ *04–76–85–19–01.* ☒ *25 frs.* ☉ *Nov.–Apr., Wed.–Mon. 10–6; May–Oct., Wed.–Mon. 10–7.*

The church of **St-Laurent,** near the Musée Dauphinois (☞ *above*), has an atmospheric 6th-century crypt—one of the country's oldest Christian monuments—supported by a row of formidable marble pillars. ☒ *2 pl. St-Laurent,* ☎ *04–76–44–78–68.* ☒ *20 frs.* ☉ *Wed.–Mon. 8–noon and 2–6.*

Place de Lavalette, on the south side of the river where most of Grenoble is concentrated, is home to the **Musée de Grenoble,** formerly the Musée de Peinture et de Sculpture (Painting and Sculpture Museum). Founded in 1796 and since enlarged, it is one of France's oldest museums and the first to concentrate on modern art (Picasso donated his *Femme Lisant* in 1921); a modern addition incorporates the medieval Tour de l'Isle (Island Tower), a Grenoble landmark. The collection includes 4,000 paintings and 5,500 drawings, among them works from the Italian Renaissance, Rubens, Flemish still lifes, Zurbaran, and Canaletto; Impressionists such as Renoir and Monet; and 20th-century works by Matisse (*Intérieur aux Aubergines*), Signac, Derain, Vlaminck, Magritte, Ernst, Miró, and Dubuffet. Modern sculpture adorns the gardens. ☒ *5 pl. de Lavalette,* ☎ *04–76–63–44–44.* ☒ *25 frs.* ☉ *Wed. 11–10, Thurs.–Mon. 11–7.*

Dining and Lodging

$$–$$$ ✕🏨 **Alpotel.** This reasonably priced chain hotel is modern and functional, comfortable rather than plush, and handily situated on a main boulevard a few minutes from the old town. The bustling restaurant's inventive menu has such delicacies as crab *saveloy* (sausage), and poached salmon with pink butter. ☒ *12 bd. du Maréchal-Joffre, 38000,* ☎ *04–76–87–88–41,* ℻ *04–76–47–58–52. 88 rooms. Restaurant, bar. AE, DC, MC, V.*

$$ ✕🏨 **Château de la Commanderie.** In a suburb of Grenoble is this
★ hotel-restaurant made up of a 13th-century building, which has been owned by the same family for 200 years, plus a 20th-century addition. In public rooms, ancestral portraits peer down on grandfather clocks. Each room in the modern section differs in design, but all share the same light color scheme and fresh feeling. Dining is a real pleasure: each dish, such as hot oysters coated with chopped watercress or venison fillet, shows chef Dennis Coutarel's flair and creativity. The restaurant doesn't serve Sunday dinner and Monday lunch. ☒ *17 av. D'Echirolles, 38320 Eybens (5 km [3 mi] south of Grenoble),* ☎ *04–76–25–34–58,* ℻ *04–76–24–07–31. 25 rooms. Restaurant, pool, meeting rooms. AE, DC, MC, V.*

Nightlife and the Arts

Look for the monthly *Grenoble-Spectacles* for a list of events around town. **Le Joker** (☒ *1 Grande-Rue*) is a lively, youthful disco. **La Soupe aux Choux** (☒ *7 rte. de Lyon*) is the spot for jazz.

Cinq Jours de Jazz is just that—five days of jazz—in February or March. In summer classical music characterizes the **Session Internationale de Grenoble-Isère.**

Outdoor Activities and Sports

The **Maison de la Randonée** (✉ 7 rue Voltaire, ☎ 04–76–51–76–00) can provide you with information on places to hike around Grenoble.

En Route If you have time only for a brief glimpse of the Alps, take N91 out of Grenoble toward Briançon, past the spectacular mountain scenery of **L'Alpe d'Huez, Les Deux Alpes,** and the **Col du Galibier.** Or take D512 north from Grenoble for 17 km (11 mi), fork left, and follow small D57-D as far as you can (only a few miles) before leaving your car for the 30-minute climb to the top of the 6,000-ft **Charmant Som peak.** Your reward will be a stunning view of the Grande Chartreuse Monastery (☞ *below*), to the north. If you're heading to Provence and using Grenoble as your gateway through the Alps, be sure to take N76, which cuts through the mountains and presents some majestic scenery. From spring through fall the valleys are lush with greenery; in winter they are snow-covered bowls attracting skiers. Along the way you'll pass many small villages tucked insidethe mountain sleeves, which guard them from winter winds.

Corps

㊹ *66 km (41 mi) south of Grenoble, 138 km (85½ mi) north of Sisteron.*

The village of Corps is one of the area's major tourist centers and a good base for skiing and hiking. Gourmets come year-round to enjoy chef Dulas's cooking at Hotel de la Poste (☞ Dining and Lodging, *below*).

Dining and Lodging

$$ ✕🏨 **Château des Herbeys.** South of Corps on the Route Napoléon is this château-hotel (off the road in a small park, so it's quiet), which, though altered many times since, began life in the 13th century. The owners, the Dulas, have decorated guest rooms with antiques and—unfortunately—occasionally with tacky modern bric-a-brac; bathrooms are ultramodern. Dinner is served in two rooms that echo the grand style of the château, though some feel the ambience is somewhat too staid. ✉ *Off N76 (10 km [6 mi] south of Corps), 05800 Chauffayer,* ☎ *04–92–55–26–83,* FAX *04–92–55–29–66. 10 rooms. Restaurant. MC, V. Closed Dec.–Jan.*

$–$$ ✕🏨 **Hôtel de la Poste.** Reservations are essential at the restaurant to enjoy Monsieur Dulas's fine cooking (he also owns the Château des Herbeys, ☞ *above*). In two rustic and intimate dining rooms, you may feast on such fare as scrumptious quail or smoked duck salad, followed by perfectly cooked roast lamb or mountain trout. Guest rooms come in varying sizes (the least expensive ones are very small), with warm, colorful fabrics and rustic furnishings. Avoid those over the road, which can be noisy at night. ✉ *Rte. N76, 38970,* ☎ *04–76–30–00–03,* FAX *04–76–30-02–73. 18 rooms. Restaurant. AE, MC, V. Closed Dec.–Jan. 15.*

Grande Chartreuse

㊺ *23 km (14 mi) north of Grenoble; head north on D512 and fork left 8 km (5 mi) on D520-B just before St-Pierre-de-Chartreuse.*

St. Bruno founded this 12-acre monastery in 1084; it later spawned 24 other charter houses in Europe. Burned, and rebuilt, several times, it was stripped of possessions during the French Revolution, when the monks were expelled. On their return they resumed making their sweet liqueur, Chartreuse, whose herb-based formulas are known today to only three monks. Today it is sold worldwide and is a main source of income for the monastery. Enclosed by wooded heights and limestone crags, the monastery is austere and serene. Although it is not open to visitors, you can see the road that goes to it.

The **Musée de la Correrie,** near the road to the monastery, has exhibits on monastic life and sells the monks' distillation. ☎ *04–76–88–60–45.* ⊡ *25 frs.* ⊙ *Easter–Oct., daily 10–noon and 2–6.*

Chartreuse is also sold in **Voiron,** 26 km (16 mi) west of St-Pierre-de-Chartreuse and 27 km (17 mi) northwest of Grenoble; free tastings are offered. ⊠ *10 bd. Edgar-Kofler,* ☎ *04–76–05–81–77.* ⊙ *Daily except winter weekends, 8:30–11:30 and 2–5:30.*

Chambéry

46   *44 km (27 mi) northeast of Voiron, 40 km (25 mi) north of St-Pierre-de-Chartreuse, 55 km (34 mi) north of Grenoble.*

Elegant old Chambéry is the region's shopping hub. Townspeople congregate for coffee and people-watching on pedestrians-only **place St-Léger.** The town's highlight is the 14th-century **Château des Ducs de Savoie.** Its Gothic Ste-Chapelle has good stained glass and houses a replica of the Turin Shroud, thought by many to have been Christ's burial wrappings but believed by others to be a hoax. ⊠ *Rue Basse du Château,* ☎ *no phone.* ⊡ *27 frs.* ⊙ *Guided tours May–June and Sept., daily at 10:30 and 2:30; July–Aug., daily at 10:30, 2:30, 3:30, 4:30, and 5:30; Mar.–Apr. and Oct.–Nov., Sat. at 2:15, Sun. at 3:30.*

Dining and Lodging

$$$$ ✕⊡ **Château de Candie.** This rambling manor on a hill east of Cham-
★   béry makes a delightful base. Owner Lhostis Didier, an avid antiques collector, spent four years renovating. Linger over a lavish breakfast in your large room—No. 106, a corner room with a view, has honey gold beams, a grandfather clock, and a carved armoire. For dinner the chef's dishes include rabbit terrine with shallot compote and *escalope de fruits de mer* (seafood arranged in the shape of a lobster). ⊠ *Rue du Bois de Candie, 73000 Chambéry-le-Vieux (6 mi [4 mi] east of Chambéry),* ☎ *04–79–96–63–00,* 🝙 *04–79–96–63–10. 16 rooms, 4 suites. Restaurant. AE, MC, V.*

Outdoor Activities and Sports

Go horseback riding in the foothills of the Alps with a horse from the **Centre Équestre** (⊠ Chenin des Bigornes, Voglans, ☎ 04–79–54–47–52).

Aix-les-Bains

47   *14 km (9 mi) north of Chambéry, 106 km (65 mi) east of Lyon.*

The family resort and spa town of Aix-les-Bains takes advantage of its position on the eastern side of **Lac du Bourget,** the largest natural freshwater lake in France, with a fashionable lakeshore esplanade. Although the lake is icy cold, you can sail, fish, play golf and tennis, or picnic on the 25 acres of parkland at the water's edge. (Try to avoid it on weekends, when it gets really crowded.) The main town of Aix is 3 km (2 mi) inland from the lake itself. Its sole reason for being is its thermal waters. Many small hotels line the streets, and streams of visitors take to the baths each day; in the evening, for a change of pace, they play the slot machines at the casino or attend tea dances.

The Roman Temple of Diana (2nd to 3rd centuries AD) now houses the **Musée Archéologique** (Archaeology Museum); enter via the tourist office on place Mollard. The ruins of the original Roman baths are underneath the present **Thermes Nationaux** (National Thermal Baths), built in 1934. ⊙ *Guided tours only Apr.–Oct., Mon.–Sat. at 3; Nov.–Mar., Wed. at 3.*

OFF THE
BEATEN PATH

ABBAYE DE HAUTECOMBE – Mass is celebrated with Gregorian chants at this picturesque spot, a half-hour boat ride from Aix-les-Bains. ☎ 04–79–54–26–12. ⌨ 65 frs. ◷ Departures from Grand Pont, Mar.–June and Sept.–Oct., daily at 2:30; July–Aug., daily at 9:30, 2, 2:30, 3, 3:30, and 4:30.

Outdoor Activities and Sports

Some brave souls pursue water sports on the lake, but most swim in the local *piscine* (pool; ⊠ Av. Daniel-Rops). There's also an attractive 18-hole **golf course** (⊠ Av. du Golf).

En Route   Fast A41 links Aix-les-Bains and Annecy. For a prettier if longer route, go 24 km (15 mi) on D911; turn left onto D912 at La Charniaz to snake the 24 km (15 mi) north to Annecy along the Montagne du Semnoz.

Annecy

★ ㊽ *33 km (20 mi) north of Aix-les-Bains, 137 km (85 mi) east of Lyon, 43 km (27 mi) southwest of Geneva.*

Jewel-like, beauteous Annecy is on crystal-clear **Lac d'Annecy** (Annecy Lake), surrounded by snow-tipped peaks. Though the canals, flower-decked bridges, and cobbled pedestrian streets are filled on market days—Tuesday and Friday—with shoppers and tourists, the town is still tranquil. Does the River Thiou seem to flow the "wrong way" (out of the lake)? You're right: It drains the lake, feeding the town's canals. Most of the old town is now a pedestrian zone lined with half-timber houses. Here is where the best restaurants are, so you'll probably be back in the evening.

Meander through the old town, starting on the small island in the River Thiou, at the 12th-century **Palais de l'Isle** (Island Palace), once home to courts of law and a prison, now a landmark and one of France's most photographed sites. It houses the **Musée d'Histoire d'Annecy** (Museum of Annecy History) and is where tours of the old prisons and cultural exhibitions begin. ☎ 04–50–33–87–30. ⌨ 30 frs. ◷ June–Sept., daily 10–6; Oct.–May, Wed.–Mon. 10–noon and 2–6.

From the towers of the medieval **Château d'Annecy,** high on a hill opposite the Palais, there are good views of the lake. This mighty castle of four towers (the oldest is from the 12th century) has a stout defensive outer wall and an inner courtyard whose several dwellings reflect different eras of Annecy history (covered in a small permanent exhibit on-site). ☎ 04–50–33–87–31. ⌨ 30 frs. ◷ June–Sept., daily 10–6; Oct.–May, Wed.–Mon. 10–noon and 2–6.

A drive around Lake Annecy—or at least along its eastern shore, which is the most attractive—is a must; set aside a half day for the 40-km (25-mi) trip. Picturesque **Talloires,** on the eastern side, has many hotels and restaurants. Just after Veyrier-du-Lac, keep your eyes open for the privately owned medieval **Château de Duingt.** Continue around the

★ eastern shore to get to the intimate-feeling **Château de Menthon-St-Bernard.** You can tour the castle, but it's really the exterior that's the stuff of fairy tales. The castle's medieval rooms—some aglow with tapestries and heraldic motifs—have been lovingly restored by the owner, who can actually trace his direct ancestry back to St. Bernard. You can get a good view of the castle by turning onto the Thones road out of Veyrier. ☎ 04–50–60–12–05. ⌨ 30 frs. ◷ July–Aug., daily 2–4:30; May–June and Sept., Tues., Thurs., and weekends 2–4:30; Oct.–Apr., Thurs. and weekends 2–4:30.

Dining and Lodging

$ ✕ **L'Estamille.** The decor is always changing at this restaurant, which also sells its furnishings and decorations in addition to the food. So it's no surprise that it feels like an antiques store—serving modern, inexpensive cuisine such as grilled river perch and *raclette* (a round of cheese baked with potatoes). ☒ *4 quai E. Chappuis,* ☎ *04–50–45–21–16. MC, V.*

$ ✕ **L'Étage.** This small, second-floor restaurant serves inexpensive local fare—from cheese and beef fondue to grilled freshwater fish from Lake Annecy, and raclette (a round of cheese baked over potatoes) made from the local Reblochon cheese. Minimal furnishings and plain wooden tables give it a rather austere look, but the often lively crowd makes up for it by creating an atmosphere of bonhomie. ☒ *13 rue Paquier,* ☎ *04–50–51–03–28. AE, DC, MC, V.*

$$$$ ✕🏨 **Impérial Palace.** Though the Palace, across the lake from the town center, is Annecy's leading hotel, it lacks character. In contrast to its Belle Epoque exterior, the spacious, high-ceiling guest rooms are done in the subdued colors so loved by contemporary designers. The better rooms face the public gardens on the lake; waking up to breakfast on the terrace is a great way to start the day. Service is professional, but you pay for it, including a 50-franc charge for making international credit card calls. Fine cuisine is served in the stylish La Voile (although jackets and ties are not required, they are not out of place here); the food in Le Jackpot Café, in the casino, is acceptable and less costly. ☒ *32 av. Albigny, 74000,* ☎ *04–50–09–30–00,* FAX *04–50–09–33–33. 98 rooms. 2 restaurants, casino. AE, DC, MC, V.* 🐾

$$$$ ✕🏨 **Père Bise.** This deluxe inn on the lake has a leafy veranda, fine views, and a classy restaurant (with less-than-perfect service). Chef Sophie Bise's grilled lobster with spicy tomato and her puff pastry with potatoes, foie gras, and truffles are memorable. You'll also find a superb wine list and the famous *marjolaine,* a multilayer chocolate-and-nut cake. Alas, some of the non-air-conditioned rooms are stuffy, and the better ones are very expensive. ☒ *Rte. du Port, 74290 Talloires,* ☎ *04–50–60–72–01,* FAX *04–50–60–73–05. 25 rooms, 9 suites. Restaurant. AE, DC, MC, V. Closed Dec.–mid-Feb.* 🐾

$$ 🏨 **Hôtel du Palais de l'Isle.** Steps away from the lake, in the heart of
★ old Annecy, is this delightful small hotel. Without destroying the building's ancient feel, rooms have a cheery, contemporary look and Philippe Starck furnishings; some have a view of the Palais de l'Isle. Rates reflect size of the room. Breakfast is served. Though the area is pedestrians only, you can drive up to unload luggage. ☒ *13 rue Perrière, 74000,* ☎ *04–50–45–86–87,* FAX *04–50–51–87–15. 26 rooms. AE, MC, V.*

Outdoor Activities and Sports

Bikes can be rented at the **train station** (☒ Pl. de la Gare). Mountain bikes are available from **Loca Sports** (☒ 37 av. de Loverchy, ☎ 04–50–45–44–33) and **Sports Passion** (☒ 3 av. du Parmelan, ☎ 04–50–51–46–28). From April through October you can take an hour-long cruise around Lake Annecy on the M.S. *Libellule* (☒ Compagnie des Bateaux du Lac d'Annecy, 2 pl. aux Bois, ☎ 04–50–51–08–40) for 57 francs.

Thonon-les-Bains

49 *74 km (46 mi) east of Annecy, 37 km (23 mi) northeast of Geneva.*

Most of the south side of **Lake Geneva** (Lac Léman in French) is French, not Swiss, and is popular for its thermal waters. However, Thonon-les-Bains, a fashionable summer resort on the lake, primarily draws Geneva residents.

Évian-les-Bains

50 *9 km (6 mi) east of Thonon-les-Bains, 83 km (52 mi) east of Annecy.*

People stay in chic Évian-les-Bains as much to be seen as to enjoy the creature comforts and spa facilities of its deluxe hotels. In late afternoon they promenade along the lake—a constitutional that precedes formal dinner parties. Its mineral waters, which are bottled for export throughout the world, began to achieve fame in the early 18th century.

En Route Many small and lesser-known Alpine **ski resorts** lie south of Lake Geneva, accessible via riverside D902: **Morzine; Avoriaz,** accessible via Thonon-les-Bains and by cable car (or D338) from Morzine; and **Cluses.** From Cluses take N205 left along the Arve Valley to get to Chamonix.

Chamonix

51 *96 km (60 mi) south of Thonon-les-Bains, 94 km (58 mi) east of Annecy, 83 km (51 mi) southeast of Geneva.*

Chamonix is the oldest and biggest of the French winter-sports resort towns. It was the site of the first Winter Olympics, held in 1924. As a ski resort, however, it has its limitations: The ski areas are spread out, none is very large, and the lower slopes often suffer from poor snow conditions. On the other hand, some runs are extremely memorable, such as the 20-km (12-mi) run through the **Vallée Blanche** or the off-trail area of **Les Grands Montets.** And the situation is getting better: many new lifts have been added, improving access to the slopes as well as lessening lines for the lifts. In summer it's a great place for hiking, climbing, and enjoying outstanding views. If you're heading to Italy via the Mont Blanc Tunnel, Chamonix will be your gateway.

The world's highest **cable car** soars 12,000 ft up the Aiguille du Midi, providing positively staggering views of 15,700-ft **Mont Blanc,** Europe's loftiest peak. Be prepared for a lengthy wait, both going up and coming down—and wear warm clothing. ▧ *290 frs round-trip.* ☉ *May–Sept., daily 8–4:45; Oct.–Apr., daily 8–3:45.*

Dining and Lodging

$$$$ ✕▥ **Le Hameau Albert Ier.** At Chamonix's most desirable hotel, rooms are furnished with elegant reproductions, and most have balconies. Many, such as No. 33, have unsurpassed views of Mont Blanc. Choose between rooms in the original building or in the Alpine lodge–style accommodations—with contemporary rustic elegance in the complex known as Le Hameau. The dining room also has stupendous Mont Blanc views. Pierre Carrier's cuisine is best characterized as perfectly prepared and presented, though sometimes not so interesting or original. ✉ *119 impasse du Montenvers, 74400,* ☎ *04–50–53–05–09,* FAX *04–50–55–95–48. 17 rooms, 12 suites, 3 chalets, 12 rooms in farmhouse. 2 restaurants, 1 outdoor pool, 1 indoor pool, hot tub, sauna. AE, DC, MC, V. Closed 2 wks in Nov.* ✤

$$$–$$$$ ✕▥ **Mont Blanc.** In the center of town, next to the tourist office, is this Belle-Epoque hotel that has catered to the rich and famous since 1878. Family owned, it is permeated by a sense of well-being and is run by an efficient and personable staff. High ceilings give guest rooms a majestic feel, accentuated by warm, pale colors and period pieces. Most rooms look onto either Mont Blanc or Mont Brevant. Dining on chef Morand's creations in the restaurant, Le Matafan, is a refined pleasure. Besides classic French dishes (try the succulent crayfish with shallots and chanterelle mushrooms), many foods available only locally are served, such as a delicious lake fish known as *fera*. ⊠ *Allée du Majestic, 74404,* ☎ *04–50–53–05–64,* FAX *04–50–55–89–44. 42 rooms. Restaurant, pool, 2 tennis courts. AE, DC, MC, V. Closed Nov.* ❧

$–$$ ✕⊞ **Auberge Croix-Blanche.** In the heart of Chamonix, this small inn has modest and tidy rooms, each with a good-size bathroom—from one you can even lie in the tub and look out the window at Mont Blanc. The hotel has no restaurant, but right next door is the Brasserie de L'M, where good-priced Savoie specialties are served. The hotel shuttle bus can take you to the slopes. ⊠ *81 rue Vallot, 74404,* ☎ *04–50–53–00–11,* FAX *04–50–53–48–83. 35 rooms. AE, DC, MC, V. Closed May.*

Nightlife

Chamonix is a lively place at night with its discos and late-night bars. A popular place to start or end the evening is at the **Casino** (⊠ Pl. de Saussure, ☎ 04–50–53–07–65), which has a bar, a restaurant, roulette, and blackjack. Entrance to the casino is 75 francs, though it's free entry to the slot machine rooms.

Outdoor Activities and Sports

Contact the **Chamonix Tourist Office** (☞ Visitor Information *in* Lyon and the Alps A to Z, *below*) for information on skiing in the area. Want to try bobsledding? Two approximately 3,000-ft-long runs are open winter and summer at **Parc de Loisirs des Planards** (☎ 04–50–53–08–07). Chamonix's indoor **skating rink** (☎ 04–50–53–12–36) is open year-round, Thursday–Tuesday 3–6 and Wednesday 3–11. Admission is 23 francs, and skates are 16 francs.

The **Sports Centre Olympide** (☎ 04–50–53–09–07) has an indoor-out-door Olympic-size pool. Hang gliding and paragliding can be arranged through **Chamonix Parapente** (☎ 04–50–55–99–22). **Espace Sensations** (☎ 04–50–55–99–49) also organizes hang gliding and paragliding for a cost of 500 francs. Mont Blanc provides the backdrop to golf at the course in **Les Praz de Chamonix** (⊠ Rte. de Tignes, ☎ 04–50–53–06–28); it's open daily May–November; greens fees are 350 francs. Horseback rides are organized by the **Club Hippique La Guérinière** (☎ 04–50–53–42–84); an hour's trek is 95 francs.

Megève

52 *35 km (22 mi) west of Chamonix, 69 km (43 mi) southeast of Geneva.*

Idyllic Alpine Megève is not only a major ski resort but also a chic winter watering hole that draws royalty, celebrities, and big wallets from all over the world. Ski passes purchased here cover the slopes not only around Megève but also in Chamonix. In summer the town is a popular spot for golfing and hiking. From Megève the drive along N212 to Albertville goes along one of the prettiest little gorges in the Alps.

Dining and Lodging

$$$$ ✕⊞ **Chalet-Hôtel du Mont d'Arbois.** This rustic but sophisticated mountain resort—part of a vast, upscale development next to the ski lifts, 3 km (2 mi) up from Megève on Mont d'Arbois—is run by Nadine de Rothschild. Most guests come here for a few days or more to ski or hike. Rooms have fine views, antiques, and down comforters. The restaurant is the most prestigious in the area and serves delicious spit-roasted meats and fish (try salmon in red-wine sauce) as well as many wines from the Rothschilds' Bordeaux vineyards. A word of caution: Most guests here seem to know others staying in the complex so it can seem very cold and impersonal to the outsider. ⊠ *447 chemin Rocaille, 74120,* ☎ *04–50–21–25–03,* FAX *04–50–21–24–79. 24 rooms, 5 suites. Restaurant, pool, hot tub, sauna, health club, 18-hole golf course, tennis courts. AE, DC, MC, V. Closed Apr.–mid-June and Oct.–mid-Dec.* ❧

$$$ ✕⊞ **Les Fermes des Maries.** By reassembling four Alpine chalets brought down from the mountains and decorating rooms with old Savoie furniture (shepherds' tables, sculptured chests, credenzas), Jocelyne and Jean-Louis Sibuet have created a luxury hotel with a delightfully rustic feel. Both a summer and winter resort, it has shuttle bus service to ski lifts in season and a spa providing a wide range of services in this most tranquil of settings. In the kitchen, chef Nicolas le Bec is a master of creativity and perfection who glorifies local produce. ✉ *Chemin de Riante Colline, 74120,* ☎ *04–50–93–03–10,* ℻ *04–50–93–09–84. 69 rooms. 3 restaurants, bar, pool, sauna, spa, exercise room, library. AE, DC, MC, V. Closed Apr.–May and Oct.–Nov.* 🕭

$$ ✕⊞ **Les Cîmes.** Friendly owners Monsieur and Madame Bourdin put their hearts into running this tiny, reasonably priced hotel with small, neat rooms and a pleasant little restaurant. Simple food is served, such as roast lamb or grilled fish. Breakfast is included in room rates. The hotel's only drawback is its location on a main street entering Megève, which can be a little noisy. ✉ *341 av. Charles Feige, 74120,* ☎ *04–50–21–01–71,* ℻ *04–50–58–70–95. 8 rooms. Restaurant. V.*

$$–$$$ ⊞ **Hôtel Mont-Blanc.** Each guest room at this hotel in the heart of Megeve's pedestrians-only zone has a different theme, from Austrian to English to Haute Savoie; half have a small balcony overlooking the courtyard—an ideal spot for summer breakfasts and evening cocktails. Wood predominates, as does artwork collected from all over Europe. Public areas are comfortable, from the lounge with huge easy chairs to the leather-bound library that doubles as a tearoom and bar. ✉ *Pl. de l'Eglise, 74120,* ☎ *04–50–21–20–02,* ℻ *04–50–21–45–28. 40 rooms. Bar, pool, library. AE, DC, MC, V. Closed May.*

Outdoor Activities and Sports

For information about skiing in the area, contact the **Megève Tourist Office** (☞ Visitor Information *in* Lyon and the Alps A to Z, *below*). In summer you can play at the 18-hole **Megève Golf Course** (✉ Golf du Mont d'Arbois, ☎ 04–50–21–29–79); it costs about 20 francs per round.

Albertville

53 *32 km (20 mi) southwest of Megève, 80 km (50 mi) northeast of Grenoble.*

Albertville, in the Arly Valley, was the site of the 1992 Winter Olympics. To the south are other serious ski resorts, where many of the Olympic competitions were held. As a result, you'll find some of France's most up-to-date ski facilities in the area, though Albertville itself is more of a transit town to the slopes around it than it is a full resort.

Courchevel, at the base of a vast north-facing Alpine amphitheater whose snows last long into spring, started out as a rustic Savoyard village; it's now oh-so-chic, composed of a quartet of planned ski villages named for their metric elevation. **Méribel,** with Courchevel, is part of the Trois Vallées (Three Valleys) area, with **Val Thorens** and **Les Menuires.**

Bourg-St-Maurice

54 *53 km (33 mi) east of Albertville on the spectacular D925 (becomes D902), 76 km (47 mi) south of Chamonix.*

In winter Bourg-St-Maurice, in the Isère Valley, is a bustling ski station. In summer it's a popular base for hiking, mountain biking, and kayaking along the Isère. **Les Arcs** ski resort is 11 km (7 mi) up the mountain peaks that rise up more than 9,900 ft from Bourg-St-Maurice. **Tignes,** another major ski resort, is 20 km (12 mi) beyond Les Arcs via D902. **Val d'Isère,** a favorite ski resort among the rich and famous, is 31 km

(19 mi) from Bourg-St-Maurice. An extensive network of chairlifts and cable cars connects Tignes and Val d'Isère with other, smaller resorts— La Daille, Les Boisses, and Les Brévières.

Outdoor Activities and Sports

A map of hiking trails and information about skiing in Les Arcs is available at the **Bourg-St-Maurice Tourist Office** (⌧ Pl. de la Gare, ☎ 04–79–07–04–92), across from the train station. **Le Lac tourist office** (☎ 04–79–40–03–13), in Tignes, can help you organize all kinds of sporting activities in the area. Mountain bikes can be rented from **Cyclo Minoret** (⌧ 66 av. Général-Leclerc, ☎ 04–79–07–70–16). **L'Espace Killy** (☎ 04–79–06–00–35) encompasses Val d'Isère and Tignes, with more than 100 lifts and endless skiing possibilities.

En Route   From Val d'Isère to Bonneval-sur-Arc (at 9,084 ft, the country's highest mountain pass, accessible only between July and late October), take **route de l'Iséran,**—D902—for some magnificent views. From Bonneval-sur-Arc continue on D902 to **Lanslevillard,** which is tucked in beneath an old church on a rocky outcrop; soon after the town, D902 broadens into N6. Farther along N6 is Modane, and just beyond is the 13-km (9-mi) **Tunnel du Fréjus,** which leads to Italy. At St-Michel de Maurienne, pick up D902 south, now called the **route du Galibier.** Usually closed from November to May, it twists between France and Italy in rugged grandeur, passing through the busy ski village of **Valloire.** Enjoy the spectacular views along the route du Galibier as you wind up the barren **Col du Galibier,** one of the French Alps' highest passes. A short walk to the 8,900-ft summit (follow signs) yields a panorama of the southern Alps. Just afterward, stop to admire a monument to Henri Desgranges, founder of the Tour de France bike race, and spare a thought for the hapless cyclists who pedal up here each July. Eight kilometers (5 miles) past the Col du Galibier, before N91, is 6,750-ft **Col du Lautaret,** alive with wildflowers in summer.

LYON AND THE ALPS A TO Z

Arriving and Departing

By Car

A6 speeds south from Paris to Lyon (463 km [287 mi]) Lyon, a distance of 463 km (287 mi). The Tunnel de Fourvière, which cuts through Lyon, is a classic hazard, and at peak times you may sit idling for hours. From Marseille, Lyon is 313 km (194 mi) north on A7. To get to Grenoble (568 km [352 mi] from Paris) from Lyon, take A43. Coming from the south, take A7 to Valence and then swing east on A49 to Grenoble. Access to the Alps is easy from Geneva or Italy (via the Tunnel du Mont Blanc at Chamonix or the Tunnel du Fréjus from Turin). Another popular route into the Alps, especially coming north from Provence, is from Sisteron via N85.

By Plane

The region's international gateway is **Lyon-Satolas Airport** (☎ 04–72–22–72–21 for information), 26 km (16 mi) east of Lyon, in Satolas. **Air France, British Airways,** and many other major carriers have connecting services from Paris into Lyon-Satolas. Only domestic airlines, such as Air France, fly into **Grenoble Airport.**

AIRPORT TRANSFERS

To get between the airport and downtown Lyon take the **Satobus** (☎ 04–72–22–71–28), a shuttle bus that goes to the city center between 5 AM and 9 PM and to the train station between 6 AM and 11 PM; journey time is 35–45 minutes, and the fare is 45 francs. There's also a bus from Satolas to Grenoble; journey time is just over an hour, and the fare is 120 francs. A **taxi** into Lyon costs about 200 francs. Taking a taxi from the small Grenoble airport to downtown Grenoble is expensive, but it may be your only alternative.

By Train

The high-speed TGV (*Train à Grande Vitesse*) to Lyon leaves from Paris (Gare de Lyon) hourly and arrives in just two hours. There are also six TGVs daily between Paris's Charles de Gaulle Airport and Lyon. The TGV also has less frequent service to Grenoble, where you can connect to local SNCF trains headed for villages in the Alps. South of Lyon, the TGV goes to Avignon and then splits and goes either to Marseille or Montpellier. The trips from Lyon to Marseille and Lyon to Montpellier take about 1½ hours.

Getting Around

By Bus

Buses cover the entire region, but Lyon and Grenoble are the two main bus stations for long-distance (national and international) routes. From these towns, buses go to the smaller towns.

By Car

Regional roads are fast and well maintained, though smaller mountainous routes can be difficult to navigate and high passes may be closed in winter.

By Métro

Lyon's good subway system serves both of the city's train stations. A single ticket costs 8 francs, and a 10-ticket book 68 francs. A day pass for bus and métro is 24 francs (available from bus drivers and the automated machines in the métro).

By Plane

There are domestic airports at Grenoble, Valence, Annecy, Chambéry, and Aix-les-Bains.

By Taxi

Lyon Espace Affaires (☎ 04–78–39–26–11) runs a fleet of well-kept taxi-vans in the city.

By Train

Major rail junctions include Grenoble, Annecy, Valence, Chambéry, and Lyon, with frequent train service to other points. Albertville is the rail station for continuing by bus up into the Alps to the ski resorts of Val d'Isère, Courchevel, and Megève.

Contacts and Resources

Car Rental

Avis (⊠ 1 av. du Dr-Desfrançois, Chambéry, ☎ 04–79–33–58–54, FAX 04–79–15–13–63; ⊠ In Aéroport de Lyon-Satolas). **Hertz** (⊠ 16 rue Émile-Gueymard, Grenoble, ☎ 04–76–43–12–92, FAX 04–76–47–97–26; ⊠ 11 rue Pasteur, Valence, ☎ 04–75–44–39–45, FAX 04–75–44–76–88).

Emergencies

In case of an emergency, call the **fire department** (☎ 18) or the **police** (☎ 17). **Samu** (☎ 04–72–33–15–15), in Lyon, provides emergency medical aid and ambulance service. Lyon has several all-night pharmacies. One of the largest, with an equivalence chart of foreign medicines, is **Pharmacie Blanchet** (⊠ 5 Pl. des Cordeliers, ☎ 04–78–37–81–31). In Grenoble contact **Europ'ambulance** (☎ 04–76–33–10–03).

Guided Tours

The **Lyon Tourist Office** (⊠ Pl. Bellecour, ☎ 04–72–77–69–69) organizes walking tours of the city in English, as well as minibus tours. To survey Lyon by air, contact the **Aéro-Club du Rhône et du Sud-Est** (⊠ Aéroport de Lyon-Bron, 69500 Bron, ☎ 04–78–26–83–97). **Navig-Inter** (⊠ 13 bis quai Rambaud, 69002 Lyon, ☎ 04–78–42–96–81) arranges daily boat trips from Lyon along the Saône and Rhône rivers. **Philibert** (⊠ 24 av. Barthélémy-Thimonier, B.P. 16, 69300 Caluire, ☎ 04–72–23–10–56, FAX 04–72–27–00–97) runs bus tours of the region from April to October starting in Lyon.

Travel Agencies

American Express (⊠ 6 rue Childebert, 69002 Lyon, ☎ 04–72–77–74–50). **Wagons-Lits** (⊠ 2 bd. des Alpes, 38240 Melan, ☎ 04–76–04–24–00, FAX 04–76–04–24–02).

Visitor Information

Contact the **Comité Régional du Tourisme Rhône-Alpes** (⊠ 78 rte. de Paris, 69260 Charbonnières-les-Bains, ☎ 04–72–59–21–59) for Lyon and the Alps. The **Maison du Tourisme** (⊠ 14 rue de la République, B.P. 227, 38019 Grenoble, ☎ 04–76–42–41–41) deals with the Isère département and the area around Grenoble.

Local tourist offices for towns mentioned in this chapter include the following: **Annecy** (⊠ Centre Bonlieu, 1 rue Jean-Jaurès, ☎ 04–50–45–00–33). **Aubenas** (⊠ Centre Ville, ☎ 04–75–89–02–03). **Bourg-en-Bresse** (⊠ 6 av. d'Alsace-Lorraine, ☎ 04–74–22–49–40). **Chambéry** (⊠ 24 bd. de la Colonne, ☎ 04–79–33–42–47). **Chamonix** (⊠ 85 pl. du Triangle de l'Amitié, ☎ 04–50–53–00–24). **Courchevel** (⊠ La Croisette, ☎ 04–79–08–00–29). **Évian-les-Bains** (⊠ Pl. d'Allinges, ☎ 04–50–75–04–26). **Grenoble** (⊠ 14 rue de la République, ☎ 04–76–42–41–41; ⊠ Train station, ☎ 04–76–54–34–36). **Lyon** (⊠ Pl. Bellecour, ☎ 04–72–77–69–69; ⊠ Av. Adolphe Max near cathedral, ☎ 04–72–77–69–69; ⊠ Perrache train station). **Megève** (⊠ Rue Monseigneur Conseil, ☎ 04–50–21–27–28). **Montélimar** (⊠ Allées Provençales, ☎ 04–75–01–00–20). **Privas** (⊠ 3 rue Elie-Reynier, ☎ 04–75–64–33–35). **Tournon** (⊠ Mairie de Tournon, ☎ 04–75–08–10–23). **Valence** (⊠ Parvis de la Gare, ☎ 04–75–44–90–40). **Vienne** (⊠ Cours Brillier, ☎ 04–74–53–80–30).

10 THE MASSIF CENTRAL

Continental France's wildest region, the Massif Central offers a top-10 medley of land, lots of land, including windswept plains, snowcapped mountains, volcanic plateaus, and romantic forests. This is a country of early to bed and early to rise, the better to take delight in the great outdoors, where unblemished landscapes and spectacular panoramas seem to appear around nearly every turn. As the most untamed part of a very civilized country, the Massif Central is a refreshing contrast to cosmopolitan France.

Updated by
George Semler

| T IS NOT FOR NOTHING THAT THEY CALL this region *massif*. Stretching over a vast landscape that manages to border both Beaune and Avignon, both Toulouse and Tours, it covers a massive portion of the nation. But what's there? Very little you've heard of. If the points of France's topographic star are outthrust limbs—Alsace, Provence, the Basque Country, Bretagne—then this is the country's underbelly: raw, unprotected, and unrevealed. Its biggest city? Clermont-Ferrand, best known as the home of the Michelin Tire Man. Its most (in)famous city? Vichy, whose dubious distinction is to bear the name of the Nazi puppet government Pétain established there.

But if the Massif Central doesn't bring to mind French culture or civilization, it is home to another side of France—usually the last one visitors choose to explore. For aside from the occasional bicycle-with-baguette ride, few outsiders know natural France, the nation of rugged country carved deep with torrential rivers and sculpted with barren and beautiful landscapes begging to be hiked, climbed, or surveyed on horseback. Windswept plains are punctuated with tiny villages in time-ravaged stone. Volcanic cones thrust above the horizon and speak of a landscape still forming, even as the rivers gouge canyons of dizzying depth. The Gorges du Tarn is one of France's most famous natural landmarks, and the volcano-top village of Puy-de-Dôme is one of its most admired phenomena.

Battles have raged across this rugged land since the dawn of history: Romans versus Arvernes (the original Celtic settlers), Gauls versus Visigoths, Charlemagne versus Saracens, the dukes of Bourbon versus Francis I, and Huguenots versus Catholics in the Wars of Religion. Small wonder, then, that the Auvergnois kept to themselves during the Revolution and managed to escape much of its mayhem. Collaborating with Hitler under Pétain's Vichy-based government spared the region from bombing in World War II. Thus little was lost—though, some might add, little was there in the first place.

This is truly *la France profonde,* or deepest France, sought by lovers of natural beauty, scorned for the most part by seekers of art museums and grand châteaux. But before you turn the page in search of a more tourist-intensive region, take note: The more rural the region, the better the cheese. And any area that boasts crusty yellow Cantal, redolent of volcanic ash; nutty-smooth St-Nectaire; mild and tangy Bleu d'Auvergne; and the world-famous Roquefort, salty-sharp and sheepy. . . well, perhaps the landscape hasn't gone to waste after all. As the lucky travelers who venture to discover the Massif Central realize, there are few greater pleasures than a day's hard hiking in France's deepest backcountry, and sitting down at night to a simple local roadhouse feast. After all, the way to France's heart is almost always through its stomach, and the Massif Central is indeed the nation's heartland.

— Nancy Coons

Pleasures and Pastimes

Dining

Food in the Massif Central is fuel for the body; fine dining it is not. But there are a few regional specialties: *aligot* (puree of potatoes with Tomme de Cantal cheese and garlic), *cousinat* (chestnut soup), *sanflorin* (fried pork and herbs in pastry), and *salmis de colvert Cévenole* (wild duck sautéed in red wine and onions). Several well-known cheeses are also made here: Roquefort, creamy Bleu d'Auvergne, Gaperon with garlic, and the delightfully nutty St-Nectaire. In summer bakers turn *myrtilles* (blueberries) into tangy pies and tarts.

CATEGORY	COST*
$$$$	over 400 frs
$$$	250 frs–400 frs
$$	125 frs–250 frs
$	under 125 frs

*per person for a three-course meal, including tax (20.6%) and tip but not drinks

🐚 *following the text of a review is your signal that the property has a Web site, where you will find details and, usually, images; for a link, visit www.fodors.com/urls.*

Lodging

Because the region was difficult to get to for so long, you won't find a broad selection of accommodations. The larger towns generally have modest hotels, the villages have small inns, and a few châteaux dot the countryside. In July and August rates are higher and rooms are at a premium, so be sure to make reservations in advance. Many hotels are closed from November to March.

CATEGORY	COST*
$$$$	over 800 frs
$$$	550 frs–800 frs
$$	300 frs–550 frs
$	under 300 frs

*All prices are for a standard double room for two, including tax (20.6%) and service charge.

Outdoor Activities and Sports

With its volcanic peaks and impressive gorges, the Massif Central is a great alternative to the Alps for outdoor adventures. Bicycling and mountain biking (mountain bikes are known as *vélos touts terrains,* or VTT) over the hills and along country roads is a good way to see the region; bikes can be rented at train stations in most towns. For serious hiking, strike out along the extensive network of trails that crisscross the large Parc National des Volcans and follow the Gorges du Tarn. Kayaking down the Gorges du Tarn is also popular. For gentler walking from village to village and valley to valley, follow the Monts du Cantal. During winter there is limited skiing around Le Mont-Dore and Mt. Aigoual in the Causses, a high limestone plateau.

Exploring the Massif Central

The Massif Central is roughly demarcated by Burgundy, the Rhône River, Languedoc-Roussillon, and the Dordogne River valley. France's central highlands offer dramatic untouched terrain, quiet medieval villages, imposing castles, and few large towns: Clermont-Ferrand (population 150,000), in the center of the region, is the major metropolis; elegant, infamous Vichy and industrial St-Étienne are two other cities. At the center of the region is the Auvergne, where the expansive Parc National des Volcans, the grand Gorges du Tarn, and the magnificent Cévennes Mountains, crisscrossed with canyons, are favorite destinations of nature lovers.

Great Itineraries

Because the Massif Central is so big, it's almost impossible to see everything in a short trip. But with 3–10 days you can get at least a fair sense of the region.

The Massif Central

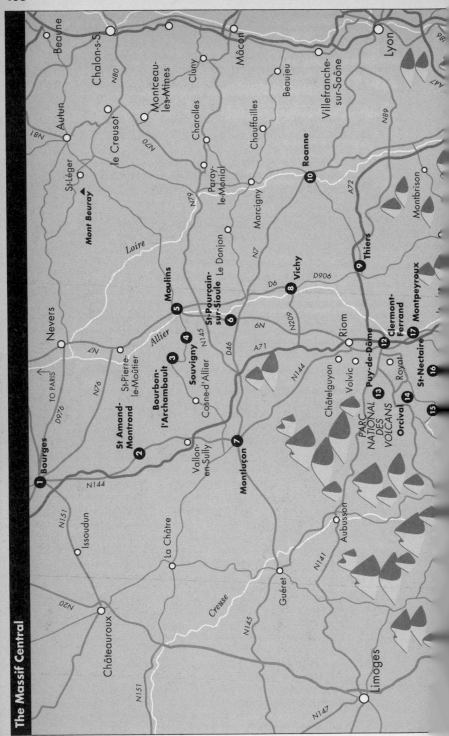

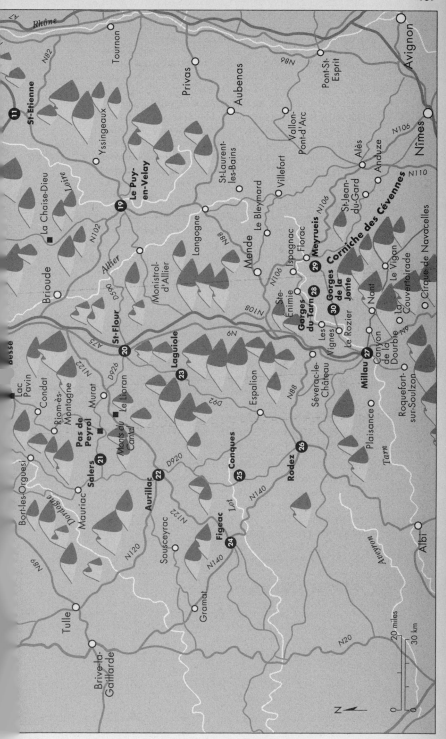

Numbers in the text correspond to numbers in the margin and on the Massif Central map.

IF YOU HAVE 3 DAYS

Begin your first day in the former, short-lived capital of France, ☷ **Bourges** ①, a medieval city that is home to the tallest Gothic cathedral in the country, and certainly one of its most beautiful; spend the night there or in nearby ☷ **St-Amand-Montrond** ② at the Château de la Commanderie. On day two explore Bourbonnais country, with stops in **Bourbon-l'Archambault** ③ and **Souvigny** ④. Head to medieval ☷ **Moulins** ⑤ for the night. On day three drive through the Parc National des Volcans to see a natural wonder, the stone formation of **Puy-de-Dôme** ⑬; then visit the Romanesque church in **Orcival** ⑭.

IF YOU HAVE 9 DAYS

You can cover much of the region by car if you don't mind a lot of driving. Begin with lunch in **Bourges** ① and then head to the Château de la Commanderie, near ☷ **St-Amand-Montrond** ②, for the night. The second day explore **Bourbon-l'Archambault** ③, **Souvigny** ④, and ☷ **Moulins** ⑤, home of the Bourbons and another good place to spend the night. On day three pass through **Vichy** ⑧ on your way to **Thiers** ⑨; stop in ☷ **Roanne** ⑩ for the night and try to dine at the superb Trois-gros restaurant. On the fourth day drive south to ☷ **Le Puy-en-Velay** ⑲ and then on to ☷ **Millau** ㉗; stay overnight there or in one of the towns closer to the ☷ **Gorges du Tarn** ㉘. On day five explore the gorge, then head for the **Gorges de la Jonte** ㉚ on your way back to Millau. On day six head over head to **Rodez** ㉖ to see its pink-sandstone cathedral en route to the basilica in **Conques** ㉕. By nightfall get to ☷ **Aurillac** ㉒ or ☷ **Salers** ㉑. Spend day seven exploring the *cols* (passes) and valleys in this area and the sparse lands around **Laguiole** ㉓ and **St-Flour** ⑳. On day eight travel through the **Parc National des Volcans** around the **Puy-de-Dôme** ⑬, perhaps spending the night in ☷ **St-Nectaire** ⑯ or ☷ **Montpeyroux** ⑰. On your last day make your way to ☷ **Clermont-Ferrand** ⑫ and then on to home.

When to Tour the Massif Central

Autumn, when the sun is still warm on the shimmering, golden trees, and early spring, especially May, when the wildflowers are in bloom, are the best times to visit central France. In summer the *canicule* (literally, dog days) can be oppressively hot, and the sky is often cloudy; in winter it's cold, and a snowstorm can make a catastrophic intrusion. Then again, getting snowed in by a cozy fire somewhere in France's central highlands may be just what you're looking for.

THE BOURBONNAIS

The northern part of the Massif Central, from Bourges south to Montluçon and east to Vichy, is known as the Bourbonnais for the dynasty of kings that it spawned.

Bourges

①   *243 km (151 mi) south of Paris, 70 km (42 mi) west of Nevers, 153 km (92 mi) east of Tours.*

Find your way to Bourges, and you'll find yourself at the center of France. Perhaps we should say medieval France, as modern times have largely passed it by, and the result is a preserved market town with an immensely high cathedral and streets lined with timber-frame houses right out of the Middle Ages. Pedestrians-only rue Mirabeau and rue Coursarlon are particularly appealing places to stroll and shop. In the early 15th century the town was home to France's most flamboyant art patron and fashion plate, Jean, Duc de Berry. Later in the 15th century, it served as temporary capital for Charles VII, who was forced to flee invading British forces. The town hero at that time was Jacques Coeur, the son of a local fur trader, who amassed a fortune as the king's finance minister. His lavish Renaissance palace still stands as one of the town's foremost sights.

★ Approaching the town, you'll see the soaring towers of the 13th-century **Cathédrale St-Étienne.** For lovers of the Middle Ages and connoisseurs of Gothic architecture, this cathedral is the skyscraper of medieval cathedrals. The architects who completed the nave in 1280 really pushed the envelope, as shown by the side aisles flanking the nave, which rise to an astonishing 65 ft—high enough to allow windows to be placed above the level of the second side aisles. The central portal is a masterpiece of sculpture: Cherubim, angels, saints, and prophets cluster in the archway. Inside, the interior is sleek, elegant, and entirely given over to heaven-seeking vertical forces. ⊠ *Off rue Porte Jaune.*

Once home to the incredibly wealthy Jacques Coeur, the **Palais Jacques-Coeur** is one of the most luxurious Gothic dwellings in France. Notice its vaulted chapel, the wooden ceilings covered with original paintings, and the dining room with its tapestries and massive fireplace—all set pieces of the International Gothic style, which was the last style type prevalent during medieval times. As well as being Charles VII's finance minister, Coeur was a great art patron and helped create a taste for Italy's new Renaissance style. ⊠ *Rue Jacques-Coeur,* ☎ *02–48–24–06–87.* ⌨ *35 frs.* ☉ *Apr.–June and Sept.–Oct., daily 9–noon and 2–6; Nov.–Mar., daily 9–noon and 2–5; July–Aug., daily 9–noon and 2–7, 45-min guided tours only, begin 15 mins after the hr.*

Dining and Lodging

$$ ✕⊞ **Hôtel d' Angleterre.** This efficient hotel in the center of town near the palace is popular with business travelers. Recently acquired by the Best Western chain, rooms have modern conveniences but little in the way of character. The restaurant, decorated in Louis XVI style, has prix-fixe menus starting at 95 francs. ⊠ *1 pl. des Quatre-Piliers, 18000 Bourges,* ☎ *02–48–24–68–51,* ℻ *02–48–65–21–41. 31 rooms. Restaurant, bar, minibars. AE, DC, MC, V.* ✍

$$ ✕⊞ **Auberge du Moulin de Chaméron.** Out in the country with only the owls to keep you awake at night, this hotel is a peaceful place to stay. Though rooms are in a modern, almost motel-like building and are small and have standard hotel furnishings that make them seem even smaller, most open out onto the lovely garden. At the other end of the garden is the restaurant, in a former mill. Dining outside on the terrace in the twilight or in either of the cozy, beamed dining rooms is a fine way to end the day. The cooking is not fancy, but the produce is fresh, and the beef is prime Charolais; menus run from 130 to 190 francs. ⊠ *18210 Bannegon (40 km [25 mi] from Bourges),* ☎ *02–48–61–83–80 for hotel; 02–48–61–84–48 for restaurant,* ℻ *02–48–61–84–92. 12 rooms, 1 apartment. Restaurant. AE, DC, MC, V. Closed mid-Nov.–Mar.*

St-Amand-Montrond

➋ *44 km (27 mi) south of Bourges, 54 km (33 mi) north of Montluçon.*

The small market town of St-Amand-Montrond is a convenient stopping point when you're heading south into the heart of the Massif Central. If time permits, visit the **town museum,** a former St-Vic mansion dating from the 16th century, for an account of the region's history from the Stone Age to the present. ✉ *Off pl. du Marché,* ☎ *02–48–96–55–20.* 🎫 *15 frs.* ☉ *Mon. and Wed.–Sat. 10–noon and 2–6, Sun. 2–6.*

Also worth exploring is the **Montrond Fortress,** once a residence of Louis II. Though it's in ruins, you can wander around and imagine its former grandeur.

OFF THE
BEATEN PATH

ABBAYE DE NOIRLAC – Twenty kilometers (12 miles) northwest of St-Amand is this abbey constructed in 1150, still one of the finest examples of medieval monastic architecture in France. The abbey church is intact, with 13th- and 14th-century arcades flanking the south cloister; also standing are the monastery, the chapter house, and the monks' hall. ✉ *18200 Bruère-Allichamps,* ☎ *02–48–62–01–01.* 🎫 *35 frs.* ☉ *Feb.–Sept., daily 9:45–noon and 1:45–5; Oct.–Jan., Wed.–Mon., 9:45–noon and 1:45–5.*

Dining and Lodging

$$$$ ✕🏠 **Château de la Commanderie.** You won't regret going out of your
★   way to reach this impressive 11th-century château-inn, where you'll stay in style in large, elegant rooms. Dinner can be arranged with the hosts, the Comte and Comtesse de Jouffrey-Gonsans, (jacket and tie required, *s'il vous plaît*) in the paneled dining room. Expect well-prepared family fare, often including perfectly aged Charolais beef. ✉ *D144 at Farges-Allichamps, 18200 Farges-Allichamps (44 km [27 mi] south of Bourges on N144 and 12 km [6 mi] northwest of St-Armand-Montrond),* ☎ *02–48–61–04–19,* ℻ *02–48–61–01–84. 7 rooms. AE, MC, V.*☜

$ ✕🏠 **La Poste - Le Relais.** The main draw is the restaurant—where reasonably priced, delicious food is prepared with loving care and fresh ingredients from imaginative recipes (note that it's closed Sunday and doesn't serve dinner Monday). Rooms are small, plainly furnished, but perfectly adequate. ✉ *9 rue du Docteur Vallet, 18200,* ☎ *02–48–96–27–14,* ℻ *02–48–96–97–74. 18 rooms. Restaurant. AE, MC, V. Closed Nov.–Mar.*

Bourbon-l'Archambault

❸ *48 km (58 mi) northeast of Montluçon.*

During the 17th–19th centuries Bourbon-l'Archambault was a ritzy thermal spa; illustrious figures such as Talleyrand, France's powerful foreign minister, took the waters here. But the fleeting fancy for fashionable spas left the town a little less noble. However, the weathered buildings and the ruined 14th-century **Château**—once the quarters of the noble tourists—still have an appealing faded glory. ✉ *Rue du Château,* ☎ *no phone.* ☉ *Mid-Apr.–mid-Oct., daily 2–6.*

Souvigny

❹ *14 km (9 mi) southeast of Bourbon-l'Archambault.*

Small, picturesque Souvigny is dominated by its surprisingly large church. Built in the 11th, 12th, and 15th centuries of pale golden stone, the **Prieuré St-Pierre** appears light compared to most other Auvergne buildings, which are made out of volcanic stone. This village was the first financial base of the Bourbon fortunes, solid enough to enable them to establish a royal dynasty.

Dining

$ ✕ **Auberge des Tilleuls.** In an old town house on a small square near
★   the priory, this little restaurant serves innovative cuisine at exceptional prices. Especially good is the hearty beef casserole with a rich, zesty sauce. ✉ *Pl. St-Eloi,* ☎ *04–70–43–60–70. MC, V. Closed Mon., 2 wks in Jan., and 2 wks in Oct. No dinner Sun. (except July–Aug.)*

Moulins

⑤ *12 km (7 mi) east of Souvigny, 291 km (182 mi) south of Paris, 98 km (61 mi) southeast of Bourges, 54 km (32 mi) southeast of Nevers.*

Once the capital of the dukes of Bourbon, Moulins has a compact, medieval center, which is dominated by its cathedral. The oldest part (1474–1507) of the **Cathédrale Notre-Dame** (⊠ Rue de Paris), in Flamboyant Gothic style, is known for its stained-glass windows. In the 15th century such windows served as picture books for illiterate peasants, enabling them to follow the story of the crusades of Louis IX. The cathedral's other medieval treasure is the triptych of the *Maître de Moulins*—one of the greatest painters of early Renaissance France—painted toward the end of the 15th century. The painter mixed classicizing style with realistic details—notice the Virgin is not as richly clothed as the duke and duchess of Bourbon, who commissioned the painting. The town's belfry, known as the **Jacquemart** (⊠ Pl. de l'Hôtel), was built in 1232 and rebuilt in 1946 after it ignited during a fireworks display. **The Musée du Folklore** (Folklore Museum), in a 15th-century mansion next door to the Jacquemart, is filled with costumes, farming implements, and other reminders of Moulins's past. ⊠ *4 pl. de l'Ancien Palais,* ☎ *04–70–44–39–03.* ⌨ *25 frs.* ☉ *Daily 10–noon and 2–6, 45-min guided tours.*

Dining and Lodging

$$$ ✕▥ **Hôtel de Paris.** This family-owned hotel, just a block from the
★ town's medieval quarter, is a genuine delight—traditional France at its best. Service is efficient and welcoming. Rooms are suitably large, with high ceilings and 19th-century antiques. The menus range from a weekday special at 150 francs to a 450-franc for a three-course combination meal, usually including a hearty portion of Charolais beef. ⊠ *21 rue de Paris, 03000 Moulins,* ☎ *04–70–44–00–58,* ⅁ *04–70–34–05–39. 23 rooms, 4 suites. Restaurant. AE, DC, MC, V. Closed 1st 3 wks Jan., last 2 wks June.*

St-Pourçain-sur-Sioule

⑥ *31 km (19 mi) south of Moulins, 59 km (37 mi) east of Montluçon, 27 km (18 mi) northwest of Vichy.*

Most of the region's wine comes from the attractive little village of St-Pourçain-sur-Sioule—one of the oldest viticulture centers in France. The wine, which varies considerably in quality and price, is generally not found in other parts of France and is often a good value.

Lodging

$$$$ ▥ **Château de Boussac.** Although the turrets and moat suggest its defensive past, this château-inn is fully modernized. It's also a working Charolais cattle ranch and is very quiet. Lovely breakfasts are served in guest rooms, which are furnished with antiques. In the evening you can enjoy an aperitif with the Marquis and Marquise de Longueil before the table d'hôte dinner (advance arrangements required) is served. ⊠ *Target, 03140 Chantelle (10 km [6 mi] from St-Pourçain on D987),* ☎ *04–70–40–63–20,* ⅁ *04–70–40–60–03. 3 rooms. AE, MC, V. Closed Dec.–Mar.*

Montluçon

⑦ *94 km (58 mi) south of Bourges, 54 km (34 mi) south of St-Amand-Montrond, 59 km (37 mi) west of St-Pourçain.*

Montluçon is best known for its Bourbon castle and its old quarter, where small 16th- and 17th-century houses line the streets. Built during the Hundred Years' War, the **Château de Montluçon** is remarkably well preserved. It houses the **Musée des Musiques Populaires** (Museum of Folk Music), with a collection of local artifacts from the 18th and 19th centuries, including a historical account of the hurdy-gurdy, a traditional stringed instrument. ☎ *04–70–02–56–56.* ⌧ *25 frs.* ☉ *Easter–Oct., Tues.–Sun. 2–7.*

Dining and Lodging

$$ ✕⛉ **Le Grenier à Sel.** On the ground floor of a private villa in the center of town, this restaurant is the meeting place for the town's bigwigs. They come for chef Morlon's classic French cuisine and the excellent service. Choose from such dishes as *foie gras chaud* (warm foie gras) or *sandre* (pike perch) poached in wine with a light beurre blanc sauce. There are also five small, pretty rooms if you want to stay the night. ⌧ *Pl. des Toiles, 8 rue St-Anne,* ☎ *04–70–05–53–79,* 𝔽𝔸𝕏 *04–70–05–87–91. 5 rooms. AE, DC, MC, V. Closed Mon., except July–Aug. No dinner Sun.*

$$ ⛉ **Château de Fragne.** The Comtesse de Montaignac has opened five rooms to guests in her 18th-century château set on sizable grounds, just 15 minutes from town. A random assortment of furniture, some from the turn of the century, gives rooms a haphazard feel, but all are quite comfortable. In the morning enjoy an excellent breakfast, and if you make advance arrangements, a table d'hôte dinner in the evening. ⌧ *03190 Verneix (northeast of Montluçon on D302 or Exit 10 of A71),* ☎ *04–70–07–88–10,* 𝔽𝔸𝕏 *04–70–07–83–73. 4 rooms, 1 suite. AE, DC, MC, V. Closed Nov.–Apr.*

En Route   Between Montluçon and Bourbon-l'Archambault is the delightful rural town of **Cosne-d'Allier** (Exit 10 off A71 to D94 east), where locals come to market. Look for the small, top-value market restaurant **Globe,** at 61 rue de la République, for bosky specialties such as hare with wild mushrooms in season.

Vichy

❽ *91 km (56 mi) southeast of Montluçon, 30 km (19 mi) south of St-Pourçain, 54 km (33 mi) north of Clermont-Ferrand, 349 km (216 mi) south of Paris.*

Vichy, one of the few large towns in the region, does not have the depth of character you'd expect from a place whose mineral waters attracted the Romans and, later, Paris haute society. Nobles such as France's greatest woman of letters, the marquise de Sévigné—who once famously wrote, "The countryside here alone would cure me"—and her friend the duchess of Angoulême started the trend in the 17th century; then the arrival of Napoléon III in the mid-19th century and the railroad in the early 20th century attracted the middle classes.

When France fell to the Germans in 1940 and the country was divided under direct and indirect German control, the Pétain government moved to Vichy, using its hotels as embassies and ministries. After the war the puppet government left a stain of infamy on the city.

Today Vichy is trying to overcome its past, as well as the perception that it's only a place for retirement. A stretch of the River Allier is being transformed into a lake, and large conference facilities and thermal baths have been built. Although there are no old, famous buildings to admire, the city has a **thermal spa** (⌧ Rue Callou, ☎ 04–70–97–39–59) that looks like a mosque and the **Grand Casino,** which contains an opera house, in the Parc des Sources. Around the park is a shopping area; the **tourist office** (⌧ 19 rue du Parc, ☎ 04–70–98–71–94) is on the western side.

Dining and Lodging

$$ ✕ **L'Alambic.** A master with local produce, chef-owner Jean-Jacques Barbot creates such dishes as fish, fresh from nearby streams, grilled with endives, and lentil salad using the famous tiny *lentilles de Puy.* ✉ *8 rue Nicolas-Larbaud,* ☎ *04–70–59–12–71. MC, V. Closed late Feb.– early Mar., late Aug.–early Sept., and Mon. No lunch Tues.*

$ ✕ **Le Piquenchagne.** Classic cooking to perfection is chef Vincent's motto—and he lives up to it. Try the *lapin* (rabbit) roasted with coriander and cumin or the sautéed fresh bream. Service is smoothly orchestrated by Madame Vincent. ✉ *69 rue de Paris,* ☎ *04–70–98–63–45. AE, MC, V. Closed Wed., during Feb. school holidays. No dinner Tues.*

$$ 🏨 **Hôtel Arverna.** This hotel in an 18th-century building in the center of town provides excellent value for the money. And the owner, who has traveled the world extensively, provides a friendly welcome. Rooms are modest but functional (Nos. 101 and 102 are the best); bathrooms are clean. ✉ *12 rue Debrest, 03200,* ☎ *04–70–31–31–19,* ℻ *04–70–97– 86–43. 22 rooms, 4 suites. AE, DC, MC, V. Closed Dec. 15–Jan. 5.* 🐝

AUVERGNE

Auvergne, the real heart of central France, is home to the Parc National des Volcans, which is characterized by *puys,* craggy lava peaks. Medieval villages perch on the hilltops, and outdoor markets make the narrow streets come alive. Many of these country villages are now being transformed into skiing and hiking resorts. Industry is also a focus in such towns as Thiers, Roanne, St-Étienne, and Clermont-Ferrand— though good restaurants, museums, and churches are to be found in these areas as well. Everywhere there is a harmony between religious architecture and the terrain from which it rises, be it a mountain crest, as at St-Nectaire, or the green hollow of a valley nestling its church, as at Orcival.

Thiers

❾ *34 km (21 mi) south of Vichy, 47 km (29 mi) northeast of Clermont-Ferrand.*

Built on a steep hill, Thiers is a slightly grimy but nonetheless fascinating 18th- and 19th-century town that is famous for its cutlery. It supplies 70% of France's cutting needs, producing everything from table knives to daggers. In the old days, while the River Durolle turned the massive grindstones, craftsmen would lie on planks over the icy water to hone their blades on the stone. Today's factories use less exotic methods, but the tourist office gives demonstrations of the old way (as well as maps and information). Be prepared for stiff walking—the streets run only up and down!

Follow rue Conchette, then rue Bourg to appealing place du Pirou, where there is a wonderful example of ancient half-timber architecture, the 15th-century **Maison du Pirou** (Pirou House). At 11 rue de Pirou is the **Maison des Sept Péchés Capitaux** (House of the Seven Deadly Sins)— look at the carvings on the ends of the beams, and you'll know why.

On rue de la Coutellerie are old knife-making workshops and the 15th-century **Maison des Coutelliers** (Cutlery House), a small museum and workshop with demonstrations covering five centuries of knife making. ✉ *58 rue de la Coutellerie,* ☎ *04–73–80–58–86.* 🎫 *25 frs.* ☉ *Oct.– May, Tues.–Sun. 10–noon and 2–6; June and Sept., daily 10–noon and 2–6:30; July–Aug., daily 10–6:30.*

Dining

$ ✕ **Le Coutelier.** Housed in a former *coutelier*'s (cutler's) shop, this restaurant is filled with old Thiers cutlery. The fare is traditional Auvergne style—dishes such as lentils with bacon and sausage, chicken cooked in wine, and, most traditional of all, *truffade* (a potato dish with ham, cheese and green salad). ✉ *4 pl. du Palais,* ☎ *04–73–80–79–59. MC, V. Closed June. No dinner Mon.–Thurs. in winter, no dinner Mon. in summer.*

Roanne

🔟 *59 km (37 mi) east of Thiers, 87 km (54 mi) west of Lyon, 98 km (61 mi) southeast of Moulins, 389 km (243 mi) south of Paris.*

The industrial city of Roanne is probably on your itinerary for only one reason—the world-famous Troisgros restaurant.

Dining and Lodging

$$$$ ✕🏨 **Troisgros.** For more than four decades one of the most revered
★ restaurants in France and one of the traditional mainstays of haute cuisine, Troisgros has a seven-course feast, the Menu dans la Tradition (540 francs), which might include lightly sautéed foie gras with grilled groundnuts, frogs'-leg lasagna, regional cheeses, and fantastic desserts. The surprisingly ordinary dining room has comfortable chairs and big windows, and service is at your table before you know you need it. The restaurant is closed Tuesday and Wednesday. The high-design guest rooms are luxurious and comfortable. ✉ *Pl. Jean Troisgros (across from train station), 42300,* ☎ *04–77–71–66–97,* 📠 *04–77–70–39–77. 9 rooms, 4 apartments, 1 suite. Restaurant. AE, DC, MC, V. Closed 3 wks during school holidays in Feb. and 1st 2 wks Aug.*

St-Étienne

⓫ *84 km (52 mi) south of Roanne, 147 km (91 mi) southeast of Clermont-Ferrand, 56 km (35 mi) southwest of Lyon.*

The former mining city of St-Étienne (population 200,000) is better known today for its soccer team (in June 1998 the city hosted some matches of the World Cup) than for its attractions, though it does have a good museum.

The fine **Musée d'Art et d'Industrie** (Art and Industry Museum) has paintings (Rubens, Whistler, Monet) as well as exhibits on local industry. Unfortunately, it's closed for renovations until late 2001. ✉ *2 pl. Louis-Comte,* ☎ *04–77–33–04–85.*

OFF THE
BEATEN PATH
LA CHAISE-DIEU – The abbey, whose name means "Chair of God," about 40 km (25 mi) north of Le Puy-en-Velay via N102 and D906, has splendid red-and-black frescoes of the *Danse Macabre* (Death dancing with the nobility, bourgeoisie, and peasants).

Clermont-Ferrand

⓬ *40 km (24 mi) west of Thiers, 400 km (248 mi) south of Paris, 178 km (110 mi) west of Lyon.*

Known to historians as the hometown of Vercingétorix, who rallied the Arvernes to defeat Julius Caesar in 52 BC and who is immortalized in Astérix comic books, Clermont-Ferrand is the only large city in Auvergne. A bustling, modern commercial center that is the Michelin tire company's headquarters, Clermont-Ferrand probably won't draw you for more than a few hours. But the city is an ideal transfer point to the rest of Auvergne. It has some good museums and a small, old quarter dominated by its cathedral.

The monolithic **Cathédrale Notre-Dame-de-l'Assomption** (⊠ Pl. de la Victoire) was constructed of a special black volcanic stone that enabled the pillars to be thinner and the interior to soar to greater heights than ever before. Originally it was built in Romanesque style in the 13th century, but a subsequent renovation gave it a much more Gothic appearance. In 1884 the two spires were added according to plans drawn up by Viollet le Duc to imitate the style of the 13th and 15th centuries.

The older **Notre-Dame-du-Port** (⊠ Rue du Port) was built of sandstone and has an entirely different feel from the cathedral. Though founded in the 6th century, renovations in the 11th and 12th centuries gave it a Romanesque look. Note the raised choir with carved capitals that illustrate such tales as the struggle between Virtue and Vice and the fall of Adam and Eve.

Housed in a former Ursuline convent, the **Musée des Beaux-Arts** (Fine Arts Museum) has a beautifully designed exhibit on the history of painting and sculpture. ⊠ *Pl. Louis-Deteix,* ☎ *04–73–16–11–30.* 🖼 *25 frs.* ☉ *Tues.–Sun. 10–6.*

The **Musée du Ranquet** houses an assortment of artifacts, from ancient musical instruments to the world's first calculating machine, invented in the 17th century by native son Blaise Pascal. ⊠ *34 rue des Gras,* ☎ *04–73–37–38–63.* 🖼 *15 frs.* ☉ *Tues.–Sun. 10–noon and 1–6.*

Dining and Lodging

$$$ ✕ **Bernard Andrieux.** Chef Bernard Andrieux cooks deceptively sim-
★ ple dishes such as salmon with truffle sauce and *escalope de foie chaud de canard* (hot scalloped duck liver). The restaurant's elegance—cream-color walls, white linens, and well-spaced tables—matches the prices (the least expensive prix-fixe menu is 165 francs) but not the suburban location. ⊠ *Rte. de la Baraque (3 km [2 mi] northwest of Clermont-Ferrand on D141A),* ☎ *04–73–19–25–00,* FAX *04–73–19–25–04. AE, DC, MC, V. Closed Sun. mid-Aug.–mid-July, and Mon.*

$$ 🏨 **Hôtel de Lyon.** With its exposed timbers, this centrally located hotel stands out in contrast to the surrounding buildings made of volcanic stone and concrete, but don't expect much more than clean rooms and efficient if perfunctory service. ⊠ *16 pl. de Jaude, 63000,* ☎ *04–73–93–32–55,* FAX *04–73–93–54–33. 32 rooms. Restaurant. AE, DC, MC, V.*

Parc National des Volcans and Puy-de-Dôme

★ ⑬ *18 km (11 mi) west of Royat on D68, 24 km (15 mi) west of Clermont-Ferrand.*

Stretching 150 km (90 mi) from north to south, the **Parc National des Volcans** (National Park of Volcanoes) contains 80 or so dormant volcanoes, with all kinds of craters, dikes, domes, prismatic lava flows, caldera cones, and basaltic plateaus. The volcanoes are (relatively) young; the most recent is only 6,000 to 8,000 years old, which explains why their shapes are so well preserved.

At 4,806 ft, the Puy-de-Dôme is the highest volcano in the Mont-Dôme range. The Romans built a temple to Mercury here; the ruins of the temple were uncovered in 1872. The number of tourists, especially in July and August, is tremendous—Puy-de-Dôme is one of the three most-visited sights in France. Count on spending most of the day here, and bring your walking shoes so that you can follow the trails up to magnificent panoramas. If you're set on a bird's-eye view, parasailing, hot-air ballooning, and hang gliding can be arranged. 🖼 *30 frs per car except July and Aug. access by shuttle bus only: 21 francs.. ☉ Mar. and Nov., daily 8–6; Apr. and Oct., daily 8–8; May–Sept., daily 7 AM– 10 PM; Dec., weekends 7–5:30.*

Orcival

⑭ *13 km (8 mi) southwest of Puy-de-Dôme, 22 km (14 mi) southwest of Clermont-Ferrand.*

Mont-Dôme was a major hurdle for pilgrims making the long walk to Santiago de Compostela in Spain. To house them, five major sanctuaries—St-Austremoine d'Issoire, Notre-Dame-du-Port, Notre-Dame d'Orcival, St-Nectaire, and St-Saturnin—were erected in the 12th century. Of these vaulted Romanesque hospices, **Notre-Dame d'Orcival** (1146–78) was the most famous. Step inside to inspect a most unusual statue of the Virgin carrying an adult-looking child.

En Route   From Orcival take D27, which joins D983, for a beautiful ride over the **Col de Guery** pass, at 4,160 ft.

Le Mont-Dore

⑮ *19 km (12 mi) south of Orcival.*

On the Dordogne River at the head of the sheltered Chaudefour Valley, Le Mont-Dore was once a Roman spa town. Today it still has hot springs, though the town now derives much of its income as a convenient, although not particularly attractive, summer and winter resort. Ski trails (mostly intermediate level) radiate from the town center and a *téléphérique* (cable car) climbs the peaks.

Dining and Lodging

$ ✕ **Le Boeuf dans l'Assiette.** This restaurant provides simple fare for ravenous skiers and hikers. With a three-course menu and a bottle of St-Pourçain wine, two people can replenish their energy for less than 175 francs. ☒ *9 av. Michel-Bertrand,* ☎ *04–73–65–01–23. MC, V. Closed Mon.*

$$–$$$ ⌂ **Château de Bassignac.** This fortified 16th-century manor has just
★   four rooms, decorated with an assortment of family antiques. Bassignac is still a working farm, but the Bessons leave that aspect of business to their children. Monsieur Besson is an artist who often gives painting classes; Madame Besson acts like everyone's mother. In the evening you can sit before the fire mellowing with a glass of Armagnac after a day of fly fishing on the nearby river Sumène. In winter the château is only open by advance arrangement. ☒ *Brousse, 15240 Bassignac (on edge of village, 14 km [9 mi] southwest of Bort-les-Orgues on D922; 55 km [34 mi] from Le Mont Dore),* ☎ FAX *04–71–40–82–82. 4 rooms. Trout fishing. No credit cards.*

St-Nectaire

⑯ *16 km (10 mi) east of Le Mont-Dore, 44 km (27 mi) southwest of Clermont-Ferrand.*

In the upper part of the village of St-Nectaire is a Romanesque hospice—you may want to give thanks here after the challenge of driving over the passes. But your true reward is St-Nectaire's superb, soft, nutty-tasting cheese, made here since the 3rd century.

Lodging

$$ ⌂ **Relais Mercure.** On the site of the former Roman baths, in a dignified 19th-century building, is this attractive, modern hotel. Soaring ceilings in the palatial public areas and picture windows in the restaurant

and bar give it a light, airy feel. Part of the reliable Mercure chain, the hotel has all the amenities, from cable TV to direct-dial phones and in-room modem lines. The grounds in back, rising protectively from the hotel, contain a tranquil arboretum. ⊠ *63710 St-Nectaire,* ☎ *04–73–88–57–00,* FAX *04–73–88–57–02. 71 rooms. Bar, restaurant, in-room modem lines, 1 indoor and 1 outdoor pool, sauna, hot tub, health club, pool tables, meeting rooms. AE, DC, MC, V.*

Montpeyroux

⑰ *20 km (12 mi) east of St-Nectaire, 23 km (13 mi) south of Clermont-Ferrand.*

This medieval village, perched on a knoll just 8 km (5 mi) off A75 Exit 7, has made a comeback. By the early 19th century, 445 inhabitants lived behind its granite walls, going out each day to tend the vineyards. Then came the phylloxera, in the later part of the century, which destroyed the vines. The village's population dwindled to 125 people, and its once proud homes fell into disrepair. In the 1970s, however, came recognition in France that its many medieval relics needed to be preserved and Montpeyroux's rebirth began. Now the village has 360 residents, restored houses, and an annual festival of flowers the third week in May. There isn't actually that much to see here, except for the 13th-century round donjon, and a restaurant or two. Nonetheless, the views from the village of the sprawling landscape and the distant volcanic mountains, and the serenity of the place, make it quite appealing.

Lodging

$–$$ 🏠 **Chez Astruc.** Owner M. Astruc's enthusiasm for the village—he is its mayor—and his knowledge of the area make staying at this charming four-story inn a pleasure. The Astrucs live on the top floor; guest rooms—not large but pleasant if a bit fussy—are on the lower three floors. Ask to stay on the second floor, where two rooms have balconies and views of the countryside. ⊠ *63720 Montpeyroux,* ☎ *04–73–96–69–42. 5 rooms. Breakfast room. No credit cards.*

Besse

⑱ *6 km (4 mi) east of St-Nectaire, 51 km (32 mi) southwest of Clermont-Ferrand.*

Besse, like many of the other small, old farming villages in the mountainous Mont-Dôme region, has become a popular spot for winter sports and for hiking in summer. If you're here on a Monday, be sure to go to the cheese market.

A favorite excursion from Besse is to nearby **Lac Pavin,** a perfectly symmetrical caldera lake. Anglers come here to fish for mammoth-size trout called *omble chevalier*—delicious in the hands of a good chef.

En Route   The route south from Besse is splendid if you take D978 through the **Monts du Cantal, Monts du Condat,** and **Riom-les-Montagnes.** The route becomes even more dramatic when, at Riom, D62 leads west from Besse, and D680 heads through the **Cirque de Falgoux,** whose tricky twists and turns will require all your attention.

Le Puy-en-Velay

⑲ *130 km (81 mi) southeast of Clermont-Ferrand, 76 km (47 mi) southwest of St-Étienne.*

Le Puy-en-Velay is a stunning sight, built up on the *puys* that rise from the fertile valley like pyramids. These solidified-lava peaks are crowned with man-made monuments: on the lowest, a statue of St. Joseph and the Infant Jesus; on the highest, the 11th-century chapel of St-Michel; on another, a huge statue of the Virgin. Most spectacular of the monuments is the Romanesque cathedral of **Notre-Dame-du-Puy,** built of polychrome lava and balanced atop the fourth narrow pinnacle, reachable only by a long flight of steps.

St-Flour

⑳ *110 km (69 mi) east of Le Puy-en-Velay, 74 km (46 mi) west of Aurillac, 141 km (87 mi) north of Millau.*

St-Flour is a medieval enclave perched on the edge of an escarpment with cliffs dropping down on three sides. The age of the town becomes even more apparent as you drive from the newer *ville basse* (lower town) up to the ancient *ville haute* (upper town). Narrow cobblestone streets meander between 16th- and 17th-century buildings.

The **Musée de la Haute-Auvergne** (Auvergne Museum), in the former bishop's palace, presents some local archaeological finds but is mostly filled with artifacts and furnishings used by residents over the last 300 years. ⊠ *1 pl. d'Armes,* ☎ *04–71–60–61–34.* 🔄 *25 frs.* ◔ *Mid-Oct.–mid-Apr., Mon.–Sat. 10–noon and 2–6; mid-Apr.–July and Sept.–mid-Oct., daily 10–noon and 2–6; July–Aug., daily 10–noon and 2–7.*

Across the square from the Musée de la Haute-Auvergne is the **Musée Alfred Douët.** The 13th-century building, renovated in the 16th century, has on display tapestries and furnishings from the 16th, 17th, and 18th centuries. The items are laid out just as they might have been when the building was occupied by the consul-general, enabling you to get a sense of that era. ⊠ *Pl. d'Armes,* ☎ *04–71–60–44–99.* 🔄 *25 frs.* ◔ *Mid-Apr.–mid-Oct., daily 9–noon and 2–6; mid-Oct.–mid-Apr., Mon.–Sat. 9–noon and 2–6.*

Dining and Lodging

$$ ✕🏠 **Grand Hôtel de l'Europe.** The choice of hotels in St-Flour's ville haute is limited; the family-run Europe is the best. A long, horizontal building on the edge of town, it overlooks the valley below and the hills beyond—a large part of the hotel's appeal. Ask for a room—and in the restaurant, a table—with a view of the valley. Rooms, though not large, are old-fashioned, homey, and comfortable. ⊠ *12–13 cours Spy des Ternes, 15100,* ☎ *04–71–60–03–64,* FAX *04–71–60–03–45. 44 rooms. Bar, breakfast room, restaurant. AE, DC, MC, V.*

En Route   At nearly 5,249 ft, the **Pas de Peyrol** is Auvergne's highest pass. Leave your car in the parking lot and take the 30-minute walk to the summit of **Puy Mary.** The views from here are tremendous: 13 valleys radiate from the mountain, funneling their streams into some of France's major rivers.

Salers

★ ㉑ *11 km (7 mi) west of the Pas de Peyrol, 20 km (12 mi) south of Mauriac, 43 km (25 mi) north of Aurillac.*

Medieval Salers, perched on a bluff above the Maronne Valley, is filled with tourists—little wonder, since this town cannot fail to seduce most visitors. In the 15th century the people of Salers, feeling isolated in the country, began building protective ramparts and subsequently won the right to govern themselves. Many 15th- and 16th-century houses of black lava stone remain and are now filled with boutiques and small restaurants. Although this was once an important cattle-market town, farming today plays a smaller role than tourism—though you st may be awakened by the sound of cowbells. On market days **Grande-Place**, in the heart of the village, is very busy.

About 15 km (9 mi) south of Salers, the valley ridges are so beautiful that you could spend a day or two exploring the tiny, winding roads. The *cols* (mountain passes) are high enough (plus or minus 3,000 ft) to have snow in the winter, but they are really quite gentle, and they provide a good view of the comely valleys below. Find your way to the small *hameau* (hamlet) of **Fontanges,** with its tiny chapel hollowed out of a limestone bluff on which stands a white Madonna. The sweet hillside village of Tournemire and its **Château Anjony** are also worth a visit. *Château:* ☎ 04–71–47–64–11. ☞ *32 frs.* ☉ *Mar.–mid-Nov., Mon.–Sat. 2–5:30.*

Lodging

$$–$$$ ★ 🏠 **Château de la Vigne.** Monsieur and Madame du Fayet de la Tour's château-inn is on a hillcrest (the Parc National des Volcans is visible in the distance). It retains elements of its past as an 8th-century Merovingian castle and a medieval fortress, though it was rebuilt in the 15th century. Family coats of arms and stained-glass windows decorate the best guest room, the large Chambre Troubadour, where Jean-Jacques Rousseau is said to have stayed in 1767. Otherwise, furnishings are sparse and bathrooms makeshift. A table d'hôte dinner of regional dishes (reservations required) is served in the splendid dining room. ☒ *15700 Ally (16 km [10 mi] mi from Salers),* ☎ ᖴᗩ᙭ *04–71–69–00–20. 4 rooms. Dining room. No credit cards. Closed mid-Oct.–late Mar.*

$$–$$$ 🏠 **Hostellerie de la Maronne.** In a tranquil valley, this converted 19th-century farmhouse has well-kept, modern rooms, some with balconies. Furnishings, however, are of the department-store variety. The lounge and bar are pleasant, but the most care has been put into the dining room and the glassed-in kitchen. Dinner provides an opportunity to savor the best Salers beef, though the cuisine itself is not worth a special trip. ☒ *Le Treil, 15140 St-Martin-Valmeroux (6 km [4 mi] from Salers),* ☎ *04–71–69–20–33,* ᖴᗩ᙭ *04–71–69–28–22. 20 rooms, 1 apartment. Restaurant, bar, lobby lounge, breakfast room. AE, DC, MC, V. Closed Nov. 1–Easter.*

$$ 🏠 **Hôtel des Ramparts.** From its position atop the ramparts, this hotel has spectacular panoramic views. Rooms are simple and functional. The management likes to quote half-pension rates, which you should resist if you are staying for more than one night. ☒ *Esplanade de Barrouze, 15410 Salers,* ☎ *04–71–40–70–33,* ᖴᗩ᙭ *04–71–40–75–32. 18 rooms. Restaurant. MC, V. Closed late Oct.–late Dec.*

Aurillac

㉒ *42 km (26 mi) south of Salers, 157 km (97 mi) southwest of Clermont-Ferrand.*

The prefecture and market town of Aurillac, at the edge of the Monts du Cantal, bustles by day and becomes a sleepy country village by night. The oldest part of town—a small area—has an old cheese market, ancient houses, and narrow streets that twist along the banks of the River Jordanne. Locals and tourists spend their days at the cafés on place du Palais-de-Justice, the main square. Stop by the tourist office here for a free walking-tour map—well worth following.

At the **Musée d'Art et d'Archéologie** (Art and Archaeology Museum), remains of a Gallo-Roman temple and various religious objects are on display. A unique collection of umbrellas from the past three centuries—about half of all French umbrellas are made in Aurillac—is also housed here. ⊠ *Centre Pierre Mendès-France, 37 rue des Carmes,* ☎ *04–71–45–46–10.* 🎫 *20 frs.* ⏰ *Apr.–Oct., Tues.–Sat. 10–noon and 2–6; July–Aug., Tues.–Sat. 10–noon and 2–6, Sun. 2–6.*

Dining and Lodging

$$ ✕ **Poivre et Sel.** This intimate, friendly bistro serves a refined version of Auvergne fare. It is a good place to try Salers beef, as well as other regional dishes such as *salmis de colvert Cévenole* (ragout of game). ⊠ *4 rue du 14-Juillet,* ☎ *04–71–64–20–20. MC, V. Closed Sun.–Mon.*

$ ✕ **Le Bistrot.** For genuine Auvergne fare come to this little bistro with Formica tables and a long bar. Two of the fine regional specialties served are *truffade* (sautéed potato slices covered with melted cheese) and *choux farcis* (stuffed cabbage). ⊠ *18 rue Gambetta,* ☎ *04–71–48–01–04. MC, V.*

$$ 🏨 **Grand Hôtel de Bordeaux.** There are advantages to this Best Western hotel—its central location, its private garage, and its professional staff. Otherwise, rooms are what you'd expect from this chain—compact but clean, functional, and adequate, though some have views of the gardens of the Palais de Justice. ⊠ *2 av. de la République, 15000,* ☎ *04–71–48–01–84,* 🆁🆇 *04–71–48–49–93. 33 rooms. Bar. AE, DC, MC, V. Closed end Dec.–early Jan.* 🐾

GORGE COUNTRY

Carved into the limestone plateaus of the Causses, a number of breathtaking gorges mark the landscape here. Millennia ago pressure caused fractures and cleavages that trapped torrential rains. Through thousands of years the swirling waters ate into the mass of stone, gouging out the canyons and caves, the underground rivers and lakes that are today such wonders to the tourist, boatman, and geologist. The most famous of these are the Gorges du Tarn, a wilderness filled with sudden views of dramatic silhouettes of red and yellow cliffs. The lovely, old, rural towns dotting the area make perfect bases for exploring the area, which also features some great medieval churches.

Laguiole

㉓ *85 km (53 mi) southeast of Aurillac, 56 km (35 mi) north of Rodez.*

On the high basalt plateau, Laguiole is more than 3,000 ft above sea level. In winter the wind roars across the land, piling up snow on ski trails; in summer the sun scorches the land; in spring and fall the angled sunlight dances on the granite outcroppings. The town is known for its hardy breed of Aubrac cattle; for its distinctive cheese made from unpasteurized cows' milk, flavored by the varied local flora; and for its spring-hinged pocket knife. You can visit the factory, the **Societé Forge de Laguiole** (☎ 05–65–48–43–34), where they make these knives, which have a slightly curved handle and a long blade; buy one here or in town

Dining and Lodging

$$$$ ✕🏨 **Michel Bras.** Despite the flowery prose used by the Bras to describe their contemporary hotel-restaurant, it does not really "mold itself perfectly to the countryside," but stands on a promontory like a space ship about to be launched. To be fair, the rooms are full of light, creature comforts are everywhere, and the views of the granite outcrop are haunting. But the main draw is Michel Bras's unique creations—foie gras with apricots and honey vinegar and asparagus with truffle vinaigrette—as well as his more classic Aubrac beef and wild boar dishes. ⊠ *Rte. de l'Aubrac, 12210,* ☎ *05–65–51–18–20,* 🆁🆇 *05–65–48–47*

02. *15 rooms. Restaurant. AE, DC, MC, V. Closed Mon. and no lunch
Tues., except July–Aug. and Nov.–Easter.* ✆

$$ ✕🏨 **Grand Hôtel Auguy.** A good alternative to the high-priced Michel
Bras (☞ *above*), the Auguy has basic rooms with just enough space
for a bed, a desk, and a couple of armchairs. Ask for one of the qui-
eter rooms, away from the street. Owner Isabelle Auguy is a creative
cook who uses her grandparents' rustic recipes but gives them a lighter
touch. The foie gras salad is a delight, as are the Aubrac beef and the
fresh trout. The restaurant is closed Monday and doesn't serve dinner
Sunday. ✉ *2 allée de l'Amicale, 12210,* ☎ *05–65–44–31–11,* FAX *05–
65–51–50–81. 27 rooms. Restaurant, bar, lobby lounge. AE, DC, MC,
V. Closed Dec.–Jan.*

Figeac

㉔ *66 km (44 mi) southwest of Aurillac, 38 km (24 mi) west of Conques,
43 km (27 mi) northwest of St-Cirq-Lapopie.*

The old town of Figeac, which has a lively Saturday-morning market,
was once a major stopping point for pilgrims heading toward Santi-
ago de Compostela in Spain. Many of the 13th-, 14th-, and 15th-cen-
tury houses in the old part of town have been carefully restored; note
their octagonal chimneys and *soleilhos* (open attics used for drying flow-
ers and wood). The elegant 13th-century **Hôtel de la Monnaie,** a block
from the Célé River, is a characteristic old Figeac house. Probably used
as a money-changing office in the Middle Ages, today it houses the **tourist
office** and a museum of relics. ✉ *Pl. Vival,* ☎ *05–65–34–06–25.* 🎫
15 frs. ☉ *July–Aug., daily 10–1 and 2–7; Sept.–June, Mon.–Sat. 11–
noon and 2:30–5:30.*

Jean-François Champollion (1790–1830), one of the first men to de-
cipher Egyptian hieroglyphics, was born in Figeac. The **Musée Cham-
pollion** (leave place Vival on rue 11-Novembre, take the first left, and
follow it as it veers right) contains a casting of the Rosetta stone, dis-
covered in the Nile River delta, which Champollion used to decode
Pharaonic dialect. A varied collection of Egyptian antiquities is also
on display. ✉ *5 impasse Champollion,* ☎ *05–65–50–31–08.* 🎫 *20 frs.*
☉ *Mar.–Oct., Tues.–Sun. 10–noon and 2:30–6:30; Nov.–Feb., Tues.–
Sun. 2–6; July–Aug., daily 10–noon and 2:30–6:30.*

Dining and Lodging

$$$$ ✕🏨 **Château du Viguier du Roy.** Everything—the tower, the cloister, the
gardens, the wooden beams, the tapestries, and the canopied beds—in
this medieval palace, once the residence of the king's *viguier* (repre-
sentative), has been painstakingly restored. Rooms throughout are
regal. The restaurant, La Dinée du Viguier, is excellent. ✉ *rue Droite,
46100,* ☎ *05–65–50–05–05,* FAX *05–65–50–06–06. 17 rooms, 4 suites.
Restaurant. AE, DC, MC, V. Closed early–mid-Dec. and early Jan.–Mar.*

$$–$$$ 🏨 **Ferme Auberge Domaine des Villedieu.** This lovely farmhouse-inn,
partly dating from the 16th century, is lovingly run by the Villedieu fam-
ily. Not only are there cozy rooms in ancient (restored) outbuildings such
as the former bakery, but you can also look forward to a fireside dinner
of cassoulet in a bubbling earthenware casserole accompanied by home-
made foie gras and a local Cahors wine. ✉ *Rte. D13, Vallée du Célé,
46100 Boussac (10 km [6 mi] from Figeac),* ☎ *05–65–40–06–63,* FAX
05–65–40–09–22. 5 rooms. Dining room, lounge, pool. DC, MC, V.

En Route Leave Figeac on the road to Rodez and take D52, a small road on your
left: It leads through the beautiful Lot Valley to D901, which goes to
Conques.

Conques

② *44 km (27 mi) east of Figeac, 39 km (24 mi) northwest of Rodez, 56 km (35 mi) south of Aurillac.*

The pretty red-ochre houses of Conques harmonize perfectly with the surrounding rocky gorge. The village was home to a Benedictine abbey whose outstanding Romanesque church was one of the principal stopping points on the pilgrimage route between Le Puy-de-Dôme and Santiago de Compostela.

★ Begun in the early 11th century, the abbey church of **Ste-Foy** had its heyday in the 12th and 13th centuries, after which the flood of pilgrims and their revenue dried up. The two centuries of success were due to the purloined relics of Ste-Foy (St. Faith), a 13-year-old Christian girl who was martyred in 303 in Agen, where her remains were jealousy guarded. A monk from Conques venerated them so highly that he traveled to Agen, joined the community of St. Faith, and won their trust. After 10 years they put him in charge of guarding the saint's relics, whereupon he stole them and brought them back to Conques. Devastated by Huguenot hordes, the church languished until the 19th century, when the writer Prosper Mérimée raised the money to salvage it. Ste-Foy clings to a hill so steep that even driving and walking—let alone building—are precarious activities. The church's interior is high and dignified; the ambulatory was given a lot of wear by medieval pilgrims, who admired the church's most precious relic, a 10th-century wooden statue of Ste-Foy encrusted with gold and precious stones. You can see it in the treasury, off the recently restored cloister.

The **Musée Docteur Joseph-Fau** (Trésor II), opposite the pilgrims' fountain near Ste-Foy, houses a collection of 17th-century furniture, neo-Gothic reliquaries, and tapestries from Ste-Foy Abbey. 🖭 *25 frs.* ☉ *Sept.–June, Mon.–Sat. 9–noon and 2–6, Sun. 2–6; July–Aug., Mon.–Sat. 9–noon and 2–7, Sun. 2–7.*

Rodez

② *39 km (24 mi) southeast of Conques, 46 km (29 mi) southeast of Rocamadour.*

Rodez, capital of the Aveyron, stands on a windswept hill. At its center is the pink-sandstone **Cathédrale Notre-Dame** (13th–15th centuries). Its sober bulk is lightened by decorative upper stories, completed in the 17th century, and by the magnificent 285-ft bell tower. The renovated **Cité Quartier,** once ruled by medieval bishops, lies behind the cathedral. On tiny place de l'Olmet, just off place du Bourg, is the 16th-century **Maison d'Armagnac,** a fine Renaissance mansion with a courtyard and an ornate facade covered with medallion emblems of the counts of Rodez. The extensively modernized **Musée Denys Puech,** an art museum, is just east of the wide boulevard that circles the old town. ⊠ *Pl. Clemenceau,* ☎ *05–65–42–70–64.* 🖭 *20 frs.* ☉ *Mon. 2–7, Wed.–Sat. 10–noon and 2–6, Sun. 2–6.*

Dining and Lodging

$ ✕ **Goûts et Couleurs.** In an intimate, pastel-color atmosphere, enjoy the seasonal menu, with such selections as pan-fried calf's liver stuffed with cabbage, or rabbit with fresh herbs. ⊠ *38 rue de Bonald,* ☎ *05–65–42–75–10. MC, V. Closed Sun.–Mon. and mid-Jan.–mid-Feb.*

$–$$ ✕🖭 **La Diligence.** Talented chef Joël Delmas makes succulent mille-
★ feuilles of lamb kidneys and a superb banana coconut tart, among other fine dishes. Equally impressive are the prices: Prix-fixe lunches start 89 francs. Except for July and August, the restaurant is closed Tue

day and doesn't serve dinner Monday. Rooms, furnished in modern style, are not luxurious, but they are adequate and modestly priced. ⊠ *12330 Vallady (10 km [6 mi] northwest of Rodez on rte. N140 near village of Nuces),* ☎ *05–65–72–60–20. 6 rooms. Restaurant. MC, V. Closed 1st 2 wks of Jan.*

En Route If you are traveling from Rodez to Millau and have time, skip N88 and treat yourself to the shorter and prettier route D28, off N88.

Millau

㉗ *66 km (41 mi) southeast of Rodez, 248 km (154 mi) south of Clermont-Ferrand.*

Millau is primarily a jumping-off point for exploring the magnificent gorges (☞ below) that cut through the limestone *causses* (plateaus). Give yourself time to wander through the old quarter, especially around place du Maréchal-Foch, with its 800-year-old arcades. Browse through the shops on place des Mandarous and place de la Tine for leather goods, by-products of all those sheep producing milk for Roquefort cheese.

In Roman times Millau produced pottery and sent its vases as far afield as Scotland. Some of these artifacts, collected from the nearby archaeological site, are in the **Musée de Millau.** ⊠ *Hôtel de Pégayrolles, Pl. Foch,* ☎ *05–65–59–01–08.* 🄲 *27 frs.* ☉ *Apr.–Sept., daily 10– noon and 2–6; Oct.–Mar., Mon.–Sat. 10–noon and 2–6.*

Dining and Lodging

$$ ✕🏨 **Château de Creissels.** This hotel, in an ancient 12th-century fort, has rooms furnished in simple country style and modern decor. A few have a terrace overlooking the small village of Creissels. Dinner is served in the medieval atmosphere of the vaulted cellar. ⊠ *Rte. de Ste-Afrique, 12100 Millau (3 km [2 mi] outside town on D992),* ☎ *05–65–60–31– 79,* 🄵🄰🄷 *05–65–61–24–63. 31 rooms, 26 with bath or shower. Restaurant. MC, V. Closed mid-Dec.–mid-Feb.*

Outdoor Activities and Sports

Mountain bikes, a good way to explore the gorges, can be rented from **William Orts** (⊠ 21 bd. de l'Ayrolle, ☎ 05–65–61–14–29).

Gorges du Tarn

★ ㉘ *Extends from Le Rozier (16 km [10 mi] northeast of Millau) to Florac, 75 km (47 mi) to the northeast.*

Though not quite as awesome as the Grand Canyon, the Gorges du Tarn (Tarn Gorge) is very beautiful and dramatic. Route D907 leads into its mouth and runs along it, 1,968 ft below the cliff top. Beginning at **Le Rozier,** the Tarn River, flowing out of the gorge, is joined by the Jonte, coming from the Gorges de la Jonte (☞ below). Follow D907B to **Les Vignes,** where the gorge opens into a little valley. Take D995 to the top, along some challenging switchbacks, and follow signs for **Point Sublime,** where you'll find views that justify the name. After Les Vignes the gorge becomes the most dramatic, with sheer cliffs and rock face dappled with grays, whites, and blues. In summer you can take a boat through this stretch; a bus takes you to the embarkation point.

At the **Cirque des Baumes,** just before the village of La Malène, the cliffs form a natural amphitheater. Continue on to **Les Détroits** (the straits), the gorge's narrowest section, where the tumbling waters barely squeeze through. After passing **La Malène,** note the 15th-century **Château de la Caze,** with its imposing array of turrets. Beyond the castle, just before the village of St-Chély-du-Tarn, is the **Cirque de**

Pournadoires and catercorner to it is another, larger natural amphitheater. On summer nights it is the site of a son-et-lumière show. But don't make a point of seeing it: The gorge looks far more beautiful under natural light.

Ste-Énimie, the gorge's major town, is mired in summer by a flood of tourists. In its little church ceramic tiles tell the 7th-century legend of Ste-Énimie, the beautiful sister of the Frankish king. When she was about to marry, she fell ill with leprosy and was scorned by her suitor. On the advice of an angel she was cured at the fountain of Burle, where she then founded a convent. Its ruins can still be seen, as can the fountain. From Ste-Énimie, the road winds through the valley, opening out just before the small market town of **Florac.**

Dining and Lodging

$ ✕▥ **Le Vallon.** Locals are drawn year-round by the simple yet good fare at this restaurant-inn in the touristy town of Ispagnac, along the gorge. Menus range from 65 to 160 francs; 95 francs buys you a very respectable four courses, which might include an omelet, a salad, a casserole, and some cheese. Rooms are simple, clean, and inexpensive. ✉ *Rte. D907B, 48320 Ispagnac,* ☎ *04–66–44–21–24,* ℻ *04–66–44–26–05, www.hotelvallon.com. 24 rooms. Restaurant, bar. AE, MC, V. Closed late Dec.–Jan.*

Outdoor Activities and Sports

For kayaking down through the Gorges du Tarn, try **Canyon Location** (✉ Rte. de Millau, Ste-Énimie, ☎ 04–66–48–50–52). Trips can be as short as 9 km (5½ mi) and as long as 72 km (50 mi). **FREMYC** (✉ Meyrueis, ☎ 04–66–45–61–54) is another outfit for kayaking the Gorges du Tarn, which also organizes horseback riding, rents mountain bikes, and sends you riding the winds in a hang glider (*parapente*).

En Route   Between Florac and St-Jean-du-Gard, the **Corniches des Cévennes** road winds its way through spectacular scenery. Follow D907 from Florac; then take a left on D983 toward St-Laurent-de-Trèves. From here the road ascends the **Col du Rey,** high above the valley.

Meyrueis

❷❾ *35 km (22 mi) southwest of Florac, 43 km (27 mi) east of Millau.*

The Jonte and Betuzon rivers join at the village of Meyrueis (2,300 ft/690 m), whose warm days and cool nights make it a perfect base for exploring the gorgeous Gorges du Tarn (☞ *above*), Gorges de la Jonte (☞ *below*), and other nearby caves, causses, and cirques. Meyrueis itself has a medieval round tower, part of ancient fortifications, which houses the tourist office, as well as a ruined château high above. The narrow streets of the oldest part of town, once within the walls, conceal a minuscule Jewish quarter and a noble house you can stay in. A self-guided walking tour will introduce you to everyone once worth knowing in Meyrueis, as well as show you where they lived, prayed, and administered justice.

Dining and Lodging

$$$ ✕▥ **Château d'Ayres.** A Benedictine monastery before the Wars of Religion, this aristocratic manor house has been transformed into a marvelous country retreat, 1½ km (1 mi) out of Meyrueis. A serene pool reflects the Virginia creeper–covered building, and spacious grounds contain a tennis court and pool. Inside are comfortable public spaces and two dining rooms where delightful Auvergne meals are served. Aubrac beef and Mt. Aigoual mushrooms are just some of the regional riches. Up the broad stone staircase are spacious, high-ceilinged guest rooms with a mix of antiques and newer, comfortable furnishings. ✉

Rte. d'Ayres, 48150, ☎ *04–66–45–60–10,* FAX *04–66–45–62–26. 20 rooms, 7 suites. Restaurant, pool, tennis court, horseback riding. AE, DC, MC, V. Closed mid-Nov.–late Mar.* ✇

$ ⊞ **La Renaissance.** Just off shady place d'Orléans is this small 16th-century *hôtel particulier* (mansion) owned by the Bourguet family since it was first built. Over the centuries they have furnished it with antiques, beautiful linen-fold paneling, and family portraits. Don't expect to find telephones in rooms (although there are TVs) or an elevator. A nice breakfast room overlooks the garden, but other meals are served at the neighboring Hôtel du St-Sauveur (also owned by the Bourguets), whose restaurant and wine list are of gastronomic note. ✉ *rue de la Ville, 48150,* ☎ *04–66–45–60–19,* FAX *04–66–45–68–81. 20 rooms. Breakfast room. AE, DC, MC, V. Closed Nov.–Mar.*

Gorges de la Jonte

③⓪ *Extends from Meyrueis (35 km [22 mi] southwest of Florac) 21 km (13 mi) west to Le Rozier (16 km [16 mi] northeast of Millau).*

The splendid Gorges de la Jonte (Jonte Gorge) is narrower than the Gorges du Tarn (☞ *above*). At its depths is the Jonte River. Start from the village of **Meyrueis** (☞ *above*), where the gorge is at its broadest. Within a short distance, the gorge narrows, and the eroded limestone cliffs form strange pinnacle shapes. A good spot to stop for a snack is **Les Douzes.** From here proceed to the deepest part of the gorge, along the cliff side. Past **Truel,** a cluster of houses clinging to the cliff face, is a lookout where for a moment the view opens to reveal two levels of cliff—**Les Terrasses de Truel**—then closes again before Le Rozier. Four kilometers (2 miles) from Rozier a sign to the right directs you up to the **Belvédère des Vautours,** a natural reserve for birds of prey. Over the past two decades these birds have been reestablished on the causse, offering you a rare chance to see them in their proper habitat—as well as marvel at the cliff-hanging views. ☎ *04–66–45–60–33 for information about bird reserve.* ▨ *35 frs.* ☉ *Apr.–Nov., daily 10–7.*

THE MASSIF CENTRAL A TO Z

Arriving and Departing

By Car
Take A10 from Paris to Orléans, then A71 into the center of France. From Paris, Bourges is 229 km (137 mi), and Clermont-Ferrand is 378 km (243 mi). Coming from Lyon it takes less than 90 minutes to drive the 179 km (111 mi) on A72 to Clermont-Ferrand. Entry into Auvergne from the south is mostly on small, curving national roads, though the new A75 will eventually link Montpellier with Clermont-Ferrand through Millau; portions of the autoroute are already completed and open to vehicles.

By Plane
The major airport for the region, at **Clermont-Ferrand** (☎ 04–73–62–71–00), has regularly scheduled flights to Paris (Orly), Bordeaux, Dijon, Lyon, Marseille, Nantes, Nice, and Toulouse on Air France and direct international flights to Geneva, Milan, and London on Air France, British Airways, and Swissair. **TAT** (Transport Aérien Transrégional) flies from Paris's Orly Airport to Rodez (☎ 01–42–79–05–05 for reservations in Paris; 05–65–42–20–30 in Rodez).

By Train
The fastest way from Paris (Gare de Lyon) to Clermont-Ferrand, the capital of Auvergne, is on the high-speed TGV (*Trains à Grande Vitesse*) via Lyon, where you change for the regular **train** to Clermont-

Ferrand (☎ 08–36–35–35–35 for information). Regular SNCF trains also go from Paris to Bourges and Clermont-Ferrand and from Nantes, Limoges, Toulouse, Brive, Bordeaux, and Nîmes to Clermont-Ferrand.

Getting Around

By Car

There is only one way to *really* explore the region, and that is by car. Although national highways will get you from one place to another fairly expediently, the region's beauty is best discovered on the small roads that twist through the mountains and along the gorges.

Contacts and Resources

Car Rental

Avis (✉ 22 bd. Etienne-Clémentel, Clermont-Ferrand, ☎ 04–73–25–72–06, FAX 04–73–25–86–34; ✉ Clermont-Ferrand Airport, ☎ 04–73–91–18–08, FAX 04–73–61–06–93; ✉ Clermont-Ferrand train station, ☎ 04–73–91–72–94, FAX 04–73–90–74–11). **Europcar** (✉ Rue Émile-Loubet, ☎ 04–73–92–70–26, FAX 04–73–90–28–10; ✉ Clermont-Ferrand Airport, ☎ 04–73–92–70–26 at airport). **Hertz** (✉ 71 av. de l'Union Soviétique, Clermont-Ferrand, ☎ 04–73–92–36–10, FAX 04–73–90–46–47; ✉ Clermont-Ferrand Airport, ☎ 04–73–62–71–93, FAX 04–73–62–71–96).

Guided Tours

Rafting trips of the Gorges du Tarn can be arranged through the following: **Service Loisirs** (✉ Haute-Loire, ☎ 05–61–09–20–80); **Association Le Merlet** (✉ Rte. de Nîmes, St-Jean du Gard, ☎ 04–66–85–18–19). From April to November float through the skies above the volcanoes in a balloon; contact **Objectif** (✉ 44 av. des Etats-Unis, 63057 Clermont-Ferrand, ☎ 04–73–29–49–49, FAX 04–73–34–11–11).

Travel Agencies

Centre Auvergne Tourisme (✉ 9 rue Ballainvilliers, 63000 Clermont-Ferrand, ☎ 04–73–90–10–20). **Voyagers Maisonneuve** (✉ 24 rue Georges-Clemenceau, 63000 Clermont-Ferrand, ☎ 04–73–93–16–72).

Visitor Information

Main regional tourist office: **Comité Régional du Tourisme D'Auvergne** (✉ 43 av. Julien, 63011 Clermont-Ferrand, ☎ 04–73–29–49–49, FAX 04–73–34–11–11).

Departmental tourist offices: **Allier** (✉ 11 rue François-Péron, 03000 Moulins, ☎ 04–70–44–14–14). **Aveyron** (✉ Pl. Maréchal-Foch, 12000 Rodez, ☎ 05–65–68–02–27). **Cantal** (✉ Pl. du Square, 15000 Aurillac, ☎ 04–71–48–46–58). **Cher** (✉ 5 rue de Séaucourt, 18000 Bourges, ☎ 02–48–67–00–18). **Haute-Loire** (✉ Pl. du Breuil, 43000 Le Puy-en-Velay, ☎ 04–71–09–38–41). **Lot** (✉ Pl. François-Mitterrand, 46000 Cahors, ☎ 05–65–53–20–65). **Lozère** (✉ 14 bd. Henri-Bourrillon, 48000 Mende, ☎ 04–66–65–60–00). **Puy-de-Dôme** (✉ 26 rue St-Esprit, 63000 Clermont-Ferrand, ☎ 04–73–42–21–21).

Local tourist offices: **Besse** (✉ Place Pipet, 63610, ☎ 04–73–79–52–84). **Bourbon-l'Archambault** (✉ 1 pl. de Thermes, 03160, ☎ 04–70–67–09–79). **Montluçon** (✉ 5 pl. Piquand, 03100, ☎ 04–70–05–11–44). **Montpeyroux** (✉ Les Pradets-Lebourg, 63114, ☎ 04–73–96–68–80). **Moulins** (✉ 11 rue François Péron, 03006, ☎ 04–70–44–14–14). **Orcival** (✉ Le Bourg, 63210, ☎ 04–73–65–92–25). **St-Amand-Montrond** (✉ Pl. de la République, 78200, ☎ 02–48–96–16–86). **St-Nectaire** (✉ Les Grands Thérmes, 63710, ☎ 04–73–88–50–86). **St-Pourçain-sur-Sioule** (✉ 13 pl. Maréchal Foch, 03500, ☎ 04–70–45–32–73). **Thiers** (✉ Pl. du Pirou, 63300, ☎ 04–73–80–10–74).

11 PROVENCE

Provence means dazzling light and arid, rocky countryside striped with vineyards, lavender, and silvery olive groves. The Romans staked their first claim here and left epic monuments behind; van Gogh and Cézanne abstracted it into vivid, geometric daubs of paint; then in the late 20th century essayist Peter Mayle bought a house and spread the word—and the rest of the world was not far behind. From the marshlands of the Camargue to the honey-gold hill towns of the Luberon, this alluring land touches something ancient in all of us.

A S YOU APPROACH PROVENCE, there is a magical moment when you finally leave the north behind: Cypresses and red-tile roofs appear; you hear the screech of the cicadas and catch the scent of wild thyme and lavender. Even along the highway, oleanders bloom on the center strip against a backdrop of austere, brightly lighted landscapes that inspired the Postimpressionists.

Updated by
Nancy Coons

Then you notice a hill town whose red roofs skew downhill at Cubist angles, sun-bleached and mottled with age. Your eye catches the rhythm of Romanesque tiles overlapping in sensual snaking rows, as alike and as varied as the reeds in a pan pipe, their broad horizontal flow forming a foil for the dark, thrusting verticals of the cypress, and the ephemeral, feminine puff of the silvery olive. Overhead, the sky is an azure prism thanks to the famous mistral—a fierce, cold wind that razors through the Rhône Valley—which often scrubs the torpid sky to crystal blue. Sheep bells tonk behind dry rock walls, while in the distance your ear picks up the pulsing roar of the sea. The Phoenicians, the Greeks, and the Romans recognized a new Fertile Crescent and founded vital civilizations here, leaving traces untouched by millennia of clean, dry air. Nowhere in France, and rarely in the Western world, can you touch antiquity with this intimacy—its exoticism, its purity, eternal and alive. This is Provence the primordial.

But there's another Provence in evidence today, a disarming culture of *pastis* (an anise-based aperitif), *pétanque* (lawn bowling), and shady plane trees, where dawdling is a way of life, where you may take root in a sidewalk café and listen to the trickling fountain, putter aimlessly down narrow cobbled alleyways, heft melons in the morning marketplace and, after a three-hour lunch, take a postprandial snooze in the cool blue shade of a 500-year-old olive tree.

Until the cell phone rings, that is. Because ever since Peter Mayle abandoned the London fog and described with sensual relish a life of unbuttoned collars and espadrilles in his best-selling 1990 *A Year in Provence,* the world has beaten a path to Provence. Now Parisians are heard in the local marketplaces passing the word on the best free-range rabbit, the purest olive oil, the lowest price on a five-bedroom *mas* (farmhouse) with vineyard and pool. And a chic new *bon-chic-bon-genre* city crowd languishes stylishly at the latest country inn and makes an appearance at the most fashionable restaurant. Ask them, and they'll agree: ever since Princess Caroline of Monaco moved to St-Rémy, Provence is the new Côte d'Azur.

But chic Provence hasn't eclipsed idyllic Provence, and it's still possible to melt into a Monday-morning market crowd, where blue-aproned *paysannes* scoop gnarled fistfuls of mesclun into a willow basket, matron-connoisseurs paw through bins containing the first Cavaillon asparagus, a knot of *pépés* in workers' blues take a pétanque break. . . and welcome you into the game.

Relax and join them—and plan to stay a while. Yes, there are plenty of sights to see: some of the finest Roman ruins in Europe, from the Pont du Gard to the arenas at Arles and Orange; the pristine Romanesque abbeys of Senanque and de Montmajour; bijoux chapels and weathered mas; the feudal châteaux at Tarascon and Beaucaire; the monolithic Papal Palace in old Avignon; and everywhere vineyards, pleasure ports, and sophisticated city museums. But allow yourself time to feel the rhythm of modern Provençal life, to listen to the pulsing *breet* of the cicadas, to breath deep the perfume of wild herbs and old stone to feel the velvet air of a summer night on your skin. To experience, slowly, sensually, the real Provence primordial.

— Nancy Coons

Pleasures and Pastimes

Architecture and Antiquities

Churches, châteaux, and abbeys sprinkle the countryside of Provence, a surprising concentration of them pure Romanesque—that is, built in the solid progression of arches and barrel vaults that marked Roman engineering and was mimicked by architects through the 12th and 13th centuries. Although you'll find Roman traces throughout Provence (in fact, the name comes from the Roman *provincia*, or the province), the most beautifully preserved are concentrated around the Rhône, their main shipping artery. There are two arenas (in Arles and Nîmes), the ancient Hellenistic settlement outside St-Rémy (Glanum), the miraculously preserved temple in Nîmes (Maison Carrée), a theater in Orange, and two villages in Vaison-la-Romaine.

Dining

Now universally emulated for its winning combination of simplicity, healthy ingredients, and vivid sun-kissed flavors, Provençal cooking glories in olive oil, garlic, tomatoes, olives, and the ubiquitous wild herbs that crunch underfoot. France's greatest chefs scour lively markets for melons still warm from the morning sun, and buy glistening olives by the pailful. You can't lose when you start with an icy pastis, that pale yellow, anise-based aperitif; smear your toast with *tapenade,* a delicious paste of olives, capers, and anchovies; heap aioli, a garlicky mayonnaise, on your fresh fish; and rub thyme and garlic on your lamb. No meal is complete without a round of goat cheese, sun-ripened fruit, and a chilled bottle of rosé from the surrounding hills.

CATEGORY	COST*
$$$$	over 400 frs
$$$	250 frs–400 frs
$$	125 frs–250 frs
$	under 125 frs

per person for a three-course meal, including tax (20.6%) and tip but not wine

✎ *following the text of a review is your signal that the property has a Web site, where you will find details and, usually, images; for a link, visit www.fodors.com/urls.*

Lodging

Accommodations in this oft-visited part of France range from luxurious villas to elegantly converted *mas* (farmhouses) to modest city-center hotels. Reservations are essential for much of the year, and many hotels are closed in winter.

CATEGORY	COST*
$$$$	over 800 frs
$$$	550 frs–800 frs
$$	300 frs–550 frs
$	under 300 frs

All prices are for a standard double room for two, including tax (20.6%) and service charge.

Markets

At Provençal markets, seafood, poultry, olives, melons, and asparagus cry out to be gathered in a basket, arranged lovingly in pottery bowls, and cooked in their purest form. For picnics, stock up on tubs of tape-

nade and *anchoïade* (anchovy spread), dried game sausage, tangy marinated seafood, and tiny pucks of withered goat cheese. In fact, you
can usually also pick up any silverware, linens, pottery, and clothing
you'll need from hawkers in nearby stalls. And antiques and *brocantes*
(collectibles) are never far away, sometimes providing the most authentic
local souvenirs.

Exploring Provence

Bordered to the west by the Languedoc and melting to the south and
east into the blue waters of the Mediterranean, Provence falls easily
into four areas. The Camargue is at the heart of the first, flanked by
Nîmes and picturesque Arles to the east. Northeast of Arles, the rude
and rocky Alpilles jut upward, their hillsides green with orchards and
olive groves; here you'll find feudal Les Baux and the Greco-Roman
enclave of St-Rémy, now fashionable with the Summer People. The third
area, which falls within the boundaries of the Vaucluse, begins at Avignon and extends north to Orange and Vaison-la-Romaine, then east
to the forested slopes of the Luberon. The fourth area encompasses
Cézanne country, east of the Rhône, starting in Aix-en-Provence, then
winding southward to Marseille and east along the Mediterranean coast
to the idyllic Iles d'Hyères.

Great Itineraries

Peter Mayle's book *A Year in Provence* prescribes just that, but even
a year might not be long enough to soak up all the charm of this captivating region. In three days you can see three representative (and very
different) towns: Arles, Avignon, and St-Rémy; with seven days you
can easily add the Camargue, the Luberon, and Aix-en-Provence; with
10 days you can add Vaison-la-Romaine and Marseille. The following are suggested itineraries for touring the area; another option is to
base yourself in one place and take day trips from there.

To make the most of your time in the region, plan to divide your days
between big-city culture, backcountry tours, and waterfront leisure.
You can "do" Provence at a if-this-is-Tuesday breakneck pace, but its
back roads and tiny villages reward a much more leisurely approach.
Provence is as much a way of life as a region charged with tourist must-
sees; allow time to enjoy the old-fashioned pace of Provençal life. Hot
afternoons tend to mean siestas, with signs of life discernible only as
the shadows under the *platanes* (plane trees) start to lengthen and locals saunter out to play *boules* (the French version of boccie, or lawn
bowling) and drink long, cooling pastis.

*Numbers in the text correspond to numbers in the margin and on the
Provence, Nîmes, Arles, Avignon, and Marseille maps.*

IF YOU HAVE 3 DAYS
The best gateway to the region is **Avignon** ㉘–㉟, where tiny, narrow
streets cluster around the 14th-century Palais des Papes as if it is still
seeking the protection afforded to them when this massive structure
represented the supreme Christian authority of the world back in the
14th century. Then make an afternoon outing west to the **Pont du Gard** ①
aqueduct, a majestic relic from the ancient Romans that is more like
a work of art than a practical construction. On day two stop briefly
in **Nîmes** ②–⑩ to see the antiquities of the Arènes and the Maison Carrée—a striking contrast to this busy and commercial center—then
head into atmospheric old ☒ **Arles** ⑭–㉓, inspiration to van Gogh, who
captured the beauty of the Arlésienne, with her delicate pointed features, in some of his finest portraits. On day three drive through the
countryside, stopping at the **Abbaye de Montmajour** ㉔—whose clois-

ters are a particularly charming spot when the oleander trees are in bloom—-and the medieval hill town of **Les Baux-de-Provence** ㉕; stay overnight in ▣ **St-Rémy-de-Provence** ㉖, with its Roman ruins and van Gogh landmarks.

IF YOU HAVE 7 DAYS

Visit **Orange** ㊲ on your first day before stopping to see the **Pont du Gard** ①—both the ancient Roman theater in Orange and the famous aqueduct will allow you to travel back two millennia in time. Spend two nights in ▣ **Avignon** ㉘–㉟ and don't forget to visit the Bridge of St-Bénézet (famed in the old song "Sur le pont d'Avignon"). In the morning stop briefly in **Nîmes** ②–⑩ on your way to the fortified town of **Aigues-Mortes** ⑪ and make a slight detour through the Camargue to ▣ **Arles** ⑭–㉓. The next morning explore Arles's Roman remains. Try to get to **Les Baux-de-Provence** ㉕ by lunchtime and then continue to ▣ **St-Rémy-de-Provence** ㉖ to see where van Gogh painted. On day five wend your way through **L'Isle-sur-la-Sorgue** ㊶ to **Gordes** ㊸, in the Luberon Mountains, one of Provence's most famous *villages perchés* (perched villages). Spend the night in the hilltop village of **Bonnieux** ㊼ and drive over the windswept spine of the Luberon on your way south to ▣ **Aix-en-Provence** ㊽–㊾; spend two days there visiting the marvelous 18th-century mansions, the museums, and its Cours Mirabeau, which is to Aix what the Champs-Élysées is to Paris.

IF YOU HAVE 10 DAYS

To the seven-day itinerary, add a day visiting ruins in the Rhône-side Roman market town of **Vaison-la-Romaine** ㊳ and drive the winding back roads of the neighboring Mont Ventoux region, where fruit lands give way to forest heights. Or make a broader sweep through the Camargue to include the eccentric seaside town of **Stes-Maries-de-la-Mer** ⑬, its gloomy Romanesque church (full of Gypsy tributes to the two St. Maries and their servant girl Sarah). Then take the time to experience the urban vitality of **Marseille** ㊺–㊻, or cool your heels at the gently gentrified seaside retreat of ▣ **Cassis** ㊽.

When to Tour Provence

Spring and fall are the best months to experience the dazzling light, rugged rocky countryside, and fruitful vineyards of Provence. Though the lavender fields show peak color in mid-July, summer is beastly hot; worst, it's always crowded on the beaches and connecting roads. Winter has some nice days, when genuine locals enjoy their cafés and their town squares tourist-free, but it often rains, and the razor-sharp mistral can cut to the bone.

NÎMES, ARLES, AND THE CAMARGUE

Though Roman remains are found throughout Provence, their presence is strongest where the rivers meander their way to the sea on the region's western flank: the beautiful Pont du Gard aqueduct and the arenas in Nîmes and Arles. Just west and south of these landmarks, the Camargue is a vast watery plain formed by the sprawling Rhône delta and extending over 800 square km (300 square mi).

Pont du Gard

★ ❶ *22 km (13 mi) southwest of Avignon, 37 km (23 mi) southwest of Orange, 48 km (30 mi) north of Arles.*

No other sight in Provence rivals the Pont du Gard, a mighty, three-tiered aqueduct midway between Nîmes and Avignon. Erected some 2,000 years ago as part of a 48-km (30-mi) canal supplying water to

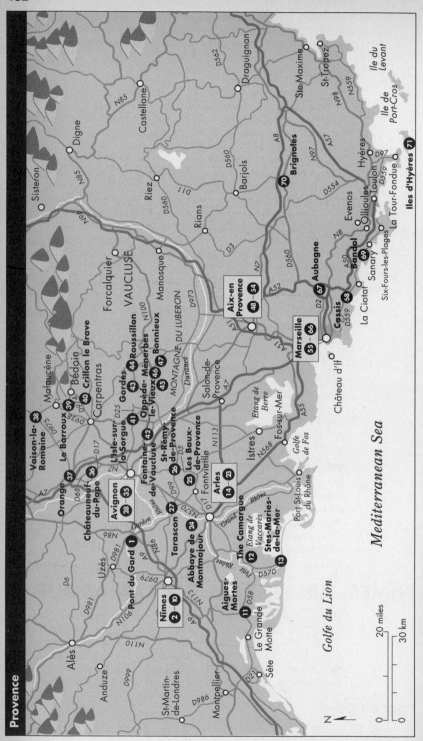

Roman Nîmes, it is astonishingly well preserved. In the early morning the site offers an amazing blend of natural and classical beauty. The rhythmic repetition of arches resonate with strength, testimony to an engineering concept relatively new in the 1st century AD, when it first was built under Emperor Claudius. Later in the day, however, crowds become a problem, even off-season. You can approach the aqueduct from either side of the Gardon River. If you choose the north side (Rive Gauche), you'll be charged 22 francs to park (stay as close to the booth as possible because unfortunately break-ins are a problem). The walk to the *pont* (bridge) is shorter and the views arguably better from here. It costs less (18 francs) to park on the south side (Rive Droite), and there's a tourist office with information and postcards—but this is also the side the tour buses prefer. Access to the spectacular walkway along the top is indefinitely blocked due to restoration work.

Nîmes

20 km (13 mi) southwest of the Pont du Gard, 43 km (26 mi) south of Avignon, 121 km (74 mi) west of Marseille, 711 km (427 mi) south of Paris.

If you've come to the south seeking Roman treasures, you need look no further than Nîmes (pronounced neem): The Arènes and Maison Carrée are among continental Europe's best-preserved antiquities. But if you have come seeking a more modern mythology—of lazy, graceful Provence—give Nîmes a wide berth. It's a feisty, run-down rat race of a town, with jalopies and Vespas roaring irreverently around the ancient temple. Its medieval old town has none of the gentrified grace of those in Arles or St-Rémy. Yet its rumpled and rebellious ways trace directly back to its Roman incarnation, when its population swelled with soldiers, arrogant and newly victorious after their conquest of Egypt in 31 BC.

Already anchoring a fiefdom of pre-Roman *oppidums* (elevated fortresses) before ceding to the empire in the 1st century BC, this ancient city grew to formidable proportions under the Pax Romana. Its next golden age bloomed under the Protestants, who established an anti-Catholic stronghold here and wreaked havoc on iconic architectural treasures—not to mention the papist minority. Their massacre of some 200 Catholic citizens is remembered as the Michelade; many of those murdered were priests sheltered in the *évêché* (bishop's house), now the Museum of Old Nîmes.

A locally produced lightweight serge (a densely woven fabric) brought fame to Nîmes more than once. Legend has it that Christopher Columbus admired its durability and used it for sails; its reputation spread, and it was exported worldwide from the ports of Genoa (Gênes in French). Levi Strauss found its sturdy texture strong enough for gold miners' pants and Americanized its name from *bleu de Gênes* to blue jeans. The now-ubiquitous fabric's name traces back to its origins: *de Nîmes*, or denim.

★ ❷ The **Arènes** (Arena) is considered the world's best-preserved Roman amphitheater. A miniature of the Colosseum in Rome, it stands more than 520 ft long and 330 ft wide, with a seating capacity of 24,000. Bloody gladiator battles and theatrical wild-boar hunts drew crowds to its bleachers. Nowadays its most colorful use is the *corrida,* the bullfight that transforms the arena (and all of Nîmes) into a sangria-flushed homage to Spain (☞ Outdoor Activities and Sports, *below*). ✉ *bd. Victor-Hugo,* ☎ *04–66–76–72–77.* 🎫 *28 frs; joint ticket to Arènes and Tour Magne 34 frs.* ☉ *May–Sept., daily 9–6:30; Oct.–Apr., daily 9–noon and 2–5.*

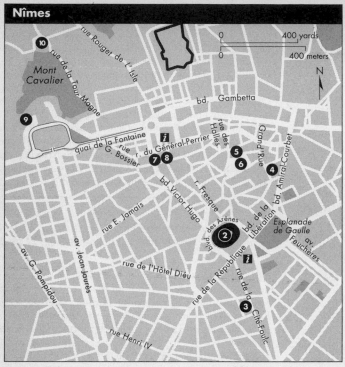

Nîmes

❸ The **Musée des Beaux-Arts** (Fine Arts Museum) contains a vast Roman mosaic; the marriage ceremony depicted provides intriguing insights into the Roman aristocratic lifestyle. Old-master paintings (by Nicolas Poussin, Pieter Brueghel, Peter Paul Rubens) and sculpture (by Auguste Rodin) form the mainstay of the collection. ⊠ *Rue de la Cité-Foulc,* ☎ *04–66–67–38–21.* ⊡ *26 frs.* ⊙ *Tues.–Sun. 11–6.*

❹ The **Musée Archéologique et d'Histoire Naturelle** (Museum of Archaeology and Natural History) is rich in local archaeological finds, mainly statues, busts, friezes, tools, coins, and pottery. ⊠ *bd. de l'Amiral-Courbet,* ☎ *04–66–67–25–57.* ⊡ *28 frs.* ⊙ *Tues.–Sun. 11–6.*

❺ Destroyed and rebuilt in several stages, with particular damage by rampaging Protestants who slaughtered eight priests from the neighboring *évêché* (bishop's house), the **Cathédrale Notre-Dame et St-Castor** (⊠ Pl. aux Herbes) still shows traces of its original construction in 1096. A miraculously preserved Romanesque frieze portrays Adam and Eve cowering in shame, the gory slaughter of Abel, and a flood-weary Noah. Inside, look for the 4th-century sarcophagus (third chapel on the right) and a magnificent 17th-century chapel (in the apse).

❻ The **Musée du Vieux Nîmes** (Museum of Old Nîmes), opposite the cathedral in the 17th-century bishop's palace, has embroidered garments in exotic and vibrant displays. Look for the 14th-century jeans jacket made of blue-serge de Nîmes, the famous fabric from which Levi-Strauss first fashioned blue jeans. ⊠ *Pl. aux Herbes,* ☎ *04–66–36–00–64.* ⊡ *28frs.* ⊙ *Tues.–Sun. 11–6.*

★ **❼** Lovely and forlorn in the middle of a busy downtown square, the exquisitely preserved **Maison Carrée** (Square House) strikes a timeless balance between symmetry and whimsy, purity of line and richness of decor. Built around 5 BC and dedicated to Caius Caesar and his grandson Lucius, it has survived subsequent use as a medieval meeting hall, an Augustine church, a storehouse for Revolutionary archives, and a horse shed. It was modeled on the Temple to Apollo in Rome. Alas, its interior now serves as a slapdash display space for temporary exhibitions. ⊠ *bd. Victor-Hugo,* ☎ *04–66–36–26–76.* ⊡ *Free.* ☉ *May–Oct., daily 9–7; Nov.–Apr., daily 9–noon and 2–6.*

The glass-fronted Carré d'Art (it's directly opposite the Maison Carrée) was designed in 1993 by British architect Sir Norman Foster as its neighbor's stark contemporary mirror: It literally reflects the Maison Carrée's creamy symmetry and figuratively answers it with a featherlight deconstructed colonnade. Homages aside, it looks like an airport (8) terminal. It serves as home to the **Musée d'Art Contemporain** (Contemporary Art Museum), featuring art dating from 1960 onward and temporary exhibits of new works. ⊠ *Pl. de la Maison Carrée,* ☎ *04–66–76–35–70.* ⊡ *28 frs.* ☉ *Tues.–Sun. 10–6.*

(9) The shattered Roman ruin known as the **Temple de Diane** (Diana's Temple) dates from the 2nd century BC. The temple's function is unknown, though it is thought to be part of a larger Roman complex that is still unexcavated. In the Middle Ages Benedictine nuns occupied the building before it was converted into a church. Destruction came during the Wars of Religion.

(10) The **Tour Magne** (Magne Tower), at the far end of the Jardin de la Fontaine, is all that remains of a tower the emperor Augustus had built on Gallic foundations; it was probably used as a lookout post. Despite a loss of 30 ft during the course of time, it still provides fine views of Nîmes for anyone energetic enough to climb the 140 steps. ⊠ *quai de la Fontaine,* ☎ *04–66–67–29–11.* ⊡ *Tour Magne 15 frs, joint ticket with Arènes 34 frs.* ☉ *May–Oct., daily 9–7; Nov.–Apr., daily 9–5.*

Dining and Lodging

$$ ✕ **Le Jardin d'Hadrien.** This enclave, with its quarried white stone, ancient plank-and-beam ceiling, and open fireplace, would be a culinary haven even without its lovely hidden garden, a shady retreat for summer meals. Fresh cod crisped in salt and olive oil, zucchini flowers filled with *brandade* (the creamy, light paste of salt cod and olive oil) and a frozen parfait perfumed with licorice all show chef Alain Vinouze's subtle skills. ⊠ *11 rue Enclos Rey,* ☎ *04–66–21–86–65. AE, MC, V.*

$ ✕ **Chez Jacotte.** Duck into an old-town back alley and into this cross-
★ vaulted grotto that embodies Nîmes's Spanish-bohemian flair. Candlelight flickering on rich tones of oxblood, ochre, and cobalt enhances the warm welcome of red-haired owner Jacotte Friand. Mouth-watering goat-cheese-and-fig gratin, mullet crisped in olive oil and basil, herb-crusted lamb, and seasonal fruit crumbles show off chef Christophe Ciantar's flair with local ingredients. ⊠ *15 rue Fresque (impasse),* ☎ *04–66–21–64–59. MC, V. Closed Sun.–Mon. No lunch Sat.*

$ ✕ **Vintage Café.** This popular old-town wine bar draws a loyal crowd of oenophiles for serious tastings and simple, compatible regional specialties—for example, hot lentil salad with smoked haddock, and pressed goat cheese terrine. Ochre, bright ceramics and warm-color lamplight enhance the artful Mediterranean decor. Summer nights on the terrace are idyllic. ⊠ *7 rue de Bernis,* ☎ *04–66–21–04–45. MC, V. Closed Sun.–Mon. No lunch Sat.*

$$ ▥ **La Baume.** In the heart of scruffy old Nîmes, this noble 17th-century *hôtel particulier* (mansion) has been reincarnated as a stylish hotel with an architect's eye for mixing ancient detail with modern design. The balustraded stone staircase is a protected historic monument, and stenciled beam ceilings, cross vaults, and archways counterbalance hot ochre tones, swagged raw cotton, leather, and halogen lights. ⊠

21 rue Nationale, 30000, ☎ *04–66–76–28–42,* FAX *04–66–76–28–45.*
33 rooms. Breakfast room, air-conditioning. AE, DC, MC, V. 🕸

$$ 🏨 **Royal Hôtel.** Jazz, Art Deco ironwork, and caged birds set the Latin
★ tone at this bohemian, shabby-chic urban hotel, where whitewash and
scrubbed concrete set off 1930s details and trendy flea-market finds.
Bathrooms are newly tiled and amenities reasonably up to date. Its Span-
ish restaurant serves tapas on the pedestrian place d'Assas, but the lobby
bar is where you'd expect to run across Picasso slumming over absinthe.
⊠ *3 bd. Alphonse Daudet, 30000,* ☎ *04–66–58–28–27,* FAX *04–66–
58–28–28. 27 rooms. Restaurant, bar. AE, MC, V.*

$ 🏨 **Amphithéâtre.** Just behind the arena, this big, solid old private
home has fortunately fallen into the hands of a loving owner, who has
stripped 18th-century double doors and fitted out rooms with re-
stored-wood details and antique bedroom sets. ⊠ *4 rue des Arènes,*
30420, ☎ *04–66–67–28–51,* FAX *04–66–67–07–79. 17 rooms. Break-*
fast room. AE, MC, V.

Outdoor Activities and Sports

The **corrida** (bullfight) is the quintessential Nîmes experience, taking
place as it does in the ancient Roman arena. There are usually three
opportunities a year, always during the carnival-like citywide *férias* (fes-
tivals): in early spring (mid-February), at Pentecost (end of May), and
during the wine harvest (end of September). For tickets and advance
information contact the Arena's *bureau de location* (ticket office; ⊠
1 rue A. Ducros, Nîmes 30900, ☎ 04–66–67–28–02).

Shopping

The only authentic commercial maker of brandade, Nîmes's signature
salt-cod-and-olive-oil paste, is **Raymond** (⊠ 24 rue Nationale, ☎ 04–
66–67–20–47). It's paddled fresh into a plastic carton or sold in sealed
jars so you can take it home.

Aigues-Mortes

⓫ *13 km (8 mi) east of La Grande Motte, 41 km (25 mi) south of Nîmes,*
48 km (30 mi) southwest of Arles.

Like a tiny illumination in a medieval manuscript, Aigues-Mortes is a
precise and perfect miniature fortress-town, contained within symmetrical
crenellated walls, with streets laid out in geometric grids. Now awash
in a flat wasteland of sand, salt, and monotonous marsh, it once was
a major port town from which no less than St-Louis himself (Louis IX)
set sail to conquer Jerusalem in the 13th century. In 1248 some 35,000
zealous men launched 1,500 ships for Cyprus, engaging the infidel on
his own turf and suffering swift defeat; Louis himself was briefly taken
prisoner. A second launching in 1270 led to more crushing loss, and
Louis succumbed to the plague.

Louis's state-of-the-art **fortress-port** remains astonishingly well preserved.
Its stout walls now contain a small Provençal village milling with
tourists, but the visit is more than justified by the impressive scale of
the original structure. ⊠ *Porte de la Gardette,* ☎ *04–66–53–61–55.*
🎫 *32 frs.* ☉ *Easter–late May, daily 10–6; late May–mid-Sept., daily*
9:30–8; mid-Sept.–Easter, daily 10–5.

It's not surprising that the town within the rampart walls has become
tourist oriented, with the usual plethora of gift shops and postcard stands.
But **place St-Louis,** where a 19th-century statue of the father of the fleur-
de-lis reigns under shady pollards, has a mellow village feel. The pretty,
bare-bones **Église Notre-Dame des Sablons,** on one corner of the
square, has a timeless air (it dates from the 13th century, but the
stained glass is ultramodern).

Dining and Lodging

$$$ ✗🏠 **Les Arcades.** Long a success as an upscale seafood restaurant, this
★ beautifully preserved 16th-century house now has big, airy rooms, some
with tall windows overlooking a green courtyard. Pristine white-stone
walls, color-stained woodwork, and rubbed-ochre walls frame an-
tiques and lush fabrics. Classic cooking features lotte (monkfish) in saf-
fron and poached turbot in hollandaise. ✉ *23 bd. Gambetta, 30220,*
☎ *04–66–53–81–13,* 🆇 *04–66–53–75–46. 9 rooms. Restaurant, air-
conditioning, pool. AE, DC, MC, V.*

$$ 🏠 **Les Templiers.** In a 17th-century residence within the ramparts, this
delightful hotel sets the stage with stone, stucco, and terra-cotta floors.
Furnishings are classically simple and softened with antiques. On the
ground floor are two small, cozy sitting areas; breakfast, weather per-
mitting, is served in the small courtyard. ✉ *23 rue de la République,
30220,* ☎ *04–66–53–66–56,* 🆇 *04–66–53–69–61. 11 rooms. Air-
conditioning, parking. MC, V. Closed Nov.–Feb.*

The Camargue

⑫ *19 km (12 mi) east of Aigues-Mortes, 15 km (9 mi) south of Arles.*

For about 800 square km (309 square mi), the vast alluvial delta of
the Rhône known as the Camargue stretches to the horizon, an austere marshland unrelievedly flat, scoured by the mistral and swarmed
over by mosquitoes. Between the endless flow of sediment from the
Rhône and the erosive force of the sea, its shape is constantly changing. Even the Provençal poet Frederic Mistral described it in bleak terms:
"Ni arbre, ni ombre, ni âme" (Neither tree, nor shade, nor a soul).

Yet its harsh landscape harbors a concentration of exotic wildlife
unique in Europe, and its isolation has given birth to an ascetic and
ancient way of life that transcends national stereotype. It's a strange
region, one worth discovering slowly, either on foot or by horseback—
especially as its wildest reaches are inaccessible by car. If people find
the Camargue interesting, birds find it irresistible. Its protected marshes
lure some 400 species, including more than 160 in migration. As you
drive the scarce roads that barely crisscross the Camargue, you'll usually be within the boundaries of the **Parc Regional de Camargue.** Unlike state and national parks in the United States, this area is privately
owned and utilized within rules imposed by the French government.
The principal owners are the *manadiers* (the Camargue equivalent of
a small-scale rancher) and their *gardians* (a kind of open-range cow-
boy), who keep it for grazing their wide-horn bulls and their dappled-
white horses. When it's not participating in a bloodless bullfight
(mounted players try to hook a red ribbon from its horns), a bull may
well end up in the wine-rich regional stew called *gardianne de taureau.*
Riding through the marshlands in leather pants and wide-rimmed
black hats and wielding long prongs to prod their cattle, the gardians
themselves are as fascinating as the wildlife. Their homes—tiny and
whitewashed—dot the countryside.

The easiest place to view bird life is in a private reserve just outside
the regional park called the **Parc Ornithologique du Pont de Gau** (Pont
du Gau Ornithological Park). On some 150 acres of marsh and salt
lands, birds are welcomed and protected (but in no way confined); in-
jured birds are treated and kept in large pens, to be released if and when
able. A series of boardwalks (including a short, child-friendly inner loop)
snakes over the wetlands, the longest leading to a blind, where a half
hour of silence, binoculars in hand, can reveal unsuspected treasures.
☎ *04–90–97–82–62.* 💰 *35 frs.* ☉ *Oct.–Mar., daily 10–sunset; Apr.–
Sept., daily 9–sunset.*

If you're an even more committed nature lover, venture into the inner sanctum of the Camargue, the **Réserve Nationale de Camargue.** This intensely protected area contains the central pond called **Le Vaccarès,** mostly used for approved scientific research. Pick up maps and information at the **Centre d'Information** (☎ 04–90–97–86–32, 𝙵𝙰𝚇 04–90–97–70–82), open April–September, daily 9–6 and October–March, Saturday–Thursday 9:30–5; it's just up D570 from the Parc Ornithologique. To explore this area, you'll have to strike out on foot, bicycle, or horseback (the **Association Camarguaise de Tourisme Equestre** publishes a list of stables where you can rent horses, available at the information center or the Stes-Maries tourist office). Note that you are not allowed to diverge from marked trails.

Stes-Maries-de-la-Mer

⑬ *32 km (20 mi) southeast of Aigues-Mortes, 129 km (80 mi) west of Marseille, 39 km (24 mi) south of Arles.*

The principal town within the confines of the Parc Régional de Camargue, Stes-Maries is a beach resort with a fascinating history. Provençal legend has it that around AD 45 a band of the very first Christians were rounded up and set adrift at sea in a boat without a sail and without provisions. Their stellar ranks included Mary Magdalene, Martha, and Mary Salome, mother of apostles James and John; Mary Jacoby, sister of the Virgin; and Lazarus, not necessarily the one risen from the dead. Joining them in their fate was a dark-skinned servant girl named Sarah. Miraculously, their boat washed ashore at this ancient site, and the grateful Marys built a chapel in thanks. The pilgrims attracted to Stes-Maries aren't all lighting candles to the two St. Marys: Sarah has been adopted as an honorary saint by the Gypsies of the world. Two extraordinary festivals celebrating the Marys take place every year in Stes-Maries, one on May 24–25 and the other on the Sunday nearest to October 22.

★ On entering the damp, dark, and forbidding fortress-church, **Église des Stes-Maries,** what is most striking is its novel character. Almost devoid of windows, its tall, barren single nave is cluttered with florid and sentimental ex-votos (tokens of blessings, prayers, and thanks) and primitive and sentimental artworks of the famous trio. Another oddity brings you back to the 20th century: A sign on the door forbids visitors to come *torso nu* (topless). For outside its otherworldly role, Stes-Maries is first and foremost a beach resort: dead flat, whitewashed, and more than a little tacky. Unless you've made a pilgrimage to the sun and sand, don't spend much time in the town center; if you've chosen Stes-Maries as a base for viewing the Camargue, stay in one of the discreet *mas* (country inns) outside its city limits.

Lodging

$$ 🏠 **Mas de Cacharel.** On 170 acres of private marshland bordering
★ the Réserve Départemental de Camargue, this low-slung, low-key haven is well set back from D85 just north of Stes-Maries. A simple retreat, it has a lodgelike central breakfast hall complete with Provençal furniture and a pleasantly smoky grand fireplace. Spartan rooms are arranged motor-court style, so most have windows that overlook the eternal stretch of reeds and birds. ✉ *13460 Stes-Maries de la Mer (4 km [2 mi] north of town on D85),* ☎ *04–90–97–95–44,* 𝙵𝙰𝚇 *04–90–97–87–97. 15 rooms. Bar, breakfast room, pool, horseback riding. MC, V.*

Arles

38 km (24 mi) north of Stes-Maries-de-la-Mer, 92 km (57 mi) north-west of Marseille, 36 km (22 mi) south of Avignon, 31 km (19 mi) east of Nîmes.

If you were obliged to choose just one city to visit in Provence, lovely little Arles would give Avignon and Aix a run for their money. It's too chic to become museumlike yet has a wealth of classical antiquities and Romanesque stonework, quarried-stone edifices and shuttered town houses, and graceful, shady old-town streets and squares. Throughout the year there are pageantry, festivals, and cutting-edge arts events. Its variety of atmospheric restaurants and picturesque small hotels makes it the ideal headquarters for forays into the Alpilles and the Camargue.

A Greek colony since the 6th century BC, little Arles took a giant step forward when Julius Caesar defeated Marseille in the 1st century BC. The emperor-to-be designated Arles a Roman colony and lavished funds and engineering know-how on it. It became an international crossroads by sea and land and a market to the world, with goods from Africa, Arabia, and the Far East. The emperor Constantine himself moved to Arles and brought with him Christianity.

The remains of this golden age are reason enough to visit Arles today, yet its character nowadays is as gracious and low-key as it once was cutting edge. Seated in the shade of the plane trees on place du Forum or strolling the rampart walkway along the sparkling Rhône, you'll see what enchanted Gauguin and drove van Gogh mad with inspiration.

Note: If you plan to visit many of the monuments and museums in Arles, buy a *visite generale* ticket for 55 francs. This covers the 35-franc entry fee to the Musée de l'Arles Antique and any and all of the other museums and monuments (except the independent Museon Arlaten), which normally charge 15 francs each per visit. It's good for the length of your stay.

★ ⑭ Though it's a hike from the center, a good place to set the tone and context for your exploration of Arles is at the state-of-the-art **Musée de l'Arles Antique** (Museum of Ancient Arles). The bold, modern triangular-shape structure was built in 1995 on the site of an enormous Roman *cirque* (chariot-racing stadium). You'll learn about all the aspects of Arles in its heyday, from the development of its monuments to the details of daily life in Roman times. Ask for the English-language guidebook. ⊠ *Presqu'île du Cirque Romain,* ☎ *04–90–18–88–88.* 🖾 *35 frs.* ☉ *Apr.–mid-Oct., daily 9–7; mid-Sept.–Mar., daily 10–5.*

⑮ A good way to plunge into post-Roman Arles is through the quirky old **Museon Arlaten** (Museum of Arles). Created by the father of the Provençal revival, turn-of-the-century poet Frédéric Mistral, it enshrines a seemingly bottomless collection of regional treasures. Following Mistral's wishes, women in full Arlésienne costume oversee the labyrinth of lovely 16th-century halls. ⊠ *29 rue de la République,* ☎ *04–90–93–58–11.* 🖾 *25 frs.* ☉ *Apr.–Sept, daily 9:30–12:30 and 2–6; Oct.–Mar., Tues.–Sun. 10–12:30 and 2–5:30.*

⑯ At the entrance to a 17th-century Jesuit college, you can access the ancient underground galleries called the **Cryptoportiques.** Dating from 30 BC to 20 BC, this horseshoe of vaults and pillars buttressed the ancient forum from underneath. Yet openings let in natural daylight, and artworks of considerable merit and worth were unearthed here, adding to the mystery of these passages' true function. ⊠ *Rue Balze,* ☎ *04–90–49–36–74.* 🖾 *15 frs.* ☉ *Apr.–Sept. daily 9–7; Oct.–Mar., daily 10–4:30.*

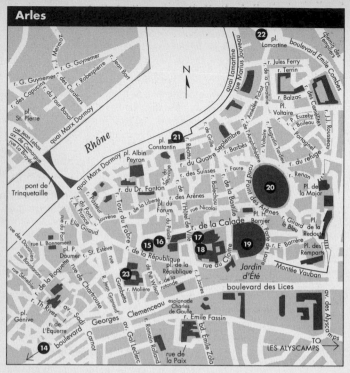

Arles

★ **17** Classed as a world treasure by UNESCO, the extraordinary Romanesque **Église St-Trophime** (⊠ Pl. de la République) alone would justify a visit to Arles, though it's continually upstaged by the antiquities around it. Its transepts date from the 11th century and its nave from the 12th; the church's austere symmetry and ancient artworks (including a stunningly Roman-style 4th-century sarcophagus) are fascinating in themselves. But it is the church's superbly preserved Romanesque sculpture on the 12th-century **portal**—its entry facade—that earns it international respect.

18 Tucked discreetly behind St-Trophime is a peaceful haven, the **Cloître St-Trophime** (St-Trophime Cloister). A Romanesque treasure worthy of the church, it's one of the loveliest cloisters in Provence. ☎ 04–90–49–36–74. ▣ 15 frs. ☉ Apr.–Sept., daily 9–7; Oct.–Mar., daily 10–4:30.

19 Directly up rue de la Calade from place de la République are the picturesque ruins of the **Théâtre Antique** (Ancient Theater), built by the Romans under Augustus in the 1st century BC. Now overgrown and a pleasant, parklike retreat, it once served as an entertainment venue to some 20,000 spectators. Today it serves as a concert stage for the Festival d'Arles (in July and August) and a venue for the Recontres Internationales de la Photographie (Photography Festival). ⊠ Rue de la Calade, ☎ 04–90–49–36–74. ▣ 15 frs. ☉ Apr.–Sept., daily 9–7; Oct.–Mar., daily 10–4:30.

20 Rivaled only by the even better-preserved version in Nîmes, the **Arènes** (Arena) dominates old Arles. Its four medieval towers are testimony to its transformation from classical sports arena to feudal fortification in the middle ages. Younger than Arles's theater, it dates from the 1st century AD, and unlike the theater, seats 20,000 to this day. Its primary function is as a venue for the traditional spectacle of the corridas, or bullfights, which take place annually during the *feria pascale,* or Easter festival. ⊠ *Rond Point des Arènes*, ☎ *04–90–49–36–74.* 🖅 *15 frs.* ☉ *Apr.–Sept., daily 9–7; Oct.–Mar., daily 10–4:30.*

Though it makes every effort today to make up for its misjudgment, Arles treated Vincent van Gogh very badly during the time he passed here near the end of his life. It was 1888 when he settled in to work in Arles with an intensity and tempestuousness that drove away his colleague and companion Paul Gauguin and alienated his neighbors. In 1889 the people of Arles circulated a petition to have him evicted, a shock that left him more and more at a loss to cope with life and led to his voluntary commitment to an insane asylum in nearby St-Rémy. Thus Arles can't boast a single van Gogh painting—but did they have to name their art museum after Jacques Réattu, a local painter of con-

㉑ firmed mediocrity? The **Musée Réattu** lavishes three rooms on his turn-of-the-19th-century ephemera but redeems itself with a decent collection of 20th-century works. The best thing about the Réattu may be the building, a Knights of Malta priory dating from the 15th century. ⊠ *Rue Grand Prieuré*, ☎ *04–90–49–36–74.* 🖅 *15 frs.* ☉ *Apr.–Sept., daily 9–7; Oct.–Mar., daily 10–4:30.*

You'll have to go to Amsterdam to view van Goghs. But the city has provided helpful markers and a numbered itinerary to guide you from one landmark to another—many of them recognizable from beloved

㉒ canvases. You can stand on **place Lamartine** (between the rail station and the ramparts), where he lived in the famous Maison Jaune (Yellow House); it was destroyed by bombs in 1944. *Starry Night* may have been painted from the quai du Rhône just off place Lamartine. The most strikingly resonant site, impeccably restored and landscaped to match one of van Gogh's paintings, is the courtyard garden of what

㉓ is now the **Espace van Gogh** (⊠ Pl. Dr. Félix Rey), featured in *Le Jardin de l'Hôtel-Dieu*. This was the hospital to which the tortured artist repaired after cutting off his earlobe (contrary to myth, he didn't cut off his entire ear and, in fact, made the desperate gesture to Gauguin, whom he had come to idolize, following the fashion in Provencal bullrings for a matador to present his lady love with an ear from a dispatched bull) and its cloistered grounds have become something of a shrine for visitors.

OFF THE **LES ALYSCAMPS –** Though this romantically melancholy Roman cemetery
BEATEN PATH lies away from the old town, it's worth the hike—certainly, vaan Gogh thought so, as several of his famous canvases prove. This long necropolis amassed the remains of the dead from antiquity to the Middle Ages. Greek, Roman, and Christian tombs line the long shady road that was once the entry to Arles—the Aurelian Way. ☎ *04–90–49–36–74.* 🖅 *15 frs.* ☉ *Apr.–Sept., daily 9–7; Oct.–Mar., daily 10–4:30.*

Dining and Lodging

$$$ ✕ **Le Vaccarès.** Claim a shaded table on place du Forum at this sought-after summer spot and enjoy an elegant lunch with other Arles elite; by night it's downright glamorous. The Dumas men—grandfather, father, and son—have been creating sophisticated Provençal specialties for aeons without going stale. ⊠ *Pl. du Forum*, ☎ 04–90–96–06–17. MC, V. Closed mid-Jan.–mid-Feb. No dinner Sun. No lunch Mon.

$$ ✕ **Brasserie Nord-Pinus.** With its tile-and-ironwork interior straight
★ out of a design magazine and its place du Forum terrace packed with all the right people, this cozy-chic retro brasserie features the superb but unpretentious cooking of Jean-André Charial, trained at the hallowed L'Oustau de la Baumanière (☞ Les Baux-de-Provence, *below*). The cuisine is light, simple, and purely Provençal. ⊠ *Pl. du Forum*, ☎

04–90–93–44–44. Reservations essential. AE, DC, MC, V. Closed Feb. and Wed. Nov.–Mar.

$$ ✕ **La Gueule du Loup.** Serving as hosts, waiters, and chefs, the ambitious couple who own this restaurant tackle serious cooking—monkfish and squid in saffron, lamb in pastry lined with tapenade, and crème brûlée perfumed with orange blossoms. Jazz music and vintage magic posters bring the old Arles stone-and-beam setting up to date. ✉ *39 rue des Arènes,* ☎ *04–90–96–96–69. MC, V. Closed Sun.–Mon. Oct.–Mar.; closed Sun. Apr.–Sept. No lunch Mon.*

$ ✕ **L'Affenage.** A vast smorgasbord of Provençal hors d'oeuvres draws loyal locals to this former fire-horse shed. They come here for heaping plates of fried eggplant, tapenade, chickpeas in cumin, and a slab of ham carved off the bone. In summer you can opt for just the first-course buffet and go back for thirds; reserve a terrace table out front. ✉ *4 rue Molière,* ☎ *04–90–96–07–67. AE, MC, V. Closed Sun. and 3 wks in Aug.*

$$$$ ✕⊞ **Le Mas de Peint.** This may be the ultimate mas experience, set as it is in a 17th-century farmhouse on some 1,250 acres of Camargue ranch land. Luxurious Provençal fabrics and antiques grace the old stone floors. Rooms are lavished with brass beds, monogrammed linens, even canopied bathtubs. At dinner time guests gather in the kitchen for sophisticated specialties using home-grown products. Diners not staying in the hotel are welcomed into the kitchen, too, for lunch or dinner; the restaurant ($$) is closed Wednesday, and advance reservations are required. ✉ *Le Sambuc, 13200 Arles (20 km [12 mi] south of town),* ☎ *04–90–97–20–62,* FAX *04–90–97–22–20. 8 rooms, 3 apartments. Restaurant, air-conditioning, pool, horseback riding. AE, DC, MC, V. Closed mid-Jan.–mid-Mar.* ✍

$$$$ ⊞ **Jules César.** This elegant landmark, once a Carmelite convent but styled like a Roman palace, anchors the lively boulevard des Lices. Low-slung, with rooms on the small side, it's not a grand luxury palace; rather, it's an intimate, traditional hotel, conservatively decorated with richly printed fabrics and burnished woodwork. Some windows look over the pool and some over the pretty cloister, where breakfast is served under a vaulted stone arcade. ✉ *Bd. des Lices, 13200,* ☎ *04–90–93–43–20,* FAX *04–90–93–33–47. 49 rooms, 5 suites. Restaurant, air-conditioning, pool. AE, DC, MC, V. Closed mid-Nov.–late Dec.*

$$$$ ⊞ **Nord-Pinus.** J. Peterman would feel right at home in this quintessen-
★ tially Mediterranean hotel on place du Forum; Hemingway did. Travel relics, kilims, oil jars, angular wrought iron, and colorful ceramics create a richly atmospheric stage set. Its scruffy art director's chic is not for everyone: Traditionalists should head for the mainstream luxuries of the Jules César (☞ *above*). ✉ *Pl. du Forum, 13200,* ☎ *04–90–93–44–44,* FAX *04–90–93–34–00. 25 rooms. Bar, brasserie. AE, DC, MC, V.* ✍

$$$ ⊞ **Arlatan.** Once home to the counts of Arlatan, this noble 15th-century stone house stands on the site of a 4th-century basilica. Rows of rooms horseshoe around a fountain courtyard, each decorated with a lovely, light hand. Recent renovations have added seven modern rooms and pretty new breakfast salons, and a pool is in the works. ✉ *26 rue du Sauvage, 13200,* ☎ *04–90–93–56–66,* FAX *04–90–49–68–45. 33 rooms, 7 suites. Bar, dining room. AE, DC, MC, V.*

$ ⊞ **Le Cloître.** Built as the private home for the head of the Cloisters, this grand old medieval building has luckily fallen into the hands of a couple devoted to making the most of its historic details—with their own bare hands. They've chipped away plaster from pristine quarried stone walls, cleaned massive beams, restored tile stairs, and mixed natural chalk and ochre to plaster the walls. ✉ *16 rue du Cloître, 13200,* ☎ *04–90–96–29–50,* FAX *04–90–96–02–88. 30 rooms. AE, MC, V.*

$
★
Muette. With 12th-century exposed stone walls, a 15th-century spiral stair, weathered wood, and an old-town setting, a hotelier wouldn't have to try very hard to please. But the couple who own this place do: Hand-stripped doors, antiques, fresh white-and-blue-tile baths, hair dryers, good mattresses, Provençal prints, and fresh sunflowers in every room show they care. ⊠ *15 rue des Suisses, 13200,* ☎ *04–90–96–15–39,* FAX *04–90–49–73–16. 18 rooms. AE, MC, V.* 🕸

Nightlife and the Arts

To find out what's happening in and around Arles (even as far away as Nîmes and Avignon), the free weekly **Le César** lists films, plays, cabarets, and jazz and rock events. It's distributed at the tourist office and in bars, clubs, and cinemas. In high season the cafés stay lively till the wee hours; in winter the streets empty out by 11. **Le Cargo de Nuit** (⊠ 7 av. Sadi-Carnot, ☎ 04–90–49–55–99) is the main venue for live jazz, reggae, and rock, with a dance floor next to the stage. Though Arles seems to be one big sidewalk café in warm weather, the place to drink is the hip bar **Le Cintra,** in the Hôtel Nord-Pinus (☞ *above*).

THE ALPILLES AND THE RHÔNE FORTRESSES

The low mountain range called the Alpilles (pronounced ahl-*pee*-yuh) forms a rough-hewn, rocky landscape that rises into nearly barren limestone hills, the flanking fields silvered with ranks of twisted olive trees and alleys of gnarled *amandiers* (almond trees). There are superb antiquities in St-Rémy and feudal ruins in Les Baux. West of the Alpilles, the fortresses of Tarascon and Beaucaire guard the Rhône between Avignon and the sea.

Abbaye de Montmajour

㉔ *5 km (3 mi) northeast of Arles, 17 km (10½ mi) south of Tarascon*

An extraordinary structure looming over the marshlands north of Arles, this magnificent Romanesque abbey stands in partial ruin. Begun in the 12th-century by a handful of Benedictine monks, it grew according to an ambitious plan of church, crypt, and cloister. Under corrupt lay monks in the 17th century, it grew more sumptuous; when those lay monks were ejected by the church, they sacked the place. After the Revolution it was sold to a junkman, and he tried to pay the mortgage by stripping off and selling its goods. A 19th-century medieval revival spurred its partial restoration, but its 18th-century portions remain in ruins. Ironically, because of this mercenary history, what remains is a spare and beautiful piece of Romanesque architecture. The **cloister** rivals that of St-Trophime in Arles for its balance, elegance, and air of mystical peace: van Gogh was drawn to its womblike isolation and came often to the abbey to paint and reflect. ☎ *04–90–54–64–17.* 🖃 *32 frs.* 🕐 *Apr.–Sept., daily 9–7; Oct.–Mar., Wed.–Mon. 10–1 and 2–5.*

Les Baux-de-Provence

★ **㉕** *18 km (11 mi) northeast of Arles, 29 km (18 mi) south of Avignon.*

When you first search the craggy hilltops for signs of Les Baux-de-Provence (pronounced lay-bo), you may not quite be able to distinguish between bedrock and building, so naturally do the ragged skyline of towers and crenellation blend into the sawtooth jags of stone. This tiny château-village ranks as one of the most visited tourist sites in France, a tour-de-force blend of natural setting and medieval ambience of astonishing beauty.

From this intimidating vantage point, the lords of Les Baux ruled throughout the 11th and 12th centuries over one of the largest fiefdoms in the south. Only in the 19th century did Les Baux find new purpose: The mineral bauxite, valued as an alloy in aluminum production, was discovered in its hills and named for its source. A profitable industry sprang up that lasted into the 20th century before fading into history.

Today Les Baux offers two faces to the world: its beautifully preserved medieval village and the ghostly ruins of its fortress, once referred to as the *ville morte* (dead town). In the village, lovely 12th-century stone houses, even their window frames still intact, shelter the shops, cafés, and galleries that line the steep cobbled streets.

The 17-acre cliff-top sprawl of ruins is contained under the umbrella name the **Château des Baux.** At the entry, the Tour du Brau contains the **Musée d'Histoire des Baux,** a small collection of relics and models. Its exit gives access to the wide and varied grounds, where Romanesque chapels and towers mingle with skeletal ruins. The tiny **Chapelle St-Blaise** shelters a permanent music-and-slide show called *Van Gogh, Gauguin, Cézanne au Pays de l'Olivier,* of artworks depicting olive orchards in their infinite variety. ☎ 04-90-54-55-56. 🖃 36 frs. ⊙ *Mar.–June and Sept.–Oct., daily 9–7; July–Aug., daily 9 AM–9:30 PM; Nov. and Feb., daily 9–6; Dec.–Jan., daily 9–5.*

Dining and Lodging

$$$$ ✕🏠 **L'Oustau de la Baumanière.** Sheltered by rocky cliffs below the ★ village of Les Baux, this long-famous hotel, with its formal landscaped terrace and broad swimming pool, has the air of a Roman palazzo. Chef Jean-André Charial's hallowed reputation continues to attract culinary pilgrims. Be sure to make reservations. Note that from November to December and in March the restaurant is closed Wednesday and doesn't serve lunch Thursday; during January and February both the hotel and restaurant are closed. In three buildings on broad landscaped grounds, rooms are breezy, private, and beautifully furnished with antiques. ⊠ *Val d'Enfer, 13520,* ☎ *04-90-54-33-07,* FAX *04-90-54-40-46. 22 rooms. Restaurant, pool, 2 tennis courts, horseback riding. AE, DC, MC, V. Closed mid-Jan.–Feb.* 🍴

$ ✕🏠 **La Reine Jeanne.** At this modest but majestically placed inn right at the entrance to the village, you can stand on balconies and look over rugged views worthy of the châteaux up the street. Rooms are small, simple, and—despite the white vinyl-padded furniture—lovingly decorated. Reserve in advance for one of the two rooms with a balcony, though even one of the tiny interior rooms gives you the right to spend an evening in Les Baux after the tourists have drained away. Good home-style cooking is served in the restaurant, which has views both from inside and outside on the pretty terrace. ⊠ *13520,* ☎ *04-90-54-32-06,* FAX *04-90-54-32-33. 10 rooms. Restaurant. MC, V.*

$$$ 🏠 **Mas de L'Oulivié.** Built to look ancient, with recycled roof tiles and hand-waxed chalk walls, this mas is clarity itself, with a cool, clean look and a low-key ambience. There's no upscale restaurant—just easy and unpretentious lunches by the pool (grilled meats, salads, and goat cheese). Eight rooms on the upper floor of the main house are pretty enough, with floral-print curtains and rich carpets, but ask for one with doors opening onto the lavender gardens and olive groves. ⊠ *Below Les Baux, D27 direction Fontvieille, Les Arcoules, 13520,* ☎ *04-90-54-35-78,* FAX *04-90-54-44-31. 22 rooms, 1 suite. Restaurant, air-conditioning, pool, tennis. AE, DC, MC, V. Closed Dec.–Feb.* 🍴

St-Rémy-de-Provence

★ **26** *8 km (5 mi) north of Les Baux, 24 km (15 mi) east of Arles, 19 km (12 mi) south of Avignon.*

Something felicitous has happened in this market town in the heart of the Alpilles—a steady infusion of style, of art, of imagination—all brought by people with a respect for local traditions and a love of Provençal ways. Here more than anywhere you can meditate quietly on antiquity, browse redolent markets with basket in hand, and enjoy urbane galleries, cosmopolitan shops, and specialty food boutiques. An abundance of choices in restaurants, mas, and even châteaux awaits you; the almond and olive groves conceal dozens of stone-and-terra-cotta gîtes, many with pools.

First established by an indigenous Celtic-Ligurian people who worshiped the god Glan, the village Glanum was adopted and gentrified by the Greeks of Marseille in the 2nd and 3rd centuries before Christ. Rome moved in to help ward off Hannibal, and by the 1st century BC Caesar had taken full control. The Via Domitia, linking Italy to Spain, passed by its doors, and the main trans-Alpine pass emptied into its entrance gate. Under the Pax Romana there developed a veritable city, complete with temples and forum, luxurious villas and baths.

The Romans eventually fell, but a town grew up next to their ruins, taking its name from their protectorate Abbey St-Remi, in Reims. It grew to be an important market town, and wealthy families built fine mansions in its center—among them the family de Sade (whose black sheep relation held forth in the Lubéron at Lacoste). Another famous native son was the eccentric doctor, scholar, and astrologist Michel Nostradamus (1503–66), who is credited by some as having predicted much of the modern age.

Perhaps the best known of St-Rémy's residents was the ill-fated Vincent van Gogh. Shipped unceremoniously out of Arles at the height of his madness (and creativity), he committed himself to the asylum St-Paul-de-Mausolé.

To approach Glanum, you must park in a dusty roadside lot on D5 south of town (in the direction of Les Baux). But before crossing, you'll be confronted with two of the most miraculously preserved classical monuments in France, simply called **Les Antiques.** Dating from 30 BC, the **Mausolée** (mausoleum), a wedding-cake stack of arches and columns, lacks nothing but its finial on top, yet it is dedicated to a Julian (as in Julius Caesar), probably Caesar Augustus. A few yards away stands another marvel: the **Arc Triomphal,** dating from AD 20.

Across the street from Les Antiques and set back from D5, a slick visitor center prepares you for entry into the ancient village of **Glanum** with scale models of the site in its various heydays. A good map and an English brochure guide you stone by stone through the maze of foundations, walls, towers, and columns that spread across a broad field; Greek sites are helpfully noted by numbers, Roman by letters. ⊠ *Off D5, direction Les Baux, info phone at Hôtel de Sade (☞ below),* ☎ *04–90–92–64–04.* ▧ *32 frs. (36 frs includes entry to Hôtel de Sade).* ☉ *Apr.–Sept., daily 9–7; Oct.–Mar., daily 9–noon and 2–5.*

You can cut across the fields from Glanum to **St-Paul-de-Mausolée,** the lovely, isolated asylum where van Gogh spent the last year of his life (1889–90). But enter it quietly: It shelters psychiatric patients to this day—all of them women. You're free to walk up the beautifully manicured garden path to the church and its jewel-box Romanesque **cloister,** where the artist found womblike peace. ⊠ *Next to Glanum, off*

D5, direction Les Baux, ☎ *04–90–92–77–00.* 🎫 *15 frs.* ⊙ *May–Sept., daily 8–7; Oct.–Apr., daily 8–5.*

Within St-Rémy's fast-moving traffic loop, a labyrinth of narrow streets leads you away from the action and into the slow-moving inner sanctum of the **Vieille Ville** (old town). Here trendy, high-end shops mingle pleasantly with local life, and the buildings, if gentrified, blend unobtrusively.

Make your way to the **Hôtel de Sade,** a 15th- and 16th-century private manor now housing the treasures unearthed with the ruins of Glanum. The de Sade family built the house around remains of 4th-century baths and a 5th-century baptistery, now nestled in its courtyard. ⊠ *Rue du Parage,* ☎ *04–90–92–64–04.* 🎫 *15 frs (36 frs includes Glanum entry).* ⊙ *Feb.–Mar. and Oct., Tues.–Sun. 10–noon and 2–5; Apr.–Sept., Tues.–Sun. 10–noon and 2–6; Nov.–Dec., Wed. and weekends 10–noon and 2–5.*

Dining and Lodging

$$–$$$ ✕ **Maison Jaune.** This modern retreat in the old town draws crowds of summer people to its pretty roof terrace, with a decor of sober stone and lively contemporary furniture both indoors and out. The look reflects the cuisine: With vivid flavors and a cool, contained touch, chef François Perraud prepares grilled sardines with crunchy fennel and lemon confit, and veal lightly flavored with olives, capers, and celery. ⊠ *15 rue Carnot,* ☎ *04–90–92–56–14. Reservations essential. MC, V. Closed Mon. No lunch Tues.*

$–$$ ✕ **L'Assiette de Marie.** Marie Ricco is a collector, and she's turned her
★ tiny restaurant into a bower of attic treasures. Seated at an old school desk, you choose from the day's specials, all made with Marie's Corsican-Italian touch—marinated vegetables with tapenade, a cast-iron casserole of superb pasta, satiny *panetone* (flan). ⊠ *1 rue Jaume Roux,* ☎ *04–90–92–32–14. Reservations essential in high season. MC, V. Closed Mon. Nov.–Easter. No lunch Tues.*

$ ✕ **La Gousse d'Ail.** Another intimate, indoor old-town hideaway, this family-run bistro lives up to its name (the Garlic Clove), serving robust, highly flavored southern dishes in hearty portions. Aim for Thursday night, when there are Gypsy music and jazz. ⊠ *25 rue Carnot,* ☎ *04–90–92–16–87. AE, MC, V. Closed Jan.–Feb. except occasional weekends.*

$$$$ ✕🏨 **Domaine de Valmouriane.** In this genteel mas-cum-resort, beauti-
★ fully isolated on a broad park, overstuffed English-country decor mixes cozily with cool Provençal stone and timber. The restaurant features chef Pierre Walter, who vies to please with fresh game, seafood, local oils, and truffles; his desserts have won him national standing. But it's the personal welcome from English owner Judith McHugo that makes you feel like a weekend guest. ⊠ *Petite rte. des Baux (D27), 13210,* ☎ *04–90–92–44–62,* FAX *04–90–92–37–32. 14 rooms. Restaurant, outdoor pool, hot tub, steam room, tennis court, billiards. AE, DC, MC, V.* 🐾

$$$$ 🏨 **Château des Alpilles.** At the end of an alley of grand old plane trees, this early 19th-century manor house lords over a vast park off D31. If its public spaces and atmosphere are cool and spare to the point of sparseness, rooms are warm and fussy, with lush Provençal prints and polished antiques. Outer buildings offer jazzy-modern apartments with kitchenettes, and the poolside grill gives you a noble perspective over the park. ⊠ *Ancienne rte. du Grès, 13210,* ☎ *04–90–92–03–33,* FAX *04–90–92–45–17. 15 rooms, 4 suites. Pool, sauna, 2 tennis courts. AE, DC, MC, V. Closed mid-Nov.–mid-Dec. and Jan.–mid-Feb.*

$$$ ⊞ **Mas de Cornud.** An American mans the wine cellar and an Egyptian runs the professional kitchen (by request only), but the attitude is pure Provence: David and Nito Carpita have turned their farmhouse, just outside St-Rémy, into a bed-and-breakfast. The house and the rooms are filled with French country furniture and objects from around the world. Without drop-in clients barging in (rooms must be reserved), you feel like. . . well, guests. Table d'hôte dinners, cooking classes, and tours can be arranged. Breakfast is included. ⊠ *Rte. de Mas-Blanc, 13210,* ☎ *04–90–92–39–32,* FAX *04–90–92–55–99. 5 rooms, 1 suite. Dining room, pool. No credit cards. Closed Jan.–Feb.*

$$ ⊞ **Château de Roussan.** In a majestic park shaded by ancient plane trees, this 18th-century château is being valiantly preserved by managers who (without a rich owner to back them) are lovingly restoring it, squatter style. Glorious period furnishings and details are buttressed by brocantes and bric-a-brac, and the bathrooms have an afterthought air about them. Cats outnumber the staff. Yet if you're the right sort for this place—backpackers, romantic couples on a budget, lovers of atmosphere over luxury—you'll blossom in this three-dimensional costume drama. ⊠ *Rte. de Tarascon, 13210,* ☎ *04–90–92–11–63,* FAX *04–90–92–50–59. 22 rooms. Restaurant. MC, V.*

Shopping

Every Wednesday morning St-Rémy hosts one of the most popular and picturesque **markets** in Provence, during which place de la République and narrow old-town streets overflow with fresh produce, herbs, and olive oil by the vat, as well as fabrics and brocantes.

Tarascon

㉗ *16 km (10 mi) west of St-Rémy, 17 km (11 mi) north of Arles, 25 km (15 mi) east of Nîmes.*

Tarascon's claim to fame is as home to the mythical Tarasque, a monster that would emerge from the Rhône to gobble up children and cattle. Luckily, Ste. Marthe, who washed up at Stes-Maries-de-la-Mer, tamed the beast with a sprinkle of holy water, after which the inhabitants slashed it to pieces. This dramatic event is celebrated on the last weekend in June with a parade and was immortalized by Alphonse Daudet, who lived in nearby Fontvieille, in his tales of a folk hero known to all French schoolchildren as *Tartarin de Tarascon.* Unfortunately, a saint has not yet been born who can vanquish the fumes that emanate from Tarascon's enormous paper mill, and the hotel industry is suffering for it.

★ Nonetheless, with the walls of its formidable **Château** plunging straight into the roaring Rhône, this ancient city on the river presents a daunting challenge to Beaucaire, its traditional enemy across the water. Begun in the 13th century by the noble Anjou family on the site of a Roman *castellum,* it grew through the generations into a splendid structure, crowned with both round and square towers and elegantly furnished. Complete with a moat, a drawbridge, and a lovely faceted spiral staircase, it retains its beautiful decorative stonework and original window frames. ☎ *04–90–91–01–93.* 🎟 *32 frs.* ☉ *Apr.–Sept., daily 9–7; Oct.–Mar., Wed.–Mon. 9–noon and 2–5.*

AVIGNON AND THE VAUCLUSE

Anchored by the magnificent papal stronghold of Avignon, the Vaucluse spreads luxuriantly east of the Rhône. Its famous vineyards— Châteauneuf-du-Pape, Gigondas, Vacqueyras, Beaumes-de-Venise—seduce connoisseurs, and its Roman ruins in Orange and Vaison-la-Romaine draw scholars and arts lovers. Arid lowlands dotted with orchards of olives, apricots, and almonds give way to a rich and wild mountain terrain around the formidable Mont Ventoux and flow into the primeval Luberon, made a household name by Peter Mayle. The hill villages around the Luberon—Gordes, Roussillon, Oppède, Bonnieux—are as lovely as any you'll find in the south of France.

Avignon

24 km (15 mi) northeast of Tarascon, 82 km (51 mi) northwest of Aix-en-Provence, 95 km (59 mi) northwest of Marseille, 224 km (140 mi) south of Lyon.

From its famous Palais des Papes (Papal Palace), where seven exiled popes camped between 1309 and 1377 after fleeing from the corruption and civil strife of Rome, to the long, low bridge of childhood song fame stretching over the river, you can beam yourself briefly into the 14th century in Avignon, so complete is the context, so evocative the setting. Yet the town is anything but a museum; it surges with modern ideas and energy and thrives within its ramparts as it did in the heyday of the popes—like those radical church lords, sensual, cultivated, cosmopolitan, with a taste for lay pleasures. Avignon remained papal property until 1791, and elegant mansions bear witness to the town's 18th-century prosperity.

★ ㉘ The colossal **Palais des Papes** creates a disconcertingly fortresslike impression, underlined by the austerity of its interior decor. Most of the furnishings were returned to Rome with the papacy, and others were dispersed during the French Revolution. Some imagination is required to picture it in medieval splendor, awash with color and with worldly clerics enjoying what the 14th-century Italian poet Petrarch called "licentious banquets." On close inspection, two different styles of building emerge at the palace: the severe **Palais Vieux** (Old Palace), built between 1334 and 1342 by Pope Benedict XII, a member of the Cistercian order, which frowned on frivolity, and the more decorative **Palais Nouveau** (New Palace), built in the following decade by the artsy, lavish-living Pope Clement VI. The Great Court, where visitors arrive, links the two.

The main rooms of the Palais Vieux are the **Consistory** (Council Hall), decorated with some excellent 14th-century frescoes by Simone Martini; the **Chapelle St-Jean** (original frescoes by Matteo Giovanetti); the **Grand Tinel,** or Salle des Festins (Feast Hall), with a majestic vaulted roof and a series of 18th-century Gobelin tapestries; the **Chapelle St-Martial** (more Giovanetti frescoes); and the **Chambre du Cerf,** with a richly decorated ceiling, murals featuring a stag hunt, and a delightful view of Avignon. The principal attractions of the Palais Nouveau are the **Grande Audience,** a magnificent two-nave hall on the ground floor, and, upstairs, the **Chapelle Clémentine,** where the college of cardinals once gathered to elect the new pope. ⊠ *Pl. du Palais,* ☎ *04–90–27–50–00.* 🎫 *45 frs entry includes choice of guided tour or individual audio guide; 55 frs includes audio guided tour to pont St-Bénézet.* ☉ *Nov.–Mar., daily 9:30–5:45; Apr.–June and Oct., daily 9–7; July (during theater festival), daily 9–9; Aug.–Sept., daily 9–8.*

㉙ The **Cathédrale Notre-Dame-des-Doms,** first built in a pure Provençal Romanesque style in the 12th century, was quickly dwarfed by the extravagant palace beside it. It rallied in the 14th century with a cupola—that promptly collapsed. As rebuilt in 1425, it's a marvel of stacked arches with a strong Byzantine flavor and is topped nowadays with a gargantuan Virgin Mary lantern—a 19th-century afterthought—whose glow can be seen for miles around. ⊠ *Pl. du Palais,* ☎ *04–90–86–81–01.* ☉ *Mon.–Sat. 7–7, Sun. 9–7.*

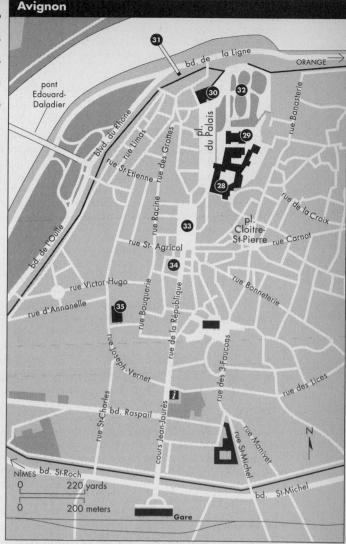

Avignon

③⓪ The **Petit Palais,** the former residence of bishops and cardinals, houses a large collection of old-master paintings. The majority are Italian works from the Renaissance schools of Siena, Florence, and Venice—styles with which the Avignon popes would have been familiar. A key piece to seek out in the 15th-century rooms is Sandro Botticelli's *Virgin and Child*; 16th-century masterworks include Venetian paintings by Carpaccio and Giovanni Bellini. ⊠ *Pl. du Palais,* ☎ 04–90–86–44–58. ⌦ 30 frs. ☉ Oct.–May, Wed.–Mon. 9:30–1 and 2–5:30; June–Sept., Wed.–Mon. 10–1 and 2–6.

★ ③① The **Pont St-Bénézet** (St. Bénézet Bridge) is the source of the famous children's song: *"Sur le pont d'Avignon on y danse, on y danse . . ."* ("On the bridge of Avignon one dances, one dances . . ."). Unlike London Bridge, this one still stretches its arches across the river but only part way: Half was washed away in the 17th century. Its first stones allegedly laid with the miraculous strength granted St-Bénézet in the 12th century, it once reached all the way to Villeneuve. ⊠ *Port du Rochre.*

③② The hilltop garden known as **Rocher des Doms** (Rock of the Domes), with statuary and swans under grand Mediterranean pines, offers extraordinary views of the palace, the rooftops of old Avignon, the Pont St-Bénézet, and formidable Villeneuve across the Rhône. On the horizon looms Mont Ventoux, the Luberon, and Les Alpilles. ⊠ *Montée du Moulin off pl. du Palais.*

③③ The **place de l'Horloge** (Clock Square) is the social nerve center of Avignon, where the concentration of bistros, brasseries, and restaurants draws swarms of locals to the shade of its plane trees.

③④ Housed in a pretty little Jesuit chapel on the main shopping street, the **Musée Lapidaire** gathers a collection of classical sculpture and stonework from Gallo-Roman times (1st and 2nd centuries), as well as items from the Musée Calvet's collection of Greek and Etruscan works. They are haphazardly labeled and insouciantly scattered throughout the noble chapel, itself slightly crumbling but awash with light. ⊠ *27 rue de la République,* ☎ *04–90–85–75–38.* 🎫 *10 frs.* ☉ *Wed.–Mon. 10–1 and 2–6.*

③⑤ Worth a visit for the beauty and balance of its architecture alone, the fine old **Musée Calvet** contains a rich collection of antiquities and classically inspired works. Recent acquisitions are Neoclassic and Romantic and almost entirely French, including works by Manet, Daumier, and David. The main building itself is a Palladian-style jewel in pale Gard stone dating from the 1740s; and the garden is so lovely that it may distract you from the paintings. ⊠ *65 rue Joseph-Vernet,* ☎ *04–90–86–33–84.* 🎫 *30 frs.* ☉ *Wed.–Mon. 10–1 and 2–6.*

Dining and Lodging

$$ ✕ **Brunel.** Stylishly redecorated in a hip, contemporary retro-bistro style in urbane shades of gray, this Avignon favorite features the passionate Provençal cooking of Avignon-born and -bred chef Roger Brunel. This is down-home bistro cooking based on a sophisticated larder: parchment-wrapped mullet with eggplant and tomatoes, chicken roasted with garlic confit (preserves), and caramelized apples in tender pastry. ⊠ *46 rue de la Balance,* ☎ *04–90–85–24–83. Reservations essential. MC, V.*

$$ ✕ **La Cuisine de Reine.** Glassed into the white-stone cloister of the trendy
★ art gallery called Les Cloître des Arts, this chic bistro sports a theatrical dell'arte decor and a young, laid-back waitstaff. The blackboard lists eclectic dishes: duck in rosemary honey and salmon tartare with eggplant caviar and citrus vinaigrette. Or join the cashmere-and-loafer set for the 120-franc Saturday brunch buffet. ⊠ *83 rue Joseph-Vernet,* ☎ *04–90–85–99–04. AE, DC, MC, V. Closed Sun.*

$ ✕ **Le Grand Café.** Behind the Papal Palace, in a massive former fac-
★ tory—a setting of carefully preserved industrial decay—this hip entertainment complex combines an international cinema, a bar, and this popular bistro. Gigantic 18th-century mirrors and dance festival posters hang on crumbling plaster and brick, and votive candles half-light the raw metal framework—an inspiring environment for intense film talk and a late supper of foie gras, goat cheese, or marinated artichokes. ⊠ *La Manutention, 4 rue des Escaliers Ste-Anne,* ☎ *04–90–86–86–77. MC, V. Closed Mon. (except Jul.).*

$ ✕ **Maison Nani.** Crowded inside and out with trendy young professionals, this pretty lunch spot serves stylish home cooking in generous portions without the fuss of multiple courses. Choose from heaping salads sizzling with fresh meat, enormous kebabs, and a creative quiche du jour. It's just off rue de la République. ⊠ *29 rue Théodore Aubanel,* ☎ *04–90–82–60–90. No credit cards. Closed Sun. No dinner Mon.–Thurs.*

$$$$ ✕⊞ **Hôtel de la Mirande.** Richly decorated with exquisite reproduc-
★   tion fabrics and beeswaxed antiques, this designer's dream of a hotel
    is just below the Papal Palace. Its enclosed garden is a breakfast and
    dinner oasis, and its central lounge is a skylighted and jazz-warmed
    haven. Rooms are both gorgeous and comfy. The costume-drama din-
    ing room and sultry summer garden provide an idyllic setting for the
    restaurant's sophisticated cuisine. Look for friendly Friday-night cook-
    ing classes in the massive downstairs "country" kitchen. ⊠ *Pl. de la
    Mirande, 84000,* ☎ *04–90–85–93–93,* FAX *04–90–86–26–85. 19 rooms,
    1 suite. Restaurant, bar. AE, DC, MC, V.*

$$$–$$$$ ✕⊞ **Hôtel d'Europe.** This splendid 16th-century home, built by the Mar-
    quis of Graveson, is discreet and classic and has a seasoned staff.
    Rooms are sizable, with two suites overlooking the Papal Palace. The
    restaurant, La Vieille Fontaine, is one of Avignon's finest. ⊠ *12 pl. Cril-
    lon, 84000,* ☎ *04–90–14–76–76,* FAX *04–90–14–76–71. 47 rooms.
    Restaurant. AE, DC, MC, V.* ✍

$$ ⊞ **Du Palais des Papes.** Despite its two-star rating, this is a remark-
    ably solid, comfortable, and charming hotel—all the more for its loca-
    tion just off the place du Palais. Recently updated with chic ironwork
    furniture and rich fabrics, the exposed-stone-and-beam decor fulfills fan-
    tasies of a medieval city, but one with good tile baths. A film-set Louis
    XIII restaurant downstairs, Le Lutrin, is more for honeymooners than
    gastronomes. ⊠ *1 rue Gérard-Philippe, 84000,* ☎ *04–90–86–04–13,*
    FAX *04–90–27–91–17. 23 rooms. Restaurant, bar. AE, DC, MC, V.* ✍

$$ ⊞ **Hôtel du Blauvac.** Just off rue de la République and place de l'Hor-
★   loge, this 17th-century nobleman's home has been divided into 16 guest
    rooms. Many have pristine exposed stonework, aged-oak details, and
    lovely tall windows that look, alas, onto backstreet walls. Pretty fab-
    rics and a warm, familial welcome more than compensate, however.
    ⊠ *11 rue de la Bancasse, 84000,* ☎ *04–90–86–34–11,* FAX *04–90–86–
    27–41. 16 rooms. Breakfast room. AE, DC, MC, V.*

$ ⊞ **Hôtel de Mons.** Tatty and almost intolerably eccentric, this is a neo-
    Gothic budget flophouse after Edward Gorey's own heart, first built
    as a 13th-century chapel. Transformation took some maneuvering, but
    guest rooms with baths (with '70s-style decor) have been fitted into
    crooked nooks and crannies, while retaining some period detail (slant-
    ing spiral stairs, quarried stone). Breakfast is served in a groin-vaulted
    crypt. Location is everything: It's two steps off place de l'Horloge. And
    it's dirt cheap. ⊠ *5 rue de Mons, 84000,* ☎ *04–90–82–57–16,* FAX *04–
    90–85–19–15. 11 rooms, 10 with bath. AE, MC, V.*

Nightlife and the Arts

Held annually in July, the Avignon festival, known officially as the **Fes-
tival Annuel d'Art Dramatique** (Annual Festival of Dramatic Art), has
brought the best of world theater to this ancient city since 1947. Some
300 productions take place every year; the main performances are at
the Palais des Papes (for tickets and information contact ☎ 04–90–
27–66–50).

Within its fusty old medieval walls, Avignon teems with modern
nightlife well into the wee hours. At **AJMI** (Association Pour le Jazz et
la Musique Improvisée, ⊠ 4 rue Escaliers Ste-Anne, ☎ 04–90–86–08–
61), in La Manutention, you can hear live jazz acts of some renown.
At the cabaret **Dolphin Blues** (⊠ Chemin de L'île Piot, ☎ 04–90–82–
46–96), a hip mix of comedy and music dominates the repertoire, and
there's a children's theater as well. **Le Rouge Gorge** (⊠ 10 bis rue Pey-
rollerie, behind palace, ☎ 04–90–14–02–54) presents a dinner show
and after-dinner dancing every Friday and Saturday night.

Shopping

Avignon has a cosmopolitan mix of French chains, youthful clothing shops (it's a college town), and a few plummy shops. **Rue des Marchands,** off place Carnot, is one shopping stretch, but **rue de la République** is the main artery.

Châteauneuf-du-Pape

36 *18 km (11 mi) north of Avignon, 23 km (14 mi) west of Carpentras.*

The countryside around this very famous wine center is a patchwork of rolling vineyards. Great gates and grand houses punctuate the scene, as symmetrical and finely detailed as the etching on a wine label, and signs beckon you to follow the omnipresent smell of fermenting grapes to their source.

Once the table wine of the Avignon popes, who kept a fortified summer house here (hence the name of the town, which means "new castle of the pope"), the vineyards of Châteauneuf-du-Pape had the good fortune to be wiped out by phylloxera in the 19th century. Its revival as a muscular and resilient mix of up to 13 varietals has moved it to the forefront of French wines. To learn more, stop in at the **Musée des Outils de Vignerons Père Anselme,** a private collection of tools and equipment displayed in the *caveau* (wine cellar) of the Brotte family. ⊠ *Rte. d'Avignon,* ☎ *04–90–83–70–07.* ✆ *Free.* ☉ *Daily 9–noon and 2–6.*

If you're disinclined to spend your holiday sniffing and sipping in a dark basement, climb the hill to the ruins of the **Château.** Though it was destroyed in the Wars of Religion and its remaining donjon blasted by the Germans in World War II, it still commands magnificent views.

Dining and Lodging

$–$$ ✕ **Le Pistou.** This friendly little inn serves sophisticated cooking by a chef in love with things Provençal, from marketing to cooking all-day daubes and marking his whims on a blackboard. The welcome is warm, and the fixed-price menus start cheap. ⊠ *15 rue Joseph-Ducos,* ☎ *04–90–83–71–75. MC, V. Closed Mon. No dinner Sun.*

$$ ✕▥ **La Garbure.** With four rooms decked in soft pastel ruffles upstairs and a new, low-price *menu terroir* (prix-fixe menu of regional specialties), this pretty inn aims to please. Look for potted quail in Carpentras truffles and stuffed rabbit with subtle thyme sauce (the restaurant is closed Sunday, October through June, and doesn't serve Sunday lunch in season.) ⊠ *3 rue Joseph-Ducos 84230,* ☎ *04–90–83–75–08,* ℻ *04–90–83–52–34. 4 rooms. Restaurant, air-conditioning. MC, V.*

Orange

37 *10 km (6 mi) north of Châteauneuf-du-Pape, 31 km (19 mi) north of Avignon, 193 km (121 mi) south of Lyon.*

Even less touristy than Nîmes and just as eccentric, the city of Orange (pronounced oh-*rawnzh*) nonetheless draws thousands every year to

★ its spectacular **Théâtre Antique,** a colossal Roman theater built in the time of Caesar Augustus. Its vast stone stage wall, bouncing sound off the facing hillside, climbs four stories high, and the niche at center stage contains the original statue of Augustus, just as it reigned over centuries of productions of classical plays. Today this theater inspires and shelters world-class theater and opera. ⊠ *Pl. des Frères-Mounet,* ☎ *04–90–34–70–88.* ✆ *30 frs, joint ticket with Musée Municipal.* ☉ *Apr.– Oct., daily 9–6:30; Nov.–Mar., daily 9–noon and 1:30–5.*

The small **Musée Municipal** (Town Museum) displays antiquities unearthed around Orange, including three detailed marble *cadastr* (land survey maps) dating from the 1st century. Upstairs are Provençal fabrics manufactured in local mills in the 18th century and a collection of faience pharmacy jars. ⊠ *Pl. des Frères-Mounet,* ☎ *04–90–34–70–88.* ⌨ *30 frs, joint ticket with theater.* ☉ *Apr.–Sept., daily 9–6:30; Oct.–Mar., daily 9–noon and 1:30–5.*

North of the city center is the **Arc de Triomphe,** which once straddled the Via Agrippa between Lyon and Arles. Three arches support a heavy double attic (horizontal top) floridly decorated with battle scenes and marine symbols, referring to Augustus's victories at Actium. The arch, which dates from about 20 BC, is superbly preserved, particularly the north side, but to view it on foot, you'll have to cross a roundabout seething with traffic. ⊠ *North of center on av. de l'Arc, in direction of Gap.*

Dining and Lodging

$ ✕ **La Yaka.** At this intimate, unpretentious bistro, you are greeted by the beaming owner, who is also your host and waiter, then pampered with an array of menu choices. Specialties are emphatically *style grand-mère* (like Grandma used to make) and include rabbit stew, *caillette* (pork-liver meat loaf), and even canned peas with bacon. It's all in a charming stone-and-beam setting. ⊠ *24 pl. Sylvain,* ☎ *04–90–34–70–03. MC, V. Closed Wed. and Nov. No dinner Tues.*

$$ ☷ **Arène.** On a quiet square in the old town center, this comfortable old hotel has attentive owners and a labyrinth of rooms done in rich colors and heavy fabrics. The nicest ones look out over the square. As it's built between several fine old houses strung together, there's no elevator, but a multitude of stairways compensates. ⊠ *Pl. de Langues, 84100,* ☎ *04–90–11–40–40,* FAX *04–90–11–40–45. 30 rooms. Air-conditioning. AE, DC, MC, V.*

The Arts

Every July **Les Chorégies d'Orange** echo tradition and present operatic and classical music spectacles under the summer stars (☎ 04–90–34–24–24, FAX 04–90–11–04–04; or write to ⊠ Chorégies, B.P. 205, 84107 Orange Cedex well in advance).

Vaison-la-Romaine

③⑧ *27 km (17 mi) northeast of Orange, 30 km (19 mi) northeast of Avignon.*

This ancient town thrives as a modern market center yet retains an irresistible Provençal charm, with medieval backstreets, lively squares lined with cafés, and, as its name implies, the remains of its Roman past. Vaison's well-established Celtic colony joined forces with Rome in the 2nd century BC and grew to powerful status in the empire's glory days. No gargantuan monuments were raised, yet the luxurious villas surpassed even those of Pompeii.

There are two broad fields of **Roman ruins,** both in the center of town: Before you pay entry at either of the ticket booths, pick up a map (with English explanations) at the **Maison du Tourisme et des Vins** (☎ 04–90–36–02–11), which sits between them; it's open July–August, daily 9–12:30 and 2—6:45; September–June, Mon.–Sat. 9–noon and 2–5:45. Like a tiny Roman forum, the **Maison des Messii** spreads over the field and hillside in the heart of town. Its skeletal ruins of villas, landscaped gardens, and museum lie below the ancient theater, all of which are accessed by the booth across from the tourist office. Closest to the entrance, the foundations of the **Maison des Messii** (Messii House) retain the outlines of its sumptuous design. A formal garden echoes a similar landscape of the time; wander under its cypresses and flowering shrubs to the **Musée Archéologique Théo-Desplans** (Théo-

Desplans Archaeology Museum). In this streamlined venue, the accoutrements of Roman life have been amassed and displayed by theme: pottery, weapons, representations of gods and goddesses, jewelry, and sculpture. Cross the park behind the museum to climb into the bleachers of the 1st-century **theater**, which is smaller than Orange's but is still used today for concerts and plays. Across the parking lot is the

★ **Quartier de la Villasse**, where the remains of a lively market town evoke images of main-street shops, public gardens, and grand private homes, complete with floor mosaics. The most evocative image of all is in the *thermes* (baths): a neat row of marble-seat toilets. ⊠ *Av. Général-de-Gaulle at pl. du 11 Novembre,* ☎ *04–90–36–02–11.* ☞ *Ruins, museum, and cloister 41 frs.* ☉ *Puymin June–Sept., daily 9:30–6; Mar.–May and Oct., daily 10–12:30 and 2–6; Nov.–Feb., daily 10–noon and 2–4:30. Museum Mar.–May and Oct., daily 10–12:30 and 2:30–6; June–Sept., daily 9:30–6; Nov.–Feb., daily 10–11:30 and 2–4. Villasse June–Sept., daily 9:30–noon and 2–6; Mar.–May and Oct., daily 10–12:30 and 2–6; Nov.–Feb., daily 10–noon and 2–4:30.*

Take the time to climb up into the **Haute Ville,** a medieval neighborhood perched high above the river valley. Its 13th- and 14th-century houses owe some of their beauty to stone pillaged from the Roman ruins below, but their charm is from the Middle Ages.

If you're in a medieval mood, stop into the sober Romanesque **Cathédrale Notre-Dame-de-Nazareth,** based on recycled fragments and foundations of a Gallo-Roman basilica. Its richly sculpted **cloister** is the key attraction. ⊠ *Av. Jules-Ferry.* ☉ *June–Sept., daily 9:30–noon and 2–5:30; Mar.–May and Oct., daily 10–noon and 2–5:30; Nov.–Feb., daily 10–noon and 2–4.*

One last highlight: The remarkable single-arch **Pont Romain** (Roman Bridge), built in the 1st century, stands firm across the Ouvèze River.

Dining and Lodging

$$$ ✕🏠 **Château de la Baude.** Just 6 km (4 mi) outside Vaison, this fortified medieval farm has been converted into a bed-and-breakfast retreat, complete with swimming, tennis, Ping-Pong, pétanque, and 9 acres of grounds. There are table d'hôte dinners and sleek beamed rooms, and breakfast is served under the grape trellis. ⊠ *La Baude, Villedieu, 84110,* ☎ *04–90–28–95–18,* ℻ *04–90–28–91–05. 4 rooms, 2 suites. Restaurant (guests only), pool, whirlpool, tennis. AE, DC, MC, V.* ✍

$$–$$$ ✕🏠 **Le Beffroi.** On a cliff top in the old town, this elegant grouping of
★ 16th-century homes makes a fine little hotel. The extravagant salon decked in period style leads to the sizable rooms with beams and antiques; the big corner rooms have breathtaking views. From April through October dine on local specialties under the fig tree in the intimate enclosed garden court. By day you can enjoy a simple salad on the garden terrace or take a dip in the rooftop pool. ⊠ *Rue de l'Évêché, 84110,* ☎ *04–90–36–04–71,* ℻ *04–90–36–24–78. 22 rooms. Restaurant. AE, DC, MC, V. Closed Feb.–mid-Mar.*

$$ 🏠 **Évêché.** In the medieval part of town, this turreted 16th-century former bishop's palace has just four small rooms. The warm welcome and rustic charm—delicate fabrics, exposed beams, wooden bedsteads—have garnered a loyal following among travelers who prefer B&B character to modern luxury. ⊠ *Rue de l'Évêché, 84110,* ☎ *04–90–36–13–46,* ℻ *04–90–36–32–43. 4 rooms. No credit cards.*

Le Barroux

③⑨ *16 km (10 mi) south of Vaison-la-Romaine, 34 km (21 mi) northeast of Avignon.*

Of all the marvelous hilltop villages stretching across the south of France, this tiny ziggurat of a town may be unique: It is 100% boutique-and-gallery-free and has only one tiny old *épicerie* (small grocery) selling canned goods, yellowed postcards, and today's *Le Provençal*. You are forced, therefore, to look around you and listen to the trickle of the ancient fountains at every labyrinthine turn.

The **Château** is its main draw, though its perfect condition reflects a complete restoration after a World War II fire. Grand vaulted rooms and a chapel date from the 12th century, and other halls serve as venues for contemporary art exhibits. ☎ 04–90–62–35–21. ⊠ 20 frs. ◷ *Apr.–May, weekends 10–7; June, weekdays 2–7, weekends 10–7; July–Sept., daily 10–7; Oct., daily 2:30–7.*

Dining and Lodging

$ ✕⌂ **Les Géraniums.** Though it has simple, pretty rooms, many with views sweeping down to the valley, this family-run auberge emphasizes its restaurant ($–$$). A broad garden terrace stretches along the cliff side, where you can sample herb-roasted rabbit, a truffle omelet, and local cheeses. Half-pension is strongly encouraged. New rooms in the annex across the street take in panoramic views. ⊠ *Pl. de la Croix, 84330,* ☎ *04–90–62–41–08,* ℻ *04–90–62–56–48. 22 rooms. Restaurant, bar. AE, DC, MC, V. Closed Jan.–Feb.*

Crillon le Brave

④⓪ *12 km (7 mi) south of Malaucène (via Caromb), 21 km (13 mi) southeast of Vaison-la-Romaine.*

The main reason to come to this tiny village, named after France's most notable soldier hero of the 16th century, is to stay or dine at its hotel, the Hostellerie de Crillon le Brave (☞ Dining and Lodging, *below*). But it's also pleasant—perched on a knoll in a valley shielded by Mont Ventoux, with the craggy hills of the Dentelles in one direction and the hills of the Luberon in another. Today the village still doesn't have even a *boulangerie* (bakery), let alone a souvenir boutique.

Dining and Lodging

$$$$ ✕⌂ **Hostellerie de Crillon le Brave.** The views from the interconnected hilltop houses of this Relais & Châteaux property are as elevated as its prices, but for this you get a rarefied atmosphere of medieval luxury. A cozy-chic southern decor informs book-filled salons and brocante-trimmed guest rooms, some with terraces looking out onto infinity. In the stone-vaulted dining room, stylish French cuisine is served. Wine tastings and regional discovery packages encourage longer stays. ⊠ *Pl. de l'Église, 84410,* ☎ *04–90–65–61–61,* ℻ *04–90–65–62–86. 23 rooms. Restaurant, pool. AE, DC, MC, V. Closed Jan.–mid-Mar.* ✎

L'Isle-sur-la-Sorgue

④① *18 km (11 mi) south of Malaucène, 41 km (25 mi) southeast of Orange, 26 km (16 mi) east of Avignon.*

Crisscrossed with lazy canals and alive with moss-covered waterwheels that once drove its silk, wool, and paper mills, this valley town retains its gentle appeal. Except on Sunday, when this easygoing old town transforms itself into a Marrakech of marketeers, its streets crammed with antiques and brocante, its cafés swelling with crowds of bargain browsers making a day of it. There are also street musicians, food stands groaning under rustic breads, vats of tapenade, cloth-lined baskets of spices, and miles of café tables offering ringside seats to the spectacle. On a nonmarket day life returns to its mellow pace, with plenty of antiques dealers holding forth year-round, as well as fabric and interior design shops, bookstores, and food stores for you to explore.

The token sight to see is L'Isle's 17th-century church, the **Collégiale Notre-Dame-des-Anges,** extravagantly decorated with gilt, faux marble, and sentimental frescoes. Its double-colonnaded facade commands the center of the old town.

Dining and Lodging

$$–$$$ ✕ **La Prévôté.** With all the money you saved bargaining on that chipped Quimper vase, splurge on lunch at this discreet, pristine spot hidden off a backstreet courtyard. The cuisine has won top awards for chef Roland Mercier—try his cannelloni stuffed with salmon and goat cheese, or tender duckling with lavender honey. Evening and à la carte meals are an investment. ✉ *4 rue Jean-Jacques-Rousseau,* ☎ *04–90–38–57–29. Reservations essential. MC, V. Closed Mon. (Dec.–June), Nov., and 2 wks in Feb. No dinner Sun.*

$ ✕ **Lou Nego Chin.** In winter you sit shoulder to shoulder in the cramped but atmospheric dining room (chinoiserie linens, brightly hued tiles), but in summer tables are strewn across the quiet street, on a wooden deck along the river. Ask for a spot at the edge so you can watch the ducks play and order the inexpensive house wine and the menu du jour, often a goat-cheese salad and a good, garlicky stew. ✉ *12 quai Jean Jaurès,* ☎ *04–90–20–88–03. MC, V. Closed Mon. No dinner Sun.*

$–$$ ✕▥ **Le Mas de Cure-Bourse.** This graceful old 18th-century postal-coach
★ stop is well outside the fray, snugly hedge-bound in the countryside amid 6 acres of fruit trees and fields. Rooms are freshly decked out in Provençal prints and painted country furniture. The Pomarèdes, the new owners of this popular landmark, have kept their kitchen team and a loyal local following: You'll be served sophisticated home cooking with a local touch. The restaurant is closed Monday, and lunch is not served Tuesday. ✉ *Rte. de Caumont 84800,* ☎ *04–90–38–16–58,* ℻ *04–90–38–52–31. 13 rooms. Restaurant, pool. MC, V. Closed 3 wks in Nov., first 2 wks in Jan.*

$ ✕▥ **La Gueulardière.** After a Sunday glut of antiquing along the canals, you can dine and sleep just up the street in a setting full of collectible finds, from the school posters in the restaurant to the oak armoires and brass beds that furnish the simple lodgings. Each room has French windows that open onto the enclosed garden courtyard, where you can enjoy a private breakfast in the shade. ✉ *1 rue d'Apt, 84800,* ☎ *04–90–38–10–52,* ℻ *04–90–20–83–70. 5 rooms. Restaurant. AE, DC, MC, V.*

Shopping

Of the dozens of antiques shops in L'Isle, one conglomerate concentrates some 40 dealers under the same roof: **L'Isle aux Brocantes** (✉ 7 av. des Quatre Otages, ☎ 04–90–20–69–93); it's open Saturday–Monday. Higher-end antiques are concentrated next door at the twin shops of **Xavier Nicod et Gérard Nicod** (✉ 9 av. des Quatre Otages, ☎ 04–90–38–35–50 or 04–90–38–07–20). **Maria Giancatarina** (✉ 4 av. Julien Guigue [across from train station], ☎ 04–90–38–58–02) features beautifully restored linens, including *boutis* (Provençal quilts).

Fontaine-de-Vaucluse

㊷ *8 km (5 mi) east of L'Isle-sur-la-Sorgue, 33 km (20 mi) east of Avignon.*

★ The **Fontaine de Vaucluse,** for which the town is named, is a strange and beautiful natural phenomenon that has been turned into a charming yet slightly tacky tourist center—like a tiny Niagara Falls—and should not be missed if you're either a connoisseur of rushing water or a fan of foreign kitsch. There's no exaggerating the magnificence of the *fontaine* itself, a mysterious spring that gushes from a deep underground source that has been explored to a depth of 1,010 ft . . . so far. Framed by towering cliffs, a broad, pure pool wells up and spews dramatically over massive rocks down a gorge to the village, where its roar soothes and cools the tourists who crowd the riverfront cafés.

You must pay to park and then run a gauntlet of souvenir shops and tourist traps on your way to the top. But even if you plan to make a beeline past the kitsch, do stop in at the legitimate and informative **Moulin Vallis-Clausa.** A working paper mill, it demonstrates a reconstructed 15th-century waterwheel that drives timber crankshafts to mix rag pulp, while artisans roll and dry thick paper *à l'ancienne* (in the old manner). Observation is fascinating and free of charge, though it's almost impossible to resist buying note cards, posters, even lampshades fashioned from the pretty stuff. Fontaine was once a great industrial mill center, but its seven factories were closed by strikes in 1968 and never recovered. ☎ 04–90–20–34–14. ⊙ *Sept.–June, daily 9–noon and 2–6; July–Aug., daily 9–7.*

Fontaine has its own ruined **Château,** perched romantically on a forested hilltop over the town and illuminated at night. First built around the year 1000 and embellished in the 13th century by the bishops of Cavaillon, it was destroyed in the 15th century and forms little more than a saw-tooth silhouette against the sky.

The Renaissance poet Petrarch, driven mad with unrequited love for a beautiful married woman named Laura, retreated to this valley to nurse his passion in a cabin with "one dog and only two servants." Sixteen years in this wild isolation didn't ease the pain, but the serene setting inspired him to poetry. The small **Musée-Bibliothèque Pétrarch,** built on the site of his stay, displays prints and engravings of the virtuous lovers. ☎ 04–90–20–37–20. ☒ *20 frs.* ⊙ *Apr.–May., Wed.–Mon. 10–noon and 2–6; June–Sept., Wed.–Mon. 10–12:30 and 1:30–6; Oct., weekends 10–noon and 2–5.*

Dining and Lodging

$$ ✕▥ **Le Parc.** In a spectacular riverside setting in the shadow of the ruined château, this solid old hotel has basic, comfortable rooms (whitewashed stucco, all-weather carpet) with clean bathrooms and no creaks; five of them offer river views. The restaurant (closed Wednesday) spreads along the river in a pretty park setting with tables shaded by trellises heavy with grapes and trumpet vine. Moderately priced daily menus include river-fresh salmon. ☒ *Rue de Bourgades, 84800,* ☎ *04–90–20–31–57,* FAX *04–90–20–27–03. 12 rooms. Restaurant. AE, DC, MC, V. Closed Jan.–mid-Feb.*

En Route Gordes is only a short distance from Fontaine de Vaucluse, but you need to wind your way south, east, and then north on D100A, D100, D2, and D15 to skirt the impassable hillside. It's a lovely drive through dry, rocky country covered with wild lavender and scrub oak and may tempt you to a picnic or a walk.

Gordes

❹❸ *16 km (10 mi) southeast of Fontaine-de-Vaucluse, 35 km (22 mi) east of Avignon.*

Gordes was once merely an unspoiled hilltop village; it is now a famous, unspoiled hilltop village surrounded by luxury vacation homes, modern hotels, restaurants, and B&Bs. No matter: The ancient stone village still rises above the valley in painterly hues of honey gold, and its mosaiclike cobbled streets—lined with boutiques, galleries, and real estate offices—still wind steep and narrow to its Renaissance château. The only way to see the interior of the **Château** is to view its ghastly collection of photo paintings by pop artist Pol Mara, who lived in Gordes. It's worth the price of admission to look at the fabulously decorated stone fireplace, created in 1541. ☎ 04–90–72–02–75. 🖽 25 frs. ⊘ Wed.–Mon. 10–noon and 2–6.

★ Just outside Gordes, on a lane heading north from D2, follow signs to the **Village des Bories.** Found throughout this region of Provence, the bizarre and fascinating little stone hovels called *bories* are concentrated some 20 strong in an ancient community. Their origins are provocatively vague: Built as shepherds' shelters with tight-fitting, mortarless stone in a hivelike form, they may date to the Celts, the Ligurians, even the Iron Age—and were inhabited or used for sheep through the 18th century. ☎ 04–90–72–03–48. 🖽 35 frs. ⊘ Daily 9–sunset or 8, whichever comes 1st.

★ In a wild valley some 4 km (2 mi) north of Gordes (via D177), the beautiful 12th-century Romanesque **Abbaye de Sénanque** floats above a redolent sea of lavender (in full bloom in July and August). Begun in 1150 and completed at the dawn of the 13th century, the **church** and adjoining **cloister** are without decoration but still touch the soul with their chaste beauty. Next door, the enormous vaulted **dormitory** contains an exhibition on the abbey's construction, and the **refectory** shelters a display on the history of Cistercian abbeys. ☎ 04–90–72–05–72. 🖽 30 frs. ⊘ Mar.–Oct., Mon.–Sat. 10–noon and 2–6, Sun. 2–6; Nov.–Feb., weekdays 2–5, weekends 2–6.

Dining and Lodging

$$$ ✕ **Comptoir du Victuailler.** Across from the château, this tiny but deluxe bistro features daily *aïoli,* a smorgasbord of fresh cod and lightly steamed vegetables crowned with the garlic mayonnaise. Evenings are reserved for intimate, formal indoor meals à la carte—roast Luberon lamb, beef with truffle sauce. The '30s-style bistro tables and architectural lines are a relief from Gordes's ubiquitous rustic-chic. ✉ Pl. du Château, ☎ 04–90–72–01–31. Reservations essential. MC, V. Closed Wed. Sept.–May. No dinner Tues. mid-Nov.–Easter.

$$ ✕🖼 **Ferme de la Huppe.** This 17th-century stone farmhouse with a well in the courtyard, a swimming pool in the garden, and rooms with pretty prints and secondhand finds is in the countryside outside Gordes. Dine poolside on three styles of roast lamb, prepared by the proprietors' son, Gerald Konings, but reserve ahead: The restaurant (closed Thursday) is as popular as the hotel. ✉ Les Pourquiers (3 km [2 mi] east of Gordes, R156), 84220, ☎ 04–90–72–12–25, FAX 04–90–72–01–83. 9 rooms. Restaurant, pool. MC, V. Closed end Dec.–Mar.

$$$ 🖼 **Domaine de l'Enclos.** This cluster of private stone cottages has newly laid antique tiles and fresh faux-patinas that keep it looking fashionably old. There are panoramic views and a pool, baby-sitting services and swing sets, and an atmosphere that is surprisingly warm and familial for an inn of this sophistication. ✉ Rte. de Sénanque, 84220, ☎ 04–90–72–71–00, FAX 04–90–72–03–03. 12 rooms, 5 apartments. Restaurant, pool. AE, MC, V. 🌫

$$$ 🖼 **Les Romarins.** At this small inn on a hilltop crossroads on the outskirts of Gordes, you can gaze across the valley at town while you breakfast on a sheltered terrace in the morning sun. Rooms are clean, well lighted, and feel spacious—ask for either No. 1, in the main building, from whose white-curtained windows you can see forever, or the room with a terrace in the atelier. Warm Oriental rugs, antique furniture around

the fireplace in the sitting room, and a pool surrounded with borielike stone add to your contentment. ⊠ *Rte. de Sénanque, 84220,* ☎ *04–90–72–12–13,* FAX *04–90–72–13–13. 10 rooms. Pool. AE, MC, V.*

Roussillon

🕢 *10 km (6 mi) east of Gordes, 45 km (28 mi) east of Avignon.*

In shades of deep rose and russet, this hilltop cluster of houses blends into the red-ochre cliffs from which its stone was quarried. The ensemble of buildings and jagged, hand-cut slopes are equally dramatic, and views from the top look over a landscape of artfully eroded bluffs.

This famous vein of natural ochre, which spreads some 25 km (15 mi) along the foot of the Vaucluse plateau, has been mined for centuries. You can visit the old **Usine Mathieu de Roussillon** (Roussillon's Mathieu Ochre Works) to learn more about ochre's extraction and its modern uses. There are explanatory exhibits, ochre powders for sale, and guided tours in English with advance request. ⊠ *On D104 southeast of town,* ☎ *04–90–05–66–69.* ⊙ *Mar.–Nov., daily 10–7.*

$$–$$$ 🏨 **Ma Maison.** In the valley 4 km (2½ mi) below Roussillon, this isolated 1850 mas has been infused with a laid-back, cosmopolitan style by its artist-owners. There's a big saltwater pool, an idyllic garden, a massive country kitchen, and views toward Bonnieux and the Luberon. ⊠ *Quartier Les Devens, 84220,* ☎ *04–90–05–74–17,* FAX *04–90–05–74–63. 6 rooms. Pool. MC, C. Closed Nov.–mid-Mar.* 🛦

Oppède-le-Vieux

🕤 *25 km (15½ mi) southeast of Avignon, 15 km (9 mi) southwest of Gordes.*

Follow signs toward Oppède; you'll occasionally be required to follow signs for Oppède-le-Village, but your goal will be marked with the symbol of *monuments historiques*: Oppède-le-Vieux. A Byronesque tumble of ruins arranged against an overgrown rocky hillside, Oppède's charm—or part of it—lies in its preservation. Taken over by writers and artists who have chosen to live here and restore but not develop it, the village has a café or two but little more. Bring a lunch, wander, and contemplate.

Cross the village square, pass through the old city gate, and climb up steep trails past restored houses to the church known as **Notre-Dame-d'Alydon.** First built in the 13th century, its blunt buttresses were framed into side chapels in the 16th century; you can still see the points of stoned-in Gothic windows above. The marvelous hexagonal bell tower sprouts a lean, mean gargoyle from each angle. It once served as part of the village's fortifications.

Head left past the cliff-edge wall, plunge into the rock tunnel, and clamber up to the ruins of the **Château,** built in the 13th century and then transformed in the 15th century. From the left side of its great square tower, look down into the dense fir forests of the Luberon's north face.

En Route As you drive along D188 between Oppède and Ménerbes, the rolling rows of grapevines are punctuated by stone farmhouses. But something is different: These farmhouses have electric gates, tall arborvitae hedges, and swimming pools. Peter Mayle isn't the only outsider to have vacationed here and contrived to stay.

Ménerbes

🕦 *5 km (3 mi) east of Oppède-le-Vieux, 30 km (19 mi) southeast of Avignon.*

The town of Ménerbes clings to a long, thin hilltop over this sought-after valley, looming over the surrounding forests like a great stone ship. At its prow juts the **Castellet,** a 15th-century fortress. At its stern rears up the 13th-century **Citadelle.** These redoubtable fortifications served the Protestants well during the War of Religions—until the Catholics wore them down with a 15-month siege.

A campanile tops the Hôtel de Ville (Town Hall), on pretty **place de l'Horloge** (Clock Square), where you can admire the delicate stonework on the arched portal and mullioned windows of a Renaissance house. Just past the tower on the right is an overlook taking in views toward Gordes, Roussillon, and Mont Ventoux.

But what you really came to see is **Peter Mayle's house,** right? Do its current owners a favor and give it a wide berth: After years of tour buses spilling the curious into the private driveway to crane their necks and snap pictures, the heirs to the stone picnic table, the pool, and Faustin's grapevines wish the books had never been written. And besides, Peter Mayle has moved to Lourmarin now, on the other side of the mountain. Do leave him in peace.

Lodging

$$$ ☷ **Le Roy Soleil.** In the imposing shadow of the Luberon, this luxurious country inn has pulled out all stops on comfort and decor: marble and granite bathrooms, wrought-iron beds, and coordinated fabrics. But the integrity of its 17th-century building, with thick stone walls and groin vaults and beams, redeems it just short of pretentiousness and makes it a lovely place to escape to. ⊠ *Rte. des Beaumettes, 84560,* ☎ *04-90-72-25-61,* FAX *04-90-72-36-55. 19 rooms. Restaurant, bar, pool, tennis court. AE, MC, V. Closed mid-Nov.–mid-Mar.* ✎

Bonnieux

47 *11 km (7 mi) south of Roussillon, 45 km (28 mi) north of Aix-en-Provence.*

The most impressive of the Luberon's hilltop villages, Bonnieux rises out of the arid hills in a jumble of honey-color cubes that change color subtly as the day progresses. The village is wrapped in crumbling ramparts and dug into bedrock and cliff. Most of its sharply raked streets take in wide-angle valley views, though you'll get the best view from the pine-shaded grounds of the 12th-century church, reached by stone steps that wind past tiny niche houses.

Dining and Lodging

$$–$$$ ✗ **Le Fournil.** In a natural grotto deep in stone, lighted by candles and arty torchères, this restaurant would be memorable even without its trendy look and stylishly presented Provençal cuisine. Try the adventurous dishes such as the crisped pigs'-feet *galette* (patty) and the informed wine list. ⊠ *5 pl. Carnot, 84480,* ☎ *04-90-75-83-62,* FAX *04-90-75-96-19. MC, V. Closed mid-Nov.–mid-Dec., mid-Jan.–mid-Feb., and Mon. No lunch Sat. July–Aug.*

$$–$$$ ☷ **Hostellerie du Prieuré.** Not every hotel has its own private chapel,
★ but this gracious inn holds forth in an 18th-century abbey, right in the village center. From the firelighted salon to the dining room glowing with Roussillon ochre, it's a pleasantly warm setting. Summer meals and breakfasts are served in the enclosed garden oasis. Rooms have plush carpets and antiques. The Coutaz family has been in the hotel business since Napoléon III, and it shows. ⊠ *In center of village, 84480,* ☎ *04-90-75-80-78,* FAX *04-90-75-96-00. 10 rooms. Restaurant. MC, V. Closed Nov.–Feb.* ✎

$$ ⊞ **Le Clos du Buis.** At this B&B, whitewash and quarry tiles, lovely
★ tiled baths, and carefully juxtaposed antiques create a regional look
in rooms. Public spaces, with scrubbed floorboards, a fireplace, and
exposed stone, are free for your use around the clock. It even has a
pool and a pretty garden, and it's all overlooking the valley from the
village center. ⊠ *Rue Victor Hugo, 84480,* ☎ *04–90–75–88–48,* FAX
04–90–75–88–57. 6 rooms. Pool. MC, V. ✆

AIX-EN-PROVENCE AND THE
MEDITERRANEAN COAST

The southeastern part of this area of Provence, on the edge of the Côte
d'Azur, is dominated by two major towns: Aix-en-Provence, consid-
ered the capital of Provence and the most cultural town in the region;
and Marseille, a vibrant port town that combines seediness with fash-
ion and metropolitan feistiness with classical grace. For a breathtak-
ing experience of the dramatic contrast between the azure Mediterranean
sea and the rocky, olive tree–filled hills, take a trip along the coast east
of Marseille and make an excursion to the Iles d'Hyères.

Aix-en-Provence

★ *48 km (29 mi) southeast of Bonnieux, 82 km (51 mi) southeast of Avi-
gnon, 176 km (109 mi) west of Nice, 759 km (474 mi) south of Paris.*

Gracious, cultivated, and made all the more cosmopolitan by the pres-
ence of some 30,000 international university students, the lovely old
town of Aix (pronounced ex) was once the capital of Provence. The
vestiges of that influence and power—fine art, noble architecture, and
graceful urban design—remain beautifully preserved today. That and
its thriving market, vibrant café life, and world-class music festival make
Aix tie with Arles and Avignon as one of the towns in Provence that
shouldn't be missed.

The Romans were first drawn here by mild thermal baths, naming the
town Aquae Sextiae (Waters of Sextius) in honor of the consul who
founded a camp near the source in 123 BC. Just 20 years later some
200,000 Germanic invaders besieged Aix, but the great Roman gen-
eral Marius flanked them and pinned them against the mountain
known ever since as Ste-Victoire. Marius remains a popular first name
to this day.

Under the wise and generous guidance of Roi René (King René) in the
15th century, Aix became a center of Renaissance arts and letters. At
the height of its political, judicial, and ecclesiastic power in the 17th
and 18th centuries, Aix profited from a surge of private building, each
grand *hôtel particulier* (mansion) vying to outdo its neighbor. Its sig-
nature *cours* (promenade) and *places* (squares), punctuated by grand
fountains and intriguing passageways, date from this time.

It was into this exalting elegance that artist Paul Cézanne (1839–1906)
was born, though he drew much of his inspiration from the raw coun-
tryside around the city and often painted Ste-Victoire. A schoolmate
of Cézanne's made equal inroads: the journalist and novelist Emile Zola
(1840–1902) attended the Collège Bourbon with Cézanne and de-
scribed their friendship as well as Aix itself in several of his works. You
can sense something of the ambience that nurtured these two geniuses
in the streets of modern Aix.

In the deep shade of tall plane trees interlacing their heavy leaves over
48 the street, **cours Mirabeau** is the social nerve center of Aix. One side

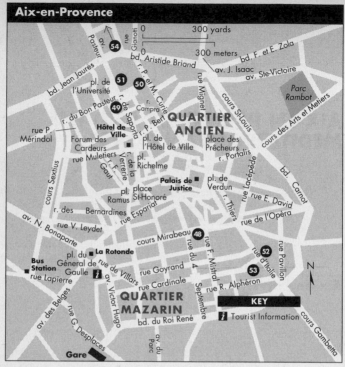

Aix-en-Provence

of the street is lined with dignified 18th-century hôtels particuliers; you can view them from a comfortable seat in one of the dozen or so cafés and restaurants that spill onto the sidewalk on the other side.

49 In the **Musée du Vieil Aix** (Museum of Old Aix), an eclectic assortment of local treasures resides in a 17th-century mansion, from faience to *santons* (terra-cotta figurines) to ornately painted furniture. The building itself is lovely, too. ✉ *17 rue Gaston-de-Saporta*, ☎ *04-42-21-43-55*. ✆ *15 frs.* ☉ *Apr.–Oct., Tues.–Sun. 10–noon and 2:30–6; Nov.–Mar., Tues.–Sun. 10–noon and 2–5.*

50 The **Musée des Tapisseries** (Tapestries Museum), housed in the 17th-century **Palais de l'Archevêché** (Archbishop's Palace), displays a sumptuous collection of tapestries that once decorated the walls of the bishop's quarters. In the broad courtyard, the main opera productions of the Festival International d'Art Lyrique take place. ✉ *Pl. de l'Ancien-Archevêché*, ☎ *04-42-23-09-91*. ✆ *10 frs.* ☉ *Wed.–Mon., 10–noon and 2–5:45.*

★ **51** The **Cathédrale St-Sauveur** (✉ Rue Gaston de Saporta) juxtaposes so many eras of architectural history, all clearly delineated and preserved, it's a survey course in itself. There are a double nave, Romanesque and Gothic side by side, and a Merovingian (5th-century) **baptistery,** its colonnade mostly recovered from Roman temples to other gods. Shutters hide the ornate 16th-century carvings on the **portals,** opened by a guide on request. The guide can also lead you into the tranquil Romanesque **cloisters** next door so you can admire the carved pillars and slender columns. As if these treasures weren't enough, the cathedral also contains an extraordinary 15th-century triptych, painted by Nicolas Froment in the heat of inspiration from his travels in Italy and Flanders. Entitled *Triptyque du Buisson Ardent* (*Burning Bush Triptych*), it depicts the generous art patrons King René and Queen Jeanne kneeling on each side of the Virgin, who is poised above a burning bush. Now, to avoid light damage, it's only opened for viewing Tuesday from 3 to 4.

52 The 12th-century **Église St-Jean-de-Malte** (⊠ At intersection of rue Cardinale and rue d'Italie) served as a chapel of the Knights of Malta, a medieval order of friars devoted to hospital care. It was Aix's first attempt at the Gothic style. It was here that the counts of Provence were buried throughout the 18th century; their tombs (in the upper left) were attacked during the Revolution and have been only partially repaired.

In the graceful Quartier Mazarin, below the cours Mirabeau, the **53** **Musée Granet** was once the Ecole de Dessin (Art School) that granted Cézanne a second prize in 1856. Cézanne's drawings and watercolors have been moved here from his studio, and there are eight of his paintings as well. You'll also find Rubens, David, Ingres, and a group of sentimental works by the museum's namesake, François Granet (1775–1849). In the archaeology section are statues and busts recovered from the early Roman settlement. ⊠ *Pl. St-Jean-de-Malte,* ☎ *04–42–38–14–70.* ◻ *10 frs.* ⊙ *Wed.–Mon., 10–noon and 2–6.*

54 Just north of the old-town loop is the **Atelier Cézanne** (Cézanne's Studio). After the death of his mother forced the sale of Paul Cézanne's (1839–1906) beloved country retreat, known as Jas de Bouffan, he had this studio built just above the town center. In the upstairs work space, the artist created some of his finest paintings, including *Les Grandes Baigneuses* (*The Large Bathers*). But what is most striking is the collection of simple objects that once featured prominently in the still lifes he created—redingote, bowler hat, ginger jar, and all. ⊠ *9 av. Paul-Cézanne,* ☎ *04–42–21–06–53.* ◻ *25 frs.* ⊙ *Apr.–Sept., daily 10–noon and 2:30–6; Oct.–Mar., daily 10–noon and 2–5. Guided tours Wed. and Sat. at 10 and 3 (English on request).*

Dining and Lodging

$$$$ ✕ **Le Clos de la Violette.** Whether you dine under the chestnut trees or
★ in the airy, pastel dining room, you'll get to experience the cuisine of one of the south's top chefs, Jean-Marc Banzo. Banzo spins tradition into gold, from pressed crab on a humble chickpea salad to langoustine tails on shortbread with coral ravioli. The restaurant isn't far from the Atelier Cézanne, outside the old-town ring. ⊠ *10 av. de la Violette,* ☎ *04–42–23–30–71. Jacket required. AE, MC, V. No lunch Mon.*

$$ ✕ **Les Bacchanales.** Despite a slightly self-important air and a position on a tourist-trap street off cours Mirabeau, this is a pleasant, intimate restaurant with inviting daub-filled beams, yellow-ochre stucco, and Louis XIII chairs. The broad range of fixed-price menus may include a delicate octopus salad, stuffed guinea hen, *rouget* (mullet) perfumed with sage and fennel, and caramelized pears over pistachio ice cream. As the name implies, wine figures large here, and the list is extensive. ⊠ *10 rue de la Couronne,* ☎ *04–42–27–21–06. AE, MC, V.*

$$ ✕ **Brasserie Les Deux Garcons.** The food is rather ordinary—stick to the *coquillages* (oysters and clams) or the smoked-duck salad—but eating isn't what you come here for. It's the linen-decked sidewalk tables facing onto the cours Mirabeau, the white-swathed waiters, and the blackboard menu. Dining inside is less glamorous, but the murals and gilt-ivory decor date to the restaurant's founding, in 1792. Cézanne, Zola, and Cocteau were devoted regulars. ⊠ *53 cours Mirabeau,* ☎ *04–42–26–00–51. MC, V.*

$$$$ ▥ **Villa Gallici.** Shaded by ancient cypress and plane trees and land-
★ scaped with jars of laurel and topiary boxwood, this luxurious hilltop garden retreat stands serenely apart from the city center—yet it's only steps away. Have breakfast on the shaded terrace, tea by the pool, then retreat to your extravagant room swagged with rich florals or plaids.

⊠ *Av. de la Violette, 13100,* ☎ *04–42–23–29–23,* FAX *04–42–96–30–45. 18 rooms, 4 suites. Restaurant, pool. AE, DC, MC, V.*

$$$ 🖭 **Augustins.** The best aspect of this old-town hotel, just a half block back from cours Mirabeau, is its reception area: The groin-vaulted stone, stained glass, and ironwork banister date from the 15th century, when the house was an Augustinian convent. The rooms are perfectly nice but a bit of a letdown, with heavy carpeting and fabric-covered walls. Bathrooms are all-white tile and marble. ⊠ *3 rue de la Masse, 13100,* ☎ *04–42–27–28–59,* FAX *04–42–26–74–87. 29 rooms. Breakfast room, air-conditioning. AE, DC, MC, V.*

$$–$$$ 🖭 **Nègre-Coste.** Its prominent cours Mirabeau position and its lavish public areas make this 18th-century town house a popular hotel. Now a fresh new Provençal decor and newly tiled bathrooms live up to the lovely ground-floor salons. It's worth the price to open your shutters in the morning and lean out over the cours Mirabeau with a cup of café crème in hand. ⊠ *33 cours Mirabeau, 13100,* ☎ *04–42–27–74–22,* FAX *04–42–26–80–93. 37 rooms. Breakfast room, air-conditioning. AE, DC, MC, V.*

$$ 🖭 **St-Christophe.** With so few midprice *hôtels de charme* in Aix and a distinct shortage of regional style, you might as well opt for this glossy Art Deco–style hotel, where the comfort and services are remarkable for the price. Rooms are slickly done in deep jewel tones, and the top-floor rooms have artisanal tiles in the bathrooms. ⊠ *2 av. Victor-Hugo, 13100,* ☎ *04–42–26–01–24,* FAX *04–42–38–53–17. 58 rooms, 7 suites. Restaurant, air-conditioning, parking (fee). AE, MC, V.* ✉

$–$$ 🖭 **Quatre Dauphins.** In the quiet Mazarin quarter, this modest but im-
★ peccable lodging inhabits a noble *hôtel particulier.* Its pretty, comfortable little rooms have been spruced up with *boutis* (Provençal quilts), Les Olivades fabrics, quarry tiles, jute carpets, and hand-painted furniture. The house-proud but unassuming owner-host bends over backward to please. ⊠ *55 rue Roux Alphéran, 13100,* ☎ *04–42–38–16–39,* FAX *04–42–38–60–19. 12 rooms. MC, V.*

Nightlife and the Arts

To find out what's going on in town, pick up a copy of the events calendar *Le Mois à Aix* or the bilingual city guide *Aix la Vivante* at the tourist office. **Le Scat Club** (⊠ 11 rue de la Verrerie, ☎ 04–42–23–00–23) is the place for live soul, funk, reggae, rock, blues, and jazz. For a night of playing roulette and the slot machines, head for the **Casino Municipal** (⊠ 2 bis av. N.-Bonaparte, ☎ 04–42–26–30–33).

Every July during the **Festival International d'Art Lyrique** (International Opera Festival; ☎ 04–42–17–34–00 for information), you can see world-class opera productions in the courtyard of the Palais de l'Archevêché.

Shopping

Aix is a market town, and a sophisticated **food and produce market** takes place every morning on place Richelme; just up the street, on place Verdun, is a good high-end **brocante** (collectibles market) Tuesday, Thursday, and Saturday mornings. A famous Aixois delicacy is *calissons,* a blend of almond paste and glazed melon in almond shapes. The most picturesque shops specializing in calissons are **Bechard** (⊠ 12 cours Mirabeau) and **Leonard Parli** (⊠ 35 av. Victor-Hugo), by the train station.

In addition to its old-style markets and jewel-box candy shops, Aix is a modern shopping town—perhaps the best in Provence. The winding streets of the Vieille Ville above cours Mirabeau—focused around **rue Clemenceau, rue Marius Reinaud, rue Espariat, rue Aude,** and **rue Maréchal Foch**—have a head-turning array of goods.

Marseille

31 km (19 mi) south of Aix-en-Provence, 188 km (117 mi) west of Nice, 772 km (483 mi) south of Paris.

Much maligned, Marseille is often given wide berth by travelers in search of a Provençal idyll. It's their loss, for they miss its Cubist jumbles of white stone rising up over a picture-book seaport, bathed in light of blinding clarity and crowned by larger-than-life neo-Byzantine churches. Its neighborhoods teem with multiethnic life, its souklike African markets reek deliciously of spices and coffees, its labyrinthine old town paints in broad strokes of saffron, cinnamon, and robin's-egg blue. Feisty and fond of broad gestures, Marseille is a dynamic city, as cosmopolitan now as when the Phoenicians first founded it and with all the exoticism of the international shipping port it has been for 2,600 years. Vital to the Crusades in the Middle Ages and crucial to Louis XIV as a military port, Marseille continued to flourish as France's market to the world—and still does today.

The heart of Marseille is clustered around the Vieux Port—immortalized in all its briny charm in the 1961 Leslie Caron film version of *Fanny.* The hills to the south of the port are crowned with megamonuments, such as Notre-Dame de la Garde and Fort St-Jean. To the north lies the ramshackle hilltop old town known as Le Panier. East of the port you'll find the North African neighborhood and, to its left, the famous thoroughfare called La Canebière. South of the city, the cliff-top waterfront highway leads to obscure and colorful ports and coves.

55 One of many museums devoted to Marseille's history as a shipping port, the **Musée de la Marine** (Marine Museum) concentrates on the 17th century to today. It's all about boats: There are steamboats and sailboats and schooners in miniature, as well as a collection of paintings and prints of the port in action. ⊠ *Palais de la Bourse, 7 La Canebière,* ☎ *04–91–39–33–33.* ⊞ *12 frs.* ☉ *Daily 10–6.*

★ **56** The modern, open-spaced **Musée d'Histoire de Marseille** (Marseille History Museum) illuminates Massalia's history by mounting its treasure of archaeological finds in didactic displays. There's a real Greek-era wooden boat in a hermetic display case. ⊠ *Centre Bourse, entrance on rue de Bir-Hakeim,* ☎ *04–91–90–42–22.* ⊞ *12 frs.* ☉ *Mon.–Sat. noon–7.*

57 The **Jardin des Vestiges** (Garden of Remains), just behind the Marseille History Museum, is on the site of the original waterfront of Marseille's classical prime and contains remains of the Greek fortifications and loading docks. It was discovered in 1967 when roadwork was being done next to the Bourse (Stock Exchange). ⊠ *Centre Bourse,* ☎ *04–91–90–42–22.* ⊞ *12 frs includes entry to Museum of History.* ☉ *Mon.–Sat. noon–7.*

★ **58** **Le Panier** is the old heart of Marseille, a maze of high shuttered houses looming over narrow cobbled streets, *montées* (stone stairways), and tiny squares. Long decayed and neglected, it is the principal focus of the city's efforts at urban renewal. Wander this atmospheric neighborhood at will, making sure to stroll along rue du Panier, the montée des Accoules, rue du Petit-Puits, and rue des Muettes.

★ **59** At the top of the Panier district, the **Centre de la Vieille Charité** (Center of the Old Charity) is a superb ensemble of 17th- and 18th-century architecture designed as a hospice for the homeless by Marseillais artist/architects Pierre and Jean Puget. Even if you don't visit the museums inside, walk around its inner court, studying the retreating perspective of triple arcades and admiring the Baroque chapel with its novel

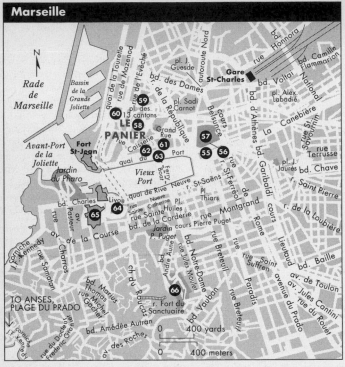

egg-peaked dome. Of the complex's two museums, the larger is the **Musée
d'Archéologie Méditerranéenne** (Museum of Mediterranean Archaeology), with a sizable collection of pottery and statuary from classical
Mediterranean civilization, erratically labeled (for example "pot").
There's also a display on the mysterious Celt-like Ligurians who first
peopled the coast, cryptically presented with the most emphasis on the
digs instead of the findings themselves. The best of the lot is the evoca-
tively mounted Egyptian collection, the second biggest in France, after
the Louvre. There are mummies, hieroglyphs and gorgeous sarcophagi,
in a tomblike setting. Also upstairs, the **Musée d'Arts Africains,
Océaniens, et Amérindiens** (Museum of African, Oceanian, and American Indian Art) provides a theatrical foil for the works' intrinsic drama:
The spectacular masks and sculptures are mounted along a pure black
wall, lighted indirectly, with labels across the aisle. ⊠ *2 rue de la Charité,* ☎ *04–91–14–58–80.* ⊡ *12 frs per museum.* ☉ *May–Sept., Tues.–
Sun. 11–6; Oct.–Apr., Tues.–Sun. 10–5.*

60 A gargantuan neo-Byzantine 19th-century fantasy, the **Cathédrale de
la Nouvelle Major** (⊠ Pl. de la Major) was built under Napoléon III—
but not before he'd ordered the partial destruction of the lovely 11th-
century original, once a perfect example of the Provençal Romanesque
style. You can view the flashy decor—marble and rich red porphyry
inlay—in the newer of the two churches; the medieval one is being
restored.

61 The **Musée du Vieux Marseille** (Museum of Old Marseille)—in the 16th-
century **Maison Diamantée** (one of the few buildings in this quarter
that would be spared by Hitler), so called because of its beveled-stone
diamondlike facade—concentrates on Marseille's Provençal personality. The collection includes beautifully carved wooden furniture, crèches,
and santons, and 19th-century clothes. Closed at press time for reno-

vations, it was slated to reopen by early 2001; check with the tourist office for new hours. ⊠ *Rue de la Prison,* ☎ *04–91–13–89–00 for information.*

In 1943 Hitler had the neighborhood along the quai du Port destroyed—some 2,000 houses—displacing some 20,000 citizens. This act of brutal urban renewal, ironically, laid open the ground for new discoveries. When Marseille began to rebuild in 1947, they dug up remains of a Roman shipping warehouse, full of terra-cotta jars and am-

㉒ phorae that once lay in the bellies of low-slung ships. The **Musée des Docks Romains** (Roman Docks Museum) created around it demonstrates the scale and range of Massalia's shipping prowess. ⊠ *Pl. de Vivaux,* ☎ *04–91–91–24–62.* ⚏ *12 frs.* ☉ *Oct.–May, Tues.–Sun. 10–5; June–Sept., Tues.–Sun. 11–6.*

㉓ Departing from the quai below the Hôtel de Ville, the **Ferry Boat** is a Marseille treasure. To hear the natives say "fer-ry bo-at" (they've adopted the English) is one of the joys of a visit here. For a pittance you can file onto this little wooden barge and chug across the Vieux Port. ⊠ *Travels between pl. des Huiles on the quai de Rive Neuve side and the Hôtel de Ville on the quai du Port.* ⚏ *3 frs.*

★ **㉔** Founded in the 4th century by St-Cassien, who sailed into Marseille's port full of fresh ideas on monasticism acquired in Palestine and Egypt, the **Abbaye St-Victor** grew to formidable proportions. With its severe exterior of crenellated stone and the spare geometry of its Romanesque church, the structure would be as at home in the Middle East as its founder. The Saracens destroyed the first structure, so the abbey was rebuilt in the 11th century and fortified against further onslaught in the 14th. By far the best reason to come: the **crypt,** St-Cassien's original, which lay buried under the medieval church's new structure. In evocative nooks and crannies you'll find the 5th-century sarcophagus that allegedly holds the martyr's remains. Upstairs look for the reliquary containing what's left of St. Victor himself, who was ground to death between millstones, probably by Romans. ⚏ *Crypt entry: 10 frs.* ☉ *Daily 8:30–6:30.*

㉕ The twinned structures of **Fort St-Nicolas and Fort St-Jean** enclose the Vieux Port's entry from both sides. In order to keep the feisty, rebellious Marseillais under his thumb, Louis XIV had the fortresses built with the guns pointing *inward.* To view them, climb up to the Jardin du Pharo.

㉖ Towering above the city and visible for miles around, the preposterously overscaled neo-Byzantine monument called **Notre-Dame-de-la-Garde** was erected in 1853 by the ever-tasteful Napoléon III. Its interior is a Technicolor bonanza of red-and-beige stripes and glittering mosaics. The gargantuan *Madonna and Child,* on the steeple (almost 30 ft high), is covered in real gold leaf. The boggling array of naive ex-votos, mostly thanking the Virgin for death-bed interventions and shipwreck survivals, make the pilgrimage worth it. ⊠ *On foot, climb up cours Pierre Puget, cross jardin Pierre Puget, cross bridge to rue Vauvenargues, and hike up to pl. Edon. Or catch Bus 60 from cours Jean-Ballard.* ☎ *04–91–13–40–80.* ☉ *May–Sept., daily 7 AM–8 PM; Oct.–Apr., daily 7–7.*

OFF THE BEATEN PATH

★ **CHÂTEAU D'IF –** François I, in the 16th century, recognized the strategic advantage of an island fortress surveying the mouth of Marseille's vast harbor, so he had one built. Its effect as deterrent was so successful, it never saw combat and was eventually converted to a prison. It was here that Alexandre Dumas locked up his most famous character, the Count of Monte Cristo. Though he was fictional, the hole Dumas had him escape through is real enough, and it's visible in the cells today. Video monitors playing relevant scenes from dozens of Monte Cristo films bring each tower and cell to life. On the other hand, the real-life Man in the Iron Mask, whose cell is still being shown, was not actually imprisoned here. The boat ride (from the quai des Belges, 50 francs) and the views from the broad terrace alone are worth the trip. ☎ 04–91–59–02–30. 🎫 *Château 25 frs.* ⊙ *Apr.–Sept., daily 9–7; Oct.–Mar., Tues.–Sun. 9–5:30.* ✎

Dining and Lodging

$$$ ✕ **Chez Fonfon.** Tucked into a storybook film set of a fishing port east
★ of the center, this landmark draws the Marseillais for plain, fresh seafood and classic bouillabaisse. Alexandre Pinna, the owner's son, has taken over for the late, great chef Fonfon, but the restaurant's cachet remains. ⊠ *140 rue du Vallon des Auffes,* ☎ *04–91–52–14–38. Reservations essential. AE, DC, MC, V. Closed 2 wks in Jan. No dinner Sun.*

$$$ ✕ **Mets de Provence.** Climb up the sleazy wharf-side stairs and enter a cosseted Provençal world. With the boats bobbing in the Vieux Port below the picture window and a landlubbing country decor, this extraordinarily romantic restaurant makes the most of Marseille's dual personality, split between land and sea. Classic Provençal hors d'oeuvres—tapenade, brandade, aïoli—lead into sophisticated seafood (dorade roasted with fennel and licorice) and meats (rack of lamb in herb pastry). There are a four-course lunch (200 francs including wine) and a six-course dinner (295 francs), artfully orchestrated but with plenty of choice. ⊠ *18 quai de Rive-Neuve,* ☎ *04–91–33–33–38. AE, MC, V. Closed Sun. No lunch Mon.*

$$ ✕ **Les Arcenaulx.** At this book-lined, red-walled haven in the stylish book-and-boutique complex of this renovated arsenal, you can have a sophisticated regional lunch—and read while you're waiting. Look for mussels in saffron with buckwheat crepes, carpaccio of cod with crushed olives, or rabbit with garlic confit. The terrace (on the Italian-scaled cours d'Estienne d'Orves) is as pleasant as the interior. ⊠ *25 cours d'Estienne d'Orves,* ☎ *04–91–59–80–30. AE, DC, MC, V. Closed Sun.*

$$ ✕ **Baie des Singes.** On a tiny rock-ringed lagoon as isolated from the nearby city as if it were a desert island, this cinematic corner of paradise was once a customs house under Napoléon III. You can rent a mattress and lounge chair, dive into the turquoise water, and shower off for the only kind of meal worthy of such a setting: fresh fish. It's all served at terrace tables overlooking the water. ⊠ *Anse des Croisettes, Les Goudes,* ☎ *04–91–73–68–87. AE, DC, MC, V. Closed Oct.–Mar.*

$$ ✕ **Le Panier des Arts.** Behind a saffron-color facade and lace-covered windows, this sophisticated neighborhood bistro welcomes regulars and visitors. The cooking is straightforward but soigné—a basket of crudités with aïoli, a simple steak with shallots, and a modest local wine—and served on unpretentious olive-print oilcloths. ⊠ *3 rue du Petit-Puits,* ☎ *04–91–56–02–32. MC, V. Closed Sun.*

$ ✕ **Etienne.** This historic Le Panier hole-in-the-wall has more than just
★ a good fresh-anchovy pizza from the wood-burning oven. There are also fried squid, eggplant gratin, a slab of rare-grilled beef big enough for two, and the quintessential *pieds et paquets*, Marseille's earthy classic of sheeps' feet and stuffed tripe. ⊠ *43 rue de la Lorette,* ☎ *no phone. No credit cards.*

$$$$ ✕🏠 **Le Petit Nice.** On a rocky promontory overlooking the sea, this
★ fantasy villa was bought from a countess in 1917 and converted to a hotel/restaurant. The Passédat family has been getting it right ever since, with father and son manning the exceptional kitchen (one of the coast's best), creating truffled brandade, sea anemone beignets, fresh fish

roasted whole, and licorice soufflé (the restaurant is closed Sunday). Most rooms are sleek and minimalist, with some Art Deco–cum–postmodern touches. ⊠ *Anse de Maldormé, corniche J.-F.-Kennedy, 13007,* ☎ *04–91–59–25–92,* 𝖥𝖠𝖷 *04–91–59–28–08. 15 rooms. Restaurant, air-conditioning, pool. AE, DC, MC, V.* 🐾

$$$ 🏨 **Mercure Beauvau Vieux Port.** The antiques are real, the woodwork
★ burnished with age; add a little marble, a touch of brass, and deep carpet underfoot, and you have an idea of this intimate urban hotel's genuine old-world charm. George Sand kept a suite here—knowing that makes the plush retro appearance of all the rooms, with paisleys and moiré, seem all the more appropriate. Port-view rooms more than justify the splurge. ⊠ *4 rue Beauvau, 13001,* ☎ *04–91–54–91–00; 800/ MERCURE for U.S. reservations,* 𝖥𝖠𝖷 *04–91–54–15–76. 71 rooms. Bar, breakfast room, air-conditioning. AE, DC, MC, V.*

$–$$ 🏨 **Alizé.** On the Vieux Port, its front rooms taking in postcard views, this straightforward lodging has been modernized to include tight double windows, slick modular baths, and a laminate-and-all-weather-carpet look. Public spaces have exposed stone and preserved details, and a glass elevator whisks you to your floor. It's an excellent value and location for the price. ⊠ *35 quai des Belges, 13001,* ☎ *04–91–33–66–97,* 𝖥𝖠𝖷 *04–91–54–80–06. 37 rooms. Air-conditioning. AE, DC, MC, V.*

$–$$ 🏨 **Hermès.** Just around the corner from the Quai du Port, this modest city hotel has been smartly renovated. Rooms are snug and modular, with all-new baths. Ask for one of the fifth-floor rooms with tiny balconies overlooking the port—or the crow's-nest *nuptiale* double with a private rooftop terrace. ⊠ *2 rue Bonneterie, 13002,* ☎ *04–96–11– 63–63,* 𝖥𝖠𝖷 *04–96–11–63–64. 29 rooms. Breakfast room, air-conditioning. AE, DC, MC, V.*

Nightlife and the Arts

With a population of more than 800,000, Marseille is a big city by French standards, with all the nightlife the name entails. Arm yourself with *Marseille Poche,* a glossy monthly events minimagazine; the monthly *In Situ,* a free guide to music, theater and galleries; *Sortir,* a weekly about film, art, and concerts in southern Provence; or *TakTik,* a hip weekly on theater and new art. They're all in French. Rock, jazz, and reggae concerts are held at the **Espace Julien** (⊠ 39 cours Julien, ☎ 04–91–24–34–10). **Le Trolleybus** (⊠ 24 quai de Rive Neuve, ☎ 04–91–54–30–45) is the most popular disco in town, with a young, *branché* (hip) crowd. Classical music concerts are given in the **Abbaye St-Victor** (☎ 04–91–05–84–48 for information). Operas and orchestral concerts take place at the **Opéra Municipal** (⊠ 2 rue Molière, pl. Ernest Reyer, ☎ 04–91–55–21–24).

Outdoor Activities and Sports

Marseille's waterfront position makes it easy to swim and sunbathe within the city sprawl. From the Vieux Port, Bus 83 or Bus 19 takes you to the vast green spread of reclaimed land called the **Parc Balnéaire du Prado.** Its waterfront is divided into beaches, all of them public and well equipped. The beach surface varies between sand and gravel.

Marseille is a major center for diving (*plongée*), with several organizations offering *baptêmes* (baptisms, or first dives) to beginners. The coast is lined with rocky inlets, grottos, and ancient shipwrecks, not to mention thronging with aquatic life. For general information contact the **Association Plongez Marseille** (⊠ 5 rue de Valmy, 13012, ☎ 𝖥𝖠𝖷 04–91–49–12–93).

Shopping

The locally famous bakery **Four des Navettes** (⊠ 136 rue Sainte, ☎ 04–91–33–32–12), up the street from Notre-Dame-de-la-Garde, makes orange-spice, shuttle-shape *navettes*. These cookies are modeled on the little boat in which Mary Magdalene and Lazarus washed onto continental shores. **Savon de Marseille** (Marseille soap) is a household standard in France, often sold as a satisfyingly crude and hefty block in odorless olive-oil green. But the chichi offspring are dainty pastel guest soaps in almond, lemon, vanilla, and other scents.

Aubagne

67 *16 km (10 mi) east of Marseille, 36 km (22 mi) south of Aix-en-Provence.*

This easygoing, plane-tree-shaded market town is an ideal spot to spend the morning browsing through the old town or basking on the broad tree-lined squares. Aubagne claims the title of the *santon*-making capital of Provence. The craft, originally from Marseille, was focused here at the turn of the 20th century, when artisans moved inland to make the most of local clay. The more than a dozen studios in town are set up for you to observe the production process. Make sure you visit Aubagne on a market day, when the sleepy center is transformed into a tableau of Provençal life. The Tuesday market is the biggest.

The town is proud of its native son, the dramatist, filmmaker, and chronicler of all things Provençal, Marcel Pagnol, best known as the author of *Jean de Florette* and *Manon des Sources* (*Manon of the Springs*) and the stories that comprise the Fanny trilogy. You can study miniature dioramas of scenes from Pagnol stories at **Le Petit Monde de Marcel Pagnol** (The Small World of Marcel Pagnol). ✉ *Esplanade de Gaulle.* 🎫 *Free.* ☉ *Daily 9–noon and 2–6.*

Even if you haven't read Pagnol's works or seen his films, you can enjoy the **Circuit Pagnol,** a hike in the raw-hewn, arid *garrigues* (scrublands) behind Marseille and Aubagne. Here Pagnol spent his idyllic summers, described in his *Souvenirs d'un Enfance* (*Memories of a Childhood*). When he grew up to be a famous playwright and filmmaker, he shot some of his best work in these hills. After Pagnol's death Claude Berri came back to find a location for his remake of *Manon des Sources* but found it so altered by brush fires and power cables, he chose to shoot in the Luberon instead. Although the trail may no longer shelter the pine-shaded olive orchards of its past, it still gives you the chance to walk through primeval Provençal countryside and rewards you with spectacular views of Marseille and the sea. ✉ *To access marked trail by yourself, drive to La Treille northeast of Aubagne and follow signs. For an accompanied tour with literary commentary, contact tourist office:* ☎ *04–42–03–49–98.*

Another claim to fame for Aubagne: It's the headquarters for the French Foreign Legion. The legion was created in 1831 and accepts recruits from all nations, no questions asked. The **Musée de la Légion Étrangère,** named after the distinctive white caps of the *légionnaires*, does its best to polish the image by way of medals, uniforms, weapons, and photographs. ✉ *Caserne Viénot (to get there, take a left off D2 onto D44A just before Aubagne),* ☎ *04–42–18–82–41.* 🎫 *Free.* ☉ *June–Sept., Tues.–Thurs. and weekends 10–noon and 3–7, Fri. 10–noon; Oct.–May, Wed. and weekends 10–noon and 2–6.*

Dining

$ ✗ **La Farandole.** In a rustic Provençal setting of lemon-print cloths, lace curtains, and the region's typical bow-legged chairs, you can enjoy good home cooking with local regulars who claim the same table every day. The inexpensive daily menu may feature panfried chicken livers on a green salad, *rascasse* (a local fish) with sorrel, or garlicky steak and *frites* (fries); wine is included. ⊠ 6 *rue Martino (just off cours Maréchal, on a narrow street leading into the old town)*, ☎ 04–42–03–26–36. *MC, V. Closed Sun. No dinner Mon.*

Cassis

68 *11 km (7 mi) south of Aubagne, 30 km (19 mi) east of Marseille, 42 km (26 mi) west of Toulon.*

Surrounded by vineyards, flanked by monumental cliffs, guarded by the ruins of a medieval castle, and nestled around a picture-perfect fishing port, Cassis is the prettiest coastal town in Provence. Stylish without being too recherché, it provides shelter to numerous pleasure-boaters, who restock their galleys at its market, replenish their nautical duds in its boutiques, and relax with a bottle of Cassis and a platter of sea urchins in one of its numerous waterfront cafés. Pastel houses at Cubist angles frame the port, and the mild rash of parking-garage architecture that scars its outer neighborhoods can't spoil the general effect, which is one of pure and unadulterated charm.

The **Château de Cassis** has loomed over the harbor since the invasions of the Saracens in the 7th century, evolving over the centuries into a walled enclosure crowned with stout watch towers. It's private property today and best viewed from a port-side café.

You can't visit Cassis without touring the **Calanques,** the fjordlike finger bays that probe the rocky coastline. Either take a sightseeing cruise or hike across the cliff tops, clambering down the steep sides to these barely accessible retreats. Or you can combine the two, going in by boat and hiking back; make arrangements at the port (☞ Outdoor Activities and Sports, *below*). The Calanque closest to Cassis is the least attractive: **Port Miou** was a stone quarry until 1982, when the Calanques became protected sites. Now this calanque is an active leisure and fishing port. **Calanque Port Pin** is prettier, with wind-twisted pines growing at angles from the white-rock cliffs. But it's the third calanque that's

★ a corner of paradise: the **Calanque En Vau** is a castaway's dream, with a tiny beach at its root and jagged cliffs looming overhead. The series of massive cliffs and calanques stretch all the way to Marseille.

Dining and Lodging

$$ ✕ **Monsieur Brun.** One of the most authentic meals you can have in Cassis is a platter of raw shellfish. At this terrace brasserie on the west side of the port, a multitier tower of shellfish on a bed of kelp is served with nothing but bread, butter, and a finger towelette. Have the nutty little *bleues*, the local oyster, but *oursins* (sea urchins) are a Cassis specialty, and these are brought in daily by the chef's fisherman friend. Omelets and salads are alternatives. ⊠ *2 quai Calendal*, ☎ 04–42–01–82–66. *No credit cards. Closed mid-Dec.–mid-Jan.*

$$ ✕▥ **Jardin d'Émile.** Tucked back from the waterfront under quarried
★ cliffs and massive parasol pines, this stylish yet homey inn takes in views of the cape. Rooms are intimate and welcoming, with rubbed-chalk walls, scrubbed pine, and weathered stone. The restaurant is atmospheric, on a permanently sheltered garden terrace surrounded by greenery and, by night, the illuminated cliffs. Regional specialties with a cosmopolitan twist—such as rascasse filled with goat cheese and wrapped in eggplant— are served on locally made pottery. ⊠ *Plage du Bestouan, 13260*, ☎ 04–42–01–80–55, ℻ 04–42–01–80–70. *7 rooms. Restaurant, air-conditioning. AE, DC, MC, V.* ✍

$$$ ▥ **Les Roches Blanches.** First built as a private home in 1887, this cliffside villa takes in smashing views of the port and the Cap Canaille, both from the best rooms and from the panoramic dining hall. The beautifully landscaped terrace is shaded by massive pines, and the horizon-line pool seems to spill into the sea. Yet the ambience is far from snooty or deluxe; rather it's friendly, low-key, and pleasantly mainstream. ⊠ *Rte. des Calanques, 13260,* ☎ *04–42–01–09–30,* FAX *04–42–01–94–23. 19 rooms, 5 suites. 2 restaurants, pool. AE, MC, V.* 🕮

Outdoor Activities and Sports

To go on a **boat ride** to Les Calanques, get to the port around 10 AM or 2 PM and look for a boat that's loading passengers. Round-trips should include visits to at least three Calanques and average 65 francs. To **hike** the Calanques, gauge your skills: The GR98 (marked with red-and-white bands) is the most scenic but requires scrambling to get down the sheer walls of En Vau. The alternative is to follow the green markers and approach En Vau from behind. If you're ambitious, you can hike the length of the GR98 between Marseille and Cassis, following the coastline.

En Route   From Cassis head east out of town and cut sharply right up the **route des Crêtes.** This road takes you along a magnificent crest over the water and up to the very top of **Cap Canaille.** Venture out on the vertiginous trails to the edge, where the whole coast stretches below.

Bandol

⑥⑨ *25 km (15½ mi) southeast of Cassis, 15 km (9 mi) west of Toulon.*

Although its name means wine to most of the world, Bandol is also a popular and highly developed seaside resort town. It has seafood snack shacks, generic brasseries, a harbor packed with yachts, and a waterfront promenade. Yet the east end of town conceals lovely old villas framed in mimosas, bougainvillea, and pine. And a port-side stroll up the palm-lined allée Jean-Moulin feels downright Côte d'Azur. But be warned: The sheer concentration of high-summer crowds can't be exaggerated. If you're not a beach lover, pick up an itinerary from the tourist office and visit a few Bandol vineyards just outside town.

Brignoles

⑦⓪ *86 km (47 mi) northwest of Bandol, 70 km (39 mi) north of Toulon-* This rambling backcountry hill town, crowned with a medieval chateau, is the market center for the wines of the Var and the crossroads of this green, ungentrified region—until now, that is. With a new Ducasse restaurant in the region, real estate has rocketed, and le tout Paris whispers that this little corner of nowheresville is The Next Luberon. The main point of interest in the region is the **Abbaye de La Celle,** a 12th-century Benedictine abbey that served as a convent until the 17th century, when it was closed because its young nuns had began to run wild and were known less for their chastity than "the color of their petticoats and the name of their lover." There's a refectory and a ruined cloister; the simple Romanesque chapel still serves as the parish church.

Dining and Lodging

$$$–$$$$ ✕▥ **Hostellerie de l'Abbaye de La Celle.** Superchef Alain Ducasse
    ★   continues to diversify and expand investments, now having opened this new country inn buried in the unspoiled backcountry north of Toulon and just southwest of Brignoles. Just up the road from the abbey, this beautifully restored 18th-century *bastide* (country house) has rooms overlooking vineyards and a park thick with chestnut and mulberry trees. Heading the formidable kitchen is chef Benoît Witz, transferred from Ducasse's Bastide at Moustiers, whose creations glorify the rustic: wild mushrooms sautéed with crayfish, rabbit with olives and po-

lenta, crisp French toast with strawberries. ⊠ *Pl. du Général-de-Gaulle, 83170 La Celle,* ☎ *04–98–05–14– 14,* FAX *04–98–05–14–15. 10 rooms. Restaurant, pool. AE, DC, MC, V.* ❧

Iles d'Hyères

⓻ *32 km (20 mi) off the coast south of Hyères. To get to the islands, follow the narrow Giens Peninsula to La Tour-Fondue, at its tip. Boats (leaving every half hour in summer, every 60 or 90 minutes the rest of the year for 80 francs round-trip) make a 20-minute beeline to Porquerolles. For Port-Cros and Levant, you'll depart from Port d'Hyères at Hyères-Plages.*

Off the southeastern point of France's star and spanning some 32 km (20 mi), this archipelago of islands could be a set for a pirate movie; in fact, it has featured in several, thanks to a soothing microclimate and a wild and rocky coastline dotted with palms. And not only film pirates made their appearance: In the 16th century the islands were seeded with convicts to work the land. They soon ran amok and used their adopted base to ambush ships heading into Toulon.

★ A more wholesome population claims the islands today, which consists of three main bodies. **Port-Cros** is a national park, with both its surface and underwater environs protected. **Levant** has been taken over, for the most part, by nudists. **Porquerolles** is the largest and best of the lot—and a popular escape from the modern world. Off-season, it's a castaway paradise of pine forests, sandy beaches, and vertiginous cliffs above rocky coastline. Inland, its preserved pine forests and orchards of olives and figs are crisscrossed with dirt roads to be explored on foot or on bikes; except for the occasional jeep or work truck, the island is car-free. In high season (April to October) day-trippers pour off the ferries and surge to the beaches.

Dining and Lodging

$$$ ✕🏨 **Mas du Langoustier.** Amid lush terrain at the westernmost point
★ of the Ile de Porquerolles, 3 km (2 mi) from the harbor, this luxurious hideout is a popular getaway. Owner Madame Richard will pick you up at the port in her Dodge; her grandmother was given the island as a wedding gift. Choose between big new California-modern rooms and cosseted old-style rooms in the original section. Chef Joël Guillet creates inspired southern French cuisine, to be accompanied by the rare island rosé. ⊠ *Pointe du Langoustier, 83400 Ile de Porquerolles,* ☎ *04–94–58–30–09,* FAX *04–94–58–36–02. 49 rooms. Restaurant, tennis courts, beach, billiards. AE, DC, MC, V. Closed Nov.–Apr.* ❧

$$–$$$ ✕🏨 **Les Glycines.** In soft shades of yellow ochre and sky blue, this sleekly modernized little bastide has an idyllic enclosed courtyard. Back rooms look over a jungle of mimosa and eucalyptus. Public salons have Provençal chairs and fabrics. The restaurant, where food is served on the terrace or in the garden, features port-fresh tuna and sardines. The inn is just back from the port in the village center. ⊠ *Pl. d'Armes, 83400 Ile de Porquerolles,* ☎ *04–94–58–30–36,* FAX *04–94–58–35–22. 11 rooms. Restaurant, bar, air-conditioning. AE, MC, V.*

Outdoor Activities and Sports

You can rent a mountain bike (*velo tout-terrain,* or VTT) for a day to pedal the paths and cliff-top trails of Porquerolles at **Cycle Porquerol** (⊠ Rue de la Ferme, ☎ 04–94–58–30–32) or **L'Indien** (⊠ Pl. d'Armes, ☎ 04–94–58–30–39). **Locamarine 75** (⊠ On port, ☎ 04–94–58–35–84) rents motorboats to amateurs with or without license.

PROVENCE A TO Z

Arriving and Departing

By Car
A6/A7 (a toll road) from Paris, known as the Autoroute du Soleil—the Highway of the Sun—takes you straight to Provence, when it divides at Orange, 659 km (412 mi) from Paris; the trip can be done in a fast five hours or so.

By Plane
Marseille is served by frequent flights from Paris and London, and daily flights from Paris arrive at the smaller airport at Nîmes, which serves Arles and the Camargue (the trip takes about an hour). There are direct flights in the summer from the United States to Nice, 160 km (100 mi) from Aix-en-Provence.

By Train
The high-speed TGV (*Trains à Grande Vitesse*) goes from Paris (Gare de Lyon) to Avignon in less than four hours. Add another hour for Marseille and Nîmes. For other destinations you must change to local trains.

Getting Around

By Bicycle
Bikes can be rented from the train stations in Aix-en-Provence, Arles, Avignon, Marseille, Nîmes, and Orange for a cost of about 40 francs per day. Contact the **Comité Départemental de Cyclotourisme** (⊠ Les Passadoires, 84420 Piolenc) for a list of scenic bike routes in Provence.

By Bus
A moderately good network of bus services links places not served, or badly served, by train. If you plan to explore Provence by bus, Avignon, Marseille, Aix-en-Provence, and Arles are good bases. Avignon is also the starting point for excursion bus tours and boat trips down the Rhône.

By Car
After route A7 divides at Orange, A9 heads west to Nîmes (723 km [448 mi] from Paris) and continues into the Pyrénées and across the Spanish border. Route A7 continues southeast from Orange to Marseille on the coast (1,100 km [680 mi] from Paris), while A8 goes to Aix-en-Provence (with a spur to Toulon) and then to the Côte d'Azur and Italy.

By Train
After the main line of the TGV divides at Avignon, the westbound link of the TGV heads to Nîmes (less than five hours from Paris by TGV) and points west. The southeast-bound link of the TGV takes in Marseille (also under five hours from Paris by TGV), Toulon, and the Côte d'Azur. There is also frequent service of daily local trains to other towns in the region from these main TGV stops.

Contacts and Resources

Bed and Breakfasts
Gîtes de France, the French national network of vacation lodging, rate participating B&Bs for comfort and lists them in a catalog (☞ Lodging *in* Smart Travel Tips A to Z). For chambres d'hotes regulated by this national network, contact the local branches, divided by *départements* (administrative regions). Addresses are listed under Vacation Rentals, *below.*

Car Rental
Avis (⊠ 11 bd. Gambetta, Aix, ☎ 04–42–21–64–16; ⊠ At train station, Avignon, ☎ 04–90–27–96–10; ⊠ At train station, Marseille, ☎

04–91–64–71–00; ⊠ 19 av. Charles de Gaulle, Orange, ☎ 04–90–34–11–00).

Budget (⊠ Bd. St-Roch, Avignon, ☎ 04–90–27–94–95; ⊠ 42 bd. Edouard Daladier, Orange, ☎ 04–90–34–00–34).

Hertz (⊠ 43 av. Victor Hugo, Aix, ☎ 04–42–27–91–32; ⊠ 2A av. Monclar, Avignon, ☎ 04–90–14–26–90; ⊠ Train station, Marseille, ☎ 04–91–90–14–03).

Guided Tours

The tourist offices in Arles, Nîmes, Avignon, Aix-en-Provence, and Marseille (☞ Visitor Information, *below*) all organize a variety of walking tours (some in summer only). For 300 francs, **Taxis T.R.A.N.** (☎ 04–66–29–40–11) can take you on a round-trip ride from Nîmes to the Pont du Gard (ask the taxi to wait while you explore for 30 minutes).

Travel Agencies

Havas (⊠ 4 bd. des Lices, Arles, ☎ 04–90–18–31–31; ⊠ 35 rue de la République, Avignon, ☎ 04–90–80–66–80; ⊠ 44 bd. Victor Hugo, Nîmes, ☎ 04–66–36–99–99; ⊠ 34 rue de la République, Orange, ☎ 04–90–11–44–44). **Nouvelle Frontières** (⊠ 14 rue Carnot, Avignon, ☎ 04–90–82–31–32). **Provence-Camargue Tours** (⊠ 1 rue Émile Fassin, Arles, ☎ 04–90–49–85–58).

Vacation Rentals

Properties for rent in Provence are listed by the national house-rental agency, **Gîtes de France** (*in* Smart Travel Tips A to Z). Regional offices include: **Bouches-du-Rhône** (⊠ Domaine du Vergon, B.P. 26, 13370 Mallemort, ☎ 04–90–59–49–40, FAX 04–90–59–16–75). **Gard** (⊠ 3 pl. des Arènes, B.P. 59, 30007 Nîmes Cedex 4, ☎ 04–66–27–94–94, FAX 04–66–27–94–95). **Var** (⊠ 1 bd. Maréchal Foch, Draguignan, ☎ 04–94–50–93–93, FAX 04–94–50–93–90). **Vaucluse** (⊠ Pl. Campana, B.P. 164, 84008 Avignon Cedex 1, ☎ 04–90–85–45–00). In addition, each of the tourist offices for towns in the region usually publishes lists of independent rentals (*locations meublés*), many of them inspected and classified by the tourist office itself.

Visitor Information

Regional tourist offices prefer written queries only. The mother lode of general information is the **Comité Regional du Tourisme de Provence-Alpes-Côte d'Azur** (⊠ 12 pl. Joliette, 13002 Marseille, ☎ 04–91–56–47–00, FAX 04–91–56–47–01). For information specific to one département, contact the following: **Comité Départemental du Tourisme des Bouches-du-Rhône** (⊠ 13 rue Roux de Brignole, 13006 Marseille, ☎ 04–91–13–84–13, FAX 04–91–33–01–82). **Comité Départemental du Tourisme du Var** (⊠ 1 bd. Maréchal Foch, 83300 Draguignan, ☎ 04–94–50–55–50, FAX 04–94–50–55–51). **Comité Départemental du Tourisme de Vaucluse** (⊠ B.P. 147, 84008 Avignon Cedex 1, ☎ 04–90–80–47–00, FAX 04–90–86–86–08).

Local tourist offices for major towns covered in this chapter can be phoned, faxed, or addressed by mail. **Aix** (⊠ 2 pl. du Général-de-Gaulle, B.P. 160, 13605 Cedex 1, ☎ 04–42–16–11–61, FAX 04–42–16–11–62). **Arles** (⊠ 35 pl. de la République, 13200, ☎ 04–90–18–41–21, FAX 04–90–93–17–17). **Avignon** (⊠ 41 cours Jean-Jaurès, 84000, ☎ 04–90–82–65–11, FAX 04–90–82–95–03). **Marseille** (⊠ 4 La Canebière, 13001, ☎ 04–91–13–89–00, FAX 03–91–13–89–20). **Nîmes** (⊠ 6 rue Auguste, 3000 Nîmes, ☎ 04–66–67–29–11, FAX 04–66–21–81–04). **Orange** (⊠ 5 cours A. Briand, 84100, ☎ 04–90–34–70–88, FAX 04–90–34–99–62). **St-Rémy** (⊠ Pl. Jean-Jaurès, 13210 St-Rémy, ☎ 04–90–92–05–22, FAX 04–90–92–38–52).

12 THE CÔTE D'AZUR

This is the Riviera of Hollywood lore, the land of sunglasses, convertibles, and palm trees waving over indigo surf. From glamorous St-Tropez and Cannes to picturesque Antibes to sophisticated Nice, this captivating sprawl of pebble beaches and ochre villas has drawn sun lovers and socialites since the days of the Grand Tour. And artists, too: Renoir, Matisse, Picasso, and Cocteau all reveled in the light and left an impressive legacy of modern art behind them. If you weary of the coast, it's three quick heel-clicks into another world—the golden hill towns of Old Provence, lie just behind the shore: St-Paul, Vence, Grasse.

WITH THE ALPS AND PRE-ALPS PLAYING bodyguard against inland winds and the sultry Mediterranean warming the sea breezes, the Côte d'Azur is pampered by a nearly tropical climate. Thus, this is where the dreamland of azure waters and indigo sky begins, with white villas with balustrades edging the blue horizon, evening air perfumed with jasmine and mimosa, and parasol pines silhouetted against sunsets of apricot and gold. Ideal as the cover of a Jazz Age sheet music tune, the image of the Côte d'Azur seems to define happiness itself in the mind of the world, a happiness the world has pursued with a vengeance.

Revised and updated by Nancy Coons

But the Jazz Age dream confronts modern reality: On the hills that undulate along the blue water, every cliff, cranny, gully, and plain bristles with hot pink cubes of cement and iron balconies skewed toward the sea and the sun. Like a rosy rash these crawl and spread, outnumbering the trees and blocking each other's views. Their owners and renters who arrive at every vacation—Easter, Christmas, Carnival, All Saints'—choke the tiered highways with their bumper cars, and on a hot day in high summer the traffic to the beach—slow-flowing any day—coagulates and blisters in the sun.

There has always been a rush to the Côte d'Azur, starting with the ancient Greeks drawn eastward from Marseille to market their goods to the natives. From the 18th-century English aristocrats who claimed it as one vast spa to the 19th-century Russian nobles who transformed Nice into a tropical St. Petersburg to the 20th-century American tycoons who cast themselves as romantic sheiks, the coast beckoned like a blank slate for their whims. Like the modern vacationers who have followed in their footsteps, they all have left their mark on the coast—their villas, their shrines, their Moroccan-fantasy castles-in-the-air—temples all to the sensual pleasures of the sun and sultry sea breeze. Artists, too, made the Côte d'Azur their own, as museum goers who've studied the sunny legacy of Picasso, Renoir, Matisse, and Chagall will attest. Today's visitors can take this all in, along with the Riviera's textbook points of interest: animated St-Tropez; the Belle Epoque aura of Cannes; the towns made famous by Picasso—Antibes, Vallauris, Mougins; the urban charm of Nice; and several spots where the per-capita population of billionaires must be among the highest on earth: Cap d'Antibes, Villefranche-sur-Mer, and Monaco. The latter, once a Belle Epoque fairyland, has for some time been known as the Hong Kong of the Riviera, a hustling community where the sounds of drills tearing up the ground to build something new has replaced the clip-clop of the horse-drawn fiacres. The ghosts of Grace Kelly and Cary Grant must be residing somewhere else.

Veterans know that the beauty of the Côte d'Azur coastline is only skin deep, a thin veneer of coddled glamour that hugs the water and hides a much more ascetic region beyond it up in the hills. These low-lying mountains and deep gorges are known as the *arriére-pays* (backcountry) for good cause: They are as aloof and isolated as the waterfront resorts are in the swim. Medieval stone villages cap rocky hills and play out scenes of Provençal life—the game of boules, the slow *pastis* (the anise-and-licorice-flavored spirit mixed slowly with water), the farmers' market—as if the ocean were a hundred miles away. Some of them—Eze, St-Paul, Vence—have become virtual Provençal theme parks, catering to busloads day-tripping from the coast. But just behind them, dozens of hill towns stand virtually untouched, and you can lose yourself in a cobblestone maze.

You could drive from St-Tropez to the Italian border in three hours and see the entire Riviera, so small is this renowned stretch of Mediterranean coast. Along the way you'll undoubtedly encounter the downside: jammed beaches, insolent waiters serving frozen seafood, gridlocked traffic. But once you dabble your feet off the docks in picturesque ports full of brightly painted boats, or drink a Lillet in a hilltop village high above the coast, or tip your face up to the sun from a boardwalk park bench and doze to the rhythm of the waves, you—like the artists and nobles who paved the way before you—will likely be seduced to linger.

— Nancy Coons

Pleasures and Pastimes

Art

Because the Côte d'Azur has long nurtured a relationship among artists, art lovers, and wealthy patrons, this region is blessed with superb art museums. Renoir, Picasso, Matisse, Chagall, Cocteau, Léger, and Dufy all left their mark here; museums devoted to their work are scattered along the coast. Formidable collections of modern masters and contemporary works can be seen in the museums of Nice and at the Fondation Maeght above St-Paul. St-Tropez has a good collection of Impressionist paintings of its port at the Musée de l'Annonciade.

Beaches

With their worldwide fame as the earth's most glamorous beaches, the real thing often comes as a shock to first-timers: Much of the Côte d'Azur is lined with rock and pebble, and the beaches are narrow swathes backed by city streets or roaring highways. Only St-Tropez and isolated bits around Fréjus and Antibes have sandy waterfront. Many beaches are private, renting parasols and mattresses to anyone who pays; if you're a guest of one of these hotels, you'll get a discount, but beach access is not included in the price of your stay. Fees for private beaches average 40–65 francs for a dressing room and mattress, between 15 and 25 francs for a parasol, and between 25 and 35 francs for a cabana to call your own. Private beaches alternate with open stretches of public frontage served by free toilets and open showers.

Dining

Typical throughout Provence but especially at home with a slab of fresh coastal fish, the garlicky mayonnaise called *aïoli* is a staple condiment. Even more pungent is the powerful paste called *anchoiade,* made of strong, salty anchovies. The Provençal version of pesto, basil-y *pistou* flavors a hearty vegetable soup called *soupe au pistou.* Fresh Mediterranean fish, such as *rouget* (mullet) and *loup* (sea bass), often are served grilled with a crunch of fennel. Your plate may be garnished with ratatouille, or zucchini flowers, stuffed and fried in batter. Niçois specialties include the *pissaladière,* the father of modern pizza, topped with a heap of caramelized onions. It's a good picnic takeout, as is a hefty *pan bagnat,* a pitalike bun with tuna, hard-boiled eggs, tomatoes, and olives. Try *socca,* a paste of ground chickpeas smeared on a griddle and scraped up like a gritty pancake; *petits farcis,* a selection of red peppers, zucchini, and eggplant stuffed with spicy sausage paste and roasted; and sardine beignets, fresh, whole sardines fried in a thick puff of spicy batter.

CATEGORY	COST*
$$$$	over 500 frs
$$$	250 frs–500 frs
$$	150 frs–250 frs
$	under 150 frs

per person for a three-course meal, including tax (20.6%) and tip but not wine

✎ *following the text of a review is your signal that the property has a Web site, where you will find details and, usually, images; for a link, visit www.fodors.com/urls.*

Lodging

If you've come from other regions in France—even western Provence—you'll notice a sharp hike in hotel prices, costly by any standard, but vertiginous in summer. In Cannes and Nice the grand hotels are big on prestige and weak on swimming pools, which are usually just big enough to dip in; their private beaches are on the other side of the busy street, and you'll have to pay for access, just as nonguests do. Up in the hills above the coast you'll find the charm you expect from France, both in sophisticated hotels with gastronomic restaurants and in friendly mom-and-pop auberges (inns); the farther north you drive, the lower the prices.

CATEGORY	COST*
$$$$	over 1,000 frs
$$$	600 frs–1,000 frs
$$	300 frs–600 frs
$	under 300 frs

All prices are for a standard double room for two, including tax (20.6%) and service charge.

Exploring the Côte d'Azur

You can visit any spot between St-Tropez and Menton in a day trip; the hilltop villages and towns on the coastal plateau are just as accessible. Thanks to the efficient raceway, A8, you can whisk at high speeds to the exit nearest your destination up or down the coast; thus, even if you like leisurely exploration, you can zoom back to your home base at day's end. Above the autoroute things slow down considerably, and you'll find the winding roads and overlooks between villages an experience in themselves.

Great Itineraries

Numbers in the text correspond to numbers in the margin and on The Côte d'Azur: St-Tropez to Cannes; The Côte d'Azur: Cannes to Menton; Nice; and Monaco maps.

IF YOU HAVE 3 DAYS

Base yourself in **Antibes** ⑩, exploring the **Cap d'Antibes** ⑪. Make a day trip west to **Cannes** ⑧, stopping in Picasso country at **Vallauris** ⑬; or head inland for **St-Paul-de-Vence** ⑱ and **Vence** ⑰. On day three explore the museums and old town of **Nice** ㉑–㊳.

IF YOU HAVE 5 DAYS

Spend your first day and night in **St-Tropez** ①, making an excursion up to the hill villages of **Ramatuelle** ② and **Gassin** ③. The next day cruise (or in high summer, crawl along) the coastal highway N98, stopping to visit **Fréjus** ⑤. Still on N98, wind around the dramatic Corniche de l'Estérel and make a triumphant entry into **Cannes** ⑧, straight down La Croisette. Spend your third morning in **Antibes** ⑩, then head inland for an afternoon in **St-Paul** ⑱ or **Vence** ⑰, both good stopovers. Day four could be spent in big-city **Nice** ㉑–㊳, escaping for a quiet night in **St-Jean-Cap-Ferrat** ㊵. On your last day bet your return ticket on the baccarat tables in **Monaco** ㊹–㊿.

IF YOU HAVE 10 DAYS

Expand the five-day itinerary with a second night in Cannes so you can make a boat trip to one of the **Iles de Lérins** ⑨. Spend two nights in Nice so you can take in the Matisse and Chagall museums and see all the Baroque churches in the old town. Then spend two nights in **Menton** ⑤ so you can visit the market and make an excursion to **Roquebrune** ⑤ to see its château and walk the length of the cape.

When to Tour

Unless you enjoy jacked-up prices, traffic jams, and sardine-style beach crowds, avoid the coast like the plague in July and August. Many of the better restaurants simply shut down to avoid the coconut-oil crowd, and the Estérel is closed to hikers during this flash-fire season. Cannes books up early for the film festival in May, so aim for another month (April, June, September, or October). Between Cannes and Menton, the Côte d'Azur's gentle microclimate usually provides moderate winters; it's protected by the Estérel from the mistral that razors through Fréjus and St-Raphaël.

ST-TROPEZ TO ANTIBES

Flanked at each end by subtropical capes and crowned by the red-rock Estérel, this stretch of the coast has a variety of waterfront landmarks. St-Tropez first blazed into fame when it was discovered by painters like Paul Signac and writers such as Colette. Since then it has never looked back and remains one of the most animated little stretches of territory on the Côte d'Azur, flooded at high season with people who like to roost at waterfront cafés and watch the passing parade of local flora and fauna. St-Tropez vies with Cannes for name recognition and glamour, but the more modest resorts—Ste-Maxime, Fréjus, and St-Raphaël—offer a more affordable Riviera experience. Historic Antibes and jazzy Juan-les-Pins straddle the subtropical peninsula of Cap d'Antibes.

St-Tropez

❶ *35 km (22 mi) southwest of Fréjus, 66 km (41 mi) northeast of Toulon.*

At first glance, it really doesn't look all that lovely: There's a moderately pretty port full of bobbing boats, a picturesque old town in sugared-almond hues, sandy beaches, and old-fashioned squares with plane trees and *pétanque* (lawn bowling) players. But what made St-Tropez a household word? In two words: Brigitte Bardot. When this *pulpeuse* (voluptuous) teenager showed up in St-Tropez on the arm of the late Roger Vadim in 1956 to film *And God Created Woman,* the heads of the world snapped around. Neither the gentle descriptions of writer Guy de Maupassant (1850–93), nor the watercolor tones of Impressionist Paul Signac (1863–1935), nor the stream of painters who followed him (including Matisse and Bonnard) could focus the world's attention on this seaside hamlet as could one voluptuous woman, in head scarf, Ray-Bans, and capri pants. With the film world following in her steps, St-Tropez became the hot spot it to some extent remains. What makes it worthwhile is if you get up early (before the 11 o'clock breakfast rush at Le Gorille Café) and wander the medieval backstreets and waterfront alone. You'll experience what the artists first found to love and what remain the village's real charms: its soft light, warm pastels, and scent of the sea wafting in from the waterfront.

★ The legacy of the artists who loved St-Tropez has been preserved in the extraordinary **Musée de l'Annonciade** (Annunciation Museum), a 14th-century chapel converted to an art museum that alone merits a visit to St-Tropez. Works by Signac, Matisse, Signard, Braque, Dufy, Vuillard, and Rouault trace the evolution of painting from Impressionism to Expressionism, many of them painted in (and about) St-Tropez. ✉ *Quai de l'Épi/pl. Georges Grammont,* ☎ *04–94–97–04–01.* ⌷ *35 frs.*

Paris, France.

Paris, Texas.

When it Comes to Getting Local Currency at an ATM, Same Thing.

Whether you're in Yosemite or Yemen, using your Visa' card or ATM card with the PLUS symbol is the easiest and most convenient way to get local currency. For example, let's say you're in France. When you make a withdrawal, using your secured PIN, it's dispensed in francs, but is debited from your account in U.S. dollars. This makes it easy to take advantage of favorable exchange rates. And if you need help finding one of Visa's 627,000 ATMs in 127 countries worldwide, visit **visa.com/pd/atm.** We'll make finding an ATM as easy as finding the Eiffel Tower, the Pyramids or even the Grand Canyon.

It's Everywhere You Want To Be.'

Savings all over the map.

Enjoy even greater savings with Hertz Affordable Europe.

Whatever direction you're headed, Hertz is there to greet you with even greater savings throughout Europe. Like 15% off Affordable Europe Non-Prepaid Weekly Rates on Intermediate cars and above. Just call **1-800-654-3001** and mention **CDP# 1209761**. Or for an even better deal, receive 20% off when you book on hertz.com and enter **CDP# 1209762**.

But, just because you're vacationing in Europe, it doesn't mean you can't feel at home. English is spoken at all Hertz European locations. Plus, you'll also receive the peace of mind that comes with our toll-free Affordable Europe Helpline and 24-Hour Emergency Roadside Assistance. For complete details call **1-800-654-3001**, or visit us on the web at hertz.com and you'll soon be on the road to savings. Another reason nobody does it exactly like Hertz.

🕐 *June–Sept., Wed.–Mon. 10–noon and 3–7; Oct.–May, Wed.–Mon. 10–noon and 2–6.*

From the quai head up rue Laugier and rue de la Citadelle to the 16th-century **Citadelle,** which stands in a lovely hilltop park. Inside its donjon, the **Musée Naval** (Naval Museum) displays ship models, cannons, and pictures of St-Tropez in its days as a naval port. ⊠ *Rue de la Citadelle,* ☎ *04–94–97–59–43.* 🎫 *25 frs.* 🕐 *Dec.–Easter, Wed.–Mon. 10–noon and 1–5; Easter–Oct., daily 10–6.*

From the citadel head back down and lose yourself in the **Quartier de la Ponche,** the old-town maze of backstreets and old ramparts, daubed in shades of gold, pink, ochre, and sky blue. Trellised jasmine and wrought-iron birdcages hang from the shuttered windows, and many of the tiny streets dead-end at the sea.

Dining and Lodging

$$$ ✕ **Les Mouscardins.** Breton-born chef Laurent Tarridec has left the Bistrot des Lices for a spectacular seaside setting with 180-degree sea views, just on the edge of St-Tropez's old town. His cooking, however, maintains the sophisticated tradition of upscale Provençal cuisine: Opt for a frothy mullet soup, an earthy *galette* of chestnuts and morel mushrooms, the house bourride, or the tender, long-simmered veal. ⊠ *Tour du Portalet,* ☎ *04–94–97–29–00. AE, DC, MC, V. Closed mid-Nov.–mid-Dec. and mid-Jan.–mid-Feb.*

$$ ✕ **Le Girelier.** Like his father before him, chef Yves Rouet makes an effort to prepare Mediterranean-only fish for his buffed and bronzed clientele, who enjoy the casual sea-shanty decor and the highly visible Vieux Port terrace tables. Grilling is the order of the day, with most fish sold by weight, but this is also a stronghold for bouillabaisse. ⊠ *Quai Jean-Jaurès,* ☎ *04–94–97–03–87. AE, DC, MC, V. Closed Oct.–Mar. (with the occasional exception).*

$$ ✕ **Lou Revelen.** Strike a pose on the throw-pillowed couch by the fireplace or people-watch from the terrace: this smart, stagy restaurant caters to the glamorous or wanna-bes. There's also, not incidentally, good Provençal cooking: Try duck carpaccio, garlicky-sweet eggplant terrine, or basil-perfumed lamb; the fennel-grilled fish of the day is a mainstay. ⊠ *4 rue des Remparts,* ☎ *04–94–97–06–34. MC, V.*

$$$$ ✕🏨 **Byblos.** Arranged like a Provençal village, with ochre-stucco cottagelike suites grouped around courtyards landscaped with palms, olive trees, and lavender, this landmark stresses fitness and beauty treatment. Chef Georges Pelissier creates artful classics with a Mediterranean touch: sea bass roasted with salsify and garlic chips or rib-sticking beef tournedos with foie gras. ⊠ *Av. Paul-Signac, 83990,* ☎ *04–94–56–68–00,* 🖷 *04–94–56–68–01. 50 rooms, 48 suites. Restaurant, air-conditioning, pool, spa, exercise room, nightclub. AE, DC, MC, V. Closed mid-Oct.–Easter.* ✆

$$–$$$ 🏨 **Ermitage.** Surrounded by mimosas and lemon trees, this big, old-fashioned hotel is on a hill above town and, from backrooms and garden, commands striking sea views. The fireplace and colonial rattan in the bar; the solid, light-bathed rooms in soft pastels; and owner Annie Bolloreis's friendly welcome make this a real charmer. ⊠ *Av. Paul-Signac, 83990,* ☎ *04–94–97–52–33,* 🖷 *04–94–97–10–43. 26 rooms. Bar. MC, V.*

$$–$$$ 🏨 **La Résidence de la Pinède.** This balustraded white villa and its broad annex sprawl elegantly along a private waterfront, wrapped around an isolated courtyard and pool shaded by parasol pines. Pay extra for the seaside rooms, where you can lean over the balustrade and take in broad views of the coast. ⊠ *Plage de la Bouillabaisse, 83991,* ☎ *04–94–55–91–00,* 🖷 *04–94–97–73–64. 39 rooms, 4 suites. Restaurant, air-conditioning, pool. AE, DC, MC, V. Closed mid-Oct.–Mar.*

$$ 🔲 **Lou Cagnard.** Inside an enclosed garden courtyard, this pretty lit-
★ tle hotel is owned by an enthusiastic young couple who are fixing it
up room by room. Five ground-floor rooms open onto the lovely man-
icured garden, where breakfast is served in the shade of a fig tree. Freshly
decorated rooms have regional tiles and Provençal fabrics. ⊠ *18 av.
Paul Roussel, 83900,* ☎ *04–94–97–04–24,* FAX *04–94–97–09–44. 19
rooms. Parking (free). MC, V. Closed Nov.–late Dec.*

Nightlife and the Arts

The most elite and sought-after nightspot in St-Tropez is the evergreen
Les Caves du Roy, in the Byblos Hotel (⊠ Av. Paul-Signac, ☎ 04–94–
97–16–02). **Le Papagayo** (⊠ Résidence du Port, ☎ 04–94–54–88–18),
a vast disco, caters to a young crowd of teens and twentysomethings.
The **VIP Room** (⊠ Residence du Port, ☎ 04–94–97–14–70) draws a
chic mix of young clients and baby boomers. Every July and August
classical music concerts take place in the gardens of the Château de la
Moutte (⊠ Rte. des Salins). For ticket information inquire at the
tourist office (☎ 04–94–97–45–21).

Outdoor Activities and Sports

The best *plages* (beaches) are scattered along a 5-km (3-mi) stretch
reached by the Route des Plages (Beach Road); the most fashionable
are **Moorea, Tahiti,** and **Club 55.** Those beaches close to town—**Plage
des Greniers** and the **Bouillabaisse**—are accessible on foot, but many
prefer the 10-km (6-mi) sandy crescent at **Les Salins** and the long
sandy stretch of the **Plage de Pampelonne,** 4 km (3 mi) from town. Bi-
cycles are an ideal way to get to the beach; try **Espace 93** (⊠ 2 av. Général-
Leclerc, ☎ 04–94–55–80–00) or **Holiday Bikes** (⊠ 14 av.
Général-Leclerc, ☎ 04–94–97–09–39).

Shopping

Rue Sibilli, behind the quai Suffren, is lined with all kinds of trendy
boutiques. The **place des Lices** overflows with produce, regional foods,
clothing, and *brocantes* (collectibles) Tuesday and Saturday mornings.
The picturesque little fish market holds forth on **place aux Herbes** every
morning.

Ramatuelle

② *12 km (7 mi) southwest of St-Tropez.*

A typical hilltop whorl of red-clay roofs and dense inner streets topped
with arches and lined with arcades, this ancient market town was de-
stroyed in the War of Religions and rebuilt as a harmonious whole in
1620. Now its souvenir shops and galleries attract day-trippers out of
St-Tropez, who enjoy the pretty drive through the vineyards as much
as the village itself.

En Route   From Ramatuelle the lovely ride to the hilltop village of Gassin takes
you through vineyards and woods full of twisted cork oaks over the
highest point of the peninsula (1,070 ft).

Gassin

③ *7 km (4 mi) north of Ramatuelle.*

Though not as picturesque as Ramatuelle, this hilltop village gives you
spectacular views over the surrounding vineyards and St-Tropez's bay.
In winter, before the summer haze drifts in and after the mistral has
given the sky a good scrub, you may be able to make out a brilliant
white chain of Alps looming on the horizon. There's less commerce
here to keep you distracted; for shops, head to Ramatuelle.

Ste-Maxime

❹ *8 km (5 mi) east of Port-Grimaud, 33 km (20 mi) east of St-Tropez.*

You may be put off by the heavily built-up waterfront, bristling with parking-garage-style apartments and hotels, and its position directly on the waterfront highway, but Ste-Maxime is an affordable family resort with fine sandy beaches. It even has a sliver of car-free old town and a stand of majestic plane trees sheltering central Place Victor-Hugo. The main beach, north of town, is the wide and sandy La Nartelle.

Fréjus

❺ *19 km (12 mi) northeast of Ste-Maxime, 37 km (23 mi) northeast of St-Tropez.*

After a stroll on the sandy curve along the tacky, overcommercial Fréjus-Plage (Fréjus Beach), turn your back on modern times and head uphill to Fréjus-Centre. Here you'll enter a maze of narrow streets lined with small shops barely touched by the cult of the lavender sachet. The farmers' market (Monday, Wednesday, and Saturday mornings) is as real and lively as any in Provence, and the cafés encircling the fountains and squares nourish an easygoing social scene.

Yet Fréjus has the honor of possessing some of the most important historic monuments on the coast. Founded in 49 BC by Julius Caesar himself and named Forum Julii, this quiet town was once a thriving Roman city of 40,000 citizens. Today you can see the remains: Just outside the old town is the Roman **Théâtre Antique**; its remaining rows of arches are mostly intact, and much of its stage works are still visible at its center. The **Arènes** (often called the Amphithéâtre) is still used today for concerts and bullfights.

★ Fréjus is also graced with one of the most impressive religious monuments in Provence: Called the **Groupe Épiscopal**, it's made up of an early Gothic **cathedral**, a 5th-century Roman-style **baptistery**, and an early Gothic **cloister**, its gallery painted in sepia and earth tones with a phantasmagoric assortment of animals and biblical characters. Off the entrance and gift shop is a small museum of findings from Roman Fréjus, including a complete mosaic and a sculpture of a two-headed Hermès. ✉ *58 rue de Fleury,* ☎ *04–94–51–26–30.* 🎫 *Cathedral free; cloister, museum, and baptistery 25 frs.* ☉ *Cathedral daily 8:30–noon and 2–6. Cloister, museum, and baptistery Apr.–Sept., daily 9–7; Oct.–Mar., Tues.–Sun. 9–noon and 2–5.*

St-Raphaël

❻ *1 km (½ mi) southeast of Fréjus, 41 km (25½ mi) southwest of Cannes.*

Right next door to Fréjus, with almost no division between, is St-Raphaël, a sprawling resort town with a busy downtown anchored by a casino. It's also a major sailing center, has five golf courses nearby, and draws the weary and indulgent to its seawater-based thalassotherapy. It serves as a major rail crossroads, the closest stop to St-Tropez. The port has a rich history: Napoléon landed at St-Raphaël on his triumphant return from Egypt in 1799; it was also from here in 1814 that he cast off in disgrace for Elba. And it was here, too, that the Allied forces landed in their August 1944 offensive against the Germans.

Dining and Lodging

$$ ✕ **La Bouillabaisse.** Enter through the beaded curtain covering the open doorway to a wood-paneled room decked out with starfish and the

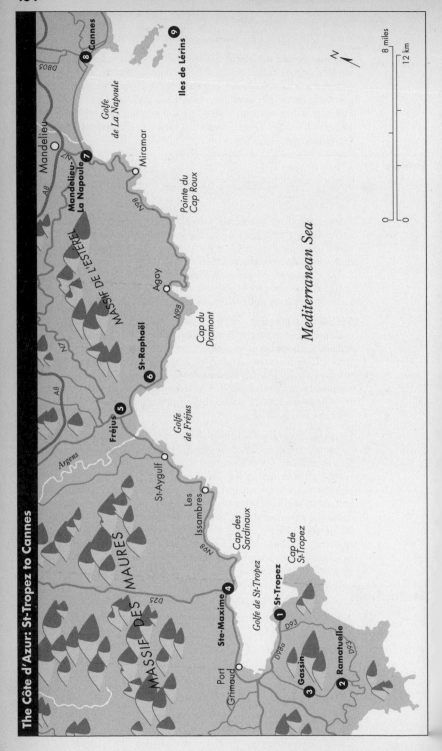

The Côte d'Azur: St-Tropez to Cannes

mounted head of a swordfish: This classic hole-in-the-wall has a brief, straightforward menu inspired by the fish markets. You might have the half lobster with spicy *rouille* (peppers and garlic whipped with olive oil), the seafood-stuffed paella, or the generous house bouillabaisse. ⊠ *50 pl. Victor-Hugo,* ☎ *04–94–95–03–57. AE, MC, V. Closed Mon.*

$$$ 🏨 **Excelsior.** This urban hotel has been under the careful management of one family for three generations. Its combination of straightforward comforts and a waterfront position in the center of town attract a regular clientele. Rooms are plush and pastel, bathrooms up to date. ⊠ *Promenade Coty, 83700,* ☎ *04–94–95–02–42,* 𝖥𝖠𝖷 *04–94–95–33–82. 36 rooms. Restaurant, café, air-conditioning. AE, DC, MC, V.* 🕏

$ ★ 🏨 **Le Thimotée.** The new owners of this bargain lodging are throwing themselves wholeheartedly into improving an already attractive 19th-century villa. They've also restored the garden, with its grand palms and pines shading the walk to the pretty little swimming pool. Though it's tucked away in a neighborhood far from the waterfront, top-floor rooms have poster-perfect sea views. ⊠ *375 bd. Christian-Lafon, 83700,* ☎ *04–94–40–49–49,* 𝖥𝖠𝖷 *04–94–19–41–92. 12 rooms. Pool. AE, MC, V.* 🕏

En Route The rugged **Massif de l'Estérel,** between St-Raphaël and Cannes, is a hiker's dream. Made up of rust-red volcanic rocks (porphyry) carved by the sea into dreamlike shapes, the harshness of the landscape is softened by patches of lavender, scrub pine, and gorse. Take N7, the mountain route to the north, to lose yourself in the desert landscape far from the sea. Or stay on N98, the **Corniche de l'Estérel** (the coastal road along the dramatic corniche), past tiny calanques and sheer rock faces plunging into the waves.

Mandelieu–La Napoule

❼ *32 km (20 mi) northeast of St-Raphaël, 8 km (5 mi) southwest of Cannes.*

La Napoule is the small, old-fashioned port village devoured by the big-fish resort town of Mandelieu. You can visit Mandelieu for a golf-and-sailing retreat and La Napoule for a port-side stroll, a meal, or a tour of its peculiar castle.

The **Château de La Napoule,** looming over the sea and the port, is a bizarre hybrid of Romanesque, Gothic, Moroccan, and Hollywood cooked up by the eccentric American sculptor Henry Clews. Working with his architect wife, he transformed the 14th-century bastion into something that suited his own expectations and filled the place with his fantastical sculptures. ⊠ *Av. Henry Clews,* ☎ *04–93–49–95–05.* 🎟 *25 frs.* ⊘ *Guided visits Mar.–June and Sept.–Nov., Wed.–Mon. at 3 and 4; July–Aug., Wed.–Mon. at 3, 4, and 5.*

Dining and Lodging

$$ ★ ✕ **Le Boucanier.** The drab, low-ceiling dining room is upstaged by wraparound plate-glass views of the marina and château at this waterfront favorite. Locals gather here for mountains of oysters and whole fish, simply grilled and served with a drizzle of fruity olive oil, a pinch of rock salt, or a brief flambé in pastis. ⊠ *Port La Napoule,* ☎ *04–93–49–80–51. AE, DC, MC, V.*

$$$ 🏨 **Le Domaine d'Olival.** Set back from the coast on its own vast landscaped grounds along the Siagne River, this inn has a Provençal feel that denies its waterfront-resort situation. Bright rooms with country-fresh fabrics have built-in furniture and small kitchenettes. Balconies, ideal for breakfast, overlook the semitropical garden. ⊠ *778 av. de la Mer, 06210,* ☎ *04–93–49–31–00,* 𝖥𝖠𝖷 *04–92–97–69–28. 18 apartments. Air-conditioning, kitchenettes, tennis court. AE, DC, MC, V. Closed Nov.–mid-Jan.*

Outdoor Activities and Sports

The **Golf Club de Cannes-Mandelieu** (⊠ rte. du Golf, ☎ 04–92–97–32–00) is one of the most beautiful in the south of France; it has two courses—one with 18 holes (par 71) and one with nine (par 33).

Cannes

❽ *73 km (45 mi) northeast of St-Tropez, 33 km (20 mi) southwest of Nice, 908 km (563 mi) southeast of Paris.*

Backed by gentle hills and flanked to the south by the Estérel, warmed by dependable sun but kept bearable in summer by the cool Mediterranean breeze, Cannes is pampered with the luxurious climate that has made it one of the most popular and glamorous resorts in Europe. For 150 years the mecca of sun worshipers, it has been further glamorized by the success of its film festival.

Its bay served as nothing more than a fishing port until in 1834 an English aristocrat, Lord Brougham, made an emergency stopover with his sick daughter and fell in love with the site. He had a home built here and returned every winter for a sun cure—a ritual quickly picked up by his peers. With the democratization of modern travel, Cannes has become a tourist and convention town. But glamour—and the perception of glamour—is self-perpetuating, and as long as Cannes enjoys its ravishing climate and setting, it will maintain its incomparable panache.

Pick up a map at the tourist office in the **Palais des Festivals,** the scene of the famous Festival International du Film, known as the Cannes Film Festival. As you leave the information center, follow the Palais to your right to see the red-carpeted stairs where the stars ascend every year. Set into the surrounding pavement, the **Allée des Etoiles** (Stars' Alley) enshrines some 300 autographed imprints of film stars' hands—of Dépardieu, Streep, and Stallone, among others.

Through the palm trees and flowers and crowds of strolling poseurs (furs coats in tropical weather, mobile phones on Rollerblades, and sunglasses at night) follow the waterfront promenade known as **La Croisette** east past the broad expanse of private beaches, glamorous shops, and luxurious hotels. Two blocks behind La Croisette lies **rue d'Antibes,** Cannes's main high-end shopping street. At its western end **rue Meynadier** is packed tight with trendy clothing boutiques and fine food shops. Just beyond, the covered **Marché Forville** is the scene of the animated morning food market.

Climb up rue St-Antoine into the picturesque old-town neighborhood known as **Le Suquet,** on the site of the original Roman *castrum*. Shops proffer Provençal goods, and the atmospheric theme-restaurants give you a chance to catch your breath; the pretty pastel shutters, Gothic stonework, and narrow passageways are lovely distractions. The hill is crowned by the 11th-century château, housing the **Musée de la Castre,** and the imposing four-sided **Tour du Suquet** (Suquet Tower), built in 1385 as a lookout against Saracen invasions. ⊠ *Pl. de la Castre,* ☎ *04–93–38–55–26.* ☞ *10 frs.* ☉ *Apr.–June, Wed.–Mon. 10–noon and 2–6; July–Sept., Wed.–Mon. 10–noon and 3–7; Oct.–Dec. and Feb.–Mar., Wed.–Mon. 10–noon and 2–5.*

Dining and Lodging

$$ ✕ **La Mère Besson.** This long-standing favorite continues to please a largely foreign clientele with regional specialties such as sweet-and-sour sardines *à l'escabèche* (marinated), monkfish Provençal (with tomatoes, fennel, and onion), and roast lamb with garlic purée. The formal setting, with damask linens and still lifes, is lightened up with clatter from the open kitchen. ⊠ *13 rue des Frères-Pradignac,* ☎ *04–93–39–59– 24. AE, DC, MC, V. Closed Sun. Sept.–June. No lunch Sat., Mon. except during festivals.*

$$ ✗ **Montagard.** This extraordinary newcomer serves elegant, imaginative vegetarian cuisine—rare in France—in a chic, low-key setting. A turnover stuffed with pumpkin and chestnuts may be trimmed with deep-fried pumpkin rings and ruby beet chips, or you may select from a choice of three fish. Strains of Keith Jarrett waft through the artful mise-en-scène, with its high-design chairs and warm shades of ochre. ⊠ *6 rue Maréchal Joffre,* ☎ *04–93–39–98–38. MC, V. Closed Sun., Mon.*

$ ✗ **Bouchon d'Objectif.** Popular and unpretentious, this tiny bistro serves inexpensive Provençal menus prepared with a sophisticated twist. Watch for terrine of hare with sultanas and Armagnac, stuffed sardines, or a trio of fresh fish with aïoli. An ever-changing gallery display of photography adds a hip touch to the simple ochre-and-aqua setting. ⊠ *10 rue Constantine,* ☎ *04–93–99–21–76. AE, MC, V. Closed Mon.*

$$$$ ⚏ **Carlton Inter-Continental.** As one of the turn-of-the-century pioneers of this resort town, this deliciously pompous Neoclassical landmark quickly staked out the best position: La Croisette seems to radiate symmetrically from its figurehead waterfront site. Seafront rooms have a retro Laura Ashley look; those on the back compensate with cheery Provençal prints. ⊠ *58 bd. de la Croisette, 06414,* ☎ *04–93–06–40– 06,* FAX *04–93–06–40–25. 310 rooms, 28 suites. 3 restaurants, bar, air-conditioning, health club, beach, casino. AE, DC, MC, V.* ✍

$$$$ ⚏ **Majestic.** Classical statuary and tapestries set the aristocratic tone at this other La Croisette "palace"; it's grand but gracious, with a quieter feel than most of its neighbors. Its romantic poolside terrace and Egyptian/Art Deco bar give a nod to cinematic glamour. Ask for one of the rooms newly redone in retro style. ⊠ *14 bd. de la Croisette, 06400,* ☎ *04–92–98–77–00,* FAX *04–93–38–97–90. 298 rooms, 24 apartments. Restaurant, bar, air-conditioning, pool, sauna, parking (fee). AE, DC, MC, V. Closed mid-Nov.–Dec..* ✍

$$–$$$ ⚏ **Splendid.** If you covet a waterfront position but can't afford the grand hotels on La Croisette, consider this traditional 1873 palace overlooking La Pantiéro and the old port. Rooms are a bit creaky but sleekly decorated, and though the bathrooms have '60s tiling, they're well maintained. There are flowers and fruit in rooms, robes and kitchenettes in those with sea views, and pretty Provençal furniture in the breakfast room. ⊠ *Allées de la Liberté, entrance on 4–6 rue Félix-Faure, 06407,* ☎ *04–93–99–53–11,* FAX *04–93–99–55–02. 64 rooms. Air-conditioning, kitchenettes. AE, DC, MC, V.*

$$ ⚏ **Molière.** Plush, intimate, and low-key, this hotel has pretty tiled baths and small rooms in cool shades of peach, indigo, and white-waxed oak. Nearly all overlook the vast, enclosed front garden, where palms and cypress shade terrace tables, and breakfast is served most of the year. ⊠ *5 rue Molière, 06400,* ☎ *04–93–38–16–16,* FAX *04–93–68–29–57. 24 rooms. AE, MC, V. Closed mid-Nov.–end Dec.*

$ ⚏ **Albert Ier.** In a quiet residential area above the Forville market—a 10-minute walk downhill to La Croisette and the beach—this neo-Deco mansion has pretty rooms in pastels, as well as tidy tile baths and an enclosed garden setting. You can have breakfast on the flowered, shady terrace or in the family-style salon. The hotel has had the same owner since 1980, and it shows. ⊠ *68 av. de Grasse, 06400,* ☎ *04–93–39– 24–04,* FAX *04–93–38–83–75. 11 rooms. MC, V.*

Nightlife and the Arts

The Riviera's cultural calendar is splashy and star-studded, and never more so than during the **International Film Festival,** in May. The film

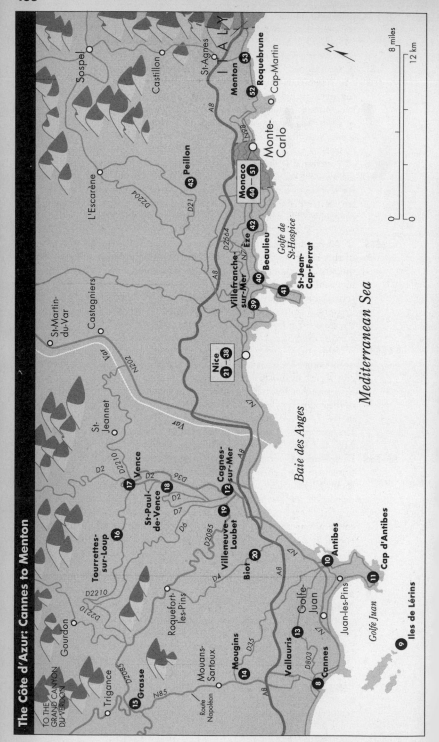

The Côte d'Azur: Cannes to Menton

screenings are not open to the public, so unless you have a pass, your star-studded glimpses will be on the streets or in restaurants (though if you hang around in a tux, a stray ticket might come your way).

As befits a glamorous seaside resort, Cannes has two casinos. The famous **Casino Croisette** (☒ In Palais des Festivals, 04–92–98–78–00) draws more crowds to its slot machines than any other casino in France. The **Carlton Casino Club** (☒ 58 bd. de la Croisette, 04–92–99–51–00) encourages an exclusive atmosphere in its posh seventh-floor hideaway.

To make the correct entrance at the popular **Le Cat Corner** (☒ 22 rue Macé, ☎ 04–93–39–31–31) have yourself whisked by limo from the steak house Le Farfalla. **Jimmy'z** (☒ Palais des Festivals, ☎ 04–93–68–00–07) cabaret shows are legendary. After many metamorphoses, **César Palace** (☒ 48 bd. de la République, ☎ 04–93–68–23–23) remains one of the main disco draws.

Outdoor Activities and Sports

Most of the **beaches** along La Croisette are owned by hotels and/or restaurants, though this doesn't necessarily mean the hotels or restaurants front the beach. It does mean they own a patch of beachfront bearing their name, from which they rent chaise longues, mats, and umbrellas to the public and hotel guests (who also have to pay). Public beaches are between the color-coordinated private beach umbrellas and offer simple open showers and basic toilets.

Sailboats can be rented from **Camper & Nicholson's** (☒ Port Canto) and the **Yacht Club de Cannes** (☒ Palm Beach Port). Windsurfing equipment is available from **Le Club Nautique La Croisette** (☒ Plage Pointe Palm-Beach) and the **Centre Nautique Municipal** (☒ 9 rue Esprit-Violet). The **Majestic Ski Club** (Ponton du Majestic; ☒ At Majestic's private beach, ☎ 04–92–98–77–47) can take you waterskiing or pull you on a ski-board, an inflatable chair, or take you up over the water on a parachute.

Iles de Lérins

⑨ *15–20 minutes by ferry off the coast of Cannes.*

When you're glutted on glamour, you may want to make a day trip to the peaceful Iles de Lérins (Lérins Islands); boats depart from Cannes's Vieux Port. Allow at least a half day to enjoy either of the islands; you can see both only if you get an early start. You have two options: **Horizon/Caribes Company** (☒ Jetée Edouard, ☎ 04–92–98–71–36) or the less comfortable **Estérel Chanteclair** (☒ Promenade La Pantiéro, ☎ 04–93–39–11–82).

It's a 15-minute, 60-franc round-trip to **Ile Ste-Marguerite.** Its Fort Royal, built by Richelieu and improved by Vauban, offers views over the ramparts to the rocky island coast and the open sea. Behind the prison buildings is the **Musée de la Mer** (Marine Museum), with its Roman boat dating from the 1st century BC and its collection of amphorae and pottery recovered from ancient shipwrecks. ☎ 04–93–43–18–17 *museum.* ☒ *10 frs.* ☉ *Oct.–Dec. and Feb.–Mar., Wed.–Mon. 10:30–12:15 and 2:15–4:30; Apr.–June and Sept., Wed.–Mon. 10:30–12:15 and 2:15–5:30; July–Aug., Wed.–Mon. 10:30–12:15 and 2:15–6:30.*

Ile St-Honorat can be reached in 20 minutes (60 francs round-trip) from the Vieux Port. Smaller and wilder than Ste-Marguerite, it's home to an active monastery and the ruins of its 11th-century predecessor.

Antibes

⑩ *11 km (7 mi) northeast of Cannes, 15 km (9 mi) southeast of Nice.*

With its broad stone ramparts scalloping in and out over the waves and backed by blunt medieval towers and a skew of tile roofs, Antibes is one of the most romantic old towns on the Mediterranean coast. Stroll Promenade Amiral-de-Grasse along the crest of Vauban's sea walls, and you'll understand why Picasso was inspired here to paint on a panoramic scale. Yet a few steps inland you'll enter a souklike maze of atmospheric old streets.

To visit old Antibes, pass through the **Porte Marine,** an arched gateway in the rampart wall. Follow rue Aubernon to **cours Masséna,** where the little sheltered market vaunts lemons, olives, and hand-stuffed sausages, and the vendors take breaks in the shoebox cafés flanking one side. From cours Masséna head up to the **Église de l'Immaculée-Conception** (✉ Pl. de la Cathédrale), which served as the region's cathedral until the bishopric was transferred to Grasse in 1244. Its stout medieval watchtower was built in the 11th century with stones "mined" from Roman structures. Inside is a Baroque altarpiece painted by the Niçois artist Louis Bréa in 1515.

Next door to the cathedral, the medieval **Château Grimaldi** rises high over the water on a Roman foundation. The Grimaldi family lived here until the Revolution, but this fine old castle was little more than a monument until in 1946 its curator offered use of its vast chambers to Picasso. Here the artist worked with a singular passion, creating vast paintings on wood, canvas, paper, and walls. This extraordinary collection of works, alive with nymphs, fauns, and centaurs, forms the
★ core of the **Musée Picasso.** It houses more than 300 works by the artist, as well as pieces by Miró, Calder, and Léger. ✉ *Pl. du Château,* ☎ *04–92–90–54–20.* 🎫 *30 frs.* ⊙ *June–Sept., Tues–Sun. 10–6; Oct.–May, Tues.–Sun. 10–noon and 2–6.*

The Bastion St-André, a squat Vauban fortress, is now home to the **Musée Archéologique** (Archaeology Museum). Its collection focuses on Antibes's classical history, displaying amphorae and sculptures found in local digs as well as in shipwrecks from the harbor. ✉ *Av. Général-Maizières,* ☎ *04–92–90–54–35.* 🎫 *20 frs.* ⊙ *Tues.–Sun. 10–noon and 2–6.*

From old Antibes you can jump on a bus or hike over the hill to **Juan-les-Pins,** the jazzy younger-sister resort town that, with Antibes, bracelets the wrist of the Cap d'Antibes. The scene along its waterfront is something to behold, with thousands of international sun seekers flowing up and down the promenade and lying flank to flank on its endless stretch of sand.

Dining and Lodging

$$$$ ✕ **La Terrasse.** At this renowned restaurant in the Juana Hotel (☞
★ *below*), Chef Christian Morisset maintains top honors with such dishes as sea bass steamed with Menton lemon or lamb roasted in Vallauris clay. ✉ *av. Georges-Gallice, Juan-les-Pins,* ☎ *04–93–61–08–70. AE, MC, V. Closed Nov.–Mar.*

$$–$$$ ✕ **La Bonne Auberge.** In a graceful inn set back from the overbuilt sprawl along N7, Chef Philippe Rostang cooks up classic, conservative specialties such as lamb slow-simmered in herbs, lobster salad with tiny ravioli, and airy fish soufflés. The dining room is a pastel haven of exposed beams, fresh flowers, and soft light. ✉ *Quartier de la Brague (4 km [2 mi] east of Antibes),* ☎ *04–93–33–36–65. AE, MC, V. Closed Mon., except July–Aug. Closed mid-Nov.–mid-Dec. No dinner Sun., except July–Aug.*

$$$ ✕ **La Jarre.** You can dine under the beams or the ancient fig tree at this lovely little garden hideaway, just off the ramparts and behind the cathedral. Open only for dinner, it has an ambitious menu of Provençal specialties filtered through an international lens: tabbouleh topped with mullet and sharp black tapenade, sweet-and-sour duck breast, shrimp grilled in ginger, and apricot nougat. ✉ *14 rue St-Esprit, Antibes,* ☎ *04–93–34–50–12. MC, V. Closed mid-Oct.–Easter. No lunch.*

$ ✕ **Le Brûlot.** One street back from the market, this bistro remains one
★ of the busiest in Antibes. Burly Chef Christian Blancheri hoists anything from pigs to apple pies in and out of his roaring wood oven, and it's all delicious. Watch for the sardines *à l'escabèche* (in a tangy sweet-sour marinade), sizzling lamb chops, or grilled fresh fish. ✉ *3 rue Frédéric Isnard, Antibes,* ☎ *04–93–34–17–76. MC, V. Closed Sun., last 2 wks of Aug., and last wk of Dec.–1st wk Jan. No lunch Mon.*

$$$$ ▥ **Juana.** This luxuriously renovated landmark, run by the Barrache
★ family since it opened in 1931, retains a Gatsby feel, with striped awnings and white balustrades. Pine trees tower over the grounds and the white-marble pool, and rooms have a cool plain-pastel decor. Though it's two blocks from the waterfront, the Juana has its own private sand beach. The restaurant is La Terrasse (☞ *above*). ✉ *Av. Georges-Gallice, 06160 Juan-les-Pins,* ☎ *04–93–61–08–70,* ℻ *04–93–61–76–60. 45 rooms, 5 suites. Restaurant, bar, air-conditioning, pool. AE, MC, V. Closed Nov.–Mar..* ✍

$$ ▥ **Le Mas Djoliba.** Tucked into a residential neighborhood on the crest between Antibes and Juan, this converted Provençal farmhouse is surrounded by greenery and well protected from traffic noise. Rooms, decked in bright colors and floral prints, have either views of the garden or the sea. Note that in summer the restaurant serves half board only. ✉ *29 av. de Provence, 06600 Antibes,* ☎ *04–93–34–02–48,* ℻ *04–93–34–05–81. 13 rooms. Restaurant, pool. AE, DC, MC, V. Closed Nov.–Jan.* ✍

$$ ▥ **Le Mimosa.** The fabulous setting, in an enclosed hilltop garden studded with tall palms, mimosa, and tropical greenery, makes up for the hike down to the beach. Rooms are small and modestly decorated in Victorian florals, but ask for a balcony: Many look over the garden and sizable pool. ✉ *Rue Pauline 06160, Antibes 06160,* ☎ *04–93–61–04–16,* ℻ *04–92–93–06–46. 34 rooms. Pool. MC, V. Closed Oct.–Apr..*

Nightlife and the Arts

The glassed-in complex of the **Eden Casino** (✉ Bd. Baudoin, Juan-les-Pins, ☎ 04–92–93–71–71) houses restaurants, bars, dance clubs, and a casino. **La Siesta** (✉ Rte. du Bord de Mer, Antibes, ☎ 04–93–33–31–31) is an enormous summer entertainment center with seven dance floors (some on the beach), bars, slot machines, and roulette. Every July the **Festival de Jazz d'Antibes-Juan-les-Pins** (☎ 04–92–90–50–00 for information) challenges Montreux for its stellar lineup and romantic venue under ancient pines.

Outdoor Activities and Sports

Antibes and Juan together claim 25 km (15½ mi) of coastline and 48 **beaches** (including Cap d'Antibes). In Antibes you can choose between small sandy inlets—such as **La Gravette,** below the port; the central **place de Ponteil;** and **Plage de la Salis,** toward the Cap—rocky escarpments around the old town; or the vast stretch of sand above the Fort Carré.

Cap d'Antibes

⓫ *2 km (1 mi) south of Antibes.*

This idyllic peninsula, protected from the concrete plague infecting the mainland coast, has been carved up into luxurious estates shaded by thick, tall pines. Since the 19th century its wild greenery and isolation have drawn a glittering guest list: Guy de Maupassant, Anatole France, Claude Monet, the Duke and Duchess of Windsor, and the cream of the Lost Generation, including Scott and Zelda Fitzgerald. Now the focal point is the famous Hotel Eden Roc, rendezvous and weekend getaway of film stars.

You can sample a little of what draws famous people to the site by walking up the chemin de Calvaire from the Plage de la Salis in Antibes (about 1 km [¾ mi]) and taking in the extraordinary views from the hill that supports the old lighthouse, the **Phare de la Garoupe** (Garoupe Lighthouse). Next to the lighthouse, the 16th-century double chapel of **Notre-Dame-de-la-Garoupe** contain ex-votos and statues of the Virgin, all in the memory, and for the protection, all in memory of and for the protection of sailors. ☎ 04–93–67–36–01. ☉ *Easter–Sept., daily 9:30–noon and 2:30–7; Oct.–Easter, daily 10–noon and 2:30–5.*

Dining and Lodging

$$$–$$$$ ✕ **Restaurant de Bacon.** Since 1948, under the careful control of the
    ★   Sordello brothers, this has been the spot for seafood on the Côte d'Azur. The catch of the day may be minced in lemon ceviche, floating in a top-of-the-line bouillabaisse, or simply grilled with fennel, crisped with hillside herbs. The warm welcome, discreet service, sunny dining room, and dreamy terrace over the Baie des Anges justify extravagance. ✉ *Bd. de Bacon,* ☎ *04–93–61–50–02. Reservations essential. AE, DC, MC, V. Closed Mon. and Nov.–Jan.*

$$$–$$$$ 🏨 **La Baie Dorée.** Clinging to the waterfront and skewed toward the
    ★   open sea, this elegant little inn provides you with private sea-view terraces off every room. The decor is plush and subdued, yet even the small standard doubles feel deluxe when you look out the window. The public grounds and terraces fall in tiers down to the water, from the shaded restaurant to the private beach on the Baie de la Garoupe. ✉ *579 bd. de la Garoupe, 06160,* ☎ *04–93–67–30–67,* 🖷 *04–92–93–76–39. 17 rooms. Restaurant, beach. MC, V. Closed Nov.–mid-Dec..* ✎

Cagnes-sur-Mer

🕛 *21 km (13 mi) northeast of Cannes, 10 km (6 mi) north of Antibes, 14 km (9 mi) southwest of Nice.*

Although from N7 you may be tempted to give wide berth to the congested sprawl of Cagnes-sur-Mer, follow the signs inland and up into **Haut-de-Cagnes.** Its steep-cobbled old town is crowned by the fat, crenellated **Château de Cagne,** built in 1310 by the Grimaldis and reinforced over the centuries. Within are vaulted medieval chambers, a vast Renaissance fireplace, and a splendid 17th-century trompe l'oeil fresco of the fall of Phaeton from his sun chariot. ✉ *Pl. Grimaldi,* ☎ *04–93–20–87–29.* 🎫 *20 frs.* ☉ *Oct. and Dec.–Easter, Wed.– Mon. 10–noon and 2–5; Easter–Sept., Wed.–Sun. 10–noon and 2–6.*

After staying up and down the coast, August Renoir (1841–1919) settled in a house in Les Collettes, just east of the old town, now the **Musée Renoir.** Here he passed the last 12 years of his life, painting the landscape around him, working in bronze, and rolling his wheelchair through the luxuriant garden of olive, lemon, and orange trees. You can view his home as it was preserved by his children, as well as 11 of his last paintings. ✉ *Av. des Collettes,* ☎ *04–93–20–61–07.* 🎫 *20 frs.* ☉ *June–Oct., Wed.–Mon. 10–noon and 2–6; Nov.–May, Wed.–Mon. 10–noon and 2–5. Guided tours in English, Thurs. July–Aug.*

THE HILL TOWNS: ON THE TRAIL OF PICASSO AND MATISSE

The hills that back the Côte d'Azur are often called the *arrière-pays*, or backcountry. This particular wedge of backcountry—behind the coast between Cannes and Antibes—has a character all its own: deeply, unself-consciously Provençal, with undulating fields of lavender and perched villages in golden stone. Many of these villages look as if they do not belong to the last century—but they do, since they played the muse to some of modern art's most famous figures, notably Pablo Picasso and Henri Matisse. A highlight here is the Maeght Foundation, in St-Paul de Vence, one of France's leading museums of modern art. Its neighbor, Vence, has the Chapelle du Rosaire, entirely designed and decorated by Matisse. It's possible to get a small taste of this backcountry on a day trip out of Fréjus, Cannes, or Antibes; even if you're vacationing on the coast, you may want to settle in for a night or two.

Vallauris

⑬ *6 km (4 mi) northeast of Cannes, 6 km (4 mi) west of Antibes.*

In the low hills over the coast, dominated by a blocky Renaissance château, this ancient village was ravaged by waves of the plague in the 14th century, then rebuilt in the 16th century by 70 Genovese families imported to repopulate the abandoned site. They brought with them a taste for Roman planning—hence the grid format in the old town—but more important, a knack for pottery making. Their skills and the fine clay of Vallauris were a marriage made in heaven, and the village thrived as a pottery center for hundreds of years.

In the 1940s Picasso found inspiration in the malleable soil and settled here in a simple stone house, creating pottery art with a single-minded passion. But he returned to painting in 1952 to create one of his masterworks in the château's Romanesque chapel, the vast multi-paneled oil-on-wood composition called *La Guerre et la Paix* (*War and Peace*). The chapel is part of the **Musée National Picasso** today, where several of Picasso's ceramic pieces are displayed. There's also a group of paintings by Picasso's contemporary, Italian artist Alberto Magnelli. ✉ *Pl. de la Libération,* ☎ *04–93–64–16–05.* 🖼 *17 frs.* ☉ *June–Sept., Wed.–Mon. 10–6:30; Oct.–May, Wed.–Mon. 10–noon and 2–6.*

Mougins

⑭ *8 km (5 mi) north of Cannes, 11 km (7 mi) northwest of Antibes, 32 km (20 mi) southwest of Nice.*

Passing through Mougins, a popular summer-house community convenient to Cannes and Nice, you may perceive little more than suburban sprawl. But in 1961 Picasso found more to admire and settled into a *mas* (farmhouse) that became a mecca for artists and art lovers; he died there in 1973.

You can find Picasso's final home and see why of all spots in the world, he chose this one, by following D35 to the ancient ecclesiastic site of **Notre-Dame-de-Vie.** This was the hermitage, or monastic retreat, of the Abbey of Lérins, and its 13th-century bell tower and arcaded chapel form a pretty ensemble in a magnificent setting. Approached through an alley of ancient cypress, the house Picasso shared with his wife, Jacqueline, overlooks the broad bowl of the countryside.

Dining and Lodging

$$$–$$$$ ✕⊡ **Moulin de Mougins.** In a 16th-century olive mill on a hill above
★ the coastal fray, this sophisticated inn houses one of the best restau-
rants in the region—even though celebrity Chef Roger Vergé gave over
most responsibility to Serge Chollet. Still, the sun-drenched Mediter-
ranean cuisine is excellent, with the freshest fish and whitest aspara-
gus. Inside are intimate beamed dining rooms; in summer dine outside
under the awnings. The restaurant is closed Monday; reservations are
always essential. Guest rooms are elegantly rustic; the apartments are
small but deluxe. ✉ *Notre-Dame-de-Vie, 06250,* ☎ *04–93–75–78–
24,* FAX *04–93–90–18–55. 3 rooms, 4 apartments. Restaurant. AE,
DC, MC, V. Closed Feb.* ✤

Grasse

⑮ *10 km (6 mi) northwest of Mougins, 17 km (10½ mi) northwest of
Cannes, 22 km (14 mi) northwest of Antibes, 42 km (26 mi) south-
west of Nice.*

High on a plateau over the coast, this busy, modern town is usually
given wide berth by anyone who isn't interested in its prime tourist in-
dustry, the making of perfume. But its unusual art museum featuring
works of the 18th-century artist Fragonard and the picturesque back-
streets of its very Mediterranean old town round out a pleasant day
trip from the coast.

It's the Côte d'Azur's hothouse climate, nurturing nearly year-round
shows of tropical-hue flowers, that fosters Grasse's perfume industry.
It takes 10,000 flowers to produce 2.2 pounds of jasmine petals and
nearly 1 ton of petals to distill 1½ quarts of essence; this helps justify
the sky-high cost of perfumes, priced by the proportion of essence in
the final blend.

You can't visit the laboratories where the great blends of Chanel, Dior,
and Guerlain are produced. But to accommodate the crowds of tourists
who come here wanting to know more, Grasse has three functioning
perfume factories that create simple blends and demonstrate produc-
tion techniques for free.

Fragonard (✉ Rte. de Cannes Les 4-Chemins, ☎ 04–93–77–94–30)
holds forth in a factory built in 1782. **Galimard** (✉ 73 rte. de Cannes)
traces its pedigree to 1747. **Molinard** (✉ 60 bd. Victor-Hugo, ☎ 04–
93–36–01–62) was established in 1849.

The **Musée International de la Parfumerie** (International Museum of
Perfume), not to be confused with the museum in the Fragonard fac-
tory, traces the 3,000-year history of perfume making. The museum
has a room equipped with potbellied copper stills and old machines,
and labels guide you through the steps of production during different
eras. ✉ *8 pl. du Cours,* ☎ *04–93–36–80–20.* ⊡ *20 frs.* ◷ *June–Sept.,
daily 10–7; Oct.–May., Wed.–Sun. 10–12:30 and 2–5:30.*

The **Musée Fragonard** features the work of Grasse's most famous son,
Jean-Honoré Fragonard (1732–1806), one of the great French artists
of the period. The lovely villa contains a collection of drawings, en-
gravings, and paintings by the artist. Other rooms in the mansion dis-
play works by Fragonard's son Alexandre-Evariste and his grandson
Théophile. ✉ *23 bd. Fragonard,* ☎ *04–93–36–02–71.* ⊡ *20 frs.* ◷
June–Sept., daily 10–7; Oct.–May, Wed.–Sun. 10–12:30 and 2–5:30.

The **Musée d'Art et d'Histoire de Provence** (Museum of the Art and
History of Provence), just down from the Fragonard perfumery, has a
large collection of faience from the region, including works from

Moustiers, Biot, and Vallauris. Also on display in this noble 18th-century mansion are *santons* (terra-cotta figurines), furniture, local paintings, and folk costumes. ⊠ *2 rue Mirabeau*, ☎ *04–93–36–01–61.* ☞ *20 frs.* ⊙ *June–Sept., daily 10–7; Oct.–May., Wed.–Sun. 10–12:30 and 2–5:30.*

Continue down rue Mirabeau and lose yourself in the dense labyrinth of the **Vieille Ville** (Old Town), its steep, narrow streets darkened on each side by shuttered houses five and six stories tall. On a cliff-top overlook at the old town's edge, the Romanesque **Cathédrale Ste-Marie** (⊠ Pl. de la Cathédrale) contains no less than three paintings by Rubens, a triptych by the Provençal painter Louis Bréa, and *Lavement des Pieds* (*Washing of the Feet*), by the young Fragonard.

Dining

$ ✕ **Arnaud.** Just off place aux Aires, this easygoing corner bistro serves up inventive home cooking under a vaulted ceiling trimmed with stenciled grapevines. Choose from an ambitious and sophisticated menu of à la carte specialties—three kinds of fish in garlic sauce, *pieds et paquets* (pigs' feet and tripe), or a hearty *confit de canard* (preserved duck). ⊠ *10 pl. de la Foux,* ☎ *04–93–36–44–88. MC, V.*

Route Napoléon

Extends 176 km (109 mi) from Grasse to Sisteron.

One of the most famous and panoramic roads in France is the Route Napoléon, taken by Napoléon Bonaparte in 1815 after his escape from imprisonment on the Mediterranean island of Elba. Napoléon landed at Golfe-Juan, near Cannes, on March 1 and forged northwest to Grasse, then through dramatic, hilly countryside to Castellane, Digne, and Sisteron. Commemorative plaques bearing the imperial eagle stud the route, inspired by Napoléon's remark, "The eagle will fly from steeple to steeple until it reaches the towers of Notre-Dame." Nowadays there are some lavender-honey stands and souvenir shacks, but they're few and far between. It's the panoramic views as the road winds its way up into the Alps that make this route so worth traveling. If you like scenic drives, follow the Route Napoléon to Trigance and on to the spectacular gorge called the **Grand Canyon du Verdon.**

Tourrettes-sur-Loup

⑯ *5 km (3 mi) west of Vence, 24 km (15 mi) west of Nice.*

In this steep-sloped old hill town, the wind blows colder, the forest around is dense and arid, and the coast seems hours—and ages—away (though it's less than an hour's drive from Nice). From the town square that doubles as a parking lot with an ongoing pétanque game on one side, to the sharp-raked, torturously twisted streets snaking down the slopes of the old town, this is old Provence without the stage makeup. Yes, there are dozens of galleries and arts-and-crafts shops, but they're owned and run by real artists and artisans, who have made a life for themselves in this intimate community.

Vence

⑰ *4 km (2 mi) north of St-Paul, 22 km (14 mi) north of Nice.*

Encased behind stone walls inside a thriving modern market town, this jewel of an old town dates from the 15th century. Though crowded with boutiques and souvenir shops, it's slightly more conscious of its history than St-Paul—plaques guide you through its historic squares and *portes* (gates). Wander past the pretty Place du Peyra, with its fountains, to place Clemenceau, with its ochre-color Hôtel-de-Ville (Town Hall), to Place du Frêne, with its ancient ash tree, planted in the 16th century.

In the old-town center, the **Cathédrale de la Nativité de la Vierge** (Cathedral of the Birth of the Virgin, on place Godeau) was built on the Roman's Champ de Mars (military drilling field) and traces bits and pieces to Carolingian and even Roman times. It's a hybrid of Romanesque and Baroque styles, expanded and altered over the centuries. In the baptistery is a ceramic mosaic by Chagall of Moses in the bulrushes.

★ On the outskirts of Vence, toward St-Jeannet, the **Chapelle du Rosaire** (Chapel of the Rosary) was decorated with beguiling simplicity and clarity by Matisse between 1947 and 1951. It reflects the reductivist style of the era: Walls, floor, and ceiling are gleaming white, and the small stained-glass windows are cool greens and blues. "Despite its imperfections I think it is my masterpiece. . . the result of a lifetime devoted to the search for truth," wrote Matisse, who designed and dedicated the chapel when he was in his eighties and nearly blind. ⊠ *Av. Henri-Matisse,* ☎ *04–93–58–03–26. 15 frs.* ⊙ *Tues. and Thurs. 10–11:30 and 2–5:30; Mon., Wed., and Sat. 2–5:30.*

Dining and Lodging

$$$ ✕ **Jacques Maximin.** This temperamental superchef has found peace
★ of mind in a gray-stone farmhouse covered with wisteria—his home and his own country restaurant. Here he devotes himself to creative country cooking, superbly prepared and unpretentiously priced—white beans in rich squid ink, Mediterranean fish grilled in rock salt and olive oil, and candied-eggplant sorbet. The yellow dining room is airy and uncluttered; the garden is a palm-shaded paradise. ⊠ *689 chemin de la Gaude,* ☎ *04–93–58–90–75. AE, MC, V. Closed Mon. and Nov. No dinner Sun. Sept.–June*

$–$$ ✕ **La Farigoule.** In a long beamed dining room that opens onto a shady terrace, this is a fine place to enjoy sophisticated Provençal cooking in an easygoing atmosphere. Watch for tangy pissaladieres with sardines marinated in ginger and lemon, salt-cod ravioli, lamb with olive polenta, and a crunchy parfait of honey and hazelnuts. ⊠ *15 rue Henri-Isnard,* ☎ *04–93–58–01–27. MC, V. Closed Wed., 1st 2 wks Nov., end Dec.–early Jan., 2 wks Feb. No lunch Tues. Oct.–Apr. and Thurs. May–Sept.*

$$ ▥ **Villa Roseraie.** This quiet little inn outside the center is a pet proj-
★ ect of the enthusiastic young owners, Monsieur and Madame Ganier, who have scoured antiques shops for regional details and invested in fine local tiles and fabrics. You can enjoy a generous breakfast on the terrace and lounge by the pool much of the year, and it's a quick walk down to old Vence. ⊠ *51 av. Henri-Giraud, 06140,* ☎ *04–93–58–02–20, ᴙ̄ 04–93–58–99–31. 12 rooms. Pool. AE, MC, V.*

St-Paul-de-Vence

⑱ *18 km (11 mi) north of Nice, 4 km (2 mi) south of Vence.*

The medieval village of St-Paul-de-Vence can be seen from afar, standing out like its mate, Vence, against the skyline. In the Middle Ages St-Paul was basically a city-state, and it controlled its own political destiny for centuries. But by the early 20th century St-Paul had faded to oblivion, overshadowed by the growth of Vence and Cagnes—until it was rediscovered in the 1920s when a few penniless artists began paying their drink bills at the local auberge with paintings. Those artists turned out to be Signac, Modigliani, and Bonnard, who met at the Auberge de la Colombe d'Or, now a sumptuous inn, where the walls are still covered with their ink sketches and daubs. Nowadays art of a sort still dominates in the myriad tourist traps that take your eyes off the beauty of St-Paul's old stone houses and its rampart views. The most commercially developed of Provence's hilltop villages, St-Paul is nonetheless a magical place when the tourist crowds thin. Artists are still drawn to its light, its pure air, its wraparound views, and its honey-color stone walls, soothingly cool on a hot Provençal afternoon. Film stars continue to love its lazy yet genteel ways, lingering on the garden-bower terrace of the Colombe d'Or and challenging the locals to a game of pétanque under the shade of the plane trees.

★ Many people come to St-Paul just to visit the **Fondation Maeght,** founded in 1964 by art dealer Aimé Maeght and set on a wooded cliff top high above the medieval town. It's not just a small modern art museum but an extraordinary marriage of the arc-and-plane architecture of José Sert; the looming sculptures of Miró, Moore, and Giacometti; and a humbling hilltop setting of pines, vines, and flowing planes of water. On display is an intriguing and ever-varying array of the work of modern masters, including the wise and funny late-life masterwork *La Vie* (*Life*), by Chagall. ☎ 04–93–32–81–63. ⊠ *50 frs.* ☉ *July–Sept., daily 10–7; Oct.–June, daily 10–12:30 and 2:30–6.*

Dining and Lodging

$$$–$$$$ ✕ **Colombe d'Or.** This idyllic old auberge was the heart and soul of St-Paul's artistic revival, and the cream of 20th-century France lounged together under its fig trees—Picasso and Chagall, Maeterlinck and Kipling, Marcel Pagnol (*Manon des Sources*) and Jacques Prévert (*Les Enfants du Paradis*). Yves Montand and Simone Signoret met and married here, and current film stars make appearances from time to time. They do so more in homage to the inn's resonant history and *pastorale* atmosphere than for its food. ⊠ *Pl. Général-de-Gaulle, 06570,* ☎ *04–93–32–80–02. AE, DC, MC, V. Closed Nov.–late Dec.*

$$$$ ✕🏨 **St-Paul.** Right in the center of the labyrinth of stone alleys, with
★ views over the ancient ramparts, this luxurious inn (a Relais & Châteaux property) fills a noble 15th-century house with Provençal furniture, quarried stone, and lush fabrics. The restaurant (closed Wednesday from October to April; no lunch Tuesday), serving sophisticated regional specialties, is rapidly climbing the gastronomic ladder, with national awards already bestowed on the chef. ⊠ *86 rue Grande, 06570,* ☎ *04–93–32–65–25,* FAX *04–93–32–52–94. 19 rooms. Restaurant, bar, airconditioning. AE, DC, MC, V. Closed early Jan.–mid-Feb.*

$$ 🏨 **Le Hameau.** Less than 1½ km (1 mi) outside St-Paul, with views of the valley and the village, this lovely little inn is a jumble of terraces, trellises, archways, and honeysuckle vines. The main hotel, built in 1920, has good-size rooms and old Provençal furniture; or you can opt for the 18th-century farmhouse, with smaller, more modern rooms but wonderful views. Friendly new owners have built a sizable new pool. ⊠ *528 rte. de La Colle, 06570,* ☎ *04–93–32–80–24,* FAX *04–93–32–55–75. 17 rooms. Pool. MC, V. Closed mid-Nov.–mid-Feb. (except Christmas–New Year's).*

Villeneuve-Loubet

⑲ *10 km (6 mi) north of Antibes, 17 km (10½ mi) southwest of Nice, 20 km (12 mi) northeast of Cannes.*

This tiny village, its medieval château heavily restored in the 19th century, is best known for its lower sprawl of overbuilt beachfront, heavily charged with concrete high-rises with all the architectural charm of a parking ramp. If you're a foodie, you may want to make a pilgrimage uphill to the eccentric **Musée de l'Art Culinaire** (Museum of

Culinary Arts), a shrine to the career of the great chef Auguste Escoffier (1846–1935), the founding father of the modern school of haute cuisine. In his birthplace are illustrations of his creations and a collection of fantastical menus. ⊠ *3 rue Escoffier,* ☎ *04–93–20–80–51.* 🖪 *25 frs.* ☉ *Sept.–June, Tues.–Sun. 2–6; July–Aug., Tues.–Sun. 2–7.*

Biot

❷⓪   *6 km (4 mi) northeast of Antibes, 15 km (9 mi) northeast of Cannes, 18 km (11 mi) southwest of Nice.*

Rising above an ugly commercial-industrial quarter up the coast from Antibes, Biot (pronounced bee-*otte*) sits neatly on a hilltop, welcoming day-trippers into its self-consciously quaint center. For centuries home to a pottery industry known for its fine yellow clay that stretched into massive, solid oil jars, it has in recent generations made a name for itself as a glass-art town. Nowadays its cobbled streets are lined with glass boutiques and galleries. Yet despite the commercialism, traces of the feel of old Provence remain, especially in the evening after the busloads of shoppers leave and the deep-shaded *placettes* (small squares) under the plane trees fall quiet.

Long a regular on the Côte d'Azur, Fernand Léger fell under Biot's spell and bought a mas here in 1955 to house an unwieldy collection of his sculptures. The modernized structure of the **Musée National Fernand-Léger** is striking, its facade itself a vast mosaic in his signature style of heavily outlined color fields. Within you can trace the evolution of Léger's technique, from his fascination with the industrial to freewheeling abstractions. ⊠ *Chemin du Val de Pomme,* ☎ *04–92–91–50–30.* 🖪 *38 frs.* ☉ *July–Sept., Wed.–Mon. 11–6; Oct.–June., Wed.–Mon. 10–12:30 and 2–5:30.*

On the edge of town follow the pink signs to **La Verrerie de Biot** (Biot Glassworks), founded in the 1950s. Here you can observe the glassblowers at work, visit the extensive galleries of museum-quality art glass, and start a collection of bubbled-glass goblets, cruets, or pitchers. ⊠ *5 chemin des Combes,* ☎ *04–93–65–03–00.* ☉ *May–Sept., daily 10–7; Oct.–Apr., Mon.–Sat. 10:30–1 and 2:30–6:30.*

Dining and Lodging

$ ✕🏨 **Galerie des Arcades.** Tucked away behind the quiet palm-lined
★   Place des Arcades in the old town, this combination hotel/restaurant/art gallery draws a loyal clientele. They come for unpretentious, authentic Provençal food: rabbit sautéed in fresh herbs, stuffed sardines, or a Friday *aïoli* (fish and crudités served with garlic mayonnaise). Ask for one of the three *grandes chambres* (large rooms) and revel in antiquity: four-poster beds, beams, and a tapestry-rich color scheme. ⊠ *14 pl. des Arcades, 06410,* ☎ *04–93–65–01–04,* 🗚 *04–93–65–01–05. 12 rooms. Restaurant. AE, DC, MC, V.*

NICE

As the fifth-largest city in France, this distended urban tangle is often avoided, but that decision is one to be rued: Nice's waterfront, paralleled by the famous Promenade des Anglais and lined by grand hotels, is one of the noblest in France. It's capped by a dramatic hilltop château–park whose slopes plunge almost into the sea and at whose base unfolds a bewitching warren of ancient Mediterranean streets.

It was in this old quarter, now Vieux Nice, that the Greeks established a market-port in the 4th century BC and named it Nikaia. After falling to the Saracen invasions, Nice regained power and developed into an important port in the early Middle Ages. In 1388 under Louis d'Anjou, Nice, along with the hill towns behind, effectively seceded from the county of Provence and allied itself with Savoie as the Comté de Nice (Nice County). It was a relationship that lasted some 500 years and stained the culture, architecture, and dialect in rich Italian hues.

Nowadays Nice strikes an engaging balance between old-world grace, port-town exotica, urban energy, whimsy, and high culture. You could easily spend your vacation here, attuned to Nice's quirks, its rhythms, and its Mediterranean tides.

Vieux Nice

Framed by the château and cours Saleya, the old town of Nice is its strongest drawing point and, should you only be passing through, the best place to capture the city's historic atmosphere.

A Good Walk

First, head for the morning flower market on the **cours Saleya** ㉑. At the center of cours Saleya is the florid, Baroque **Chapelle de la Miséricorde** ㉒. Thread your way into the old-town maze to the extravagant **Chapelle de l'Annonciation** ㉓. Continue up Poissonerie to rue de la Place Vieille, then head right to rue Droite; the **Chapelle St-Jacques-Jesu** ㉔ looms large and spare. Turn left on rue Rossetti and cross the square to the **Cathédrale Ste-Réparate** ㉕. Now take a break from the sacred, doubling back up rue Rossetti and continuing left up narrow rue Droite to the magnificent **Palais Lascaris** ㉖. Head next to boulevard Jean-Jaurès, which empties onto the grand, arcaded **place Garibaldi** ㉗; one of its five street spokes points straight to the **Musée d'Art Moderne** ㉘. From place Garibaldi and boulevard Jean-Jaurès, wind your way up to the ruins of the castle, now a park called the **Colline de Château** ㉙.

TIMING

Aim for morning on this walk, so you'll see the market on cours Saleya at its liveliest. If you include a visit to the Palais Lascaris and a visit to the Musée Terra Amata, this would make a full-day's outing.

Sights to See

㉕ **Cathédrale Ste-Réparate.** An ensemble of columns, cupolas, and symmetrical ornaments dominates the old town, flanked by its own 18th-century bell tower and capped by its glossy ceramic tile dome. The cathedral's interior, restored to a bright color palette of ochre golds and rusts, has elaborate plasterwork and decorative frescoes on every surface. ⊠ *Rue Ste-Réparate.*

㉒ **Chapelle de la Miséricorde.** A superbly balanced *pièce-montée* (wedding cake) of half domes and cupolas, this chapel is decorated within an inch of its life with frescoes, faux marble, gilt, and crystal chandeliers. A magnificent Bréa altarpiece crowns the ensemble. ⊠ *Cours Saleya.*

㉓ **Chapelle de l'Annonciation.** This 17th-century Carmelite chapel is a classic example of pure Niçoise Baroque, from its sculpted door to its extravagant marble work and the florid symmetry of its arches and cupolas. ⊠ *Rue de la Poissonerie.*

㉔ **Chapelle St-Jacques-Jesu.** If the old town's other chapels are jewel boxes, this 17th-century chapel is a barn: Broad, open, and ringing hollow, this church seems austere by comparison. That's only because the theatrical decoration is spread over a more expansive surface. ⊠ *Corner of rue Droite and rue Gesu.*

㉙ **Colline de Château** (Château Hill). Though nothing remains of this once-massive medieval stronghold but a few ruins left after its 1706 dis-

Nice

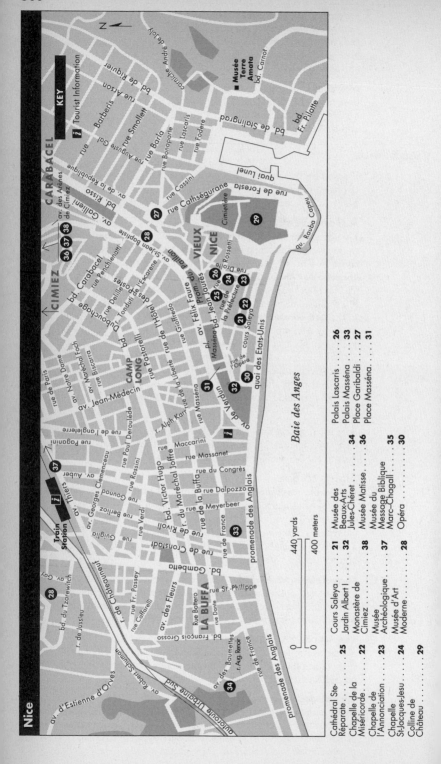

KEY

i Tourist Information

■ Musée Terre Amata

CARABACEL

CIMIEZ

CAMP LONG

VIEUX NICE

LA BUFFA

Train Station

Baie des Anges

440 yards
400 meters

Cathédral Ste-Réparate	**25**	Cours Saleya	**21**
Chapelle de la Miséricorde	**22**	Jardin Albert I	**32**
Chapelle de l'Annonciation	**23**	Monastère de Cimiez	**38**
Chapelle St-Jacques-Jesu	**24**	Musée Archéologique	**37**
Colline de Château	**29**	Musée d'Art Moderne	**28**

Musée des Beaux-Arts Jules-Chéret	**34**
Musée Matisse	**36**
Musée du Message Biblique Marc-Chagall	**35**
Opéra	**30**

Palais Lascaris	**26**
Palais Masséna	**33**
Place Garibaldi	**27**
Place Masséna	**31**

mantling, this park still bears its name. From here take in extraordinary views of the Baie des Anges, the length of the Promenade des Anglais, and the red-ochre roofs of the old town. ☉ *Daily 7–7.*

㉑ **Cours Saleya.** This street is framed with 18th-century houses and shaded by plane trees. The tall yellow-stone building at the far-east end was home to Henri Matisse from 1921 to 1938.

㉘ **Musée d'Art Moderne.** The assertive contemporary architecture of the Modern Art Museum makes a bold and emphatic statement of Nice's presence in the modern world. The art collection inside focuses intently and thoroughly on contemporary art from the late 1950s onward. ⊠ *Promenade des Arts,* ☎ *04–93–62–61–62.* ▧ *25 frs.* ☉ *Mon., Wed.– Thurs., and weekends 11–6; Fri. 11–10.*

㉖ **Palais Lascaris.** The aristocratic Lascaris Palace was built in 1648 for Jean-Baptiste Lascaris-Vintimille, *marechal* to the duke of Savoy. The magnificent vaulted staircase, with its massive stone balustrade and niches filled with classical gods, is only surpassed in grandeur by the Flemish tapestries (after Rubens) and the extraordinary trompe l'oeil fresco of the fall of Phaeton. ⊠ *15 rue Droite,* ☎ *04–93–62–05–54.* ▧ *25 frs.* ☉ *Tues.–Sun. 10–noon and 2–6.*

㉗ **Place Garibaldi.** Encircled by grand vaulted arcades stuccoed in rich yellow, the broad pentagon of this square could have been airlifted out of Turin. In the center, the shrinelike fountain sculpture of Garibaldi seems to survey you as you walk by, strolling under the arcades and lounge in its cafés.

Along the Promenade des Anglais

The original Promenade des Anglais was built as a walkway for the flocks of British Victorians drawn to Nice's warm climate. Nowadays it's a wide multilane boulevard thick with traffic, the last gasp of the coastal highway N98. Beside it runs the famous paved pedestrian walkway, which has intermittent steps leading down to the smooth-rock beach.

A Good Walk

From the west end of cours Saleya, walk down rue St-François-de-Paule past the Belle Epoque **Opéra** ㉚. Continue up the street, then head right up rue de l'Opéra to **Place Masséna** ㉛, framed in broad arcades and opening onto the vast, green **Jardin Albert I** ㉜. Three long blocks past the Casino Ruhl, you'll reach the gates and park of the imposing **Palais Masséna** ㉝. Walk along the waterfront for a few blocks, past busy boulevard Gambetta, then head inland up tiny rue Sauvan. Cross boulevard Grosso and head diagonally up the hill on avenue des Baumettes. In this quiet, once luxurious neighborhood is the **Musée des Beaux-Arts Jules-Chéret** ㉞, built in extravagant Italianate style.

TIMING

This walk covers a long stretch of waterfront, so it may take up to an hour to stroll the length of it. Allow a half day if you explore the Palais Massena or the Musée des Beaux Arts.

Sights to See

㉜ **Jardin Albert I** (Albert I Garden). Along the Promenade des Anglais, this luxurious garden stands over the delta of the River Paillon, underground since 1882. Every kind of flower and palm tree grows here, thrown into exotic relief by night illumination.

㉞ **Musée des Beaux-Arts Jules-Chéret** (Jules-Chéret Fine Arts Museum). In a 19th-century Italianate mansion, the museum has a fine collection of paintings by Nice artists of the era, including works by the museum's namesake. It also has a small collection of Impressionist works, two pieces by Rodin, and some ceramic pieces by Picasso. ⊠ *33 av. des Baumettes,* ☎ *04–92–15–28–28.* 🎫 *25 frs.* ⊙ *Oct.–Apr., Tues.– Sun. 10–noon and 2–5; May–Sept., Tues.–Sun. 10–noon and 2–6.*

③⓪ **Opéra.** A half block west of the cours Saleya stands a flamboyant Italian-style theater designed by Charles Garnier, architect of the Paris Opéra. It's home today to the Opéra de Nice, with a permanent chorus, orchestra, and ballet corps (☞ Nightlife and the Arts, *below*). ⊠ *4 rue St-François-de-Paul,* ☎ *04–92–17–40–40.*

③③ **Palais Masséna** (Masséna Palace). This handsome Belle Epoque building, housing the **Musée d'Art et d'Histoire** (Museum of Art and History), is undergoing a complete renovation and will reopen only mid-2001. ⊠ *Entrance at 65 rue de France,* ☎ *04–93–88–11–34.*

③① **Place Masséna.** As cours Saleya is the heart of the old town, so this broad square is the heart of the city as a whole. It's framed by an ensemble of Italian-style arcaded buildings first built in 1815, their facades stuccoed in rich red ochre.

Cimiez

Once the site of the powerful Roman settlement Cemenelum, the hilltop neighborhood of Cimiez—4 km (2 mi) north of cours Saleya—is Nice's most luxurious quarter (use Bus 15 from place Massena or avenue Jean-Médecin to visit its sights).

A Good Walk
Begin at the **Musée du Message Biblique Marc-Chagall** ㉟, which houses one of the finest collections of Chagall's works based on biblical themes. Then make the pilgrimage to the center of Cimiez and the **Musée Matisse** ㊱, where an important collection of Matisse's life work is amassed in an Italianate villa. Just behind, the **Musée Archéologique** ㊲ displays a wealth of Roman treasures. Slightly east of the museum is the thriving **Monastère de Cimiez** ㊳, a Franciscan monastery.

TIMING
Between bus connections and long walks from sight to sight, this walk is a half-day commitment at minimum. If you plan to really spend time in the Matisse Museum and the Chagall Museum, this could easily be a day's outing.

Sights to See
㊳ **Monastère de Cimiez.** This fully functioning monastery is worth the pilgrimage. You'll find a lovely **garden,** replanted along the lines of the original 16th-century layout; the **Musée Franciscain,** a didactic museum tracing the history of the Franciscan order; and a 15th-century **church** containing three works of remarkable power and elegance by Bréa. ⊠ *Pl. du Monastère,* ☎ *04–93–81–00–04.* 🎫 *Free.* ⊙ *Mon.–Sat. 10–noon and 3–6.*

㊲ **Musée Archéologique** (Archaeology Museum). This museum, next to the Matisse Museum, has a dense and intriguing collection of objects extracted from the digs around the Roman city of Cemenelum, which flourished from the 1st to the 5th centuries. ⊠ *160 av. des Arènes-de-Cimiez,* ☎ *04–93–81–59–57.* 🎫 *25 frs.* ⊙ *Apr.–Sept., Tues.–Sun. 10–noon and 2–6; Oct.–Mar., Tues.–Sun. 10–1 and 2–5.*

★ ㊱ **Musée Matisse.** A lovely, light-bathed 17th-century villa is home to this large collection of Henri Matisse's works. Matisse settled in Nice in 1917, seeking a sun cure after a bout of pneumonia, and remained here until his death in 1954. ⊠ *164 av. des Arènes-de-Cimiez,* ☎ *04–93–81–08–08.* ☜ *25 frs.* ☉ *Apr.–Sept., Wed.–Mon. 10–6; Oct.–Mar., Wed.–Mon. 10–5.*

★ ㉟ **Musée du Message Biblique Marc-Chagall** (Marc Chagall Museum of Biblical Themes). This museum has one of the finest permanent collections of Chagall's (1887–1985) late works. Superbly displayed, 17 vast canvases depict biblical themes, each in emphatic and joyous color schemes. ⊠ *Av. du Dr-Ménard (head up av. Thiers, then take a left onto av. Malausséna, cross railway tracks, and take first right up av. de l'Olivetto),* ☎ *04–93–53–87–20.* ☜ *30 frs, in summer 38 frs.* ☉ *July–Sept., Wed.–Mon. 10–6; Oct.–June, Wed.–Mon. 10–5.*

Dining and Lodging

$$ ✕ **Grand Café de Turin.** Whether you crowd onto a banquette in the dark, low-ceiling bar or win a coveted table under the arcaded porticoes on Place Garibaldi, this is *the* place to go for shellfish in Nice: sea snails, clams, plump *fines de claires* and salty *bleues* oysters, and urchins by the dozen. It's packed noon and night. ⊠ *5 pl. Garibaldi,* ☎ *04–93–62–29–52. AE, DC, MC, V. Closed June.*

$$ ✕ **La Mérenda.** The back-to-bistro boom climaxed here when Dominique
★ Le Stanc retired his crown at the Negresco to take over this tiny, unpretentious landmark of Provençal cuisine. Now he and his wife work in the miniature open kitchen, creating the ultimate versions of stuffed sardines, pistou, and slow-simmered *daubes* (beef stews). Stop by in person to reserve entry to the inner sanctum. ⊠ *4 rue de la Terrasse,* ☎ *no phone. No credit cards. Closed weekends, last wk in July, 1st 2 wks in Aug., and school holidays.*

$–$$ ✕ **L'Olivier.** In this hole-in-the-wall bistro on Place Garibaldi, two brothers have gone back to their roots, and all of Nice has followed. Frank Musso, trained at the Tour d'Argent in Paris, concentrates his sophisticated gifts on simple dishes: tripe simmered in tomatoes, daubes and pork confits, and crêpes with homemade bitter-orange marmalade. His brother Christian provides the cheery welcome. ⊠ *2 pl. Garibaldi,* ☎ *04–93–26–89–09. Reservations essential. AE, MC, V. Closed Sun. and Aug. No lunch Wed.*

$ ✕ **Chez René/Socca.** This back-alley landmark is the most popular dive in town for socca, the snack food unique to Nice. Rustic olive-wood tables line the street, and curt waiters splash down your drink order. For the food, you get in line and carry it steaming to the table yourself. It's off Place Garibaldi on the edge of the old town, across from the *gare routière* (bus station). ⊠ *2 rue Miralhetti,* ☎ *04–93–92–05–73. No credit cards.*

$ ✕ **Lou Pilha Leva.** Not as well known as Chez René (☞ *above*) but much more serious about the food it serves, this street stand just south of place St-François offers good, fresh-cooked versions of petits farcis, chickpea socca, quichelike *tourta de blea,* and pissaladières as well as full meals of homemade pasta, pizza, stockfish, and polenta, all made on the premises. Order food at the window, drinks at the table. ⊠ *10 rue du Collet on pl. Centrale,* ☎ *04–93–13–99–08. MC, V.*

$$$$ ✕🏨 **La Perouse.** Just past the old town, at the foot of the château, this hotel is a secret treasure cut into the cliff (an elevator takes you up to reception). Some of the best rooms not only overlook the azure sea but also look down into an intimate garden with lemon trees and a cliff-side pool. The restaurant serves meals in the candlelighted garden May–September. ⊠ *11 quai Rauba-Capeau, 06300,* ☎ *04–93–62–34–63,* ℻ *04–93–62–59–41. 64 rooms. Restaurant, air-conditioning, pool, sauna. AE, DC, MC, V.* ✍

$$$-$$$$ ✕▣ **Beau Rivage.** Occupying an imposing late-19th-century town house near cours Saleya, this hotel is just a few steps from the best parts of old Nice and the beach, though buildings have long since blocked its sea views. The room decor is standard and a bit stuffy, done in a color scheme of pinks and teals; corner rooms have big windows and are by far the best. ✉ *24 rue St-François-de-Paule, 06000,* ☎ *04–93–80–80–70,* ℻ *04–93–80–55–77. 118 rooms. Restaurant, air-conditioning, beach. AE, DC, MC, V.*

$$ ▣ **La Fontaine.** Downtown and a block from the waterfront, this immaculate, simply designed hotel offers a friendly welcome from its house-proud owners. Rooms are small and comfortable, in cheery blues and yellows and with bathrooms freshly tiled. It even has a pretty little courtyard where breakfast is served. ✉ *49 rue de France, 06000,* ☎ *04–93–88–30–38,* ℻ *04–93–88–98–11. 29 rooms. Breakfast room, air-conditioning. AE, DC, MC, V.*

$$ ▣ **Windsor.** This is a memorably eccentric hotel with a vision: Most
★ of its white-on-white rooms either have frescoes of mythic themes or are works of artists' whimsy. But the real draw of this otherworldly place is its astonishing city-center garden—a tropical paradise of lemon, magnolia, and palm trees. You can breakfast or dine here by candle-light (guests only) and dip into the small, shrub-screened pool. ✉ *11 rue Dalpozzo, 06000,* ☎ *04–93–88–59–35,* ℻ *04–93–88–94–57. 57 rooms. Restaurant, bar, pool. AE, DC, MC, V.*❧

$ ▣ **Felix.** On popular, pedestrian rue Masséna and a block from the beach, this tiny hotel is owned by a hard-working couple (both fluent in English) who make you feel welcome. Rooms are compact but neat and bright, so they don't feel as small, and four have tiny balconies with ringside seats over the pedestrian thoroughfare. ✉ *41 rue Masséna, 06000,* ☎ *04–93–88–67–73,* ℻ *04–93–16–15–78. 14 rooms. Air-conditioning. AE, DC, MC, V.*

Nightlife and the Arts

The **Casino Ruhl** (✉ 1 Promenade des Anglais, 04–93–87–95–87), gleaming neon-bright and modern, is a sophisticated Riviera landmark. If you're all dressed up and have just won big, invest in a drink in the intimate walnut-and-velour **Bar Anglais** (✉ 37 Promenade des Anglais, ☎ 04–93–88–39–51), in the landmark Hôtel Negresco.

In July the **Nice Jazz Festival** (☎ 04–92–17–77–77 for information) draws international performers from around the world. Classical music and ballet performances take place at Nice's convention center, the **Acropolis** (✉ Palais des Congrès, Esplanade John F. Kennedy, ☎ 04–93–92–83–00). The season at the **Opéra de Nice** (✉ 4 rue St-François-de-Paul, ☎ 04–92–17–40–40) runs from September to June.

Outdoor Activities and Sports

Nice's **beaches** extend all along the Baie des Anges, backed full-length by the Promenade des Anglais. Public stretches alternate with posh private beaches that feature restaurants—and bar service, mattresses and parasols, waterskiing, parasailing, windsurfing, and jet skiing. Some of the handiest private beaches are the **Beau Rivage** (☎ 04–92–47–82–83), across from the cours Saleya; and the **Ruhl** (☎ 04–93–87–09–70), across from the casino.

Shopping

Olive oil by the gallon in cans sporting colorful, old-fashioned labels is sold at tiny **Alziari** (✉ 14 rue St-François-de-Paule). A good source for crystallized fruit, a Nice specialty, is the **Confiserie du Vieux Nice** (✉ 14 quai Papacino), on the west side of the port. The venerable old **Henri Auer** (✉ 7 rue St-François-de-Paule) has sold crystallized fruit since 1820.

Seafood of all kinds is sold at the **fish market** (⊠ Pl. St-François) every morning except Monday. At the daily **flower market** (⊠ Cours Saleya) you can find all kinds of plants and fruits and vegetables. The **antiques and brocante market** (⊠ Pl. Robilante), by the old port, is held from Tuesday through Saturday.

En Route The lay of the land east of Nice is nearly vertical, as the coastline is one great cliff, a corniche terraced by three parallel highways—the **Basse Corniche,** the **Moyenne Corniche,** and the **Grande Corniche**—that snake along its graduated crests. The lowest (*basse*) is the slowest, following the coast and crawling through the main streets of resorts—including downtown Monte Carlo. The highest (*grande*) is the fastest, but its panoramic views are blocked by villas, and there are few safe overlooks. The middle (*moyenne*) offers views down over the shoreline and villages and passes through a few picturesque towns.

THE EASTERN CÔTE D'AZUR

You may build castles in Spain or picture yourself on a South Sea island, but when it comes to serious speculation about how to spend that first $10 million and slip easily into the life of the idle rich, most people take out a map of France and highlight, then head for the stretch of coast that covers the eastern Côte d'Azur. Here, backed by the mistral-proof Alps and coddled by mild Mediterranean breezes, waterfront resorts—Villefranche and Menton—draw energy from the thriving city of Nice, while jutting tropical peninsulas—Cap Ferrat, Cap Martin—frame the tiny principality of Monaco. Here the corniche highways snake above sparkling waters, pink and white villas turning faces toward the sun. Cliffs bristle with palm trees and parasol pines, and mimosa, bougainvillea, jasmine and even cactus bloom in the hothouse climate. Crowded with sunseekers, the Riviera still reveals quiet corners with heart-stopping views of sea, sun, and mountains—all in one memorable frame.

Villefranche-sur-Mer

★ ㊴ *10 km (6 mi) east of Nice.*

Nestled discreetly along the deep scoop of harbor between Nice and the Cap Ferrat, this pretty watercolor of a fishing port seems surreal, flanked as it is by the big city of Nice and the assertive wealth of Monaco. Genuine fishermen actually skim up to the docks here in weathered-blue *barques,* and the streets of the old town flow directly to the waterfront, much as they did in the 13th century. Behind towering gates and secluded groves are the private vacation villas of some of the wealthiest people on earth.

So enamored was Jean Cocteau of this painterly fishing port that he decorated the 14th-century **Chapelle St-Pierre** with images from the life of St. Peter and dedicated it to the village's fishermen. ⊠ *Pl. Pollanais,* ☎ *04–93–76–90–70.* ▧ *12 frs.* ⊙ *Mid-June–mid-Sept., Tues.–Sun. 10– noon and 4–8:30; mid-Sept.–mid-Nov., Tues.–Sun. 9:30–noon and 2– 6; end Dec.–Mar., Tues.–Sun. 9:30–noon and 2–5:30; Apr.–mid-June, Tues.–Sun. 9:30–noon and 3–7.*

Running parallel to the waterfront, the extraordinary 13th-century **rue Obscure** (literally, Dark Street) is entirely covered by vaulted arcades; it sheltered the people of Villefranche when the Germans fired their parting shots—an artillery bombardment—near World War II's end.

The stalwart 16th-century **Citadelle St-Elme,** restored to perfect condition, anchors the harbor with its broad, sloping stone walls. Beyond its drawbridge lie the city's offices and a group of minor gallery-museums. Whether or not you stop into these private collections of local art (all free of charge), you are welcome to stroll around the inner grounds and to circle the imposing exterior.

Lodging

$$–$$$ 🏨 **Hôtel Welcome.** When Villefranche harbored a community of artists
★   and writers, this waterfront landmark was their adopted headquarters. Somerset Maugham holed up in one of the tiny crow's-nest rooms at the top, and Jean Cocteau moved into one of the corners. Evelyn Waugh and Richard Burton used to tie one on in the bar. It's comfortable and modern, with the best rooms brightened with vivid colors and stenciled quotes from Cocteau. ⊠ *Quai Courbet, 06230,* ☎ *04–93–76–27–62,* 🖷 *04–93–76–27–66. 32 rooms. 2 restaurants, bar, air-conditioning. AE, DC, MC, V. Closed mid-Nov.–mid-Dec.*

Beaulieu

④⓪ *4 km (2 mi) east of Villefranche, 14 km (9 mi) east of Nice.*

With its back pressed hard against the cliffs of the corniche and sheltered between the peninsulas of Cap Ferrat and Cap Roux, this once-grand resort basks in a tropical microclimate that earned its central neighborhood the name *Petite Afrique.* The town was the pet of 19th-century society, and its grand hotels welcomed Empress Eugénie, the Prince of Wales, and Russian nobles.

One manifestation of Beaulieu's Belle Epoque excess is the extravagant
★ **Villa Kerylos,** a mansion built in 1902 in the style of classical Greece. It was the dream house of the amateur archaeologist Théodore Reinach, who commissioned an Italian architect so he could surround himself with Grecian delights: cool Carrara marble, rare fruitwoods, and a dining room where guests reclined to eat, *à la Greque.* ⊠ *Rue Gustave-Eiffel,* ☎ *04–93–01–01–44.* 🖼 *43 frs.* ۞ *Mid-Feb.–mid–Nov., daily 10:30–6; mid-Dec.–mid-Feb., weekdays 2–6, weekends 10:30–6; July–Aug., daily 10:30–7.*

St-Jean-Cap-Ferrat

④① *2 km (1 mi) south of Beaulieu on D25.*

This luxuriously sited pleasure port moors the peninsula of Cap Ferrat; from its port-side walkways and crescent of beach you can look over the sparkling blue harbor to the graceful green bulk of the corniches. Yachts purr in and out of port, and their passengers scuttle into cafés for take-out drinks to enjoy on their private decks.

★ Between the port and the mainland, the gaudily beautiful **Villa Ephrussi de Rothschild** stands as witness to the wealth and worldly taste of the baroness who had it built. Constructed in 1905, the house was created around the precious artworks, tapestries, and furniture Beatrice de Rothschild collected. The grounds are landscaped with no less than seven theme gardens. The extraordinary ensemble reigns over a hilltop at the crest of the peninsula, taking in spectacular views of the coastline. ⊠ *Av. Ephrussi,* ☎ *04–93–01–33–09.* 🖼 *Access to ground floor and gardens 49 frs; guided tour upstairs 14 frs extra.* ۞ *Feb.-June and Sept.–Nov., daily 10–6; July–Aug., daily 10–7; Nov.–Jan., weekdays 2–6, weekends 10–6.*

Dining and Lodging

$$ ✕ **Le Sloop.** This sleek port-side restaurant caters to the yachting crowd and sailors who cruise into dock for lunch. The focus is fish, of course: *Soupe de poisson* (fish soup), *St-Pierre* (John Dory) steamed with asparagus, or whole, roasted whole sea bass. Its outdoor tables surround a tiny "garden" of potted palms. ⊠ *Port de Plaisance,* ☎ *04–93–01–48–63. AE, MC, V. Closed Wed. mid-Sept.–mid-Apr. No lunch Wed.–Thurs. mid-Apr.–mid-Sept.*

$$$ ⊡ **Brise Marine.** This golden-ochre 1878 villa, brightened with sky blue
★ shutters and a frieze of frescoed lemons, opens onto a broad balustraded
terrace and unbroken views of the sea. Pretty little pastel guest rooms
feel like bedrooms in a private home. ⊠ *58 av. Jean Mermoz, 06230,*
☎ *04–93–76–04–36,* FAX *04–93–76–11–49. 16 rooms. Bar, air-condi-
tioning. AE, DC, MC, V. Closed Nov.–Jan.* ⊜

Eze

㊷ *2 km (1 mi) east of Beaulieu, 12 km (7 mi) east of Nice, 7 km (4 mi)
west of Monte Carlo.*

Towering like an eagle's nest above the coast and crowned with ram-
parts and the ruins of a medieval château, Eze (pronounced ehz) is un-
fortunately the most accessible of all the perched villages. Consequently,
it's by far the most commercialized, surpassing St-Paul-de-Vence for
the tackiness of its souvenir shops and the indifference of its waiters.
It is, nonetheless, spectacularly sited; if you can manage to shake the
crowds and duck off to a quiet overlook, the village commands splen-
did views up and down the coast.

Dining and Lodging

$$$$ ✕⊡ **Château de la Chèvre d'Or.** Though it's directly on the main
★ tourist thoroughfare, this extraordinary conglomerate of weathered-
stone houses allows you to turn your back on the world and drink in
unsurpassed sea views. More than half the creamy white rooms look
over the water, and the others compensate with exposed stone, beams,
and burnished antiques. The three restaurants all take in the views, too,
as does the Louis XIII–style bar. It's a member of the Relais & Châteaux
group. ⊠ *rue du Barri, 06360,* ☎ *04–92–10–66–66,* FAX *04–93–41–
06–72. 22 rooms, 8 apartments. 3 restaurants, bar, pool. AE, DC, MC,
V. Closed Dec.–Feb.* ⊜

Peillon

★ ㊸ *15 km (9 mi) northeast of Nice via D2204 and D21.*

Perhaps because it's difficult to reach and not on the way to or from
anything else, this idyllic village has maintained the magical ambience
of its medieval origins. You can hear the bell toll here, walk in silence
up its weathered cobblestones, and smell the thyme crunching under-
foot if you step past its minuscule boundaries onto the unspoiled hill-
sides. And its streets are utterly and completely commerce free; the citizens
have voted to vaccinate themselves against the plague of boutiques, gal-
leries, and cafés that have infected its peers along the coast.

Dining and Lodging

$–$$$ ✕⊡ **Auberge de la Madone.** With its shaded garden terrace and its
★ impeccable bright-colored rooms, this inn is a charming oasis. A lunch
of sea bass, pigeon, and goat cheese on the flowery veranda is everything the south of France should be. The inn has a tennis court on the
slope above it and, in the village annex Lou Pourtail, six little rooms
offering shelter at bargain rates. ⊠ *06440 Peillon Village,* ☎ *04–93–
79–91–17,* FAX *04–93–79–99–36. 18 rooms, 2 suites. Restaurant, tennis court. MC, V. Closed late Oct.–late Dec. and Jan.*

Monaco

7 km (4 mi) east of Eze, 21 km (13 mi) east of Nice.

It's positively feudal, the idea that an ancient dynasty of aristocrats could
still hold fast to its patch of coastline, the last scrap of a once-vast domain. But that's just what the Grimaldi family did, clinging to a few

acres of glory and maintaining their own license plates, their own telephone area code (377), and their own highly forgiving tax system. Yet the Principality of Monaco covers just 473 acres and would fit comfortably inside New York's Central Park or a family farm in Iowa. And its 5,000 pampered citizens would fill only a small fraction of the seats in Yankee Stadium.

The present ruler, Prince Rainier III, traces his ancestry to Otto Canella, who was born in 1070. The Grimaldi dynasty began with Otto's great-great-great-grandson, Francesco Grimaldi, also known as Frank the Rogue. Expelled from Genoa, Frank and his cronies disguised themselves as monks and in 1297 seized the fortified medieval town known today as Le Rocher (the Rock). Except for a short break under Napoléon, the Grimaldis have been here ever since, which makes them the oldest reigning family in Europe.

In the 1850s a Grimaldi named Charles III made a decision that turned the Rock into a giant blue chip. Needing revenues but not wanting to impose additional taxes on his subjects, he contracted with a company to open a gambling facility. The first spin of the roulette wheel was on December 14, 1856. Almost overnight, a threadbare principality became an elegant watering hole for European society. Profits were so great that Charles eventually abolished all direct taxes.

But it's the tax system, not the gambling, that's made Monaco one of the most sought-after addresses in the world. It bristles with gleaming glass-and-concrete corncob-towers 20 and 30 stories high and with vast apartment complexes, their terraces, landscaped like miniature gardens, jutting over the sea. You now have to look hard to find the Belle Epoque grace of yesteryear—but if you spend some time at the Casino, Opéra, or the Louis XV restaurant, you may be able to conjure up Monaco's elegant past and the much-missed spirit of Princess Grace.

★ ④④ Place du Casino is the center of Monte Carlo, and the **casino** is a must-see, even if you don't bet a sou. Into the gold-leaf splendor of the casino, the hopeful traipse from tour buses to tempt fate beneath the gilt-edged rococo ceiling. Jacket and tie are required in the back rooms, which open at 3 PM. Bring your passport (under-21s not admitted). ⊠ *Pl. du Casino,* ☎ *377/92–16–20–00.* ◷ *Noon–4 AM.*

④⑤ In the true spirit of the town, it seems that the **Opéra** (⊠ Pl. du Casino), with its 18-ton gilt-bronze chandelier and extravagant frescoes, is part of the casino complex. The designer, Charles Garnier, also built the Paris Opéra.

④⑥ Some say the most serious gamblers play at **Sun Casino,** in the Monte Carlo Grand Hotel, by the vast convention center that juts over the water. ⊠ *12 av. des Spélugues,* ☎ *92–16–21–23.* ◷ *Tables open weekdays at 5 PM and weekends at 4 PM; slot machines open daily at 11 AM.*

④⑦ From Place des Moulins an elevator descends to the Larvotto Beach complex, artfully created with imported sand, and the **Musée National,** housed in a Garnier villa within a rose garden. It has a beguiling collection of 18th- and 19th-century dolls and mechanical automatons. ⊠ *17 av. Princesse Grace,* ☎ *93–30–91–26.* ▣ *30 frs.* ◷ *Easter–Aug., daily 10–6:30; Sept.–Easter, daily 10–12:15 and 2:30–6:30.*

④⑧ West of Monte Carlo stands the famous Rock, crowned by the **Palais Princier,** where the royal family resides. A 40-minute guided tour (summer only) of this sumptuous chunk of history, first built in the 13th century and expanded and enhanced over the centuries, reveals an extravagance of 16th- and 17th-century frescoes, as well as tapestries,

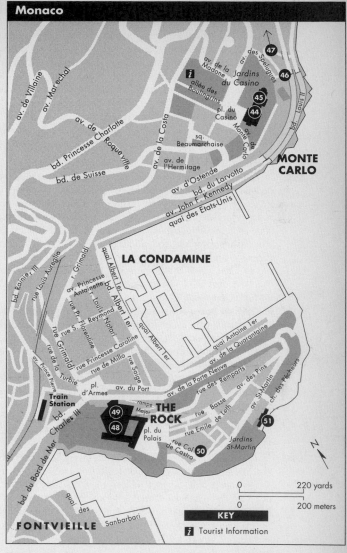

gilt furniture, and paintings on a grand scale. ⊠ *Pl. du Palais,* ☎ *93–25–18–31.* ⊡ *30 frs; joint ticket with Musée Napoléon 40 frs.* ☉ *June–Oct., daily 9:30–5.*

④⑨ One wing of the palace, open throughout the year, is taken up by the **Musée Napoléon,** filled with Napoléonic souvenirs—including The Hat and a tricolor scarf—and genealogical charts. ⊠ *In Palais Princier,* ☎ *93–25–18–31.* ⊡ *20 frs; joint ticket with palace apartments 40 frs. (☞ above).* ☉ *June–Sept., daily 9:30–6:30; Oct.–mid-Nov., 10–5; Dec.–May, Tues.–Sun. 10:30–12:30 and 2–5.*

⑤⓪ Follow the flow of crowds down the last remaining streets of medieval Monaco to the **Cathédrale de l'Immaculée-Conception** (⊠ av. St-Martin), an uninspired 19th-century version of Romanesque. Nonetheless, it harbors a magnificent altarpiece, painted in 1500 by Bréa, and the tomb of Princess Grace.

★ ☙ ⑤ At the prow of the Rock, the grand **Musée Océanographique** (Oceanography Museum) perches dramatically on a cliff. It's a splendid Edwardian structure, built under Prince Albert I to house specimens collected on amateur explorations. Jacques Cousteau (1910–97) led its missions from 1957 to 1988. The main floor displays skeletons and taxidermy of enormous sea creatures; early submarines and diving gear dating to the Middle Ages; and a few interactive science displays. The main draw is the famous **aquarium,** a vast complex of backlighted tanks containing every imaginable variety of fish, crab, and eel. ⊠ *Av. St-Martin,* ☎ *93–15–36–00.* 🎫 *60 frs.* ☉ *July–Aug., daily 9–8; Sept. and Apr.–June, daily 9–7; Oct. and Mar., daily 9:30–7; Nov.–Feb., daily 10–6.*

Dining and Lodging

$$$$ ✕ **Le Louis XV.** This sumptuous neo-Baroque restaurant, in the Hôtel
★   de Paris (☞ *below*), stuns with royal decor that is nonetheless upstaged by its product: the superb cuisine of Alain Ducasse, one of Europe's most celebrated chefs. Ducasse often refers to his deceptively simple style as "country cooking," where caviar and truffles slum happily with stockfish (stewed salt cod) and tripe. In short, it's a panoply of Mediterranean delights. If you can afford it, this is a must. ⊠ *Hôtel de Paris, pl. du Casino,* ☎ *92–16–30–01. AE, DC, MC, V. Closed Tues. and Wed. (except Wed. dinner mid-June–Aug.), 2 wks in Feb.–early Mar., and late Nov.–late Dec.*

$$ ✕ **Café de Paris.** This landmark Belle Epoque brasserie, across from the Casino, offers a wide variety of classic dishes (shellfish, steak tartare, matchstick frites, and fish boned table-side). Supercilious, super-pro waiters fawn gracefully over old-world preeners, gentlemen, jet-setters, and tourists alike. Happily, there's good hot food until 2AM. ⊠ *Place du Casino,* ☎ *92–16–20–20. AE, DC, MC, V.*

$$ ✕ **Castelroc.** With its tempting pine-shaded terrace just across from the entrance to the Prince's Palace, this popular local lunch spot serves up specialties of cuisine Monegasque, ranging from anchoiade to stockfish. ⊠ *Pl. du Palais,* ☎ *93–30–36–68. AE, MC, V. Closed Sat. and Dec.–Jan.*

$$$$ 🏨 **Hermitage.** A riot of frescoes and plaster flourishes embellished with gleaming brass, this landmark 1900 hotel nonetheless maintains a relatively low profile, set back a block from the Casino scene. Even if you're not staying, come to see the glass-dome Art Nouveau vestibule, designed by Gustav Eiffel. The best rooms face the sea or angle toward the port. ⊠ *Sq. Beaumarchais, 98005,* ☎ *92–16–40–00,* FAX *92–16–38–52. 195 rooms, 14 junior suites, 18 suites. Restaurant, bar, air-conditioning, pool. AE, DC, MC, V.* ☙

$$$$ 🏨 **Hôtel de Paris.** Built in 1864 on an extravagant scale, this vestige of the Belle Epoque has one of the most prestigious addresses in Europe. The cavernous lobby is a veritable crossroads of the buffed and befurred Euro-gentry, and rooms—fresh, pretty, and not in the least grandiose—overlook the Casino, the gardens, and from above, the sea. ⊠ *Pl. du Casino, 98000,* ☎ *92–16–30–00,* FAX *92–16–38–50. 141 rooms, 40 suites, and 19 junior suites. 4 restaurants, air-conditioning, pool, indoor pool, spa. AE, DC, MC, V.* ☙

$$$$ 🏨 **Monte Carlo Grand Hotel.** Sprawling long and low along the waterfront at Monte Carlo's base, this ultramodern airport-scale complex is so vast it commands a full-time staff of upholsterers. Bright rooms decked in vivid hues angle onto the open sea. The bars, casino, boutiques, and mall-size lobby easily contain megaconventions, but vacationers will feel at home, too. ⊠ *12 av. des Spélugues, 98000,* ☎ *93–50–65–00,* FAX *93–30–01–57. 619 rooms, 69 apartments. 3 restaurants, 1 bar, air-conditioning, pool, hot tub, health club,casino. AE, DC, MC, V.* ☙

$$$ 🖭 **Alexandra.** The friendly proprietress, Madame Larouquie, makes you feel right at home at this central, comfortable spot, just north of the casino. Though the color schemes clash and the decor is spare, bathrooms are big and up to date, and insulated windows shut out traffic noise. ✉ *35 bd. Princesse-Charlotte, 98000,* ☎ *93–50–63–13,* 🆊 *92–16–06–48. 56 rooms. Air-conditioning. AE, DC, MC, V.*

Nightlife and the Arts

There's no need to go to bed before dawn in Monte Carlo when you can go to the **casinos** (☞ *above*).

Monte Carlo's spring arts festival, **Printemps des Arts,** takes place from early April to mid-May and includes the world's top ballet, operatic, symphonic, and chamber performers. Year-round, ballet and classical music can be enjoyed at the **Salle Garnier** (✉ Pl. du Casino, ☎ 92–16–22–99), the main venue of the Opéra de Monte-Carlo and the Orchestre Philharmonique de Monte-Carlo, both worthy of the magnificent hall.

Outdoor Activities and Sports

The **Monte Carlo Tennis Tournament** is held during the spring arts festival. When the tennis stops, the auto racing begins: The **Grand Prix de Monaco** (☎ 93–15–26–00 for information) takes place in mid-May.

Roquebrune–Cap-Martin

㉒ *5 km (3 mi) east of Monaco.*

In the midst of the frenzy of overbuilding that defines this last gasp of the coast before Italy, two twinned havens have survived, each in its own way: The perched old town of Roquebrune, which gives its name to the greater area, and Cap-Martin—luxurious, isolated, and exclusive. With its tumble of raked tile roofs and twisting streets, fountains, archways, and quiet squares, Roquebrune retains many of the charms of a hilltop village, but it's heavily gentrified and commercialized.

Roquebrune's main attraction is its **Château Féodal** (Feudal Castle): Around the remains of a 10th-century tower, the Grimaldis erected an impregnable fortress that was state of the art in the 16th century, with crenellation, watch towers, and a broad moat. 🔳 *20 frs.* ☉ *Oct.–Jan., daily 10–12:30 and 2–5; Feb.–May 10–12:30 and 2–6; June–Sept. 10–12:30 and 3–7:30.*

In the **cemetery** Swiss-French architect Le Corbusier lies buried with his wife in a tomb of his own design. He kept a humble *cabanot* (beach bungalow) on the rocky shores of the Cap-Martin, where he drowned while swimming in 1965.

★ You can visit Le Corbusier's bungalow and see the glorious fauna of the cape by walking the **Promenade Le Corbusier.** It leads over chalk cliffs and through dense Mediterranean fauna to his tiny retreat, as much indoors as out and designed along the rigorous lines he preferred. Park at the base of the cape on avenue Winston-Churchill and follow the signs.

Menton

㉓ *1 km (¾ mi) east of Roquebrune, 9 km (5½ mi) east of Monaco.*

Menton, the most Mediterranean of the French resort towns, rubs shoulders with the Italian border and owes its balmy climate to the protective curve of the Ligurian shore. Its picturesque harbor skyline seems to beg artists to immortalize it, while its Cubist skew of terra-cotta roofs and yellow-ochre houses, Baroque arabesques capping the church facades, and ceramic tiles glistening on their steeples all evoke the villages of the Italian coast. Menton is the least pretentious of the Côte d'Azur resorts and all the more alluring for its modesty.

The **Basilique St-Michel** (⊠ Parvis St-Michel), a majestic Baroque church, dominates the skyline of Menton with its bell tower. Beyond the beautifully proportioned facade—a 19th-century addition—the richly frescoed nave and chapels contain several works by Genovese artists and a splendid 17th-century organ.

Just above the main church, the smaller **Chapelle de l'Immaculée-Conception** answers St-Michel's grand gesture with its own pure Baroque beauty, dating from 1687. Between 3 and 5 you can slip in to see the graceful trompe-l'oeil over the altar and the ornate gilt lanterns the penitents carried in processions.

Two blocks below the square, **rue St-Michel** serves as the main commercial artery of the Vieille Ville, lined with shops, cafés, and orange trees. Between the lively pedestrian rue St-Michel and the waterfront, the marvelous **Marché Couvert** (Covered Market) sums up Menton style with its Belle Epoque facade decorated in jewel-tone ceramics. Inside, it's just as appealing, with merchants vaunting chewy bread, mountain cheeses, oils, fruit, and Italian delicacies in Caravaggio-esque disarray.

On the waterfront opposite the market, a squat medieval bastion crowned with four tiny watchtowers houses the **Musée Jean-Cocteau.** Built in 1636 to defend the port, it was spotted by the artist-poet-filmmaker Jean Cocteau (1889–1963) as the perfect site for a group of his works. There are bright, cartoonish pastels of fishermen and wenches in love, and a fantastical assortment of ceramic animals in the wrought-iron windows he designed himself. ⊠ *Vieux Port,* ☎ *04–93–57–72–30.* ☞ *20 frs.* ☉ *Wed.–Mon. 10–noon and 2–6.*

The 19th-century Italianate **Hôtel de Ville** conceals another Cocteau treasure: He decorated the **Salle des Mariages** (Marriage Room), the room in which civil marriages take place, with vibrant allegorical scenes. ⊠ *17 av. de la République.* ☞ *10 frs.* ☉ *Weekdays 8:30–12:30 and 1:30–5.*

At the far-west end of town stands the 18th-century **Palais Carnolès** (Carnoles Palace) in vast gardens luxuriant with orange, lemon, and grapefruit trees. It was once the summer retreat of the princes of Monaco; nowadays it contains a sizable collection of European paintings from the Renaissance to the present day. ⊠ *3 av. de la Madone,* ☎ *04–93–35–49–71.* ☞ *Free.* ☉ *Wed.–Mon. 10–noon and 2–6.*

Dining and Lodging

$$–$$$ ✕ Aiglon. Sweep down the curving stone stair to the terrazzo mo-
★   saic lobby of this lovely 1880 garden villa and wander out for a drink or a meal by the pool. Or settle onto your little balcony overlooking the grounds and a tiny wedge of sea. The poolside restaurant, Le Riaumont, serves classic seafood by candlelight; breakfast is served in a shady garden shelter. It's a three-minute walk to the beach. ⊠ *7 av. de la Madone, 06502,* ☎ *04–93–57–55–55,* FAX *04–93–35–92–39. 28 rooms, 2 apartments. Restaurant, bar. AE, MC, V.* ✍

Nightlife and the Arts

In August the **Festival de Musique de Chambre** (Chamber Music Festival) takes place on the stone-paved plaza outside the church of St-Michel. The **Fête du Citron** (Lemon Festival), at the end of February, celebrates the lemon with Rose Bowl Parade–like floats and sculptures, all made of real fruit.

THE CÔTE D'AZUR A TO Z

Arriving and Departing

By Car

A8 parallels the coast from above St-Tropez to Nice to the resorts on the Grand Corniche; N98 follows the coast more closely. From Paris the main southbound artery is A6/A7, known as the Autoroute du Soleil; it passes through Provence and joins the eastbound A8 at Aix-en-Provence.

By Plane

The **Nice–Côte d'Azur Airport** (⊠ 7 km [4 mi] from Nice, ☎ 04–93–21–30–30) sits on a peninsula between Antibes and Nice. There are frequent flights between Paris and Nice on Air Liberté, AOM, and Air France, as well as direct flights on Delta Airlines from New York. The flight time between Paris and Nice is about one hour.

By Train

Nice is the major rail crossroads for trains arriving from Paris and other northern cities, as well as from Italy. This coastal line, working eastward from Marseille and west from Ventimiglia, stops at Fréjus, Antibes, Monaco, and Menton. There is no rail access to St-Tropez; St-Raphaël is the nearest stop. To get from Paris to Nice, you can take the TGV, though it only maintains high speeds to Valence before returning to conventional rails and rates.

Getting Around

By Bus

If you want to penetrate deeper into villages and backcountry spots not on the rail line, you can take a bus out of Fréjus, Nice, Antibes, or Menton to the most frequented spots. Pick up a schedule for local and commercial excursion buses at the train station, at tourist offices, and at the local *gare routière* (bus station). Many hotels and excursion companies organize day trips into St-Paul-de-Vence and Vence.

By Car

The best way to explore the secondary sights in this region, especially the backcountry hill towns, is by car. It also allows you the freedom to zip along A8 between the coastal resorts and to enjoy the tremendous views from the three Corniches that trace the coast from Nice to the Italian border. N98, which connects you to coastal resorts in between, can be extremely slow, though scenic.

By Train

You can easily move along the coast by train on the Côte d'Azur line, a dramatic and highly tourist-pleasing route that offers panoramic views as it rolls from one famous resort to the next. But train travelers will have difficulty getting up to St-Paul, Vence, Peillon, and other backcountry villages; that you must accomplish by bus or car.

Contacts and Resources

Car Rentals

Most likely you'll want to rent your car at one of the main rail stops, either St-Raphäel, Nice, Monaco, or Menton, or at the airport in Nice, where all major companies are represented.

Avis (⊠ 2 av. des Phocéens, Nice, ☎ 04–93–80–63–52; ⊠ Nice Airport, ☎ 04–93–21–42–80; ⊠ 190 pl. Pierre Coullet, St-Raphaël (gare), ☎ 04–94–95–60–42). **Budget** (⊠ 23 rue de Belgique, Nice, ☎ 04–93–

16–24–16; ⊠ Nice Airport, ☎ 04–93–21–36–50; ⊠ 40 rue Waldeck, St-Raphaël, ☎ 04–94–82–24–44). **Europcar** (⊠ 3 av. Gustave, Nice, ☎ 04–92–14–44–50; ⊠ Nice Airport, ☎ 04–93–21–43–54; ⊠ 47 av. de Grande-Bretagne, Monaco, ☎ 377–93–50–74–95; ⊠ 54 pl. Pierre Coullet, St-Raphaël, ☎ 04–94–95–56–87). **Hertz** (⊠ 1 prom. Anglais, Nice, ☎ 04–93–87–11–87; ⊠ Nice Airport, ☎ 04–93–21–36–72; ⊠ 32 rue Waldeck, St-Raphaël, ☎ 04–94–95–48–68; ⊠ 27 bd. Albert I, Monaco, ☎ 377–93–50–79–60).

Guided Tours

Santa Azur (⊠ 11 av. Jean-Médecin, Nice, ☎ 04–93–85–46–81) organizes all-day or half-day bus excursions to sights near Nice, including Monaco, Cannes, and nearby hill towns, either leaving from its offices or from several stops along the Promenade des Anglais, mainly in front of the big hotels. In Antibes, **Phocéens Voyages** (⊠ 8 pl. de Gaulle, Antibes, ☎ 04–93–34–15–98) organizes similar bus explorations of the region. The city of Nice arranges individual guided tours on an à la carte basis according to your needs. For information contact the **Bureau d'Acceuil** (☎ 04–93–14–48–00) and specify your dates and language preferences. A small **tourist train** (☎ 04–93–92–45–59) goes along the waterfront from in front of the Casino Ruhl, along cours Saleya, and up to the Château.

Outdoor Activities and Sports

This is **golf** country, and you can pick up the brochure and map *Les Golfs du Soleil* (*Golf Courses of the Sun*) and *Destination Golf* at local tourist offices to get a complete listing of golf courses and facilities from St-Tropez to Monaco.

Travel Agencies

American Express Voyages (⊠ 11 Promenade des Anglais, Nice, ☎ 04–93–16–53–51; ⊠ 35 bd. Princess Charlotte, Monte Carlo, ☎ 377/ 93–25–74–45; ⊠ 8 rue des Belges, Cannes, ☎ 04–93–38–15–87). **Havas Voyages** (⊠ 12 av. Félix Faure, Nice ☎ 04–93–62–76–30; ⊠ 64 av. Commandant Guilbaud, St-Raphael, ☎ 04–94–19–82–20; ⊠ 17 bd. Louis Blanc, St-Tropez, ☎ 04–94–56–64–64).

Vacation Rentals

The tourist offices of individual towns often publish lists of *locations meublés* (furnished rentals), sometimes vouched for by the tourist office and rated for comfort. **Gîtes de France** is a nationwide organization that rents *gîte ruraux* (rural vacation lodgings) by the week, usually of outstanding regional character. The headquarters for the regions covered in this chapter are **Gîtes de France Var** (⊠ Rond-Point du 4 Décembre 1974, B.P. 215, 83006 Draguignan Cedex, ☎ 04–94–50–93–93, ⅎ̶A̶X̶ 04–94–50–93–90) and **Gîtes de France des Alpes-Maritimes** (⊠ 55 Promenade des Anglais, B.P. 1602, 06011 Nice Cedex 01, ☎ 04–92–15–21–30, ⅎ̶A̶X̶ 04–93–86–01–06, ✍). Write or call for a catalog, then make a selection and reservation.

Visitor Information

For information on travel within the department of Var (St-Tropez to La Napoule), write to the **Comité Départemental du Tourisme du Var** (⊠ 1 bd. Maréchal Foch, 83300 Draguignan, ☎ 03–94–50–55–50, ⅎ̶A̶X̶ 04–94–50–55–51). The **Comité Régional du Tourisme Riviera Côte d'Azur** (⊠ 55 Promenade des Anglais, B.P. 1602, 06011 Nice Cedex 1, ☎ 04–93–37–78–78, ✍) provides information on tourism throughout the department of Alpes-Maritimes, from Cannes to the Italian border.

Local tourist offices in major towns discussed in this chapter are as follows: **Antibes/Juan-les-Pins** (⊠ 11 pl. de Gaulle, 06600 Antibes, ☎ 04–92–90–53–00, ⅎ̶A̶X̶ 04–92–90–53–01). **Cannes** (⊠ Palais des Festivals, Esplanade G. Pompidou, B.P. 272, ☎ 04–93–39–24–53, ℻ 04–92–99–84–23). **Fréjus** (✉ 325 rue Jean-Jaurès, B.P. 8, 83601, ☎ 04–94–51–83–83, ℻ 04–94–51–00–26). **Grasse** (✉ Palais des Congrés, 22 Cours Honoré Cresp, ☎ 04–93–36–66–66, ℻ 04–93–36–86–36). **Menton** (✉ Palais de l'Europe, av. Boyer, 06500, ☎ 04–92–41–76–76, ℻ 04–92–41–76–78). **Monaco** (✉ 2a bd. des Moulins, 98000 Monte Carlo, ☎ 377–92–16–61–66, ℻ 377–92–16–60–00). **Nice** (✉ 5 Promenade des Anglais, 06000, ☎ 04–92–14–48–00, ℻ 04–92–14–48–03; or in person at the train station or airport). **St-Paul-de-Vence** (✉ 2 rue Grande, 06570, ☎ 04–93–32–86–95, ℻ 04–93–32–60–27). **St-Raphaël** (✉ Rue Waldeck-Rousseau, 83700, ☎ 04–94–19–52–52, ℻ 04–94–83–85–40). **St-Tropez** (✉ Quai Jean-Jaurès, B.P. 183, F-83992, ☎ 04–94–97–45–21, ℻ 04–94–97–82–66). **Vence** (✉ Pl. du Grand Jardin, 06140, ☎ 04–93–58–06–38, ℻ 04–93–58–91–81).

13 CORSICA

Just an overnight ferry ride from Marseille, this Mediterranean-bound "mountain in the sea" off the coast of Monaco is known for its unspoiled scenery, villages out of the Middle Ages, and Ajaccio—the birthplace of one Napoléon Bonaparte. Come here to visit the rough and tumble port of Bastia, to explore the *castagniccia* chestnut forest and the tiny harbor at Centuri, or to laze the day away on a beach in Calvi—you'll find that everywhere houses and boats sparkle with the wild, bright Corsican reds, greens, yellows, and blues. At sunset the natural bounty of Corsican cuisine can sometimes take second fiddle to a haunting accompaniment of half-French, half-Genoese folk songs.

Updated by
George Semler

F ORMING A VERTICAL GRANITE WORLD of its own in the Mediterranean between Provence and Tuscany, Corsica is France's wild west: a powerful natural setting and, literally, a breath of fresh air. Corsica is where you go to clear your head, to get away from it all and find your magnetic north, a microcosmic anthology of mountains, beaches, fishing ports, wilderness, and generic Mediterranean culture. Mountain people by nature, Corsicans have historically distrusted the sea and the cosmopolitan coastal landing points for invading forces. The true Corsican is a highland spirit, at home in the dense undergrowth of the maquis, the all-sustaining chestnut forest, or the Laricio pines that climb the upper reaches of what Guy de Maupassant christened his "mountain in the sea."

Corsica's artistic and archaeological treasures, crystalline waters, granite peaks, and pine forests all add up to one of France's wildest and most unspoiled sanctuaries. The island's strategic location 168 km (105 mi) south of Monaco and 81 km (50 mi) west of Italy has made Corsica a prize hotly contested by a succession of Mediterranean powers, notably Genoa, Pisa, and France. Their vestiges remain: the city-state of Genoa ruled Corsica for more than 200 years, leaving impressive citadels, churches, bridges, and nearly 100 medieval watchtowers around the island's coastline. The Italian influence is also apparent in village architecture and in the Corsican language, a combination of Italian, Tuscan dialect, and Latin.

Corsica seems immense, far larger than its 215 km (133 mi) length and 81 km (50 mi) width, partly because rugged, mountainous terrain makes for slow traveling and partly because the landscape and the culture vary so much from one "microregion" to another. Much of the part of Corsica that is not wooded or cultivated is covered with a dense thicket of undergrowth called the *maquis,* a variety of wild and aromatic plants including lavender, myrtle, and heather that gave Corsica one of its sobriquets, "the perfumed isle." The maquis, famous for harboring fugitives, became the term used for the French underground Resistance movement during World War II. In Corsica going underground meant taking to the maquis.

Vendetta is, along with *maquis,* Corsica's other great contribution to world lexicography. The rough and ready legend associated with the island comes from a long tradition of apparent lawlessness and deeply entrenched clannishness. As justice from "the Continent," whether France or Italy, was usually slow and often unsatisfying, Corsican clans frequently fought each other in blood feuds of honor and revenge.

Famous as the birthplace of Napoléon Bonaparte (who never returned to the island after beginning his military career), Corsica's real national hero is Pasquale Paoli, who framed the world's first republican constitution for his independent Corsican nation in 1755. Paoli's ideas significantly influenced the French Revolution, as well as the founding fathers of the United States.

Inspiration for generations of literati from Homer to Mérimée, Boswell, Dumas and Balzac, Corsica has always been, in Greek, *Kallisté,* "the most beautiful," a sylvan paradise and repository for romantic characters from Mérimée's Robin Hood–like *bandit d'honneur* Colomba to comic-book Asterix's pal Ocatarinetabellatchitchix. In the end, you'll find Corsica composed of equal parts vendetta, witchcraft, dream hunters, shepherds improvising the rough and haunting Corsican polyphony, megalithic menhirs, chestnuts, free-range livestock, powerful cheeses, and—always—the bittersweet, lemon-pepper fragrance of the maquis—an aroma like no other, described by Dorothy Carrington in her award-winning *Granite Island* as "akin to incense" and the only fitting perfume for Balzac's "back of beyond."

— George Semler

Pleasures and Pastimes

Dining

Authentic Corsican fare based on free-range livestock, game (especially wild boar), herbs, and wild mushrooms is best found October–June in the tiny villages of the mountainous interior. *Civets* (delicious meaty stews) feature prominently on menus, as do many versions of the prototypical, hearty Corsican soup (alternately known as *soupe paysanne, soupe corse,* and *soupe de montagne*), made from herbs and vegetables simmered for hours with a ham bone. Seafood dishes are available on the coast: particularly good is *aziminu,* a rich bouillabaisse. Everywhere you'll find all kinds of *charcuterie* (pork products): *lonzu* (shoulder), *coppa* (fillet), and *figatelli* (liver sausage) are standard cuts, along with *prisuttu* (cured ham). Among Corsican cheeses, the most emblematic is really not a cheese at all: *brocciu* (pronounced broach) is similar to ricotta and is used in omelets, *fiadone* (cheesecake), *fritelli* (chestnut-flour doughnuts), and as stuffing for trout or rabbit. Cheeses from Corsica's microregions include *bastelicaccia,* a soft, creamy sheep cheese, and the harder and sharper *sartenais.* Many of the most powerful cheeses are simply designated as *brebis* (sheep) or *chèvre* (goat). Chestnuts and chestnut flour also play an important part in Corsican gastronomy: in *castagna* (Corsican for chestnut), a cake; *panetta,* a kind of bread; *canistrelli,* dry cookies; beignets (fried dough), often made of chestnut flour; *pulenta,* a doughy chestnut-flour bread; and *pietra,* chestnut beer. Be sure, too, to try some of Corsica's fine wines: Arenas, Orenga de Gaffory or Gentile, from the Patrimonio vineyards; Domaine Peraldi, Clos de Capitoro, or Clos Alzeto, from Ajaccio; Fiumicicoli, from Sartène; or Domaine de Torracia, from Porto-Vecchio.

CATEGORY	COST*
$$$$	over 350 frs
$$$	250 frs–350 frs
$$	125 frs–250 frs
$	under 125 frs

per person for a three-course meal, including tax (20.6%)

✍ *following the text of a review is your signal that the property has a Web site, where you will find details and, usually, images; for a link, visit www.fodors.com/urls.*

Lodging

The amount of building around Porto-Vecchio in the 1950s was so horrifying to Corsicans that, with some extra encouragement from separatist bombers, they resolved to avoid excessive tourist-driven development. Instead, *fermes-auberges* (farmhouse-inns) are being restored at a rapid clip, and tastefully designed new hotels are being built. During the peak season (from July to mid-September) prices are higher, and some hotels insist breakfast and dinner be included as part of the price. The best seaside hotels are priced only marginally lower than in the Riviera, but lodging in the interior villages remains substantially cheaper. Off-season, good prices can be found all over.

CATEGORY	COST*
$$$$	over 750 frs
$$$	400 frs–750 frs
$$	250 frs–400 frs
$	under 250 frs

*All prices are for a standard double room for two, including tax (20.6%) and service charge.

Outdoor Activities

From the wild, undeveloped strands of the northern Cap Corse (Cape Corsica) to the Riviera-like tourist beaches near Calvi and Propriano, the island's coastline is astonishingly varied. In summer, during the *canicule* (literally, dog days), Corsicans take to the rivers, always cooler than the Mediterranean. Others take on the rugged GR 20 (Grande Randonnée 20); considered one of Europe's greatest hiking trails, it requires from 70 to 100 hours to complete. Planned in stages from one mountain refuge to another, the well-marked GR 20 is the ultimate way to see Corsica. If you are traveling by car, short probes along the GR 20 are easily feasible. Check with tourist offices or bookstores for guides.

Exploring Corsica

Leaving Marseille (on the excellent SNCM *Ferryterranée,* which also departs from Toulon and Nice) at sunset, and arriving in Ajaccio at sunrise are among the finest moments of any trip to Corsica. Napoléon claimed he could identify the fragrance of the Corsican maquis at sea from many miles out; approaching the island by airplane seems like heresy. The northern half of the island (Haute Corse) is generally wilder than the southern half (Corse du Sud), which is hotter and more barren. On the other hand, southern Corsica's archaeological sites at Filitosa and Pianu de Levie, the Col de Bavella and its majestic Laricio pine forest, and the towns of Sartène and Bonifacio all rank indisputably among the island's finest treasures. The least interesting part of the island is the coast road between Porto-Vecchio and Bastia, while one of the prettiest drives is the tour around the northward-pointing finger of Cap Corse. Don't hesitate to drive into the interior highlands, the true Corsica; if you spend too much time at sea level, you'll miss the dramatic heights for which the island is famous.

Great Itineraries

Three days is barely sufficient time to visit Corsica's three main cities and some of the island's prettiest scenery. In five days you can cover most of Haute Corse, and in 10 days it is possible, though not necessarily advisable, to see the whole island. The danger is spending too much time car-bound. One approach is to settle in Corte, near the island's center, setting out each day on a quest to see different attractions.

Numbers in the text correspond to numbers in the margin and on the Corsica and Ajaccio maps.

IF YOU HAVE 3 DAYS

Ajaccio ①–⑧ is a good place to start. A two-hour drive over the Vizzavona Pass to 🔳 **Corte** ⑱ will place you at the island's historical heart for the night. Explore the town and the nearby Restonica gorges the next day. On day three drive through the chestnut-covered La Castagniccia region, visiting the small villages along the way. Find your way out of La Castagniccia via Folelli, stopping for lunch (call ahead for reservations) in **Murato** ㉟. Save the afternoon and evening for exploring **Bastia** ㊶ before shipping out for the mainland.

IF YOU HAVE 5 DAYS

Follow the three-day itinerary in a more leisurely fashion and spend the fourth and fifth nights in or near 🔳 **Bastia** ㊶. Tour Cap Corse on day four, starting out on the eastern side, stopping for lunch in the fishing port of **Centuri** ㉟, and visiting **Nonza** ㊳, **St-Florent** ㊱, and the vineyards of the **Patrimonio** ㊲ before driving up over the Col de Teghime (at sunset, if possible). Spend day five exploring Bastia and then continue overnight to the French or Italian mainland.

IF YOU HAVE 10 DAYS

Start in **Ajaccio** ①–⑧, visiting the market and the Musée Fesch and reaching the megalithic site at **Filitosa** ⑩ by midday. Have a look through **Sartène** ⑪ and drive into ⚄ **Bonifacio** ⑭ as the sun sets into the sea. The next day get to the Laricio pine forest, near the **Col de Bavella** ⑯, to see or even walk to the famous granite peaks. Tiny D268 comes out on the east coast at N198, which will take you up to **Aléria** ⑰ and into ⚄ **Corte** ⑱ on N200. Make Corte your base: Devote day three to Corte and the Restonica gorges, day four to the **Asco** ㉒, day five to the small villages in **La Castagniccia.** On day six take **La Scala di Santa Regina** road through the Aitone Forest. Spend the night in ⚄ **Ota** ㉔. Pass through the Scandola Natural Reserve on day seven, reaching the Riviera-like ⚄ **Calvi** ㉗ by evening. Go to the beach in Calvi on day eight. In the evening drive through La Balagne to **L'Ile Rousse** ㉝ and medieval ⚄ **Lama** ㉞. On the ninth day drive around Cap Corse and spend the night in ⚄ **Erbalunga** ㊵ or in ⚄ **Bastia** ㊶. On the morning of day 10 hike up to the Bocca di Santo Lunardo or go to the beach at Erbalunga; in the afternoon explore Bastia and then head back to the mainland.

When to Tour Corsica

The best time to visit Corsica is fall or spring, when the weather is cool. Most Corsican culinary specialties are at their best between October and June. Try to avoid July and August, when French and Italian vacationers fill hotels and push up prices. In winter the island has the best weather in France, but a majority of the hotels and restaurants are closed.

CORSE DU SUD

Corse du Sud includes the French administrative capital of Ajaccio, the mountainous zones of the Cinarca and Alta Rocca, megalithic treasures at Filitosa and Levie, and the fortresslike towns of Sartène, Bonifacio, and Porto-Vecchio. Perhaps because southern Corsica is on the French side of the island, it seems more Continentalized. Forest fires and the resulting flooding scarred much of the southern part of the island in the mid-'90s, though the irrepressible maquis has quickly regrown.

Ajaccio

40 mins by plane, 5–10 hrs by ferry from Marseille, Nice, or Toulon.

Ajaccio, Napoléon's birthplace and Corsica's modern capital, is a busy, French-flavored town with a bustling port, beautiful beaches, ancient streets, and in the Musée Fesch, five centuries of Italian master-
❶ pieces. Start at the spectacular **food market,** held every morning except Monday in place Campinchi across the quai from the ferry port, an opportunity to admire an enticing array of Corsican cheeses, pastries, sausages, and everything from traditional chestnut-flour beignets to prehistoric *rascasse* (red scorpion fish) at the fish market tucked in under the Hôtel de Ville across from the southeast corner of the square.

Rows of stately palm trees lead up to a marble statue of Napoléon on
❷ ❸ **Place Maréchal-Foch,** the city's main square. The **Hôtel de Ville** (Town Hall) has an Empire-style grand salon hung with portraits of a long

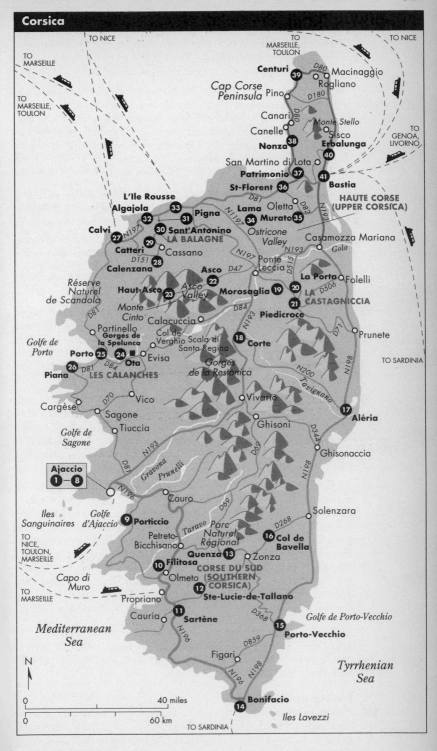

Corsica

TO NICE

TO MARSEILLE,
TOULON

TO NICE

TO MARSEILLE

TO MARSEILLE,
TOULON

Centuri ③⑨ Macinaggio
Rogliano

*Cap Corse
Peninsula* Pino

TO GENOA,
LIVORNO

Canari

Monte Stello

Canelle Sisco

Nonza ③⑧ **Erbalunga**

San Martino di Lota ④⓪

Patrimonio ③⑦

St-Florent ③⑥ ④① **Bastia**

Lama Oletta **HAUTE CORSE
(UPPER CORSICA)**

L'Ile Rousse ③③ **Pigna** ③④ **Murato** ③⑤

Algajola ③② ③① Ostricone
Valley Casamozza Mariana

Calvi ②⑦ ③⓪ **Sant'Antonino** Ponte- *Golo*
Leccia

Catteri ②⑨ **Cassano** **La Porta** Folelli

Calenzana ②⑧ **Asco** ②② **LA
CASTAGNICCIA**

*Réserve
Naturel
de Scandola* **Haut-Asco** ②③ *Asco
Valley* **Morosaglia** ①⑨ ②⓪

*Monte
Cinto* Calacuccia ②① **Piedicroce**

*Golfe de
Porto* Partinello
**Gorges de
la Spelunca** Col de
Verghio Scala di
Santa Regina ①⑧ **Corte** Prunete

Porto ②⑤ ②④ **Ota**
Evisa *Gorges
de la Restonica* TO SARDINIA

Piana ②⑥ **LES CALANCHES**

Cargèse Vico **Vivario**

*Golfe de
Sagone* Sagone **Ghisoni** Aléria ①⑦

Tiuccia Ghisonaccia

Ajaccio
① — ⑧ Cauro Solenzara

*Iles
Sanguinaires* *Golfe
d'Ajaccio* ⑨ **Porticcio** Parc
Naturel
Régional

TO NICE,
TOULON,
MARSEILLE

Petreto-
Bicchisano **Col de
Bavella** ①⑥

Quenza ①③ Zonza

Filitosa ①⓪ **CORSE DU SUD
(SOUTHERN
CORSICA)**

Olmeto ①②

*Capo di
Muro* **Ste-Lucie-de-Tallano**

TO
MARSEILLE

Propriano

Cauria **Sartène** ①① ①⑤ *Golfe de Porto-Vecchio*

Porto-Vecchio

*Mediterranean
Sea*

Figari

*Tyrrhenian
Sea*

N

0   40 miles

0   60 km **Bonifacio**

TO SARDINIA ①④ *Iles Lavezzi*

line of Bonapartes. You'll find a fine bust of Letizia, Napoléon's formidable mother; a bronze death mask of the emperor himself; and a frescoed ceiling that depicts Napoléon's meteoric rise. ⊠ *Pl. Maréchal-Foch,* ☎ *04–95–21–48–17.* ☞ *12 frs.* ◷ *Apr.–Oct., weekdays 9–noon and 2:30–5:30; Nov.–Mar., weekdays 9–noon and 2–5.*

❹ Two short blocks left of the statue of Napoléon on place Maréchal-Foch, is the **Maison Bonaparte** (Bonaparte House). Here Napoléon was born on August 15, 1769. Today this large (once middle-class) house contains a museum with portraits and cameos of the entire Bonaparte clan. Search out the two genealogical documents that are family trees actually woven out of human hair. ⊠ *rue St-Charles,* ☎ *04–95–21–43–89.* ☞ *25 frs.* ◷ *Mon. 2–5, Tues.–Sat. 10–noon and 2–5, Sun. 10–noon.*

❺ At the corner of rue St-Charles and rue Roi de Rome are the city's oldest houses, opposite the tiny church of **St-Jean Baptiste.** They were built shortly after the town was founded in 1492.

For a look at the Citadelle, walk east down rue Roi de Rome to boulevard Danielle Casanova. At the corner, the **Musée du Capitellu** is a fascinating private museum tracing the history of Ajaccio through the life of a single family. ⊠ *18 bd. Danielle Casanova,* ☎ *04–95–21–50–57* ☞ *15 frs.* ◷ *Tues.–Sat. 10–12:30 and 3–7.*

❻ The 16th-century Baroque **Cathédrale** where Napoléon was baptized is at the end of rue St-Charles. The interior is covered with trompe l'oeil frescoes, and the high altar, from an old church in Lucca, Italy, was donated by Napoléon's sister Eliza after he made her princess of Tuscany. Above the altar, look for Eugène Delacroix's famous painting *Virgin of Sacré Coeur.* ⊠ *rue F.-Conti.*

❼ The Renaissance-style **Chapelle Imperial** (Imperial Chapel) was built in 1857 by Napoléon's nephew, Napoléon III, to accommodate the tombs of the Bonaparte family (Napoléon Bonaparte himself is buried in the Hôtel des Invalides in Paris). A Coptic crucifix taken from Egypt during the general's 1798 campaign hangs over the chapel's main altar. ⊠ *50 rue Fesch,* ☞ *15 frs.* ◷ *Tues.–Sat. 10–12:30 and 3–7.*

★ **❽** Adjacent to the Chapelle Impérial, the **Musée Fesch** houses a fine collection of Italian masters, ranging from Botticelli, Canaletto, to De Tura—part of a massive collection of 30,000 paintings bought at bargain prices following the French Revolution by Napoléon's uncle, Cardinal Fesch, the archbishop of Lyon. Thanks to his nephew's military conquests, the cardinal was able to amass (steal, some would say) many celebrated old-master paintings, the most famous of which are now in the Louvre. ⊠ *50 rue Fesch,* ☎ *04–95–21–48–17.* ☞ *35 frs.* ◷ *Apr.–June and Sept.–Oct., Wed.–Mon. 9:30–noon and 3–6:30; Jul.–Aug., Tues.–Sat. 9–midnight, Sun.–Mon. 9:30 noon and 3–6:30; Nov.–Mar., Wed.–Mon. 9:30–noon and 2:30–6.*

NEED A
BREAK?   After visiting the old quarter, walk down to the Plage St-François to the **Café Fesch** for coffee while you contemplate the Golfe d'Ajaccio. **Le Cohiba,** next door, is another good choice.

Dining and Lodging

$$–$$$ ✕ **A La Funtana.** A fountain greets diners at the door of this gourmet restaurant, named for a popular Corsican folk song. Fresh flowers and Oriental carpets are the only touch of decoration in the simple white dining room. The house specialty is homemade foie gras; other items worth sampling include *morilles* (morels) in foie gras and homemade sorbets. ⊠ *7 rue Notre-Dame,* ☎ *04–95–21–78–04. AE, DC, MC, V. Closed June and Sun.–Mon.*

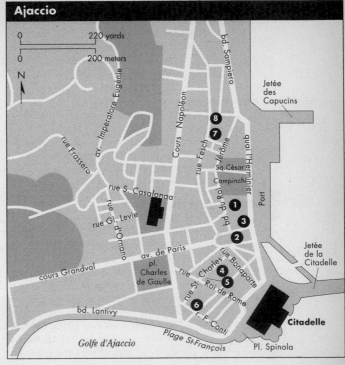

Ajaccio

\$\$ ✕ Auberge de Prunelli. This cheerful riverside inn overlooking the
★ Prunelli River has a good-value, three-course prix-fixe menu for 110
francs. You can also choose from such regional specialties as sea urchin
beignets with brocciu, brocciu omelets, trout, roast *cabrit* (kid), or figatelli sausage from the excellent à la carte menu. ⊠ *Pisciatellu (11
km [7 mi] south of Ajaccio just off N196; look for the turnoff onto
D55B just before crossing the river)*, ☎ 04–95–20–02–75. Reservations essential. MC, V. Closed Tues.

\$\$ ✕ Le Maximilien. Across from the cathedral, at this stylish spot chef-
owner Serge Alain Gros serves Continental cuisine to a fashionable crowd
interested in something more than local cooking. The cassoulet *périgord* (with duck, sausage, and white beans) and the *lotte au foie gras
de canard* (monkfish with duck liver) are interesting combinations of
maritime and upland products. ⊠ *Rue Eugène-Macchini*, ☎ 04–95–
51–36–39. AE, DC, MC, V. Closed Mon.

\$ ✕ Da Mamma. Just after 13 rue Fesch, turn into the Passage de la
Guinguetta, where there is a small, shady square of the same name.
Under a leafy rubber tree you might, in season, try such specials as *civet
de sanglier* (wild boar stew) with *trompettes de la mort* (wild mushrooms) served in a bubbling earthenware casserole. ⊠ *2 passage
Guinguetta*, ☎ 04–95–21–39–44. MC, V. Closed Sun. Nov.–Mar. No
lunch Sun.–Mon., Apr.–Oct.

\$\$\$\$ ✕⊡ Eden Roc. The modern Eden Roc overlooks the gulf in Ajaccio's
most exclusive suburb. Gardens surround the swimming pool, and a
tiny beach lies across the road. Rooms are large and luxurious, each
with a terrace and sea view. The restaurant is a favorite gourmet outing for Ajaccio residents. ⊠ *Rte. des Iles Sanguinaires, 20000 (8 km
[5 mi] from center of town)*, ☎ 04–95–51–56–00, FAX 04–95–52–05–
03. 45 rooms. Restaurant, piano bar, pool, private beach, health club,
parking (fee). AE, DC, MC, V. ✎

$$$–$$$$ ✕⊡ **La Dolce Vita.** Spread out over flower-filled terraces at the edge of the Gulf of Ajaccio, this hotel-restaurant is lavishly Italianate. The spectacular swimming pool overlooks the sea, and the restaurant ranks as one of the island's best for gourmet interpretations of traditional Corsican dishes. ⊠ *Rte. des Iles Sanguinaires, 20000 (8 km [5 mi] from center of town),* ☎ *04–95–52–42–42,* ⨳ *04–95–52–07–15. 32 rooms. Restaurant, bar, pool. AE, DC, MC, V.*

$$–$$$ ⊡ **Hôtel San Carlu.** On the edge of the old town, this friendly hotel over-
★ looking the ramparts and the sea is an ideal base for exploring Ajaccio. Rooms are clean and comfortable; those on the Golfe d'Ajaccio side (east) on the third floor get an abundance of morning sunshine streaming across the beds and into the bathtubs, not a bad way to greet a new day on the Isle de la Beauté. ⊠ *8 bd. Danielle Casanova, 20000,* ☎ *04–95–21–13–84,* ⨳ *04–95–21–09–99. 40 rooms. AE, DC, MC, V.*

Nightlife and the Arts

Most of Ajaccio's top nightspots are 4 km (2½ mi) north of town, in the new Santalino District along route des Iles Sanguinaires. **La Cinquième Avenue** (⊠ Rte. des Iles Sanguinaires) is the reigning dance-until-dawn venue for all ages, the younger the better. **Le Satélite** (⊠ Rte. des Iles Sanguinaires) and **L'Interdit** (⊠ Rte. des Iles Sanguinaires) are other nearby hot spots. For in-town action, **Le Pigale** (⊠ Pl. Charles de Gaulle) and **L'Entreacte** (⊠ Bd. Lantivy [next to the casino]) are the spots to hit. For one of the new stars in the Ajaccion night scene head to **La Privilège** (⊠ Rue Macchini [pl. Charles-de-Gaulle]). **Le Cohiba** (⊠ Bd. Lantivy, 1 Résidence Diamant) is a very popular bar. **La Place** (⊠ Bd. Lantivy) is another well-known boîte (night club) and piano bar.

The **Fête de la Miséricorde** (Feast of Our Lady of Mercy), on March 18, features the Procession de la Madunnuccia (Procession of the Madonna), Ajaccio's patron saint. In May Ajaccio celebrates during its festive **Carnival.** In July you can attend the **Rencontres Internationales de Musique,** a gathering of classical and operatic musicians. A major festival, the **Fêtes Napoléoniennes,** is held on August 15, Napoléon's birthday.

Outdoor Activities and Sports

NAVE VA (⊠ 2 rue J.B. Marcaggi, ☎ 04–95–21–83–98) operates boating excursions to the Iles Sanguinaires, Reserve Naturelle de Scandola, Girolata, Calanches de Piana, and the chalk cliffs of Bonifacio. **BMS** (⊠ quai de la Citadelle, ☎ 04–95–21–33–75) rents bicycles year-round. **Locacorse** (⊠ 10 av. Bévérini-Vico, ☎ 04–95–20–71–20) has bike rentals from April through September. Horseback riding is ideal along the former mule paths; the **Centre de Randonnées Équestres de St-Georges** (⊠ Domaine de Campiccioli, rte. de Vigna Piana, ☎ 04–95–25–34–83) rents horses and organizes outings. The **Poney-Club d'Ajaccio** (⊠ Campo dell' Oro, ☎ 04–95–23–03–10) also rents horses. For fishing, swimming, underwater diving, kayaking, or windsurfing, head to **Club des Calanques** (⊠ Hôtel des Calanques, rte. des Sanguinaires, ☎ 04–95–21–39–65). **Les Dauphins** (⊠ Rte. des Sanguinaires, Plage de Barbicaja, ☎ 04–95–52–07–78) also has water-sports gear. For information about sailing, contact the **Ligue Corse de Voile** (⊠ Port de la Citadelle, ☎ 04–95–21–07–79). Or you can rent a sailboat at the **Tahiti Nautic Club d'Ajaccio** (⊠ Plage du Ricanto, ☎ 04–95–20–05–95).

Shopping

Much more than just a bookstore specializing in books about Corsica, **Librairie la Marge** (⊠ 7 rue Emmanuelle-Arène) is a hub of Corsican culture, where you can buy music and attend poetry readings. **Paese Nostru** (⊠ Passage Guinguetta) sells Corsican crafts of all kinds. **U Tilaghju** (⊠ rue Forcioli Conti), one of several artisan shops near the cathedral, has an impressive collection of ceramics.

Porticcio

❾ *17 km (10½ mi) south of Ajaccio on N196.*

Across the Prunelli River south of Ajaccio, Porticcio is the capital's fancy suburb and luxurious beach resort town. It's primarily notable for its seawater cures at the **Institut de Thalassothérapie** (Institute of Thalassotherapy), on the Punta di Porticcio, and the *grand luxe* Le Maquis hotel (☞ *below*).

Dining and Lodging

$$$–$$$$ ✕⊡ **Le Maquis.** The Maquis ranks as one of the island's (even Europe's)
★ finest *hôtels de charme.* The quaint, ivy-covered building reaches down to a private beach. Rooms have views of the sea or the hills. At the candlelighted restaurant L'Arbousier, with its ancient beams taken from what was once the Ajaccio prison, a blend of traditional and nouvelle cuisine is served: fish tartare, scrambled eggs with truffles, and fresh tagliatelle. ⊠ *D55, 20166 Porticcio,* ☎ *04–95–25–05–55,* 𝔽𝔸𝕏 *04–95–25–11–70. 27 rooms. Restaurant, 1 indoor and 1 outdoor pool, tennis court, beach. AE, DC, MC, V.* 🕸

Outdoor Activities and Sports

Bikes are a great way to explore the beach; **Avis** (⊠ In Hôtel Marina Viva) rents them. Kids love **Aqua Cyrné Gliss** (⊠ Follow signs in Porticcio, ☎ 04–95–25–17–48), a water park with water slides and swimming pools. Admission is 70 francs, and it's open mid-June–mid-September, daily 10:30–7, plus two nights a week (usually Tuesday and Friday).

Filitosa

★ ❿ *71 km (43 mi) southeast of Ajaccio off N196.*

Filitosa is the site of Corsica's largest grouping of megalithic menhir statues. Bizarre, life-size stone figures of ancient warriors rise up mysteriously from the undulating terrain, many with human faces that have been eroded and flattened over time. A small museum on the site houses archaeological finds, including the menhir known as *Scalsa Murta,* whose delicately carved spine and rib cage make it difficult to believe the statue dates from some 5,000 years ago. Be sure to buy the excellent guidebook in English (30 francs) by experts Cesari and Acquaviva. You can study it over a snack at the pleasant museum café. *Contact Centre Préhistorique Filitosa,* ☎ *04–95–74–00–91 for information.* 📧 *Guided tours in English 30 frs.* ☉ *June–Aug., daily 8–7.*

Sartène

⓫ *27 km (16 mi) southeast of Filitosa on N196.*

The hillside town of Sartène was called the "most Corsican of all Corsican towns" by French novelist Prosper Mérimée. Dorothy Carrington, author of *Granite Island,* the definitive work (in English and probably in any language) on Corsica, described it as one of the least changed places on Corsica. Founded in the 16th century, Sartène has survived pirate raids and bloody feuding among the town's families. The word "vendetta" is believed to have originated here as the result of a 19th-century family feud so serious that French troops were brought in as a peace-keeping buffer force. Centuries of fighting have left the town with a somewhat eerie and menacing atmosphere. Perhaps adding to this is the annual Good Friday *catenacciu* (enchaining) procession in which an anonymous penitent, dragging ankle chains, lugs a heavy cross through the village streets.

The most interesting part of town is **Vieux Sartène** (Old Sartène), surrounded by ancient ramparts. Start at place de la Libération, the main square. To one side is the **Hôtel de Ville** (Town Hall), in the former Genoese governor's palace. For a taste of the Middle Ages, slip through the tunnel in the Town Hall to place du Maggiu and the old quarter of **Santa Anna,** a warren of narrow, cobbled streets lined with granite houses. Scarcely 100 yards from the Hôtel de Ville, down a steep and winding street, a 12th-century *tour de guet* (watchtower) stands out in sharp contrast to the modern apartment buildings behind.

Sartène is the center for research into Corsica's prehistory, due to its proximity to Pianu de Levie and numerous dolmens and megalithic statues. For a look at some of the island's best prehistoric relics, head to the **Musée Départemental de Préhistoire Corse** (Regional Museum of Corsican Prehistory), in the town's former prison. ✉ *rue Croce,* ☎ *04–95–77–01–09.* 🎫 *25 frs.* ☉ *Apr.–Oct., Mon.–Sat. 10–noon and 2–6; Nov.–Mar., weekdays 10–noon and 2–5.*

Dining

$$ ✕ **Auberge de Santa Barbara.** This excellent restaurant is just 1 km (½ mi) north of Sartène. Known as one of the top specialists in authentic Corsican cuisine, chef Giselle Lovighi also serves innovative seafood specialties such as shrimp soufflé and crayfish salad. ✉ *Alzone, Sartène,* ☎ *04–95–77–09–06. MC, V. Closed Mon. and Nov.–Easter.*

Outdoor Activities and Sports

Horses can be rented from the **Ferme Équestre de Baracci** (✉ Propriano, ☎ 04–95–76–08–02), just north of Sartène; 5- to 15-day seaside and mountain outings are also arranged. Another way to see the area is to hike along the **Tra Mare a Mare** (Sea-to-Sea Trail) from Propriano to Porto-Vecchio. Roadside information points suggest itineraries.

Ste-Lucie-de-Tallano

⑫ *15 km (9 mi) northeast of Sartène, 12 km (7 mi) southeast of Levie on D268.*

The pretty little village of Ste-Lucie-de-Tallano is in the heart of Mérimée country, the setting for *Colomba,* the tale of a beautiful young Corsican woman caught in an Andromaque-like web of love, honor, vendetta, and death. Driving up the Rizzanese Valley, the *Spin' a Cavallu* (Horse's Back) Bridge, one of the oldest and loveliest Genoese bridges on the island, is the first important sight. The St-François convent and the church of Ste-Lucie are the main religious buildings in town.

Dining

$$ ✕ **Vecchiu Mulinu.** This restored mill serves simple but delicious *cuisine du terroir* (regional country cooking). The local Fiumicicoli red is the perfect match. ✉ *Bains de Caldanes,* ☎ *04–95–77–00–54. Reservations essential. MC, V. Closed Mon. Oct.–Easter.*

En Route   Five kilometers (3 miles) east of Ste-Lucie-de-Tallano on the Zonza road (D268), the 3-km (2-mi) walk up to the **Pianu de Levie** (Levie Plateau) offers a look at one of Corsica's best archaeological sites. The **Castellu de Cucurruzzu** is a Torréen fortress, 3,500 years old. A 20-minute additional walk from Cucurruzzu is another Torréen fortress, the **Castellu de Capula.** In **Levie,** the **Musée Archeologique** (archaeology museum) (☎ 04–95–78–46–34. 🎫 25 frs.) displays prehistoric discoveries; it's open July–September, daily 9:30–6, and October–June, weekdays 10–noon and 2–4.

Quenza

⑬ *8 km (5½ mi) west of Zonza on D420.*

Quenza is known for its 10th-century chapel of **Santa Maria.** It's also the headquarters of the **I Muntagnoli Corsi** (☎ 04–95–78–64–05), which organizes guided hikes into the Coscione Forest.

Dining and Lodging

$$–$$$ ✕⬚ **Auberge Sole e Monti.** One of southern Corsica's best gourmet options for authentic Corsican cooking and a standout as a hotel as well, this place is worth a detour. Rooms are modern and well-kept, and the staff is friendly. Try the local version of *soupe corse* (Corsican soup) and, in summer, trout with wild mint and brocciu (reservations essential). ⌧ *Quenza 20122 (1 km [½ mi] east of town on the Zonza rd.),* ☎ *04–95–78–62–53,* 𝔽𝔸𝕏 *04–95–78–63–88. 20 rooms. Restaurant, bar. MC, V. Closed Dec.–Mar.*

Bonifacio

★ ⑭ *54 km (33 mi) southeast of Sartène via N196.*

The ancient fortress town of Bonifacio occupies a spectacular cliff-top setting above a harbor carved from limestone cliffs. It is just 13 km (8 mi) from Sardinia, and local speech is heavily influenced by the accent and idiom of this nearby Italian island. Established in the 12th century as Genoa's first Corsican stronghold, Bonifacio remained Genoese through centuries of battles and sieges. As you wander the narrow streets of the **Haute Ville** (Upper Village) inside the walls of the citadel, think of Homer's *Odyssey.* It was here, in the harbor, that classics scholars have placed the catastrophic encounter (Chapter X) between Ulysses's fleet and the Laestrygonians, who hurled lethal boulders down from the cliffs.

From place d'Armes at the city gate, enter the **Bastion de l'Étendard** (Bastion of the Standard); you can still see the system of weights and pulleys used to pull up the drawbridge. The former garrison now houses life-size dioramas of Bonifacio's history. ⬚ *25 frs.* ⌓ *Mid-June–mid-Sept., daily 9–7.*

In the center of the maze of cobbled streets that makes up the citadel is the 12th-century church of **Ste-Marie-Majeure,** with buttresses attaching it to surrounding houses. Inside the church, note the Renaissance baptismal font, carved in bas-relief, and the 3rd-century white-marble Roman sarcophagus. Walk around the back to see the loggia, which is built above a huge cistern that contained water for use in times of siege, as were the circular silos throughout the town.

From Bonifacio you can take a **boat trip** to the **Dragon Grottoes** and **Venus's Bath** (the trip takes one hour on boats that set out every 15 minutes during July and August) or the **Lavezzi Islands.** (⌧ Boats leave from outside Hôtel La Caravelle; ☎ 04–95–75–05–93 for information).

Dining and Lodging

$$ ✕ **U Ceppu.** Just outside of Bonifacio, this rustic, barn-size restaurant
★ features grilled meats and seafood prepared in the dining room on a big open hearth—for instance, smoked salmon and wild boar stew. Picture windows look out on lobster pots bobbing in the bay and scattered over the beach. ⌧ *L'Auberge de Santa Manza (5 km [3 mi] east of Bonifacio on road to Plage de Santa Manza),* ☎ *04–95–73–02–34. MC, V. No lunch Mon.–Sat.*

$–$$ ✕ **Les 4 Vents.** This friendly restaurant near the Sardinia boat termi-
nal is popular with the yachting crowd and with families. In winter
the kitchen serves up Alsace specialties like sauerkraut and sausages.
In summer the focus is on barbecued fish and meats, as well as typical Corsican dishes. ✉ *29 quai Bando di Ferro,* ☎ *04–95–73–07–50.
MC, V. Closed mid–late Nov., and Tues. Nov.–June*

$ ✕ **Restaurant du Pêcheur.** People often line the sidewalk waiting to dine
at this tiny, authentic seafood spot. True to its name, the restaurant is
run by fishermen who serve the catch of the day straight from the sea.
There's no written menu, so ask what's available. ✉ *14 rue Doria,* ☎
*04–95–73–12–56. Reservations not accepted. MC, V. Closed Nov.–
Easter.*

$$$–$$$$ 🏨 **Hôtel le Genovese.** This small, intimate hotel is built into the
ramparts of the upper town's citadel. Rooms glow with peach-fab-
ric wall coverings. Upstairs rooms have superb views over the cliffs
and out to Sardinia. ✉ *Quartier de Citadelle, Haute Ville, 20169,*
☎ *04–95–73–12–34,* FAX *04–95–73–09–03. 14 rooms. Bar. AE, DC,
MC, V.* 🐾

Nightlife and the Arts

Party until dawn at **Le Langoustier** (✉ Quai Comparetti, ☎ 04–95–
73–01–44), in the port. Or drive out to **Amnesia** (✉ 10 km [6 mi] from
town on the Porto-Vecchio road, ☎ 04–95–72–12–27), the dance club
of choice.

The **Fête Millénaire de Bonifacio,** Bonifacio's celebration of the 1,000th
anniversary of its founding, has been held in late August for the last
few years and is threatening to become an annual event, with concerts,
processions, and street dances.

Outdoor Activities and Sports

The area around Bonifacio is ideal for water sports; contact **Club Atoll**
(✉ Rte. de Porto-Vecchio, ☎ 04–95–73–02–83). The best golf course
on Corsica (and one of the best in the Mediterranean), a 20,106-ft par-
72 gem designed by Robert Trent Jones, is at **Sperone** (✉ Domaine de
Sperone, ☎ 04–95–73–17–13), just east of Bonifacio.

Shopping

Pierres de Cade (✉ Haute Ville) has a good selection of beautiful ob-
jects carved from Corsica's rich forests of chestnut and juniper.

Porto-Vecchio

⑮ *27 km (16 mi) north of Bonifacio via N198.*

The old walled town of Porto-Vecchio has become synonymous
with mass tourism dominated by tour operators from Italy, so you
might want to consider skipping it. The town's network of me-
dieval streets has now been largely given over to bistros, boutiques,
and cafés. Nonetheless, the Gulf of Porto-Vecchio is lined with
beautiful beaches.

Dining and Lodging

$$$$ ✕🏨 **Grand Hôtel de Cala Rossa.** This famous hotel and restaurant
built over the water merits a look, even though the luxurious sur-
roundings and overdeveloped Porto-Vecchio tourist scene are proba-
bly not the Corsica you had in mind. Nouvelle Mediterranean cuisine
with a Corsican flair is featured in the restaurant, long considered one
of the island's premier dining spots. ✉ *Rte. de Cala Rossa, 20137 (8
km [5 mi] north of Porto-Vecchio),* ☎ *04–95–71–61–51,* FAX *04–95–
71–60–11. 55 rooms. Restaurant, tennis court. AE, DC, MC, V. Closed
Nov.–Apr.* 🐾

$$–$$$ ✕⊞ **Moby Dick.** Stuck out on a spit of land between the Golfe de Santa Giulia and the Tyrrhenian Sea, this sophisticated modern hotel is nearly surrounded by water and sandy beaches. The rooms, decorated in blue and white, make you feel like part of the seascape. The restaurant serves a good-value buffet lunch and both a regular and a gourmet menu at dinner. The crayfish in oil of fresh basil is delicious. ⊠ *Baie de Santa Giulia, 20137 (8 km [5 mi] south of town),* ☎ *04–95–70–70–00,* FAX *04–95–70–71–01. 113 rooms. Restaurant, beach, 2 tennis courts. AE, DC, MC, V. Closed Nov.–Apr.* ❧

En Route Porto-Vecchio backs onto Corsica's largest cork oak forest, **L'Ospédale.** An excursion across the forest on D368, climbing 49 km (30 mi) to the mountain pass of **Col de Bavella,** is one of the island's most magical tours and shouldn't be missed. Only opt in favor of the alternative—a flat, straight road up the east coast—if you have a boat leaving Bastia in two hours.

Col de Bavella

⑯ *50 km (31 mi) northeast of Porto-Vecchio on D368 and D268.*

The granite peaks known as the **Aiguilles de Bavella** (Needles of Bavella) tower some 6,562 ft overhead as you reach the Col de Bavella (Bavella Pass). Hiking trails are well marked. The narrow but mostly well-paved roadway over the pass will take you back to the coast along the Solenzara River. If you stop and peer carefully into its depths, you may be able to see wild Corsican trout dining on aquatic insects.

Dining

$ ✕⊞ **Le Refuge.** Near the top of the spectacular drive from Porto-Vec-
★ chio to the Col de Bavella, follow signs for Le Refuge, an inexpensive little *gîte d'étape* (hikers' inn). Here, by a roaring fire, you can enjoy a hearty lunch or dinner of Corsican mountain fare or spend a night in simple but adequate accommodations under immense laricio pines. ⊠ *Cartalavonu (2 km [1½] mi off D368 to the left),* ☎ *04–95–70–00–39. 4 double rooms, 30 single dormitory bunks without bath. MC, V.*

Aléria

⑰ *32 km (20 mi) north of Solenzara on N198; 70 km (63 mi) north of Porto-Vecchio; 48 km (29 mi) southeast of Corte.*

Just before the village of Aléria are the ruins of the Roman city of the same name. On a pine-studded plateau is the carefully restored 16th-century **Fort de Matra,** which houses the **Musée Jérôme Carcopino.** On display are pottery and tools found on the site, as well as Etruscan, Greek, and Roman artifacts dating from as far back as 500 BC. ⊠ *25 frs.* ☉ *Apr.–Oct., daily 8–noon and 2–7; Nov.–Mar., Mon.–Sat. 8–noon and 2–5.*

Dining

$$ ✕ **Chez Mathieu.** This beach-side restaurant, open year-round, specializes in very fresh *loup* (sea bass) and *dorade* (sea bream). In summer if you have dinner on the beach at sunset (before driving back up into the mountains at Corte), you can get—aside from the best fresh fish—a sense of Corsica's unique geographical diversity. ⊠ *Plage Padulone,* ☎ *04–95–57–12–03. MC, V.*

Outdoor Activities and Sports

At Aléria's **beach** you can go surf casting, swimming, or sailing. The beach stretches north from the mouth of the Tavignano River and gets wilder the farther north you go. **Camping-Bungalows Marina d'Aléria** (⊠ At intersection of N200 and the beach, ☎ 04–95–57–01–42) rents all kinds of nautical equipment.

HAUTE CORSE

Haute Corse (Upper Corsica) encompasses the northeastern end of the island and is, indeed, higher in mean altitude than Corse du Sud, topped by the 8,876-ft Monte Cinto. Most Corsica enthusiasts agree that Haute Corse is richer than other parts of the island in what is most Corsican about this "mountain in the sea": highland forests, remote villages, hidden cultural gems, and alpine lakes and streams. In the center of Haute Corse is the city of Corte, Corsica's historic heart. To the east is the chestnut-forested region of La Castagniccia, named for the abundance of *châtaigniers* (chestnut trees). This is one of Corsica's treasures, especially in the fall, when leaves and chestnuts cover the ground. The forest's tiny roadways go through villages with stunning Baroque churches and houses still roofed in traditional blue-gray slate. To the north is Cap Corse: The 105-km (65-mi) drive along the coastal route D80, from the town of Patrimonio to the city of Bastia, takes about three hours (four with lunch in Centuri and five with a run up the Col de Ste-Lucie). Bastia is Corsica's most Italianate city, a dramatic contrast to the tidier and more "Continental" Ajaccio.

Corte

⑱ *48 km (30 mi) northwest of Aléria on N200, 83 km (51 mi) northeast of Ajaccio, 70 km (43 mi) southwest of Bastia.*

Among spectacular cliffs and gorges at the confluence of the Tavignano, Restonica, and Orta rivers, Corte is the spiritual heart and soul of Corsica. Capital of Pasquale Paoli's government from 1755 to 1769, it was also where Paoli established the Corsican University in 1765. Closed by the victorious French in 1769, the university, always a symbol of Corsican identity, was reopened in 1981.

To reach the upper town and the 15th-century château overlooking the rivers, walk up the cobblestone ramp from place Pasquale-Paoli. Stop in lovely **place Gaffori** at one of the cafés or restaurants. Note the bullet-pocked house where the Corsican hero Gian Pietro Gaffori and his wife, Faustina, held off the Genoese in 1750.

★ The **Citadelle,** a Vauban-style fortress (1769–78), is built around the original 15th-century fortification at the highest point of the cliff, with the river below. It contains the **Musée de la Corse** (Corsica Museum), dedicated to the island's history and ethnography. ☎ *04–95–45–25–45.* 🖂 *35 frs.* ☉ *Nov.–Apr., Tues.–Sat. 10–5; May–Oct., daily 10–8.*

The **Palais National** (National Palace), just outside the citadel and above place Gaffori, is the ancient residence of Genoa's representatives in Corsica and was the seat of the Corsican parliament from 1755 to 1769. The building is now part of the Corsican University. 🖂 *Pl. du Poilu.* ☉ *Weekdays 2–6.*

For an unforgettable view of the river junction and the Genoese bridge below, the citadel's tiny watchtower above and the mountains behind, walk left along the citadel wall to the **Belvedere.**

Leave the Haute Ville and go through the tiny alleys of the **Quartier de Chiostra.** Follow the cobblestone path (as you look down) to the right from the Belvedere, bearing right and across at the **Chapelle St-Théophile.** Coming into the tiny square on your left, don't miss the open stone staircase on the opposite wall, or the prehistoric fertility goddess carved into the wall to the left next to the pottery artisans' shop. After leaving this little space, continue downhill, and you will rejoin the ramp leading into place Pasquale-Paoli.

The **Gorges de la Restonica** (Restonica Gorges) make a spectacular day hike. At the top of the Restonica Valley, leave your car in the parking area at the end of the road. A two-hour climb will take you to **Lac de Mélo,** a trout-filled mountain lake 6,528 ft above sea level. Surrounded by a circle of craggy granite peaks, the mountain is the site of a classical concert in early August. Another hour up is the usually snow-bordered **Lac de Capitello.** Information on trails is available from the tourist office (☞ Corsica A to Z, *below*) or the Parc Naturel Régional (☞ Corsica A to Z, *below*). At the Restonica Gorge, in the stone shepherds' huts at the **Bergeries de Grotelle,** light meals are served.

Dining and Lodging

$$$ **✕⊞ Auberge de la Restonica** Over the crystalline Restonica River, this
★ cozy inn—known for its hearty Corsican fare—has seven charming rooms (one of which is a duplex apartment) in a hunting lodge–like building over rushing water. The cuisine is well known in and around Corte. ⊠ *Vallée de la Restonica, 20250,* ☎ *04–95–45–25–25,* 𝖥𝖠𝖷 *04–95–61–15–79. 7 rooms. Restaurant, pool.. AE, DC, MC, V.*

$$–$$$ **✕⊞ Hôtel Dominique Colonna.** Originally the modern annex across the parking lot from the Auberge de la Restonica, this comfortable spot has sliding glass and screen doors leading directly out to breakfast nooks next to the stream. Owner Dominique "Dumé" Colonna, one of France's (and certainly Corsica's) greatest soccer stars, drops by from time to time. ⊠ *Vallée de la Restonica, 20250,* ☎ *04–95–45–25–65,* 𝖥𝖠𝖷 *04–95–61–03–91. 28 rooms. Restaurant. AE, DC, MC, V.*

En Route **Ponte Leccia,** 24 km (15 mi) north of Corte on N193, is the entry point to La Castagniccia: take D71 southeast into the forest. A rail, road, and river crossing with gas stations and a supermarket, the town has little else to recommend it.

Morosaglia

⑲ *14 km (9 mi) southeast of Ponte Leccia, 9 km (5 mi) east of La Porta.*

The town of Morosaglia is the birthplace of Pasquale Paoli. Letters, portraits, and memorabilia from Paoli's life are on display at the **Maison de Pasquale Paoli** (Pasquale Paoli House). ☎ *04–95–61–04–97.* ▣ *25 frs.* ☉ *Spring–fall, daily 9–noon and 2:30–7:30; winter, daily 1–5.*

La Porta

⑳ *9 km (5 mi) west of Morosaglia, 14½ km (9 mi) north of Piedicroce on D515.*

As the name of the village suggests, La Porta (the Door) is an entranceway to La Castagniccia. The **St-Jean-Baptiste** church here is widely accepted as the crowning glory of Corsican Baroque art. The bright ochre facade and the five-story bell tower are feasts for the eyes, as are the paintings inside. Look for the *Martyrdom of Saint Eulalie of Barcelona* (1848), by Louis Destouches (1819–81), just inside on the left.

Dining

$$ **✕ L'Ampugnani–Chez Elisabeth.** This excellent restaurant is known throughout Corsica as a treasury of fine local cooking. Specializing in *cuisine du terroir* (local country cooking), you'll find such dishes as a superb leg of lamb with herbs and *figatellu* (liver sausage). ⊠ *La Porta,* ☎ *04–95–39–22–00. Reservations essential. MC, V. Closed Mon. Oct.–Easter.*

Piedicroce

㉑ *14 km (9 mi) south of La Porta on D515, 66 km (40 mi) south of Bastia.*

Piedicroce's panoramic view of La Castagniccia is superb. Be sure to stop in the vividly painted Baroque church of **St-Pierre-et-St-Paul,** one of the finest of its type in the area. The nearby mineral springs of **Orezza** are reputed to have miraculous powers. The **Fium Alto Stream,** running along the road that goes northeast to Folelli, is one of Corsica's best trout streams. To exit La Castagniccia, follow signs for **Folelli** (37 km [22 mi] north) or Bastia (66 km [40 mi] north).

Dining and Lodging

$$ ✕ **U Fragnu.** After you've exited La Castagniccia at Folelli, head north to this restaurant for some exquisite local country cooking. The Garelli family has cooked for the French premier as representatives of Corsican gastronomy, and Madame Garelli is a specialist in *soupe de berger* (shepherd's soup)—made from an original recipe, recovered after much research. ✉ *Rte. de Vescovato, Venzolasca (7 km [4 mi] north of Folelli on N198, then 2 km [1 mi] up D37),* ☎ *04–95–36–62–33. Reservations essential. No credit cards. No lunch Thurs.–Sat. Nov.–Mar.*

$$ ✕🏠 **Le Refuge.** A handy midway point in the labyrinthine La Castag-
★   niccia, this hotel-restaurant is a good place for a superb meal based on the Rafalli family's home-processed charcuterie and a night's sleep in the small but cozy quarters overlooking the Castagniccia and the valley of the Fium Alto stream. ✉ *20229 Piedicroce,* ☎ *04–95–35–82–65,* ℻ *04–95–35–84–42. 20 rooms. Restaurant. MC, V. Closed Nov.*

Asco

㉒   *22 km (13 mi) west of Ponte Leccia: 2 km (1 mi) north of Ponte Leccia, D147 turns off N197 toward the village of Asco, 16 km (10 mi) away.*

The Asco Valley is studded with beehives, and honey and cheese abound in Asco's shops. Don't miss the Genoese bridge below Asco or, even better, a swim in the river. Above Asco the granite gorge becomes a cool pine forest, perfect for hiking. Follow the road for another 12 km (7 mi) past the village, ending at the top against a wall of mountains.

The Asco Valley runs west to an awe-inspiring barrier of mountains crowned by **Monte Cinto,** rising to 8,795 ft, the highest point in Corsica. As you travel up the valley, the maquis-covered slopes give way to a sheer granite gorge hung with sweet-smelling juniper. This is certainly a drive well worth making in daylight, although if you must make the trip up at night, you can see it on the way down the next day.

Haut-Asco

㉓   *13 km (8 mi) west of Asco.*

Haut-Asco is the starting point for the eight- to nine-hour (round-trip) walk up **Monte Cinto.** On a clear day, from the top you can see the entire island and even the Appennines on the Italian mainland. Clouds and mist gather after about 10 AM, however, particularly in summer. For this reason a 4 AM start is recommended. Questions can be answered at Le Chalet (☞ *below*).

Dining and Lodging

$ ✕🏠 **Le Chalet.** This tidy hideaway at the very top of the island has a simple, no-frills restaurant serving Corsican cuisine. Walls are covered with photographs of famous mountaineers. Along with the 22 private rooms there are also a hikers' dormitory, a bar, and a store selling supplies to trekkers, who use the chalet as a way station from the GR 20. ✉ *20276 Haut-Asco,* ☎ ℻ *04–95–47–81–08. 22 rooms, plus dormitory without bath. Restaurant, bar, shop. MC, V. Closed early Nov.–early May.*

Outdoor Activities and Sports

From at least December to April Corsica's upper reaches are snowed in, creating opportunities for both alpine and cross-country skiing; consult the **Club Alpin Français** (☎ 04–95–22–73–81) in Ajaccio. For information about hiking up Monte Cinto, in Bastia contact the **Office National des Forets** (☎ 04–95–32–81–90.

La Scala di Santa Regina

★ *9 km (5 mi) south of Ponte Leccia, D84 leaves N193, starts up the Golo River, and turns into La Scala di Santa Regina.*

This road, known as La Scala di Santa Regina (Stairway of the Holy Queen), is one of the most spectacular on the island. It's also one of the most difficult to navigate, especially in winter. The route follows the twisty path of the Golo River, which has carved its way through layers of red granite, forming dramatic gorges and waterfalls. Be prepared for herds of animals to cross the road. Follow the road to the **Col de Verghio** (Verghio Pass) for superb views of Tafunatu, the legendary perforated mountain, and Monte Cinto. On the way up you'll pass through the **Valdo Niello Forest,** Corsica's most important woodlands, filled with pines and beeches. The col is considered the border between Haute Corse and Corse du Sud. As you descend from the Verghio Pass through the **Forêt d'Aitone** (Aitone Forest), note how well manicured it is—the pigs, goats, and sheep running rampant through the tall Laricio pines keep it this way. As you pass the village of Evisa, with its orange roofs, look across the impressive **Gorges de Spelunca** (Spelunca Gorge) to see the hill village of Ota. A small road on the right will take you across the gorge, where there's an ancient Genoese-built bridge.

Ota

㉔ *16 km (10 mi) northwest of Evisa on La Scala di Santa Regina.*

The tiny village of Ota, overlooking the **Gorges de Spelunca,** has traditional stone houses that seem to be suspended on the mountainside, an amazing view of the surrounding mountains, and a number of trailheads. It's an excellent base for hiking in the area.

Dining and Lodging

$ ✕🏨 **Chez Félix.** This homey place serves as dining room, taxi stand, and town hall. Cheerful owner Marinette Ceccaldi cooks up heaping portions of Corsican specialties ranging from wild boar to chestnut-flour beignets. Suites are decorated with curios and antiques, each with a balcony overlooking the gorge. Rooms are comfortable and rustic; some have private bathrooms, others share. The hotel has a van that will transport you out to hiking routes. ✉ *Pl. de la Fontaine, 20150,* ☎ 🄵🄰🄷 *04–95–26–12–92. 4 2-bedroom apartments, 36 beds in 4- and 6-bed rooms with shared bath. Restaurant. No credit cards.*

Porto and Les Calanches

㉕ *5 km (3 mi) west of Ota, 30 km (19 mi) south of Calvi.*

The flashy resort town of Porto doesn't have much character, but its setting on the crystalline **Golfe de Porto** (Gulf of Porto), surrounded by massive pink-granite mountains, is superb. Activity focuses on the small port, where there is a boardwalk with restaurants and hotels. A short hike from the boardwalk will bring you to a 16th-century Genoese tower that overlooks the bay. Boat excursions leave daily for the **Réserve Naturel de Scandola** (☞ *below*).

Detour south of Porto on D81 to get to **Les Calanches,** jagged out-croppings of red rock considered among the most extraordinary natural sites in France. Look for arches and stelae, standing rock formations shaped like animals and phantasmagoric human faces.

Piana

★ **㉖**   *11 km (7 mi) south of Porto, 71 km (44 mi) north of Ajaccio.*

Piana overlooks Les Calanches and the Golfe de Porto. Explore the crooked streets of the old town and climb up to the old fortress at the top of **Capo Rosso** to admire the craggy rocks that jut out from the water.

Dining and Lodging

$$ ✕🏨 **Les Roches Rouges.** On the hillside just below the Capo Rosso, this rambling old mansion has a distinctive British flavor. The vast Imperial-style restaurant is classified as a historic monument. Try the fish soup or grilled lobster. ⊠ *Rte. de Porto, 20115,* ☎ *04–95–27–81–81,* 🇫🇦🇽 *04–95–27–81–76. 20 rooms. Restaurant. AE, DC, MC, V. Closed Nov.–Mar.*

$$$–$$$$ 🏨 **Capo Rosso.** The Capo Rosso sits high in the hills overlooking the gulf, just yards from Les Calanches. The views—whether seen from your room, the outdoor pool, or the restaurant's terrace—are dramatic. Rooms are modern and functional more than charming, but all the comforts are guaranteed. ⊠ *20115 Piana,* ☎ *04–95–27–82–40,* 🇫🇦🇽 *04–95–27–80–00. 57 rooms. Restaurant, pool. AE, DC, MC, V. Closed mid-Oct.–Easter.*

Calvi

㉗   *92 km (58 mi) north of Piana, 159 km (100 mi) north of Ajaccio.*

Calvi, Corsica's slice of the Riviera, has been described by author Dorothy Carrington as "an oasis of pleasure on an otherwise austere island." Calvi grew rich by supplying products to Genoa; its citizens remained loyal supporters of Genoa long after the rest of the island declared independence. Calvi also claims to be the birthplace of Christopher Columbus. During the 18th century the town endured assaults from Corsican nationalists, including celebrated patriot Pasquale Paoli. Today Calvi sees a summertime invasion of tourists, drawn to the 6-km (4-mi) stretch of sandy white beach, the citadel, and the buzzing nightlife.

The Genoese **Citadelle,** perched on a rocky promontory at the tip of the bay, competes with the beach as a major attraction. An inscription above the drawbridge—CIVITAS CALVI SEMPER FIDELIS (The citizens of Calvi always faithful)—reflects the town's unswerving allegiance to Genoa. At the welcome center, just inside the gates, you can see a video on the city's history and arrange to take a guided tour in English (three times a day) or a self-guided walking tour. ⊠ *Up the hill off av. de l'Uruguay,* ☎ *04–95–65–36–74.* 🎟 *Guided tour and video show 50 frs.* 🕙 *Tour Easter–early Oct., daily at 10, 4:30, and 6:30.*

Stop in at the 13th-century church of **St-Jean-Baptiste** (⊠ Pl. d'Armes.); it contains an interesting Renaissance baptismal font. Look up to see the rows of pews screened by grillwork: the chaste young women of Calvi's upper classes sat here.

Dining and Lodging

$$$ ✕ **Chez Tao.** At Chez Tao, a mandatory stop on almost everyone's
★   itinerary, you can rub elbows with the town's glitterati on the ochre-color 16th-century terraces that look out over the bay. Seafood is what everyone eats, but food plays second fiddle to the atmosphere, which includes

Corsican folk singing and piano until the wee hours. ✉ *Pl. de la Citadelle,* ☎ *04–95–65–00–73. AE, DC, MC, V. Closed mid-Sept.–Easter.*

$$$ ✕ **L'Île de Beauté.** One of Calvi's most celebrated restaurants, it has been pulling in crowds since 1929. Metal suns adorn the walls of the dining room, where the menu features a variety of seafood and upland dishes ranging from lobster fricassee to wild boar stew. ✉ *Quai Landry,* ☎ *04–95–65–00–46. AE, DC, MC, V. Closed Oct.–Apr. No lunch Wed.*

$–$$ ✕ **U San Carlu.** Good, classic Corsican and French cooking at reasonable prices makes U San Carlu a favorite. The brick-vaulted dining room is in a 16th-century building that was once a hospital. In summer you can eat outdoors on the palm-shaded patio. Specialties include steak in Roquefort sauce and prawns flamed in brandy; there's also an excellent daily menu. ✉ *10 pl. St-Charles,* ☎ *04–95–65–92–20. AE, DC, MC, V. Closed Wed. mid-Oct.–mid-May. No dinner Tues.*

$$$ ✕🏨 **Le Signoria.** This 17th-century country manor (and annex) has
★ homey bedrooms and large bathrooms. From the pool and patio there are panoramic views of the mountains and the bay. The renowned restaurant serves imaginative, regional cuisine (it's closed for lunch, except for weekends from July through August). ✉ *Rte. de la Forêt de Bonifato, 20260 (5 km [3 mi] from Calvi),* ☎ *04–95–65–23–73,* FAX *04–95–65–33–20. 10 rooms. Restaurant, bar, pool, Turkish bath. AE, MC, V. Closed Nov.–Easter.*

$$$$ 🏨 **La Villa.** On a hill with marvelous views of the town and the citadel, this Relais & Châteaux hotel feels like a modern Italian villa. The architecture leans heavily toward arched loggias and wrought iron; fountains, paintings, and sculpture abound. Rooms are large and have terra-cotta floors and balconies. The canopied dining area overlooks the pool, surrounded by a fragrant garden. ✉ *Chemin de Notre Dame de la Serra, 20260,* ☎ *04–95–65–10–10,* FAX *04–95–65–10–50. 25 rooms. Restaurant, bar, pool, beauty salon, Turkish bath. AE, DC, MC, V. Closed Jan.–Mar.*

$$ 🏨 **Le Magnolia.** Rooms in this cozy 19th-century former mansion between the church and the marketplace are named after French literary figures: the Verlaine overlooks rooftops to the port. Cupids and cherubs perch over beds. The restaurant is in the garden under a giant magnolia tree—thus the name of the hotel. ✉ *Pl. du Marché 20260,* ☎ *04–95–65–19–16,* FAX *04–95–65–34–52. 12 rooms. Restaurant, air-conditioning, minibars. DC, MC, V. Closed Jan.–Feb.*

Nightlife and the Arts

The cabaret-restaurant **Chez Tao** (✉ Pl. de la Citadelle, ☎ 04–95–65–00–73) is the "in" spot in town. On the quai Landry next to the port Captaincy is the piano bar **L'Eden Port** (✉ Quai Landry, ☎ 04–95–62–10–32). On the outskirts of town, **La Camargue** and **L'Acapulco** (✉ On N167) are the town's biggest dance clubs; a free *navette* (shuttle bus) cruises downtown Calvi until dawn collecting and returning club goers.

The **Calvi Jazz Festival** is held the last week in June. **Rencontres Polyphoniques,** an international choral festival, is held in mid-September. **Les Recontres d'Art Contemporain de Calvi** shows contemporary painting and sculpture under the arcades of the Citadelle from mid-June to the end of August. **Festiventu,** a celebration of wind-powered sports, musical instruments, and scientific artifacts, happens in late October.

Outdoor Activities and Sports

The **GR 20** begins near Calvi and follows the watershed line on the crests of the mountains northwest–southeast to Ste-Lucie de Porto-Vecchio. Contact the tourist office (☞ Corsica A to Z, *below*) for information. For water-sports, diving, and boating information and equipment rental, contact **Calvi Nautique Club** (✉ Port de Plaisance, ☎ 04–95–

65–10–65). The **Centre Équestre de Calvi** (✉ Rte. de Pietramaggiore, ☎ 04–95–65–22–22) arranges tours on horseback.

Shopping

The major shopping streets are rue Clemenceau and boulevard Wilson. Look for pottery, for which the region is known. Corsican knives are another specialty item, as are regional charcuterie, cheeses, and jams.

Calenzana

㉘ *13 km (8 mi) from Calvi: Head east on N197 for 5 km (3 mi), then south on D151.*

Leaving Calvi via the rose-color hill towns of La Balagne, "the garden of Corsica," will take you through some memorable towns and villages. Calenzana is the jumping-off point for the GR 20, Corsica's challenging 20-day hike over the crest of its mountainous interior. It's also the home of the spectacular wine cellar of the Orsini vineyards, the **Cave du Domaine Orsini** (✉ Clos Rochebelle, ☎ 04–95–62–81–01; visits by appointment).

The 11th-century church of **Ste-Restitute,** about 1 km (½ mi) beyond town, has an altar backed by medieval frescoes depicting the life of St. Restitute. Legend has it that the saint was martyred here in the 3rd century, and when the people of the town began building a church on another site, the stone blocks were moved here each night by two huge white bulls. Apparently, this happened several times before the townsfolk finally got the divine message and changed building sites.

En Route From Calenzana serpentine D151 winds around hillsides dotted with picturesque villages. Most are surrounded by walls and have the same layout: a central area surrounded by short streets radiating out like the spokes of a wheel, ending with a final house built into the village walls.

Catteri

㉙ *18 km (11 mi) north of Calenzana on D151.*

The cheese-making center of Catteri, in La Balagne, is known for its unique bell-tower church facade, a scrolled and pilastered miniature replica of Notre-Dame-des-Anges.

Dining

$ ✕ **Restaurant A Lataria.** This little spot just beyond the crossroads of Catteri has a flower-filled terrace with views of the village and the sea. The Corsican and Mediterranean fare, such as paella and brocciu lasagna, is a good value. ✉ *Just outside Catteri on D51,* ☎ *04–95–61–71–44. No credit cards. Closed Oct.–May.*

Sant'Antonino

㉚ *7 km (4 mi) north of Cateri on D13 and across the gorge.*

The medieval, stone hilltop village of Sant'Antonino, believed to date from the 9th century, is one of the oldest still-inhabited places on the island. The view over La Balagne from here is spectacular.

Pigna

㉛ *7 km (4 mi) northeast of Sant'Antonino on D151.*

The unusual village of Pigna is dedicated to bringing back traditional Corsican music and crafts. Here you can listen to folk songs in cafés, visit workshops, and buy handmade musical instruments. The Casa Musicale (☞ *below*), a concert hall, auberge, and restaurant, is at the center of it all. During the first half of July, the Casa Musicale hosts a Festivoce (song festival) of vocalists and a capella groups.

Dining and Lodging

$ ✕⌂ **Casa Musicale.** This unique spot has traditional local cuisine, music of all kinds—often authentic Corsican polyphonic singing— and a lovely view over La Balagne down to Calvi. Rooms are simple but elegant, with whitewashed walls and rustic furniture; they sleep two, three, or four. ⊠ *20220 Pigna,* ☎ *04–95–61–77–31,* FAX *04–95– 61–77–81. 7 rooms. MC, V. Closed Jan.–Feb. No dinner Sun.–Mon.*

Shopping

The **Casa di l'Artigiani** (☎ 04–95–61–77–29) sells a wide range of local crafts, from jam and honey to musical instruments and hand-knit sweaters.

Algajola

③② *8 km (5 mi) east of Pigna, 10 km (6 mi) southwest of L'Ile Rousse on N197.*

Built in the 16th century, the village of Algajola is another ancient fortress, the last and smallest of the seven citadel towns built by the Genoese on Corsica's shores. A low-key and friendly resort, it has a perfect crescent beach that attracts crowds.

Dining and Lodging

$$ ✕⌂ **L'Ondine.** Nestled into the rocks at the edge of a sandy cove, L'Ondine is part of a pleasantly landscaped village of single-story beige-stucco buildings. The dining room, serving typical Corsican maritime cuisine, commands a million-dollar view of the beach and Algajola. ⊠ *7 rue à Marina, 20220,* ☎ *04–95–60–70–02,* FAX *04–95–60–60–36. 53 rooms. Restaurant, bar, pool. MC, V. Closed late Oct.–late Mar.*

L'Ile Rousse

③③ *10 km (6 mi) northeast of Algajola, 37 km (22 mi) southwest of St-Florent.*

L'Ile Rousse, named for the mass of reddish rock now connected to the town by a causeway, is a favorite spot of French vacationers who come to bask in its Riviera-like atmosphere. A small two-car train runs from here along the coast to Calvi, delivering sun worshipers to beaches not accessible by road.

Dining and Lodging

$$ ✕⌂ **A Pasturella.** This picturesque hotel has simple rooms with modern furnishings and geranium-filled window boxes overlooking the mountains. The widely admired restaurant specializes in seafood and Corsican dishes. ⊠ *Monticello 20220 (5 km [3 mi] outside L'Ile Rousse),* ☎ *04–95–60–05–65,* FAX *04–95–60–21–78. 14 rooms. Restaurant, bar. AE, MC, V. Closed mid-Nov.–mid-Dec.*

$$$ ⌂ **La Pietra.** This modern building is one of those places that is more pleasurable to be inside of looking out: the views from its windows are stunning. Built into the red-granite rocks across from the port of L'Ile Rousse, this comfortable spot combines contemporary taste, friendly service, and unbeatable seascapes. ⊠ *Chemin du Phare, 20217,* ☎ *04–95–63–02–30,* FAX *04–95–60–15–92. 40 rooms. Restaurant, parking (free). AE, MC, V.*

Outdoor Activities and Sports

Two of the best **beaches** in the area are the **Plage d'Ostriconi,** at the mouth of the Ostriconi River (20 km [13 mi] north of town), and the wilder and much-frequented-by-nudists **Plage Saleccia,** used in the 1960s filming of *The Longest Day.*

Shopping

Baked goods, local wines, and herbs from the maquis can be bought at the **market** (⊠ Pl. Paoli) every morning except Monday.

Lama

㉞ *15 km (9 mi) southeast of L'Ile Rousse, 57 km (24 mi) north of Corte.*

The charmingly restored medieval village of Lama is only 10 minutes up the Ostriconi Valley and is a handy place to spend a night on your way to Cap Corse. Everyone from the mayor to the local children works to accommodate visitors; people say hello in the streets and seem to know where you are staying. Once a prosperous olive-growing town, the village was nearly deserted after a 1971 fire destroyed 35,000 olive trees in one afternoon. Carefully cultivated tourism has put Lama back on the map.

Dining and Lodging

$$ ✕ **U Campu Latinu.** Skillfully built into an ancient *bergerie,* using old stones and drywall construction, this flower-festooned restaurant overlooks Lama, the sea, and the mountains. Try an omelet or lasagna prepared with mint and brocciu or lamb grilled over coals with maquis herbs. ⊠ *At top of village of Lama; walk or drive up from main square,* ☎ 04–95–48–23–83. *DC, MC, V. Closed Sept.–June.*

$$–$$$ ✕⊞ **Auberge de Lama.** Pierre-Jean and Françoise Costa make you part of their life, whether on horseback, on a wild boar hunt, or by showing you Lama's hidden corners and secret spots. Lodgings are scattered throughout the village in small stone cottages that sleep from two to eight. The lively restaurant, open year-round, is the town's informal nerve center. Excellent Corsican specialties are served, such as a mint-and-brocciu omelet or roast kid. ⊠ *20218 Lama,* ☎ 04–95–48–22–99, ℻ 04–95–48–21–49. *50 cottages. Restaurant, kitchenettes. DC, MC, V.*

Outdoor Activities and Sports

Riding along the old mule trails on horseback is an excellent way to see the countryside; for this and nearly any other outdoor activity you can imagine, from hang gliding to canyoning to a wild boar hunt, contact Pierre-Jean Costa at **Corse Escapades** (⊠ Village de Lama, 20218 Lama, ☎ 04–95–48–22–99, ℻ 04–95–48–23–77).

Murato

㉟ *15 km (9 mi) west of Lama, 12 km (7 mi) south of Bastia: Take N193 to D82 to D305 at Rutalli.*

The village of Murato has two excellent restaurants (Le Monastère and Le Ferme Campo di Monte, ☞ Dining, *below*) as well as a remarkable 12th-century Pisan church, one of Corsica's finest and foremost architectural treasures.

The polychrome, green-marble, and white-limestone **Église Mosaïque de San Michele de Murato** (Mosaic Church of San Michele of Murato) suggests many interpretations. Look for the relief depicting Eve tempted by a serpent, covering her nakedness with an oversize hand. The site overlooks the Golfe de St-Florent. When the *libecciu* (a powerful and persistent wind) is blowing hard from the west, even the continent (the mainland) is sometimes visible.

Dining

$$ ✕ **Le Ferme Campo di Monte.** The Julliard sisters prepare what is
★   widely regarded as Corsica's best, most authentic cuisine at this lovely 350-year-old stone farmhouse. Especially good are the *storzapreti* (brocciu croquettes). ⊠ *D305 Rutali-Murato,* ☎ 04–95–37–64–60. *Reservations essential. AE, DC, MC, V. Closed weekdays Sept.–June.*

$$ ✕ **Le Monastère.** This handsome stone structure in the middle of town,
★ within walking distance from the church, serves excellent roast kid and
lamb cooked in herbs. If the Campo di Monte is booked, this is a great
alternative. ⊠ *D305 Rutali-Murato,* ☎ *04–95–37–64–18. Reservations
essential. AE, DC, MC, V. Open only for specific reservations Oct.–June.*

St-Florent

㊱ *28 km (17 mi) northeast of the exit for Lama on D81, 46 km (28½
mi) northeast of L'Ile Rousse.*

St-Florent is a postcard-perfect village nestled into the crook of the Golfe
de St-Florent between the rich Nebbio Valley and the desert of Agri-
ates. The town has a crumbling citadel and a yacht basin ringed by shops
and restaurants.

Be sure to seek out the interesting Romanesque **Santa Maria Assunta**
(⊠ Rue Agostino Giustiniani), just outside the village. Standing in iso-
lated splendor among the vineyards, this 12th-century white-limestone
church is one of only two Pisan churches remaining on the island. The
facade and interior columns support a menagerie of sculpted human
faces, snakes, snails, and mythical animals.

Dining and Lodging

$$$ ✕ **La Rascasse.** This fine restaurant overlooking the port is known for
its excellent fish stews and fresh seafood dishes. Try to get an upstairs
table for a better view of the gulf. The *civet de lotte* (stewed monkfish)
and the warm scallop salad are especially good. ⊠ *Esplanade du Port,*
☎ *04–95–37–06–69. AE, DC, MC, V. Closed Mon. Apr.–June and Sept.*

$$$ 🏨 **Hôtel de l'Europe.** This central, old, and elegant spot is open nearly
all winter and has spectacular views over the sea. Rooms are spacious
and well decorated, and the café downstairs is the town nerve center.
⊠ *Pl. du Village, 20217,* ☎ *04–95–37–00–03,* FAX *04–95–37–17–36.
22 rooms. AE, MC, V. Closed Jan.–Feb.*

Patrimonio

㊲ *5 km (3 mi) northeast of St-Florent, 18 km (11 mi) west of Bastia.*

Patrimonio lies at the base of the Cap Corse Peninsula, among vine-
yards that produce most of Corsica's best wines. The most prestigious
of the vineyards are **Antoine Arena** (☎ 04–95–37–08–27), **Dominique
Gentile** (☎ 04–95–37–01–54), and **Orenga de Gaffory** (☎ 04–95–30–
11–38). Tours of the vineyards and of the Orenga de Gaffory gallery
can be arranged; all are open weekdays 9–noon and 3–6.

Nightlife and the Arts

The **Nuits de la Guitare** music festival during the third week of July is
one of Corsica's top musical events, featuring blues, jazz, and fla-
menco guitarists from all over the world.

Outdoor Activities and Sports

One of the most spectacular mountain **hiking** routes in Corsica follows
the crest of Cap Corse over the 4,287-ft Monte Stello, from which you
can see the hills of Tuscany and Provence. Contact the Parc Naturel
Régional de la Corse (☞ Corsica A to Z, *below*) for details.

Nonza

㊳ *14 km (9 mi) north of Patrimonio, 8 km (5 mi) south of Canelle.*

On your way along Cap Corse, be sure to stop in Nonza. This vertig-
inous crag seems impossibly high over its famous black beach, the legacy

of a former asbestos mine down the coast at Canari. The beach is accessible only by trudging down the 600 steps from Nonza, and no doubt this is the reason it's usually deserted. The chapel is dedicated to the martyred St. Julie, whose severed breasts, it is said, became the double fountain known as the *Fontaine aux Mamelles* (Fountain of Mammaries) on the way down to the beach. The spectacular gravity-defying tower was constructed by Pasquale Paoli in 1760. Its squared corners made it easier to defend, as famed Captain Casella proved in 1768 when he stood off 1,200 French troops.

Dining and Lodging

$$ ✕🏠 **Auberge Patrizi.** On a shady terrace in the center of town, this place serves excellent Corsican cuisine in a lively setting. It also has rooms—small and a little too close to the road—but with spectacular views. ✉ *Pl. du Village, 20217,* ☎ *04–95–37–82–16,* FAX *04–95–37–86–40. 13 rooms. AE, MC, V. Closed Nov.–Mar.*

Centuri

③⑨ *55 km (34 mi) north of Patrimonio, 41 km (25 mi) north of Nonza.*

Centuri (pronounced *chen*-toori), Cap Corse's top fishing port, is a good place for lunch on your way around the cape. The late afternoon arrival and unloading of the fishing boats is also an event for which it is worth staying around.

Dining and Lodging

$$–$$$ ✕🏠 **Le Vieux Moulin.** Old-world charm and authentic Corsican flavor characterize this place. The main house was built in 1870 as a private residence; the eight-room annex is more recent but no less inviting, with bougainvillea cascading from its balconies. Boat rides and fishing trips can be arranged, and tennis courts and golf are nearby. The restaurant specializes in Centuri's famous seafood. ✉ *Rte. de Cap Corse, 20238 Centuri Port,* ☎ *04–95–35–60–15,* FAX *04–95–35–60–24. 14 rooms. Restaurant. AE, DC, MC, V. Closed Nov.–Mar.*

En Route From Centuri continue along the D80 coastal road to the **belvedere** near the Moulin Mattei Windmill at Col de Serra on the tip of the peninsula. As you round the tip, you can see some of Corsica's 90 **Genoese watchtowers,** as well as Giraglia Island, with its lighthouse. Take D253 north to reach the fishing village of **Barcaggio.** A long, sandy beach extends east from the village, ending in a path leading to the 16th-century Tour D'Agnello. The **Finocchiarola Islands,** a protected aviary reserve that can be visited by boat from Macinaggio, are visible off the northeast corner of the peninsula. As you head down the east coast of Cap Corse on D80, you might want to make a detour on D180 through the **Col de Ste-Lucie** to the **Tour de Sénèque,** home of the Roman philosopher and writer Seneca after he was exiled for seducing the niece of Emperor Claudius. Farther south on D80, a drive up D32 to the town of **Sisco** will take you to within a 2-km (1-mi) walk of the Romanesque church of San Michele, built in 1030.

Erbalunga

④⓪ *40 km (25 mi) southeast of Centuri, 10 km (6 mi) north of Bastia.*

Erbalunga is one of the most charming villages on Cap Corse's east coast, with stone houses sloping gently down to a Genoese tower built into a rock ledge. Probably as a result of Erbalunga's aesthetic grace, though possibly because it was French poet Paul Valéry's ancestral home, a colony of artists settled here in the '20s.

Lodging

$$–$$$ **Castel' Brando.** This 19th-century mansion has dark green shutters
★ and terra-cotta tiles. The large rooms are furnished with country-style
antiques and dried flowers. The large pool and the terrace, where
breakfast is served, are in the garden. ⊠ *Off D80 (mailing address:
B.P. 20), 20222 Erbalunga,* ☎ *04–95–30–10–30,* FAX *04–95–33–98–
18. 27 rooms. Air-conditioning, kitchenettes, pool. AE, MC, V. Closed
late Oct.–Apr.* ⊛

Bastia

41 *10 km (6 mi) south of Erbalunga, 23 km (14 mi) east of St-Florent,
93 km (58 mi) northeast of Calvi, 170 km (105 mi) north of Bonifacio, 153 km (95 mi) northeast of Ajaccio.*

Bastia (bastion) was named for the fortress the Genoese built here in
the 14th century as a stronghold against rebellious islanders and potential invaders. Today the city is Corsica's business center and largest
town. Despite sprawling suburbs the center of Bastia retains the timeless, salty flavor of an ancient Mediterranean port.

The **Terra Vecchia** (Old Town) is best explored on foot. Start at the wide,
palm-filled **place St-Nicolas,** bordered on one side by docked ships looming large in the port and on the other by two blocks of popular cafés
along boulevard Général-de-Gaulle. Head south on boulevard Général-
de-Gaulle, which becomes rue Napoléon, for two blocks to the **Église
de la Conception** (Church of the Conception; ⊠ Rue Napoléon), occupying a pebble-studded square. Step inside to admire the church's
ornate 18th-century interior, although the lighting is poor, requiring a
bright day to see much. The walls are covered with a riot of wood carvings, gold, and marble, and the ceiling is painted with vibrant frescoes.
Place du Marché, the market square, behind the church, buzzes with
activity every morning except Monday. The warren of tiny streets that
make up the old fishermen's quarter begins at the far side of the square.

To the south is the picturesque **Vieux Port** (Old Port), along quai des
Martyrs de la Libération, dominated by the hilltop citadel. The harbor, lined with excellent seafood restaurants, is home to million-dol-
lar yachts, but you can still find many bright red-and-blue fishing
boats and tangles of old nets and lines. A walk around the port takes
you to **Terra Nova** (New Town), a maze of not-so-new streets and houses
at the base of the 15th-century fortress. Climb the Escalier Romieu stairway beside the leafy Jardins Romieu for a sweeping view of the Italian islands of Capraia, Elba, and Montecristo.

The **Palais des Nobles Douzes** (also known as the Palais des Gouverneurs
Genois, or Genoese Governors' Palace), whose vaulted, colonnaded galleries once held the **Musée d'Ethnographie Corse** (Corsican Ethnographic
Museum) is presently closed. If visits are allowed, don't miss the
Casablanca, a French submarine used by the Resistance with swastikas
on the turret representing downed Nazi aircraft. ⊠ *Pl. du Donjon,* ☎
04–95–31–09–12.

A network of cobbled alleyways rambles across the citadel to the 15th-
century **Cathédrale Ste-Marie** (⊠ Rue Notre-Dame). Inside, classic
Baroque abounds in an explosion of gilt decoration. The 18th-century
silver statue of the Assumption is paraded at the head of a religious
procession every August 15.

The sumptuous Baroque style of the **Chapelle Ste-Croix** (Chapel of the
Holy Cross), behind the cathedral, makes it look more like a theater
than a church. The chapel owes its name to a blackened oak crucifix,

dubbed "Christ of the Miracles," discovered by fishermen at sea in 1428 and venerated to this day by Bastia's fishing community.

Dining and Lodging

$$–$$$ ✕ **La Citadelle.** This rustic and intimate spot, arranged around an ancient oil press, is near the Governor's Palace on the heights of the Terra Nova. The cuisine is carefully and elegantly prepared and presented; especially tasty is the rockfish soup, a delicious dark and thick potage. ⊠ *5 rue du Dragon,* ☎ *04–95–31–44–70. AE, MC, V. Closed Sun.*

$$ ✕ **A Scaletta.** Enjoy the view of the Old Port as you choose from a host ★ of fish and seafood specials at this popular spot. (Lavezzi, next door, has the same view, fine cuisine, and higher prices.) The cuisine in this rollicking little bistro is traditional Corsican with maritime leanings. ⊠ *4 rue St-Jean,* ☎ *04–95–32–28–70. AE, DC, MC, V. Closed Sun.*

$$$ 🏨 **Pietracap.** Perched on a hillside five minutes north of Bastia, Pietracap is a strikingly modern hotel nestled into a fragrant garden. The large rooms have stark, white modern furnishings and balconies. The lobby and hallways are decorated with bold canvases painted by the amiable owner's brother. ⊠ *20 rte. de San Martino di Lota, 20200 Pietranera-Bastia,* ☎ *04–95–31–64–63,* FAX *04–95–31–39–00. 42 rooms. Bar, restaurant, pool, bicycles. AE, DC, MC, V. Closed mid-Dec.–early Mar.*

$$ 🏨 **Posta Vecchia.** The greatest feature of this hotel in an old building not far from place St-Nicolas is its quai-side location. The unpretentious rooms have floral wallpaper and wood-beam ceilings; some are quite small. Ask for one in the main house facing the port. ⊠ *quai des Martyrs-de-la-Libération, 20200,* ☎ *04–95–32–32–38,* FAX *04–95–32–14–05. 49 rooms. AE, DC, MC, V.*

Nightlife and the Arts

L'Alba (⊠ 22 quai des Martyrs-de-la-Libération, ☎ 04–95–31–13–25) is a piano bar with occasional cabaret and floor shows. **Apocalypse** (⊠ In La Marana, 10 km [6 mi] south of Bastia, ☎ 04–95–33–36–83) is *the* place to go dancing. A younger set gathers at **Mayflower** (⊠ Port de Plaisance, ☎ 04–95–32–33–14) to hear loud rock and roll. Musicians fill the lively patio of the **Pub Chez Assunta** (⊠ Pl. Fontaine Nueve 4, ☎ 04–95–34–11–40) on most summer nights. For a night of traditional Corsican music, head to **U-Fanale** (⊠ Vieux Port, ☎ 04–95–32–68–38).

One of Corsica's major carnivals, the **Fête du Christ Noir** (Feast of the Black Christ), dedicated to Bastia's most important religious icon, is on May 3. The **Fête de St-Jean,** on Midsummer's Eve (June 23), means concerts in all of Bastia's Baroque spaces. A **Film Festival of Mediterranean Cultures** is held every November. An **International Music Festival** is in early December.

Outdoor Activities and Sports

Golf at the nine-hole **Bastia Golf Club** (⊠ Castellarèse, rte. de l'aéroport, Borgo, 12 km [7 mi] south of Bastia, ☎ 04–95–38–33–99). **Corsica Loisirs** (⊠ 31 av. Émile-Sari, ☎ 04–95–32–54–34) organizes fishing outings and rents equipment. Bikes can be rented from **Objectif Nature** (⊠ 3 rue Notre-Dame-de-Lourdes, ☎ 04–95–32–54–34). Horses are available at the **Société Hippique Urbaine de Bastia La Marana** (☎ 04–95–33–53–08 or 04–95–30–37–62) and go, and you can take them galloping along the coast.

Shopping

Casa di l'Artigiani (⊠ 5 rue des Terrasses) has a wide selection of local crafts. The **Mattei Cap Corse** store (⊠ Pl. St-Nicolas) sells the Mattei family's special Cap Corse liqueur (made from grapes). At the **market** (⊠ Pl. du Marché, behind St-Jean-Baptiste), everything from local cheeses to charcuterie to myrtle liqueur is sold on weekday mornings

CORSICA A TO Z

Arriving and Departing

By Ferry

Regular car ferries run from Marseille, Nice, and Toulon to Ajaccio, Bastia, Calvi, L'Ile Rousse, and Propriano. These crossings take from 5 to 10 hours, with sleeping cabins available. The high-speed ferry from Nice to either Calvi or Bastia takes about three hours. Package deals, which include making the crossing with a car, an onboard cabin, and a hotel in Corsica, are available from SNCM. **CMN** (✉ Compagnie Méridionale de Navigation, Ajaccio, ☎ 04–95–21–20–34; ✉ Bastia, ☎ 04–95–31–63–38). **SNCM** (Société Nationale Maritime Corse-Méditérranée; ✉ Paris, ☎ 01–49–24–24–24; ✉ Marseille, ☎ 04–91–56–30–30; ✉ Nice, ☎ 04–93–13–66–99; ✉ Toulon, ☎ 04–94–16–66–66; ✉ Ajaccio, ☎ 04–95–29–66–99; ✉ Bastia, ☎ 04–95–54–66–88; ✉ Calvi, ☎ 04–95–65–01–38; ✉ L'Île Rousse, ☎ 04–95–60–09–56).

Connections from the Italian mainland are run by **Corsica Ferries** (✉ Bastia, ☎ 04–95–32–95–95; ✉ Genoa, Italy, ☎ 010–59–33–01). **Moby Lines** (✉ Bastia, ☎ 04–95–31–46–29; ✉ Bonifacio, ☎ 04–95–73–00–29; ✉ Genoa, Italy, ☎ 010–20–56–51) also runs Italian mainland connections. Sardinia can be reached by ferry from Bastia or Bonifacio on **Navarma Lines** (✉ 4 rue Luce-de-Casablanca, 20200 Bastia, ☎ 04–95–31–46–29). **Saremar** (✉ Gare Maritime, 20169 Bonifacio, ☎ 04–95–73–06–75) also runs ferries to Sardinia.

By Plane

Corsica has four major airports: Ajaccio, Bastia, Calvi, and Figari. **Air France** (☎ 04–95–29–45–45 Ajaccio; 01–45–46–90–00 Paris) has daily service connecting Paris and Lyon with Ajaccio, Bastia, and Calvi. **Compagnie Corse Méditérranée** (☎ 04–95–29–05–00 Ajaccio) connects Ajaccio and Bastia to Nice and Marseille, with several flights a day. **Delta** (☎ 800/241–4141) connects with Air France for flights from the United States to Corsica from May to October. **TAT** (Transport Aérien Transrégional; ☎ 05–05–50–05 toll free in France; 04–95–71–01–20 in Figari) flies to Figari from Paris.

AIRPORT TRANSFERS

The airports at Ajaccio and Bastia run regular **shuttle-bus** services to and from town. At Figari a bus meets all incoming flights and will take passengers as far as Bonifacio and Porto-Vecchio for about 100 francs. From Calvi the best way to get into town is to take a **taxi** for about 100 francs.

Getting Around

By Bus

The local bus network is geared to residents who take it to school and work. At least two buses a day connect all the southern towns with Ajaccio, while northern towns are connected by bus to Bastia.

By Car

Though driving is undoubtedly the best way to explore the island's scenic stretches, note that winding, mountainous roads and uneven surfaces can actually double or triple your expected travel time. The Michelin 1/200,000 map No. 90 is essential. Be prepared for spelling anomalies, many of which are Corsican not French. Drive defensively: Drivers tend to circulate at terrifying speeds.

By Plane

Following are airlines with intraisland flights: **Air Balagne** (☎ 04–95–65–02–97). **ATM** (Air Transport Méditérranée; ☎ 04–95–76–04–99). **Kyrnair** (☎ 04–95–20–52–29).

By Train

The main line of Corsica's simple rail network runs from Ajaccio, in the west, to Corte, in the central valley, then divides at Ponte Leccia. From here one line continues to L'Ile Rousse and Calvi, in the north, and the other to Bastia, in the northeast. Another service runs four times daily between Ajaccio and Bastia. In summer a small train connects Calvi and L'Ile Rousse, stopping at numerous beaches and resorts. Following are numbers for local train stations: **Ajaccio** (☎ 04–95–23–11–03); **Bastia** (☎ 04–95–32–60–06); **Calvi** (☎ 04–95–65–00–61); and **Corte** (☎ 04–15–46–00–87).

Contacts and Resources

Car Rental

Avis Ollandini (✉ Ajaccio Airport, ☎ 04–95–23–25–14). **Europcar** (✉ 1 rue du Nouveau Port, Bastia, ☎ 04–95–31–59–29). **Hertz** (✉ Ajaccio Airport, ☎ 04–95–22–14–84; ✉ 8 cours Grandval, Ajaccio, ☎ 04–95–21–70–94; ✉ Sq. St-Victor, Bastia, ☎ 04–95–31–14–24; ✉ Quai du Commerce, Bonifacio, ☎ 04–95–73–02–47; ✉ 2 rue Maréchal-Joffre, Calvi, ☎ 04–95–65–06–64) serves the entire island with 18 offices at all the airports, harbors, and major towns. Be sure to reserve at least two weeks in advance in July and August.

Guided Tours

Most of Corsica's spectacular scenery is best viewed from the water. **Colombo Line** (✉ Quai Landry, ☎ 04–95–65–32–10) and **Promenades en Mer** (✉ Porto Marine, ☎ 04–95–26–15–16), in Calvi, organize whole-day glass-bottom-boat tours of Girolata, the Scandola Nature Reserve, and the Golfe de Porto. **Promenades en Mer** (✉ Port de l'Amirauté, 20000 Ajaccio, ☎ 04–95–23–23–38) organizes daily trips (at 9 and 2) to the Iles Sanguinaires. **Vedettes Christina** (☎ 04–95–73–14–69) and **Vedettes Méditérranée** (☎ 04–95–73–07–71) arrange outings from Bonifacio to the Iles Lavezzi, Les Calanches, and Les Grottes. Canoeing, kayaking, and rafting are popular pastimes on the inland mountain rivers in the area; for details write the **Association Municipale de Ponte-Leccia** (✉ 20218 Ponte Leccia). Two- and three-day guided hikes through the mountains and lake region are organized by the **Associu di Muntagnoli Corsi** (✉ Quartier Pentaniedda, 20122 Quenza, ☎ 04–95–78–64–05). **Ollandini** (✉ 1 rte. d'Alata, Ajaccio, ☎ 04–95–21–10–12) arranges whole- and half-day bus tours of the island, leaving from Ajaccio. **ATM** (☎ 04–95–76–04–99) and **Kyrnair** (☎ 04–95–20–52–29) arrange sightseeing tours by plane.

Travel Agencies

Corse Itineraries (✉ 32 cours Napoléon, Ajaccio, ☎ 04–95–51–01–10, FAX 04–45–21–52–30). **Corse Voyages** (✉ Immeuble Les Remparts, bd. Wilson, Calvi, ☎ 04–95–65–26–71). **Cyrnea Tourisme** (✉ 9 av. Xavier-Luciani, Corte, ☎ 04–95–46–24–62, FAX 04–95–46–11–22). **Kallistour** (✉ 6 av. Maréchal-Sebastiani, Bastia, ☎ 04–95–31–71–49, FAX 04–95–32–35–73).

Visitor Information

The **Agence du Tourisme de la Corse** (✉ 17 bd. Roi-Jérôme, 20000 Ajaccio, ☎ 04–95–51–77–77, FAX 04–95–51–14–40) can provide information about the whole island. The **Parc Naturel Régional de la Corse** (✉ Rue du Général-Fiorella, ☎ 04–95–21–56–54; ✉ Mailing ad dress: B.P. 417, 20100 Ajaccio), Corsica's wildlife and natural-resource management authority, controlling well over a third of the island, can provide trail maps, booklets, and a wide range of information.

Local tourist offices are as follows: **Ajaccio** (✉ Hôtel de Ville, pl. Foch, ☎ 04–95–51–53–03). **Bastia** (✉ Pl. St-Nicolas, ☎ 04–95–31–00–89). **Bonifacio** (✉ Rue des deux moulins, ☎ 04–95–73–11–88). **Calvi** (✉ Port de Plaisance, ☎ 04–95–65–16–67). **Corte** (✉ La Citadelle, ☎ 04–95–46–24–20).**L'Île Rousse** (✉ Pl. Paoli, ☎ 04–95–60–04–35). **Levie–Alta Rocca** (✉ Rue Sorba, ☎ 04–95–78–41–95). **Piana** (✉ Hôtel de Ville, ☎ 04–95–27–84–42). **Piedicroce–Castagniccia** (✉ Piedicroce, ☎ 04–95–35–82–54).**Porticcio** (✉ 428 bd. Rive Sud, ☎ 04–95–25–01–00). **Porto Vecchio** (✉ Rue du Député de Rocca Serra, ☎ 04–95–70–09–58). **Propriano** (✉ Port de Plaisance, ☎ 04–95–76–01–49). **Sartène** (✉ Rue Borgo, ☎ 04–95–77–15–40). **Sollacaro–Filitosa** (✉ Filitosa, ☎ 04–95–74–07–64).

14 THE MIDI-PYRÉNÉES AND THE LANGUEDOC-ROUSSILLON

The Midi-Pyrénées and the Languedoc-Roussillon form the main body of France's traditional southwestern region. Sports and nature lovers flock here to enjoy the natural beauty of the area, while Toulouse—a university town of rosy pink brick—is the cultural star. Here, too, are Albi and its wonderful Toulouse-Lautrec Museum, Moissac and its famous Romanesque cloister, once-upon-a-timefied Carcassonne, and the spa towns that enliven the Pyrénées. And when you see picturesque Collioure's stunning Mediterranean setting, you'll know why artists such as Matisse and Derain were so inspired.

Revised and
updated by
George Semler

LIKE THE MOST CELEBRATED DISH OF THIS AREA in southwestern France, the cassoulet, the region itself is an amazingly tasty feast. It would be sacrilegious to refer to cassoulet as simply baked beans, as so many ingredients besides beans go into it. Likewise, southwestern France is more than just Toulouse, the famous peaks of the Pyrénées, and frozen-in-time Carcassonne. There are rolling sunbaked plains and stone-and-shrub-covered hills spiked with ruins of ancient civilizations paralleling the burning coastline; once-great cities like Béziers and Narbonne, with their fortifications and cathedrals, dreaming in a Mediterranean haze; and the celebrated Côte Vermeille, immortalized by Picasso and Matisse. But as *cassoulet toulousain* (made with goose) is the variety you are most apt to find all over France, so the city of Toulouse, in turn, tops the tourist bill of fare here.

The gateway to the region, alive with music, sculpture, and architectural gems, vibrant with students, Toulouse is all that more famous regional capitals would like to have remained. Sinuously spread along the romantic banks of the Garonne as it meanders north and west from the Catalan Pyrénées on its way to the Atlantic, *la ville en rose*—so-called for its redbrick buildings—has a Spanish sensuality unique in all Gaul, a feast for eyes and ears alike. Toulouse was the ancient capital of the province called Languedoc, which was so christened when it became royal property in 1270, signifying the country where *oc,* instead of the *oil* or *oui* of northern France, meant yes.

Outside Toulouse, the countrysides of the Midi-Pyrénées and Languedoc-Roussillon are studded with highlights, like so many raisins sweetening up a spicy stew. Albi, with its Toulouse-Lautrec legacy, is a star attraction while outlying towns—from Montauban to Moissac to Auch, Mirepoix, or Cordes-sur-Ciel—each has artistic and architectural secrets to reveal. Besides Albi's Toulouse-Lautrec Museum, other art museums not to missed here are Montauban's Musée Ingres, devoted to France's most accomplished Neoclassical painter, and Ceret's Musée d'Art Moderne, which is packed with Picassos, Braques, and Chagalls.

There is also an "open-air museum" prized by artists and poets: the Côte Vermeille, or Vermilion Coast, a region centered around the fishing village of Collioure, where Matisse, Derain, and the Fauvistes committed chromatic mayhem in the early years of the 20th century. To write unrestrainedly about the Côte Vermeille would make pretty maudlin reading. With admirable restraint we shall say, in a muffled voice, that you'll like it. You'll like its red hills rolling into the sea over which Hannibal marched with his elephants—and so did everyone else, from Pompey to Louis XIV. You will like its Mediterranean, smooth and opalescent at five o'clock in the morning. You will like its people dancing in the streets to music of raucous, ancient *tenores* and curious brass horns. The whole region is flooded with the lovely golden light peculiar to the Mediterranean shores, so its villages are sheer heaven for painters. Picasso and Gris worked for years in Céret, on the Tech River, recapturing a vigor they imparted to Cubism. In fact, they imbued modern art with the style of the Romanesque sculpture of Roussillon churches and cloisters. The heart of this region is Collioure, with its narrow, cobbled streets and pink-and-mauve houses. A town of espadrille merchants and fishing boats and adorned with an ancient Crusader fort, it functions more as a muse for tourists than for artists these days.

With their mountains, lakes, rivers, wide green valleys, and arid limestone plateaus, many of these areas in this chapter are also ideal for outdoor activities. The Ariège Valley and the Pyrénées Orientales provide a dramatic route through Cathar country and the Cerdagne Valley on the way to the Mediterranean at Collioure. For the *sportif,* options run from kayaking or windsurfing to climbing up to high Pyrenean lakes and peaks, exploring mountain monasteries such as St-Martin de Canigou, fly-fishing the upper Segre river, or walking up to the Spanish border at the Gorges de Carança above Thuès-entre-Valls or the Col de Nuria above Eyne.

— George Semler

Pleasures and Pastimes

Dining

Languedoc is known for powerful and strongly seasoned cooking. Garlic and goose fat are generously used in traditional recipes. though modern chefs are skilled at producing traditional tastes in lighter formats. Be sure to try some of the renowned *foie gras* (goose liver) and *confit de canard* (duck preserves). The most famous regional dish is cassoulet, a succulent white-bean stew with *confit d'oie* (goose preserves) or *confit de canard,* spicy sausage, pork, and sometimes lamb. Other specialties might include *farci du lauragais,* a kind of pork pancake, or *gigot de sept heures,* a leg of lamb cooked for seven hours. In the Gers *département* (province) finish your meal with a glass of Armagnac, the local brandy distilled throughout the province. In the Pyrénées look for rich, dark *civet d'isard* (stewed mountain goat) or *trinchat,* a Cerdagne Valley specialty of mashed half-frozen cabbage, potato, and bacon. In the Roussillon and along the Mediterranean coast from Collioure up through Perpignan to Narbonne, the prevalent Catalan cuisine features olive-oil-based cooking and sauces such as the classic aïoli (crushed and emulsified garlic and olive oil).

CATEGORY	COST*
$$$$	over 400 frs
$$$	250 frs–400 frs
$$	125 frs–250 frs
$	under 125 frs

per person for a three-course meal, including tax (20.6%) and tip but not wine

✆ following the text of a review is your signal that the property has a Web site, where you will find details and, usually, images; for a link, visit www.fodors.com/urls.

Lodging

Hotels range from Mediterranean modern to medieval baronial to Pyrenean chalet; most are small and cozy rather than luxurious. Toulouse has the usual range of big-city hotels; make reservations well in advance if you plan to visit in spring or fall. Look for *gîtes d'étape* (hikers' way stations) and table d'hôtes (bed-and-breakfasts), which offer excellent value and a chance to meet local and international travelers and sample life on the farm, as well as the delights of *cuisine du terroir* (country cooking).

CATEGORY	COST*
$$$$	over 800 frs
$$$	550 frs–800 frs
$$	300 frs–550 frs
$	under 300 frs

All prices are for a standard double room, including tax (20.6%) and service charge.

Outdoor Activities and Sports

The Pyrénées Orientales (Eastern Pyrénées) between Prades and Foix offer great and relatively easy walking, though sturdy legs come in handy. The rough waters of the Tarn and Aveyron gorges are perfect for canoeing and kayaking; the peaceful Quercy River is better for a gentler trip. Skiing—downhill or cross-country—is excellent in the Pyrénées, with more than two dozen ski resorts along the central and eastern part of the range. There are also equestrian tours, fishing opportunities, and several superb golf courses.

Exploring the Midi-Pyrénées and the Languedoc-Roussillon

France's largest region, Midi-Pyrénées spreads from the Dordogne in the north to the Spanish border along the Pyrénées. Radiating out from Toulouse to the surrounding towns of Albi, Carcassonne, Montauban, Auch and up through the Ariège Valley into the Pyrénées Orientales, the central and southern parts of the Midi-Pyrénées are rich in history, natural resources, art, and architecture. Languedoc-Roussillon fits in along the Mediterranean from Collioure north through Perpignan, Narbonne, Beziers, and Montpellier, all once part of Catalonia and the crown of Aragon's medieval Mediterranean empire.

This chapter divides the region into three areas. The first covers the lively city of Toulouse. The second encompasses the area to the north and west of Toulouse, including the Gers *département,* Albi, the Lot Valley, Montauban, and verdant Gascony. The third extends southeast into the Languedoc-Roussillon and up the Mediterranean coast to the now-inland crossroads of Narbonne.

Great Itineraries

Getting to know this vast region would take several weeks, or even years. But it is possible to sample its finest offerings in three to seven days, if that's all you have.

Numbers in the text correspond to numbers in the margin and on the Midi-Pyrénées and the Languedoc-Roussillon and Toulouse maps.

IF YOU HAVE 3 DAYS

Bask in the rich rose color of ▦ **Toulouse** ①–㉔ for a day, and then head to **Cordes** ㉖, a fortified medieval village. Make Toulouse-Lautrec's hometown, ▦ **Albi** ㉕, your home for the night. On day three explore the medieval citadel at ▦ **Carcassonne** ㉝.

IF YOU HAVE 7 DAYS

Spend the first day and a half in ▦ **Toulouse** ①–㉔; then drive west to ▦ **Auch** ㉜, the capital of the Gers département. Next, head north to **Fleurance** ㉛ and the old Roman town of **Lectoure** ㉚. Next up is a true high point of the trip: the famous Romanesque sculptures of the abbey church at ▦ **Moissac** ㉘. On day three study up on the university town of **Montauban** ㉗ before stepping back in time in medieval **Cordes** ㉖. Spend the night in ▦ **Albi** ㉕. On the fourth day go south to **Carcassonne** ㉝ for more medieval history, before heading to **Mirepoix** ㉞, near the castle town of ▦ **Foix** ㉟ for the night. The next day drive into the Pyrénées, passing through **Tarascon-sur-Ariège** ㊱ to see the Grotte de Niaux, the mountain resorts of **Ax-les-Thermes** ㊲ and **Font-Romeu** ㊳, and the Vauban fortress town of **Mont-Louis** ㊵. Spend the night in nearby ▦ **Eyne** ㊴ before continuing east out of the Pyrénées toward the Mediterranean. Stop in the fortified town of **Villefranche-de-Conflent** ㊶ and the Abbaye de St-Martin-de-Canigou. Pass through the spa town of **Vernet-les-Bains** ㊷ on your way to **Prades** ㊸ and the Abbaye de St-Michel-de-Cuxa, and to **Céret** ㊹. Spend the sixth night in Roussillon's historic capital, ☷ **Perpignan** ㊻, or the fishing village of ☷ **Collioure** ㊺. On the final day drive north to **Salses** ㊼, which Hannibal once passed through, before leaving this region at **Narbonne** ㊽.

TOULOUSE

The ebullient city of Toulouse is the capital of the Midi-Pyrénées and the fourth-largest city in France. Just 96 km (60 mi) from the border with Spain, Toulouse's flavor is in many ways closer to southern European Spanish than to northern European French. Weathered redbrick buildings line sidewalks, giving the city its nickname, La Ville Rose (the Pink City). Downtown, the sidewalks and restaurants pulse late into the night with tourists, workers, college students, and technicians from the giant Airbus aviation complex headquartered outside the city.

The city was founded in the 4th century BC and quickly became an important part of Roman Gaul. In turn, it was made into a Visigothic and Carolingian capital before becoming a separate county in 843. Ruling from this Pyrenean hub and one of the great artistic and literary capitals of medieval Europe, the counts of Toulouse held sovereignty over nearly all of the Languedoc and maintained a brilliant court known for its fine troubadours and literature. In the early 13th century an alliance between the northern French nobility and the papacy, ostensibly to wipe out the Albigensian heresy (Catharism) but more realistically as an expansionist move, plundered Toulouse. The counts toppled, but Toulouse experienced a cultural and economic rebirth thanks to the *woad* (dye) trade; wealthy merchants' homes constitute Toulouse's main architectural patrimony.

In 1659 the Roussillon region was officially ceded to France by Spain in the Treaty of the Pyrénées, 17 years after Louis XIII conquered the area from Spain. Toulouse, at the intersection of the Garonne and the Canal du Midi, midway between the Massif Central and the Pyrénées, became an important nexus between Aquitania, Languedoc, and the Roussillon. Today Toulouse is France's second-largest university town after Paris and the center of France's aeronautical industry.

The huge garage beneath place du Capitole is a good place to park, and offers easy walking distance to all the major sites. If you leave your car in another garage, you can take the subway that runs east–west to central Toulouse; it costs 7 francs for one zone, 9.50 francs for two.

Old Toulouse

The area between the boulevards and the Garonne forms the historic nucleus of Toulouse. Originally part of Roman Gaul and later capital for Visigoths and Carolingians, by AD 1000 Toulouse was one of the artistic and literary centers of medieval Europe. Despite the 13th-century defeat by the lords of northern France, Toulouse quickly reemerged as a cultural and commercial power and has remained so ever since. The religious and civil structures bear witness to this illustrious past, even as the city's booming student life mirrors a dynamic present. This is the heart of Toulouse, with place du Capitole at its center.

A Good Walk

Start on **place du Capitole** ①, stopping at the donjon (keep) next to the **Capitole/Hôtel de Ville** ②, where there is a tourist office with maps. Rue du Taur, off the square, leads to **Notre-Dame du Taur** ③. Continue along rue du Taur to the **Ancien Collège de Périgord** ④ to see the oldest part of the medieval university. Toulouse's most emblematic church, **St-Sernin** ⑤, is at the end of rue du Taur on place St-Sernin. Next door is the **Musée St-Raymond** ⑥, the city's archaeological museum.

Leave place St-Sernin and cut out along rue Bellegarde to the boulevard de Strasbourg, site of the vegetable and produce market. Take the boulevard to rue Victor-Hugo and the **Marché Victor Hugo** ⑦, the large market hall. Find your way back to place du Capitole, cross the square, and take rue Gambetta past the colorfully restored Art Nouveau facade on the left to rue Lakanal. To the right is the **Église des Jacobins** ⑧, one of the city's most important architectural sites.

Back on rue Gambetta is the opulent **Hôtel de Bernuy** ⑨. Cut through rue Jean Suau to **place de la Daurade** ⑩. **Notre-Dame de la Daurade** ⑪ is the nonsteepled and domeless church on your left; the Café des Artistes is to the right. After a pause here, continue up quai de La Daurade past the sculpted goddesses on the facade of the École des Beaux-Arts to the **Pont Neuf** ⑫. Here you can cross the Garonne to the **Château d'Eau** ⑬, the water tower once used to store and pressurize the city's water system, now an excellent photographic gallery-museum. Or you can turn left on rue de Metz to the **Hôtel d'Assézat** ⑭, home of the Fondation Bemberg and its excellent collection of paintings. The nearby **Musée des Augustins** ⑮ has one of the world's best collections of Romanesque sculpture and is a de rigueur visit, especially on a rainy day.

Take a left on rue des Changes, once part of the Roman road that sliced through Toulouse from north to south; now it's a chic pedestrians-only shopping area. Stop to admire the **Hôtel d'Astorg** ⑯, the **Hôtel d'Arnault Brucelles** ⑰, and the **Hôtel Delpech** ⑱. Continue along rue des Changes to the intersection with rue de Temponières. Note the handsome wood-beam and brick building on the far right corner and the faux granite at the near left, complete with painted lines between the "stones" and trompe l'oeil windows (a reminder of the legendary window tax all good citizens struggled to avoid). The next street to the left, rue Tripière, loops through place du May onto rue du May, which leads to the **Musée du Vieux Toulouse** ⑲, housed in the Hôtel Dumay.

TIMING
This walk covers some 3 km (2 mi) and should take 3–4 hours depending on how long you spend at each sight. Most sights close punctually at noon, so it is essential that you get an early start. Or better yet, take a long lunch at some lovely spot and continue on again after 1 or 2, when places reopen.

Sights to See

❹ **Ancien Collège de Périgord** (Old Périgord College). This wooden structure, on the street side of the courtyard, is the oldest remnant of the 14th-century residential college. ✉ *56–58 rue du Taur.*

❷ **Capitole/Hôtel de Ville** (Capitol/Town Hall). The 18th-century Capitole is home to the Hôtel de Ville and the city's highly regarded opera company. The reception rooms are open when not in use for official functions or weddings. Halfway up the **Grand Escalier** (Grand Staircase) hangs a large painting of the *Jeux Floraux* (*Floral Games*), organized by a literary society created in 1324 to promote the local language, Langue d'Oc. The festival continues to this day: Poets give public readings here each May, and the best are awarded silver- and gold-plated violets, one of the emblems of Toulouse. At the top of the stairs is the **Salle Gervaise**, a hall used for weddings, beneath a series of paintings inspired by the themes of love and marriage. The mural at the far end of the room portrays the Isle of Cythères, where Venus received her lovers, alluding to a French euphemism for getting married: *embarquer pour Cythères* (to embark for Cythères). More giant paintings in the **Salle Henri-Martin**, named for the artist (1860–1943),

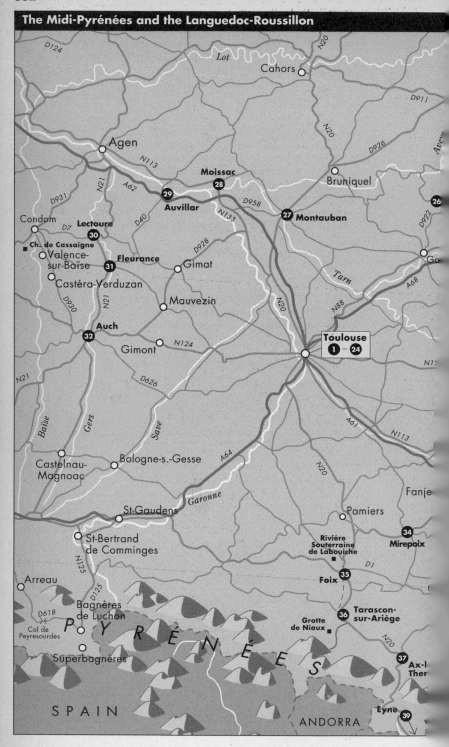

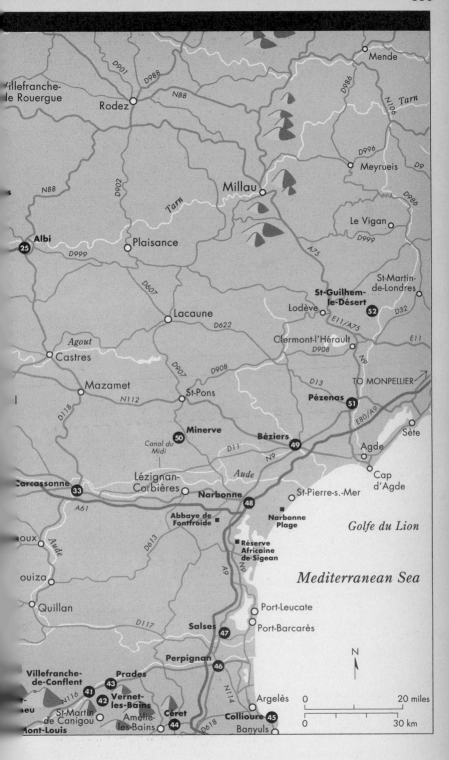

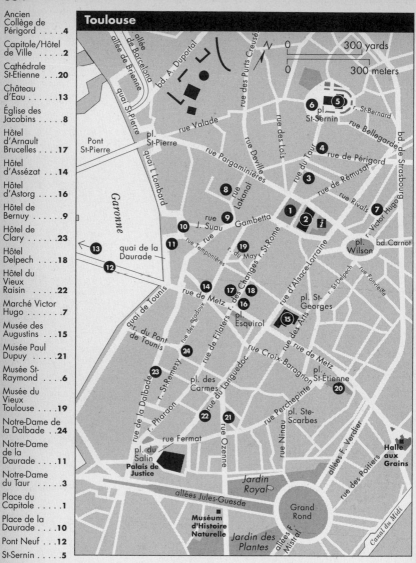

show the passing seasons set against the eternal Garonne. Look for Jean Jaurès, one of France's greatest socialists (1859–1914), in *Les Rêveurs* (*The Dreamers*); he's wearing a boater and a beige coat. At the far left end of the elegant **Salle des Illustres** (Hall of the Illustrious) is a large painting of a fortress under siege, portraying the women of Toulouse killing Simon de Montfort, leader of the Albigensian crusade against the Cathars, during the siege of Toulouse in 1218. ⊠ *Pl. du Capitole,* ☎ *05–61–11–34–12.* ▨ *Free.* ☉ *Weekdays 8:30–5, weekends 10–6.*

⑬ **Château d'Eau.** This 19th-century water tower at the far end of the Pont Neuf, once used to create water pressure, is now used for photography exhibits. ⊠ *1 pl. Laganne,* ☎ *05–61–77–09–40.* ▨ *15 frs.* ☉ *Wed.– Mon. 1:30–6.*

⑧ **Église des Jacobins.** An extraordinary structure built in the 1230s for the Dominicans (dubbed Jacobins in 1217 for their Parisian base in rue St-Jacques), this church has two rows of columns running the length of the nave—a standard feature of Dominican churches. The column on the right farthest from the entrance is one of the world's two or three finest examples of palm-tree vaulting. The original refectory is used for temporary art exhibitions. The cloister is one of the city's gems and in summer hosts piano concerts. ⊠ *Rue Lakanal.*

ⓘ **Hôtel d'Arnault Brucelles.** One of the tallest and best of Toulouse's 49 towers can be found at this 16th-century mansion. ⊠ *19 rue des Changes.*

ⓘ **Hôtel d'Assézat.** Built in 1555 by Toulouse's top Renaissance architect, Nicolas Bachelier, this mansion, considered the city's most elegant, has arcades and ornately carved doorways. It is now home to the **Fondation Bemberg**, an exceptional collection of paintings ranging from Tiepolo to Toulouse-Lautrec. Climb to the top of the tower for splendid views over the city's rooftops. ⊠ *Rue de Metz.* 🎫 *25 frs.* ⊙ *Daily 10–noon and 2–6.*

ⓘ **Hôtel d'Astorg.** This 16th-century mansion is notable for its lovely wooden stairways and galleries and for its top-floor *mirande,* a wooden balcony. ⊠ *16 rue des Changes.*

ⓘ **Hôtel de Bernuy.** Now part of a school, this mansion, around the corner from the Église des Jacobins, was built for Jean de Bernuy in the 16th century, when Toulouse was at its most prosperous. De Bernuy made his fortune exporting woad, the dark blue dye that made 18th-century Toulouse wealthy. De Bernuy's success is reflected in the use of stone, a costly material in this region of brick, and by the octagonal stair tower, the highest in the city. You may wander freely around the courtyard. ⊠ *Rue Gambetta.*

ⓘ **Hôtel Delpech.** Look for the biblical inscriptions in Latin carved in stone under the windows. ⊠ *20 rue des Changes.*

ⓘ **Marché Victor Hugo** (Victor Hugo Market). This hangarlike indoor market is always a refreshing stop. Consider eating lunch at one of the seven upstairs restaurants. **Chez Attila,** just to the left at the top of the stairs, is the best of them. ⊠ *Pl. Victor-Hugo.*

ⓘ **Musée des Augustins** (Augustinian Museum). In a former medieval Augustinian convent, the museum uses the sacristy, chapter house, and cloisters for displaying an outstanding array of Romanesque sculpture and religious paintings. ⊠ *Rue de Metz,* ☎ *05–61–22–21–82.* 🎫 *Museum 12 frs, exhibit 15 frs, museum and exhibit 20 frs; free Sun.* ⊙ *Wed. 10–9, Thurs.–Mon. 10–6.*

ⓘ **Musée St-Raymond.** The city's archaeological museum, next to the basilica of St-Sernin (☞ *below*), has an extensive collection of imperial Roman busts, as well as ancient coins, vases, and jewelry. ⊠ *Pl. St-Sernin,* ☎ *05–61–22–21–85.* 🎫 *12 frs.* ⊙ *Mon. and Wed.–Sat. 8–noon and 2–6, Sun. noon–6.*

ⓘ **Musée du Vieux Toulouse** (Museum of Old Toulouse). This museum is worthwhile for the building itself as much as for its collection of Toulouse memorabilia, paintings, sculptures, and documents. Be sure to note the ground floor fireplace and wooden ceiling. ⊠ *7 rue du May,* ☎ *05–61–13–97–24.* 🎫 *15 frs.* ⊙ *June–Sept., Mon.–Sat. 3–6.*

ⓘ **Notre-Dame de la Daurade.** Overlooking the Garonne is this 18th-century church. The name *Daurade* comes from *doré* (gilt), referring to the golden reflection given off by the mosaics decorating the 5th-century temple to the Virgin Mary that once stood on this site. ⊠ *Pl. de la Daurade.*

❸ **Notre-Dame du Taur.** Built on the spot where St. Saturnin (or Sernin), the martyred bishop of Toulouse, was dragged to his death in AD 257 by a rampaging bull, this church is famous for its *cloche-mur*, or wall tower. The wall looks like an extension of the facade and has inspired many similar versions throughout the region. ⊠ *Rue du Taur.*

❶ **Place du Capitole.** This vast, open square lined with shops and cafés in the city center is a good spot for getting your bearings or for soaking up some spring or winter sun. A very convenient parking lot is underneath.

❿ **Place de la Daurade.** On the Garonne, this is one of Toulouse's nicest squares. A stop at the Café des Artistes is almost obligatory. The corner of the quai offers a romantic view of the Garonne, the Hôtel Dieu across the river, and the Pont Neuf.

⓬ **Pont Neuf** (New Bridge). Despite its name, the graceful span of the Pont Neuf opened to traffic in 1632. The remains of the old bridge—one arch and the lighter-color outline on the brick wall of the **Hôtel-Dieu** (hospital)—are visible across the river. The 16th-century hospital was used for pilgrims on their way to Santiago de Compostela. Just over the bridge, on a clear day in winter, the snowcapped peaks of the Pyrénées are often visible in the distance, which is said to be a sign of imminent rain.

★ ❺ **St-Sernin.** Toulouse's most famous landmark and the world's largest Romanesque church once belonged to a Benedictine abbey, built in the 11th century to house pilgrims on their way to Santiago de Compostela in Spain. When illuminated at night, St-Sernin's five-tier octagonal tower glows red against the sky. Not all the tiers are the same: The first three, with their rounded windows, are Romanesque; the upper two, with their pointed Gothic windows, were added around 1300. ⊠ *Rue du Taur,* ☎ *05–61–21–70–18.* 🎫 *Crypt 15 frs.* ☉ *Daily 10–11:30 and 2:30–5:30.*

South of Rue de Metz

South of rue de Metz, you'll discover the cathedral of St-Étienne Cathedral, the antiques district along rue Perchepinte, and the town houses and palaces along the way on rue Ninau, rue Ozenne, and rue de la Dalbade—all among the top sights in Toulouse.

A Good Walk

From the **Cathédrale St-Étienne** ⑳ walk down rue Fermat to place Stes-Scarbes and the 17th-century Hôtel du Bourg, at No. 6. Rue Perchepinte, the old antiques district, is lined with noble 16th- to 18th-century houses all the way down to place du Salin. Take a left on rue Ninau; at No. 15 is the 16th-century Hôtel d'Ulmo, with its graceful tower, front stairs, courtyard, and interior garden; at No. 19 is the 18th-century Hôtel Castagnier. Place Montoulieu opens into rue Vélane, passing brick and timber-frame houses and the narrow 14th-century rue Neuve. At 16 rue Velane is the 17th-century Hôtel Penautier, with an elegant courtyard, stairway, and garden through the entryway next to the Laure Bandet antiques shop. Rue Vélane emerges back out on rue Perchepinte. Take a left on Perchepinte and a quick right onto rue de la Pléau to get to the **Musée Paul Dupuy** ㉑, a museum of medieval arts. Head right on rue Ozenne to No. 9, the 15th-century Hôtel de Dahus. Go left on rue du Languedoc; at No. 36 is the 15th- and 16th-century mansion **Hôtel du Vieux Raisin** ㉒, with its unusual octagonal tower. Continue back down rue du Languedoc to place du Salin, where farmers sell homemade foie gras on market mornings. Rue de la Dalbade, parallel to the Garonne, leads past one stately facade after another. The finest is No. 25, the **Hôtel de Clary** ㉓, also known as the Hôtel de Pierre (not for Peter but for the *pierre* (stone) used in its construction. Continue up the street to the church of **Notre-Dame de la Dalbade** ㉔. From here cut through rue Pont de Tounis, past the doorway on the left with the sculpted Gambrinus, legendary Flemish inventor of beer, and over the bridge (which used to span a branch of the Garonne) and out to quai de Tounis. The Pont Neuf is just up to the right.

TIMING
This walk will take you about three hours.

Sights to See

㉔ **Cathédrale St-Étienne.** The cathedral was erected in stages between the 13th and 17th centuries, though the nave and choir languished unfinished because of a lack of funds. A fine collection of 16th- and 17th-century tapestries traces the life of St. Stephen. In front of the cathedral is the city's oldest fountain, dating from the 16th century. ⊠ *Pl. St-Étienne.*

㉓ **Hôtel de Clary.** This mansion, known as the Hôtel de Pierre because of its unusual solid *pierre* (stone) construction—at the time considered a sign of great wealth—is one of the finest 17th- and 18th-century mansions on the street. The ornately sculpted stone facade was built in 1608 by parliamentary president François de Clary. ⊠ *25 rue de la Daurade.*

㉒ **Hôtel du Vieux Raisin.** Officially the Hôtel Maynier, for the original owner, the house became the Vieux Raisin (Old Grape) after the early name of the street and even earlier inn. Built in 1550, the mansion has an octagonal tower, male and female figures on the facade, and allegorical sculptures of the three ages of life—infancy, maturity, and old age—over the windows to the left. ⊠ *36 rue de Languedoc.*

㉑ **Musée Paul Dupuy.** This museum, dedicated to medieval applied arts, is housed in the Hôtel Pierre Besson, a 16th-century mansion. ⊠ *13 rue de la Pleau,* ☎ *05–61–14–65–50.* 🖼 *15 frs.* ⏲ *Wed. 10–9, Thurs.– Mon. 10–5.*

OFF THE
BEATEN PATH
MUSÉUM D'HISTOIRE NATURELLE – Surrounded by gardens, the Natural History Museum has a varied collection of stuffed birds and prehistoric exhibits. ⊠ *35 allée Jules-Guesde,* ☎ *05–61–52–00–14.* 🖼 *15 frs.* ⏲ *Wed.–Mon. 10–5.*

㉔ **Notre-Dame de la Dalbade.** Originally Sancta Maria de Ecclesia Alba, in Langue d'Oc (Ste-Marie de l'Église Blanche, in French, or St. Mary of the White Church—*alba* meaning "white" as in "albino"), the name of the church evolved into "de Albata" and later "Dalbade." Ironically, one of its outstanding features today is the colorful 19th-century ceramic tympanum over the Renaissance door. ⊠ *Pl. de la Dalbade.*

Dining and Lodging

$$$$ ✕ **Jardins de l'Opéra.** One of the most fashionable restaurants in town is in the Grand Hôtel de l'Opéra (☞ *below*). Intimate dining rooms and a covered terrace around a little pond make for undeniable, if slightly overformal, charm. The food is an innovative departure from local fare, with Gascon touches, such as the ravioli stuffed with foie gras. ⊠ *1 pl. du Capitole,* ☎ *05–61–23–07–76. Reservations essential. AE, DC, MC, V.*

$$$ ✕ **Au Pois Gourmand.** A good 40-minute walk (down the right bank of the river to the Pont des Catalanes, cross to the left bank, and continue along the gravel walkway to the fourth bridge downstream) or

a 15-minute cab ride from the Pont Neuf brings you to one of the best restaurants in Toulouse, in a lovely wooden house overlooking the Garonne. Colossally good-natured chef Jean-Claude Plazzotta, a specialist in wild mushrooms and spices, takes you on a memorable gastronomical tour of foie gras, lamb, *magret de canard* (duck breast), and squab. In summer dine in the garden or on the balcony with views of the river. ⊠ *3 rue Heybrard,* ☎ *05–61–31–95–95. AE, DC, MC, V. Closed Sun. No lunch Sat. and Mon.*

$$$ ✕ **Brasserie des Beaux-Arts.** Overlooking the Pont Neuf, this elegant brasserie is the place to be at sunset. Watch the colors change over the Garonne from a quayside window or a sidewalk table while enjoying delicious seafood, including a dozen varieties of oyster. The house white wine, a local St-Lannes from the nearby Gers region, is fresh and fruity, yet dry, and the service is impeccable. ⊠ *1 quai de la Daurade,* ☎ *05–61–21–12–12. AE, DC, MC, V.*

$$–$$$ ✕ **La Corde.** This little hideaway is worth taking the time to find. Built ★ into a lovely 15th-century corner tower hidden in the courtyard of the 16th-century Hôtel Bolé, La Corde claims the distinction of being the oldest restaurant in Toulouse. Try the *effiloché de canard aux pêches* (shredded duck with caramelized peach). ⊠ *4 rue Jules-Chalande,* ☎ *05–61–29–09–43. AE, DC, MC, V. Closed Sun. No lunch Mon.*

$$ ✕ **Au Bon Vivre.** This intimate bistro lined with tables with red-checked tablecloths is filled up at lunch and dinner every day. Quick, unpretentious, and always good, the house specialties include such dishes as roast monkfish in garlic, venison and cassoulet. ⊠ *15 pl. Wilson,* ☎ *05–61–23–07–17. AE, DC, MC, V.*

$$ ✕ **Chez Emile.** Downstairs you'll find a seafood menu that changes daily; if it's available, have the turbot in ginger. Upstairs is a cozy hideaway for a more traditional taste of Toulouse with classical specialties such as cassoulet and magret de canard. ⊠ *13 pl. St-Georges,* ☎ *05–61– 21–05–56. Reservations essential. AE, DC, MC, V. Closed last wk in Aug. and Sun.–Mon.*

$$$$ ⊞ **Grand Hôtel de l'Opéra.** This downtown doyen has an old-world ★ feel. Rooms are plush, with rich fabrics and painted headboards in many; some have views of place du Capitole. The three restaurants range from provincial bistro to international gourmet to Indian curry. ⊠ *1 pl. du Capitole, 31000,* ☎ *05–61–21–82–66,* FAX *05–61–23–41–04. 49 rooms. 3 restaurants, café, pool, health club. AE, DC, MC, V.*

$$$ ⊞ **Grand Hôtel d'Orléans.** This picturesque former stagecoach relay station was built in 1867 and still retains a certain 19th-century charm. Four floors of wooden balustrades with hanging plants center over a central patio. Rooms are small but cozy. ⊠ *72 rue Bayard 31000 (near Matabiau railroad station),* ☎ *05–61–62–98–47,* FAX *05–61–62–78– 24. 56 rooms. Restaurant, breakfast room. AE, DC, MC, V.*

$$$ ⊞ **Hôtel des Beaux-Arts.** In the thick of the most Toulousain part of ★ town, over the Pont Neuf and next to the Hôtel d'Assézat, this cozy place has small but tasteful rooms; the best have a tiny terrace overlooking the Garonne. The staff is attentive. ⊠ *1 pl. du Pont-Neuf, 31000,* ☎ *05–61–23–40–50,* FAX *05–61–22–02–27. 20 rooms. Breakfast room. AE, DC, MC, V.*

$–$$ ⊞ **Hôtel Albert I.** The building may seem undistinguished and the reception hall is no Versailles, but the rooms are cheerful and spacious (especially the older ones with giant fireplaces and mirrors). The extremely warm and personable owner, Madame Hilaire, is on hand to give suggestions of all kinds. A Continental breakfast is served, and nearby parking can be arranged by the hotel. ⊠ *8 rue Rivals, 31000,* ☎ *05–61–21–17–91,* FAX *05–61–21–09–64. 50 rooms. Breakfast room. AE, DC, MC, V.*

$ 🖼 **Hôtel du Grand Balcon.** This charmingly down-at-the-heels spot has
★ views of place du Capitole from some of its corner rooms. As the spot
where Antoine de St-Exupéry, author of *The Little Prince*, stayed with
his fellow aviators early in the 20th century, the hotel has a cult following and has been used as a film location for several French films.
⊠ *8 rue Romiguières, 31000,* 🕾 *05–61–21–48–08,* FAX *05–61–21–59–
98. 54 rooms. Breakfast room. AE, DC, MC, V.*

Nightlife and the Arts

For a schedule of events contact the city tourist office. If you want to
stay up late—and they do in Toulouse—a complete list of clubs and
discos can be found in the weekly *Toulouse Pratique,* available at any
newsstand.

The main music venues and theaters in Toulouse are the **Halle Aux
Grains** (⊠ Pl. Dupuy, 🕾 05–61–63–18–65); **Théâtre du Capitole** (⊠ Pl.
du Capitole, 🕾 05–61–23–21–35); **Théâtre Daniel Sorano** (⊠ 35 allée
Jules-Guesde, 🕾 05–61–25–66–87); **Théâtre de la Digue** (⊠ 3 rue de la
Digue, 🕾 05–61–42–97–79); and **Théâtre du Taur** (⊠ 69 rue du Taur,
🕾 05–61–21–77–13). So many opera singers perform at the **Théâtre du
Capitole** and the **Halle aux Grains** that the city is known as the *capitale
du bel canto.* The opera season lasts from October until late May, with
occasional summer presentations. A wide variety of dance companies
perform in Toulouse: The **Ballet du Capitole** stages classical ballets; **Bal-
let-Théâtre Joseph Russillo** and **Compagnie Jean-Marc Matos** put on
modern dance concerts. The **Centre National Chorégraphique de Toulouse**
welcomes international companies each year in the St-Cyprien quarter.

For general carousing and carrying on, the **Bagamoyo** (⊠ 27 rue des
Couteliers, 🕾 05–62–26–11–36) is a lively spot for nocturnal snacks of
simple but delicious African fare. **Bar Basque** (⊠ 7 pl. St-Pierre, 🕾 05–
61–21–55–64) is one of the many good watering holes around place St-
Pierre. **Le Bistro à Vins** (⊠ 5 rue Riguepels, 🕾 05–61–25–20–41), near
the church of St-Étienne, is a hot spot for the third-Thursday-in-Novem-
ber Beaujolais Nouveau blowout. Brazilian guitarists perform at **La
Bonita** (⊠ 112 Grand-Rue St-Michel, 🕾 05–62–26–36–45). For jazz try
Le Café des Allées (⊠ 64 allée Charles-de-Fitte, 🕾 05–62–27–14–46),
a hothouse for local musicians. **Café Le Griot** (⊠ 34 rue des Blanchers,
🕾 05–62–36–41–56) features a number of American duos and trios.

At **El Mexicano** (⊠ 37 rue de l'Industrie, 🕾 05–61–63–17–36) a crush
of people inhales tequila and 3-inch steaks. **La Péniche** (⊠ Canal de Bri-
enne, 90 allée de Barcelone, 🕾 05–61–21–13–40) is a local gay bar. Begin
your night on the town at **Père Louis** (⊠ 45 rue des Tourneurs, 🕾 05–
61–21–33–45), an old-fashioned winery (and restaurant) with barrels
for tables and vintage photographs. **Puerto Habana** (⊠ 12 port St-Étienne, 🕾 05–61–54–45–61) is the place for salsa music. If you're looking for onion soup and other treats in the wee hours, head for **St-André**
(⊠ 39 rue St-Rome, 🕾 05–61–22–56–37), open 7 PM to dawn (closed
Sunday). Local glitterati and theater stars go to **L'Ubu** (⊠ 16 rue St-Rome,
🕾 05–61–23–97–80), the city's top nightspot for 20 years.

Outdoor Activities and Sports

Toulouse is just 100 km (60 mi) from the nearest peaks. For information about hiking, skiing, mountain refuges, and just about anything
having to do with the Pyrénées, check with the **Pyrénées Club** (⊠ 29
rue du Taur, 🕾 05–61–21–11–44). There are two good 18-hole golf
courses near Toulouse: **Golf Club de Toulouse** (⊠ Vieille Toulouse, 🕾
05–61–73–45–48) and **Golf Club de Toulouse Palmola** (⊠ Rte. d'Albi,

☎ 05–61–84–20–50). If you want to go horseback riding, try **Pony City** (✉ St-Paul, 40 km [25 mi] east of Toulouse, ☎ 05–63–42–06–45).

Shopping

Toulouse is a chic design outlet for clothing and artifacts of all kinds. **Rue St-Rome, rue Croix Baragnon, rue des Changes,** and **rue d'Alsace-Lorraine** are all good shopping streets.

ALBI AND THE GERS

Along the banks of the Tarn to the northeast of Toulouse is Albi, Toulouse's rival in rose colors. West from Albi, along the river, the land opens up to the rural Gers *département,* home of the heady brandy Armagnac and heart of the former dukedom of Gascony. Studded with châteaux—from simple medieval fortresses to ambitious classical residences—and with tiny, isolated villages, the Gers is an easy place to fall in love with, or in.

Albi

★ **㉕** *75 km (47 mi) northeast of Toulouse.*

Toulouse-Lautrec's native Albi is a well-preserved and busy provincial market town. In its heyday, Albi was a major center for Cathars, members of a dualistic and ascetic religious movement critical of the hierarchical and worldly ways of the Catholic Church. Pick up a copy of the excellent visitor booklet (in English) from the **tourist office** (✉ Pl. Ste-Cécile, ☎ 05–63–49–48–80), and follow the walking tours—of the old city, the old ramparts, and the banks of the River Tarn.

The huge **Cathédrale Ste-Cécile,** with its intimidating clifflike walls, resembles a cross between a castle and an ocean liner. It was constructed as a symbol of the church's return to power after the 13th-century Crusade that wiped out the Cathars. The interior is an astonishingly ornate reply to the massive austerity of the outer walls. Maestro Donnelli and a team of 16th-century Italian artists covered every possible surface with religious scenes and brightly colored patterns. The most striking fresco is a 15th-century depiction of the Last Judgment, on the west wall. ✉ *Pl. Ste-Cécile.*

★ The **Musée Toulouse-Lautrec** occupies the **Palais de la Berbie** (Berbie Palace), set between the cathedral and the Pont Vieux (Old Bridge) in a garden designed by the famed André Le Nôtre (who created the famous "green geometries" at Versailles). Built in 1265 as a defensive fortress, the fortress was transformed in 1905 into a museum to honor Albi's most famous son: Belle Epoque painter Henri de Toulouse-Lautrec (1864–1901). Toulouse-Lautrec left Albi for Paris in 1882 and soon became famous for his colorful and tumultuous evocations of the bohemian glamour in and around Montmartre. Son of a wealthy and aristocratic family (Lautrec is a town not far from Toulouse), the young Henri suffered from a genetic bone deficiency and broke both legs as a child, which stunted his growth. The artist's fascination with the decadent side of life led to an early grave at the age of 37 and Hollywood immortalization in the 1954 John Huston film *Moulin Rouge.* With more than 1,000 of the artist's works, the Albi exhibit is the country's largest Toulouse-Lautrec collection. ✉ *Just off pl. Ste-Cécile,* ☎ *05–63–49–48–70.* 💶 *25 frs, gardens free.* ☉ *May–Sept., daily 10–noon and 2–6; Oct.–Apr., Wed.–Mon. 10–noon and 2–5.*

Leaving the Palais de la Berbie behind you, walk to the 11th- to 15th-century college and **Cloître de St-Salvy** (cloister; ✉ Rue St-Cécile). Next, visit Albi's finest restored traditional house, the **Maison du Vieil Albi** (Old Albi House; ⊠ On corner of rue de la Croix-Blanche and Puech-Bérenguer). If you're a real fan of Toulouse-Lautrec, stop by his birth-place, the **Maison Natale de Toulouse-Lautrec** (⊠ 14 rue Henri de Toulouse-Lautrec). Rue de l'Hôtel de Ville, two streets west of the Maison Natale, leads past the *Mairie* (City Hall), with its hanging globes of flowers, to Albi's main square, **place du Vigan.** Take a break in one of the two main cafés, Le Pontie or Le Vigan.

Dining and Lodging

$$$ ✕ **Le Moulin de la Mothe.** This onetime mill on the banks of the Tarn is neatly tucked into the river, surrounded by lush vegetation. Chef-owner Michel Pellaprat specializes in inventive cooking based on high-quality local products. ⊠ *Rue de Lamothe,* ☎ *05–63–60–38–15. AE, MC, V. Closed Wed. Sept.–June. No dinner Sun. Sept.–June.*

$$ ✕ **Le Jardin des Quatre Saisons.** A good-value menu and superb fish dishes are the reasons for this restaurant's excellent reputation. Chef-owner Georges Bermond's house specialties include mussels baked with leeks and *suprême de sandre* (a freshwater fish cooked in wine). ⊠ *19 bd. de Strasbourg,* ☎ *05–63–60–77–76. AE, MC, V. Closed Mon.*

$$–$$$ ✕🏠 **Hostellerie St-Antoine.** Founded in 1734, this hotel in the center of town is one of the oldest in France. Modern renovations have made it eminently comfortable. Room 30 has a pleasing view of the garden; pristine white furnishings give it a spacious feel. The superb restaurant serves classical cuisine, such as *foie gras de canard* (duck liver) and sad-dle of hare with a foie gras–based sauce. ⊠ *15 rue St-Antoine, 81000,* ☎ *05–63–54–04–60,* 𝖥𝖠𝖷 *05–63–47–10–47. 50 rooms. Restaurant, parking (fee). AE, DC, MC, V.*

$$ ✕🏠 **Hôtel Chiffre.** In a centrally located town house, this hotel has im-peccable rooms overlooking a cozy garden. The restaurant, the Bateau Ivre, run by chef Michel Gouty, is one of Albi's finest. ⊠ *50 rue Séré-de-Rivières, 81000,* ☎ *05–63–54–04–60,* 𝖥𝖠𝖷 *05–63–47–20–61. 40 rooms. Restaurant. AE, DC, MC, V.*

$$ ✕🏠 **Mercure Albi Bastides.** This converted 18th-century *vermicellerie* (noodle mill), across the river from the old center of Albi, has rooms that are functional and modern, if somewhat cramped. The views of the Tarn and the Pont Vieux are spectacular, however. In the stylish restaurant (which doesn't serve lunch weekends), try chef Gérard Bel-bèze's regional specialties or his "Toulouse-Lautrec menu." ⊠ *41 rue Porta, 81000,* ☎ *05–63–47–66–66; 800/637–2873 U.S. reservations; 0181/741–3100 U.K. reservations,* 𝖥𝖠𝖷 *05–63–46–18–40. 56 rooms. Restaurant, free parking. AE, DC, MC, V.*

$$–$$$ 🏠 **La Pérouse.** This intimate and tasteful enclave is centrally located and supremely quiet. Rooms are comfortable, and the garden is a lush and shady spot to rest between sorties in and around Albi. There's also a secluded swimming pool. ⊠ *21 pl. Lapérouse, 81000,* ☎ *05–63–54–69–22,* 𝖥𝖠𝖷 *05–63–38–03–69. 22 rooms. Pool, tennis court. AE, DC, MC, V.*

$$ 🏠 **Le George V.** This little in-town B&B is near the cathedral and the train station. Each room is unique, and the garden makes for a pleasant retreat in summer. ⊠ *29 av. Maréchal-Joffre 81000,* ☎ *05–63–54–24–16,* 𝖥𝖠𝖷 *05–63–49–90–78. 9 rooms. Pool, tennis court. AE, DC, MC, V.*

Outdoor Activities and Sports

Eighteen-hole golf courses can be found at **Golf d'Albi** (⊠ Château de Lasbordes, ☎ 05–63–54–98–07) and **Golf de Florentin** (⊠ Le Bosc, Florentin, 29 km [17 mi] from Albi, ☎ 05–63–55–20–50).

Shopping

Around **place Ste-Cécile** are numerous clothing, book, music, and antiques shops. The finest foie gras in town is found at **Albi Foie Gras** (✉ 29 rue Mariès, ☎ 05–63–38–21–23). **L'Artisan Chocolatier** (✉ 4 rue Dr- Camboulives, on pl. du Vigan, ☎ 05–63–38–95–33) is famous for its chocolate.

Albi has many **produce markets:** One takes place Tuesday through Sunday in the market halls near the cathedral; another is held on Sunday morning on place Ste-Cécile. A Saturday-morning **flea and antiques market** is held in the Halle du Castelviel (✉ Pl. du Castelviel).

Cordes

★ ㉖   *25 km (15 mi) northwest of Albi, 80 km (50 mi) northeast of Toulouse.*

The picture-book hilltop village of Cordes, built in 1222 by Count Raymond VII of Toulouse, is one of the most impressively preserved *bastides* (fortified medieval towns built along a strict grid plan) in France. When mists steal up from the Cérou Valley and enshroud the hillside, Cordes appears to hover in midair, hence its nickname, Cordes-sur-Ciel (Cordes-on-Sky/Heaven). Many of the restored medieval houses are occupied by artisans and craftspeople; the best crafts shops are found along the main street, Grande-Rue. The village's venerable covered market, supported by 24 octagonal stone pillars, is also noteworthy, as is the nearby well, which is more than 300 ft deep.

Dining and Lodging

$$$ ✕⊞ **Le Grand Écuyer.** The dramatic hilltop setting of this hotel suits it
★   well—it's a perfectly preserved medieval mansion. Rooms have period furnishings; the best, Planol, Horizon, and Ciel, have grand views of the rolling countryside. Yves Thuriès is one of the region's best chefs and chocolatiers; sample his salmon and sole twist in vanilla or the guinea fowl supreme in pastry. Menus begin around 200 francs and culminate in a seven-course gourmet extravaganza that costs more than 500 francs. ✉ *Rue Voltaire, 81170,* ☎ *05–63–53–79–50,* FAX *05–63–53–79–51. 13 rooms. Restaurant. AE, DC, MC, V. Closed mid-Oct.–early Apr.*

$$ ✕⊞ **L'Hostellerie du Vieux Cordes.** This magnificent 13th-century house is built around a lovely courtyard shaded by a 200-year-old wisteria and dotted with tiny white tables. Guest rooms are richly decorated but not nearly as opulent as the vast crimson dining rooms. There are no fixed menus; each dish costs 50 francs (the restaurant is closed Monday from November to Easter and also the month of January). ✉ *Rue St-Michel, 81170,* ☎ *05–63–53–79–20,* FAX *05–63–56–02–47. 21 rooms. Restaurant. AE, DC, MC, V. Closed Jan. 1–mid-Feb.*

Montauban

㉗   *59 km (37 mi) west of Cordes, 52 km (32 mi) north of Toulouse.*

Montauban, built in 1144, was one of the first bastides in France. The town is best known as the birthplace of the great painter Jean-Auguste-Dominique Ingres (1780–1867) and is home to a superb collection of his works.

★   The **Musée Ingres,** overlooking the Tarn River, is housed in what was originally the château of Edward the Black Prince (1330–76), who was briefly ruler of the English principality of Aquitaine. The château was later converted into a bishop's palace in the 17th century. Ingres has the second floor to himself; note the contrast between his love of myth (*Ossian's Dream*) and his deadpan, uncompromising portraiture (*Madame Gonse*). Ingres was the last of the great French Classicists, who favored line over color and used classical antiquity as a source for subject matter. However, Ingres fell out of favor with the strict Neo-classicists of his day as a result of his unusual combination of superb draftsmanship and sensuality. Later, artists such as Degas, Renoir, and Picasso acknowledged their debt to Ingres. Most paintings here are from Ingres's excellent private collection, ranging from his followers (Théodore Chassériau) and precursors (Jacques-Louis David) to old masters. ⊠ *19 rue de l'Hôtel de Ville,* ☎ *05–63–22–12–92.* ⊡ *20 frs.* ☉ *July–Aug., Mon.–Sat. 9:30–noon and 1:30–6, Sun. 1:30–6; Sept.–June, Tues.–Sat. 10–noon and 2–6.*

The 14th-century **Pont Vieux** (Old Bridge), with its seven pointed arches, is another of Montauban's attractions. A chapel dedicated to St. Catherine, protector of mariners (Montauban had some 3,000 river men during the 18th century), used to stand on the fourth piling until washed away by a flood in the 18th century.

In the 12th-century arcaded and brick-vaulted **place National,** in the center of Montauban, look for the simple wooden cross marking the medieval execution and pillory site (it's in front of the Brasserie des Arts, a good spot for lunch or coffee). Note the sundial on the north side of the square with its carpe diem inscription UNA TIBI ("one for you"— meaning, your hour will come). Markets are held on the square almost every day; Wednesday markets are held across the river on place Lalaque.

The mid-13th-century **Église St-Jacques** (⊠ Pl. Victor Hugo), with its Toulouse-style steeple, is a dark, single-nave church of austere dignity.

The 17th- to 18th-century **Notre-Dame Cathedral** (⊠ Pl. Franklin Roosevelt) was built of white stone to contrast with the city's redbrick architecture and to proclaim Catholicism's triumph over Protestantism. On display here is a poorly illuminated Ingres masterpiece, *Vow of Louis XIII.*

Dining and Lodging

$$ ✕ **Le Rabelais.** The fresh ingredients and graceful vaulted dining room make this a top midtown dining choice. Especially good is the *galinail de Montauban au millas* (farmyard hen with polenta). ⊠ *13 rue de l'Hôtel de Ville,* ☎ *05–63–63–21–09. AE, DC, MC, V. Closed Sun.–Mon.*

$$–$$$ ⊞ **Hôtel du Midi–Mercure.** Refurbished in 1999 by the Mercure chain, the Hôtel du Midi combines old-world elegance with modern comforts. A plaque on the hotel's facade attests that Manuel Azaña, last president of the Spanish Republic, died here in exile in 1940. ⊠ *12 rue Notre-Dame 82000,* ☎ *05–63–63–17–23,* 𝖥𝖠𝖷 *05–63–66–43–66. 40 rooms. Restaurant, bar. AE, DC, MC, V.*

Moissac

★ ㉓ *29 km (18 mi) west of Montauban, 72 km (45 mi) northwest of Toulouse.*

Moissac has the largest and probably the most beautiful still-standing Romanesque cloisters and one of the region's most remarkable abbey churches. The port—at the confluence of the Tarn, Aveyron, and Garonne rivers, and the lateral canal—is a surprising sight so far from the sea. For a spectacular view over this Mississippi-like riverine expanse, France's widest, head to the lookout point at Boudou, 2 km (1 mi) west of Moissac off route N113.

★ Little is left of the original 7th-century **Abbaye St-Pierre,** and religious wars laid waste its 11th-century replacement. Today's abbey, dating mostly from the 15th century, narrowly escaped demolition early in the 20th century when the Bordeaux-Sète railroad was rerouted within feet of the cloisters. Each of the 76 capitals has a unique pattern of animals, geometric motifs, and religious or historical scenes. Look for the Cain and Abel story on the 19th column to the right of the entry point. The 63rd column (fourth back from the northeast corner) shows St-Sernin being dragged to his death by a bull. The highlight of the abbey church is the 12th-century south portal, topped with carvings illustrating the Apocalypse. Especially noteworthy is the representation of a sweetly mournful Jeremiah, author of the Old Testament Book of Lamentations, on the lower part of the door. The **Musée des Arts et Traditions Populaires** (Folk Art Museum), in the abbey, contains regional treasures and a room of local costumes. ⊠ *6 bis rue de l'Abbaye,* ☎ *05–63–04–05–73.* 🖾 *Cloisters and museum 25 frs.* ☉ *Oct.–Mar., Tues.–Sun. 9–noon and 2–5; Apr.–June and Sept., Tues.–Sun 9–noon and 2–6; July–Aug., Tues.–Sun. 9–noon and 2–7.*

Dining and Lodging

$$–$$$ ✕🖾 **Le Pont Napoléon.** One of France's rising culinary stars, Michel
★ Dussau, who trained with Alain Ducasse (and others), is a master of refined simplicity and innovative combinations of regional products. Try such dishes as scallops with chestnut-flour pasta or *foie gras pôelé* (sautéed goose liver), and anything made with Moissac's *chasselas* grape (the restaurant is closed Wednesday). Guest rooms are furnished with elegant, authentic antiques and have lovely views of the Tarn and the bridge. ⊠ *2 allée Montbello, 82200,* ☎ *05–63–04–01–55,* 🖃 *05–63–04–34–44. 12 rooms. Restaurant, bar. AE, DC, MC, V.*

$$–$$$ 🖾 **Château St-Roch.** Thirty minutes west of Moissac, this turreted neo-Renaissance château is an eye-stopper; public rooms are on display to nonguests for 25 francs. Guest rooms are huge, with coffered ceilings and French doors leading onto terraces. Two drawbacks: the barrackslike bar and the dining room, in a separate, modern building. The food is just acceptable, so consider eating elsewhere. On the plus side, breakfasts—brought to your room—include good coffee and fresh bread. ⊠ *82340 Le Pin (19 km [12 mi] west of Moissac; 5 km [3 mi] east of Auvillar),* ☎ *05–63–95–95–22,* 🖃 *05–63–94–85–54. 15 rooms. Restaurant, bar. MC, V. Closed Jan.–Apr.*

Auvillar

㉙ *23 km (14 mi) west of Moissac.*

Formally classified as one of France's most beautiful villages, Auvillar is centered on a circular, covered **Halle aux Grains** (Grain Market) built in 1825. Most other buildings in the town are equally lovely, including the stone-and-brick **Tour de l'Horloge** (Clock Tower). The 18th-century brick-and-beam **Maison des Consuls** (Consuls' House) was the local magistrate's home; it is now a hotel.

Lectoure

㉚ *57 km (35 mi) southwest of Moissac, 94 km (58 mi) northwest of Toulouse.*

Once a Roman city and a fortified Gallic town, Lectoure stands on a promontory above the Gers Valley in the heart of the former dukedom of Gascony. Lectoure was ravaged in 1473 when Louis XI attacked its fortress and established direct royal rule by killing the last count of Armagnac, but there's still plenty to see in its old arched streets. The 13th-century **Fontaine Diane** (Diana's Fountain; ⊠ Rue Fontélie) is the town's most interesting monument, as well as a visual feast. The 15th-to 16th-century **Cathédrale St-Gervais et St-Protais** (⊠ Pl. de la Cathédrale) is an enormous structure for a town of this size and is an immense trove of art and architectural treats.

The **Musée Municipal** (Town Museum), near the cathedral, is in the vaulted cellars of the former **Palais Épiscopal** (Bishop's Palace), now the Town Hall. Its collection contains an array of 2,000-year-old Gallo-Roman artifacts ranging from tweezers and hairbrushes to Latin-engraved pre-Christian altars and heads of sacrificial bulls. Ask about the sculpture of Priapus, god of fertility, and what happened to his allegedly heroic virility. ✉ *Pl. de la Cathédrale, in the Hôtel de Ville,* ☎ *05–62–68–70–22.* 🎫 *25 frs.* ☉ *Daily 9–noon and 2–6.*

Dining and Lodging

$$–$$$ ✕🏨 **Hôtel de Bastard.** This elegant hotel and restaurant on an 18th-
★ century estate is the creation of chef Jean-Luc Arnaud and his wife, Anne (who speaks excellent English). The rooms, while not spacious, are modern and comfortable and have fine views over the fields. The innovative cuisine is prepared with fresh local produce; try the *il était trois foies,* foie gras prepared three ways—raw, steamed, and grilled—all with herbs and vegetables. ✉ *Rue Lagrange, 32700,* ☎ *05–62–68–82–44,* 🅵🅰🅇 *05–62–68–76–81. 28 rooms. Restaurant, pool. AE, DC, MC, V. Closed mid-Dec.–early Feb.*

Fleurance

③① 20 km (12 mi) southeast of Lectoure, 83 km (50 mi) northwest of Toulouse, 24 km (14 mi) north of Auch.

Fleurance is one of several bastide towns in the Armagnac region. Founded in 1272, the town's grid street plan centers on place de la République, with its handsome vaulted *halle* (covered market hall), built in 1834. The bronze maidens at the four corners of the market hall represent the four seasons. Markets are held here Tuesday and Saturday. The Gothic church of **St-Laurent** (✉ Pl. de l'Église) has three stained-glass windows by Arnaud de Moles, whose most famous windows are in Auch (☞ *below*).

Auch

③② 24 km (14 mi) south of Fleurance, 77 km (46 mi) west of Toulouse, 73 km (44 mi) northeast of Tarbes.

Auch, the capital of the Gers département, is best known for its stunning Gothic **Cathédrale de Ste-Marie.** Most of the stained-glass windows in the choir were done by Arnaud de Moles; vividly colorful, they portray biblical figures and handsome pre-Christian sibyls, or prophetesses. The oak choir stalls are intricately carved with more than 1,500 biblical and mythological figures that took 50 years and three generations of artisans to complete. In June classical music concerts are held here. ✉ *Pl. Salinis.* 🎫 *15 frs.* ☉ *Daily 8–noon and 2–6.*

On the first floor of the 15th-century brick and wood-beam Maison Fedel, on the other side of the cathedral, is the **tourist office** (✉ 1 rue Dessoles), where you can obtain maps and information.

Across place Salinis is a terrace overlooking the Gers River. A monumental flight of 370 steps leads down to the riverbank. Halfway down is the **Statue of D'Artagnan,** the musketeer immortalized by Alexandre Dumas. Although Dumas set the action of his historical drama *The Three Musketeers* in the 1620s, the true D'Artagnan—Charles de Batz—was born in 1620, probably in Castlemore, near Lupiac, and did not become a musketeer until 1645.

Off place Salinis, in a wood-beam and brick house known as the **Maison d'Henri IV** (✉ 32 rue d'Espagne), the French and Navarran monarch is said to have cavorted with several of his 57 mistresses. A left at the end of rue d'Espagne will take you through one of the *pouster-les*, steep and narrow alleys leading up from the river.

The **Musée des Jacobins,** behind the former Archbishop's Palace (now the Préfecture), has a fine collection of Latin-American art, pre-Columbian pottery, and Gallo-Roman relics. Look for the white-marble epitaph in Latin dedicated by a grief-stricken Roman mistress to her dog Myia, for whose *"douces morcures"* ("sweet love bites") she mourned. ⊠ *Rue Daumesnil,* ☎ *05–62–05–74–79.* ☞ *25 frs.* ⊙ *May–Oct., Tues.–Sun. 10–noon and 2–6; Nov.–Apr., Tues.–Sat. 10–noon and 2–5.*

Dining and Lodging

$$ ✕ **Café Gascon.** This ramshackle and romantic little spot is right over
★   the Halles aux Herbes. The fare is typical country Gascon with inno-vative personal touches such as the *salade folle* (duck prepared three different ways) with apples, tomatoes, and raspberries on lettuce). Chef, poet, and painter Georges Nosella is likely to come out to your table and make your *café gascon* (coffee, whipped cream, and flam-ing Armagnac) with grace and humor. ⊠ *5 rue Lamartine,* ☎ *05–62–61–88–08. AE, DC, MC, V. Closed Sun. No dinner Mon.–Wed.*

$$$ ✕▥ **Hôtel de France.** Roland Garreau has taken over the restaurant
★   at this classic central Auch hotel; his specialty is gourmet interpreta-tions of country cooking. The brasserie serves simpler but still excel-lent fare. The duplex suite behind the circular dormer window on the facade facing the square is worth a look, even if you resist the temp-tation to spend the $350 it costs to sleep there. Other rooms are cozy, if a little small and overly fabric filled. ⊠ *Pl. de la Libération, 32000,* ☎ *05–62–61–71–71,* ᴲᴬˣ *05–62–61–71–81. 29 rooms. 2 restaurants, bar, shop. AE, DC, MC, V. Closed Jan.*

Shopping

Caves de l'Hôtel de France (⊠ Rue d'Étigny) sells a wide selection of Armagnac.

LANGUEDOC-ROUSSILLON

Draw a line between Toulouse and Narbonne, on the Mediterranean: The area to the south down to the Pyrénées, long part of the Catalo-nia-dominated House of Aragón, is known as the Roussillon. Rolling plains sweep along the northern border; the Pyrénées line the south-ern end; and craggy hills, divided by gorges, lie in between. On the east-ern side are the Mediterranean and the Côte Vermeille (Vermilion Coast)—home to the villages once so beloved by Matisse, Picasso, and other great artists of the early 20th century; on the western side is the Ariège Valley. The Languedoc begins south of Narbonne at Salses.

Carcassonne

★ ㉝ *88 km (55 mi) southeast of Toulouse, 105 km (65 mi) south of Albi.*

Set atop a hill overlooking lush green countryside and the Aude River, Carcassonne is a medieval town that looks lifted from the pages of a storybook—literally, perhaps, as its circle of towers and battlements (comprising the longest city walls in Europe) is said to be the setting for Charles Perrault's *Puss in Boots.* The oldest sections of the walls, built by the Romans in the 1st century AD, were later enlarged by the Visigoths in the 5th century. Charlemagne once set siege to the settle-ment in the 9th century, only to be outdone by one Dame Carcas, a clever woman who boldly fed the last of the city's wheat to a pig in full view of the conqueror; Charlemagne, thinking this indicated end-less food supplies, promptly decamped, and the exuberant townsfolk named their city after her. During the 13th century Louis IX (St. Louis) and his son Philip the Bold strengthened Carcassonne's fortifications— so much so that the town became considered inviolable by marauding armies and was duly nicknamed "the virgin of Languedoc." A town that can never be taken in battle is often abandoned, however, and for centuries Carcassonne fell under a Sleeping Beauty spell. It was only awakened in the mid-19th century by the painter and historian Viollet-le-Duc (who found his greatest fame restoring Paris's Notre-Dame) during the 19th-century craze for chivalry and the Gothic style. Today the town is more Viollet than authentic medieval, but it still remains one of the most romantic sights in France.

The town is divided by the river into two parts—La Cité, the fortified upper town, and the lower, newer city (the *ville basse*), known simply as Carcassonne. Unless you are staying at a hotel in the upper town, private vehicles are not permitted; you must park in the lot (15 francs) across the road from the drawbridge. Be aware that the train station is in the lower town, which means a cab ride or a 45-minute walk up to the old city. Plan on spending at least a couple of hours exploring the walls and peering over the battlements across sun-drenched plains toward the distant Pyrénées.

Today the 1844 renovation done by Viollet-le-Duc is considered almost as much a work of art as the actual medieval town. In 1835, when the historic-monument inspector (and poet) Prosper Mérimée arrived, he was so appalled by the dilapidated state of the walls he commissioned Viollet-le-Duc to restore the town. Once inside the walls of the upper town, however, 21st-century tourism takes over. The streets are lined with souvenir shops, crafts boutiques, and restaurants. Staying overnight within the ancient walls lets you savor the timeless atmosphere after the daytime hordes are gone.

The 12th-century **Château Comtal** is the last inner bastion of Carcassonne. It has a drawbridge and a museum, the **Musée Lapidaire,** where stone sculptures found in the area are on display. ☎ 04–68–25–01–66. ⌨ 32 frs. ⊙ June–Sept., daily 9–6; Oct.–May, daily 9–noon and 2–5.

The best part about the the ville basse, built between the Aude and the Canal du Midi, is the **Musée des Beaux-Arts** (Fine Arts Museum). It houses a nice collection of porcelain, 17th- and 18th-century Flemish paintings, and works by local artists—including some stirring battle scenes by Jacques Gamelin (1738–1803). ⊠ *Rue Verdun,* ☎ 04–68–72–47–22. ⌨ *Free.* ⊙ *Mon.–Sat. 10–noon and 2–5.*

Dining and Lodging

$$ ✕ **Le Languedoc.** This restaurant in the ville basse serves up light versions of the region's specialties, from confit to game. The flowery patio is a perfect spot for a long evening dinner in summer. Be sure to try the quail with foie gras, if available. ⊠ *32 allée d'Iéna,* ☎ 04–68–25–22–17. MC, V. Closed mid-Dec.–mid-Jan. and Mon. No dinner Sun. July–Oct.

$$$$ ✕▦ **Domaine d'Auriac.** Former rugby player Bernard Rigaudis and his family maintain a countrified atmosphere in this 19th-century manor house southwest of Carcassonne. Room prices vary according to the size and view; the largest look out over the magnificent park and vineyards. In the dining room, festooned with copper pots, traditional Languedoc cuisine is served. A Relais & Châteaux property, it tends to charge even more than top dollar—a superior room runs more than 1,500 francs, and a good after-dinner brandy can cost 400 francs— but the quality is undeniable. ⊠ *Rte. de St-Hilaire, 11330 Auriac (4 km [2½ mi] southwest of Carcassonne),* ☎ 04–68–25–72–22, FAX 04–

68–47–35–54. 28 rooms. Restaurant, air-conditioning, pool, 18-hole golf course, tennis court. AE, MC, V. Closed last 2 wks of Feb., last 2 wks of Nov., 1st wk of Dec.

$$$$ 🏨 **La Cité.** This is *the* spot for royalty and celebrities in Carcassonne. Enter the ivy-covered building, and you'll be surrounded by the kind of luxurious creature comforts the ascetic Cathars would have decried. Have afternoon tea in the library or in the garden. Change for dinner in your spacious, high-ceiling room. No. 21 is a good choice for views of the sun hitting the snow-covered Pyrenean peaks or dropping down behind them. ⊠ *Pl. de l'Église, 11000 La Cité de Carcassonne,* ☎ *04–68–25–03–34,* ℻ *04–68–71–50–15. 60 rooms, 3 suites. Restaurant, pool. AE, DC, MC, V. Closed early Jan.–mid-Feb.*

$$$ 🏨 **Château de Garrevaques.** Equidistant (50 km/31 mi) from Toulouse, Carcassonne, and Albi, this château on 8 acres of parkland makes a great base. Built in 1470 and rebuilt in the early 19th century, it is owned by Madame Combes, who will happily guide you through the family heirlooms and antiques. Rooms are spacious, baronial, and furnished with antiques. Continental breakfast is included in room rates. The table d'hôte dinner is a good chance to sample the local country cooking (advance reservations are required). ⊠ *81700 Garrevaques (5 km [3 mi] northwest of Revel),* ☎ *05–63–75–04–54,* ℻ *05–63–70–26–44. 7 rooms, 2 suites. Pool, tennis court, billiards. AE, DC, MC, V.*

$$ 🏨 **Hôtel Montségur.** With its ville basse location, this hotel is especially convenient. Rooms on the first two floors have Louis XV and Louis XVI furniture, some of it genuine; those above are more romantic, with gilt-iron bedsteads under sloping oak beams. ⊠ *27 allée d'Iéna, 11000,* ☎ *04–68–25–31–41,* ℻ *04–68–47–13–22. 21 rooms. Restaurant. AE, DC, MC, V. Closed mid-Dec.–mid-Jan.*

The Arts

Carcassonne hosts a major arts festival in July, with dance, theater, classical music, and jazz; for details contact the **Théâtre Municipal** (⊠ B.P. 236, rue Courtejaire, 11005, ☎ 04–68–25–33–13; 04–68–77–71–26 for reservations).

Mirepoix

㉞   *48 km (29 mi) southwest of Carcassonne, 88 km (53 mi) southeast of Toulouse, 35 km (22 mi) northeast of Foix.*

The 13th-century walled town of Mirepoix is in the heart of Cathar country. A good time to come here is during Mirepoix's Medieval Festival, in July, when a historical procession is held on the third Sunday of the month. The town is built around the lovely, medieval main square, **place Général-Leclerc,** surrounded by 13th- to 15th-century houses with intricately carved timbers forming arcades or porticoes called *couverts.*

Dining and Lodging

$$–$$$ ✕ **La Porte d'Aval.** Next to one of Mirepoix's key monuments, a fortified entryway, this elegant spot serves quail, wild pigeon, fresh fish, and a sampling of cuisine du terroir (local country cooking). The terrace is the place to be in summer. ⊠ *Cours Maréchal de Mirepoix,* ☎ *05–61–68–19–19. AE, DC, MC, V. Closed Mon. and early-mid-Jan.*

$$$ 🏨 **La Maison des Consuls.** This extraordinary hotel on the central
★   square is a classified historic site. The 500-year-old carved timber gargoyles concentrated around the hotel facade make the exquisitely restored interior even more surprising. Each room is decorated in a different color, most with exposed beams. The Chambre de Dame Louise and the Chambre du Maréchal, both overlooking the square, are the best. ⊠ *Pl. des Couverts, 09500 Mirepoix,* ☎ *05–61–68–81–81,* ℻ *05–61–68–81–15. 7 rooms. MC, V.*

Foix

③⑤ *16 km (10 mi) north of Tarascon-sur-Ariège, 84 km (52 mi) south of Toulouse, 35 km (22 mi) southwest of Mirepoix, 138 km (86 mi) west of Perpignan.*

Nestled in the Ariège Valley, Foix is the capital of the Ariège département. Notice the fancy 19th-century administrative buildings south of avenue Fauré, the town's major thoroughfare.

The **Château de Foix,** sitting impregnably on a promontory above the town and river, has three enormous towers reaching skyward like sentinels. The castle **museum** details regional history and archaeological finds. ✉ *Rue Mercadal,* ☎ *05–61–65–56–05.* 🎫 *25 frs.* ⊙ *Daily 10–noon and 2–5:30.*

A 5-km (3-mi) drive northwest from Foix along D1 leads to the **Rivière Souterraine de Labouiche** (Labouiche Subterranean River), a mysterious underground river whose waters have tunneled a 5-km (3-mi) gallery through the limestone. The 75-minute boat trip covers a 1½-km (1-mi) stretch, past weirdly shaped, subtly lighted stalactites and stalagmites, ending with a subterranean waterfall. Dry land is 230 ft overhead. ☎ *05–61–65–04–11.* 🎫 *45 frs.* ⊙ *Apr.–mid-June and mid-Sept.–mid-Nov., daily 2–5; mid-June–mid-Sept., daily 10–noon and 2–5.*

Dining and Lodging

$$–$$$ ✗ **Le Phoebus.** The views across the Ariège and over the Château de Foix, which once belonged to the illustrious Gaston Phoebus himself, the most famous of the counts of Foix, are superb. The Phoebus is known for game specialties in season and cuisine du terroir, such as *foie de canard mi-cuit* (half-cooked duck liver) and *rable de lièvre au poivrade* (hare in pepper sauce). ✉ *3 cours Irénée Cros,* ☎ *05–61–65–10–42. AE, DC, MC, V. Closed Mon. and mid-July–mid-Aug. No lunch Sat.*

$$ ✗🏠 **Audoye-Lons.** This former post house in the town center has comfortable, modernized rooms that vary in size. The restaurant is reasonably priced and overlooks the Ariège; it is closed Saturday in winter. ✉ *4 pl. Georges-Duthil, 09000,* ☎ *05–61–65–52–44,* 🗚 *05–61–02–68–18. 35 rooms, 24 with bath or shower. Restaurant. AE, DC, MC, V. Closed mid-Dec.–mid-Jan.*

Outdoor Activities and Sports

The rivers and mountain lakes here are excellent trout habitat. Beginner and advanced fishing courses are run by **Loisirs Accueil** (✉ Service Pêche, 14 rue Lazéma, 09000, ☎ 05–61–65–01–15).

Tarascon-sur-Ariège

③⑥ *16 km (10 mi) south of Foix.*

Tarascon is best known for its superb, extensive grotto, with its collection of prehistoric art second only to Lascaux (☞ Chapter 16). As you enter Tarascon, veer left along D8 to the **Grotte de Niaux,** which contains scores of red-and-black Magdalenian rock paintings done in charcoal and iron oxide. Stylized horses, goats, deer, and bison, dating from about 20,000 BC, gallop around a naturally circular underground gallery (known as the Salon Noir, or Black Room) 1 km (½ mi) inside the entrance. Now that the famous caves at Lascaux in the Dordogne can be seen only in reproduction, this is the finest assembly of prehistoric art open to the public anywhere in France. ☎ *05–61–05–88–37 (guided tours only; call ahead for reservations and to check schedule).* 🎫 *45 frs.* ⊙ *July–Sept., tours daily every 45 mins 8:30–11:30 and 1:30–5:15; Oct.–June, tours daily at 11, 3, and 4:30.*

Ax-les-Thermes

㊲ *26 km (15 mi) southeast of Tarascon-sur-Ariège, 104 km (64 mi) southwest of Carcassonne.*

A summer and winter resort town, Ax-les-Thermes has more than 80 mineral springs—at one, in the middle of town, you can often see local merchants on a coffee break or lunch hour reading the newspaper with trousers rolled to the knees and legs immersed. There are ski stations in Ax-Bonascre and Ascou-Pailhères, 5 km (3 mi) from town, and cross-country skiing at the Plateau de Beille and Domaine de Chioula, 10 km (6 mi) from town; for more information contact the **tourist office** (☎ 05–61–64–60–60). After a day of skiing, come back to Ax for a thermal hot bath—an unbeatable winter combination. Crisscrossing the surrounding heights are 400 km (248 mi) of hiking trails.

Font-Romeu

㊳ *75 km (45 mi) southeast of Ax-les-Thermes, 87 km (54 mi) southeast of Tarascon-sur-Ariège, 88 km (55 mi) southwest of Perpignan.*

A high-altitude vacation spot since 1920, French Olympians trained in Font Romeu for the Mexico City games of 1968. The views over the Cerdagne Valley from the balcony across from the tourist office should not be missed. Sports facilities include various ski lifts (one leaving from the center of town), an ice rink, a riding school, a swimming pool, tennis courts, and a nine-hole golf course. Known for the sunniest slopes and best snow-making machines in the area, the skiing can get very crowded during peak Christmas and Easter vacation weekends. For more information contact the tourist office (☎ 04–68–30–68–30) or the École de Ski Français (☎ 04–68–30–03–74).

Dining and Lodging

$$–$$$ ✕🏠 **Pyrénées.** This modern hotel perched above the Cerdagne Valley offers stunning views over the sunniest and widest highland space in the Pyrénées. A five-minute walk from the gondola ski lift up to the snow (or to hiking trails in summer), this handy spot is also next to Font Romeu's best restaurant, Le Chalet à Fondue. The rooms are small but command unforgettable panoramas, while the hotel pool seems all but suspended over the valley. ⊠ *Pl. des Pyrénées, 66120,* ☎ *04–68–30–01–49,* FAX *04–68–30–35–98. 37 rooms. Restaurant, bar, brasserie, pool, sauna. AE, DC, MC, V.*

Outdoor Activities and Sports

The knowledgeable and English-speaking Roy van der Groen at **Sport 2000** (⊠ 102 av. Emmanuel Brousse, ☎ 04–68–30–15–99, FAX 04–68–30–09–34) can provide ski equipment and plenty of good advice about where to ski, dine, or slide into a sunny thermal bath.

Font Romeu's nine-hole golf course, at **Golf de Font-Romeu** (⊠ Espace Sportif Colette Besson, ☎ 04–68–30–38–09), is a rare high-altitude (3,720 km [6,000 ft]) course offering excellent views and some challenging mountaineering as well. For fly-fishing contact **Marc Ribot**(⊠ 6 impasse des Lutins, ☎ 04–68–30–30–93, FAX 04–68–30–06–75) for guides, equipment, and fly-fishing courses.

Eyne

㊴ *12 km (7 mi) southeast of Font-Romeu, 5 km (3 mi) southwest of Mont-Louis.*

Eyne Village, with a grand total of zero in-town commercial establishments—not a café or a bakery—is one of the purest and best-preserved villages remaining in the broad Pyrenean valley of the Cerdagne. Nestled below a nationally classified botanical park, the **Réserve Naturelle d'Eyne** has been famous since the 17th century as the point where Atlantic and Mediterranean weather systems and vegetation converge. Information about the park can be obtained at the park headquarters and museum (☎ 04–68–04–08–05),a in Eyne Village. There are also archaeological walks to megalithic menhirs and dolmens, a ski station uphill (2 km [1 mi] away), and hiking trails to neighboring villages and thermal springs; to find out more contact the *mairie* (Town Hall; ☎ 04–68–04–77–07) or the ski station (☎ 04–68–04–08–01) at Eyne-Station.

Dining and Lodging

$$ ✕⊞ **Cal Pai.** In a lovely 17th-century farmhouse filled with heavy
★ wooden beams and massive granite pillars, this *gîte d'étape* (way station for hikers and skiers) has all kinds of accommodations (doubles, dormitory-style beds, with bathrooms, without) and table d'hôte (communal, prix-fixe dinners) of uncommon quality. Manager and chef Françoise Massot knows every wild mushroom and raspberry in the valley and puts them to delicious use in memorable breakfasts and dinners. ⊠ *Eyne Village,* ☎ *04–68–04–06–96. 15 rooms without bath. Dining room. No credit cards.*

Mont-Louis

40 *30 km (18 mi) west of Villefranche-de-Conflent, 5 km (3 mi) east of Eyne, 118 km (73 mi) south of Carcassonne.*

This fortified village, at 5,200 ft—France's highest—was set up as a border stronghold by Vauban in 1679 and commands views over the Cerdagne Valley to the west, the Capcir to the north, and the Conflent to the east. The ramparts and the citadel, never attacked, are perfectly preserved. A solar oven—over the bridge and inside the portal in the town—is the only one in France in commercial use and is a key attraction.

Dining and Lodging

$$ ✕⊞ **Lou Rouballou.** Famed as the best value and top cuisine in Mont Louis, mother and daughter Christiane and Christine Bigorre's tiny flower-covered hideaway is the place to go. Rooms are simple, small, and cozy. The cuisine is rich in sauces based on Pyrenean herbs, wild mushrooms, and game; try the *chartreux de perdreaux* (partridge with winter cabbage) or the *ouillade* (a soup of potatoes, pork, and cabbage). ⊠ *Rue des Écoles Laïques, 66210,* ☎ *04–68–04–23–26,* FAX *04–68–04–14–09. 14 rooms, 7 with bath. Restaurant. AE, DC, MC, V. Closed May and Oct.–Dec.*

Villefranche-de-Conflent

41 *6 km (4 mi) west of Prades, 30 km (18 mi) east of Mont-Louis, 49 km (30 mi) southwest of Perpignan.*

Named for its location at the confluence of the Têt and Cady rivers, this village has remnants of an 11th-century fortress, with Vauban improvements from the 17th century. Cross the tiny St-Pierre Bridge over the Têt and use the pink-marble "stairway of a thousand steps" to climb up to Fort-Liberia for views of the village, the Canigou, and the valleys east to Prades.

Dining and Lodging

$$$ ✕ **Auberge St-Paul.** One of the best-known tables in the area, this warm stone-surrounded refuge is known for its fine Catalan and Roussillon cuisine, such as *truite à la llosa* (trout on slate slabs), and *civet d'isard*

(stewed mountain goat). ⌧ *7 pl. de l'Église,* ☎ *04–68–96–30–95. Reservations essential. MC, V. Closed Mon.*

$$ ✕⊡ **Auberge du Cèdre.** This comfortable little inn over the river commands fine views of the fortress. Rooms are small but cozy. Pyrenean and Catalan specialties are served on a little glassed-in porch suspended over the Têt. Reservations are essential at the restaurant; call before you go to make sure it's open. ⌧ *Domaine Ste-Eulalie, 66500,* ☎ *04–68–96–37–37,* FAX *04–68–05–35–32. 10 rooms. Restaurant. AE, DC, MC, V. Closed Nov. and early Jan.*

Vernet-les-Bains

㊷ *12 km (7 mi) southwest of Prades, 55 km (34 mi) west of Perpignan.*

English writer Rudyard Kipling came to take the waters in Vernet-les-Bains, a long-established spa town. The hilltop village church is dwarfed by the imposing Mont Canigou behind. Even higher up is the medieval abbey.

Leave your car in Casteil, 2 km (1 mi) farther on, and complete the journey to the **Abbaye St-Martin du Canigou** on foot. Brace yourself for the steep half-hour climb; the abbey is perched on a triangular promontory at an altitude of nearly 3,600 ft. Although the abbey was diligently restored by the bishop of Perpignan early in the 20th century, part of the cloisters, along with the higher (and larger) of the two churches, date from the 11th century. The lower church, dedicated to Notre-Dame-sous-Terre, is even older. Rising above is a stocky, fortified bell tower. ☎ *04–68–05–50–03.* ⌧ *20 frs.* ☉ *Daily 10–12:30 and 2:30–5.*

Prades

㊸ *6 km (4 mi) east of Villefranche-de-Conflent, 43 km (27 mi) west of Perpignan.*

Once home to Catalan cellist Pablo Casals, the market town of Prades is famous for its annual summer music festival (from late July to mid-August), the **Festival Pablo Casals.**

★ Founded by Pablo Casals in 1950, the music festival is primarily held at the medieval **Abbaye de St-Michel de Cuxa,** (⌧ *Km 3 on D-7 south of Prades and Codalet,* ☎ *04–68–96–15–35.* ⌧ *20 frs.* ☉ *Daily 9:30–11:30; 2–5.*) One of the gems of the Pyrénées, the abbey's sturdy, crenellated four-story bell tower is visible from afar. If the remains of the cloisters here seem familiar, it may be because you have seen the missing pieces at New York City's Cloisters Museum; they first were purchased in 1907 by American sculptor George Grey Barnard and then in 1925 by the Metropolitan Museum. The 10th-century pre-Romanesque church is a superb aesthetic and acoustical venue for the summer cello concerts. The six-voice Gregorian vespers service held at 7 PM in the monastery next door is hauntingly simple and medieval in tone and texture.

Céret

㊹ *68 km (41 mi) southeast of Prades, 35 km (21 mi) west of Collioure, 31 km (19 mi) southwest of Perpignan.*

The "Barbizon of Cubism," Céret achieved immortality when Picasso, Juan Gris, and many other artists found this small Pyrenean town irresistible at the beginning of this century. Adorned by cherry orchards, the town landscapes have been captured in paintings by Picasso, Gris, Dufy, Braque, Chagall, Kisling, and others. Some of these are on view
★ in the fine collection of the **Musée d'Art Moderne** (Modern Art Mu-

seum). ⊠ *8 bis Maréchal-Joffre,* ☎ *04–68–87–27–76.* ⊡ *20 frs.* ☾ *May–Sept., Wed.–Mon. 10–6.*

After visiting the Modern Art Museum, stroll through pretty **Vieux Céret** (Old Céret): Find your way through **place des Neufs Jets** (Nine Fountains Square), around the church, and out to the lovely fortified **Porte de France** gateway. Then walk over the single-arched **Vieux Pont** (Old Bridge).

Dining

$$$ ✕ **Les Feuillants.** Widely known as one of the top restaurants in the
★   area, this elegant place combines cuisine, wine, and traditional design in another manifestation of Céret's superb and surprising artistic endowment. Marie Louise and Didier Banyols, sommelier and chef, respectively, produce spectacular fare, such as *rouelles de homard Bretagne au Banyuls et châtaignes* (sliced Brittany lobster in sweet wine and chestnuts). ⊠ *1 bd. La Fayette,* ☎ *04–68–87–37–88. AE, DC, MC, V. No lunch Sat.*

Collioure

④⑤ *35 km (21 mi) east of Céret, 27 km (17 mi) southeast of Perpignan.*

The heart of Matisse Country, this pretty seaside fishing village with a sheltered natural harbor has become a summer magnet for tourists (so much so it should be strenuously avoided in July and August). Painters such as Henri Matisse, André Derain, Henri Martin, and Georges Braque—who were dubbed Fauves for their "savage" (*fauve* means "wild animal") approach to color and form—were among the early discoverers of Collioure. The view they admired remains largely unchanged today: To the north, the rocky Ilot St-Vincent juts out into the sea, a modern lighthouse at its tip, while inland the Albères Range rises to connect the Pyrénées with the Méditerranean. Collioure continues to play the muse to the entire Côte Vermeille—after all, it gave rise to the name of the Vermilion Coast because Matisse daringly painted Collioure's yellow-sand beach using a bright red terra-cotta hue.

Near the old Quartier du Mouré is the 17th-century church of **Notre-Dame-des-Anges** (⊠ Pl. de l'Église). It has exuberantly carved altarpieces and a pink-dome bell tower that doubled as the original lighthouse.

A slender jetty divides the Boramar Beach, beneath the church, from the small landing area at the foot of the **Château Royal,** a 15th-century castle remodeled by Vauban 200 years later. ☎ *04–68–82–06–43.* ⊡ *20 frs.* ☾ *Mar.–Oct., daily 10–noon and 2–5.*

Dining and Lodging

$$–$$$ ✕⊞ **Relais des Trois Mas.** Overlooking Collioure from the cliffs south of town, this hotel has small but interestingly furnished rooms—headboards, for example, are made from antique Spanish doors. Rooms are named for painters whose work appears on the bathroom tiles. The views are spectacular. Below is a pebbled beach, though you may prefer the small pool (hewn from rock) or the huge Jacuzzi. Dine at the restaurant, La Balette, on the terrace or in one of the two small dining rooms looking over the harbor. ⊠ *Rte. de Port-Vendres, 66190,* ☎ *04–68–82–05–07,* 𝖥𝖠𝖷 *04–68–82–38–08. 19 rooms, 4 suites. Restaurant, 2 dining rooms, pool, hot tub, exercise room, beach. AE, DC, MC, V. Closed mid-Nov.–mid-Dec.*

$$ ✕⊞ **Les Templiers.** Universally considered the "soul" of Collioure, no
★   visit is complete without a stop here. Owner Jojo Pous, son of the force behind Collioure's art colony, has more than 2,500 original works hanging from every nook and cranny. The bar itself is a work of art, curved

like the hull of a skiff and ending with a wood sculpture of a mermaid suckling an infant sailor. The mostly Catalan cuisine is excellent, and the rooms overlooking the château are cozy. ⊠ *Quai de l'Amirauté, 66190,* ☎ *04–68–98–31–10,* ℻ *04–68–98–01–24. 43 rooms. Restaurant, bar, café. AE, DC, MC, V. Closed early Jan.–early Feb.*

Perpignan

46 *27 km (17 mi) northwest of Collioure, 64 km (40 mi) south of Narbonne, 204 km (126 mi) southeast of Toulouse.*

During medieval times Perpignan was the second city of Catalonia (after Barcelona), before falling to Louis XIII's French army in 1642. The Spanish influence is evident in Perpignan's leading monument, the fortified **Palais des Rois de Majorque** (King of Majorca Palace), begun in the 14th century by James II of Majorca. Highlights here are the majestic **cour d'Honneur** (Courtyard of Honor), the two-tier Flamboyant Gothic chapel of **Ste-Croix,** and the **Grande Salle** (Great Hall) with its monumental fireplaces. ⊠ *Rue des Archers,* ☎ *04–68–34–48–29.* 🎫 *10 frs.* ☉ *Daily 9–5.*

The center of town is marked by a medieval monument, the 14th-century **Le Castillet,** with its tall, crenellated twin towers. Originally this hulking brick building was the main gate to the city; later it was used as a prison. Now the **Casa Pairal,** a museum devoted to Catalan art and traditions, is housed here. ⊠ *Pl. de Verdun,* ☎ *04–68–35–42–05.* 🎫 *Free.* ☉ *Wed.–Mon. 9–noon and 2–6.*

The **Promenade des Plantanes,** across boulevard Wilson from Le Castillet, is a cheerful place to stroll among flowers, plane trees, and fountains. To see more interesting medieval buildings, walk along the streets—the **Petite Rue des Fabriques d'En Nabot** is the best—near Le Castillet and the adjacent place de la Loge, the town's nerve center. Note the frilly wrought-iron campanile and dramatic medieval crucifix on the **Cathédrale St-Jean** (⊠ Pl. Gambetta).

The **Loge de Mer** (Maritime Exchange; ⊠ Rue de la Loge), a graceful 14th-century building, was once the chamber of commerce for maritime trade.

The 15th-century **Palais de la Députation** (⊠ Rue de la Loge) was once the seat of the permanent deputy, or representative of the Catalan Corts (parliament). The massive arched entryway is typical of the Catalonian, or House of Aragon, civil design of that period.

Dining and Lodging

$$$–$$$$ ✕ **Chapon Fin.** An upscale crowd pours into this excellent restaurant in the Park hotel (☞ *below*) to sample the subtle, understated cuisine. Three prix-fixe menus showcase authentic Mediterranean food. ⊠ *18 bd. Jean-Bourrat,* ☎ *04–68–35–14–14. AE, DC, MC, V. Closed Sun. No lunch Mon.*

$$ ✕ **La Casa Sansa.** This very Catalan, very popular restaurant serves
★ fine regional specialties in an atmosphere thick with tastefully designed local color. Paintings crowd the walls with Roussillon themes. ⊠ *2 rue Fabrique d'en Nadal,* ☎ *04–68–34–21–84. Reservations essential. AE, DC, MC, V. Closed Sun. No lunch Mon.*

$$$ 🏨 **Park.** Don't be deceived by the undistinguished facade: This fam-
★ ily-run hotel enjoys ironclad prestige in Perpignan. Although some rooms are small, most are luxurious, soundproof, and air-conditioned. ⊠ *18 bd. Jean-Bourrat, 66000,* ☎ *04–68–35–14–14,* ℻ *04–68–35–48–18. 67 rooms. Restaurant. AE, DC, MC, V.*

$–$$ ⌂ **Hôtel de la Poste et de la Perdrix.** If you're looking for an inexpensive place with old French charm in the center of town next to Le Castillet, don't miss this little spot. Rooms, like the hotel, are simple and poetic, as opposed to overcomfortable and prosaic. The cuisine is Catalan. ⊠ *6 rue Fabriques Nabot, 66000,* ☎ *04–68–34–42–53,* FAX *04–68–34–58–20. 38 rooms. Restaurant. AE, DC, MC, V.*

Shopping

Rue des Marchands, near Le Castillet, is thick with chic shops. **Maison Quinta** (⊠ Rue Louis Blanc) is a top design and architectural artifacts store. Excellent local ceramics can be found at the picturesque **Sant Vicens crafts center** (⊠ Rue Sant Vicens, off D22 east of town center).

Salses

47 *16 km (10 mi) north of Perpignan, 48 km (30 mi) south of Narbonne.*

Salses has a history of sieges. Hannibal stormed through the town with his elephants on his way to the Alps in 218 BC, though no trace of his passage remains. The colossal and well-preserved **Fort de Salses,** built by Ferdinand of Aragon in 1497 and equipped for 300 horses and 1,000 soldiers, fell to the French under Cardinal Richelieu in 1642 after a three-year siege. Bulky round towers ring the rectangular inner fort, and the five-story keep, with its narrow corridors and small-scale drawbridges, was designed to keep the fort's governor safe to the last. ☎ *04–68–38–60–13.* ▣ *25 frs.* ⊙ *July–Aug., daily 9–6; Sept.–June, daily 9:30–11:30 and 2–5:30; Nov.–Easter, 9:30–11:30 and 2–4.*

Narbonne

48 *64 km (40 mi) north of Perpignan, 60 km (37 mi) east of Carcassonne, 94 km (58 mi) south of Montpellier.*

In Roman times, bustling, industrial Narbonne was the second-largest town in Gaul (after Lyon) and an important port, though today little remains of its Roman past. Until the sea receded during the Middle Ages, Narbonne prospered.

The town's former wealth is evinced by the 14th-century **Cathédral St-Just** (⊠ Rue Armand-Gauthier); its vaults rise 133 ft from the floor, making it the tallest cathedral in southern France. Only Beauvais and Amiens, in Picardy, are taller, and as at Beauvais, the nave at Narbonne was never built.

Richly sculpted cloisters link the cathedral to the former **Palais des Archevêques** (Archbishops' Palace), now home to museums of archaeology, art, and history. Note the enormous palace kitchen and the late-13th-century keep, the Donjon Gilles-Aycelin; climb the 180 steps to the top for a view of the region and the town. ⊠ *Palais des Archevêques,* ☎ *04–68–90–30–30.* ▣ *28 frs (includes all town museums).* ⊙ *May–Sept., daily 9–noon and 2–6; Oct.–Apr., Tues.–Sun. 10–noon and 2–5:30.*

On the south side of the Canal de la Robine is the **Musée Lapidaire** (Sculpture Museum), in the handsome 13th-century former church of **Notre-Dame de la Mourguié.** Classical busts, ancient sarcophagi, lintels, and Gallo-Roman inscriptions await you. ⊠ *Pl. Lamourguier,* ☎ *04–68–65–53–58.* ▣ *28 frs (includes all town museums).* ⊙ *May–Sept., daily 9–noon and 2–6; Oct.–Apr., Tues.–Sun. 10–noon and 2–5:30.*

For the nearest decent beach, follow pretty D168 as it winds its way over the Montagne de la Clape to **Narbonne-Plage,** 15 km (9 mi) away. Just up the coast in St-Pierre-sur-Mer is the curious **Gouffre de l'Oeil-Doux,** an inland lake fed by seawater.

Dining and Lodging

$$$ ✕☐ **Le Relais du Val d'Orbieu.** Good hotels are scarce in Narbonne. The most commodious, though a bit overpriced, is this hostelry west of town. Owner Jean-Pierre Gonsalvez speaks English and is extremely helpful. Designed around a courtyard, most rooms are reached through covered arcades. The better ones are pleasantly simple, with bare tile floors and large French windows leading onto terraces; the standard ones (100 francs less) are slightly smaller and do not have terraces or views. The restaurant (no luncheon served November–March) lacks intimacy, but the wine list has good local wines at reasonable prices. ⊠ *D24, 11200 Ornaisons (14 km [8 mi] west of Narbonne),* ☎ *04–68–27–10–27,* [FAX] *04–68–27–52–44. 13 rooms, 7 apartments. Restaurant, pool, tennis court. AE, DC, MC, V.*

$$ ✕☐ **Languedoc.** In this old-fashioned, turn-of-the-last-century hotel downtown, the smallish rooms vary in style and comfort; a full bath is an extra 100 francs. La Coupole restaurant (closed Monday, no dinner Sunday) serves inexpensive regional dishes,a with menus starting at 90 francs; ⊠ *22 bd. Gambetta, 11100,* ☎ *04–68–65–14–74,* [FAX] *04–68–65–81–48. 38 rooms, 34 with bath or shower; 2 suites. Restaurant, piano bar. AE, DC, MC, V.*

Béziers

㊾ *20 km (12 mi) northeast of Narbonne, 54 km (33 mi) southwest of Montpellier.*

Capital of the Canal du Midi, Béziers owes its reputation to the genius of native son and royal salt-tax collector Pierre-Paul Riquet. In 1666 he realized his dream of linking the Atlantic to the Mediterranean by canal, a project inherited from the Romans. Few would have predicted much of a future for Béziers in July of 1209 after Simon de Montfort, leader of the crusade against the Cathars, scored his first major victory here, massacring 20,000. Today the Canal du Midi hosts mainly pleasure cruisers, and Béziers sits serenely on its perch overlooking the distant Mediterranean and the foothills of the Cévennes Mountains.

Presiding over the allées Paul Riquet in the center of town is the corroded bronze figure of **Pierre-Paul Riquet.** It was Riquet who came up with the idea of using mountain streams as the canal's water source, channeled through *rigoles* (channels). A visionary at a time when roads were in deplorable shape and grain was transported on the backs of mules, Riquet invested so much of his fortune on the project that he was brought nearly to ruin; the project was nicknamed "La Rigole à Riquet" ("Riquet's Laugh") by Louis XIV's minister Colbert, who nevertheless approved it in 1666. Riquet died a pauper in 1680, a year before the canal's completion and the revolutionizing of commerce in the south of France.

Just off allées Paul Riquet on place G. Péri is a statue that has come to represent Béziers's other local hero, the mythical figure **Pépézuc** (the statue is actually made up of the body of one Roman emperor, topped by the head of another). Legend has it that Pépézuc defended the town against the onslaught of the English under the Black Prince. At one corner of place G. Péri, Béziers's only **12th-century house** (⊠ Rue du Chapeau Rouge), with arcaded windows and carved heads, survives as testament to a time before the Crusade.

The heavily restored **Église de la Madeleine** (⊠ Off rue de la République), with its distinctive octagonal tower, was the site of the beginning of the massacre, which occurred in 1209. About 7,000 townspeople who had sought refuge from Simon de Montfort inside were burned alive before he turned his attention to sacking the town; the event is known as *"le grand mazel"* ("the great bonfire"). Restoration work means that you may only be able to admire the crenellations, gargoyles, floral frieze, and crooked arches of the late 11th-century pentagon-shape apse.

Béziers's late-19th-century **Les Halles** (Market Hall) was done in the style of the architect Baltard, who built the original Les Halles in Paris. This is a particularly beautiful example, with large stone cabbages gracing the entrance like urns. ⊠ *Entrances on rue Paul Riquet, pl. Pierre Sémard.* ☉ *Daily 6:30–12:30.*

The **Cathédrale St-Nazaire** (⊠ Pl. des Albigeois) was rebuilt over several centuries after the sacking of Béziers. Note the medieval wall along rue de Juiverie, which formed the limit between the cathedral precincts and the Jewish quarter of town. The western facade resembles a fortress for good reason: it served as a warning to would-be invaders. The truncated transept is in the form of the Greek cross and contributes to the disproportionate feel of the interior. Look for the magnificent 17th-century walnut organ and the frescoes about the life of St. Stephen and others. Adjoining the cathedral is a 14th-century cloister and the **Jardin des Evêques** (Bishops' Garden), conceived of as a terraced garden descending to the banks of the Orb; only two tree-shaded levels were ever built. The views from here, which take in Béziers's five bridges, are magnificent. ⊠ *Pl. des Albigeois.* ☉ *Oct.– Apr., daily 10–noon and 2–5:30; May–Sept., daily 10–7.*

Just 2 km (1 mi) outside Béziers are the **Neuf Écluses de Fonséranes** (Nine Locks of Fonséranes), one of Riquet's engineering masterpieces. This series of oval locks permits boats navigating the Canal du Midi to descend a steep gradient. Take A9 toward Valras and follow the signs.

Dining and Lodging

$$$ ✕⌂ **Château de Lignan.** Tiled rooftops top the four narrow towers of this hotel and give it a vaguely Italianate feel, as does the austere stucco facade; the pool and wooded park complete the pleasant ensemble. Pity that rooms have little to distinguish them from standard chain hotels except their size and louvered windows. But the sauna and whirlpool are appealing and light filled, and the restaurant is exceptional. The octagonal sprawl of the skylighted dining room is bright and welcoming, if a bit tacky; enjoy simple, elegant fare like strongly flavored *loup en papillote* (sea perch cooked in foil) and finish with vanilla ice cream–filled baked pears. ⊠ *Pl. de l'Église, 34490 Lignan-sur-Orb (6 km [4 mi] northwest of Béziers),* ☏ *04–67–37–91–47,* ⅂⅃ *04–67–37–99–25. 49 rooms. Restaurant, pool, exercise room, meeting rooms. AE, MC, V.*

Outdoor Activities

Daylong excursions on the Canal du Midi include passage over the canal bridge spanning the Orb and through the nine locks; some go to the Mediterranean resort town of Agde, 21 km (14 mi) away. Contact the following canal-boat operators: **Les Bâteaux du Soleil** (⊠ 6 rue Chassefière, Agde 34300, ☏ 04–67–94–08–79, ⅂⅃ 04–67–21–28–38) and **Crosières Cathy** (⊠ Regimont, Poilhes 34310, ☏ 04–67–03–72–16).

Minerve

⑤⓪ *40 km (25 mi) west of Béziers, 30 km (19 mi) northwest of Narbonne.*

Surrounded by the meandering, juniper-covered limestone gorges of the Vallée de la Cesse, Minerve is the quintessential medieval hilltop village. The town sheltered a large number of heretics at the start of the Albigensian Crusade. But its defensive position was no match for Simon de Montfort's army in July 1210, when after a seven-week siege, the dehydrated citizens capitulated, and 180 Cathar prefects were burned. De Montfort's army had blocked the village well with the aid of a catapult called La Malvoisine (the Evil Neighbor), which has been reconstructed on its original strategic position. Stroll around the remaining fortifications and try to imagine the assault. Around Minerve are a number of geological curiosities, including *ponts naturels* (natural bridges), enormous tunnels in the rock cut by the path of the Cesse River, prehistoric grottoes, and dolmens.

Maps and information are available from the somewhat hidden **Syndicat d'Initiative** (✉ Pl. du Monument aux Morts, ☎ 04–68–91–81–43), the tourist office in the center of the village. You can also get addresses of local winemakers who produce the classed wine Minervois (a rough, fruity red) from grapes grown in arid, pebbly soil.

The austere, Romanesque **Église St-Etienne** has one of the oldest altar tables in Europe, dating from AD 456. Next to the church is a carving of a dove, a monument to the village's resistance during the Crusades. The château was destroyed by Simon de Montfort. Only the curious, candlelike **Tour du Guet** (Watchtower) remains on a ledge at the far end of the village.

The **Musée Hurepel** re-creates the events of the Albigensian Crusade in a series of figurine-populated dioramas and does a good job of explaining how villagers would have interacted with the Cathars they sheltered. ✉ *5 rue des Martyrs,* ☎ *04–68–91–12–26.* ⊠ *20 frs.* ☉ *Apr.–late Sept., daily 10:30–12:30 and 2–6:30; other times by appointment only.*

Dining and Lodging

$$ ✕🏠 **Relais Chantovent.** Overlooking the gorges of the Brian River, this oak-beamed, terra-cotta-tile restaurant and inn is decorated with exceptional paintings by local artists. Rooms are basic but quaint, with old lamps, framed prints, and wooden furniture. Owners Maïté and Loulou Evenou serve up delicious, elegantly garnished local fare, including strong, salty *jambon de la Montagne Noire* (Black Mountain ham) and trout in a cream, bouillon, and red pepper sauce. The 95-franc menu is a bargain. The restaurant is closed Monday, and there is no dinner Sunday. ✉ *17 Grande-Rue, 34210 Minerve,* ☎ *04–68–91–14–18,* FAX *04–68–91–81–99. 10 rooms. Restaurant. MC, V. Mid-Dec.–late Mar.*

$$–$$$ 🏠 **Les Aliberts.** Tucked away among the vine- and asphodel-covered hills
★ just outside Minerve, with stunning views of the Pyrénées and the Montagne Noire, this *gîte* (rustic inn or hiker's way station) is in a renovated set of 12th- to 17th-century farm buildings. Internationally traveled, cosmopolitan owners Pascal and Monique Bourgogne treat guests like friends. The majestic main farmhouse has common rooms with an enormous fireplace, library, and piano. The five cozy houses, without phones, range in style from Scandinavian to Asian to French contemporary; all have full kitchens and fireplaces. Meals and breakfasts can be ordered in advance. ✉ *Les Aliberts, 34210 Minerve (off D10 south toward Olonzac),* ☎ *04–68–91–81–72,* FAX *04–68–91–22–95. 5 houses with 13 rooms total. Pool, library, laundry facilities. No credit cards.*

Pézenas

51 *23 km (14 mi) northeast of Béziers, 52 km (32 mi) southwest of Montpellier.*

Pézenas retains the courtly appearance and feel it acquired in the 16th century, when the Estates General of the Languedoc, the regional administrative body, governed from here. The town made its fortune with 16th- to 18th-century textile fairs, at which denim was sold. Hence you have Pézenas's architectural richness: Around every picturesque corner is another *hôtel particulier* (town-house mansion)—and architectural competition among the wealthy means they are all unique. Some notable streets are rue Triperie Vieille; rue de la Foire, where you'll find the Maison Carrion de Nizas and the Hôtel de Wicque; cour Jean-Jaurès, famous for its Maison Émile Mâzuc, at No. 10; place du 14 Juillet and its outstanding Hôtel des Barons de Lacoste; and rue Émile Zola, home to the Maison de Jacques Coeur. At the end of rue Émile Zola is a rounded archway leading into the rue Juiverie, also called La Carriera, which in the Occitan language denotes a Jewish ghetto.

The tourist office, which organizes a variety of tours of Pézenas, is in the **Maison du Barbier Gély** (⊠ 1 pl. Gambetta), once home to Molière's barber and friend, Monsieur Gély. Pézenas's most impressive hôtel particulier is the **Hôtel d'Alfonce,** with its twisted Baroque columns, three-tiered balustraded loggia overlooking the garden, and vinelike corner staircase. This was the residence of the Prince de Conti, who sponsored visits by Molière and his acting troupe in 1650, 1653, and 1655. *Le Médecin Volant* (*The Flying Doctor*) may have premiered here shortly before Conti, mad from syphilis, purged his illustrious court. The owners, Monsieur Aubert and his daughter, give private tours of their family home. ⊠ *Rue Conti,* 🖃 *10 frs.* ☉ *June–Sept., Mon.–Sat. 10–noon and 2–6.*

Nightlife and the Arts

As part of **La Mirondela Del Arts** festival in July and August, Molière's spirit comes alive with performances by comedy troupes; there are also Occitan-language music and poetry events. In February the town's medieval mascot, **Le Poulain** (a giant horse made out of chestnut and cloth), gets toted around in honor of Carnival.

St-Guilhem-le-Désert

52 *44 km (28 mi) north of Pézenas, 40 km (25 mi) northwest of Montpellier.*

The name of this ancient abbey on the St-Jacques de Compostella pilgrimage route conjures up visions of windswept sands. Actually, it's nowhere near the desert—the term refers to its isolated, inhospitable location. Poised at the top of the Verdus Estuary in the Gellone Valley among the heather-covered Hérault gorges, the abbey was founded in 804 by Guilhem d'Orange, count of Toulouse and cousin of Charlemagne. St. Guilhem was seeking to retire from war with the Saracens and to live a monastic life when his cousin presented him with a piece of the true cross. The remote site chose itself: Guilhem was a devout follower of Benoît d'Aniane, founder of the Benedictine order and abbot in nearby Aniane.

A massive 140-year-old plane tree dominates place de la Liberté, on which sits all that remains of the Abbaye St-Guilhem-le-Désert, the **abbey church,** and some beautiful arcaded medieval houses; look for large, dried *cardabelle* flowers, native to the region, decorating people's homes. The nave of the somber church, with its austere tower, dates to the 11th century and the apse to the 12th, built over a Carolingian crypt: Note the unusual tribunes in the transept. What's left of St-Guilhem's remains are in a reliquary in the wall, recovered from an 1817 flood. Another niche contains the fragment of the cross. But the **altar** in the chapel is the real attraction here: Thought to be from the 12th century, it's made entirely of white marble, with a black marble base, and the tracings of Christ were once filled with colored glass.

Around a square pool filled with carp, the **cloître** is a place of reflection for the nine young Carmelite nuns who live here and cultivate the garden encircling the apse. The beautiful sculptures that once decorated the cloister, including *Daniel in the Lion's Den,* were bought in the early 20th century by art collector George Ray Barnard for New York's Cloisters. ⊠ *In abbey church.* ⊘ *Sept.–Mar., daily 10:30–12:30 and 2–5; Apr.–Aug., daily 9:30–7.*

The abbeys of St-Guilhem and Aniane built the impressive **Pont du Diable** (Devil's Bridge) in the mid-11th century to straddle the Hérault at the entrance to its gorges. Legend has it that the devil, wanting to prevent St-Guilhem from building the bridge, threatened to damn the first man who crossed it. A dog was prudently sent instead. ⊠ *Just south of St-Guilhem on D4, heading toward D27 and Aniane.*

THE MIDI-PYRÉNÉES AND THE LANGUEDOC-ROUSSILLON A TO Z

Arriving and Departing

By Car

The fastest route from Paris to Toulouse (700 km [435 mi] southwest) is via Bordeaux on A10, then A62; the journey time is about nine hours. If you choose to head south over the Pyrénées to Barcelona, the Tunnel du Puymorens saves a half hour of switchbacks between Hospitalet and Porta, but in good weather and with time to spare, the drive over the Puymorens Pass is spectacular. Plan on taking three hours between Toulouse and Font-Romeu and another three to Barcelona. The fastest route from Toulouse to Barcelona is the four-hour, 421-km (253-mi) drive via Carcassonne and Perpignan on A61 and A9, which becomes A7 at Le Perthus.

By Plane

All international flights arrive at Toulouse's **Blagnac Airport** (☎ 05–61–42–44–65), a 20-minute drive from the center of the city. **Air France** (☎ 08–02–80–28–02) has regular flights between Toulouse and most European capitals. **TAT** (Transport Aérien Transrégional) has direct flights from Paris's Orly Airport to Rodez (reservations: ☎ 01–42–79–05–05 Paris; 05–65–42–20–30 Rodez).

AIRPORT TRANSFERS

Airport shuttles run regularly (every half hour between 8:15 AM and 8:45 PM) from the airport to the bus station in Toulouse (at the train station; fare 25 francs) and also at 9:20 PM, 10 PM, and 10:45 PM. From the Toulouse bus station to the airport, buses leave every half hour 5:30 AM–8:30 PM.

By Train

Trains for the southwest leave from Paris (Gare d'Austerlitz). There are direct trains to Toulouse (six to seven hours), Carcassonne (seven to eight hours), and Montauban (six hours). For Rodez (seven to eight hours), change in Brive, and for Auch (more than eight hours), in Toulouse. Seven trains leave Paris (Gare de Lyon) daily for Narbonne (six hours) and Perpignan (seven hours); a change at Montpellier is often necessary. Note that at least three high-speed TGV (*Train à Grande Vitesse*) per day leave Paris (Gare Montparnasse) for Toulouse; journey time is five hours.

Getting Around

By Car

A62/A61 slices through the region on its way through Carcassonne to the coast at Narbonne, where A9 heads south to Perpignan. At Toulouse, where A62 becomes A61, various highways fan out in all directions: N124 to Auch; N117/E80 to St-Gaudens, Tarbes, and Pau; A62/N20 to Montauban and Cahors; N20 south to Foix and the Ariège Valley; N88 to Albi and Rodez.

By Train

The regional French rail network in the southwest provides regular services to many towns, though not all. Béziers is linked by train to Carcassonnne, Perpignan, Narbonne, and Montpellier, as well as Paris (but via slow trains that take hours not TGVs). Agde is linked to Béziers by train (12 minutes). There's no train service to Pézenas, Minerve, and St-Guilhem.

Contacts and Resources

Car Rental

Avis (⊠ 13 bd. Conflent, Perpignan, ☎ 04–68–34–26–71; ⊠ Blagnac Airport, Toulouse, ☎ 05–61–30–04–94). **Hertz** (⊠ Pl. Lagarrasic, Auch, ☎ 05–62–05–26–26; ⊠ 5 av. Chamier, Montauban, ☎ 05–63–20–29–00).

Guided Tours

Contact the **Toulouse tourist office** (⊠ Donjon du Capitole, ☎ 05–61–11–02–22) for information about walking tours and bus tours in and around Toulouse. Ask for the encyclopedic, superbly entertaining, and English-speaking Gilbert Casagrande for a nonpareil tour of Toulouse.

The **Comité Régional du Tourisme** (CRT; ⊠ 54 bd. de l'Embouchure, 31200 Toulouse, ☎ 05–61–13–55–55) has a brochure, "1,001 Escapes in the Midi-Pyrénées," with descriptions of weekends and short organized package vacations.

Music Festivals

Fifty music festivals a year take place in the smaller towns throughout the region; the Comité Régional du Tourisme (CRT) and larger tourist offices can provide a list of dates and addresses, or contact the **Délégation Musicale Régionale** (⊠ 56 rue du Taur, 31080 Toulouse, ☎ 05–61–29–21–00).

Outdoor Activities and Sports

For information on canoeing or kayaking, contact the **Ligue de Canoë-Kayak** (⊠ 16 rue Guillemin-Tarayre, 31000 Toulouse, ☎ 05–61–62–65–05). For information on hiking or horseback riding, contact the **Comité de Randonnées Midi-Pyrénées** (CORAMIP; ⊠ 14 rue Bayard, 31000 Toulouse, ☎ 05–61–99–44–00). Local tourist offices also have detailed maps of more than 3,220 km (2,000 mi) of marked trails. The **Comité Regional du Tourisme du Languedoc-Roussillon** (☞ Visitor Information, *below*) publishes a brochure on golf courses in the area and sells a pass honored at 14 courses.

Travel Agencies

Havas (✉ 73 rue d'Alsace-Lorraine, Toulouse, ☎ 05–61–23–16–35). **Wagons-Lits** (✉ Voyages Dépêche, 42 bis rue d'Alsace-Lorraine, Toulouse, ☎ 05–62–15–42–70).

Visitor Information

The regional tourist office for the Midi-Pyrénées is the **Comité Régional du Tourisme** (CRT; ✉ 54 bd. de l'Embouchure, 31200 Toulouse, ☎ 05–61–13–55–55). For Pyrénées-Roussillon information contact the **Comité Départemental de Tourisme** (✉ Quai de Lattre de Tassigny, B.P. 540, 66005 Perpignan, ☎ 04–68–34–29–94). For the Languedoc-Roussillon contact the **Comité Régional du Tourisme du Languedoc-Roussillon** (✉ 20 rue de la République, 34000 Montpellier, ☎ 04–67–22–81–00, FAX 04–67–58–06–10, ✇).

Local tourist offices are as follows: **Albi** (✉ Pl. Ste-Cécile, ☎ 05–63–49–48–80). **Auch** (✉ 1 rue Dessoles, ☎ 05–62–05–22–89). **Béziers** (✉ Palais des Congrès, 29 av. St-Saëns, ☎ 04–67–76–47–00). **Carcassonne** (✉ 15 bd. Camille-Pelletan, ☎ 04–68–25–07–04). **Céret** (✉ 1 bd. Clemenceau, ☎ 04–68–87–00–53). **Collioure** (✉ Pl. 18-juin, ☎ 04–68–82–15–47). **Cordes** (✉ Maison Fonpeyrouse, ☎ 05–63–56–00–52). **Fleurance** (✉ Pl. de la République 2, ☎ 05–62–64–00–00). **Larressingle** (✉ Syndicat D'Initiative, ☎ 05–62–28–37–02). **Lectoure** (✉ Pl. de l'Église, ☎ 05–62–68–76–98). **Minerve** (✉ Pl. du Monument aux Morts, ☎ 04–68–91–81–43). **Montauban** (✉ Ancien College, B.P. 201, ☎ 05–63–63–60–60). **Moissac** (✉ 6 Pl. Durand de Bredon, ☎ 05–63–04–01–85). **Mont-Louis** (✉ Rue Vauban, ☎ 04–68–04–21–97). **Narbonne** (✉ Pl. Roger-Salengro, ☎ 04–68–65–15–60). **Perpignan** (✉ Quai de Lattre de Tassigny, ☎ 04–68–66–30–30). **Pézenas** (✉ 1 pl. Gambetta, ☎ 04–67–98–36–40). **Prades** (✉ 4 rue Victor-Hugo, ☎ 04–68–05–41–02). **St-Guilhem-le-Désert** (✉ 2 rue de la Font du Portal, ☎ 04–67–57–44–33). **Toulouse** (✉ Donjon du Capitole, ☎ 05–61–11–02–22).

15 THE BASQUE COUNTRY, THE BÉARN, AND THE HAUTES-PYRÉNÉES

Travel here, and you'll want to buy a pair of those wonderfully comfortable Basque espadrilles, with rope soles and cloth uppers—you'll need them if you dance the native fandango in the streets all night as the locals sometimes do. If sightseeing tops your list, this tempting region is filled with pleasures—from scenic Bay of Biscay resorts like Biarritz to picturesque villages like St-Jean-de-Luz to the dramatic reaches of the Hautes-Pyrénées, which are one of France's most spectacular natural wonders.

Revised and
updated by
George Semler

RECENTLY, A PELOTA-PLAYING MAYOR IN THE PROVINCE OF SOULE welcomed a group of travelers by telling them blithely, in one breath, that the Basque Country is the most beautiful in the world, that his ancestors fought in the Crusades, and that Christopher Columbus was certainly a Basque. There, in short order, was a composite picture of the pride, dignity, and humor of the people of the Basque. And if Columbus was not a Basque (a claim historians very much doubt), at least we know that whalers of the regional village of St-Jean-de-Luz sailed with their three-masted ships as far as America, and that Juan Sebastián Elkano, from the Spanish Basque village of Guetaria, did indeed complete Magellan's voyage around the world.

From berets and pelota matches to Basque cooking, the culture of this little "country" that straddles the French and Spanish Pyrénées has cast its spell over peoples around the world. And continues to do so—just witness the best-seller status of Mark Kurlansky's 1999 *The Basque History of the World*. Today, travelers bruised by the crowding and commerce of more-frequented parts of France are increasingly heading to this southwest corner to discover the region's amazing variety of rich cultures and landscapes—from the scenic seaside resorts of the Basque coast to the verdant rolling Béarn region in the east to the towering granite majesty of the Hautes-Pyrénées stretching along the border with Spain.

Center stage is held by the three French Basque provinces—Labourd, Soule, and Basse Navarre—which share a singularly distinct culture with their four cousin Basque provinces in Spain: jai alai, whaleboat regattas, stone lifting, world-famous cuisine, and a mysterious and ancient non-Indo-European language all its own. In fact, the origins of this culture remain obscure. The resemblance of the Basque evening (or war) call, the *irrinzina,* to that of the Upper Amazon Indians does not solve the mystery; nor does the fact that the Basque reckon in twenties, like the ancient Maya. Some trace Basque origins back to the Berbers of North Africa, while others whisper about the survivors of the lost city of Atlantis. Some parish priests even refer to a direct line from Adam and Eve. The most tenable and logical theory on the origin of the Basques is that they were aboriginal tribes of Iberian peoples who best protected their cultural identity and language by settling the distant, mountainous northern reaches of the Iberian Peninsula.

At the Basque Country's eastern edge, the ski and spelunking town of Pierre-St-Martin marks the start of the Béarn, with its splendid capital city of Pau and the pristine valleys of Aspe, Ossau, and Barétous descending from the Pyrénées. Sauveterre-de-Béarn's medieval drawbridge, Navarrenx and its *bastide* over the rushing Gave d'Oloron, and the Romanesque and Mudejar Ste-Croix church at Oloron-Ste-Marie provide stepping-stones into the limestone heights surrounding the 8,263-ft Pic d'Anie, the highest point in the Béarn. The European brown-bear refuge at Etsaut and the Chemin de la Mâture trace carved into the rock wall by chain gangs lead up to Somport, the Roman *summus portus,* or "highest pass," over the central Pyrénées. Farther east in the Vallée d'Ossau, the *petit train d'Artouste,* Europe's highest railroadtrain, chugs up to a series of remote Pyrenean lakes and tarns.

East through the Aubisque Pass, at the Béarn's eastern limit, is the heart of the Hautes-Pyrénées, where France's highest Pyrenean peaks at Vignemale (10,820 ft) and Balaïtous (10,321 ft) compete with some of the Pyrénées' most legendary natural treasures: The Cirque de Gavarnie is the world's most spectacular natural amphitheater, centered around a 1,400-ft waterfall. The nearby Brèche de Roland is a dramatic breach, or cleft, in the rock wall between France and Spain, while to the east, the Cirque de Troumouse is the largest in all the Pyrénées.

But when you get your fill of mountaintop vistas and Basque peaks, you can always head to regional spa-towns and coastal cities refined enough to have once welcomed half the crowned heads of Europe. It was Empress Eugènie who gave Biarritz its coming-out party, changing it from a simple bourgeois town into an international favorite in the era of Napoléon III. Today you can still enjoy the Second Empire trimmings by winding down from sightseeing with a try at the roulette table in the town casino.

— George Semler

Pleasures and Pastimes

Basque Sports
Perhaps the best known and most spectacular of Basque sports is the ancestral ball game of pelota, a descendant of the medieval *jeux de paume* (literally, palm games), a fundamental part of rural Basque culture. A Basque village without a fronton (backboard and pelota court) is as unimaginable as an American town without a baseball diamond. There are many versions and variations on this graceful and rapid sport, played with the bare hand, with wooden bats, or with curved basketlike gloves; a real wicker *chistera*—the wicker bat used in the game—is an interesting souvenir to buy (and a very pretty fruit basket, but let no Basque hear that bit of heresy). Other rural Basque sports include scything, wood chopping and sawing, sack hauling, stone lifting, long-distance racing, tug-of-war, whaleboat rowing competitions, and, for those who really want to take the bull by the horns, oxen pulling.

Dining
Dining in this region is invariably a feast, whether it's seafood or up-land dishes ranging from beef to lamb to game birds such as the famous migratory *palombes* (wood pigeons). Dishes to keep in mind include *ttoro* (hake stew), *pipérade* (tomatoes and green peppers cooked in olive oil, and often scrambled eggs), *bakalao al pil-pil* (cod cooked in oil *"al pil-pil"*—at the precise temperature so that oil makes this bubbling noise as the fish creates its own sauce), *marmitako* (tuna and potato stew), and *zikiro* (roast lamb). Béarn is famous for its *garbure*, thick vegetable soup with *confit de canard* (preserved duck) and *fèves* (broad beans). *Civets* (stews) made with *isard* (wild goat) or wild boar are other specialties. La Bigorre and the Hautes-Pyrénées are equally dedicated to garbure, though they may call it *soupe paysanne bigourdane* (Bigorran peasant soup) to distinguish their cuisine from their neighbors.

CATEGORY	COST*
$$$$	over 400 frs
$$$	250 frs–400 frs
$$	125 frs–250 frs
$	under 125 frs

*per person for a three-course meal, including tax (20.6%) and tip but not wine

✑ following the text of a review is your signal that the property has a Web site, where you will find details and, usually, images; for a link, visit www.fodors.com/urls.

Hiking
The Pyrénées are best explored on foot—and after a day of hiking along the gorges and into the mountains the hearty regional cuisine makes

perfect sense. The lengthy GR (Grande Randonnée) 10, a trail marked by discreet red-and-white paint markings, runs all the way from the Atlantic at Hendaye to Banyuls-sur-Mer on the Mediterranean, through villages and up and down the mountains. Along the way are mountain refuges. The HRP (Haute Randonnée Pyrénéenne, High Pyrenean Hike) stays closer to the border crest, following the terrain through both France and Spain, irrespective of national borders. Local trails are also well indicated, usually with blue or yellow markings. Some of the classic walks in the Basque Pyrénées include the Iparla Ridge walk between Bidarrai and St-Étienne-de-Baïgorry, the Santiago de Compostela Trail's dramatic St-Jean-Pied-de-Port to Roncesvalles walk over the Pyrénées, and the Holçarté Gorge walk between Larrau and Ste-En-grâce. Trail maps are available from local tourist offices.

Lodging

From palatial beachside splendor in Biarritz to simple mountain auberges in the Basque Country to Pyrenean refuges in the Hautes-Pyrénées, the gamut of lodging in southwest France is ample. For top value and camaraderie, look for *gîtes* or *tables d'hôtes* (rustic bed-and-breakfasts and way stations for hikers and skiers) where all guests dine together. Be sure to book summer lodging on the Basque coast well in advance, particularly for August. In the Hautes-Pyrénées only Gavarnie during its third-week-of-July music festival presents a potential booking problem. Even better: Make it up as you go along; the surprises are usually very pleasant.

CATEGORY	COST*
$$$$	over 800 frs
$$$	550 frs–800 frs
$$	300 frs–550 frs
$	under 300 frs

All prices are for a standard double room, including tax (20.6%) and service charge.

Exploring Basque Country and the Hautes-Pyrénées

Bayonne and Pau are the urban bookends for this southwest corner of France. But whether you approach from the Atlantic or the Mediterranean, you won't want to miss Gavarnie, Ste-Engrâce, St-Jean-Pied-de-Port, Sauveterre-de-Béarn, Ainhoa, or St-Jean-de-Luz. Trans-Pyrenean hikers (and drivers) generally prefer moving west to east for a variety of reasons, especially the excellent lighting provided by the late afternoon and evening sunlight during the prime months of May to October.

Great Itineraries

Consider Dax and Eugénie-les-Bains as excellent side trips to the basic itinerary outlined here. Begin in Bayonne, exploring the Basque coast, and then head east into the Atlantic Pyrénées. Explore the Béarn as carefully as time permits—Sauveterre-de-Béarn, Oloron-Ste-Marie, and Pau—before continuing on to La Bigorre, the Hautes-Pyrénées, and Gavarnie.

Numbers in the text correspond to numbers in the margin and on the Basque Country and the Hautes-Pyrénées maps.

IF YOU HAVE 3 DAYS

There is nothing leisurely about this three-day tour, nor is there time to do much walking, which is why it's recommended only if you have limited time and unlimited curiosity. Begin in **Bayonne** ①, spending a morning exploring the town. See the cathedral and the Bonnat Museum before hitting **Biarritz** ④ for afternoon tea. Spend the night in ▦

St-Jean-de-Luz ⑤. On day two drive through **Sare** ⑥ and **Ainhoa** ⑦ and past **Pas de Roland** ⑧ on the way up the Nive River to **St-Jean-Pied-de-Port** ⑨ for lunch. Explore the Haute Soule during the afternoon: Drive through the Irati Forest to **Larrau** ⑩ and **Ste-Engrâce** ⑫ on the way through **Oloron-Ste-Marie** ⑮ to ⊞ **Pau** ⑱ for the night. On day three have a look around Pau, see **Lourdes** ⑳ at midday, and get up to ⊞ **Gavarnie** ㉒ in time to see the sunset from the legendary Hôtel du Cirque et de la Cascade.

IF YOU HAVE 7 DAYS

Begin in **Bayonne** ①, spending a morning exploring the town. See the cathedral and the Bonnat Museum before going to **Dax** ② for a bull-fight and ⊞ **Eugénie-les-Bains** ③ for dinner and the night. The next day head back to the coast at **Biarritz** ④ for some time at the beach. Spend the night in ⊞ **St-Jean-de-Luz** ⑤. On day three climb La Rhune (or take the little train to the top) for a stunning view over the entire Basque coast. Drive through **Sare** ⑥ and **Ainhoa** ⑦ and past **Pas de Roland** ⑧ on the way up the Nive River to ⊞ **St-Jean-Pied-de-Port** ⑨ for the night. Explore the town and the Haute Soule the next morning: Drive through the Irati Forest to ⊞ **Larrau** ⑩ and do the Holçarté Gorges walk to ⊞ **Ste-Engrâce** ⑫ if there is time; return to Larrau if not. On day five explore the lower Soule, **Oloron-Ste-Marie** ⑮, and ⊞ **Pau** ⑱. On day six walk around Pau, tour the château, see **Lourdes** ⑳ at lunchtime, and get up to ⊞ **Gavarnie** ㉒ in time to see the sunset from the Hôtel du Cirque et de la Cascade. On day seven explore around Gavarnie.

When to Tour the Basque Country and the Hautes-Pyrénées

From early May through late October is the best time to explore this region. June and September are the height of the season. July is the only month you can be nearly 100% sure of being to able to, say, walk safely over the glacier to the Brèche de Roland. In winter beach life is over, and the Pyrénées are snowed in; many hotels and restaurants close. Only for skiing and the pleasure of the nearly total absence of tourism is winter recommended.

THE BASQUE COAST

The French Basque coast—a world of its own with its own language, sports, and folklore—occupies France's southwesternmost corner along the Spanish border. Inland, the area is laced with rivers: The Bidasoa River border with Spain marks the southern edge of the region, and the Adour River, on its northern edge, separates the Basque country from the neighboring Les Landes. The Nive River flows through the heart of the verdant Basque littoral to join the Adour at Bayonne, and the smaller Nivelle River flows into the Bay of Biscay at St-Jean-de-Luz. Bayonne, Biarritz, and St-Jean-de-Luz are the main towns along the coast, all less than 40 km (25 mi) from the first peak of the Pyrénées.

Bayonne

❶ *48 km (30 mi) southwest of Dax, 184 km (114 mi) south of Bordeaux, 295 km (183 mi) west of Toulouse.*

At the confluence of the Adour and Nive rivers, Bayonne, France's most Basque city, was in the 4th century a Roman fort, or *castrum,* and for 300 years (1151–1451) a British colony. With a name that comes from the term (and the weapon) *bayonet,* itself derived from the French *baïonnette,* today's Bayonne is more famous for its *jambon de Bayonne* ham and the annual Basque pelota world championships held in Septem-

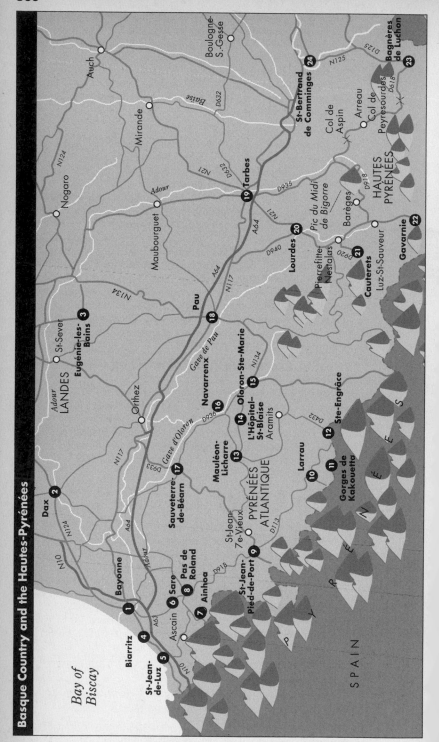

Basque Country and the Hautes-Pyrénées

Bay of Biscay

SPAIN

LANDES

PYRÉNÉES ATLANTIQUE

HAUTES PYRÉNÉES

PYRÉNÉES

Bayonne
Biarritz
St-Jean-de-Luz
Dax
Ascain
Sare
Ainhoa
Pas de Roland
St-Jean-Pied-de-Port
St-Jean-le-Vieux
Aramits
Mauléon-Licharre
Sauveterre-de-Béarn
Navarrenx
Oloron-Ste-Marie
L'Hôpital-St-Blaise
Ste-Engrâce
Larrau
Gorges de Kakouetta
Pau
Tarbes
Lourdes
Cauterets
Luz-St-Sauveur
Gavarnie
Bagnères-de-Luchon
St-Bertrand-de-Comminges
Pierrefitte-Nestalas
Barèges
Arreau
Col de Aspin
Col de Peyresourde
Pic du Midi de Bigorre
Gave de Pau
Gave d'Oloron
Gave de Pau
Adour
Adour
Adour
Baïse
Boulogne-S.-Gesse
St-Sever
Eugénie-les-Bains
Nogaro
Mirande
Auch
Maubourguet
Orthez

N10
N124
A63
A64
N117
N134
N124
N10
D918
D113
D432
D936
D933
N134
D940
D935
N21
N21
A64
N117
D632
D262
D632
D920
D921
D918
D918
D618
D125
N125

ber. Even though the port is spread out along the Adour estuary leading out to the sea, 5 km (3 mi) away, the two rivers and five bridges lend this small gem of a city a definite maritime feel. The quai-front houses, the intimate place Pasteur, the Château-Vieux, the elegant 18th-century homes along rue des Prébendés, the 17th-century ramparts, and the cathedral are some of the town's not-to-be-missed sights. The **Cathédrale** (called both Ste-Marie and Notre-Dame) was predominantly built in the 13th century and is one of France's southernmost examples of Gothic architecture. Its 13th- to 14th-century cloisters are one of the cathedral's best elements. The airy, modernized **Musée Bonnat,** in itself reason enough to visit Bayonne, has a notable treasury of 19th-century paintings collected by French portraitist and historical painter Léon Bonnat (1833–1922). ⊠ *5 rue Jacques-Lafitte,* ☎ *05–59–59–08–52.* ⊠ *20 frs.* ☉ *Wed.–Mon. 10–noon and 2:30–6:30.*

Dining and Lodging

$$ ✕ **Euskalduna.** This profoundly Basque establishment serves the best
★ *cuisine du terroir* (home-style regional cooking) in rustic-nautical surroundings. The food is authentic and hearty, featuring fresh fish dishes as well as upland specialties from the Basque hills. ⊠ *61 rue Pannecau,* ☎ *05–59–59–28–02. MC, V. Closed Sun.–Mon. and early–mid-June and mid-Oct.–late Oct.*

$$$ ✕🛏 **Le Grand Hôtel.** Just down the street from the Château-Vieux, this central spot has pleasant, comfortable rooms with an old-world feel. The restaurant, Les Carmes, built in a former Carmelite convent, is excellent. ⊠ *21 rue Thiers, 64100,* ☎ *05–59–59–62–00,* ﬁﬁ *05–59–59–62–01. 54 rooms. Restaurant. AE, DC, MC, V.*

Dax

❷ *143 km (89 mi) south of Arcachon, 145 km (90 mi) south of Bordeaux.*

Known by Romans as Aquae Tarbellicae, Dax has been famous for its thermal springs for 2,000 years. Caesar Augustus's daughter came here to soothe her aches and pains, the first in a long line of seasonal guests. No fewer than 18 thermal establishments are active still; call the **tourist office** (☎ 05–58–86–86) for information. Be sure to stroll through the parks and gardens and along the banks of the Adour. The church of **St-Paul-les-Dax** (⊠ Rue Victor-Hugo) is known for the 11th-century bas-reliefs decorating the apse. The cathedral of **Notre-Dame** (⊠ Pl. Ducos) is a Classical replacement for a previous Gothic structure.

Eugénie-les-Bains

❸ *68 km (42 mi) east of Dax, 140 km (87 mi) south of Bordeaux.*

Empress Eugénie popularized Eugénie-les-Bains at the end of the 19th century, for which the villagers renamed the town. Michel and Christine Guérard brought the village back to life in 1973 by putting together one of France's most fashionable thermal retreats, which became the birthplace of nouvelle cuisine, thanks to the great talents of chef Michel. The 13 therapeutic treatments address everything from weight loss to rheumatism. Two springs are certified by the French Ministry of Health: L'Impératrice and Christine-Marie, whose 39°C (102°F) waters come from nearly 1,300 ft below the earth's surface.

Dining and Lodging

$$ ✕ **La Ferme aux Grives.** Nature's bounty is the theme at the Guérards' delightfully re-created old coaching inn. A banquet table is laid out with vegetables and breads, darkened beams give a rich hue, and hunting paintings cover the walls. The three-course fixed menu may include a vinaigrette of grilled pears over locally cured ham, lamb roasted in a pastry shell, or a meringue with Chantilly sauce. ⊠ *Eugénie-les-Bains,* ☎ *05–58–51–19–08. MC, V. Closed Jan.–mid-Feb.*

$$$$ ✕⌧ **Les Prés d'Eugénie.** The birthplace of nouvelle cuisine, Michel
★   Guérard's excellent restaurant is all but a regional institution. Grandeur
prevails here. Rooms are formal; those in the former 18th-century con-
vent have an understated luxury. The cuisine remains an inventive and
cosmopolitan approach to local produce. ⊠ *40320 Eugénie-les-Bains,*
☎ *05–58–05–06–07; 05–58–05–05–05 for restaurant reservations,* FAX
*05–58–51–10–10. 44 rooms. Restaurant, pool, 9-hole golf course, 2
tennis courts, exercise room. AE, DC, MC, V.*

Biarritz

❹ *8 km (5 mi) south of Bayonne, 190 km (118 mi) southwest of Bordeaux,
50 km (31 mi) north of San Sebastián, 115 km (69 mi) west of Pau.*

Biarritz rose to prominence in the 19th century when upstart emperor
Napoléon III took to spending his holidays here on the prompting of
his Spanish wife, Eugénie. Carlist exiles from Spain first put Biarritz
on the map in 1838. Unable to visit San Sebastian on the Spanish coast,
they sought a recreation spot as close as possible to their old stamp-
ing ground. Among the exiles was Eugénie de Montijo, soon destined
to become empress of France. Half the crowned heads of Europe slept
in Eugénie's villa, now the Hôtel du Palais. No matter whether you
consider Napoléon III's bombastic architectural legacies an eyesore or
part of the fun—at least they have the courage of their convictions.
Biarritz no longer lays claim to the title "the resort of kings and the
king of resorts"—but there is no shortage of deluxe hotel rooms or
bow-tied gamblers ambling over to the casino. Yet the old, down-to-
earth charm of the former fishing village remains to counterbalance
the Second Empire ambience.

Although not as drop-dead stylish as it once was, the town is making
a comeback as a swank surfing capital with its new casino and con-
vention center. The **beaches** attract crowds—particularly the fine,
sandy beaches of **Grande Plage** and the neighboring **Plage Miramar,**
both amid craggy natural beauty. The narrow streets around the cozy
16th-century church of **St-Martin** are delightful to stroll. The harbor
of the **Port des Pêcheurs** (Fishing Port) provides a tantalizing glimpse
of the Biarritz of old. A walk along the beach promenades gives a view
of the foaming breakers that beat constantly upon the sands, giving
the name *Côte d'Argent* (Silver Coast) to the length of this part of the
French Basque coast.

Dining and Lodging

$$ ✕ **Les Platanes.** Chef-owner Arnaud Daguin specializes in adapting country recipes and giving them a personal touch. Be sure to try his foie
gras, which he gets from Auch, his hometown in Gers. The decor of
the restaurant, in an old Basque town house, is comfortably formal.
⊠ *32 av. Beau-Soleil,* ☎ *05–59–23–13–68. AE, DC, MC, V. No lunch
Mon.–Tues., June 1–10 and Nov. 1–10.*

$$$$ ✕⌧ **Hôtel du Palais.** This majestic redbrick hotel, with immense driveway, lawns, and semicircular dining room, still exudes an opulent, aristocratic air, no doubt left by Empress Eugénie a century ago when she
built it as her Biarritz palace. Rooms are spacious; the 2,000-franc ones
facing the ocean are especially grand. In the restaurant, La Rotonde,
chef Jean-Marie Gautier creates deft, innovative fare using local Atlantic and Pyrenean resources. Specialties range from lobster gazpa-
cho to roast lamb. Lunch is served beside the curved pool above the
Atlantic. ⊠ *1 av. de l'Impératrice, 64200,* ☎ *05–59–41–64–00,* FAX *05–
59–41–67–99. 137 rooms, 20 suites. 3 restaurants, 2 bars, outdoor*

heated saltwater pool, sauna. AE, DC, MC, V. Closed 2 wks in winter; dates vary.

$$$ ✕🖾 **Café de Paris.** This well-known hotel is also a popular Biarritz
★ restaurant—in fact, two. One is an elegant (and expensive) gourmet
restaurant featuring such items as *ris de veau* (veal sweetbreads) and
fish served with an imaginative nouvelle touch. The other is a less for-
mal brasserie (with the same chefs). The haute cuisine restaurant is closed
for lunch, as well as for dinner on Sunday; the brasserie is always open.
Rooms are luxurious and have ocean views. ☒ *5 pl. Bellevue, 64200,*
🕾 *05–59–24–19–53,* 🖷 *05–59–24–18–20. 19 rooms. Restaurant.
AE, MC, DC, V.*

$$–$$$ ✕🖾 **Windsor.** This hotel, built in the 1920s, is close to the casino and
the beach. Rooms are modern and cozy; those with sea views cost about
twice as much as the ones facing the inner courtyard. The restaurant
serves a variety of dishes, including terrine de foie gras with Armagnac
and ravioli stuffed with crab. ☒ *19 bd. du Général-de-Gaulle, 64200,*
🕾 *05–59–24–08–52,* 🖷 *05–59–24–98–90. 49 rooms. Restaurant.
AE, MC, V. Closed Jan.–mid-Mar.*

Nightlife and the Arts

At the **Casino de Biarritz** (☒ 1 av. Edouard-VII, 🕾 05–59–22–77–77)
you can play the slots or blackjack, or go dancing at the Flamingo. **Le
Queen's Bar** (☒ 25 pl. Clemenceau, 🕾 05–59–24–70–65) is a com-
fortable hangout both day and night. To keep your connections in cyber-
space, **Internet & Café** (☒ 5 rue Jauerry, 🕾 05–59–24–03–31), behind
the post office, provides the link.

Outdoor Activities and Sports

Désertours Aventure (☒ 65 av. Maréchal-Juin, 🕾 05–59–41–22–02)
organizes rafting trips on the Nive River and four-wheel-drive vehicle
tours through the Atlantic Pyrénées. **Golf de Biarritz** (☒ 2 av. Edith-Cavell,
🕾 05–59–03–71–80) has an 18-hole, par-69 course. **Pelote Basque: Biar-
ritz Athletic-club** (☒ Parc des Sports d'Aguilera, 🕾 05–59–23–91–09)
offers instruction in every type of Basque pelota including *main nue* (bare-
handed), *pala* (paddle), *chistera* (with a basketlike racket), and *cesta punta*
(another game played with the same curved basket).

On Wednesday and Saturday at 9 PM in July, August, and September,
you can watch pelota games at the **Parc des Sports d'Aguilera** (🕾 05–
59–23–91–09).

St-Jean-de-Luz

★ **⑤** *23 km (16 mi) southwest of Bayonne, 24 km (18 mi) northeast of San
Sebastián, 54 km (32 mi) west of St-Jean-Pied-de-Port, 128 km (77 mi)
west of Pau.*

Along the coast between Biarritz and the Spanish border, St-Jean-de-
Luz is memorable for its colorful harbor (scenes of which grace the cel-
ebrated New York City restaurant La Côte Basque), old streets, curious
church, and elegant beach. The tree-lined **place Louis-XIV,** alongside
the Hôtel de Ville (Town Hall), with its narrow courtyard and dainty
statue of Louis XIV on horseback, is the hub of the town. The church
of **St-Jean-Baptiste** (☒ Pl. des Corsaires) has unusual wooden galleries
lining the walls, creating a theaterlike effect.

Of particular note is the **Maison de l'Infante** (Princess's House), be-
tween the harbor and the bay, where Maria Teresa of Spain stayed prior
to her wedding to the Sun King. The foursquare mansion now houses
the **Musée Grévin**, which contains 17th-century furnishings and pe-
riod costumes. ☒ *quai de l'Infante,* 🕾 *05–59–51–24–88.* 🖾 *33 frs.*

☉ *July–Aug., 10–10; Apr.–Oct., daily 10:30–noon and 2–6:30; Nov.–Mar., by appointment.*

Dining and Lodging

$$$ ✕ **La Coupole.** This semicircular gourmet restaurant, in the Grand Hôtel (☞ *below*), looks over the bay and serves excellent regional specialties: confit of lobster, baby lamb from the Pyrénées, and fresh fish from the Bay of Biscay. ⊠ *43 bd. Thiers,* ☎ *05–59–26–35–36. AE, DC, MC, V. Closed late Oct.–early Apr.*

$$$ ✕ **Txalupa.** The name is Basque for "skiff" or "small boat," and you feel like you're in one when you're this close to the bay—yachts and fishing vessels go about their business just a few yards away. This well-known haunt with a terrace over the port serves the famous *jambon de Bayonne* (Bayonne ham) in vinegar and garlic sauce, as well as fresh fish and natural products such as wild mushrooms. ⊠ *Pl. Louis-XIV,* ☎ *05–59–51–85–52. AE, DC, MC, V.*

$ ✕ **Chez Pablo.** The simple, home-style menu is based on what the fishing fleet caught that morning; try the *marmitako,* a hearty fisherman's tuna stew. Long tables covered with red-and-white tablecloths, benches, and plastered walls make for a casual meal. ⊠ *Rue M. Etcheto,* ☎ *05–56–26–37–81. No credit cards. Closed Sun.*

$$$–$$$$ ⊞ **Le Grand Hôtel.** Although it's the town's leading hotel, it's not as grand as you might expect—rooms have seen better days. But a major plus is its location, on the waterfront; Suites 301 and 302 have terraces over the bay. ⊠ *43 bd. Thiers, 64500,* ☎ *05–59–26–35–36,* 𝖥𝖠𝖷 *05–59–51–19–91. 43 rooms, 3 suites. Restaurant. AE, DC, MC, V. Closed late Oct.–early Apr.*

THE ATLANTIC PYRÉNÉES

The Atlantic Pyrénées extend east from the Atlantic to the Col du Pourtalet and encompass Béarn and the mountainous part of the Basque Country. Watching the Pyrénées grow from rolling green foothills in the west to jagged limestone peaks to glacier-studded granite massifs in the Hautes-Pyrénées is an exciting process. The Atlantic Pyrénées' first major height is at La Rhune (2,969 ft), known as the Balcon du Côte Basque (Balcony of the Basque Coast). The highest Basque peak is at Orhi (6,617 ft); the Béarn's highest is Pic d'Anie (8,510 ft). Not until Balaïtous (10,381 ft) and Vignemale (10,820 ft), in the Hautes-Pyrénées, does the altitude surpass the 10,000-ft mark. Starting east from St-Jean-de-Luz up the Nivelle River, a series of picturesque villages such as Ascain, Sare, Ainhoa and Bidarrai lead up to St-Jean-Pied-de-Port and the Pyrénées.

This journey ends in Pau, far from the Pays Basque and set in Béarn, akin in temperament to the larger region of which it is an enclave, Gascony. Gascony is purse-poor but certainly rich in scenery and lore. Its proud and touchy temperament is typified in literature by the character d'Artagnan of Dumas's *Three Musketeers* and in history by the lords of the château of Pau. An inscription over its entrance, TOUCHEZ-Y, SI TU L'OSES—"Touch this if you dare"—was that of Gaston Phoebus, a golden-haired and volatile count of Foix. An arts lover, he also had a hasty temper, which led him to murder his brother and his only son.

Sare

❻ *14 km (8 mi) southeast of St-Jean-de-Luz; 9 km (5½ mi) southwest of Ainhoa on D118: Take the first left.*

The gemlike village of Sare is built around a large fronton, or backboard, where a permanent pelota game habitually rages around the clock.

Not surprisingly, the Hôtel de Ville (Town Hall) offers a permanent exhibition on Pelote Basque (open July–August, daily 9–1 and 2–6:30; September–June, daily 3–6). Sare was a busy smuggling hub throughout the 19th century. Its chief attractions are colorful wood-beam and whitewashed Basque architecture, the 16th-century late Romanesque church with its lovely triple-decked interior, and the **Ospitale Zaharra** pilgrim's hospice behind the church. More than a dozen tiny chapels sprinkled around Sare were built as ex-votos by seamen who survived Atlantic storms. Up the Sare Valley is the panoramic Col de Lizarrieta and the **Grottes de Sare,** where you can study up on Basque culture and history at a **Musée** Ethnographique (Ethnographical Museum) and take a guided tour (in five languages) for 1 km (½ mi) underground and see a son-et-lumière show. ☎ *05–59–54–21–88.* 🎫 *30 frs.* ⊙ *Mid-Feb.–Dec. Tues.–Sun. 11–7*

🐄 West of Sare on D4, at the Col de St-Ignace, take the **Petit Train de la Rhune,** a tiny wood-paneled cogwheel train that reaches the dizzying speed of 5 mph while climbing up La Rhune peak. The views of the Bay of Biscay, the Pyrénées, and the grassy hills of the Basque farmland are wonderful. ☎ *05–59–54–20–26.* 🎫 *45 frs.* ⊙ *Round-trip (1 hr): Easter vacation and May–June, daily 10 and 3; July–Sept., daily every 35 mins.*

Dining and Lodging

$$ ✕🏨 **Baratxartea.** This little inn 1 km (½ mi) from the center of Sare in one of the town's prettiest and most ancient *quartiers* is a find. Monsieur Fagoaga's family-run hotel and restaurant occupy a 16th-century town house complete with *colombiers* (pigeon roosts) and is surrounded by some of the finest rural Basque architecture in Labourd. ⊠ *Quartier Ihalar, 64310 Itxassou,* ☎ *05–59–54–20–48,* 🆂 *05–59–47–50–84 22 rooms. Restaurant. MC, V. Closed Jan.–Feb.*

Ainhoa

➐ *9 km (5½ mi) east of Sare, 23 km (14 mi) southeast of St-Jean-de-Luz, 31 km (19 mi) northwest of St-Jean-Pied-de-Port.*

The Basque village of Ainhoa is officially registered among the villages selected by the national tourist ministry as the prettiest in France. The streets are lined with one lovely 16th- to 18th-century house after another, complete with whitewashed walls, flower-filled balconies, brightly painted shutters, and carved master beams. The church of **Notre-Dame de l'Assomption** has a traditional Basque three-tiered wooden interior with carved railings and ancient oak stairs.

Lodging

$$ 🏨 **Hôtel Ohantzea.** Across from the church, this classical Basque house, with a beautiful facade and garden, was a farm in the 17th century. The original antiques and the many paintings by artists who traded them for lodging all make this comfortable space as much a museum as a hotel. Ask for a room with a balcony overlooking the garden. ⊠ *Rue Principale, 64250,* ☎ *05–59–29–90–50. 9 rooms. MC, V. Closed Dec.–Jan.*

Pas de Roland

➑ *15 km (9 mi) east of Ainhoa; 30 km (18 mi) northwest of St-Jean-Pied-de-Port; follow signs for Itxassou and proceed past the town up to the pass.*

Legend has it that the Pas de Roland (Roland's Footprint) was where the legendary medieval French hero Roland allowed Charlemagne's troops to pass by cutting a passageway through an impeding boulder with his mystical sword, Durandal. In the process he purportedly left his footprint in the rock, where the "evidence" remains to this day. The drive along this bend in the Nive river is a scenic detour off the D-918 road up to St-Jean-Pied-de-Port.

St-Jean-Pied-de-Port

9 *54 km (33 mi) east of Biarritz, 46 km (28 mi) west of Larrau.*

St-Jean-Pied-de-Port, a fortified town on the Nive River, got its name from its position at the foot (*pied*) of the *port* (mountain pass) of Roncevaux (Roncesvalles). The pass was the setting for *La Chanson de Roland* (*The Song of Roland*), the 11th-century epic poem considered the real beginning of French literature. The bustling town center, a major stop for pilgrims en route to Santiago de Compostela, seems, after a tour through the Soule, like a frenzied metropolitan center—even in winter. In summer, especially around the time of Pamplona's San Fermin blowout (the running of the bulls, July 7–14), the place is filled to the gills and is somewhere between exciting and unbearable.

Walk into the old section through the Porte de France just behind and to the left of the tourist office, climb the steps on the left up to the walkway circling the ramparts, and walk around to the stone stairway down to the rue de l'Église. The street leads down to the magnificent doorway of **Notre-Dame-du-Bout-du-Pont** (Our Lady of the End of the Bridge), a characteristically Basque three-tier structure: women on the ground floor, the men in the first balcony, and the choir in the loft above. From the **Pont Notre-Dame** (Notre-Dame Bridge) you can watch the wild trout in the Nive (also an Atlantic salmon stream) as they sip mayflies off the surface. Note that fishing is *défendu* (forbidden) in town. Upstream, along the left bank, is another wooden bridge. Cross it and then walk around and back through town, crossing back to the left bank on the main road.

The **Relais de la Nive** bar and café—hanging over the river at the north end of the bridge in the center of town—is the perfect spot to admire the reflection of the pont de Notre-Dame upstream and watch the trout working in the current while having a coffee.

On **rue de la Citadelle** are a number of sights of interest: the **Maison Arcanzola** (Arcanzola House), at No. 32 (1510); the **Maison des Évêques** (Bishops' House), at No. 39; and the famous **Prison des Évêques** (Bishops' Prison), next door to it. Continue up along rue de la Citadelle to get to the **Citadelle,** a classic Vauban fortress, now occupied by a school. The views from the Citadelle, complete with maps identifying the surrounding heights and valleys, are panoramic.

Dining and Lodging

$$–$$$ ✕ **Chez Arbillaga.** Tucked inside the citadel ramparts, this lively bistro is a sound choice for lunch or dinner. The food represents what the Basques do best: simple cooking of excellent quality, such as *agneau de lait à la broche* (roast lamb), in winter, or *coquilles St-Jacques au lard fumé* (scallops with bacon), in summer. ⊠ *8 rue de l'Église,* ☎ *05–59–37–06–44. MC, V. Closed 1st 2 wks of June and Oct. and Wed. Jan.–May.*

$$$ ✕▥ **Les Pyrénées.** This inn has the best restaurant in town, specializing in nouvelle Basque cuisine such as ravioli and prawns with caviar sauce and hot wild-mushroom terrine. Rooms are modern and vary in size; four have balconies. ⊠ *19 pl. du Général-de-Gaulle, 64220,* ☎ *05–59–37–01–01,* ℻ *05–59–37–18–97. 18 rooms, 2 apartments. Restaurant, pool. AE, DC, MC, V. Closed last 3 wks of Jan., late Nov.–late Dec.*

$$ ✕⛩ **Central Hôtel.** Get the best quality for price in town at this family-run hotel and restaurant over the Nive, where trout could be literally (though illegally) caught from rooms. The wonderful 200-year-old oak staircase is another nice touch. The owners speak Basque, Spanish, French, English, and some German, so communicating is no problem. The cuisine is superb, especially the lamb and *magret de canard* (duck breast). ✉ *1 pl. Charles-de-Gaulle, 64220,* ☎ *05–59–37–00–22,* FAX *05–59–37–27–79. 14 rooms. Restaurant. AE, DC, MC, V. Closed mid-Dec.–early Mar.*

En Route   The road between St-Jean-Pied-de-Port and Larrau twists through mountain passes, **Col de Burdinkurutzeta** and **Col de Organbideska,** offering views north over the Arbailles Forest and the sweeping Basque hills as it enters the vast **Iraty Forest** to the south. The forest, one of Europe's largest stands of beech, provided masts for the Spanish and French fleets up through the 18th century.

Larrau

❿ *46 km (28 mi) east of St-Jean-Pied-de-Port, 20 km (12 mi) west of Ste-Engrâce, 42 km (26 mi) southwest of Oloron-Ste-Marie.*

Larrau is a cozy way station on the road over the pass into Spain. The town has several hotels of distinction and a number of extraordinarily ancient, rustic mountain houses. Once known for its 19th-century forges, Larrau is now a winter base camp for hunters and a summer center for hikers. It's a good departure point for the **Holçarté Gorges walk.** This classic trek is a 90-minute round-trip hike, including a spectacular bridge that hangs 561 ft above the rocky stream bed. The full tour looping back around to the Logibar is a four-hour walk, while the hike over to Ste-Engrâce is a seven-hour trip each way, a good two-day project over and back. The well-marked trail begins at the Logibar Inn (☞ Dining and Lodging, *below*), 3 km (2 mi) east of Larrau.

Dining and Lodging

$$$ ✕⛩ **Hôtel Etxemaïté.** This sophisticated country inn has spectacular views
★ and is one of the area's top dining spots (closed Sunday dinner and Monday from mid-November to mid-May). The dining room seems suspended over the garden and is often full in summer. The inn is well endowed with Basque antiques, including several *susulia* chair-and-table combinations allowing two to dine comfortably by the fire. The Basque cooking is excellent: Terrine *de poule au foie gras* (hen with duck liver) is just one good choice. Rooms are done in light woods and cheery colors. ✉ *Rte. D26, 64560 Larrau,* ☎ *05–59–28–61–45,* FAX *05–59–28–72–71. 16 rooms. Restaurant. DC, MC, V. Closed mid–late Jan.*

$ ✕⛩ **Logibar.** This simple inn with a *gîte d'étape* (way station) for hikers serves nonpareil garbure and an even better *omelette aux cèpes* (wild mushroom omelet). Rooms are tiny but cozy, and the Quihilliry family, in its fourth generation running this well-known spot, has a knack for making you feel at home. ✉ *Rte. D26, 64560 Larrau,* ☎ *05–59–28–61–14,* FAX *05–59–28–61–14. 12 rooms. Restaurant. MC, V. Closed early Dec.–early Mar.*

Gorges de Kakuetta

⓫ *13 km (8 mi) east of Larrau, 3 km (2 mi) west of Ste-Engrâe.*

A right turn onto D113 at the junction of the Uhaitxa and Larrau rivers will take you toward Ste-Engrâce and past one of the area's great natural phenomena, the Gorges de Kakuetta (the Basque spelling). A famous canyon cut through the limestone cliffs by the Uhaitxa River, the gorge is at times as narrow as 12 ft across and reaches depths of more than 1,155 ft. Stairways are cut into the rock, and hanging bridges span the watercourse. A waterfall and a grotto mark the end of the climb, a two-hour walk round-trip. This hike is recommended only during low-water conditions, normally between June and October. Good hiking shoes are indispensable. ☏ *05–59–28–73–44.* ✉ *25 frs.* ⊙ *Mid-Mar.–mid-Nov., daily 8 AM–dark*

Ste-Engrâce

⑫   *66 km (40 mi) east of St-Jean-Pied-de-Port, 37 km (23 mi) southwest of Oloron-Ste-Marie, 100 km (62 mi) southwest of Pau.*

Ste-Engrâce is at the eastern edge of the Basque Country in the Haute Soule (Upper Soule). Soule is the smallest of the three French Basque provinces. Nearly all the inhabitants speak Euskera (Basque), a non-Indo-European language of uncertain (though probably native Pyrenean and Iberian) origins.

Medieval pilgrims on the way to Santiago de Compostela in northwest Spain once flocked to the village's lovely 11th-century church of **Ste-Engrâce** to venerate the arm of Sancta Gracia, a young Portuguese noblewoman martyred around the year 300. When pillaging Calvinists removed the cherished relic in 1569, a ring finger was sent from the scene of her martyrdom in Zaragoza to replace the stolen arm. The church has an asymmetrical, slanting roof, redolent of *maison Basque* (Basque house) design. Its gray stone contrasts eerily with the green hills and fields behind. The ornate interior is a surprising contrast to the church's stark exterior. The town remains a key crossroads for pilgrims traveling to Santiago and trans-Pyrenean trekkers going east across the "dragon's back," as generations of Pyreneists have respectfully dubbed the mountain range's jagged profile.

Lodging

$ ⊞ **Auberge Elichalt.** This cozy *gîte d'étape* (hikers' way station) and table d'hôte (bed and breakfast) has 50 beds in varying situations. There are double rooms, dormitory beds, and an apartment for rent, all in the shadow of the church. Monsieur and Madame Burguburu (Euskera for "head of town") can recommend hikes into the mountains. ⊠ *64560 Ste-Engrâce,* ☏ *05–59–28–61–63,* ᴲᴬˣ *05–59–28–75–54. 5 double rooms, 1 apartment for 5, 40 dormitory beds without bath. MC, V.*

Outdoor Activities and Sports

The nearby ski station, 10 km (6 mi) away in **Pierre-St-Martin,** has alpine and Nordic skiing. If you're interested in fly-fishing, the **Gave d'Oloron** (*gave* is the word for river in the language of the Béarn), flowing through Sauveterre-de-Béarn, is a trout and Atlantic salmon fishery. On D919 between Aramits and Oloron-Ste-Marie, look for the Vert River and the nearby town of **Féas.** The gentle Vert Valley, with a meadow brook running through it, is well populated with trout.

En Route   The **Basse Soule** (Lower Soule), also known as the Barétous region, is a transitional zone between the Basque Country and Béarn characterized by rolling green hills and corn fields. To explore the Basse Soule, take D132 from Pierre-St-Martin down to Arette. Drive the loop beginning west toward the hometown of the legendary Aramis of Three Musketeers at **Aramits,** continuing through **Lannes, Trois-Villes, and Gotein** with its characteristic *clocher-calvaire,* a three-peaked bell tower designed as an evocation of Calvary. Just short of Mauléon-Licharre on D918 is the rustic 11th-century **Chapelle St-Jean-de-Berraute,** built by the Order of Malta for pilgrims on the way to Santiago de Compostela.

Mauléon-Licharre

⑬ *16 km (10 mi) southwest of Navarrenx, 40 km (24 mi) northeast of St-Jean-Pied-de-Port.*

Mauléon-Licharre, capital of the Soule, is the upland Basque Country's only industrial city, thanks to the manufacture of rope-soled espadrilles. Spread along the banks of the Saison River, the 16th-century **Hôtel de Maytie** (also known as the Château d'Andurain), the 17th-century **Hôtel de Montréal** and the remains of the 12th-century **château fort** fortress are the main spots to seek out.

L'Hôpital-St-Blaise

⑭ *13 km (8 mi) east of Mauléon-Licharre, 18 km (11 mi) west of Oloron-Ste-Marie.*

L'Hôpital-St-Blaise, a village of some 75 inhabitants, is notable for its 12th-century church combining Romanesque and Mozarabic (Christian artesans in Moorish Spain) characteristics. Possibly the work of the same architect who designed the church of Ste-Croix in Oloron-Ste-Marie, L'Hôpital-St-Blaise is remarkable for its Greek cross format and for its striated cupola crowned by a central bell tower. Once an important way station for pilgrims on their way to Santiago de Compostela, L'Hôpital-St-Blaise is on the very edge of the Basque country, as shown by the typically Basque discoidal grave marker next to the church.

En Route From L'Hôpital-St-Blaise a right on D936 will take you into Oloron-Ste-Marie. A left on D936 will take you to **Navarrenx** and **Sauveterre-de-Beárn,** two spectacular towns in the Soule region.

Oloron-Ste-Marie

⑮ *33 km (20½ mi) southwest of Pau on N134.*

Oloron-Ste-Marie straddles the confluence of two rivers, the Gave d'Aspe and the Gave d'Ossau. Trout and even the occasional Atlantic salmon can be spotted when the sun is out. Originally an Iberian and later a Roman military outpost, the town was made a stronghold by the viscounts of Béarn in the 11th century.

The **Quartier Ste-Croix** occupies the once fortified point between the two rivers and is the most interesting part of town. The fortresslike church of **Ste-Croix,** with its Moorish-influenced cupola; the two Renaissance buildings nearby; and the 14th-century **Tour Grède** (Grède Tower) are the main attractions. A walk around the **Promenade Bellevue** along the ramparts below the west side of the church will give you a view down the Aspe Valley and into the mountains behind.

Dining and Lodging

$–$$ ✗ **Le Biscondau.** Come here to sample one of the finest garbures, the hearty peasant vegetable soup, in Oloron. The view over the Gave d'Ossau is at its best from the terrace in summer. ✉ *7 rue de la Filature,* ☎ *05–59–39–06–15. DC, MC, V. Closed Mon.*

$$–$$$ ✗▥ **Hôtel Darroze.** This traditional hotel is on a quiet corner next to the Town Hall. Rooms overlook the Oloron rooftops and the Pyrénées. The restaurant, one of the town's best, is decorated with old murals depicting Oloron's confluence of *gaves,* or rivers. Be sure to try the *tourtière Gasconne flambé à l'Armagnac* (Gascon pigeon in flaming Armagnac). The restaurant is closed Monday, and there's no dinner Sunday. ✉ *4 pl. de la Mairie 64400,* ☎ *05–59–39–00–99,* ℻ *05–59–39–17–88. 30 rooms. Restaurant. AE, DC, MC, V.*

$ 🏠 **Chambre d'Hôtes Paris.** This bed-and-breakfast in Féas, run by Christian and Marie-France Paris, is a great deal, especially if you like fly-fishing. Christian, a registered guide, knows every trout in the Barétous—by name. ✉ *64570 Féas (7½ km [5 mi] past Oloron-Ste-Marie),* ☎ *05–59–39–01–10. 3 rooms. No credit cards. Closed late Dec.–early Jan.*

Navarrenx

⑯ *19 km (11 mi) northwest of Oloron-Ste-Marie.*

Perched over the Gave d'Oloron, Navarrenx was built in 1316 as a *bastide* (fortified town) at an important crossroads on the Santiago de Compostela pilgrimage route. Henri d'Albret, king of Navarre, constructed the present ramparts in 1540. The bastion of Porte St-Antoine, with its miniature turret, is one of the Soule's best-known sights. The town motto, *Si You Ti Baou* (Bearnais for "If I should see you"), refers to the cannon guarding the approach to the town across the bridge. The Gave d'Oloron is an excellent trout and salmon river. Salmon angling is an important part of Navarrenx tradition: Every year a salmon-fishing championship takes place, during which spectators line the banks of the legendary salmon pool 985 ft upstream from the bridge.

Dining and Lodging

$$ ✗🏠 **Le Commerce.** As the best restaurant and most traditional lodging in Navarrenx, the Commerce is an easy choice. Rooms are old-fashioned and cozy and have renovated, spacious bathrooms. The exquisite menu features such items as *pigeonneau au style bécasse* (woodcock-style squab), fragrant dark meat in a Madeira sauce, or *foie gras frais au myrtille* (fresh duck liver in a berry sauce). ✉ *Pl. des Casernes, 64190,* ☎ *05–59–66–50–16,* 𝖥𝖠𝖷 *05–59–66–52–67. 38 rooms. Restaurant. AE, DC, MC, V.*

Sauveterre-de-Béarn

⑰ *19 km (11 mi) northwest of Navarrenx, 39 km (23 mi) northwest of Oloron-Ste-Marie, 39 km (23 mi) northeast of St-Jean-Pied-de-Port.*

Make your first stop the terrace next to the church: The view of the Gave d'Oloron, the fortified 12th-century drawbridge, the lovely Montréal Tower, and the Pyrénées rising in the distance is among the finest in the region. The bridge, known both as the **Vieux Pont** (Old Bridge) and the Pont de la Légende (Bridge of the Legend), was named after the legend of Sancie, widow of Gaston V de Béarn. Accused of murdering a child after her husband's death in 1170, Sancie was subjected to the "Judgment of God" and thrown, bound hand and foot, from the bridge by order of the king of Navarre, her brother. When the river carried her safely to the bank, she was deemed to be exonerated on all charges.

Dining and Lodging

$$–$$$ ✗🏠 **Hôtel du Vieux Pont.** Former British journalists Paul and Sandie Williams have beautifully restored this medieval manor house built into the town's fortified 12th-century drawbridge. The views over the river and up to the ramparts of Sauveterre are superb. Rooms range from cozy and comfortable to grand and baronial (ask for the one in the corner, which has two views of the river and an immense bathroom). Excellent cuisine is served in the restaurant (especially if you bring back fresh trout or salmon for them to cook), including such dishes as magret de canard and *poulet Basquaise* (Basque chicken) and a good choice of local wines. ✉ *Rue du Pont de la Légende, 64390 Sauveterre-de-Béarn,* ☎ *05–59–38–95–11,* 𝖥𝖠𝖷 *05–59–38–99–10. 7 rooms. Restaurant. AE, DC, MC, V.*

Pau

18 *106 km (63 mi) east of Bayonne and Biarritz.*

The busy and elegant town of Pau is the historic capital of Béarn, a state annexed to France in 1620. Pau was "discovered" in 1815 by British officers returning from the Peninsular War in Spain, and it soon became a prominent winter resort town. Fifty years later English-speaking inhabitants made up one-third of Pau's population. They started the Pont-Long Steeplechase, still one of the most challenging in Europe, in 1841; created France's first golf course here, in 1856; and introduced fox hunting to the region.

Pau's regal past is commemorated at its **château,** begun in the 14th century by Gaston Phoebus, the flamboyant count of Béarn. The building was transformed into a Renaissance palace in the 16th century by Marguerite d'Angoulême, sister of François I. A woman of diverse gifts, her pastorales were performed in the château's sumptuous gardens. Her bawdy *Heptameron*—written at age 60—furnishes as much sly merriment today as it did when read by her doting kingly brother. Marguerite's grandson, the future king of France, Henri IV, was born in the château in 1553. Exhibits connected to Henri's life and times are displayed regularly, along with portraits of the most significant of his alleged 57 lovers and mistresses. His cradle, a giant turtle shell, is on exhibit in his bedroom, one of the sumptuous, tapestry-lined royal apartments. ✉ *Rue du Château,* ☎ *05–59–82–38–00.* 🎟 *28 frs, Sun. 15 frs.* ☉ *Apr.–Oct., daily 9:30–11:30 and 2–5:45; Nov.–Mar., daily 9:30–11:30 and 2–4:30.*

The **Musée Béarnais,** on the fourth floor of the château, gives an overview of the region, encompassing everything from fauna to furniture to festival costumes. ☎ *05–59–27–07–36.* 🎟 *10 frs.* ☉ *Apr.–Oct., daily 9:30–12:30 and 2:30–6:30; Nov.–Mar., daily 9:30–12:30 and 2:30–5:30.*

Dining and Lodging

$$–$$$ ✕ **Gousse d'Ail.** In the Hédas district, the deep mid-city canyon in the oldest part of Pau, this lovely hideaway is tucked under the stairway at the end of the street. Traditional Béarn cooking and international cuisine are served; try the magret de canard cooked over coals. ✉ *12 rue du Hédas,* ☎ *05–59–27–31–55,* 🖷 *05–59–06–10–53. MC, V. Closed Sun. No lunch Sat.*

$$ 🏨 **Hôtel de Gramont.** Five minutes from the château, the Gramont is a cozy and convenient base for exploring Pau. Ask for one of the *chambres mansardées* (dormered bedrooms) under the eaves overlooking the Hédas. ✉ *3 pl. de Gramont, 64000,* ☎ *05–59–27–84–04,* 🖷 *05–59–27–62–23. 36 rooms. Breakfast room. AE, DC, MC, V.*

Nightlife and the Arts

During the music and arts **Festival de Pau,** theatrical and musical events take place almost every evening from mid-July to late-August, nearly all of them gratis. Nightlife in Pau revolves around the Hédas district, where bars and restaurants line the alleys down into this one-time river gorge. The streets around the château are also sprinkled with cozy pubs and dining spots, while Pau's **casino**(✉ Parc Beaumont, ☎ 05–59–27–06–92) offers racier entertainment.

Outdoor Activities and Sports

Pau Golf Club (✉ Rue du Golf, Billère, ☎ 05–59–32–02–33) France's first golf course, is a lush 18-hole beauty. The **Haras National** (✉ 1 rue Mal-Leclerq, Gélos, ☎ 05–59–06–60–57) displays a stunning community of thoroughbreds. **Hippodrome du Pont-Long** (✉ 462 blvd. Cami-

Salié, ☎ 05–59–32–02–33) runs one of the best steeplechases in Europe and has horse races from October to May.

THE HAUTES-PYRÉNÉES

The Hautes-Pyrénées includes the highest and most spectacular natural resources in the cordillera. Although mountain peaks soar in this region, there are also centers of more civilized charms—notably, the towns of Cauterets and Bagnères-de-Luchon, set in a spa region that once attracted such formidable guests as Montaigne, Madame de Maintenon, Henri IV, and the composer Rossini. Traditionally known as La Bigorre, the border with the Béarn is at the Col d'Aubisque southeast of Oloron-Ste-Marie, while the eastern border with the Haute Garonne is at the Col de Peyresourde just west of Bagnères-de-Luchon. The legendary Cirque de Gavarnie (natural mountain amphitheater), the Vignemale peak (10,817 ft) and glacier, the Balaïtous peak (10,312 ft), the Brèche de Roland, and the Cirque de Troumouse are the main attractions in the Hautes-Pyrénées.

Tarbes

⑲ *40 km (24 mi) east of Pau, 152 km (94 mi) southwest of Toulouse, 214 km (133 mi) southeast of Bordeaux.*

Tarbes is the commercial and administrative center of the Bigorre region and the Hautes-Pyrénées Département. If Tarbes is your point of entry into the Hautes-Pyrénées, stop by the **tourist office** (⊠ 3 cours Gambetta, ☎ 05–62–51–30–31) for information, brochures, and maps of the region. The **Halle Marcadieu** is the commercial center. Thursday market day offers a chance to check out widely acclaimed local products ranging from the *choux-fleurs* (cauliflower) of Arros to the carrots of Asté, from the onions of Trébons to the famed *haricot tarbais*, a delicate-skinned kidney bean required in any authentic garbure.

Tarbes was the **birthplace of Marshal Ferdinand Foch** (⊠ 2 rue de la Victoire, ☎ 05–62–93–19–02), the general most responsible for the 1918 Allied victory. The town is also home to the **Haras National** (⊠ 70 av. du Régiment-de-Bigorre, ☎ 05–62–34–44–59), an equestrian stud farm and dressage academy. A nice place for a walk on a warm day is the **Jardin Massey** (Massey Garden), a luxuriant park filled with ducks and an abundance of flowers in summer.

Dining and Lodging

$$ ✕🛏 **L'Isard.** This handy spot in the center of Tarbes near the Massey Garden and the train station is a good choice for a night in town. It's comfortably Old World and has a good staff and a restaurant specializing in simple local fare. ⊠ *70 av. du Mal-Joffre, 65100,* ☎ *05–62–93–06–69,* ℻ *05–62–93–99–55. 8 rooms. Breakfast room. MC, V.*

Lourdes

⑳ *41 km (27 mi) southeast of Pau, 19 km (12 mi) southwest of Tarbes.*

Five million pilgrims flock to Lourdes annually, many in quest of a miraculous cure for sickness or disability. A religious pilgrimage may be one thing, but a sightseeing expedition is another question. The famous churches and grotto and the area around them are woefully lacking in beauty. Off-season, acres of empty parking lots echo. Shops are shuttered, restaurants closed. In season a mob jostles to see the grotto behind a forest of votive candles.

In February 1858 Bernadette Soubirous, a 14-year-old miller's daughter, saw the Virgin Mary in the **Grotte de Massabielle,** near the Gave de Pau (actually she had 18 visions). Bernadette dug in the grotto, releasing a gush of water from a spot where no spring existed. From then on, pilgrims thronged the Massabielle rock for the water's supposed healing powers, though church authorities reacted skeptically. It took four years for the miracle to be authenticated by Rome and a sanctuary erected over the grotto. In 1864 the first organized procession was held. Today there are six official annual pilgrimages between Easter and All Saints' Day, the most important on August 15.

Lourdes celebrated the centenary of Bernadette Soubirous's visions by building the world's largest underground church, the **Basilique St-Pie X,** with space for 20,000 people—more than the town's permanent population. Above St-Pie X stands the unprepossessing neo-Byzantine **Basilique Rosaire** (1889). The **Basilique Supérieure** (1871), tall and white, hulks nearby.

The **Pavillon Notre-Dame,** across from St-Pie X, houses the **Musée Bernadette,** with mementos of Bernadette's life and an illustrated history of the pilgrimages. In the basement is the **Musée d'Art Sacré du Gemmail** (Museum of Stained-Glass Mosaic Religious Art). ⊠ *72 rue de la Grotte,* ☎ *05–62–94–13–15.* ⌸ *Free.* ⊙ *July–Nov., daily 9:30–11:45 and 2:30–6:15; Dec.–June, Wed.–Mon. 9:30–11:45 and 2:30–5:45.*

Across the river is the **Moulin de Boly** (Boly Mill), where Bernadette was born on January 7, 1844. ⊠ *12 rue Bernadette-Soubirous.* ⌸ *Free.* ⊙ *Easter–mid-Oct., daily 9:30–11:45 and 2:30–5:45.*

The **cachot,** a tiny room where, in extreme poverty, Bernadette and her family took refuge in 1856, can also be visited. ⊠ *15 rue des Petits-Fossés,* ☎ *05–62–94–51–30.* ⌸ *Free.* ⊙ *Easter–mid-Oct., daily 9:30–11:45 and 2:30–5:30; mid-Oct.–Easter, daily 2:30–5:30.*

The **Château** on the hill above town can be reached by escalator, by 131 steps, or by the ramp up from rue du Bourg (from which a small Basque cemetery with ancient discoidal stones can be seen). Once a prison, the castle now contains the **Musée Pyrénéen,** one of France's best provincial museums, devoted to the popular customs, arts, and history of the Pyrénées. ⊠ *25 rue du Fort,* ☎ *05–62–94–02–04.* ⌸ *32 frs.* ⊙ *Easter–mid-Oct., daily 9–noon and 2–7 (last admission at 6); mid-Oct.–Easter, Wed.–Mon. 9–noon and 2–7 (last admission at 6).*

Dining and Lodging

$$ ✕☂ **Hôtel Albert/La Taverne de Bigorre.** The Moreau family's popular establishment serves traditional French mountain cooking, such as the hearty garbure. Rooms are clean and comfortable, with a personal touch that is very welcome in Lourdes. ⊠ *21 pl. du Champ Commun, 65100,* ☎ *05–62–94–75–00,* FAX *05–62–94–78–45. 27 rooms. Restaurant. AE, DC, MC, V. Closed mid-Nov.–mid-Dec. and Jan.*

Cauterets

㉑ *30 km (19 mi) south of Lourdes, 49 km (30 mi) south of Tarbes.*

Cauterets (which derives from the word for hot springs in the local *bigourdan* dialect) is a spa and resort town (for long-term treatments) high in the Pyrénées. It has been revered since Roman times for thermal baths thought to cure maladies ranging from back pain to female sterility. Novelist Victor Hugo (1802–85) womanized here; Lady Aurore Dudevant—better known as the writer George Sand (1804–76)—is said to have discovered her feminism here. Other famous visitors include Gastón Fébus, Chateaubriand, Sarah Bernhardt, King Edward VII of England, and Spain's King Alfonso XIII.

En Route   Two kilometers (1 mile) south of Cauterets is the parking lot for the thermal baths where the red-and-white marked GR10 *Sentier des Cascades* (Path of the Waterfalls) departs for Pont d'Espagne. This famous walk (three hours round-trip) reveals stunning views of the waterfalls and abundant *marmottes* (Pyrenean groundhogs). From **Pont d'Espagne,** to which you can also drive, continue on foot or by chairlift to the plateau and a view over the bright blue **Lac de Gaube,** fed by the river of the same name. Above is **Le Vignemale** (10,817 ft) France's highest Pyrenean peak. Return via Cauterets to Pierrefitte-Nestalas and turn right on D921 up Luz-St-Saveur and Gavarnie.

Gavarnie

㉒ *30 km (19 mi) south of Cauterets on D921, 50 km (31 mi) south of Lourdes.*

The village of Gavarnie is a good base for exploring the mountains in the region. For starters, it's at the foot of the **Cirque de Gavarnie,** one of the world's most remarkable examples of glacial erosion and a daunting challenge to mountaineers. Horses and donkeys, rented in the village, are the traditional way to reach the head of the valley (though walking is preferable) where the Hôtel du Cirque (☞ Dining and Lodging, *below*) has hosted six generations of visitors. When the upper snows melt, numerous streams tumble down from the cliffs to form spectacular waterfalls; the greatest of them, Europe's largest, is the **Grande Cascade,** dropping nearly 1,400 ft.

Another dramatic sight is 2 km (7 mi) west of the village of Gavarnie. Take D921 up to the Col de Boucharo, where you can park and walk five hours up to the **Brèche de Roland** glacier (you cross it during the last two hours). For a taste of mountain life, have lunch high up at the Club Alpin Français's **Refuge de Sarradets ou de la Brèche.** This is a serious climb, only feasible from mid-June to mid-September, for which you need (at least) good hiking shoes and sound physical conditioning. Crampons and ice axes are available for rent in Gavarnie; check with the Gavarnie tourist office (☞ Visitor Information, *below*) for weather reports and for information about guided tours.

Dining and Lodging

$$ ✕ **Hôtel du Cirque.** With its legendary views of the Cirque de Gavarnie, this spot is magic at sunset. Despite its name, it's just a restaurant, but not just any one: The garbure here is as delicious as the sunset. Seventh-generation owner Pierre Vergez claims his recipe using water from the Cirque and *cocos de Tarbes* (Tarbes broad beans) is unique. ✉ *1-hr walk above the village of Gavarnie,* ☎ *05–62–92–48–02. MC, V. Closed mid-Sept.–mid-June.*

$$ ✕▣ **Hôtel Marboré.** This multigabled house over a rushing mountain brook offers all the history and tradition of Gavarnie along with delightful creature comforts. Rooms are bright and pleasant and look out onto lush hillside meadows. The kind and lively owner-manager Roselyne Fillastre attends to her guests with great warmth and vivacity. The restaurant, too, is excellent: Look forward to fine cuisine prepared with the freshest ingredients. ✉ *Village de Gavarnie, 65120,* ☎ *05–62–92–40–40,* ℻ *05–62–92–40–30. 13 rooms. Restaurant. MC, V.*

Nightlife and the Arts

Every July Gavarnie holds an outdoor ballet and music performance **La Fête des Pyrénées,** using the Cirque de Gavarnie as a backdrop; show time is at sunset. For information contact the tourist office (☎ 05–62–92–49–10).

En Route The dramatic mountain scenery is impressive all along D921 between Gavarnie and **Luz-St-Sauveur.** Continuing east from Luz-St-Sauveur along D918 toward Arreau, the road passes through the lively little spa town of **Barèges** and under the brow of the mighty **Pic du Midi de Bigorre,** a mountain peak towering nearly 10,000 ft above the Col du Tourmalet pass. The finest views—and the sharpest curves—are found toward the Col d'Aspin pass. Another spectacular road is D618 from Arreau over the **Col de Peyresourde** to Bagnères de Luchon.

Bagnères de Luchon

❷❸ *150 km (93 mi) east of Gavarnie.*

The largest and most fashionable Pyrenean spa is Bagnères de Luchon (simply known as Luchon), at the head of a lush valley. Dubbed the *Reine des Pyrénées* (Queen of the Pyrénées), Luchon was considered by the Romans to rank second as a spa only to Naples. Thermal waters here cater to the vocal cords: Opera singers, lawyers, and politicians hoarse from electoral promises all pile in to breathe in the healing vapors on a long-term basis. The **Parc des Quinconces** is a pretty stroll in summer. Look for the beautiful Couteillas sculpture *Le Baiser à la Source* (*The Kiss at the Spring*), hidden under a pine tree.

On display at the **Musée du Pays de Luchon** (⊠ 18 allée d'Étigny, ☎ 05–61–79–21–21) are exhibits about Pyrenean history and lore and artifacts such as a curious sculpture portraying a woman and a serpent.

Dining and Lodging

$$$–$$$$ ✕▥ **Hôtel Corneille.** This elegant spot with a lovely terrace and park has all the comforts you could want and then some. Most furniture is original Napoléon III. The staff is very helpful and pleasant. ⊠ 5 av. A. Dumas, 65100, ☎ 05–61–79–36–22, ℻ 05–61–79–81–11. 56 rooms. Restaurant. AE, DC, MC, V. Closed end-Nov.–mid-Dec.

St-Bertrand de Comminges

❷❹ *32 km (20 mi) north of Bagnères de Luchon, 57 km (35 mi) southeast of Tarbes, 107 km (66 mi) southwest of Toulouse.*

A Roman road once led directly from Luchon to St-Bertrand de Comminges (then a huge town of 60,000). Today this delightful village, whose inhabitants number just over 200, is dwarfed beneath the imposing (mostly) 12th-century **Cathédrale Ste-Marie** (⊠ Rue des Gouverneurs); don't miss the cloisters and the intricately and playfully sculpted wood choir stalls. Described as a land-bound Mont-St-Michel, St-Bertrand's old houses, sloping alleyways, and crafts shops add to its charm. The summer music festival held here and in neighboring villages in July and August is excellent.

BASQUE COUNTRY AND THE HAUTES-PYRÉNÉES A TO Z

Arriving and Departing

By Car

A64 connects Pau and Bayonne in under an hour, and A63 runs up and down the Atlantic coast. N117 connects Hendaye with Toulouse via Pau and Tarbes. N134 connects Bordeaux, Pau, Oloron-Ste-Marie, and Spain via the Col de Somport and Jaca.

By Plane

Biarritz–Parme Airport (☎ 05–59–43–83–83) serves Bayonne and Biarritz and has several daily flights to and from Paris and several weekly to London, Marseille, Geneva, Lyon, Nice, and Pau. **Pau-Pyrénées International Airport** (☎ 05–59–33–33–00) has 10 flights daily to and from Paris as well as flights to Nantes, Lyon, Marseille, Nice, Biarritz, Madrid, Rome, Venice, Milan, and Geneva. **Air France** (☎ 05–59–27–27–28) flies from Paris and other major European destinations to Biarritz and Pau.

By Train

High-speed trains (TGVs, Trains à Grande Vitesse) cover the 800 km (500 mi) from Paris to Bayonne in 4½ hours. To get to Pau, take the TGV to Bordeaux (three hours) and connect to Pau (two hours). Bayonne and Toulouse are connected by local SNCF trains via Pau, Tarbes, Lourdes, Lannemezan, and St-Gaudens. A local train runs along the Nive from Bayonne to St-Jean-Pied-de-Port.

Getting Around

By Car

Roads are occasionally slow and tortuous in the more mountainous areas, but valley and riverside roads are generally quite smooth and fast. D132, which goes between Arette and Pierre-St-Martin, can be snowed in between mid-November and mid-May, as can N134 through the Valley d'Aspe and the Col de Somport into Spain.

By Plane

Air France (☎ 05–59–33–34–35) flies to Pau, Bayonne, Biarritz. **Air Littoral** (☎ 05–59–33–26–64) flies between Biarritz, Pau, Toulouse, Nice, and Marseille.

By Train

Bayonne is the central train hub for this region; the TGV arrives here from Paris. Local trains go between Bayonne and Biarritz and from Bayonne into the Atlantic Pyrénées, a slow but picturesque trip. Hendaye is connected to Bayonne and to San Sebastián via the famous *topo* (mole) train, so-called for the number of tunnels it passes through.

Contacts and Resources

Car Rental

BAYONNE
The following are in the train station: **Ada Location** (☎ 05–59–55–71–96). **Alfa Citer** (☎ 05–59–55–10–50). **Aquitaine Location** (☎ 05–59–55–30–55). **Europcar** (☎ 05–59–55–38–20).

BIARRITZ
The following are in the Biarritz-Parme Airport: **Alfa Citer** (☎ 05–59–23–67–95). **ALS Eurorent** (☎ 05–59–23–05–96). **Avis** (☎ 05–59–23–67–92). **Budget** (☎ 05–59–23–58–62). **Eurodollar** (☎ 05–59–41–21–12). **Europcar** (☎ 05–59–23–90–68). **Hertz** (☎ 05–59–43–92–92).

HENDAYE
Avis (107 bd. Général-de-Gaulle, ☎ 05–59–20–79–04).

PAU
The following are in the Pau-Pyrénées International Airport: **Alfa Citer** (☎ 05–59–33–25–00). **Avis** (☎ 05–59–33–27–13). **Budget** (☎ 05–59–33–77–45). **Europcar** (☎ 05–59–33–24–31). **Hertz** (☎ 05–59–33–16–38).

ST-JEAN-DE-LUZ
Avis (in train station, ☎ 05–59–26–76–66).

Guided Tours

In Biarritz, **Aitzin** (☎ 05–59–24–36–05) organizes tours of Bayonne, Biarritz, the Basque coast, and the Basque Pyrénées. The **Association des Guides** (☎ 05–59–30–44–01), in Pau, arranges tours with guides of the city, the Pyrénées, and Béarn and Basque Country. The **Bayonne tourist office** (☎ 05–59–46–01–46) gives guided tours of the city. **Guides Culturels Pyrénéens** (☎ 05–62–44–15–44), in Tarbes, arranges a variety of tours, including such themes as cave painting, art and architecture, Basque sports, hiking, and horseback riding.

Travel Agencies

BAYONNE
Agence Garrouste (✉ 10 rue Thiers, ☎ 05–59–59–02–35). **Havas Voyages** (✉ 5 rue Lormand, ☎ 05–59–46–29–26).

BIARRITZ
Adour Voyages (✉ 3 rue Gardères, ☎ 05–59–24–14–25). **Saga Tours** (✉ 4 av. du Maréchal-Foch, ☎ 05–59–24–39–39).

LOURDES
L'Accueil Pyrénéen (✉ 26 av. Maransin, ☎ 05–62–94–15–62). **American Express** (✉ 14 Chausée du Bourg, ☎ 05–62–94–40–84); note that they receive mail but don't do any banking transactions. **Maison du Pélérin** (✉ 12 av. Maransin, ☎ 05–62–94–70–05).

Visitor Information

The addresses of tourist offices in towns mentioned in this chapter are as follows: **Ainhoa** (✉ Mairie, ☎ 05–59–29–92–60). **Bagnères-de-Luchon** (✉ 18 allée d'Etigny, ☎ 05–61–79–21–21). **Bayonne** (✉ Pl. des Basques, ☎ 05–59–46–01–46). **Biarritz** (✉ 1 sq. Ixelles, ☎ 05–59–23–37–00). **Cauterets** (✉ 15 Cauterets, ☎ 05–62–92–50–27). **Dax** (✉ Pl. Thiers, ☎ 05–58–56–86–86). **Gavarnie** (✉ In center of village, ☎ 05–62–92–49–10). **Lourdes** (✉ Pl. Beyramalu, ☎ 05–62–42–77–40). **Navarrenx** (✉ Mairie, ☎ 05–59–66–10–22). **Oloron-Ste-Marie** (✉ Pl. de la Résistance, ☎ 05–59–39–98–00). **Pau** (✉ Pl. Royale, ☎ 05–59–27–27–08). **St-Bertrand-de-Comminges** (✉ Mairie, ☎ 05–61–88–33–12). **St-Jean-de-Luz** (✉ Pl. Foch, ☎ 05–59–26–03–16). **St-Jean-Pied-de-Port** (✉ 14 pl;. Charles-de-Gaulle, ☎ 05–59–37–03–57). **Sare** (✉ Mairie, ☎ 05–59–54–20–14). **Sauveterre-de-Béarn** (✉ Mairie, ☎ 05–59–38–50–17).

16 BORDEAUX, DORDOGNE, AND POITOU-CHARENTES

From the grand châteaux of Bordeaux country to the stone-cottage pastorale of Dordogne, from the chic white-sand beaches of Royan to the watery bower of the Marais Poitevin, this region offers a marvelous mix of high culture and gentle nature. And, in the land of foie gras and cognac, you'll eat (and drink) like the kings (and queens) who disputed this coveted southwest corner, staking it out with châteaux-forts and blessing it with Romanesque churches.

Revised and
updated by
Simon Hewitt

IF YOU'RE LOOKING FOR THE GOOD LIFE, look no farther. No other region of France packs such a concentration of fine wine, extraordinary spirits, superb culinary delicacies, and rib-sticking country cooking. It's almost too much to ask that it be lovely, too—but it is. Viewed for generations of British as the quintessential French escape, Dordogne is a picture-postcard fantasy of green countryside, stone cottages, and cliff-top châteaux, crowned by the enchanting medieval wine town of St-Emilion. The Atlantic beaches north of Bordeaux offer elite enclaves of white-sand beach; the vineyards of Medoc stretch lush green row after row to their south. And in the fertile outreaches of Charente, the canal-laced Marais Poitevin—France's "Green Venice"—is a luxuriant, watery bower.

It's no wonder the English fought for it so hard throughout the Hundred Years' War. This coveted corner of France was home (and name) to Eleanor of Aquitaine, and when she left her first husband, France's Louis VII, to marry Henry II of England, it came under English rule. Henry Plantagenet was, after all, a great-grandson of William the Conqueror, and the Franco-English ambiguity of the age exploded in a war that defined much of modern France and changed its face forever. Southwestern France was the stage upon which much of the war was acted. Hence the region fairly bristles with defensive châteaux-forts, hence no end of Romanesque churches were dedicated to the noble families' cause, and hence the steady flow of Bordeaux wines to England, who still dub it "claret" after *clairet*, a light-red version from earlier days.

What they sought, the world still seeks. The wines of Bordeaux tower as a standard against which all wines are measured, especially the burgeoning worldwide range of cabernets. From the grandest *premiers grands crus*—the Lafite-Rothschilds, the Margaux—to the modest *supérieur* in your picnic basket, the rigorously controlled Bordeaux commands respect. Fans and oenophiles come from around the world to pay homage; to gaze at the noble symmetry of estate châteaux, with their rows of green-and-black vineyards radiating in every direction; to sink a nose deep into a well-swirled glass, sucking in heady vapors of oak and almond and leather; and to reverently pack a few blood-lined bottles into a trunk or a suitcase for home.

The rest you will drink on site, from the mouthful of golden Graves that washes down the oysters to the syrupy sip of sauternes that slips down with the foie gras to the last glass of Médoc with the salt-marsh lamb that leads to pulling the cork on a Pauillac—because there is, after all, cheese to come . . .

But brace yourself: You've barely scratched the culinary surface. Take a deep breath and head inland, following the winding sprawl of the Dordogne River into Duck Country. This is the land of the *gavé* goose, force-fed extravagantly to plump its liver into one of the world's delicacies. Duck and goose fat glisten on potatoes, on salty confits, on *rillettes d'oie,* a spread of potted duck that melts on the tongue as no butter ever could. Wild mushrooms and truffles weave their musky perfume through dense game pâtés. The wines, such as Bergerac and Cahors, are coarser here, as if to stand up to such an onslaught of earthy textures and flavors. And a snifter of amber cognac, locally made, is de rigueur for the digestion.

Dining thus, in a vine-covered stone *ferme auberge* deep in the green wilds of Dordogne, the day's châteaux and chapel tours blurring pleasantly into a parade of picturesque history, you'll see what the Plantagenets were fighting for.

— Nancy Coons

Pleasures and Pastimes

Beaches
French families concentrate on the resort towns of Royan and Arcachon, but there are plenty of other huge beaches where you can escape the crowds: along the forest-girdled Côte Sauvage (Wild Coast) north of Royan; along the coast of the islands of Ré, Aix, and Oléron; and beneath the huge dunes south of Arcachon.

Boat Trips
Although the region's two main islands, the Ile de Ré and the Ile d'Oléron, are now linked to the mainland by bridges, boats still ply the Atlantic waters south of La Rochelle, visiting Fort Boyard and docking at the Ile d'Aix. Explore the oyster beds of the Baie de Seudre or make an excursion across the Gironde to the Cordouan Lighthouse, stranded on a sandbank in midestuary. Ferries ply the Gironde from Royan and Blaye; punts, steered with long poles, float peacefully along the canals of the Marais Poitevin; and the Dordogne River is a favorite with canoers.

Dining
Truffles, foie gras, walnuts, plums, trout, eel, oysters, and myriad succulent species of mushrooms jostle for attention on restaurant menus. The hearty food of Dordogne, the rich dairy produce of Poitou-Charentes, and shoals of succulent seafood from the Atlantic make for diversified tables. The versatile wines of Bordeaux make fine accompaniments to most regional dishes. Cognac is de rigueur at the end of a meal; sweet, tangy *pineau des Charentes*—made from cognac and unfermented grape juice—at the start.

CATEGORY	COST*
$$$$	over 400 frs
$$$	250 frs–400 frs
$$	125 frs–250 frs
$	under 125 frs

per person for a three-course meal, including tax (20.6%) and tip but not wine

🐾 *following the text of a review is your signal that the property has a Web site, where you will find details and, usually, images; for a link, visit www.fodors.com/urls.*

Lodging
Vacationers flock to the coast and islands, and for miles around hotels are booked solid months in advance. Farther inland—except for the Dordogne Valley—the situation is easier, but there aren't as many places to stay. Advance booking is particularly desirable in Bordeaux and Dordogne, where hotels fill up quickly in midsummer. Many country or small-town hotels expect you to have at least one dinner there, and if you can have two meals a day with lodging and stay several nights, it will save you money. Prices off-season (October–May) often drop as much as 20%

CATEGORY	COST*
$$$$	over 800 frs
$$$	600 frs–800 frs
$$	300 frs–600 frs
$	under 300 frs

All prices are for a standard double room for two, including tax (20.6%) and service charge.

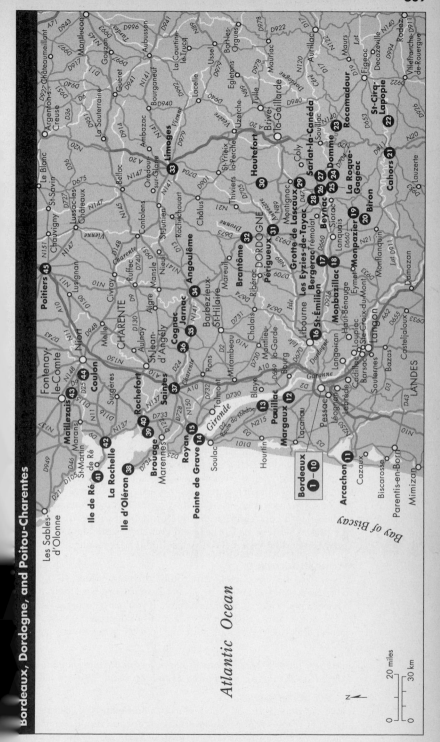

Atlantic Ocean

Bay of Biscay

Bordeaux 1 – 10

Wine

No other part of France has such a concentrated wealth of top-class vineyards. The versatile Bordeaux region yields sweet and dry whites and fruity or full-bodied reds from a huge domain extending on either side of the Gironde (Blaye and Bourg to the north, Médoc and Graves to the south) and inland along the Garonne (Sauternes) and Dordogne (St-Émilion, Fronsac, Pomerol) or in between these two rivers (Entre-Deux-Mers). Farther north, the rolling hills of Cognac produce the world's finest brandy. Less familiar appellations are also worth seeking out, including Bergerac, Pécharmant, and Monbazillac, along the Dordogne River, and the lighter whites and reds of the Fiefs Vendéens, northeast of La Rochelle.

Exploring Bordeaux, Dordogne, and Poitou-Charentes

For three centuries during the Middle Ages, this region was a battlefield in the wars between the French and the English. Of the castles and châteaux dotting the area, those at Biron, Hautefort, and Beynac are among the best. Robust Romanesque architecture is more characteristic of this area than the airy Gothic style found elsewhere in France: Poitiers showcases the best examples, notably Notre-Dame-la-Grande, with its richly worked facade. Romanesque can also be admired at the nearby abbey of St-Savin, in Angoulême and Périgueux, and in countless village churches.

If there is a formula for enjoying this region, it should include exploring cultural spots, relaxing by the sea, tasting wine, and treating yourself to oysters, truffles, and foie gras. Swaths of sandy beaches line the Atlantic coast: Well-heeled resorts, like Royan and Arcachon, are thronged with glistening bodies baking in the sun. The world-famous vineyards of Médoc, Sauternes, Graves, Entre-Deux-Mers, Pomerol, and St-Émilion surround the elegant 18th-century city of Bordeaux, set on the southwest edge of the region near the foot of the Gironde Estuary.

But if you prefer solitude, you won't have any trouble discovering vast, underpopulated stretches inland toward the east in the rolling countryside of Dordogne, also chockfull of riverside châteaux, medieval villages, and prehistoric sites. To the north, the rural region of Poitou-Charentes stretches from Angoulême through cognac country to the Atlantic coast, and back inland through the canals around Niort to Poitiers. Between La Rochelle and Poitiers lies the Marais Poitevin, a marshy area known as "Green Venice" for its crisscrossing small canals.

Great Itineraries

To see all of the region in one trip would be overambitious, so you need to be selective. If you love the beach and the outdoors, head to the Royan Peninsula or the islands of Ré and Oléron. If you're a gourmet, go straight to Dordogne; if wine is your passion, use Bordeaux as your base. For nature, seek out the Marais-Poitevin. Following are some suggested itineraries.

Numbers in the text correspond to numbers in the margin and on the Bordeaux, Dordogne, and Poitou-Charentes map.

IF YOU HAVE 5 DAYS

Have a morning tour and pleasant lunch in **Bordeaux** ①–⑩ before heading on to medieval ☒ **St-Émilion** ⑯ during the afternoon. On the second day visit the fortified medieval village of **Monpazier** ⑲ and the mighty château in **Biron** ⑳, before veering north to overnight at ☒ **La Roque Gageac** ㉕, huddled beneath a towering gray cliff. On day three head along the Dordogne River to the castle at **Beynac** ㉖, lunch on foie gras and truffles in the medieval market town of ☒ **Sarlat** ㉗, then check out the cave paintings at the **Grotte de Lascaux** ㉙ or the archeological findings at the Musée Nationale de Préhistoire in **Les Eyzies-de-Tayac** ㉘. Rest up near 🖼 **Hautefort** ㉚. On day four leave Dordogne via quaint **Brantôme** ㉜ en route to hilltop **Angoulême** ㉞. Try to get to 🖼 **Jarnac** ㉟ or 🖼 **Cognac** ㊱ by afternoon so you have time to visit a *chai* (brandy warehouse), then continue along the Charente Valley before spending the night in stately 🖼 **Saintes** ㊲. On your final day head up to **Coulon** ㊹ to explore the Marais Poitevin, a verdant, marshy area crisscrossed by canals, then continue to **Poitiers** ㊺, known for its Romanesque churches and an easy drive from the Loire Valley.

IF YOU HAVE 7 DAYS

Follow the above itinerary as far as 🖼 **Saintes** ㊲. On day five drive up to 🖼 **La Rochelle** ㊷, passing through historic **Brouage** ㊳ and **Rochefort** ㊵ along the way. Next day explore the old town and picturesque harbor at La Rochelle and cross to the bucolic 🖼 **Ile de Ré** ㊶ after lunch. On your final day head east to the Marais Poitevin, visiting the ruined abbey of **Maillezais** ㊸, lunching in the pretty village of **Coulon** ㊹, and continuing to **Poitiers** ㊺ to end your tour.

When to Tour Bordeaux, Dordogne, and Poitou-Charentes

Spring and autumn are the best times to visit—there aren't as many tourists around, and the weather is still pleasant. The *vendanges* (grape harvests) usually begin about mid-September in the Bordeaux region (though you can't visit the wineries at this time), and two weeks later in the Cognac region, to the north. A number of hotels close from the end of October through March.

THE BORDEAUX REGION

Bordeaux, the commercial and cultural center of southwest France, is ringed by renowned vineyards: Graves and pretty Sauternes, to the south; Pomerol and St-Émilion, to the east; and to the northwest, the dusty Médoc Peninsula, looking across the Gironde Estuary at the vineyards of Bourg and Blaye. Head southwest, and you'll find great swaths of pine forest, huge sand dunes, and the fancy resort of Arcachon, with its lagoon.

Bordeaux

580 km (360 mi) southwest of Paris, 240 km (150 mi) northwest of Toulouse, 190 km (118 mi) northeast of Biarritz.

Bordeaux as a whole, rather than any particular points within it, is what you'll want to visit in order to understand why Victor Hugo described it as Versailles plus Antwerp and why the great painter Goya chose it as his home until his death in 1828. The capital of southwest France and the region's largest city, Bordeaux is still trying to diversify its tourist appeal—its May music festival pulls in the crowds—but the city remains synonymous with the wine trade: Wine shippers have long based their headquarters along the banks of the Garonne. An aura of 18th-century elegance permeates downtown Bordeaux, where fine shops invite exploration. To the south of the city center are the old docklands, targeted for renewal but still a bit shady. As a whole, Bordeaux is a less exuberant city than most others in France. To get a feel for the historic port of Bordeaux, take the 90-minute boat trip that leaves quai Louis-XVIII every weekday afternoon.

❶ For a view of the picturesque quayside, stroll across the Garonne on the **pont de Pierre** (Stone Bridge), the only bridge across the river until

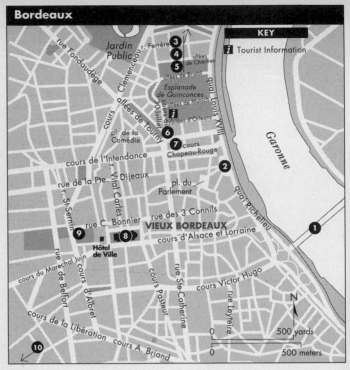

2 1965. Then head along the left bank to **place de la Bourse,** an open square (built 1730–55) ringed with large-windowed buildings designed by the era's most esteemed architect, Jacques-Ange Gabriel. Continue along the Garonne, past the sprawling Esplanade des Quinconces, to **3** explore the **Croiseur Colbert,** a 1950s battleship withdrawn from service in 1991. ⊠ *Quai des Chartrons,* ☎ *05–53–44–96–11.* 🎫 *42 frs.* ☉ *Apr.–Sept., daily 10–6, Oct.–Mar., Tues.–Sun. 10–6.*

Nearby are the **Cité Mondiale du Vin** (World of Wine Center; ⊠ 25 quai des Chartrons), part office building, part shopping mall, and part **4** cultural center, all focusing on the world of wine; and the **Musée des Chartrons,** in an 18th-century vintner's house, retracing the history of the wine trade with a fine collection of old barrels and antique bottles. ⊠ *41 rue Borie,* ☎ *05–57–87–50–60.* 🎫 *20 frs.* ☉ *Weekdays 2–6.*

A half mile (¼ km) farther down the quayside is the massive, bunker-**5** like **Base Sous-Marine** (Submarine Base), built by the Nazis in 1941. ⊠ *Bd. Alfred-Daney,* ☎ *05–56–11–11–50.* 🎫 *20 frs.* ☉ *Wed., Thurs. and weekends 1–6.*

Turn back along the Garonne and cross Esplanade des Quinconces to **6** tree-lined cours du XXX-Juillet and the **CIVB** (Counseil Interprofessionne des Vins de Bordeaux), headquarters of the Bordeaux wine trade. You can get information and samples here, you can make purchases at the **Vinothèque** opposite.

One block south is the city's leading 18th-century monument: the **7** **Grand Théâtre,** designed by Victor Louis and built between 1773 and 1780. The pride of the city, it is a building so magnificent that Charles Garnier did not hesitate to borrow major elements from its design when he built the Opéra in Paris. Its elegant exterior is ringed by graceful

Corinthian columns, while the majestic foyer features a two-winged staircase and cupola. The theater-hall has a frescoed ceiling, a shimmering chandelier composed of 14,000 Bohemian crystals, and, it is said, perfect acoustics. ⊠ *Pl. de la Comédie,* ☎ *05–56–00–85–95.* ⊡ *30 frs. Contact tourist office for guided tours.*

⑧ Continue south on rue Ste-Catherine, then turn right on cours d'Alsace to reach the **Cathédrale St-André** (⊠ Pl. Pey-Berland). This hefty edifice isn't one of France's better Gothic cathedrals, but the soaring 14th-century chancel makes an interesting contrast with the earlier, more severe nave. Excellent stone carvings adorn the facade. You can climb the 15th-century, 160-ft **Tour Pey-Berland** for a view of the city; the admission is 25 francs, and it's open Tuesday–Sunday 10–noon and 2–5.

⑨ The nearby **Musée des Beaux-Arts,** across tidy gardens behind the ornate Hôtel de Ville (Town Hall), has a notable collection of works spanning the 15th–20th centuries, with important paintings by Paolo Veronese (*Apostle's Head*), Camille Corot (*Bath of Diana*), and Odilon Redon (*Chariot of Apollo*) and sculptures by Auguste Rodin. ⊠ *20 cours d'Albret,* ☎ *05–56–10–20–56.* ⊡ *30 frs.* ☉ *Wed.–Mon. 11–6.*

One of the region's most famous wine-producing châteaux is actually within the city limits: Follow N250 southwest from central Bordeaux (in the direction of Arcachon) for 3 km (2 mi) to the district of Pessac, **⑩** home to **Haut-Brion,** producer of the only non-Médoc wine to be ranked a *premier cru* (the most elite wine classification). The classical white château looks out over the celebrated pebbly soil. The wines produced at **La Mission–Haut Brion,** across the road, are almost as sought after.

Dining and Lodging

Old Bordeaux has many small restaurants, particularly around the 18th-century place du Parlement, like bustling L'Ombrière (No. 14), with fairly priced steaks, and pricey Chez Philippe (No. 1), one of the city's top fish restaurants. What is lacking is charming hotels. You may want to consider staying outside Bordeaux, at the Château Lamothe in St-Sulpice et Cameyrac, 20 km (12 mi) east of the city (☞ St-Émilion Lodging, *below*), for instance.

$$ ✕ **Vieux Bordeaux.** This lively, much-acclaimed nouvelle-cuisine haunt
★ lies on the fringe of the old town. Chef Michel Bordage's menu is short but of high quality, complemented by three prix-fixe menus. His fish dishes are particularly tasty, such as the grilled *bar* (bass) on a peppery galette of crab. ⊠ *27 rue Buhan,* ☎ *05–56–52–94–36. AE, DC, MC, V. Closed Sun., Aug., and first half of Feb. No lunch Sat.*

$$ ✕ **Gravelier.** Anne-Marie, daughter of Pierre Troisgros of Roanne (☞ Chapter 10), married Yves Gravelier, and they combined their culinary talents. In sparse decor, full of light and openness, imaginative cuisine is served: fillets of *rouget* (red mullet) with foie gras and pigeon pot-pie with Chinese cabbage. The 110-franc lunch menu is a good deal. ⊠ *114 cours de Verdun,* ☎ *05–56–48–17–15. AE, DC, MC, V. Closed Sun. and 1st 3 wks in Aug. No lunch Sat.*

$$$ ✕⊡ **Burdigala.** Of the three luxury hotels in Bordeaux, Burdigala (Latin for "Bordeaux") is the only one within walking distance of the center of town. The modern exterior is extremely unappealing, but the inside is comfortable. The soundproof rooms are smart and neat; No. 416 is especially quiet and sunny. Deluxe rooms have marble bathrooms with whirlpool baths. The Jardin du Burdigala restaurant serves nouvelle haute cuisine. ⊠ *115 rue Georges-Bonnac, 33000,* ☎ *05–56–90–16–16,* FAX *05–56–93–15–06. 68 rooms, 15 suites. Restaurant, meeting rooms. AE, DC, MC, V.*

$$$ ✕🏨 **Sainte-Catherine.** This hotel is in a 19th-century building in the old part of town. Service is limited, but the reception staff is helpful. The compact rooms are decorated with light floral fabrics. Beautifully presented, light nouvelle cuisine is served in the dining room, with its 12th-century vaulted ceilings. ✉ *27 rue du Parlement-Ste-Catherine, 33000,* ☎ *05–56–81–95–12,* FAX *05–56–44–50–51. 84 rooms, 3 suites. Restaurant, piano bar. AE, DC, MC, V.*

$$ 🏨 **Quatre Soeurs.** In an elegant 1840 town house near the Grand Théâtre, this hotel has well-kept rooms of varying sizes and prices. The adjoining Art Nouveau café has carved woodwork and plush velvet seats and often hosts classical concerts; the jolly owner, Ernestine Defalque, has a wonderful voice. ✉ *6 cours du XXX-juillet, 33000,* ☎ *05–57–81–19–20,* FAX *05–56–01–04–28. 35 rooms. Bar, café. MC, V.*

Nightlife and the Arts

A respected and long-established Bordeaux hangout, **Les Argentiers** (✉ 33 rue des Argentiers) is the place for jazz. **L'Aztécal** (✉ 61 rue du Pas-St-Georges) is a comfortable spot for a drink. **Sénéchal** (✉ 57 bis quai de Paludate) is the place to dance the night away.

The **Grand Théâtre** (✉ Pl. de la Comédie, ☎ 05–56–00–85–95) puts on performances of French plays and occasionally operas. Bordeaux's **International Musical May** is a leading event on France's cultural calendar for classical concerts.

Shopping

Between the cathedral and the Grand Théâtre are numerous pedestrian streets where stylish shops abound. For an exceptional selection of cheeses, go to **Jean d'Alos** (✉ 4 rue Montesquieu). The **Vinothèque** (✉ 8 cours du XXX-Juillet) sells more than 250 top-ranking Bordeaux wines.

Arcachon

🟓 *64 km (40 mi) southwest of Bordeaux via N250.*

In the midst of the sandy pine forest of Les Landes, along the Atlantic coast southwest of Bordeaux, is the resort town of Arcachon. (It became a resort in the 1850s when the new railroad connected it with Bordeaux.) These days Arcachon is a lively, busy boating center, with three jetties protruding over its sandy beaches. From boulevard de la Mer there are good views toward Cap Ferret, across the narrow straits that mark the divide between lagoon and ocean.

The highlight of a visit to Arcachon (actually 6 km [4 mi] to the south) is probably the mighty **Dune du Pyla,** a wall of sand that, at more than 370 ft high, counts as Europe's highest sand dune.

The **Bassin d'Arcachon** is a lagoon renowned both for its variety of migratory birds and for its excellent oysters, clustered around the **Ile aux Oiseaux** (Island of Birds), a small island in the middle. Arcachon stands at the southernmost tip of a chain of lakes connected by streams and canals. In the center of this chain, linked to the Bassin d'Arcachon by the **Canal de Lège,** is the small **Lac de Lacanau,** teeming with pike, perch, and eel. Farther north is the 19-km-long (12-mi-long) **Lac d'Hourtin-Carcans.** The small town of **Hourtin,** with a marina and 450-yard jetty, stands on its northernmost shore. The D101 heads through the forest to **Soulac,** a small resort town overlooking the Atlantic. The 12th-century basilica of **Notre-Dame de la Fin-des-Terres** deserves to have an outlandish history, given its name—Our Lady of the Ends of the Earth—and it does. By 1800 it had been almost completely embedded in drifting sands and was dug out and restored only 100 years ago.

Nightlife and the Arts

Activities are ongoing at Arcachon's **casino** (⊠ 163 bd. de la Plage). Arcachon's major festival, celebrating the sea, is the **Fêtes de la Mer,** held in mid-August.

Outdoor Activities and Sports

Both Arcachon and Lacanau, to the north, have 18-hole **golf courses** (⊠ Arcachon, ☎ 05–56–54–44–00; ⊠ Lacanau, ☎ 05–56–03–92–92).

Route du Médoc

North of Bordeaux, the Route du Médoc wine road (D2) winds through the Médoc Peninsula, a strange, dusty region. Even the vines in Médoc look dusty, and so does the ugly town of **Margaux,** the area's unofficial capital, 27 km (17 mi) northwest of Bordeaux. Yet **Château Margaux,** an elegant, coolly restrained classical building of 1802, is recognized as a producer of premiers crus, whose wine qualifies with Graves's Haut-Brion as one of Bordeaux's top five reds.

Continue to Cussac, visit the winery and carriage museum at **Château Lanessan,** then stop in **Pauillac,** home to three wineries—Lafite-Rothschild, Latour, and Mouton-Rothschild—that produce Médoc's other top reds. Of all the towns and villages in the Médoc, Pauillac is the prettiest; you may want to stroll along the riverfront and stop for refreshments at one of its restaurants.

At the tip of the peninsula, near a memorial commemorating the landing of U.S. troops in 1917, is the **Pointe de Grave,** where you can take the *bac* (ferry) across the Gironde to Royan; it runs at least four times daily and costs 125 francs per car and 18 francs per passenger. During the half-hour crossing, keep an eye out for the **Phare de Cordouan** on your left, a lighthouse that looks as if it's emerging from the sea (it's actually built on a sandbank, exposed at low tide).

Dining and Lodging

$$$$ ╳🗹 **Château Cordeillan-Bages.** This 17th-century château just outside Pauillac is surrounded by the vines that produce its own *cru bourgeois.* Paris-trained chef Thierry Marx is one of the most highly rated in the region, and his fortes range from local salt-meadow lamb and spit-roasted kid with shallots to crisp potato slices layered with oxtail and truffles (the restaurant is closed Monday and doesn't serve lunch Saturday). ⊠ *61 rue des Vignerons, 33250 Pauillac (1½ km [1 mi] south of town),* ☎ *05–56–59–24–24,* 🅵🅰🆇 *05–56–59–01–89. 25 rooms. Restaurant. AE, DC, MC, V. Closed Dec.–Jan.*

Outdoor Activities and Sports

The **Médoc Marathon,** on the first Saturday of September, is more than just a 42-km (26-mi) race through the vineyards: 50 groups of musicians turn out to serenade the runners, who can indulge in no fewer than 20 giant buffets en route, and drink free wine from two dozen estates along the way. Speed is not exactly of the essence for most competitors.

Royan

104 km (65 mi) north of Bordeaux, 40 km (25 mi) south of Rochefort, 38 km (24 mi) southwest of Saintes.

Royan is a commercialized resort town on the Atlantic whose vast seafront is packed to the gills in summer, although there are prettier beaches just north—in Pontaillac, St-Palais, and La Palmyre (also home to France's largest zoo). Boats leave Royan in summer for trips down the Gironde Estuary and across to the Phare de Cordouan (☞ *above*).

★ Royan was tastefully rebuilt after being destroyed by German bombing in 1945. The imaginative domed, octagonal, concrete **Marché Central** (Central Market) merits a visit. In the **Église Notre-Dame,** an enormous concrete church with a breathtaking oval interior, the huge, unsupported sweep of the curved ceiling is a technical tour de force. The elegant church tower dominates the town skyline.

En Route   From Royan, follow the Route Verte (Green Route) up the Gironde Estuary. Take D25 to the pleasant resort town of **St-Georges-de-Didonne** then continue south through pine forests and chalky cliffs to **Meschers** and Les Grottes de Matata, where you can sip tea or eat ice cream on a flower-bedecked terrace overlooking the estuary (from June through September). Farther south, **Talmont** is an unspoiled, car-free village renowned for its gently proportioned 12th-century church jutting out over the waters. Staying on D145, pause at the cheerful little harbor of **Mortagne-sur-Gironde;** then continue through rolling hills, with beguiling views over the Gironde Estuary and vineyards, which produce cognac and then Bordeaux wines, as you progress south. **Blaye** is home to a vast Vauban citadel and a ferry that crosses to Lamarque, in the Médoc (four times a day for 90 francs per car and 25 francs per passenger). A scenic riverside road continues to **Bourg,** famed for its lightish red wines and classical château facing the river. From Bourg head southwest toward **Libourne,** skirting the town to the north to explore the vineyards of Fronsac, Pomerol, and Lalande-de-Pomerol, close to St-Émilion.

St-Émilion

★ ⓰   *128 km (80 mi) southeast of Royan, 35 km (23 mi) east of Bordeaux.*

Suddenly the sun-fired flatlands of Pomerol break into hills and send you tumbling into St-Émilion. This jewel of a town has old buildings of golden stone, ruined town walls, well-kept ramparts offering pleasing views, and a church hewn into a cliff. Sloping vineyards invade from all sides, and thousands of tourists invade down the middle. The medieval streets are filled with wine stores (St-Émilion reaches maturity earlier than other Bordeaux reds and often offers a better value for the money than Médoc or Graves), crafts shops, and bakeries selling macaroons, a local specialty.

Tours of the pretty local vineyards—Château Pétrus and Cheval Blanc, among others—including wine tastings, and train rides through the vineyards, are organized by the tourist office, the **Syndicat d'Initiative** (⊠ Pl. des Créneaux, ☎ 05–57–55–28–28).

A stroll along the 13th-century ramparts takes you to the **Château du Roi** (King's Castle), built by occupying sovereign Henry III of England (1216–72). From the castle ramparts steps lead down to **place du Marché,** a wooded square where cafés remain open late into the balmy summer night. Beware of the inflated prices at the café tables.

The **Église Monolithe** (Monolithic Church) is one of France's largest underground churches, hewn out of the rock face between the 9th and 12th centuries. Its handsome spire-topped bell tower emerges from the bedrock, dominating the center of town. ⊠ *Pl. du Marché.* ⊡ *33 frs.* ⊙ *Tours leave every 45 mins from tourist office, daily 10–11:30 and 2–5.*

Just south of the town walls is the **Château Ausone,** an estate that is ranked with Cheval Blanc as producing the finest wine of St-Émilion.

Dining and Lodging

$$ ✕ **Chez Germaine.** Family cooking and regional dishes are the focus at this central St-Émilion eatery. The candlelit upstairs dining room and the terrace are both pleasant places to enjoy the reasonably priced se

menus. Grilled meats and fish are house specialties; for dessert, go for the almond macaroons. ⊠ *13 rue du Clocher,* ☎ *05–57–74–49–34. DC, V. Closed Sun.–Mon. and mid-Dec.–mid-Jan.*

$$$$ ✕⊞ **Grand Barrail.** This turn-of-the-century estate just outside St-Émilion has been converted into a luxury hotel, albeit a little stiff and Germanic. Rooms are unusually large for a French hotel and are smartly furnished; about half are in the former stables. The talented young chef serves traditional regional fare in the small dining room (no dinner Sunday; closed Monday out of season). St-Émilions constitute at least 60% of the impressive wine list. ⊠ *5 rue Marzelle, 33330 (4 km [2½] mi northwest of St-Émilion),* ☎ *05–57–55–37–00,* ℻ *05–57–55–37–49. 28 rooms. Restaurant, pool. AE, DC, MC, V. Closed part of Feb.*

$$$ ✕⊞ **Hostellerie de Plaisance.** Across from the tourist office in the upper
★ part of town is this sought-after hotel. Rooms are warm and appealing; the Descault Room has an excellent view of the vineyards. Dinner matches the St-Émilion wines; if you are not staying here, make this your number one choice for a leisurely lunch or dinner. The restaurant tends to be overbooked, so be ready to be turned away or fight for your rights. ⊠ *5 pl. du Clocher, 33330,* ☎ *05–57–55–07–55,* ℻ *05–57–74–41–11. 16 rooms. Restaurant. AE, DC, MC, V. Closed Jan.*

$$ ✕⊞ **Auberge de la Commanderie.** Close to the ramparts, this two-story, 19th-century two-story hotel has a garden and a view of the vineyards. Rooms are small but clean and individually decorated. The attractive restaurant, often frequented by nonguests, serves hearty regional fare, such as confit de canard, steaks, and gizzard salad, and a good selection of local wines; it's closed Tuesday, except in July and August. ⊠ *2 rue de la Porte-Brunet, 33300,* ☎ *05–57–24–70–19,* ℻ *05–57–74–44–53. 17 rooms. Restaurant. MC, V. Closed late Dec.–Feb.*

$$$ ⊞ **Château Lamothe.** St-Émilion's hotels are mostly in-and-out tourist stops and Bordeaux's lack charm; a nice alternative is this private manor house (advance reservations required) halfway between the two. The large guest rooms have big four-poster beds with soft cotton sheets; you may find them a little too frilly, but they are very comfortable. Invariably the friendly hosts, Monsieur and Madame Bastide, will join you for an aperitif or breakfast. Jacques Bastide speaks English and is extremely helpful with suggestions. ⊠ *6 rte. du Stade, 33450 St-Sulpice et Cameyrac (25 km [16 mi] northeast of St-Émilion, 20 km [12 mi] west of Bordeaux),* ☎ *05–56–30–82–16,* ℻ *05–56–30–88–33. 3 rooms. MC, V.*

Vineyards Around Bordeaux

Cross the Dordogne at Brannes, 8 km (5 mi) south of St-Émilion, and head southwest along D11, via Targon, through the region known as **Entre-Deux-Mers** (between two seas—that is, the Dordogne and Garonne rivers), whose dry white wine is particularly flavorsome if made from the vineyards near the ruins of the **Château de Haut-Bénauge.** Soon after the ruined castle, D11 collides with the Garonne at **Cadillac** and its 17th-century château. Turn left along D10 to the picturesque villages of **Loupiac** and **Sainte-Croix-du-Mont,** sandwiched between the river and hillside vineyards producing sweet white wine.

At Langon, cross the Garonne and head west on D8 into the **Sauternes** vineyards, home to what is generally acclaimed as the finest sweet wine in the world. Nothing in the grubby village of Sauternes would tell you that mind-boggling wealth lurks amid the picturesque vine-laden slopes and hollows. The village has a wine shop where bottles gather dust on rickety shelves, next to handwritten price tags demanding 1,000 francs (about $160) and more. Making Sauternes is a tricky business. Autumn mists steal up the valleys to promote *Botrytis cinerea,* a form of "noble rot" called *pourriture noble,* which sucks moisture out of the grapes, leaving a high proportion of sugar. Not all grapes achieve the required degree of over-ripeness simultaneously; up to seven successive harvests are undertaken at **Château d'Yquem,** a little more than 1½ km (1 mi) north of Sauternes, to assure the optimum selection. This painstaking attention to detail, added to a centuries-old reputation and soil ideally suited to making sweet white wine, enables bottles of Yquem to obtain prices more appropriate to liquid gold. If you do splurge on a recent vintage, you may as well lock it away; Yquem needs to wait at least 10 years before coming into its own and will reward decades of patience.

Heading northwest toward Bordeaux, you encounter the vineyards of the **Graves** region, so called because of its gravelly soil. This is the region's most historic appellation: A lightish-red wine known as *clairet* was esteemed by English occupiers during the Middle Ages.

White wine—mainly dry—is also produced, some of the best at the Domaine de Chevalier in **Léognan,** 10 km (6 mi) southwest of Bordeaux.

DORDOGNE

Stretching along the Dordogne, Isle, Dronne, and Auvezère rivers, this wooded region's rolling hills and valleys are full of romantic riverside châteaux, small medieval villages, and prehistoric sites, including the incomparable Lascaux cavern paintings (and the not so incomparable Lascaux 2). You may want to spend a week exploring the small country roads and picnicking on the riverbanks.

Bergerac

⑰ *87 km (54 mi) east of Bordeaux, 57 km (36 mi) east of St-Émilion.*

Bergerac is a lively town with ancient half-timber houses, narrow alleys, and colorful Wednesday and Saturday (the larger of the two) markets. Guided walking tours of the old town (one hour, 25 francs) leave from the **tourist office** (⊠ 97 rue Neuve d'Argenson, ☎ 05–53–57–03–11). There are also hour-long cruises along the Dordogne (40 francs); check with the tourist office or the **cruise company** (☎ 05–53–24–58–80) for information.

The **Cloître des Récollets,** a former convent, is in the wine business. The convent's stone-and-brick buildings range in date from the 12th to the 17th centuries and include galleries, a large vaulted cellar, and a cloister, where the **Maison du Vin** (Wine Center) dishes out information on—and samples of—local vintages. ⊠ *Quai Salvette,* ☎ *05–53–63–57–55.* ⌦ *25 frs.* ◷ *Daily 10–12:30 and 1:30–6.*

You can learn about another local industry—tobacco growing—from its pre-Columbian origins to its spread worldwide, at the **Musée du Tabac** (Tobacco Museum). It's housed in the 17th-century Maison Peyrarède, near the quayside. ⊠ *Pl. de Feu,* ☎ *05–53–63–04–13.* ⌦ *15 frs.* ◷ *Tues.–Fri. 10–noon and 2–6, Sat. 10–noon and 2–5, Sun. 2:30–6:30.*

Dining and Lodging

$$ ✕▥ **Bordeaux.** One of the better hotels in town, the family-owned Bordeaux has contemporary furnishings and neat rooms. Request one on the garden-courtyard or No. 22, which is slightly more spacious. Though you're not obliged to eat at the restaurant, it's difficult to refuse the marinated salmon in anisette and lime or the panfried *escalope de foie gras* (sautéed foie gras). The owner, Monsieur Maury, speaks fluent English. ⊠ *38 pl. Gambetta, 24100,* ☎ *05–53–57–12–83,* ℻ *05–53–57–72–14. 40 rooms. Restaurant, bar, pool. AE, DC, MC, V. Closed mid-Dec.–Jan.*

$$ ╳⛉ **Petite Auberge.** Head south to Razac d'Eymet to find this modernized, English-run country house. Rooms are tidy and cozy; for an extra 100 francs you might be tempted to stay in No. 7, the spacious ground-floor suite with a fireplace. Locals come to dine on the light version of regional cooking, particularly confit de canard, foie gras, and walnut tart, as well as vegetarian dishes. (The restaurant is usually closed to nonguests November–March.) ⊠ *Le Royère, 24500 Razac d'Eymet (18 km [11 mi] south of Bergerac, 4 km [2 mi] east of D933, before the town of Eymet),* ☎ *05–53–24–69–27,* ⬛ *05–53–61–02–63. 7 rooms, 2 suites. Restaurant, pool. MC, V.*

Monbazillac

⑱ *6 km (4 mi) south of Bergerac via D13.*

From the hilltop village of Monbazillac are spectacular views of the sweet-wine-producing vineyards tumbling toward the Dordogne. The squat corner towers of the beautifully proportioned 16th-century gray-stone **Château de Monbazillac** pay tribute to the fortress tradition of the Middle Ages, but the large windows and sloping roofs reveal the Renaissance influence. Regional furniture and an ornate early 17th-century bedchamber enliven the interior. A wine tasting is provided at the end of your tour to tempt you into buying a case or two of the famous but expensive bottles. The restaurant on the grounds serves expensive meals. ☎ *05–53–61–52–52.* ⬛ *35 frs.* ◷ *June–Sept., daily 10–12:30 and 2–7:30; mid-Feb.–May, Oct.–Dec., daily 10–noon and 2–5.*

En Route   Southeast of Monbazillac is **Issigeac,** a well-preserved old town with numerous medieval houses. From Issigeac, follow D207 to **Villeréal,** another small *bastide* (fortified medieval town with regimented street plans) of note.

Monpazier

⑲ *16 km (10 mi) southeast of Bergerac.*

Monpazier, on the tiny Drot River, is one of France's best-preserved bastide towns. It was built in ochre-color stone by English king Edward I in 1284 to protect the southern flank of his French possessions. The bastide has three stone gateways (of an original six), a large central square, and the church of **St-Dominique,** housing 35 carved wooden choir stalls and a would-be relic of the True Cross. Opposite the church is the finest medieval building in town, the **Maison du Chapître** (Chapter House), once used as a barn for storing grain. Its wood-beam roof is constructed of chestnut to repel web-spinning spiders.

Dining and Lodging

$ ╳⛉ **France.** Once an outbuilding on the estates of the Château de Biron, the Hôtel de France has never capitalized on its 13th-century heritage or its 15th-century staircase (a historical monument). Instead, it has remained a small, modest family-run hotel that caters more to locals at its bar and restaurant, serving rich regional food, than to tourists. Rooms are a clutter of old furniture (with a plastic cabinet shower and toilet squeezed into the corner); some are quite large. ⊠ *21 rue St-Jacques, 24540,* ☎ *05–53–22–60–01,* ⬛ *05–53–22–07–27. 17 rooms. Restaurant, bar. MC, V.*

Biron

⑳ *8 km (5 mi) south of Monpazier via D53.*

Stop in Biron to see its massive hilltop castle, the **Château de Biron.** Highlights of the château, which, along with the keep, square tower,

and chapel, dates from the Middle Ages, include monumental staircases and the kitchen with its huge stone slabs. The classical buildings
were completed in 1730. English Romantic poet Lord Byron (1788–
1824) is claimed as a distant descendant of the Gontaut-Biron family,
who lived here for 14 generations. ☎ *05–53–63–13–39.* 🗪 *28 frs.* ☉
*Apr.–June and Sept., Tues.–Sun. 10–noon and 2–6; Oct.–Mar., Tues.–
Sun. 2–5; July–Aug., daily 10–7.*

Cahors

㉑ *60 km (38 mi) southeast of Monpazier via D660, 108 km (67 mi) northwest of Albi.*

Once an opulent Gallo-Roman town, Cahors, sitting snugly within a
loop of the Lot River, is famous for its tannic red wine, known to the
Romans as black wine. Many of the small estates in the area have tastings. The town's finest sight is the 14th-century **Pont Valentré,** a bridge
with three elegant towers that counts as a spellbinding feat of medieval
engineering. Also look for the fortresslike **Cathédrale St-Étienne** (⌖ off
rue du Mar. Joffre), with its cupolas and cloisters connecting to the
courtyard of the archdeaconry, which is awash with Renaissance decoration and thronged with visitors who come for art exhibits.

Dining and Lodging

$$$$ ✕🏨 **Château de Mercuès.** Just outside town, this hotel in the former
home of the Counts of Cahors has older rooms in baronial splendor
(ask for one of these), as well as unappealing modern ones (which tend
to attract mosquitoes). One of the best is "Tour," with a ceiling that
slides back to expose the turret. Duck, lamb, and truffles reign in the
restaurant, but the high prices lead you to expect more creativity from
chef Philip Combet than is produced. Service also tends to be rather
slack until you make the staff aware that you expect your needs ful-
filled immediately. The restaurant is closed Wednesday, except July and
August. ⌖ *46090 Mercuès (6 km [4 mi] west of Cahors on the road
to Villeneuve-sur-Lot),* ☎ *05–65–20–00–01,* ℻ *05–65–20–05–72. 24
rooms, 6 suites. Restaurant, pool, 2 tennis courts, helipad. AE, DC,
MC, V. Closed Nov.–Easter.*

$$–$$$ ✕🏨 **Terminus.** At this small ivy-covered hotel, only a two-minute walk
from the train station, the Marré family goes out of its way to help.
Rooms are tastefully done and up to date; those on the first floor are
the largest. The restaurant, La Balandre, is the town's best; truffles as
well as exceptional *brandade* (puree of cod and potatoes) are served
(closed Monday, no dinner Sunday). ⌖ *5 av. Charles-de-Freycinet,
46000,* ☎ *05–65–35–24–50,* ℻ *05–65–22–06–40. 22 rooms. Restaurant. AE, DC, MC, V. Closed 2 wks in Feb., 1 wk in June.*

St-Cirq-Lapopie

㉒ *25 km (16 mi) east of Cahors via D653 and D662.*

The beautiful 13th-century village of St-Cirq (pronounced san-*sare*) is
on a rocky spur 262 ft up, with nothing but a vertical drop to the Lot
River below. Filled with artisans' workshops and not yet renovated à
la Disney, the town has so many dramatic views you may end up
spending several hours here. A mostly ruined château can be reached
by a stiff walk along the path that starts near the Hôtel de Ville. Stop
by the tourist office in the center of town for information.

Lodging

$$ 🏨 **La Pelerissa.** This jewel of a hotel is very small and simple, but the
ancient building has all the atmosphere you'd expect. Room No. 3 has
a view of the village; No. 4 has a view of the valley and the river; some

rooms in the garden have less grand views. The lounge is a snug place to relax in the evening, in front of the fire. ✉ *46330 St-Cirq-Lapopie,* ☎ *05–65–31–25–14,* FAX *05–65–30–25–52. 8 rooms. Restaurant. MC, V. Closed Nov.–Mar.*

Rocamadour

★ ㉓ *62 km (39 mi) north of St-Cirq, 46 km (29 mi) northwest of Figeac.*

Rocamadour is a medieval village that seems to defy the laws of gravity; it surges out of a cliff 1,500 ft above the Alzou River gorge. The town got its name after the discovery in 1166 of the 1,000-year-old body of St. Amadour "quite whole." The body was moved to the cathedral, where it began to work miracles. Pilgrims flocked to the site, climbing the 216 steps to the church on their knees. Making the climb on foot is sufficient reminder of the medieval penchant for agonizing penance; today an elevator lifts weary souls. The village is especially mobbed with pilgrims and tourists in summer. Cars are not allowed; park in the lot below the town.

The staircase and elevator up to the **Cité Religieuse** start from place de la Carreta; if you walk, pause at the landing 141 steps up to admire the fort. Once up, you'll see tiny place St-Amadour and its seven sanctuaries: the basilica of **St-Sauveur** opposite the staircase; the **St-Amadour crypt** under the basilica; the chapel of **Notre-Dame** to the left; the chapels of **John the Baptist, St-Blaise,** and **Sainte-Anne** to the right; and the Romanesque chapel of **St-Michel,** built into an overhanging cliff. St-Michel's two 12th-century frescoes—depicting the Annunciation and the Visitation—have survived in superb condition. ✉ *Centre d'Accueil Notre-Dame.* ☎ *Tips at visitors' discretion.* ☉ *Guided tours Mon.–Sat. 9–5 ; English-speaking guide available.*

The village itself, though very touristy, is full of beautifully restored medieval houses. One of the finest is the 15th-century **Hôtel de Ville,** near the Porte Salmon, which houses the **tourist office** and an excellent collection of tapestries. ☎ *Free.* ☉ *Mon.–Sat. 10–noon and 3–8.*

Dining and Lodging

$$$–$$$$ ✕▥ **Château de la Treyne.** Part of the Relais & Châteaux group, this small hotel 3½ km (6 mi) northwest of Rocamadour serenely guards the Dordogne, as it has since the 14th century. Dinner is served in a paneled room with old portraits and a roaring fire. The spacious rooms are traditionally furnished with 19th-century paintings and country antiques. During high season you are expected to have dinner. ✉ *La Treyne, 46200 Lacave,* ☎ *05–65–32–60–60,* FAX *05–65–37–60–70. 15 rooms. Restaurant, pool, sauna, tennis court. AE, DC, MC, V. Closed mid-Nov.–Feb.*

$$ ✕▥ **Le Beau Site.** This is the best of the few old-town hotels. The charm of the ancient beams, exposed stone, and open hearth in the foyer ends as you climb the stairs, however; rooms are modern and functional. The dining room overlooks the canyon, and best of all, you can park inside Rocamadour if you stay here. ✉ *Cité Médiévale, 46500,* ☎ *05–65–33–63–08,* FAX *05–65–33–65–23. 43 rooms. Restaurant. AE, DC, MC, V. Closed mid-Nov.–mid-Feb.*

Domme

㉔ *50 km (31 mi) west of Rocadamour.*

The historic cliff-top village of Domme is famous for its **grottoes,** where prehistoric bison and rhinoceros bones have been discovered. You can visit the 500-yard-long illuminated galleries, which are lined with stalagmites and stalactites. ✉ *Entrance on pl. de la Halle.* ☎ *30 frs.* ☉ *Apr.–Sept., daily 9:30–noon and 2–6; Mar. and Oct., daily 2–6.*

Dining and Lodging

$$ ✕⊞ **Esplanade.** Make sure your room overlooks the Dordogne—the expansive view makes this hotel special. Rooms are small but modern, and the location on the edge of the square is perfect. Worthy chef René Gillard creates such specialties as foie de canard in pot-au-feu, and all kinds of truffle-filled dishes. The restaurant doesn't serve dinner Monday February–April and doesn't serve lunch Monday September–June. ⊠ *Rue du Pont-Carrat, 24250 Domme,* ☎ *05–53–28–31–41,* FAX *05–53–28–49–92. 25 rooms. Restaurant. AE, DC, MC, V. Closed mid-Nov.–mid-Feb.*

La Roque-Gageac

㉕ *5 km (3 mi) northwest of Domme via D703.*

Across the Dorodgne from Domme, in the direction of Beynac, huddled beneath a cliff, is La Roque-Gageac, one of the best-restored villages in the valley. Crafts shops line its narrow streets, dominated by the outlines of the 19th-century mock-medieval Château de Malartrie and the Manoir de Tarde, with its cylindrical turret.

Dining and Lodging

$$ ✕⊞ **Plume d'Oie.** This small inn overlooks the river and the limestone cliffs. Rooms, in light fabrics and wicker furniture, vary in size and price. La Plume d'Oie's major raison d'être, however, is the stone-walled restaurant, at which you are expected to have at least one meal. Chef-owner Marc-Pierre Walker prepares classical regional cuisine, such as fillet of beef cooked in red wine and ragout of foie gras (the restaurant is closed Monday and doesn't serve lunch Tuesday). ⊠ *24250 La Roque-Gageac,* ☎ *05–53–29–57–05,* FAX *05–53–31–04–81. 4 rooms. Restaurant. MC, V. Closed late Nov.–mid-Dec. and early Mar.*

Beynac-et-Cazenac

㉖ *5 km (3 mi) west of La Roque-Gageac, 63 km (39 mi) east of Bergerac.*

The main reason to stop in Beynac is to see its medieval castle. Daringly perched atop a sheer cliff face beside an abrupt bend in the Dordogne, the 13th-century **Château de Beynac** has unforgettable, muscular architecture and staggering views from its battlements. ☎ *05–53–29–50–40.* 🎫 *40 frs.* ☉ *Apr.–June and Sept.–mid-Nov, daily 10–noon and 2–5; July–Aug., daily 10–7; mid-Nov.–Jan. and Mar., daily noon–5.*

Cross the Dordogne just upstream from Beynac and then turn right on D53 to pass the ruined castle of **Castlenaud,** containing a large collection of medieval warfare; it's open May–November, daily 10–7 and admission is 38 francs. Five kilometers (3 miles) farther is the turreted **Château des Milandes** (☎ *05–53–59–31–21*), which is open mid-February–December, daily 10–noon and 2–5 (43 francs). It was once owned by the American-born cabaret star of Roaring '20s Paris, Josephine Baker, and there's a museum devoted to her memory. In summer there are falconry displays. From here D53 (via Belvès) leads southwest to Monpazier.

Sarlat-la-Canéda

★ ㉗ *10km (6 mi) northeast of Beynac, 74 km (46 mi) east of Bergerac.*

The small town of Sarlat-la-Canéda is filled most days with tour groups, and especially hectic on Saturday, market day: All the geese on sale are proof of the local addiction to foie gras. To do justice to the town's golden-stone splendor, wander through its medieval streets in the later afternoon or early evening, aided by the tourist office's walking map. The tourist office also organizes walking tours, which for 25 francs gives you an in-depth look at the town's medieval buildings.

Of particular note is rue de la Liberté, which leads to **place du Peyrou,** occupied on one corner by the pointed-gable Renaissance house where writer-orator Étienne de la Boétie (1530–63) was born. The elaborate turret-topped tower of the **Cathédrale St-Sacerdos** (⊠ Pl. du Peyrou), begun in the 12th century, is the oldest part of the building and, along with the choir, all that remains of the original Romanesque cathedral. The sloping garden behind the cathedral, the **Cour de l'Évêché** (Bishop's Courtyard), contains a strange, conical tower known as the Lanterne des Morts (Lantern of the Dead), which was occasionally used as a funeral chapel.

Rue d'Albusse, adjoining the garden behind the cathedral, and rue de la Salamandre are narrow, twisty streets that head to place de la Liberté and the 17th-century **Hôtel de Ville.** Opposite the town hall is the rickety former church of **Sainte-Marie,** overlooking place des Oies. Ste-Marie points the way to Sarlat's most interesting street, **rue des Consuls.** Among its medieval buildings are the Hôtel Plamon, with broad windows that resemble those of a Gothic church, and, opposite, the 15th-century Hôtel de Vassal.

Dining and Lodging

$$ ✕🖫 **St-Albert et Montaigne.** The Garrigou family has two hotels on ★ this delightful square in the center of town. The Montaigne is in a manor; ask for lovely Room 33, with exposed beams. The St-Albert has simply furnished rooms of varying size. Hearty regional fare is served in the restaurant (closed Sunday dinner and Monday from November to Easter). Over dinner discuss your next day's itinerary with Monsieur Garrigou: He not only knows the region well but is also the town's backroom politician. ⊠ 10 pl. Pasteur, 24200, ☎ 05–53–31–55–55, FAX 05–53–59–19–99. 60 rooms. Restaurant. AE, MC, V.

En Route The road between Sarlat and Les Eyzies (twisty D47) goes past the elegant **Château de Puymartin** (☎ 05–53–59–29–97); it's open April–October, daily 10–noon; admission is 32 francs.

Les Eyzies-de-Tayac

❷❽ *21 km (13 mi) northwest of Sarlat via D47.*

Many signs of prehistoric man have been discovered in the vicinity of Les Eyzies; a number of excavated caves and grottoes, some with wall paintings, are open for public viewing. At the **Grotte du Grand-Roc,** you can view weird-shape crystalline stalactites and stalagmites. ⊠ *Rte. de la Gare,* ☎ 05–53–06–92–70. 🎟 *38 frs.* ☉ *Feb.–May and Sept.–Dec., daily 10–5; June–Aug., daily 9–7.*

The **Musée National de Préhistoire** (National Museum of Prehistory), in a Renaissance château, attracts 300,000 visitors a year with its renowned collection of prehistoric artifacts, including primitive sculpture, furniture, and tools. You can also get ideas at the museum about excavation sites to visit in the region. ⊠ *Le Bourg,* ☎ 05–53–06–45–45. 🎟 *22 frs.* ☉ *Apr.–Oct., Wed.–Mon. 9:30–noon and 2–6; Nov.–Mar., Wed.–Mon. 9:30–noon and 2–5.*

Dining and Lodging

$$$–$$$$ ✕🖫 **Vieux Logis.** A member of the Relais & Châteaux group, this vine-★ clad manor house at the edge of Trémolat is one of the best hotels in Dordogne. The warm rooms vary in size; most face the well-tended

garden and a rushing brook. One favorite, No. 22, has a terra-cotta tile floor, exposed beams, stone walls, and a suitelike bathroom. For dinner, the five-course Menu Vieux Logis (270 francs) might include the chef's forte, pigeon terrine (the restaurant is closed Tuesday from mid-January through May). ⊠ *24510 Trémolat (24 km [15 mi] west of Les Eyzies)*, ☎ *05–53–22–80–06*, FAX *05–53–22–84–89. 19 rooms, 5 suites. Restaurant, pool. AE, DC, MC, V.*

$$$ ✕⌂ **Centenaire.** Though it's also a stylish, modern, comfortable hotel, Le Centenaire is known first as a restaurant. Chef Roland Mazère adds flair to the preparation of local specialties: risotto with truffles or snails with ravioli and gazpacho. The dining room, with its gold-color stone and wooden beams, retains local character (the restaurant doesn't serve lunch Tuesday or Wednesday; a jacket is required). Rooms, especially at the lower end of the price scale, are fairly small. ⊠ *24620 Les Eyzies-de-Tayac*, ☎ *05–53–06–68–68*, FAX *05–53–06–92–41. 19 rooms. Restaurant, pool, sauna, health club. AE, DC, MC, V. Closed Nov.–Mar.*

$$ ✕⌂ **Auberge du Noyer.** This inn, in a small 18th-century building west of Les Eyzies, is owned by two expats from England. The comfortable, provincial-style rooms are in the main building and in the former barn (avoid those on the ground floor: you can hear the upstairs plumbing). The good four-course prix-fixe dinner menu is made up of soup, appetizer, main dish, such as *magret de canard* (duck breast) or fresh trout, and cheese or dessert. ⊠ *Le Reclaud-de-Bouny-Bas, 24260 Le Bugue (5 km [3 mi] outside village; 11 km [7 mi] west of Les Eyzies)*, ☎ *05–53–07–11–73*, FAX *05–53–54–57–44. 10 rooms. Restaurant, pool. MC, V. Closed Nov.–Mar.*

Grotte de Lascaux

㉙ *27 km (17 mi) northeast of Les Eyzies via D706.*

The famous **Grotte de Lascaux** (Lascaux Caves), just outside Montignac, contain hundreds of prehistoric wall paintings—thought to be at least 20,000 years old. They were discovered by chance in 1940. Although the caves have been sealed off to prevent irreparable damage, two of the galleries and many of the paintings have been reproduced in vivid detail in the Lascaux II exhibition center nearby. Purchase tickets at the tourist office in Montignac before setting off. ⊠ *Rte. de la Grotte*, ☎ *05–53–51–95–03.* 🎫 *50 frs.* ☉ *Tues.–Sun. 10–noon and 2–5:30.*

Dining and Lodging

$$$ ✕⌂ **Manoir d'Hautegente.** This old, ivy-covered manor is in a pastoral
★ setting with a lily pond, sheep, and a 13th-century windmill. Inside, the simple rooms have beige-fabric wallpaper and colorful curtains matching bedspreads. Regional fare, such as homemade foie gras, is excellent, though as with all Dordogne cuisine, it's a little heavy. ⊠ *Haute Gente, 24120 Coly (25 km [15 mi] south of Hautefort, 26 km [16 mi] north of Sarlat, 12 km [7 mi] east of Lascaux)*, ☎ *05–53–51–68–03*, FAX *05–53–50–38–52. 10 rooms. Restaurant, pool. MC, V. Closed Nov.–Mar.*

Hautefort

㉚ *28 km (18 mi) north of Lascaux.*

The reason to come to Hautefort is to see its castle, which presents a
★ disarmingly arrogant face to the world. The skyline of the **Château de Hautefort** bristles with high roofs, domes, chimneys, and cupolas. The square-lined Renaissance left wing clashes with the muscular, round towers of the right wing as the only surviving section of the original medieval castle—the gateway and drawbridge—referees in the middle.

Adorning the inside are 17th-century furniture and tapestries. ✉ *Le Bourg,* ☎ *05–53–50–51–23.* 🎟 *35 frs.* ⏲ *Easter–Nov., daily 2–6; Dec.–Easter, Sun. 2–5.*

Lodging

$$ **Enclos.** Out of a group of 250-year-old farm buildings on 4 acres of land, some 9 km (5 mi) west of Hautefort, Americans Robert and Dana Ornsteen have created a charming and comfortable base in the country. They live in the main house, where there are also a living room for guests and two small guest rooms. The *granges* (outbuildings) include five more guest rooms and one cottage in the garden. Exposed walls and beams, a restored bread oven, and fireplaces are some of the elements in the unique rooms. Table d'hôte dinners are served once or twice a week. ✉ *Pragelier, 24390 Tourtoirac,* ☎ *05–53–51–11–40,* FAX *05–53–50–37–21. 7 rooms. Pool. No credit cards.*

Périgueux

31 *40km (24 mi) west of Hautefort via D5, 121 km (75 mi) northeast of Bordeaux, 85 km (53 mi) southeast of Angoulême.*

Périgueux is best known for its weird-looking cathedral. Finished in 1173 and restored in the 19th century, the **Cathédrale St-Front** looks like it might be on loan from Istanbul, given its shallow-scale pattern domes and elongated conical cupolas sprouting from the roof like baby minarets. You may be struck by similarities with the Byzantine-style Sacré-Coeur in Paris (☞ Chapter 1); that's no coincidence—architect Paul Abadie (1812–84) worked on both. ✉ *Pl. de la Clarté.*

Brantôme

32 *27 km (17 mi) northwest of Périgueux via D939, 59 km (37 mi) southeast of Angoulême.*

The beautiful old town of Brantôme, with its waterside abbey, entirely ringed by the sparkling Dronne River, is often considered the gateway to (or from) the Dordogne region. It deserves a stop, even if you just take a walk along the river or through the old, narrow streets. At night the abbey is romantically floodlighted.

Dining and Lodging

$$ **Château Laborie.** This country château is a step above your usual B&B. A long avenue of *tilleuls* (linden trees) leads to the moat and the impressive facade. Owner Micheline "Dizzy" Duseau is an amiable hostess who chats with guests and offers advice on where to dine (one of these suggestions, the Terrace des Jardins, is well below par). Rooms, furnished with hand-me-down antiques, are comfortable if a little stilted, though two rooms on the first floor are warmer and have less bourgeois pretense. ✉ *La Borie, 24530 Champagnac-de Belair (5 km [3 mi] north of Brantôme),* ☎ *05–53–54–22–99,* FAX *05–53–08–53–78. 5 rooms. Breakfast room, pool. No credit cards. Closed early Nov.–Easter.*

POITOU-CHARENTES

Poitou-Charentes occupies the northern part of the region covered in this chapter. Rural, rolling Poitou is named for the ancient town of Poitiers. Charentes refers to two départements linked by the Charente River: Charente-Maritime, with its islands and sandy Atlantic beaches, and inland Charente. Highlights of Poitou-Charentes include the museums in Poitiers, the "Green Venice" of the Marais Poitevin, and the towns of Cognac and Limousin, famed for their liqueur and porcelain, respectively.

Limoges

 87 km (54 mi) northeast of Brantôme, 120 km (75 mi) southeast of Poitiers.

The city of porcelain and enamel, Limoges is a large town somewhat off the beaten track. It seems that every other shop, especially on rue Jean-Jaurès, rue du Clocher, rue du Consulat, and rue St-Michel, sells the prized porcelain, fabled for its delicacy and translucency. The manufacturers utilize a pure white clay found in St-Yviex, south of Limoges. This clay, called kaolin, had been known for centuries in China but was only discovered in Europe in the 18th century. Americans fell in love with Limoges porcelain thanks to one David Havilland, who, after arriving in the mid-19th century, opened his own factory after native producers refused to adapt their designs for tastes overseas.

You can get a good overview of what is produced by the factories at the **Limoges-Castel Centre de Démonstration** (a demonstration center with museum, video on the process, and shop). ⌧ *Pavillon de la Porcelaine, 40 av. du Président-Kennedy,* ☎ *05–55–30–26–23.* ☉ *Mid-Apr.–mid-Oct., daily 8:30–6; mid-Oct.–mid-Apr., Mon.–Sat. 8:30–6.*

The best porcelain made over the last two centuries is on display at the **Musée National Adrien-Dubouché.** It also has a good technical section introducing the process that gave rise to the four principal ceramic groups: terra-cotta, glazed earthenware, stoneware, and porcelain. ⌧ *8 pl. Winston-Churchill,* ☎ *05–55–33–08–50.* ⌧ *22 frs.* ☉ *Wed.–Mon. 10–12:30 and 2–5:45.*

The **Musée de l'Évêché** (Town Museum), in the 18th-century Bishop's Palace, has an extensive array of ceramics—from the 12th to the 20th centuries—and an archaeological section on Limoges Roman history. Look, too, for the few works of Renoir; Limoges was his birthplace. ⌧ *Pl. de l'Évêché,* ☎ *05–55–34–44–09.* ⌧ *Free.* ☉ *Oct.–June, Wed.–Mon. 10–11:45 and 2–5; July–Sept., Wed.–Mon. 10–11:45 and 2–6.*

The **Cathédrale St-Étienne** (⌧ Pl. de la Cathédrale), across from the Bishop's Palace, was begun in 1273 and closely resembles the cathedrals of Narbonne and Clermont-Ferrand, with their extremely high vaults—the trademark of architect Jean Deschamps.

OFF THE BEATEN PATH **ORADOUR-SUR-GLANE –** This village 22 km (14 mi) northwest of Limoges stands as a chilling reminder of Nazi barbarism. On the night of June 10, 1944, the Germans stormed the village, herded the men into a barn, the women and children into the church, and slew nearly everyone. Some believe they mistook it for another town, reputed to harbor members of the Resistance. Some 642 people, including 205 children, were murdered. Ten villagers survived by hiding under the corpses. A new town was established with the same name 1 km (½ mi) away, leaving this village just as it was that evening. ⌧ *Donation of 30 frs to visit village.* ☉ *Daily 9–sunset.*

Dining and Lodging

$ ✕⍁ **La Roche.** In the hilly, lake-filled countryside east of Limoges, near the small town of Eymoutiers, is this former coaching inn, which Josette and Michel Jaubert have renovated with flair. Michel is an artist, which is why paintings and sculptured lamps embellish the two guest rooms and lounge. Josette cooks a hearty three-course dinner with wine—for under 100 francs. ⌧ *La Roche, 87210 Eymoutiers (44 km [27 mi] east of Limoges),* ☎ *05–55–69–61–88. 2 rooms. Restaurant. No credit cards.*

Angoulême

④ *100 km (62 mi) west of Limoges, 116 km (72 mi) south of Poitiers, 86 km (54 mi) northwest of Périgueux.*

Angoulême is divided, like many other French towns, between an old, picturesque section around a hilltop cathedral and a modern, industrial part sprawling along the valley and railroad below. The 19th-century novelist Honoré de Balzac is one of the town's adopted sons; Balzac described Angoulême in his meaty novel *Lost Illusions*. The Ville Haute (Upper Town), known as Le Plateau, has a warren of quaint old streets around the Hôtel de Ville (Town Hall) and stunning views from the ramparts.

The 12th-century **Cathédrale St-Pierre** (⊠ Pl. St-Pierre) bears little resemblance to the majority of its French counterparts because of the cupolas topping each of its three bays. The cathedral was partly destroyed by Calvinists in 1562, then restored in a heavy-handed manner in 1634 and 1866. Its main attraction is its magnificent Romanesque facade, whose layers of rounded arches bear 70 stone statues and bas-reliefs illustrating the Last Judgment.

Dining and Lodging

$ ✕ **Tour des Valois.** Diagonally across from the market, this restaurant has a good choice of regional food. Sample one of the veal dishes—the one using the local mustard from Jarnac is particularly good—and the locally made foie gras. ⊠ *7 rue Massillon,* ☎ *05–45–95–23–64. AE, MC, V. Closed late Feb., mid-Aug.–early Sept., and Sun. No lunch Mon.*

$$$ ✕🏨 **Château de Nieuil.** An avenue of trees opening onto a circular lawn leads to this former hunting lodge—a huge Renaissance château with towers. Rooms vary: Some have traditional furnishings and pastel blue fabric; others have a *petit salon* (small sitting area) or a garden view. Unfortunately, the reception area is small. The formidable dining room (no dinner Sunday; September to June closed Monday) has a large stone fireplace with sculpted family crests and a multifaceted chandelier. Enjoy superb lamb (a regional specialty) or scallop of milk-fed veal with grapes. The wine list is impressive, but you need to search for an affordable bottle. ⊠ *16270 Nieuil (40km east of Angoulême),* ☎ *05–45–71–36–38,* 𝔽𝔸𝕏 *05–45–71–46–45. 11 rooms, 3 suites. Restaurant, pool, tennis court, fishing, helipad. AE, DC, MC, V. Closed Nov.–Mar.*

$$ 🏨 **Mercure Hôtel de France.** On the edge of the Ville Haute, across from the covered market, this hotel has a traditional air. From the garden there are fine views of the city. Rooms are decorated in light blues with striped curtains and bedspreads. The staff is professional and accustomed to speaking English. In the restaurant (closed for lunch at weekends), solid, unpretentious regional cuisine is served. ⊠ *1 pl. des Halles, 16000,* ☎ *05–45–95–47–95; 0181/741–3100 in U.K.; 800/637–2873 in U.S.;* 𝔽𝔸𝕏 *05–45–92–02–70. 89 rooms. Restaurant, bar. AE, DC, MC, V.*

Jarnac

㉟ *28 km (17 mi) west of Angoulême via N141.*

The village of Jarnac is primarily known as the birthplace of the late president François Mitterrand, who is buried in the local cemetery. Several excellent cognac firms are found here as well. **Hine** (⊠ quai de l'Orangerie, ☎ *05–45–35–59–59*), one of Jarnac's oldest cognac firms, organizes visits of its riverbank premises. **Courvoisier** (⊠ Pl. du Château, ☎ *05–45–35–55–55*), in a bombastic redbrick factory, gives tours of its premises and its chais.

Dining and Lodging

$$ **✕▥ Maison Karina.** Co-owner Niki Legon is an Englishwoman who
★ describes herself as a cupboard cook: She starts with a recipe, then looks
into her cupboard to see what to add. The result is a dish that is dif-
ferent each time it's prepared, whether it be canard *à la pineau* (with
pineau, a sweet, cognac-based aperitif) or *côtes de porc* (pork chops).
Rooms in this former distillery have exposed beams and walls. In the
cozy bar you'll find Jarnac cognac. ✉ *Bois Faucon, 16200, Les Mé-
tairies (off D736, 3 km [2 mi] north of Jarnac),* ☎ *05–45–36–26–26,*
▥ *05–45–81–10–93. 7 rooms, 2 suites. Restaurant, bar, pool, 18-hole
golf course, tennis court, horseback riding. MC, V.*

Cognac

36 *14 km (9 mi) west of Jarnac via N141.*

The black-walled town of Cognac seems an unlikely home for one of
the world's most successful drink trades. You may be disappointed ini-
tially by the town's unpretentious appearance, but like the drink, it tends
to grow on you. Cognac owed its early development to the transport
of salt and wine along the Charente River. When 16th-century Dutch
merchants discovered that the local wine was both tastier and easier
to transport if distilled, the town became the heart of the brandy in-
dustry. Most cognac houses organize visits of their premises and chais.
Wherever you decide to go, you will literally soak up the atmosphere
of cognac—3% of the precious cask-bound liquid evaporates every year.
This has two consequences: Each chais smells delicious, and a small,
black fungus, which feeds on cognac's alcoholic fumes, forms on walls
throughout the town.

The leading monument in Cognac is the former **Château François-Ier,**
now the premises of Otard Cognac. Volatile Renaissance monarch
François I was born here in 1494. The remaining buildings are some-
thing of a hodgepodge, though the chunky towers recall the site's for-
tified origins. The tour of Otard Cognac combines its own propaganda
with historical comment on the drink itself. At the end you get to sam-
ple free cognac, and you can buy some at reduced prices. ✉ *127 bd.
Denfert-Rochereau,* ☎ *05–45–36–88–88.* ▤ *15 frs.* ☉ *Guided tours
on the hr, Apr.–Oct., daily 10–noon and 2–5.*

Hennessy, along the banks of the Charente and easily recognized by
the company's mercenary emblem—an ax-wielding arm carved in
stone—includes in its tour a cheerful jaunt across the Charente in old-
fashioned boats. ✉ *Quai Richard-Hennessy,* ☎ *05–45–35–72–68.* ▤
30 frs. ☉ *June–Sept., Mon.–Sat. 9–6; Oct.–Dec. and Mar.–May, week-
days 10–5.*

Martell gives the most polished guided tour of the Cognac houses, and
its chais are perhaps more picturesque than Hennessy's. ✉ *7 pl.
Édouard-Martell,* ☎ *05–45–36–33–33.* ▤ *25 frs.* ☉ *July–Aug., week-
days 9:30–5, weekends 10–5; June and Sept., weekdays 9:30–11 and
2–5; Oct.–May, Mon.–Thur. 9:30–11 and 2:30–5.*

Rue Saulnier, alongside the Hennessy premises, is the most atmo-
spheric of the somber, sloping cobbled streets that compose the core
of Cognac, dominated by the tower of **St-Léger** (✉ Pl. d'Armes), a church
with a notably large Flamboyant Gothic rose window.

Busy boulevard Denfert-Rochereau twines around the old town, pass-
ing the town hall and the neighboring **Musée Municipal** (Town Mu-
seum) with its collection of cognac posters, glasses and other marketing
artifacts. ✉ *48 bd. Denfert-Rochereau,* ☎ *05–45–32–07–25.* ▤ *13*

frs. ⊙ *June–Sept., Wed.–Mon. 10–noon and 2–6; Oct.–May, Wed.–Mon. 2–5:30.*

Dining and Lodging

$$
★ ✕⌂ **Pigeons Blancs.** "White Pigeons," a modernized coaching inn on spacious grounds 1½ km (1 mi) from the center of Cognac, has been owned by the same family since the 17th century. Each room is different: No. 32 has a gabled ceiling supported by an ancient beam and a skylight. The major draw, though, is chef Jacques Tachet's cuisine: Try his milk-fed lamb with *jus d'ail doux* (sweet garlic juice) or grilled escargots. The three-course prix-fixe menu is a find at 140 francs. You can arrange to have two meals per day with your room rate (there's no dinner Sunday). ✉ *110 rue Jules-Brisson, 16100,* ☎ *05–45–82–16–36,* ⅎₐₓ *05–45–82–29–29. 7 rooms. Restaurant. AE, DC, MC, V. Closed 1st half Jan.*

Nightlife and the Arts

La Maison Blanche (✉ 2 impasse de Moulins) is the place to party every night. Each September Cognac hosts a **crime film festival.**

Outdoor Activities and Sports

Hit the greens at the local 18-hole **golf course** (✉ in the village of St-Brice, 5 km [3 mi] east of Cognac, ☎ 05–45–32–18–17); fees range from 300 francs in peak season to 200 francs off-season.

Shopping

A bottle of old cognac makes a fine souvenir; try **La Cognathèque** (✉ 8 pl. Jean-Monnet), in Cognac itself, though you can sometimes find the same item infinitely cheaper at a local producer.

Saintes

③⑦ *27 km (17 mi) northwest of Cognac via D24.*

On the banks of the Charente River, Saintes, littered with religious edifices and Roman ruins dating from the 1st century, exudes stately serenity. The town owes its development to the salt marshes that first attracted the Romans to the area some 2,000 years ago.

The Romans left their mark with the impressive **Arènes** (Amphitheater). There are several better-preserved examples in France, but few as old. You'll find it to the west of the town center, close to the church of St-Eutrope with its mighty spire. On the banks of the Charente stands a grand Roman triumphal arch, the **Arc de Germanicus,** built in AD 19. Boats leave alongside for river trips in summer (☎ 05–46–91–12–92 for details).

Climbing above the red roofs of the old town is the **Cathédrale St-Pierre** (✉ Pl. du Synode), which seems to stagger beneath the weight of its stocky tower. Engineering caution foiled plans for the traditional pointed spire, so the tower was given a shallow dome—incongruous, perhaps, but distinctive. The austere 16th-century interior is lined with circular pillars of formidable circumference. The narrow pedestrians-only streets clustered around the cathedral contrast with the broad boulevards that slice through the town and over the river.

Saintes's ecclesiastical pride and joy is the **Abbaye aux Dames** (Ladies' Abbey), consecrated in 1047. The abbey church is fronted by an exquisite intricately carved, arcaded facade. Although the Romanesque choir remains largely in its original form, the rest of the interior is less harmonious, as the abbey fell on hard times after the death of the last abbess—the 30th—in 1792. It became a prison, then a barracks, and now it is a cultural center for expositions. The brasserie opposite the abbey portals has inexpensive lunch menus (65–100 francs). ⊠ *7 pl. de l'Abbaye,* ☎ *05–46–97–48–48.* ☉ *Apr.–Sept., daily 10–12:30 and 2–7; Oct.–Mar., Wed. and Sat. 10–12:30 and 2–6, Sun.–Tues. and Thurs.–Fri. 2–6.*

Dining and Lodging

$$–$$$ ✕⊞ **Relais du Bois St-Georges.** Rooms in this hotel vary; some have contemporary furnishings, others traditional; some are miniduplexes with loft beds, others small with fold-down beds (one is named "Count de Monte Cristo's Prison Cell"); many have separate sitting areas. Service is enthusiastic because the staff has input in running the hotel. In the restaurant overlooking gardens and a lake, seafood and specialties from the Charente region and become eye-catching creations in the hands of chef Jérôme Emery. ⊠ *Le Pinier, cours Genêt, 17100,* ☎ *05–46–93–50–99,* ⅎⅩ *05–46–93–34–93. 27 rooms, 3 suites. Restaurant, bar, indoor pool, croquet, meeting rooms. MC, V.*

$$–$$$ ✕⊞ **Moulin de Marcouze.** You, too, can feast like a brandy baron—if you make the 30-minute drive from Saintes to Mosnac, where an old water mill has been transformed into a sophisticated restaurant and inn. The style is understated: spacious layout, artwork, and food that is innovative but not flashy (sautéed sole fillet, duck pie with truffles). At midday local executives whirl in for power lunches; dinner is more low-key. ⊠ *Rte. de St-Georges, 17240 Mosnac (33 km [20 mi] south of Saintes, 34 km [21 mi] southwest of Cognac),* ☎ *05–46–70–46–16,* ⅎⅩ *05–46–70–48–14. 10 rooms. Restaurant, pool, helipad. AE, DC, MC, V. Closed Nov.–mid-Mar.*

En Route From Saintes take N150 24 km (15 mi) southwest to **Saujon,** at the foot of the Baie de Seudre, home to a **steam train** (☎ 05–46–36–64–59 for times, 🚂 60 frs) that chugs up a disused branch line to La Tremblade on Wednesday and Sunday from mid-June through mid-September. Armed with a good map (best is the blue IGN map No. 1332ET), you can explore the west side of the bay by car. Stop first in the picturesque village of **Mornac,** with its quaint market hall, foursquare church tower, and tumbling main street. Then visit the brightly colored huts and fishing boats used by oyster farmers in the villages of **Chaillevette** and **Arvert** en route to **La Tremblade,** where boats leave daily in summer for tours of the bay and nearby islands. Take the toll bridge across the Baie de Seudre to **Marennes** and climb its elegant 250-ft church spire. Another toll bridge leads past the offshore **Fort Louvois,** built in 1691, to Ile d'Oléron.

Ile d'Oléron

③⑧ *48 km (10 mi) northwest of Saintes via D728.*

Sand dunes ring the Ile d'Oléron (Isle of Oléron) to the north and west, and oyster beds line the eastern shores. On the west coast, visit **La Cotinière,** home to the island's most colorful harbor. On the south side of the island, the town of **Le Château d'Oléron** has a mighty Vauban citadel. Head up the east coast to Boyardville to enjoy the astonishing sight of **Fort Boyard**—an oval 19th-century fort that appears to rise from the waves like a marooned ocean liner. The fort, conceived as a stationary battleship, is built on a sandbank that's hidden below sea level; it was soon converted into an escape-proof prison, then abandoned early in the 20th century. The fort was restored in the 1980s and has been used since as a giant stage for a popular French TV games show. Boats leave Boyardville daily in summer for Ile d'Aix, hovering admiringly in front of Fort Boyard along the way (☎ 05–46–47–01–45 for details).

Brouage

39 *16 km (10 mi) east of Ile d'Oléron via D26 and D3.*

The ancient walls of Brouage loom defiantly above desolate marshland. Come on a grim day, and it looks like a stage set of funereal grandeur: a crumbling fortress in the middle of nowhere, with turrets and parapets piercing the skyline. Once, unbelievably, Brouage was France's richest Atlantic port—in the late 16th century, when Samuel de Champlain was growing up here before sailing off to found Quebec in 1608. The main street is aflutter with the fleur-de-lised white-and-blue flags of *la belle province* (Quebec), in honor of Champlain.

In the shambling village church, the **Église St-Pierre** (rue de Québec), you can learn about Champlain's tale. The elegantly vaulted **Maison aux Vivres** (Food Storehouse; ⊠ rue de Québec) is now a museum with exhibits on local geography—for instance, you'll learn that, in medieval times, all the surrounding region was underwater.

If you're wearing good shoes, walk along the top of the **town walls.** Try to imagine grand galleons sailing up the Havre de Brouage, now a slimy, narrow mud channel, and docking beneath the imposing **Porte Royale** (Royal Gateway), named for Louis XIV (his sweetheart, Maria Mancini, spent three months moping in Brouage after being dumped in favor of the Infanta of Spain in 1659). The sea melts into the distance 3 km (2 mi) to the west; the ruined 12th-century castle, the **Donjon de Broue,** which you can spot 8 km (5 mi) inland, was once on the water.

Rochefort

40 *12 km (7 mi) northeast of Brouage via D3.*

Rochefort was built from scratch in the 1660s as a naval base for Louis XIV's fleet to defend France's Atlantic coast from English attack. Facing the Charente River, the extraordinary 400-yard long **Corderie Royale** (Rope Factory) is the most significant survivor from the 17th century. Rope making stopped in 1926, and the building fell into disrepair. But it was beautifully restored and reopened in 1985 as the **Centre International de la Mer** (Marine Center), hosting temporary exhibitions. It's surrounded by immaculately tended lawns and gardens. ⊠ *Rue Jean-Baptiste-Audebert,* ☎ *05–46–87–01–90.* 🎟 *30 frs.* ۩ *Daily 9–6.*

Right next to the Corderie Royale, on the riverfront, is the former royal arsenal. After decades of neglect, one of its dry docks is once again in use: for the painstaking, decade-long reconstruction of the **Hermione** frigate in which La Fayette made his 38-day trip across the Atlantic in 1780. You can see carpenters at work and learn about old-time shipbuilding techniques. Once completed, the new *Hermione* will sail to the United States before returning to Rochefort and a permanent mooring along the Charente. ⊠ *Pl. Amiral-Dupont,* ☎ *05–46–87–01–90.* 🎟 *25 frs.* ۩ *Daily 10–1 and 2–6.* Rochefort's claim to 20th-century fame rests on being the sun-drenched setting for the French movie industry's best-loved musical, Jacques Demy's 1968 *Les Demoiselles de Rochefort,* starring Gene Kelly and Catherine Deneuve. Much of the action takes place on the main square, **place Colbert.** The opening titles were shot at the **Pont Transbordeur,** a magnificent turn-of-the-century iron transporter bridge just south of the town, the last of its kind in France to remain operational before being replaced by a modern road bridge in the late 1960s. It's now open again, to pedestrians only.

Although his books are little known to English speakers, don't miss the former home of Pierre Loti (1850–1923), whose exotic novels (set everywhere from Angkor Wat to Japan) helped make Orientalism a fashionable new art movement in turn-of-the-century France. As befits a son of Rochefort, Loti was an avid sailor and explorer, and his exotic tales are reflected in the **Maison Pierre-Loti.** From the outside this looks just like any other house in an unremarkable street. Inside, however, not only is it full of Persian silks and Turkish silverware, but, using Arabic arches, colored tiles, and carved ceilings, entire rooms have been transformed into chambers from a mosque or an Ottoman palace. ⊠ *141 rue Pierre-Loti,* ☎ *05–46–99–16–88.* ⊠ *45 frs.* ☉ *Guided tours only, Wed.–Mon. at 11, noon, 2, 3, and 4. Call tourist office to book a tour in English.*

Ile de Ré

④ *44 km (28 mi) northwest of Rochefort via N137 and the Pont-Via-duc.*

A toll bridge curves across just north of La Rochelle to the cheerful Ile de Ré, an island just 26 km (16 mi) long and never more than 6 km (4 mi) wide. Vineyards sweep over the eastern part of the island; oyster beds straddle the shallow waters to the west.

The first village on the north coast reached from the mainland is **La Flotte.** The rectangular harbor hiding tiny fishing boats is surrounded by sturdy houses ready to stand against Atlantic gales. Ten km (6 mi) farther on is the largest village on the island, **St-Martin de Ré** (population 3,000). It has a lively harbor and a citadel built by ace military architect Sébastien de Vauban in 1681. Many of its streets also date from the 17th century, and the villagers' low, white houses are typical of that period. **Ars,** a smaller village 10 km (6 mi) farther west, has a black-and-white church spire, fine street market, and cute harbor.

If you go all the way to the northwestern end of Ile de Ré, be sure to climb up the **Phare de la Baleine** (Whale Lighthouse) for sweeping views of the Atlantic. At its foot is the **Café de la Phare,** which has a surprising Art Deco setting full of artsy '30s lamps and serves a good *poutargue,* a local specialty made from smoked cod roe accompanied by shallots and sour cream.

Dining and Lodging

$$$ ✕⊡ **Le Richelieu.** Eat chef Dominique Bourgeois's seafood as you gaze at the ocean. Let lobster and smoked oysters spark your taste buds for the excellent grilled turbot in beurre blanc and superb wine. Guest rooms are innocuously furnished but have all the amenities, from bathrobes to balconies. A separate building houses masseurs, beauticians, and thalassotherapy equipment. A beach fronts the hotel, but it's better for strolling than lounging. ⊠ *44 av. de la Plage, 17630 La Flotte-en-Ré,* ☎ *05–46–09–60–70,* ⬚ *05–46–09–50–59. 39 rooms, 3 suites. Restaurant, pool, beauty salon, massage, spa, 2 tennis courts, beach. AE, DC, MC, V. Closed early Jan.–mid-Feb.*

Outdoor Activities and Sports

A good way to get around this flattish island is on a bicycle; rent one in St-Martin from **Ile de Ré Vélo** (⊠ 17 rue de l'Amiral-Macquin, ☎ 05–46–09–36–90).

La Rochelle

★ **㊷** *11 km (7 mi) east of Ile de Ré, 32 km (20 mi) northwest of Rochefort.*

La Rochelle is a vibrant, appealing town, with ancient streets and a picture-postcard harbor, the Vieux Port. Standing sentinel on either side of the harbor are two fortresslike 14th-century towers, the **Tour St-**

Nicolas (to the left) and the **Tour de la Chaîne** (right); a third tower, the 15th-century **Tour de la Lanterne**, emerges a little further along the quayside. You can climb to the top of any of them for a view of the bay toward Ile d'Aix. ☜ *Each tower 25 frs; 45 frs all 3.* ⊙ *Apr.– Sept., daily 10–7; Oct.–Mar., daily 10–12:30 and 2–5:30.*

Cours des Dames, a spacious avenue lined with sturdy trees and 18th-century houses, leads along the west side of the Vieux Port to the **Porte de la Grosse Horloge** (Gate of the Big Clock), a massive stone gate marking the entrance to the narrow, bustling streets of the old town. From the gate head down rue du Palais and onto rue Gargoulleau: Halfway down on the left is the 18th-century Bishop's Palace, now the **Musée des Beaux-Arts** (Museum of Fine Arts). ⊠ *28 rue Gargoulleau,* ☎ *05– 46–41–64–65.* ☜ *22 frs, joint tickets for all town museums 42 frs.* ⊙ *Mon. and Wed.–Sat. 10:30–12:30 and 1:30–6, Sun. 3–6.*

The **Muséum d'Histoire Naturelle** (Museum of Natural History), housed in an elegant mansion, contains extensive collections of rocks, coral, and shell work. Other items range from a tribal idol from Easter Island to a giraffe (now stuffed) given as a gift to King Charles X (reigned 1824–30). ⊠ *28 rue Albert-I,* ☎ *05–46–41–18–25.* ☜ *22 frs, joint tickets for all town museums 42 frs.* ⊙ *Apr.–Oct., Tues.–Sun. 10–noon and 2–6; Nov.–Mar., Tues.–Sat. 10–noon and 2–5, Sun. 2–5.*

At the **Musée du Nouveau-Monde** (New World Museum), in an 18th-century building, old maps, engravings, watercolors, and even wallpaper evoke the commercial links between La Rochelle and the New World. ⊠ *10 rue Fleuriau,* ☎ *05–46–41–46–50.* ☜ *22 frs, joint tickets for all town museums 42 frs.* ⊙ *Wed.–Mon. 10:30–12:30 and 1:30–6, Sun. 3–6.*

In summer boats operated by **Ré Croisières** leave La Rochelle harbor daily for cruises to the nearby islands, **Ile de Ré** and **Ile d'Aix**, and to **Fort Boyard**. ⊠ *Bassin d'Échouage, Vieux Port,* ☎ *05–46–41–50–40.* ☜ *Round-trip: Ile de Ré, 75 frs; Ile d'Aix and Fort Boyard, 100 frs; buy tickets from Agence de La Rochelle.* ⊙ *Departure times vary; it's best to call ahead.*

Dining and Lodging

$$$ ✕ **Richard Coutanceau.** Widely acknowledged as the region's premier
★ chef, Richard Coutanceau deals imaginatively in fish and seafood in this sober, modern restaurant overlooking the bay and old port. Lobster, eel, bass with basil, and spider crab with asparagus number among his specialties. ⊠ *Plage de la Concurrence,* ☎ *05–46–41–48–19. AE, DC, MC, V. Closed Sun.*

$$ ✕ **André.** The salty decor is a bit excessive—fishing nets and posters of ocean liners. But the food and service have such gusto that you'll be caught up in the mood, especially if you order the monumental seafood platter and wash it down with white Charente wine. The three prix-fixe menus are priced from 125 to 190 francs. ⊠ *5 rue St-Jean-du-Pérot,* ☎ *05–46–41–28–24. AE, DC, MC, V.*

$–$$ ✕ **Les Quatre Sergents.** On a street on the north side of the Vieux Port, where good restaurants abound, this place serves excellent, traditional seafood with distinctive sauces. Plants grow in every nook and cranny, shielding one table from another—it's like dining in a winter garden. ⊠ *49 rue St-Jean du Pérot,* ☎ *05–46–41–35–80. AE, DC, MC, V. Closed Mon. No dinner Sun.*

$$–$$$ ⌑ **Hôtel de la Monnaie.** This 17th-century house by the Vieux Port has a wonderful lobby and cobblestone courtyard. Rooms are less inspiring; the quietest overlook the courtyard. Free parking is available adjacent to the hotel, a definite plus as it's only a few minutes' walk from the harbor and town. ✉ *3 rue de la Monnaie, 17000,* ☎ *05–46–50–65–65,* FAX *05–46–50–63–19. 31 rooms, 4 suites. Free parking. AE, DC, MC, V.*

$$ ⊡ **33 rue Thiers.** Amiable Maybelle Iribe, an expatriate American who
★   has a wealth of local knowledge, owns this inn in a private town house. With advance notice, she'll prepare a splendid dinner from fresh market products. You're likely to eat in the kitchen and, if you want, pick up some cooking tips (Maybelle teaches cooking classes). Rooms are large and wonderfully furnished, expressing the owner's idiosyncrasies: The Mexican Room is gaily decorated with cheerful colors; the Blue Room is also a delight. ✉ *33 rue Thiers, 17000,* ☎ *05–46–41–62–23,* FAX *05–46–41–10–76. 8 rooms. Dining room. MC, V.*

$$ ⊡ **Tour de Nesle.** This foursquare white-wall 19th-century hotel is around the corner from quai Valin and close to the old port. Rooms are a bit cramped but up to date; some have a view across the Canal Maubert. Breakfast is served. ✉ *2 quai Louis-Durand, 17000,* ☎ *05–46–41–30–72,* FAX *05–46–41–95–17. 28 rooms. AE, DC, MC, V.*

Nightlife and the Arts

Held over Pentecost, La Rochelle's major festival, the **Fêtes de la Mer,** is a celebration inspired by the sea, with regattas and sailboats on display in the harbor.

Shopping

La Rochelle will impress you as more than a port town if you are here on a Wednesday or Saturday for the **market** in the old town.

En Route   Head inland from La Rochelle along D9 and D20 northeast toward Marans, once a thriving seaport but now linked to the sea only by canal. The landscape is flat, barren, almost eerie: This is the **Marais Desséché** (Dry Marsh), and your first encounter with the Marais Poitevin. The verdant, tree-lined waterways that form the more scenic **Marais Mouillé** (Wet Marsh) gradually take over as you continue east. Take D114 from Marans, then a left on D116 just before Courçon, to La Ronde and on to Maillezais.

Maillezais

④③   *48 km (30 mi) northeast of La Rochelle.*

Maillezais is a good base for waterborne exploration of the Marais Poitevin—France's "Green Venice". Willow, ash, and alder trees line the rivers and canals of the Marais; artichokes, onions, melons, and garlic are grown in the fields alongside. Boats depart from the **Embarcadère de l'Abbaye** (☎ 02–51–87–21–87 for information).

The town was once a bishop's seat and a powerful Benedictine monastery; all that remains of the **Abbaye St-Pierre** are the 14th-century cloister and refectory, the 11th-century church, and the ruined castle nearby. ☎ *02–51–00–70–11.* ⊡ *15 frs.* ☉ *Nov.–Mar., daily 9–noon and 2–6; Apr.–Oct., daily 9–12:30 and 2–7.*

Coulon

④④   *18 km (11 mi) southeast of Maillezais.*

The photogenic village of Coulon is the best base for exploring the Marais Poitevin. The best way to explore the Marais is by rowboat—or, more typically, on a *pigouille* (a flat, narrow boat maneuvered with a long pole), which you can find in Coulon. They cost about 90 francs per hour per boat, maximum six persons, or you can hire a boat with a guide (for 45 minutes at 120 francs). If your French is decent, you'll probably get an earful of local lore as well as a ride. The town also has a lovely medieval church and a privately-run folk museum, the **Musée Maraichin** (⊠ rue de l'Église). There are no regular hours: Just show up and see if it's open; donations are accepted.

Dining and Lodging

$$ ✕⛿ **Central.** Just opposite the church on the town square, the restaurant (closed Monday, no dinner Sunday) here is a favorite haunt of the local bourgeoisie, who enjoy an almost obsequious welcome from the blue-blazered owner. The fine choice of regional fare includes succulent lamb, eel fricassee, and warm oysters cooked with nettle leaves. Rooms are plain and small, but reasonably priced. ⊠ *4 rue d'Autremont, 79510,* ☎ *05–49–35–90–20,* ⅿ *05–49–35–81–07. 11 rooms. Restaurant. MC, V. Closed part of Oct., part of Jan.*

Outdoor Activities and Sports

One of the best ways to explore the area is by bicycle (a detailed map is advisable), rented from **La Libellule** (⊠ 94 quai Louis-Tardy, ☎ 05–49–35–83–42).

Poitiers

★ ㊺ *72km (45 mi) northeast of Niort, 120 km (75 mi) northwest of Limoges, 340 km (212 mi) southwest of Paris.*

Thanks to its majestic hilltop setting above the Clain River and its position halfway along the Bordeaux–Paris trade route, Poitiers became an important commercial, religious, and university town in the Middle Ages. Life quieted down after the 17th century, but tranquillity has resulted in excellent architectural preservation. Thirty thousand students perk things up when school is in session.

The church of **Notre-Dame-la-Grande** (⊠ Pl. Charles-de-Gaulle), in the town center, is an impressive example of the Romanesque architecture so common in western France. Its 12th-century facade, framed by rounded arches and decorated with a multitude of bas-reliefs and sculptures, was meticulously restored in 1994; a 15-minute light show highlights the details in color every evening from mid-June through September. The dark interior is enlivened with murals painted in 1851.

The **Cathédrale St-Pierre** (⊠ Pl. de la Cathédrale), a few hundred yards beyond Notre-Dame-la-Grande, was built between the 12th and the 14th centuries. With a huge portal showing plump gargoyles without and tremendous open space and luminosity within, the largest church in Poitiers has a distinctive facade marked by two asymmetrical towers. The imposing interior is noted for its late 18th-century organ, stained glass, and 13th-century wooden choir stalls, claimed as the oldest in France.

The **Musée Ste-Croix** houses archaeological discoveries, traditional regional crafts, and European paintings from the 15th to the 19th centuries, all of good though not outstanding quality. The museum is part of a triad of museums. The **Musée de Chièvres** (⊠ 9 rue Victor-Hugo, ☎ 05–49–41–42–21) displays Renaissance furniture, ceramics, and old-master paintings. The **Hypogée Martyrium** (⊠ 44 rue du Père-de-la-Croix, ☎ 05–49–01–68–85), a subterranean chapel with ancient sarcophagi and sculptures, was closed for restoration at press time. ⊠ *61 rue St-Simplicien,* ☎ *05–49–41–07–53.* ⛿ *15 frs (joint ticket for all museums); free Tues.* ☉ *Museums: Tues.–Fri. 10–noon and 1–5, weekends 10–noon and 2–6.*

The 4th-century **Baptistère St-Jean** is the oldest Christian building in France. Its heavy stone bulk, some 12 ft beneath ground level, includes a rectangular baptismal chamber; go inside to see the octagonal basin for baptism by total immersion. ⊠ *Rue Jean-Jaurès.* 🎫 *4 frs.* ⊙ *Easter–Oct., daily 10–12:30 and 2–4:30; Nov.–Easter, Thurs.–Tues. 2–4:30.*

St-Hilaire-le-Grand (⊠ Rue St-Hilaire) dates partly from the early 11th century. Inside, a semicircular, mosaic-floor choir rises high above the level of the nave, and striking frescoes ornament the chapels around the east end.

★ ☕ At **Futuroscope,** just north of Poitiers, a bevy of futuristic cinemas provides a variety of high-tech, interactive thrills. A combination of giant movie screens, 3-D effects, video games, and a children's amusement park have rapidly established this as western France's leading tourist attraction. ⊠ *Jaunay-Clan (Exit 28 off A10),* ☎ *05–49–49–59–84.* 🎫 *140–195 frs, according to season.* ⊙ *Mid-June–Aug., daily 9 AM–11 PM; Sept.–mid-June, weekdays 9–6, weekends 9 AM–10 PM.*

Dining and Lodging

$$–$$$ ✕ **Maxime.** Reasonable prix-fixe menus and chef Christian Rougier's cooking have made Maxime a crowd pleaser. Enjoy foie gras and duck salad in the pastel dining room lined with '30s-style frescoes. ⊠ *4 rue St-Nicolas,* ☎ *05–49–41–09–55. Reservations essential. AE, DC, MC, V. Closed weekends and part of July–Aug.*

$$ 🏨 **Europe.** An early 19th-century building with a modern extension houses this unpretentious hotel in the middle of town. Because it's off the main street and has a forecourt, rooms are quiet. It also has a pleasant garden in the back for an afternoon tea or an evening aperitif. ⊠ *39 rue Carnot, 86000,* ☎ *05–49–88–12–00,* 🅵🅰🆇 *05–49–88–97–30. 85 rooms. AE, DC, MC, V.*

Nightlife and the Arts

For a night of dancing, head to **Black House** (⊠ 195 av. du 8-mai-1945, ☎ 05–49–57–08–21). **La Grand'Goule** (⊠ 46 rue du Pigeon-Blanc, ☎ 05–49–50–41–36) is a split-level disco with a good ambience. At the **Théâtre de Poitiers (Scène Nationale)** (⊠ 1 pl. du Maréchal-Leclerc, ☎ 05–49–39–29–29), mainly French works are performed.

BORDEAUX, DORDOGNE, AND POITOU-CHARENTES A TO Z

Arriving and Departing

By Car

As the capital of southwest France, Bordeaux has superb transport links with Paris, Spain, and even the Mediterranean (A62 expressway via Toulouse). The A10, the Paris–Bordeaux expressway, passes close to Poitiers, Niort (Exit 33 for La Rochelle), and Saintes before continuing toward Spain as A63.

By Plane

Frequent daily flights on **Air France** (☎ 08–02–80–28–02) link Bordeaux and the domestic airport at Limoges with Paris.

By Train

Superfast TGV (*Trains à Grande Vitesse*) Atlantique service links Paris (Gare Montparnasse) to Bordeaux—584 km (365 mi) in three hours—with stops at Poitiers and Angoulême (change for Jarnac, Cognac, and Saintes); and to La Rochelle—467 km (292 mi) in three hours—with a stop in Niort. Trains link Bordeaux to Lyon 8–9 hours) and Nice (eight hours) via Toulouse. Six trains daily make the 3½-hour, 400-km (250 mi) trip from Paris to Limoges.

Getting Around

By Car

Fast N137 connects La Rochelle with Saintes via Rochefort; Angoulême is linked to Bordeaux and Poitiers by N10 and to Limoges by N141; and D936 runs along the Dordogne Valley to Bergerac. N89 links Bordeaux to Périgueux, continuing to Limoges as N21.

By Train

Bordeaux is the region's major train hub (☞ Arriving and Departing by Train, *above*). Trains run regularly from Bordeaux to Bergerac (80 minutes), with occasional stops at St-Émilion, and three times daily to Sarlat (nearly three hours). At least six trains daily make the 90-minute journey from Bordeaux to Périgueux, and four continue to Limoges (2 hours, 20 minutes). Poitiers is the connecting point for Niort, La Rochelle, and Rochefort; Angoulême is the connecting point for Jarnac, Cognac, and Saintes.

Contacts and Resources

Car Rental

Avis (✉ Gare St-Jean, Bordeaux, ☎ 05–56–91–65–50; ✉ 133 bd. du Grand-Cerf, Poitiers, ☎ 05–49–58–13–00; ✉ 166 bd. Joffre, La Rochelle, ☎ 05–46–41–13–55). **Hertz** (✉ Pl. de la Gare, Bergerac, ☎ 05–53–57–19–27; ✉ 105 bd. du Grand-Cerf, Poitiers, ☎ 05–49–58–24–24).

Guided Tours

The **Office de Tourisme** in Bordeaux (✉ 12 cours du XXX-Juillet, 33080 Bordeaux cedex, ☎ 05–56–00–66–00) organizes four-hour coach tours of the surrounding vineyards every Wednesday and Saturday afternoon.

Travel Agencies

American Express (✉ 14 cours de l'Intendance, Bordeaux, ☎ 05–56–00–63–33). **Carlson-Wagonlits** (✉ 43 rue de la Porte-Dijeaux, Bordeaux, ☎ 05–56–52–92–70).

Visitor Information

Information on wine tours and tastings and local and regional sights is available at the **Bordeaux Office de Tourisme** (✉ 12 cours du XXX-Juillet, ☎ 05–56–00–66–00), which also has round-the-clock phone service in English.

The addresses of other tourist offices in towns mentioned in this chapter are as follows: **Angoulême** (✉ 7 bis rue du Chat, ☎ 05–45–95–16–84). **Bergerac** (✉ 97 rue Neuve d'Argenson, ☎ 05–53–57–03–11). **Cognac** (✉ 16 rue du XIV-Juillet, ☎ 05–45–82–10–71). **La Rochelle** (✉ Pl. de la Petite-Sirène, ☎ 05–46–41–14–68). **Limoges** (✉ 8 bd. Fleurus, ☎ 05–55–34–46–87). **Niort** (✉ Rue Ernest-Pérochon, ☎ 05–49–24–18–79). **Poitiers** (✉ 8 rue des Grandes-Écoles, ☎ 05–49–41–21–24). **Rochefort** (✉ Av. Sadi-Carnot, ☎ 05–46–99–08–60). **Royan** (✉ Palais des Congrès, ☎ 05–46–23–00–00). **St-Émilion** (✉ 15 rue du Clocher, ☎ 05–57–55–28–28). **Saintes** (✉ 62 cours National, ☎ 05–46–74–23–82). **Sarlat** (✉ Pl. de la Liberté, ☎ 05–53–31–45–45).

17 BACKGROUND & ESSENTIALS

Portraits of France

Books and Videos

France at a Glance: A Chronology

Smart Travel Tips A to Z

French Vocabulary

Menu Guide

BON APPÉTIT!: THE ART OF FRENCH COOKING

Born British, naturalized American, I am an unabashed chauvinist about French food. To wander through a French open market, the vegetables overflowing from their crates, the fruits cascading in casual heaps on the counter, is a sensual pleasure. To linger outside a bakery in the early morning, watching the fresh breads and croissants being lined up in regimental rows, must awaken the most fickle appetite. Just to read the menu posted outside a modest café alerts the imagination to pleasures to come.

Best of all, the French are happy to share their enthusiasm for good food with others. There are more good restaurants and eating places in France than in any other European country; the streets are lined with delicatessens, butchers, cheese shops, bakeries, and pastry shops. And I have yet to find a Frenchman, cantankerous though he may be, who does not warm to anyone who shows an interest in his national passion for wines and fine cuisine.

Fine cuisine does not necessarily mean fancy cuisine. Masters though French chefs are of the soufflé and the butter sauce, the salmon in aspic, and the strawberry *feuilleté* (puff pastry), such delicacies are reserved for celebration. Everyday fare is much more likely to be roast chicken, steak and *frites* (fries), an omelet, or a pork chop. Bread, eaten without butter, is mandatory at main meals, while the bottle of mineral water is almost as common as wine.

Where the French do score is in the variety and quality of their ingredients. Part of the credit must go to climate and geography—just look at the length of the French coastline and the part seafood plays in the cooking of Normandy, Brittany, and Provence. Count the number of rivers with fertile valleys for cattle and crops. Olives and fruit flourish in the Mediter-

ranean sun, while the region from southwest of Paris running up north to the Belgian border is one of the great breadbaskets of Europe.

No one but the French identifies three basic styles of cuisine—classical, nouvelle, and regional. No other European nation pays so much attention to menus and recipes.

Most sophisticated are the sauces and soufflés, the mousselines and *macédoines* of classical cuisine. Starting in the 17th century, successive generations of chefs have lovingly documented their dishes, developing an intellectual discipline from what is an essentially practical art. As a style, classical cuisine is now outmoded, but its techniques form the basis of rigorous professional training in French cooking. In some measure, all other styles of cooking are based on its principles.

Nouvelle cuisine, for instance, is directly descended from the classics. Launched with great fanfare more than 20 years ago, it takes a fresh, lighter approach, with simpler sauces and a colorful view of presentation. First-course salads, often with hot additions of shellfish, chicken liver, or bacon, have become routine. For a while, cooks experimented with such way-out combinations as vanilla with lobster and chicken with raspberries, but now new-style cooking has its own classics. Typical are *magrets de canard* (boned duck breast) sautéed like steak and served with a brown sauce of wine or green peppercorns and pot-au-feu made of fish rather than the usual beef.

M any cooks have made a refreshing return toward country-style cooking. Indeed, many cooks never left it, for classical and nouvelle cuisines are almost exclusively the concern of professionals. However, regional dishes are cooked by everyone—at restaurants, at home, and in the café on the corner.

The city of Lyon exemplifies the best of regional cuisine. It features such local specialties as poached eggs in *meurette* (red-wine sauce), *quenelles* (fish dumplings) in crayfish sauce, sausage with pistachios, and chocolate gâteau (cake). The Lyonnais hotly dispute Paris's title as gastronomic capital of France, pointing to the number of prestigious restaurants in their city. What is more, some of the world's finest wines are produced only 90 miles north, in Burgundy.

Lyon may represent the best of French regional cooking, but there's plenty to look for elsewhere. Compare the sole of Normandy, cooked with mussels in cream sauce, with the sea bass of Provence, flamed with dried fennel or baked with tomatoes and thyme. Contrast the butter cakes of Brittany with the yeast breads of Alsace, the braised endive of Picardy with the gratin of cardoons (a type of artichoke) found in the south.

Authentic regional specialties are based on local products. They have a character that may depend on climate (cream cakes survive in Normandy but not in Provence) or geography (each mountain area has its own dried sausages and hams). History brought spice bread to Dijon, a legacy of the days when the dukes of Burgundy controlled Flanders and the spice trade. Ethnic heritage explains ravioli around Nice on the Italian border, waffles in the north near Belgium, and dumplings close to Germany. Modern ethnic influences show up in cities, with many an Arab pastry shop started by Algerian immigrants and many a restaurant run by Vietnamese.

Fundamental to French existence is the baker, the *boulanger*. From medieval times legislation has governed the weight and content of loaves of bread, with stringent penalties for such crimes as adulteration with sand or sawdust. Today the government pegs the price of white bread, and you'll find the famous long loaves a bargain compared with the price of brioche, croissants, or loaves of whole wheat (*pain complet*), rye (*pain de seigle*), and bran (*pain de son*). White bread can be bought as thin *flûtes* to slice for soup; as baguettes; or as the common, thicker loaves known simply as *pains*.

Since French bread stays fresh for only a few hours, it is baked in the morning for midday and baked again in the afternoon. A baker's day starts at 4 AM to give the dough time to rise. Sadly, there is a lack of recruits, so more and more French bread is being produced industrially, without the right nutty flavor and chew to the crisp crust. The clue to bread baked on the spot is the heady smell of fermenting yeast, so sniff out a neighborhood bakery before you buy.

If bread is the staff of French life, pastry is the sugar icing. The window of a city pastry shop (in the country, bakery and pastry shop are often combined) is a wonderland of éclairs and meringues, madeleines, and puff pastry, spun sugar, and caramel. You'll find pies laden with seasonal fruit, nut cakes, and chocolate cakes, plus the baker's specialty, for he is certain to have one. Survey them with a sharp eye; they should be small (good ingredients are expensive) and impeccably alike in color and size (the sign of an expert craftsman). Last, the window should not be overflowing; because of the high cost, the temptation to cram the shelves with leftovers from the day before is strong.

The charcuterie is almost as French an institution as the bakery. *Chair cuite* means "cooked meat," and a charcuterie is a kind of delicatessen, specializing in pâtés, terrines, ham, and sausages. A charcuterie also sells long-lasting salads, such as cucumber, tomato, or grated carrot vinaigrette and root celery (celeriac) *rémoulade* (with mustard mayonnaise). Cooked "dishe of the day" may include coq au vin and *choucroute alsacienne* (sauerkraut with smoked pork hock). Often you'll also find such condiments as pickles, plus a modest selection of wines, cheeses, and desserts—rice pudding or baked apple, for example. Only bread is needed to complete the meal, and you're set for the world's best picnic!

French cheese deserves, and gets, close attention. Choosing a cheese is as delicate a matter as deciding on the right wine. In a good cheese shop you will be welcome to sample any of the cut cheeses, and assistants will gladly offer advice. One cardinal rule is to look for *fromage fermier* (farmhouse cheese), a rough equivalent of château-bottled wine. If the label says *lait cru* (raw milk)—even better; only when milk is unpasteurized does the flavor of some cheeses, Camembert, for example, develop properly. Try to keep a cheese cool without refrigeration and eat it as soon as you can. Delicate soft cheeses like Brie can become overripe within a matter of hours, one reason it is rare to find a wide-ranging selection of cheeses in a restaurant.

Many other kinds of specialty stores exist, often for local products. In Dijon, for instance, you'll find shops selling mustards in ornamental pots; in Gascony (near Bordeaux), it's foie gras and canned confit (preserved duck or goose). But the most famous concentration of food shops in the world must be clustered around Place de la Madeleine in Paris. On one corner stands Fauchon, the dean of luxury food emporiums. Just across the square stands Hédiard, specializing in spices, rare fruits, and preserves.

The Madeleine crossroads may be unique, but with a bit of persistence, a more modest version can be found in most French towns in the weekly market, often held in a picturesque open hall that may be centuries old. Markets start early, typically around 8 AM, and often disband at noon. In Paris, street markets continue to thrive in almost every quarter, and although

the main wholesale market of Les Halles has moved to the suburbs, the area around rue Coquillière is still worth exploring for its maze of truffle vendors, game purveyors, and professional kitchen-equipment outlets.

French markets are still dominated by the season—there is little or no sign of frozen produce and meats. The first baby lamb heralds Christmas; little chickens arrive around Easter, together with kid and asparagus. Autumn excitement comes with game—venison, pheasant, and wild boar. Even cheeses look and taste different according to the time of year.

If you're an early riser, there's a long wait until lunch, for snacks are not a French habit. The structure of a meal, its timing, and its content are taken seriously. The "grazing" phenomenon—minimeals snatched here and there throughout the day—is almost unheard of, and snacks are regarded as spoiling the appetite, not to mention being nutritionally unsound.

Still, the French light breakfast can come as no surprise; its unbeatable wake-up combination of croissant, brioche, or crusty roll with coffee has swept much of the world. Traditionally, the coffee comes as café au lait, milky and steaming in a wide two-handled bowl for dipping the bread.

At noon you'll be rewarded by what, for most French people, remains the main meal of the day. In much of the country, it is still true that everything stops for two hours; children return from school, and museums and businesses lock their doors. The pattern is much the same in provincial cities: Restaurants, bistros, and cafés are crammed with diners, most of whom eat at least two and often three or more courses. Unfortunately, however, quick lunches are becoming more and more the norm in larger cities like Paris.

A big lunch keeps French adults going until evening, but you may want to follow the example of schoolchildren, who are allowed a treat on the way home. Often it is a *pain au chocolat* (chocolate croissant). By 8 PM, you'll be ready for dinner and one of the greatest pleasures France has to offer.

The choice of restaurants in France is a feast in itself. At least once during your trip you may want to indulge in an outstanding occasion. But restaurants are just the beginning. You can also eat out in cafés, bistros, brasseries, fast-food outlets (they, too, have reached France), or auberges, which range from staid country inns to sybaritic hideaways.

Simplest is the café (where the espresso machine is king), offering drinks and such snacks as *croque monsieur* (toasted ham and cheese sandwich), *oeufs sur le plat* (fried eggs), *le hot dog*, and foot-long sandwiches of French bread. Larger-city cafés serve hot meals, such dishes as onion soup and braised beef with vegetables, consumed on marble-top tables to a background of cheerful banter. Like English pubs, French cafés are a way of life, a focal point for gossip and dominoes in practically every village.

The bistro, once interchangeable with the café, has taken a fashionable turn. In cities, instead of sawdust on the floor and a zinc-topped counter, you may find that a bistro is designer-decorated, serving new-style or fusion cuisine to a trendy, chattering crowd. If you're lucky, the food will be as witty and colorful as the clientele.

With few exceptions, brasseries remain unchanged—great bustling places with white-aproned waiters and hearty food. Go to them for oysters on the half shell and other fine seafood, garlic snails, *boudin* (black pudding), sauerkraut, and vast ice cream desserts. Originally a brasserie brewed beer, and since many brewers came from Alsace on the borders of Germany, the cooking reflects their origins.

Training is an important factor in maintaining the standards of French cooking. Professional chefs begin their three-year apprenticeship at age 16, starting in baking, pastry, or cuisine and later branching out into such specialties as aspic work and sugar sculp-

ture. To be a *chocolatier* is a career in itself. Much more than a manual trade, cooking in France aspires to being an art, and its exponents achieve celebrity status. Each decade has its stars, their rise and fall a constant source of eager speculation in the press and at the table.

The importance placed on food in France is echoed by the number of gastronomic societies, from the Chevaliers du Tastevin to the Chaîne des Rôtisseurs and the Confrérie des Cordons Bleus, to mention only three. The French believe that good eating, at whatever level, is an art that merits considerable time and attention. They have done the hard work, and as a traveler, you can reap the benefits.

— Anne Willan

Anne Willan is president and founder of the École de Cuisine La Varenne in Paris. She has a series on PBS, *Look and Cook with Anne Willan*, and has written numerous books, including *Cook It Right* and *La France Gastronomique*.

Splendid Stones: A Survey of French Architecture

It is a commonplace to describe the French as a people of *measure*. The national genius is held not to exaggerate. The high points in France's artistic history are not individual peaks, Shakespeare or Beethoven, but plateaus, inhabited by whole schools of art. One field where France has been a land of measure *par excellence* is architecture. Despite the ravages of wars throughout the centuries, France retains examples of nearly every historic and regional style.

Each region has its own characteristics. The dark red brick of the north stands in contrast to the pink brick of Toulouse, as does the white, chalky stone of the Cognac and Champagne regions when compared with the pink sandstone of the Vosges. Roofs vary as well, from the steep slopes of Alsace to the flat, orange-tile expanse of the Midi and the colorful slate patterns of Burgundy.

Medieval black-and-white timber frame houses survive in towns north of the Loire, such as Troyes, Dinan

Rennes, and the Petite France sector of Strasbourg. Castles perch grandly on cliffs throughout the southwest; hilltop villages survey the vineyards and olive groves of Provence in the southeast. Grim gateways repel strangers in the Charente region, whereas flower-strewn balconies welcome them to Alsace. Flemish belfries and Spanish gables flourish in the north, while the Germans, armed with their heavy Gothic Renaissance style, transformed parts of Strasbourg into a Gallic Berlin.

Although the cave paintings at Lascaux in the Dordogne and the freestanding *menhirs* of Brittany prove that the French (or their ancestors) have created and constructed since prehistoric times, the first great builders were the Romans. Their efforts—mostly in ruins—are found throughout France, especially in the south. The amphitheaters of Nîmes and Arles, the theater of Orange, and the Pont du Gard aqueduct are masterpieces equal to anything in Italy. Autun, Saintes, and Reims have proud Roman arches, and even the sprawling cities of Lyon and Paris house Roman remains.

With occasional exceptions, such as the 5th-century chapel at La Pépiole, near Toulon, the next architectural style of note was the Carolingian, in the 9th and 10th centuries. Surviving examples include the Basse-Oeuvre at Beauvais and the octagonal abbey church of Ottmarsheim, in Alsace. The massive Romanesque style that succeeded Carolingian differed in various ways—with its stone (as opposed to wood) ceilings or vaults, its introduction of windows high up the walls, and its preference for stone sculpture over such superficial ornament as mosaic and painting. Many 10th- and 11th-century Romanesque buildings survive in Burgundy, Alsace, the Auvergne, and western France, notably Poitiers, with the intricately carved west front of the church of Notre-Dame-la-Grande.

The airier Gothic of the great French cathedrals built between the 12th and 16th centuries represented a fundamental departure from Romanesque. The most obvious visual change: Pointed arches replaced round ones. Just as important, though, was a new vaulting structure based on intersecting ribbed vaults, which sprang across the roof from column to column. Outward thrust was borne by flying buttresses, slender arches linking the outer walls to freestanding columns, often topped by spiky pinnacles. While Romanesque architecture had thick, blocky walls with little room for window space, Gothic architecture, technically more sophisticated, replaced stone with stained glass.

Most medieval churches were built in the form of a cross, often topped by a tower in Romanesque churches. The nave, divided into bays (the spaces between columns) and flanked on either side by aisles, formed the main body of the church, with the east end, known as the chancel, containing the choir and altar. Many Gothic churches also have a number of small chapels behind the high altar, forming an outline known as the *chevet*, or apse.

Romanesque and Gothic churches are divided into three or four distinct vertical sections, like strata. Forestlike rows of pillars, topped by carved capitals, spring from the ground either to a gallery or triforium (an arcade of small columns and arches, originally of stone, later filled with glass), then to a clerestory (row of windows) above. The Romanesque facade was intended as an ornate screen and was sometimes fronted by a large porch (or narthex). The tympanum, a large sculpted panel above the central doorway (usually representing Christ in Judgment or Glory), was retained in the Gothic facade, which also featured huge portals, a circular rose window, a statue gallery, and lofty towers. Other towers, over the crossing or alongside the transepts, gradually lost favor: The stone bulls on top of the many-towered cathedral of Laon mourn a dying breed.

Pointed arches and ribbed vaults were first used during the 1130s at Sens and St-Denis—home of Abbot Suger, the leading political figure of the day. Within a decade, local bishops had followed Suger's lead, and huge Gothic cathedrals were under way at Noyon, Senlis, and Laon. As France expanded during the early Middle Ages from its Parisian epicenter, Gothic went with it. But the Gothic style did not displace the Romanesque overnight. Many Romanesque churches survive as crypts beneath later buildings (as at Dijon Cathedral, for example). Similarly, Romanesque naves were conserved at Mont-St-Michel, Vézelay, and Le Mans despite the addition of new Gothic chancels. At Strasbourg Cathedral, the reverse is true and a Romanesque chancel survives.

As the Gothic style evolved, less and less stone was used, and churches became delicate, almost skeletal. Paris's Ste-Chapelle is the most famous example, though as a stained-glass showcase, its scale doesn't match that of Metz Cathedral or St-Urbain in Troyes. The circular rose window spans through the Middle Ages like a leitmotif, evolving from 13th-century geometric splendor at St-Denis and Notre-Dame in Paris to a petal-like fluidity during the first half of the 16th century.

Height was another Gothic quest. Roofs soared higher and higher—until the one atop Beauvais Cathedral came crashing down in 1284. Notre-Dame of Paris is 106 ft high, but later cathedrals are even taller: Chartres climbs 114 ft; Bourges, 120; Reims, 124; Amiens, 137; and Beauvais, an ill-fated 153.

The Chambiges family, last in a long line of medieval master masons and star glaziers, played a major role in the development of the Flamboyant style. When the bishop of Beauvais was planning a grandiose transept, he sent for Martin Chambiges, tempting him away from Sens and keeping him jealously at Beauvais for 30 years. Some see in the flamelike Flamboyant style the last shrieks of Gothic decadence. But while its decorative profusion smacks of sculptural self-indulgence (St-Pierre in Caen is a good example), there are some admirable Flamboyant churches—take St-Séverin (Paris) and St-Nicolas de Port, near Nancy.

In the 16th century Gothic architecture was subject to the influx of Renaissance ideas, given official encouragement when François I (1515–47) invited Italian painters and architects Il Rosso, Primaticcio, and Leonardo da Vinci to his court. Renaissance architecture, marked by a stylistic return to ancient Rome, existed side by side with Gothic throughout the 16th century. In a number of Paris churches you will see classical columns and ornaments superimposed on Gothic structures (St-Étienne-du-Mont, St-Gervais, and St-Eustache are the best examples). Although Gothic was essentially an ecclesiastical style, the chief creations of Renaissance architecture were the châteaux of noblemen, princes, and kings. In the Loire Valley, medieval castles (like Chinon) gradually yielded to ideals of comfort and luxury (like Cheverny). Along the way, Renaissance proportion and daintiness were mingled with medieval massiveness, as at Azay-le-Rideau and Amboise.

To contrast the Renaissance style with the Baroque, its successor, compare the pink-brick arcades of the Place des Vosges in Paris (1612) with the grand, solemn stonework of the Place Vendôme, built in 1685 across town. A similar difference can be observed between the intimate château of Fontainebleau (mid-16th century) and the immense palace of Versailles (late 17th century).

Baroque imbued the classical style with drama and a sense of movement. Take a look at Mansart's dome surging above Paris's Hôtel des Invalides or the powerful rhythms of Charles Perrault's Louvre facade. Yet only in northern France, under the temporary influence of Spanish occupiers, did Latin exuberance find an outlet typified in the soaring curls on th colossal belfry of St-Amand-les-Eaux, near Lille. The overblown fantasies of Baroque in Italy, Spain, southern Germany, and Austria—wild curves, broken outlines, and sculptural overkill—were held firmly in check by the French love of discipline. Whole towns survive to remind us: The rigid plan and identical houses of Richelieu, south of Chinon, are restrained and austere.

The 18th century saw several major provincial building programs in the Neoclassical style—a more literal, toned-down interpretation of antique precedent. The state rooms of Strasbourg's Château des Rohan, the charming Place Stanislas, in Nancy, and the Grand Théâtre and Place de la Bourse, in Bordeaux, are top examples. Baroque, however, continued to dominate church building until the early 19th century (witness the cathedrals of Nancy and Arras). Many clerics commissioned architects to dress up Gothic buildings in classical apparel, sticking pilasters on columns or transforming pointed arches into rounded ones. Louis XIV set the tone by remodeling the choir of Notre-Dame in Paris in 1708, but Autun Cathedral—revamped throughout—is the most extreme example of such architectural rethink.

Napoléon ushered in the 19th century with the Arc de Triomphe, which remained unfinished for 20 years—typifying the hesitations of a century bereft of original ideas. Iron made its appearance then—most obviously at the Eiffel Tower, most frequently accompanied by glass in train stations and covered markets.

The 19th century bequeathed us Paris as we know it, with Baron Haussmann carving boulevards through the city. Luckily, Haussmann's seven-story buildings have proved sufficiently large and imposing to withstand the rapacious onslaughts of modern developers, and central Paris has remained unchanged for 100 years. But it's not surprising that the showpiece of Haussmann's Paris, the Opéra, is a pompous jumble of styles.

Things perked up in the 20th century. Although such Paris landmarks as the Grand and Petit Palais and opulent town halls throughout the country were faithful to conservative taste, Émile Gallé and Hector Guimard led an artistic revolution known as Art Nouveau, with sinuous, nature-based forms. The Paris métro, ornamented by iron railings and canopies, is the most familiar example. A reaction occurred in the straighter lines of Art Deco, which first turned up at the Théâtre des Champs-Élysées in 1913. At the same time, the French developed a taste for reinforced concrete that they have never lost. Its most imaginative exponent was Swiss-born Le Corbusier, an architectural Picasso whose best work (like the chapel at Ronchamp in eastern France) obeys few established rules.

In the first half of the 20th century, much energy was spent repairing the damage of two world wars: Many towns had to be rebuilt almost from scratch. At its worst, the result was bland and hurried (Amiens, Reims); at its best, spacious, rational, and monumentally austere (Le Havre). Official buildings—like town halls and train stations—number among the most significant buildings of the period.

The most visited postwar building in France is Paris's futuristic Pompidou Center (thus requiring it be renovated for the new millennium). Its pipes and workings are on the outside, ensuring that the interior is uncluttered to a fault. Paris's latter-day skyscrapers have—with the exception of the Tour Montparnasse—been banished to the city outskirts, notably to La Défense. There, the giant glass-and-concrete arch known as La Tête Défense has cemented a vista that stretches along avenue de la Grande Armée, past the Arc de Triomphe, down the Champs-Élysées, across Place de la Concorde, and over the Tuileries to the gleaming glass pyramid of the Louvre.

— Simon Hewitt

WHAT TO READ & WATCH BEFORE YOU GO

The best introduction to modern France is John Ardagh's *France Today*. A witty but less complete survey of the country and its people is Theodore Zeldin's *The French*. Another entry on the list is Richard Bernstein's *Fragile Glory*. An immensely popular, if slightly satiric, introduction to French country life is provided by Peter Mayle's two autobiographical books on Provence, *A Year in Provence* and *Toujours Provence*, as well as his novel *Chasing Cézanne*.

Nancy Mitford's readable *The Sun King* covers the regal grandeur of the 17th century, while Alfred Cobban's workmanlike *History of Modern France* describes trends and events from the death of Louis XIV up to 1962. Another readable and fascinating book about French history is Barbara Tuchman's *A Distant Mirror*. Dorothy Carrington's classic work on Corsica, *Granite Island: A Portrait of Corsica,* is available at the library. For a history of Paris from the Revolution to the Belle Epoque, look for Johannes Willms's *Paris: Capital of Europe.* For modern French history, particularly the Vichy era, a good bet is Robert Paxton's *Vichy France and the Jews*. For a scholarly study of Romanesque and Gothic architecture, read Henri Focillon's thoughtfully illustrated *The Art of the West*, available at the library.

Charles Dickens in *A Tale of Two Cities*, George Orwell in *Down and Out in Paris and London,* Ernest Hemingway, notably in *A Moveable Feast,* F. Scott Fitzgerald in *Tender Is the Night,* and Gertrude Stein in *Paris, France* are just some of the authors who have written about Paris in English. The novels of Émile Zola—*La Curée, L'Assommoir, Nana,* and *La Débâcle*—are mostly set in Provence or in Paris, emerging from mid-19th-century reconstruction amid backstreet squalor and brash glamour.

As for books about French wine and cuisine, Patricia Wells's *The Food Lover's Guide to Paris* and *The Food Lover's Guide to France* provide a good beginning. Waverly Root's *The Food of France* is a great accompaniment to any trip. Alexis Lichine's *Guide to Wines and Vineyards of France* is still the classic wine guide, though it's now only available from the library. For more books about French wine, try Robert M. Parker's *Bordeaux: A Comprehensive Guide to the Wines Produced from 1961–1990* and *Wines of the Rhône Valley*. A. J. Liebling's *Between Meals* provides a more literary and entertaining look at the fine art of eating in France.

Further listings of hotels and inns in France can be found in *Rivages: Hotels and Country Inns of Character and Charm in France, Rivages: Bed and Breakfasts of Character and Charm in France, Karen Brown's France: Charming Bed and Breakfasts,* and *Karen Brown's France: Charming Inns and Itineraries.* For more expanded, in-depth coverage of Provence and the Côte d'Azur, look for *Fodor's Provence and the Côte d'Azur,* 4th edition. If you're interested in finding out more about vineyards in France, *Rivages: Wines and Vineyards of Character and Charm in France* is a good resource.

If you want to see France on film before you go, consider renting one of the following films: Louis Malle's *Au Revoir les Enfants* (1987), which takes place during World War II in Provins in Ile-de-France; Krzysztof Kieslowski's *The Double Life of Véronique* (1991), a mysterious drama set in Paris and Poland; *Everyone Says I Love You* (1996), a Woody Allen comedy with Paris as a backdrop; *Jean de Florette* (1986) or *My Father's Glory* (1990), Claude Berri's and Yves Robert's views of rural Provençal life; *My Favorite Season* (1993), André Techiné's family drama set in southwestern France; *Mr. Hulot's Holiday* (1953), Jacques Tati's classic comedy on the beach in Brittany; *Ready to Wear* (1994), Robert Altman's send-up of the fashion industry in Paris; *The Return of Martin Guerre* (1982), Daniel Vigne's vision of 16th-century village life; *A Sunday in the Country* (1984), Bertrand Tavernier's story of a day in the life of an elderly painter on his country estate; *To Catch a Thief* (1955), and Alfred Hitchcock's mystery set on the French Riviera, with Grace Kelly and Cary Grant; and *When the Cat's Away* (1996).

FRANCE AT A GLANCE

Here's a mini-history of France—an *aide mémoire* to monarchs and moments.

ca. 3500 BC Megalithic stone complexes erected at Carnac, Brittany.

ca. 1500 BC Lascaux cave paintings executed (Dordogne, southwestern France).

ca. 600 BC Greek colonists found Marseille.

after 500 BC Celts appear in France.

58–51 BC Julius Caesar conquers Gaul; writes up the war in *De Bello Gallico*.

52 BC Lutetia, later to become Paris, is built by the Gallo-Romans.

46 BC Roman amphitheater built at Arles.

14 BC Pont du Gard aqueduct at Nîmes is erected.

AD 406 Invasion by the Vandals (Germanic tribes).

451 Attila invades and is defeated at Châlons.

The Merovingian Dynasty

486–511 Clovis, king of the Franks (481–511), defeats the Roman governor of Gaul and founds the Merovingian dynasty. Great monasteries, such as those at Tours, Limoges, and Chartres, become centers of culture.

497 Franks convert to Christianity.

567 Frankish kingdom is divided into three parts—the eastern countries (Austrasia), later to become Belgium and Germany; the western countries (Neustria), later to become France; and Burgundy.

The Carolingian Dynasty

768–78 Charlemagne (768–814) becomes king of the Franks (768); conquers northern Italy (774); and is defeated by the Moors at Roncesvalles, Spain, after which he consolidates the Pyrénées border (778).

800 The pope crowns Charlemagne Holy Roman Emperor in Rome. Charlemagne expands the French kingdom far beyond its present borders and establishes a center for learning at his capital, Aix-la-Chapelle (Aachen, in present-day Germany).

814–987 Death of Charlemagne. The Carolingian line continues through a dozen or so monarchs, leading to a batch called Charles (the Bald, the Fat, the Simple) and a sprinkling of Louises over the centuries. Under the Treaty of Verdun (843), the empire is divided in two—the eastern half becoming Germany, the western half, France.

The Capetian Dynasty

987 Hugh Capet (987–996) is made king of France and establishes the principle of hereditary rule for his descendants. Settled conditions and the increased power of the church see the flowering of Romanesque architecture in the cathedrals of Autun and Angoulême.

1066 Norman conquest of England by William the Conqueror (1028–87).

1067 Work begins on the Romanesque Bayeux Tapestry, celebrating the Norman Conquest.

ca. 1100 First universities in Europe include one in Paris. Development of European vernacular verse: *Chanson de Roland.*

1140 The Gothic style of architecture first appears at St-Denis and later becomes fully developed at the cathedrals of Chartres, Reims, Amiens, and Paris's Notre-Dame.

ca. 1150 Struggle between the Anglo-Norman kings (Angevin Empire) and the French; when Eleanor of Aquitaine switches husbands (from Louis VII of France to Henry II of England), her extensive lands pass to English rule.

1257 Sorbonne University is founded in Paris.

1270 Louis IX (1226–70), the only French king to achieve sainthood, dies in Tunis on the seventh and last Crusade.

1302–07 Philippe IV the Fair (1285–1314) calls together the first States-General, predecessor to the French Parliament. He disbands the Knights Templars in order to gain their wealth (1307).

1309 Pope, under pressure, leaves a corrupt and disorderly Rome to take up residence in Avignon in southern France, which becomes the seat of the papacy for nearly 70 years.

The Valois Dynasty

1337–1453 Hundred Years' War between France and England: fighting for control of those areas of France gained by the English crown following the marriage of Eleanor of Aquitaine and Henry II.

1348–50 Black Death (plague) rages in France.

1428–31 Joan of Arc (1412–31), the Maid of Orléans, sparks the revival of French fortunes in the Hundred Years' War but is captured by the English and burned at the stake at Rouen.

1434 Johannes Gutenberg invents the printing press in Strasbourg, Alsace.

1453 France finally defeats England, terminating the Hundred Years' War and English claims to the French throne.

1475 Burgundy is at the height of its power under Charles the Bald.

1494 Italian wars: beginning of Franco-Hapsburg struggle for hegemony in Europe.

1515–47 Reign of François I, who imports Italian artists, including Leonardo da Vinci (1452–1519), and brings the

Renaissance to France. The château of Fontainebleau is begun (1528).

1558   France captures Calais, England's last territory on French soil.

1562–98   Wars of Religion: Catholics versus Huguenots (French Protestants).

The Bourbon Dynasty

1589   The first Bourbon king, Henri IV (1589–1610), is a Protestant who converts to Catholicism and achieves peace in France. He signs the Edict of Nantes, giving limited freedom of worship to Protestants. The development of Renaissance Paris begins.

ca. 1610   Scientific revolution in Europe begins, marked by the discoveries of mathematician and philosopher René Descartes (1596–1650).

1643–1715   Reign of Louis XIV, the Sun King, a monarch who builds the Baroque power base of Versailles and presents Europe with a glorious view of France. With his first minister, Colbert, Louis makes France, by force of arms, the most powerful nation-state in Europe. He persecutes the Huguenots, who emigrate in great numbers, nearly ruining the French economy.

1660   Classical period of French culture: dramatists Pierre Corneille (1606–84), Molière (1622–73), and Jean Racine (1639–99), and painter Nicolas Poussin (1594–1665).

ca. 1715   Rococo art and decoration develop in Parisian boudoirs and salons, typified by the painter Antoine Watteau (1684–1721) and, later, François Boucher (1703–70) and Jean-Honoré Fragonard (1732–1806).

1700–onward   Writer and pedagogue Voltaire (1694–1778) is a central figure in the French Enlightenment, along with Jean-Jacques Rousseau (1712–78) and Denis Diderot (1713–84), who in 1751 compiles the first modern encyclopedia. The ideals of the Enlightenment—for reason and scientific method and against social and political injustices—pave the way for the French Revolution. In the arts, painter Jacques-Louis David (1748–1825) reinforces revolutionary creeds in his Neoclassical works.

1756–63   The Seven Years' War results in the loss by France of most of its overseas possessions and in the ascension of England as a world power.

1776   The French assist the Americans in the Revolutionary War. Ideals of liberty cross the Atlantic with the returning troops to reinforce new social concepts.

The French Revolution

1789–1804   The Bastille is stormed on July 14, 1789. Following upon early Republican ideals comes the Reign of Terror and the administration of the Directory under Robespierre. There are widespread political executions—Louis XVI and Marie Antoinette are guillotined in 1793. Reaction sets in, and the instigators of the Terror are themselves executed (1794).

Napoléon Bonaparte enters Champion of the Directory (1795–99) and is installed as First Consul during the Consulate (1799–1804).

The First Empire

1804 Napoléon crowns himself emperor of France at Notre-Dame in the presence of the pope.

1805–12 Napoléon conquers most of Europe. The Napoleonic Age is marked by a Neoclassical artistic style called Empire as well as by the rise of Romanticism—characterized by such writers as François-Auguste-René de Chateaubriand (1768–1848) and Marie-Henri Stendhal (1783–1842) and the painters Eugène Delacroix (1798–1863) and Théodore Géricault (1791–1824)—which is to dominate the arts of the 19th century.

1812–14 Winter cold and Russian determination defeat Napoléon outside Moscow. The emperor abdicates and is transported to Elba.

Restoration of the Bourbons

1814–15 Louis XVIII, brother of the executed Louis XVI, regains the throne after the Congress of Vienna settles peace terms.

1815 The Hundred Days: Napoléon returns from Elba and musters an army on his march to the capital but lacks national support. He is defeated at Waterloo (June 18) and exiled to the island of St-Helena, in the south Atlantic.

1821 Napoléon dies in exile.

1830 Bourbon king Charles X, locked into a pre-Revolutionary state of mind, abdicates. A brief upheaval (called Three Glorious Days) brings Louis-Philippe, the Citizen King, to the throne.

1840 Napoléon's remains are brought back to Paris.

1846–48 Severe industrial and farming depression contributes to Louis-Philippe's abdication (1848).

Second Republic and Second Empire

1848–52 Louis-Napoléon (nephew and step-grandson of Napoléon I) is elected president of the short-lived Second Republic. He makes a successful attempt to assume supreme power and is declared emperor of France, taking the title Napoléon III.

ca. 1850 The ensuing period is characterized in the arts by the emergence of realist painters, such as Jean-François Millet (1814–75), Honoré Daumier (1808–79), and Gustave Courbet (1819–77), and late-Romantic writers, among them Victor Hugo (1802–85), Honoré de Balzac (1799–1850), and Charles Baudelaire (1821–87).

1863 Napoléon III inaugurates the Salon des Refusés in response to critical opinion. It includes work by Édouard Manet (1832–83), Claude Monet (1840–1926), and Paul Cézanne (1839–1906) and is commonly regarded as the birthplace of Impressionism and of modern art in general.

Chronology

Chronology

The Third Republic

1870–71 The Franco-Prussian War sees Paris besieged by and then fall to the Germans. Napoléon III takes refuge in England. France loses Alsace and Lorraine to Prussia before the peace treaty is signed.

1871–1914 Before World War I, France expands its industries and builds vast colonial empires in North Africa and Southeast Asia. Sculptor Auguste Rodin (1840–1917), composers Maurice Ravel (1875–1937) and Claude Debussy (1862–1918), and poets such as Stéphane Mallarmé (1842–98) and Paul Verlaine (1844–96) set the stage for Modernism.

1870s Emergence of the Impressionist school of painting: Claude Monet, Auguste Renoir (1841–1919), Camille Pissarro (1830–1903), and Edgar Degas (1834–1917).

1889 The Eiffel Tower is built for the Paris World Exhibition. Centennial of the French Revolution.

1894–1906 Franco-Russian Alliance (1894). Dreyfus affair: The spy trial and its anti-Semitic backlash shock France.

1900 Paris holds World Exposition.

1904 The Entente Cordiale: England and France become firm allies.

1914–18 During World War I France fights with the Allies, opposing Germany, Austria-Hungary, and Turkey. Germany invades France; most of the big battles (Vimy Ridge, Verdun, Somme, Marne) are fought in trenches in northern France. French casualties exceed 5 million. With the Treaty of Versailles (1919), France regains Alsace and Lorraine and attempts to exact financial and economic reparations from Germany.

1918–39 Between wars, Paris attracts artists and writers, including Americans Ernest Hemingway (1899–1961) and Gertrude Stein (1874–1946). France nourishes major artistic and philosophical movements: Constructivism, Dadaism, Surrealism, and Existentialism.

1939–45 At the beginning of World War II, France sides with the Allies until invaded and defeated by Germany in 1940. The French government, under Marshal Philippe Pétain (1856–1951), moves to Vichy and cooperates with the Nazis. French overseas colonies split between allegiance to the legal government of Vichy and declaration for the Free French Resistance, led (from London) by General Charles de Gaulle (1890–1970).

1944 D-Day, June 6: The Allies land on the beaches of Normandy and successfully invade France. Additional Allied forces land in Provence. Paris is liberated in August 1944, and France declares full allegiance to the Allies.

1944–46 A provisional government takes power under General de Gaulle; American aid assists French recovery.

The Fourth Republic

1946 France adopts a new constitution; French women gain the right to vote.

1946–54 In the French-Indochina War, France is unable to regain control of its colonies in Southeast Asia. The 1954 Geneva

Agreement establishes two governments in Vietnam: one in the north, under the Communist leader Ho Chi Minh, and one in the south, under the emperor Bao Dai. U.S. involvement eventually leads to French withdrawal.

1954–62 The Algerian War leads to Algeria's independence from France. Other French African colonies gain independence.

1957 The Treaty of Rome establishes the European Economic Community (now known as the European Union—EU), with France as one of its members.

The Fifth Republic

1958–69 De Gaulle is the first president under a new constitution; he resigns in 1969, a year after widespread disturbances begun by student riots in Paris.

1976 The first supersonic transatlantic passenger service begins with the Anglo-French Concorde.

1981 François Mitterrand (1916–1996) is elected the first Socialist president of France since World War II.

1988 Mitterrand is elected for a second term.

1990 TGV (*Train à Grande Vitesse*) clocks a world record—515 kph (322 mph)—on a practice run. Channel Tunnel linkup between France and England begins.

1993 After nine years of painstaking renovations by I. M. Pei, American-Chinese architect, the Richelieu Wing of the Louvre is opened to the public, doubling the museum's exhibition space.

1994 The Channel Tunnel (or Chunnel) opens; trains link London to Paris in three hours.

1995 Jacques Chirac, mayor of Paris, is elected president.

1997 The world's largest library, the Bibliothèque Nationale François-Mitterrand, is inaugurated in Paris. President Jacques Chirac calls early elections, a Socialist coalition wins a majority, and Lionel Jospin is appointed prime minister.

1998 Amid scenes of popular fervor not seen since the liberation from Germany in 1944, France hosts and wins the Soccer World Cup at the state-of-the-art Stade de France in St-Denis, a suburb just north of Paris. A new museum of Jewish art and history opens in Paris, and the art museum in Lille reopens after six years of renovation. Métro line 14 opens, linking central Paris to the Bibliothèque François-Mitterrand and the Bercy district.

1999 The launch of the euro—the single European currency—sees prices in shops and restaurants commonly posted in both francs and euros; euro bills and coins will not be introduced until 2002.

2000 The Pompidou Center reopens at midnight on December 31, 1999, after two years of renovation, heralding the onset of millennium festivities in Paris and across France.

ESSENTIAL INFORMATION

AIR TRAVEL

As one of the premier destinations in the world, Paris is serviced by many international carriers and a surprising number of U.S.-based companies. **Air France** is the French flag carrier and offers numerous flights (often several per day) between Paris's Charles de Gaulle airport and New York City's JFK airport; Newark, New Jersey; Washington, D.C.'s Reagan airport; Miami; Chicago; Houston; San Francisco; Los Angeles; Toronto; Montréal; and Mexico City. American-based carriers are usually less expensive but offer, on the whole, fewer nonstop flights. **TWA** offers daily nonstop flights to Paris from New York City's JFK; in peak season, flights from Boston's Logan International airport, Washington, D.C., and St. Louis are offered as well as connecting flights from Los Angeles. **Delta Airlines** is a popular U.S.–France carrier; departures to Paris leave Atlanta, Cincinnati, and New York City's JFK, while Delta's regional flights link airports through the southeast U.S and the Midwest with its main international hub in Atlanta. Travelers in the northeast and southwest of the U.S. often use **Continental Airlines,** whose nonstop Paris flights generally depart from Newark and Houston; in peak season, they often offer daily departures. Another popular carrier is **United Airlines,** with nonstop flights to Paris from Chicago, Washington, D.C., and San Francisco. **American Airlines** also offers daily nonstop flights to Paris's Orly airport from numerous cities, including New York City's JFK, Boston, Miami, Chicago, and Dallas/Fort Worth. **Northwest** offers a daily departure to Paris from their hub in Detroit; connections from Seattle, Minneapolis, and numerous other airports link up to Detroit. In Canada, Air France and **Air Canada** are the leading choices for departures from Toronto and Mont-

réal; in peak season, departures are often on a daily basis. From London, Air France, **British Airways, British Midland,** and **Air U.K.** are the leading carriers, with up to 15 flights daily in peak season. In addition, direct routes link Manchester, Edinburgh, and Southampton with Paris. Considering the expense of this short flight, however, more and more travelers are using train transport via the Eurostar Express through the Channel Tunnel (☞ The Channel Tunnel and Train Travel to and from Paris, *below*). Options are more limited for travelers to Paris from Australia and New Zealand, who usually wind up taking British Airways and **Qantas** flights to London, then connections to Paris.

BOOKING

When you book **look for nonstop flights** and **remember that "direct" flights stop at least once.** Try to avoid connecting flights, which require a change of plane.

CARRIERS

➤ MAJOR AIRLINES: **Air Canada** (☎ 800/776–3000 in the U.S. and Canada). **Air France** (☎ 800/237–2747 in the U.S.; 08-02-80-28-02 in France). **American Airlines** (☎ 800/433–7300 in the U.S.; 01-69-32-73-07 in France). **British Airways** (☎ 800/247-9297 in the U.S.; 0345/222111 in the U.K.; 08-25-82-54-00 in France). **Continental** (☎ 800/231-0856 in the U.S.; 01-42-99-09-09 in France). **Delta** (☎ 800/241-4141 in the U.S.; 01-47-68-92-92 in France). **Northwest** (☎ 800/225-2525 in the U.S.; 01-42-66-90-00 in France). **Qantas** (☎ 800/227-4500 in the U.S.; 08-03-84-68-46 in France). **TWA** (☎ 800/892-4141 in the U.S.; 08-01-89-28-92 in France). **United** (☎ 800/538-2929 in the U.S.; 08-01-72-72-72 in France). **US Airways** (☎ 800/428-4322 in the U.S.; 01-49-10-29-00 in France).

➤ DOMESTIC AIRLINES: **Air France** (☞ *below*). **Air Liberté** (☎ 08–03–80–58–05). **AOM** (☎ 01–49–79–12–34 or 08–03–00–12–34).

➤ U.K. TO FRANCE: **Air France** (☎ 020/8742–6600 in the U.K.; 08–02–80–28–02 in France). **British Airways** (☎ 0345/222–111 in the U.K.; 08–02–80–29–02 in France). **Air U.K.** (☎ 0345/666–777 in the U.K.; 01–44–56–18–08 in France). **British Midland** (☎ 020/8754–7321; 0345/554–554 in the U.K.; 01–48–62–55–65 in France). **Easyjet** (☎ 0990/292–929 in the U.K.; 04–93–21–48–33 in France) runs scheduled services to Nice from Luton.

CHECK-IN & BOARDING

Assuming that not everyone with a ticket will show up, airlines routinely overbook planes. When everyone does, airlines ask for volunteers to give up their seats. In return, these volunteers usually get a certificate for a free flight and are rebooked on the next flight out. If there are not enough volunteers, the airline must choose who will be denied boarding. The first to get bumped are passengers who checked in late and those flying on discounted tickets, so **get to the gate and check in as early as possible,** especially during peak periods. Be sure to **bring a government-issued photo I.D. to the airport.** You are usually asked to show it before you are allowed to check in.

CUTTING COSTS

The least expensive airfares to France must usually be purchased in advance and are non-refundable. It's smart to **call a number of airlines, and when you are quoted a good price, book it on the spot**—the same fare may not be available the next day. Always **check different routings** and look into using different airports. Travel agents, especially low-fare specialists (☞ Discounts & Deals, *below*), are helpful.

Consolidators are another good source. They buy tickets for scheduled international flights at reduced rates from the airlines, then sell them at prices that beat the best fare available directly from the airlines, usually without restrictions. Sometimes you can even get your money back if you need to return the ticket. Carefully read the fine print detailing penalties for changes and cancellations, and **confirm your consolidator reservation with the airline.**

When you **fly as a courier,** you trade your checked-luggage space for a ticket deeply subsidized by a courier service. There are restrictions on when you can book and how long you can stay.

➤ CONSOLIDATORS: **Cheap Tickets** (☎ 800/377–1000). **Discount Airline Ticket Service** (☎ 800/576–1600). **Unitravel** (☎ 800/325–2222). **Up & Away Travel** (☎ 212/889–2345). **World Travel Network** (☎ 800/409–6753).

➤ COURIERS: **Air Courier Association** (✉ 15000 W. 6th Ave., Suite 203, Golden, CO 80401, ☎ 800/282–1202, ✎). **International Association of Air Travel Couriers** (✉ 220 South Dixie Highway #3, P.O. Box 1349, Lake Worth, FL, 33460, ☎ 561/582–8320, ℻ 561/582–1581, ✎). **Now Voyager Travel** (✉ 74 Varick St., Suite 307, New York, NY 10013 ☎ 212/431–1616, ℻ 212/219–1753 or 212/334–5243, ✎).

➤ DISCOUNT PASSES: **Air France** (☞ Major Carriers, *above*).

FLYING TIMES

Flying time to Paris is 7½ hours from New York, 9 hours from Chicago, 11 hours from Los Angeles, and 1 hour from London. Flying time between Paris and Nice is 1 hour.

HOW TO COMPLAIN

If your baggage goes astray or your flight goes awry, complain right away. Most carriers require that you **file a claim immediately.**

➤ AIRLINE COMPLAINTS: U.S. Department of Transportation **Aviation Consumer Protection Division** (✉ C-75, Room 4107, Washington, DC 20590, ☎ 202/366–2220, ✎). **Federal Aviation Administration Consumer Hotline** (☎ 800/322–7873).

AIRPORTS

There are two major gateway airports to France, located just outside the capital: Orly, 16 km (10 mi) south of

Paris, and Charles de Gaulle—also known as Roissy—which is 26 km (16 mi) northeast of the city. Orly has two terminals: Orly Ouest (domestic flights) and Orly Sud (international, regular and charter flights). Roissy has three terminals: Aérogare 1 (foreign flights), Aérogare 2 (Air France flights), and Aérogare T-9 (charter flights). Terminal information should be noted on your ticket. The three Orly terminals are connected with a free shuttle service, called the *navette*. At Roissy there's a TGV station (from terminal 2) where you can connect to trains going all over the country. Many airlines have less-frequent flights to Lyon, Nice, Marseille, Bordeaux, and Toulouse. Or you can fly to Paris and get a connecting flight to other destinations in France.

➤ AIRPORT INFORMATION: **Charles de Gaulle/Roissy** (☎ 01–48–62–22–80 in English). **Orly** (☎ 01–49–75–15–15).

DUTY-FREE SHOPPING

As of July, 1999, duty-free shopping at French airports is no longer available for those traveling within the European Community. Only travelers leaving Europe will benefit from duty-free prices.

BARGE AND YACHT TRAVEL

Canal and river trips are popular in France, particularly along the picturesque waterways in Brittany, Burgundy, and the Midi. For further information, contact a travel agent; ask for a "Tourisme Fluvial" brochure in any French tourist office; or get in touch with one of the companies that organizes barge trips. It's also possible to rent a bare railboat or one with a crew to travel around the coast of France, particularly along the Côte d'Azur.

➤ DOMESTIC BARGE COMPANIES: **Bourgogne Voies Navigables** (✉ 1 quai de la République, 89000 Auxerre, ☎ 03–86–72–92–10). **Connoisseur Cruisers** (Halye Nautique, Ile Sauzay, 70100 Gray, ☎ 03–84–64–95–20).

➤ INTERNATIONAL BARGE COMPANIES: **Abercrombie & Kent** (✉ 1520 Kensington Rd, Oak Brook, IL 60521, ☎ 630/954–2944 or 800/323–7308, FAX 630/954–3324). **Étoile de Champagne**

(88 Broad St., Boston, Massachusetts 02110, ☎ 800/280–1492, FAX 617/426–4689). **European Waterways** (140 E. 56th St., Suite 4C, New York, NY 10022, ☎ 212/688–9489 or 800/217–4447, FAX 212/688–3778 or 800/296–4554). **French Country Waterways** (Box 2195, Duxbury, Massachusetts 02331, ☎ 781/934–2454 or 800/222–1236, FAX 781/934–9048). **KD River Cruises of Europe** (2500 Westchester Ave., Purchase, NY 10577, ☎ 914/696–3600 or 800/346–6525, FAX 914/696–0833, ✍). **Kemwel's Premier Selections** (106 Calvert St., Harrison, NY 10528, ☎ 914/835–5555 or 800/234–4000, FAX 914/835–5449).

➤ YACHT CHARTERS AND TOURS: **Club Voyages** (43 Hooper Ave., Atlantic Highlands, NJ, 07716, ☎ 732/291–8228 or 888/842–2122). **The Moorings** (19345 U.S. Hwy. 19 N, 4th floor, Clearwater, FL 34624-3193, ☎ 813/530–5424 or 800/535–7289, FAX 813/530–9474). **Ocean Voyages** (1709 Bridgeway, Sausalito, CA 94965, ☎ 415/332–4681 or 800/299–4444, FAX 415/332–7460).

BEACHES

Along the miles of French coast you'll find broad-brimmed hats, parasols, and opaque sunglasses—their modesty and discretion charmingly contradictory in view of (and we mean full view of) the frankly bare flesh that bobbles up and down the miles of seashore. And not just the famous *seins nus* (topless women), but the bellies of gastronome *pépés* (grandfathers) as well. Naked children crouch over sand châteaux, their unselfconsciousness a reflection of their elders' own. For the French the summer beach holiday is a sacred ritual, a counterbalance to the winter ski trip.

To avoid the July–August stampede, **go in June or September.** Ironic as it may be, France's most famous coastline possesses the country's worst beaches: sand along the Côte d'Azur is in shorter supply than pebbles. By far the finest French beaches are those facing north (toward the Channel) and west (toward the Atlantic). Many are so vast that you can spread out even at the most popular resorts (like Biarritz, Royan, Dinard, or Le Touquet). Brittany's beaches are the most picturesque, though the water can be chilly, even in summer.

If you're planning to devote a lot of time to beaches and haven't tackled the French coast before, get to **know the distinction between private and public.** France's waterfront is carved up into private frontage, often roped off and advertised by color-coordinated awnings, parasols, and mattresses. These private beaches frequently offer full restaurant and bar service, and rent mattresses, umbrellas, and lounge chairs by the day and half-day. Dressing rooms and showers are included; some even rent private cabanas. Prices can run from 60 francs a day to 120 or more. Interspersed between these commercial beaches is plenty of public space.

BIKE TRAVEL

The French are great bicycling enthusiasts—witness the Tour de France—and there are many good bicycling routes in France. For about 45 francs a day (55 francs for a 10-speed touring bike) **you can rent a bike from one of 30 train stations throughout the country;** you need to show your passport and leave a deposit of 1,000 francs or a Visa or MasterCard. Mountain bikes (known as VTT or Vélos Touts Terrains) can be rented from many shops as well as from some train stations. Tourist offices supply details on the more than 200 local shops that rent bikes and the SNCF has a brochure entitled the "Guide du Train et du Vélo," available at any train station. Bikes may be taken as accompanied luggage from any station in France; some trains in rural areas don't even charge for this.

For information about good bike routes, contact the Fédération Française de Cyclotourisme. The yellow Michelin maps (1:200,000 scale) are fine for roads, but for off-road bicycling you may want to get one of the Institut Géographique National's detailed, large-scale maps. Try their blue series (1:25,000) or orange series (1:50,000).

➤ BIKE MAPS: **Institut Géographique National** (IGN, 107 rue La Boétie, 75008 Paris, ☎ 01–42–56–06–68).

➤ BIKE RENTALS: **SNCF** (☞ Train Travel, *below*).

➤ BIKE ROUTES: **Fédération Française de Cyclotourisme** (✉ 8 rue Jean-Marie-Jégo, 75013 Paris, ☎ 01–44–16–88–88).

➤ BIKE TOURS: **Backroads** (801 Cedar St., Berkeley, CA 94710-1800, ☎ 510/527–1555 or 800/462–2848, 𝕱𝔸𝕏 510-527–1444, 🖳). **Bike Riders Tours** (✉ P.O. Box 130254, Boston, Massachusetts 02113, ☎ 617/723–2354 or 800/473–7040, 𝕱𝔸𝕏 617/723–2355). **Butterfield & Robinson** (70 Bond St., Toronto, Ontario, Canada M5B 1X3, ☎ 416/864–1354 or 800/678–1147, 𝕱𝔸𝕏 416/864–0541, 🖳). **Chateaux Bike Tours** (Box 5706, Denver, CO 80217, ☎ 303/393–6910 or 800/678–2453, 𝕱𝔸𝕏 303/393–6801). **Discover France Biking** (✉ 1603 E. Gardenia Ave., Phoenix, AZ 85020, ☎ 800/960–2221, 𝕱𝔸𝕏 602/944–5934, 🖳). **Euro-Bike Tours** (Box 990, De Kalb, IL 60115, ☎ 815/758–8851 or 800/321–6060, 𝕱𝔸𝕏 815/758–8822). **Europeds** (761 Lighthouse Ave., Monterey, CA 93940, ☎ 800/321–9552, 𝕱𝔸𝕏 831/655–4501). **RMF** (✉ 1342 Birchcliff Dr., Oakville, Ontario, L6M2A4 Canada, ☎ 905/825–0796 or 800/530–5957, 𝕱𝔸𝕏 905/825–4177).

BIKES IN FLIGHT

Most airlines accommodate bikes as luggage, provided they are dismantled and boxed. For bike boxes, often free at bike shops, you'll pay about $5 from airlines (at least $100 for bike bags). International travelers can sometimes substitute a bike for a piece of checked luggage at no charge; otherwise, the cost is about $100. Domestic and Canadian airlines charge $25–$50.

BOAT & FERRY TRAVEL

BETWEEN THE U.K. AND FRANCE

A number of ferry and hovercraft routes link the United Kingdom and France. Driving distances from the French ports to Paris are as follows: from Calais, 290 km (180 mi); from Boulogne, 243 km (151 mi); from Dieppe, 193 km (120 mi); from Dunkerque, 257 km (160 mi). The fastest routes to Paris from each port are via the N43, A26, and A1 from Calais and the Channel Tunnel; via the N1 from Boulogne; via the N15 from Le Havre; via the D915 and N1 from Dieppe; and via the A25 and A1 from Dunkerque.

➤ DOVER–CALAIS: **Hoverspeed** (✉ International Hoverport, Marine Parade, Dover CT17 9TG, ☎ 01304/ 240241) operates up to 15 crossings a day by Hovercraft and catamaran. The crossings take 35 minutes (Hovercraft) or 55 minutes (catamaran). **P&O European Ferries** (✉ Channel House, Channel View Rd., Dover, Kent CT17 9TJ, ☎ 020/8575–8555, ✆) has up to 25 sailings a day; the crossing takes about 75 minutes. **Seafrance** (✉ 23 rue Louis le Grand Paris, France 75002, ☎ 01–44–94–40–40, ✆) operates up to 15 sailings a day; the crossing takes about 90 minutes.

➤ FOLKESTONE–BOULOGNE: **Hoverspeed** (☞ Dover–Calais, *above*) is the sole operator on this route, with ten 35-minute crossings a day.

➤ NEWHAVEN–DIEPPE: **Seafrance** (☞ Dover–Calais, *above*) has as many as four sailings a day, and the crossing takes four hours.

➤ PORTSMOUTH–LE HAVRE: **P&O European Ferries** (☞ Dover–Calais, *above*) has up to three sailings a day, and the crossing takes 5½ hours by day, 7½ by night.

FARES & SCHEDULES

Sample fare: Dover/Calais, round-trip (within 5 days): 1 person 240 francs, two adults plus car, 1450 francs (this price doubles if the visit exceeds 5 days). Schedules and tickets are available at any travel agency throughout France or via Internet. Means of payment: traveler's checks, major credit cards, cash.

BUS TRAVEL

France's excellent train service means that long-distance buses are rare; **regional buses are found mainly where train service is spotty.** Excursions and bus tours are organized by the SNCF and other tour companies. Ask for a brochure at any major travel agent or contact the French Tourism Office (☞ Visitor Informa-

tion, *below*). Bus tours from the U.K. generally depart from London, for Paris, the Atlantic Coast, Chamonix and the Alps, Grenoble, Lyon, and the Côte d'Azur. Note that **reservations are necessary on most buses.**

There is no central bus network servicing France but the largest operator is Eurolines France, whose main terminal is located in the Parisian suburb of Bagnolet (a half-hour métro ride from central Paris, at the end of métro line 3). Eurolines is obliged by law to run many international routes, including a route from London to Paris, usually departing at 9 AM, arriving at 6 PM; noon, arriving at 9 PM; and 10 PM, arriving at 7 AM. Fares are £60 round-trip (under-25 youth pass £56), £35 one-way. Other Eurolines routes include: Amsterdam (7 hours/400 francs); Barcelona (15 hours/1040 francs); and Berlin (10 hours/930 francs). There are also international-only arrival/departures from Avignon, Bordeaux, Lille, Lyon, Toulouse, and Tours. Local bus information to the rare rural areas where trains do not have access can be obtained from the SNCF.

➤ FROM THE U.K.: **Eurolines** (28 av. Général-de-Gaulle, Bagnolet, ☎ 08–36–69–52–52 in France; 020/7730–3499 in the U.K.).

➤ WITHIN FRANCE: **Paris Vision** (1 rue d'Auber, 75009 Paris, ☎ 01–47–42–27–40). **SNCF** (88 rue St-Lazare, 75009 Paris, ☎ 08–36–35–35–39 in English).

BUSINESS HOURS

BANKS & OFFICES

Generally, **banks are open weekdays, from 9:30 to 4:30** (note that the Banque de France closes at 3:30), and some banks are also open on Saturday. Most take a one-hour, or even a 90-minute, lunch break, except for those in Paris. In general government offices and businesses are open 9–5. For information about post office hours, *see* Mail & Shipping, *below.*

GAS STATIONS

Gas stations in cities and towns are generally open 8 AM–8 PM, Monday–Saturday. Those along the highways are open 24 hours, seven days a week.

MUSEUMS & SIGHTS

Usual opening times are from 9:30 to 5 or 6. Many close for lunch (noon–2). Most are closed one day a week (generally Monday or Tuesday) and on national holidays: **check museum hours before you go.**

PHARMACIES

Pharmacies are generally open Monday–Saturday 8:30 AM–8 PM; on the door of every pharmacy is a list of those closest that are open on Sunday or 24 hours.

SHOPS

Large stores in big towns are open from 9 or 9:30 until 7 or 8. Smaller shops often open earlier (8 AM) and close later (8 PM) but take a lengthy lunch break (1–4), particularly in the south of France. Corner groceries frequently stay open until around 10 PM. Some Paris stores are beginning to stay open on Sunday, although it's still uncommon.

CAMERAS & PHOTOGRAPHY

If you need to get your camera repaired, your best bet in Paris and other major cities is to go to a FNAC (a book, record, and electronics store). You should be able to find a small camera repair shop in most small towns. Note that you may have to wait some time to get your camera fixed.

➤ PHOTO HELP: **Kodak Information Center** (☎ 800/242–2424). *Kodak Guide to Shooting Great Travel Pictures,* available in bookstores or from Fodor's Travel Publications (☎ 800/533–6478; $16.50 plus $5.50 shipping).

EQUIPMENT PRECAUTIONS

Always **keep your film and tape out of the sun.** Carry an extra supply of batteries, and **be prepared to turn on your camera or camcorder** to prove to security personnel that the device is real. Always **ask for hand inspection of film,** which becomes clouded after repeated exposure to airport X-ray machines, and **keep videotapes away from metal detectors.**

FILM & DEVELOPING

In Paris and most major cities, the easiest place to get film developed and printed is at a FNAC store. If you're in a smaller town and want your film developed, look for a store with a Kodak sign outside its door. Keep in mind that **it's expensive to develop and print film in France**—around $20 per 36-exposure roll.

VIDEOS

France uses SECAM, which is a different system than is used in the U.S. (NTSC) or the U.K. (PAL). This means that you won't be able to play the videotapes that you bring from home on French equipment. In addition, you probably won't be able to use SECAM videotapes in your camera, so it's a good idea to **bring extra videotapes from home.**

CAR RENTAL

Though renting a car in France is expensive—about twice as much as in the United States—as is gas (5.80 francs to 6.80 francs per liter), it can pay off if you're traveling with two or more people. In addition, renting a car gives you a kind of freedom that the train does not. Rates in Paris begin at about $70 a day and $200 per week for an economy car with air conditioning, a manual transmission, and unlimited mileage. The price doesn't usually take into account the 20.6% VAT tax or, if you pick it up from the airport, the airport tax. You won't need a car in the capital, so **wait to pick up your rental until the day you leave Paris.**

➤ MAJOR AGENCIES: **Alamo** (☎ 800/522–9696; 0181/759–6200 in the U.K.). **Avis** (☎ 800/331–1084; 800/879–2847 in Canada; 02/9353–9000 in Australia; 09/525–1982 in New Zealand). **Budget** (☎ 800/527–0700; 0144/227–6266 in the U.K.). **Dollar** (☎ 800/800–6000; 0181/897–0811 in the U.K., where it is known as Eurodollar; 02/9223–1444 in Australia). **Hertz** (☎ 800/654–3001; 800/263–0600 in Canada; 0181/897–2072 in the U.K.; 02/9669–2444 in Australia; 03/358–6777 in New Zealand). **National InterRent** (☎ 800/227–3876; 0845/722–2525 in the U.K., where it is known as Europcar InterRent). **SNAC** (☎ 01–44–05–33–99).

➤ LOCAL AGENICES: **ACAR** (⊠ 99 bd. Auguste-Blanqui, 75013 Paris,

☎ 01–45–88–28–38). **Locabest** (✉ 104 bd. Magenta, 75010 Paris, ☎ 01–44–72–08–05). **Rent-A-Car** (✉ 79 rue de Bercy, 75012 Paris, ☎ 01–43–45–98–99).

CUTTING COSTS

Renting a car through a local French agency has a number of serious disadvantages, notably price, as they simply cannot compete with the larger international companies. These giants combine bilingual service, the security of name recognition, extensive services (such as 24-hour hot lines), and automatic vehicles. However, SNAC—a France-based agency—can be useful if you are interested in luxury cars (convertible BMWs) or large family vans (Renault Espace, for example). Note that the big international agencies, like Hertz and Avis, offer better prices to their clients who make reservations in their home countries before they arrive in France; if you need to rent a car while in France, it even pays to call home and have a friend take care of it for you from there. So, to get the best deal **reserve a car before you leave home.**

Do **look into wholesalers,** companies that do not own fleets but rent in bulk from those that do and often offer better rates than traditional car-rental operations. Payment must be made before you leave home. Also **look into long-term leasing**; Renault rents new cars for a minimum of 17 days.

➤ LONG-TERM LEASING: **Renault Eurodrive** (☎ 800/221–1052 east; 800/477–7716 west; 800/777–7131 FL and Puerto Rico).

➤ WHOLESALERS: **Auto Europe** (☎ 207/842–2000 or 800/223–5555, FAX 800–235–6321, 🖳). **Europe by Car** (☎ 212/581–3040 or 800/223–1516, FAX 212/246–1458, 🖳). **DER Travel Services** (✉ 9501 W. Devon Ave., Rosemont, IL 60018, ☎ 800/782–2424, FAX 800/282–7474 for information; 800/860–9944 for brochures, 🖳). **Kemwel Holiday Autos** (☎ 800/678–0678, FAX 914/825–3160, 🖳).

INSURANCE

When driving a rented car you are generally responsible for any damage to or loss of the vehicle. Before you rent see what coverage your personal auto-insurance policy and credit cards already provide.

Collision policies that car-rental companies sell for European rentals usually do not include stolen-vehicle coverage. Before you buy it, check your existing policies—you may already be covered.

REQUIREMENTS & RESTRICTIONS

In France you must be 21 to rent a car, though rates may be higher if you're under 25. Your own driver's license is acceptable. (☞ Rules of the Road *in* Car Travel, *below*).

SURCHARGES

Before you pick up a car in one city and leave it in another, **ask about drop-off charges or one-way service fees,** which can be substantial. Note, too, that some rental agencies charge extra if you return the car before the time specified in your contract. To avoid a hefty refueling fee, **fill the tank just before you turn in the car,** but be aware that gas stations near the rental outlet may overcharge.

CAR TRAVEL

In France, **you may use your own driver's license,** but you must be able to prove you have third-party insurance. You don't need an International Driver's Permit unless you are planning on a long-term stay; they are available from the American or Canadian automobile association, and, in the United Kingdom, from the Automobile Association or Royal Automobile Club. You must be 18 years old to drive but there is no top age limit (if your faculties are intact).

EMERGENCY SERVICES

If your car breaks down on an expressway, **go to a roadside emergency telephone.** If you have a breakdown anywhere else, find the nearest garage or contact the police. There are also 24-hour assistance hotlines valid throughout France (available through rental agencies and supplied to you when you rent the car), but do not hesitate in calling the police in case of any roadside emergency, for they are quick, reliable, and the phone call is free. There are special phones just for this purpose on all highways—just pick up the phone and dial 17. The French equivalent of the AAA is the Club Automobile de l'Ile de France, but it only takes care of its members and is of little use to international travelers.

➤ CONTACTS: **Police** (☎ 17).

FROM THE U.K.

If you're driving from the U.K., you have a choice of either the Channel Tunnel or the ferry services when traveling to the continent. Reservations are essential at peak times and always a good idea, especially when going via the Chunnel. Cars don't drive in the Chunnel, but are loaded onto trains. ☞ Channel Tunnel, Ferry & Boat Travel, and Train Travel, *below.*

GASOLINE

Gas is expensive, especially on expressways and in rural areas. When possible, **buy gas before you get on the expressway** and keep an eye on pump prices as you go. These vary enormously; anything from 6.5 to 8 francs per liter. The cheapest gas can be found at *hypermarchés* (large supermarkets). Credit cards are accepted in every gas station. It's possible to go for miles in the country without passing a gas station—**don't let your tank get too low in rural areas.**

PARKING

Parking is a nightmare in Paris and often difficult in other large towns. Meters and ticket machines (pay and display) are common: Make sure you **have a supply of 1-, 2-, 5-, and 10-franc coins.** If you're planning on spending a lot of time in Paris with a car, **it might be a good idea to buy a parking card** (*carte de stationnement*) for 100 francs at any café sporting the red TABAC sign. This card works like a credit card in the parking meters, allowing you to avoid the inconvenience of finding exact change. Whether you are paying with coins or with a parking card, do not forget to display the green receipt that you receive from the machine inside the front window of your car so that it is clearly visible to the meter patrol.

Note that in August, parking is free in certain residential areas; however, **only parking meters sporting a dense yellow circle indicate a free parking zone;** if you do not see the circle, pay. Parking tickets are expensive and there is no shortage of the blue-uniformed parking police. Parking lots, indicated by a blue sign with a white "P" are usually underground and are generally expensive. In smaller towns, parking may be permitted on one side of the street only—alternating every two weeks—so pay attention to signs.

ROADS

For the fastest roads between two points, **look for roads marked A for autoroutes.** A *péage* (toll) must be paid on most expressways: The rate varies but can be steep. The *N* (Route Nationale) roads—which are sometimes divided highways—and *D* (Route Départementale) roads are usually also wide and fast. Don't be daunted by smaller (*C* and *V*) roads, either.

There are excellent links between Paris and most French cities, but poor ones between the provinces (the principal exceptions being A26 from Calais to Reims, A62 between Bordeaux and Toulouse, and A9/A8 the length of the Mediterranean coast).

Though routes are numbered, **the French generally guide themselves from city to city and town to town by destination name.** When reading a map, keep one eye on the next big city toward your destination as well as the next small town; most snap decisions will have to be based on town names, not road numbers.

When traveling in and out of Paris, note there are two major rings that run parallel to each other and encircle the city: the *périphérique intérieur,* the inside ring also known as the *grands boulevards* (not to be confused with the major avenue layout in the center of Paris's Right Bank), and also the *périférique extérieur,* the outside ring which is a major highway. From this ring there are *portes* (gates) which connect to the major highways of France. The names of these highways function on the same principal as the Paris métro, with the final destination as the determining point in the direction you must take. These directions are indicated by major cities and the major highways connect to Paris at these points. For instance, heading north, look for Porte de la Chapelle (direction Lille and Charles de Gaulle Airport); east, for Porte de Bagnolet (direction Metz and Nancy); south, for Porte d'Orléans (direction Lyon and Bordeaux); and west, for Porte d'Auteuil (direction Rouen and Chartres) or Porte de St-Cloud. Other portes include Porte de la Villette; Porte de Pantin; Porte de Bagnolet (A3 to CDG); Porte de Bercy (A4 to Reims); Porte d'Italie; and Porte de Maillot (A14 to Rouen).

The major expressways into Paris are the A1 from the north/Great Britain; the A13 from Rouen, Normandy, and northwest France; the A6 from Lyon, the French Alps, the Riviera, and Italy; the A10 from France's southwest andf the Pyrénées; and the A4 from Nancy and Strasbourg in eastern France.

ROAD MAPS

If you plan to drive through France, **get a yellow Michelin map** for each region you'll be visiting. The maps are available from most bookshops and magazine stores.

RULES OF THE ROAD

Drive on the right and **yield to drivers coming from streets to the right.** However, this rule does not necessarily apply at roundabouts, where you should watch out for just about everyone. You must **wear your seat belt,** and children under 12 may not travel in the front seat. Speed limits are 130 kph (80 mph) on expressways (*autoroutes*), 110 kph (70 mph) on divided highways (*routes nationales*), 90 kph (55 mph) on other roads (*routes*), 50 kph (30 mph) in cities and towns (*villes et villages*). French drivers break these limits and police dish out hefty on-the-spot fines with equal abandon. Do not expect to find traffic lights in the center of the road, as French lights are usually located on the right and left hand sides of the lane.

Some important traffic terms and signs to note: *Sortie* (Exit); *Sens Unique* (One Way); *Stationnement Interdite* (No Parking); *Cul de Sac* (Dead End). Blue rectangular signs indicate a highway; green rectangular signs indicate a major direction; triangles carry illustrations of a particular traffic hazard; speed limits are indicated in a cirle with the maximum limit encircled in red.

➤ AUTO CLUBS: **American Automobile Association** (☎ 800/564–6222). **Australian Automobile Association** (☎ 02/6247–7311). **Canadian Automobile Association** (CAA, ☎ 613/247–0117). **Club Automobile de l'Ile de France** (☎ 01–40–55–43–00). **New Zealand Automobile Association** (☎ 09/377–4660). **Royal Automobile Club** (RAC, ☎ 0990/722–722 for membership; 0345/121–345 for insurance). **U.K. Automobile Association** (AA, ☎ 0990/500–600).

THE CHANNEL TUNNEL

Short of flying, the "Chunnel" is the fastest way to cross the English Channel: 35 minutes from Folkestone to Calais, 60 minutes from motorway to motorway, or 3 hours from London's Waterloo Station to Paris's Gare du Nord.

Motorists from the U.K. have a choice of either the Channel Tunnel or ferry services (☞ Ferry Travel, *below*) when traveling to the continent. Reservations are essential at peak times and always a good idea, especially when going via the Chunnel. Cars don't drive in the Chunnel, but are loaded onto trains (☞ Train Travel, *below*). Cars without reservations, if they can get on at all, are charged 20 percent extra.

➤ CAR TRANSPORT: **Le Shuttle** (☎ 0870/535–3535 in the U.K.).

➤ PASSENGER SERVICE: In the U.K.: **Eurostar** (☎ 0870/518–6186), **Inter-City Europe** (✉ Victoria Station, London, ☎ 0870/584–8848 for credit-card bookings). In the U.S.: **BritRail Travel** (☎ 800/677–8585), **Rail Europe** (☎ 800/942–4866).

CHILDREN IN FRANCE

Be sure to plan ahead and **involve your youngsters** as you outline your trip. When packing, include things to keep them busy en route. On sightseeing days try to schedule activities of special interest to your children.

Getting around Paris and other major cities with a stroller can be a challenge, so **take your lightest folding stroller.** Many museums require you to check strollers at the entrance. In Paris, not all métro stations have escalators; you're better off taking the bus in off-peak hours.

➤ FAMILY-FRIENDLY TOUR OPERATORS: **Grandtravel** (✉ 6900 Wisconsin Ave., Suite 706, Chevy Chase, MD 20815, ☎ 301/986–0790 or 800/247–7651) for people traveling with grandchildren ages 7–17. **Families Welcome!/Great Destinations** (✉ 92 N. Main St., Ashland, OR 97520, ☎ 541/482–6121 or 800/326–0724, FAX 541/482–0660). **A Touch of France** (660 King Rd., Fords, NJ 08863, ☎ 800/738–5240).

➤ LOCAL INFORMATION: **CIDJ** (Centre d'Information et de Documentation pour la Jeunesse, 101 quai Branly, 75015 Paris, ☎ 01–44–49–12–00).

CAR TRAVEL

If you're renting a car don't forget to **arrange for a car seat** when you reserve. Playgrounds can be found off of many highways. Most rest stop bathrooms have changing tables.

FLYING

If your children are two or older, **ask about children's airfares.** As a general rule, infants under two not occupying a seat fly at greatly reduced fares or even for free. When booking, **confirm carry-on allowances** if you're traveling with infants. In general, for babies charged 10% of the adult fare you are allowed one carry-on bag and a collapsible stroller; if the flight is full, the stroller may have to be checked or you may be limited to less.

Experts agree that it's a good idea to use safety seats aloft for children weighing less than 40 pounds. Airlines set their own policies: U.S. carriers usually require that the child be ticketed, even if he or she is young enough to ride free, since the seats must be strapped into regular seats. Do **check your airline's policy about using safety seats during takeoff and landing.** And since safety seats are not allowed just everywhere in the plane, get your seat assignments early.

When reserving, **request children's meals or a freestanding bassinet** if you need them. But note that bulkhead seats, where you must sit to use the bassinet, may lack an overhead bin or storage space on the floor.

FOOD

The best restaurants in France generally do not welcome small children; except for the traditional family Sunday-noon dinner, fine dining is considered an adult pastime. Aim for more modest *auberges* (country inns), and if there's a choice **consider having your meal in the café or bar** rather than in the linen-and-goblet filled dining room. In cities, brasseries and cafés offer a casual option and the flexible meal times that children often require. If you get desperate, France has its share of McDonald's, Pizza Huts, and other fast-food restaurants.

Very few mainstream restaurants have highchairs but some do serve children's portions *(menu enfant)*, usually spaghetti or the ubiquitous *steak-frites*, a mountain of fries with a thin steak or fat patty of ground beef, usually extremely rare. If you're queasy about this, ask for it *bien cuit* (well done). If your children go to bed early, **opt for your hot meal at noon** (there are cheaper prix-fixe menus, too) and consider having a sandwich, quiche, a *croque monsieur* (a grilled egg and cheese sandwich), or pizza at a café or brasserie in the early evening; full-service restaurants usually do not serve before 7 PM.

or pizza at a café or brasserie in the early evening; full-service restaurants usually do not serve before 7 PM.

LODGING

If you're planning to stay in hotels, be sure to book ahead. Many small hotels have only one or two rooms that sleep four (triples are much more common); if there are more of you, you'll have to book two neighboring rooms or a suite. Larger hotels often provide cribs free to guests with young children, which is not usually the case at inns and smaller hotels. Older children are charged at adult rates unless the hotel offers a special family rate. Be sure to **ask about the cutoff age for children's discounts** when booking.

Some hotel chains offer discounts for families and programs for children. Club Med is particularly family friendly: it has a "Baby Club" (from age four months) at its resort in Chamonix, and "Mini Clubs" (for ages four to six or eight, depending on the resort), and "Kids Clubs" (for ages eight and up during school holidays) at all its resort villages in France except in Val d'Isère. Some clubs are only French-speaking. The Novotel chain allows up to two children under 15 to stay free in their parents' room. Sofitel hotels offer a free second room for children during July and August and over the Christmas period.

Another option: **consider a gîte, a short-term apartment or house rental,** or a home exchange (☞ Lodging, *below*).

➤ FAMILY-FRIENDLY LODGING: **Club Med** (40 W. 57th St., New York, NY 10019, ☎ 800/258–2633). **Novotel** (☎ 800/221–4542). **Sofitel** (☎ 800/221–4542).

SIGHTS & ATTRACTIONS

Places that are especially good for children are indicated by a rubber duckie icon in the margin. There are plenty of diversions for the young and **almost all museums and movie theaters have discounted rates.**

SUPPLIES & EQUIPMENT

Supermarkets carry several major brands of diapers (*couches à jeter*), universally referred to as Pampers (pawm-paires). Junior sizes are hard to come by, as the French toilet-train early. Baby formula is available in grocery stores or pharmacies. There are two types of formulas: *lait prémier age,* for infants 0–4 months, and *lait deuxieme age,* for 4 months or older. French formulas come in powder form and need to be mixed with a pure, low mineral content bottled water like Evian or Volvic (the French *never* mix baby formula with tap water). American formulas do not exist in France. If you're looking for treats for your little ones, some items to keep in mind are: *coloriage* (color-

ing books); *crayons de couleur* (crayons);*pate à modeler* (modeling clay); and *feutres* (magic markers).

TRANSPORTATION

SNCF allows children under 4 to travel free (provided they don't occupy a seat) or for 50 francs for a seat, and children 4 to 12 to travel at half fare with an accompanying adult. The Carte "Enfant Plus" (350 francs) allows children under 12 and as many as four accompanying adults to make an unlimited number of trips at as much as half the cost (though you are only guaranteed at least 25% off on all trains). This card is worth your while only if you are planning on traveling extensively in France—it is valid for one year.

When traveling by train with children you may want to travel first class, as there is more space and it's calmer. Another option is to request an "*espace famille*" ("family space") in second class (when you make reservations), which consists of two sets of seats facing each other. For more information, *see* Train Travel, *below.*

COMPUTERS ON THE ROAD

If you use a major internet provider, getting online in France shouldn't be difficult. Some hotels even have in-room modem lines. You may, however, need an adapter for your computer for the European-style plugs (☞ Electricity, *below*). As always, if you're traveling with a laptop, carry a spare battery and adapter. Never plug your computer into any socket before asking about surge protection. IBM sells a pen-size modem tester that plugs into a telephone jack to check if the line is safe to use.

➤ ACCESS NUMBERS IN PARIS: **AOL** (☎ 01–41–45–81–00). **Compuserve** (☎ 08–03–00–60–00, 08–03–00–80–00, or 08–03–00–90–00).

CONSUMER PROTECTION

Whenever shopping or buying travel services in France, **pay with a major credit card** so you can cancel payment or get reimbursed if there's a problem. If you're doing business with a particular company for the first time, **contact your local Better Business**

Bureau and the attorney general's
offices in your own state and the
company's home state, as well. Have
any complaints been filed? Finally, if
you're buying a package or tour,
always **consider travel insurance** that
includes default coverage (☞ Insurance, *below*).

➤ BBBs: **Council of Better Business
Bureaus** (✉ 4200 Wilson Blvd., Suite
800, Arlington, VA 22203, ☎ 703/
276–0100, FAX 703/525–8277 ✍).

CUSTOMS & DUTIES

When shopping, **keep receipts** for all
purchases. Upon reentering the country, **be ready to show customs officials
what you've bought.** If you feel a
duty is incorrect or object to the way
your clearance was handled, note the
inspector's badge number and ask to
see a supervisor. If the problem isn't
resolved, write to the appropriate
authorities, beginning with the port
director at your point of entry.

IN FRANCE

There are two levels of duty-free
allowance for travelers entering
France: one for goods obtained (tax
paid) within another European Union
(EU) country and the other for goods
obtained anywhere outside the EU or
for goods purchased in a duty-free
shop within the EU.

In the first category, you may import
duty-free: 300 cigarettes or 150
cigarillos or 75 cigars or 400 grams
of tobacco; 5 liters of table wine and
(1) 1½ liters of alcohol over 22%
volume (most spirits), (2) 3 liters of
alcohol under 22% by volume (fortified or sparkling wine), or (3) 3 more
liters of table wine; 90 milliliters of
perfume; 375 milliliters of toilet
water; and other goods to the value of
2,400 francs (620 francs for those
under 15).

In the second category, you may
import duty-free: 200 cigarettes or
100 cigarillos or 50 cigars or 250
grams of tobacco (these allowances
are doubled if you live outside Europe); 2 liters of wine and (1) 1 liter
of alcohol over 22% volume (most
spirits), (2) two liters of alcohol under
22% volume (fortified or sparkling
wine), or (3) 2 more liters of table
wine; 60 milliliters of perfume; 250

milliliters of toilet water; and other
goods to the value of 300 francs (150
francs for those under 15).

➤ INFORMATION: **Direction des
Douanes** (✉ 16 rue Yves Toudic, 10ᵉ,
☎ 01–40–40–39–00).

IN AUSTRALIA

Australian residents who are 18 or
older may bring home $A400 worth
of souvenirs and gifts (including
jewelry), 250 cigarettes or 250 grams
of tobacco, and 1,125 ml of alcohol
(including wine, beer, and spirits).
Residents under 18 may bring back
$A200 worth of goods. Prohibited
items include meat products. Seeds,
plants, and fruits need to be declared
upon arrival.

➤ INFORMATION: **Australian Customs
Service** (Regional Director, ✉ Box 8,
Sydney, NSW 2001, ☎ 02/9213–
2000, FAX 02/9213–4000).

IN CANADA

Canadian residents who have been
out of Canada for at least 7 days may
bring home C$500 worth of goods
duty-free. If you've been away less
than 7 days but more than 48 hours,
the duty-free allowance drops to
C$200; if your trip lasts 24–48 hours,
the allowance is C$50. You may not
pool allowances with family members. Goods claimed under the C$500
exemption may follow you by mail;
those claimed under the lesser exemptions must accompany you. Alcohol
and tobacco products may be included in the 7-day and 48-hour
exemptions but not in the 24-hour
exemption. If you meet the age requirements of the province or territory through which you reenter
Canada, you may bring in, duty-free,
1.14 liters (40 imperial ounces) of
wine or liquor *or* 24 12-ounce cans or
bottles of beer or ale. If you are 16 or
older you may bring in, duty-free,
200 cigarettes and 50 cigars. Check
ahead of time with Revenue Canada
or the Department of Agriculture for
policies regarding meat products,
seeds, plants, and fruits.

You may send an unlimited number
of gifts worth up to C$60 each dutyfree to Canada. Label the package
UNSOLICITED GIFT—VALUE UNDER $60.
Alcohol and tobacco are excluded.

➤ INFORMATION: **Revenue Canada**
(✉ 2265 St. Laurent Blvd. S, Ottawa, Ontario K1G 4K3, ☎ 613/993–0534; 800/461–9999 in Canada, FAX 613/957–8911, ✎).

IN NEW ZEALAND

Homeward-bound residents 17 or older may bring back $700 worth of souvenirs and gifts. Your duty-free allowance also includes 4.5 liters of wine or beer; one 1,125-ml bottle of spirits; and either 200 cigarettes, 250 grams of tobacco, 50 cigars, or a combination of the three up to 250 grams. Prohibited items include meat products, seeds, plants, and fruits.

➤ INFORMATION: **New Zealand Customs** (Custom House, ✉ 50 Anzac Ave., Box 29, Auckland, New Zealand, ☎ 09/359–6655, FAX 09/359–6732).

IN THE U.K.

If you are a U.K. resident and your journey was wholly within the European Union (EU), you won't have to pass through customs when you return to the United Kingdom. If you plan to bring back large quantities of alcohol or tobacco, check EU limits beforehand. From countries outside the EU, you may bring home, duty-free, 200 cigarettes or 50 cigars; 1 liter of spirits or 2 liters of fortified or sparkling wine or liqueurs; 2 liters of still table wine; 60 ml of perfume; 250 ml of toilet water; plus £136 worth of other goods, including gifts and souvenirs. If returning from outside the EU, prohibited items include meat products, seeds, plants, and fruits.

➤ INFORMATION: **HM Customs and Excise** (✉ Dorset House, Stamford St., Bromley, Kent BR1 1XX, ☎ 0171/202–4227).

IN THE U.S.

U.S. residents who have been out of the country for at least 48 hours (and who have not used the $400 allowance or any part of it in the past 30 days) may bring home $400 worth of foreign goods duty-free.U.S. residents 21 and older may bring back 1 liter of alcohol duty-free. In addition, regardless of your age, you are allowed 200 cigarettes and 100 non-Cuban cigars. Antiques, which the U.S. Customs Service defines as objects more than 100 years old, enter duty-free, as do original works of art done entirely by hand, including paintings, drawings, and sculptures.

You may also send packages home duty-free: up to $200 worth of goods for personal use, with a limit of one parcel per addressee per day (except alcohol or tobacco products or perfume worth more than $5); label the package PERSONAL USE and attach a list of its contents and their retail value. Do not label the package UNSOLICITED GIFT or your duty-free exemption will drop to $100. Mailed items do not affect your duty-free allowance on your return.

➤ INFORMATION: **U.S. Customs Service** (✉ 1300 Pennsylvania Ave. NW, Washington, DC 20229, www.customs.gov; inquiries ☎ 202/354–1000; complaints c/o ✉ Office of Regulations and Rulings; registration of equipment c/o ✉ Resource Management, ☎ 202/927–0540).

DINING

All establishments must post their menus outside, so study them carefully before deciding to enter. Most restaurants have two basic types of menu: à la carte and fixed price (prix fixe, or *un menu*). The prix-fixe menu is usually the best value, though choices are more limited. Most menus begin with a first course (*une entrée*), often subdivided into cold and hot starters, followed by fish and poultry, then meat; it's rare today that anyone orders something from all three. However, outside brasseries, wine bars, and other simple places, it's inappropriate to order just one dish, as you'll understand when you see the waiter's expression. The restaurants we review in this book are the cream of the crop in each price category.

A few pointers on French dining etiquette: Diners in France don't negotiate their orders much, so don't expect serene smiles when you ask for sauce on the side. Order your coffee after dessert, not with it. When you're ready for the check, ask for it: No professional waiter would dare put a bill on your table while you're still enjoying the last sip of coffee. And don't ask for a doggy bag; it's just not done. The French usually drink wine or mineral water—not soda or coffee—with their food. You may ask for a carafe of tap water, but not always: In general, diners order mineral water if they don't order wine.

MEALS & SPECIALTIES

What's the difference between a bistro and a brasserie? Can you order food at a café? Can you go to a restaurant just for a snack? The following definitions should help.

A **restaurant** traditionally serves a three-course meal (first, main, and dessert) at both lunch and dinner. Although this category includes the most formal, three-star establishments, it also applies to humble neighborhood spots. Don't expect to grab a quick snack. In general, restaurants are what you choose when you want a complete meal and when you have the time to linger over it.

Many say that **bistros** served the world's first fast food. After the fall of Napoléon, the Russian soldiers who occupied Paris were known to bang on zinc-topped café bars, crying "*bistro*"—"quickly" in Russian. In the past, bistros were simple places with minimal decor and service. Although many nowadays are quite upscale, with beautiful interiors and chic clientele, most remain cozy establishments serving straightforward, frequently gutsy cooking.

Brasseries—ideal places for quick, one-dish meals—originated when Alsatians fleeing German occupiers after the Franco-Prussian War came to Paris and opened restaurants serving specialties from home. Pork-based dishes, *choucroute* (sauerkraut), and beer (*brasserie* also means brewery) were—and still are—mainstays here. The typical brasserie is convivial and keeps late hours. Some are open 24 hours a day—a good thing to know, since many restaurants stop serving at 10:30 PM.

Like bistros and brasseries, **cafés** come in a confusing variety. Often informal neighborhood hangouts, cafés may also be veritable showplaces attracting chic, well-heeled crowds. At most cafés, regulars congregate at the bar, where coffee and drinks are cheaper than at tables. At lunch, tables are set and a limited menu is served. Sandwiches, usually with *jambon* (ham), *fromage* (cheese, often Gruyère or Camembert), or *mixte* (ham and cheese), are served throughout the day. *Casse croûtes* (snacks) are also offered. Cafés are for lingering, for people-watching, and for daydreaming. If none of these options fit the bill, head to the nearest **traiteur** (deli) for picnic fixings.

See the Menu Guide at the end of the book for guidance with menu items that appear frequently on French menus and throughout the reviews in this book.

MEALTIMES

Breakfast is usually served from 7:30–10 AM; lunch from noon–2; and dinner from 8–10 PM. Restaurants in Paris usually serve dinner until 10:30 PM. Unless otherwise noted, the restaurants listed in this guide are open daily for lunch and dinner.

PAYING

By French law, prices must include tax and tip (*service compris* or *prix nets*), but pocket change left on the table in basic places, or an additional 5% in better restaurants, is always appreciated. Beware of bills stamped "Service Not Included" in English or restaurants slyly using American-style credit-card slips, hoping that you'll be confused and add the habitual 15% tip.

RESERVATIONS & DRESS

Reservations are always a good idea: we mention them only when they're essential or not accepted. Book as far ahead as you can, and reconfirm as soon as you arrive. We mention dress only when men are required to wear a jacket or a jacket and tie.

DISABILITIES & ACCESSIBILITY

Though the French government is doing much to ensure that public facilities provide for visitors with disabilities, it still has a long way to go.

➤ LOCAL RESOURCES: **Association des Paralysés de France** (17 bd. Auguste-Blanqui, 75013 Paris, ☎ 01–40–78–69–00) for a list of Paris hotels.

Comité Nationale Français de Liaison pour la Réadaptation des Handicapés (236-B rue de Tolbiac, 75013 Paris, ☎ 01–53–80–66–66).

LODGING

Only some hotels—particularly more modern ones—are equipped with ramps, elevators, and special toilet facilities. Lists of regional hotels include a symbol to indicate which hotels have rooms that are accessible to people using wheelchairs.

RESERVATIONS

When discussing accessibility with an operator or reservations agent, **ask hard questions.** Are there any stairs, inside *or* out? Are there grab bars next to the toilet *and* in the shower/tub? How wide is the doorway to the room? To the bathroom? For the most extensive facilities meeting the latest legal specifications, **opt for newer accommodations.**

SIGHTS & ATTRACTIONS

Only some monuments and museums—especially those constructed within the past decade—are equipped with ramps, elevators, and special toilet facilities.

TRANSPORTATION

Work began in 1999 to make all major public transportation systems in Europe accessible by 2002. Currently the SNCF has special cars on some trains that have been reserved exclusively for people using wheelchairs; arrangements can be made for those passengers to be escorted on and off trains and assisted in making connections (this service must be requested in advance).

Unfortunately, at this time very few métro stations in Paris that are wheelchair accessible and only some RER stations. For information about accessibility, **get the RER and métro access guide,** available at most stations and from the Paris Transit Authority.

The Airhop shuttle company runs adapted vehicles to and from the airports; Orly–Paris costs 180F and Charles de Gaulle–Paris costs 250F; this service is available Monday through Friday only. Reservations (in French) must be made in advance. Note that you must pay 15 francs for every 15 minutes there is a delay.

➤ COMPLAINTS: **Disability Rights Section** (✉ U.S. Department of Justice, Civil Rights Division, Box 66738, Washington, DC 20035-6738, ☎ 202/514–0301 or 800/514–0301; TTY 202/514–0301 or 800/514–0301, ⅎ 202/307–1198) for general complaints. **Aviation Consumer Protection Division** (☞ Air Travel, *above*) for airline-related problems. **Civil Rights Office** (✉ U.S. Department of Transportation, Departmental Office of Civil Rights, S-30, 400 7th St. SW, Room 10215, Washington, DC 20590, ☎ 202/366–4648, ⅎ 202/366–9371) for problems with surface transportation.

➤ LOCAL RESOURCES: **Airhop** (☎ 01–41–29–01–29). **Paris Transit Authority** (RATP) kiosk (54 Quai de la Rapée, 75599 Cedex 12, ☎ 08–36–68–77–14).

TRAVEL AGENCIES

In the United States, the Americans with Disabilities Act requires that travel firms serve the needs of all travelers. Some agencies specialize in working with people with disabilities.

➤ TRAVELERS WITH MOBILITY PROBLEMS: **Access Adventures** (✉ 206 Chestnut Ridge Rd., Rochester, NY 14624, ☎ 716/889–9096), run by a former physical-rehabilitation counselor. **CareVacations** (✉ 5-5110 50th Ave., Leduc, Alberta T9E 6V4, ☎ 780/986–6404 or 877/478–7827, ⅎ 780/986–8332, ✍), for group tours and cruise vacations. **Flying Wheels Travel** (✉ 143 W. Bridge St., Box 382, Owatonna, MN 55060, ☎ 507/451–5005 or 800/535–6790, ⅎ 507/451–1685, ✍).

DISCOUNTS & DEALS

Be a smart shopper and **compare all your options** before making decisions. A plane ticket bought with a promotional coupon from travel clubs, coupon books, and direct-mail offers may not be cheaper than the least expensive fare from a discount ticket agency. And always keep in mind that what you get is just as important as what you save.

In Paris, Lyon, Arles, and other cities in France, tourist offices sell museum and monument passes, which give you a discount or unlimited access. Railroad and métro stations also often sell these passes.

In Paris, the *Carte Musées et Monuments* (Museums and Monuments Pass) offers unlimited access to more than 65 museums and monuments in Paris over a one-, three-, or five-consecutive day period; the cost, respectively, is 80, 160, and 240 francs. Temporary exhibitions are not included in this pass. This pass is beneficial if you are going to visit many museums and monuments in a short amount of time; also, it may allow you access to museums and monuments without having to wait on line. However, if don't plan on seeing that many museums or monuments, you may be better off paying per sight. *See also* Train Travel, *below,* for information on train passes.

DISCOUNT RESERVATIONS

To save money, **look into discount reservations services** with toll-free numbers, which use their buying power to get a better price on hotels, airline tickets, even car rentals. When booking a room, always **call the hotel's local toll-free number** (if one is available) rather than the central reservations number—you'll often get a better price. Always ask about special packages or corporate rates.

When shopping for the best deal on hotels and car rentals, **look for guaranteed exchange rates,** which protect you against a falling dollar. With your rate locked in, you won't pay more, even if the price goes up in the local currency.

➤ AIRLINE TICKETS: ☎ **800/FLY–4–LESS.** ☎ **800/FLY–ASAP.**

➤ HOTEL ROOMS: **Hotel Reservations Network** (☎ 800/964–6835, ✉). **International Marketing & Travel Concepts** (☎ 800/790–4682). **Steigenberger Reservation Service** (☎ 800/223–5652, ✉). **Travel Interlink** (☎ 800/888–5898, ✉).

PACKAGE DEALS

Don't confuse packages and guided tours. When you buy a package, you travel on your own, just as though you had planned the trip yourself. Fly/drive packages, which combine airfare and car rental, are often a good deal. If you **buy a rail/drive pass,** you may save on train tickets and car rentals. All Eurail- and Europass holders get a discount on Eurostar fares through the Channel Tunnel.

ELECTRICITY

To use your U.S.-purchased electric-powered equipment, **bring a converter and adapter.** The electrical current in France is 220 volts, 50 cycles alternating current (AC); wall outlets take wall outlets take continental-type plugs, with two round prongs.

If your appliances are dual-voltage, you'll need only an adapter. Don't use 110-volt outlets marked FOR SHAVERS ONLY for high-wattage appliances such as blow-dryers. Most laptops operate equally well on 110 and 220 volts and so require only an adapter.

EMBASSIES

If you need assistance in an emergency, you can go to your country's embassy. Proof of identity and citizenship are generally required to enter. If your passport has been stolen, get a police report then contact your embassy for assistance.

➤ AUSTRALIA: **Australian Embassy** 4 rue Jean-Rey, Paris, 15ᵉ, ☎ 01–40–59–33–00, métro Bir Hakeim, ◷ weekdays 9:15–12:15.

➤ CANADA: **Canadian Embassy** 35 av. Montaigne, Paris, 8ᵉ, ☎ 01–44–43–29–00, métro Franklin-D.-Roosevelt, ◷ weekdays 8:30–11.

➤ NEW ZEALAND: **New Zealand Embassy** 7 ter rue Léonardo da Vinci, Paris, 16ᵉ, métro Victor Hugo, ☎ 01–45–00–24–11, ◷ weekdays 9–1.

➤ UNITED KINGDOM: **British Embassy** 35 rue du Faubourg-St-Honoré, Paris, 8ᵉ, ☎ 01–44–51–31–00, , ◷ métro Madeleine weekdays 9:30–12:30 and 2:30–5; 24 av. du Prado, Marseille, ☎ 04–91–15–72–10, ◷ weekdays 9–noon and 2–5.

➤ UNITED STATES: **US Embassy** 2 rue St-Florentin, Paris, 1ᵉʳ, ☎ 01–43–12–22–22 in English; 01–43–12–23–47 in emergencies, métro Concorde,

⊘ weekdays 9–3; 12 bd. Paul Peytral, Marseille, ☎ 04–91–54–92–00, ⊘ weekdays 8:30–12:30 and 1:30–5:30 (until 4:30 Fri.).

EMERGENCIES

France's emergency services are conveniently streamlined and universal, so no matter where you are in the country, you can dial the same phone numbers, listed below. Every town and village has a *médecin de garde* (on-duty doctor) for flus, sprains, tetanus shots, etc. To find out who's on any given evening, call any *généraliste* (general practitioner) and a recording will refer you. If you need an x-ray or emergency treatment, call the ambulance and you'll be whisked to the hospital of your choice—or the nearest one. Note that outside of Paris it's very difficult to find English-speaking doctors.

Pharmacies in France can be very helpful with minor health problems and remedies. In case of fire, hotels are required to post emergency exit maps inside every room door and multilingual instructions. On the street, the French phrases that may be needed in an emergency are: *Au secours!* (Help!), *urgence* (emergency), *samu* (ambulance), *pompiers* (firemen), *poste de station* (police station), *médicin* (doctor), and *hôpital* (hospital).

See also Emergencies *in* A to Z sections *in* individual chapters for information on local hospitals.

➤ CONTACTS: **Ambulance** (☎ 15). **Fire Department** (☎ 18). **Police** (☎ 17).

ENGLISH-LANGUAGE MEDIA

BOOKS

Paris has many bookstores selling English-language books (☞ Shopping *in* Chapter 1) and you can probably find at least one bookstore in other major cities with English-language books. However, in most smaller towns, you won't have much luck.

NEWSPAPERS & MAGAZINES

Besides a large variety of French newspapers and magazines, all kinds of English-language newspapers and magazines can be found at newsstands in larger cities and even in smaller towns, including: *The International Herald Tribune, USA Today, The New York Times, The European Financial Times, The London Times, Newsweek, The Economist, Vogue,* and *Elle.* In Paris, a number of free magazines in English, with all kinds of listings, including events, bars, restaurants, shops, films, and museums, are available: Look for *Time Out Paris, FUSAC, The Paris Free Voice,* and *Irish Eyes.*

RADIO & TELEVISION

Turn on the television and you'll notice many American shows dubbed into French (Canal Jimmy, Channel 8, shows American shows in their original, undubbed format). France has both national stations (TF1, France 2, France 3, La Cinq/Arte, and M6) and cable stations (most notably Canal+, France's version of HBO). Every morning at 7:05 AM, ABC News (from the night before) is aired. You can also find CNN, BBC World, and BBC Prime on cable.

You'll find all kinds of music on French radio stations: some focus on one type of music and others play different kinds of music, from rock to jazz to classical, depending on the time of day.

GAY & LESBIAN TRAVEL

The largest gay and lesbian communities in France are in Paris. A number of informative newspapers and magazines that cover the Parisian gay/lesbian scene are available at stores and kiosks in the city: *Gai Guide, Gai Pied Hebdo, Lesbia,* and *Tetu.*

➤ GAY- & LESBIAN-FRIENDLY TRAVEL AGENCIES: **Different Roads Travel** (✉ 8383 Wilshire Blvd., Suite 902, Beverly Hills, CA 90211, ☎ 323/651–5557 or 800/429–8747, ℻ 323/651–3678). **Kennedy Travel** (✉ 314 Jericho Turnpike, Floral Park, NY 11001, ☎ 516/352–4888 or 800/237–7433, ℻ 516/354–8849, ✍). **Now Voyager** (✉ 4406 18th St., San Francisco, CA 94114, ☎ 415/626–1169 or 800/255–6951, ℻ 415/626–8626, ✍). **Skylink Travel and Tour** (✉ 1006 Mendocino Ave., Santa Rosa, CA 95401, ☎ 707/546–9888 or 800/225–5759, ℻ 707/546–9891, ✍), serving lesbian travelers.

➤ ORGANIZATIONS: **Agora** (33 bd. Picpus, 12ᵉ, ☎ 01–43–42–19–02). **Association des Médecins Gais** (☎ 01–48–05–81–71). **Centre Gai et Lesbien** (3 rue Keller, 11ᵉ, ☎ 01–43–57–21–47).

HEALTH

For information about emergencies and hospitals, ☞ Emergencies, *above*.

HIKING AND WALKING

France has many good places to hike and an extensive network of mapped-out *Grandes Randonnées* (GRs or Long Trails) that range from easy to challenging. For details on hiking in France and guides to GRs in specific areas, contact the Club Alpin Français or the Fédération Française de la Randonnée Pédestre, which also publishes good topographical maps. The IGN maps sold in many bookshops are also invaluable (☞ Bike Travel, *above*).

➤ HIKING ORGANIZATIONS: **Club Alpin Français** (✉ 24 av. Laumière, 75019 Paris, ☎ 01–53–72–87–00). **Fédération Française de la Randonnée Pédestre** (✉ 14 rue de Riquet, 75019 Paris, ☎ 01–44–89–93–93).

➤ HIKING AND WALKING TOURS: **Abercrombie & Kent** (☞ Barge Travel, *above*). **BCT Scenic Walking** (✉ 703 Palomar Airport Rd, Suite 200, Carlsbad, CA 92009-1042, ☎ 760/431–7306, ℻ 760/431–7782). **Butterfield & Robinson** (☞ Bike Travel, *above*). **Classic Adventures** (☞ Bike Travel, *above*). **Country Walkers** (✉ Box 180, Waterbury, VT 05676-0180, ☎ 802/244–1387 or 800/464–9255, ℻ 802/244–5661). **Mountain Travel-Sobek** (✉ 6420 Fairmount Ave., El Cerrito, CA 94530, ☎ 510/527–8100 or 800/227–2384, ℻ 510/525–7710). **Wilderness Travel** (✉ 1102 Ninth St., Berkeley, CA 94710, ☎ 510/558–2488 or 800/368–2794, ℻ 510/558–2489, ✍).

HOLIDAYS

With 11 national *jours feriés* (holidays) and 5 weeks of paid vacation, the French have their share of repose. In May, there is a holiday nearly every week, so be prepared for stores, banks, and museums to shut their

doors for days at a time. Be sure to **call museums, restaurants, and hotels in advance to make sure they will be open.**

The following dates are for 2001: January 1 (New Year's Day); April 15 (Easter Monday); May 1 (Labor Day); May 8 (VE Day); May 24 (Ascension); June 4 (Pentecost Monday); July 14 (Bastille Day); August 15 (Assumption); November 1 (All Saints); November 11 (Armistice); December 25 (Christmas).

INSURANCE

The most useful travel insurance plan is a comprehensive policy that includes coverage for trip cancellation and interruption, default, trip delay, and medical expenses (with a waiver for preexisting conditions).

Without insurance you will lose all or most of your money if you cancel your trip, regardless of the reason. Default insurance covers you if your tour operator, airline, or cruise line goes out of business. Trip-delay covers expenses that arise because of bad weather or mechanical delays. Study the fine print when comparing policies.

If you're traveling internationally, a key component of travel insurance is coverage for medical bills incurred if you get sick on the road. Such expenses are not generally covered by Medicare or private policies. U.K. residents can buy a travel insurance policy valid for most vacations taken during the year in which it's purchased (but check pre-existing-condition coverage). British and Australian citizens need extra medical coverage when traveling overseas. Always **buy travel policies directly from the insurance company**; if you buy them from a cruise line, airline, or tour operator that goes out of business you probably will not be covered for the agency or operator's default, a major risk. Before making any purchase, **review your existing health and homeowner's policies** to find what they cover away from home.

➤ TRAVEL INSURERS: In the U.S.: **Access America** (✉ 6600 W. Broad St., Richmond, VA 23230, ☎ 804/285–3300 or 800/284–8300, ℻ 804/

673–1583, ✆), **Travel Guard International** (✉ 1145 Clark St., Stevens Point, WI 54481, ☎ 715/345–0505 or 800/826–1300, ℻ 800/955–8785, ✆).In Canada: **Voyager Insurance** (✉ 44 Peel Center Dr., Brampton, Ontario L6T 4M8, ☎ 905/791–8700; 800/668–4342 in Canada).

LANGUAGE

Although many French people, especially in major tourist areas, speak some English, it's important to remember that you are going to France and that people speak French. However, generally at least one person in most hotels can explain things to you in English (unless you are in a very rural area). Be patient, and speak English slowly.

The French may appear prickly at first to English-speaking visitors. But it usually helps if you **make an effort to speak a little French.** So even if your own French is terrible, try to master a few words. A simple, friendly *bonjour* (hello) will do, as will asking if the person you are greeting speaks English ("Parlez-vous anglais?"). *See* the French Vocabulary and Menu Guide at the back of the book for more suggestions.

LANGUAGES FOR TRAVELERS

A phrase book and language-tape set can help get you started.

➤ PHRASE BOOKS & LANGUAGE-TAPE SETS: *Fodor's French for Travelers, Fodor's German for Travelers, Fodor's Italian for Travelers, Fodor's Spanish for Travelers* (☎ 800/733–3000 in the U.S.; 800/668–4247 in Canada; $7 for phrasebook, $16.95 for audio set).

LODGING

The lodgings we list are the cream of the crop in each price category. We always list the facilities that are available—but we don't specify whether they cost extra: When pricing accommodations, always ask what's included and what costs extra. Properties indicated by a ✕🏠 are lodging establishments whose restaurant warrants a special trip.

Assume that hotels operate on the **European Plan** (EP, with no meals). On occasion, hotels (generally in the rural countryside) offer rates that include full or half board; inquire when making your reservation.

APARTMENT & VILLA RENTALS

If you want a home base that's roomy enough for a family or group and comes with cooking facilities **consider a furnished rental.** Renting an apartment or a *gîte rural*—a furnished house in the country—for a week or month can also save you money.

The national rental network, the Fédération Nationale des Gîtes de France, rents rural homes with regional flavor. Gîtes are nearly always maintained by on-site owners, who greet you on your arrival and provide information on groceries, doctors, and nearby attractions. A nationwide catalogue (105 francs) is available from the Fédération Nationale des Gîtes de France listing gîtes ruraux for rent. Called "Nouveaux Gîtes Ruraux," the catalogue only lists the newest additions to the network because a comprehensive nationwide listing of all gîtes would make an unwieldy volume. If you know what region you want to stay in, contact the departmental branch directly and order a photo catalogue that lists every property. If you specify which dates you plan to visit, the office will narrow down the choice to rentals available for those days.

Individual tourist offices often publish lists of *locations meublés* (furnished rentals); these are often inspected by the tourist office and rated by comfort standards. Usually they are booked directly through the individual owner, which generally requires some knowledge of French. Rentals that are not classified or rated by the tourist office should be undertaken with trepidation, and can fall well below your minimum standard of comfort.

Vacation rentals in France always book from Saturday to Saturday (with some offering weekend rates off-season). Most do not include bed linens and towels, but make them available for an additional fee. Always check on policies on pets and children, and specify if you need an enclosed garden for toddlers, a washing machine, a fireplace, etc. If you plan to have overnight guests during your stay, let the owner know; there may be additional charges. Insurance restrictions prohibit loading in guests beyond the specified capacity.

➤ INTERNATIONAL AGENTS: **At Home Abroad** (✉ 405 E. 56th St., Suite 6H, New York, NY 10022, ☎ 212/421–9165, FAX 212/752–1591, ✎). **Drawbridge to Europe** (✉ 5456 Adams Rd., Talent, OR 97540, ☎ 541/512–8927 or 888/268–1148, FAX 541/512–0978, ✎). **Hideaways International** (✉ 767 Islington St., Portsmouth, NH 03801, ☎ 603/430–4433 or 800/843–4433, FAX 603/430–4444 www.hideaways.com; membership $99).

Hometours International (✉ Box 11503, Knoxville, TN 37939, ☎ 865/690–8484 or 800/367–4668, ✎). **Interhome** (✉ 1990 N.E. 163rd St., Suite 110, N. Miami Beach, FL 33162, ☎ 305/940–2299 or 800/882–6864, FAX 305/940–2911, ✎). **Vacation Home Rentals Worldwide** (✉ 235 Kensington Ave., Norwood, NJ 07648, ☎ 201/767–9393 or 800/633–3284, FAX 201/767–5510, ✎). **Villanet** (✉ 12600 S.E. 38th St., Suite 202, Bellevue, WA 98006, ☎ 425/653–7733 or 800/964–1891, FAX 425/653–3866, ✎). **Villas and Apartments Abroad** (✉ 1270 Avenue of the Americas, 15th floor, New York, NY 10020, ☎ 212/897–5045 or 800/433–3020, FAX 212/897–5039, ✎). **Villas International** (✉ 950 Northgate Dr., Suite 206, San Rafael, CA 94903, ☎ 415/499–9490 or 800/221–2260, FAX 415/499–9491, ✎).

➤ LOCAL AGENTS: **Fédération Nationale des Gîtes de France** (59 rue St-Lazare, 75009 Paris, ☎ 01–49–70–75–75, FAX 01–42–81–28–53). **French Government Tourist Office** (☞ Visitor Information, *below*).

➤ RENTAL LISTINGS:

B&BS

Chambres d'hôtes (bed & breakfasts) offer simple lodging, usually in the hosts' home, with breakfast. They are most common in rural France, though they are becoming more so in Paris and other major cities. Check with local tourist offices or contact Gîtes de France, a national organization that lists B&Bs all over the country, or private reservation agencies. Often table d'hôte dinners (meals cooked by and eaten with the owners) can be arranged for an extra, fairly nominal fee. Note that at B&Bs, unlike at hotels, it's more likely that the owners will only speak French.

➤ RESERVATION SERVICES: **Gîtes de France** (✉ 59 rue St-Lazare, 75439 Cedex 09 Paris, ☎ 01–49–70–75–75, FAX 01–42–81–28–53). **Paris Bed & Breakfast** (☎ 800/872–2632).

CAMPING

French campsites have a good reputation for organization and amenities but are crowded in July and August. Many campsites welcome reservations, and in summer, it makes sense to book in advance. The Fédération Française de Camping et de Caravaning publishes a guide to France's campsites (100 francs, plus shipping).

➤ CAMPSITE GUIDE: **Fédération Française de Camping et de Caravaning** (✉ 78 rue de Rivoli, 75004 Paris, ☎ 01–42–72–84–08).

HOME EXCHANGES

If you would like to exchange your home for someone else's, **join a home-exchange organization,** which will send you its updated listings of available exchanges for a year and will include your own listing in at least one of them. It's up to you to make specific arrangements.

➤ EXCHANGE CLUBS: **HomeLink International** (✉ Box 650, Key West, FL 33041, ☎ 305/294–7766 or 800/638–3841, FAX 305/294–1448, www.homelink.org; $98 per year). **Intervac U.S.** (✉ Box 590504, San Francisco, CA 94159, ☎ 800/756–4663, FAX 415/435–7440, www.intervac.com; $89 per year includes two catalogues).

➤ EXCHANGE LISTINGS: **FUSAC** (✉ 26 rue Bénard, Paris 75014, ☎ 01–56–53–54–54, FAX 01–56–53–54–55; ✉ Box 115, Cooper Station, New York, NY, 10276).

HOSTELS

No matter what your age, you can **save on lodging costs by staying at hostels.** In some 5,000 locations in more than 70 countries around the world, Hostelling International (HI), the umbrella group for a number of national youth-hostel associations, offers single-sex, dorm-style beds and, at many hostels, rooms for couples and family accommodations. Membership in any HI national hostel association, open to travelers of all ages, allows you to stay in HI-affiliated hostels at member rates; one-year membership is about $25 for adults (C$26.75 in Canada, £9.30 in the U.K., $30 in Australia, and $30 in New Zealand); hostels run about $10–$25 per night. Members have priority if the hostel is full; they're also eligible for discounts around the world, even on rail and bus travel in some countries.

Paris's major public hostels are run by the Fédération Unie des Auberges de Jeunesse (FUAJ)—for about 130 francs, a bed, sheets, shower, and breakfast are provided, with beds usually three to four to a room. Maisons Internationales des Jeunes Étudiants (MIJE) have the plushest hostels, sometimes in historic mansions. Private hostels have accommodations that run from pleasant, if spartan, double rooms to dormlike arrangements.

➤ BEST OPTIONS IN PARIS: Near the Eiffel Tower: **Aloha Hostel** (✉ 1 rue Borromée,, 75015, ☎ 01–42–73–03–03, 🖷 01–42–73–14–14). Near Montmartre: **Village** (✉ 20 rue d'Orsel, 75018, ☎ 01–42–64–22–02, 🖷 01–42–64–22–04).In the Latin Quarter: **Young and Happy Youth Hostel** (✉ 80 rue Mouffetard, 75005, ☎ 01–45–35–09–53).In the Marais: **Hôtel le Fauconnier MIJE** (✉ 11 rue de Fauconnier, 75004, ☎ 01–42–74–23–45, 🖷 01–42–74–08–93). **Hôtel Maubuisson MIJE** (✉ 12 rue des Barnes, 75004, ☎ 01–42–74–23–45, 🖷 01–42–74–08–93).

➤ ORGANIZATIONS: **Féderation Unie des Auberges de Jeunesse (FUAJ/Hostelling International)** (✉ FUAJ Beaubourg: 9 rue Brantôme, 3ᵉ, Paris, ☎ 01–48–04–70–40; Centre National: ✉ 27 rue Pajol, 18ᵉ, Paris, ☎ 01–44–89–87–27). **Hostelling International—American Youth Hostels** (✉ 733 15th St. NW, Suite 840, Washington, DC 20005, ☎ 202/783–6161, 🖷 202/783–6171, 🖳). **Hostelling International—Canada** (✉ 400–205 Catherine St., Ottawa, Ontario K2P 1C3, ☎ 613/237–7884, 🖷 613/237–7868, 🖳). **Youth Hostel Association of England and Wales** (✉ Trevelyan House, 8 St. Stephen's Hill, St. Albans, Hertfordshire AL1 2DY, ☎ 01727/855215 or 01727/845047, 🖷 01727/844126, 🖳). **Australian Youth Hostel Association** (✉ 10 Mallett St., Camperdown, NSW 2050, ☎ 02/9565–1699, 🖷 02/9565–1325, 🖳). **Youth Hostels Association of New Zealand** (✉ Box 436, Christchurch, New Zealand, ☎ 03/379–9970, 🖷 03/365–4476, 🖳).

HOTELS

Hotels in France are officially classified from one-star to four-star-deluxe and stars appear on a shield on the facade of most hotels. The grading system is based on a notoriously complicated evaluation of amenities and services. At the bottom end of the scale are the one-star hotels, where you might have to share a bathroom and do without an elevator. You can expect two- and three-star hotels to have private bathrooms, elevators, and in-room televisions. At the high end are the luxurious four-star hotels, which have excellent amenities and prices to match. The ratings are sometimes misleading, however, since many hotels prefer to be under-starred for tax reasons.

Rates are always by room, not per person. Prices must, by law, be posted at the hotel entrance and should include taxes and service. You might try negotiating rates if you're planning on staying for a week or longer or are coming off season.

All hotels listed have private bath unless otherwise noted. You should always **check what bathroom facilities the price includes.** When making your reservation, state your preference for shower (*douche*) or tub (*baignoire*)—the latter always costs more. Also when booking, **ask for a grand lit if you want a double bed.**

If you're counting on air-conditioning you should **make sure, in advance, that your hotel room is** *climatisé* (air-conditioned). If air-conditioning is not noted in a hotel review, don't assume there will be air-conditioning. And when you throw open the windows, **don't expect screens** *(moustiquaires)*. Nowhere in Europe are they standard equipment.

The quality of accommodations, particularly in older properties and even in luxury hotels, can vary greatly from room to room; **if you don't like the room you're given, ask to see another.**

Breakfast is not always included in the price, but you're sometimes expected to have it and are occasionally charged for it regardless. Make sure to **inform the hotel if you are not going to be breakfasting there**; you may want to find the nearest café anyway. In smaller rural hotels you may be expected to have your evening meal at the hotel, too.

It's always a good idea to **make hotel reservations in Paris and other major tourist destinations as far in advance as possible,** especially in late spring, summer, or fall. Faxing is the easiest way to contact the hotel (the staff is probably more likely to read English than to understand it over the phone long distance), though calling also works. In your fax (or over the phone), specify the exact dates that you want to stay at the hotel; the size of the room you want and how many people will be sleeping there; what kind of bed you want (two twins, double, etc.); and what kind of bathroom (private with shower or bath, or both). You might also ask if a deposit (or your credit card number) is required and, if so, what happens if you cancel. Request that the hotel fax you back so that you have a written confirmation of your reservation.

If you arrive without a reservation, the tourist offices in major train stations and most towns can probably help you find a room.

Many hotels in France are small, often independently-owned or family-run establishments. Some are affiliated with hotel groups, such as Logis de France, which can be relied on for comfort, character, and regional cuisine (look for its distinctive yellow-and-green sign). A Logis de France paperback guide is widely available in bookshops (100 frs) or from Logis de France. Two prestigious international groups with numerous converted châteaux and manor houses among its members are Relais & Châteaux and Small Luxury Hotels of the World; booklets listing members are available from these organizations. France also has some hotel chains. Examples in the upper price bracket are Frantel, Novotel, Sofitel as well as Inter-Continental, Marriott, Hilton, Hyatt, Westin, and Sheraton. The Best Western, Campanile, Climat de France, Ibis, and Timhotel chains are more moderate. Typically, chains offer a consistently acceptable standard of modern features (modern bathrooms, TV, etc.), but tend to lack atmosphere, with some exceptions (Best Western, for instance, tries to maintain the local character of the hotels it takes over).

➤ TOLL-FREE NUMBERS: **Best Western** (☎ 800/528–1234, 🖎). **Clarion** (☎ 800/252–7466, 🖎). **Hilton** (☎ 800/445–8667, 🖎). **Hyatt Hotels & Resorts** (☎ 800/233–1234, 🖎).**Le Meridien** (☎ 800/543–4300, 🖎). **Renaissance Hotels & Resorts** (☎ 800/468–3571, 🖎). **Sheraton** (☎ 800/325–3535, 🖎). **Westin Hotels & Resorts** (☎ 800/228–3000, 🖎). **Wyndham Hotels & Resorts** (☎ 800/ 822-4200, 🖎).

MAIL & SHIPPING

Post offices, or PTT, are found in every town and are recognizable by a yellow LA POSTE sign. They are usually open weekdays 8 AM–7 PM, Saturday 8 AM–noon, but the **main Paris post office** (✉ 52 rue du Louvre, 1ᵉʳ) is open 24 hours seven days a week.

OVERNIGHT SERVICES

Sending overnight mail from major cities in France is relatively easy. Besides DHL, Federal Express, and UPS, the French post office has overnight mail service called Chronopost.

➤ MAJOR SERVICES: **DHL** (✉ 6 rue des Colonnes, 7ᵉ, ☎ 01–55–35–30– 30; ✉ 59 rue Iéna, 16ᵉ, ☎ 01–45–01–

91–00). **Federal Express** (✉ 63 bd. Haussmann, 8ᵉ, Paris, ☎ 01–40–06–90–16, ✉ 2 rue 29 Juillet, 1ᵉʳ, Paris, ☎ 01–49–26–04–66; 08–00–12–38–00 for information about pick ups all over France). **UPS** (✉ 34 bd. Malesherbes, 8ᵉ, Paris, ✉ 107 rue Réaumur, 2ᵉ, Paris, ☎ 08–00–87–78–77 for information all over France).

POSTAL RATES

Letters and postcards to the United States and Canada cost 4.40 francs (about 80¢) for 20 grams. Letters and postcards to the United Kingdom cost 3 francs (about 33p) for up to 20 grams. Letters and postcards within France cost 3 francs. Stamps can be bought in post offices (La Poste) and cafés sporting a red TABAC sign outside. It takes, on the average, 5 days for a letter to reach the U.S., 5-6 days for Australia, 4-5 days for Canada, and 3 days for any location in Europe.

RECEIVING MAIL

If you're uncertain where you'll be staying, **have mail sent to the local post office,** addressed as "poste restante," or to American Express, but remember that during peak seasons, American Express may refuse to accept mail. The French postal service has a 3 franc per item service charge.

MONEY MATTERS

Prices throughout this guide are given for adults. Substantially reduced fees are almost always available for children, students, and senior citizens. For information on taxes, *see* Taxes, *below.*

The following prices are for Paris; other cities and areas are often cheaper (with the notable exception of the Côte d'Azur). Keep in mind that it's less expensive to eat or drink standing at a café or bar counter than it is to sit at a table. Two prices are listed, *au comptoir* (at the counter) and *à salle* (at a table); sometimes items cost even more if you're seated a terrace table). Coffee in a bar: 6–7 francs (standing), 10–30 francs (seated); beer in a bar: 10 francs (standing), 15–40 francs (seated); Coca-Cola: 6–10 francs a can; ham sandwich: 15–25 francs; one-mile taxi ride: 35 francs; movie-theater seat: 58 francs (15%–33% cheaper on Mon-

day and Wednesday); foreign newspaper: 10–15 francs.

ATMS

Fairly common in Paris and other big towns as well as in airports and train stations, **ATMs are one of the easiest ways to get francs.** Don't, however, count on finding ATMs in smaller towns and rural areas. Banks usually offer excellent, wholesale exchange rates through ATMs.

To get cash at ATMs in France, **your PIN must be four digits long.** Note that the machine will give you two chances to enter your correct PIN number; if you make a mistake on the third try, your card will be held and you'll have to return to the bank the next morning to retrieve it. You may have better luck with ATMs with a credit or debit card that is also a Visa or MasterCard, rather than just your bank card. Note, too, that you may be charged by your bank for using ATMs overseas; inquire at your bank about charges.

Before you go, it's a good idea to **get a list of ATM locations that you can use** in France from your bank.

CREDIT CARDS

Many restaurants and stores take both credit and debit cards, though there is often a 100-franc minimum.

Throughout this guide, the following abbreviations are used: **AE,** American Express; **DC,** Diner's Club; **MC,** Master Card; and **V,** Visa.

➤ REPORTING LOST CARDS: **American Express** (☎ 336/939–1111 or 336/668–5309) call collect. **Diner's Club** (☎ 303/799–1504) call collect. **Mastercard** (☎ 0800/90–1387). **Visa** (☎ 0800/90–1179; 410/581–9994 collect).

CURRENCY

Up to January 1st, 2002, the French franc (fr) and the centime will remain the main units of currency in France but after that date, the new single European Union (EU) currency, the euro, will take over. Until then, people will use the franc in their day-to-day transactions and travelers will continue to exchange their money for its colorful 500-, 200-, 100-, 50-, and

20-franc banknotes; 20-, 10-, 5-, 2-, and 1-franc coins will weigh down their pockets and the tiny 20-, 10-, and 5-centime coins will find their way inevitably to the bottom of their luggage as they always do. At press time (summer 2000), the exchange rate was about 7.30 francs to the U.S. dollar, 4.90 to the Canadian dollar, 10.00 to the pound sterling, 4.15 to the Australian dollar, 3.40 to the New Zealand dollar, and 8.30 to the Irish punt. For the euro denomination, the exchange rate was about 1.12 euros to the U.S dollar, 0.74 to the Canadian dollar, 0.63 to the Australian dollar, 0.51 to the New Zealand dollar, and 1.26 to the Irish punt.

At this point, francs are actually mere denominations of the euro— any transaction not involving cash may currently be transacted in euros. Remaining francs will stay in circulation up to July 1, 2002, the date of the final demise of the franc (and many other currencies of the European Union, including the Italian lira, the Irish punt, and the Austrian schilling). After January 1st, 2002, participating European national currencies will no longer be listed on foreign exchange markets. The rates of conversion between the euro and local currencies have already been irrevocably fixed (1 euro = 6.55957 francs), eliminating commission charges in currency exchange. Please note that prices in euros correspond generally to the U.S. dollar as their exchange rates are relatively close.

Slowly but surely, the euro is becoming a part of daily European life; for every item purchased—be it a piece of gum or a car—the price in both francs and euros has to be, by law, listed to familiarize the French and you to this monumental change. Under the euro system, there are eight coins: 1 and 2 euros, plus 1, 2, 5, 10, 20, and 50 centimes, or cents, of the euro. All coins have one side that has the value of the euro on it and the other side with each countries' own unique national symbol. There are seven notes: 5, 10, 20, 50, 100, 200, and 500 euros. Notes are the same for all countries. The euro's weakness on the exchange markets has made France a cheaper destination for American and British travelers—even though (at press date, summer 2000) the French economy has been in excellent shape, with falling unemployment and minimal inflation.

CURRENCY EXCHANGE

These days, **the easiest way to get francs is through ATMs** (☞ *above*).

If you're concerned that you may not be able to use your bank or debit card at the airport or train station when you first arrive, or you want to avoid lines at airport or train station exchange booths, **consider getting a bit of local currency before you leave home.** It's also a good idea to have some cash and traveler's checks as back up.

For the best deal, **compare rates at banks and booths** and **look for exchange booths that clearly state "no commission."** At exchange booths always confirm the rate with the teller before exchanging money. If you're exchanging a large amount of money, you may be able to get a better deal; it's worth asking. Exchange booths in airports, train stations, hotels, and stores generally offer the worst rates, though you may find their hours more convenient. In general, the **Banque de France has the best rates** (which is why there are huge lines at its branches all year long). Note also that all Banque de France agencies close at 3:30 PM. Other banks might offer pretty good exchange rates but they make up for it by adding a commission.

➤ EXCHANGE SERVICES: **International Currency Express** (☎ 888/278–6628 for orders, ✎). **Thomas Cook Currency Services** (☎ 800/287–7362 for telephone orders and retail locations, ✎).

TRAVELER'S CHECKS

Do you need traveler's checks? It depends on where you're headed. If you're going to rural areas and small towns, go with cash; traveler's checks are best used in cities. Lost or stolen checks can usually be replaced within 24 hours. To ensure a speedy refund, buy your own traveler's checks— don't let someone else pay for them: irregularities like this can cause delays. The person who bought the checks should make the call to request a refund.

PACKING

CHECKING LUGGAGE

How many carry-on bags you can bring with you is up to the airline. Most allow two, but not always, so make sure that everything you carry aboard will fit under your seat or in the overhead bin, and get to the gate early. Note that if you have a seat at the back of the plane, you'll probably board first, while the overhead bins are still empty.

If you are flying internationally, note that baggage allowances may be determined not by piece but by weight—generally 88 pounds (40 kilograms) in first class, 66 pounds (30 kilograms) in business class, and 44 pounds (20 kilograms) in economy.

Airline liability for baggage is limited to $1,250 per person on flights within the United States. On international flights it amounts to $9.07 per pound or $20 per kilogram for checked baggage (roughly $640 per 70-pound bag) and $400 per passenger for unchecked baggage. You can buy additional coverage at check-in for about $10 per $1,000 of coverage, but it excludes a rather extensive list of items, shown on your airline ticket.

PACKING LIST

Although you'll usually have no trouble finding a baggage cart at the airport, luggage restrictions on international flights are tight and baggage carts at railroad stations are not always available; so **pack light.**

Over the years, **casual dress has become more acceptable in France,** though Paris is still the world's fashion capital and people dress accordingly (and they bring this fashion sense to other major French cities and resorts). There is no need to wear a tie and jacket at most restaurants (unless specified), even fancy ones. For beach resorts, take a cover-up, as wearing bathing suits on the street is frowned upon. Most casinos and nightclubs along the Côte d'Azur require jackets and ties.

Most of France is hot in summer and cool in winter. Since it rains all year round, **bring a raincoat and umbrella.** You'll need a sweater or warm jacket for the Mediterranean in winter.

To protect yourself against purse snatchers and pickpockets, **take a handbag with long straps that you can sling across your body,** bandolier-style, with a zippered compartment for your money and some form of identification—French law requires that you carry identification at all times. It may be best, however, to leave your passport in your hotel safe, and just carry your license or a copy of your passport.

If you're staying in budget hotels, take along soap; many hotels either do not provide it or give you a very limited number.

In your carry-on luggage **bring an extra pair of eyeglasses or contact lenses** and **enough of any medication** you take to last the entire trip. You may also want your doctor to write a spare prescription using the drug's generic name, since brand names may vary from country to country. **Never put prescription drugs or valuables in luggage to be checked.** To avoid customs delays, carry medications in their original packaging.

PASSPORTS & VISAS

When traveling to France, you must **carry a passport.** It's a good idea to **make two photocopies of the data page** (one for someone at home and another for you, carried separately from your passport). If you lose your passport promptly call the nearest embassy or consulate and the local police.

ENTERING FRANCE

All Australian, Canadian, New Zealand, U.K, and U.S. citizens, even infants, need only a valid passport to enter France for stays of up to 90 days.

PASSPORT OFFICES

The best time to apply for a passport or to renew is in fall and winter. Before any trip, check your passport's expiration date, and, if necessary, renew it as soon as possible.

➤ AUSTRALIAN CITIZENS: **Australian Passport Office** (☎ 131–232, 🖎).

➤ CANADIAN CITIZENS: **Passport Office** (☎ 819/994–3500 or 800/567–6868, 📠).

➤ NEW ZEALAND CITIZENS: **New Zealand Passport Office** (☎ 04/494–0700, 📠).

➤ U.K. CITIZENS: **London Passport Office** (☎ 0990/210–410) for fees and documentation requirements and to request an emergency passport.

➤ U.S. CITIZENS: **National Passport Information Center** (☎ 900/225–5674; calls are 35¢ per minute for automated service, $1.05 per minute for operator service).

PUBLIC TRANSPORTATION

For information about public transportation in France *see* A to Z sections *in* individual chapters.

REST ROOMS

Although, in general, most cafés reserve the right to use their bathroom facilities for the paying customer, most French are willing to ignore the frustrated glare of the waiter in an emergency. Bathrooms are often located downstairs, are usually unisex (which means that you may have to walk by urinals in use), are often just holes in the ground surrounded by porcelain pads for your feet, and to top it all off, you'll probably have to pay one or two francs—exact change only. They are not the cleanest places in the world, especially for children, so it is in your best interest to be prepared and always carry a small box of tissues with you. In cities, your best bet may be fast-food chains and large department stores. Do not be alarmed if you do not see any light switches—once the bathroom door is shut and locked, the lights will go on. You can also find pay-per-use toilet units on the street in Paris, which require 2 francs (small children, however, should not use these alone, as the self-sanitizing system works with weight-related sensors that might not sense the presence of a child). There are bathrooms in the larger métro stations and in all train stations for a cost of 1–2 francs. There are also bathrooms at highway rest stops which are equipped with changing tables for babies and even showers during summer months.

SAFETY

Beware of petty theft—purse snatching, pickpocketing, and pilfering from automobiles—throughout France, particularly in Paris and along the Côte d'Azur. Use common sense: Avoid pulling out a lot of money in public; wear a handbag with long straps that you can sling across your body, bandolier-style, with a zippered compartment for your money and passport. It's also a good idea to wear a money belt. Men should keep their wallets up front. Car break-ins, especially in isolated parking lots where hikers set off for the day, are on the rise. It makes sense to **take valuables with you or leave your luggage at your hotel.**

WOMEN IN FRANCE

Overall statistics show that France is relatively safe. However, you should take the same precautions you would anywhere, especially in large cities. Avoid walking alone in dark, unknown areas at night and be very careful on public transportation late at night. Note that a smile or steady eye contact is often seen as an invitation. If someone is making you uncomfortable, ignore the person and walk quickly into the nearest, busiest, brightest area. Also, be careful when taking money out of ATMs, particularly at night.

SENIOR-CITIZEN TRAVEL

Older travelers (60+) can take advantage of many discounts, such as reduced admissions of 20%–50% to museums and movie theaters. For rail travel in France, the Carte Senior entitles travelers 60 years or older to discounts (☞ Train Travel, *below*).

To qualify for age-related discounts, **mention your senior-citizen status up front** when booking hotel reservations (not when checking out) and before you're seated in restaurants (not when paying the bill). When renting a car, ask about promotional car-rental discounts, which can be cheaper than senior-citizen rates.

➤ EDUCATIONAL PROGRAMS: **Elderhostel** (✉ 75 Federal St., 3rd floor,

Boston, MA 02110, ☎ 877/426–8056, FAX 877/426–2166, ✆). **Interhostel** (✉ University of New Hampshire, 6 Garrison Ave., Durham, NH 03824, ☎ 603/862–1147 or 800/733–9753, FAX 603/862–1113, ✆).

SHOPPING

While it is somewhat disconcerting to see Gap stores gracing almost every major street corner in Paris and other urban areas in France, if you take the time to peruse smaller specialty shops you can find rare original gifts—be it an antique brooch from the 1930s or a modern vase crafted from Parisian rooftop-tile zinc. It is true that the traditional gifts of silk scarves, perfume, and wine can often be purchased for less in the shopping mall back home, but you can make an interesting twist by purchasing a vintage Hermès scarf, or a unique perfume from an "artisan perfumer." Take the time to explore and you will find that France still remains one of the shopping capitals of the world.

When in France, think gourmet. For those who love to cook—or just love to taste—there are some simple gifts available in grocery stores or one of the many city and countryside outdoor markets: Delicious mustard in a ceramic jar made following a traditional recipe from the 18th century costs about 18 francs; organic jams made with whole cherries or figs from the south cost about 15 francs; organic olive oils (with flavors ranging from thyme to truffle) will run about 80–100 francs; and a pot of organic lavender honey goes for 30 francs. There is even gourmet salt called *fleur de sel* that comes from the coast of Brittany. Wonderful liqueurs include cognacs, armagnacs, or calvados—the fiery apple after-dinner *digestif* from Normandy—or one of the various fruit flavored *eaux de vie* that Hemingway and Fitzgerald loved so much. These liquors can be found in any grocery or liquor store and cost from 100–300 francs. For the best quality, look for the tall slender bottles with handwritten labels and red wax seals. For the champagne lover, there are wonderful organic champagnes produced by smaller vineyards.

For other unique gift ideas, look to the museums. The Louvre, for example, has a museum shop that sells beautiful reproductions of a variety of masterpieces from Greek figures to Egyptian heads, and ceramic buddhas using the original molds. You can also purchase here t-shirts with charming vintage illustrations of Parisian life. Or look—surprise!—in the larger pharmacies for gift ideas from small French companies. For example, you could buy a small pot of all-natural Nuxe honey lip balm, or the increasingly popular skin care products by Claudelie made from grapeseed extracts—French actresses swear by these. But it's always most interesting to look to the past: Flea markets and *brocantes* (second-hand shops) sell Art Deco brooches, tiny eau-de-vie glasses, and evocative old copies of *Paris Match*. And there's always the chance of finding a stray bit of Quimper faience. Another good bet is purchasing regional specialties, though your exports must be legal—madeleines, say, or nougat—as those savory sausages and glass jars of foie gras may be confiscated by customs.

People don't usually bargain in shops where **prices are clearly marked,** but at outdoor and flea markets, and in antiques stores, bargaining is accepted. If you're thinking of buying several items, you've nothing to lose by cheerfully suggesting to the proprietor, *"Vous me faites un prix?"* ("How about a discount?").

A number of shops offer VAT tax refunds to foriegn shoppers (☞ Taxes, *below*).

SMOKING

The French are smokers, there's no way around it. And they're notorious for disregarding the few no-smoking laws that do exist, with little retribution. Even in restaurants, cafés, and train and métro stations that have no-smoking sections, you'll see people smoking. Even if you ask people to move or not to smoke, don't expect them to respond or respect your request. Your best bet for finding as smoke-free an environment as possible is to stick to the larger cafés and restaurants where there might be the possibility of having more clearly defined smoking and no-smoking areas.

SNCF trains have cars designated for smoking and no-smoking (specify when you make reservations), and these are some of the few places where the laws are respected. Some hotels, too, have designated no-smoking rooms; ask for these when reserving.

STREET ADDRESSES

Addresses in France are fairly straightforward: the number and the street name. However, you may see an address with a number plus "bis," for instance, 20 bis rue Vavin: This indicates that 20 bis is the next entrance or door down from 20 rue Vavin. In small towns a street number may not be given as the site will be the dominant (or only) building on the block or square. In rural areas, often only the route name or number off which the site is located is given, and sometimes only the name of the small village in which the site is located.

In Paris, a site's location in one of the city's 20 arrondissements is also noted: for instance, by Paris 75010 or, simply, the last two digits, 10ᵉ, both of which indicate that the address is in the 10th arrondissement. Due to its large size, Paris's 16th arrondissement has two numbers assigned to it: 75016 and 75116. Note that in France you enter a building on the *rez-de-chaussée* (RC or 0) and go up one floor to the first floor or *premier étage*.

STUDENTS IN FRANCE

Studying in France is the perfect way to shake up your perception of the world, make international friends, and improve your language skills. You may choose to study through a U.S.-sponsored program, usually through an American university, or to enroll in a program sponsored by a French organization. Do your homework: programs vary greatly in expense, academic quality, exposure to language, amount of contact with locals, and living conditions. Working through your local university is the easiest way to find out about study-abroad programs in France. Most universities have staff members who distribute information on programs at European universities, and they might be able to put you in touch with program participants.

Student bargains can be found almost everywhere—on train and plane fares, and for movie and museum tickets. Note, however, that you must be 26 or under.

➤ RESOURCES: **American Institute for Foreign Study** (102 Greenwich Ave., Greenwich, CT 06830, ☎ 203/869–9090 or 800/727–2437, ℻ 203/863–6180). **American Council of International Studies** (ACIS; 19 Bay State Rd., Boston, Massachusetts 02215, ☎ 617/236–2051 or 800/888–2247). **Council on International Educational Exchange** (CIEE; 205 E. 42nd St., 14th fl., New York, NY 10017, ☎ 212/822–2600 or 888/268–6245, ℻ 212/822–2699). **Institute of International Education** (IIE; 809 U.N. Plaza, New York, NY 10017, ☎ 212/984–5413). **World Learning** (Kipling Rd., Box 676, Brattleboro, VT 05302, ☎ 802/257–7751 or 800/336–1616, ℻ 802/258–3248).

TRAVEL AGENCIES

To save money, **look into deals available through student-oriented travel agencies.** To qualify you'll need a bona fide student I.D. card. Members of international student groups are also eligible.

➤ I.D.s & SERVICES: **Council Travel** (CIEE; ✉ 205 E. 42nd St., 14th floor, New York, NY 10017, ☎ 212/822–2700 or 888/268–6245, ℻ 212/822–2699, ✉) for mail orders only, in the U.S. **Travel Cuts** (✉ 187 College St., Toronto, Ontario M5T 1P7, ☎ 416/979–2406 or 800/667–2887, ✉) in Canada.

➤ STUDENT TOURS: **Contiki Holidays** (✉ 300 Plaza Alicante, Suite 900, Garden Grove, CA 92840, ☎ 714/740–0808 or 800/266–8454, ℻ 714/740–2034). **AESU Travel** (✉ 2 Hamill Rd., Suite 248, Baltimore, MD 21210-1807, ☎ 410/323–4416 or 800/638–7640, ℻ 410/323–4498).

TAXES

All taxes must be included in posted prices in France. The initials TTC (*toutes taxes comprises*—taxes included) sometimes appear on price lists but, strictly speaking, are superfluous. By law, **restaurant and hotel prices must include 20.6% taxes and a service charge.** If they show up as extra charges on your bill, complain.

VALUE-ADDED TAX

A number of shops offer VAT refunds to foreign shoppers. You are entitled to an Export Discount of 20.6%, depending on the item purchased, but it is often applicable only if your purchases in the same store reach a minimum of 2,800 francs (for U.K. and EU residents) or 1,200 francs (other residents, including U.S. and Canadian residents). Remember to **ask for the refund, as some stores—especially larger ones—offer the service only upon request.**

Global Refund is a V.A.T. refund service that makes getting your money back hassle-free. The service is Europe-wide and has 130,000 affiliated stores. In participating stores, **ask for the Global refund form** (called a Shopping Cheque). Have it stamped like any customs form by customs officials when leaving the European Union. Then take it to the Global Refund counter—conveniently located at more than 700 airports and border crossings—and your money will be refunded on the spot in the form of cash, check, or a refund to your credit card account.

➤ V.A.T. REFUNDS: **Global Refund** (✉ 707 Summer St., Stamford, CT. 06901, ☎ 800/566–9828, FAX 203/674–8709, taxfree@us.globalrefund.com, www.globalrefund.com.).

TELEPHONES

AREA & COUNTRY CODES

The country code for France is 33. The first two digits of French numbers are a prefix determined by zone: Paris and Ile-de-France, 01; the northwest, 02; the northeast, 03; the southeast, 04; and the southwest, 05. Numbers beginning with 08 can either be toll-free calls or calls that you are charged for (it depends on how the company has set up the number).

CALLING FRANCE

Note that **when dialing France from abroad, drop the initial 0 from the number.** For instance, to call a telephone number in Paris from the United States, dial 011–33 plus the phone number minus the initial 0 (phone numbers in this book are listed with the full 10 digits, which you use to make local calls). To call France from the United Kingdom, dial 00–33, then dial the number in France minus the initial 0.

DIRECTORY & OPERATOR ASSISTANCE

To find a number **in France, dial 12 for information.** For international inquiries, dial 00–33 plus the country code.

Another source of information is the Minitel, an online network similar to the Internet. You can find one—they look like a small computer terminal—in most post offices. Available free is an online phone book covering the entire country. To find information, hit the *appel* (call) key, then, when prompted, type the name you are looking for and hit *envoi* (return). It is also useful for tracking down services: choose *activité* (activity), tap in *piscine* (swimming pool), then Chartres, for example, and it will give you a list of all the pools in Chartres. Go to other lines or pages by hitting the *suite* (next) key. Newer models will connect automatically when you hit the book-icon key. To disconnect, hit *fin* (end).

INTERNATIONAL CALLS

To make a direct international call out of France, dial 00 and wait for the tone, then dial the country code (1 for the United States and Canada, 44 for the United Kingdom, 61 for Australia, and 64 for New Zealand) and the area code (minus any initial 0) and number.

Expect to be overcharged if you make calls from your hotel. Approximate daytime rates, per minute, are 2.25 francs to the United States and Canada (8:00 AM–9:30 PM), and 2.10 francs for the United Kingdom (2:00 PM–8:00 PM); reduced rates at other time intervals, per minute, are 1.80 francs to the United States and Canada and 1.65 francs to the United Kingdom.

To call home with the help of an operator, dial 00–33 plus the country

code. There is an automatic 44.5
franc service charge. Telephone cards
(☞ *below*) are sold that enable you to
make long-distance and international
calls from pay phones.

LOCAL CALLS

To make calls in the same city or
town, or in the same region, dial the
full 10-digit number.

LONG-DISTANCE CALLS

To call any region in France from
another region, just dial the full 10-
digit number.

LONG-DISTANCE SERVICES

AT&T, MCI, and Sprint access codes
make calling long distance relatively
convenient, but you may find the
local access number blocked in many
hotel rooms. First ask the hotel operator to connect you. If the hotel operator balks, ask for an international
operator, or dial the international
operator yourself. One way to improve your odds of getting connected
to your long-distance carrier is to
travel with more than one company's
calling card (a hotel may block Sprint,
for example, but not MCI). If all else
fails, call from a pay phone.

➤ ACCESS CODES: **AT&T Direct** (☎
08–00–99–00–11; 08–00–99–01–11;
800/874–4000 for information). **MCI
WorldPhone** (☎ 08–00–99–00–19;
800/444–4444 for information).
Sprint International Access (☎ 08–
00–99–87; 800/793–1153 for information).

PHONE CARDS

Most **French pay phones are operated
by *télécartes*** (phone cards), which
you can buy from post offices, tabacs,
and métro stations. These phone
cards will save you money and hassle,
since it's hard to find phones that
take change these days. There are two
types of cards: the *télécarte international*, which allows you to make
local calls and offers greatly reduced
rates on international calls (instructions are in English and the cost is 50
francs for 60 units and 100 francs for
120 units); and the simple *télécarte*,
which allows you to make calls in
France (the cost is 49 francs for 50
units; 97.5 francs for 120 units). You
can also use your credit card in much

the same way as a télécarte but be
careful, its much more expensive.

PUBLIC PHONES

Telephone booths **can almost always
be found at post offices, train stations,
on the street, and often in cafés.** A
local call costs 74 centimes for every
three minutes; half-price rates apply
weekdays between 9:30 PM and 8 AM,
from 1:30 PM Saturday, and all day
Sunday. Most French pay phones are
operated by phone cards (☞ *above*).
In a few cafés you may still be able to
find pay phones that operate with 1-,
2,- and 5-franc coins (1.5 francs for
local calls). Lift the receiver, place
your coin(s) in the appropriate slots,
and dial.

TIME

The time difference between New
York and Paris 6 hours (so when it's 1
PM in New York, it's 7 PM in Paris).
The time difference between London
and Paris is 1 hour; between Sydney
and Paris, 8–9 hours; and between
Auckland and Paris, 12 hours. France,
like the rest of Europe, uses the 24-
hour (or "military") clock, which
means that after 12 noon you continue
counting forward: 13h00 is 1 PM,
14h00 is 2 PM, 22h30 = 10:30 PM, etc.

TIPPING

The French have a clear idea of when
they should be tipped. Bills in bars
and restaurants include a service
charge, but **it is customary to round
out your bill with some small change**
unless you're dissatisfied. The amount
of this varies: anywhere from 50
centimes if you've merely bought a
beer, to 10 francs after a meal. Tip
taxi drivers and hairdressers about
10%. Give ushers in theaters and
movie theaters 1 or 2 francs. In some
theaters and hotels, coat check attendants may expect nothing (if there is a
sign saying POURBOIRE INTERDIT—tips
forbidden); otherwise give them 2–5
francs. Washroom attendants usually
get 2 francs, though the sum is often
posted.

If you stay in a hotel for more than
two or three days, it is customary to
leave something for the chambermaid—about 10 francs per day. In
expensive hotels you may well call on
the services of a baggage porter (bell

boy) and hotel porter and possibly the telephone receptionist. All expect a tip: Plan on about 10 francs per item for the baggage porter, but the other tips will depend on how much you've used their services—common sense must guide you here. In hotels that provide room service, give 5 francs to the waiter (this does not apply to breakfast served in your room). If the chambermaid does some pressing or laundering for you, give her 5 francs on top of the charge made. If the concierge has been very helpful, it is customary to leave a tip of 50–100 francs, depending on the type of hotel and the level of service.

Gas-station attendants get nothing for gas or oil, and 5 or 10 francs for checking tires. Train and airport porters get a fixed 6–10 francs per bag, but you're better off getting your own baggage cart if you can (a 10-franc coin—refundable—is necessary in train stations only). Museum guides should get 5–10 francs after a guided tour, and it is standard practice to tip tour guides (and bus drivers) 10 francs or more after an excursion, depending on its length.

TOURS & PACKAGES

Because everything is prearranged on a prepackaged tour or independent vacation, you'll spend less time planning—and often get it all at a good price.

BOOKING WITH AN AGENT

Travel agents are excellent resources. But it's a good idea to collect brochures from several agencies as some agents' suggestions may be influenced by relationships with tour and package firms that reward them for volume sales. If you have a special interest, **find an agent with expertise in that area**; ASTA (☞ Travel Agencies, *below*) has a database of specialists worldwide.

Make sure your travel agent knows the accommodations and other services of the place they're recommending. Ask about the hotel's location, room size, beds, and whether it has a pool, room service, or programs for children, if you care about these. Has your agent been there in person or sent others whom you can contact?

Do some homework on your own, too: local tourism boards can provide information about lesser-known and small-niche operators, some of which may sell only direct.

BUYER BEWARE

Each year consumers are stranded or lose their money when tour operators—even large ones with excellent reputations—go out of business. So **check out the operator**. Ask several travel agents about its reputation, and try to **book with a company that has a consumer-protection program**. (Look for information in the company's brochure.) In the United States, members of the National Tour Association and the United States Tour Operators Association are required to set aside funds to cover your payments and travel arrangements in the event that the company defaults. It's also a good idea to choose a company that participates in the American Society of Travel Agents' Tour Operator Program (TOP); ASTA will act as mediator in any disputes between you and your tour operator.

Remember that the more your package or tour includes the better you can predict the ultimate cost of your vacation. Make sure you know exactly what is covered, and **beware of hidden costs.** Are taxes, tips, and transfers included? Entertainment and excursions? These can add up.

➤ TOUR-OPERATOR RECOMMENDATIONS: **American Society of Travel Agents** (☞ Travel Agencies, *below*). **National Tour Association** (NTA; ✉ 546 E. Main St., Lexington, KY 40508, ☎ 606/226–4444 or 800/682–8886, ✈). **United States Tour Operators Association** (USTOA; ✉ 342 Madison Ave., Suite 1522, New York, NY 10173, ☎ 212/599–6599 or 800/468–7862, FAX 212/599–6744, ✈).

THEME TOURS

The following tour companies specialize in trips to France. The French Government Tourist Office (☞ Visitor Information, *below*) publishes brochures on theme trips in France including "In the Footsteps of the Painters of Light in Provence" and "France for the Jewish Traveler." Also *see* Barge & Boat Travel, Bike Travel, Hiking and Walking, and Children in France, *above,* for more information about theme tours.

➤ FOOD AND WINE: **Cooking with Friends** (✉ 29 Commonwealth Ave., Boston Massachusetts, ☎ 617/350–3837, FAX 617/247–6149, ✆). **DuVine Adventures** (✉ 635 Boston Ave., Suite 2, Boston, Massachusetts 02144, ☎ 781/395–7440 or 888/396–5383, FAX 781/395–8472, ✆). **European Culinary Adventures** (✉ 5 Ledgewood Way, Suite 6, Peabody, Massachusetts 01960, ☎ 978/535–5738 or 800/852–2625). **France In Your Glass** (✉ 814 35th Ave., Seattle, WA 98122, ☎ 206/325–4324 or 800/578–0903, FAX 206/325–1727 or 800/578–7069, ✆). **The International Kitchen** (✉ 1209 N. Astor, #11-N, Chicago, IL, ☎ 800/945–8606, FAX 847/295–0945, ✆). **Le Cordon Bleu** (✉ 8 rue Léon Delhomme, 75015 Paris, ☎ 01–53–68–22–50, FAX 01–48–56–03–77). **Ritz-Escoffier** (☎ 800/966–5758) in Paris's Ritz hotel. **La Varenne** (✉ P.O. Box 25574, Washington, DC 20007, ☎ 202/337–0073 or 800/537–6486, FAX 703/823–5438, ✆).

➤ MUSIC: **Dailey-Thorp Travel** (✉ 330 W. 58th St., #610, New York, NY 10019-1817, ☎ 212/307–1555 or 800/998–4677, FAX 212/974–1420).

TRAIN TRAVEL

The SNCF, France's national rail service, is fast, punctual, comfortable, and comprehensive. Traveling across France, you have various options: local trains, overnight trains with sleeping accommodations, and the high-speed TGV, the *Trains à Grande Vitesse* (Very Fast Trains).

TGVs average 255 kph/160 mph on the Lyon/southeast line, and 300 kph/190 mph on the Lille and Bordeaux/southwest lines, and are the best and the fastest domestic trains. They operate between Paris and Lille/Calais, Paris and Brussels, Paris and Amsterdam, Paris and Lyon/Switzerland/the Côte d'Azur, and Angers/Nantes, and Tours/Poitiers/Bordeaux. As with other main-line trains, a small supplement may be assessed at peak hours.

It's possible to get from one end of France to the other without traveling overnight, especially on TGVs. Otherwise, you have the choice between high-priced *wagons-lits* (sleeping cars) and affordable *couchettes* (bunks, six to a compartment in second class, four to a compartment in first, with sheets and pillow provided, priced at around 90 francs).

Try to **get to the station half an hour before departure** to ensure that you'll have a good seat. Before boarding, you must **punch your ticket (but not Eurailpass) in one of the orange machines** at the entrance to the platforms, or else the ticket collector will fine you 100 francs on the spot.

In Paris there are six international rail stations: Gare du Nord (northern France, northern Europe, and England via Calais or Boulogne); Gare St-Lazare (Normandy, England via Dieppe); Gare de l'Est (Strasbourg, Luxembourg, Basel, and central Europe); Gare de Lyon (Lyon, Marseille, the Côte d'Azur, Geneva, Italy); and Gare d'Austerlitz (Loire Valley, southwest France, Spain). Note that Gare Montparnasse has taken over as the main terminus for trains bound for southwest France.

BETWEEN THE U.K. AND FRANCE

Short of flying, the "Chunnel" is the fastest way to cross the English Channel (☞ Channel Tunnel, *above*). It's a good idea to **make a reservation if you're traveling with your car on a Chunnel train**; cars without reservations, if they can get on at all, are charged 20 percent extra.

British Rail also has four daily departures from London's Victoria Station, all linking with the Dover-Calais/Boulogne ferry services through to Paris. There is also an overnight service on the Newhaven-Dieppe ferry. Journey time is about eight hours. Credit-card bookings are accepted by phone or in person at a British Rail Travel Centre.

➤ CAR TRANSPORT: **Le Shuttle** (☎ 0990/353–535 in the U.K.; 03–21–00–61–00; 01–43–18–62–22 in France).

> PASSENGER SERVICE: In the U.K.:
Eurostar (☎ 0990/186–186), Inter-
City Europe (✉ Victoria Station,
London, ☎ 0990/848–848 for credit-
card bookings). In the U.S.: BritRail
Travel (☎ 800/677–8585), Rail
Europe (☎ 800/942–4866).

CLASSES

There are two classes on French
trains: first and second. The main
difference between the two classes
(besides the fact that first class costs
about 50% more) is that first class
has larger, more comfortable seats,
three to a row, whereas second class
has smaller seats with less leg room
and four to a row.

CUTTING COSTS

To save money **look into rail passes**
(☞ Rail Passes, *below*). But be aware
that if you don't plan to cover many
miles, you may come out ahead by
buying individual tickets.

FARES, SCHEDULES & RESERVATIONS

You can **call for train information
from any station or reserve tickets in
any station.** Train schedules are
available at stations or on the multilingual, computerized schedule information network, found at many
stations. You can also make reservations and buy your ticket at the
computer. Go to the Grandes Lignes
counter for travel within France and
to the Billets Internationaux desk if
you're heading out of the country.
Note that calling the SNCF's 08
number (*below*) costs money (you're
charged per minute), so it's better to
go to the nearest station.

You must **always make a seat reservation for the TGV**—easily obtained at
the ticket window or from an automatic machine. Seat reservations are
reassuring but seldom necessary on
other main-line French trains, except
in summer and at certain busy holiday times. You also need a reservation for sleeping accommodations.

> TRAIN INFORMATION: BritRail
Travel (☎ 800/677–8585 in the U.S.;
020/7834–2345 in the U.K.). Eu-
rostar (☎ 08–36–35–35–39 in
France; 0345/881881 in the U.K., ✆).
InterCity Europe (✉ Victoria Station,

London, ☎ 020/7834–2345; 020/
7828–0892; 0990/848–848 for credit-
card bookings). **Rail Europe** (☎ 800/
942–4866 in the U.S., ✆). **SNCF** (88
rue St-Lazare, 75009 Paris, ☎ 08–
36–35–35–35, ✆).

LUGGAGE DELIVERY SERVICE

With an advance arrangement, SNCF
will pick up and deliver your luggage
at a given time. For instance, if you're
planning on spending a weekend in
Nice, SNCF will pick up your luggage
at your hotel in Paris in the morning
before check out and deliver it to
your hotel in Nice, where it will be
awaiting your arrival. The cost is 95
francs for the first bag, and 60 francs
two additional bags, with a maximum
of three bags per person.

> CONTACT: **SNCF Luggage Deliver**
Service (☎ 08–03–84–58–45).

RAIL PASSES

There are two kinds of rail passes:
those you must purchase at home
before you leave for France, including
the France Rail Pass, the EurailPass,
and the EuroPass, and those available
in France from SNCF. Eurail- and
Europasses are available through
travel agents and a few authorized
organizations. SNCF rail passes are
available at any train station in
France.

If you plan to travel outside of Paris
by train, **consider purchasing a France**
Rail Pass, which allows three days of
unlimited train travel in a one-month
period. If you travel solo, first class
will run you $210, while second class
will come to $180: you can add up to
6 days on this pass for $30 a day. For
two people traveling together—called
a "Saver Pass," it's $171, while in
second class, the cost is $146. Again,
additional days (up to 6) costs $30
each. Other options include the
France Rail 'n Drive Pass (combining
rail and rental car), France Rail 'n Fly
Pass (rail travel and one air travel
journey within France), and the
France Fly Rail 'n Drive Pass (a rail,
air, and rental car program all in one

France is one of 17 countries in which
you can use EurailPasses, which
provide unlimited first-class rail trave
in all of the participating countries,

for the duration of the pass. If you plan to rack up the miles, get a standard pass. These are available for 15 days ($554), 21 days ($718), one month ($890), two months ($1,260), and three months ($1,558). If your plans call for only limited train travel, **look into a Europass,** which costs less money than a EurailPass. Unlike EurailPasses, however, you get a limited number of travel days, in a limited number of countries, during a specified time period. For example, a two-month Europass ($348–$728) allows between 5 and 15 days of rail travel, but costs around $200 less than the least expensive EurailPass. Keep in mind, however, that the Europass is good only in France, Germany, Italy, Spain, and Switzerland, and the number of countries you can visit is further limited by the type of pass you buy.

In addition to standard EurailPasses, **ask about special rail-pass plans.** Among these are the Eurail Youthpass (for those under age 26), the Eurail Saverpass (which gives a discount for two or more people traveling together), a Eurail Flexipass (which allows a certain number of travel days within a set period), the Euraildrive Pass and the Europass Drive (train and rental car).

The SNCF offers a number of discount rail passes available only for purchase in France. When traveling together, **two people (who don't have to be a couple) can save money with the Prix Découverte à Deux,** purchased in France. You'll get a 25% discount during "périodes bleus" (blue periods; weekdays and not on or near any holidays). Note that you have to be with the person you said you would be traveling with.

You can **get a reduced fare if you're a senior citizen (over 60).** There are two options: For the Prix Découverte Senior, all you have to do when you travel in France is to show a valid ID with your age and you're entitled to up to a 25% reduction in fares in first and second class. The second, the Carte Senior, is better if you're planning on spending a lot of time traveling; it costs 285F, is valid for one year, and entitles you to up to a 50%

reduction on most trains with a guaranteed minimum reduction of 25%. It also entitles you to a 30% discount on trips outside of France.

With the Carte Enfant Plus, for 350F **children under 12 and up to 4 accompanying adults can get 50% off on most trains for an unlimited number of trips.** This card is perfect if you're planning on spending a lot of time traveling in France with you're children, as it's valid for one year. You can also opt for the Prix Découverte Enfant Plus: When you buy you ticket, simply show a valid ID with your child's age and you can get a significant discount for your child and a 25% reduction for up to four accompanying adults.

If you purchase an individual ticket from SNCF in France and you're under 26, you automatically get a 25% reduction (a valid ID, such as an ISIC card or your passport, is necessary). If you're going to be using the train quite a bit during your stay in France and **if you're under 26, consider buying the Carte 12–25** (270F), which offers unlimited 50% reductions for one year (provided that there's space available at that price, otherwise you'll just get the standard 25% discount).

If you don't benefit from any of these reductions and **if you plan on traveling at least 200 km minimum roundtrip and don't mind staying over a Saturday night, look into the Prix Découverte Séjour.** This ticket gives you a 25% reduction.

Don't assume that your rail pass guarantee you a seat on the train you wish to ride. You need to **book seats ahead even if you're using a rail pass.**

➤ RAIL PASS AGENTS: CIT Tours Corp. (✉ 15 West 44th St., 10th Floor, New York, NY 10036, ☎ 800/248–7245 for rail; 800/248–8687 for tours and hotels). **DER Travel Services** (9501 W. Devon Ave., Rosemont, IL 60018, ☎ 800/782–2424). **Rail Europe** (☞ *above*).

TRAVEL AGENCIES

A good travel agent puts your needs first. Look for an agency that has been in business at least five years, emphasizes customer service, and has someone on staff who specializes in your destination. In addition, **make sure the agency belongs to a professional trade organization.** The American Society of Travel Agents (ASTA), with 27,000 agents in some 170 countries, is the largest and most influential in the field. Operating under the motto "Integrity in Travel," it maintains and enforces a strict code of ethics and will step in to help mediate any agent-client disputes if necessary. ASTA also maintains a Web site that includes a directory of agents. (If a travel agency is also acting as your tour operator, *see* Buyer Beware *in* Tours & Packages, *above.*)

In France, there are a number of good local agencies with offices in Paris as well as in other major cities. Nouvelles Frontiéres has offices in France as well as the U.S.

➤ LOCAL AGENT REFERRALS: **American Society of Travel Agents** (ASTA; ☎ 800/965–2782 24-hr hot line, FAX 703/684–8319, ✉). **Association of British Travel Agents** (✉ 68–71 Newman St., London W1P 4AH, ☎ 0171/637–2444, FAX 0171/637–0713, ✉). **Association of Canadian Travel Agents** (✉ 1729 Bank St., Suite 201, Ottawa, Ontario K1V 7Z5, ☎ 613/521–0474, FAX 613/521–0805). **Australian Federation of Travel Agents** (✉ Level 3, 309 Pitt St., Sydney 2000, ☎ 02/9264–3299, FAX 02/9264–1085, ✉). **Travel Agents' Association of New Zealand** (✉ Box 1888, Wellington 10033, ☎ 04/499–0104, FAX 04/499–0827).

➤ LOCAL AGENCIES: **Access Voyages** (✉ 6 rue Pierre Lescot, 1ᵉ, métro Châtelet–Les Halles, ☎ 01–44–76–84–50). **American Express** (✉ 11 rue Scribe, 8ᵉ, ☎ 01–47–77–77–07; ✉ 38 av. de Wagram, 8ᵉ, ☎ 01–42–27–58–80). **Nouvelles Frontières** (✉ 5 ave. de l'Opéra, 1ᵉʳ, métro Pyramides, ☎ 08–03–33–33–33; ✉ 14 Av. de Verdun, 06000 Nice,; ✉ 12 E. 33rd St. New York, NY 10016,, FAX 212/779–1007). **Soltours** (✉ 48 rue de Rivoli, 4ᵉ, métro Hôtel-de-Ville, ☎ 01–42–71–24–34).

VISITOR INFORMATION

➤ FRANCE TOURISM INFORMATION: **France On-Call** (☎ 410/286–8310 Mon.–Fri. 9–7, ✉). **Chicago** (✉ 676 N. Michigan Ave., Chicago, IL 60611). **Los Angeles** (✉ 9454 Wilshire Blvd., Suite 715, Beverly Hills, CA 90212). **New York City** (✉ 444 Madison Ave., 16th floor, New York, NY 10022). **Canada** (✉ 1981 Ave. McGill College, Suite 490, Montréal, Québec H3A 2W9). **U.K.** (✉ 178 Piccadilly, London W1V OAL, ☎ 171/6399–3500, FAX 171/6493–6594.

➤ LOCAL TOURIST OFFICES: *See* the A to Z sections *in* individual chapters for local tourist office telephone numbers and addresses.

➤ U.S. GOVERNMENT ADVISORIES: **U.S. Department of State** (✉ Overseas Citizens Services Office, Room 4811 N.S., 2201 C St. NW, Washington, DC 20520, ☎ 202/647–5225 for interactive hot line, 301/946–4400 for computer bulletin board, FAX 202/647–3000 for interactive hot line); enclose a self-addressed, stamped, business-size envelope.

WEB SITES

Do check out the World Wide Web when you're planning. You'll find everything from current weather forecasts to virtual tours of famous cities. Fodor's Web site, www.fodors.com, is a great place to start your on-line travels. When you see a ✉ in this book, go to www.fodors.com/urls for an up-to-date link to that destination's site. For more information specifically on France, visit the following:

➤ RECOMMENDED WEB SITES: **Bordeaux Tourist Office** (✉). **Eurail** (✉). **Eurostar** (✉). **French Embassy** (✉). **French Government Tourist Office** (✉). **French Ministry of Culture** (✉). **French Youth Hostel Federation** (✉). **International Youth Hostel Organization** (✉). **Louvre Museum** (✉). **Lyon Tourist Office** (✉). **Monaco Tourist Office** (✉). **Paris Tourist Office** ✉). **Provence Tourist Office** (✉). **Rail Europe** (✉). **Riviera Tourist Office** (✉). **SNCF** (✉). **Strasbourg Tourism Office** (✉).

WHEN TO GO

June and September are the best months to be in France, as both are free of the midsummer crowds. June offers the advantage of long daylight hours, while cheaper prices and frequently warm weather (often lasting well into October) make September attractive. Try to avoid the second half of July and all of August, when almost all of France goes on vacation. Huge crowds jam the roads and beaches, and prices are jacked up in resorts. Don't travel on or around July 14 and August 1, 15, and 31. July and August in southern France can be stifling. Paris can be stuffy and uncomfortable in August, especially with the problems that have arisen recently with the record highs in pollution. However, the city is pleasantly deserted. Many restaurants, theaters, and small shops close, but enough stay open these days to make a low-key, unhurried visit a pleasure.

The ski season in the Alps and Pyrénées lasts from Christmas to Easter; if you can, avoid February, when school holidays mean crowds. Anytime between March and November will offer you a good chance to soak up the sun on the Côte d'Azur. If Paris and the Loire are among your priorities, remember that the weather is unappealing before Easter. If you're dreaming of Paris in the springtime, May is your best bet, not rainy April. But the capital remains a joy during midwinter, with plenty of things to see and do.

CLIMATE

What follows are average daily maximum and minimum temperatures for Paris and Nice.

➤ FORECASTS: **Weather Channel Connection** (☎ 900/932–8437), 95¢ per minute from a Touch-Tone phone.

NICE

Jan.	55F	13C	May	68F	20C	Sept.	77F	25C
	39	4		55	13		61	16
Feb.	55F	13C	June	75F	24C	Oct.	70F	21C
	41	5		61	16		54	12
Mar.	59F	15C	July	81F	27C	Nov.	63F	17C
	45	7		64	18		46	8
Apr.	64F	18C	Aug.	81F	27C	Dec.	55F	13C
	46	8		64	18		41	5

PARIS

Jan.	43F	6C	May	68F	20C	Sept.	70F	21C
	34	1		49	10		53	12
Feb.	45F	7C	June	73F	23C	Oct.	60F	16C
	34	1		55	13		46	8
Mar.	54F	12C	July	76F	25C	Nov.	50F	10C
	39	4		58	15		40	5
Apr.	60F	16C	Aug.	75F	24C	Dec.	44F	7C
	43	6		58	15		36	2

FESTIVALS AND SEASONAL EVENTS

France is a festival all year round, with special events taking place throughout the country. In Paris, check the listings in *Pariscope* (which includes *Time Out,* a section with reviews in English of the week's main events), *L'Officiel des Spectacles,* or *Figaroscope* to find out what's going on around town. The *International Herald Tribune* also lists special events in its weekend edition, but not in great detail. The most complete listing of festivals comes in a small pamphlet published by the French Government Tourist Office (☞ Visitor Information *above*).

➤ DEC.: On the 24th, a Christmas celebration known as the **Shepherd's Festival,** featuring midnight Mass and picturesque "living crèches," is held in Les Baux, Provence. From the end of November through the New Year, Strasbourg mounts its famous **Christmas Market,** with echoes of German gemütlichkeit. **Christmas in Paris** spells celebrations, especially for children, from late December to early January. A giant crèche is set up on the square in front of the Hôtel de Ville.

➤ JAN.: The **International Circus Festival,** featuring top acts from around the world, and the **Monte Carlo Motor Rally,** one of the motoring world's most venerable races, are held in Monaco. Wine-producing villages throughout France celebrate **St. Vincent's Day** with festivities on January 22 in honor of their patron saint. The **Tournament St-Vincent,** a colorful Burgundy wine festival, takes place on the third weekend in a different wine village each year. Angoulême hosts the world's biggest and most popular comic-book festival, the **Fête de la Bande Dessinée.**

➤ FEB.: The **Carnival de Nice** is a period of parades and revelry in the weeks leading up to Lent. Other cities and villages also have their own smaller versions. **The Carnival de Dunkerque** on the weekend before Shrove Tuesday is the most rambunctious street carnival in northern France. **L'École de Paris**—a major retrospective featuring paintings, photographs, and sculptures of artists from the Paris School (1905–1929), including Chagall, Modigliani, and Man Ray, will be on view at the Musée d'Art Moderne in Paris. The **Festival de Film Fantastique** is the international horror film festival held in Gerardmer.

➤ MAR.: The **Salon de Mars,** an art and antiques fair, and the **Salon du Livre,** France's biggest book festival, take place in Paris. **La Foire à la Brocante et au Jambon** is an important, high quality antique fair held every year in Chátou, a beautiful village outside Paris.

➤ APR.: The **Monte Carlo Open Tennis Championships** get under way at the Monte Carlo Country Club.

➤ MAY: The **Cannes Film Festival** sees two weeks of star-studded events. Classical concert festivals get under way throughout the country. The **Foire de Paris** is a giant fair with food and agricultural products from all over France; it's held at the Porte de Versailles in Paris. At the end of the month, the **French Open Tennis Championships** are held at Roland Garros Stadium in Paris.

➤ JUNE: From now until September you will find **son-et-lumière** (sound-and-light) shows—historical pageants featuring special lighting effects—at many French châteaux and churches in the Loire. Throughout France, there's dancing in the streets during the **Fête de la Musique,** a musical festival on June 21. Strasbourg's **Fête de la Musique** features concerts in the Cathédrale Notre-Dame and various halls. This is a popular time for horse races: The **Prix du Président de la République** is run at the Hippodrome de Vincennes, the **Grand Steeplechase de Paris** is at the Auteuil Racecourse, and the **Grand Prix de Paris** is at Longchamp Racecourse. The **24 Heures du Mans,** the famous 24-hour car race, is held in Le Mans. The **Paris Air Show** is a display of planes at Le Bourget Airport near Paris. On the last weekend in June, the **Fête du Cinéma** allows you to take in as many movies as you can for the price of a single ticket. **The International Wine and Liquor Fare** will be held in Bordeaux from the June 18 to June 22.

➤ JULY: The **summer arts festival season** gets into full swing, particularly in Provence. Avignon offers a month of top-notch theater, Aix-en-Provence specializes in opera, Carpentras in religious music, Nice holds a big Jazz Festival, and Arles mounts a big photography festival. Northern France's spectacular **Fête de Gayant** (festival of the *giant,* in local patois) is held in Douai on the first Sunday after July 5. The **Tour de France,** the world's most famous bicycle race, dominates national attention for three weeks before crossing the finish line on the Champs-Élysées on the last Sunday of the month. The **Festival de l'Art Lyrique** brings over one million music lovers to Aix-en-Province to hear music spanning several centuries. On **Bastille Day** (July 14) all of France commemorates the Storming of the Bastille in 1789—the start of the French Revolution. Look out for fireworks, free concerts, and street festivities beginning the evening of the 13th with the **Bal des Pompiers** (Firemen's Ball) organized by local firemen.

➤ AUG.: On **Assumption** (August 15) many towns, notably Chartres and Lisieux, hold religious festivals and processions dedicated to the Virgin Mary. On the first Sunday following August 15, the **Festival de la Force Basque** in St-Palais brings together participants from eight villages to compete in contests of strength. The most famous annual religious festival in Brittany is the *pardon* in Ste-Anne-la-Palud, near Quimper, on the last Sunday of August.

➤ SEPT.: The **vendanges** (grape harvests) begin and festivals are held in the country's wine regions. The **Grande Braderie** turns Lille into one giant street fair on the month's first weekend. The **Fête de Musique de Besançon et Franche-Comté** consists of a series of chamber music concerts in and around Besançon during the month. The **Fête d'Automne**, a major arts and film festival, opens in Paris and continues until December. The **Rencontres Polyphoniques** in Calvi is an excellent chance to hear authentic Corsican music. The **Journée du Patrimoine,** on the Sunday nearest to September 21, opens the doors of many official and private buildings usually closed to the public. The **American Film Festival** in Deauville is one of the most important international events (second to Cannes) for American film.

➤ OCT.: The **Prix de l'Arc de Triomphe,** horseracing's most prestigious flat race, is held at Longchamp Racecourse in Paris on the first Sunday of the month. A giant contemporary art exhibition called **FIAC** takes place in Paris early in the month. The week-long **Paris Indoor Open** attracts the world's top tennis players at the end of the month.

➤ NOV.: **Les Trois Glorieuses,** Burgundy's biggest wine festival, includes the year's most important wine auction and related merriment in several Burgundy locations. The **Festiventu** in Calvi (Corsica) is a celebration of wind-related activities ranging from Windsurfers to woodwinds. Nation-wide **Armistice Day** ceremonies on November 11 commemorate veterans of World Wars I and II; in Paris, there's a military parade down the Champs-Élysées. On the third Thursday in November, France—especially Paris—celebrates the arrival of the **Beaujolais Nouveau.** The **Salon des Caves Particulières,** a giant wine fair is held in Paris at the end of the month.

WORDS AND PHRASES

One of the trickiest French sounds to pronounce is the nasal final *n* sound (whether or not the *n* is actually the last letter of the word). You should try to pronounce it as a sort of nasal grunt—as in "huh." The vowel that precedes the *n* will govern the vowel sound of the word, and in this list we precede the final *n* with an *h* to remind you to be nasal.

Another problem sound is the ubiquitous but untransliterable *eu*, as in *bleu* (blue) or *deux* (two), and the very similar sound in *je* (I), *ce* (this), and *de* (of). The closest equivalent might be the vowel sound in "put," but rounded.

English	French	Pronunciation
Basics		
Yes/no	Oui/non	wee/nohn
Please	S'il vous plaît	seel voo **play**
Thank you	Merci	mair-**see**
You're welcome	De rien	deh ree-**ehn**
That's all right	Il n'y a pas de quoi	eel nee ah pah de **kwah**
Excuse me, sorry	Pardon	pahr-**dohn**
Sorry!	Désolé(e)	day-zoh-**lay**
Good morning/ afternoon	Bonjour	bohn-**zhoor**
Good evening	Bonsoir	bohn-**swahr**
Goodbye	Au revoir	o ruh-**vwahr**
Mr. (Sir)	Monsieur	muh-**syuh**
Mrs. (Ma'am)	Madame	ma-**dam**
Miss	Mademoiselle	mad-mwa-**zel**
Pleased to meet you	Enchanté(e)	ohn-shahn-**tay**
How are you?	Comment ça va?	kuh-mahn-sa-**va**
Very well, thanks	Très bien, merci	tray bee-ehn, mair-**see**
And you?	Et vous?	ay **voo**?
Numbers		
one	un	uhn
two	deux	deuh
three	trois	twah
four	quatre	**kaht**-ruh
five	cinq	sank
six	six	seess
seven	sept	set
eight	huit	wheat
nine	neuf	nuff
ten	dix	deess
eleven	onze	ohnz

twelve	douze	dooz
thirteen	treize	trehz
fourteen	quatorze	kah-**torz**
fifteen	quinze	kanz
sixteen	seize	sez
seventeen	dix-sept	deez-**set**
eighteen	dix-huit	deez-**wheat**
nineteen	dix-neuf	deez-**nuff**
twenty	vingt	vehn
twenty-one	vingt-et-un	vehnt-ay-**uhn**
thirty	trente	trahnt
forty	quarante	ka-**rahnt**
fifty	cinquante	sang-**kahnt**
sixty	soixante	swa-**sahnt**
seventy	soixante-dix	swa-sahnt-**deess**
eighty	quatre-vingts	kaht-ruh-**vehn**
ninety	quatre-vingt-dix	kaht-ruh-vehn-**deess**
one-hundred	cent	sahn
one-thousand	mille	meel

Colors

black	noir	nwahr
blue	bleu	bleuh
brown	brun/marron	bruhn/mar-**rohn**
green	vert	vair
orange	orange	o-**rahnj**
pink	rose	rose
red	rouge	rooje
violet	violette	vee-o-**let**
white	blanc	blahnk
yellow	jaune	zhone

Days of the Week

Sunday	dimanche	**dee**-mahnsh
Monday	lundi	**luhn**-dee
Tuesday	mardi	**mahr**-dee
Wednesday	mercredi	**mair**-kruh-dee
Thursday	jeudi	**zhuh**-dee
Friday	vendredi	**vawn**-druh-dee
Saturday	samedi	**sahm**-dee

Months

January	janvier	**zhahn**-vee-ay
February	février	**feh**-vree-ay
March	mars	marce
April	avril	a-**vreel**

Vocabulary

May	mai	meh
June	juin	zhwehn
July	juillet	**zhwee**-ay
August	août	oot
September	septembre	sep-**tahm**-bruh
October	octobre	awk-**to**-bruh
November	novembre	no-**vahm**-bruh
December	décembre	day-**sahm**-bruh

Useful Phrases

Do you speak . . . English?	Parlez-vous . . . anglais?	par-lay **voo** **ahn**-glay
I don't speak . . . French	Je ne parle pas . . . français	zhuh nuh parl **pah** frahn-**say**
I don't understand	Je ne comprends pas	zhuh nuh kohm-prahn **pah**
I understand	Je comprends	zhuh kohm-**prahn**
I don't know	Je ne sais pas	zhuh nuh say **pah**
I'm American/ British	Je suis américain/ anglais	zhuh sweez a-may-ree-**kehn**/ahn-**glay**
What's your name?	Comment vous appelez-vous?	ko-mahn voo za-pell-ay-**voo**
My name is . . .	Je m'appelle . . .	zhuh ma-**pell** . . .
What time is it?	Quelle heure est-il?	kel air eh-**teel**
How?	Comment?	ko-**mahn**
When?	Quand?	kahn
Yesterday	Hier	yair
Today	Aujourd'hui	o-zhoor-**dwee**
Tomorrow	Demain	duh-**mehn**
This morning/ afternoon	Ce matin/cet après-midi	suh ma-**tehn**/set ah-pray-mee-**dee**
Tonight	Ce soir	suh **swahr**
What?	Quoi?	kwah
What is it?	Qu'est-ce que c'est?	kess-kuh-**say**
Why?	Pourquoi?	**poor**-kwa
Who?	Qui?	kee
Where is . . .	Où se trouve . . .	oo suh **troov**
the train station?	la gare?	la gar
the subway?	la station de?	la sta-**syon** duh
station?	métro?	may-**tro**
the bus stop?	l'arrêt de bus?	la-**ray** duh **booss**
the airport?	l'aérogare?	lay-ro-**gar**
the post office?	la poste?	la post
the bank?	la banque?	la bahnk
the hotel?	l'hôtel?	lo-**tel**
the store?	le magasin?	luh ma-ga-**zehn**

the cashier?	la caisse?	la **kess**
the museum?	le musée?	luh mew-**zay**
the hospital?	l'hôpital?	lo-pee-**tahl**
the elevator?	l'ascenseur?	la-sahn-**seuhr**
the telephone?	le téléphone?	luh tay-lay-**phone**
Where are the rest rooms?	Où sont les toilettes?	oo sohn lay twah-**let**
Here/there	Ici/là	ee-**see**/la
Left/right	A gauche/à droite	a goash/a drwaht
Straight ahead	Tout droit	too drwah
Is it near/far?	C'est près/loin?	say pray/lwehn
I'd like . . .	Je voudrais . . .	zhuh voo-**dray**
a room	une chambre	ewn **shahm**-bruh
the key	la clé	la clay
a newspaper	un journal	uhn zhoor-**nahl**
a stamp	un timbre	uhn **tam**-bruh
I'd like to buy . . .	Je voudrais acheter . . .	zhuh voo-**dray ahsh**-tay
a cigar	un cigare	uhn see-**gar**
cigarettes	des cigarettes	day see-ga-**ret**
matches	des allumettes	days a-loo-**met**
dictionary	un dictionnaire	uhn deek-see-oh-**nare**
soap	du savon	dew sah-**vohn**
city map	un plan de ville	uhn plahn de **veel**
road map	une carte routière	ewn cart roo-tee-**air**
magazine	une revue	ewn reh-**vu**
envelopes	des enveloppes	dayz ahn-veh-**lope**
writing paper	du papier à lettres	dew pa-pee-**ay** a **let**-ruh
airmail writing paper	du papier avion	dew pa-pee-**ay** a-vee-**ohn**
postcard	une carte postale	ewn cart pos-**tal**
How much is it?	C'est combien?	say comb-bee-**ehn**
It's expensive/cheap	C'est cher/pas cher	say share/pa share
A little/a lot	Un peu/beaucoup	uhn peuh/bo-**koo**
More/less	Plus/moins	plu/mwehn
Enough/too (much)	Assez/trop	a-say/tro
I am ill/sick	Je suis malade	zhuh swee ma-**lahd**
Call a doctor	Appelez un médecin	a-play uhn mayd-**sehn**
Help!	Au secours!	o suh-**koor**
Stop!	Arrêtez!	a-reh-**tay**
Fire!	Au feu!	o fuh
Caution!/Look out!	Attention!	a-tahn-see-**ohn**

Dining Out

A bottle of . . .	une bouteille de . . .	ewn boo-**tay** duh
A cup of . . .	une tasse de . . .	ewn **tass** duh
A glass of . . .	un verre de . . .	uhn **vair** duh
Ashtray	un cendrier	uhn sahn-dree-**ay**
Bill/check	l'addition	la-dee-see-**ohn**
Bread	du pain	dew pan
Breakfast	le petit-déjeuner	luh puh-**tee** day-zhuh-**nay**
Butter	du beurre	dew burr
Cheers!	A votre santé!	ah vo-truh sahn-**tay**
Cocktail/aperitif	un apéritif	uhn ah-pay-ree-**teef**
Dinner	le dîner	luh dee-**nay**
Special of the day	le plat du jour	luh plah dew **zhoor**
Enjoy!	Bon appétit!	bohn a-pay-**tee**
Fixed-price menu	le menu	luh may-**new**
Fork	une fourchette	ewn four-**shet**
I am diabetic	Je suis diabétique	zhuh swee dee-ah-bay-**teek**
I am on a diet	Je suis au régime	zhuh sweez oray-**jeem**
I am vegetarian	Je suis végé-tarien(ne)	zhuh swee vay-zhay-ta-ree-**en**
I cannot eat . . .	Je ne peux pas manger de . . .	zhuh nuh **puh** pah mahn-**jay** deh
I'd like to order	Je voudrais commander	zhuh voo-**dray** ko-mahn-**day**
I'm hungry/thirsty	J'ai faim/soif	zhay fahm/swahf
Is service/the tip included?	Le service est-il compris?	luh sair-**veess** ay-teel com-**pree**
It's good/bad	C'est bon/mauvais	say bohn/mo-**vay**
It's hot/cold	C'est chaud/froid	say sho/frwah
Knife	un couteau	uhn koo-**toe**
Lunch	le déjeuner	luh day-zhuh-**nay**
Menu	la carte	la cart
Napkin	une serviette	ewn sair-vee-**et**
Pepper	du poivre	dew **pwah**-vruh
Plate	une assiette	ewn a-see-**et**
Please give me . . .	Merci de me donner . . .	Mair-**see** deh meh doe-**nay**
Salt	du sel	dew sell
Spoon	une cuillère	ewn kwee-**air**
Sugar	du sucre	dew **sook**-ruh
Waiter!/Waitress!	Monsieur!/Mademoiselle!	muh-**syuh**/mad-mwa-**zel**
Wine list	la carte des vins	la **cart** day van

MENU GUIDE

French	English
General Dining	
Entrée	Appetizer/Starter
Garniture au choix	Choice of vegetable side
Selon arrivage	When available
Supplément/En sus	Extra charge
Sur commande	Made to order
Breakfast	
Confiture	Jam
Miel	Honey
Oeuf à la coque	Boiled egg
Oeufs au bacon	Bacon and eggs
Oeufs sur le plat	Fried eggs
Oeufs brouillés	Scrambled eggs
Tartine	Bread with butter or jam
Appetizers/Starters	
Anchois	Anchovies
Andouille(tte)	Chitterling sausage
Assiette de charcuterie	Assorted pork products
Crudités	Mixed raw vegetable salad
Escargots	Snails
Jambon	Ham
Jambonneau	Cured pig's knuckle
Pâté	Liver puree blended with meat
Quenelles	Light dumplings
Saucisson	Dried sausage
Terrine	Pâté in an earthenware pot
Soups	
Bisque	Shellfish soup
Bouillabaisse	Fish and seafood stew
Julienne	Vegetable soup
Potage/Soupe	Soup
Potage parmentier	Thick potato soup
Pot-au-feu	Stew of meat and vegetables
Soupe du jour	Soup of the day
Soupe à l'oignon gratinée	French onion soup
Soupe au pistou	Provençal vegetable soup
Velouté de . . .	Cream of . . .
Vichyssoise	Cold leek and potato cream soup
Fish and Seafood	
Bar	Bass
Bourride	Fish stew from Marseilles
Brandade de morue	Creamed salt cod
Brochet	Pike
Cabillaud/Morue	Fresh cod
Calmar	Squid
Coquilles St-Jacques	Scallops

Crabe	Crab
Crevettes	Shrimp
Daurade	Sea bream
Écrevisses	Prawns/crayfish
Harengs	Herring
Homard	Lobster
Huîtres	Oysters
Langouste	Spiny lobster
Langoustine	Prawn/lobster
Lotte	Monkfish
Lotte de mer	Angler
Loup	Catfish
Maquereau	Mackerel
Matelote	Fish stew in wine
Moules	Mussels
Palourdes	Clams
Perche	Perch
Poulpe	Octopus
Raie	Skate
Rascasse	Scorpion-fish
Rouget	Red mullet
Saumon	Salmon
Thon	Tuna
Truite	Trout

Meat

Agneau	Lamb
Ballotine	Boned, stuffed, and rolled
Blanquette de veau	Veal stew with a white-sauce base
Boeuf	Beef
Boeuf à la Bourguignonne	Beef stew
Boudin blanc	Sausage made with white meat
Boudin noir	Sausage made with pig's blood
Boulettes de viande	Meatballs
Brochette	Kabob
Cassoulet	Casserole of white beans, meat
Cervelle	Brains
Châteaubriand	Double fillet steak
Côtelettes	Chops
Choucroute garnie	Sausages and cured pork served with sauerkraut
Côte de boeuf	T-bone steak
Côte	Rib
Cuisses de grenouilles	Frogs' legs
Entrecôte	Rib or rib-eye steak
Épaule	Shoulder
Escalope	Cutlet
Foie	Liver
Gigot	Leg
Langue	Tongue
Médaillon	Tenderloin steak
Pavé	Thick slice of boned beef
Pieds de cochon	Pig's feet

Porc	Pork
Ragoût	Stew
Ris de veau	Veal sweetbreads
Rognons	Kidneys
Saucisses	Sausages
Selle	Saddle
Tournedos	Tenderloin of T-bone steak
Veau	Veal
Viande	Meat

Methods of Preparation

À point	Medium
À l'étouffée	Stewed
Au four	Baked
Bien cuit	Well-done
Bleu	Very rare
Bouilli	Boiled
Braisé	Braised
Frit	Fried
Grillé	Grilled
Rôti	Roast
Saignant	Rare
Sauté/poêlée	Sautéed

Game and Poultry

Blanc de volaille	Chicken breast
Caille	Quail
Canard/Caneton	Duck/duckling
Cerf/Chevreuil	Venison
Coq au vin	Chicken stewed in red wine
Dinde/Dindonneau	Turkey/Young turkey
Faisan	Pheasant
Lapin	Rabbit
Lièvre	Wild hare
Oie	Goose
Pigeon/Pigeonneau	Pigeon/Squab
Pintade/Pintadeau	Guinea fowl/Young guinea fowl
Poularde	Fattened pullet
Poulet/Poussin	Chicken/Spring chicken
Sanglier/Marcassin	Wild boar/Young wild boar
Volaille	Fowl

Vegetables

Artichaut	Artichoke
Asperge	Asparagus
Aubergine	Eggplant
Carottes	Carrots
Champignons	Mushrooms
Chou-fleur	Cauliflower
Chou (rouge)	Cabbage (red)
Choux de Bruxelles	Brussels sprouts
Courgette	Zucchini
Cresson	Watercress
Épinard	Spinach
Haricots blancs/verts	White kidney/green beans
Laitue	Lettuce

Lentilles	Lentils
Maïs	Corn
Oignons	Onions
Petits pois	Peas
Poireaux	Leeks
Poivrons	Peppers
Pomme de terre	Potato
Pommes frites	French fries
Tomates	Tomatoes

Sauces and Preparations

Béarnaise	Vinegar, egg yolks, white wine, shallots, tarragon
Béchamel	White sauce
Bordelaise	Mushrooms, red wine, shallots, beef marrow
Bourguignon	Red wine, herbs
Chasseur	Wine, mushrooms, shallots
Diable	Hot pepper
Forestière	Mushrooms
Hollandaise	Egg yolks, butter, vinegar
Indienne	Curry
Madère	With Madeira wine
Marinière	White wine, mussel broth, egg yolks
Meunière	Brown butter, parsley, lemon juice
Périgueux	With goose or duck liver puree and truffles
Poivrade	Pepper sauce
Provençale	Onions, tomatoes, garlic

Fruits and Nuts

Abricot	Apricot
Amandes	Almonds
Ananas	Pineapple
Cacahouètes	Peanuts
Cassis	Black currants
Cerises	Cherries
Citron/Citron vert	Lemon/Lime
Figues	Figs
Fraises	Strawberries
Framboises	Raspberries
Fruits secs	Dried fruit
Groseilles	Red currants
Marrons	Chestnuts
Melon	Melon
Mûres	Blackberries
Noisettes	Hazelnuts
Noix de coco	Coconut
Noix	Walnuts
Pamplemousse	Grapefruit
Pêche	Peach
Poire	Pear
Pomme	Apple
Pruneaux	Prunes
Prunes	Plums

| Raisins blancs/noirs | Grapes green/purple |
| Raisins secs | Raisins |

Desserts

Coupe (glacée)	Sundae
Crêpe	Thin pancake
Crème brûlée	Custard with caramelized topping
Crème caramel	Caramel-coated custard
Crème Chantilly	Whipped cream
Gâteau au chocolat	Chocolate cake
Glace	Ice cream
Mousse au chocolat	Chocolate mousse
Sabayon	Egg-and-wine-based custard
Tarte aux pommes	Apple pie
Tarte tatin	Caramelized apple tart
Tourte	Layer cake

Alcoholic Drinks

À l'eau	With water
Avec des glaçons	On the rocks
Kir	Chilled white wine mixed with black-currant syrup
Bière	Beer
blonde/brune	*light/dark*
Calvados	Apple brandy from Normandy
Eau-de-vie	Brandy
Liqueur	Cordial
Poire William	Pear brandy
Porto	Port
Vin	Wine
sec	*dry/neat*
brut	*very dry*
léger	*light*
doux	*sweet*
rouge	*red*
rosé	*rosé*
mousseux	*sparkling*
blanc	*white*

Nonalcoholic Drinks

Café	Coffee
noir	*black*
crème	*with steamed milk/cream*
au lait	*with steamed milk*
décaféiné	*caffeine-free*
Express	Espresso
Chocolat chaud	Hot chocolate
Eau minérale	Mineral water
gazeuse/non gazeuse	*carbonated/still*
Jus de . . .	. . . juice
Lait	Milk
Limonade	Lemonade
Thé	Tea
au lait/au citron	*with milk/lemon*
glacé	*Iced tea*
Tisane	Herb tea

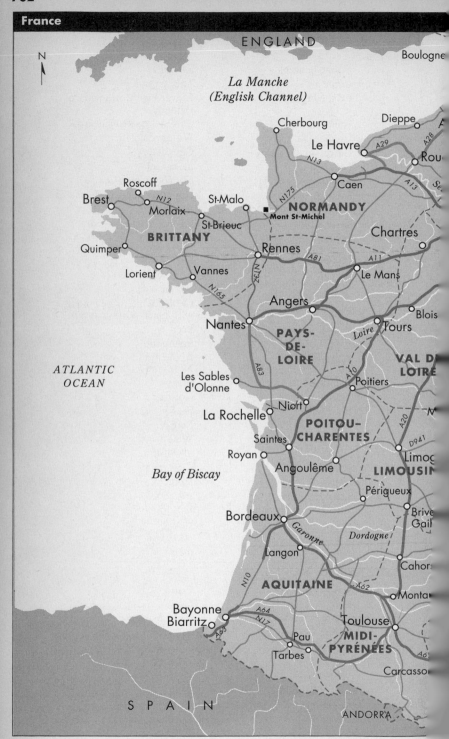

ENGLAND

Boulogne

La Manche
(English Channel)

N

Cherbourg

Dieppe

Le Havre

A29

A28

Rou

N13

A13

Se

Caen

N175

Roscoff

St-Malo

NORMANDY

Mont St-Michel

Chartres

Brest

N12

Morlaix

St-Brieuc

BRITTANY

Quimper

Rennes

A81

A11

Le Mans

Lorient

Vannes

N165

Angers

Blois

Nantes

Tours

Loire

VAL DE
LOIRE

PAYS-
DE-
LOIRE

N137

A83

A10

Les Sables
d'Olonne

Poitiers

M

Niort

La Rochelle

POITOU-
CHARENTES

A20

Saintes

Limo

Royan

Angoulême

D941

LIMOUSIN

Bay of Biscay

Périgueux

ATLANTIC
OCEAN

Brive
Gail

Bordeaux

Garonne

Dordogne

Langon

Cahor

N10

AQUITAINE

A62

Monta

Bayonne
Biarritz

A64

N17

Toulouse

N165

Pau

MIDI-
PYRÉNÉES

A6

Tarbes

Carcasso

S P A I N

ANDORRA

Mediterranean Sea

ICELAND

⊛ Reykjavík

NORWAY

Bergen ○

NORTHERN
IRELAND

SCOTLAND

⊛ Edinburgh

*North
Sea*

Skage

⊛ Belfast

DENMARK

IRELAND

*Irish
Sea*

Dublin ⊛

U N I T E D
K I N G D O M

WALES

Hambur

ENGLAND

NETHERLANDS

Cardiff ○

London ○

The Hague ○

Amsterdam ○

GER

*ATLANTIC
OCEAN*

English Channel

Rotterdam ○

Brussels ⊛

BELGIUM

Bonn ○

Paris ⊛

Frankfurt ○

LUXEMBOURG

F R A N C E

Zürich ○

Mu

Bern ⊛

SWITZERLAND

LIECHTEN

Lyon ○

Milan ○

PORTUGAL

Monte
Carlo

Nice ○

Marseille ○

MONACO

Floren

Madrid ⊛

ANDORRA

Corsica

Lisbon ○

Barcelona ○

S P A I N

*Balearic
Islands*

Sardinia

Seville ○

Granada ○

Tyrr

Gibraltar ○

Mediterranean Sea

MOROCCO

ALGERIA

0 — 400 miles

0 — 600 km

TUNISIA

INDEX

Icons and Symbols

★   Our special recommendations

✕   Restaurant

▦   Lodging establishment

✕▦   Lodging establishment whose restaurant warrants a special trip

🐥   Good for kids (rubber duck)

☞   Sends you to another section of the guide for more information

✉   Address

☎   Telephone number

🕐   Opening and closing times

💳   Admission prices

💸   Sends you to www.fodors.com/urls for up-to-date links to the property's Web site

Numbers in white and black circles ③ ❸ that appear on the maps, in the margins, and within the tours correspond to one another.

A

FODOR'S FRANCE 2001

EDITOR: Robert I. C. Fisher

Editorial Contributors: Nancy Coons, Simon Hewitt, Nicola Keegan, Alexander Lobrano, Christopher Mooney, Ian Phillips, George Semler, Brandy Whittingham

Editorial Production: Tom Holton

Maps: David Lindroth, *cartographer;* Robert Blake, *map editor*

Design: Fabrizio La Rocca, *creative director;* Guido Caroti, *art director;* Jolie Novak, *photo editor;* Melanie Marin, *photo researcher*

Cover Design: Pentagram

Production/Manufacturing: Robert B. Shields

COPYRIGHT

ISBN 0–679–00554–4

ISSN 0532–5692

SPECIAL SALES

Fodor's Travel Publications are available at special discounts for bulk purchases for sales promotions or premiums. Special editions, including personalized covers, excerpts of existing guides, and corporate imprints, can be created in large quantities for special needs. For more information, contact your local bookseller or write to Special Markets, Fodor's Travel Publications, 280 Park Avenue, New York, NY 10017. Inquiries from Canada should be directed to your local Canadian bookseller or sent to Random House of Canada, Ltd., Marketing Department, 2775 Matheson Boulevard East, Mississauga, Ontario L4W 4P7. Inquiries from the United Kingdom should be sent to Fodor's Travel Publications, 20 Vauxhall Bridge Road, London SW1V 2SA, England.

PRINTED IN THE UNITED STATES OF AMERICA

10 9 8 7 6 5 4 3 2 1

IMPORTANT TIP

Although all prices, opening times, and other details in this book are based on information supplied to us at press time, changes occur all the time in the travel world, and Fodor's cannot accept responsibility for facts that become outdated or for inadvertent errors or omissions. So **always confirm information when it matters,** especially if you're making a detour to visit a specific place.

PHOTOGRAPHY

Tony Stone Images: Suzanne and Nick Geary, cover. (Normandy)

Comité Regional du Tourisme de Bourgogne: *Alain Doire, 29 bottom right.*

Corbis: *3 top left, 3 top right, 3 center, 3 bottom left, 26A, 27B, 28D, 29F.*

DIAF: *Tristan Deschamps, 4-5, 10B. Daniel Faure, 11C. Arnaud Fevrier, 19B. J.C. Gerard, 13F, 22A. François Le Divenah, 11D. Rosine Mazin, 8C, 9C. Eric Planchard, 17D. Pratt-Pries, 19C. Erwan Quemere, 10A. Daniel Thierry, 8B, 19A.*

Fondation Maeght, *3 bottom right.*

Owen Franken, *11E, 13E, 17B, 20B, 20C, 25A.*

French Government Tourist Office: *Gea Koenig, 28E. Le Jeune, 2 top right. Perret, 30A. Daniel Thierry, 7E, 27C.*

Hôtel du Palais, *2 bottom center.*

The Image Bank: *Daniel Barbier, 6A, 7C. Bullaty & Lomeo, 20A. Luis Castañeda, 21B. Alain Choisnet, 10 center, 12C, 15A, 24C, 30C. Chris Close, 9B. Color Day Productions, 25C. Gary Cralle, 30I. Grant V. Faint, 9A. FotoWorld, 22C. Larry Dale Gordon, 25B. Romilly Lockyer, 12A. Malcom, 32. Timothy Murphy, 30H. M.E. Newman, 30D. J.P. Pieuchot, 13D, 18B. Andrea Pistolesi, 22B. Bernard Roussel, 18A. Bernard Van Berg, 17C, 23A. Raphael Van Butsele, 8A. Hans Wolf, 24A, 24B.*

Catherine Karnow, *12B, 14A, 14B, 14C, 20D, 21A.*

Bob Krist, *6B, 7D, 15C, 16A.*

La Cour des Loges, *30B.*

La Maison des Consuls: *Marc Mesplié Photographie, 30F.*

L'Ami Fritz: *Eric Bouvet, 30J.*

La Treille Muscate, *2 bottom left, 18C, 30E.*

Musée Condé: *Ph. Giraudon, 2 top left, 30G.*

Musée Matisse, *2 bottom right.*

Nik Wheeler, *1, 15B, 23 top, 23B.*

ABOUT OUR WRITERS

Every trip is a significant trip. Acutely aware of that fact, we've pulled out all stops in preparing *Fodor's France*. To help you zero in on what to see in France, we've gathered some great color photos of the key sights in every region. To show you how to put it all together, we've created great itineraries and neighborhood walks. And to direct you to the places that are truly worth your time and money, we've rallied the team of endearingly picky know-it-alls we're pleased to call our writers. Having seen all corners of the regions they cover for us, they're real experts. If you knew them, you'd poll them for tips yourself.

Based in a 300-year-old farmhouse in Lorraine, **Nancy Coons** covers much of northeastern France while satisfying her long-distance love affair with the luscious south of the country. Author of *Fodor's Provence and the Côte d'Azur*, as well as two of Fodor's new color-photograph guide books—*Escape to Provence* and *Escape to the French Riviera*—she has become adept at describing the golden light of Arles from under the iron-gray skies back home. For this edition, she crafted many of our new chapter introductions, as well as updating three chapters.

Editor of *France 2001*, **Robert I. C. Fisher** succeeded in getting one foot in the caviar when he traveled to Paris to write up the noted Ile St-Louis mansion of Baron and Baroness Guy de Rothschild for the April 1988 issue of *Town & Country*. His favorite French memory? A pre-dawn hike up to the basilica of Sacré-Coeur, atop Montmartre, to watch the sun come up over Paris.

Simon Hewitt, who updated eight chapters of this book, headed to Paris straight from studying French and art history at Oxford. When not contemplating the Sun King's bicep-flexing baroque palace at Versailles, his thoughts often turn to cricket—he is captain of the French national team. He also writes reguarly about antiques and the art market.

Nicola Keegan was born in Ireland and raised in Iowa. But after spending one year at the Sorbonne university, she knew Paris was going to be her home forever. In Smart Travel Tips from A to Z, she advises you on how to make your trip to France easier.

Now European correspondent for *Gourmet,* **Alexander Lobrano,** who updated the Paris dining and nightlife sections, has lived in Paris for 14 years. Along with reporting on French food and style for many publications—including *Departures* and *Paris Time Out*—he has also been editor of the *Paris Zagat's Survey*. His most recent best meal in Paris? At Guy Savoy.

Christopher Mooney came to Paris to study French philosophy and hang out in cafés. A born-again Epicurean, he herein devotes his efforts to finding the best accommodations in Paris, along with a complete update of our Burgundy chapter.

Ian Phillips, who updated the Outdoor Activities and Sports and Shopping sections of the Paris chapter, is a freelance journalist, writing on culture and fashion for publications in Paris, London, and New York.

George Semler lives over the border in Spain, but he has skied, hiked, fly-fished, and explored both sides of the Pyrénées. He's acquainted with every trout—of Spanish *and* French persuasion—as well as each wild mushroom and Romanesque chapel. For this edition, he updated five chapters, including Corsica—his second love and his mountain in the sea.

We'd especially like to thank the staff at the French Government Tourist Office in New York for fact-finding assistance.

Don't Forget to Write

We love feedback—positive and negative—and follow up on all suggestions. So contact the France editor at editors@ fodors.com or c/o Fodor's, 280 Park Avenue, New York, New York 10017. Have a wonderful trip!

Karen Cure
Editorial Director